K

HANDBOOK OF DEPRESSION

HANDBOOK
OF
DEPRESSION

Edited by

Ian H. Gotlib
Constance L. Hammen

THE GUILFORD PRESS
New York   London

© 2002 The Guilford Press
A Division of Guilford Publications, Inc.
72 Spring Street, New York, NY 10012
www.guilford.com

Printed in the United States of America

This book is printed on acid-free paper.

Last digit is print number: 9   8   7   6   5   4   3   2   1

Library of Congress Cataloging-in-Publication Data

Handbook of depression / edited by Ian H. Gotlib, Constance L. Hammen.
    p. cm.
Includes bibliographical references and index.
   ISBN 1-57230-725-0 (alk. paper)
   1. Depression, Mental—Handbooks, manuals, etc.   I. Gotlib, Ian H.   II.
Hammen, Constance L.
   RC537 .H3376 2002
   616.85'27—dc21   2002003553

About the Editors

Ian H. Gotlib, PhD, is Professor of Psychology at Stanford University and Director of the Stanford Mood and Anxiety Disorders Laboratory. Dr. Gotlib is very active in clinical research, which has been supported by grants from the National Institute of Mental Health and the Medical Research Council of Canada. In his research, Dr. Gotlib examines information-processing styles of depressed children, adolescents, and adults; patterns of brain activation of depressed patients in response to different emotional stimuli; and the emotional, cognitive, behavioral, and biological functioning of children of depressed mothers. He has published over 150 scientific articles and has written or cowritten several books in the areas of depression and stress. In addition, he has been Associate Editor of *Cognition and Emotion, Cognitive Therapy and Research,* and the *Journal of Social and Personal Relationships,* and has served on the Editorial Boards of the *British Journal of Clinical Psychology,* the *Journal of Abnormal Psychology,* and *Psychological Assessment.* Dr. Gotlib is a Fellow of the American Psychological Association, the American Psychological Society, and the American Psychopathological Association.

Constance L. Hammen, PhD, is Professor of Psychology and Psychiatry and Biobehavioral Sciences at the University of California, Los Angeles (UCLA). She is also Chair of the clinical psychology area and Director of Clinical Training at UCLA, and is affiliated with the Mood Disorders Clinic at the UCLA Neuropsychiatric Institute. Dr. Hammen is a clinical researcher specializing in mood disorders, with an emphasis on stress, family factors, and individual vulnerability factors predicting depression in adults and adolescents, and course of disorder in adults with bipolar illness. Her research has been supported by the William T. Grant Foundation and the National Institute of Mental Health. She has written or cowritten nearly 200 articles, books, and textbooks, and has served as President of the Society for Research in Psychopathology, as Associate Editor of *Cognitive Therapy and Research,* and on the editorial boards of the *Journal of Abnormal Psychology, Journal of Social and Clinical Psychology,* and the *British Journal of Clinical Psychology.*

Contributors

Lyn Y. Abramson, PhD, Department of Psychology, University of Wisconsin, Madison, Wisconsin

Lauren B. Alloy, PhD, Department of Psychology, Temple University, Philadelphia, Pennsylvania

Steven R. H. Beach, PhD, Department of Psychology and the Institute for Behavioral Research, University of Georgia, Athens, Georgia

Robert J. Boland, MD, Department of Psychiatry and Human Behavior, Brown University, Providence, Rhode Island

Bruce Bongar, PhD, ABPP, Pacific Graduate School of Psychology, Stanford University School of Medicine, Palo Alto, California

Laurel L. Brown, PhD, Department of Psychiatry, Vanderbilt University, Nashville, Tennessee

Yulia Chentsova-Dutton, MA, Department of Psychology, Stanford University, Stanford, California

David C. Clark, PhD, Rush Medical College, Rush-Presbyterian–St. Luke's Medical Center, Chicago, Illinois

Gregory Clarke, PhD, Kaiser Permanente Center for Health Research, Portland, Oregon

Arin M. Connell, MA, Department of Psychology, Emory University, Atlanta, Georgia

Richard J. Davidson, PhD, W.M. Keck Laboratory for Functional Brain Imaging and Behavior, Waisman Center, University of Wisconsin, Madison, Wisconsin

C. Emily Durbin, MA, Department of Psychology, State University of New York at Stony Brook, Stony Brook, New York

Cecilia A. Essau, PhD, Westfalische Wilhelms-Universität Münster, Münster, Germany

Andrew Futterman, PhD, Department of Psychology, Holy Cross College, Worcester, Massachusetts

Dolores Gallagher-Thompson, PhD, Veterans Affairs Palo Alto Health Care System and the Department of Psychiatry and Behavioral Sciences, Stanford University School of Medicine, Palo Alto, California

Judy Garber, PhD, Department of Psychology and Human Development, Vanderbilt University, Nashville, Tennessee

Brandon E. Gibb, MA, Department of Psychology, Temple University, Philadelphia, Pennsylvania

Michael J. Gitlin, MD, Department of Psychiatry, University of California, Los Angeles, Los Angeles, California

Sherryl H. Goodman, PhD, Department of Psychology, Emory University, Atlanta, Georgia

Ian H. Gotlib, PhD, Department of Psychology, Stanford University, Stanford, California

Katholiki Hadjiyannakis, MS, Department of Psychology, University of Oregon, Eugene, Oregon

Gerald J. Haeffel, MA, Department of Psychology, University of Wisconsin, Madison, Wisconsin

Kirsten L. Haman, PhD, Developmental Psychopathology Training Program, Vanderbilt University, Nashville, Tennessee

Constance L. Hammen, PhD, Department of Psychology, University of California, Los Angeles, Los Angeles, California

Benjamin L. Hankin, PhD, Department of Psychology, University of Illinois, Chicago, Illinois

Steven D. Hollon, PhD, Department of Psychology, Vanderbilt University, Nashville, Tennessee

Jason L. Horowitz, MS, Department of Psychology and Human Development, Vanderbilt University, Nashville, Tennessee

Robert H. Howland, MD, Department of Psychiatry, University of Pittsburgh School of Medicine, Pittsburgh, Pennsylvania

Rick E. Ingram, PhD, Department of Psychology, Southern Methodist University, Dallas, Texas

Lisa Jaycox, PhD, RAND Health, Arlington, Virginia

Ripu Jindal, MD, Department of Psychiatry, University of Pittsburgh School of Medicine, Pittsburgh, Pennsylvania

Sheri L. Johnson, PhD, Department of Psychology, University of Miami, Coral Gables, Florida

Thomas E. Joiner, Jr., PhD, Department of Psychology, Florida State University, Tallahassee, Florida

Deborah J. Jones, PhD, Cardiovascular Behavioral Medicine, Department of Psychiatry, University of Pittsburgh School of Medicine, Pittsburgh, Pennsylvania

Nadine J. Kaslow, PhD, Department of Psychiatry, Emory University–Grady Hospital, Atlanta, Georgia

Martin B. Keller, MD, Department of Psychiatry and Human Behavior, Brown University, Providence, Rhode Island

Ronald C. Kessler, PhD, Department of Health Care Policy, Harvard Medical School, Boston, Massachusetts

Amy Kizer, BA, Department of Psychology, University of Miami, Coral Gables, Florida

Daniel N. Klein, PhD, Department of Psychology, State University of New York at Stony Brook, Stony Brook, New York

Huynh-Nhu Le, PhD, Department of Psychology, George Washington University, Washington, DC

Peter M. Lewinsohn, PhD, Oregon Research Institute, Eugene, Oregon

Donal G. MacCoon, MA, Department of Psychology, University of Wisconsin, Madison, Wisconsin

John C. Markowitz, MD, Payne Whitney Clinic, The New York–Presbyterian Hospital, Weill Medical College, Cornell University, New York, New York

Erin B. McClure, PhD, Department of Psychology, Emory University, Atlanta, Georgia

Kelly S. McClure, PhD, Division of Oncology, Children's Hospital of Philadelphia, Philadelphia, Pennsylvania

Peter McGuffin, PhD, Social, Genetic, and Developmental Psychiatry Research Centre, Institute of Psychiatry, King's College, London, United Kingdom

Scott M. Monroe, PhD, Department of Psychology, University of Oregon, Eugene, Oregon

Ricardo F. Muñoz, PhD, Department of Psychiatry at San Francisco General Hospital, University of California, San Francisco, San Francisco, California

Arthur M. Nezu, PhD, Department of Clinical and Health Psychology, MCP Hahnemann University, Philadelphia, Pennsylvania

Christine Maguth Nezu, PhD, Department of Clinical and Health Psychology, MCP Hahnemann University, Philadelphia, Pennsylvania

Jack B. Nitschke, PhD, W.M. Keck Laboratory for Functional Brain Imaging and Behavior, Waisman Center, University of Wisconsin, Madison, Wisconsin

Susan Nolen-Hoeksema, PhD, Department of Psychology, University of Michigan, Ann Arbor, Michigan

Diego Pizzagalli, PhD, W.M. Keck Laboratory for Functional Brain Imaging and Behavior, Waisman Center, University of Wisconsin, Madison, Wisconsin

David V. Powers, PhD, Department of Psychology, Loyola College, Baltimore, Maryland

Neil J. Santiago, BA, Department of Psychology, State University of New York at Stony Brook, Stony Brook, New York

Tiffany Schneider, BA, Social, Genetic, and Developmental Psychiatry Research Centre, Institute of Psychiatry, King's College, London, United Kingdom

Stewart A. Shankman, MA, Department of Psychology, State University of New York at Stony Brook, Stony Brook, New York

Greg J. Siegle, PhD, Department of Psychiatry, University of Pittsburgh School of Medicine, Pittsburgh, Pennsylvania

Ronald A. Stolberg, PhD, Pacific Graduate School of Psychology, Palo Alto, California; The Winston School, Del Mar, California

Michael E. Thase, MD, Department of Psychiatry, University of Pittsburgh School of Medicine, Pittsburgh, Pennsylvania; Western Psychiatric Institute, Pittsburgh, Pennsylvania

Larry Thompson, PhD, Pacific Graduate School of Psychology and Division of Gerontology, Endocrinology, and Metabolism, Stanford University School of Medicine, Palo Alto, California

Jeanne L. Tsai, PhD, Department of Psychology, Stanford University, Stanford, California

John Wallace, MRCPsych, Social, Genetic, and Developmental Psychiatry Research Centre, Institute of Psychiatry, King's College, London, United Kingdom

Myrna M. Weissman, PhD, College of Physicians and Surgeons of Columbia University and the New York State Psychiatric Institute, New York, New York

Marni L. Zwick, MA, Department of Clinical and Health Psychology, MCP Hahnemann University, Philadelphia, Pennsylvania

Contents

HANDBOOK OF DEPRESSION

Introduction

Ian H. Gotlib and Constance L. Hammen

Depression is among the most prevalent of all psychiatric disorders. Recent estimates indicate that almost 20% of the U.S. population, primarily women, will experience a clinically significant episode of depression at some point in their lives. In fact, the rates of depression are so high that the World Health Organization Global Burden of Disease Study ranked depression as the single most burdensome disease in the world in terms of total disability-adjusted life years among people in the middle years of life (Murray & Lopez, 1996). In epidemiological studies, depression has been found to be associated with poor physical health, in particular, high rates of cardiac problems and higher rates of smoking (e.g., Roy, Mitchell, & Wilhelm, 2001; Sullivan, LaCroix, Russo, & Walker, 2001). There is also a significant economic cost of depression. In a recent analysis of depression in the workplace, Greenberg, Kessler, Nells, Finkelstein, and Berndt (1996) estimated that the annual salary-equivalent costs of depression-related lost productivity in the United States exceeds $33 billion. And because this figure does not take into account the impact of depression on such factors as the performance of coworkers, turnover, and industrial accidents, it is likely to be an underestimate of the overall costs of depression in the workplace.

Perhaps not surprisingly, given these findings concerning the impact of depression on health and workplace productivity, there is now mounting evidence that depression adversely affects the quality of interpersonal relationships, in particular, relationships with spouses and children. Not only is the rate of divorce higher among depressed than among nondepressed individuals (e.g., Wade & Cairney, 2000), but the children of depressed parents have themselves been found to be at elevated risk for psychopathology (see Gotlib & Goodman, 1999, for a review of this literature).

Depression is a highly recurrent disorder. Over 75% of depressed patients have more than one depressive episode (Keller & Boland, 1998), often developing a relapse of depression within 2 years of recovery from a depressive episode. This high recurrence rate in depression suggests that there are specific factors that serve to increase people's risk for developing repeated episodes of this disorder. In this context, therefore, in trying to understand mechanisms that increase risk for depression, investigators have examined biological and genetic factors and psychological and environmental characteristics that may lead individuals to experience depressive episodes.

The enormous costs of depression, combined with the recent documentation of increasing rates of depressive disorders, have led to an exponential increase in research over the past decade examining factors that are involved in the onset, course, and maintenance of depression, and addressing the effectiveness of psychological and biological treatments for depression. This research has resulted in significant advances in our understanding of virtually all aspects of this debilitating disorder. Unfortunately, there is not a single source to which scientists and other interested readers can turn to learn about recent important developments in different areas of depression research. Consequently, we decided to assemble this handbook, with each chapter written by leading scientists in the field.

We have organized this book into four broad parts. The authors of the chapters in the first part discuss descriptive and definitional aspects of depression, including epidemiology, course and outcome, assessment, personality, methodological issues in the study of depression, and the relation between unipolar and bipolar depression. The second part contains chapters dealing with vulnerability, risk, and models of depression. Three chapters in this part describe advances in the genetics, the biology, and the neurobiology of depression. The four other chapters in this part discuss developments in our understanding of cognitive and interpersonal aspects of depression, and the importance of stress and of early adverse experiences. The third part of this handbook is devoted to issues involving the prevention and treatment of depression. Here the authors describe recent developments in the prevention of major depression and advances in pharmacotherapy, cognitive-behavioral therapy, interpersonal psychotherapy, and marital and family therapy for depression. This part also includes an important chapter discussing innovations in the treatment of depression in children and adolescents. The final part of the volume includes chapters describing advances in our understanding of depression as it occurs in specific populations. These chapters discuss depression in different cultures; gender differences in depression; depression in children, adolescents, and the elderly; and the relation between depression and suicide. All of the authors in this handbook were asked to conclude their chapters with a section on future directions, in order that the reader would have a sense not only of the advances that have been made in each field so far, but also of the important issues that are likely to take center stage in the years to come.

We selected these specific areas of research for inclusion in this handbook because they are the major areas of depression research in which significant advances have been made over the past decade in increasing our understanding of the nature of this disorder. These areas cover descriptive aspects of depression, mechanisms of risk for this disorder, prevention and treatment of depression, and the nature of depression in various specific populations. To set the stage for the chapters in this handbook, in the sections below we briefly discuss topics in each these four areas.

DESCRIPTIVE ASPECTS OF DEPRESSION

Epidemiology of Depression

In the past decade we have seen dramatic increases in the rates of depression reported in the general population. In the United States, the most recent epidemiological survey of adults between the ages of 15 and 54, using the Composite International Diagnostic Interview (CIDI; Robins et al., 1988), reported a prevalence of 4.9% for current major depression and 17% for lifetime major depression (Kessler et al., 1994). Earlier surveys using the Diagnostic Interview Schedule (DIS; Robins, Helzer, Croughan, Williams, & Spitzer, 1981) had reported substantially lower rates. Experts have attributed these substantial prevalence inconsistencies to methodological differences between these two interviews. In fact, the CIDI was developed, in part, to include additional initial probes designed to reduce denial of symptoms (Blazer, Kessler, McGonagle, & Swartz, 1994). To some extent, however, the rates may also reflect a trend that was first reported in the late 1980s and later confirmed in international epidemiological studies: an increase in rates of depression among young people (e.g., Weissman, Bland, Joyce, & Newman, 1993). Although some investigators have attributed these secular changes to methodological issues such as an increased willingness to report depressive symptoms, it does appear that young people are in fact now experiencing higher rates of depression than was the case in previous decades.

Findings from investigations examining secular increases in depression and birth cohort shifts are consistent with a further development: the recognition that depression is a disorder of young onset. Improvements in diagnostic evaluations of children and increased longitudinal research on community populations of youth are among the methodological contributions that have raised awareness of the strikingly high rates of major depression among adolescents, and of the likelihood that it will recur in adulthood (e.g., Weissman, Wolk, Goldstein, et al., 1999; Weissman, Wolk, Wickramaratne, et al., 1999).

These epidemiological trends have a number of implications, many of which are discussed in various chapters in this volume. Increased recognition of the high prevalence of depression goes hand in hand with a growing appreciation of its enormously debilitating public health burden and its impact on individuals and families. The magnitude of the problem in personal and social costs has stimulated further research to understand, and eventually improve treatment or prevention of, depression. The greater recognition of the costs and burdens of mood disorders has led to more effective and more widely disseminated treatments, and to an exponential increase in basic research in depression.

At the same time that recent epidemiological research has clarified the magnitude of the problem, it has also raised awareness of *comorbidity*, a no-longer-hidden "secret" that has been variously viewed as a reflection of the inadequacy of contemporary diagnostic schemes, as a troublesome obstacle to the elucidation of etiological factors, as an intriguing developmental and conceptual problem to unravel, as a challenge to effective treatment, or as all of the above. In the past decade, diagnostic comorbidity of depression with Axis I conditions has been shown to be present in half of adult cases (e.g., Blazer et al., 1994) and in the great majority of cases of child and adolescent depression (e.g., Angold, Costello, & Erkanli, 1999). The association of depression and Axis II phenomena appears to be even higher (e.g., Shea, Widiger, & Klein, 1992). Clearly, therefore, the phenomenon of comorbidity must be dealt with in all research contexts, and is discussed throughout this volume.

Diagnosis and Assessment of Depression

The past decade has also witnessed the extensive development of assessment tools for depression and refinements in diagnostic criteria for depressive disorders, as well as wide dissemination of DSM-IV criteria and categories. Diagnosed "clinical" depression has become the "gold standard" for defining populations for study, in preference to samples selected by self-reported symptoms and high scores on questionnaire measures. Despite the advantages of clinical diagnosis, however, it also has its drawbacks, including the reification of the construct of "depression" as an entity that may be treated like diseases that people are believed to have or not have. Similarly, the use in research of diagnoses of common constructs like major depressive episode may unwittingly obscure the enormous heterogeneity of depression, likely oversimplifying the true complexity of our research tasks. Overreliance on diagnostic benchmarks may also greatly distort perceptions of the effectiveness of treatments to the extent that they detract from appreciation of the importance of subsyndromal symptoms, a point to which we return below.

Alternative strategies for conceptualizing depression phenomena have begun to emerge, including a focus on broadband concepts such as "internalizing" disorders, on underlying traits and personality styles, on constructs such as positive and negative affectivity, or even on individual symptoms. Research focused on elucidating the spectrum of mood disorder phenomena and the functional relationships among relevant constructs has expanded considerably in recent years, as discussed by Klein, Durbin, Shankman, and Santiago (Chapter 5, this volume). Furthermore, it is important not to forget the task of subdividing, or subtyping, different phenomenological or etiological forms of depression. It is also vitally important not to bring premature closure to the question of developmental issues of symptom expression and assessment in depression and bipolar disorders in children.

It is worth noting a recent trend in depression research to draw attention to the importance of "subsyndromal" symptoms. Investigators studying adults and children have commented on the fundamentally arbitrary line between "having" a diagnosis and falling short of meeting criteria (e.g., Angold et al., 1999; Gotlib, Lewinsohn, & Seeley, 1995). Several chapters in this volume discuss the continuity between milder and more severe levels of symptoms in terms of impairment of current functioning and prediction of future dysfunction.

Course of Depression

Over the past decade we have witnessed a significant shift from viewing and treating depression as entailing one or two episodes to recognizing that depression is a often a chronic or recurrent disorder. Striking a parallel to how bipolar disorder is conceptualized, unipolar depression is increasingly viewed for most people as a disorder of early onset that is potentially lifelong. It is now recognized that the probability of recurrence is high, and that most adults will experience multiple episodes (e.g., Judd, 1997). There is much speculation, and some empirical evidence, that the median time to recurrence decreases with subsequent episodes in clinical samples (e.g., Post, 1992; Solomon et al., 2000). Moreover, studies of the natural history of the disorder in treated populations reveal that even after individuals "recover" from an episode of major depression, they typically continue to exhibit both symptoms and psychosocial impairment (e.g., Judd et al., 1998, 2000).

It is worth reiterating here the recent focus on the early onset of most depression. Only a few decades ago depression was often seen in middle-aged samples, and was frequently viewed as a disorder with adult onset. Recently, however, stimulated both by improved diagnoses of children and inclusion of adolescents in epidemiological samples, data have clearly supported what depressed adults have often claimed: first depressive experiences frequently occur in adolescence (e.g., Burke, Burke, Reigler, & Rae, 1990). Because of the particular impact of depression on attainment of important life transitions during adolescence and early adulthood, this high-risk period calls for preventive interventions as well as treatments tailored to and disseminated among youth populations.

Unipolar versus Bipolar Depression

Although the distinction between unipolar and bipolar depression emerged in the 1970s, there has been increasing interest in the similarities and differences between these two disorders. Recent research has examined questions such as: "Do different processes trigger manic and depressive episodes?" "How are bipolar I and II disorders distinct in their etiology, and how might they be related to unipolar depression?" "What are the best treatments for bipolar depression?" In the past, psychologists have contributed relatively little to understanding and treating bipolar disorder, but this situation is changing rapidly. Psychologists have contributed to the development of psychotherapies for bipolar disorder to supplement pharmacotherapy; to the understanding of cognitive, social, and stress factors that affect the course of bipolar disorder; and to the application of neuroscience techniques and paradigms to gain a better understanding of the etiological mechanisms of this disorder. Although the volume contains only one chapter that explicitly addresses bipolar depression (Johnson & Kizer, Chapter 6), many of the other chapters include some discussion of bipolar disorder. Indeed, several of the authors in this book have contributed to the bipolar literature, in terms of methods, theoretical paradigms, treatments, and understanding of developmental features of mood disorders.

Methodological Advances in Depression Research

As we will document in more detail below, the past decade has witnessed key advances in methods and designs of studies in the area of mood disorders. There have been significant advances in methods of brain imaging that have sparked major developments in neuroscience in general and in psychopathology more specifically. Other developing methodologies in genetic analysis, cellular processes involved in neurotransmitters and neurohormones, and other biological processes—based on both human and animal research, and on research with both clinical and nonclinical samples—have enhanced opportunities for further understanding of mood disorders and the fuller integration of biological and psychosocial variables. There have also been new developments in tools for assessing information processing, cognition, and infant and young child development, and in methods for defining key variables in depression and testing hypotheses about mechanisms of transmission of risk for this disorder.

With respect to research designs, there has been increasing emphasis on, and financial support for, longitudinal investigations in the area of depression. These prospective studies permit analyses of the course of mood disorder in both adults and children, of assessments of emerging patterns of adjustment in children at risk due to parental mood disorder, and of the depression-related sequelae of early exposure to both chronic and episodic stressors. Indeed, it is to some extent the case that investigators in the area of adult depression have increasingly become interested in the childhood origins of depressive vulnerability; consequently, the longitudinal study of depression in children and adolescents has expanded considerably. The past decade has also witnessed increased use of epidemiological methods with large and representative samples to test important hypotheses about mood disorders. For example, recognizing the limitations and possible distortions of conclusions based entirely on clinical samples of depressed people, the past overreliance on clinical populations has now been complemented by studies of appropriate nonclinical samples.

These changes and developments in tools and research designs permit growth in knowledge, but at the same time, they involve increased "costs" in terms of complexity—multiple variables operating at several levels of biological and psychosocial functioning, with reciprocal and dynamic effects over time. There are new challenges to the task of designing appropriate studies to test ever-elaborated hypotheses, of implementing studies capable of collecting valid data at many levels of analysis, and of rendering meaningful and appropriate conclusions about complex variables and their associations with hypothesized outcomes.

VULNERABILITY, RISK, AND MODELS OF DEPRESSION

Genetic Research in Mood Disorders

As the new millennium ushered in the fruits of the Human Genome Project, psychopathologists moved closer to achieving a long-standing goal of establishing the genetic basis for major mental illness. It had long been anticipated that bipolar disorder might be the first to yield a comprehensive understanding of the genetic basis of the severe and cyclic mood shifts defined as bipolar I disorder. Now, however, because of the heterogeneity and apparent multiple causal pathways of unipolar depression, including psychological and social precursors, it has become clear to genetic researchers and epidemiologists that this disorder is unlikely to be a good candidate in searching for a single (or a few) major genetic locus. Nevertheless, the enormous recent interest in genetic factors in psychopathology has contributed to significant advances in our appreciation that unipolar depression does have a significant genetic aspect, estimated to be in the range of 20–45%, as noted by Wallace, Schneider, and McGuffin (Chapter 7, this volume).

Much of the work advancing knowledge of the genetics of unipolar depression has been based on behavioral genetics methods of biometric modeling in populations of family members. In particular, there have been significant contributions stemming from studies of large populations of twins or other relatives. Twin studies in both community and clinical populations have demonstrated that genetic and nonshared environmental factors each contribute to the risk for unipolar depression (e.g., Kendler, Neale, Kessler, Heath, & Eaves, 1993; Lyons et al., 1998; McGuffin, Katz, Watson, & Rutherford, 1996). These studies have calculated heritability estimates, but have not identified gene loci or modes of transmission of depression. Moreover, the question of whether some forms of depression—such as early-onset or more severe or melancholic depressions—have a stronger genetic component than do other forms has not yet been answered definitively, largely because of the inconsistent findings of these studies. Of course, answering this question will be facilitated by greater diagnostic precision and reliability of identifying possible subtypes of depression.

It is clear that individuals do not inherit a "disease" of depression; instead, they appear to inherit a susceptibility, or a vulnerability, to develop depression. There have been intriguing findings in recent years that suggest what the nature of this susceptibility might be, such as a tendency to experience (or report or cause or react to) stressful life events (e.g., Silberg et al., 1999; Thapar, Harold, & McGuffin, 1998) or to experience lower social support (Henderson, 1998). And, of course, depression susceptibility may also be related to traits, temperaments, or dispositions such as neuroticism (negative affectivity) that are themselves heritable.

The development of new molecular techniques for analyses of genetic linkage has provided the impetus for studies of genes with small effects (rather than major gene effects). Because of the nature of unipolar depression, such methods may prove fruitful in the years to come. Such studies would be advanced by additional knowledge of potential mechanisms of depression that provide molecular "candidates" to facilitate the search for relevant genes.

Developments in the Biology and Neuroscience of Depression

Since the time of Hippocrates, scientists have contemplated the role of biological processes in the onset and maintenance of depression. Over the past 50 years, a number of theories have been formulated that have implicated various forms of biological dysfunction in explaining the etiology and course of depression. Interestingly, many of these theories grew out of observations that patients who either suffered from diseases involving deficiencies in particular neurotransmitters (e.g., hyperthyroidism) or who were receiving medications that depleted specific neurotransmitters (e.g., reserpine for the treatment of hypertension) often exhibited abnormalities in their mood (Golden & Janowsky, 1990). These observations led, for example, to catecholamine theories of depression (e.g., Schildkraut, 1965), which implicated a deficiency in norepinephrine, or in its major metabolite, 3-methoxy-4-hydroxyphenylglycol (MHPG), in the onset of depression. Investigators have now demonstrated not only that depressed individuals are characterized by relatively low levels of norepinephrine (e.g., Schatzberg et al., 1989), but further, that pharmacologic agents that act to increase levels of norepinephrine elevate the mood of depressed patients (see Potter, Grossman, & Rudorfer, 1993). Strikingly similar patterns of findings have also been demonstrated for serotonin (Malone & Mann, 1993) and dopamine (Muscat, Sampson, & Wilner, 1990).

Whereas these approaches to understanding the biology of depression have focused on dysfunctions in neurotransmitter production and uptake, a number of investigators have examined other biological abnormalities that characterize depressed individuals. Considerable attention, for example, has been paid to disturbances in sleep (e.g., Nofzinger, Buysse, Reynolds, & Kupfer, 1993), with a particular focus on REM sleep dysfunctions (e.g., Kupfer, Ehlers, Frank, Grochocinski, & McEachran, 1991). Indeed, the results of recent studies in this area suggest that sleep disturbances may not only be a symptom of depression, but more important, may be related to relapse of this disorder (e.g., Buysse et al., 1996). New developments in the role played by biological factors in the onset, maintenance, and relapse of depression are reviewed in this volume in Chapter 8 by Thase, Jindal, and Howland, with an important focus on the influence of both gender and age in moderating the relation between biological functioning and depression.

Other investigators have examined waking EEG rhythms in depression, and have found consistent evidence of a hemispheric asymmetry in the alpha power of the frontal lobes. Spurred in large part by Davidson's pioneering work (e.g., Davidson, 1998), scientists have documented that depressed individuals are characterized by relatively lower left than right hemispheric activation (e.g., Debener et al., 2000), and, moreover, that this hemispheric asymmetry continues to differentiate depressed individuals from never-depressed controls even following recovery from a depressive episode (e.g., Gotlib, Ranganath, & Rosenfeld, 1998). Davidson (1998) has argued that this asymmetry reflects a deficit in the approach-related motivational system of depression-vulnerable individuals, a position supported by recent evidence of lowered levels of self-reported responses in the behavioral activation system of depressed persons (e.g., Kasch, Rottenberg, Arnow, & Gotlib, 2001).

This focus on the patterns of brain activation that characterize depressed individuals is particularly timely given recent advances in brain imaging technology. Using magnetic resonance imaging to measures aspects of the brain and neural functioning, investigators have examined both structural and functional correlates of depression. From a structural perspective, the results of these studies indicate that depressed individuals may have relatively small volumes of the caudate nucleus, the prefrontal cortex, and the hippocampus (e.g., Coffey et al., 1993; Drevets et al., 1997; Krishnan et al., 1992). More recently, investigators have examined the patterns of brain activation of depressed individuals in response to emotional stimuli. Interestingly, findings from these studies implicate the prefrontal cortex, the amygdala, and the anterior cingulate cortex as playing a role in the emotional dyregulation that characterizes depressed individuals. As Davidson, Pizzagalli, and Nitschke nicely describe in Chapter 9 in this volume, these studies form the foundation of the emerging field of affective neuroscience. This is an especially exciting time to be conducting research examining brain functioning in different forms of psychopathology. In particular, we believe that recent attempts to integrate and understand the interaction of biological and psychological aspects of depressive functioning will yield information that will provide the direction for more comprehensive studies over the next decade (e.g., Benson et al., 2000).

Cognitive and Interpersonal Models of Depression

Psychological models of depression have focused largely on the nature of cognitive and interpersonal functioning in depressed individuals. Much of the early work in these areas was designed to elucidate the nature of the cognitive and interpersonal dysfunctions that characterize depressed individuals. For example, the development of Beck's (1967, 1976) cognitive theory of depression, and of Abramson, Seligman, and Teasdale's (1978) attributional formulation of depression, provided the impetus for an enormous number of studies demonstrating that depressed persons are indeed characterized by dysfunctional attitudes and attributions and by specific distortions in their thought processes.

These early studies were important in delineating the specific cognitive deficits and biases that distinguish depressed persons from their nondepressed counterparts. They were limited, however, both by their reliance on self-report measures of cognitive functioning and by their predominant use of cross-sectional designs. More recent studies of the relation of cognitive dysfunction and depression have addressed both of these shortcomings. Investigators now are increasingly using information-processing methodologies, initially developed by experimental cognitive psychologists, to examine the cognitive functioning of depressed individuals (e.g., Gotlib & Neubauer, 2000). Moreover, these methodologies are being utilized in studies that include a sample of remitted depressed persons and in longitudinal studies of individuals at high risk for developing a depressive episode (e.g., Alloy & Abramson, 1999). These recent studies have considerable promise for illuminating the nature of the association between cognitive dysfunction and depression.

We have known for some time now that depression is also associated with significant impairment in interpersonal functioning. Considerable research has painted a bleak picture of the quality of the marriages of depressed persons. There is evidence of higher rates of psychopathology in the spouses of depressed persons (see Mathews & Reus, 2001); not surprisingly, perhaps, the interactions of couples with a depressed spouse have been found to be characterized by anger, hostility, and high levels of general negative affect (Basco, Prager, Pita, Tamir, & Stephens, 1992; Ruscher & Gotlib, 1988). Finally, the children of depressed parents, exposed to parental psychopathology and high levels of environmental stress and marital dissatisfaction, have themselves been found to develop episodes of depression and anxiety at rates significantly higher than those of matched controls.

Against this backdrop, recent work examining interpersonal aspects of depression has focused more explicitly on the role of interpersonal functioning in depressive disorders. As is the case with research examining cognitive functioning and depression, investigators have begun to extend previous work in the area of interpersonal functioning by designing and conducting longitudinal prospective studies of interpersonal dysfunction and depression. These investigations are beginning to document the possibility that impairments in social skills predict the development of depressive symptoms when individuals encounter stressful life events (e.g., Segrin & Flora, 2000). Similar prospective studies are now being reported indicating that specific interpersonal characteristics, such as shyness or dependency, may also predispose individuals to experience depression (e.g., Joiner, 1997; Mazure, Bruce, Maciejewski, & Jacobs, 2000). Finally, researchers are now documenting that the experience of depression can lead to subsequent difficulties in interpersonal functioning (e.g., Gotlib, Lewinsohn, & Seeley, 1998).

Early Adversity and the Childhood Origins of Depression

The search for early origins of depression has a long history. Almost a century ago, Freud theorized that the loss of a parent early in life predisposed an individual to experience depression later in adulthood. Since Freud's formulation, other theorists have implicated exposure to prenatal stress, inadequate parenting, and early abuse or neglect as risk factors for the subsequent development of depression. Until recently, there has been relatively little empirical research conducted to test these theories. Now, however, with advances in neurobiology and experimental research designs, studies using rats, monkeys, and humans are being carried out to explore early potential precursors of depression.

These recent studies are characterized by a focus on the mechanisms through which various early experiences might predispose individuals to develop depression later in their lives, as adolescents or adults, and often, by the adoption of a developmental perspective in understanding these mechanisms of risk. Thus, there are now investigations of behavioral and biological factors occurring during pregnancy, as well as during infancy and early childhood, that might serve to increase an individual's risk for subsequent depression. These studies include examinations of the impact on the offspring of stress in pregnant animals, with an attendant focus on levels of cortisol and corticotropin-releasing factor as possible mechanisms of this effect (e.g., Glover, Teixeira, Gitau, & Fisk, 1998; Schneider, Roughton, Koehler, & Lubach, 1999), as well as explorations of factors occurring after birth that might increase the risk for depression, such as neglectful or harsh parenting, abuse, and early loss or parental separation (see Goodman & Gotlib, 1999, for a detailed review of these factors).

It is becoming increasingly clear that considerable progress can be made in this area by integrating findings from animal studies with results from investigations using human participants. In Chapter 10 in this volume, Goodman takes an important step in this direction by describing biological and psychological mechanisms through which early adverse experience may place individuals at increased risk for subsequent depression.

Stress and the Social Environment of Depressed Persons

For decades now, a considerable number of theorists have attributed the onset of unipolar depression to difficulties in people's social environments. It seemed obvious to many that people become depressed in response to stress and life difficulties. Indeed, early investigations of the social environments of depressed persons simply asked depressed participants to evaluate their levels of stress and rate their satisfaction with their interpersonal relationships. Not surprisingly, given what we have learned about the reporting styles of depressed persons, substantial correlations were found in these studies among depression, stress, and the experience of difficult social environments (see Mazure, 1998, for a review of this literature).

As research in this area developed, theoretical models of the relation between depression and the social environment became more sophisticated. Building on Zubin and Spring's (1977) formulation of the nature of the interaction of diatheses and stressor in the development of schizophrenia, investigators began to integrate stress and environmental factors with constitutional and other individual-difference variables in the generation of diathesis–stress models of depression (e.g., Monroe & Simons, 1991). These diathesis–stress models of depression served to move the field forward in large part by broadening the scope of cognitive models of depression to include a consideration of the role of environmental stressors in the onset of depressive episodes.

Even with these advances in the conceptualization of stress and the social environment, there were significant limitations to the research in this area. For example, assessments of both stress and the nature of the social environment most often continued to rely on the self-reports of depressed individuals. Similarly, depression was typically assessed as a homogeneous entity, with little regard for the specific symptoms or subtypes of depression that may be most strongly affected by stress. Finally, conceptualizations of the association between depression and elevated stress and/or a difficult social environment typically emphasized a unidirectional relationship, in which depression was viewed as arising from high stress or adverse environmental conditions.

More recent theoretical and empirical work in this area has both addressed these limitations and offered more sophisticated conceptualizations of stress, the social environment, depression, and the nature of their interactions. As Monroe and Hadjiyannakis clearly detail in Chapter 13 in this volume, self-report measures of stress are slowly being replaced by less subjective interview-based assessments of life events and the social environment. In addition, recent formulations of stress and depression are recognizing their bidirectional influences (e.g., Hammen, 1991), and are examining the ways in which the experience of depression can generate high levels of stress and/or difficulties in the individual's social environment. These advances, combined with more refined assessments and classifications of the constructs of depression and stress, and of aspects of the social environment, promise to further our understanding of the social context of depression.

PREVENTION AND TREATMENT OF DEPRESSION

Psychopharmacology of Depression

One of the biggest stories in the treatment of depression in recent years is, of course, the widening stream of new medications coming to market. Based on novel chemical structures compared to the original tricyclic antidepressants, these new medications are increasingly targeted to have effects on a specific (or on several specific) neurotransmitter(s). For example, the selective serotonin reuptake inhibitors (SSRIs) transformed the practice of prescribing medication, providing nonpsychiatrists with simple dosing procedures and treatments that were relatively free of side effects. Ease of use—not superior effects—contributed to the widespread prescribing of these medications for a variety of emotional and behavioral disorders. The availability and medical acceptance of these medications may have also played a role in making "depression" better recognized, whatever the downside of such developments might be.

As depression became increasingly viewed as a recurrent or chronic disorder, it became necessary to investigate the effectiveness of long-term treatment with medications, resulting in the development of protocols for continuing and maintaining pharmacotherapy after resolution of the acute depressive symptoms. Only in recent years have practice guidelines been disseminated for such applications. At the same time, lack of evidence that new treatments improved outcomes compared to earlier antidepressants has meant that many individuals do not respond—or respond only temporarily—to the new antidepressants. "Treatment-resistant" patients are currently commonly treated with combinations of medications, with guidelines emerging to assist in making treatment choices.

For bipolar patients, the dominance of lithium monotherapy has given way in the past decade or so as a consequence of greater availability of alternative mood stabilizers or combinations of medications. As is the case with unipolar disorder, bipolar disorder is either treated relatively easily, or not at all. Indeed, many severely ill individuals seemingly respond incompletely or unstably to pharmacotherapy, a challenge that continues to stimulate research to identify the mechanisms that contribute to the causes and features of mood disorders that might help to identify or refine treatment options.

Psychotherapies for Depression

The relatively successful performances of interpersonal psychotherapy (IPT) and cognitive-behavioral therapy (CBT) in the NIMH Treatment of Depression Collaborative Study in 1989 (Elkin et al., 1989) provided the impetus for new developments in these therapies in the 1990s. These brief therapies for major depressive episodes have continued to be evaluated in clinical trials, and to expand their range of application to other clinical problems and populations, including dysthymic disorder and persons with personality disorders, older (and younger) patients, and many others. Although these therapies were spurred in part by theoretical models that emphasize cognitive vulnerability or interpersonal stressors, the increasing dissemination and use of these therapies may be attributed to several other factors, including growing attention by managed care providers, by prospective patients learning of their merits in the media and via the Internet, and by treatment providers and patients seeking effective treatments for the life problems and personal difficulties that are not changed by medication. Clinical use of the treatments has been paralleled by considerable new research activity with increasingly sophisticated designs and methods.

In addition to these two dominant short-term treatments, there has been expansion and testing of other modalities for their relevance to depression. Behavioral marital therapy and other behavioral interventions have built on the observation that marital and relationship difficulties are common precipitants of depression—and that depression may erode healthy and pleasurable couple and family functioning (see Beach and Jones, Chapter 18, this volume).

Treatments for Depressed Children

Effective treatments for youngsters have lagged behind the recognition that children and adolescents could experience depression. Over the past decade, however, great advances have been made in developing and demonstrating the effectiveness of treatments for children and adolescents. Psychotherapies that had been proven effective with adults were reworked and applied to children and adolescents, with relatively good outcomes. For instance, behavioral and cognitive-behavioral treatments have now been shown to be effective in reducing depressive symptoms in children and adolescents (e.g., Brent et al., 1997; reviews by Birmaher et al., 1996; Hammen, Rudolph, Weisz, Rao, & Burge, 1999). Weissman and colleagues have also expanded interpersonal psychotherapy to adolescents, and have reported good outcomes with this treatment (Mufson, Weissman, Moreau, & Garfinkel, 1999).

As pointed out in Kaslow, McClure, and Connell in Chapter 19, this volume, investigators have now formulated novel treatments for young children, developmentally appropriate interventions for children of depressed mothers, and treatments that involve family processes. An additional important development is the translation of "lab-based" treatments that work well in university settings into procedures that can be applied in community clinics and agencies that typically deal with more difficult, complex, and multiproblem cases (e.g., Weisz, Thurber, Sweeney, Proffitt, & LeGagnoux, 1997).

At the same time that there has been a proliferation of psychotherapies adapted for children and adolescents, research on the effectiveness of pharmacotherapy has demonstrated fairly convincingly that tricyclic medications do not work well in reducing depression in youngsters (e.g., review in Birmaher, 1996). In contrast, the 1990s have seen the increased use and study of SSRIs and atypical antidepressant medications for children and adolescents, with growing evidence of their effectiveness. For instance, Emslie et al. (1997) have demonstrated that fluoxetine (Prozac) reduces depressive symptoms in youngsters with major depressive episodes; other investigators have also demonstrated some success with different nontricyclic agents, as reviewed by Kaslow et al. (Chapter 19, this volume). Considerable effort is underway to test the suitability and safety of such medications for youth.

Prevention of Depression

The sheer magnitude of the problem of depression—and its typical emergence in adolescence and among women of childbearing ages—would seem to demand substantial efforts to prevent the development of initial depression or its recurrence. Identification of risk factors (e.g., parental depression, cognitive vulnerability) has also progressed to the point of attempting experimental intervention to prevent depression outcomes. Nevertheless, the prevention field has developed relatively slowly compared to the treatment field, but evidence has been mounting for the success of efforts that may have significant long-range effects.

In fact, evidence of preventive effects appears to be stronger for children and adolescents than it is for adults, as reviewed by Muñoz, Le, Clarke, and Jaycox (Chapter 14, this volume; see also Kaslow et al., Chapter 19, this volume). In addition, novel programs for targeted groups under high-risk conditions are being tested, and this field offers much promise for further development.

DEPRESSION IN SPECIFIC POPULATIONS

Overall, there has been increasing interest in the past decade in understanding what may be the unique experiences of depression in individuals of different ages, gender, and cultures. As the field of mood disorders research has expanded, so too has research broadened to include various groups that had been either excluded from typical studies or whose characteristics may have been lost in broad generalizations about depression in general.

Gender and Depression

It has been long recognized, of course, that women's rates of depression exceed those of men by about 2:1. In recent years this pattern has been found to apply in nearly every culture studied with systematic diagnostic evaluation (Weissman & Olfson, 1995). It has also become established relatively recently that the gender difference, at least in industrialized nations, appears to emerge in early adolescence.

Research on this topic over the past decade has generally taken one of two forms: an effort to account for gender differences and exploration of the implications of these patterns. Developments in improved methods of measuring hormones, and the interactions among gonadal hormones and neuroregulatory processes, have contributed to increased study of female hormones and their possible association with depression, as reviewed in this volume by Nolen-Hoeksema (Chapter 21). At the same time, considerable work has attempted to explore the unique psychological and social experiences of women that may create a risk for depression onset or for its severity and likelihood of recurrence. Increasingly, models of the etiology of depression have been responsive to the need to account for gender differences.

There have also been significant advances in the study of gender-related implications of women's depression. Recognizing the enormous toll of depression on family functioning, there has been a vast amount of research on the mother–infant and mother–child relationship decrements that may be a consequence of depression, and on the ways in which such dysfunctional patterns may contribute to the risk of cognitive and social dysfunction in children, potentially portending diagnosable disorders and maladjustment in the offspring (e.g., Cicchetti & Toth, 1998; Goodman & Gotlib, 2002). The focus on women's experiences with depression in their social milieus has also helped to identify interpersonal components of depression (such as marital discord, reassurance seeking, dependency, social conflict) as significant contributors to the onset and course of depressive disorders (e.g., Gotlib & Hammen, 1992). Finally, women's unique vulnerability to severe adversity such as sexual victimization has contributed to the increased interest in the effects of stress exposure and reactivity to stress as components of depressive reactions (e.g., Heim et al., 2000).

Cultural Differences in Depression

Until the last decade, there was surprisingly little research examining depression in different cultures. More recently, however, there has been increasing interest in exploring the unique aspects of disorders in different cultural contexts. Although depression is recognized as a universal human condition, its variations in experience and expression—and indeed, in incidence—have prompted increased research interest in recent years. Both international and domestic studies have attempted to address questions such as whether depression occurs at different rates in different populations that vary by ethnicity or cultural experience, whether its meaning and manifestations are the same or different, and how depression is viewed and treated across cultures.

Cross-cultural research on depression has probably seen more explosive growth to date than has been the case for other disorders. In fact, there are now major cross-national collaborations exploring the epidemiology and course of depression (Weissman et al., 1996; Thornicroft & Sartorius, 1993). Although such studies employed Western-defined diagnostic constructs, it is increasingly becoming recognized that depression has different meanings and manifestations in different cultures. For instance, findings of lower incidence of depression in Asian cultures (e.g., Simon, VonKorff, Picvinelli, Fullerton, & Ormel, 1999) is consistent with Asians viewing less separation of emotional and physical symptoms than do Westerners, resulting in a stronger focus on somatic complaints and a greater stigma being attached to mental disorders.

The increasing diversity of the U.S. culture has, of course, prompted investigators to address the unique aspects of disorders in different groups. In a belated recognition of the perils of overgeneralizing from primarily Caucasian research samples, the National Institutes of Health have mandated inclusion of ethnically and culturally diverse (as well as varied gender and age) study samples in funded research. Such a policy change, in addition to the growing interest in examining cultural variations in mental health and treatment, will undoubtedly affect how we study and understand depression in the years to come.

Depression in Children and Adolescents

Arguably one of the most active areas of research on mood disorders in the past decade, the study of depression in children and adolescence has proliferated almost exponentially. Indeed, there have been important advances in almost every topic in this area: epidemiology, diagnosis, course and continuity, biological and psychosocial models of risk and outcome, and somatic and psychosocial treatment.

As we noted earlier, investigators have now documented the emergence of higher rates of depression among females starting in early adolescence, and have identified adolescence broadly as the typical age of onset of major depression. It has become clear that depression is largely a disorder of young people, with apparently higher rates among teenagers born in recent decades than in earlier eras (Weissman et al., 1993). Although the use of DSM criteria for diagnosis of major depression and dysthymic disorder in children is well established, recent years have witnessed considerable controversy in the application of adult criteria for mania (bipolar disorder) for children, with considerable interest in research that will help to resolve important issues in this area.

During the past decade, longitudinal studies have yielded results confirming the continuity of depression from childhood or adolescence into adulthood (e.g., Reinherz, Giaconia, Hauf, Wasserman, & Paradis, 2000; Lewinsohn, Rohde, Klein, & Seeley, 1999; Weissman, Wolk, Goldstein et al., 1999; Weissman, Wolk, Wickramaratne et al., 1999). Such findings, combined with the observation of typical adolescent onset of depression, add to the impetus for early detection of risk for depression and early intervention or prevention.

Biological and psychosocial models of depression etiology are increasingly applying developmentally appropriate methods and hypotheses to study potential vulnerabilities, rather than simply using downward extensions of adult models. For instance, the effects of stress on the developing brain and the consequences of dysregulation of the hypothalamic–pituitary–adrenal axis as a model of depression are attracting great interest in both preclinical and human studies (e.g., reviewed in Plotsky, Owens, & Nemeroff, 1998).

Depression in Older Adults

Emerging demographic trends in the United States and most industrialized nations make it apparent that study of the psychological disorders of older adults is of compelling interest. It has been noted that ours is an aging society, with individuals over the age of 65 comprising the largest growing segment of the population. Often this group has been omitted or seriously underrepresented in epidemiological studies of psychopathology; when studied, their rates of depression have been seen to be relatively low compared to those of young adults. However, recent research attempting to use methods of assessment and diagnosis appropriate to the mobility and health status of elders has suggested that depression is a significant issue for elders. Moreover, as Powers, Thompson, Futterman, and Gallagher-Thompson point out in Chapter 24 in this volume, there may be phenomenological subtypes of depression that require developmentally sensitive assessment methods (e.g., a "depression syndrome" vs. a "depletion syndrome").

Certainly, increased interest in late-life depression involves a practical issue of recognizing and serving the needs of a large and growing population. In addition, however, this topic also presents important etiological considerations that might help further understand the origins and mechanisms of depressive disorders, as well as their associations with health and medical conditions. Thus, research on the link between depression and neurodegenerative conditions, for instance, is helping to clarify brain processes in mood disorders. At the same time, associations between depression and mortality from strokes and myocardial infarctions (e.g., Frasure-Smith, Lesperance, & Talajic, 2000) may eventually contribute to our understanding of the mechanisms linking mood and physical functioning.

Finally, recognition of depression in older adults has also stimulated applications of psychotherapies and pharmacotherapy in this group. Intriguing applications of treatments to depressed elderly individuals who also have dementia have enormous potential implications for improved care and management of a commonly neglected population (e.g., Teri, Logsdon, Uomoto, & McCurry, 1997).

Suicide

Suicidality is a significant challenge to all who study and treat mood disorders. Suicidal individuals represent a "special population" as well as a special challenge to the questions of causes and interventions in mood disorders. While it has long been known that suicidality varies with culture, gender, and age, and that patterns of association are different for completers and attempters, there have also been new developments in this field in recent years.

It has become increasingly apparent that while suicidal thoughts and motivations are a symptom of the depression syndrome, suicide is by no means invariably associated with this disorder. Depression is estimated to be a factor in about one-third or more of suicides, but other mental disorders such as alcoholism and schizophrenia are alternative pathways to suicide. And although the construct of "hopelessness" appears to cut across diagnostic boundaries, and often emerges as an important predictor of potential suicidal risk, no risk-prediction method has proven to be infallible, especially in predicting imminent risk of suicide. Interestingly, although much of the research on suicidality has focused on the psychological and environmental factors with which it is often associated, there has also been new research on biological predictors or possible mechanisms of suicide. Suicidality appears to have a familial component consistent with a genetic predisposition, possibly associated with defective serotonergic processes (also linked to impulsivity and violence; Mann, Brent, & Arango, 2001).

The demographics of suicidality have also apparently shifted somewhat in recent years, marked particularly by huge increases in deaths among adolescent males (e.g., Fombonne, 1998), and somewhat lessened rates among older males. Overall, however, the observation that more males *commit* suicide and more females *attempt* suicide has remained true.

Finally, in recent years there has also been increased recognition of a distinction between parasuicidal behaviors such as self-mutilation and truly suicidal-intent behaviors. For example, research on Axis II borderline personality disorder has helped clinicians to recognize such distinctions, even though suicidal threats and actions are also common among borderline patients (Dulit, Fyer, Leon, Brodsky, & Frances, 1994).

CONCLUDING REMARKS

It is clear from this overview not only that we have made significant progress in our understanding of depression, but that we are embarking on a number of exciting new directions in the study of affective disorders. Without exception, the contributors to this volume have captured the excitement of this growth. In each chapter, they have conveyed to readers their vision of how research in this field might unfold over the next decade. We hope that the insights and formulations presented in these chapters will stimulate readers to integrate these ideas into their own research and practice in the area of depression, and that they will bring us closer to understanding, treating, preventing, and ultimately eliminating this debilitating disorder.

REFERENCES

Abramson, L. Y., Seligman, M. E. P., & Teasdale, J. D. (1978). Learned helplessness in humans: Critique and reformulation. *Journal of Abnormal Psychology, 87,* 49–74.

Alloy, L. B., & Abramson, L. Y. (1999). The Temple–Wisconsin Cognitive Vulnerability to Depression (CVD) Project: Conceptual background, design, and methods. *Journal of Cognitive Psychotherapy: An International Quarterly, 13,* 227–262.

Angold, A., Costello, J. E., & Erkanli, A. (1999). Comorbidity. *Journal of Child Psychology and Psychiatry and Allied Disciplines, 40*, 57–87.

Basco, M. R., Prager, K. J., Pita, J. M., Tamir, L. M., & Stephens, J. (1992). Communication and intimacy in the marriages of depressed patients. *Journal of Family Psychology, 6*, 184–194.

Beck, A. T. (1967). *Depression: Clinical, experimental, and theoretical aspects.* New York: Harper & Row.

Beck, A. T. (1976). *Cognitive therapy and the emotional disorders.* New York: International Universities Press.

Benson, E. S., Sivers, H., Canli, T., Keane, M., Gotlib, I. H., & Gabrieli, J. D. E. (2000). FMRI of cognitive bias in depression and social phobia. *Society for Neuroscience Abstracts, 26*, 754.1.

Birmaher, B., Ryan, N. D., Williamson, D. E., Brent, D. A., Kaufman, J., Dahl, R. E., Perel, J., & Nelson, B. (1996). Childhood and adolescent depression: A review of the past 10 years: Part 1. *Journal of the American Academy of Child and Adolescent Psychiatry, 35*, 1427–1439.

Blazer, D. G., Kessler, R. C. McGonagle, K. A., & Swartz, M. S. (1994). The prevalence and distribution of major depression in a national community sample: The National Comorbidity Survey. *American Journal of Psychiatry, 151*, 979–986.

Brent, D., Holder, D., Kolko, D., Birmaher, B., Baugher, M., Roth, C., Iyengar, S., & Johnson, B. (1997). A clinical psychotherapy trial for adolescent depression comparing cognitive, family, and supportive therapy. *Archives of General Psychiatry, 54*, 877–885.

Burke, K. C., Burke, J. D., Reigler, D. A., & Rae, D. S. (1990). Age at onset of selected mental disorders in five community populations. *Archives of General Psychiatry, 47*, 511–518.

Buysse, D. J., Reynolds, C. F., III, Hoch, C. C., Houck, P. R., Kupfer, D. J., Mazumdar, S., & Frank, E. (1996). Longitudinal effects of nortriptyline on EEG sleep and the likelihood of recurrence in elderly depressed patients. *Neuropsychopharmacology, 14*, 243–252.

Cicchetti, D., & Toth, S. L. (1998). The development of depression in children and adolescents. *American Psychologist, 53*, 221–241.

Coffey, C. E., Wilkinson, W. E., Weiner, R. D., Parashos, I. A., Djang, W. T., Webb, M. C., Figiel, G. S., & Spritzer, C. E. (1993). Quantitative cerebral anatomy in depression: A controlled magnetic resonance imaging study. *Archives of General Psychiatry, 50*, 7–16.

Davidson, R. J. (1998). Anterior electrophysiological asymmetries, emotion and depression: Conceptual and methololological conundrums. *Psychophysiology, 35*, 607–614.

Debener, S., Beauducel, A., Nessler, D., Brocke, B., Heilemann, H., & Kayser, J. (2000). Is resting anterior EEG alpha asymmetry a trait marker for depression?: Findings for healthy adults and clinically depressed patients. *Neuropsychobiology, 41*, 31–37.

Drevets, W. C., Price, J. L., Simpson, J. R. J., Todd, R. D., Reich, T., Vannier, M., & Raichle, M. E. (1997). Subgenual prefrontal cortex abnormalities in mood disorders. *Nature, 386*, 824–827.

Dulit, R. A., Fyer, M. R., Leon, A. C., Brodsky, B. S., & Frances, A. J. (1994). Clinical correlates of self-mutilation in borderline personality disorder. *American Journal of Psychiatry, 151*, 1305–1311.

Elkin, I., Shea, M. T., Watkins, J. T., Imber, S. D., Sotsky, S. M., Collins, J. F., Glass, D. R., Pilkonis, P. A., Leber, W. R., Docherty, J. P., Fiester, S. J., & Parloff, M. B. (1989). National Institute of Mental Health treatment of depression collaborative research program: General effectiveness of treatments. *Archives of General Psychiatry, 46*, 971–982.

Emslie, G. J., Rush, A. J., Weinberg, W. A., Kowatch, R. A., Hughes, C. W., Carmody, T., & Rintelmann, J. (1997). A double-blind, randomized, placebo-controlled trial of fluoxetine in children and adolescents. with depression. *Archives of General Psychiatry, 54*, 1031–1037.

Fombonne, E. (1998). Interpersonal psychotherapy for adolescent depression. *Child Psychology and Psychiatry Review, 3*, 169–175.

Frasure-Smith, N., Lesperance, F., & Talajic, M. (2000). The prognostic importance of depression, anxiety, anger, and social support following myocardial infarction: Opportunities for improving survival. In P. M. McCabe, N. Schneiderman, T. Field, & A. Wellens (Eds.), *Stress, coping, and cardiovascular disease* (pp. 203–228). Mahwah, NJ: Erlbaum.

Glover, V., Teixeira, J., Gitau, R., & Fisk, N. (1998, April). *Links between antenatal maternal anxiety and the fetus.* Paper presented at the 11th Biennial Conference on Infant Studies, Atlanta, GA.

Golden, R. N., & Janowsky, D. S. (1990). Biological theories of depression. In B. B. Wolman & G. Stricker (Eds.), *Depressive disorders: Facts, theories and treatment methods* (pp. 3–21). New York: Wiley.

Goodman, S. H., & Gotlib, I. H. (1999). Risk for psychopathology in the children of depressed mothers: A developmental model for understanding mechanisms of transmission. *Psychological Review, 106,* 458–490.

Goodman, S. H., & Gotlib, I. H. (Eds.). (2002). *Children of depressed parents: Mechanisms of risk and implications for treatment.* Washington, DC: APA Books.

Gotlib, I. H., & Goodman, S. H. (1999). Children of parents with depression. In W. K. Silverman & T. H. Ollendick (Eds.), *Developmental issues in the clinical treatment of children* (pp. 415–432). Boston: Allyn & Bacon.

Gotlib, I. H., & Hammen, C. L. (1992). *Psychological aspects of depression: Toward a cognitive-interpersonal integration.* Chichester, UK: Wiley.

Gotlib, I. H., Lewinsohn, P. M. & Seeley, J. R. (1995). Symptoms versus a diagnosis of depression: differences in psychosocial functioning. *Journal of Consulting and Clinical Psychology, 63*(1), 90–100.

Gotlib, I. H., Lewinsohn, P. M., & Seeley, J. R. (1998). Consequences of depression during adolescence: Marital status and marital functioning in early adulthood. *Journal of Abnormal Psychology, 107,* 686–690.

Gotlib, I. H., & Neubauer, D. L. (2000). Information-processing approaches to the study of cognitive biases in depression. In S. L. Johnson, A. M. Hayes, T. M. Field, N. Schneiderman, & P. M. McCabe (Eds.), *Stress, coping, and depression* (pp. 117–143). Mahwah, NJ: Erlbaum.

Gotlib, I. H., Ranganath, C., & Rosenfeld, J. P. (1998). Frontal EEG alpha asymmetry, depression, and cognitive functioning. *Cognition and Emotion, 12,* 449–478.

Greenberg, P., Kessler, R., Nells, T., Finkelstein, S. & Berndt, E. R. (1996). Depression in the workplace: An economic perspective. In J. P. Feighner & W. F. Boyer (Eds.), *Selective serotonin reuptake inhibitors: Advances in basic research and clinical practice* (pp. 327–363). New York: Wiley.

Hammen, C. (1991). Generation of stress in the course of unipolar depression. *Journal of Abnormal Psychology, 100,* 555–561.

Hammen, C., Rudolph, K., Weisz, J., Rao, U., & Burge, D. (1999). The context of depression in clinic-referred youth: Neglected areas in treatment. *Journal of the American Academy of Child and Adolescent Psychiatry, 38,* 64–71.

Heim, C., Newport, D. J., Heit, S., Graham, Y. P. Wilcox, M., Bonsall, R., Miller, A. H., & Nemeroff, C. B. (2000). Pituitary–adrenal and autonomic responses to stress in women after sexual and physical abuse in childhood. *Journal of the American Medical Association, 284,* 592–597.

Henderson, A. S. (1998). Social support: Its present significance for psychiatric epidemiology. In B. P. Dohrenwend (Ed.), Adversity, stress, and psychopathology (pp. 390–397). New York: Oxford University Press.

Joiner, T. E., Jr. (1997). Shyness and low social support as interactive diatheses, and loneliness as mediator: Testing an interpersonal–personality view of depression. *Journal of Abnormal Psychology, 106,* 386–394.

Judd, L. L. (1997). The clinical course of unipolar major depressive disorders. *Archives of General Psychiatry, 54,* 989–991.

Judd, L. L., Akiskal, H. S., Maser, J. D., Zeller, P. J., Endicott, J., Coryell, W., Paulus, M. P., Kunovac, J. L., Leon, A. C., Mueller, T. I., Rice, J. A., & Keller, M. B. (1998). Major depressive disorder: A prospective study of residual subthreshold depressive symptoms as predictor of rapid relapse. *Journal of Affective Disorders, 50,* 97–108.

Judd, L. L., Paulus, M. J., Schettler, P. J., Akiskal, H. S., Endicott, J., Leon, A. C., Maser, J. D., Mueller, T., Solomon, D. A., & Keller, M. B. (2000). Does incomplete recovery from first lifetime major depressive episode herald a chronic course of illness? *American Journal of Psychiatry, 157,* 1501–1504.

Kasch, K. L., Rottenberg, J., Arnow, B. A., & Gotlib, I. H. (2001). *Behavioral activation and inhibition systems and the severity and course of depression.* Manuscript under editorial review.

Keller, M. B., & Boland, R. J. (1998). Implications of failing to achieve successful long-term maintenance treatment of recurrent unipolar major depression. Biological Psychiatry, 44, 348–360.

Kendler, K. S., Neale, M. C., Kessler, R. C., Heath, A. C., & Eaves, L. J. (1993). A longitudinal twin
study of personality and major depression in women. *Archives of General Psychiatry, 50,*
853–862.

Kessler, R. C., McGonagle, K. A., Zhao, S., Nelson, C. B., Hughes, M., Eshleman, S., Wittchen, H.-U.
& Kendler, K. S. (1994). Lifetime and 12-month prevalence of DSM-III-R psychiatric disorders
in the United States: Results from the National Comorbidity Survey. *Archives of General Psychiatry, 51,* 8–19.

Krishnan, K. R. R., McDonald, W. M., Escalona, P. R., Doraiswamy, P. M., Na, C., Husain, M. M.,
Figiel, G. S., Boyko, O. B., Ellinwood, E. H., & Nemeroff, C. B. (1992). Magnetic resonance of
the caudate nuclei in depression. *Archives of General Psychiatry, 49,* 553–557.

Kupfer, D. J., Ehlers, C. L., Frank, E., Grochocinski, V. J., & McEachran, A. B. (1991). EEG sleep
profiles and recurrent depression. *Biological Psychiatry, 30,* 641–655.

Lewinsohn, P. M., Rohde, P., Klein, D. N., & Seeley, J. R. (1999). Natural course of adolescent major
depressive disorder: 1. Continuity into young adulthood. *Journal of the American Academy of
Child and Adolescent Psychiatry, 38,* 56–63.

Lyons, M. J., Eisen, S. A., Goldberg, J., True, W., Lin, N., Meyer, J. M., Toomey, R., Faraone, S. V.,
Merla-Ramos, M., & Tsuang, M. T. (1998). A registry-based twin study of depression in men.
Archives of General Psychiatry, 55, 468–472.

Malone, K., & Mann, J. J. (1993). Serotonin and major depression. In J. J. Mann & D. J. Kupfer
(Eds.), *Biology of depressive disorders: Part A. A systems perspective* (pp. 29–49). New York:
Plenum Press.

Mann, J. J., Brent, D. A., & Arango, V. (2001). The neurobiology and genetics of suicide and attempted suicide: A focus on the serotonergic system. *Neuropsychopharmacology, 24,* 467–477.

Mathews, C. A., & Reus, V. I. (2001). Assortative mating in the affective disorders: A systematic review and meta-analysis. *Comprehensive Psychiatry, 42,* 257–262.

Mazure, C. M. (1998). Life stressors as risk factors in depression. *Clinical Psychology: Science and
Practice, 5,* 291–313.

Mazure, C. M., Bruce, M. L., Maciejewski, P. K., & Jacobs, S. C. (2000). Adverse life events and cognitive-personality characteristics in the prediction of major depression and antidepressant response. *American Journal of Psychiatry, 157,* 896–903.

McGuffin, P., Katz, R., Watkins, S., & Rutherford, J. (1996) A hospital based twin register of heritability of DSM-IV unipolar depression. *Archives of General Psychiatry, 53,* 129–136.

Monroe, S. M., & Simons, A. D. (1991). Diathesis stress in the context of life stress research: Implications for the depressive disorders. *Psychological Bulletin, 110,* 406–425.

Mufson, L., Weissman, M. M., Moreau, D., & Garfinkel, R. (1999). Efficacy of interpersonal psychotherapy for depressed adolescents. *Archives of General Psychiatry, 56,* 573–579.

Murray, C. J. L., & Lopez, A. D. (Eds.). (1996). *The global burden of disease: A comprehensive assessment of mortality and disability from diseases, injuries, and risk factors in 1990 and projected to 2020.* Cambridge, MA: Harvard University Press.

Muscat, R., Sampson, D., & Wilner, P. (1990). Dopaminergic mechanism of imipramine action in an
animal model of depression. *Biological Psychiatry, 28,* 223–230.

Nofzinger, E. A., Buysse, D. J., Reynolds, C. F., III, & Kupfer, D. J. (1993). Sleep disorders related to
another mental disorder (nonsubstance/primary): A DSM-IV literature review. *Journal of Clinical
Psychiatry, 54,* 244–255.

Plotsky, P. M., Owens, M. J., & Nemeroff, C. B. (1998). Psychoneuroendocrinology of depression:
Hypothalamic–pituitary–adrenal axis. *Psychiatric Clinics of North America, 21,* 293–307.

Post, R. (1992). Transduction of psychosocial stress into the neurobiology of recurrent affective disorder. *American Journal of Psychiatry, 149,* 999–1010.

Potter, W. Z., Grossman, F., & Rudorfer, M. V. (1993). Noradrenergic function in depressive disorders. In J. J. Mann & D. J. Kupfer (Eds.), *Biology of depressive disorders: Part A. A systems perspective* (pp. 1–27). New York: Plenum Press.

Reinherz, H. Z., Giaconia, R. M., Hauf, A. M. C., Wasserman, M. S., & Paradis, A. D. (2000). General and specific childhood risk factors for depression and drug disorders by early adulthood. *Journal of the American Academy of Child and Adolescent Psychiatry, 39,* 223–231.

Robins, L. N., Helzer, J. E., Croughan, J., Williams, J. B. W., & Spitzer, R. L. (1981). *NIMH Diagnostic Interview Schedule: Version III.* Rockville, MD: National Institute of Mental Health.

Robins, L. N., Wing, J., Wittchen, H. U., Helzer, J. E., Babor, T. F., Burke, J., Farmer, A., Jablenski, A., Pickens, R., & Regier, D. A. (1988). The Composite International Diagnostic Interview. An epidemiologic instrument suitable for use in conjunction with different diagnostic systems and in different cultures. *Archives of General Psychiatry, 45,* 1069–1077.

Roy, K., Mitchell, P., & Wilhelm, K. (2001). Depression and smoking: Examining correlates in a subset of depressed patients. *Australian and New Zealand Journal of Psychiatry, 35,* 329–335.

Ruscher, S. M., & Gotlib, I. H. (1988). Marital interaction patterns of couples with and without a depressed partner. *Behavior Therapy, 19,* 455–470.

Schatzberg, A. F., Samson, J. A., Bloomingdale, K. L., Orsulak, P. J., Gerson, B., Kizuka, P. P. Cole, J. O., & Schildkraut, J. J. (1989). Toward a biochemical classification of depressive disorders. *Archives of General Psychiatry, 46,* 260–268.

Schildkraut, J. J. (1965). The catecholamine hypothesis of affective disorder: A review of supporting evidence. *American Journal of Psychiatry, 122,* 509–522.

Schneider, M. L., Roughton, E. C., Koehler, A. J., & Lubach, G. R. (1999). Growth and development following prenatal stress exposure in primates: An examination of ontogenetic vulnerability. *Child Development, 70,* 263–274.

Segrin, C., & Flora, J. (2000). Poor social skills are a vulnerability factor in the development of psychosocial problems. *Human Communication Research, 26,* 489–514.

Shea, M. T., Widiger, T. A., & Klein, M. H. (1992). Comorbidity of personality disorders and depression: Implications for treatment. *Journal of Consulting and Clinical Psychology, 60,* 857–868.

Silberg, J., Pickles, A., Rutter, M., Hewitt, J., Simonoff, E., Maes, H., Carbonneau, R, Murrelle, L., Foley, D., & Eaves, L. (1999). The influence of genetic factors and life stress on depression among adolescent girls. *Archives of General Psychiatry, 56,* 225–232.

Simon, G. E., VonKorff, M., Picvinelli, M., Fullerton, C., & Ormel, J. (1999). An international study of the relation between somatic symptoms and depression. *New England Journal of Medicine, 18,* 1329–1335.

Solomon, D. A., Keller, M. B., Leon, A. C., Mueller, T. I., Lavori, P. W., Shea, M. T., Coryell, W., Warshaw, M., Turvey, C., Maser, J. D., & Endicott, J. (2000). Multiple recurrences of major depressive disorder. *American Journal of Psychiatry, 157,* 229–233.

Sullivan, M. D., LaCroix, A. Z., Russo, J. E., & Walker, E. A. (2001). Depression and self-reported physical health in patients with coronary disease: Mediating and moderating factors. *Psychosomatic Medicine, 63,* 248–256.

Teri, L., Logsdon, R. G., Uomoto, J., & McCurry, S. M. (1997). Behavioral treatment of depression in dementia patients: A controlled clinical trial. *Journals of Gerontology, 52B,* 159166.

Thapar, A., Harold, G., & McGuffin, P. (1998). "Life events and depressive symptoms in childhood—shared genes or shared adversity?: A research note. *Journal of Child Psychology and Psychiatry, 39,* 1153–1158.

Thornicroft, G., & Sartorius, N. (1993). The course and outcome of depression in different cultures: 10-year follow-up of the WHO collaborative study on the assessment of depressive disorders. *Psychological Medicine, 23,* 1023–1032.

Wade, T. J., & Cairney, J. (2000). Major depressive disorder and marital transition among mothers: Results from a national panel study. *Journal of Nervous and Mental Disease, 188,* 741–750.

Weissman, M. M., Bland, R., Joyce, P. R., & Newman, S. (1993). Sex differences in rates of depression: Cross-national perspectives. *Journal of Affective Disorders Special Issue: Toward New Psychobiology of Depression in Women, 29,* 77–84.

Weissman, M. M., & Olfson, M. (1995). Depression in women: implications for health care research. *Science, 269,* 799–801.

Weissman, M. M., Wolk, S., Goldstein, R. B., Moreau, D., Adams, P., Greenwald, S., Klier, C. M., Ryan, N. D., Dahl, R. E., & Wickramaratne, P. (1999). Depressed adolescents grown up. *Journal of the American Medical Association, 281,* 1707–1713.

Weissman, M. M., Wolk, S., Wickramaratne, P., Goldstein, R. B., Adams, P., Greenwald, S., Ryan, N. D., Dahl, R. E., & Steinberg, D. (1999). Children with prepubertal-onset major depressive disorder and anxiety grown up. *Archives of General Psychiatry, 56,* 794–801.

Weisz, J., Thurber, C., Sweeney, L., Proffitt, V., & LeGagnoux, G. (1997). Brief treatment of mild to moderate child depression using primary and secondary control enhancement training. *Journal of Consulting and Clinical Psychology, 65,* 703–707.

Zubin, J., & Spring, B. (1977). Vulnerability: A new view of schizophrenia. *Journal of Abnormal Psychology, 86,* 103–126.

PART I

DESCRIPTIVE ASPECTS
OF DEPRESSION

Depression is one of the most common psychiatric disorders and, from a societal perspective, is perhaps the most costly. Depression is also a highly recurrent disorder with an increasingly younger age of onset for the initial episode. In the six chapters in this part, the authors discuss issues concerning the onset and course of depression, its prevalence and societal costs, and important factors involved in studying this disorder. Kessler (Chapter 1) describes epidemiological aspects of depression: its prevalence and its economic cost. Boland and Keller (Chapter 2) discuss the course and outcome of this disorder, describing the results of several large-scale longitudinal investigations that have monitored the course of depression over many years. Nezu, Nezu, McClure, and Zwick (Chapter 3) describe the most widely used interview-based and self-report measures of depression, and discuss important issues involved in the assessment of this disorder. Extending this discussion, Ingram and Siegle (Chapter 4) describe a number of methodological issues in the study of depressive disorders, and make several noteworthy recommendations concerning how research in this area might proceed most fruitfully. Klein, Durbin, Shankman, and Santiago (Chapter 5) then describe the nature of the relation between depression and various aspects of personality functioning. Finally, Johnson and Kizer (Chapter 6) discuss similarities and differences in the clinical phenomenology and psychosocial predictors of unipolar and bipolar depression.

1

Epidemiology of Depression

Ronald C. Kessler

The first modern North American general population epidemiological surveys that included information about depression were carried out in the late 1950s in the Midtown Manhattan Study (Srole, Langner, Michael, Opler, & Rennie, 1962) and the Stirling County Study (Leighton, Harding & Macklin, 1963). These early surveys used dimensional screening scales of nonspecific psychological distress to pinpoint respondents with likely mental disorders and then administered clinical interviews to these respondents. The outcome of primary interest was a global measure of mental disorder rather than individual diagnoses. No prevalence estimates of depression were reported. However, the screening scales in these studies included a number of items that assessed depressed mood and other symptoms that have subsequently come to be seen as part of the depressive syndrome. It is possible to make rough estimates about the prevalence and correlates of depressive disorders from these data (Murphy, Laird, Monson, Sobol, & Leighton, 2000).

In later surveys, variants on the screening scales used in the Midtown Manhattan and Stirling County studies were generally used without clinical follow-up. (See Link & Dohrenwend, 1980, for a review.) Scale scores were sometimes dichotomized in order to define "cases" of mental disorder based on some external standard of a clinically relevant cutpoint, although there was ongoing controversy about the appropriate decision rules for defining cases (Seiler, 1973). In order to resolve this controversy, structured diagnostic interviews appropriate for use in community surveys were developed in the late 1970s. The Diagnostic Interview Schedule (DIS; Robins, Helzer, Croughan, Williams, & Spitzer, 1981) was the first of these instruments. Dimensional screening scales continued to be widely used to screen for mental illness in primary care (Goldberg, 1972) and to assess symptom severity and treatment effectiveness among patients in treatment for mental disorders (Derogatis, 1977) even after the introduction of the DIS. However, psychiatric epidemiologists, influenced by the widely published results of the Epidemiologic Catchment Area Study (Robins & Regier, 1991), which was based on the DIS, abandoned the study of dimensional distress measures in favor of dichotomous caseness classifications in general population surveys.

We now have had 2 decades of experience with community epidemiological surveys using fully structured diagnostic interviews like the DIS and the more recently developed CIDI (Robins et al., 1988), PRIME-MD (Spitzer et al., 1994), and MINI (Sheehan, Lecrubier,

Sheehan, Amorim, & Janavs, 1998). It is clear from this experience that fully structured diagnostic interviews, while very useful, are inadequate by themselves to provide the information needed by health policy planners on the magnitude of the problem of untreated serious depression. The reason for this is that the DSM and ICD criteria are so broad that close to half of the people in the general population receive one or more diagnoses on a lifetime basis (Kessler et al., 1994) and close to one-fifth at any one point in time (Kessler & Frank, 1997). With prevalences as high as these, the dichotomous caseness data provided in diagnostic interviews need to be supplemented with dimensional information on severity to be useful to health policy planners (Regier et al., 1998).

Unfortunately, the most recently available adult general population epidemiological data on the prevalence of major depression do not include dimensional severity measures. This is an especially important omission in light of the suggestion by some commentators that the majority of community cases who meet criteria for major depression have fairly mild disorders (Regier, Narrow, Rupp, Rae, & Kaelber, 2000). The World Health Organization (WHO) is currently carrying out a massive worldwide epidemiological survey of mental disorders, known as the World Mental Health 2000 (WMH2000) Initiative, that aims to correct this problem by evaluating a wide range of mental disorders both with dichotomous diagnostic measures and with dimensional clinical severity measures (Kessler & Ustun, 2000). However, WMH2000 results will not be available for another 2 years.

The first section of this chapter presents a broad overview of the main findings in the literature regarding the descriptive epidemiology of major depression. The overview is brief because much of this literature has recently been reviewed elsewhere (Lewinsohn, Rohde, Seeley, Klein, & Gotlib, 2000; Merikangas, 2000; Blazer, 2000; Horwath & Weissman, 1995; Bland, 1997). The second section of the chapter addresses the issue of severity by reviewing available data on the consequences of depression as assessed in community surveys. The third section, finally, reviews epidemiological data on patterns of help seeking for depression.

DESCRIPTIVE EPIDEMIOLOGY

Point Prevalence

Community surveys that assess depression with symptom screening scales find that up to 20% of adults and up to 50% of children and adolescents report depressive symptoms during recall periods between 1 week and 6 months (Kessler, Avenevoli, & Merikangas, 2001). There is a U-shaped distribution of mean scores in these surveys in relation to age, with the highest scores found among the youngest and the oldest respondents and the lowest scores found among people in midlife (Kessler, Foster, Webster, & House, 1992). Point prevalence estimates for DSM major depression in surveys that use structured diagnostic interviews are considerably lower. Rates of current major depression are typically less than 1% in samples of children (reviewed by Merikangas & Angst, 1995), as high as 6% in samples of adolescents (reviewed by Kessler, Avenevoli, & Merikangas, 2001), and in the range 2–4% in samples of adults (WHO International Consortium in Psychiatric Epidemiology, 2000).

The discrepancy between the high prevalence of symptoms in screening scales and the comparatively low prevalence of depressive disorders means that many people have subsyndromal depressive symptoms. Recent epidemiological studies have started to investigate these subsyndromal symptoms using the diagnostic criteria for minor depression and recurrent brief depression (RBD) stipulated in DSM-IV-TR (American Psychiatric Association, 2000). Major depression (MD) requires 2 weeks of clinically significant dysphoria or anhedonia (or irritability among children) along with a total of five symptoms. Minor depression (mD), in comparison, requires two to four symptoms with the same severity and duration requirements as MD, while RBD requires the repeated occurrence of the same number and severity of symptoms as MD for several days each month over the course of a full year. These recent studies have documented rates of subsyndromal depression among both adolescents (Gotlib, Lewinsohn, & Seeley, 1995; Kessler & Walters, 1998) and adults (Judd, Akiskal, & Paulus, 1997; Kessler, Zhao, Blazer, & Swartz, 1997) that are as high as, if not higher than, the rates of MD. In addition, a longitudinal study of adolescents followed into adulthood found that subsyndromal depression is a powerful predictor of the subsequent onset of MD (Angst, Sellaro, & Merikangas, 2000).

Subtypes

A number of proposals have been made to subtype the diagnosis of MD based on symptom profiles (reviewed by Kendell, 1976). The only stable subtyping distinction that has emerged consistently in empirical epidemiological studies, however, is between depression with vegetative symptoms (e.g., weight loss, insomnia, appetite loss) and reverse vegetative symptoms (e.g., weight gain, hypersomnia, appetite increase) (Davidson, Woodbury, Pelton, & Krishnan, 1988; Eaton, Dryman, Sorenson, & McCutcheon, 1989). Between one-fourth and one-third of all people with MD have a reverse vegetative symptom profile, with some evidence that this atypical depression is more common among women than men and more strongly associated than vegetative depression with a family history of depression. There is little evidence, in comparison, that atypical depression is more persistent or severe than typical depression. Indeed, in one recent analysis of depression subtyping, typicality and severity emerged as separate and largely independent subtyping dimensions (Sullivan, Kessler, & Kendler, 1998).

Another important subtyping distinction concerns the existence of cyclical depression. Two cycling depressive subtypes have been identified: seasonal affective disorder (SAD; Rosenthal et al., 1984) and premenstrual mood disorder (PMD; Halbreich, 1997). Community surveys find that 10% or more of people in the general population report seasonal variations in depressed mood and related symptoms (e.g., Booker & Hellekson, 1992; Rosen et al., 1990). Seasonal depression is typically most common in the winter months and more prevalent in northern than southern latitudes. However, the prevalence of narrowly defined DSM seasonal affective disorder, which requires a lifetime diagnosis of recurrent MD or mD and at least two-thirds of all episodes following a seasonal pattern, is much less common. Blazer, Kessler, and Swartz (1998) found that only 1% of the population meet narrowly defined criteria for SAD, representing only about 5% of all people with mD or MD. Among people with clinical depression, Blazer et al. found that SAD was somewhat more common among men than women and older than younger respondents.

Community surveys show that the majority of women report experiencing some symptom changes associated with their menstrual cycles (Pearlstein & Stone, 1998; Olive, 1991). Only between 4 and 6%, however, report what appears to be a PMD (Sveindottir & Backstrom, 2000). A diagnosis of PMD requires a clear and recurring pattern of onset and offset of five or more mood and related symptoms at specific points in the majority of menstrual cycles over the course of a full year. Assessments with daily mood diaries over two or more menstrual cycles (Freeman, DeRubeis, & Rickels, 1996) typically show that only about half of the women who report cyclical mood problems actually suffer from PMD. The others have more chronic syndromal or subsyndromal mood disorders that are sometimes exacerbated by menstrual symptoms. There is currently a great deal of interest in PMD among depression researchers based on evidence of family aggregation with major depression

(Yonkers, 1997) and responsiveness to selective serotonin reuptake inhibitors but not tricyclic antidepressants (Freeman, Rickels, Sondheimer, & Polansky, 1999). However, there is also controversy regarding appropriate diagnostic and assessment criteria (Severino, 1996). Community epidemiological data are scant due to the logistic complications created by the fact that a definitive diagnosis requires the collection of daily mood diaries across two or more menstrual cycles. Such diaries are typically collected only in clinical samples, although there are a few small community surveys that have collected diary data as well (e.g., Sveindottir & Backstrom, 2000). Given the existence of so many uncertainties in this area of investigation, a large representative epidemiological survey of PMS using dairy methods would be very valuable.

Lifetime Prevalence

Epidemiological surveys that administer diagnostic interviews generally assess lifetime prevalences of MD and estimate age of onset distributions from retrospective reports (e.g., Christie et al., 1988). Lifetime prevalence estimates of MD in U.S. surveys have ranged widely, from as low as 6% (Weissman, Bruce, Leaf, Florio, & Holzer, 1991) to as high as 25% (Lewinsohn, Rohde, Seeley, & Fischer, 1991). The only nationally representative general population data in the United States based on a structured diagnostic interview come from the National Comorbidity Survey (NCS; Kessler et al., 1994), where 15.8% of respondents met criteria for a lifetime MD episode and an additional 10.0% of respondents met criteria for lifetime mD (Kessler, Zhao, et al., 1997).

The wide variation in prevalence estimates across surveys is probably due to a combination of at least three factors. First, as discussed in more depth below, the prevalence of depression has probably increased in recent cohorts. This means that earlier surveys would be expected to have lower prevalence estimates than more recent surveys. Second, reluctance to admit depression has decreased in recent cohorts, which will also increase prevalences in more recent surveys. The third factor involves an important methodological difference between the diagnostic interviews that were used in early surveys based on the Epidemiologic Catchment Area (ECA) program (Robins & Regier, 1991), which uniformly produced very low prevalence estimates, and the more refined diagnostic interviews used in recent surveys such as the NCS, the Mental Health Supplement to the Ontario Health Survey (Offord et al., 1994), and the Mexican-American Prevalence and Services Survey (Vega et al., 1998). Both types of interviews use a stem–branch structure to assess mental disorders. In this approach, respondents are first asked one or more initial questions about core symptoms of the disorder under investigation. For example, a stem question for MD might be "Did you ever have a time lasting 2 weeks or longer when you felt sad or depressed most of the day nearly every day"? The respondents who are affirmative are then administered a more detailed set of follow-up questions that assess all criteria of the disorder. This same stem–branch approach is used to assess each of the dozen or more diagnoses evaluated in the surveys.

While both the type of interview used in the ECA and the type of interview used in the NCS were based on this stem–branch structure, only the NCS interview was designed to minimize the underreporting problems that methodological studies have shown to occur in interviews of this sort. A detailed discussion of the instrument design issues is presented elsewhere (Kessler, Wittchen, Abelson, & Zhao, 2000). In brief, methodological studies show that stem–branch questions are prone to two types of underreporting bias (Bradburn, Sudman, & Associates, 1979; Turner & Martin, 1984). One is that some respondents underreport stem questions once they recognize that positive responses lead to more detailed questions. The other is that most respondents fail to appreciate the cognitive complexity of the memory search involved in answering stem questions that require lifetime recall. These problems were addressed in the NCS by developing a Life Review Section near the beginning of the interview that included the stem questions for all the disorders assessed in the survey. The respondent instructions in this section were designed to facilitate and motivate active memory search. This entire section was administered before probing any positive stems, thus avoiding conscious nondisclosure once respondents recognized that positive stem responses led to further questioning. A field experiment carried out after the completion of the NCS randomly assigned respondents to either asked stem-and-branch questions in sequence throughout the interview or a version that included the Life Review Section and then validated diagnoses with clinician-administered reinterviews. Two important results emerged from this experiment. First, the Life Review Section was found to increase the prevalence estimates of depression and other disorders enough to explain the large observed differences in prevalence estimates between the ECA and the NCS. Second, the clinical reinterviews showed that the additional cases discovered with the Life Review Section were genuine cases of depression rather than false positives (Kessler, Wittchen, et al., 1998).

Based on these results, it seems safe to conclude that at least one out of every six adults in the U.S. population has met criteria for an MD episode at some time in their life and one in four has met criteria for either MD, mD, or recurrent brief depression. It is important to recognize, though, that these are estimates of prevalence-to-date risk rather than lifetime risk. Kaplan–Meier (KM) age-of-onset curves can be used to generate lifetime risk estimates. As shown in Figure 1.1, which presents KM curves separately for MD and mD based on the NCS data, the lifetime risk projections based on these curves are considerably higher than the lifetime-to-date prevalence estimates.

In evaluating the KM curves in Figure 1.1, it is important to recognize that the lifetime risk projections they generate are based on the assumption that conditional risk of first onset at given ages is constant across cohorts. This assumption is incorrect. As shown in

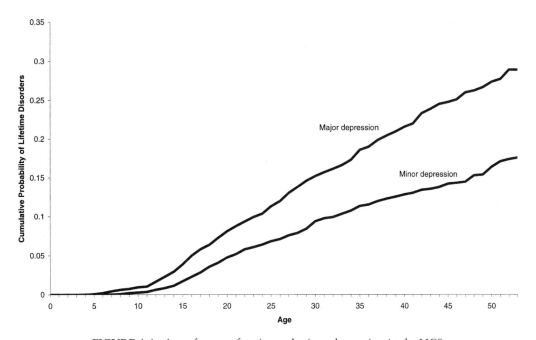

FIGURE 1.1. Age of onset of major and minor depression in the NCS.

Figure 1.2, the KM curves for MD and mD combined in the NCS differ substantially by cohort. The same general pattern holds when we examine MD and mD separately (Kessler,
Zhao, et al., 1997). This pattern of intercohort variation could be due to the risk of depression increasing in successively more recent cohorts. Other possible causes are that willingness to admit depression in a survey might have increased in recent cohorts (Kessler, 2000a)
and that forgetting a past history of depression might increase with age (Giuffra & Risch,
1994). There is no way to adjudicate among these contending interpretations definitively
with available data, although indirect evidence strongly suggests that at least part of the apparent cohort effect is due to a true increase in risk of depression in recent cohorts (Weissman & Klerman, 1992).

Course

Little longitudinal research has been done to study the course of depression in general population samples (but for important exceptions, see Angst & Merikangas, 1997; Lewinsohn
et al., 2000). However, cross-sectional surveys consistently find that the prevalence ratio of
12-month MD versus lifetime MD is in the range between .5 and .6 (Kessler, McGonagle,
Swartz, Blazer, & Nelson, 1993; Weissman et al., 1991). This means that between half and
two-thirds of people who have ever been clinically depressed will be in an episode in any
given year over the remainder of their lives. At least three separate processes contribute to
the size of this ratio: the probability of a first episode becoming chronic; the probability of
episode recurrence among people with a history who are not chronically depressed; and
speed of episode recovery among people with recurrent episodes.

Epidemiological studies show that the first of these three processes is quite small, with
only a small fraction of 1% of people in the population reporting a single lifetime depressive episode that persists for many years (Kessler et al., 1993). The prevalences of dysthymia

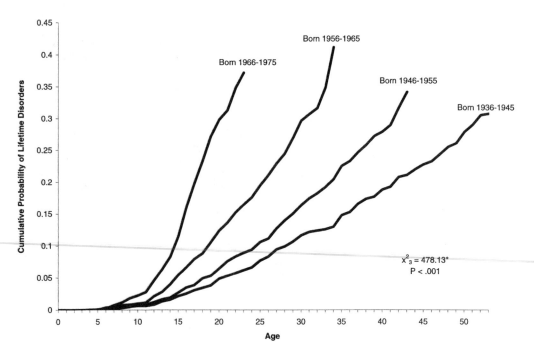

FIGURE 1.2. Age of onset of major and minor depression by cohort in the NCS.

and chronic mD are somewhat higher, but still only in the range 3–4% combined in the total population (Kessler et al., 1994). Episode recurrence, in comparison, is very common, with more than 80% of people with a history of MD having recurrent episodes. In the NCS, the median number of episodes was seven among respondents with an age of first onset more than a decade prior to the interview. Moreover, over 90% of all episodes in the year prior to the interview were recurrences rather than first onsets. Speed of episode recovery, finally, appears to be highly variable, although the epidemiological evidence is slim. Only two large community surveys have studied speed-of-episode recovery. One found that 40% of cases of MD recovered by 5 weeks and over 90% by 1 year (McLeod, Kessler, & Landis, 1992). The other found that the median time to recovery was 6 weeks, with over 90% recovered within a year (Kendler, Walters, & Kessler, 1997). Very few of the people with short episodes ever come to clinical attention, which means that time to recovery is considerably longer in clinical samples (e.g., Brugha et al., 1990).

Distinguishing First Onset from Recurrence

It is important to distinguish between first onset and recurrence in studying the predictors of depression episode onset because the two types of episodes have different predictors (Lewinsohn, Allen, Seeley, & Gotlib, 1999). For example, women are nearly twice as likely as men to become depressed for the first time, while most epidemiological studies find no sex difference in recurrence risk (Kessler et al., 1993). History of depression is not only a powerful predictor of episode onset, but it is also strongly related to stressful events such as divorce and job loss and to presumed stress buffers such as social support and neuroticism (Kessler & Magee, 1993). Because of these relationships with all three of the main variables in models of the relationship between stress and depression (i.e., stress, stress buffers, and depression), failure to control for history of depression can lead to substantial bias in stress models. Yet most epidemiological studies that attempt to discover risk factors for episode onset of depression fail to include a control for history of prior episodes (Kessler, 1997a). A complicating factor is that risk of spontaneous recurrence of depressive episodes increases with number of prior episodes (Ghaziuddin, Ghaziuddin, & Stein, 1990). This means that it is important not only to control for history of depression in studies of the predictors of episode onset, but also to control for number of prior episodes and to estimate interactions between number of prior episodes and other predictors (Hammen & Gitlin, 1997).

Comorbidity

Studies of diagnostic patterns in community samples show that there is substantial lifetime and episode comorbidity between depression and other mental and substance use disorders. Indeed, comorbidity is the norm among people with depression. The ECA study found that 75% of respondents with lifetime MD also met criteria for at least one of the other DSM-III disorders assessed in that survey (Robins, Locke, & Regier, 1991), while the comparable proportion of DSM-III-R (American Psychiatric Association, 1987) comorbidity in the NCS was 74% (Kessler, 1995). There is controversy concerning the extent to which these high rates of comorbidity are artifacts of changes in the diagnostic systems used in almost all recent studies of comorbidity (Frances et al., 1992). In the United States, these systems, beginning with DSM-III (American Psychiatric Association, 1980) and continuing through DSM-IV-TR (American Psychiatric Association, 2000), dramatically increased the number of diagnostic categories and reduced the number of exclusion criteria so that many people who would have received only a single diagnosis in previous systems now receive multiple diagnoses. The intention was to retain potentially important differentiating information that could be useful in refining understanding of etiology, course, and likely treatment response (First, Spitzer, & Williams, 1990). However, it could also be argued that it had the unintended negative consequence of artificially inflating the estimated prevalence of comorbidity.

This uncertainty will presumably be resolved in the future by using established criteria to determine the validity of diagnostic distinctions (Cloninger, 1989). Until that time, though, we are left with a situation in which it appears that depression is highly comorbid with a number of other disorders. The strength of these comorbidities is remarkably consistent between the ECA and NCS surveys, the two largest general population surveys in the United States that have estimated comorbidities among DSM disorders (Kessler, 1995). The strongest lifetime comorbidities (odds ratios) of depression in both these surveys are with anxiety disorders, especially generalized anxiety disorder (6.0), panic disorder (4.0), and posttraumatic stress disorder (4.0), although less powerful but still significant comorbidities are found with a wide range of other mental disorders (Kessler, 1997b). Episode comorbidities are generally somewhat stronger, indicating that comorbidity is associated with recurrence risk (Kessler, 1995).

The majority of comorbid depression is temporally secondary in the sense that the first onset of depression occurs subsequent to the first onset of at least one other comorbid disorder, although this is more true among men than among women. Survival analysis of the cross-sectional NCS data using retrospective age-of-onset reports to determine temporal priority shows that a wide range of temporally primary anxiety, substance abuse, and other disorders predict the subsequent first onset of depression (Kessler et al., 1996). Time-lagged effects are strongest for generalized anxiety disorder (7.6) and simple phobia (4.2). There is little evidence of change in these odds ratios as a function of time since onset of the primary disorder. This absence of a time gradient is inconsistent with the hypothesis that secondary depression is a general exhaustion response to unremitting anxiety (Akiskal, 1990). At the same time, most of these odds ratios are confined to effects of active primary disorders as opposed to remitted primary disorders. This means that people who currently have these other disorders are at risk of depression. The fact that history of remitted anxiety is generally not associated with risk of depression suggests indirectly that anxiety is a risk factor rather than a risk marker. Two important exceptions, though, are early-onset simple phobia and panic, both of which appear to be markers rather than risk factors. The key evidence here is that people with a history of these disorders have elevated risk of subsequent first onset of depression even when the primary disorders are no longer active (Kessler et al., 1996).

THE CONSEQUENCES OF DEPRESSION

Psychiatric epidemiologists have traditionally been much more interested in estimating prevalences and discovering modifiable risk factors (e.g., Eaton & Weil, 1955) than in studying the consequences of mental illness (e.g., Faris & Dunham, 1939). This situation has changed in the past decade, though, as the managed care revolution and the rise of evidence-based medicine have made it necessary to document the societal costs of illness (Gold, Siegel, Russell, & Weinstein, 1996). Depression has emerged as an important disorder in this new work. Indeed, the World Health Organization Global Burden of Disease (GBD) Study ranked depression as the single most burdensome disease in the world in terms of total disability-adjusted life years among people in the middle years of life (Murray & Lopez, 1996). This top ranking was due to a unique combination of high lifetime prevalence, early age of onset, high chronicity, and high role impairment (Kessler, 2000c).

Role Impairment

It was noted in the introduction that the estimated prevalence of depression and other mental disorders in recent epidemiological surveys has been so high that some commentators have speculated that most must be mild cases (e.g., Regier et al., 2000). This speculation is superficially inconsistent with the GBD conclusion that depression is associated with more societal burden than any other condition. However, the GBD relied on expert opinion rather than epidemiological data to rank-order the impairments of chronic conditions. The expert raters were most familiar with clinical cases. It is possible that the cases found in community surveys are less seriously impaired.

The Medical Outcomes Study (Wells et al., 1989) collected data on this issue by screening samples of primary care patients for a small number of sentinel conditions that included MD and following these patients over time to evaluate their medical costs and role functioning. The role impairments caused by depression were comparable to those caused by seriously impairing chronic physical disorders. Similar results were found in the nationally representative general population sample assessed in the MacArthur Foundation's Midlife Development in the United States (MIDUS) survey. The MIDUS results suggest that the role impairments caused by depression are comparable to those caused by such chronic physical disorders as arthritis, asthma, diabetes, and hypertension (Kessler, Mickelson, Barber, & Wang, 2001).

A substantial part of the role impairment caused by depression involves reduced work performance. A recent economic analysis of the costs of depression in the workplace estimated that the annual salary-equivalent costs of depression-related lost productivity in the United States exceeds $33 billion (Greenberg, Kessler, Nells, Finkelstein, & Berndt, 1996). This is an underestimate of the overall workplace costs of depression because it excludes such potentially important components as the effects of depression on the performance of coworkers, industrial accidents, and turnover. It is important to note that these effects of depression on work performance disappear among remitted cases (Kessler & Frank, 1997), suggesting that effective depression treatment would reduce workplace costs. Simulations suggest that employers could recover between 45% and 90% of the direct treatment costs of depression in improved salary-equivalent work performance over the course of a single year (Kessler, Barber, et al., 1999). It is plausible to imagine that a complete cost accounting that considered the effects of depression on a broader set of workplace outcomes would show that the direct costs of depression treatment are fully offset by decreased indirect workplace costs. A definitive effectiveness trial to evaluate this hypothesis has not yet been carried out, although depression treatment trials have consistently documented significant effects of treatment on work outcomes (Mintz, Mintz, Arruda, & Hwang, 1992; Wells et al., 2000).

Role Transitions

It was noted in the discussion of the GBD study that depression has a unique constellation of characteristics leading to its rating by the World Health Organization as the single most burdensome chronic condition in the world among people in the middle years of life. Perhaps the most important of these is early age of onset. The median age of onset of MD (see Figure 1.1) is in the mid-20s. This is at least 2 decades earlier than the median ages of onset of the chronic physical disorders that have prevalences and impairments comparable to those of depression. One important implication of this early age of onset is that depression, unlike most chronic physical disorders, occurs at a time in the life course when it can have a profound effect on critical life course role transitions. The latter include educational attainment, entry into the labor force, parenting, and marital timing and stability.

A series of analyses based on the NCS used retrospectively dated age of onset reports to estimate the effects of depression and other mental disorders on early life role transitions. An investigation of the effects of early-onset depression on educational attainment found that depression prior to completing high school significantly predicted (odds ratio) high school dropout (1.5) and, among high school graduates, predicted failure to enter college (1.6) (Kessler, Foster, Saunders, & Stang, 1995). Depression as of the age of high school completion powerfully predicted college dropout among respondents who went to college (2.9). A separate investigation of the effects of early-onset depression on teen childbearing found that depression is associated with a 2.2 relative odds of teenage pregnancy among both girls and boys as well as with elevated rates of failure to contracept (Kessler, Berglund, et al., 1997). An investigation of the effects of early-onset depression on marital timing and stability, finally, found that prior depression predicts both teenage marriage (2.3) and subsequent divorce (1.7) (Kessler, Walters, & Forthofer, 1998).

It is important to appreciate that this constellation of truncated education, early childbearing, and marital instability are central components of welfare dependency. It is little wonder, then, that the welfare-to-work experiments that have been carried out in conjunction with recent state welfare reform programs have documented high rates of depression among welfare mothers and significant adverse effects of maternal depression on making a successful transition from welfare to work (Danziger et al., 2000; Olson & Pavetti, 1996). This is another example of a case in which the societal costs of not treating depression may be greater than the costs of treatment. We are unaware, though, of any trial to evaluate the cost-effectiveness of providing mental health treatment as a component of the services provided to welfare mothers to facilitate the transition from welfare to work.

Other Adverse Consequences of Depression

It was noted in the last subsection that the financial savings to the employer due of increased work productivity with the remission of depression might approach or exceed the direct costs of treating depressed workers. The critical experiment needed to test this hypothesis has not yet been carried out. However, another type of experiment has been carried out that documents a cost saving of depression treatment for managed care. Specifically, services research shows that people with untreated depression are often heavy users of primary care medical services for vaguely defined physical complaints. This observation has led some clinical researchers to speculate that systematic screening, detection, and treatment of primary care patients with depression might lead to an overall reduction in primary care costs. A series of experiments have shown that a partial offset effect of this sort exists (Katon et al., 1996; Katzelnick et al., 2000). The vast majority of depressed patients detected in primary care screening accept treatment for their depression. The average total cost of these patients to the managed care system exclusive of the cost of their depression treatment decreases significantly after their depression is treated. This reduction partially offsets the cost of depression treatment over a follow-up period of 1 year. It is conceivable that the total costs of depression treatment are recovered over a longer time period, but long-term follow-up studies have not yet been carried out to determine whether this is the case.

EPIDEMIOLOGICAL STUDIES OF HELP SEEKING

Speed of Initial Treatment Contact

The findings reviewed above concerning the adverse effects of early-onset depression on role transitions raise an obvious question: Would timely treatment prevent these effects? We do not know the answer because the critical experiment has never been carried out. We do know, though, that timely treatment is the exception rather than the rule and that this is especially true for early-onset cases. This evidence comes from parallel studies of speed of initial treatment contact based on analysis of the NCS (Kessler, Olfson, & Berglund, 1998) and the Mental Health Supplement to the Ontario Health Survey (Olfson, Kessler, Berglund, & Lin, 1998). Both of these surveys asked respondents with a history of depression if they had ever sought treatment and, if so, their age of first obtaining treatment. Comparisons of reported ages of onset with ages of first obtaining treatment were used to study patterns and correlates of delay in seeking treatment. The results were consistent in the two surveys in showing that delays in initial help seeking are pervasive. Only about one-third of the people who ever sought treatment did so in the same years as the first onset of their MD, while the median delay among those who did not seek immediate treatment was more than 5 years. Even more striking was the consistent finding that speed of contact is strongly related to age of onset. The vast majority of respondents who reported first onsets of depression in middle age or later sought treatment soon after the onset. Respondents with first onsets in early adulthood, in comparison, were much slower to seek treatment. Respondents with child or adolescent onsets, finally, were by far the slowest of all, with median delays of more than a decade. It is not clear why this is the case, but one plausible hypothesis is that youngsters must rely on adults to initiate a treatment referral. Whatever the case may be, this is an especially disturbing pattern for two reasons. First, early-onset depression is often more severe than later-onset depression. Second, as noted above, early-onset depression has powerful effects on critical developmental transitions that affect well-being throughout life. These results strongly suggest that special efforts are needed to reach out to children and adolescents with depression

Current Service Use

Turning from speed of initial lifetime help-seeking to treatment at a point in time, data from two nationally representative epidemiological surveys in the United States show that between one-third and one-half of the people who meet criteria for MD in a given year obtain some type of treatment for their depression during that year (Kessler, Zhao, et al., 1999; Wang, Berglund, & Kessler, 2000). A substantial proportion of this treatment occurs in the general medical sector. Unfortunately, analysis of the content of this treatment in comparison to published treatment guidelines (Agency for Health Care Policy and Research, 1993; American Psychiatric Association, 1993) shows that no more than 30% of these patients receive even minimally acceptable treatment (Katz, Kessler, Lin, & Wells, 1998; Wang et al., 2000). There is clear evidence that depression treatment that fails to conform with treatment guidelines is associated with incomplete recovery and increased risk of recurrence (Melfi et al., 1998). These results show that advances in the development and implementation of treatment quality improvement programs are clearly needed.

Another development of great importance in depression treatment involves the rise of complementary and alternative (CAM) therapies. Three recently completed national surveys have documented that a substantial proportion of people with depression use a variety of CAM therapies, such as St. John's wort and relaxation therapy, to treat their depression

(Eisenberg et al., 1993; Eisenberg et al., 1998; Unutzer et al., 2000). In the most detailed of these surveys, which was carried out in 1997–1998, 54% of the respondents with self-defined "serious depression" in the year prior to the interview reported that they used some form of CAM for their depression (Kessler et al., 2001). An alternative medicine professional, such as an energy healer or herbalist, was seen during that same year for the treatment of depression by 19% of the respondents with self-defined serious depression. This compares to 36% who reported seeing any conventional physician or mental health professional for their depression during that same time period. The patients who used CAM were more likely to see a conventional provider than those who did not use CAM, with 66% of the patients who saw a conventional professional for their depression also using CAM.

Importantly, only a small minority of CAM users who are also in treatment with a conventional provider tell the latter about their CAM use (Eisenberg et al., 1998). It is important to recognize that this type of unsupervised joint use of CAM and conventional therapy can be dangerous, as case studies show that some types of CAM can create potentially dangerous interactions with pharmacotherapies (Yager, Siegfried, & DiMatteo, 1999; Almeida & Grimsley, 1996). For example, recent case reports suggest that the mixture of St. John's wort with selective serotonin reuptake inhibiters can induce a mild serotonin syndrome (Ernst, 1999). *In vitro* studies also suggest that hypericum extracts, which are commonly used herbal treatments for depression, are potent inducers of hepatic enzymes that can reduce plasma concentrations of a variety of concomitant prescription medications (Fugh-Berman, 2000). Opening up lines of communication between conventional mental health professionals and patients with regard to CAM use is consequently of great importance.

FUTURE DIRECTIONS

Developmental Epidemiology

There is an increased interest in developmental studies of the onset and course of depression as part of a larger interest in developmental epidemiology (Angold & Costello, 1995). The realization that first onset of depression often occurs early in life and that gender differences in depression begin to emerge in midadolescence are fueling this interest. It is likely that future developmental epidemiological studies will collect blood or saliva samples that can be used to measure sex hormones in an effort to tease out the biological and social effects of pubertal status and timing. Two epidemiological studies of adolescents have already collected data of this type and has shown that increases in sex hormones appear to explain much of the emerging sex difference in depression in midpuberty (Angold, Costello, & Worthman, 1998; Patton et al., 1996). It is also important, though, that these future studies give equal attention to social changes that occur at about the same time. The importance of this equal treatment is illustrated nicely in a recent report from the National Longitudinal Study of Adolescent Health (Bearman, Jones, & Udry, 1998), which showed that the greater increase in exposure to stresses associated with dating among girls than boys can explain much of the increasing sex difference in depression in midpuberty without reference to hormonal changes (Joyner & Udry, 2000).

Genetic Epidemiology

Psychiatric epidemiologists have been greatly interested in behavioral genetic studies of depression and other major mental disorders, with most of the focus being on twin and twin–family designs. Such studies use structural equation models to partition variances and covariances into genetic and environmental components (Neale & Cardon, 1992). Although convincing data have been presented in these studies that depression is clearly heritable (Kendler et al., 1996), behavioral genetic studies have been disappointing in not advancing far beyond this basic fact. Some commentators on the future of psychiatric epidemiology have suggested that our greatest hope for a breakthrough in understanding the etiology of depression is likely to come from genetic epidemiology (Robins, 1992). However, there is no indication that this promise has begun to be fulfilled in the nearly two decades since epidemiological studies based on genetically informative designs (i.e., twin–family and adoption designs) have been actively pursued. Linkage studies have been unable to identify a single specific gene or gene marker for any mood disorder. If such markers can be identified, integration of psychiatric epidemiology with population genetics would be valuable in a number of ways (Risch & Merikangas, 1996). It is not clear, though, when and if such markers will be identified.

Experimental Epidemiology

Epidemiology has played a major part in the development of many public health interventions. Important epidemiological contributions along these same lines are beginning to emerge in psychiatric epidemiology as well. Included here are studies that have documented effects of obstetrical complications on childhood-onset schizophrenia (Nicholson et al., 1999), of childhood nutritional deficits on conduct disorder (Neugebauer, Hoek, & Susser, 1999), and of childhood lead exposure on early-onset Alzheimer's disease (Prince, 1998). However, the enormous complexity of environmental etiological processes in bringing about mental disorders has led most psychiatric epidemiologists to focus their efforts on broad nonspecific risk factors such as stress, social support, social class, and gender that do not have clear intervention implications. As a result, psychiatric epidemiologists have been less actively involved in targeting interventions than epidemiologists working in other areas of research. (For an important exception, see Harris, Brown, & Robinson, 1999a, 1999b.) As described in more detail elsewhere (Kessler, 2000b), the way in which analytic epidemiological research is carried out differs in important ways depending on whether the researcher sees the work as important for hypothesis testing or for guiding intervention development and targeting. If future psychiatric epidemiologists are to become closely involved in intervention work, changes will be needed in the types of questions asked, the kinds of analyses carried out, and the standards of proof required for epidemiological studies.

ACKNOWLEDGMENTS

I appreciate the helpful comments of Kathleen Merikangas, Ellen Walters, and the editors on an earlier version of this chapter. Preparation of this chapter was supported by grants from the U.S. Public Health Service Grant Nos. MH46376, MH49098, and MH528611, and by the W.T. Grant Foundation (90135190).

REFERENCES

Agency for Health Care Policy and Research. (1993). *Treatment of major depression: Vol. 2. Depression in primary care.* Rockville, MD: U.S. Department of Health and Human Services.

Akiskal, H. S. (1990). Toward a clinical understanding of the relationship of anxiety and depressive disorders. In J. D. Maser & C. R. Cloninger (Eds.), *Comorbidity of mood and anxiety disorders* (pp. 597–607). Washington, DC: American Psychiatric Press.

Almeida, J. C., & Grimsley, E. W. (1996). Coma from the health food store: Interaction between kava and alprazolam [letter]. *Annals of Internal Medicine, 125*(11), 940–941.

American Psychiatric Association. (1980). *Diagnostic and statistical manual of mental disorders* (3rd ed.). Washington, DC: Author.

American Psychiatric Association. (1987). *Diagnostic and statistical manual of mental disorders* (3rd ed., rev.). Washington, DC: Author.

American Psychiatric Association. (1993). Practice guideline for major depressive disorder in adults. *American Journal of Psychiatry, 150*(4, Suppl.), 1–26.

American Psychiatric Association. (2000). *Diagnostic and statistical manual of mental disorders* (4th ed., text rev.). Washington, DC: Author.

Angold, A., & Costello, E. J. (1995). Developmental epidemiology. *Epidemiologic Reviews, 17*(1), 74–82.

Angold, A., Costello, E. J., & Worthman, C. M. (1998). Puberty and depression: The roles of age, pubertal status and pubertal timing. *Psychological Medicine, 28*(1), 51–61.

Angst, J., & Merikangas, K. (1997). The depressive spectrum: Diagnostic classification and course. *Journal of Affective Disorders, 45*(1–2), 31–39; discussion, 39–40.

Angst, J., Sellaro, R., & Merikangas, K. R. (2000). Depressive spectrum diagnoses. *Comprehensive Psychiatry, 41*(2, Suppl. 1), 39–47.

Bearman, P., Jones, J., & Udry, J. R. (1998). *The National Longitudinal Study of Adolescent Health: Research design.* Chapel Hill, NC: Carolina Population Center.

Bland, R.C. (1997). Epidemiology of affective disorders: a review. *Canadian Journal of Psychiatry, 42*(4), 367–377.

Blazer, D. G. (2000). Mood disorders: Epidemiology. In B. J. Sadock & V. A. Sadock (Eds.), *Kaplan and Sadock's comprehensive textbook of psychiatry* (7th ed., pp. 1298–1308). Philadelphia: Lippincott Williams & Wilkins.

Blazer, D. G., Kessler, R. C., & Swartz, M. S. (1998). Epidemiology of recurrent major and minor depression with a seasonal pattern: The National Comorbidity Survey. *British Journal of Psychiatry, 172,* 164–167.

Booker, J. M., & Hellekson, C. J. (1992). Prevalence of seasonal affective disorder in Alaska. *American Journal of Psychiatry, 149*(9), 1176–1182.

Bradburn, N., Sudman, S., & Associates (1979). *Improving interview method and questionnaire design: Response effects to threatening questions in survey research.* San Francisco: Jossey-Bass.

Brugha, T. S., Bebbington, P. E., MacCarthy, B., Sturt, E., Wykes, T., & Potter, J. (1990). Gender, social support and recovery from depressive disorders: A prospective clinical study. *Psychological Medicine, 20,* 147–156.

Christie, K. A., Burke, J. D., Jr., Regier, D. A., Rae, D. S., Boyd, J. H., & Locke, B. Z. (1988). Epidemiologic evidence for early onset of mental disorders and higher risk of drug abuse in young adults. *American Journal of Psychiatry, 145*(8), 971–975.

Cloninger, C. R. (1989). Establishment of diagnostic validity in psychiatric illness: Robins and Guze's method revised. In L. N. Robins & J. Barrett (Eds.), *Validity of psychiatric diagnosis* (pp. 9–18). New York: Raven Press.

Danziger, S. K., Corcoran, M., Danziger, S., Heflin, C., Kalil, A., Levine, J., Rosen, D., Seefeldt, K., Siefert, K., & Tolman, R. (2000). Barriers to the employment of welfare recipients. In R. Cherry & W. Rodgers (Eds.), *Prosperity for all?: The economic boom and African Americans* (pp. 245–278). New York: Russell Sage Foundation.

Davidson, J., Woodbury, M. A., Pelton, S., & Krishnan, R. (1988). A study of depressive typologies using grade of membership analysis. *Psychological Medicine, 18*(1), 179–189.

Derogatis, L. R. (1977). *SCL-90 administration, scoring and procedures manual for the revised version.* Baltimore: Johns Hopkins University Press.

Eaton, J. W., & Weil, R. J. (1955). *Culture and mental disorders.* Glencoe, IL: Free Press.

Eaton, W. W., Dryman, A., Sorenson, A., & McCutcheon, A. (1989). DSM-III major depressive disorder in the community: A latent class analysis of data from the NIMH Epidemiologic Catchment Area programme. *British Journal of Psychiatry, 155,* 48–54.

Eisenberg, D., Davis, R. B., Ettner, S. L., Appel, S., Wilkey, S., van Rompay, M., & Kessler, R. C.

(1998). Trends in alternative medicine use in the United States, 1990–1997: Results of a follow-up national survey. *Journal of the American Medical Association, 280,* 1569–1575.

Eisenberg, D. M., Kessler, R. C., Foster, C., Norlock, F. E., Calkins, D. R., & Delbanco, T. L. (1993). Unconventional medicine in the United States: Prevalence, costs, and patterns of use. *New England Journal of Medicine, 328*(4), 246–252.

Ernst, E. (1999). Second thoughts about safety of St. John's wort. *Lancet, 354*(9195), 2014–2016.

Faris, R., & Dunham, H. (1939). *Mental disorders in urban areas.* Chicago: University of Chicago Press.

First, M. B., Spitzer, R. L., & Williams, J. B. W. (1990). Exclusionary principles and the comorbidity of psychiatric diagnoses: A historical review and implications for the future. In J. D. Maser & C. R. Cloninger (Eds.), *Comorbidity of mood and anxiety disorders* (pp. 83–109). Washington, DC: American Psychiatric Press.

Frances, A., Manning, D., Marin, D., Kocsis, J., McKinney, K., Hall, W., & Kline, M. (1992). Relationship of anxiety and depression. *Psychopharmacology, 106,* S82–S86.

Freeman, E. W., DeRubeis, R. J., & Rickels, K. (1996). Reliability and validity of a daily diary for premenstrual syndrome. *Psychiatry Research, 65*(2), 97–106.

Freeman, E. W., Rickels, K., Sondheimer, S. J., & Polansky, M. (1999). Differential response to antidepressants in women with premenstrual syndrome/premenstrual dysphoric disorder: A randomized controlled trial. *Archives of General Psychiatry, 56*(10), 932–939.

Fugh-Berman, A. (2000). Herb–drug interactions. *Lancet, 355*(9198), 134–138.

Ghaziuddin, M., Ghaziuddin, N., & Stein, G. S. (1990). Life events and the recurrence of depression. *Canadian Journal of Psychiatry, 35*(3), 239–242.

Giuffra, L. A., & Risch, N. (1994). Diminished recall and the cohort effect of major depression: A stimulation study. *Psychological Medicine, 24,* 375–383.

Gold, M. R., Siegel, J. E., Russell, L. B., & Weinstein, M. C. (1996). *Cost-effectiveness in health and medicine.* New York: Oxford University Press.

Goldberg, D. P. (1972). *The detection of psychiatric illness by questionnaire: A technique for the identification and assessment of non-psychotic psychiatric illness.* London: Oxford University Press.

Gotlib, I. H., Lewinsohn, P. M., & Seeley, J. R. (1995). Symptoms versus a diagnosis of depression: Differences in psychosocial functioning. *Journal of Consulting and Clinical Psychology, 63*(1), 90–100.

Greenberg, P., Kessler, R., Nells, T., Finkelstein, S., & Berndt, E. R. (1996). Depression in the workplace: An economic perspective. In J. P. Feighner & W. F. Boyer (Eds.), *Selective serotonin reuptake inhibitors: Advances in basic research and clinical practice* (pp. 327–363). New York: Wiley.

Halbreich, U. (1997). Premenstrual dysphoric disorders: A diversified cluster of vulnerability traits to depression. *Acta Psychiatrica Scandinavica, 95*(3), 169–176.

Hammen, C., & Gitlin, M. (1997). Stress reactivity in bipolar patients and its relation to prior history of disorder. *American Journal of Psychiatry, 154*(6), 856–857.

Harris, T., Brown, G. W., & Robinson, R. (1999a). Befriending as an intervention for chronic depression among women in an inner city: 1. Randomised controlled trial. *British Journal of Psychiatry, 174,* 219–224.

Harris, T., Brown, G. W., & Robinson, R. (1999b). Befriending as an intervention for chronic depression among women in an inner city: 2. Role of fresh-start experiences and baseline psychosocial factors in remission from depression. *British Journal of Psychiatry, 174,* 225–232.

Horwath, E., & Weissman, M. M. (1995). Epidemiology of depression and anxiety disorders. In M. T. Tsuang, M. Tohen, & G. E. P. Zahner (Eds.), *Textbook in psychiatric epidemiology* (pp. 317–344). New York: Wiley.

Joyner, K., & Udry, J. R. (2000). You don't bring me anything but down: Adolescent romance and depression. *Journal of Health and Social Behavior, 41*(4), 369–391.

Judd, L. L., Akiskal, H. S., & Paulus, M. P. (1997). The role and clinical significance of subsyndromal depressive symptoms (SSD) in unipolar major depressive disorder. *Journal of Affective Disorders, 45*(1–2), 5–17; discussion, 17–18.

Katon, W., Robinson, P., Von Korff, M., Lin, E., Bush, T., Ludman, E., Simon, G., & Walker, E.

(1996). A multifaceted intervention to improve treatment of depression in primary care. *Archives of General Psychiatry, 53*(10), 924–932.

Katz, S. J., Kessler, R. C., Lin, E., & Wells, K. B. (1998). Medication management of depression in the United States and Ontario. *Journal of General Internal Medicine, 13*(2), 77–85.

Katzelnick, D. J., Simon, G. E., Pearson, S. D., Manning, W. G., Helstad, C. P., Henk, H. J., Cole, S. M., Lin, E. H., Taylor, L. H., & Kobak, K. A. (2000). Randomized trial of a depression management program in high utilizers of medical care. *Archives of Family Medicine, 9*(4), 345–351.

Kendell, R. E. (1976). The classification of depressions: A review of contemporary confusion. *British Journal of Psychiatry, 129*, 15–28.

Kendler, K. S., Eaves, L. J., Walters, E. E., Neale, M. C., Heath, A. C., & Kessler, R. C. (1996). The identification and validation of distinct depressive syndromes in a population-based sample of female twins. *Archives of General Psychiatry, 53*, 391–399.

Kendler, K. S., Walters, E. E., & Kessler, R. C. (1997). The prediction of length of major depressive episodes: Results from an epidemiological sample of female twins. *Psychological Medicine, 27*(1), 107–117.

Kessler, R. C. (1995). The epidemiology of psychiatric comorbidity. In M. T. Tsaung, M. Tohen, & G. E. P. Zahner (Eds.), *Textbook in psychiatric epidemiology* (pp. 179–197). New York: Wiley.

Kessler, R. C. (1997a). The effects of stressful life events on depression. *Annual Review of Psychology, 48*, 191–214.

Kessler, R. C. (1997b). The prevalence of psychiatric comorbidity. In S. Wetzler & W. C. Sanderson (Eds.), *Treatment strategies for patients with psychiatric comorbidity* (pp. 23–48). New York: Wiley.

Kessler, R. C. (2000a). Gender difference in major depression: Epidemiological findings. In E. Frank (Ed.), *Gender and its effect in psychopathology* (pp. 61–84). Washington, DC: American Psychiatric Press.

Kessler, R. C. (2000b). Psychiatric epidemiology: Selected recent advances and future directions. *Bulletin of the World Health Organization, 78*(4), 464–474.

Kessler, R. C. (2000c). Burden of depression. In S. Kasper & A. Carlsson (Eds.), *Selective serotonin reuptake inhibitors 1990–2000: A decade of developments.* Copenhagen, Denmark: H. Lundbeck A/S.

Kessler, R. C., Avenevoli, S., & Merikangas, S. K. (2001). Mood disorders in children and adolescents: An epidemiological perspective. *Biological Psychiatry, 49*, 1002–1014.

Kessler, R. C., Barber, C., Birnbaum, H. G., Frank, R. G., Greenberg, P. E., Rose, R. M., Simon, G. E., & Wang, P. (1999). Depression in the workplace: Effects on short-term disability. *Health Affairs, 18*(5), 163–171.

Kessler, R. C., Berglund, P. A., Foster, C. L., Saunders, W. B., Stang, P. E., & Walters, E. E. (1997). Social consequences of psychiatric disorders: II. Teenage parenthood. *American Journal of Psychiatry, 154*(10), 1405–1411.

Kessler, R. C., Foster, C. L., Saunders, W. B., & Stang, P. E. (1995). Social consequences of psychiatric disorders: I. Educational attainment. *American Journal of Psychiatry, 152*(7), 1026–1032.

Kessler, R. C., Foster, C., Webster, P. S., & House, J. S. (1992). The relationship between age and depressive symptoms in two national surveys. *Psychology and Aging, 7*(1), 119–126.

Kessler, R. C., & Frank, R. G. (1997). The impact of psychiatric disorders on work loss days. *Psychological Medicine, 27*(4), 861–873.

Kessler, R. C., & Magee, W. J. (1993). Childhood adversities and adult depression: Basic patterns of association in a U.S. national survey. *Psychological Medicine, 23*, 679–690.

Kessler, R. C., McGonagle, K. A., Swartz, M., Blazer, D. G., & Nelson, C. B. (1993). Sex and depression in the National Comorbidity Survey: I. Lifetime prevalence, chronicity and recurrence. *Journal of Affective Disorders, 29*(2–3), 85–96.

Kessler, R. C., McGonagle, K. A., Zhao, S., Nelson, C. B., Hughes, M., Eshleman, S., Wittchen, H.-U., & Kendler, K. S. (1994). Lifetime and 12–month prevalence of DSM-III-R psychiatric disorders in the United States: Results from the National Comorbidity Survey. *Archives of General Psychiatry, 51*, 8–19.

Kessler, R. C., Mickelson, K. D., Barber, C. B., & Wang, P. (2001). The association between chronic medical conditions and work impairment. In A. S. Rossi (Ed.), *Caring and doing for others: Social responsibility in the domains of the family, work, and community* (pp. 403–426). Chicago: University of Chicago Press.

Kessler, R. C., Nelson, C. B., McGonagle, K. A., Liu, J., Swartz, M. S., & Blazer, D. G. (1996). Comorbidity of DSM-III-R major depressive disorder in the general population: Results from the U.S. National Comorbidity Survey. *British Journal of Psychiatry, 168*, 17–30.

Kessler, R. C., Olfson, M., & Berglund, P. A. (1998). Patterns and predictors of treatment contact after first onset of psychiatric disorders. *American Journal of Psychiatry, 155*(1), 62–69.

Kessler, R. C., Soukup, J., Davis, R. B., Foster, D. F., Wilkey, S. A., Van Rompay, M. I., & Eisenberg, D. M. (2001). The use of complementary and alternative therapies to treat anxiety and depression in the United States. *American Journal of Psychiatry, 158*(2), 289–294.

Kessler, R. C., & Ustun, T. B. (2000). The World Health Organization World Mental Health 2000 (WMH2000) initiative: Editorial. *Hospital Management International.*

Kessler, R. C., & Walters, E. E. (1998). Epidemiology of DSM-III-R major depression and minor depression among adolescents and young adults in the National Comorbidity Survey. *Depression and Anxiety, 7*, 3–14.

Kessler, R. C., Walters, E. E., & Forthofer, M. S. (1998). The social consequences of psychiatric disorders. III. Probability of marital stability. *American Journal of Psychiatry, 155*(8), 1092–1096.

Kessler, R. C., Wittchen, H.-U., Abelson, J., Kendler, K., Knauper, B., McGonagle, K. M., Schwarz, N., & Zhao, S. (1998). Methodological studies of the Composite International Diagnostic Interview (CIDI) in the U.S. National Comorbidity Survey. *International Journal of Methods in Psychiatric Research, 7*, 33–55.

Kessler, R. C., Wittchen, H.-U., Abelson, J., & Zhao, S. (2000). Methodological issues in assessing psychiatric disorder with self-reports. In A. A. Stone, J. S. Turrkan, C. A. Bachrach, J. B. Jobe, H. S. Kurtzman, & V. S. Cain (Eds.), *The science of self-report: Implications for research and practice* (pp. 229–255). Mahwah, NJ: Erlbaum.

Kessler, R. C., Zhao, S., Blazer, D. G., & Swartz, M. (1997). Prevalence, correlates and course of minor depression and major depression in the National Comorbidity Study. *Journal of Affective Disorders, 45*(1–2), 19–30.

Kessler, R. C., Zhao, S., Katz, S. J., Kouzis, A. C., Frank, R. G., Edlund, M., & Leaf, P. (1999). Past year use of outpatient services for psychiatric problems in the National Comorbidity Survey. *American Journal of Psychiatry, 156*, 115–123.

Leighton, D. C., Harding, J. S., & Macklin, D. B. (1963). *Stirling County Study: Vol. 3. The character of danger.* New York: Basic Books.

Lewinsohn, P. M., Allen, N. B., Seeley, J. R., & Gotlib, I. H. (1999). First onset versus recurrence of depression: Differential processes of psychosocial risk. *Journal of Abnormal Psychology, 108*(3), 483–489.

Lewinsohn, P. M., Rohde, P., Seeley, J. R., & Fischer, S. A. (1991). Age and depression: Unique and shared effects. *Psychology and Aging, 6*(2), 247–260.

Lewinsohn, P. M., Rohde, P., Seeley, J. R., Klein, D. N., & Gotlib, I. H. (2000). Natural course of adolescent major depressive disorder in a community sample: Predictors of recurrence in young adults. *American Journal of Psychiatry, 157*(10), 1584–1591.

Link, B. G., & Dohrenwend, B. P. (1980). Formulation of hypotheses about the true relevance of demoralization in the United States. In B. P. Dohrenwend, B. S. Dohrenwend, M. Schwarz-Gould, B. Link, R. Neugebauer, & R. Wunsch-Hitzig (Eds.), *Mental illness in the United States: Epidemiological estimates* (pp. 114–132). New York: Praeger.

McLeod, J. D., Kessler, R. C., & Landis, K. R. (1992). Speed of recovery from major depressive episodes in a community sample of married men and women. *Journal of Abnormal Psychology, 101*(2), 277–286.

Melfi, C. A., Chawla, A. J., Croghan, T. W., Hanna, M. P., Kennedy, S., & Sredl, K. (1998). The effects of adherence to antidepressant treatment guidelines on relapse and recurrence of depression. *Archives of General Psychiatry, 55*(12), 1128–1132.

Merikangas, K. R. (2000). Epidemiology of mood disorders in women. In M. Steiner, K. A. Yonkers, & E. Eriksson (Eds.), *Mood disorders in women* (pp. 1–14). London: Martin Dunitz.

Merikangas, K. R., & Angst, J. (1995). The challenge of depressive disorders in adolescence. In M. Rutter (Ed.), *Psychosocial disturbances in young people: Challenges for prevention* (pp. 131–165). Cambridge, UK: Cambridge University Press.

Mintz, J., Mintz, L. I., Arruda, M. J., & Hwang, S. S. (1992). Treatments of depression and the functional capacity to work. *Archives of General Psychiatry, 49*(10), 761–768.

Murphy, J. M., Laird, N. M., Monson, R. R., Sobol, A. M., & Leighton, A. H. (2000). A 40–year perspective on the prevalence of depression: The Stirling County Study. *Archives of General Psychiatry, 57*(3), 209–215.

Murray, C. J. L., & Lopez, A. D. (Eds.). (1996). *The global burden of disease: A comprehensive assessment of mortality and disability from diseases, injuries, and risk factors in 1990 and projected to 2020.* Cambridge, MA: Harvard University Press.

Neale, M. C., & Cardon, L. R. (1992). *Methodology for genetic studies of twins and families.* Dordrecht, The Netherlands: Kluwer Academic Press.

Neugebauer, R., Hoek, H. W., & Susser, E. (1999). Prenatal exposure to wartime famine and development of antisocial personality disorder in early adulthood. *Journal of the American Medical Association, 282*(5), 455–462.

Nicolson, R., Malaspina, D., Giedd, J. N., Hamburger, S., Lenane, M., Bedwell, J., Fernandez, T., Berman, A., Susser, E., & Rapoport, J. L. (1999). Obstetrical complications and childhood-onset schizophrenia. *American Journal of Psychiatry, 156*(10), 1650–1652.

Offord, D. R., Boyle, M., Campbell, D., Cochrane, J., Goering, P. N., Lin, E., Rhodes, A., & Wong, M. (1994). *Mental health in Ontario: Selected findings from the Mental Health Supplement to the Ontario Health Survey.* Toronto: Queen's Printer for Ontario.

Olfson, M., Kessler, R. C., Berglund, P. A., & Lin, E. (1998). Psychiatric disorder onset and first treatment contact in the United States and Ontario. *American Journal of Psychiatry, 155*(10), 1415–1422.

Olive, D. L. (1991). The prevalence and epidemiology of luteal-phase deficiency in normal and infertile women. *Clinical Obstetrics and Gynecology, 34*(1), 157–166.

Olson, K., & Pavetti, L. (1996). *Personal and family challenges to the successful transition from welfare to work.* Washington, DC: Urban Institute.

Patton, G. C., Hibbert, M. E., Carlin, J., Shao, Q., Rosier, M., Caust, J., & Bowes, G. (1996). Menarche and the onset of depression and anxiety in Victoria, Australia. *Journal of Epidemiology and Community Health, 50*(6), 661–666.

Pearlstein, T., & Stone, A. B. (1998). Premenstrual syndrome. *Psychiatric Clinics of North America, 21*(3), 577–590.

Prince, M. (1998). Is chronic low-level lead exposure in early life an etiologic factor in Alzheimer's disease? *Epidemiology, 9*(6), 618–621.

Regier, D. A., Kaelber, C. T., Rae, D. S., Farmer, M. E., Knauper, B., Kessler, R. C., & Norquist, G. S. (1998). Limitations of diagnostic criteria and assessment instruments for mental disorders: Implications for research and policy. *Archives of General Psychiatry, 55*(2), 109–115.

Regier, D. A., Narrow, W. E., Rupp, A., Rae, D. S., & Kaelber, C. T. (2000). The epidemiology of mental disorder treatment need: Community estimates of "medical necessity." In G. Andrews & S. Henderson (Eds.), *Unmet need in psychiatry: Problems, resources, responses* (pp. 41–58). Cambridge, UK: Cambridge University Press.

Risch, N., & Merikangas, K. R. (1996). The future of genetic studies of complex human diseases. *Science, 273,* 1516–1517.

Robins, L. N. (1992). The future of psychiatric epidemiology. *International Journal of Methods in Psychiatric Research, 2,* 1–3.

Robins, L. N., Helzer, J. E., Croughan, J., Williams, J. B. W., & Spitzer, R. L. (1981). *NIMH Diagnostic Interview Schedule: Version III.* Rockville, MD: National Institute of Mental Health.

Robins, L. N., Locke, B. Z., & Regier, D. A. (1991). An overview of psychiatric disorders in America. In L. N. Robins & D. A. Regier (Eds.), *Psychiatric disorders in America: The Epidemiologic Catchment Area Study* (pp. 328–366). New York: Free Press.

Robins, L. N., & Regier, D. A. (Eds.). (1991). *Psychiatric disorders in America: The Epidemiologic Catchment Area Study.* New York: Free Press.

Robins, L. N., Wing, J., Wittchen, H. U., Helzer, J. E., Babor, T. F., Burke, J., Farmer, A., Jablenski, A., Pickens, R., Regier, D. A., et al. (1988). The Composite International Diagnostic Interview: An epidemiologic instrument suitable for use in conjunction with different diagnostic systems and in different cultures. *Archives of General Psychiatry, 45*(12), 1069–1077.

Rosen, L. N., Targum, S. D., Terman, M., Bryant, M. J., Hoffman, H., Kasper, S. F., Hamovit, J. R., Docherty, J. P., Welch, B., & Rosenthal, N. E. (1990). Prevalence of seasonal affective disorder at four latitudes. *Psychiatry Research, 31*(2), 131–144.

Rosenthal, N. E., Sack, D. A., Gillin, J. C., Lewy, A. J., Goodwin, F. K., Davenport, Y., Mueller, P. S., Newsome, D. A., & Wehr, T. A. (1984). Seasonal affective disorder: A description of the syndrome and preliminary findings with light therapy. *Archives of General Psychiatry, 41*(1), 72–80.

Seiler, L. H. (1973). The 22–item scale used in field studies of mental illness: A question of method, a question of substance, and a question of theory. *Journal of Health and Social Behavior, 14*(3), 252–264.

Severino, S. K. (1996). Premenstrual dysphoric disorder: Controversies surrounding the diagnosis. *Harvard Review of Psychiatry, 3*(5), 293–295.

Sheehan, D., Lecrubier, Y., Sheehan, K., Amorim, P., & Janavs, J. (1998). The Mini-International Neuropsychiatric Interview (MINI): The development and validation of a structured diagnostic psychiatric interview for DSM-IV and ICD-10. *Journal of Clinical Psychiatry, 59*(Suppl. 20), 22–33.

Spitzer, R. L., Williams, J. B., Kroenke, K., Linzer, M., deGruy, F. V., 3rd, Hahn, S. R., Brody, D., & Johnson, J. G. (1994). Utility of a new procedure for diagnosing mental disorders in primary care: The PRIME-MD 1000 study. *Journal of the American Medical Association, 272*(22), 1749–1756.

Srole, L., Langner, T. S., Michael, S. T., Opler, M. K., & Rennie, T. A. C. (1962). *Mental health in the metropolis: The Midtown Study.* New York: McGraw-Hill.

Sullivan, P. F., Kessler, R. C., & Kendler, K. S. (1998). Latent class analysis of lifetime depressive symptoms in the National Comorbidity Survey. *American Journal of Psychiatry, 155*(10), 1398–1406.

Sveindottir, H., & Backstrom, T. (2000). Prevalence of menstrual cycle symptom cyclicity and premenstrual dysphoric disorder in a random sample of women using and not using oral contraceptives. *Acta Obstetrica et Gynecologica Scandinavica, 79*(5), 405–413.

Turner, C. F., & Martin, E. (1984). *Surveying subjective phenomena* (Vol. I). New York: Russell Sage Foundation.

Unutzer, J., Klap, R., Sturm, R., Young, A. S., Marmon, T., Shatkin, J., & Wells, K. B. (2000). Mental disorders and the use of alternative medicine: Results from a national survey. *American Journal of Psychiatry, 157*(11), 1851–1857.

Vega, W. A., Kolody, B., Aguilar-Gaxiola, S., Alderete, E., Catalano, R., & Caraveo-Anduaga, J. (1998). Lifetime prevalence of DSM-III-R psychiatric disorders among urban and rural Mexican Americans in California. *Archives of General Psychiatry, 55*(9), 771–778.

Wang, P. S., Berglund, P., & Kessler, R. C. (2000). Recent care of common mental disorders in the United States: Prevalence and conformance with evidence-based recommendations. *Journal of General Internal Medicine, 15*(5), 284–292.

Weissman, M. M., Bruce, M. L., Leaf, P. J., Florio, L. P., & Holzer, C. III. (1991). Affective disorders. In L. N. Robins & D. A. Regier (Eds.), *Psychiatric disorders in America* (pp. 53–80). New York: Free Press.

Weissman, M. M., & Klerman, G. L. (1992). Depression: Current understanding and changing trends. *Annual Review of Public Health, 13,* 319–339.

Wells, K. B., Sherbourne, C., Schoenbaum, M., Duan, N., Meredith, L., Unutzer, J., Miranda, J., Carney, M. F., & Rubenstein, L. V. (2000). Impact of disseminating quality improvement programs for depression in managed primary care: A randomized controlled trial. *Journal of the American Medical Association, 283*(2), 212–220.

Wells, K., Stewart, A., Hays, R., Burnam, M., Rogers, W., Daniels, M., Berry, S., Greenfield, S., & Ware, J. (1989). The functioning and well-being of depressed patients: Results from the Medical Outcomes Study. *Journal of the American Medical Association, 262,* 914–919.

WHO International Consortium in Psychiatric Epidemiology. (2000). Cross-national comparisons of the prevalences and correlates of mental disorders. *Bulletin of the World Health Organization*, *78*(4), 413–426.

Yager, J., Siegfreid, S. L., & DiMatteo, T. L. (1999). Use of alternative remedies by psychiatric patients: Illustrative vignettes and a discussion of the issues. *American Journal of Psychiatry*, *156*(9), 1432–1438.

Yonkers, K. A. (1997). The association between premenstrual dysphoric disorder and other mood disorders. *Journal of Clinical Psychiatry*, *58*(Suppl. 15), 19–25.

2

Course and Outcome of Depression

Robert J. Boland and Martin B. Keller

In the past two decades we have gained an increasing understanding of the course of depression. Previously viewed as an acute and self-limiting illness, it is now clear that, for many individuals, depression is a lifelong illness. Furthermore, we now increasingly appreciate the importance of course in affecting associated psychosocial outcomes, comorbidities, and treatment. This increased understanding is the result of several factors. First, a paradigmatic shift in our conception of depression had to occur. This paradigm shift then allowed for a number of important investigations, including long-term naturalistic studies of depression, that have been conducted over the last two decades. This chapter reviews these studies and their implications for understanding depression. Limitations in the data from these studies will be discussed and future directions for research will be suggested.

HISTORICAL PERSPECTIVE AND THE IMPORTANCE OF COURSE

Historically, mood disorders have been viewed from a variety of perspectives, depending on the period and the theoretical approach. Using such perspectives, depression was usually categorized either by its severity or by its presumed cause. In Europe during the 19th century, major mood disorders were thought to be either congenital or degenerative in origin. Alternatively, a phenomenological approach grew under such figures as Falret and Kraepelin that was primarily concerned with careful description of a particular disorder. This latter approach, though important in its emphasis on symptom classification, was primarily cross-sectional in its description.

Such etiological approaches were evident in 20th century attempts to classify psychiatric disease. The first edition of the American Psychiatric Association's *Diagnostic and Statistical Manual of Mental Disorders* (DSM-I; American Psychiatric Association, 1952) divided mood disorders into those that were "organic" and those that were "reactions" to, presumably, some environmental circumstance. The second edition (DSM-II; American Psychiatric Association, 1968), though softening this stance, perpetuated the same basic distinction, dividing mood disorders into those that were "psychotic" and those that were "neurotic" in nature. The difference involved both presumed etiology (the psychotic disorders being more a type of "brain disease," the neurotic disorders being more "diseases of the mind") and severity. These distinctions were important, as DSM-II was roughly contemporaneous with the development of somatic treatments. Diagnoses had important treatment implications, and the psychotic/neurotic distinction presupposed a division between those who would be helped by drugs and those who would be helped by therapy.

Assumptions about the course of disease and length of treatment also proceeded from these theoretical stances. For individuals whose disease was "reactive" or "neurotic," the presumption was that the individual would remain at risk for mood disturbances until the underlying stress, conflict, or defensive style was removed or altered. For patients with "organic" or "psychotic" disorders, the presumptions were less clear. It seems from the practice of this time that patients who were put into this category were presumed to have a "brain disorder." This disorder was assumed to be chronic. Treatments followed from that assumption, consisting of long-term institutionalization and ongoing somatic treatment. The result was, for many, a black-and-white distinction regarding course, in which some mood disorders were either chronic or "curable."

The DSM's third edition (DSM-III; American Psychiatric Association, 1980) represented a break with etiological divisions in favor of a descriptive approach. One result of this change was a new view of mood disorders, in which patients were no longer categorized by presumed etiology, but rather by severity of symptoms. Presumptive dichotomies about course and treatment were challenged as well. Decisions about treatment became based less on etiological assumptions, and more on cross-sectional criteria. Patients who were sufficiently ill to meet criteria for major depression were more likely to receive somatic treatment, regardless of the presumed etiology. In clinical practice, however, somatic treatment was usually aimed at symptom relief. Once patients improved to the point of being symptom-free or near symptom-free, the patient was usually withdrawn from treatment over a relatively brief time.

This cross-sectional approach left unclear a number of longitudinal treatment decisions. For example, it was not clear how long treatment should be continued following symptomatic improvement. Research in the 1970s and 1980s suggested that many patients for whom treatment was discontinued after symptomatic improvement were likely to relapse back into depression (NIMH Consensus Development Conference Statement, 1985). It seemed that, though symptoms were no longer evident, there remained a period of time following treatment response in which the mood disorder was still present, though controlled. By the mid-1980s, the general wisdom was to continue a patient on medications for a certain period following symptomatic improvement; this period was referred to as the *continuation period*. Although the proper length of continuation was not clear, it seemed likely that it should be as long as a usual episode of untreated depression. Recommendations for the continuation period could vary widely. For example, the 1993 U.S. Department of Health's Clinical Practice Guidelines for the treatment of depression in primary care (Depression Guideline Panel, 1993) recommended a continuation interval of 4–9 months—a rather wide range.

The treatment period, therefore, became extended beyond the point of simple symptom relief. However, the approach toward depression was still basically a cross-sectional one. That is, episodes of depression were viewed singly, with ongoing treatment aimed at preventing a relapse of the acute episode. Treatment usually consisted of an acute period of 6–9 weeks, followed by a continuation period of anywhere from 4 months to a year.

Even with adequate continuation treatment, it was clear that some patients had a recurrence of symptoms when treatment was discontinued, even though the discontinuation was well beyond the period assumed for a single episode. Other patients never seemed to fully recover at all. Understanding the likelihood of such outcomes and potential risk factors for them became paramount for guiding treatment recommendations.

With the advent of more valid and reliable diagnostic and treatment assessment instruments, investigators were able to ask questions that could not be addressed before. Most important was the need to understand the proper length of treatment and the need to determine which individuals were most likely to have a chronic or recurrent depression.

To shed light on these questions, one had to understand the natural course of depression. Treatment studies alone were not adequate. That is, although treatment studies could establish the effectiveness of a medication at various stages of the illness, one had to understand the natural course of the illness before one could investigate the effect of interventions on that course. It is easy to see how earlier assumptions about mood disorders did not lend themselves to such investigations. Thus, it has been relatively recent research that has elucidated these questions.

Much of the groundwork was laid in the pioneering work of Angst and his colleagues in Zurich (Angst, 1986). Beginning in the early 1960s, they identified 173 patients who were originally hospitalized with major depression, and evaluated this group every 5 years for up to 21 years of follow-up. This study provided some of the first information regarding the relation between course and outcome of depression, much of which has been supported by subsequent studies.

Much of what we now accept regarding the course of depression is derived from the Collaborative Depression Study (CDS; Katz & Klerman, 1979). The CDS is a prospective, long-term, naturalistic study of the course of depression that built on the work of Angst, using a larger sample from multiple centers and more up-to-date diagnostic methods. Subjects in the CDS were recruited from patients with depression seeking outpatient or inpatient psychiatric treatment at one of five sites (university or teaching hospitals in Boston, Chicago, Iowa City, New York, and St. Louis). This study included programs in biological and clinical studies. The data presented here are from the clinical studies program. Five hundred and fifty-five subjects in the clinical studies program had an index episode of unipolar major depression. Subjects were examined at 6-month intervals for 5 years and then annually for a minimum of 18 years. Recent NIMH funding will extend the follow-up to at least 23 years on all participants. This study represents the most rigorous study of the course of depression to date.

It should be emphasized from the start, however, that there are limitations of such studies. These studies are investigations of clinical samples, that is, subjects already seeking treatment for depression. Thus, they are not a random sample, nor are they necessarily typical of how depression acts in the community. The studies were naturalistic: data about their treatment were collected and considered as a variable, but the investigators did not attempt to influence treatment decisions. One cannot assume, however, that patients treated at specialty centers will be treated in a manner typical of the depressed patient in the general population.

DEFINITION OF TERMS: THE CHANGE POINTS IN DEPRESSION

For studies such as the CDS to be useful, some agreement had to be reached in defining the key change points in a depressive course. Early studies were hindered by the lack of any such consensus, making the results difficult to interpret and compare. Terms such as *remission* or *recovery* were used inconsistently and sometimes interchangeably. It was for this reason that a MacArthur Foundation task force (Frank et al., 1991) recommended that the change points be described with the following terms: *episode, remission, response, relapse* and *recurrence*. These terms and change points are described below, and are illustrated in Figure 2.1.

An *episode* is defined on the basis of having a certain number of symptoms for a certain period of time. This sort of definition is typical of the types of definitions that would be embraced by researchers on depression. The presence or absence of a disease here is conceptualized not in absolute terms—in which a gold-standard definition can establish without doubt whether or not a person has an episode of a disorder—but rather in statistical terms. The decision must be made as to where to place "the bar" for a disorder: whether it should be conservative or liberal, and what type of error one is willing to accept. This type of decision making must be made at each change point of the disorder, both in terms of number of symptoms and length of time.

Remission, conceptually, is the point at which an episode ends. It is defined by a period of time in which an individual no longer meets criteria for the disorder. Such remission can be partial or full. In *partial remission*, an individual still has more than minimal symptoms. *Full remission* is defined as the point at which an individual no longer meets criteria for the disorder and has no more than minimal symptoms.

A remission may or may not be related to an intervention. *Response*, however, is a remission that is due to a treatment intervention. Response is, in reality, an "apparent" response, due to the inherent difficulty in establishing causality between treatment and response. The assumption is made that a remission that occurs at or near the time of a treatment intervention is most likely causally related. Such an assumption is difficult to prove.

Episode, response, and *remission* are all acute phenomena. Of concern to the investigator of disease course is the point at which an illness has ended: When has the patient *recovered*? Such a definition is important in differentiating *relapse* from *recurrence*.

Recovery is defined as a full remission that lasts for a defined period of time. Conceptually, it implies the end of an episode of an illness, not the end of the illness itself. A *relapse* is defined as the early return of symptoms following an apparent response. Conventionally, *continuation treatment* means treatment during the initial 4–6 months after response. Episodes that occur during this period are relapses. *Recurrence* refers to a new episode occurring after recovery from a previous episode. During continuation treatment, one expects a relapse to occur soon after discontinuation of treatment, as the treatment is presumably suppressing a disease that is still present. For recurrence, reemergence of symptoms does not

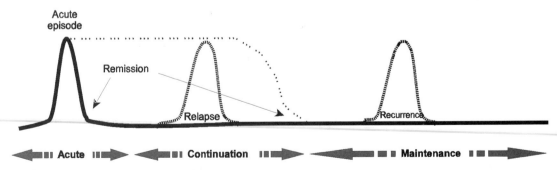

FIGURE 2.1. The changes points of depression. The course is divided into the acute, continuation, and maintenance periods. The triple dotted line (... ... ...) line illustrates the acute and continuation course of an untreated episode, the solid a treated episode. The points at which relapse and recurrence would occur are illustrated with dotted lines. If conceptualized as a graph, the *x* axis would be *time* and the *y* axis would be *number of depressive symptoms*.

necessarily occur soon after stopping treatment, as the patient presumably has been brought into a state of well-being.

These definitions rely on a number of assumptions that cannot be proven because we lack valid biological markers for major depression. Though not independently validated, these definitions represent reasonable working definitions, and are used by most of the studies that are reviewed here.

RESULTS OF NATURAL STUDIES

Recovery

Early studies suggested that, for many patients, the course of depression might extend beyond the normally accepted periods for an acute major depressive episode. Kerr and colleagues (1972), following initially hospitalized patients, found that 6% remained ill for the 4 years of the study. In a prospective follow-up of 96 patients with major depression, Rounsaville and colleagues (1980) found that 12% of subjects had not recovered after 16 months.

Other studies show comparable data. In the Zurich study, Angst and colleagues (1973) reported that during the follow-up evaluations, about 13% of patients did not recover from their episode of major depression. In the CDS, approximately 70% of patients recovered from the index episode of major depression within the first year (Keller, Shapiro, Lavori, & Wolfe, 1982). However, for those patients who did not recover in the first year, most still had not recovered after a much longer time. By 2 years, about 20% of the original sample was still depressed; thus two-thirds of those still depressed at 1 year were still in their index episode of depression at 2 years. At 5 years, 12% of patients had still not recovered (Keller et al., 1992), by 10 years 7% had not recovered (Mueller et al., 1996), and by 15 years the number seems to have leveled off at 6% (Keller & Boland, 1998). These data are presented in Figure 2.2.

The long duration of the CDS allowed the investigators to observe subsequent episodes

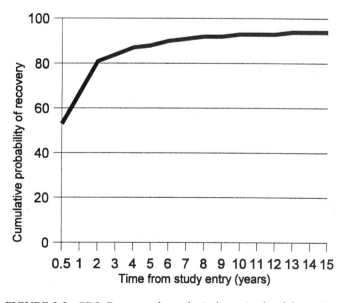

FIGURE 2.2. CDS: Recovery from the index episode of depression.

of major depression beginning during the study. This was particularly useful, as the onset of symptoms could be identified more accurately than when retrospectively judging the beginning of an index episode. It was found that for each new episode of depression, the rates of recovery were similar to those seen during the index episode. For the second episode (first prospectively observed episode), approximately 8% of subjects did not recover after 5 years. An analysis of subsequent episodes (second, third, and fourth prospectively observed episodes) showed similar findings (Figure 2.3). By the fifth episode, the rate decreases, but not significantly so (Solomon et al., 1997). It appears that for each episode of depression, some individuals—about 10%—remain ill for at least 5 years.

The seemingly high rate of chronicity was surprising. A reasonable concern about this result was that this patient population may have been unusually treatment-resistant—as already noted, this was a group of patients seeking treatment at one of five major medical centers and, as such, they may not truly represent the general population. However, most patients in this study received either no treatment or subtherapeutic doses given for inadequate durations (Keller, Klerman, et al., 1982). The problem, therefore, does not seem to be simply one of unusually strong treatment resistance.

Overall, then, the results from the CDS and from other studies suggest that most patients with a major depressive episode will recover within a year. However, a substantial number do not recover, and many of these individuals will still not have a remission after 5 years. Once recovered, each new episode of depression contains the disturbing chance that, this time, the individual may develop a chronic disorder.

Relapse

For the 141 patients in the CDS who recovered from their index episode of major depression, 22% relapsed within 1 year of follow-up (Keller, Lavori, et al., 1983). Factors predicting a relapse included the following:

- Multiple episodes of major depression.
- Older age.

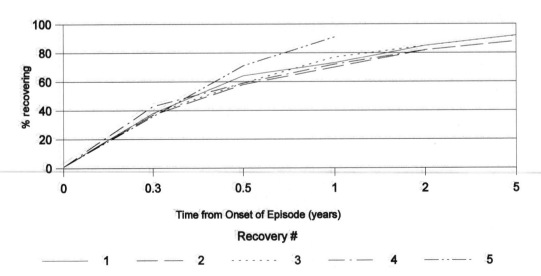

FIGURE 2.3. CDS: Proportion of subjects recovering from subsequent episodes of depression.

- History of nonaffective psychiatric illness.
- Double depression.

The number of previous episodes of depression was a particularly strong predictor of a relapse. When the characteristics of this relapsed group were examined, it was found that the likelihood of remaining depressed for at least a year after a relapse was 22%. Predictors of prolonged time to recovery included a longer length of the index episode, older age, and a lower family income.

Many studies examine relapses in terms of how patients are affected by treatment; this topic will be considered later in this chapter. Here, however, the overall message appears to be that, again, a sizable minority of patients (about 20%) experience a relapse of symptoms after initial recovery. For some of these patients, again, about 20%, achieving a subsequent remission will be more difficult.

Recurrence

A number of early studies have found high rates of recurrence of depression. Weissman and Kasl (1976) found that two-thirds of women seen for more than 1 year had a recurrence of depression. Rao and Nammalvar (1977), examining more than 100 cases of depression in India for a follow-up of between 3 and 13 years, found that only about 25% of the original group reported no recurrence of symptoms. Angst (1992), reporting on a 10-year follow-up of patients in the Zurich study, found that only 25% of patients had no more than a single episode of depression. Thus, three-quarters of the sample had one or more recurrences of depression. Though Angst examined a number of sociodemographic variables, he found none that significantly predicted the likelihood of recurrence of depression.

In the CDS there was a 25–40% rate of recurrence after 2 years. These rates of recurrence in the CDS group increased over time: to 60% after 5 years (Lavori, Keller, Mueller, & Scheftner, 1994), to 75% after 10 years, and to 87% after 15 years (Keller & Boland, 1998). This suggests that, in contrast to rates of recovery (which level off after 5–10 years), individuals continue to be at a high risk for recurrence after 5 and even 10 years. Such a finding was unanticipated.

The rates of recurrence tended to increase with subsequent episodes. In addition, with each subsequent episode of depression, the length of time to recurrence tended to shorten. These differences, however, were not statistically significant. These findings are summarized in Figure 2.4. Consistent with the relapse data, the time to recurrence was also strongly predicted by the number of previous episodes (Figure 2.5). For the first episode of recurrence (following recovery from the index episode), the first onset group had a median of 4 years to recurrence, compared with 1.5 years in the recurrent group. Apparently, once individuals are prone to recurrence (by virtue of having several prior episodes), the time to recurrence continues to decrease. This decrease seems to level off between the third and fourth episode.

The rate and timing of recurrence seem most dependent on the type of recovery. Patients in the CDS who fully recovered (i.e., who were asymptomatic on follow-up evaluation) had a much lower rate of recurrence (66%) than did those who had some residual symptoms (87% recurrence rate). The time to recurrence was also much longer in the asymptomatic group (M = 180 weeks in the asymptomatic group; M = 33 weeks in the group with residual symptoms).

Some risk factors for recurrent depression are summarized below:

- History of frequent and/or multiple episodes.
- Double depression (major depression plus dysthymia).

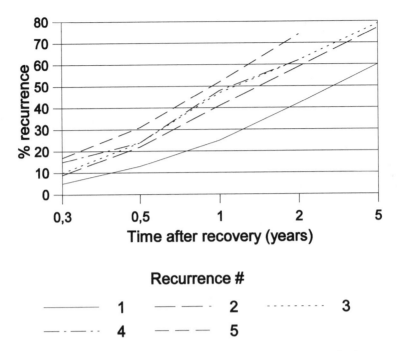

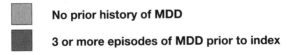

FIGURE 2.4. Probability of recurrence following recovery from the index and subsequent episodes of depression.

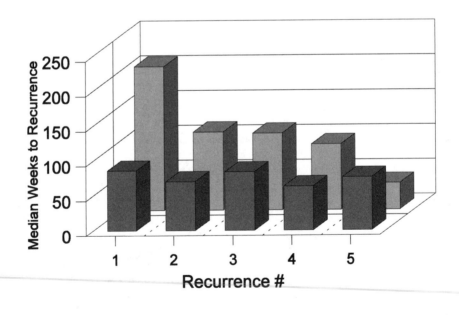

FIGURE 2.5. Median time to recurrence and history of unipolar major depression episodes.

- Onset after age 60.
- Long duration of individual episodes.
- Family history of affective disorder.
- Poor symptom control during continuation therapy.

The overall conclusion from these findings is that, although the risks of nonrecovery and of relapse are of equal concern, recurrence is a particularly oppressive problem: most patients will experience a recurrence by 5 years, and the rate of recurrence continues upward beyond that time. Thus, although most patients would be safe to expect a recovery after an episode of depression, and can remain reasonably assured that they will probably not experience a relapse of symptoms during the continuation period, the same patients should expect that, given enough time, they most likely will have a recurrence of their depression.

COMORBIDITY AND ITS EFFECT ON THE COURSE OF DEPRESSION

The comorbid presence of other illnesses, be they psychiatric or medical, has a negative effect on outcome. This was demonstrated in a study by Keitner and colleagues (1991) who examined inpatients with major depression who also had a comorbid nonaffective psychiatric or medical illness. They referred to patients with one of these comorbid disorders as having "compound depression" (vs. "pure" depression). They found that patients with compound depression had both significantly poorer function during the 12-month follow-up of the study and lower recovery rates.

These findings are important for several reasons. As the population ages, psychiatrists will deal increasingly with geriatric depression, and medical-psychiatric comorbidity will be common in this group. Furthermore, nonpsychiatric physicians are often the "first defense" against depression and, for them, complex interactions between the "mind" and the "body" are the rule.

Some specific comorbidities, and their effect on the course of depression, are considered below.

Double Depression

Double depression—the concurrent presence of both dysthymia and major depression (Keller & Shapiro, 1982)—appears to be an important course modifier. By definition, patients with this disorder have a chronic course. The effect on major depressive episodes is notable as well: patients with double depression seem to recover more rapidly from episodes of major depression than do patients with major depression alone. This was observed most dramatically in the CDS. A large percentage of patients in the study—approximately 25%—had double depression. On 1-year follow-up, 88% of the patients with double depression had recovered from their index episode of depression, whereas only 69% of patients with major depression alone had recovered. This pattern continued through 2 years of follow-up, by which time it was found that 97% of patients with double depression had recovered from the index episode of major depression, whereas only 79% of the group with major depression alone had recovered (Keller, Lavori, Endicott, Coryell, & Klerman, 1983).

Interestingly, the patients do not appear to recover to a level of complete normalcy, but rather to a level of dysthymia. In the CDS, of the subjects with double depression who recovered from their major depressive episode, 58% had not recovered from their underlying dysthymia by the second year of follow-up.

Patients with double depression appear to be more likely to relapse than those patients with major depression alone. In the CDS group described above, patients with double depression were twice as likely as patients without double depression to relapse to major depression during the study period.

In sum, patients who suffer from dysthymia and then experience major depression may exhibit a different course of illness than what would be expected for depression alone. Recovery may be quicker, but may not be as stable as in the case of "pure depression," where relapses are more common, as is incomplete recovery.

Comorbid Medical Illness

Comorbid medical illness may predispose patients with major depression to a more chronic course of disease. This has been suggested in a number of studies, but little research has examined this question directly. The Medical Outcomes Study (Wells et al., 1989) examined the course of several diseases (myocardial infarction, congestive heart failure, hypertension, diabetes, and depression) in a variety of outpatient health care settings, including large medical group practices, small group practices, and solo practices, in three cities (Los Angeles, Boston, and Chicago). This was a large naturalistic study with more than 20,000 subjects. Wells et al. found that medical and psychiatric illness had a combined effect on patient functioning, suggesting a worse overall outcome for patients with medical-psychiatric comorbidity.

Anxiety Disorders

Coryell and colleagues (1988) found that depressed patients with panic disorders were more likely to have been depressed for longer periods of time. They also noted that the symptoms of depression were more severe in patients with comorbid anxiety disorders. Similarly, in the CDS, Clayton and colleagues (1991) found that patients with major depression who also had a higher rating of anxiety had a longer time to recovery. Because anxiety disorders are commonly found with depression, presumably this is one of the more common examples of the deleterious effect of comorbid psychiatric illness on the course of depression.

Personality Disorders

There is a commonly held belief that personality disorders negatively affect the outcome of depression. Although this impression is based more on clinical experiences than on actual data, most studies examining this tend to confirm this belief. Reich and Green (1991) reviewed a number of inpatient and outpatient studies. They reported that all of the studies found outcome to be poorer in patients with depression and a comorbid personality disorder. However, these studies were mostly naturalistic in design, and the patients with comorbid illness tended to be more depressed than were the "pure" depressed patients. Hirschfeld and colleagues (1998) examined predictors of response to acute treatment in patients from the chronic major depression and double depression study, a double-blind study of treatment for chronic depression, and found that the presence of a personality disorder did not influence the rate of response. However, the presence of depressive personality traits did predict a poorer response to pharmacotherapy. Thus, although we generally assume that personality disorders have a negative effect on the course of depression, this bears more investigation.

Substance Abuse

The comorbid presence of alcoholism can exert a deleterious effect on the course of major depression. Mueller and colleagues (1994), examining the CDS cohort, found that depressed subjects with alcoholism, as defined by Research Diagnostic Criteria, were half as likely as other patients to recover from their episode of major depression. Add to this finding the increased risk of suicide when depressed and alcoholic, and it becomes clear that comorbid substance abuse and depression is one of the more insalubrious combinations of disorders.

TREATMENT AS A COURSE VARIABLE

A great deal of data exist to support the contention that treatment of depression can shorten the time to recovery. Such data represent the primary justification for the use of antidepressant medications and several psychotherapies. The efficacy of antidepressant treatment will not be specifically reviewed here, except to note that the primary challenge in treating acute episodes of depression is not so much in finding newer and better treatments, but in ensuring that patients receive such treatment. The CDS and other naturalistic studies continue to support the assertion that only a minority of patients with major depression will receive adequate treatment for their disorder.

Beyond the acute phase of antidepressant treatment, there is substantially less information to support the role of antidepressants in shortening the course of depression. As discussed earlier, the goal of continuation therapy is to prevent a relapse of depression. There are some data to indicate that antidepressants do just that. At least one supportive study exists for most of the serotonin reuptake inhibitors, including fluoxetine (Montgomery et al., 1988), paroxetine (Montgomery & Dunbar, 1993), sertraline (Doogan & Calliard, 1992), and citalopram (Montgomery, Rasmussen, & Tanghol, 1993). Mirtazapine (Montgomery, Reimitz, & Zivkov, 1998) and nefazodone (Feiger et al., 1999) have also been shown to be efficacious in continuation treatment. Though limited for any one agent, the weight of these studies together does suggest that antidepressants lessen the risk for relapse during the continuation period.

When looking beyond continuation therapy to the maintenance treatment of recurrent depression, however, less data exist. Prien and colleagues (1984) conducted a 2-year maintenance trial for depression, comparing lithium carbonate, imipramine, both, or placebo. Treatments were continued for 2 years with doses maintained at acute treatment levels. Of 150 patients beginning maintenance treatment, 36% were successfully treated. The groups treated with imipramine (alone or with lithium) had the lowest rate of recurrence.

Kocsis and colleagues (1996) examined the maintenance treatment in a placebo-controlled trial of desipramine for the treatment of chronic depression. Patients who were initially successfully treated during an acute phase and 16-week continuation treatment were then randomized to receive either desipramine or placebo for up to 2 years of maintenance treatment. During this maintenance period, patients treated with desipramine had one-quarter the recurrence rate of patients receiving a placebo.

The longest study of maintenance treatment to date is the Pittsburgh study of maintenance treatment for recurrent depression (Kupfer et al., 1992). This study reported on up to 5 years of maintenance treatment. Patients first underwent open treatment for acute depression, using imipramine with interpersonal therapy (IPT). Patients who achieved recovery for at least 4 months were then randomized to medication, IPT, placebo, or a combination of two of these, and then were treated for 3 years. In this study, patient selection was highly biased toward recurrent depression in order to increase the likelihood of finding a statistically significant effect size for the interventions. This, therefore, is a study of maintenance treatment for highly recurrent depression. Kupfer et al. found that patients who received imipramine (with or without IPT), had an approximately 20% risk of recurrence after 3 years. This is significantly lower than the other conditions: IPT alone had a 60% risk of recurrence and the placebo condition had an 80% risk.

This study was extended, with a smaller sample, for another 2 years, using subjects who had remained well during the first 3 years. By the end of the study, only 20 patients remained. However, for this small group, the treatment intervention was much more effective in preventing recurrence than was the placebo.

A similar study was conducted by Reynolds and colleagues (1999) using a geriatric population (60 years or older). The major difference in the design was that nortriptyline was used instead of imipramine because of its greater tolerability in the elderly. Maintenance treatment was continued for 3 years in more than 100 patients. Recurrence rates over this period were as follows: combined treatment, 20%; medication alone, 43%; IPT plus placebo, 64%; placebo alone, 90%.

The good news here is that all available studies support the efficacy of antidepressants in the maintenance period of treatment. That is, they do appear to successfully prevent recurrence of major depression. The bad news, however, is that the studies are both few and small. For data beyond 2 years, we have only a few hundred patients to look at. Beyond 3 years, we have only 20. Furthermore, the available studies use tricyclic antidepressants: imipramine and nortriptyline. Because most clinicians are now using agents from different classes, it is a leap of faith to assume that what we have learned from the tricyclic antidepressants can be generalized to patients receiving serotonin reuptake inhibitors or other newer agents.

Specific Subtypes of Major Depression

As noted above, the Pittsburgh maintenance study targeted one specific group of patients with major depression: those with recurrent depression. Others studies have chosen to target other specific groups. For example, in the chronic major depression and double depression study, Keller and his colleagues (1998) examined the effect of treatment on both these chronic disorders. In this study, 161 patients who were successfully treated for major depression (acute and continuation phase treatment) were then randomized to receive either sertraline or placebo for a 76-week maintenance period. The study included patients with chronic major depression and patients with double depression in roughly equal numbers; because the results did not differ between the groups, the data from these two groups were combined. Keller et al. found that the placebo-treated patients were four times more likely to have a recurrence of depression than were those who received sertraline. Moreover, for those patients receiving sertraline who did have a recurrence, the time to recurrence was significantly delayed compared to those treated with the placebo.

Keller and colleagues (2000) also examined the use of combination therapy in the treatment of chronic depression. In this study, 681 patients from 12 different sites were randomly assigned to receive acute therapy for depression. The treatment conditions consisted of nefazodone and psychotherapy, alone and in combination. The psychotherapy was the cognitive behavioral-analysis system of psychotherapy developed by McCullough (1995), a structured form of cognitive behavioral therapy that includes elements of IPT.

Results from the acute phase portion of the study lend strong support for the efficacy of combined treatment in mitigating the outcome of chronic depression. The group receiving both psychotherapy and pharmacotherapy had the highest remission rate: 85% compared with 55% in the medication-only group and 52% in the psychotherapy group. Using an intention-to-treat analysis, the results were just as striking: 73% of the combination group showed a total response, compared to 48% for the medication alone group and 47% for the psychotherapy alone group. These combination treatment response rates are the highest reported to date in a large-scale controlled trial for major depression. Data from the continuation, crossover, and maintenance phases should be available for publication by the fall of 2001 and should answer several critical hypotheses about combination treatment in the longer term.

Though again limited data exist, the evidence remains positive for the ability of antidepressants to both speed recovery and delay recurrence in patients with chronic depression. Several features of these studies make them particularly welcome. First, they use agents more commonly used in contemporary clinical practice. Most interesting, however, is the strong result found for psychotherapy, something that has been noticeably lacking in previous studies. Though the effect size is surprising when compared to previous combination therapy studies, this may be explained by the high intensity and frequency of the therapy (usually two times a week or more in the acute phase of treatment).

Other Subtypes of Depression

Few data exist concerning the treatment of subsyndromal depression and forms of minor depression. What data do exist are primarily on the treatment of dysthymia, though even there the number and scope of treatment studies are quite limited. This may be somewhat surprising, given that psychotherapy has been the traditional treatment for all nonmajor forms of depression. The ability of psychotherapy to reduce the chronicity of dysthymia remains hypothetical. The few studies that have been conducted tend to have methodological limiations (e.g., small samples, lack of a control group) (Conte & Karasu, 1992; Markowitz, 1994), and only a few concentrate specifically on relapse or recurrence prevention as goals. Cognitive therapy has been studied most extensively, but some data exist for a variety of other treatments, including interpersonal therapy, marital therapy, group therapy, and family therapy (Conte & Karasu, 1992; Markowitz, 1994; Paykel, 1994).

Pharmacotherapy studies examining the treatment of dysthymia are also limited. Most show at least a modest response to medication (Howland, 1991). Overall, randomized controlled studies demonstrate efficacy for most available agents, including tricyclic antidepressants (Kocsis et al., 1985; Stewart et al., 1993), serotonin reuptake inhibitors (Hellerstein et al., 1993; Thase et al., 1996; Ravindran, Bialik, & Lapierre, 1994; Vanelle, 1997) and such atypical agents as ritanserin (Bakish, Ravindran, Hooper, & Lapierre, 1994), moclobemide (Botte, Evrard, Gilles, Stenier, & Wolfrum, 1992) and amisulpride (Boyer & Lecrubier, 1996). Some attempts have been made to investigate whether some agents are preferentially efficacious. For example, some earlier data suggested that monoamine oxidase inhibitors were more useful for dysthymia (Howland, 1991). However, there are no definitive data to suggest that any one agent is more efficacious than other agents.

FUTURE DIRECTIONS

We have been greatly helped in the last two decades by natural studies of depression and by clinical investigations of depression treatment. On the one hand, natural studies have encouraged us to view depression as, for many, a chronic disorder, with three stages (or phases) of the illness. On the other hand, clinical studies have established the efficacy of a variety of potent treatments for depression. What we must now accomplish is a bridging of the gap between these two knowledge bases. We still cannot adequately predict who will develop what type of depression: who will get only a single episode, who will go on to experience recurrent episodes with interepisode recovery, and who will become chronically depressed. Consequently, many patients are fated to suffer the morbidity of major depressive episodes as a result of premature treatment withdrawal and inadequate treatment. Furthermore, treatment efficacy data have only begun to take into account natural history data; as one gets further from the acute phase of the illness, the number of treatment studies available dramatically diminishes. Clearly, we need to better target which patients should have long-term treatment, and then better understand which treatments will best prevent future episodes. Only long-term prospective studies that take into account the patient's natural course of illness *and* the longitudinal treatment response will persuasively enlighten these issues.

To truly alter the course of major depression, we also need to better understand other factors apart from natural history and traditional treatment efficacy data. For example, perhaps the greatest barrier to treatment efficacy is patient adherence; yet most of the studies discussed in this review do not collect data on adherence or on variables that may explain problems with adherence. Clearly, one of the most important reasons for treatment failures (and, hence, a worse course of depression) lies not in the pharmacodynamics of individual medications, but in the complex interactions between patients and their doctors. We still do not understand why some patients choose to not receive treatment, once offered, or why they terminate treatment prematurely. Most current studies of adherence (regardless of particular disease) are cross-sectional or of short duration. However, to truly understand how adherence affects the long-term course of depression we need to better incorporate adherence data into long-term intervention and natural history studies.

Perhaps even less is understood about the behaviors of physicians. What little information there is on the decision-making processes of physicians suggests that more than mere education will be needed to improve the process of initiating and maintaining treatment in patients with depression.

The problems of comorbidity, and its effect on the course of depression, also are important areas in need of investigation. As already discussed, there are few studies investigating how medical illness and depression interact. What information does exist suggests that depressed patients with medical illnesses have a much worse course. However, important questions remain unanswered. Is the effect simply additive, or does the interaction of medical and psychiatric illness confer additional risk? Furthermore, we know that certain illnesses are more predisposed to depression. Whether these are also more likely to deleteriously affect the course of depression remains an interesting question. Future long-term studies of depression will have to collect more precise data on patients' medical histories and illnesses, as well as their history of treatments for the same in order to better answer these questions.

The role of the environment in depression, particularly the importance of adverse life events and their effect on depression, is another important area of study. As noted earlier, prior to DSM-III, depressive illnesses were largely divided into those that were presumed to be organic and those that were "reactive." Now, we generally accept the notion that the etiology of depression is much more complex. Recent research, both genetic and sociological, has begun to explore the relationship between behavior and the environment in a sophisticated way. It will be interesting and important to expand this research longitudinally. For example, if future long-term natural studies of depression used "cutting-edge" methodologies for tracking life events, the results could greatly enhance our understanding of the interplay between nature and nurture, and of how adding the dimension of time affects that interplay.

Finally, we cannot ignore the issue of economics. A number of large-scale studies, including the CDS and the Medical Outcomes Study, have suggested that the cost of depression in loss of work productivity more than justifies the cost of treatment. Most of these data are based on extrapolations or suppositions from cross-sectional studies. It is not clear whether such information has been persuasive enough to influence economic decisions in medicine, particularly those of third-party payers. As noted earlier, we are beginning to find that early and intensive interventions using both medication and psychotherapy may be the most effective strategy to affect the outcome of a depressive illness. We will have to work hard to convince others of this. Particularly influential would be data showing that such improvement translates directly into a measurable cost savings. Similarly important will be the need to demonstrate that the cost offsets occur in a reasonable time. This is needed to better combat the often short-sighted business models of many third-party payers. Future long-term studies of depression should make sophisticated collection of economic variables a priority.

REFERENCES

American Psychiatric Association. (1952). *Diagnostic and statistical manual of mental disorders.* Washington, DC: Author.

American Psychiatric Association. (1968). *Diagnostic and statistical manual of mental disorders* (2nd ed.). Washington, DC: Author.

American Psychiatric Association. (1980). *Diagnostic and statistical manual of mental disorders* (3rd ed.). Washington, DC: Author.

American Psychiatric Association. (1987). *Diagnostic and statistical manual of mental disorders* (3rd ed. rev.). Washington, DC: Author.

American Psychiatric Association. (1994). *Diagnostic and statistical manual of mental disorders* (4th ed.). Washington, DC: Author.

Angst, J. (1986). The course of major depression, atypical bipolar disorder, and bipolar disorder. In H. Hippius, G. L. Klerman, & N. Matussek (Eds.), *New results in depression research* (pp. 26–35). Berlin/Heidelberg: Springer-Verlag.

Angst, J. (1992). How recurrent and predictable is depressive illness? In S. Montgomery & F. Rouillon (Eds.), *Long-term treatment of depression* (pp. 1–15). New York: Wiley.

Angst, J., Baastrup, P., Grof, P., Hippius, H., Poldinger, W., & Weis, P. (1973). The course of monopolar depression and bipolar psychoses. *Psychiatria, Neurologia Neurochirurgia, 76,* 489–500.

Bakish, D., Ravindran, A., Hooper, C., & Lapierre, Y. (1994). Psychopharmacological treatment response of patients with a DSM-III diagnosis of dysthymia disorder. *Psychopharmacology Bulletin, 30,* 53–59.

Botte, J., Evrard, J. L., Gilles, C., Stenier, P., & Wolfrum, C. (1992). Controlled comparison of RO-11-1163 (moclobemide) and placebo in the treatment of depression. *Acta Psychiatry Belgium, 92,* 355–369.

Boyer, P., & Lecrubier, Y. (1996). Atypical antipsychotic drugs in dysthymia: Placebo controlled studies of amisulpride versus imipramine, versus amineptine. *European Psychiatry, 11*(Suppl. 3), 135S–140S.

Clayton, P. F., Grove, W. M., Coryell, W., Keller, M., Hirschfeld, R., & Fawcett, J. (1991). Follow-up and family study of anxious depression. *American Journal of Psychiatry, 148,* 1512–1517.

Conte, H. R., & Karasu, T. B. (1992). A review of treatment studies of minor depression: 1980–1991. *American Journal of Psychotherapy, 46,* 58–74.

Coryell, W., Endicott, J., Andreasen, N. C., Keller, M. B., Clayton, P. J., Hirschfeld, R. M. A., Schefner, W. A., & Winokur, G. (1998). Depression and panic attacks: the significance of overlap as reflected in follow-up and family study data. *American Journal of Psychiatry, 145,* 293–300.

Depression Guideline Panel. (1993). *Depression in primary care: Vol. 2. Treatment of major depression* (Clinical Practice Guideline, No. 5). Rockville, MD: U.S. Department of Health and Human Services, Public Health Service, Agency for Health Care Policy and Research.

Doogan, D. P., & Caillard, V. (1992). Sertraline in the prevention of depression. *British Journal of Psychiatry, 160,* 217–222.

Feiger, A. D., Bielski, R. J., Bremner, J., Heiser, J. F., Trivedi, M., Wilcox, C. S., Roberts, D. L., Kensler, T. T., McQuade, R. D., Kaplita, S. B., & Archibald, D. G. (1999). Double-blind placebo-substitution study of nefazodone in the prevention of relapse during continuation treatment of outpatients with major depression. *Clinical Psychopharmacology, 14,* 19–28.

Frank, E., Prien, R. F., Jarrett, R. B., Keller, M. B., Kupfer, D. J., Lavori, P. W., Rush, A. J., & Weissman, M. M. (1991). Conceptualization and rationale for consensus definitions of terms in major depressive disorder: Remission, recovery, relapse, and recurrence. *Archives of General Psychiatry, 48,* 851–855.

Hellerstein, D. J., Yanowitch, P., Rosenthal, J., Samstag, L. W., Maurer, M., Kasch, K., Burrows, L., Poster, M., Cantillon, M., & Winston, A. (1993). A randomized double-blind study of fluoxetine versus placebo in the treatment of dysthymia. *American Journal of Psychiatry, 150,* 1169–1175.

Hirschfeld, R. M., Russell, J. M., Delgado, P. L., Fawcett, J., Friedman, R. A., Harrison, W. M., Koran, L. M., Miller, I. W., Thase, M. E., Howland, R. H., Connolly, M. A., & Miceli, R. J. (1998). Predictors of response to acute treatment of chronic and double depression with sertraline or imipramine. *Journal of Clinical Psychiatry, 59,* 669–675.

Howland, R. H. (1991). Pharmacotherapy of dysthymia: A review. *Journal of Clinical Psychopharmacology, 11,* 83–92.

Katz, M., & Klerman, G. L. (1979). Introduction: Overview of the clinical studies program. *American Journal of Psychiatry, 136,* 49–51.

Keitner, G. I., Ryan, C. E., Miller, I. W., Kohn, R., & Epstein, N. B. (1991). 12-month outcome of patients with major depression and comorbid psychiatric or medical illness (compound depression). *American Journal of Psychiatry, 148,* 345–350.

Keller, M. B. (1990). Depression underrecognition and undertreatment by psychiatrists and other health care professionals. *Archives of Internal Medicine, 150,* 946–948.

Keller, M. B. (1993). The difficult depressed patient in perspective. *Journal of Clinical Psychiatry, 54*(Suppl. 2), 4–9.

Keller, M. B., & Boland, R. J. (1998). Implications of failing to achieve successful long-term maintenance treatment of recurrent unipolar major depression. *Biological Psychiatry, 44,* 348–360.

Keller, M. B., Klerman, G. L., Lavori, P. W., Fawcett, J. A., Coryell, W., & Endicott J. (1982). Treatment received by depressed patients. *Journal of the American Medical Association, 248*(15), 1848–1855.

Keller, M. B., Kocsis, J. H., Thase, M. E., Gelenberg, A. J., Rush, A. J., Koran, L., Schatzberg, A., Russell, J., Hirschfeld, R., Klein, D., McCullough, J. P., Fawcett, J. A., Kornstein, S., La Vange, L., & Harrison, W. (1998). Maintenance phase efficacy of sertraline for chronic depression: a randomized controlled trial. *Journal of the American Medical Association, 280,* 1665–1672.

Keller, M. B., Lavori, P. W., Endicott, J., Coryell, W., & Klerman, G. L. (1983). "Double depression": Two-year follow-up. *American Journal of Psychiatry, 140,* 689–694.

Keller, M. B., Lavori, P. W., Klerman, G. L., Andreasen, N. C., Endicott, J., Coryell, W., Fawcett, J., Rice, J. P., & Hirschfield, R. M. (1986). Low levels and lack of predictors of somatotherapy and psychotherapy received by depressed patients. *Archives of General Psychiatry, 43,* 458–466.

Keller, M. B., Lavori, P. W., Lewis, C. E., & Klerman, G. L. (1983). Predictors of relapse in major depressive disorder. *Journal of the American Medical Association, 250L,* 3299–3304.

Keller, M. B., Lavori, P. W., Mueller, T. I., Endicott, J., Coryell, W., Hirschfeld, R. M., & Shea, T. (1992). Time to recovery, chronicity, and levels of psychopathology in major depression: A 5-year prospective follow-up of 431 subjects. *Archives of General Psychiatry, 49,* 809–816.

Keller, M. B., McCullough, J. P., Klein, D. N., Arnow, B., Dunner, D. L., Gelenberg, A. J., Markowitzz, J. C., Nemeroff, C. B., Russell, J. M., Thase, M. E., Trivedi, M. H., & Zajecka, J. (2000). A comparison of nefazodone, the cognitive behavioral-analysis system of psychotherapy, and their combination for the treatment of chronic depression. *New England Journal of Medicine, 342,* 1462–1470.

Keller, M. B., & Shapiro, R. W. (1982). "Double depression": Superimposition of acute depressive episodes on chronic depressive disorders. *American Journal of Psychiatry, 139,* 438–442.

Keller, M. B., Shapiro, R., Lavori, P. W., & Wolfe, N. (1982). Recovery in major depressive disorder: Analysis with the life table and regression models. *Archives of General Psychiatry, 39*(8), 905–910.

Kerr, T. A., Roth, M. Schapira, K., & Gurney, C. (1972). The assessment and prediction of outcome in affective disorders. *British Journal of Psychiatry, 121,* 167–174.

Kocsis, J. H., Frances, A. J., Voss, C., Mann, J. J., Mason, B. J., & Sweeney, J. (1985). Imipramine treatment for chronic depression. *Archives of General Psychiatry, 45,* 253–257.

Kocsis, J. H., Friedman, R. A., Markowitz, J. C., Leon, A. C., Miller, N. L., Gniwesch, L., & Parides, M. (1996). Maintenance therapy for chronic depression: A controlled clinical trial of desipramine. *Archives of General Psychiatry, 53,* 769–774.

Kupfer, D. J., Frank, E., Perel, J. M., Cornes, C., Mallinger, A. G., Thase, M. E., McEachran, A. B., & Grochocinski, V. J. (1992). Five-year outcome for maintenance therapies in recurrent depression. *Archives of General Psychiatry, 49,* 769–773.

Lavori, P. W., Keller, M. B., Mueller, T. I., & Scheftner, W. (1994). Recurrence after recovery in unipolar major depressive disorder: An observational follow-up study of clinical predictors and somatic treatment as a mediating factor. *International Journal of Methods in Psychological Research, 4,* 211–229.

Markowitz, J. C. (1994). Psychotherapy of dysthymia. *American Journal of Psychiatry, 151,* 1114–1121.

McCullough, J. P. (1995). *Therapist manual for cognitive behavioral analysis system of psychotherapy.* Richmond, VA: Commonwealth University.

Montgomery, S. A., & Dunbar, G. (1993). Paroxetine is better than placebo in relapse prevention and the prophylaxis of recurrent depression. *International Clinical Psychopharmacology, 8,* 189–195.

Montgomery, S. A., Dunfour, H., Brion, S., Gailledreau, J., Laqueille, X., Ferry, G., Moron, P., Parant-Lucena, N., Singer, L., & Danion, J. H. M. (1988). The prophylactic efficacy of fluoxetine in unipolar depression. *British Journal of Psychiatry, 153*(Suppl. 3), 69–76.

Montgomery, S. A., Rasmussen, J. G., & Tanghol, P. (1993). A 24-week study of 20 mg citalopram, 40 mg citalopram and placebo in the prevention of relapse of major depression. *International Clinical Psychopharmacology, 8,* 181–188.

Montgomery, S. A., Reimitz, P.-E., & Zivkov, M. (1998). Mirtazapine versus amitriptyline in the long-term treatment of depression: a double-blind placebo-controlled study. *International Clinical Psychopharmacology, 13,* 63–73.

Mueller, T. I., Keller, M. B., Leon, A., Solomon, D. A., Shea, M. T., Coryell, W., & Endicott, J. (1996). Recovery after five years of unremitting major depressive disorder. *Archives of General Psychiatry, 53,* 794–799.

Mueller, T. I., Lavori, P. W., Keller, M. B., Swatz, A., Warshaw, M., Hasin, D., Coryell, W., Endicott, J., Rice, J., & Akiskal, H. (1994). Prognostic effect of the variable course of alcoholism on the 10-year course of depression. *American Journal of Psychiatry, 151,* 701–706.

NIMH Consensus Development Conference Statement. (1985). Mood disorders: Pharmacologic prevention of recurrences. *American Journal of Psychiatry, 142,* 469–476.

Paykel, E. S. (1994). Dysthymia in clinical practice: Psychological therapies. *Acta Psychiatrica Scandinavica, 383*(Suppl.), 35–41.

Prien, R. F., Kupfer, D. J., Mansky, P. A., Small, J. G., Tuason, V. B., Voss, C. B., & Johnson, W. E. (1984). Drug therapy in the prevention of recurrences in unipolar and bipolar affective disorders, *Archives of General Psychiatry, 41,* 1096–1104.

Rao, A. V., & Nammalvar, N. (1977). The course and outcome in depressive illness: A follow-up study of 122 cases in Madurai, India. *British Journal of Psychiatry, 130,* 392–396.

Ravindran, A. V., Bialik, R. J., & Lapierre, Y. D. (1994). Therapeutic efficacy of specific serotonin reuptake inhibitors (SSRIs) in dysthymia. *Canadian Journal of Psychiatry, 39,* 21–26.

Reich, J. H., & Green, A. I. (1991). Effect of personality disorders on outcome of treatment. *Journal of Nervous and Mental Disease, 179,* 74–82.

Reynolds, C. F., Frank, E., Perel, J. M., Imber, S. D., Corens, C., Miller, M. D., Mazumday, S., Houck, P. R., Dew, M. A., Stack, J. A., Pollock, B. G., & Kupfer, D. J. (1999). Nortriptyline and interpersonal psychotherapy as maintenance therapies for recurrent major depression: a randomized controlled trial in patients older than 59 years. *Journal of the American Medical Association, 281,* 39–45.

Rounsaville, B. J., Prusoff, B. A., & Padian, N. (1980). Chronic mood disorders in depression outpatients: Aa prospective 16-month study of ambulatory patients. *Journal of Nervous and Mental Disorders, 168,* 406–411.

Solomon, D. A., Keller, M. B., & Leon, A. C. (1997). Recovery from major depression: A 10-year prospective follow-up across multiple episodes. *Archives of General Psychiatry, 54,* 1001–1006.

Stewart, J. W., McGrath, P. J., Quitkin, F. M., Rabkin, J. G., Harrison, W., Wager, S., Nunes, E., Ocepek-Welikson, K., & Tricamo, E. (1993). Chronic depression: Response to placebo, imipramine and phenelzine. *Journal of Clinical Psychopharmacology, 13,* 391–396.

Thase, M. E., Fava, M., Halbreich, U., Kocsis, J. H., Koran, L., Davidson, J., Rosenbaum, J., & Harrison, W. (1996). A placebo-controlled, randomized clinical trial comparing sertraline and imipramine for the treatment of dysthymia. *Archives of General Psychiatry, 53,* 777–784.

Vanelle, J. M. (1997). Controlled efficacy study of fluoxetine in dysthymia. *British Journal of Psychiatry, 170,* 345–350.

Weissman, M. M., & Kasl, S. V. (1976). Help-seeking in depressed out-patients following maintenance therapy. *British Journal of Psychiatry, 129,* 252–260.

Wells, K. B., Stewart, A., Hays, R. D., Burnam, A., Rogers, W., Daniel, M., Berry, S., Greenfield, S., & Ware, J. (1989). The functioning and well-being of depressed patients: Results of the Medical Outcomes Study. *Journal of the American Medical Association, 262,* 914–919.

3

Assessment of Depression

Arthur M. Nezu, Christine Maguth Nezu,
Kelly S. McClure, and Marni L. Zwick

This chapter describes state-of-the-art assessment procedures and measures of depression. We begin with the notion that the decision to use specific procedures, inventories, methods, or questionnaires depends on several key issues—the specific goals of the assessment, the amount of time one has to accomplish an evaluation, and the specific population one is evaluating—to name just a few. Therefore, we devote the first section of this chapter to describing various clinical decision-making issues as they apply to the task of assessing depression. In the remaining sections we offer a brief overview of specific depression assessment measures, including structured clinical interviews and self-report inventories.

DECISION-MAKING ISSUES

As one approaches the assessment of depression for clinical purposes or contemplates the optimal depression assessment strategy for a research design, the need for effective decision making clearly emerges (C. M. Nezu, Nezu, & Foster, 2000). Many choices regarding depression measures and tools are available—Where does one begin when faced with the range of possible alternatives? Because so many assessment approaches exist, and because each depressed patient's difficulties are unique, no definitive cookbook or strategy exists that applies to all problem areas (Nezu & Nezu, 1989). Nonetheless, a few guidelines are generally applicable across patients and problem areas regarding the development of an overall assessment plan. As an aid to decision making, we recommend that the following questions should be considered when choosing assessment tools (see also Nezu & Nezu, 1993, C. M. Nezu & Nezu, 1995):

1. What are the goals of assessment?
2. Who is to be assessed?
3. What is the value of a given measure?
4. Who is the source of the information?

What Are the Goals of Assessment?

Many different possible contexts, reasons, or goals for assessment exist regarding depression, including (1) screening, (2) diagnosis and classification, (3) description of problem areas and symptoms, (4) case formulation and clinical hypothesis testing, (5) treatment planning, (6) prediction of behavior, and (7) outcome evaluation.

Screening

Screening provides for a timely indication of whether further assessment is warranted in clinical situations. For research purposes, it helps to determine whether a given individual might meet initial inclusion criteria. To be useful, scores from screening instruments should correlate highly with scores engendered by more comprehensive assessments regarding the presence or absence of the disorder being assessed. This requirement involves evaluating the criterion-related validity of the screening instrument. Cutoff scores are often required when using screening instruments, along with information about the types of errors made when using such cutoffs. *Sensitivity* refers to the ability of a measure to accurately identify persons who have a given characteristic in question using a given cutoff score—for example, the proportion of people with major depression who are correctly identified as depressed by their score on a given measure. *Specificity*, on the other hand, refers to the degree to which a measure accurately identifies individuals who do *not* have the characteristic being measured—for example, the proportion of people who do not have a diagnosis of major depressive disorder and who are correctly identified as *not* depressed by their score on a given depression measure.

Diagnosis and Classification

Accurate diagnostic grouping serves two important purposes: (1) it provides for a common clinical language; and (2) it offers specific "content area" or index terms by which to search the scientific literature for accurate, reliable, and valid evaluation and treatment procedures. With regard to research activities, such classifications provide for important demarcations among clinical samples, and thus can improve the validity and replicability of findings across studies. Instruments that are designed specifically for formulating diagnoses warrant particular scrutiny for their content validity. In other words, a diagnostic instrument should contain content that clearly corresponds to the criteria required for diagnosis by a formal diagnostic system, such as the *Diagnostic and Statistical Manual of Mental Disorders* (e.g., DSM-IV-TR; American Psychiatric Association, 2000). The content should exclude extraneous material and weight symptoms as required by the classification system. Further, the diagnosis that the instrument points to should be reliable over time. When clinical judgment is involved, it should demonstrate good interclinician agreement when the system is implemented by independent raters evaluating the same patient. Further, such a measure should also lead to an accurate *differential* diagnosis, that is, not only should it correctly denote what diagnosis a person qualified for, but also which diagnoses he or she does *not* qualify for, especially when symptom overlap across diagnoses exists.

Description of Symptoms

Many assessment tools attempt to provide measurement of symptom topography, range, severity, and/or frequency. These measures often provide specific idiographic information for persons within a specific diagnostic group. Severity of depressive symptomatology is likely to be a frequent target of assessment in both clinical and research settings, given that such evaluations are important with regard to treatment success. To be useful in providing such information, measures of symptom severity especially need to be documented as reliable over time.

Clinical Hypothesis Testing

In order to develop an accurate case formulation, it is important to understand the etiology, function, and maintaining factors of an individual's complaints (Nezu, Nezu, Friedman, & Haynes, 1997). Consequently, in this context, assessment focuses on hypothesized *mechanisms of action*. Such variables may involve cognitive, emotional, behavioral, social, or biomedical factors that are theoretically or empirically connected to the symptoms or complaints for which an individual is seeking treatment. Rosen and Proctor (1981) referred to these variables as *instrumental outcomes*. In other words, such factors serve as "instruments" to effect or influence change in the major problem areas or the major reasons for seeking treatment. These latter types of goals or objectives are referred to by Rosen and Proctor as *ultimate outcomes*. From a research perspective, instrumental outcomes can be thought of as *independent variables*, whereas ultimate outcomes can be viewed as *dependent variables*. Clinically, changes in instrumental outcomes (e.g., problem-solving ability) are hypothesized to lead to changes in the ultimate outcomes (e.g., depressive symptoms).

Treatment Planning

Assessing such instrumental variables helps the therapist to develop a treatment plan for depression (see C. M. Nezu & Nezu, 1989). For example, a clinician following a cognitive model of depression might first test for the presence and extent of cognitive distortions in an individual experiencing depressive symptoms. Such a measure might be the Dysfunctional Attitude Scale (Weissman & Beck, 1978) or the Automatic Thoughts Questionnaire—Revised (Kendall, Howard, & Hays, 1989). In this situation, the therapist is not only measuring depression (i.e., the referral complaints or ultimate reason for seeking treatment), but also a cognitive mediational style that is hypothesized to serve as an important causal factor of depression (an instrumental outcome). Therefore, the clinician would be able to determine if, in fact, the cognitive model of depression is applicable to this patient. If so, then a cognitive therapy approach may be recommended (e.g., Beck, 1987). If not, such an intervention might be inappropriate, and thus potentially ineffective. Therefore, measures of instrumental outcomes can be useful for evaluating the idiographic importance of various mechanisms of action that are nomothetically linked to the clinical phenomena of interest. Measurement of both types of variables also underscore the importance of outcomes assessment in both clinical and research settings (Nezu, 1996). To be especially useful for predicting which treatments are likely to work and which will not, a measure should ideally provide some evidence that its use leads to more effective or efficient treatment than would occur in its absence.

Additional examples of measures aimed at assessing hypothesized mechanisms of action that are tied to a particular psychosocial treatment approach for depression include (1) the Frequency of Self-Reinforcement Questionnaire (Heiby, 1983), a measure of self-control skills, which is connected to self-control therapy (e.g., Rehm, 1977); (2) the Pleasant Events Schedule (MacPhillamy & Lewinsohn, 1982), an inventory assessing the frequency and subjective enjoyability of pleasurable events, which is connected to Lewinsohn's (1974) behavior therapy approach; and (3) the Social Problem-Solving Inventory—Revised (D'Zurilla, Nezu, & Maydeu-Olivares, 2002), a measure of social problem-solving ability, which is related to Nezu's (e.g., Nezu, 1987, Nezu, Nezu, & Perri, 1989) problem-solving therapy for depression.

Prediction

Assessment is also used for behavioral prediction in academic, research, and clinical settings. Particularly relevant to clinical situations is the prediction of behavior that carries a high risk of danger to self or others. Examples include assessment of the likelihood of suicide or violence. Other examples include evaluating the likelihood that an individual will benefit from an educational or therapeutic experience. In this case, previous studies of predictive validity are important, for they allow the clinician to determine how well the assessment tool actually predicts the outcome for which it was intended, and they also enable the clinician to note the nature and range of errors of prediction that occur.

Treatment Outcome

Assessment devices also help to monitor patient progress and evaluate the efficacy of treatment. To be successful in this goal requires, first, that the content of the measure actually address the behaviors targeted by the treatment plan. Second, the measure should be stable in the absence of conditions that produce change (i.e., it should demonstrate acceptable test–retest reliability in the absence of treatment or changes in the client's circumstances). Third, the measure should be sufficiently sensitive to detect change. This criterion generally requires data demonstrating that scores on the measure change significantly during treatment but not in the absence of treatment. Investigations of whether changes in scores on the measure following treatment correlate highly with changes in scores on other measures of the same construct provide further evidence of treatment sensitivity, as well as convergent validity. With regard to depression, measures that assess symptom severity can also serve as instruments that provide information concerning the effects of treatment (e.g., a decrease in symptom severity).

Multiple Goals

Finally, there may be several goals of assessment for a given patient. An example involves a situation when both diagnosis and treatment recommendations are desired. Such goals require assessment tools that classify, as well as instruments that might increase the therapist's understanding of patient problem areas. Consequently, a crucial initial step toward effective selection of assessment instruments rests in the accurate determination of assessment goals.

Who Is to Be Assessed?

People suffering from depression are a heterogeneous group. Therefore, in addition to determining an assessment plan based on particular goals, it is imperative to use measures for a given individual that were developed specifically for that particular subgroup of "depressed" people.

Age Differences

One patient difference of consequence is age. For example, not only would adult measures of depression be inappropriate for children due to language differences, but also with regard to the potential divarications in the overall constellation of symptoms and their behavioral expression. A variety of depression measures have been developed for children and adolescents, many of them modeled after adult instruments. For example, the Children's Depression Inventory (CDI, Kovacs, 1992), a self-report measure of depressive symptoms developed for children and adolescents, was patterned after the Beck Depression Inventory. Other child measures of depression include the Children's Depression Rating Scale—Revised (Poznanski & Mokros, 1996), the Multiscore Depression Inventory for Children (Berndt & Kaiser, 1996), and the Reynolds Child Depression Inventory (Reynolds, 1989). Reynolds (1987) also developed a self-report measure of depression specifically for adolescents, where the age range includes ages 13–18 years, whereas his child version addresses the age range of 8–12 years.

With regard to the other end of the life span spectrum, measures have been specifically developed for older persons. A popular measure is the Geriatric Depression Scale (Yesavage et al., 1983), which is self-report questionnaire geared for adults 65 years and older. A related measure, the Depression Rating Scale (Cohen-Mansfield & Marx, 1988), was developed to assess depression, as well as social functioning, among a population of elderly nursing home residents. Although not necessary restricted to the elderly, the Cornell Scale for Depression in Dementia (Alexopoulos, Abrams, Young, & Shamoian, 1988) is geared to assess depression among people with dementia.

Presence of Multiple Diagnoses or Problems

Another potential interpatient difference is the presence of additional psychiatric or medical diagnoses. In certain cases, these concomitant problems can limit the validity of depression measures not able to take these problems into account. Examples include the Calgary Depression Scale for Schizophrenia (Addington, Addington, & Maticka-Tyndale, 1993), a clinician-rated protocol, which was developed in response to the observation that other assessment instruments for depression did not accurately represent depressive symptoms or syndromes in persons with schizophrenia. The Medical-Based Emotional Distress Scale (Overholser, Schubert, Foliart, & Frost, 1993) was developed to provide for a more valid assessment of distress, including dysphoria, such that the results are not biased by physical symptoms of the co-occurring medical disorder. Another medically related measure is the Primary Care Evaluation of Mental Disorders (PRIME-MD, Spitzer et al., 1993). This instrument was designed to identify mood, anxiety, somatoform, alcohol, and eating disorders in adults in primary care settings.

Stern (1997) developed the Visual Analogue Mood Scales specifically for persons with neurological impairment and requests respondents to indicate their current mood state along a series of eight 100-mm vertical lines, where one anchor is always "neutral," and the other anchor represents a given mood (e.g., sadness).

Although the prevalence of psychopathology in persons with mental retardation is significantly greater than among persons with normal intellectual functioning (C. M. Nezu, Nezu, & Gill-Weiss, 1992), the availability of psychometrically sound instruments to assess such problems is limited. The Psychopathology Inventory for Mentally Retarded Adults (Matson, 1988) includes eight clinical scales, one of which is an "affective disorders" scale. This interview-based instrument was developed and normed specifically on populations of mentally retarded adults. The author of this measure strongly suggests that only professionals who are trained to work with mentally retarded persons should administer this measure, underscoring the importance of our notion of always using instruments specifically designed for a given population.

Cultural Differences

Other important interindividual differences arise from ethnic and cultural backgrounds. It is not enough to ensure that a given self-report measure has been competently back-translated into another language (e.g., Spanish, Chinese), it is also important that a given instrument addresses constructs that have meaning within a given culture. Research has shown that whereas some similarities are evident in the expression of depression across various cultures, specific differences do exist (Kaiser, Katz, & Shaw, 1998). Such differences in the expression of depression (e.g., headaches and "nerves" in Latino and Mediterranean cultures, fatigue and "imbalance" among Asian cultures, "problems of the heart" in Middle Eastern countries; American Psychiatric Association, 2000) may be a function of varying values among cultures or of the manner in which Western society interprets these values. Cultures also vary in the manner in which they judge the seriousness or appropriateness of dysphoria.

The importance of considering cultural background when conducting a differential diagnosis is emphasized in DSM-IV-TR (American Psychiatric Association, 2000). In addition to the five standard diagnostic axes, it is recommended that the clinician consider five additional categories when working with multicultural environments: (1) the cultural identity of the individual (e.g., what is the person's self-identified cultural group, his or her degree of acculturation, and his or her current involvement in the host culture?); (2) cultural explanations of the individual's disorder (e.g., what are the causal attributions and significance of the "condition" that is promulgated by the individual's culture?); (3) cultural factors related to psychosocial environment and levels of functioning (e.g., what is the availability of social support? what is the cultural interpretation of social stressors?); (4) cultural elements of the relationship between the person and the clinician (e.g., what are the differences in both culture and social status between the clinician and the patient?); and (5) overall assessment for diagnosis and care (e.g., what are the cultural factors that might impact upon the patient's diagnosis and treatment?).

Coming from a cognitive-behavioral perspective, Tanaka-Matsumi, Seiden, and Lam (1996) suggest a similar approach when conducting a "culturally informed functional analysis." Specifically, they suggest eight concrete steps: (1) assess cultural identity and degree of acculturation; (2) assess and evaluate clients' presenting problems with reference to their cultural norms; (3) evaluate clients' causal attributions regarding their problems; (4) conduct a functional analysis; (5) compare one's case formulation with a patient's belief system; (6) negotiate treatment objectives and methods with the patient; (7) discuss with the patient the need for data collection to assess treatment progress; and (8) discuss treatment duration, course, and expected outcome with the client.

Various measures of depression, initially developed in Western cultures, have been demonstrated to be applicable across a variety of cultures and have been translated into numerous languages, such as the BDI and the Zung Self-Rating Depression Scale (SDS; Zung, 1965). An example of a measure of depression specifically developed for a non-Western culture is the Vietnamese Depression Scale (VDS, Kinzie et al., 1982). The VDS was developed in conjunction with Vietnamese mental health professionals and cultural group norms were considered at every stage of its development.

What Is the Value of a Given Measure?

We define the *value* of a measure in this context as a joint function of (1) the likelihood that a given measure will provide the type of information appropriate for a given goal; and (2) the cost–benefit ratio regarding practical concerns. The first component focuses on the strength of the reliability and validity of a measure, especially in relation to the specific goal at hand. As noted in the previous section, in addressing assessment goals, certain psychometric properties are particularly important relative to a given objective—for example, the need for a measure of depressive symptom severity to be especially reliable over time. In addition to evaluating a measure's test–retest stability, other forms of reliability to take into consideration when judging the value of the assessment tool include (1) *internal consistency* (the extent to which different item groupings yield consistent scores on a measure); and (2) *interrater reliability* (the degree to which two raters evaluating a given person or characteristic score consistently).

Various parameters of validity to consider include (1) *concurrent validity* (the extent to which scores of a given measure actually predict scores on a similar measure collected at the same time); (2) *construct validity* (the degree to which scores on a measure actually assess theoretically what it purports to measure); (3) *content validity* (the extent to which a measure appropriately samples the domain being assessed); (4) *convergent validity* (the degree to which scores on a measure correlate with scores on measures of the same construct); (5) *criterion-related validity* (the degree to which scores can be used to predict a person's performance regarding an important behavior); (6) *discriminant validity* (the extent to which scores on a measure are unrelated to scores on measures of theoretically unrelated constructs); (7) *discriminative validity* (the degree to which scores on a measure distinguish between groups known to differ on the construct being assessed); and (8) *predictive validity* (the extent to which scores on a measure can be used to predict a person's score on a performance measure collected at a latter time).

A cost–benefit analysis of various practical concerns should address the following issues: (1) the amount of time required by both the patient and the assessor; (2) potential risks or dangers associated with a given assessment procedure; (3) potential ethical violations associated with a given measure; (4) the effects of a given procedure on others involved (e.g., family members); (5) short-term versus long-term benefits or liabilities related to a given assessment procedure; and (6) the incremental utility of the measure (e.g., how much unique information does this measure offer?).

The obvious notion is that researchers and clinicians should choose those measures that have strong psychometric properties and are associated with a positive benefit-to-cost ratio if implemented. The final consideration in choosing assessment measures concerns the *source* of the information.

Who Is the Source of the Information?

Measures of depression can be divided into two categories pertaining to the source of the information: self-report and clinician-rated measures. Each method has its advantages and disadvantages. For example, whereas self-report questionnaires are relatively brief and require less time to complete than do clinician-rated measures, they are more vulnerable to respondent bias (e.g., patients may be less than truthful or wish to present themselves in a particularly "good or bad light"). Clinician-rated measures are likely to produce more reliable results than self-report inventories, but often require special training in the structured interviews that can accompany such procedures. All else being equal, a combination of both procedures will likely yield the most valid and comprehensive picture of a given patient. However, the reader should view all the questions posed by this decision-making guide as equally important when choosing among the various depression measures.

Although a plethora of both types of measures of depression exist, it is beyond the scope of this chapter to describe and review them all. We refer the reader to Nezu, Ronan, Meadows, and McClure (2000) for a review of over 90 depression-related measures (see Appendix 3.1 for an abridged list). In the remainder of this chapter, we provide a brief overview of several of these instruments according to the following categories: screening instruments, measures for diagnostic classification; measures of depressive symptom severity; and measures of depressive affect. Some of these measures were chosen based on their popularity (e.g., BDI), whereas others were chosen based on their recent appearance in the literature (e.g., Harvard Department of Psychiatry/National Depression Screening). However, in all cases, our choices reflect instruments of sound psychometric properties. In addition, we offer general recommendations and comments concerning each of these categories.

SCREENING MEASURES

Although it is hypothetically possible to use many of the measures described in this chapter as "screening devices" for depression, usually a researcher or clinician would be interested in an instrument that is relatively brief and user-friendly, as the purpose for screening is to determine whether further assessment is warranted or whether a person meets certain inclusion criteria. In addition to being brief, such measures should also be characterized by strong criterion-related validity. Two such examples include the Reynolds Depression Screening Inventory (RDSI; Reynolds & Kobak, 1998) and the Harvard Department of Psychiatry/National Depression Screening Day questionnaire (HANDS; Baer et al., 2000).

Reynolds Depression Screening Inventory

The RDSI (Reynolds & Kobak, 1998) is a 19-item self-report inventory designed to measure depressive symptom severity in adults. It was specifically developed to be consistent with DSM-IV (American Psychiatric Association, 1994) diagnostic criteria for major depressive disorder and to be easy to administer and score. In order to meet these goals, the manual provides three case illustrations to demonstrate how to interpret RDSI scores in a clinical setting.

The RDSI takes approximately 5–10 minutes to complete. Each item asks a question about specific depressive symptoms and is followed by a Likert-type scale with specific anchor points for each possible response. Raw scores are tallied by summing the scores of each item, and a table with corresponding T-scores and percentile scores is contained in the manual (Reynolds & Kobak, 1998). The manual also provides norms based on a community sample of 450 adults, along with cutoff scores that guide the comparison between RDSI scores and clinical severity levels. Scores between 0 and 10 indicate that a respondent is either not depressed or experiencing subclinical levels of depression; scores between 11 and 25 indicate mild clinical severity; scores between 16 and 24 represent moderate clinical severity; and scores greater than 24 indicate severe clinical depression. According to the manual for the RDSI, a cutoff score of 16 and above to identify persons with major depression has a sensitivity rate of 95% and a specificity rate of 95%.

The RDSI has additional sound psychometric properties. Based on a sample of 855 adults, internal consistency was found to be .93. Test–retest reliability in a sample of 190 adults was .94. The developers of the RDSI also conducted several stringent analyses to demonstrate the validity of this instrument. First, all of the items of the RDSI correspond with DSM-IV (American Psychiatric Association, 1994) diagnostic criteria for major depressive disorder, thus supporting the content validity of the instrument. The criterion-related validity of this instrument was supported by its high correlation ($r = .93$) with the clinician-rated Hamilton Rating Scale for Depression (Hamilton, 1960) in a group of 405 adults. The construct validity of the RDSI was also supported by its high convergent validity with instruments such as the BDI ($r = .93$) and the Beck Hopelessness Scale (Beck & Steer, 1988, $r = .80$). Furthermore, the RDSI showed a low correlation with the Marlowe–Crowne Social Desirability Scale—Short Form (Crowne, 1979, $r = -.37$), supporting the divergent validity of this measure.

Harvard Department of Psychiatry/National Depression Screening Day

This 10-item self-report questionnaire was developed specifically to be used in the National Depression Screening Day in the United States (Baer et al., 2000). It is intended to be a brief, easy-to-score scale that provides guidelines for referral to mental health services. Scores provide for the likelihood that a respondent is suffering from clinically significant depression or depressive symptomatology.

This instrument is characterized by strong psychometric properties. The items were derived from other psychometrically sound depression inventories, such as the BDI and the Zung SDS, using item response theory. The developers of the HANDS were careful to test the properties of the HANDS with participants reflecting the group that may attend National Depression Screening Day.

As noted earlier, sensitivity and specificity are critical to maximizing the validity of screening instruments. The HANDS is able to detect truly depressed individuals and minimizes the likelihood of false positives. Studies show that 93–95% of respondents scoring 9 or higher met criteria for a DSM-IV diagnosis of major depressive episode. Therefore, the authors of the HANDS recommend that respondents scoring 9 or higher be referred for further evaluation. This instrument also has good internal consistency (coefficient alpha = .87).

Comments

Because both these instruments have strong sensitivity and specificity properties, either would be effective for screening purposes in clinical settings. The HANDS is somewhat quicker to complete. For research purposes, however, we suggest a different strategy. If an investigator's purpose is to screen out depressed individuals from a study (i.e., depression is an *exclusion* criteria), than, once again, we would recommend either instrument. On the other hand, if depression is an *inclusion* criteria, whereby the goal is to eventually have clinically depressed persons as participants, then we would suggest that the researcher chose a measure of depressive symptom severity (see later section entitled *Measures of Depressive Symptom Severity*) that would also serve as one of the major dependent or outcome measures. In addition, however, a second administration of this same measure should be conducted at a later time (which would serve as the pretreatment assessment score) in order to reduce the probability of false positives that may occur due to transitory distress (Kendall, Hollon, Beck, Hammen, & Ingram, 1987). For example, in a study that evaluated the efficacy of problem-solving therapy for major depressive disorder, Nezu and Perri (1989) used a "multiple gate" system of screening, whereby persons who eventually met inclusion criteria were required to report high levels of depression (i.e., BDI score of 20) at *both* the initial screening and 4 weeks later. This second BDI score, and not the original screening score, then, served as the actual pretreatment assessment of depression level.

MEASURES FOR DIAGNOSTIC CLASSIFICATION

Schedule for Affective Disorders and Schizophrenia and Research Diagnostic Criteria

The Schedule for Affective Disorders and Schizophrenia (SADS; Endicott & Spitzer, 1978) is a clinician-administered interview designed to aid the process of diagnosis and to assess the severity of psychiatric symptoms as specified by Research Diagnostic Criteria (RDC; Spitzer, Endicott, & Robins, 1978). There are several versions of the SADS, some which were constructed to measure change in psychiatric status. In addition, there is a lifetime version and versions modified for specific syndromes like bipolar mood disorders. The standard version is completed in two parts. The first part assesses the severity of *current* psychopathology and impairment of functioning. It is organized to facilitate clinical diagnostic decision making. The manual provides follow-up questions and probes to obtain symptom severity information. The second part of the interview consists of questions that evaluate the frequency, intensity, and duration of previous episodes of psychopathology. The content of these symptom scales reflects major psychiatric constructs, such as formal thought disorders and manic syndromes.

The current version of the SADS covers 24 major psychiatric disorders, as well as disorder-specific subtypes (e.g., recurrent major depressive disorder, endogenous major depressive disorder). The structured interview takes between 90 and 120 minutes to complete and requires the interviewers to be trained mental health professionals.

General normative data are not available, although large-scale epidemiological studies evaluating the prevalence and incidence of psychiatric disorders can be applied as a useful framework. Coefficient alpha estimates for the SADS scale range from .47 (formal thought disorder) to .97 (manic syndrome). Interrater reliability estimates for the joint administration of the original version of the SADS ranged from .82 to .99. For the depression summary scale, interrater reliability was estimated to be .95. Test–retest estimates range from .49 to .93. With regard to the reliability of diagnoses made through SADS interviews, Spitzer et al. (1978) report a kappa value of .90 regarding the diagnosis of major depressive disorder and .81 for minor depressive disorder. The SADS has been translated into several languages and has been widely used in clinical research since its development. Therefore, it has a substantial body of empirical data to support its utility.

Diagnostic Interview Schedule

The Diagnostic Interview Schedule–IV (DIS-IV) is the sixth version of the Diagnostic Interview Schedule, which was initially developed in 1978 for use in the National Institute of Mental Health's Epidemiologic Catchment Area (ECA) Program (Robins, Helzer, Croughan, & Ratcliff, 1981). The goal of the ECA program was to determine the prevalence and incidence rates of various psychiatric disorders in the United States. Given the incredibly large number of diagnostic interviews that was required to meet this goal, the need arose for an interview that could be conducted by trained laypeople. This need was the impetus for the development of the DIS, which allowed for the assessment of specific diagnostic categories within the DSM-III (the then-current DSM version).

The DIS has been revised during the past several years to meet the needs of changing diagnostic systems in general. The major goal is to keep the DIS compatible with the current DSM, thus, the DIS-IV is compatible with DSM-IV. Other changes have been made as well. For example, categories not included in earlier DIS versions, such as diagnoses arising in childhood (e.g., separation anxiety disorder), are included in the DIS-IV. Also, additional questions have been added to allow for more specificity regarding the course of a disorder, treatment seeking, and links with physical causes, among other areas. Other changes removed aspects of the previous DIS, such as questions related to non-DSM diagnostic systems, so as to limit the length of the interview.

The DIS-IV is a highly structured interview designed to allow laypersons to determine DSM diagnoses. It consists of 22 individual modules, most of which focus on specific diagnoses (e.g., generalized anxiety disorder) or groups of diagnoses (e.g., specific phobia, social phobia, agoraphobia). Several modules focus on other areas such as demographics and a summary of the interview. Questions are structured so that the interviewer can exit the module at various points as it becomes apparent that the disorder in question is not present. All answers are coded according to explicitly stated guidelines, with the coded answers entered into a computer to yield specific diagnoses.

The DIS requires between 90 and 120 minutes for completion, although the authors list several ways in which the interview may be shortened without compromising its validity (e.g., dropping modules not of interest). Note that extensive training of lay interviewers is required. The DIS-IV does not include specific interpretation guidelines. It yields DSM-IV diagnoses, as well as additional information regarding related areas (e.g., treatment utilization and health behaviors).

Test–retest reliability was calculated for the depression module of the DIS-IV in a sample of 140 persons each of whom was interviewed twice about depression. Of this sample, 35% were positive for a major depressive episode, and the test–retest kappa was found to be .63 (range of .49–.77). The sample was 56% African American, 44% female, with a mean age of 36.

Because few measures cover the full range of DSM diagnoses, comparing the DIS to other measures has been difficult. Therefore, the validity of the DIS has been estimated in studies that compare DIS diagnoses with those obtained by trained professionals, such as psychiatrists. Unfortunately, results have been somewhat disappointing. For example, Anthony et al. (1985), with regard to a sample of 810 community residents, found kappa values of agreement between lay-administered DIS diagnoses and those made by psychiatrists to be relatively low (mean across diagnoses of .15).

Structured Clinical Interview for DSM-IV Axis I Disorders

The Structured Clinical Interview for DSM-IV Axis I Disorders (SCID-I; First, Spitzer, Gibbon, & Williams, 1997) provides a standardized clinical interview to determine DSM-IV (American Psychiatric Association, 1994) diagnoses and differential diagnoses. It consists of an open-ended interview, a semistructured interview, and questions pertaining to specific symptoms that determine differential diagnosis. Whereas this instrument is structured to match the specific diagnostic criteria defined in the DSM-IV, it also utilizes the skills of trained clinicians by allowing them to probe, restate questions, challenge respondents, and ask them for clarification. Results provide very specific diagnostic categorization that distinguishes current versus lifetime prevalence, severity (e.g., mild, moderate, severe), and 5th-digit specifiers. Administration of the entire SCID-I takes from 45 to 90 minutes. In certain cases, however, it is possible to administer specific modules, including the mood disorder module, if time is a factor.

The SCID-I was first published in 1983 and has evolved along with the revisions of the DSM-III, DSM-III-R, and DSM-IV. The psychometric properties of the most current version of the SCID-I have not yet been published and are commonly estimated based upon the previous version. The validity of this instrument can be evaluated in terms of how well it reflects the DSM-IV (American Psychiatric Association, 1994) diagnostic criteria and how well it measures the constructs they purport to represent.

Segal, Hersen, and Van Hasselt (1994) provide a review of studies reported until 1994 which suggest that the SCID-III-R demonstrates fair to good reliability across studies. There is some evidence to suggest that this instrument is more reliable among clinical samples than among nonpatients (Williams et al., 1992).

The SCID-I is designed for adults and can be used for clinical or research purposes. Interestingly, one study shows that this instrument may have a positive effect on study participants by decreasing their anxiety and depression (Scarvalone et al., 1996). As research expands to include participants from lower income levels, as well as persons with concomitant medical illnesses, more structured interviews are being conducted over the telephone to overcome transportation or mobility problems. The SCID-I can be conducted over the telephone. However, one study found that participants were more likely to receive a lifetime diagnosis of major depressive disorder after an in-person interview than after a telephone interview (Cacciola, Alterman, Rutherford, McKay, & May, 1999).

Comments

In general, these types of structured interview approaches are very time-intensive, although the SCID, unlike the DIS, does not require all questions to be asked and answered. For example, if a probe question on the SCID is not answered with a "yes" answer, the interviewer skips to the next section. In contrast, on the DIS, interviewers are required to ask all questions regardless of the answer, and the items are read verbatim to the respondent in a standardized order. Therefore, especially because it was originally developed for epidemiological research with normative samples, the SCID would be more useful than the DIS for clinical purposes with individual patients. Further, since the SADS was not kept up to date with the DSM system, we would also recommend the SCID over the SADS in situations in which there is a need to confirm a DSM-IV-TR differential diagnosis in a clinical setting.

MEASURES OF DEPRESSIVE SYMPTOM SEVERITY

Clinician-Rated Measures

Hamilton Rating Scale for Depression

The Hamilton Rating Scale for Depression (HRSD, Hamilton, 1960) was designed to evaluate the severity of depressive symptoms among patients who had previously been diagnosed with a depressive disorder. It has been used extensively in clinical research evaluating the effects of antidepressant medications and psychosocial treatments. Developers of other rating scales of depression tend to view the HRSD as a "gold standard," and thus use it to assess the concurrent validity of their own measures. It is historically the most widely used clinician rating of depression in psychiatric settings and has also been found to be valid for assessing depressive symptoms among primary care patients (Brown, Schulberg, & Madonia, 1995).

The HRSD is a 21-item clinician-rated measure that takes approximately 10 minutes to complete following a 30-minute interview. Of the 17 items actually scored (four items are omitted from scoring), the patient is requested to respond to questions concerning symptoms of depression that have been experienced during the past few days or week. Nine items include 5-point scales ranging from 0 to 4, representing ascending levels of symptom severity. The remaining eight items include 3-point scales ranging from 0 to 2, also representing ascending levels of severity. Hamilton (1967) recommended that all available information from others (e.g., family, friends, nurses) be used whenever the accuracy of a patient's report is questioned. Although Hamilton did not provide specific probes for interviewing patients, he recommended that clinicians limit their questions, but present them in an objective manner (e.g., ask "How badly do you sleep?" as well as "How well do you sleep?").

There has been some difficulty integrating the many research findings concerning the HRSD because different versions (i.e. three "cognitive" items, assessing hopelessness, helplessness, and worthlessness, respectively, have been added) have been developed and published studies often lack information indicating which version was implemented. Therefore, it is important to note the method employed for scoring when reporting results of studies using the HRSD. Scores on the HRSD of 6 and below (scoring only the original 17 items) are considered to represent normal, or nondepressed, levels of functioning. Additional guidelines include the following: scores of 7–17 reflect mild depression, scores of 18–24 reflect moderate depression, and scores of 25 or more represent severe depression. To place such scores in context, a score of 14 or more was required for outpatients to be entered into the National Institute of Mental Health Treatment of Depression Collaborative Research Program (Stosky & Glass, 1983).

Most interrater reliability coefficients for the HRSD have been found to be .84 or higher (Hedlund & Vieweg, 1979). Its internal consistency has been found to range from .45–.78 (Schwab, Bialon, & Holzer, 1967). Three studies with depressed patients have reported high correlations (.84, .89, .90) between HRSD scores and global clinical ratings of severity at the time of hospital admission (Hamilton, 1960; Lascelles, 1966; Paykel, Prusoff & Tanner, 1976). Studies addressing the relationship between the BDI and the HRSD reported correlations ranging from .61 to .86 in psychiatric populations and from .41 to .80 in nonpsychiatric populations (Brown et al., 1995). Similar correlations were found between the HRSD and the Zung SDS (.38 to .62; Zung, 1965). At least two relatively stable factors emerge from studies conducting factor analyses of the HRSD (Hedlund & Vieweg, 1979). The first factor to be extracted reflects retarded, or endogenous, depression, a general measure of the severity of symptoms. The second factor is a bipolar variable that reflects anxious, agitated (reactive) depression at one end, and retarded, endogenous depression at the other.

The popularity and respect by which it is held by depression researchers is evidenced by the variety of self-report measures of depression that are based on the HRSD. Such measures include the Carroll Rating Scale for Depression (Carroll, Feinberg, Smouse, Rawson, & Greden, 1981), the Hamilton Depression Inventory (Reynolds & Kobak, 1995), and the Revised Hamilton Rating Scale for Depression (Warren, 1994).

Self-Report Measures

Beck Depression Inventory

The Beck Depression Inventory (BDI; Beck, Ward, Mendelson, Mock, & Erbaugh, 1961) is one of the most widely used, reliable, and valid self-report measures of depression for both psychiatrically diagnosed patients and normal populations. The original BDI was developed as a clinician's rating scale and published by Beck and colleagues in 1961, revised as a self-report instrument in 1971, and subsequently modified in 1987 by Beck and Steer (BDI-IA) to eliminate alternative wordings for the same symptoms and to avoid the use of double negatives.

Several published studies have addressed the psychometric properties of the BDI-IA. Most reviews report average coefficient alphas of .86 for psychiatric patients and .81 for nonpsychiatric samples and a three-factor solution (negative attitudes toward self, performance impairment, and somatic disturbance) has been most frequently identified in the literature (Dozois, Dobson, & Ahnberg, 1998). The BDI has demonstrated adequate internal consistency, test–retest reliability, construct validity, and factorial validity. However, Dozois et al. (1998) suggest that one of the limitations of the BDI concerns its content validity as the instrument covers only six of nine DSM-IV diagnostic criteria—items measuring the more physical symptoms of depression (e.g., psychomotor agitation) are not included.

Thus, in response, the BDI-IA has been recently "upgraded" to the Beck Depression Inventory–II (BDI-II; Beck, Steer, & Brown, 1996) to make its symptom content more reflective of the diagnostic criteria as contained in the DSM-IV for major depressive disorders (Steer, Clark, Beck, & Ranieri, 1998). Twenty-three items were changed in the revised edition of the BDI. Although it is still composed of 21 items, it now contains four new symptoms: agitation, worthlessness, concentration difficulty, and loss of energy. The symptoms eliminated from the BDI-IA included weight loss, body image change, work difficulty, and somatic preoccupation. Each BDI-II item now has a header that is meant to focus the respondent on the overall purpose of the statement. In addition, the BDI-II now inquires about sleep and appetite increases, as compared to only decreases. Finally, the time frame was changed from 1 week to 2 weeks to be temporally compatible with the DSM-IV.

The BDI-II is scored by summing the highest ratings for each of the 21 symptoms. Each symptom is rated on a 4-point scale ranging from 0 to 3, so total scores can range from 0 to 63 (higher scores indicate more severe depressive symptoms). According to Beck et al. (1996), higher cutoff scores were determined for the BDI-II, as compared to the BDI, for defining minimal, mild, moderate, and severe depressive symptomatology. However, it is recommended that scores should not be used as the sole source of information for diagnostic purposes. The BDI-II requires 5–10 minutes to complete and it can be self-administered or interviewer-assisted.

The overall psychometric properties of the BDI-II and the BDI-IA are similar for psychiatric outpatients in general. For example, Beck et al. (1996) found that coefficient alphas of the BDI-II and the BDI-IA were .91 and .89, respectively, among 140 outpatients who were diagnosed with various DSM-IV psychiatric disorders. The correlations of both instruments' total scores for these outpatients with sex, ethnicity, age, and the diagnosis of a mood disorder were within a hundredth of 1 point of each other for the same variables. The mean BDI-II total score, however, was approximately 2 points higher than it was for the BDI-IA and approximately one more symptom on average was endorsed on the BDI-II than it was on the BDI-IA (Steer, Rissmiller, & Beck, 2000).

Evidence of convergent validity is provided by its significant correlation with the Beck Hopelessness Scale (Beck & Steer, 1988; $r = .68$) and the Scale for Suicide Ideation (Beck, Kovacs, & Weissman, 1979; $r = .37$), both constructs generally viewed to be conceptually related to depression. Further, evidence suggests that the BDI-II is positively correlated ($r = .71$) with the clinician-rated HRSD. In a normative sample of 500 outpatients with various psychiatric disorders (Beck et al., 1996), the BDI-II was described as being composed of two positively correlated dimensions reflecting a noncognitive (somatic-affective) factor and a cognitive factor composed of psychological symptoms. These results were confirmed in a sample of 210 adult outpatients who were diagnosed with DSM-IV depressive disorders. A further study confirmed this two-factor structure among geriatric outpatients diagnosed with major depressive disorder (Steer et al., 2000). In general, the factor structure of the BDI-II appears to be more clearly delineated than the original BDI. Thus, it appears that the revisions made to the BDI have improved its factorial validity.

Zung Self-Rating Depression Scale

The Zung Self-Rating Depression Scale (SDS; Zung, 1965) is also among the most popular self-rating depression scales. This 20-item questionnaire was developed to quickly assess the cognitive, behavioral, and affective symptoms of depression. Each item presents a statement describing either positive (e.g., "I feel hopeful about the future") or negative (e.g., "I have crying spells or feel like it") feelings, thoughts, or behaviors. Respondents are requested to indicate how much each statement describes how they have been feeling during the past several days. Responses are indicated along a 4-point Likert-type scale where 1 = little or none of the time and 4 = most of the time.

The psychometric properties of the SDS have been examined in a number of different cultures including Dutch, Finnish, and Japanese populations. Several factor analyses of the SDS have been conducted. In general, whereas three factors tend to emerge from these analyses, they have been interpreted differently. For example, Sakamoto, Kijima, Tomoda, and Kambara (1998) assigned the following labels to the factors that emerged in their principal components analysis: (1) cognitive symptoms, (2) affective symptoms, and (3) somatic symptoms. The analysis was conducted based on a sample of 2,187 Japanese college students and resulted in a goodness of fit index (GFI) of .94. It was further supported by a confirmatory factor analysis in a sample of 597 Japanese undergraduates (GFI = .92). On the other hand, while Kivelae and Pahkala (1987) also found three factors, they labeled them differently as (1) depressed mood, (2) loss of self-esteem, and (3) irritability and agitation. This study was conducted in Finland with a sample of 290 depressed adults aged 60 and older. It is possible that age or culturally related factors contributed to the differences among these factors.

The SDS shows good psychometric properties. One study of 85 depressed and 28 nondepressed patients in a Dutch day clinic (de Jonghe & Baneke, 1989) found the internal consistency to be .82 and the split-half reliability to be .79. The concurrent validity of the SDS has also been supported. For example, the SDS was significantly correlated with the Geriatric Depression Scale (Brink et al., 1982).

Carroll Rating Scale for Depression

In 1981, Carroll, Feinberg, Smouse, Rawson, and Greden published the Carroll Rating Scale for Depression (CRS) as a self-rating instrument that closely matches the information content and items of the 17-item clinician-rated HRSD. In 1998, the CRS was revised as the Carroll Depression Scales—Revised (CDS-R; Carroll, 1998) as a 61-item questionnaire, building upon the original CRS, in order to be compatible with the DSM-IV. A 12-item version, the Brief CDS, is also available.

The CDS-R is designed to have a maximum possible score of 61. Each of the 61 statements is written in a self-descriptive format (e.g., "I feel in good spirits") and individuals answer the questions in a "yes" or "no" response format based on their feelings over the past few days. The scoring of the CDS-R is constructed so that it can be compared with the clinician-rated HRSD. A study conducted with 72 German-speaking adults completing the CRS in both a computerized version and a paper-and-pencil format found that the overall acceptance of the computerized version was very good and did not depend on previous computer experience (Merten & Ruch, 1996).

The psychometric properties of the original CRS are strong and are directly applicable to the CDS-R. Carroll et al. (1981) reported the internal consistency in the form of split-half coefficients to be .87 using 3,725 CDS scores obtained from the University of Michigan. Internal consistency was examined in a sample of 559 depressed patients and 129 community controls, alphas for both the CDS and the Brief CDS were high, .95 and .90, respectively. These authors also reported a correlation coefficient of .80 between the CRS and the HRSD in a sample of 97 patients diagnosed with major depression and a correlation of .71 with a sample of psychiatric inpatients with a range of disorders. The CRS correlated .86 with the BDI. Overall, the CDS-R related well to the HRSD and is another instrument to measure depression that does not require a clinician interview.

Hamilton Depression Inventory

The Hamilton Depression Inventory (HDI; Reynolds & Kobak, 1995) is a self-report revision and extension of the 17-item clinician-rated HRSD (Hamilton, 1960). The HDI was developed to improve assessment of symptoms of depression in accord with the DSM-IV. It includes a broader range of depressive symptomatology and uses multiple questions for items to ensure the validity of its evaluation of symptoms. Initially, the HDI was developed as a computerized version to be used with psychiatric outpatient samples. Based on strong findings of reliability, validity, and its equivalence with the clinician-rated HRSD, a paper-and-pencil format was designed.

Similar to the clinician-rated HRSD, the HDI does not provide DSM-IV diagnoses, although users can obtain clinical information specific to aspects of depression. To enhance the clinical and research utility of this measure, several versions and scale configurations of the HDI are available. The full-scale HDI consists of 23 items that are evaluated by 38 questions, with some items having between two and four questions that are weighted to provide an item score. A melancholia subscale is also derived to evaluate all symptoms included within the melancholic features subtype of depressive disorders as specified by DSM-IV, along with a checklist of symptoms specific to the DSM-IV diagnosis of major depression. In addition to the basic 23-item HDI, a 17-item form is derived from the HDI that is consistent in content and scoring with the standard 17-item, clinician-rated HRSD.

The HDI manual provides normative data based on 506 adults (235 men, 271 women) living in a variety of community settings from the midwestern and western parts of the United States. Internal consistency estimates range from .90 to .93. With regard to test–retest reliability, a correlation was found to be .95 over a 1-week period. Regarding estimates of validity, the HDI was found to correlate .94 with scores using the clinician-rated HRSD based on a sample of 403 interviews with adults. The measure's convergent validity is further demonstrated by its high correlation to the BDI (.93) and depression-related constructs (e.g., suicide questionnaire, hopelessness).

Center for Epidemiological Studies Depression Scale

The Center for Epidemiological Studies developed a 20-item self-report symptom rating scale—the CES-D—to measure the current level of depressive symptomatology among the general population (Radloff, 1977). The CES-D can be a tool for epidemiological studies of depression, screening for treatment studies, and measuring change over time in symptom severity.

The scale items were chosen from previously developed scales in order to represent the major symptoms of clinical depression (e.g., BDI, Zung SDS, depression scale of the Minnesota Multiphasic Personality Inventory). Each item provides a statement representing a symptom characteristic of depression and respondents are asked to rate how much the statement best describes how often they have felt this way during the past week. Answers range from 0 to 3. For all but four questions higher scores indicate more impairment; the other four questions are reversed scored. The total score ranges from 0 to 60. The cutoff score for differentiating depressed from nondepressed patients is 16. The instrument was designed to be brief and takes less than 10 minutes to complete.

The CES-D has been used in many countries and has been adapted to be utilized in computer-assisted and telephone interviews. Studies have indicated that the psychometric properties of the computerized version are equivalent to that of the paper-and-pencil format (Ogles, France, Lunnen, Bell, & Goldfarb, 1998). Using the CES-D for voice recognition computer-assisted interviews has been advantageous for overcoming language barriers and disabilities, and for educating underserved populations. This system recognizes voices and administers verbal responses (Muñoz, McQuaid, González, Dimas, & Rosales, 1999). González et al. (2000) studied the effectiveness of a bilingual speech recognition IBM-compatible prototype to screen for depressive symptoms in adult public-sector primary care patients using the CES-D. This screening method can also be used to collect data regarding vocal patterns related to depressed mood.

Radloff (1977) has provided norms and psychometric properties based on three community samples and two psychiatric patient samples. Coefficient alpha estimates, with regard to internal consistency, were found to be .85 for the general population and .90 for the patient samples. The stability of the measure over 2, 4, 6, or 8 weeks with 419 participants ranged from .51 to .67. The CES-D has been found to correlate highly with a number of other depression and mood scales, indicating good concurrent validity. For example, the CES-D was found to be significantly correlated with the clinician-rated HRSD (.44), the BDI (.81), and the Zung SDS (.90). It has also been found to discriminate between psychiatric inpatient groups and the general population.

Based on a principal components analysis of data from the general population samples, four major factors were identified. These factors have been described as depressed affect, positive affect, somatic and retarded activity, and an interpersonal factor. This factor structure has been replicated in many subgroups and with the general population. More recently, Wong (2000) found this factor structure to exist in a homeless adult population. The CES-D has also been found to be a reliable and valid measure in a sample of females with breast cancer (Hann, Winter, & Jacobsen, 1999).

Comments

In both clinical and research settings, it is often useful to have data from multiple sources in order to better understand the process of change. Consequently, we would recommend that the clinician-rated HRSD, in addition to a self-report instrument, be administered. Our choice for the particular self-report measure is the BDI-II, in part because it was revised to better reflect the entire range of depressive symptoms in concert with the DSM-IV, and in part because of its widespread use, providing a plethora of samples for comparison. Although the BDI-II was published in 1996, some recently published studies continue to use the original BDI, rather than the BDI-II. We strongly urge researchers, as well as clinicians, to use the more recent version. If the targeted sample is a nonclinical population, then we would recommend the CES-D.

MEASURES OF DEPRESSIVE AFFECT AND MOOD

State–Trait Depression Adjective Checklists

Several measures exist that assess depressive affect or mood. Such instruments are of interest to clinicians or researchers who are more concerned with specifically measuring mood and affect rather than the entire range of depressive symptoms. The Depression Adjective Checklist (ST-DACL; Lubin, 1994) is an example of this type of measure. It contains a series of adjectives related to dysphoria, sadness, and psychological distress. Respondents are instructed to place check marks next to those words that describe their feelings. The ST-DACL can be used to measure a state of depression by asking respondents to indicate "how you feel now—today" or trait symptoms by indicating "how you feel today and in general." Seven lists comprise the ST-DACL, each containing either 32 or 34 adjectives. Some adjectives represent negative emotions (e.g., "sad"), whereas other adjectives are positive in nature (e.g., "joyous").

The ST-DACL has been used with adolescent, adult, and elderly populations. It is brief, easy to comprehend, and retains high face validity. It has been widely used in research and the manual provides age-related norms. The scores can be converted into percentile or *T*-scores, *T*-scores greater than 64 are believed to represent greater than normal depressed mood. Internal consistency estimates for both the State and Trait versions have been found to be relatively high (range of .82 to .94 for the State scale, range of .79 to .91 for the Trait scale). ST-DACL scores have also been found to correlated highly with the BDI and the CES-D.

Additional examples of measures geared to assess depressive mood include the Profile of Mood States (McNair, Lorr, & Droppleman, 1992) and the Positive and Negative Affect Scales (PANAS; Watson, Clark, & Tellegen, 1988). Both instruments contain scales measuring both negative (e.g., depressive) and positive (e.g., vigor) mood states.

Comments

It is important for the clinician or researcher to remember that these measures assess depressive mood and affect, not depression per se. Using such measures in lieu of other self-report inventories, such as the BDI-II and the Zung SDS, will not provide similar information. If mood is the construct of interest, however, these measures have high face validity, are easy to administer, and are psychometrically sound. The PANAS in particular may be useful when both positive and negative mood states are of interest.

FUTURE DIRECTIONS

We conclude this chapter with a brief discussion of what we consider to be important areas of future research and conceptual focus regarding the assessment of depression. These include (1) diversity issues, (2) depression in primary care, (3) advances in technology, and (4) conceptualizing depression as a public health issue.

Diversity Issues

As mentioned earlier in this chapter, the phenomenology and expression of depression can vary across cultures (Kaiser et al., 1998), thus calling into question the validity of measures that were originally developed using samples of white, middle-class adults. In addition, various ethnically diverse populations in the United States, because of their minority status, may have had limited access to traditional mental health services, thus creating further obstacles to this validation process. For example, Latinos in the United States are frequently underserved. One study found that only 11% of Mexican Americans who met diagnostic criteria for major depression had sought mental health services (Muñoz et al., 1999). Spanish-speaking patients may experience a language barrier inhibiting them from seeking services. In general, we need to better understand how depression is conceptualized in both its experience and expression across different cultures and then develop psychometrically sound measures to better assess depression among such ethnically diverse populations.

Future research also should focus on improving the assessment of depression among (1) individuals residing in rural areas, (2) individuals who have lower economic status and literacy rates, (3) the elderly, and (4) the disabled. Increasing the number of valid and reliable assessment modalities for such populations can lead to two important outcomes: (1) the degree and amount of treatment interventions aimed at reducing depression for these groups will expand; and (2) the accuracy of the estimates of the incidence and prevalence of depression in the general population will also be improved.

Depression in Primary Care

Healthcare reorganization is changing the manner in which psychological assessments are being conducted. For example, a greater emphasis is being placed on the primary care physician as the gatekeeper of mental health referrals in the United States. However, there appears to be an underdiagnosis of depression among primary care patients (Coyne, Schwenk, & Fechner-Bates, 1995). Therefore, it will become increasingly imperative that primary care physicians recognize depressive symptoms and learn how to make a depression referral. Overall, these changes can affect (1) the setting in which the assessment takes place, (2) the training of the professional who conducts the assessment, and (3) the purpose for which the assessment is conducted (i.e., for screening and referral as compared to differential diagnosis and treatment planning). Consequently, assessment protocols that require minimal training and provide for a quick reference to aid the referral process appear warranted. Although some assessments are being developed with these issues in mind (e.g., PRIME-MD; Spitzer et al., 1993), additional research is needed.

Advances in Technology

After considering the varied populations in need of future research and some of the obstacles faced by clinicians and medical settings, it is not surprising that recent research efforts have been aimed at reducing these barriers by expanding beyond the traditional paper-and-pencil or interview techniques. Computerized voice recognition programs have the capability of evaluating depression among non-English-speaking persons, disabled patients, low literacy populations, and geriatric samples (González et al., 2000). In addition, they can record and chart a patient's weekly assessment, increase the public's awareness of depression, and improve the detection and treatment of depression in the general population; moreover, they can objectify assessments and they are cost-and-time efficient (Ogles et al., 1998).

However, such technologically advanced protocols are not without their own unique problems. For example, it has been suggested that state anxiety can increase as a result of the computerized testing situation and potentially confound results (Merten & Ruch, 1996). Further, computerized screening poses the dilemma of treating patients who are suicidal or have acute crises (Ogles et al., 1998). Therefore, substantial research is needed to improve upon this technology, as well as to identify, and subsequently resolve, important ethical dilemmas.

Depression as a Public Health Issue

The recent report on mental health by the surgeon general of the United States (National Institute of Mental Health, 2000) underscored the need to view mental health as a public health issue. In addition, researchers have also called for a greater synthesis between psychological and public health research in order to develop broad-based community interventions for depression (Nezu, Nezu, Trunzo, & McClure, 1998). In this context, assessment procedures will need to be developed in order to examine the impact that depression has on public health and the efficacy and effectiveness of community-based interventions. The HANDS (Baer et al., 2000) is one of the first measures to move in this direction by focusing on screening the general public for clinically significant depression. Future research should focus on the validity of using depression measures for public health purposes, the social and financial impact of depression on the community, and the likelihood of accessing and/or maintaining effective treatment as a result of public health assessment, prevention, and intervention.

In addition, the field is increasingly recognizing that depression is a recurrent condition. In their review of treatment maintenance for unipolar depression, Nezu et al. (1998) recommended that maintenance of treatment effects should to be measured frequently in order to understand how changes in depression are related to other variables. It will be important to validate measures for the purpose of measuring treatment maintenance and, more importantly, to identify residual symptoms that may increase risk of relapse. This may require further examination of the sensitivity and specificity of various measures, as well as a more specific understanding and definition of residual symptoms (Rafanelli, Park, & Fava, 1999).

APPENDIX 3.1. MEASURES OF DEPRESSION, DEPRESSIVE SYMPTOMATOLOGY, AND DEPRESSIVE MOOD

Structured Interviews and Clinician Rating Scales

Diagnostic Interview Schedule
Hamilton Rating Scale for Depression
Manual for the Diagnosis of Major Depression
Revised Hamilton Rating Scale for Depression—Clinician Rating Form
Schedule for Affective Disorders and Schizophrenia
Structured Clinical Interview for Axis I DSM-IV Disorders

Self-Report Inventories

Beck Depression Inventory–II
Brief Psychiatric Rating Scale
Brief Symptom Inventory
Carroll Rating Scale for Depression
Center for Epidemiologic Studies Depression Scale
Depression Anxiety Stress Scales
Depression Questionnaire
Depression 30 Scale
Diagnostic Inventory for Depression
Hamilton Depression Inventory
Hopelessness Depression Symptom Questionnaire
Inventory of Depressive Symptomatology
IPAT Depression Scale
Minnesota Multiphasic Personality Inventory—Depression Scale
Montgomery–Ashberg Depression Rating Scale
Multiple Affect Adjective Check List
Multiscore Depression Inventory for Adolescents and Adults

Newcastle Scales
Positive and Negative Affect Scales
Profile of Mood Scales
Raskin Three-Area Depression Scale
Revised Hamilton Rating Scale for Depression—Self-Report Problem Inventory
Reynolds Depression Screening Inventory
Rimon's Brief Depression Scale
State–Trait Depression Adjective Check List
Symptom Checklist 90—Revised
Zung Self-Rating Depression Scale

Measures of Depression: Special Populations

Calgary Depression Scale for Schizophrenia
Children's Depression Inventory
Children's Depression Rating Scale—Revised
Cornell Scale for Depression in Dementia
Depression Rating Scale (for nursing home residents)
Geriatric Depression Inventory
Hospital Anxiety and Depression Scale
Kiddie-SADS (Schedule for Affective Disorders and Schizophrenia for School-Aged Children)
Medical-Based Emotional Distress Scale
Medical Care Outcomes Screener
Multiscore Depression Inventory for Children
Postpartum Depression Interview Schedule
Primary Care Evaluation of Mental Disorders
Psychopathology Instrument for Mentally Retarded Adults
Reynolds Adolescent Depression Scale
Reynolds Child Depression Scale
Visual Analogue Mood Scales
Youth Depression Adjective Check Lists

REFERENCES

Addington, D., Addington, J., & Maticka-Tyndale, E. (1993). Rating depression in schizophrenia: A comparison of a self-report and an observer report scale. *Journal of Nervous and Mental Disease, 181*, 561–565.

Addington, D., Addington, J., & Maticka-Tyndale, E. (1994). Specificity of the Calgary Depression Scale for schizophrenics. *Schizophrenia Research, 6*, 201–208.

Alexopoulos, G. S., Abrams, R. C., Young, R. C., & Shannon, C. A. (1988). Cornell Scale for Depression in Dementia. *Biological Psychiatry, 23*, 271–284.

American Psychiatric Association. (1994). *Diagnostic and statistical manual of mental disorders* (4th ed.). Washington, DC: Author.

American Psychiatric Association. (2000). *Diagnostic and statistical manual of mental disorders* (4th ed., text rev.). Washington, DC: Author.

Anthony, J. C., Folstein, M., Romanoski, A. J., Von Korff, M. R., Nestadt, G. R., Chahal, R., Merchant, A., Brown, C. H., Shapiro, S., & Kramer, M. (1985). Comparison of the lay Diagnostic Interview Schedule and a standardized psychiatric diagnosis: Experience in eastern Baltimore. *Archives of General Psychiatry, 42*, 667–675.

Baer, L, Jacobs, D. G., Meszler-Reizes, J. Blais, M., Fava, M., Kessler, R., Magruder, K., Murphy, J., Kopans, B., Cukor, P., Leahy, L., & O'laughlen, J. (2000). Development of a brief screening instrument: The HANDS. *Psychotherapy and Psychosomatics, 69*, 35–41.

Beck, A. T. (1987). Cognitive model of depression. *Journal of Cognitive Psychotherapy, 1*, 2–27.

Beck, A. T., Kovacs, M., & Weissman, A. (1979). Assessment of suicidal intention: The Scale for Suicide Ideation. *Journal of Consulting and Clinical Psychology, 47,* 343–352.

Beck, A. T., & Steer, R. A. (1988). *Manual for the Beck Hopelessness Scale.* San Antonio, TX: Psychological Corporation.

Beck, A. T., Steer, R. A., & Brown, G. K. (1996). *Manual for the BDI-II.* San Antonio, TX: Psychological Corporation.

Beck, A. T., Ward, C. H., Mendelson, M., Mock, J., & Erbaugh, J. (1961). An inventory for measuring depression. *Archives of General Psychiatry, 4,* 561–571.

Berndt, D. J., & Kaiser, C. F. (1996). *Multiscore Depression Inventory for Children manual.* Los Angeles: Western Psychological Services.

Brink, T. L., Yesavage, J. A., Lum, O., Heersema, P. H., Adey, M., & Rose, T. L. (1982). Screening tests for geriatric depression. *Clinical Gerontologist, 1,* 37–43.

Brown, C., Schulberg, H. C., & Madonia, M. J. (1995). Assessing depression in primary care practice with the Beck Depression Inventory and the Hamilton Rating Scale for Depression. *Psychological Assessment, 7,* 59–65.

Cacciola, J. S., Alterman, A. I., Rutherford, M. J., McKay, J. R., & May, D. J. (1999). Comparability of telephone and in-person structured clinical interview for DSM-III-R (SCID) diagnoses. *Assessment, 6,* 235–242.

Carroll, B. (1998). *Carroll Depression Scales—Revised (CDS-R): Technical manual.* North Tonawanda, NY: Multi-Health Systems.

Carroll, B. J., Feinberg, M., Smouse, P. E., Rawson, S. G., & Greden, J. F. (1981). The Carroll Rating Scale for Depression: I. Development, reliability, and validation. *British Journal of Psychiatry, 138,* 194–200.

Cohen-Mansfield, J., & Marx, M. S. (1988). Relationship between depression and agitation in nursing home residents. *Comprehensive Gerontology, Section B: Behavioral, Social, and Applied Sciences, 2,* 141–146.

Coyne, J. C., Schwenk, T. L., & Fechner-Bates, S. (1995). Nondetection of depression by primary care physicians reconsidered. *General Hospital Psychiatry, 16,* 267–276.

Crowne, D. P. (1979). *The experimental study of personality.* Hillsdale, NJ: Erlbaum.

de Jonghe, J. F., & Baneke, J. J. (1989). The Zung Self-Rating Depression Scale: A replication study on reliability, validity and prediction. *Psychological Reports, 64,* 833–834.

Dozois, D. J. A., Dobson, K. S., & Ahnberg, J. L. (1998). A psychometric evaluation of the Beck Depression Inventory—II. *Psychological Assessment, 10,* 83–89.

D'Zurilla, T. J., Nezu, A. M., & Maydeu-Olivares, A. (2002). *Social Problem-Solving Inventory— Revised (SPSI-R): Technical manual.* North Tonawanda, NY: Multi-Health Systems.

Endicott, J., & Spitzer, R. L. (1978). A diagnostic interview: The Schedule for Affective Disorders and Schizophrenia. *Archives of General Psychiatry, 35,* 837–844.

First, M. B., Spitzer, R. L., Gibbon, M., & Williams, J. B. (1997). *User's guide for the Structure Clinical Interview for DSM-IV Axis I Disorders.* Washington, DC: American Psychiatric Press.

González, G. M., Winfrey, J., Sertic, M., Salcedo, J., Parker, C., & Mendoza, S. (2000). A bilingual telephone-enabled speech recognition application for screening depression symptoms. *Professional Psychology: Research and Practice, 31,* 398–403.

Hamilton, M. (1960). Development of a rating scale for depression. *Journal of Neurology, Neurosurgery and Psychiatry, 23,* 56–62.

Hamilton, M. (1967). Development of a rating scale for primary depressive illness. *British Journal of Social and Clinical Psychology, 6,* 278–296.

Hann, D., Winter, K., & Jacobsen, P. (1999). Measurement of depressive symptoms in cancer patients: Evaluation of the Center for Epidemiological Studies Depression Scale (CES-D). *Journal of Psychosomatic Research, 46,* 437–443.

Hedlund, J. L., & Vieweg, B. W. (1979). The Hamilton Rating Scale for Depression: A comprehensive review. *Journal of Operational Psychiatry, 10,* 149–165.

Heiby, E. M. (1983). Assessment of frequency of self-reinforcement. *Journal of Personality and Social Psychology, 44,* 1304–1307.

Kaiser, A. S., Katz, R., & Shaw, B. F. (1998). Cultural issues in the management of depression. In S. S.

Kazarian & D. E. Evans (Eds.), *Cultural clinical psychology: Theory, research, and practice* (pp. 177–214). New York: Oxford University Press.

Kendall, P. C., Hollon, S. D., Beck, A. T., Hammen, C. L., & Ingram, R. E. (1987). Issues and recommendations regarding use of the Beck Depression Inventory. *Cognitive Therapy and Research, 11*, 289–299.

Kendall, P. C., Howard, B. L., & Hays, R. C. (1989). Self-referent speech and psychopathology: The balance of positive and negative thinking. *Cognitive Therapy and Research, 13*, 583–598.

Kinzie, J. D., Manson, S. M., Vino, T. D., Tolan, N. T., Anh, B., & Pho, T. N. (1982). Development and validation of a Vietnamese language rating scale. *American Journal of Psychiatry, 139*, 1276–1281.

Kivelae, S., & Pahkala, K. (1987). Factor structure of the Zung Self-Rating Depression Scale among a depressed elderly population. *International Journal of Psychology, 22*, 289–300.

Kovacs, M. (1992). *Children's Depression Inventory manual.* North Tonawanda, NY: Multi-Health Systems.

Lascelles, R. G. (1966). Atypical facial pain and depression. *British Journal of Psychiatry, 112*, 651–659.

Lewinsohn, P. M. (1974). A behavioral approach to depression. In R. J. Friedman & M. M. Katz (Eds.), *The psychology of depression: Contemporary theory and research* (pp. 157–185). New York: Wiley.

Lubin, B. (1994). *State–Trait Depression Adjective Check Lists: Professional manual.* Odessa, FL: Psychological Assessment Resources.

MacPhillamy, D. J., & Lewinsohn, P. M. (1982). The Pleasant Events Schedule: Studies on reliability, validity, and scale intercorrelation. *Journal of Consulting and Clinical Psychology, 50*, 363–380.

Matson, J. L. (1988). *The PIMRA manual.* New Orleans, LA: International Diagnostic Systems.

McNair, D. M., Lorr, M., & Droppleman, L. F. (1992). *EdITS manual for the Profile of Mood States.* San Diego, CA: EdITS.

Merten, T., & Ruch, W. (1996). A comparison of computerized and conventional administration of the German versions of the Eysenck Personality Questionnaire and the Carroll Rating Scale for Depression. *Personality and Individual Differences, 20*, 281–291.

Muñoz, R. F., McQuaid, J. R., González, G. M., Dimas, J., & Rosales, V. A. (1999). Depression screening in a women's clinic using automated Spanish and English language voice recognition. *Journal of Consulting and Clinical Psychology, 67*, 502–510.

National Institute of Mental Health. (2000). *Mental health: A report of the surgeon general* (DSL 2000–0134–P). Washington, DC: U.S. Government Printing Office.

Nezu, A. M. (1987). A problem-solving formulation of depression: A literature review and proposal of a pluralistic model. *Clinical Psychology Review, 7*, 121–144.

Nezu, A. M. (1996). What are we doing to our patients and should we care if anyone else knows? *Clinical Psychology: Science and Practice, 3*, 160–163.

Nezu, A. M., & Nezu, C. M. (Eds.). (1989). *Clinical decision making in behavior therapy: A problem-solving perspective.* Champaign, IL: Research Press.

Nezu, A. M., & Nezu, C. M. (1993). Identifying and selecting target problems for clinical interventions: A problem-solving model. *Psychological Assessment, 5*, 254–263.

Nezu, A. M., Nezu, C. M., Friedman, S. H., & Haynes, S. N. (1997). Case formulation in behavior therapy: Problem solving and functional analytic strategies. In T. D. Eells (Ed.), *Handbook of psychotherapy case formulation* (pp. 368–401). New York: Guilford Press.

Nezu, A. M., Nezu, C. M., & Perri, M. G. (1989). *Problem solving therapy for depression: Theory, research, and clinical guidelines.* New York: Wiley.

Nezu, A. M., Nezu, C. M., Trunzo, J. J., & McClure, K. S. (1998). Treatment maintenance for unipolar depression: Relevant issues, literature review, and recommendations for research and clinical practice. *Clinical Psychology: Science and Practice, 5*, 496–512.

Nezu, A. M., & Perri, M. G. (1989). Problem-solving therapy for unipolar depression: An initial dismantling investigation. *Journal of Consulting and Clinical Psychology, 57*, 408–413.

Nezu, A. M., Ronan, G. F., Meadows, E. A., & McClure, K. S. (2000). *Practitioner's guide to empirically based measures of depression.* New York: Kluwer Academic/Plenum.

Nezu, C. M., & Nezu, A. M. (1989). Unipolar depression. In A. M. Nezu & C. M. Nezu (Eds.), *Clinical decision making in behavior therapy: A problem-solving perspective* (pp. 117–156). Champaign, IL: Research Press.

Nezu, C. M., & Nezu, A. M. (1995). Clinical decision making in everyday practice: The science in the art. *Cognitive and Behavioral Practice, 2,* 5–25.

Nezu, C. M., Nezu, A. M., & Foster, S. L. (2000). A 10–step guide to selecting assessment measures in clinical and research settings. In A. M. Nezu, G. F. Ronan, E. A. Meadows, & K. S. McClure (Eds.), *Practitioner's guide to empirically based measures of depression* (pp. 17–24). NY: Kluwer Academic/Plenum.

Nezu, C. M., Nezu, A. M., & Gill-Weiss, M. J. (1992). *Psychopathology of persons with mental retardation: Clinical guidelines for assessment and treatment.* Champaign, IL: Research Press.

Ogles, B. M., France, C. R., Lunnen, K. M., Bell, M. T., & Goldfarb, M. (1998). Computerized depression screening and awareness. *Community Mental Health Journal, 34,* 27–38.

Overholser, J. C., Schubert, D. S. P., Foliart, R., & Frost, F. (1993). Assessment of emotional distress following a spinal cord injury. *Rehabilitation Psychology, 38,* 187–198.

Paykel, E. S., Prusoff, B. A., & Tanner, J. (1976). Temporal stability of symptom patterns in depression. *British Journal of Psychiatry, 128,* 369–374.

Poznanski, E. O., & Mokros, H. B. (1996). *Children's Depression Rating Scale—Revised: Manual.* Los Angeles: Western Psychological Services.

Radloff, L. S. (1977). The CES-D Scale: A self-report depression scale for research in the general population. *Applied Psychological Measurement, 1,* 385–401.

Rafanelli, C., Park, S. K., & Fava, G. A. (1999). New psychotherapeutic approaches to residual symptoms and relapse prevention in unipolar depression. *Clinical Psychology and Therapy, 6,* 194–201.

Rehm, L. P. (1977). A self-control model of depression. *Behavior Therapy, 8,* 787–804.

Reynolds, W. M. (1987). *Reynolds Adolescent Depression Scale: Professional manual.* Odessa, FL: Psychological Assessment Resources.

Reynolds, W. M. (1989). *Reynolds Child Depression Scale: Professional manual.* Odessa, FL: Psychological Assessment Resources.

Reynolds, W. M., & Kobak, K. A. (1995). *Hamilton Depression Inventory (HDI): Professional manual.* Odessa, FL: Psychological Assessment Resources.

Reynolds, W. M., & Kobak, K. A. (1998). *Reynolds Depression Screening Inventory: Professional manual.* Odessa, FL: Psychological Assessment Resources.

Robins, L. N., Helzer, J. E., Croughan, J. L., & Ratcliff, K. S. (1981). National Institute of Mental Health Diagnostic Interview Schedule: Its history, characteristics, and validity. *Archives of General Psychiatry, 38,* 381–389.

Rosen, A., & Proctor, E. K. (1981). Distinctions between treatment outcomes and their implications for treatment evaluation. *Journal of Consulting and Clinical Psychology, 49,* 418–425.

Sakamoto, S., Kijima, N., Tomoda, A., & Kambara, M. (1998). Factor structures of the Zung Self-Rating Depression Scale (SDS) for undergraduates. *Journal of Clinical Psychology, 54,* 477–487.

Scarvalone, P. A., Cloitre, M., Spielman, L. A., Jacobsberg, L., Fishman, B., & Perry, S. W. (1996). Distress reduction during the Structured Clinical Interview for DSM-III-R. *Psychiatry Research, 59,* 245–249.

Schwab, J., Bialon, M. R., & Holzer, C. E. (1967). A comparison of two rating scales for depression. *Journal of Clinical Psychology, 23,* 94–96.

Segal, D. L., Hersen, M., & Van Hasselt, V. B. (1994). Reliability of the Structured Clinical Interview for DSM-III-R: Evaluative review. *Comprehensive Psychiatry, 35,* 316–327.

Spitzer, R. L., Endicott, J., & Robins, E. (1978). Research diagnostic criteria. *Archives of General Psychiatry, 35,* 773–782.

Spitzer, R. L., Williams, J. B. W., Kroenke, K., Linzer, M., deGruy, F. V., 3rd, Hahn, S. R., & Brody, D. (1993). *PRIME-MD: Clinician evaluation guide.* New York: Pfizer.

Steer, R. A., Clark, D. A., Beck, A. T., & Ranieri, W. F. (1998). Common and specific dimensions of self-reported anxiety and depression: The BDI-II versus the BDI-IA. *Behaviour Research and Therapy, 37,* 183–190.

Steer, R. A., Rissmiller, D. J., & Beck, A. T. (2000). Use of Beck Depression Inventory-II with depressed geriatric inpatients. *Behaviour Research and Therapy, 38*, 311–318.

Stern, R. A. (1997). *Visual Analogue Mood Scales: Professional manual.* Odessa, FL: Psychological Assessment Resources.

Stosky, S., & Glass, D. (1983). *The Hamilton Rating Scale: A critical appraisal and modification for psychotherapy research.* Paper presented at the annual convention of the Society for Psychotherapy Research, Sheffield, England.

Tanaka-Matsumi, J., Seiden, D. Y., & Lam, K. N. (1996). The Culturally-Informed Functional Assessment (CIFA) Interview: A strategy for cross-cultural behavioral practice. *Cognitive and Behavioral Practice, 3*, 215–234.

Warren, W. L. (1994). *Revised Hamilton Rating Scale for Depression (RHRSD): Manual.* Los Angeles: Western Psychological Services.

Watson, D., Clark, L. A., & Tellegen, A. (1988). Development and validation of brief measures of positive and negative affect: The PANAS scales. *Journal of Personality and Social Psychology, 54*, 1063–1070.

Weissman, A., & Beck, A. T. (1978, November). *Development and validation of the Dysfunctional Attitude Scale.* Paper presented at the annual meeting of the Association for Advancement of Behavior Therapy, Chicago.

Williams, J. B. W., Gibbon, M., First, M. B., Spitzer, R. L., Davies, M., Borus, J., et al. (1992). The Structured Clinical Interview for DSM-III-R (SCID): Multisite test–retest reliability. *Archives of General Psychiatry, 49*, 630–636.

Wong, Y. I. (2000). Measurement properties of the Center for Epidemiologic Studies Depression Scale in a homeless population. *Psychological Assessment, 12*, 69–76.

Yesavage, J. A., Brink, T. L., Rose, T. L., Lum, O., Huang, V., Adey, M., & Leirer, V. O. (1983). Development and validation of a geriatric depression screening scale: A preliminary report. *Journal of Psychiatric Research, 17*, 37–49.

Zung, W. W. K. (1965). A self-rating depression scale. *Archives of General Psychiatry, 12*, 63–70.

4

Contemporary Methodological Issues in the Study of Depression
Not Your Father's Oldsmobile

Rick E. Ingram and Greg J. Siegle

Interest in understanding the core features of depression continues to be an important pursuit for many mental health professionals. Indeed, understanding depression is arguably necessary for all mental health professionals, whether this necessity stems from research pursuits or from a clinical practice perspective. All mental health professionals need access to information about depression that is both accurate and current, information that cannot be obtained without the use of sound methodological strategies and research tactics to study depression. Accordingly, the purpose of this chapter is to examine methodologies for depression research. No single chapter, or even a book devoted to methodology, can articulate all the details that are important to consider in every study of depression. Nor can a single chapter examine all the basic methodological issues that must guide the conduct of scientific research (e.g., issues such as random selection and internal and external validity). Therefore, this chapter focuses on several major issues that are especially relevant to efforts to adequately conduct research on depression.

We assume that researchers will employ sound general methodological techniques; consequently, we do not comment on these unless they are particularly germane to a topic of depression research (readers who seek information on these principles as they broadly apply to clinical research should consult Kazdin, 1998; Kendall, Butcher, & Holmbeck, 1999; or Sher & Trull, 1996). In this chapter, therefore, we address questions about the definition of depression and about how different definitions may affect methodological decisions; about some common methodological problems in depression research; about methodological issues in the study of vulnerability to depression; and about issues pertaining to the establishment of causality in depression research.

86

DEFINING THE CONSTRUCT FOR RESEARCH: WHAT IS DEPRESSION?

In examining some of the methodological issues involved in the study of psychopathology, Alloy, Abramson, Raniere, and Dyller (1999) note that investigators should start with a clearly defined theory. We could not agree more, but we take this one step further to suggest that investigators begin with a clearly defined type of depression in which they are interested. Different definitions of depression can dramatically affect investigators' methodological decision making, including how they operationally define the construct for the purposes of research. Investigators must therefore begin with a clear definition of the construct of depression. To examine the impact on methodological decisions of how depression is construed, we examine both conceptual and operational definitions of depression.

Depression as a Theoretical Construct

Historically, depression has been conceived of as encompassing a range of states and symptoms from melancholia to despondency. Major depressive disorder (MDD) is currently conceptualized as a group of related symptoms, some of which are recognized by official sources as representing the disorder (e.g., sad mood) and some of which are not (e.g., being discouraged about the future). Moreover, DSM requires that a certain number, but not a certain constellation, of symptoms be present for a diagnosis, suggesting that very different conditions can receive the same diagnostic label of depression (Beckham, Leber, & Youll, 1995). The fact that some symptoms are formally recognized while others are not underscores the idea that what we view as depression is constructed from a group of symptoms (each of which themselves are constructs) that the scientific community has collectively decided to label "depression." Depression is thus a theoretical construct that is part of a broader class of psychological ideas. Should the scientific community decide that depression is constructed from a different group of symptoms (e.g., that suicidal ideation rather than sad mood is the defining feature of depression), the nature of depression itself would change, as would the characteristics of people who are diagnosed with depression.

Consider another example that illustrates the constructed nature of depression and that has particular relevance for methodological decision making in depression studies. As several investigators have noted, the label "depression" has been used to discuss a mood state, a symptom, a syndrome consisting of a constellation of symptoms, a mood disorder, or a disease that is associated with biochemical or structural abnormalities (Kendall, Hollon, Beck, Hammen, & Ingram, 1987; Nurcombe, 1992). Although we may be tempted to ask, "Will the real depression please stand up," the fact is that each of these constructs can legitimately lay claim to the term *depression*. Thus, depression is a construct that can mean very different things, which has important implications for decision making in research.

The Current Classification System

In North America, the *Diagnostic and Statistical Manual of Mental Disorders* (DSM-IV-TR; American Psychiatric Association, 2000) is recognized by most researchers as the classification system that defines depression for research and clinical purposes. DSM-IV-TR employs a categorical approach to the description of psychological disorder; disorders are viewed as discrete entities that occur independently of other discrete disorders, although these discrete problems can occur and give rise to comorbidity. Depression is thus one of many distinct categories of disorders. Additionally, DSM-IV-TR defines disorders such as depression as mental disorders, or mental illnesses, rather than as behavioral or psychological problems.[1]

The manner in which depression is characterized in official sources such as the DSM-IV-TR has important implications, not only for how depression is conceptualized by researchers (both implicitly and explicitly), but also for how it is measured. For example, the study of MDD as defined by the DSM-IV-TR requires the selection of subjects who meet inclusion criteria but who do not meet exclusion criteria. To aid in selection of subjects, a number of procedures have been developed that correspond to criteria specified in DSM-IV-TR (see Nezu, Nezu, McClure, & Zwick, Chapter 3, this volume, for a detailed description of these procedures). These assessment strategies, such as the Structured Clinical Interview for DSM (SCID; Spitzer, Williams, Gibbon, & First, 1989), provide a series of structured questions that allow trained interviewers to determine whether a given individual meets the symptom pattern specified by DSM-IV-TR, and to then make a decision as to whether the individual fits one of the diagnostic categories described in DSM-IV-TR. Meeting the categorical inclusion and exclusion diagnostic criteria established in DSM-IV-TR provides one way for researchers to operationally define and then study depression.

Methodological Issues Informed by Continuity versus Discontinuity Assumptions in Depression

The categorical assumptions about depression that we just described can be contrasted to dimensional assumptions; the assumption to which an investigator adheres can have a dramatic impact on the qualities of subject samples and on the results that are obtained from such samples. Such differing assumptions have sparked controversy about the proper way to construe and assess depression, and about what kinds of generalizations are appropriate. In brief, this controversy focuses on whether depression is a continuous phenomenon, with MDD and mild depression/negative mood representing different ends of a continuum, or alternatively, a qualitative phenomenon where MDD reflects a state that is fundamentally different from a mild negative mood state (Ruscio & Ruscio, 2000).

The manner in which depression is characterized in official sources such as The continuity controversy has several methodological implications. One of the foremost of these is whether subclinical depressive states can be used as proxies in studies intended to understand clinically significant depression. These studies typically select college students who obtain high scores on a depression measure. This practice that has been the subject of vigorous argument in the literature. For example, a number of researchers have questioned the advisability of attempting to understand clinical depression by using subclinical samples (Gotlib, 1984; Kendall & Flannery-Schroeder, 1995; Tennen, Ebehardt, & Affleck, 1999; Tennen, Hall, & Affleck, 1995a, 1995b), with some researchers suggesting that doing so not only runs the risk of trivializing depression research, but also of diminishing the contributions of psychology in the eyes of psychiatry (Coyne, 1994). Although some researchers have argued for the validity of this practice (Weary, Edwards, & Jacobson, 1995), others have noted the problems and offered methodological suggestions for dealing with some of these issues (Haaga & Soloman, 1993; Ingram & Hamilton, 1999; Kendall et al., 1987).

What, then, is the evidence in this regard? There seems to be a growing body of evidence, if not a consensus, that depression has at least some dimensional qualities (Flett, Vredenburg, & Krames, 1997; Ruscio & Ruscio, 2000; Vredenburg, Flett, & Krames, 1993). Does this suggest that it is wise to attempt to understand clinically significant depression by studying subclinical depression? Probably not. We come to this conclusion for several reasons. First, the research specifically addressing this issue, although suggestive, is not yet definitive. We may yet see evidence indicating that the underlying structure of these states has important qualitative differences. Second, questions of continuity focus on addressing depressive syndromes of differing severity; as we note later in this chapter, however, symptom-focused methodologies are, in some cases, a better alternative to this approach. Third, even if depression does fall on a continuum, some correlates may be so small in magnitude at the low end as to escape detection. To give a very simple illustration, an investigator interested in how depression is related to interpersonal disturbance might very well find little interpersonal disturbance when studying very mild depressive states. However, given the widespread recognition that clinically significant depression is accompanied by problematic interpersonal functioning, generalization of such a subclinical finding to severe depression would be inappropriate and misleading. Fourth, and in a somewhat related fashion, even though the features of depression may be dimensional, they may potentiate categorical processes at the severe end of the spectrum. Consider an example of vegetative disturbances as seen in eating disruptions. Suppose that eating disturbances are dimensional themselves, and thus mild in mild depression and severe in severe depression. However, if they cause disruptions in the individual's nutrition intake that disrupt biological regulation at the severe end, this may also cause qualitatively different problems at severe levels of the disorder that are completely absent at the mild end. Studying subclinical depression to understand the implications of eating disturbances in clinical depression would be misguided, even if the research could demonstrate the eating disturbances themselves were on a continuum of severity.

These are merely hypothetical examples, and we could go on. The point is that a sample-to-population matching strategy will always be the most appropriate approach to studying depression. The prudent course is to study those samples who map most directly on to the population in which the researcher is interested. We think that there are legitimate reasons to study subclinical depression and, if investigators decide to do so, they may be justified in using subclinical samples (indeed, they should probably screen out clinical depression). On the other hand, investigators who are interested in clinical depression can avoid questions concerning generalizability and appropriateness altogether by confining their research to clinically significant depressive states. With this in mind, we turn to the issues involved in operationally defining depressed individuals for the purposes of research.

Clinical States: DSM-IV-TR-Defined Depression

A decision to try to understand the features of MDD requires the selection of subjects who meet the criteria for MDD. As we have noted, although it is theoretically possible to use other criteria, for all practical intents and purposes these criteria will be those specified in DSM-IV-TR.[2] As we have also noted, diagnostic measures such as the SCID are available to determine whether subjects meet inclusion and exclusion criteria (the SCID as well as other diagnostic measures are discussed in more detail by Nezu et al., Chapter 3, this volume).

The manner in which depression is characterized in official sources such as MDD is not, however, the only diagnostic category codified by the DSM-IV-TR and assessed with measures such as the SCID. Dysthymia is defined by DSM-IV-TR as the presence of at least two depressive symptoms lasting for at least 2 years. As with MDD, investigators interested in this construct are obligated to provide a clear operational definition of the construct for research purposes and, if not relying on DSM-IV-TR criteria, they need to make a case for how the measure they use maps onto this construct. For all practical purposes, however, these criteria are most likely to be those detailed in DSM-IV-TR. Bipolar disorder, along with its division into bipolar I (characterized by the presence of a manic episode) and bipolar II (the presence of a hypomanic episode) require similar attention to both conceptual and operational clarity.[3]

Subclinical States as the Target of Research

There are several reasons why an investigator might choose to study subclinical depression. For example, milder forms of depression represent the majority of affective conditions that occur throughout the world. Moreover, such mild states often represent more than just ordinary unhappiness, sad mood, or simply having a bad mood day (Gotlib, Lewinsohn, & Seeley, 1995). Indeed, it is possible for these states to be accompanied by the presence of at least some clear depressive symptoms (e.g., mild to moderate levels of motivational and cognitive deficits, vegetative signs, disruptions in interpersonal relationships, etc.). Such symptoms, though less serious than their clinical counterparts, may also interfere with significant aspects of individuals' lives. Thus, the emotionally problematic, disruptive, and common nature of mild depressive states would appear to justify their study.

Before discussing some of the methodological issues involved in studying subclinical depression, however, it is important to note that there is some confusion surrounding the concept and terminology of subclinical depression. Most broadly, *subclinical depression* tends be operationalized as any state in which depressive symptoms are present, but in which they are not present in either sufficient number or severity to qualify as clinical depression/MDD, or in which they have not been assessed in a manner that would allow for a determination of whether a diagnosis of MDD is warranted (e.g., self-report questionnaires).[4] Procedures that define depression in this way are so broad that they obscure a number of important conceptual and methodological issues, and are therefore not particularly useful. We will thus briefly discuss several concepts that seem to fall under the label "subclinical depression," each of which has received some focus of research attention, and each of which has some unique methodological issues to which attention should be directed.

Subclinical Depression Defined by DSM-IV-TR

DSM-IV-TR includes minor depressive disorder as a proposal for a new category of psychological problem and specifies that this disorder is identical to MDD with the exception that one must experience only two depressive symptoms rather than five, and that less impairment be present. Such a condition seems to clearly fall under the rubric of subclinical depression, although it is rarely appears as such in the research literature. Nevertheless, an investigator who wishes to study this type of depression has an available conceptual and operational definition of the disorder at hand in DSM-IV-TR.

Subclinical Depression Defined by Elevated Scores on Depression Questionnaires

By far the most common approach to studying subclinical depression is to select individuals (almost always college students) on the basis of scores elevated above some cutoff on a depression questionnaire. In the vast majority of these cases the questionnaire used is the Beck Depression Inventory (BDI; Beck, 1967). Although we will confine our comments to subclinical depression defined by the BDI, our comments generally apply to other questionnaire procedures as well. Because this approach is so widely used, we will briefly examine some of the issues involved in operationally defining depression with the BDI.

Aside from the considerable reliability and validity data that have accrued on the BDI (Beck, Steer, & Garbin, 1988), an important feature of this measure is the specification of cutoff points; Beck (1967) has defined the cutoff for mild depressive states as a score of 10. The availability of cutoff points raises two related questions pertaining to how subclinical depression is operationalized. The first is whether this cutoff captures the essential features of the subclinically depressed state, and the second is whether this minimum cutoff is adequate for defining a sufficiently depressed subclinical sample.

It is probably safe to assume that investigators of subclinical depression are interested in studying individuals who, even at a mild level, are experiencing one of the two cardinal features of depression: either sad mood or a loss of interest. Is a cutoff score of 10 sufficient for determining that these essential features are present? Several investigators have expressed skepticism. For example, Tennen et al. (1995a, 1995b) have argued that such scores may be obtained even though the essential features of sad mood or loss of interest may not be endorsed by many respondents.

A related consideration is the intensity of the endorsed critical symptoms. For instance, to count as endorsing a critical symptom, one only needs to check "I feel sad" on the BDI rather than the other available options such as: "I am so sad or unhappy that I can't stand it." Clearly, on a measure with scores that can range as high as 63, a score of 10 may be obtained by individuals who are either not experiencing the central features of depression or who are not experiencing them with much intensity. Fortunately, the solution for this problem is relatively straightforward; selecting only participants who, depending upon the investigator's interest, endorse either or both of the essential features of depression. Investigators who are interested in more problematic subclinical states may want to require not only the endorsement of these items, but that they be endorsed at the higher levels available on the BDI.

The second question is whether the use of this minimum cutoff ensures a sufficiently depressed subclinical sample. Although a cutoff of 10 will yield a sample that has higher average BDI scores than this minimum, this cutoff nevertheless will result in lower sample averages and fewer symptoms than will higher cutoffs. Depending upon the conceptual question and the type of depressive state of interest to the researcher, a cutoff score of 10 (or even lower) may be appropriate. In this vein, we would encourage researchers to specify precisely the "kind" of depression in which they are interested, a practice that is currently uncommon. Indeed, as Haaga and Solomon (1993) noted, some studies evidence a tendency to conceptualize the affective problem of interest on the basis of clinical theories and data on depression, with many of the implications attached to clinical depression as a background (e.g., therapy implications), but then shift their terminology and methodology to an emphasis on dysphoria when it comes time to select subjects and collect data.

In general (and with some exceptions that we note later), it would be wise for investigators to choose higher cutoff scores. What, then, is a proper cutoff point? Unfortunately, this question is not easily answered. Kendall et al. (1987) recommended that scores higher than 16 on the BDI would be reasonable in studying depressive symptomatology under the heading of dysphoria. Likewise, while arguing for increased precision in the measurement of depressive states, Kendall and Flannery-Schroder (1995) have cogently cautioned against adherence to a methodological procedure that rigidly sets cutoff points. As a general principle (but see the exceptions we discuss later in this chapter), researchers would be wise to consider increasing cutoff scores, particularly if they are interested in depressive states that are genuinely problematic for individuals. Hence, the original recommendations of Kendall et al. (1987) seem quite sound in this regard. Such procedures not only enhance the likelihood that a depressive mood state is being experienced, but also increase the probability that the state being studied is a meaningful one.

METHODOLOGICAL ISSUES AND CHALLENGES RELATED TO THE STUDY OF DEPRESSION

Having now considered some of the issues involved in operationally defining depression, we turn to a consideration of methodological issues for the purposes of adequately studying one of these depressive states. In particular, we examine some common problems in depression research and suggest some possible solutions to these difficulties.

Third-Variable Confounding

Selection of individuals who are either clinically or subclinically depressed may potentially create problems of third-variable, or "nuisance variable," confounding (Meehl, 1978), particularly in ex-post-facto studies (see Campbell & Stanley, 1966). The major problem in this regard is that depression is correlated with other emotionally dysfunctional states (Gotlib, 1984; Smith & Rhodewalt, 1991), thus making it difficult to know if results are largely a function of depression alone, of some correlated state, or of a combination of depression and other states. This is true even in the case of clinical depression defined on the basis of DSM-IV-TR criteria. Even when investigators adhere to exclusion criteria that rule out comorbid diagnoses, a significant amount of anxiety, or other problems that do not reach a diagnostic threshold, may nevertheless still be present in depressed subjects.

The methodological strategy that is most susceptible to such confounding follows the well-established research tradition of selecting depressed participants and then comparing them to a nondepressed control group on some measure of theoretical or empirical interest. The problem is that the selection of research participants on the basis of depression scores also quite likely selects for high levels of other dysfunctional conditions such as anxiety (Gotlib, 1984). Such a procedure is thus highly susceptible to confounding by a third variable (Ingram, 1989a, 1989b).

In theory, solutions to such confounding problems are relatively straightforward. Such procedures are commonly used in studies of cognitive specificity (Ingram, Kendall, Smith, Donnel, & Ronan, 1987) but engender unique methodological considerations. For example, a researcher interested in depression could assess possibly correlated nuisance variables such as anxiety and then statistically control for them in subsequent results. However, if the controlled third variable strongly covaries with depression, this strategy may decrease power to find relationships with depression.

A second method also involves assessing the nuisance variable, for example, anxiety, and then selecting only those research participants who endorse depressive symptoms but who do not endorse more than an average number of anxiety symptoms. An objection to such a restriction is that because the covariation between depression and other types of dysfunction is common, attempts to decouple naturally co-occurring affective states may be artificial. Indeed, this natural covariation can be seen in the growing body of theory and research on negative affectivity and mixed depressive/anxious states, which has consistently documented such high correlations (Clark & Watson, 1991; Kendall & Watson, 1989).

Depending upon the theoretical context that guides the work, covariation is not necessarily a problem, and may in fact lead to a more precise description of the causes and correlates of depression, as well as of other symptom patterns (Ingram, 1990). Natural covariation in and of itself, however, is not a sufficient justification for research practices that simply fail to distinguish between depressed states and other conditions. For example, Tennen et al. (1995a) note a growing body of research that has demonstrated important distinctions in the correlates of depression and anxiety despite their high correlation (Clark, Beck, & Brown, 1989; Ingram, 1989a, 1989b; Ingram et al., 1987; Kendall & Watson, 1989). Moreover, a number of researchers have begun to suggest that just as bipolar disorder represents a qualitatively different disorder from unipolar depression, so too should mixed anxiety–depression be considered a separate diagnostic category (e.g., Angst & Merikangas, 1998; Barlow & Campbell, 2000). Failing a precise definition of the affective condition or conditions in which an investigator is interested, these differences belie the idea that not empirically distinguishing between these states is appropriate.

Stability Considerations

Issues concerning depression stability have important methodological implications. Part of the significance of depressive states is that they endure over some period of time; consequently, it would seem wise to focus our research efforts on those states that evidence this stability. This is especially important in studies of subclinical depression because the milder nature of these states suggest that they will be less stable than MDD or (by definition) dysthymia. The meaningfulness of research with subclinical populations is thus enhanced by showing that the depressed state being studied endures over some period of time rather than remitting quickly.

Stability considerations bring with them some important methodological requirements. Most research on depression is pragmatically a two-step process, the first of which involves measuring the presence of depressive symptoms on one occasion, and then conducting the research on a second occasion with those individuals who met the initial criteria for depression. Again, owing to the severity and typical course of a state such as MDD, in most cases it can be assumed that these individuals will continue to evidence significant depression at the time of experimental testing (although it is still wise to empirically verify this). Subclinical states, however, have few assurances of stability. For example, depression self-report scores of the sort frequently used to assess subclinical depression can change, sometimes dramatically, over even relatively short periods of time. Thus, a group of individuals initially selected for high levels of depression may include a substantial number of people who no longer fall into a depressed range when experimental testing commences. Functionally, such research is testing hypotheses in a "depressed" sample in which not everyone is depressed. The best-case scenario in such a situation is that error variance increases, rendering detection of differences more difficult. A worse-case scenario is that such a procedure may produce misleading or erroneous results.

Researchers are thus well advised to establish the stability of the depressive state in which they are interested. Kendall et al. (1987) and Tennen et al. (1995a) have argued for the use of multiple-gating procedures in which researchers establish appropriate depression scores at selection, readminister the depression measure at testing, and then analyze data only from those who score in the specified range as depressed on both occasions. This helps to ensure that (1) this phenomenon has been stable over some period of time; and (2) participants are actually depressed at the time of testing. Of course, if the topic of interest is explicitly in the correlates of depressive symptoms on a given occasion, it is appropriate to assess such correlates based on the single administration of a depression measure as long as they are administered concurrently.

Assumptions of Continuity and Distribution in Subclinical Samples

One strategy to assess the association between depression and variables of theoretical interest is to examine the correlation between these variables in a relatively large sample, with scores typically ranging from very low to reasonably high on a measure of depressive symptomatology such as the BDI. Studies employing this strategy are based on assumptions that both depression and its association with some other variable is continuous and normally distributed, and that the associations between these variables are linear.

How reasonable are such assumptions? Not very. Because most research participants in such studies are not depressed, the majority of any given sample will score in the nondepressed range of a depression measure. Thus, studies that adopt this correlational strategy are assessing the relationship between depression and some other variable in a largely non-depressed sample. Indeed, it has been demonstrated that results can vary in important ways depending on whether associations are examined in the entire sample versus those who had exceeded the cutoff for a depressed subsample according to recommendations suggested by Kendall et al. (1987) (see Ingram & Hamilton, 1999).

Which, then, is the appropriate strategy: assessing potential bivariate relationships through the entire range of scores or evaluating a more restricted sample above a specified minimum cutoff? As we have stressed several times, the answer to this question depends upon the precisely stated interests of the researcher. Conceptual questions that focus on factors associated with depression itself, whether defined clinically or subclinically will be ill-served by analytic approaches that examine an entire range of symptoms in samples in which the majority have few or no symptoms. Alternatively, questions concerned less about depression per se and more about the experience and correlates of different degrees of symptomatology can be examined more appropriately by using the entire range of reported symptoms. Even here, however, to draw valid conclusions from this type of design, it is necessary to ensure that the full range of depressive symptoms is represented in the sample. For example, rather than administering a depression questionnaire to a sample and then studying the correlation of depressive symptoms with another measure in the entire sample (which ensures that the modal response on a measure such as the BDI will be 0), the researcher interested in this type of question could adopt a stratified sampling approach of selecting equal numbers of subjects falling within equal intervals on the depression measure (e.g., on the BDI, selecting the same number of subjects who score 0, 1, 2, etc., up to some cutoff), or in analyses using the entire sample, of weighting cases inversely proportional to the number of individuals within relevant ranges of scores. Because these strategies can provide misleading estimates of covariance when multiple correlated independent variables are used (Pedhauzer, 1982), analytic strategies must be decided on a case-by-case basis. Again, more precise specification of the conceptual question in reference to a particular sample will aid not only an investigator's evaluation of a research hypothesis, but also the broader field of depression theory and research.

RECOGNIZING DEPRESSION SUBTYPES: METHODOLOGICAL IMPLICATIONS

Although there is general agreement that depression is phenotypically diverse, the research strategies and issues discussed so far rely on studying individuals who evidence some constellation of depressive symptoms (i.e., a syndrome approach is used to define and then study depression). Several investigators have pointed out, however, the limitations of the syndrome-based approach (Costello, 1992, 1993; Ingram, Miranda, & Segal, 1998; Kendall & Brady, 1995; Persons, 1986). These limitations stem from the fact that this approach implicitly assumes that individuals with the same syndrome are equivalent in all important psychological ways—an assumption that is clearly not correct. For example, Kendall and Brady (1995) note that the symptoms of psychological disorders are so diverse that two people could be diagnosed with the same disorder but actually have very few symptoms in common. Of the nine criteria detailed in DSM-IV-TR, only five are necessary; therefore, it is possible that two depressed individuals can have very few symptoms in common.

Noting the same issue but in a somewhat different way, Costello (1992, 1993) suggests that the idea of a depressive syndrome is simultaneously complex and imprecisely defined, so much so that its true nature is difficult for investigators to agree upon. This lack of agreement makes it unclear what the observed correlates of the syndrome may mean. Moreover, relying solely on the concept of a syndrome to study a problem such as depression may miss important information (Persons, 1986). A sample of "depressed" individuals, selected only because they have enough symptoms to qualify as depressed, thus represents an extremely phenotypically heterogeneous group.

Is depression also genotypically diverse? That is, are there different causal processes that give rise to various symptom patterns that are clustered under the label "depression"? Few would dispute at least some causal heterogeneity, yet little empirical data are available to help sort out the parameters of the different causal pathways that are both possible and potentially numerous. Indeed, although the possible subtypes of depression may not be endless, they are potentially so diverse that they may functionally defy complete conceptual classification and empirical scrutiny. Nevertheless, to conceptually disregard the possibility of different subtypes, or to methodologically acquiesce to the complexity of possible causal heterogeneity by ignoring the implications of lumping together various subtypes in research studies, degrades the integrity of our efforts to understand the true nature of depression. Given this state of affairs, we believe that there are at least two broad sets of assumptions that can guide methodological decision making: conceptual proposals for various subtypes and a more empirically derived approach that focuses on examination of different subsets of symptoms.

Conceptual Approaches: Specifying Different Subtypes

Virtually all investigators operate from a theoretical framework that specifies at least some idea about the causal processes that underlie depression. Unless they propose that all cases that meet the criteria for depression are caused by the same factors, it is possible to conceptually stipulate different subtypes and to then proceed to test subtypes based on the predictions derived from a given model. These predictions would presumably involve proposals about the kinds of symptoms and features that should follow from the causal process being proposed, along with prevention and treatment implications. In theory, it should be possible to identify empirically those individuals who exhibit the proposed subtype and to then determine whether they become depressed when the "right" circumstances occur as specified by the particular subtype model (e.g., certain kinds of life events; see Monroe & Hadjiyannakis, Chapter 13, this volume).

Abramson, Alloy, and Metalsky (1988) and Alloy, Hartlage, and Abramson (1988) have laid out similar logic in their discussion of adequate methodologies to test their proposals for a negative cognition subtype of depression. Inasmuch as some of the symptoms that typify certain subtypes may occur in various types of depression, they noted that studies may not do justice to possible subtypes if they lump all research participants together on the basis of exceeding a symptom threshold; in essence this obscures the ability to find the possible casual pathways occurring in only a subset of the larger sample. Alloy and Abramson (1999) empirically followed this logic in their Temple–Wisconsin Cognitive Vulnerability to Depression Project. To test their proposed negative cognition subtype of depression, Alloy and Abramson selected college students who were not depressed but who evidenced the kind of negative thinking patterns and attributional tendencies specified by the model, and followed them over the course of several years, assessing their likelihood of becoming depressed as well as symptom patterns and features that should follow from their causal model. In a different application of this type of reasoning, Drevets (1999) developed a biological model of a novel subtype, "familial pure depression" (depression with no family history of alcoholism, antisocial personality, or mania) and subsequently selected individuals for neuroimaging assessment who were depressed and had relevant family histories to test his theory. We mention these projects to illustrate that, rather than lumping all individuals into studies based on a pure symptom approach, investigators can specify the types of casual processes that underlie their model, select individuals for whom the model seems to apply (i.e., the particular depression subtype), and then assess the kinds of clinical symptoms and features that should follow from the model. Such an approach may help move the field forward in important ways.

Symptom Profile Research Strategies

Depending upon the precise conceptual questions posed by investigators, a symptom-based conceptualization may also be a viable alternative to the pure syndrome approach. A specific symptom or symptom profile approach targets the specific symptoms, or clusters of symptoms, that are considered important, rather than grouping all "depressed" people together because they have met some threshold of depressive symptoms regardless of the composition of the symptoms. For example, negative affect is a variable that is critical to the definition of depression and is also thought to play a significant role in determining the psychological and social functioning of depressed people. Investigators who are interested in negative affect might choose to study this variable in the context of a depressive state, yet it is important to realize that depressed (clinical, subclinical, dysthymia), anxious (general anxiety states as well as more specific anxious states such as phobia and obsessive–compulsive problems), and physically ill (acute and chronically ill) people all experience negative affect. If negative affect is studied only in the context of a depressive syndrome, then important aspects of this phenomenon may be missed. Alternatively, a specific focus on negative affect rather than the syndrome of depression allows for the study of individuals who share this state and are thus similar in important respects.

Using symptom clusters to select research participants does not rule out obtaining other information from participants. For instance, if a specific measure of negative affect is used, a depression syndrome measure or an interview may still be administered. Indeed, in the case of a variable such as negative affect, such a procedure allows investigators to determine whether a depressive syndrome (or other syndromes), or some pattern of depressive (or other) symptoms, contributes to explaining variance over and above that associated with negative affect. Hence, a specific focus on negative affect allows investigators to determine the correlates and possible causes of a process that is fundamental to many types of psychopathology, and also to examine how this variable is associated with other symptoms and behaviors. Negative affect is, of course, merely an example. Investigators may decide to focus on other target symptoms or clusters of similar symptoms.

It may therefore be worthwhile for researchers to consider investigating depressive symptom profiles or clusters rather than (or perhaps in addition to) the aggregation of symptoms represented by classifying people as depressed. Of course, if researchers are interested in a depression construct characterized by the experience of a variety of symptoms (and are uninterested in specific subtypes), then the syndrome approach is warranted. Clearly, though, the symptom profile approach encompasses a high degree of flexibility and potentially allows a number of questions to be addressed that are simply not possible when participants are only selected for high versus low scores on a depression self-report measure, or when they exceed some clinical threshold of depressive symptoms. It also allows for more precise and focused conceptual questions to be addressed. In all cases, however, it is necessary for investigators to specify clearly the nature of their theoretical question with explicit reference to the population they wish to understand.

ISSUES IN UNDERSTANDING CAUSALITY

Understanding causal issues is important, if not essential, for most research efforts. Yet, what is causality? The simplest view refers to the onset of depression—the transition from a relatively normal state into a state of psychological disorder. However, because depression can develop over time, is not static after its onset, and recurs in a great many cases, a causal cycle may be a better formulation of this idea.

The Causal Cycle of Depression: Vulnerability, Onset, Maintenance, Remission, Recovery, and Vulnerability

One cause of depression can be seen in the idea of vulnerability to the disorder. Definitions of vulnerability vary, but Ingram et al. (1998) and Ingram and Price (2001) suggest several core features that characterize most accounts of vulnerability to depression. A core feature of vulnerability is that it is a *trait* rather than the kind of *state* that characterizes the actual appearance of the depression.[5] Depending upon the level of analysis used, vulnerability can be seen as residing in genetic factors, biological substrates, or psychological variables. In addition, vulnerability is usually conceptualized as an endogenous process that is latent but reactive to the effects of stress. Vulnerability is synonymous with the diathesis in the diathesis–stress approach that is common among current models of depression.

Onset

Following vulnerability, onset of the disorder is the next stage of the causal sequence. Onset is perhaps the most easily conceptualized aspect of causality because it tends to be treated as synonymous with causality. However, onset is more precisely defined as the appearance of depressive symptoms. If the type of major depressive disorder specified by DSM-IV-TR is of interest, then onset is defined as the appearance of at least five out of nine symptoms with at least one of these symptoms consisting of sad mood or loss of pleasure, and all symptoms persisting for at least 2 weeks.

Course or Maintenance of Depression

The third aspect of the causal sequence is maintenance of the depressed state. Depression is a persistent disorder with symptoms lasting months (sometimes even with effective treatment), and years in some cases (e.g., dysthymia). There is some consensus among investigators that untreated depression lasts between 6 months to a year, although for more severe cases the disorder may last for up to 2 years (Keller, Shapiro, Lavori, & Wolfe, 1982; see Boland & Keller, Chapter 2, this volume, for a detailed discussion of the course of depression). In fact, symptoms that endure for an extended period of time are most likely linked to the disruption and personal turmoil that accompany depression. Moreover, because sad mood is ubiquitous in the human condition, factors that maintain and intensify this mood may indeed be a "cause" of depression. Thus, the factors involved in the perpetuation of depression can be considered to have very real casual significance.

Remission and Recovery

Remission is defined as a significant reduction in or total disappearance of depressive symptoms. Remission, however, implies that the variables underlying the disorder may still be present. This is particularly the case when some symptoms, although diminished below clinical significance, are still present. On the other hand, *recovery* implies the complete disappearance of the disorder. In practice, differentiating between remission and recovery can be quite difficult, with probably the best indicators being the presence of some mild to moderate symptoms, or, in the case where symptoms are no longer present, the length of time since the symptoms disappeared.

Vulnerability Once More: Recurrence and Relapse

Vulnerability occurs at the beginning of the causal chain, and also at the end. Although cases of depression can and do occur where no inordinate vulnerability is present, once depression has subsided, those who are at risk are left with vulnerability to future episodes (at least barring the introduction of some intervening factor). This is the essence of the core features of vulnerability; vulnerability is a trait. This continuing vulnerability underscores the general fact that depression is a recurrent disorder for many people (Boland & Keller, Chapter 2, this volume; Hammen, 1991), and highlights the more specific ideas of recurrence and relapse. *Depressive relapse* is signified by the return of symptoms and implies the continuation of the initial episode, whereas *recurrence* suggests the onset of a new episode and would be expected to follow some time after recovery from the previous episode (see Boland & Keller, Chapter 2, this volume; Frank et al., 1991).

Necessary, Sufficient, and Contributory Causality

An important factor in assessing casual models of depression is the distinction among necessary, sufficient, and contributory casual variables. *Necessary* casual factors are those that must occur in order for symptoms to develop (Abramson et al., 1988; Alloy et al., 1988). If certain variables are necessary, then symptoms cannot occur in the absence of these causal factors. *Sufficient* causes are those whose presence assures symptom onset; conversely, if symptoms have not occurred, then the causal factor cannot be present. *Contributory* causal factors are those whose presence enhances the probability that symptoms will occur, but which in themselves are neither necessary nor sufficient variables.

As should be evident from the preceding discussion, causality is a tricky concept. In this context, what kind of methodological insights can we glean from a consideration of the conceptual issues revolving around the idea of causality? We examine several issues, especially those that pertain to the study of vulnerability to depression.

METHODOLOGICAL ISSUES IN THE STUDY
OF VULNERABILITY TO DEPRESSION

Understanding vulnerability is arguably the most important aspect of contemporary depression research (Ingram et al., 1998; Ingram & Price, 2001). There are many reasons for this, but chief among them is that vulnerability research speaks most directly to issues of causality. Understanding what makes people vulnerable to depression provides not only extremely important clues about why people become (or stay) depressed, but also has important implications for prevention and treatment. Many contemporary studies of depression have implications for understanding vulnerability, and an increasing number of studies are being conducted in which vulnerability is the stated primary concern. The methodological considerations that guide vulnerability research are thus becoming increasingly important for depression researchers. We are not able to cover all these issues, but do highlight several methodological concerns that we think are particularly critical for researchers to consider if they intend to examine vulnerability. Before doing so, however, we note three conceptual issues that are relevant to the context of empirical investigations of depression vulnerability: differentiating risk from vulnerability, differentiating between distal and proximal vulnerability factors, and defining vulnerability itself.

Differentiating Risk Factors from Risk Mechanisms

Although vulnerability and risk are sometimes treated as synonymous, they are not. A *risk factor* is any variable associated with an increased likelihood of depression (e.g., poverty). Such predictors, or risk factors, however, do not reveal anything about the mechanisms of depression. For example, knowing that poverty places people at a heightened risk for depression does not tell us much about *how* depression does or does not come about in these circumstances, or why some people who live in poverty develop depression and others do not. It is thus important to differentiate between risk factors and risk mechanisms. We use "vulnerability" to connote *risk mechanisms*, that is, factors that are informative about processes that bring about or maintain depression. We differentiate these processes from the broader concept of risk (see Ingram et al., 1998).[6]

Differentiating between Distal and Proximal Vulnerability Factors

Vulnerability factors can be either distal or proximal. *Proximal factors* precede depression relatively shortly before its onset. *Distal factors*, on the other hand, are less temporally close in time to the appearance of depression, but nevertheless contribute to vulnerability. This distinction is important not only for conceptual reasons, but also because it necessitates different methodological requirements for vulnerability research. To demonstrate this distinction, consider Beck's (1967) cognitive model, which focuses on factors such as childhood events, negative cognitive schemas, and the negative cognitive triad in the development of depression. According to this view, the most distal vulnerability factors would be those that occur during critical developmental periods that lead to the creation of a negative cognitive schema, along with a sensitivity to a set of environmental events that will activate this schema. Once developed, the presence of a schema and its likelihood of being activated is considered a more proximal vulnerability factor. Yet, when the schema is activated by some environmental event, the cognitive triad emerges, meaning that the person begins to view him- or herself, his or her world, and his or her future in a negative, quite likely distorted, way. These distortions give rise to depression by initiating a spiral from an ordinary or "normal" negative mood state into a serious episode of depression. All these factors can be considered vulnerability factors, and all are worthy of study, but they fall at different ends of the vulnerability continuum, with developmental antecedents being distal vulnerability factors that occur considerably before the appearance of a depressive disorder, and the negative cognitive triad being the most proximal factor. Just as distal and proximal vulnerability must be distinguished to appreciate the full range of vulnerability, so too must the research designs that are appropriate to study these processes. We therefore examine these designs here (a more detailed examination is available in Ingram et al., 1998).

How Do We Define Risk?: Operational Definitions of Vulnerability

The study of risk mechanisms in vulnerable individuals obviously requires some type of operational definition of vulnerability. Indeed, it is difficult to overestimate the importance of credible operational definitions inasmuch as the entire empirical enterprise rests on the accurate definition, identification, and selection of vulnerable individuals for study.

Remission Operational Definitions

Some studies operationally define vulnerability on the basis of a previously experienced depressive episode. The underlying assumption behind this strategy is that individuals who have experienced depression in the past must, by definition, have encountered the variables that led to this state. However, a concern that follows from this approach is that studies that rely solely on remission to define risk are most likely selecting a group of individuals exhibiting heterogeneous causal pathways. Depending on the degree of heterogeneity in the sample, such a strategy may still be acceptable, although at the very least sample heterogeneity may obscure some potentially important vulnerability factors (Ingram et al., 1998).

Theoretically Guided Operational Definitions: The Behavioral High-Risk Paradigm

An alternative approach to operationally defining vulnerability is a theory-based, behavioral high-risk definition. Numerous examples of theoretically defined vulnerability factors are available, including *attachment* (Hammen et al., 1995) *dependency and self-criticism* (Rude & Burnham, 1993; Zuroff, Koestner, & Powers, 1994), *inferential style* (Abramson & Alloy, 1990), *parental bonding patterns* (Parker, 1979, 1983), and *sociotropy/autonomy* (Hammen, Ellicott, Gitlin, & Jamison, 1989; Robins & Luten, 1991). In each of these cases of theoretically defined vulnerability factors, some measure of the construct is used to select research participants.

Empirically Guided Operational Definitions

Although it is preferable for operational definitions of vulnerability to be theory-guided, it is not absolutely necessary. Even though the ultimate goal is to develop theoretical models of vulnerability processes, any empirical method that shows promise for detecting vulnerable individuals can be useful whether or not it is linked to particular theoretical considerations. For instance, by using a self-report measure of characteristics that were shown to be related to bipolar disorder, Depue, Krauss, Spoont, and Arbisi (1989) identified individuals at risk for the disorder. Of course, when individuals are identified as at risk in this fashion, investigators must then seek to verify independently that risk is in fact present, and at least to eventually demonstrate how this risk is associated with some theoretical framework.

Methodological Strategies and Issues in the Study of Proximal Vulnerability

In this section we examine several designs that have been used to assess proximal vulnerability, including (1) cross-sectional designs, (2) remission designs, and (3) priming designs. In view of their emerging prominence in vulnerability research, we devote more attention in this section to priming designs.

Cross-Sectional Designs

Cross-sectional designs follow the established research tradition of comparing depressed and nondepressed subjects on some dependent variable thought to reflect a vulnerability process, with the assumption that, to the extent that these groups differ, this variable may play a causal role in depression. Although cross-sectional designs have generated an enormous amount of data, their ability to uncover vulnerability, at least vulnerability to the onset of depression, is significantly limited because cross-sectional studies are explicitly correlational in nature. Consequently, they do not allow for differentiation among causal variables, consequential variables, or third variable causality (Barnett & Gotlib, 1988; Garber & Hollon, 1991; Gotlib & Lewinsohn, 1992). *Temporal antecedence* must be demonstrated to infer onset, that is, the features must *precede* the onset of the disorder if they are to be considered a cause of the disorder (Garber & Hollon, 1991), and correlational studies do not allow for such an assessment. An exception to this limitation is that cross-sectional designs may be used to demonstrate causality for features that are believed to be constant throughout the lifespan (e.g., family history, genetic factors, or aspects of brain morphology), since these factors existed before the onset of the depression.

Remission Designs

The remission approach assesses individuals who were once, but who are no longer, depressed. This strategy assumes that remitted individuals, by virtue of their previous depression, possess some characteristics that place them at risk for depression. Remission can be identified either through longitudinal analyses where depressed individuals are followed from the depressed state to the nondepressed state (e.g., Gotlib & Cane, 1987), or retrospectively where individuals are identified who at some point in the past experienced a depressive disorder (Miranda & Persons, 1988).

For obvious reasons it is inappropriate for subjects in remission studies to be currently experiencing depression, and it is inadvisable that they be currently experiencing any other psychopathological condition. Correspondingly, it is also wise to exclude remitted subjects if they *ever* experienced another psychopathological state. This exclusion criterion parallels the procedures of many cross-sectional studies that exclude subjects if they evidence significant comorbidity (e.g., psychotic disorder). Remission studies tend to be cross-sectional in that they evaluate differences between formerly depressed and nondepressed individuals. As they pertain to vulnerability, the intent of most remission studies is to examine the stability of potentially causative factors, with the assumption that these factors should be stable and, if stable, empirically detectable.

The remission approach provides information about vulnerability factors that are both stable *and* accessible after remission. However, a remission design is a poor methodological choice to test the postulates of a model in which there is theoretical reason to believe that vulnerability factors may be stable but not easily accessible. Such assumptions are made by diathesis–stress models, in which the diathesis is only accessible under stress. To appropriately test such a theory, studies must model the complexity of diathesis–stress models (Hollon, 1992), and investigators must therefore either simulate the stress activation of vulnerability factors in the lab or find a way to assess such activating features naturalistically.

Priming Designs

Priming designs follow the logic of the diathesis–stress formulation and, in many cases, can be considered a subset of remission designs because they expose remitted depressed individuals to an experimental stimulus and then examine subsequent reactions. By incorporating triggering agents into empirical evaluations, such procedures model the relationships among variables that are specified by diathesis–stress theories. Indeed, many hypothesized psychopathology variables are assumed to be discernible only within the context of stimuli that challenge the homeostasis of the person. In this context, Segal and Ingram (1994) have emphasized that the empirical search for markers of depression is methodologically predicated on the need to understand how various systems respond when challenged, regardless of which system is of interest to the investigator. Indeed, Hollon (1992) has pointed out the remarkable similarity between the biological dysregulation models that currently dominate psychiatry research and the assumptions of psychologically based priming studies.

A strong argument for the construct validity of priming designs is that they closely model the actual complexities of the diathesis–stress assumptions that are fundamental to contemporary depression models. Priming designs thus enable the study of key variables when symptoms are not currently present, allowing a distinction to be made between processes that are symptomatic of depression and those that may precede it, and thus constitute vulnerability. Thus, vulnerability research efforts are strengthened when the hypothesized risk factors are carefully specified and activated prior to assessment, thereby allowing for more rigorous tests of vulnerability hypotheses (Segal & Ingram, 1994).

TYPE OF PRIME

Priming studies most frequently use mood inductions to prime individuals, at least in psychologically based approaches, but there is no reason to believe that other variables cannot be used as well (Segal & Ingram, 1994). For example, depression models that argue that certain interpersonal events are critical stress components in a diathesis–stress model should be able to model in the laboratory the kinds of interpersonal situations that would lead to the activation of depressotypic processes (e.g., expressed emotion; see Hooley & Gotlib, 2000). Alternatively, some theoretical models may be so general that no specific type of activating event needs be specified; for example, some biological challenge models do not rely on specific stresses, but instead focus on "generic" stresses to study the onset of affective dysregulation (e.g., exposing subjects to stressful math problems; see Depue & Kleiman, 1979). The key issue is for researchers to specify precisely what kind of stress should activate a diathesis if indeed a diathesis–stress model provides the guiding framework for the research.

ASSESSING THE ADEQUACY OF PRIMING PROCEDURES

Regardless of the type of priming induction, investigators must demonstrate changes on the variables specified to be a function of the prime (e.g., pre–post differences), or at least differences between randomly assigned primed versus nonprimed groups. For example, if a mood prime is used, changes or differences in mood must be demonstrated. This is the basic logic underlying manipulation checks; investigators must demonstrate that the intended state was in fact created (Ingram, 1991).

If control groups are used in a priming design, both groups must evidence the independently derived priming effects; otherwise, the data are inherently confounded. For instance, if a mood-priming procedure is used, both the vulnerable and the control group should show similar levels of sad mood after exposure to the induction. If only one group experiences sad mood (e.g., formerly depressed subjects), it is impossible to disentangle effects due to differences in mood from differences due to underlying vulnerability factors. This can be a particularly difficult problem in research relying on formerly depressed clinical samples because they tend to report greater levels of negative mood at baseline than do never-depressed samples (Miranda, Gross, Persons, & Hahn, 1998).

Methodological Strategies and Issues in the Study of Distal Vulnerability

We begin our discussion of distal vulnerability designs by examining the high-risk offspring design and the high-risk parental design. We then examine various longitudinal approaches. We conclude with a discussion of retrospective designs and a subcategory of these designs, experimental retrospective strategies.

High-Risk Research: The Offspring Design

Studying the offspring of individuals possessing a disorder is a well-known research approach that has its empirical roots in the first investigations of vulnerability to schizophrenia (e.g., Mednick, & Schulsinger, 1968). A crucial assumption of this strategy is that the offspring of depressed parents should possess factors that make them more likely to develop depression than the offspring of nondepressed parents. Moreover, beyond assessing risk factors for the development of a specific disorder, offspring designs are capable of providing a wealth of additional data such as whether those offspring who do not emerge with the disorder are at risk for some other manner of psychological distress, or alternatively, whether there are other factors that protect high-risk children from psychological problems.

A number of considerations are essential to the conduct of well-executed offspring designs. Some of these represent variations on basic research principles while others are relatively unique to this kind of approach to vulnerability. Hammen (1991) has examined a number of these considerations in her excellent work on the social context of risk in children of depressed mothers. We summarize these here.

DIAGNOSTIC AND DEMOGRAPHIC STATUS OF PARENTS AND THEIR CHILDREN

It is critical for investigators who assess the offspring of depressed parents to explicitly describe how depression in parents is defined and measured, and to rule out possible comorbidity if the design calls for assessing relatively "pure" depression. Explicit operational definitions also allow for selecting appropriate comparison groups (e.g., Hammen [1991], included the children of medically ill patients as a comparison group for the offspring of depressed mothers).

There are a number of variables beyond depression that are important to assess in high-risk offspring designs. For example, studies should report which (or if both) parent(s) met criteria for which type of depression (Hammen, 1991). Likewise, other psychiatric characteristics are important to examine in offspring studies (e.g., the severity of the disorder, acute vs. chronic disorder, and past psychiatric history). In a similar fashion, demographic characteristics such as parents' socioeconomic status, age, education level, and ethnicity are also important to assess for their possible impact on the development of vulnerability. Of course, the same clarity and precision that are needed to adequately assess parents in offspring studies are also needed in the assessment of the children in such studies.

MEDIATING PROCESSES IN BOTH PARENTS AND CHILDREN

Although demographic and diagnostic status are quite important, such data by themselves do not tell us much about the actual processes of vulnerability; that is, these data are informative about risk factors but not about risk mechanisms (Goodman & Gotlib, 1999; Hammen, 1991). This is true even if a particular theory specifies that offspring are at increased risk for depression for a given set of reasons. For example, some theories predict that the children of depressed parents are more likely to develop depression because of the genetic transmission of vulnerability. However, even though it is well documented that the children of depressed parents are more likely to experience depression (Garber & Flynn, 2001a; Gotlib & Goodman, 1999), this does not tell us what the genetic mechanism is, or even if it is a genetic mechanism rather than some other variable.

Thus, finding that the children of depressed parents are more likely to become depressed does not in itself validate a particular theory; additional strategies are necessary to examine potential mediating factors within the context of offspring designs. To illustrate an example of this approach, Garber and Flynn (2001b) found having a depressed mother to be associated with children's attributional styles, perceptions of self-worth, and hopelessness. However, Garber and Flynn went beyond this and also examined the parenting *behaviors* of depressed mothers and how these behaviors were associated with these variables in their children. This strategy illustrates the fact that data on the behaviors that are linked to risk are more informative then is the mere fact that a parent is depressed. Such approaches are thus advisable if researchers want to move closer to understanding possible risk mechanisms rather than just risk factors.

High-Risk Paradigm: Parental Designs

If offspring designs suggest that it may be informative to study the offspring of depressed parents, the reverse is also true. It is important to study the parents of depressed offspring and of offspring who are thought to be at risk for developing depression. Of course, the same methodological considerations that apply to offspring designs also apply to these designs (e.g., careful consideration of the descriptive characteristics of the sample, etc.). In contrast to high-risk designs defined by depressed parents, such methodologies can address a number of additional issues, such as determining whether the parental characteristics differ between depressed and nondepressed child samples, whether the interactions between children and their parents are different between samples, and so forth.

Longitudinal Designs

Longitudinal designs comprise a group of strategies that assess cohorts at different points in time, the goal being to determine which variables predict the subsequent occurrence of depressive symptoms. The length of longitudinal designs can vary considerably, ranging from hours to days to months to years (for an example of a longitudinal study spanning almost 20 years, see Zuroff et al., 1994). Likewise, assessment intervals can also vary considerably. Variables such as length and timing of assessment are determined by the theoretical context for the research and the corresponding empirical questions of interest to the researcher. Pragmatic factors such as the resources available for the research can also play a role in determining the type, length, and timing of assessments.[7]

Before discussing the different types of longitudinal designs, it is important to note that the methodological considerations in other designs apply equally to longitudinal designs. That is, in all but rare cases, theoretical considerations must guide the choice of variables to be studied and go hand in hand with the choice of samples. In addition, explicit operational definitions and assessment of diagnostic, psychological, and demographic status of samples, as well as the assessment of mediational variables, are critical to consider if longitudinal designs are to yield useful information. Likewise, depending upon the conceptual questions addressed, additional considerations will need to be taken into account, such as developmental stages, ages, and sex differences. Several types of longitudinal designs can be used to study distal vulnerability factors. These designs include prospective designs and catch-up designs (for an excellent in-depth discussion of issues in longitudinal research as well as a discussion of some additional designs, readers are referred to Rutter, 1988).[8]

PROSPECTIVE DESIGNS

Prospective longitudinal designs seek to identify variables that are thought to be linked to risk in individuals who are not yet depressed. Prior to the onset of depression, participants are assessed and then followed over some period of time. Prospective longitudinal designs are ideal for examining the temporal antecedents of variables that are vital for demonstrating at least some types of causality (Garber & Hollon, 1991). Prospective designs can take a number of forms. For instance, investigators may identify a high-risk sample and then follow them over some period of time. Likewise, some treatment studies can be considered to be prospective longitudinal designs if they examine not only the efficacy of the treatment, but of variables that are presumed to mediate this efficacy (i.e., presumed vulnerability factors) both before and after treatment.

CATCH-UP DESIGNS

Catch-up designs use data previously collected for another purpose to examine whether these data can predict depression. Thus, for example, data that may be informative about vulnerability when individuals in the sample were younger might be examined at a later date to determine if depression can be predicted. Such an approach is illustrated in a study reported by Zuroff et al. (1994), who examined data from a study of 5-year-olds first reported by Sears, Maccoby, and Leven in 1957. At later ages (i.e., 12, 18, and 31), data on self-criticism, interpersonal relationships, achievement, and general adjustment were collected. If data on depression had been collected in this sample at some point, this design could have determined whether any of the variables examined during earlier assessments (several of which have been proposed to be vulnerability factors for depression) predicted later depression.

The theoretical and empirical limitations of longitudinal studies are few, although the practical limitations of longitudinal designs can be daunting. That is, given the complexity of issues to be addressed over time, longitudinal vulnerability designs are difficult to adequately conduct, are time-consuming, and are expensive in both resources and labor. This is the case even when data were previously collected, as in catch-up designs. Longitudinal designs are also prone to problems in the retention of subjects; the longer the time frame, the greater the inevitable attrition. Such issues raise problems for the treatment of data and the interpretation of results, and thus suggest that longitudinal designs are not for researchers without adequate funding, who are untenured, or who tend to be faint of heart.

CROSS-SEQUENTIAL DESIGNS

Cross-sequential designs represent a combination of longitudinal and cross-sectional research (Vasta, Haith, & Miller, 1992). As in cross-sectional designs, different groups or cohorts are compared with one another, but as in longitudinal designs these different cohorts are also followed over time. To illustrate a developmentally based, cross-sequential design, groups of 2-year-olds might be assessed along with groups of 4-year-olds and 6-year-olds on measures that are thought to reflect risk for depression. Using this kind of design with depressed parents, for example, cross-sequential designs would allow investigators to track changes over time in the children of depressed parents. Such designs would provide a potent method for tracking changes in possible risk processes over time, determining if some of these changes are associated with later depression, and assessing whether variables that become prominent at certain times in the developmental process are related to vulnerability and depression.

RETROSPECTIVE DESIGNS

Retrospective designs seek to understand the influence of vulnerability factors through recall of information relevant to vulnerability. For example, research participants might be asked to recall earlier events from childhood or adolescence that the investigator hypothesizes are related to vulnerability. Individuals who are asked to recall these events are either currently depressed, or are not depressed but are thought to be vulnerable. An example of such a methodology can be seen in the recall of information on traumatic events that are thought to be linked to later vulnerability (e.g., Kuyken & Brewin, 1995). Likewise, if some parenting behaviors are thought to induce a vulnerability for depression, then recall of these behaviors would be assessed retrospectively (e.g., Gerlsma, Emmelkamp, & Arrindell, 1990).

EXPERIMENTAL RETROSPECTIVE DESIGNS: PRIMING STUDIES OF PAST
DEPRESSION AND POSSIBLE VULNERABILITY FACTORS

Retrospective designs can be supplemented by experimental conditions to examine somewhat different aspects of presumed vulnerability. Thus far, such experimental conditions have pertained to priming paradigms, although other conditions are possible. To illustrate this idea, consider the fact that disrupted bonding experiences with parents have been hypothesized to serve as a vulnerability factor for depression (Parker, 1979, 1983), yet such disrupted patterns may be difficult to detect for vulnerable individuals. Examination of such recollections under priming conditions may represent one way to assess the presence of vulnerability; stated simply, vulnerable individuals who have been primed may be more able to recall these disrupted interactions. In principle, such a procedure has the potential to generate data that might not be available otherwise.

SOME POSSIBLE LIMITATIONS OF RETROSPECTIVE DESIGNS

Although potentially providing a wealth of information, these designs are also vulnerable to criticisms that retrospective reports are likely to be unreliable and thus invalid. Based on an extensive review of research, Brewin, Andrews, and Gotlib (1993) classified several concerns over memory reliability, but argued that data generally do not substantiate these concerns. Nevertheless, they also suggested that retrospective reports are unlikely to ever be completely free of possible problems, and they offered several suggestions to strengthen the validity of such data. For example, they suggest that retrospective reports be supplemented with information from other informants (although they caution against using parents as these other informants). Even though they do not solve all problems, siblings may provide a better informant group, ideally, similar aged siblings, and preferably of the same sex. In addition, independent records obtained by other sources may also provide a reliable account of childhood circumstances (this is similar to the follow-back longitudinal design). Brewin et al. (1993) argue that carefully structuring the fashion in which recall is assessed can improve the validity of these reports.

CONCLUSIONS AND A CAUTIONARY NOTE
ON DEMONSTRATING CAUSALITY

As we noted earlier, vulnerability research is aimed at uncovering the potentially causative features of various processes. The designs and methodological issues we have examined can provide important clues about causality, but we must note some important cautions and limitations before any conclusions about causality can be drawn. We can illustrate this difficulty in several ways. For example, consider priming studies. A number of these studies have demonstrated that individuals who are vulnerable to depression respond in "depressive-like" ways when they are primed (Gotlib & Krasnoperova, 1998; Segal & Ingram, 1994). Although these responses tend to be in accordance with the predictions of various theoretical models, with few exceptions (see Segal, Gemar, & Williams, 1999) they have not shown that cognitive responses actually predict the eventual onset of depression. Thus, findings supporting a theoretical prediction do not in and of themselves demonstrate that a causal process has been tapped.

In a similar vein, consider the interpretational difficulty in priming studies that is raised by the "scar hypothesis." Although priming studies informed by diathesis–stress models suggest that the primed variable has causal significance, the scar hypothesis (Lewinsohn, Steinmetz, Larson, & Franklin, 1981) suggests that deficits observed after priming may represent an effect of having been depressed at some point in the past, rather than reflecting a casual feature (Ingram et al., 1998). Priming studies alone have no way to disentangle what may be a scar from what may be a genuine vulnerability feature. Although we note the scar hypothesis in the context of priming studies, similar rival hypotheses affect studies at numerous levels of analysis, ranging from the psychological to the biological research.

The problem of demonstrating causality afflicts all the methodological designs we have examined, even longitudinal research. Recall that such designs are uniquely equipped to demonstrate temporal antecedence. Yet, it is important to note that temporal antecedence is necessary but not sufficient to show causality. That is, as a prerequisite to showing that a variable is causal, data must demonstrate that the variable in question predicts depressive symptomatology, but satisfying this prerequisite is not enough; showing that a variable predicts the occurrence of depression does not in and of itself establish a cause and effect. Hence, even if a longitudinal design shows that certain responses predict subsequent depression, there is little way to determine if these are the *actual* causal variables. For example, it may be that other processes that are correlated with the target variables serve as the actual causative factors for depression. To further illustrate, consider the example of treatment studies within the context of the longitudinal design. Even though treatment targeted at a specific process may yield improvement in depression and change the process at which it was targeted (see Segal et al., 1999, for a demonstration), this does not prove that the targeted variable was the process responsible for the improvement (or was responsible for the depression to begin with). There are many reasons why treatment may work, some of which may have little to do with the processes that are targeted by treatment. Thus, the problem of demonstrating causality applies to virtually all research designs, regardless of their theoretical framework. We can move closer to understanding casualty in depression through well-conducted designs that adequately address the various issues we and others (e.g., Kazdin, 1998; Kendall et al., 1999) have discussed, but proving causality is a goal that is likely to elude the field for some time to come.

Future Directions

The methodological cautions and suggestions we have made throughout this chapter lead naturally to a number of potential future directions that may help to yield useful insights into the nature of depression. We began this chapter by discussing lay notions of depression as an amalgam of many theoretical constructs. Such divergence in ideas about depression leads quite naturally to the idea of different types of depression. Following from this, if different factors operate in the onset (or course) of different types of depression, their identification and differentiation will be increasingly important to understand. New techniques for distinguishing truly categorical subtypes of depression (e.g., taxometric techniques capable of detecting noncontinuous distinctions within populations; Meehl, 1995; Meehl & Yonce, 1994), along with recognition of more continuously varying aspects of depression in formal diagnostic systems, could facilitate such investigations, and thus represent an important future methodological direction.

As we have noted, inasmuch as anxiety and depression tend to be highly correlated, comorbidity represents a significant challenge for depression research. However, closer attention to relationships between anxiety and depression may also lead to advances in understanding causal interactions between these disorders. In so doing, this may move us closer to understanding the nature of each individual disorder. Similarly, future research on subclinical depressive states, conducted with the explicit goal of better understanding mechanisms of these states as independent entities, could be very valuable; we encourage researchers of subclinical depression to clearly proclaim their intent to study such states. As we have noted, although such research may lead to interesting clinical investigations, this need not be its end goal. A final direction in understanding the functioning of depression involves recent trends toward integrating traditionally separate areas of depression research including physiology, psychoneuroimmunology, cognitive-clinical research, and psychosocial research. Recognition of the interplay between biological, cognitive, and social aspects of depression could lead away from symptom-based categorizations of subtypes of depression, to rich feature-based descriptions (e.g., consideration of a perseverative depression subtype characterized by rumination, prefrontal inactivity, NK-cell depletion, and decreased social responsivity).

Another set of future directions could lead to clues, if not conclusive evidence, regarding the causes of onset, maintenance, and recovery. As we have suggested, establishing causality is difficult when potential antecedents of depression co-occur with other factors that might also (or instead) cause depression. A number of strategies are becoming increasingly available to deal with these problems. For example, thorough examination of large samples of depressed and never-depressed individuals over time, employing wide arrays of behavioral, social, and cognitive measures, could help counter problems by allowing for an examination of factors that might covary. Additionally, computational modeling of relevant factors can allow for an a priori quantitative prediction of how various factors can interact to produce aspects of depression, reducing the threat of capitalizing on chance covariation. Examination of genetic aspects of depression, and biological features that are not assumed to change over time, also helps get past many of these concerns. Finally, as new treatments are being developed that narrowly target specific aspects of depression (e.g., Wells, 2000), a new type of design is becoming available, involving the assessment of individuals on a variety of measures before and after such treatments. To the extent that depressive symptomatology is reduced by these treatments, without changes in factors traditionally thought of as correlates of depression, new understanding of the mechanisms of depression can be inferred. Such are the future methodological directions that may move us closer to our goal of understanding the essential features and causes of depression.

Summary

We end this chapter with a call that we have noted several times throughout this chapter, but that nevertheless warrants repeated emphasis. The appropriateness of many of the strategies and tactics that we and others have discussed in the conduct of depression research depends on the precise conceptual questions and hypotheses proposed. Some strategies may be perfectly appropriate for one type of question concerning depression, but grossly inappropriate for another question. Far too infrequently, however, do investigators elaborate the specific conceptual question in which they are interested with precise reference to a given depressed population. As we have noted, for example, we think that there are legitimate reasons to study subclinical depression, but the field would be well served if investigators always stated exactly why the question they are posing in *this* group is important. Similarly, investigators interested in a "pure" major depressive state that is not associated with the conditions that typically co-occur with clinical depression would serve the field well by explicitly addressing why *only* this sample is of interest. Overall, precisely proposing conceptual and empirical questions will guide a more precise choice of research procedures and samples that will ultimately benefit our understanding of depression (Ingram & Hamilton, 1999).

In a very general sense, we believe that the field has for too long implicitly labored under a uniformity myth, wherein depression is viewed as a single phenomenon, that can always, or virtually always, be investigated with one straightforward research strategy. The best example of such a uniformity myth was the practice of selecting depressed subjects on the basis of some indicator of depression, administering to both the depressed group and a control group a measure representing some theoretical construct, and if differences were found then concluding that information on the cause of depression had been found. This example is perhaps too simplistic but it does nevertheless represent an assumption under which many early studies operated.

This uniformity myth is giving way to a much more complex understanding of depression, and with it the need to employ complex research strategies. Depression research was simpler when the field implicitly adhered to this uniformity myth, but more sophisticated strategies are beginning to reveal important aspects of the processes that underlie depression in ways that earlier and simpler studies could not. To continue this progress, we must appreciate the complexity of the specific phenomena that characterize what we broadly call "depression," state very clearly our theoretical questions with precise reference to the depression type and phenomena to which they are to be applied, and then select a research strategy that matches the type of depression that we want to understand. We must thus confront both the complexity of depression and the methodological strategies that can be used to investigate it, and then make the best choices possible.

Given this increasing complexity and difficulty, it is natural for some researchers to yearn to return to an earlier time when depression research was simply a matter of comparing depressed and nondepressed participants' responses on a questionnaire. But this is no longer our father's Oldsmobile. That car was cheaper and easy to service, but was not all that reliable. New cars are more expensive to buy and operate, and much more complicated and difficult to service. Yet the ride is better, more reliable, and we are therefore more assured of getting to our ultimate destination. It's time to trade up.

NOTES

1. DSM-IV-TR is careful to point out that mental disorders are not necessarily true categorical variables: "DSM-IV-TR is a categorical classification that divides mental disorders into types based on criteria sets with defining features . . . . [T]here is no assumption that each category of mental disorder is a completely discrete entity with absolute boundaries dividing it from other mental disorders or from no mental disorder. There is also no assumption that all individuals described as having the same mental disorder are alike in all important ways" (p. xxxi). Although this qualification in the "Preface" of DSM-IV-TR is important, the DSM nevertheless promulgates a categorical framework for understanding psychological distress.

2. For ease of communication, and unless otherwise noted, the term *clinical depression* is used to refer to major depressive disorder as specified in DSM-IV-TR. Likewise, and unless otherwise noted, we refer to all states of less than clinical depression as *subclinical depression*.

3. DSM-IV-TR also includes a category of clinically significant disorder that is virtually identical to MDD in important respects, but that is not classified as a mood disorder. Bereavement falls under the category of "Other Conditions That May Be a Focus of Clinical Attention" and is differentiat-

ed from MDD on the basis of precipitating stressors rather than on symptom patterns. Other DSM-IV-TR disorders include adjustment disorder with depressed mood and depressive disorder not otherwise specified. Other possible depressive disorders that are proposed for further study or are included in diagnostic interviews include premenstrual dysphoric disorder, minor depressive disorder, and depressive personality disorder. Because these are the focus of limited research attention, they are not discussed here.

4. DSM-IV-TR includes a category of depression that appears to fall somewhere between clinical and subclinical depression. *Adjustment disorder with depressed mood* is defined as the appearance of clinically significant symptoms following a stressor, but that do not meet the criteria for MDD. The precise nature of the symptoms, and how they differ from those for MDD, are unclear.

5. It is also important to note that even though vulnerability is conceptualized as a trait according to some conceptualizations, vulnerability is not necessarily permanent or unalterable (although psychological vulnerability is nevertheless stable and relatively resistant to change). Corrective experiences can occur that may attenuate the vulnerability, or alternatively, certain experiences may increase vulnerability factors.

6. Although conceptually separate, it is important to note that risk and vulnerability are not empirically unrelated; vulnerability and risk interact to produce and maintain disorders such as depression (Luthar & Zigler, 1991; Rutter, 1987). Thus, the person who is "at risk" because he or she lives in a particularly stressful environment will see this risk realized in disorder if he or she *also* possesses the vulnerability mechanisms. This is, of course, the essence of the diathesis–stress approach that characterizes numerous models of depression.

7. Longitudinal designs can be applied to the study of either proximal or distal factors, but we examine them only in the context of distal research.

8. Two other designs, follow-back and registrar, are also possible; for a description of these designs, and more detail on prospective and catch-up designs, see Ingram et al. (1998) and Rutter (1988).

REFERENCES

Abramson, L. Y., & Alloy, L. B. (1990). Search for the "negative cognition" subtype of depression. In D. C. McCann & N. Endler (Eds.), *Depression: New directions in theory, research, and practice* (pp. 77–109). Toronto: Wall & Thompson.

Abramson, L. Y., Alloy, L. B., & Metalsky, G. I. (1988). The cognitive diathesis–stress theories of depression: Toward an adequate evaluation of the theories' validities. In L. B. Alloy (Ed.), *Cognitive processes in depression* (pp. 3–30). New York: Guilford Press.

Alloy, L. B., & Abramson, L. Y. (1999). The Temple–Wisconsin Cognitive Vulnerability to Depression Project: Conceptual background, design, and methods. *Journal of Cognitive Psychotherapy, 13*, 227–262

Alloy, L. B., Abramson, L. Y., Raniere, D., & Dyller, I. M. (1999). Research methods in adult psychopathology. In P. C. Kendall, J. N. Butcher, & G. N. Holmbeck (Eds.), *Handbook of research methods in clinical psychology* (2nd ed., pp. 466–498). New York: Wiley.

Alloy, L. B., Hartlage, S., & Abramson, L. Y. (1988). Testing the cognitive diathesis–stress theories of depression: Issues of research design, conceptualization, and assessment. In L. B. Alloy (Ed.), *Cognitive processes in depression* (pp. 31–73). New York: Guilford Press.

American Psychiatric Association. (2000). *Diagnostic and statistical manual of mental disorders* (4th ed., text rev.). Washington, DC: Author.

Angst, J., & Merikangas, K. R. (1998). Mixed anxiety depression. *Psychiatria Hungarica, 13*, 263–268.

Barlow, D. H., & Campbell, L. A. (2000). Mixed anxiety-depression and its implications for models of mood and anxiety disorders. *Comprehensive Psychiatry, 41*, 55–60.

Barnett, P. A., & Gotlib, I. H. (1988). Psychosocial functioning in depression: Distinguishing among antecedents, concomitants, and consequences. *Psychological Bulletin, 104*, 97–126.

Beck, A. T. (1967). *Depression: Causes and treatment.* Philadelphia: University of Pennsylvania Press.

Beck, A. T., Steer, R. A., & Garbin, M. G. (1988). Psychometric properties of the Beck Depression Inventory: Twenty-five years of evaluation. *Clinical Psychology Review, 8,* 77–100.

Beckham, E. E., Leber, W. R., & Youll, L. K. (1995). The diagnostic classification of depression. In E. E Beckham & W. R. Leber (Eds.), *Handbook of depression* (2nd ed., pp. 36–60). New York: Guilford Press.

Brewin, C. R., Andrews, B., & Gotlib, I. (1993). Psychopathology and early experience: A reappraisal of retrospective reports. *Psychological Bulletin , 113,* 82–98.

Campbell, D. T., & Stanley, J. C. (1966). *Experimental and quasi-experimental designs for research.* Chicago: Rand-McNally.

Clark, D. A., Beck, A. T., & Brown, G. (1989). Cognitive mediation in general psychiatric outpatients: A test of the content-specificity hypothesis. *Journal of Personality and Social Psychology, 56,* 958–964.

Clark, L., & Watson, D. (1991). Tripartite model of anxiety and depression: Psychometric evidence and taxonomic implications. *Journal of Abnormal Psychology, 100,* 316–336.

Costello, C. G. (1992). Conceptual problems in current research in cognitive vulnerability to psychopathology. *Cognitive Therapy and Research, 16,* 379–390.

Costello, C. G. (1993). From symptoms of depression to syndromes of depression. In C. G. Costello (Ed.), *Symptoms of depression* (pp. 291–300). New York: Wiley.

Coyne, J. C. (1994). Self-reported distress: Analog or ersatz depression? *Psychological Bulletin, 116,* 29–45.

Depue, R. A., & Kleiman, R. M. (1979). Free cortisol as a peripheral index of central vulnerability to major forms of unipolar depressive disorders: Examining stress–biology interactions in subsyndromal high risk persons. In R. A. Depue (Ed.), *The psychobiology of depressive disorders* (pp. 177–204). New York: Academic Press.

Depue, R. A., Krauss, S., Spoont, M., & Arbisi, P. (1989). Identification of unipolar and bipolar affective conditions in a university population with the General Behavior Inventory. *Journal of Abnormal Psychology, 98,* 117–126.

Drevets, W. C. (1999). Emerging neuroscience approaches to understanding cognition and psychopathology: Positron-emission tomography imaging. In C. R. Cloninger (Ed.), *Personality and psychopathology* (pp. 369–408). Washington, DC: American Psychiatric Press.

Flett, G. L., Vredenburg, K., & Krames, L. (1997). The continuity of depression in clinical and nonclinical samples. *Psychological Bulletin, 121,* 395–416.

Frank, E., Prien, R. F., Jarret, R. B., Keller, M. B., Kupfer, D. J., Lavori, P. W., Rush, A. J., & Weissman, M. M. (1991). Conceptualization and rationale for consensus definitions of terms in major depressive disorder: Remission, recovery, relapse, and recurrence. *Archives of General Psychiatry, 48,* 851–855.

Garber, J., & Flynn, C. (2001a). Vulnerability to depression in children and adolescents. In R. E. Ingram & J. M. Price (Eds.), *Vulnerability to psychopathology: Risk across the lifespan* (pp. 175–225). New York: Guilford Press.

Garber, J., & Flynn, C. (2001b). Predictors of depressive cognitions in young adolescents. *Cognitive Therapy and Research, 25,* 353–376.

Garber, J., & Hollon, S. D. (1991). What can specificity designs say about causality in psychopathology research? *Psychological Bulletin, 110,* 129–136.

Gerlsma, C., Emmelkamp, P. M. G., & Arrindell, W. A. (1990). Anxiety, depression, and perception of early parenting: A meta-analysis. *Clinical Psychology Review, 10,* 251–277.

Goodman, S. H., & Gotlib, I. H. (1999). Risk for psychopathology in the children of depressed mothers: A developmental model for understanding mechanisms of transmission. *Psychological Review, 106,* 458–490.

Gotlib, I. H. (1984). Depression and general psychopathology in university students. *Journal of Abnormal Psychology, 93,* 19–30.

Gotlib, I. H., & Cane, D. B. (1987). Construct accessibility and clinical depression: A longitudinal investigation. *Journal of Abnormal Psychology, 96,* 199–204

Gotlib, I. H., & Goodman, S. H. (1999). Children of parents with depression. In W. K. Silverman &

T. H. Ollendick (Eds.), *Developmental issues in the clinical treatment of children* (pp. 415–432). Boston: Allyn & Bacon.

Gotlib, I. H., & Lewinsohn, P. M. (1992). Cognitive models of depression: Critique and directions for future research. *Psychological Inquiry, 3,* 241–244.

Gotlib, I. H., Lewinsohn, P. M., & Seeley, J. R. (1995). Symptoms versus a diagnosis of depression: Differences in psychosocial functioning. *Journal of Consulting and Clinical Psychology, 63,* 90–100.

Gotlib, I. H., & Krasnoperova, E. (1998). Biased information processing as a vulnerability factor for depression. *Behavior Therapy, 29,* 603–617

Haaga, D. F., & Solomon, A. (1993). Impact of Kendall, Hollon, Beck, Hammen, and Ingram (1987) on treatment of the continuity issue in "depression" research. *Cognitive Therapy and Research, 17,* 313–324.

Hammen, C. (1991). *Depression runs in families: The social context of risk and resilience in children of depressed mothers.* New York: Springer-Verlag.

Hammen, C., Burge, D., Daley, S., Davila, J., Paley, B., & Rudolph, D. (1995). Interpersonal attachment cognitions and prediction of symptomatic responses to interpersonal stress. *Journal of Abnormal Psychology, 104,* 436–443.

Hammen, C., Ellicott, A., Gitlin, M., & Jamison, K. R. (1989). Sociotropy/autonomy and vulnerability to specific life events in patients with unipolar depression and bipolar disorders. *Journal of Abnormal Psychology, 98,* 154–160.

Hollon, S. D. (1992). Cognitive models of depression from a psychobiological perspective. *Psychological Inquiry, 3,* 250–253.

Hooley, J. M., & Gotlib, I. H. (2000). A diathesis–stress conceptualization of expressed emotion and clinical outcome. *Journal of Applied and Preventive Psychology, 9,* 135–151.

Ingram, R. E. (1989a). Affective confounds in social-cognitive research. *Journal of Personality and Social Psychology, 57,* 715–722.

Ingram, R. E. (1989b). Unique and shared cognitive factors in social anxiety and depression. *Journal of Social and Clinical Psychology, 8,* 198–208.

Ingram, R. E. (1990). Self-focused attention in clinical disorders: Review and a conceptual model. *Psychological Bulletin, 107,* 156–176.

Ingram, R. E. (1991). Tilting at windmills: A response to Pyszczynski, Greenberg, Hamilton, and Nix. *Psychological Bulletin, 110,* 544–550.

Ingram, R. E., & Hamilton, N. A. (1999). Evaluating precision in the social psychological assessment of depression: Methodological considerations, issues, and recommendations. *Journal of Social and Clinical Psychology, 18,* 160–180.

Ingram, R. E., Kendall, P. C., Smith, T. W., Donnell, C., & Ronan, K. (1987). Cognitive specificity in emotional distress. *Journal of Personality and Social Psychology, 53,* 734–742.

Ingram, R. E., Miranda, J., & Segal, Z. V. (1998). *Cognitive vulnerability to depression.* New York: Guilford Press.

Ingram, R. E., & Price, J. M. (2001). The role of vulnerability in understanding psychopathology. In R. E. Ingram & J. M. Price (Eds.), *Vulnerability to psychopathology: Risk across the lifespan* (pp. 3–19). New York: Guilford Press.

Kazdin, A. E. (Ed). (1998). *Methodological issues and strategies in clinical research* (2nd ed.). Washington, DC: American Psychological Association.

Keller, M. B., Shapiro, R. W., Lavori, P. W., & Wolfe, N. (1982). Relapse in RDC major depressive disorders: Analysis with the life table. *Archives of General Psychiatry, 39,* 911–915.

Kendall, P. C., & Brady, E. U. (1995). Comorbidity in the anxiety disorders of childhood: Implications for validity and clinical significance. In K. D. Craig & K. S. Dobson (Eds.), *Anxiety and depression in adults and children* (pp. 3–35). Thousand Oaks, CA: Sage.

Kendall, P. C., Butcher, J. N., & Holmbeck G. N. (Eds.), (1999). *Handbook of research methods in clinical psychology* (2nd ed.). New York: Wiley.

Kendall, P. C., & Flannery-Schroeder, E. C. (1995). Rigor, but not rigor mortis, in depression research. *Journal of Personality and Social Psychology, 68,* 892–894.

Kendall, P. C., Hollon, S. D., Beck, A. T., Hammen, C. L., & Ingram, R. E. (1987). Issues and recommendations regarding use of the Beck Depression Inventory. *Cognitive Therapy and Research, 11*, 289–299.

Kendall, P. C., & Watson, D. (Eds.). (1989). *Anxiety and depression: Distinctive and overlapping features.* San Diego: Academic Press.

Kuyken, W., & Brewin, C. R. (1995). Autobiographical memory functioning in depression and reports of early abuse. *Journal of Abnormal Psychology, 104*, 585–591.

Lewinsohn, P. M., Steinmetz, L., Larson, D. W., & Franklin, J. (1981). Depression-related cognitions: Antecedent or consequence? *Journal of Abnormal Psychology, 90*, 213–219.

Luthar, S. S., & Zigler, E. (1991). Vulnerability and competence: A review of research on resilience in childhood. *American Journal of Orthopsychiatry, 61*, 6–22.

Mednick, S. A., & Schulsinger, F. (1968). Some premorbid characteristics related to breakdown in children of schizophrenic mothers. In D. Rosenthal & S. S. Kety (Eds.), *Transmission of schizophrenia* (pp. 267–291). Oxford, UK: Pergamon Press.

Meehl, P. E. (1978). Theoretical risks and tabular asterisks: Sir Karl, Sir Ronald, and the slow progress of soft psychology. *Journal of Consulting and Clinical Psychology, 46*, 806–834.

Meehl, P. E. (1995). Bootstraps taxometrics: Solving the classification problem in psychopathology. *American Psychologist, 50*, 266–275.

Meehl, P. E. & Yonce, L. J. (1994). Taxometric analysis: I. Detecting taxonicity with two quantitative indicators using means above and below a sliding cut (MAMBAC procedure). *Psychological Reports, 74*, 1059–1274.

Miranda, J., Gross, J., Persons, J. B., & Hahn, J. (1998). Mood matters: Negative mood induction activates dysfunctional attitudes in women vulnerable to depression. *Cognitive Therapy and Research, 22*, 363–376.

Miranda, J., & Persons, J. B. (1988). Dysfunctional attitudes are mood-state dependent. *Journal of Abnormal Psychology, 97*, 76–79.

Nurcombe, B. (1992). The evolution and validity of the diagnosis of major depression in childhood and adolescence. In D. Cicchetti & S. L. Toth (Eds.), *Developmental perspectives on depression* (pp. 1–28). Rochester, NY: University of Rochester Press.

Parker, G. (1979). Parental characteristics in relation to depressive disorders. *British Journal of Psychiatry, 134*, 138–147.

Parker, G. (1983). Parental "affectionless control" as an antecedent to adult depression: A risk factor delineated. *Archives of General Psychiatry, 40*, 956–960.

Pedhazur, E. (1982). *Multiple regression in behavioral research* (2nd ed.). New York: Holt, Rinehart, & Winston.

Persons, J. B. (1986). The advantages of studying psychological phenomena rather than psychiatric diagnoses. *American Psychologist, 41*, 1252–1260.

Robins, C. J., & Luten, A. G. (1991). Sociotropy and autonomy: Differential patterns of clinical presentation in unipolar depression. *Journal of Abnormal Psychology, 100*, 74–77.

Rude, S. S., & Burnham, B. L. (1993). Do interpersonal and achievement vulnerabilities interact with congruent events to predict depression?: Comparison of DEQ, SAS, DAS, and combined scales. *Cognitive Therapy and Research, 17*, 531–548.

Ruscio, J., & Ruscio, A. (2000). Informing the continuity controversy: A taxometric analysis of depression. *Journal of Abnormal Psychology, 109*, 473–487.

Rutter, M. (1987). Psychosocial resilience and protective mechanisms. *American Journal of Orthopsychiatry, 57*, 316–331.

Rutter, M. (1988). Longitudinal data in the study of casual processes: Some uses and some pitfalls. In M. Rutter (Ed.), *Studies of psychosocial risk: The power of power of longitudinal data* (pp. 1–28). Cambridge, UK: Cambridge University Press.

Sears, R. R., Maccoby, E. E., & Leven, H. (1957). *Patterns of childrearing.* Evanston, IL: Row-Peterson.

Segal, Z. V., Gemar, M., & Williams, S. (1999). Differential cognitive response to a mood challenge following successful cognitive therapy or pharmacotherapy for unipolar depression. *Journal of Abnormal Psychology, 108*, 3–10.

Segal, Z. V., & Ingram, R. E. (1994). Mood priming and construct activation in tests of cognitive vulnerability to unipolar depression. *Clinical Psychology Review, 14*, 663–695.

Sher, K., & Trull, T. (1996). Methodological issues in psychopathology research. *Annual Review of Psychology, 47,* 371–400.

Spitzer, R. L., Williams, J. B., Gibbon, M., & First, M. B. (1989). *Instruction manual for the Structured Clinical Interview for DSM-III-R.* New York: Biometrics Research Department, Columbia University.

Smith, T., & Rhodewalt, F. (1991). In C. R. Snyder & D. R. Forsyth (Eds.), *Handbook of social and clinical psychology: The health perspective* (pp. 739–756). New York: Pergamon Press.

Tennen, H., Ebehardt, T. L., & Affleck, G. (1999). Depression research methodologies at the social-clinical interface: Still hazy after all these years. *Journal of Social and Clinical Psychology, 18,* 121–159.

Tennen, H., Hall, J. A., & Affleck, G. (1995a). Depression research methodologies in the *Journal of Personality and Social Psychology*: A review and critique. *Journal of Personality and Social Psychology, 68,* 870–884.

Tennen, H., Hall, J. A., & Affleck, G. (1995b). Rigor, rigor mortis, and conspiratorial views of depression research. *Journal of Personality and Social Psychology, 68,* 895–900.

Vasta, R., Haith, M. M., & Miller, S. A. (1992). *Child psychology: The modern science.* New York: Wiley.

Vredenburg, K., Flett, G. L., & Krames, L. (1993). Analogue versus clinical depression: A critical reappraisal. *Psychological Bulletin, 113,* 327–344.

Weary, G., Edwards, J. A., & Jacobson, J. A. (1995). Depression research methodologies in the *Journal of Personality and Social Psychology*: A reply. *Journal of Personality and Social Psychology, 68,* 885–891.

Zuroff, D. C., Koestner, R., & Powers, T. A. (1994). Self-criticism at age 12: Longitudinal study of adjustment. *Cognitive Therapy and Research, 18,* 267–386.

5

Depression and Personality

Daniel N. Klein, C. Emily Durbin,
Stewart A. Shankman, and Neil J. Santiago

The hypothesis that there is an association between personality and depression can be traced to antiquity, when Hippocrates, and later Galen, argued that particular "humors" were responsible for specific personality types and forms of psychopathology. For example, an excess of black bile was thought to be the basis for a melancholic temperament, which in turn predisposed individuals to melancholic depression (Jackson, 1986).

Personality is generally conceptualized as an individual's characteristic pattern of thinking, feeling, behaving, and relating to others. Many theorists view personality as comprising two components: temperament and character. While there are differences in opinion regarding how to define temperament, it is generally assumed to have a substantial genetic component. In contrast, character is often considered to be the part of personality that is learned, generally from early socialization experiences.

Personality is a broad field, and space limitations preclude considering all of the work that is relevant to the mood disorders. For example, there has been considerable research on the roles of cognitive styles (e.g., attributional style), coping styles (e.g., ruminative response style), and self-esteem in the mood disorders (see Abramson et al., Chapter 11, this volume). Our discussion will be limited to more traditional constructs such as personality traits and types.

The chapter topic presupposes that it is possible to distinguish between mood and personality. This is a challenging distinction. Dispositions to experience particular affects are part of the construct of personality; the structure of personality and affect have significant parallels (Clark & Watson, 1999); temperament is increasingly being viewed as having an affective core (Rothbart & Bates, 1998); and there is disagreement over whether a number of forms of psychopathology (e.g., cyclothymia, dysthymia, depressive personality) should be considered mood disorders or personality disorders.

In this chapter, we discuss a number of models that have been proposed to explain the association between personality and depression, note some of the important conceptual and methodological issues in this area, and selectively review the empirical literature bearing on the relationship between personality and the mood disorders. This literature has developed along several distinct lines. The first developed from the observations of the classic European descriptive psychopathologists in the early part of the 20th century, and is rooted in clinical psychiatry. The second is more closely tied to developments in the field of personality theory, and includes one stream following research on personality structure and another deriving from clinical theories of personality and psychotherapy. A third area that is just beginning to develop, but has considerable potential, is based on temperament research in developmental psychology. Finally, in the past 20 years there has been a surge of interest in personality disorders and their comorbidity with mood disorders. In each of these areas, there has been more research on major depressive disorder (MDD) than bipolar disorder. Therefore we will place greater emphasis on the former. Interested readers are encouraged to consult several excellent earlier reviews of personality and mood disorders (Akiskal, Hirschfeld, & Yerevanian, 1983; Clark, Watson, & Mineka, 1994; Enns & Cox, 1997; Farmer & Nelson-Gray, 1990).

MODELS OF PERSONALITY AND DEPRESSION

A variety of models of the relationship between personality and mood disorders have been proposed (see Klein, Wonderlich, & Shea, 1993). They include (1) personality and mood disorders have common causes; (2) personality is a precursor of mood disorders; (3) personality predisposes to developing mood disorders; (4) personality has pathoplastic effects on mood disorders; (5) personality features are state-dependent concomitants of mood disorder episodes; and (6) personality features are complications (or scars) of mood disorders (see Table 5.1). When pushed, the distinctions between some of these models can be problematic. Moreover, other models, as well as combinations of these models, are plausible. However, these six models provide a useful conceptual framework for approaching the issue. In the first and second models, there is no direct causal relationship between personality and mood disorder; in the third and fourth models, personality has a direct causal impact on mood disorder; in the fifth and sixth models, conversely, mood disorders have a direct causal impact on personality.

The common cause model views personality and mood disorders as arising from the same, or at least an overlapping, set of etiological processes. The precursor model views personality as an early manifestation or "*formes frustes*" of mood disorder. Like the common cause model, it views personality and mood disorders as being caused by the same set of etiological factors. However, the precursor model differs from the common cause model in that it assumes that the personality features are phenomenologically similar to, although milder in severity than, the mood disorder, and precede the mood disorder temporally.

The predisposition model is similar to the precursor model in that personality features are assumed to precede the onset of mood disorder. However, in the precursor model, per-

---

TABLE 5.1. Models of the Relationship between Personality and the Mood Disorders

1. *Common cause*. Personality and mood disorders arise from the same, or overlapping, etiological processes.
2. *Precursor*. Personality is an early manifestation of mood disorder.
3. *Predisposition*. Personality increases the risk of developing mood disorder.
4. *Pathoplasticity*. Personality influences the expression or course of mood disorder.
5. *State dependence*. Mood states color or distort the assessment of personality.
6. *Complications* (or scar). Episodes of mood disorder have an enduring impact on personality that persists after recovery.

sonality and mood disorder derive from the same set of etiological processes. In contrast, in the predisposition model, personality is determined by a different set of processes than those that lead to mood disorders, and personality subsequently has a direct causal impact on affective psychopathology by increasing the risk of developing a mood disorder. In addition, the predisposition model differs from the precursor model in that phenomenological similarity between the personality features and mood disorder symptoms is not assumed.

The pathoplasticity model is similar to the predisposition model in that personality is viewed as having a direct impact on mood disorders. However, rather than causing, or increasing the risk of, mood disorder, personality has an impact on the expression of the mood disorder after onset. This can take the form of personality influencing the severity or pattern of symptomatology, response to treatment, or the course of the mood disorder.

The final two models reverse the direction of temporal sequencing. In the concomitants (or state-dependent) model, individuals' reports (and observers' ratings) of personality are colored, or distorted, by their current mood state. This model implies that personality returns to its baseline form after recovery from the episode. In contrast, the complications (or scar) model holds that mood disorder has an enduring effect on personality, such that changes in personality persist after recovery.

METHODOLOGICAL ISSUES

A number of methodological issues must be considered in reviewing the literature on personality and mood disorders (see Widiger, 1993), including (1) study design, (2) the heterogeneity of mood disorders, and (3) methods of assessing personality.

Study Design

A number of research designs can be useful in studying the relationship between personality and the mood disorders. The concomitants model can be tested through cross-sectional studies of patients in remission, or through longitudinal studies assessing patients when they are in an episode and again after they have recovered. If personality abnormalities persist after remission, it would suggest that they are trait markers rather than concomitants of the depressed state.

The common cause, precursor, and predisposition models can be tested using family, twin, and adoption studies. Demonstrating that the never-depressed relatives of patients with mood disorders have higher levels of a personality trait than the healthy relatives of controls would provide preliminary support for all three models. These models would receive further support if the relatives of never-depressed individuals with the personality feature had an elevated rate of mood disorders (see Klein & Riso, 1993, for a more extensive discussion in another context).

The most compelling approach to testing the precursor and predisposition models is to conduct longitudinal studies of participants with no prior history of mood disorder. Finding that particular personality features prospectively predict the first onset of mood disorders in a unselected or high-risk sample would provide strong support for both models.

It is challenging to try to distinguish the common cause, precursor, and predisposition models. If the personality feature is typically evident prior to the onset of the mood disorder, it would favor the precursor and predisposition models. Moreover, the greater the similarity between the personality trait or type and the phenomenology of the mood disorder, the more plausible the precursor model is. However, definitively distinguishing between these models requires knowledge of the etiological pathway(s). For example, demonstrating a common genetic basis between a personality trait and a mood disorder would favor the common cause and precursor models, while finding that the trait is only associated with mood disorder in the presence of another variable (e.g., stressful life events) would favor the predisposition model. However, even in these examples, the distinction can be difficult. For example, it is unclear exactly how much genetic variance must be shared in order to consider two conditions to have a common cause, and life events might increase the likelihood that precursors develop into full-blown episodes.

The complications (or scar) hypothesis can be evaluated by assessing persons before and after a mood disorder episode. If personality abnormalities are absent prior to the episode, but are evident after the episode, it would support this model.

Finally, the pathoplasticity model can be evaluated in cross-sectional and longitudinal studies correlating personality with clinical features, course, and treatment response. However, these studies are susceptible to third-variable explanations such as the existence of etiologically distinct subtypes, as discussed below.

Heterogeneity

The mood disorders are clinically, and probably etiologically, heterogeneous. Hence, it is likely that the role of personality factors differs in different forms of mood disorder. The current nosology of mood disorders is based on clinical features, and is probably a poor approximation of etiological distinctions. Nonetheless, it is important to consider whether the role of personality varies as a function of the specific form of mood disorder (e.g., bipolar disorder, MDD, dysthymic disorder), subtype of mood disorder (e.g., psychotic, melancholic, atypical), and key clinical characteristics such as age of onset, recurrence, chronicity, and symptom severity. In addition, due to the substantial comorbidity between mood disorders and other Axis I conditions, it is also important to consider whether an apparent association between personality and mood disorders may actually be due to an association between personality and a co-occurring nonmood Axis I disorder. Unfortunately, few studies of personality and mood disorders have taken heterogeneity and comorbidity into account, other than the unipolar–bipolar distinction. In addition, finding associations between personality and specific subtypes and clinical characteristics raises the question of whether the differences reflect heterogeneity or pathoplasticity. The former implies that there are etiological differences between the subgroups, while the latter suggests that although personality influences symptom presentation and/or course, the primary etiological process is the same.

Assessment

Personality traits and disorders can be assessed using a variety of methods, including self-report inventories, semistructured interviews, reports of knowledgeable informants, ratings of trained observers, laboratory tasks, and combinations of data sources. The use of multiple methods is important, as the assessment of personality can be complicated by current state, limited insight, response styles, and the difficulty of distinguishing personality traits from the effects of stable environmental contexts. However, studies using different methods or instruments can produce different findings even when examining the same construct. While there is moderate to good agreement between self-reports and informants' reports for many personality dimensions in adults (Funder, 1995), the level of concordance between interviews with participants and informants, and between self-report inventories and diagnostic interviews, is poor for personality disorders (Zimmerman, 1994). Similarly, there is often poor agreement between parents' reports and laboratory and home observations of temperament in children (Rothbart & Bates, 1998). Indeed, even measures assessing similar constructs using similar methods can differ in subtle ways that have a dramatic impact on concordance (Blaney & Kutcher, 1991; Zimmerman, 1994).

Some assessment approaches may have greater validity than others in detecting associations between personality and mood disorders. For example, self-report inventories may be more susceptible to mood state biases than diagnostic interviews (Loranger et al., 1991). In addition, clinical interviews may be more sensitive than self-report inventories in detecting differences in personality between relatives of probands with mood disorders and relatives of controls (Klein, 1999).

THE CLINICAL TRADITION: THE AFFECTIVE TEMPERAMENTS

The classical European descriptive psychopathologists in the late 19th and early 20th centuries observed that many patients with major mood disorders, as well as their relatives, exhibited particular patterns of premorbid personality that appeared to be attenuated versions of their affective illnesses (Kraepelin, 1921; Kretschmer, 1925). Kraepelin (1921) described four patterns of personality that he considered to be the "fundamental states" underlying manic–depressive illness: depressive, manic, irritable, and cyclothymic temperament. He believed that these were precursors, or "rudimentary forms," of the major mood disorders. Schneider (1958) described similar types; however, he viewed them as personality disorders that were not necessarily related to the mood disorders.

In 1980 two variants of these types, cyclothymic disorder and dysthymic disorder, were included in the mood disorders section of DSM-III (American Psychiatric Association, 1980). However, in DSM-III and subsequent editions, the categories of cyclothymia and dysthymia were defined as fairly severe conditions, with the criteria emphasizing symptomatology rather than personality traits. As a result, these categories appear to be limited to the more severe, symptomatic manifestations of the affective temperaments described by Kraepelin and Schneider (Akiskal, 1989).

Most of the research in this area has focused on depressive personality (although see Klein, Lewinsohn, & Seeley, 1996, and Kwapil et al., 2000, for recent studies of hypomanic personality). A number of investigators have questioned whether depressive personality can be meaningfully distinguished from dysthymic disorder (e.g., Ryder & Bagby, 1999). However, empirical studies indicate that while there is a moderate degree of overlap between the two constructs, a substantial number of individuals who meet criteria for one of these conditions do not meet criteria for the other (e.g., Klein & Shih, 1998; Phillips et al., 1998). Patients who meet criteria for dysthymia but not depressive personality are more likely to be female, to exhibit higher levels of depressive symptoms at entry into treatment and at 6-month follow-up, and to have a higher rate of depression in their relatives than patients who meet criteria for depressive personality but not dysthymia (Klein, 1990).

Family and follow-up studies provide support for the precursor model. Individuals with depressive personality have an increased rate of major mood disorders in their first-degree relatives (Klein, 1990). Moreover, these findings hold even when probands with a lifetime history of mood disorder are excluded (Klein & Miller, 1993). In addition, patients with MDD, and particularly those with MDD superimposed on dysthymic disorder (double depression), have an increased rate of depressive personality in their first-degree relatives (Klein, 1999; Klein, Clark, Dansky, & Margolis, 1988). Finally, Kwon et al. (2000) recently reported that young women with depressive personality and no comorbid Axis I and II disorders had a significantly increased risk of developing dysthymic disorder (but not MDD) over the course of a 3-year follow-up.

These data support the Kraepelinian hypothesis that depressive personality/temperament shares overlapping familial etiological factors with, and may be a precursor of, Axis I mood disorders (Akiskal, 1989). However, it appears that the depressive personality/mood disorder spectrum may be limited to chronic (and possibly highly recurrent) Axis I depressive disorders, such as dysthymia and double depression (Klein, 1999; Kwon et al., 2000). As discussed above, the common cause, precursor, and predisposition models are difficult to distinguish. However, the phenomenological similarity, differences in severity, and temporal relationships between depressive personality and the depressive disorders are most consistent with a precursor conceptualization.

THE PSYCHOMETRIC TRADITION: PERSONALITY DIMENSIONS

A second line of research on personality and mood disorders is rooted in personality and clinical psychology. Unlike the literature on affective temperaments, which employs categorical models and is largely based on clinical interviews and observations, this approach tends to utilize dimensional models and self-report questionnaires. This literature derives from two sources: (1) research on the structure of personality, derived largely from factor analyses of data from large nonclinical samples; and (2) the clinical literature, from both psychoanalytic and cognitive perspectives.

Most contemporary models of personality structure conceptualize personality as being organized hierarchically, with a small number of "superfactors" (typically three to five) at the upper tier, each of which is divisible into a larger number of narrower traits, or "facets." The two personality superfactors included in all the major structural models of personality are neuroticism (N)/negative emotionality (NE) and extraversion (E)/positive emotionality (PE). N/NE reflects sensitivity to negative stimuli, resulting in a range of negative moods, including sadness, fear, anxiety, guilt, and anger. P/PE includes positive affect (joy, enthusiasm), energy, affiliation, dominance, and, in some conceptualizations, venturesomeness. These are also the two personality dimensions that have been most widely studied in the mood disorders, and are closely related to the affective temperament types discussed in the previous section. For example, Watson and Clark (1995) have argued that the melancholic (or depressive) temperament represents the combination of low PE and high NE. Indeed, individuals with depressive personality do exhibit a low level of PE and a high level of NE. However, Klein and Shih (1998) found that depressive personality accounted for significant variance in the lifetime history of mood disorders over and above PE and NE, suggesting that the two sets of constructs may not be entirely equivalent (although it could also reflect differences between interview vs. self-report approaches to assessing personality).

N/NE and E/PE

Individuals with MDD report higher levels of N and lower levels of E than controls and normative samples (e.g., Kendell & DiScipio, 1968; Reich, Noyes, Hirschfeld, Coryell, & O'Gorman, 1987). These differences are not specific to MDD, as most forms of psychopathology are associated with elevated NE (Clark et al., 1994). Low PE is somewhat more specific to depression, although it is also evident in other conditions, such as schizophrenia, anorexia nervosa, and social phobia. This apparent lack of specificity may indicate that there are broad temperament dimensions that underlie a variety of forms of psychopathology and contribute to the high rates of comorbidity between psychiatric disorders (Clark & Watson, 1999).

Studies of personality and psychopathology are complicated by evidence that participants' clinical state influences reports of their personalities (the concomitants model). Numerous studies have found that individuals with MDD report significantly higher levels of N when depressed than nondepressed (e.g., Boyce et al., 1989; Hirschfeld et al., 1983b; Kendler, Neale, Kessler, Heath, & Eaves, 1993). In contrast, most studies report that levels of E do not change after recovery (e.g., Boyce et al., 1989; Kendler et al., 1993; Liebowitz, Stallone, Dunner, & Fieve, 1979).

To determine whether depressed individuals continue to exhibit personality abnormalities outside of MDD episodes, a number of studies have compared persons with a history of depression when they are euthymic or significantly improved to nondepressed controls or population norms. These studies indicate that even when remitted, depressives report diminished levels of E (e.g., Hirschfeld & Klerman, 1979; Hirschfeld, Klerman, Clayton, & Keller, 1983a; Reich et al., 1987). The data for N are less consistent, however, with some studies reporting higher levels of N in recovered depressives than in controls or population norms (e.g., Hirschfeld & Klerman, 1979; Kendell & DiScipio, 1968; Reich et al., 1987), and others failing to find a significant difference (Hirschfeld et al., 1983a; Liebowitz et al., 1979). Many of these studies can be criticized for using insufficiently stringent criteria for recovery, raising the possibility of confounding between personality and residual symptoms. In addition, a number of studies compared patients to normative data collected by other investigators, raising the possibility of sample differences on demographic and sociocultural factors. Nonetheless, taken together with the data on state effects, these results indicate that the decreased E observed in individuals with depression has a substantial trait component. In contrast, the increased N in depressives has a strong state component, but may also have a trait element. The weaker findings for N may, at least in part, be due to selection effects. As N is associated with a poorer course (see below), samples of remitted depressives may include a disproportionate number of low N individuals.

The presence of personality abnormalities in the remitted state is consistent with the complications, common cause, precursor, and predisposition models, so more sophisticated designs are required to provide more specific tests of these models. Only two studies have tested the complications hypothesis by comparing personality measures in depressed individuals before and after a MDD episode. Kendler et al. (1993) reported a 1-year follow-up of a large community sample of female twins with no lifetime history of MDD. After controlling for baseline personality scores, participants who experienced a first lifetime major depressive episode during the follow-up interval exhibited a significantly higher level of N, but not E, at follow-up compared to participants who remained well throughout the study. In contrast, in a 6-year follow-up of a large sample of persons with no lifetime history of psychopathology, Shea et al. (1996) found no evidence of differential change over time on a comprehensive battery of personality measures (including N and E) between participants who developed a first lifetime episode of MDD during the follow-up and those who remained well throughout the study. The difference between these studies may be due to several factors, including (1) the more stringent criteria for recovery employed by Shea et al. (1996), raising the possibility that Kendler et al.'s (1993) findings may be due to residual depressive symptoms; and (2) the longer duration of follow-up in Shea et al. (1996), suggesting that any "scars" are short-lived and dissipate over time. Interestingly, if "scarring" occurs, there do not appear to be cumulative effects with a greater number or duration of episodes, as Duggan, Sham, Lee, and Murray (1991) reported that depressed inpatients with good versus poor outcome exhibited similar changes in N over the course of an 18-year follow-up.

A number of studies have tested the precursor and predisposition models by examining personality traits in the never-depressed relatives of patients with MDD. While several studies found significantly higher levels of N in the never-depressed relatives of probands with mood disorders than in controls (e.g., Lauer et al., 1997; Maier, Lichtermann, Minges, & Heun, 1992a), the majority of studies found no differences (e.g., Duggan, Sham, Lee, Minne, & Murray, 1995; Hecht, van Calker, Berger, & von Zerssen, 1998; Ouimette, Klein, & Pepper, 1996). Similarly, several studies reported significantly lower levels of E or related traits in the never-depressed relatives of probands with mood disorders compared to controls or population norms (Hecht et al., 1998; Hirschfeld et al., 1983a). However, most studies failed to find significant differences (e.g., Duggan et al., 1995; Lauer et al., 1997; Maier et al., 1992a; Ouimette et al., 1996).

Unfortunately, these studies suffer from several limitations. First, the results may not generalize to nonfamilial forms of depression, as personality may play a different role in familial and nonfamilial MDD (see Joffe & Regan, 1991). Second, there may be selection biases in samples using relatives who are already partly through the risk period for mood disorder, as individuals with personality vulnerabilities may have already developed the disorder, hence be excluded from the analyses. Finally, existing studies have failed to adjust for differences in personality between patient and control probands in order to rule out the possibility that any differences between groups of relatives are simply due to the familial transmission of E and N.

A more direct approach to testing the precursor and predisposition models is to conduct prospective studies of personality in never-depressed community or high-risk samples to determine whether personality predicts the subsequent onset of MDD. To our knowledge, there have been five such studies examining N, E, and related traits.

In a 6-year follow-up of a large sample with no lifetime history of psychopathology, Hirschfeld et al. (1989) reported that N-like traits, but not E, predicted the first onset of MDD among subjects between the ages of 31 and 41. Personality did not predict onset of MDD in individuals aged 17 to 30. Boyce, Parker, Barnett, Cooney, and Smith (1991) studied 140 nondepressed primiparous women in an obstetric practice. After excluding women with a previous history of depression and controlling for baseline scores on the Beck Depression Inventory (BDI), neither N nor E predicted which women would exhibit at least mild depressive symptoms (BDI $\geq$ 11) 6-months postpartum. However, elevated BDI scores were significantly predicted by baseline levels of interpersonal sensitivity, a construct that overlaps with N, but also includes elements of dependency and low E (shyness). In a large community sample of female twins with no lifetime history of MDD, Kendler et al. (1993) found that N, but not E, predicted the onset of MDD within the next year. These results were replicated in subsequent waves of follow-ups (Roberts & Kendler, 1999). In a 15-year follow-up of a large community sample, Rorsman, Grasbeck, Hagnell, Isberg, and Otterbeck (1993) reported that asthenia (reduced energy—a component of low PE) and trait anxiety (an aspect of NE) predicted the first lifetime episode of MDD in males, whereas emotional lability (an element of NE) predicted first-onset MDD in females. Clayton, Ernst, and Angst (1994) conducted an 11–16 year follow-up of a large sample of male military recruits using questionnaires and medical records. Participants who subsequently developed a first lifetime episode of MDD obtained significantly higher scores on several scales reflecting depressive and anxious traits that overlap considerably with NE, but may also include a component of low PE.

Finally, a sixth study is noteworthy even though it may have included some participants with a history of MDD prior to the initial assessment. Krueger (1999) studied a New Zealand birth cohort that had been assessed for personality and psychopathology at age 18 and followed up at age 21. After controlling for mood disorder in the year prior to the initial assessment, a higher level of NE, but not PE, significantly predicted the presence of a mood disorder at age 21. Three subscales predicted mood disorders at follow-up: lower well-being (a subscale of PE), greater stress reactivity, and less aggression (both subscales of NE). These findings were not specific to mood disorders, however, as NE at age 18 also predicted anxiety disorders, substance dependence, and antisocial personality disorder at age 21.

As discussed earlier, it is very difficult to distinguish between the common cause, precursor, and predisposition models. However, the weight of the evidence appears to support the precursor model, at least with respect to NE. In biometric analyses of twin data, Kendler et al. (1993) found that the majority (55%) of the liability to MDD was shared with N. Moreover, of the liability that was common to both N and MDD, 70% was due to shared genetic risk factors, 20% was due to shared environmental risk factors, and only 10% was due to a direct causal effect of MDD on N (the combination of state and scar effects). These data are more consistent with the common cause and precursor models than with the predisposition model. At the same time, there is stronger evidence for N preceding MDD in time than for MDD leading to increases in N, supporting the precursor and predisposition models over the common cause model. Finally, the phenomenological similarity between N/NE and MDD favors the precursor model over the common cause and predisposition models. However, it is also possible that NE serves as both a precursor and a predisposition, as there is evidence that N generates stressful life events that interact with personality in producing symptomatology (van Os & Jones, 1999).

N/NE and E/PE may also have a pathoplastic influence on depression. Several studies have reported that N is positively and E is negatively correlated with affective, cognitive, and motivational symptoms, but not with vegetative symptoms of depression (Parker, Blignault, & Manicasvasagar, 1988; Serra & Pollitt, 1975). Unfortunately, it is difficult to ascertain the direction of the effect, and these studies did not take into account the possible overlap between personality items and symptoms.

Numerous studies have reported that N predicts a poorer course and outcome of depression over follow-up periods ranging from 6 months to 18 years (e.g., Hirschfeld, Klerman, Andreasen, Clayton, & Keller, 1986a; Kendler, Walter, & Kessler, 1997; Weissman, Prusoff, & Klerman, 1978). Importantly, these results appear to hold even after controlling for severity of depression at baseline (Duggan, Lee, & Murray, 1990; Scott, Williams, Brittlebank, & Ferrier, 1995; Surtees & Barkley, 1994). Fewer studies have examined the prognostic impact of E, and the results have been less consistent. Kerr, Roth, and Schapira (1974) found that low E was associated with poorer outcome, and Kendler et al. (1997) found that high E predicted early ($\leq$ 28 days), but not later recovery. However, van Londen, Molenaar, Goekoop, Zwinderman, and Rooijmans (1998) and Weissman et al. (1978) reported that E was not significantly related to subsequent course. Finally, N and E have failed to predict response to pharmacotherapy and psychotherapy in several studies (Joyce, Mulder, & Cloninger, 1999; Zuckerman, Prusoff, Weissman, & Padian, 1980).

Studies examining the relationship between personality and clinical features/course cannot exclude the possibility that any associations reflect diagnostic heterogeneity, with personality dysfunction serving as a marker for a more severe or etiologically distinct group, rather than pathoplasticity. Indeed, there is evidence that different forms of depression differ on N/NE and E/PE. For example, several studies have reported that the melancholic (or endogenous) subtype is characterized by lower N than nonmelancholic patients (Benjaminsen, 1981; Paykel, Klerman, & Prusoff, 1976). In addition, Klein, Taylor, Harding, and Dickstein (1988a) reported that patients with dysthymic disorder exhibited higher N and lower E than patients with episodic MDD, and Hirschfeld (1990) obtained similar results in participants who had recovered from dysthymia and MDD.

To summarize, consistent with the concomitants model, N/NE is influenced by clinical state. However, it also appears to be a precursor of MDD, and may have a pathoplastic influence on the course of MDD. E/PE appears to be less influenced by clinical state. There are hints that at least some components of E/PE may be a precursor of, or predispose to, MDD, and may also have pathoplastic effects on course, although the evidence is weaker than for N/NE. Finally, evidence for the complications model is mixed with respect to N/NE and negative for E/PE.

In light of Clark and Watson's (1995) theory that the depressive temperament is a function of high NE and low PE, it is unfortunate that studies have not examined the joint (or interactive) effects of these two dimensions. However, it is interesting that some of the stronger findings in the prospective longitudinal studies were based on personality constructs that were composites of high N/NE and low E/PE. Along similar lines, the majority of studies have examined N/NE and E/PE at the superfactor level. However, several of the studies reviewed above suggest that only particular facets may play a role in the development of MDD (Boyce et al., 1991; Clayton et al., 1994; Krueger, 1999; Rorsman et al., 1993). This is particularly relevant to E/PE, which encompasses a range of loosely intercorrelated constructs (e.g., positive mood, approach/appetitive behavior, sociability, dominance, venturesomeness). Hence, it is important that future studies conduct finer grained analyses. In addition, in attempting to parse the broad domains of N/NE and E/PE, it may be important to draw on interview, informant, observational, and laboratory-based methods to complement traditional self-report inventory assessments.

Cloninger's Model

Cloninger (1987; Cloninger, Svrakic, & Przybeck, 1993) has also proposed a structural model of personality. Unlike the theories discussed above, which were developed largely on the basis of empirical research on the structure of personality, Cloninger's model was derived on theoretical grounds from research on personality structure, psychopathology, and the neurobiology of learning. The initial version of Cloninger's (1987) model consisted of three dimensions: novelty seeking (an appetitive/approach system that responds to signals of novelty and potential reward); harm avoidance (an inhibition/avoidance system that responds to aversive stimuli); and reward dependence (a behavior maintenance system that is particularly responsive to signals of social approval and attachment). However, subsequent studies indicated that a fourth dimension, persistence, should be split off from reward dependence. In a reformulation of the model, Cloninger et al. (1993) argued that these four constructs reflected basic dimensions of temperament, and added three character dimensions: self-directedness (responsible, goal-directed), cooperativeness (helpful, empathic vs. hostile, alienated), and self-transcendence (imaginative, unconventional). Although Cloninger's model overlaps with the other major structural models of personality, it does not appear to be an alternative description of the same dimensions (Heath, Cloninger, & Martin, 1994).

Initially, Cloninger (1987) proposed that cyclothymic personality was characterized by low novelty seeking, low harm avoidance, and high reward dependence. More recently, Cloninger, Bayon, and Svrakic (1998) attempted to translate Kraepelin's affective personality types into configurations of their three character dimensions. Cloninger et al. (1998) proposed that the melancholic (or depressive) type is characterized by low levels of all three character dimensions; the creative (or manic) type is characterized by high levels of all three character dimensions; the cyclothymic type is characterized by high self-transcendence and cooperativeness, but low self-directedness; and the dependent (or irritable) type is characterized by high cooperativeness and low self-transcendence and self-directedness.

A number of studies have indicated that patients with MDD are characterized by high harm avoidance and low self-directedness and cooperativeness (e.g., Cloninger et al., 1998;

Joffe, Bagby, Levitt, Regan, & Parker, 1993; Richter, Eisemann, & Richter, 2000), although these differences are not specific to MDD (Ampollini et al., 1999). Harm avoidance has a substantial state component, with scores decreasing after recovery from a depressive episode (e.g., Hellerstein, Kocsis, Chapman, Stewart, & Harrison, 2000; Joffe et al., 1993; Richter et al., 2000). There is also some evidence for state effects on reward dependence, self-directedness, and cooperativeness (e.g., Hellerstein et al., 2000; Richter et al., 2000). However, even after recovery, depressed patients appear to exhibit elevated harm avoidance and decreased self-directedness (e.g., Joffe et al., 1993; Richter et al., 2000). We are unaware of studies explicitly testing the common cause, precursor, predisposition, and complications hypotheses for Cloninger's model. However, there has been support for the pathoplasticity hypothesis. In particular, a number of studies have reported that low harm avoidance and self-directedness are associated with a poor response to antidepressant medication (e.g., Hellerstein et al., 2000; Joffe et al., 1993; Joyce et al., 1999; Sato et al., 1999; but see Newman et al., 2000, for negative results).

Dependency and Obsessionality

In addition to the literature based on structural models of personality, a separate line of research on personality and depression has developed from clinical observations and theories. Since Abraham, psychoanalysts have emphasized the role of dependent and obsessional traits in predisposing to the development of mood disorders (Chodoff, 1972). In addition, recent theorists have proposed distinctions between a dependent/sociotropic subtype of depression and a self-critical/autonomous subtype that has some conceptual overlap with obsessionality. As these ideas have produced distinct literatures, we review them separately below. With the exception of self-criticism, these constructs exhibit little overlap with the core symptoms of depression; therefore, they have been viewed more as predispositions than as precursors.

Studies of the role of dependent personality traits in depression indicate that, consistent with the concomitants model, depressed patients' scores on a variety of measures of dependency decrease after recovery (Birtchnell, Deahl, & Falkowski, 1991; Boyce et al., 1989; Hirschfeld et al., 1983b). Research examining whether recovered depressives differ from controls on dependent traits have yielded mixed findings (Hirschfeld et al., 1983a; Pilowsky & Katsikitis, 1983). Dependent traits appear to increase as a complication of MDD in adolescents (Rohde, Lewinsohn, & Seeley, 1994), but not adults (Rohde, Lewinsohn, & Seeley, 1990; Shea et al., 1996). Prospective longitudinal studies have provided some support for a predisposition model. Hirschfeld et al. (1989) found that dependency predicted a first lifetime MDD episode in participants over the age of 30 (but not aged 17–30). In a prospective study of older adults, Rohde et al. (1990) found that participants experiencing a first lifetime episode of MDD had exhibited elevated levels of dependent traits 2–3 years earlier. Consistent with the predisposition model, the dependency–MDD association was limited to participants with a high level of stress. As noted above, Boyce et al. (1991) found that interpersonal sensitivity, a construct that overlaps with dependency, predicted mild depressive symptoms in women with no prior history of depression 6 months after childbirth. However, Rohde et al. (1994) reported that adolescents who had developed a first lifetime episode of MDD during a 1-year follow-up period did not differ from adolescents who remained depression-free on baseline dependent traits. Finally, there is some evidence for the pathoplasticity model, as melancholic depressives exhibit lower levels of interpersonal sensitivity than nonmelancholics (Boyce et al., 1993), and dependent traits predict lower recovery and higher relapse rates in MDD (Alnaes & Torgerson, 1997; Lewinsohn, Rohde, Seeley, Klein, & Gotlib, 2000).

Studies examining the role of obsessional traits in depression have produced mixed findings, in part due to differences between the various measures employed (Enns & Cox, 1997). Obsessionality does not appear to be influenced by clinical state (Hirschfeld et al., 1983b). While some studies have found elevated levels of obsessional traits in remitted depressives (Hirschfeld & Klerman, 1979; Reich et al., 1987), others have not (Hirschfeld et al., 1983a). Obsessionality does not appear to increase as a consequence of MDD (Shea et al., 1996). The results of family studies examining the predisposition model have been mixed, with some studies reporting increased levels of obsessionality/rigidity in the never-depressed relatives of patients with MDD (Lauer et al., 1997; Maier et al., 1992a), and others finding no differences (Hecht et al., 1998; Ouimette, Klein, Clark, & Margolis, 1992). Longitudinal studies have not supported the predisposition model (Hirschfeld et al., 1989). Finally, obsessional traits do not predict the course of MDD (Duggan et al., 1990; Hirschfeld et al., 1986a).

Dependency/Self-Criticism and Sociotropy/Autonomy

Building on this clinical tradition, investigators from both the psychoanalytic and cognitive-behavioral traditions have independently proposed similar personality-based theories of MDD (Beck, 1983; Blatt, 1974). Blatt (1974) distinguished between anaclitic (or dependent) and introjective (or self-critical) forms of depression; the former is characterized by interpersonal concerns involving care and approval, and the latter by concerns of self-definition and self-worth. Similarly, Beck (1983) proposed a distinction between sociotropic depressives, who have an intense need for close relationships, and autonomous depressives, who have a high need for independence and achievement. For both theorists, these traits are hypothesized to predispose individuals to depression in the face of "matching" life events (interpersonal loss for dependent/sociotropic individuals, and threats to autonomy and achievement for self-critical/autonomous individuals). In addition, both theorists posit that dependent/sociotropic individuals and self-critical/autonomous individuals exhibit different patterns of symptomatology when depressed; the former being characterized by helplessness, tearfulness, and mood reactivity, and the latter by guilt, sense of worthlessness, anhedonia, social withdrawal, and lack of reactivity. Blatt and Beck are inconsistent in whether they regard dependency/sociotropy and self-criticism/autonomy as distinct types or independent dimensions. Hence, it is unclear whether these differences in symptom profiles should be viewed as reflecting the pathoplastic influence of personality on the expression of depression or the existence of qualitatively distinct subtypes (for evidence against a typological view, see Haslam & Beck, 1994).

Several studies have examined the associations between dependency/self-criticism and sociotropy/autonomy and the major structural models of personality. Self-criticism is highly correlated, and dependency and sociotropy are moderately correlated, with N, whereas autonomy is not consistently associated with any of the major personality superfactors (e.g., Bagby & Rector, 1998; Cappeliez, 1993; Zuroff, 1994). Thus, it is important to determine whether these constructs contribute over and above the effects of N.

Patients with MDD differ from healthy controls on both sets of constructs (e.g., Bagby et al., 1994; Fairbrother & Moretti, 1998; Franche & Dobson, 1992), but they do not differ from patients with anxiety disorders (Bagby et al., 1992; Cox et al., 2000). While autonomy does not appear to be influenced by clinical state, the evidence for state effects on dependency, sociotropy, and self-criticism is mixed, with some studies reporting effects (Klein, Taylor, Harding, & Dickstein, 1988b; Moore & Blackburn, 1996), but not others (Bagby et al., 1994; Fairbrother & Moretti, 1998; Franche & Dobson, 1992). Patients who have recovered from MDD differ from controls on these dimensions in most studies (Bagby et al.,

1994; Fairbrother & Moretti, 1998; Franche & Dobson, 1992; but not Rosenfarb, Becker, Khan, & Mintz, 1998). No studies have addressed the complications model. Family studies have not supported the common cause and predisposition models (Ouimette et al., 1992, 1996).

The majority of studies testing the predisposition model have focused on the personality–life events congruence (or "matching") hypothesis. Unfortunately, most of these studies suffer from methodological limitations, including the exclusion of participants with high scores on both personality dimensions; using arbitrary cutoffs to create personality subgroups; studying dysphoria rather than clinically significant depression or studying symptom severity rather than onset of episodes; using retrospective designs and suboptimal assessments of life events; and the difficulty of distinguishing between interpersonal and achievement events (Coyne & Whiffen, 1995). Moreover, none of these studies have focused on first lifetime episodes. Thus, they may actually be more relevant to the pathoplasticity model than to the predisposition model, as they address the course of an already established disorder rather than the onset of the disorder.

These studies have yielded inconsistent results. Among studies using prospective designs, some have obtained support for personality–event congruence (Hammen, Ellicott, Gitlin, & Jamison, 1989; Segal, Shaw, Vella, & Katz, 1992); others have provided partial support, finding the predicted associations for only one of the two dimensions (e.g., Hammen, Ellicott, & Gitlin, 1989; Segal, Shaw, & Vella, 1989); and some have failed to support the hypothesis for either dimension (e.g., Kwon & Whisman, 1998; Robins, Hayes, Block, Kramer, & Villena, 1995).

A number of studies have tested the hypothesis that dependency/sociotropy and self-criticism/autonomy are associated with different symptom profiles. Again, the findings have been mixed. Some studies have supported this hypothesis (e.g., Robins & Luten, 1991; Robins et al., 1995); others found support for only one of the two constructs (e.g., Robins, Block, & Peselow, 1989; Persons, Burns, Perloff, & Miranda, 1993); and some have failed to support either construct (e.g., Klein, Taylor, et al., 1988b; Robins, Bagby, Rector, Lynch, & Kennedy, 1997).

Finally, a number of studies have reported data bearing on the pathoplasticity hypothesis with respect to naturalistic course and treatment response. Unfortunately, the findings have been markedly inconsistent (Klein, Taylor, et al., 1988b; Mazure, Bruce, Maciejewski, & Jacobs, 2000; Peselow, Robins, Sanfilipo, Block, & Fieve, 1992; Rector, Bagby, Segal, Joffe, & Levitt, 2000; Scott, Harrington, House, & Ferrier, 1996).

PERSONALITY IN BIPOLAR DISORDER

Most of the work on personality and bipolar disorder has focused on E/PE and N/NE. Most studies have reported that remitted patients with bipolar disorder do not differ from never-ill controls or population norms on measures of E/PE (e.g., Hecht et al., 1998; Hirschfeld, Klerman, Keller, Andreasen, & Clayton, 1986b; Solomon et al., 1996). In contrast, comparisons on N/NE have yielded mixed results, with some studies reporting no differences (e.g., Hecht et al., 1998; Hirschfeld & Klerman, 1979; Liebowitz et al., 1979), and others finding that remitted bipolars have higher levels of N/NE (Hirschfeld et al., 1986b; Solomon et al., 1996).

A number of studies have reported that remitted bipolars have higher levels of E/PE than remitted patients with MDD (e.g., Bagby et al., 1996; Sauer et al., 1997), although several studies have failed to find a significant difference (Hecht et al., 1998; Liebowitz et al., 1979), and one study found differences for males but not for females (Hirschfeld et al.,

1986b). Most studies have failed to find differences between remitted bipolar and MDD patients on N/NE (e.g., Bagby et al., 1996; Hecht et al., 1998; Hirschfeld et al., 1986b), although several have reported that MDD is associated with greater N/NE (Hirschfeld & Klerman, 1979; Liebowitz et al., 1979).

In the one prospective study examining precursors/predispositions to bipolar disorder, Clayton et al. (1994) reported that the premorbid personalities of young men who later developed bipolar disorder did not differ from those who remained well on a broad range of personality measures. Finally, Maier, Minges, Lichtermann, and Heun (1995) found that never-depressed relatives of bipolar patients exhibited significantly higher levels of rigidity, but not N or E, than relatives of normal controls.

Interestingly, there is evidence suggesting that N/NE and E/PE may have a pathoplastic influence on the course of bipolar and nonbipolar mood disorders, with higher levels of NE being associated with more and longer periods of depression, and higher levels of PE being associated with more and longer episodes of mania/hypomania (Depue, Krauss, & Spoont, 1987; Hecht et al., 1998). However, as these data are from are cross-sectional studies, it is also possible that the relative amount of depression versus mania in the course of mood disorders influences personality.

TEMPERAMENT RESEARCH IN DEVELOPMENTAL PSYCHOLOGY

The clinical, and increasingly the psychometric (Clark & Watson, 1999), tradition emphasizes the role of temperament in mood disorders. As these literatures have focused on adults, however, they have been unable to test the critical assumption that these temperamental vulnerabilities are evident in early childhood. In addition, it is unlikely that the affective temperaments described by Kraepelin (1921), and more recently by Akiskal (1989), actually reflect basic temperamental processes. Rather, the many cognitive and interpersonal characteristics included in these temperament types are likely to be intermediate outcomes reflecting the interaction of basic temperament processes with early socialization and the environment. Research that is grounded in the child temperament literature in developmental psychology can help to identify the actual manifestations of temperamental vulnerabilities to mood disorders in young children, and trace their development, including their influence on subsequent cognitive and interpersonal processes that may also play an important role in the pathogenesis of mood disorders.

Contemporary models of child temperament typically emphasize the centrality of individual differences in emotionality (Goldsmith & Campos, 1982). Most major models of child temperament include the superordinate traits of PE, NE, sociability, and activity (Rothbart & Bates, 1998). The two temperament traits that have received the most attention with regard to risk for mood disorders in the developmental literature are low PE and behavioral inhibition, which refers to wariness/fear, diminished activity, and a lack of approach in novel situations (Kagan, Reznick, & Snidman, 1987). Using self-report measures similar to those tapping PE adults, cross-sectional studies of child clinical and nonclinical samples have replicated the finding that low PE is associated with depression (e.g., Joiner, Catanzaro, & Laurent, 1996; Lonigan, Carey, & Finch, 1994). Observational studies of the children of depressed mothers also indicate that low PE may be part of a behavioral profile of risk for depression. For example, Field (1992) demonstrated that the infants of mothers with elevated depressive symptoms exhibit diminished PE, increased social withdrawal, and low activity level. Neff and Klein (1992) found that the toddlers of mothers with a history of MDD exhibited lower PE and appetitive behavior than the offspring of never-depressed mothers in home observations. In addition, children's low PE and appetitive behavior were significantly associated with the chronicity of their mothers' depression.

Developmental researchers have also suggested that inhibition is a possible diathesis for mood and anxiety disorders (Gest, 1997; Harrist, Zaia, Bates, Dodge, & Pettit, 1997). Rosenbaum et al. (2000) found an elevated rate of behavioral inhibition in a standardized laboratory task among 2- to 6-year-old offspring of parents with MDD. Similarly, Kochanska (1991) reported that toddlers of mothers with a history of mood disorders displayed more inhibition on a battery of laboratory tasks than children of nondepressed mothers, and degree of inhibition was correlated with the recency of the mother's depression and lifetime severity of MDD.

This literature is consistent with a growing body of work linking asymmetry in frontal EEG to MDD (see Davidson, Pizzagalli, & Nitschke, Chapter 9, this volume). A number of studies have suggested that low relative left frontal activation in adults is related to low PE/approach behavior, and may serve as a trait marker for MDD. Importantly, reduced left frontal activation has also been linked to behavioral inhibition in preschoolers (Davidson, 1998; Fox et al., 1995), and has been observed in the infants and young children of depressed mothers (e.g., Dawson, Frey, Panagiotides, Osterling, & Hessl, 1997; Field, Fox, Pickens, & Nawrocki, 1995). However, as behaviorally inhibited children have been described as displaying many features of diminished PE (e.g., Fox et al., 1995; Gest, 1997; Harrist et al., 1997) and Davidson and Fox argue that the fundamental difference between inhibited and noninhibited children is a deficit in approach-related behaviors, it is unclear whether "inhibition" reflects diminished PE, heightened anxiety/NE, or an interaction of these two systems.

Finally, there is direct evidence that personality traits assessed in childhood predict the development of mood disorders in adults. Caspi, Moffit, Newman, and Silva (1996) reported that children who were rated as socially reticent, inhibited, and easily upset at age 3 had elevated rates of depressive (but not anxiety or substance use) disorders at age 21. Similarly, van Os, Jones, Wadsworth, and Murray (1997) found that physicians' ratings of behavioral apathy at ages 6, 7, and 11 were predictive of both adolescent mood disorder and chronic depression in middle adulthood. Lastly, Gjerde (1995) examined the relationship between ratings of children's behavior and personality at ages 3–4 and self-reported chronic depressive symptoms at age 23. Women with higher levels of chronic depression in young adulthood were described as shy and withdrawn during childhood. However, men with greater chronic depression exhibited elevated levels of undercontrolled/externalizing behavior as children, raising the possibility that gender moderates the temperament/mood disorder relationship.

COMORBIDITY BETWEEN MOOD AND PERSONALITY DISORDERS

Since the introduction of Axis II into the DSM-III in 1980, there has been a great deal of interest in the relationship between personality disorders (PDs) and Axis I disorders, with comorbidity between PDs and mood disorders receiving particular attention (for reviews, see Corruble, Ginestat, & Guelfi, 1996; Farmer & Nelson-Gray, 1990; Gunderson, 1999). As self-report measures appear to overestimate the prevalence of personality disorders (Zimmerman, 1994), in this section we emphasize studies using semistructured diagnostic interviews.

Rates of PDs reported in patients with MDD have varied, with most studies falling within the range of 50–85% for inpatient and 20–50% for outpatient samples (Corruble et al., 1996; Gunderson, 1999). These rates do not appear to be inflated by biases associated with treatment seeking, as Zimmerman and Coryell (1989) found that 47% of a nonpatient MDD sample also had PDs. Conversely, individuals with PDs exhibit similarly high rates of mood disorders. In most studies, cluster C (dependent, avoidant, and obsessive–compulsive) PDs are the most common Axis II conditions in MDD, and cluster A (paranoid, schizoid, schizotypal) PDs are the least common. While early studies suggested that the rate of PDs was higher in nonmelancholic than melancholic MDD (e.g., Charney, Nelson, & Quinlan, 1981), this finding has not been adequately examined using semistructured interviews.

Paralleling the differences on personality traits reviewed above, dysthymic disorder appears to be associated with an even higher rate of PDs than MDD (Garyfallos et al., 1999; Markowitz, Moran, Kocsis, & Frances, 1992; Pepper et al., 1995). Cluster B (antisocial, borderline, histrionic, narcissistic) and cluster C PDs are both common in dysthymia. However, the greatest difference between dysthymia and episodic MDD is on rates of cluster B (especially borderline) PD. Rates of PDs are also greater in early-onset than late-onset forms of dysthymia (Garyfallos et al., 1999) and MDD (Fava et al., 1996).

Due to the difficulty of assessing PDs when patients are in an acute manic state, the most valid prevalence rates in bipolar disorder derive from euthymic samples. Studies using semistructured diagnostic interviews to assess Axis II conditions in euthymic patients with bipolar I disorder or mixed bipolar I–bipolar II samples have generally reported rates in the 35–48% range (e.g., Kay, Altschuler, Ventura, & Mintz, 1999; Peselow, Sanfilipo, & Fieve, 1995; Ucok, Karaveli, Kundakci, & Yazici, 1998). The one study that focused exclusively on bipolar II disorder found a rate of PDs that was in the lower end of this range (Vieta, Colom, Martinez-Aran, Benabarre, & Gasto, 1999). The most common PDs in bipolar disorder are from cluster B and cluster C.

Few studies have attempted to explore the reasons for the high comorbidity between mood disorders and PDs. There is some evidence for mood state effects on patients' reports of PDs; however, this appears to be attenuated when interviews, rather than self-report inventories, are employed (Loranger et al., 1991). Moreover, state effects cannot entirely account for the high comorbidity between mood disorders and PDs as knowledgeable informants also report high rates of PDs in patients with mood disorders (e.g., Pepper et al., 1995; Peselow et al., 1995).

To our knowledge, only one study has examined the direction of the effects between depression and PDs using a longitudinal design. In a 2-year study of a community sample of adolescent and young adult women, Daley et al. (1999) found that baseline PD traits predicted subsequent depressive symptoms after controlling for baseline depression. In contrast, baseline depression did not predict subsequent PD traits after controlling for baseline PD. Although few of these participants met criteria for diagnoses of mood disorders or PD, these data suggest that PD traits may play a role in the etiology and/or maintenance of depressive symptoms.

In contrast to the limited data available on the common cause, precursor, predisposition, and scar models, a number of studies have addressed the possibility of pathoplastic effects of PDs on the course and treatment of mood disorders. While there have been a number of negative findings (e.g., Joyce et al., 1999), the majority of studies indicate that comorbid PDs are associated with an earlier onset, longer and more frequent episodes, and a poorer response to treatment (Reich & Vasile, 1993; Shea, Widiger, & Klein, 1992).

The one Axis II condition whose relationship to the mood disorders has received extensive consideration is borderline personality disorder (BPD). A number of studies have compared BPD and the mood disorders on phenomenology, biological correlates, family history, and treatment response (Gunderson & Phillips, 1991). Mood disorders and BPD are both characterized by affective dysregulation and an increased risk for suicidal behavior. However, they appear to exhibit subtle differences in phenomenology, as BPD patients are more likely to experience feelings of emptiness, loneliness, and neediness, while MDD patients are more likely to report feelings of guilt and remorse, and social withdrawal (Westen et al., 1992).

A number of early studies reported that patients with BPD and MDD were similar on biological variables typically associated with MDD, such as shortened REM latency. While these findings may have been due to the inclusion of patients with co-occurring MDD in the BPD group (Gunderson & Phillips, 1991), shortened REM latencies have been reported in never-depressed individuals with BPD (Battaglia, Ferini-Strambi, Smirne, Bernardeschi, & Bellodi, 1993). Similarly, early family studies reported an increased rate of mood disorders in the relatives of patients with BPD, but this was largely due to the inclusion of BPD participants with comorbid MDD (Gunderson & Phillips, 1991). However, more recent studies have found that the rate of mood disorders in relatives of never-depressed subjects with BPD was significantly higher than in the relatives of normal controls, and did not differ from the relatives of patients with mood disorders (Gasperini et al., 1991; Riso, Klein, Anderson, & Ouimette, 2000). Comparisons of rates of PDs in the relatives of patients with mood disorders and healthy controls have yielded inconsistent results, with some studies reporting increased rates of BPD in the relatives of MDD probands (Klein et al., 1995) and other studies finding no differences (Coryell & Zimmerman, 1989; Maier, Lichtermann, Minges, & Heun, 1992b). However, in the only study that focused on dysthymic disorder, Riso et al. (1996) found that the relatives of dysthymic patients without co-occurring BPD had significantly higher rates of BPD (both with and without comorbid dysthymia) than the relatives of normal controls.

Finally, the mood disorders and BPD differ in response to antidepressant medication. The core features of BPD generally do not respond to the cyclic antidepressants. Although there is some evidence suggesting that the selective serotonin reuptake inhibitors may be more effective, thymoleptic medications are still of only limited efficacy in treating BPD (Soloff, 2000).

These data suggest that the mood disorders and BPD are distinct conditions with some shared etiological factors (Gunderson & Phillips, 1991). An important area for future research is to identify the common causal processes, with leading candidates including genes, serotonergic dysregulation, and early childhood maltreatment.

CONCLUSIONS AND FUTURE DIRECTIONS

The topic of the relationship between personality and mood disorders has produced a sprawling literature, with many gaps and inconsistent findings. Nonetheless, it is possible to draw a number of tentative conclusions. First, reports of many traits (e.g., N/NE, harm avoidance, dependency) are influenced by clinical state, although some traits (e.g., E/PE, obsessionality, autonomy) appear to be independent of mood state. Further work is needed to determine whether mood state biases can be reduced by using interviews rather than self-report inventories. Second, there appear to be common causes/shared etiological factors between some personality disorders, such as BPD, and mood disorders, although further research is needed to determine what these shared factors are. Third, there is substantial support for the view that depressive personality is closely etiologically related to, and may be a precursor of, Axis I depressive disorders, particularly more chronic forms such as dysthymic disorder and double depression. However, more work is needed on the other affective temperament types. Fourth, there is mounting evidence that N/NE is a precursor of MDD, as well as some intriguing hints that low E/PE and dependency may play roles as precursors or predisposing factors. This needs to be pursued along the lines described below. Fifth, although further data addressing the complications model are needed, it appears unlikely that mood disorders produce enduring changes in personality. A possible exception, however, is that MDD episodes in adolescents and young adults (but not older adults) may increase the level of dependent traits. Sixth, many personality traits and disorders appear to have pathoplastic effects on the course of mood disorders, and may also influence treatment response. However, greater attention needs to be paid to the confound of heterogeneity. Finally, although the issue of diagnostic specificity has not been investigated for all of the personality types and dimensions reviewed here, the available evidence suggests that many of the personality features associated with mood disorders are also evident in other forms of psychopathology, particularly anxiety disorders.

To make further progress in elucidating the relationship between personality and the mood disorders, future studies should be guided by four broad considerations. These include (1) examining personality and temperament constructs at a greater level of specificity; (2) going beyond the traditional self-report inventory assessment methodology; (3) considering the heterogeneity of mood disorders; and (4) conducting prospective longitudinal studies that begin prior to the period of risk for mood disorders.

First, the literatures on affective temperament types, personality trait dimensions, and child temperament appear to be converging on the potential role of NE and PE as precursors or predisposing factors in the mood disorders. However, much of this work has been conducted at the superfactor level. It is important to determine whether a more specific level of analysis will yield more powerful effects, and increase the specificity of associations between personality constructs and particular forms of psychopathology. This will require finer grained analyses that parse the key components of the two personality/temperament superfactors. For example, within E/PE, it is critical to distinguish between positive affect, appetitive/approach behavior, sociability, dominance, and venturesomeness. In addition, it is important to explore combinations of traits (e.g., high NE and low PE) and to break trait-relevant behaviors down into more specific parameters (e.g., the frequency, intensity, duration, reactivity, and congruence to situational context of emotional experience and expression).

Second, self-report inventories may not be capable of the fine-grained analyses necessary to make these distinctions. Thus, it is important to develop semistructured interviews for personality traits that can reduce the effects of mood state biases and response styles, and make subtle distinctions between related constructs. It is also important to explore the utility of supplementing self-report data with informants' reports. Finally, it is noteworthy that the studies reporting prospective associations between childhood personality and adult mood disorders employed observational measures of personality/temperament (Caspi et al., 1996; van Os et al., 1997). This highlights the value of developing and refining observational measures of affect and behavior in naturalistic and structured laboratory settings.

Third, the role of personality/temperament may vary for different forms of mood disorders. For example, there is suggestive evidence that personality plays an especially important role in early-onset, chronic, and highly recurrent depressive conditions (e.g., Duggan et al., 1990; Fava et al., 1996; Garyfallos et al., 1999; Kwon et al, 2000; van Os et al., 1997; although see Hirschfeld et al., 1989, for an exception). Examining the relationship between personality/temperament and broad categories of mood disorder such as MDD may obscure important associations with particular forms of depression. Hence future studies need to give greater consideration to the heterogeneity of mood disorders.

Finally, there is a critical need for prospective, longitudinal studies. Unfortunately, most existing studies have employed adolescents or adults. In recent years, it has become evident that many cases of mood disorder have already developed by mid-adolescence. Hence, in order to test the precursor and predisposition models, and to trace the development and impact of potential personality/temperamental vulnerabilities, it is necessary to conduct longitudinal studies that start in childhood in order to obtain a sufficient number of first-onset cases and avoid selection biases caused by excluding participants who already have a history of mood disorder at initial assessment.

REFERENCES

Akiskal, H. S. (1989). Validating affective personality types. In L. Robins & J. Barrett (Eds.), *The validity of psychiatric diagnosis* (pp. 217–227). New York: Raven Press.

Akiskal, H. S., Hirschfeld, R. M. A., & Yerevanian, B. I. (1983). The relationship of personality to affective disorders: A critical review. *Archives of General Psychiatry, 40*, 801–810.

Alnaes, R., & Torgersen, S. (1997). Personality and personality disorders predict development and relapses of major depression. *Acta Psychiatrica Scandinavica, 81*, 197–200.

American Psychiatric Association. (1980). *Diagnostic and statistical manual of mental disorders* (3rd ed.). Washington, DC: Author.

Ampollini, P., Marchesi, C., Signifredi, R., Chinaglia, E., Scardovi, F., Codeluppi, S., & Maggini, C. (1999). Temperament and personality features in patients with major depression, panic disorder and mixed condition. *Journal of Affective Disorders, 52*, 203–207.

Bagby, R. M., Cox, B. J., Schuller, D. R., Levitt, A. J., Swinson, R. P., & Joffe, R. T. (1992). Diagnostic specificity of the dependent and self-critical personality dimensions in major depression. *Journal of Affective Disorders, 26*, 59–64.

Bagby, R. M., & Rector, N. A. (1998). Self-criticism, dependency, and the five-factor model of personality in depression: Assessing construct overlap. *Personality and Individual Differences, 24*, 895–897.

Bagby, R. M., Schuller, D. R., Parker, D. A. J., Levitt, A., Joffe, R. T., & Shafir, M. S. (1994). Major depression and the self-criticism and dependency personality dimensions. *American Journal of Psychiatry, 151*, 597–599.

Bagby, R. M., Young, L. T., Schuller, D. R., Bindseil, K. D., Cooke, R. G., Dickens, S. E., Levitt, A. J., & Joffe, R. T. (1996). Bipolar disorder, unipolar depression and the five-factor model of personality. *Journal of Affective Disorders, 41*, 25–32.

Battaglia, M., Ferini-Strambi, L., Smirne, S., Bernardeschi, L., & Bellodi, L. (1993) Ambulatory polysomnography of never-depressed borderline subjects: A high-risk approach to rapid eye-movement latency. *Biological Psychiatry, 33*, 326–334.

Beck, A. T. (1983). Cognitive therapy of depression: New approaches. In P. Clayton & J. Barrett (Eds.), *Treatment of depression: Old and new approaches* (pp. 265–290). New York: Raven Press.

Benjaminsen, S. (1981). Primary non-endogenous depression and features attributed to reactive depression. *Journal of Affective Disorders, 3*, 245–259.

Birtchnell, J., Deahl, M., & Falkowski, J. (1991). Further exploration of the relationship between depression and dependence. *Journal of Affective Disorders, 22*, 221–233.

Blaney, P. H., & Kutcher, G. S. (1991). Measures of depressive dimensions: Are they interchangeable? *Journal of Personality Assessment, 56*, 502–512.

Blatt, S. J. (1974). Levels of object representation in anaclitic and introjective depression. *Psychoanalytic Study of the Child, 29*, 107–157.

Boyce, P., Hadzi-Pavlovic, D., Parker, G., Brodaty, H., Hickie, I., Mitchell, P., & Wilhelm, K. (1989). Depressive type and state effects on personality measures. *Acta Psychiatrica Scandinavica, 81*, 197–200.

Boyce, P., Hickie, I., Parker, G., Mitchell, P., Wilhelm, K., & Brodaty, H. (1993). Specificity of interpersonal sensitivity to non-melancholic depression. *Journal of Affective Disorders, 27*, 101–105

Boyce, P., Parker, G., Barnett, B., Cooney, M., & Smith, F. (1991). Personality as a vulnerability factor to depression. *British Journal of Psychiatry, 159*, 106–114.

Cappeliez, P. (1993). The relationship between Beck's concepts of sociotropy and autonomy and the NEO-Personality Inventory. *British Journal of Clinical Psychology, 32*, 78–80.

Caspi, A., Moffitt, T. E., Newman, D. L., & Silva, P. A. (1996). Behavioral observations at age 3 years predict adult psychiatric disorders. *Archives of General Psychiatry, 53,* 1033–1039.

Charney, D. S., Nelson, J. C., & Quinlan, D. M. (1981). Personality traits and disorder in depression. *American Journal of Psychiatry, 138,* 1601–1604.

Chodoff, P. (1972). The depressive personality. *Archives of General Psychiatry, 27,* 666–677.

Clark, L. A., & Watson, D. (1999). Temperament: A new paradigm for trait psychology. In L. A. Pervin & O. P. John (Eds.), *Handbook of personality: Theory and research* (2nd ed., pp. 399–423). New York: Guilford Press.

Clark, L. A., Watson, D., & Mineka, S. (1994). Temperament, personality, and the mood and anxiety disorders. *Journal of Abnormal Psychology, 103,* 103–116.

Clayton, P. J., Ernst, C., & Angst, J. (1994). Premorbid personality traits of men who develop unipolar or bipolar disorders. *European Archives of Psychiatry and Clinical Neuroscience, 243,* 340–346.

Cloninger, C. R. (1987). A systematic method for clinical description and classification of personality variants: A proposal. *Archives of General Psychiatry, 44,* 573–588.

Cloninger, C. R., Bayon, C., & Svrakic, D. M. (1998). Measurement of temperament and character in mood disorders: A model of fundamental states as personality types. *Journal of Affective Disorders, 51,* 21–32.

Cloninger, C. R., Svrakic, D. M., & Przybeck, T. R. (1993). A psychobiological model of temperament and character. *Archives of General Psychiatry, 50,* 975–990.

Corruble, E., Ginestet, D., & Guelfi, J. D. (1996). Comorbidity of personality disorders and unipolar major depression: A review. *Journal of Affective Disorders, 37,* 157–170.

Coryell, W. H., & Zimmerman, M. (1989). Personality disorder in the families of depressed, schizophrenic, and never-ill probands. *American Journal of Psychiatry, 146,* 496–502.

Cox, B. J., Rector, N. A., Bagby, R. M., Swinson, R. P., Levitt, A. J., & Joffe, R. T. (2000). Is self-criticism unique for depression? A comparison with social phobia. *Journal of Affective Disorders, 57,* 223–228.

Coyne, J. C., & Whiffen, V. E. (1995). Issues in personality as diathesis for depression: The case of sociotropy–dependency and autonomy–self-criticism. *Psychological Bulletin, 118,* 358–378.

Daley, S. E., Hammen, C., Burge, D., Davila, J., Paley, B., Lindberg, N., & Herzberg, D. S. (1999). Depression and Axis II symptomatology in an adolescent community sample: Concurrent and longitudinal associations. *Journal of Personality Disorders, 13,* 47–59.

Davidson, R. J. (1998). Affective style and affective disorders: Perspectives from affective neuroscience. *Cognition and Emotion, 12,* 307–330.

Dawson, G., Frey, K., Panagiotides, H., Osterling, J., & Hessl, D. (1997). Infants of depressed mothers exhibit atypical frontal brain activity: A replication and extension of previous findings. *Journal of Child Psychology and Psychiatry and Allied Disciplines, 38,* 179–186.

Depue, R. A., Krauss, S. P., & Spoont, M. R. (1987). A two-dimensional threshold model of seasonal bipolar affective disorder. In D. Magnuson & A. Ohman (Eds.), *Psychopathology: An interactional perspective* (pp. 95–123). San Diego: Academic Press.

Duggan, C. F., Lee, A. S., & Murray, R. M. (1990). Does personality predict long-term outcome in depression? *British Journal of Psychiatry, 157,* 19–24.

Duggan, C., Sham, P., Lee, A., Minne, C., & Murray, R. (1995). Neuroticism: A vulnerability marker for depression evidence from a family study. *Journal of Affective Disorders, 35,* 139–143.

Duggan, C., Sham, P., Lee, A., & Murray, R. (1991). Does recurrent depression lead to a change in neuroticism? *Psychological Medicine, 21,* 985–990.

Enns, M. W., & Cox, B. J. (1997). Personality dimensions and depression: Review and commentary. *Canadian Journal of Psychiatry, 42,* 274–284.

Fairbrother, N., & Moretti, M. (1998). Sociotropy, autonomy, and self-discrepancy: Status in depressed, remitted depressed and control participants. *Cognitive Therapy and Research, 22,* 279–297.

Farmer, R., & Nelson-Gray, R. O. (1990). Personality disorders and depression: Hypothetical relations, empirical findings, and methodological considerations. *Clinical Psychology Review, 10,* 453–476.

Fava, M., Alpert, J. E., Borus, J. S., Nierenberg, A. A., Pava, J. A., & Rosenbaum, J. F. (1996). Patterns of personality disorder comorbidity in early-onset versus late-onset major depression. *American Journal of Psychiatry, 10,* 1308–1312.

Field, T. (1992). Infants of depressed mothers. *Development and Psychopathology, 4,* 9–66.

Field, T., Fox, N. A., Pickens, J., & Nawrocki, T. (1995). Relative right frontal EEG activation in 3–to 6–month-old infants of depressed mothers. *Developmental Psychology, 31,* 358–363.

Fox, N. A., Coplan, R. J., Rubin, K. H., Porges, S. W., Calkins, K. H., Long, J. M., Marshall, T. R., & Stewart, S. (1995). Frontal activation asymmetry and social competence at four years of age. *Child Development, 66,* 1770–1784.

Franche, R.-L., & Dobson, K. (1992). Self-criticism and interpersonal dependency as vulnerability factors to depression. *Cognitive Therapy and Research, 16,* 419–435.

Funder, D. C. (1995). On the accuracy of personality judgment: A realistic approach. *Psychological Review, 102,* 652–670.

Garyfallos, G., Adamopoulou, A., Karastergiou, A., Voikli, M., Sotiropoulou, A., Donias, S., Giouzepas, J., & Paraschos, A. (1999). Personality disorders in dysthymia and major depression. *Acta Psychiatrica Scandinavica, 99,* 332–340.

Gasperini, M., Battaglia, M., Scherillo, P., Sciuto, G., Diaferia, G., & Bellodi, L. (1991). Morbidity risk for mood disorders in the families of borderline patients. *Journal of Affective Disorders, 21,* 265–272.

Gest, S. (1997). Behavioral inhibition: Stability and associations with adaptation from childhood to early adulthood. *Journal of Personality and Social Psychology, 72,* 467–475.

Gjerde, P. F. (1995). Alternative pathways to chronic depressive symptoms in young adults: Gender differences in developmental trajectories. *Child Development, 66,* 1277–1300.

Goldsmith, H. H., & Campos, J. J. (1982). Toward a theory of infant temperament. In R. N. Emde & R. J. Harmon (Eds.), *The development of attachment and affiliative systems* (p. 161–193). New York: Plenum Press.

Gunderson, J. G. (1999). Personality and vulnerability to affective disorders. In C. R. Cloninger (Ed.), *Personality and psychopathology* (pp. 3–32). Washington, DC: American Psychiatric Press.

Gunderson, J. G., & Phillips, K. A. (1991). A current view of the interface between borderline personality disorder and depression. *American Journal of Psychiatry, 148,* 967–975.

Hammen, C., Ellicott, A., & Gitlin, M. (1989). Vulnerability to specific life events and prediction of course of disorder in unipolar depressed patients. *Canadian Journal of Behavioural Science, 21,* 377–388.

Hammen, C., Ellicott, A., Gitlin, M., & Jamison, K. R. (1989). Sociotropy/autotropy and vulnerability to specific life events in patients with unipolar depression and bipolar disorders. *Journal of Abnormal Psychology, 98,* 154–160.

Harrist, A. W., Zaia, A. F., Bates, J. E., Dodge, K. A., & Pettit, G. S. (1997). Subtypes of social withdrawal in early childhood: Sociometric status and social-cognitive differences across four years. *Child Development, 68,* 278–294.

Haslam, N., & Beck, A. T. (1994). Subtyping major depression: A taxometric analysis. *Journal of Abnormal Psychology, 103,* 686–692.

Heath, A. C., Cloninger, C. R., & Martin, N. G. (1994). Testing a model for the genetic structure of personality: A comparison of the personality systems of Cloninger and Eysenck. *Journal of Personality and Social Psychology, 66,* 762–775.

Hecht, H., van Calker, D., Berger, M., & von Zerssen, D. (1998). Personality in patients with affective disorders and their relatives. *Journal of Affective Disorders, 51,* 33–43.

Hellerstein, D. J., Kocsis, J. H., Chapman, D., Stewart, J. W., & Harrison, W. (2000). Double-blind comparison of sertaline, imipramine, and placebo in the treatment of dysthymia: Effects on personality. *American Journal of Psychiatry, 157,* 1436–1444.

Hirschfeld, R. M. A. (1990). Personality and dysthymia. In S. W. Burton & H. S. Akiskal (Eds.), *Dysthymic disorder* (pp. 69–77). London: Gaskell.

Hirschfeld, R. M. A., & Klerman, G. L. (1979). Personality attributes and affective disorders. *American Journal of Psychiatry, 136,* 67–70.

Hirschfeld, R. M. A., Klerman, G. L., Andreasen, N. C., Clayton, P. J. & Keller, M. B. (1986a). Psychosocial predictors of chronicity in depressed patients. *British Journal of Psychiatry, 148,* 648–654.

Hirschfeld, R. M. A., Klerman, G. L., Clayton, P. J., & Keller, M. B. (1983a). Personality and depression: Empirical findings. *Archives of General Psychiatry, 40,* 993–998.

Hirschfeld, R. M. A., Klerman, G. L., Clayton, P. J., Keller, M. B., McDonald-Scott, P., & Larkin, B. H. (1983b). Assessing personality: Effects of the depressive state on trait measurement. *American Journal of Psychiatry, 140,* 695–699.

Hirschfeld, R. M. A., Klerman, G. L., Andreasen, N. C., & Clayton, P. J., & Keller, M. B. (1986a). Psychosocial predictors of chronicity in depressed patients. *British Journal of Psychiatry, 148,* 648–654.

Hirschfeld, R. M. A., Klerman, G. L., Keller, M. B., Andreasen, N. C., & Clayton, P. J. (1986b). Personality of recovered patients with bipolar affective disorder. *Journal of Affective Disorders, 11,* 81–89.

Hirschfeld, R. M. A., Klerman, G. L., Lavori, P., Keller, M. B., Griffith, P., & Coryell, W. (1989). Premorbid personality assessments of first onset of major depression. *Archives of General Psychiatry, 46,* 345–350.

Jackson, S. W. (1986). *Melancholia and depression: From Hippocratic times to modern times.* New Haven, CT: Yale University Press.

Joffe, R. T., Bagby, R. M., Levitt, A. J., Regan, J. J., & Parker, J. D. A. (1993). The Tridimensional Personality Questionnaire in major depression. *American Journal of Psychiatry, 150,* 959–960.

Joffe, R. T., & Regan, J. J. (1991). Personality and family history of depression in patients with affective illness. *Journal of Psychiatric Research, 25,* 67–71.

Joiner, T. E., Catanzaro, S. J., & Laurent, J. (1996). Tripartite structure of positive and negative affect, depression, and anxiety in child and adolescent psychiatric inpatients. *Journal of Abnormal Psychology, 105,* 401–409.

Joyce, P. R., Mulder, R. T., & Cloninger, C. R. (1999). Temperament and the pharmacotherapy of depression. In C. R. Cloninger (Ed.), *Personality and psychopathology* (pp. 457–473). Washington, DC: American Psychiatric Press.

Kagan, J., Reznick, J. S., & Snidman, N. (1987). The physiology and psychology of behavioral inhibition in children. *Child Development, 55,* 1459–1473.

Kay, J. H., Altshuler, L. L., Ventura, J., & Mintz, J. (1999). Prevalence of Axis II comorbidity in bipolar patients with and without alcohol use disorders. *Annals of Clinical Psychiatry, 11,* 187–195.

Kendell, R. E., & DiScipio, W. J. (1968). Eysenck Personality Inventory scores of patients with depressive illness. *British Journal of Psychiatry, 114,* 767–770.

Kendler, K. S., Neale, M. C., Kessler, R. C., Heath, A. C., & Eaves, L. J. (1993). A longitudinal twin study of personality and major depression in women. *Archives of General Psychiatry, 50,* 853–862.

Kendler, K. S., Walter, E. E., & Kessler, K. S. (1997). The prediction of length of major depressive episodes: Results from an epidemiological sample of female twins. *Psychological Medicine, 27,* 107–117.

Kerr, T. A., Roth, M., & Schapira, K. (1974). Prediction of outcome in anxiety states and depressive illness. *British Journal of Psychiatry, 124,* 125–133.

Klein, D. N. (1990). Depressive personality: Reliability, validity, and relation to dysthymia. *Journal of Abnormal Psychology, 99,* 412–421.

Klein, D. N. (1999). Depressive personality in the relatives of outpatients with dysthymic disorder and episodic major depressive disorder and normal controls. *Journal of Affective Disorders, 55,* 19–27.

Klein, D. N., Clark, D. C., Dansky, L., & Margolis, E. T. (1988). Dysthymia in the offspring of parents with primary unipolar affective disorder. *Journal of Abnormal Psychology, 97,* 265–274.

Klein, D. N., Lewinsohn, P. M., & Seeley, J. R. (1996). Hypomanic personality traits in a community sample of adolescents. *Journal of Affective Disorders, 38,* 135–143.

Klein, D. N., & Miller, G. A. (1993). Depressive personality in nonclinical subjects. *American Journal of Psychiatry, 150,* 1718–1724.

Klein, D. N., & Riso, L. P. (1993). Psychiatric diagnoses: Problems of boundaries and co-occurrences. In C. G. Costello (Ed.), *Basic issues in psychopathology* (pp. 19–66). New York: Guilford Press.

Klein, D. N., Riso, L. P., Donaldson, S. K., Schwartz, J. E., Anderson, R. L., Ouimette, P. C., Lizardi, H., & Aronson, T. A. (1995). Family study of early-onset dysthymia: Mood and personality disorders in relatives of outpatients with dysthymia and episodic major depression and normal controls. *Archives of General Psychiatry, 52*, 487–496.

Klein, D. N., & Shih, J. H. (1998). Depressive personality: Associations with DSM-III-R mood and personality disorders and negative and positive affectivity, 30–month stability, and prediction of course of Axis I depressive disorders. *Journal of Abnormal Psychology, 107*, 319–327.

Klein, D. N., Taylor, E. B., Harding, K., & Dickstein, S. (1988a). Primary early-onset dysthymia: Comparison with primary nonbipolar non-chronic major depression on demographic, clinical, familial, personality, and socioenvironmental characteristics and short-term outcome. *Journal of Abnormal Psychology, 97*, 387–398.

Klein, D. N., Taylor, E. B., Harding, K., & Dickstein, S. (1988b). Dependency and self-criticism in depression: Evaluation in a clinical population. *Journal of Abnormal Psychology, 97*, 399–404.

Klein, M. H., Wonderlich, S., & Shea, M. T. (1993). Models of the relationships between personality and depression: Toward a framework for theory and research. In M. H. Klein, D. J. Kupfer, & M. T. Shea (Eds.), *Personality and depression: A current view* (pp. 1–54). New York: Guilford Press.

Kochanska, G. (1991). Patterns of inhibition to the unfamiliar in children of normal and affectively ill mothers. *Child Development, 62*, 250–263.

Kraepelin, E. (1921). *Manic depressive insanity and paranoia*. Edinburgh: E. & S. Livingstone.

Kretschmer, E. (1925). *Physique and character*. New York: Harcourt, Brace.

Krueger, R. F. (1999). Personality traits in late adolescence predict mental disorders in early adulthood: A prospective-epidemiological study. *Journal of Personality, 67*, 39–65.

Kwapil, T. R., Miller, M. B., Zinser, M. C., Chapman, L. J., Chapman, J., & Eckblad, M. (2000). A longitudinal study of high scorers on the Hypomanic Personality Scale. *Journal of Abnormal Psychology, 109*, 222–226.

Kwon, J. S., Kim, Y.-M., Chang, C.-G., Park, B.-J., Kim, L., Yoon, D. J., Han, W.-S., Lee, H.-J., & Lyoo, I. K. (2000). Three-year follow-up of women with the sole diagnosis of depressive personality disorder: Subsequent development of dysthymia and major depression. *American Journal of Psychiatry, 157*, 1966–1972.

Kwon, P., & Whisman, M. A. (1998). Sociotropy and autonomy as vulnerabilities to specific life events: Issues in life event categorization. *Cognitive Therapy and Research, 22*, 353–362.

Lauer, C. J., Bronisch, T., Kainz, M., Schreiber, W., Holsboer, F., & Krieg, J.-C. (1997). Pre-morbid psychometric profile of subjects at high familial risk for affective disorder. *Psychological Medicine, 27*, 355–362.

Lewinsohn, P. M., Rohde, P., Seeley, J. R., Klein, D. N., & Gotlib, I. H. (2000). The natural course of adolescent major depressive disorder: II. Predictors of depression recurrence in young adults. *American Journal of Psychiatry, 157*, 1584–1591.

Liebowitz, M. R., Stallone, F., Dunner, D. L., & Fieve, R. F. (1979). Personality features of patients with primary affective disorder. *Acta Psychiatrica Scandinavica, 60*, 214–224.

Lonigan, C. J., Carey, M. P., & Finch, A. J. (1994). Anxiety and depression in children and adolescents: Negative affectivity and the utility of self-reports. *Journal of Consulting and Clinical Psychology, 62*, 1000–1008.

Loranger, A. W., Lenzenweger, M. F., Gartner, A. F., Susman, V. L., Herzig, J., Zammit, G. K., Gartner, J. D., Abrams, R. C., & Young, R. C. (1991). Trait–state artifacts and the diagnosis of personality-disorders. *Archives of General Psychiatry, 48*, 720–728.

Maier, W., Lichtermann, D., Minges, J., & Heun, R. (1992a). Personality traits in subjects at risk for unipolar major depression: A family study perspective. *Journal of Affective Disorders, 24*, 153–163.

Maier, W., Lichtermann, D., Minges, J., & Heun, R. (1992b). The familial relation of personality disorders (DSM-III-R) to unipolar major depression. *Journal of Affective Disorders, 26*, 151–156.

Maier, W., Minges, J., Lichtermann, D., & Heun, R. (1995). Personality disorders and personality variations in relatives of patients with bipolar affective disorders. *Journal of Affective Disorders, 35*, 173–181.

Markowitz, J. C., Moran, M. E., Kocsis, J. H., & Frances, A. J. (1992). Prevalence and comorbidity of dysthymic disorder among psychiatric outpatients. *Journal of Affective Disorders, 24*, 63–71.

Mazure, C. M., Bruce, M. L., Maciejewski, P. K., & Jacobs, S. C. (2000). Adverse life events and cognitive-personality characteristics in the prediction of major depression and antidepressant response. *American Journal of Psychiatry, 157*, 896–903.

Moore, R. G., & Blackburn, I.-M. (1996). The stability of sociotropy and autonomy in depressed patients undergoing treatment. *Cognitive Therapy and Research, 20*, 69–80.

Neff, C., & Klein, D. N. (1992). *The relationships between maternal behavior and psychopathology and offspring adjustment in depressed mothers of toddlers.* Paper presented at the annual meeting of the Society for Research in Psychopathology, Palm Springs, CA.

Newman, J. R., Ewing, S. E., McColl, R. D., Borus, J. S., Nierenberg, A. A., Pava, J., & Fava, M. (2000). Tridimensional Personality Questionnaire and treatment response in major depressive disorder: A negative study. *Journal of Affective Disorders, 57*, 241–247.

Ouimette, P. C., Klein, D. N., Clark, D. C., & Margolis, E. T. (1992). Personality traits in offspring of parents with unipolar affective disorder: An exploratory study. *Journal of Personality Disorders, 6*, 91–98.

Ouimette, P. C., Klein, D. N., & Pepper, C. M. (1996). Personality traits in the first degree relatives of outpatients with depressive disorders. *Journal of Affective Disorders, 39*, 43–53.

Parker, G., Blignault, I., & Manicavasagar, V. (1988). Neurotic depression: Delineation of symptom profiles and their relation to outcome. *British Journal of Psychiatry, 152*, 15–23.

Paykel, E. S., Klerman, G. L., & Prusoff, B. A. (1976). Personality and symptom pattern in depression. *British Journal of Psychiatry, 129*, 327–334.

Pepper, C. M., Klein, D. N., Anderson, R. L., Riso, L. P., Oimette, P. C., & Lizardi, H. (1995). DSM-III-R Axis II comorbidity in dysthymia and major depression. *American Journal of Psychiatry, 152*, 239–247.

Persons, J. B., Burns, D. D., Perloff, J. M., & Miranda, J. (1993). Relationships between symptoms of depression and anxiety and dysfunctional beliefs about achievement and attachment. *Journal of Abnormal Psychology, 102*, 518–524.

Peselow, E. D., Robins, C. J., Sanfilipo, M. P., Block, P., & Fieve, R. R. (1992). Sociotropy and autonomy: Relationship to antidepressant drug treatment response and endogenous–nonendogenous dichotomy. *Journal of Abnormal Psychology, 101*, 479–486.

Peselow, E. D., Sanfilipo, M. P., & Fieve, R. R. (1995). Relationship between hypomania and personality disorders before and after successful treatment. *American Journal of Psychiatry, 152*, 232–238.

Phillips, K. A., Gunderson, J. G., Triebwasser, J., Kimble, C. R., Faedda, G., Lyoo, I. K., & Renn, J. (1998). Reliability and validity of depressive personality disorder. *American Journal of Psychiatry, 155*, 1044–1048.

Pilowsky, I., & Katsikitis, M. (1983). Depressive illness and dependency. *Acta Psychiatrica Scandinavica, 68*, 11–14.

Rector, N. A., Bagby, R. M., Segal, Z. V., Joffe, R. T., & Levitt, A. (2000). Self-criticism and dependency in depressed patients treated with cognitive therapy or pharmacotherapy. *Cognitive Therapy and Research, 24*, 571–584.

Reich, J., Noyes, R., Hirschfeld, R., Coryell, W., & O'Gorman, T. (1987). State and personality in depressed and panic patients. *American Journal of Psychiatry, 144*, 181–187.

Reich, J. H., & Vasile, R. G. (1993). Effect of personality disorders on the treatment outcome of Axis I conditions: An update. *Journal of Nervous and Mental Disease, 181*, 475–484.

Richter, J., Eisemann, M., & Richter, G. (2000). Temperament and character during the course of unipolar depression among inpatients. *European Archives of Psychiatry and Clinical Neuroscience, 250*, 40–47.

Riso, L. P., Klein, D. N, Anderson, R. L., & Oiumette, P. G. (2000). A family study of outpatients with borderline personality disorder and no history of mood disorder. *Journal of Personality Disorders, 14,* 208–217.

Riso, L. P., Klein, D. N, Ferro, T., Kasch, K. L., Pepper, C. M., Schwartz, J. E., & Aronson, T. A. (1996). Understanding the comorbidity between early-onset dysthymia and cluster B personality disorders: A family study. *American Journal of Psychiatry, 153,* 900–906.

Roberts, S. B., & Kendler, K. S. (1999). Neuroticism and self-esteem as indices of the vulnerability to major depression in women. *Psychological Medicine, 29,*1101–1109.

Robins, C. J., Bagby, R. M., Rector, N. A., Lynch, T. R., & Kennedy, S. H. (1997). Sociotropy, autonomy, and patterns of symptoms in patients with major depression: A comparison of dimensional and categorical approaches. *Cognitive Therapy and Research, 21,* 285–300.

Robins, C. J., Block, P., & Peselow, E. D. (1989). Relations of sociotropic and autonomous personality characteristics to specific symptoms in depressed patients. *Journal of Abnormal Psychology, 98,* 86–88.

Robins, C. J., Hayes, A. M., Block, P., Kramer, R. J., & Villena, M. (1995). Interpersonal and achievement concerns and the depressive vulnerability and symptom specificity hypothesis: A prospective study. *Cognitive Therapy and Research, 19,* 1–20.

Robins, C. J., & Luten, A. G. (1991). Sociotropy and autonomy: Differential patterns of clinical presentation in unipolar depression. *Journal of Abnormal Psychology, 100,* 74–77.

Rohde, P., Lewinsohn, P. M., & Seeley, J. R. (1990). Are people changed by the experience of having an episode of depression? A further test of the scar hypothesis. *Journal of Abnormal Psychology, 99,* 264–271.

Rohde, P., Lewinsohn, P. M., & Seeley, J. R. (1994). Are adolescents changed by an episode of major depression? *Journal of the American Academy of Child and Adolescent Psychiatry, 33,* 1289–1298.

Rorsman, B., Grasbeck, A., Hagnell, O., Isberg, P.-E., & Otterbeck, L. (1993). Premorbid personality traits and psychometric background factors in depression: The Lundby Study, 1957–1972. *Neuropsychobiology, 27,* 72–79.

Rosenbaum, J. F., Biederman, J., Hirshfeld-Becker, D. R., Kagan, J., Snidman, N., Friedman, D., Nineberg, A., Gallery, D. J., & Faraone, S. V. (2000). A controlled study of behavioral inhibition in children of parents with panic disorder and depression. *American Journal of Psychiatry, 157,* 2002–2010.

Rosenfarb, I. S., Becker, J., Khan, A., & Mintz, J. (1998). Dependency and self-criticism in bipolar and unipolar depressed women. *British Journal of Clinical Psychology, 37,* 409–414.

Rothbart, M. K., & Bates, J. E. (1998). Temperament. In N. Eisenberg (Ed.), *Handbook of child psychology: Vol. 3. Social, emotional, and personality development* (5th ed., pp. 105–176). New York: Wiley.

Ryder, A. G., & Bagby, R. M. (1999). Diagnostic viability of depressive personality disorder: Theoretical and conceptual issues. *Journal of Personality Disorders, 13,* 99–117.

Sato, T, Shigeki, H., Narita, T., Kusunoki, K., Kato, J., Goto, M., Sakado, K., & Uehara, T. (1999). Temperament and character inventory dimensions as a predictor of response to antidepressant treatment in major depression. *Journal of Affective Disorders, 56,* 153–161.

Sauer, H., Richter, P., Czernik, A., Ludwig-Mayerhofer, W., Schochlin, C., Greil, W., & von Zerssen, D. (1997). Personality differences between patients with major depression and bipolar disorder: The impact of minor symptoms on self-ratings of personality. *Journal of Affective Disorders, 42,* 169–177.

Schneider, K. (1958). *Psychopathic personalities.* London: Cassell.

Scott, J., Harrington, J., House, R., & Ferrier, I. N. (1996). A preliminary study of the relationship among personality, cognitive vulnerability, symptom profile, and outcome in major depressive disorder. *Journal of Nervous and Mental Disease, 184,* 503–505.

Scott, J., Williams, J. M. G., Brittlebank, A., & Ferrier, I. N. (1995). The relationship between premorbid neuroticism, cognitive dysfunction and persistence of depression: A 1-year follow-up. *Journal of Affective Disorders, 33,* 167–172.

Segal, Z. V., Shaw, B. F., & Vella, D. D. (1989). Life stress and depression: A test of the congruency hypothesis for life event content and depressive subtype. *Canadian Journal of Behavioural Science, 21*, 389–400.

Segal, Z. V., Shaw, B. F., Vella, D. D., & Katz, R. (1992). Cognitive and life stress predictors of relapse in remitted unipolar depressed patients: Test of the congruency hypothesis. *Journal of Abnormal Psychology, 101*, 26–36.

Serra, A. V., & Pollitt, J. (1975). The relationship between personality and the symptoms of depressive illness. *British Journal of Psychiatry, 127*, 211–218.

Shea, M. T., Leon, A. C., Mueller, T. I., Solomon, D. A., Warshaw, M. G., & Keller, M. B. (1996). Does major depression result in lasting personality change? *American Journal of Psychiatry, 153*, 1404–1410.

Shea, M. T., Widiger, T. A., & Klein, M. H. (1992). Comorbidity of personality disorders and depression: Implications for treatment. *Journal of Consulting and Clinical Psychology, 60*, 857–868.

Soloff, P. H. (2000). Psychopharmacology of borderline personality disorder. *Psychiatric Clinics of North America, 23*, 169–192.

Solomon, D. A., Shea, M. T., Leon, A. C., Mueller, T. I., Coryell, W., Maser, J. D., Endicott, J., & Keller, M. B. (1996). Personality traits in subjects with bipolar I disorder in remission. *Journal of Affective Disorders, 40*, 41–48.

Surtees, P. G., & Barkley, C. (1994). Future imperfect: The long-term outcome of depression. *British Journal of Psychiatry, 164*, 327–341.

Ucok, A., Karaveli, D., Kundakci, T., & Yazici, O. (1998). Comorbidity of personality disorders with bipolar mood disorders. *Comprehensive Psychiatry, 39*, 72–74.

van Londen, L., Molenaar, R. P. G., Goekoop, J. G., Zwinderman, A. H., & Rooijmans, H. G. M. (1998). Three- to 5–year prospective follow-up of outcome in major depression. *Psychological Medicine, 28*, 731–735.

van Os, J., & Jones, P. B. (1999). Early risk factors and adult person–environment relationships in affective disorder. *Psychological Medicine, 29*, 1055–1067.

van Os, J., Jones, P., Lewis, G., Wadsworth, M., & Murray, R. (1997). Developmental precursors of affective illness in a general population birth cohort. *Archives of General Psychiatry, 54*, 625–631.

Vieta, E., Colom, F., Martinez-Aran, A., Benabarre, A., & Gasto, C. (1999). Personality disorders in bipolar II patients. *Journal of Nervous and Mental Disease, 187*, 245–248.

Watson, D., & Clark, L. A. (1995). Depression and the melancholic temperament. *European Journal of Personality, 9*, 351–366.

Weissman, M. M., Prusoff, B. A., & Klerman, G. L. (1978). Personality and the prediction of long-term outcome of depression. *American Journal of Psychiatry, 135*, 797–800.

Westen, D., Moses, M. J., Silk, K. R., Lohr, N. E., Cohen, R., & Segal, H. (1992). Quality of depressive experience in borderline personality disorder and major depression: When depression is not just depression. *Journal of Personality Disorders, 6*, 382–393.

Widiger, T. A. (1993). Personality and depression: Assessment issues. In M. H. Klein, D. J. Kupfer, & M. T. Shea (Eds.), *Personality and depression: A current view* (pp. 77–118). New York: Guilford Press.

Zimmerman, M. (1994). Diagnosing personality disorders: A review of issues and research models. *Archives of General Psychiatry, 51*, 225–245.

Zimmerman, M., & Coryell, W. (1989). DSM-III personality disorder diagnoses in a nonpatient sample: Demographic correlates and comorbidity. *Archives of General Psychiatry, 46*, 682–689.

Zuckerman, D. M., Prusoff, B. A., Weissman, M. M., & Padian, N. S. (1980). Personality as a predictor of psychotherapy outcome for depressed outpatients. *Journal of Consulting and Clinical Psychology, 48*, 730–735.

Zuroff, D. C. (1994). Depressive personality styles and the five-factor model of personality. *Journal of Personality Assessment, 63*, 453–472.

6

Bipolar and Unipolar Depression
A Comparison of Clinical Phenomenology and Psychosocial Predictors

Sheri L. Johnson and Amy Kizer

Since depression occurs in both bipolar and unipolar mood disorder, an obvious question is whether these depressions are similar or different. This chapter presents research on clinical features, etiological issues, and psychosocial triggers for depressive episodes. Our particular emphasis on psychosocial factors reflects both a growing research literature and the possibility that unipolar and bipolar depressions may share similar mechanisms in the genesis of episodes.

Before proceeding, it is important to note a clinical reality of bipolar disorder that may have implications for understanding the nature of depression. Although clinical lore and the very name of the disorder both suggest that bipolar disorder necessarily involves depression, this is not the case. Rather, the diagnosis of bipolar I disorder is based on one lifetime manic episode and does not require an episode of depression (American Psychiatric Association, 2000). In nontreatment samples, as many as 20–33% of individuals with bipolar disorder report no lifetime episode of major depression (Depue & Monroe, 1978; Kessler, Rubinow, Holmes, Abelson, & Zhao, 1997). Indeed, in one small epidemiological study, less than half of the individuals with bipolar I disorder met lifetime depression criteria (Karkowski & Kendler, 1997). Although some authors have suggested that depression may emerge over the life span for all persons with bipolar disorder, empirical analyses suggest that the presence or absence of depression is not related to the duration of illness (Kessler et al., 1997). Rather, it appears that there is a subset of individuals with bipolar disorder who do not experience depressive episodes.

Among individuals with bipolar disorder who do experience depressive episodes, there is dramatic variability in the expression and course of depression. For example, some individuals experience depressive episodes that last for years, whereas others may experience only one brief episode. What predicts this variability in the expression of depression within bipolar disorder? In this chapter, we focus on the psychosocial predictors of bipolar depression and we evaluate whether bipolar and unipolar depression are predicted by similar psychosocial variables.

Why focus on psychosocial triggers? A burgeoning literature has suggested that psychosocial variables have a robust impact on the course of bipolar disorder (without differentiating mania vs. depression). For example, expressed emotion has been found to predict (depressive or manic) relapse (Miklowitz, Goldstein, Nuechterlein, & Snyder, 1998; Priebe, Wildgrube, & Müller-Oerlinghausen, 1989). Negative life events have been found to be associated with a 4.5-fold increase in the risk of relapse (Ellicott, 1989; see also Hunt, Bruce-Jones, & Silverstone, 1992) and a slower time to recovery from episodes (Johnson & Miller, 1997). Personality and cognitive variables also appear to predict symptom severity in bipolar disorder (cf. Hammen, Ellicott, & Gitlin, 1992; Hammen, Ellicott, Gitlin, & Jamison, 1989). These findings suggest that psychosocial variables may be quite relevant to the course of bipolar disorder.

Much of the research on bipolar disorder, including psychosocial research, has tended to focus on the illness as a whole, without differentiating mania and depression. Our own research and that of several other teams suggests, however, that the predictors of depression and mania within bipolar disorder may differ (Johnson, Winters, & Meyer, in press). In this light, then, we focus on those studies that have disentangled depression and mania.

Episodes of depression are a common feature across unipolar and bipolar disorders. Nonetheless, it is unknown whether unipolar and bipolar depression should be considered distinct illnesses. In this chapter, we review several literatures that suggest that unipolar and bipolar depression share many more commonalities than distinctions. First, we compare the course and phenomenology of unipolar and bipolar depression. Then, we turn toward models of vulnerability and triggers. As backdrop, we briefly review biological models of vulnerability to bipolar and unipolar depression. Although a comprehensive review of this topic is far beyond the scope of this chapter (for reviews, see Goodwin & Jamison, 1990; Goodnick, 1997), this overview highlights current genetic and neurotransmitter models. Finally, we turn to our major focus, psychosocial predictors of bipolar and unipolar depression.

COURSE OF DISORDER

Studies have often found that bipolar disorder tends to have a more rapidly fluctuating course than unipolar disorder. In this section, we examine different course parameters, such as episode frequency, duration, and severity, separately (see Table 6.1). In doing so, we note whether comparisons of bipolar and unipolar disorder blend mania and depression or examine depression separately.

Compared to patients with unipolar disorder, patients with bipolar disorder appear to experience significantly more mood episodes if one sums episodes of mania and depression together (Berghöfer, Kossmann, & Müller-Oerlinghausen, 1996; Coryell, Andreasen, Endicott, & Keller, 1987; Roy-Byrne, Post, Uhde, Porcu, & Davis, 1985; Winokur, Coryell, Endicott, & Akiskal, 1993; Winokur, Coryell, Keller, Endicott, & Akiskal, 1993). Nevertheless, the question of whether patients with bipolar and unipolar disorder differ in their frequency of *depressive* episodes is unclear. Roy-Byrne et al. (1985) found that patients with bipolar disorder suffered from more episodes of depression than did patients with unipolar disorder based on retrospective data, yet two prospective analyses suggest no difference in numbers of depressive episodes (Roy-Byrne et al., 1985; Winokur, Coryell, Keller, et al., 1993). The disparate findings are difficult to weigh, as retrospective reports may be more biased, but the shorter time spans of prospective studies may limit power to detect differences. The extant data, then, are unclear. Preliminary

TABLE 6.1. Course of Disorder

Author	Year	N	Sample description	Prospective or retrospective?	Symptom measures
Berghöfer, Kossmann, & Müller-Oerlinghausen	1996	86	Outpatients	15-year retrospective analysis	"Confirmed diagnosis" and "complete documentation"
Coryell, Andreasen, Endicott, & Keller	1987	372	Inpatients and outpatients with primary major depression	2-year longitudinal study	LIFE at 6 month intervals
Goldberg, Harrow, & Grossman	1995a	100	Inpatients	4.5-year longitudinal study	Hospitalization rates
Goldberg, Harrow, & Grossman	1995b	84	Inpatients	4.5-year longitudinal study	SADS at follow-up
Kessing, Andersen, Mortensen, & Bolwig	1998	20,350	Inpatients	22-year case register study	Chart review
Kessing & Mortensen	1999	9174	Inpatients	22-year case register study	Chart review for hospitalization rates
Mitchell et al.	1992	54	Inpatients and outpatients	Current	Semi-structured interview to evaluate present episode and mental state signs; previous medical records
Roy-Byrne, Post, Uhde, Porcu, & Davis	1985	95	Inpatients	Retrospective and 6-year prospective follow-up	Retrospective data from chart review and informants; prospective data based on hospitalization observation
Winokur, Coryell, Endicott, & Akiskal	1993	407	Inpatients	5-year prospective follow-up	LIFE at 6 month intervals
Winokur, Coryell, Keller, Endicott, & Akiskal	1993	320	Inpatients	5-year prospective follow-up	LIFE at 6 month intervals

Note. SADS, Schedule for Affective Disorders and Schizophrenia; LIFE, Longitudinal Interval Follow-up Examination.

evidence, though, suggests that bipolar disorder is characterized by more depressive episodes than is unipolar disorder.

Some studies have attempted to understand how episode patterns change over time. Persons with more episodes may experience faster relapses. In one of the largest longitudinal studies, Kessing and his colleagues recently published findings from a study of 20,350 bipolar and unipolar patients recruited after a first hospital admission (Kessing, Andersen,

Mortensen, & Bolwig, 1998). They tracked time to recurrence, using hospitalization for either mania or depression as the index of recurrence. Following a first episode, individuals with unipolar depression were slower to experience a recurrence (median = 12.8 years) than individuals with bipolar disorder were (median = 3.8 years). The median time to recurrence became shorter after each successive episode for individuals with either disorder. For unipolar disorder, number of previous episodes was strongly associated with speed of recurrence. As a result, by the fifth episode, the median time to recurrence was less than 18 months for both unipolar and bipolar disorder, and the two disorders did not differ on speed of recurrence. Unfortunately, no separate analyses of depression versus mania recurrence were reported. Nonetheless, it will be important to consider potential developmental changes to understand the course parameters of unipolar and bipolar disorder.

Other studies have focused on the timing within episodes. Roy-Byrne and his colleagues (1985) described bipolar depressions as "switching on and off"—that is, more frequent and shorter than unipolar depressions. With respect to the full duration of episodes, findings have been inconsistent. Findings from a few studies suggest that bipolar depressions are shorter than unipolar depressions (Mitchell et al., 1992; Roy-Byrne et al., 1985), but two large-scale studies did not find differences in the time from onset to recovery of depressive episodes (Coryell et al., 1987; Kessing & Mortensen, 1999). As with studies of timing between episodes, some of the cross-study discrepancies may reflect changes in the pattern of episodes over the life course. In a retrospective analysis, Berghöfer, Kossmann, and Müller-Oerlinghausen (1996) found that the length of bipolar depressive episodes shortened over a 15-year period.

Beyond timing, do unipolar and bipolar depression episodes differ in severity? Most studies of severity have used hospitalization rates to index episode severity. Although bipolar disorder has been associated with more frequent hospitalization than unipolar disorder (Berghöfer et al., 1996; Goldberg, Harrow, & Grossman, 1995a, 1995b; Roy-Byrne et al., 1985), most studies have not distinguished hospitalizations for mania versus hospitalizations for depression. In one study, unipolar depressions appeared more likely than bipolar depressions to result in hospitalization (Roy-Byrne et al., 1985).

As shown in Table 6.1, the methodological approaches used to study course parameters are quite varied. Even among studies that differentiate episodes of depression and mania, a number of methodological issues limit the interpretability of findings. A fundamental issue involves the measurement of episodes and their duration. Especially in case-register studies, data are often limited to the number and duration of hospitalizations, and these indices are assumed to index number and duration of episodes. A variety of factors beyond symptom status, however, influence the decision to hospitalize patients, such as the quality of social support networks or ongoing relationships with mental health care providers. Indeed, Roy-Byrne et al. (1985) found no predictive relationship between number of hospitalizations and number of episodes.

Another issue involves the heterogeneity of diagnoses in these studies. Some researchers use more stringent diagnostic criteria (e.g., endogenous depressive episodes; Mitchell et al., 1992), whereas most include diagnoses that fall within a disorder spectrum (e.g., bipolar II disorder), and some even include related disorders, such as schizoaffective disorder (Berghöfer et al., 1996; Winokur, Coryell, Endicott, et al., 1993; Winokur, Coryell, Keller, et al., 1993). Little is known about how these sampling decisions influence the pattern of findings.

A third issue is the lack of attention to confounds. Few studies control for background characteristics (see Goldberg et al., 1995a, 1995b; Berghöfer et al., 1996, for exceptions), such as the number of previous episodes. Differences in the medication regimen used to treat bipolar and unipolar disorder are perhaps the largest confound. Other than one study that recruited individuals from a lithium clinic (Berghöfer et al., 1996), this issue has not been addressed. More research is needed to address the methodological questions. Evidence to date, however, suggests that bipolar depression may have a more rapid onset and possibly a more rapid offset compared to unipolar depression.

SYMPTOMATOLOGY

One method of assessing the similarity of unipolar and bipolar depression is a comparison of symptomatology. We focus specifically on comparisons of symptoms in bipolar depression, setting aside the question of the types of symptoms displayed during mania. Early research and clinical lore on symptom profiles suggested that unipolar depression was characterized by more classic vegetative features and affective symptoms, whereas bipolar depression involved more atypical vegetative features than unipolar depression. More specifically, compared to bipolar depression, unipolar depression was characterized by relatively greater anger, anxiety, hypochondriasis, insomnia, and psychomotor agitation, as well as less psychomotor retardation and hypersomnia (for a review, see Depue & Monroe, 1978). Congruently, a series of studies found that unipolar depression was characterized by more anxiety and agitation than bipolar depression (Katz, Robins, Croughan, Secunda & Swann, 1982), greater weight loss (Abrams & Taylor, 1980), and initial insomnia (Brockington, Altman, Hillier, Meltzer, & Nand, 1982).

Subsequent research, however, has provided discrepant results. For example, in direct contrast to the above findings, two studies have found that patients in unipolar depressive episodes exhibit more psychomotor retardation, less hostility, and less psychomotor agitation compared to patients in bipolar depressive episodes (Gurpegui, Casanova, & Cervera, 1985; Mitchell et al., 1992). In one large study, bipolar and unipolar depression appeared remarkably similar on 31 different symptoms (Mitchell et al., 1992), and Coryell and his colleagues (1989) also found no difference in research diagnostic criteria (RDC) criteria between bipolar and unipolar depression. Indeed, a comprehensive review suggests no consistent patterns of symptom differences (Mitchell et al., 1992).

Nonetheless, in a recent analysis of 39 matched pairs of individuals with bipolar and unipolar depression, bipolar depression did appear associated with greater psychomotor retardation and hypersomnia (Mitchell et al., 2001). Findings from this study, then, are somewhat congruent with early theory. However, in this sample, individuals with bipolar depressions were more likely than those with unipolar depression to report psychotic depressive symptoms during their lifetimes. It seems possible that some of the symptom profile qualities identified with bipolar disorder may be tied to issues of severity. Samples with more severe bipolar depression, characterized by greater psychosis levels, may demonstrate the hypothesized pattern of greater atypical vegetative symptoms. Most recent samples, however, have not demonstrated the hypothesized pattern.

Other studies have focused on specific symptoms, particularly psychosis, sleep patterns, and suicidality. Levels of psychosis have not consistently been higher in studies of one group compared to the other (Black & Nasrallah, 1989; Breslau & Meltzer, 1998; Endicott et al., 1985; Guze, Woodruff, & Clayton, 1975; Mitchell et al., 1992). In regard to sleep patterns, studies that have matched individuals on age and gender have not identified differences between unipolar and bipolar depression (Giles, Rush, & Roffwarg, 1986; Kuhs & Reschke, 1992), and a review of studies on sleep patterns in unipolar and bipolar depression suggests no consistent differences (Goodwin & Jamison, 1990, p. 550). Finally, a review of 23 studies on suicidality among unipolar and bipolar disorders also suggests inconsistent findings (Lester, 1993), although few studies differentiate manic and depressive episodes within bipolar disorder. In sum, the early findings of symptom pattern differences have not been replicated.

One might wonder if symptom profile differences have been harder to detect in newer studies because of the increasing use of complicated medication regimens. Studies that have included a drug washout period before assessing symptoms, however, do not appear much more congruent. In these studies, findings have been inconsistent in regard to the relative frequency of anxiety and hostility (Beigel & Murphy, 1971; Gurpegui et al., 1985; Kupfer et al., 1974). Patients with unipolar disorder have appeared to have higher activity levels, more weight loss, and less appetite disturbance compared to patients with bipolar disorder in some but not all studies (Beigel & Murphy, 1971; Gurpegui et al., 1985; Kupfer et al., 1974). Hence, medication profile differences do not appear to account for the null findings.

The inconsistency of findings in this literature may reflect other methodological issues. As with studies of the course of disorder, potential confounds have received limited attention, with only two studies controlling for previous illness or demographic characteristics (Beigel & Murphy, 1971; Mitchell et al., 1992). One significant question is whether the occasionally documented patterns of vegetative symptoms in bipolar depression are related to a more severe lifetime course.

Beyond the need to attend to potential confounds, studies have varied greatly in the measures used to assess symptoms. Many investigators have focused on clinical characteristics of particular theoretical interest, and some studies do not assess the atypical vegetative symptoms initially hypothesized to be characteristic of bipolar depression. Finally, most studies in this area have conducted a large number of statistical tests without correcting alpha levels; Type I errors may yield artificially elevated reports of differences between the two conditions. In sum, the literature addressing symptom profiles is quite limited. More research is needed to determine the degree of similarity in the symptomatology of unipolar and bipolar depression.

Nonetheless, a review of the literature suggests that any differences identified in symptom profiles between unipolar and bipolar depression appear inconsistent. In most studies, atypical vegetative symptoms do not appear more common in bipolar depression than unipolar depression. Summarizing across studies, unipolar and bipolar depression symptom profiles appear similar.

BIOLOGICAL VULNERABILITY

Compared with other mental illnesses, genetic influences play an especially important role in the etiology of bipolar disorder. Across studies, the concordance rate for bipolar I disorder in monozygotic twins ranges from 33 to 80% compared to a range from 0 to 8% for dizygotic twins, with estimates of heritability ranging from 30 to 80% (National Institute of Mental Health, 1998). These studies, however, have focused on the genetic transmission of mania rather than depression.

What do we know about the transmission of depression among families of bipolar individuals? Surprisingly, most family history studies do not differentiate between bipolar disorder with and without depression. More studies have examined the familial associations between bipolar disorder (defined as mania with or without depression) and unipolar disorder. Relatives of unipolar depression probands do not appear at elevated risk for mania (Winokur & Tsuang, 1996). In contrast, relatives of bipolar probands (again, either with or without depression) are at elevated risk of unipolar depression; approximately 11% of the relatives of bipolar probands meet criteria for major depression (Plomin, DeFries, McClearn, & Rutter, 1997), compared to 3% of the relatives of nonaffectively disordered probands. In one recent epidemiological study, relatives of bipolar and unipolar probands were equivalent in their rates of depression (Karkowski & Kendler, 1997). Rates of depression among family members in these studies appear somewhat low overall in the context of epidemiological estimates that approximately 17% of the U.S. population meets lifetime criteria for major depression (Kessler et al., 1994). Given the lower rates of depression identified within the family history studies, concordance rates from these studies may be specific to more severe depression (Plomin et al., 1997).

Because depression is not associated with elevated risk of mania in family members, but mania is associated with elevated risk of familial depression, some have suggested that these genetic data demonstrate that the distinction between bipolar disorder and unipolar depression is one of severity, in which unipolar depression is a milder form of disorder than bipolar disorder (Plomin et al., 1997). Such a model based on genetic data would explain why the relatives of bipolar probands are at increased risk for unipolar disorder, whereas family members of probands with unipolar disorder are not at increased risk for bipolar disorder.

There is little direct research addressing links between severity and heritability. We identified only one study that begins to address this issue, and it was not supportive. Winokur (1984) found that relatives of probands with more severe illnesses (defined as bipolar disorder with psychotic features) actually had a lower risk of mood disorders than relatives of less severe probands (defined as nonpsychotic unipolar depression). It may well be that other models of severity, incorporating a broader array of parameters, such as rates of relapse and perniciousness of course, could accommodate the family history findings. With limited data on severity and heritability, fundamental questions remain unresolved. For example, why should mania be associated with an elevated personal or family risk of depression? Little is known about the answer to this question.

One way in which genetic vulnerability for a mood disorder may manifest itself is in brain pathology associated with mood disorders. Indeed, neuroimaging studies suggest that the same brain regions are involved in unipolar and bipolar depression. Both unipolar and bipolar depression have been associated with reduced blood flow to the cerebral cortex (Videbech, 2000), especially in the prefrontal cortex ventral to the genu of the corpus callosum (Drevets et al., 1997).

On a neurotransmitter level, irregularities have also been found to be associated with affective disturbances. To date, most research on neurotransmitters and mood episodes has focused on deficient levels of the monoamines, particularly dopamine and serotonin. We focus here on a comparison of dopaminergic and serotonergic deficits during depressive episodes of bipolar and unipolar disorder. A range of studies suggest that both bipolar and unipolar depression are associated with a decrease in the functional levels of serotonin (5-HT$_2$) activity (Yatham et al., 2000).

Given evidence that serotonin exerts negative feedback over dopamine levels (Depue & Zald, 1993; Winters, Scott, & Beevers, 2000), it is not surprising that dopamine levels also have been tied to both unipolar and bipolar depression. Indeed, 10 out of 11 studies suggested that bipolar and unipolar depression were associated with comparable cerebrospinal fluid levels of the dopamine metabolite homovanillic acid (Goodwin & Jamison, 1990). Similarly, dopamine 4 (D4) receptor genes have been associated with bipolar disorder and unipolar depression (Manki et al., 1996). A recent review suggests that increases in functional levels of dopamine may mediate sleep deprivation effects (Ebert & Berger, 1998). Experimentally induced sleep deprivation appears to produce temporary symptom relief for both bipolar depression (Barbarini et al., 1998) and unipolar depression (Wu & Bunney, 1991). In sum, studies of serotonin and dopamine levels utilizing various methodologies suggest commonalities for bipolar and unipolar depression.

Despite similarities between bipolar and unipolar depression in the serotonin and dopamine systems, differences in the levels of other neurotransmitters, enzymes, and metabolites have been found. Plasma norepinephrine, plasma norepinephrine metabolites, and norepinephrine and epinephrine excretions in urine have been found to be lower during bipolar compared to unipolar depressions (Bowden et al., 1987; Roy, Pickar, Linnoila, & Potter, 1985; Roy, Jimerson, & Pickar, 1986; Schatzberg et al., 1989). However, cerebrospinal fluid levels of norepinephrine, a more proximal measure of brain norepinephrine, have not been found to differ between bipolar and unipolar depressions (Post et al., 1978). Blood platelet monoamine oxidase enzyme activity has been found to be lower in bipolar than unipolar depression (Mann, 1979; Murphy & Weiss, 1972). Basal platelet intracellular calcium has also been found to be higher in bipolar than unipolar depression (Bowden et al., 1988; Dubovsky, Lee, Christiano, & Murphy, 1991; Dubovsky et al., 1989; Dubovsky, Thomas, Hijazi, & Murphy, 1994). However, in a review of over 80 studies on the biology of unipolar and bipolar depressive episodes, Yatham, Srisurapanont, Zis, and Kusumakar (1997) report that differences have not been replicated.

In evaluating the null findings and nonreplications within this field, it is important to note several methodological issues. In regard to sampling, studies use varying criteria for diagnosis, with no apparent consensus on whether to include diagnoses such as bipolar II disorder and minor depression. Further, most studies do not control for symptom profiles or severity. In addition, studies have varied greatly in their methods of sampling neurotransmitters and their metabolites. More sophisticated neurobiological models of depression are now emerging, and many researchers are tackling models of membrane and receptor characteristics, gene expression models, and second-messenger system regulation to explain neurotransmitter dysregulation in mood disturbances. For these more sophisticated biological assays, direct comparisons of bipolar and unipolar depression are not yet available.

Bipolar and unipolar depression may share many biological features, as considerable overlap appears to exist in genetic vulnerability, brain pathology, and functional levels of dopamine and serotonin during depressive episodes. Differences between bipolar and unipolar disorder that have emerged in some studies, such as in blood platelet monoamine oxidase and intracellular calcium levels, have not been replicated. In contrast to the apparent parallels between bipolar and unipolar depression, mania appears tied to elevated dopamine levels (Kaplan & Sadock, 1998), hyperpolarization in transmembrane potentials (El Mallakh, Li, Worth, & Peiper, 1996), and changes in dopamine sub–3 receptor mechanisms (Chiaroni et al., 2000). Mania, then, might be tied to biological characteristics that are distinct compared to those involved with either unipolar or bipolar depression. Nevertheless, due to the limited nature and number of studies, more research is needed to determine to what extent mania, unipolar depression, and bipolar depression share biological features. Tentatively, results of neuroimaging and neurotransmitter studies suggest that bipolar and unipolar depression are remarkably similar.

PSYCHOSOCIAL ANTECEDENTS TO DEPRESSION

The psychosocial antecedents to *unipolar* depression have been well studied. Among socioenvironmental variables, robust evidence has emerged for negative life events, marital distress, and expressed emotion as predictors of unipolar depression (Brown & Harris, 1978, 1989; Butzlaff & Hooley, 1998; Davila & Bradbury, 1998). Personality traits have also received considerable attention (Clark, Watson, & Mineka, 1994; Coyne & Whiffen, 1995; Klein, Durbin, Shankman, & Santiago, Chapter 5, this volume). Cognitive styles have been studied extensively, and findings are described in more detail in other places in this volume (see Abramson et al., Chapter 11). In the following sections, we describe studies examining whether these same variables predict bipolar depression. First, though, we review methodological issues that must be addressed to understand the nature of antecedents to bipolar depression.

Methodological Issues

One of the key differences across studies in this field is the use of cross-sectional versus prospective designs. Although retrospective or cross-sectional designs have been criticized across most psychopathology research (cf. Coyne, 2000), the problems with cross-sectional designs are magnified when comparing mania with depression. Depression is associated with more insight and treatment seeking than mania is. Further, the timing of episodes for the two poles contrasts sharply. For example, in our samples of individuals with bipolar I disorder, the average mania lasts less than 7 months, whereas the average depression lasts 11 months. Given this, retrospective studies of antecedents of episodes typically require recall of more distal periods for depression than for mania. Some triggers may be profound enough for people to remember them accurately for a long time; for example, individuals appear to remember severe life events for approximately 1 year (Brown & Harris, 1982). Minor changes, such as daily life events and shifts in sleep schedules, appear to be forgotten more quickly. Given these issues, prospective studies have a major advantage for differentiating the predictors of depression and mania.

Even within prospective studies, the choice of an appropriate outcome variable is complicated. Many prospective studies in this field, including our initial publications, have focused on episodes. These studies are helpful in planning treatment duration, as they provide information regarding the percentage of individuals who recover or relapse within a given time period. These studies would also seem highly relevant for understanding processes involved in the generation and maintenance of depressive and manic symptoms, as separate analyses can be conducted to contrast mania versus depression. However, categorizing an episode as "manic" or "depressive" may obscure a surprisingly significant degree of symptoms from the opposite pole. Some detail on the course parameters of our participants with bipolar disorder may help illustrate this issue.

In our studies, 149 individuals with bipolar I disorder have been recruited during an initial index episode and administered structured symptom severity interviews monthly through recovery. In our sample, 13% of index episodes met full criteria for *both* depression *and* mania on the Structured Clinical Interview for DSM-IV (SCID; First, Spitzer, Gibbon, & Williams, 1996). Even among the 85 individuals who entered the study in a "pure" manic episode according to DSM-IV criteria, 22% obtained a Modified Hamilton Rating Scale for Depression score (MHRSD; Miller, Bishop, Norman, & Maddever, 1985) in the mild range (10 or higher) and 10% obtained a score in the clinically significant range (17 or higher). Many "manias," then, are accompanied by marked depressive symptoms.

Symptom polarity also changes over time within an episode. That is, even if an episode begins with a relatively pure and stable mania, many individuals appear to experience depressive symptoms before achieving recovery. For initially manic individuals, the maximum level of depressive (MHRSD) symptoms displayed at some point before recovery averaged 14.03 ($SD = 9.44$, $N = 77$), approaching the clinical cutoff score of 17. These results suggest that individuals often experience a switch from manic to depressive symptoms before remission. In parallel, in our sample many "depressed" episodes include substantial manic symptoms during the acute episode or the recovery process.

In short, categorizing an episode as "manic" or "depressed" may obscure important variance. Depressive symptoms may have an important influence on the severity and duration of manic episodes, even when episodes do not meet criteria for mixed episodes. Given the complexity of these symptom profiles, studies in which the degree of change in depressive and manic symptom severity were estimated separately are more informative for this chapter than are studies of episodes. Relatively few studies have met this criterion.

Studies that have addressed psychosocial factors and bipolar depression can be categorized into three designs: (1) cross-sectional (or retrospective) studies, (2) prospective studies of episodes, and (3) prospective studies of symptom severity. Very few of the prospective studies have compared unipolar and bipolar depression directly. We now discuss the findings from these studies.

Socioenvironmental Predictors

Although a relatively large number of studies have focused on life events in bipolar disorder, few studies are prospective, and few evaluated whether events were caused by a person's illness (see Johnson & Roberts, 1995, for a review). More importantly, many studies included only individuals in a manic episode. As a result, they could not provide information about bipolar depression. At least six studies, though, have examined how life events contribute to depression within bipolar disorder. Two life event studies have examined rates of severe, independent life events occurring before depression episodes within bipolar disorder. Both found that 27–28% of individuals experienced life events before depressions, compared to approximately 8% of individuals who experienced life events during control periods (Hunt et al., 1992; McPherson, Herbison, & Romans, 1993).

As described by Norman and Malla (1993), designs for studying life events have varied greatly and often address quite different questions. In the studies just described, researchers examined the proportion of depressive episodes preceded by life events. Within-subject designs control for individual differences in vulnerability by comparing each person's symptoms before and after life events (see Norman & Malla, 1993, for a more detailed discussion; see Ellicott, Hammen, Gitlin, Brown, & Jamison, 1990, for such analyses within bipolar disorder). Our team (Johnson, Winett, Meyer, Greenhouse & Miller, 1999) conducted a prospective study to examine life events and social support as predictors of changes in the severity of depression and mania. Results suggested that both negative life events and low social support predicted depression, but neither predicted mania.

Given evidence that life events predict bipolar depression, one might wonder whether the links between negative life events and depression are comparable between unipolar and bipolar depression. Indeed, this does appear to be the case. Individuals with bipolar disorder and those with unipolar disorder have been found to report comparable rates of severe, independent life events before an episode of depression (Perris, 1984; Hammen, 1995). The Hammen study is notable for use of a prospective design and interview-based measures of life events. In this study, individuals with unipolar disorder appeared to generate a higher level of dependent events than individuals with bipolar disorder, although both groups appeared to experience substantial amounts of stress generation.

Isometsa, Heikinen, Henriksson, Aro, and Lonnquist (1995) compared the prevalence of life events preceding completed suicides of individuals with bipolar and unipolar disorder. Next-of-kin completed the Recent Life Change survey regarding stressors experienced by the deceased person before his or her death. Negative life events appeared to be equally common precipitants to suicide, in that 64% of bipolar individuals and 66% of unipolar individuals had experienced at least one negative life event shortly before their death.

In sum, the social environment appears to be important for understanding the course of bipolar depression. That is, negative life events frequently precede depression episodes and changes in depressive severity. Moreover, individuals with unipolar and bipolar disorder appear to experience comparable rates of independent life events before episode onsets or suicidal acts. Low social support also predicts increases in bipolar depression over time, as it does for unipolar depression. This body of evidence suggests strong overlap between the socioenvironmental factors that precede unipolar and bipolar depression.

Many of the socioenvironmental factors that have received attention within the unipolar literature, such as marital distress and expressed emotion, have not been examined as predictors of bipolar depression. Given well-replicated findings that expressed emotion predicts the course of bipolar disorder (Miklowitz et al., 1998; Priebe et al., 1989), family variables seem to be an important target for research on bipolar depression. The utility of exploring family and marital variables is supported by a recent finding that gender differences in the rates of bipolar depression are closely associated with marital status differences (Looby & Johnson, 2000), as has also been found in unipolar depression (Turner, 1994; Wu & DeMarris, 1996).

Personality Traits

Personality traits have been a focus in bipolar disorder for the better part of 100 years, as early psychodynamic theory hypothesized higher achievement-striving levels in this population. Most studies have tended to focus on whether individuals with bipolar disorder report elevated levels of certain personality traits compared to normal controls (cf. Solomon et al., 1996). Compared to individuals with unipolar depression, euthymic individuals with bipolar disorder appear to experience comparably elevated levels of neuroticism (Bagby et al., 1996; Goodwin & Jamison, 1990). Not surprisingly, individuals with bipolar disorder also appear to report high levels of positive affect and extraversion compared to individuals with unipolar depression (Bagby et al., 1996; Goodwin & Jamison, 1990). The distribution of neuroticism and positive affect within bipolar disorder appears correlated with the relative rate of episodes of depression and mania, respectively (Hecht, van Calker, Berger, & von Zerssen, 1998). These cross-sectional attempts to document personality disturbance associated with bipolar disorder, however, have been criticized for failing to attend to the toll of illness on personality measures (cf. Hirschfeld et al., 1983; Akiskal, Hirschfeld, & Yerevanian, 1983; Strakowski, Stoll, Tohen, Faedda, & Goodwin, 1993).

Despite potential changes in personality traits consequent to symptoms, a key question is whether relative levels of personality variables predict course. One study found that sociotropy predicted increases in symptom severity over time (summing across manic and depressive symptoms) in bipolar disorder (Hammen et al., 1992). But relatively few studies have examined how personality predicts depression within bipolar disorder. Recently, neuroticism was found to predict increases in bipolar depressive symptoms (but not manic symptoms) over time in one study of 39 individuals (Lozano & Johnson, 2001) and in another study of six individuals (Heerlein, Richter, Gonzalez, & Santander, 1998). These findings are remarkably congruent with those of five longitudinal studies in which neuroticism was the trait most consistently predictive of unipolar depression (Gunderson, Triebwasser, Phillips, & Sullivan, 1999). Overall, then, findings are congruent in suggesting that neuroticism is a predictor of unipolar and bipolar depression.

Cognitive Styles

The study of cognition in bipolar disorder has an interesting history. For decades, clinical writings on bipolar disorder emphasized unique cognitive styles. For example, Adler and other psychodynamic authors hypothesized that individuals with bipolar disorder have excessively high expectations. Adler also suggested that individuals with bipolar disorder use success to ward off an underlying feeling of insecurity (for a review, see Peven & Shulman, 1983).

During the 1970s, more specific studies of cognitive processes began to emerge. A set of studies focused on the effects of lithium on attention (Judd, Hubbard, Janowsky, Huey, & Takahashi, 1977; Johnson, 1988), as well as basic deficits in the selective attention of individuals with bipolar disorder (Johnson, 1986). One book reviewed evidence for attentional deficits as the potential pathophysiology of bipolar disorder (Johnson, 1984). Other investigators focused on information-processing bias for affectively relevant stimuli. For example, Weingartner, Miller, and Murphy (1977) published compelling data on how the valence of autobiographical recall shifted with the polarity of episodes in rapid cycling bipolar disorder. Their findings helped spur a large interest in mood-congruent and mood-dependent memory (Blaney, 1986; Bower, 1981), and replications have continued to establish that mood state influences the content of autobiographical recall among individuals with bipolar disorder (Eich, Macaulay, & Lam, 1997). Despite these intriguing findings, research on cognition in bipolar disorder seemed to enter a dry spell until recently, when several research teams returned to the topic. Indeed, a set of treatment manuals and articles on cognitive therapy for bipolar disorder have been published (Basco & Rush, 1996; Newman, Leahy, Beck, Reilly-Harrington, & Gyulai, 2002; Scott, 1995), as well as papers describing cognitive models of bipolar disorder (Leahy, 1999).

Current research on cognition is richly varied in methodology and designs. We describe studies focused on negative cognitive styles, as these studies appear to have the greatest overlap with studies of unipolar depression. We distinguish between studies that examine cognitive style during depression, cognitive style during remission, and those that use cognitive indices to predict depression.

Cognition during Depressive Episodes

Comparable to unipolar disorder, bipolar disorder is associated with a range of negative cognitive styles during depression, including elevated scores on the Attributional Style Questionnaire (Seligman et al., 1988), the Automatic Thoughts Questionnaire (Hill, Oei, & Hill, 1989; Hollon, Kendall, & Lumry, 1986), and the Dysfunctional Attitudes Scale (DAS; Hollon et al., 1986). Patients with bipolar depression also appear to demonstrate marked discrepancies between their descriptions of their actual selves and their "ideal" and "ought" selves (Bentall, Kinderman, & Manson, in press), and low self-esteem (Ashworth, Blackburn, & McPherson, 1982; Roy, 1991). Within both bipolar and unipolar disorder, attributions regarding failure have been found to correlate with depression severity (Seligman et al., 1988).

Cognition during Remission

Many of the negative cognitive facets documented during bipolar depression diminish with recovery. During remission, individuals with bipolar and unipolar disorder have been shown to obtain scores on the Automatic Thoughts Questionnaire within the normal range (Hollon et al., 1986) and to report self–ideal discrepancies, self-esteem levels, and attributions for negative events that are comparable to normal controls (Bentall et al., in press; Bentall & Thompson, 1990; Lyon, Startup, & Bentall, 1999; Tracy, Bauewens, Martin, Pardoen, & Mendlowicz, 1992; Winters & Neale, 1985). In some studies of remitted individuals, individuals with bipolar disorder make less stable attributions for negative events and report higher self-esteem than individuals with unipolar disorder (Ashworth, Blackburn, & McPherson, 1985; Tracy et al., 1992; Winters & Neale, 1985). Although these studies do not support cognitive vulnerability in bipolar disorder, other studies suggest that during remission individuals with bipolar disorder appear comparable to those with unipolar disorder on indices of a negative cognitive style. These cross-study discrepancies may be explained by heterogeneity in depression history among individuals with bipolar disorder, as well as by differences in the methods used to assess cognition.

UNDERSTANDING THE ROLE OF DEPRESSION HISTORY

As noted at the outset, not all individuals with bipolar disorder will experience depression. Given this, one might expect individuals with bipolar disorder to vary in their vulnerability for depression. In keeping with this, Alloy and her colleagues found that negative cognitive styles were associated with lifetime history of depression among a large study of undergraduates with lifetime hypomanic symptoms. That is, participants with no history of depression appeared similar to normal controls in their cognitive styles; those with a history of depression endorsed more negative cognitive styles than did controls (Alloy, Reilly-Harrington, Fresco, Whitehouse, & Zechmeister, 1999). Unfortunately, most other examinations of cognitive vulnerability have not considered lifetime history of depression.

METHODOLOGICAL ISSUES IN THE ASSESSMENT
OF COGNITION DURING REMISSION

Psychodynamic authors, including Helene Deutsch and Melanie Klein, described the "manic defense" in the 1930s (cf. Klein, 1994). This construct has continued to receive attention, as a series of later authors have suggested that defensiveness among individuals with bipolar disorder may interfere with the assessment of negative cognitive styles. Indeed, during remission, individuals with bipolar disorder have been found to report higher social desirability scores and greater defensiveness on MMPI validity indicators compared to individuals with unipolar disorder (Donnelly & Murphy, 1973; Donnelly, Murphy, & Goodwin, 1976). These results are difficult to interpret, however, because unipolar disorder has been characterized by a lack of positive illusions regarding the self (Alloy & Abramson, 1988; Taylor & Brown, 1988). Compared to normal controls, individuals with bipolar disorder in remission have not been found to appear defensive on standard personality measures (Hirschfeld, Klerman, Keller, Andreasen, & Clayton, 1986; Lumry, Gottesman, & Tuason, 1982), nor have those with a history of hypomanic symptoms (Bentall & Thompson, 1990).

Other evidence regarding defensiveness and bipolar disorder stems from the pattern of findings across different cognitive tasks. In an early study, Winters and Neale (1985) noted that individuals with bipolar disorder appeared similar to normal controls on overt measures of self-esteem. However, on a task described as more subtle, the Pragmatic Inference Task (PIT), individuals with bipolar disorder in remission obtained scores reflecting internal attributions for failure that were comparable to those of individuals with unipolar disorder. In addition, although PIT and self-esteem scores were correlated for individuals with unipolar disorder and those with no disorder, these scores were not correlated among individuals with bipolar disorder. In short, during remission, individuals with bipolar disorder appear to describe themselves more positively than those with unipolar disorder on some, but not all, measures. Across measures, there is greater inconsistency in the self-descriptions of individuals with bipolar disorder.

Given these findings, Bentall et al. (in press) have recommended that bipolar cognition should be measured with more subtle cognitive tasks, such as the PIT and an emotion Stroop task, rather than the Rosenberg Self-Esteem scale or the Attributional Style Questionnaire (ASQ). In two studies of undergraduates, a history of hypomanic symptoms has been related to interference for depressive words on an emotion Stroop task (Bentall & Thompson, 1990), even after controlling for anxiety levels (French, Richards, & Scholfield, 1996). In one study, individuals with bipolar I disorder did not appear biased in their attention to negative chimeric faces, although power in that study was limited (David, 1993).

In an examination of the subtle–overt distinction, Lyon et al. (1999) administered a battery of cognitive measures to patients during mania. As predicted, self-esteem scores and ASQ scores appeared comparable to those of nondisturbed controls during mania. Congruent with theory, individuals with unipolar and bipolar depression were comparable on internal attributions for failure on the PIT and information-processing bias for depressive words on an emotion Stroop task.

At this early stage of bipolar research, then, some measures appear more sensitive to negative cognitive style than others, particularly during remission. This appears to parallel the early literature on unipolar depression and cognition. As reviewed by Haaga, Dyck, and Ernst (1991), cognitive style failed to differentiate individuals with remitted unipolar depression from normal controls in many early studies. Indeed, some of these early studies suggested that individuals with remitted unipolar depression actually displayed less negative cognition than normal controls (see Segal & Ingram, 1994, p. 671).

In the unipolar research literature, there has been increasing recognition that schemas theoretically are quiescent until activated (Beck, 1967, 1976). Although various schema-activation strategies have been used, mood induction procedures have been particularly common (Williams, Watts, MacLeod, & Mathews, 1997). Even among individuals without a diagnostic history, anxious and depressed moods appear to increase the efficiency of information processing for negative stimuli (Mathews & MacLeod, 1994). Among individuals with a history of depression or anxiety, mood state appears to play an even more powerful role in information-processing biases. That is, a series of studies of unipolar depression and anxiety have shown that differences between remitted clinical populations and nondisturbed controls can be documented when individuals are in a negative mood state (Gotlib & Neubauer, 2000; Ingram, Bernet, & McLaughlin, 1994).

To date, most of the studies on bipolar disorder have not involved any schema-activation manipulation. We are aware of only one study that appeared to manipulate negative affect. After a period of self-focus, patients with remitted bipolar disorder demonstrated decreased latency to both sad and happy word sets on an emotion Stroop task, as well as significantly elevated DAS scores compared to normal controls (Lex, 2000). Findings from this study suggest that schema-activation manipulations may enhance the ability to detect underlying negative *and* positive information-processing biases.

In an early study bearing on this issue, Stern and Berrenberg (1979) identified undergraduates who obtained high scores on a hypomania symptom scale and tested them 6 weeks later. Undergraduates with a history of mild hypomanic symptoms were more likely to attribute success to their own skill and to expect success on future lab tasks than were other participants. These differential attributions emerged only after success feedback; after failure and even-handed success–failure feedback, hypomania-prone individuals could not be differentiated from control participants. It is unclear, however, whether the failure feedback induced a negative mood. These early findings suggest that both negative and positive mood primes will be important to consider in evaluating the information-processing biases of individuals with bipolar disorder.

In sum, there is a growing body of evidence regarding cognition in bipolar disorder. During depression, individuals with bipolar and unipolar disorder manifest strikingly parallel cognitive styles. Much of the research suggests that cognitive styles are relatively state-dependent in bipolar disorder, in that many negative cognitive style parameters observed during depression are less demonstrable with recovery. In this way, findings regarding unipolar and bipolar depression appear similar.

It seems important to attend to the lessons from the literature on unipolar depression, which suggests methodological and conceptual issues that must be addressed to document cognitive vulnerability during remission. Key methodological issues with respect to research on bipolar disorder include (1) heterogeneity in depression history, (2) defensiveness, and (3) priming to activate cognitive schemas. We are unaware of any one study that addresses all of these issues. Nonetheless, a series of studies address each point independently, and the findings from these studies are promising for identifying a depressogenic cognitive style during periods of remission from bipolar disorder.

Cognitive Styles as Predictors of Depression

As the cross-sectional evidence regarding these cognitive styles has expanded, there is a need to understand the importance of these styles for course. Among undergraduates with a life-time diagnosis of a mood disorder (either bipolar spectrum disorder or unipolar depression), one study found that DAS, ASQ, and self-referential encoding of negative information each interacted with negative events to predict increases in depressive symptoms across a 1-month period (Reilly-Harrington, Alloy, Fresco, & Whitehouse, 1999). Unfortunately, separate analyses were not reported for individuals with bipolar spectrum versus unipolar disorders.

Few other studies have studied the prospective role of cognition in the prediction of bipolar depression. To the extent that self-esteem measures have bearing for understanding cognition, one other study appears relevant. We found that low self-esteem predicted greater increases in depression over time, but not greater increases in mania (Johnson, Meyer, Winett, & Small, 2000). Hence, early data suggest that negative cognitive styles may help predict bipolar depression.

PSYCHOSOCIAL TREATMENT

Given the concordance between the risk factors for bipolar and unipolar depression, one might expect that treatment strategies that are effective for unipolar disorder would be helpful in alleviating bipolar depression. This is a particularly important question, as many of the traditional mood stabilizers for bipolar disorder appear to be less effective for depression than for mania (Hlastala et al., 1997). To date, two of the most carefully researched psychotherapies for bipolar disorder—family therapy and interpersonal psychotherapy—appear to relieve bipolar depression but not mania (Frank, Kupfer, et al., 2000; Miklowitz et al., 2000). Given evidence for the effectiveness of these approaches for unipolar depression (DeRubeis & Crits-Cristoph, 1998; Frank, Grochocinski, et al., 2000; Kolko, Brent, Baugher, Bridge, & Birmaher, 2000), bipolar depression might be similar to unipolar depression in psychotherapy responsiveness.

SUMMARY AND CONCLUSIONS

Many of the variables that contribute to the course of unipolar depression also appear to contribute to the course of bipolar depression. That is, negative life events, low social support, neuroticism, negative cognitive styles, and low self-esteem may each help predict depression within bipolar disorder. Given this, psychosocial models from unipolar depression appear to have robust applicability for understanding bipolar depression. One unanswered question is whether other variables that have been important in unipolar depression, such as marital and family functioning, will also play a specific role in the prediction of depression within bipolar disorder.

Throughout this chapter we have emphasized the similarities between unipolar and bipolar depression. Obviously, any comprehensive model of bipolar disorder as a whole must consider mania. Theories regarding the differences between mood disorders with and without mania abound, dating back to the early 1900s (Kraepelin, 1921; Whybrow & Mendels, 1969). In this regard, it is of interest that many of the psychosocial variables that predict unipolar and bipolar depression appear less important in the prediction of mania (Johnson et al., 1999, Johnson, Meyer, et al., 2000; Miklowitz et al., 2000). In a recent review, we have suggested that the variables that predict mania may be integrally tied to an underlying biological diathesis (Johnson et al., in press). A consideration of mania is beyond the scope of this chapter; the interested reader is referred to a series of articles focused on unique biological (Chiaroni et al., 2000; El Mallakh et al., 1996), personality (Meyer, Johnson, & Winters, 2001; Strakowski et al., 1993; von Zerssen, 1996; Young et al., 1995), and life event (Johnson, Sandrow, et al., 2000; Malkoff-Schwartz et al., 1998) predictors of mania.

Setting aside the prediction of mania, are the depressive episodes of bipolar and unipolar disorder entirely similar? Clinical intuition and preliminary data suggest that there is a unique aspect of the pathology of bipolar disorder that has importance in considering depression. Bipolar disorder appears to be fundamentally characterized by marked extremes and fluctuations. The shift from depression to mania is the most commonly noted manifestation of an underlying dysregulation. However, mood lability and cyclothymia also appear to be precursors of the development of mania (Egeland, Hostetter, Pauls, & Sussex, 2000; von Zerssen, 1993), and after the onset of bipolar disorder mood variability continues to predict the course of disorder (Goodnick, Fieve, Schlegel, & Kaufman, 1987). Family members of probands with mania are at elevated risk for cyclothymia and rapid mood fluctuations (Maier, Minges, Lichtermann, Franke, & Gansicke, 1995). Depue's model has emphasized dysregulation as a core component of the neurobiology of bipolar disorder, and individuals with bipolar spectrum disorders do appear to have greater difficulties in mood and cortisol regulation following challenges than do controls (Depue, Krauss, & Spoont, 1987). The theme of dysregulation, then, appears to emerge in a series of studies on the biology, precursors, and symptoms patterns of bipolar disorder.

We believe that this dysregulation has relevance for understanding depression within bipolar disorder as well as mania. Although Hollon (1992) has noted the importance of dysregulation in cognitive and biological models of unipolar depression, we noted above that bipolar disorder appears to contain more frequent episodes and more abrupt depression onsets than unipolar disorder. Hence, bipolar disorder may be associated with greater dysregulation than unipolar disorder, and this greater dysregulation may explain many of the differences between unipolar and bipolar depression.

Aside from the possible differences in dysregulation, our review suggests that bipolar and unipolar depression share marked commonalities in neurotransmitter levels, course, clinical features, and psychosocial antecedents. Historically, bipolar depression has been viewed as fundamentally more biologically driven than unipolar depression. This may be true, but our review suggests that traditional assumptions about how biological vulnerability unfolds are worth challenging. That is, bipolar depression appears to be influenced by the same psychological and environmental variables that influence the course of unipolar depression. If commonalities are supported in ongoing research, we believe this suggests strong hope for applying psychological treatments for unipolar disorder as adjunctive treatments for bipolar disorder.

FUTURE DIRECTIONS

Our current model suggests three testable tenets: (1) bipolar and unipolar depression are predicted by comparable psychosocial variables, (2) mania and depression are predicted by separate psychosocial variables within bipolar disorder, and (3) bipolar disorder (including both depressive and manic poles) is characterized by more dysregulation than unipolar disorder. However, the evidence for each of these tenets is quite limited, and much more careful research is needed for each.

At a basic level, there is a need to replicate early findings on the predictors of bipolar depression and to conduct comprehensive longitudinal studies to assess how predictors interact with each other. While this may seem to be a straightforward task, a myriad of issues are likely to complicate these studies. Of most importance, investigators must begin to address issues that undermine the ability to differentiate the underlying characteristics of disorders from the aftermath of symptoms and treatment patterns. This involves a number of considerations in sample definition, measurement, and study design.

In regard to sample definition, recruiting carefully controlled samples of individuals with bipolar and unipolar disorder is an ambitious task. We hope our review has highlighted the importance of considering confounds such as the duration of illness, number of episodes, and medication profiles. Given the difficulty in identifying well-matched samples of individuals with bipolar and unipolar depression, we suspect that studies will often rely on statistical matching on these important illness and treatment parameters.

Beyond sample definition, there is a fundamental need for more careful assessment strategies for both predictors and outcomes. Perhaps the best illustration of the difficulties in assessing predictors comes from the set of issues facing researchers in the area of cognition. By addressing these issues, however, the field is likely to gain a much more certain understanding of commonalities between bipolar and unipolar disorder. We hope that researchers will be intrigued enough by the parallels to conduct the next generation of studies.

Beyond possible overlap between unipolar and bipolar depression, there are also likely to be unique facets associated with each disorder. One of the more intriguing questions is the nature of dysregulation across disorders, and the implications of dysregulation for understanding the relative vulnerability to psychosocial challenges. Capturing this dysregulation mandates careful, time-dependent analyses of prospective, repeated measures data. Observing slices of functioning and risk at one point in time may obscure a fundamental dynamic process. How does such dysregulation influence symptom expression in the face of negative life events, social isolation, or maladaptive cognitive styles? If bipolar disorder is associated with greater dysregulation than unipolar disorder, one might expect more dramatic responses to psychosocial challenges in bipolar disorder compared to unipolar disorder. Addressing this question could be facilitated by studies comparing effect sizes for predictor variables in unipolar and bipolar depression. Unfortunately, we were unable to locate a single study that specifically provided such contrasts. Without such a study, our conclusions about the commonalities in bipolar and unipolar depression remain surprisingly tentative.

In sum, there is evidence to suggest that drawing from the literature on unipolar depression will foster greater understanding of the depressive pole of bipolar disorder. We hope that others will be encouraged to consider the intriguing comparisons between unipolar and bipolar depression. The results of such investigations are expected to yield new insights into etiological models and treatment strategies.

REFERENCES

Abrams, R., & Taylor, M. A. (1974). Unipolar and bipolar depressive illness. *Archives of General Psychiatry, 30,* 320–321.

Abrams, R., & Taylor, M. A. (1980). A comparison of unipolar and bipolar affective illness. *American Journal of Psychiatry, 137,* 1084–1087.

Akiskal, H. S., Hirschfeld, R. M. A., & Yerevanian, B. I., 1983. The relationship of personality to affective disorders. *Archives of General Psychiatry, 40,* 801–810.

Alloy, L. B., & Abramson, L. Y. (1988). Depressive realism: Four theoretical perspectives. In L.B. Alloy (Ed.), *Cognitive processes in depression* (pp. 223–265). New York: Guilford Press.

Alloy, L. B., Reilly-Harrington, N., Fresco, D. M., Whitehouse, W. G., & Zechmeister, J. S. (1999). Cognitive styles and life events in subsyndromal unipolar and bipolar disorders: Stability and prospective prediction of depressive and hypomanic mood swings. *Journal of Cognitive Psychotherapy, 13*(1), 21–40.

American Psychiatric Association. (2000). *Diagnostic and statistical manual of mental disorders* (4th ed., text rev.). Washington, DC: Author.

Ashworth, C. M., Blackburn, I. M., & McPherson, F. M. (1982). The performance of depressed and manic patients on some repertory grid measures: A cross-sectional study. *British Journal of Medical Psychology, 55,* 247–255.

Ashworth, C. M., Blackburn, I. M., & McPherson, F. M. (1985). The performance of depressed and manic patients on some repertory grid measures: A longitudinal study. *British Journal of Medical Psychology, 58,* 337–342.

Bagby, R. M., Young, L. T., Schuller, D. R., Bindseil, K. D., Cooke, R. G., Dickens, S. E., Levitt, A. J., & Joffe, R. T. (1996). Bipolar disorder, unipolar depression and the five-factor model of personality. *Journal of Affective Disorders, 41,* 25–32.

Barbarini, B., Colombo, C., Benedetti, F., Campori, E., Bellodi, L., & Smeraldi, E. (1998). The unipolar–bipolar dichotomy and the response to sleep deprivation. *Psychiatry Research, 79,* 43–50.

Basco, M. R., & Rush, A. J. (1996). *Cognitive-behavioral therapy for bipolar disorder.* New York: Guilford Press.

Beck, A. T. (1967). *Depression: Clinical, experimental, and theoretical aspects.* New York: Harper & Row.

Beck, A. T. (1976). *Cognitive therapy and the emotional disorders.* New York: International Universities Press.

Beigel, A., & Murphy, D. L. (1971). Unipolar and bipolar affective illness: Differences in clinical characteristics accompanying depression. *Archives of General Psychiatry, 24,* 215–230.

Bentall, R. P., Kinderman, P., & Manson, K. (in press). Self-discrepancies in bipolar disorder. *Cognitive Therapy and Research.*

Bentall, R. P., & Thompson, M. (1990). Emotional Stroop performance and the manic defense. *British Journal of Clinical Psychology, 29,* 235–237.

Berghöfer, A., Kossmann, B., & Müller-Oerlinghausen, B. (1996). Course of illness and pattern of recurrences in patients with affective disorders during long-term lithium prophylaxis: A retrospective analysis over 15 years. *Acta Psychiatrica Scandinavica, 93,* 349–354.

Bertelsen, A., Harvald, B., & Hauge, M. (1977). A Danish twin study of manic–depressive disorders. *British Journal of Psychiatry, 130,* 330–351.

Black, D. W., & Nasrallah, A. (1989). Hallucinations and delusions in 1,715 patients with unipolar and bipolar affective disorders. *Psychopathology, 22,* 28–34.

Blaney, P. H. (1986). Affect and memory: A review. *Psychological Bulletin, 99*(2), 229–246.

Bowden, C. L., Huang, L. G., Javors, M. A., Johnson, J. M., Seleshi, E., McIntyre, K., Contreras, S., & Maas, J. W. (1988). Calcium function in affective disorders and healthy controls. *Biological Psychiatry, 23,* 367–376.

Bowden, C. L., Koslow, S., Maas, J. W., Davis, J., Garver, D. L., & Hanin, I. (1987). Changes in urinary catecholamines and their metabolites in depressed patients treated with amitriptyline or imipramine. *Journal of Psychiatric Research, 21,* 111–128.

Bower, G. H. (1981). Mood and memory. *American Psychologist, 36,* 129–148.

Breslau, N., & Meltzer, H. Y. (1998). Validity of subtyping psychotic depression: Examination of phenomenology and demographic characteristics. *American Journal of Psychiatry, 145,* 35–40.

Brockington, I. F., Altman, E., Hillier, V., Meltzer, H. Y., & Nand, S. (1982). The clinical picture of bipolar affective disorder in its depressive phase: A report from London and Chicago. *British Journal of Psychiatry, 141,* 558–562.

Brown, G. W., & Harris, T. O. (1978). *Social origins of depression: A study of psychiatric disorder in women.* New York: Free Press.

Brown, G. W., & Harris, T. O. (1982). Fall-off in the reporting of life events. *Social Psychiatry, 17,* 23–28.

Brown, G. W., & Harris, T. O. (Eds.). (1989). *Life events and illness.* New York: Guilford Press.

Butzlaff, R. L., & Hooley, J. M. (1998). Expressed emotion and psychiatric relapse: A meta-analysis. *Archives of General Psychiatry, 55,* 547–552.

Chiaroni, P., Azorin, J. M., Dassa, D., Henry, J. M., Giudicelli, S., Malthiery, Y., & Planells, R. (2000). Possible involvement of the dopamine D_3 receptor locus in subtypes of bipolar affective disorder. *Psychiatric Genetics, 10,* 43–49.

Clark, L., Watson, D., & Mineka, S. (1994). Temperament, personality, and the mood and anxiety disorders. *Journal of Abnormal Psychology, 103,* 103–116.

Coryell, W., Andreasen, N. C., Endicott, J., & Keller, M. (1987). The significance of past mania or hypomania in the course and outcome of major depression. *American Journal of Psychiatry, 144,* 309–315.

Coryell, W., Endicott, J., Keller, M., Andreasen, N., Grove, W., Hirschfeld, R. M. A., & Scheftner, W. (1989). Bipolar affective disorder and high achievement: A familial association. *American Journal of Psychiatry, 146,* 983–988.

Coryell, W., Keller, M., Endicott, J., Andreasen, N., Clayton, P., & Hirschfeld, R. (1989). Bipolar II illness: Course and outcome over a five-year period. *Psychological Medicine, 19,* 129–141.

Coyne, J. C. (2000). Thinking interactionally about depression: A radical restatement. In T. Joiner and J. C. Coyne (Eds.), *The interactional nature of depression: Advances in interpersonal approaches* (pp. 365–369). Washington, DC: American Psychological Association.

Coyne, J. C., & Whiffen, V. E. (1995). Issues in personality as a diathesis for depression: The case of sociotropy–dependency and autonomy–self-criticism. *Psychological Bulletin, 118,* 358–378.

David, A. S. (1993). Spatial and selective attention in the cerebral hemispheres in depression, mania, and schizophrenia. *Brain and Cognition, 23,* 166–180.

Davila, J., & Bradbury, T. N. (1998). Psychopathology and the marital dyad. In L. L'Abate (Ed.), *Family psychopathology: The relational roots of dyfunctional behavior* (pp. 127–157). New York: Guilford Press.

Depue, R. A., Krauss, S. P., & Spoont, M. R. (1987). A two-dimensional threshold model of seasonal bipolar affective disorder. In D. Magnuson & A. Ohman (Eds.), *Psychopathology: An interactional perspective* (pp. 95–123). San Diego: Academic Press.

Depue, R. A., & Monroe, S. M. (1978). The unipolar–bipolar distinction in the depressive disorders. *Psychological Bulletin, 85,* 1001–1029.

Depue, R. A., & Zald, D. H. (1993). Biological and environmental processes in nonpsychotic psychopathology: A neurobiological perspective. In C.G. Costello (Ed.), *Basic issues in psychopathology* (pp. 127–237). New York: Guilford Press.

DeRubeis, R. J., & Crits-Christoph, P. (1998). Empirically supported individual and group psychological treatments for adult mental disorders. *Journal of Consulting and Clinical Psychology, 66,* 37–52.

Donnelly, E. F., & Murphy, D. L. (1973). Social desirability and bipolar affective disorder. *Journal of Consulting and Clinical Psychology, 41,* 469.

Donnelly, E. F., Murphy, D. L., & Goodwin, F. K. (1976). Cross-sectional and longitudinal comparisons of bipolar and unipolar depressed groups on the MMPI. *Journal of Consulting and Clinical Psychology, 44,* 233–237.

Drevets, W. C., Price, J. L, Simpson, J. R., Jr., Todd, R. D., Reich, T., Vannier, M., & Raichle, M. E. (1997). Subgenual prefrontal cortex abnormalities in mood disorders. *Nature, 386,* 824–827.

Dubovsky, S. L., Christiano, J., Daniell, L. C., Franks, R. D., Murphy, J., Adler, L., Baker, N., & Harris, R. A. (1989). Increased platelet intracellular calcium concentration in patients with bipolar affective disorders. *Archives of General Psychiatry, 46,* 632–638.

Dubovsky, S. L., Lee, C., Christiano, J., & Murphy, J. (1991). Elevated platelet intracellular calcium concentration in bipolar depression. *Biological Psychiatry, 29,* 441–450.

Dubovsky, S. L., Thomas, M., Hijazi, A., & Murphy, J. (1994). Intracellular calcium signalling in peripheral cells of patients with bipolar affective disorder. *European Archives of Psychiatry and Clinical Neuroscience, 243*(5), 229–234.

Ebert, D., & Berger, M. (1998). Neurobiological similarities in antidepressant sleep deprivation and psychostimulant use: A psychostimulant theory of antidepressant sleep deprivation. *Psychopharmacology, 140,* 1–10.

Egeland, J. A., Hostetter, A. M., Pauls, D.L., & Sussex, J. N. (2000). Prodromal symptoms before onset of manic–depressive disorder suggested by first hospital admission histories. *Journal of the American Academy of Child and Adolescent Psychiatry, 39,* 1245–1252.

Eich, E., Macaulay, D., & Lam, R. W. (1997). Mania, depression, and mood-dependent memory. *Cognition and Emotion, 11,* 607–618.

Ellicott, A. G. (1989). A prospective study of life stress and bipolar illness (doctoral dissertation, University of California, 1989). *Dissertation Abstracts International, 49,* 2851–2852.

Ellicott, A. G., Hammen, C., Gitlin, M., Brown, G., & Jamison, K. (1990). Life events and the course of bipolar disorder. *American Journal of Psychiatry, 147*(9), 1194–1198.

El-Mallakh, R. S., Li, R., Worth, C. A., & Peiper, S. C. (1996). Leukocyte transmembrane potential in bipolar illness. *Journal of Affective Disorders, 41,* 33–37.

Endicott, J., Nee, J., Andreasen, N., Clayton, P., Keller, M., & Coryell, W. (1985). Bipolar II: Combine or keep separate? *Journal of Affective Disorders, 8,* 17–28.

First, M. B., Spitzer, R. L., Gibbon, M., & Williams, J. B. W. (1996). *Structured Clinical Interview for DSM-IV Axis I Disorders: Patient edition (SCID-I-I/P Version 2.0).* (Available from the Biometrics Research Department, New York State Psychiatric Institute, 722 West 168th Street, New York, NY, 10032)

Frank, E., Grochocinski, V. J., Spanier, C. A., Buysse, D. J., Cherry, C. R., Houck, P. R., Stapf, D. M., & Kupfer, D. J. (2000). Interpersonal psychotherapy and antidepressant medication: Evaluation of a sequential treatment strategy in women with recurrent major depression. *Journal of Clinical Psychiatry, 61,* 51–57.

Frank, E., Kupfer, D. J., Gibbons, R., Houck, P., Kostelnik, B., Mallinger, A., Swartz, H. A., & Thase, M. E. (2000). Interpersonal and social rhythm therapy prevents depressive symptoms in patients with bipolar I disorder. In D. Miklowitz (Chair.), *Is the course of manic–depressive illness influenced by psychosocial factors?: Lessons from observational and treatment studies.* Symposium conducted at the fifteenth annual meeting of the Society for Research on Psychopathology, Boulder, CO.

French, C. C., Richards, A., & Scholfield, E. J. C. (1996). Hypomania, anxiety and the emotional Stroop. *British Journal of Clinical Psychology, 35,* 617–626.

Giles, D. E., Rush, A.J., & Roffwarg, H.P. (1986). Sleep parameters in bipolar I, bipolar II, and unipolar depressions. *Biological Psychiatry, 21,* 1340–1343.

Goldberg, J. F., Harrow, M., & Grossman, L. S. (1995a). Course and outcome in bipolar affective disorder: A longitudinal follow-up study. *American Journal of Psychiatry, 152,* 379–384.

Goldberg, J. F., Harrow, M., & Grossman, L. S. (1995b). Recurrent affective syndromes in bipolar and unipolar mood disorders at follow-up. *British Journal of Psychiatry, 166,* 382–385.

Goodnick, P. J. (1997). *Mania: Clinical and research perspectives.* Washington, DC: American Psychiatric Press.

Goodnick, P. J., Fieve, R. R., Schlegel, A., & Kaufman, K. (1987). Inter-episode major and subclinical symptoms in affective disorder. *Acta Psychiatrica Scandinavica, 75,* 597–600.

Goodwin, F. K., & Jamison, K. R. (1990). *Manic–depressive illness.* Oxford, UK: Oxford University Press.

Gotlib, I. H., & Neubauer, D. L., (2000). Information-processing approaches to the study of cognitive biases in depression. In S. L. Johnson, A. M. Hayes, T. Field, N. Schneiderman, & P. McCabe

(Eds.), *Stress, coping and depression: Proceedings of the Fifteenth Annual Stress and Coping Conference* (pp. 117–144). Mahwah, NJ: Erlbaum.

Gunderson, J. G., Triebwasser, J., Phillips, K. A., & Sullivan, C. N. (1999). Personality and vulnerability to affective disorders. In R. C. Cloninger (Ed.), Personality and psychopathology (pp. 3–32). Washington, DC: American Psychiatric Press.

Gurpegui, M., Casanova, J., & Cervera, S. (1985). Clinical and neuroendocrine features of endogenous unipolar and bipolar depression. *Acta Psychiatrica Scandinavica, 72*(Suppl. 320), 30–37.

Guze, S. B., Woodruff, R. A., & Clayton, P. J. (1975). The significance of psychotic affective disorders. *Archives of General Psychiatry, 32,* 1147–1150.

Haaga, D., Dyck, M. J., & Ernst, D. (1991). Empirical status of cognitive theory of depression. *Psychological Bulletin, 110,* 215–236.

Hammen, C. L. (1995). Stress and the course of unipolar and bipolar disorders. In C. M. Mazure (Ed.), *Progress in psychiatry: No. 46. Does stress cause psychiatric illness?* (pp. 87–110). Washington, DC: American Psychiatric Press.

Hammen, C. L., Ellicott, A., & Gitlin, M. (1992). Stressors and sociotropy/autonomy: A longitudinal study of their relationship to the course of bipolar disorder. *Cognitive Therapy, 16,* 409–418.

Hammen, C. L., Ellicott, A., Gitlin, M., & Jamison, K. (1989). Sociotropy/autonomy and vulnerability to specific life events in patients with unipolar depression and bipolar disorders. *Journal of Abnormal Psychology, 98,* 154–160.

Hecht, H., van Calker, D., Berger, M., & von Zerssen, D. (1998). Personality in patients with affective disorders and their relatives. *Journal of Affective Disorders, 51,* 33–43.

Heerlein, A., Richter, P., Gonzalez, M., & Santander, J., 1998. Personality patterns and outcome in depressive and bipolar disorders. *Psychopathology, 31,* 15–22.

Hill, C. V., Oei, T. P., & Hill, M. A. (1989). An empirical investigation of the specificity and sensitivity of the Automatic Thoughts Questionnaire and Dysfunctional Attitudes Scale. *Journal of Psychopathology and Behavioral Assessment, 11,* 291–311.

Hirschfeld, R. M. A., Klerman, G. L., Clayton, P. J., Keller, M. B., Mcdonald-Scott, P., & Larkin, B. H. (1983). Assessing personality: Effects of the depressive state on trait measurement. *American Journal of Psychiatry, 140,* 695–699.

Hirschfeld, R.M.A., Klerman, G. L., Keller, M. B., Andreasen, N. C., & Clayton, P. J. (1986). Personality of recovered patients with bipolar affective disorder. *Journal of Affective Disorders, 11,* 83–89.

Hlastala, S. A., Frank, E., Mallinger, A., Thase, M. E., Ritenour, A., & Kupfer, D. J. (1997). Bipolar depression: An underestimated treatment challenge. *Depression and Anxiety, 5,* 73–83.

Hollon, S. D. (1992). Cognitive models of depression from a psychobiological perspective. *Psychological Inquiry, 3,* 250–253.

Hollon, S. D., Kendall, P. C., & Lumry, A. (1986). Specificity of depressotypic cognitions in clinical depression. *Journal of Abnormal Psychology, 95,* 52–59.

Hunt, N., Bruce-Jones, W. D., & Silverstone, T. (1992). Life events and relapse in bipolar affective disorder. *Journal of Affective Disorders, 25*(1), 13–20.

Ingram, R. E., Bernet, C. Z., & McLaughlin, S. C. (1994). Attentional allocation processes in individuals at risk for depression. *Cognitive Therapy and Research, 18,* 317–332.

Isometsa, E., Heikinen, M., Henriksson, M., Aro, H., & Lonnquist, J. (1995). Recent life events and completed suicide in bipolar affective disorder: A comparison with major depressive suicides. *Journal of Affective Disorders, 33,* 99–106.

Johnson, F. N. (1984). The psychopharmacology of lithium. London: Macmillan.

Johnson, F. N. (1986). Different treatment modalities for recurrent bipolar affective disorders: An integrative approach. *Psychotherapy and Psychosomatics, 46,* 13–22.

Johnson, F. N. (1988). Signal detection analysis of information processing in patients receiving prophylactic lithium therapy. *Human Psychopharmacology Clinical and Experimental, 3,* 95–100.

Johnson, S. L., Meyer, B., Winett, C., & Small, J. (2000). Social support and self-esteem predict changes in bipolar depression but not mania. *Journal of Affective Disorders, 58,* 79–86.

Johnson, S. L., & Miller, I. (1997). Negative life events and recovery from episodes of bipolar disorder. *Journal of Abnormal Psychology, 106,* 449–457.

Johnson, S. L., & Roberts, J. R. (1995). Life events and bipolar disorder: Implications from biological theories. *Psychological Bulletin, 117,* 434–449.

Johnson, S. L., Sandrow, D., Meyer, B., Winters, R., Miller, I., Keitner, G., & Solomon, D. (2000). Increases in manic symptoms after life events involving goal attainment. *Journal of Abnormal Psychology, 109,* 721–727.

Johnson, S. L., Winett, C., Meyer, B., Greenhouse, W., & Miller, I. (1999). Social support and the course of bipolar disorder. *Journal of Abnormal Psychology, 108,* 558–566.

Johnson, S. L., Winters, R., & Meyer, B. (in press). The role of the social environment in bipolar disorder: A polarity-specific model. In Thomas Joiner (Ed.), *A festschrift for J. Hokanson.* Washington, DC: American Psychological Association.

Judd, L. L., Hubbard, B., Janowsky, D. S., Huey, L. Y., & Takahashi, K. I. (1977). The effect of lithium carbonate on the cognitive functions of normal subjects. *Archives of General Psychiatry, 34,* 355–377.

Kaplan, H. I., & Sadock, B. J. (1998). *Synopsis of psychiatry: Behavioral sciences/clinical psychiatry* (8th ed.). Philadelphia: Lippincott Williams & Wilkins.

Karkowski, L. M., & Kendler, K. S. (1997). An examination of the genetic relationship between bipolar and unipolar illness in an epidemiological sample. *Psychiatric Genetics, 7,* 159–163.

Katz, M. M., Robins, E., Croughan, J., Secunda, S., & Swann, A. (1982). Behavioural measurement and drug response characteristics of unipolar and bipolar depression. *Psychological Medicine, 12,* 25–36.

Kessing, L. V., Andersen, P. K., Mortensen, P. B., & Bolwig, T. G. (1998). Recurrence in affective disorder: I. Case register study. *British Journal of Psychiatry, 172,* 23–28.

Kessing, L. V., & Mortensen, P. B. (1999). Recovery from episodes during the course of affective disorder: A case-register study. *Acta Psychiatrica Scandinavica, 100,* 279–287.

Kessler, R. C., McGonagle, K. A., Zhao, S., Nelson, C. B., Hughes, M., Eshelman, S., Wittchen, H., & Kendler, K. S. (1994). Lifetime and 12-month prevalence of DSM-III-R psychiatric disorders in the United States: Results from the National Comorbidity Survey. *Archives of General Psychiatry, 51,* 8–19.

Kessler, R. C., Rubinow, D. R., Holmes, C., Abelson, J. M., & Zhao, S. (1997). The epidemiology of DSM-III-R bipolar I disorder in a general population survey. *Psychological Medicine, 27,* 1079–1089.

Klein, M. (1994). Mourning and its relation to manic–depressive states. In R. V. Frankiel (Ed.), *Essential papers on object loss. Essential papers in psychoanalysis* (pp. 95–122). New York: State University of New York Press.

Kolko, D. J., Brent, D. A., Baugher, M., Bridge, J., & Birmaher, B. (2000). Cognitive and family therapies for adolescent depression: Treatment specificity, mediation, and moderation. *Journal of Consulting and Clinical Psychology, 68,* 603–614.

Kraepelin, E. (1921). *Manic–depressive insanity and paranoia* (R. M. Barclay & G. M. Robertson, Trans.). Edinburgh: E. & S. Livingston.

Kuhs, H., & Reschke, D. (1992). Psychomotor activity in unipolar and bipolar depressive patients. *Psychopathology, 25,* 109–116.

Kupfer, D. J., Weiss, B. L., Foster, F. G., Detre, T. P., Delgado, J., & McPartland, R. (1974). Psychomotor activity in affective states. *Archives of General Psychiatry, 30,* 765–768.

Leahy, R. L. (1999). Decision-making and mania. *Journal of Cognitive Psychotherapy, 13,* 83–105.

Lester, D. (1993). Suicidal behavior in bipolar and unipolar affective disorders: A meta-analysis. *Journal of Affective Disorders, 27,* 117–121.

Lex, C. (2000). *Kognitive Verarbeitung bei Bipolarer Depression* [Cognitive processing in bipolar depression]. (Unpublished master's thesis, University of Vienna, Vienna, Austria).

Looby, S., & Johnson, S. L. (2000). *Marital status and the gender difference in bipolar depression.* Manuscript submitted for publication.

Lozano, B., & Johnson, S. L. (2001). Personality traits on the NEO-V as predictors of depression and mania. *Journal of Affective Disorders, 63,* 103–111.

Lumry, A. E., Gottesman, I. I., & Tuason, V. B. (1982). MMPI state dependency during the course of bipolar psychosis. *Psychiatry Research, 7,* 59–67.

Lyon, H. M., Startup, M., & Bentall, R. P. (1999). Social cognition and the manic defense: Attributions, selective attention, and self-schema in bipolar affective disorder. *Journal of Abnormal Psychology, 108,* 273–282.

Maier, W., Minges, J., Lichtermann, D., Franke, P., & Gansicke, M. (1995). Personality patterns in subjects at risk for affective disorders. *Psychopathology, 28*(Suppl. 1), 59–72.

Malkoff-Schwartz, S., Frank, E., Anderson, B., Sherrill, J. T., Siegel, L., Patterson, D., & Kupfer, D. J. (1998). Stressful life events and social rhythm disruption in the onset of manic and depressive bipolar episodes. *Archives of General Psychiatry, 55,* 702–707.

Manki, H., Kanba, S., Muramatsu, T., Higuchi, S., Suzuki, E., Matsushita, S., Ono, Y., Chiba, H., Shintani, F., Nakamura, M., Yagi, G., & Asai, M. (1996). Dopamine D_2, D_3, and D_4 receptor and transport gene polymorphisms and mood disorders. *Journal of Affective Disorders, 40,* 7–13.

Mann, J. (1979). Altered platelet monoamine oxidase activity in affective disorders. *Psychological Medicine, 9,* 729–736.

Mathews, J. M. G., & MacLeod, C. (1994). Cognitive approaches to emotion and emotional disorders. *Annual Review of Psychology, 45,* 25–50.

McPherson, H., Herbison, P., & Romans, S. (1993). Life events and relapse in established bipolar affective disorder. *British Journal of Psychiatry, 163,* 381–385.

Meyer, B., Johnson, S. L., & Winters, R. (2001). Responsiveness to threat and incentive in bipolar disorder: Relations of the BIS/BAS scale with symptoms. *Journal of Psychopathology and Behavioral Assessment, 23,* 133–143.

Miklowitz, D. J., Goldstein, M. J., Nuechterlein, K. H., & Snyder, K. S. (1998). Family factors and the course of bipolar affective disorder. *Archives of General Psychiatry, 45,* 225–231.

Miklowitz, D. J., Simoneau, T. L., George, E. L., Richards, J. A., Kalbag, A., Sachs-Ericsson, N., & Suddath, R. (2000). Family-focused treatment of bipolar disorder: 1-year effects of a psychoeducational program in conjunction with pharmacotherapy. *Biological Psychiatry, 48,* 582–592.

Miller, I. W., Bishop, S., Norman, W. H., & Maddever, H. (1985). The Modified Hamilton Rating Scale for Depression: Reliability and validity. *Psychiatry Research, 14,* 131–142.

Mitchell, P., Parker, G., Jamieson, K., Wilhelm, K., Hickie, I., Brodaty, H., Boyce, P., Hadzi-Pavlovic, D., & Roy, K. (1992). Are there any differences between bipolar and unipolar melancholia? *Journal of Affective Disorders, 25,* 97–106.

Mitchell, P., Wilhelm, K., Parker, G., Austin, M. P., Rutgers, P., & Malhi, G. S. (2001). The clinical features of bipolar depression: A comparison with matched major depressive disorder patients. *Journal of Clinical Psychiatry, 62,* 212–216.

Murphy, D. L., & Weiss, R. (1972). Reduced monoamine oxidase activity in blood platelets from bipolar depressed patients. *American Journal of Psychiatry, 128,* 1351–1357.

National Institute of Mental Health (1998). Genetics and mental disorders: Report of the NIMH genetics workgroup (NIMH Publication No. NIH-98-4268). Bethesda, MD: Author.

Newman, C., Leahy, R. L., Beck, A. T., Reilly-Harrington, N., & Gyulai, L. (2001). *Bipolar disorder: A cognitive therapy approach.* Washington, DC: American Psychological Association.

Norman, R. M., & Malla, A. K. (1993). Stressful life events and schizophrenia: II. Conceptual and methodological issues. *British Journal of Psychiatry, 162,* 166–174.

Perris, H. (1984). Life events and depression: 2. Results in diagnostic subgroups and in relation to the recurrence of depression. *Journal of Affective Disorders, 7,* 25–36.

Peven, D. E., & Shulman, B. H. (1983). The psychodynamics of bipolar affective disorder: Some empirical findings and their implications for cognitive theory. *Individual Psychology: Journal of Adlerian Theory, Research and Practice, 39,* 2–16.

Plomin, R., DeFries, J. C., McClearn, G. E., & Rutter, M. (1997). *Behavioral genetics* (3rd ed.). New York: Freeman.

Post, R. M., Lake, C. R., Jimerson, D. C., Bunney, W. E., Jr., Wood, J. R., Ziegler, M. G., & Goodwin, F. K. (1978). Cerebrospinalfluid norepinephrine in affective illness. *American Journal of Psychiatry, 135,* 907–912.

Priebe, S., Wildgrube, C., & Müller-Oerlinghausen, B. (1989). Lithium prophylaxis and expressed emotion. *British Journal of Psychiatry, 154,* 396–399.

Reilly-Harrington, N. A., Alloy, L. B., Fresco, D. M., & Whitehouse, W. G. (1999). Cognitive styles and life events as predictors of bipolar and unipolar symptomatology. *Journal of Abnormal Psychology, 108,* 567–578.

Roy, A. (1991). Personality variables in depressed patients and normal controls. *Neuropsychobiology, 23,* 119–123.

Roy, A., Jimerson, D. C., & Pickar, D. (1986). Plasma MHPG in depressive disorders and relationship to the dexamethasone suppression test. *American Journal of Psychiatry, 143,* 220–225.

Roy, A., Pickar, D., Linnoila, M., & Potter, W. Z. (1985). Plasma norepinephrine level in affective disorders: Relationship to melancholia. *Archives of General Psychiatry, 42,* 1181–1185.

Roy-Byrne, P., Post, R. M., Uhde, T. W., Porcu, T., & Davis, D. (1985). The longitudinal course of recurrent affective illness: Life chart data from research patients at the NIMH. *Acta Psychiatrica Scandinavica, 71*(Suppl. 317), 1–34.

Schatzberg, A. F., Samson, J. A., Bloomingdale, K. L., Orsulak, P. J., Gerson, B., Kizuka, P. P., Cole, J. O., & Schildkraut, J. J. (1989). Toward a biological classification of depressive disorders: X. Urinary catecholamines, their metabolites, and D-type scores in subgroups of depressive disorders. *Archives of General Psychiatry, 46,* 260–268.

Scott, J. (1995). Cognitive therapy for clients with bipolar disorder: A case example. *Cognitive and Behavioural Practice, 3,* 1–23.

Segal, Z., & Ingram, R. (1994). Mood priming and construct activation in tests of cognitive vulnerability to unipolar depression. *Clinical Psychology Review, 14,* 663–695.

Seligman, M. E. P., Castellon, C., Cacciola, J., Schulman, P., Luiborsky, L., Ollove, M., & Downing, R. (1988). Explanatory style change during cognitive therapy for unipolar depression. *Journal of Abnormal Psychology, 97,* 13–18.

Solomon, D. A., Shea, M. T., Leon, A. C., Mueller, T. I., Coryell, W., Maser, J. D., Endicott, J., & Keller, M. B. (1996). Personality traits in subjects with bipolar I disorder in remission. *Journal of Affective Disorders, 40,* 41–48.

Stern, G. S., & Berrenberg, J. L. (1979). Skill-set, success outcome, and mania as determinants of the illusion of control. *Journal of Research in Personality, 13,* 206–220.

Strakowski, S. M., Stoll, A. L., Tohen, M., Faedda, G. L., & Goodwin, D. C. (1993). The Tridimensional Personality Questionnaire as a predictor of 6-month outcome in first episode mania. *Psychiatry Research, 48,* 1–8.

Taylor, S. E., & Brown, J. D. (1988). Illusion and well-being: A social psychological perspective on mental health. *Psychological Bulletin, 103,* 193–210.

Tracy, A., Bauwens, F., Martin, F., Pardoen, D., & Mendlowicz, J. (1992). Attributional style and depression: A controlled comparison of remitted unipolar and bipolar patients. *British Journal of Clinical Psychology, 31,* 83–84.

Turner, H. (1994). Gender and social support: Taking the bad with the good? *Sex Roles, 30,* 521–541.

Videbech, P. (2000). PET measurements of brain glucose metabolism and blood flow in major depressive disorder: A critical review. *Acta Psychiatrica Scandinavica, 101,* 11–20.

von Zerssen, D. (1993). Normal and abnormal variants of premorbid personality in functional mental disorders: Conceptual and methodological issues. *Journal of Personality Disorders, 7,* 116–136.

von Zerssen, D. (1996). "Melancholic" and "manic" types of personality as premorbid structures in affective disorders. In C. Mundt, M. J. Goldstein, K. Hahlweg, & P. Fiedler (Eds.), *Interpersonal factors in the origin and course of affective disorders* (pp. 65–85). London: Gaskell/Royal College of Psychiatrists.

Weingartner, H., Miller, H., & Murphy, D. L. (1977). Mood-state dependent retrieval of verbal associations. *Journal of Abnormal Psychology, 86,* 276–284.

Whybrow, P., & Mendels, J. (1969). Toward a biology of depression: Some suggestions from neurophysiology. *American Journal of Psychiatry, 125,* 1491–1500.

Williams M. G., Watts, F. N., MacLeod, C., & Mathews, A. (1997). *Cognitive psychology and emotional disorders* (2nd ed.). London: Wiley.

Winokur, G. (1984). Psychosis in bipolar and unipolar affective illness with special reference to schizo–affective disorder. *British Journal of Psychiatry, 145,* 236–242.

Winokur, G., Coryell, W., Endicott, J., & Akiskal, H. (1993). Further distinctions between manic–depressive illness (bipolar disorder) and primary depressive disorder (unipolar depression). *American Journal of Psychiatry, 150*(8), 1176–1181.

Winokur, G., Coryell, W., Keller, M., Endicott, J., & Akiskal, H. (1993). A prospective follow-up of patients with bipolar and primary unipolar affective disorder. *Archives of General Psychiatry, 50*, 457–465.

Winokur, G., & Tsuang, M. T. (1996). *The natural history of mania, depression, and schizophrenia.* Washington, DC: American Psychiatric Press.

Winters, K. C., & Neale, J. (1985). Mania and low self-esteem. *Journal of Abnormal Psychology, 94*, 282–290.

Winters, R., Scott, W., & Beevers, C. (2000). Affective distress as a central and organizing symptom in depression: Neurobiological mechanisms. In S. L. Johnson, A. M. Hayes, T. Field, N. Schneiderman, & P. McCabe (Eds.), *Stress, coping and depression: Proceedings of the Fifteenth Annual Stress and Coping Conference* (pp. 177–222). Mahwah, NJ: Erlbaum.

Wu, J., & Bunney, W. E. (1991). The biological basis of an antidepressant response to sleep deprivation and relapse: Review and hypothesis. *American Journal of Psychiatry, 147*, 14–21.

Wu, X., & DeMarris, A (1996). Gender and marital status differences in depression: The effects of chronic strain. *Sex Roles, 34*, 299–319.

Yatham, L. N., Liddle, P. F., Shiah, I., Scarrow, G., Lam, R. W., Adam, M. J., Zis, A. P., & Ruth, T. J. (2000). Brain serotonin$_2$ receptors in major depression: A positron emission tomography study. *Archives of General Psychiatry, 57*, 850–858.

Yatham, L. N., Srisurapanont, M., Zis, A. P., & Kusumakar, V. (1997). Comparative studies of the biological distinction between unipolar and bipolar depressions. *Life Sciences, 61*(15), 1445–1455.

Young, L. T., Bagby, R. M., Cooke, R. G., Parker, J. D. A., Levitt, A. J., & Joffe, R. T. (1995). A comparison of Tridimensional Personality Questionnaire dimensions in bipolar disorder and unipolar depression. *Psychiatry Research, 58*, 139–143.

PART II

VULNERABILITY, RISK, AND MODELS OF DEPRESSION

Many approaches have been taken by theorists in attempts to understand the origins of depression. Whereas some of these theories involve genetics and biological functioning, other approaches focus on the personal characteristics of individuals who are believed to be vulnerable to experiencing depressive episodes, and on aspects of the social environments that are hypothesized to increase risk for depression. The seven chapters in this part describe approaches and models that have been developed to explain vulnerability and risk for unipolar depression. Wallace, Schneider, and McGuffin (Chapter 7) describe the genetic foundations of depression, and discuss the results of studies that have examined the heritability of depression. Continuing with a focus on biological factors in depression, Thase, Jindal, and Howland, and Davidson, Pizzagalli, and Nitschke describe biological aspects of depressive disorders. Whereas Thase et al. (Chapter 8) focus on the role of neurotransmitters in the onset and maintenance of depression, Davidson et al. (Chapter 9) describe the function of neuroanatomical structures that have recently been implicated in this disorder. Goodman (Chapter 10) also touches on biological aspects of vulnerability to depression, but broadens her focus to also include psychosocial factors occurring early in life that appear to increase risk for depression. Abramson, Alloy, Hankin, Haeffel, MacCoon, and Gibb (Chapter 11) describe the large body of research examining cognitive models of vulnerability to depression, and Joiner (Chapter 12) parallels this description with a focus on the interpersonal context of this disorder. Finally, Monroe and Hadjiyannakis (Chapter 13) adopt a diathesis–stress perspective in examining the social environment of depressed individuals.

7

Genetics of Depression

John Wallace, Tiffany Schneider, and Peter McGuffin

As described elsewhere in this volume, major depression is a common, costly, and recurrent disorder that is associated with considerable morbidity and excess mortality (see Kessler, Chapter 1, this volume). After ischemic heart disease, depression will be the major cause of disability worldwide by 2020 (Murray & Lopez, 1996). The causes of depression are of considerable concern to the sufferer and of overriding significance in clinical psychiatry.

Perhaps surprisingly therefore, the genetics of major, or unipolar, depression has been, until recently, a neglected area in comparison with other severe forms of psychiatric disorder, such as bipolar affective disorder (manic–depression) or schizophrenia, despite depression being a much more common condition. Possibly this is because the role of the environment is often very apparent in the etiology of depressive illness. That is, the fact that, based on our own general experience, we can so readily understand the "reactive" nature of some forms of depression, causes a difficulty in acknowledging the genetic contribution to the disorder. Furthermore, because depression seldom if ever shows a simple, easily recognizable pattern of Mendelian inheritance, this again tends to obscure its genetic basis. Despite all of this, however, the clustering of depression within families is a consistent finding in research. Recent studies suggest that the genetic contribution to depression is, in fact, quite substantial.

In this chapter we first explore some of the basic methodologies used by psychiatric geneticists. Next we examine the different models of transmission of depression and the important role of gene–environment interplay on the manifestation of the disorder. Finally, we address the contribution of molecular genetics to our current understanding of the etiology of depression before going on to consider the likely impact of our increasing knowledge of the genetics of depression on the future diagnosis and treatment of this very common and debilitating disorder.

METHODOLOGY IN PSYCHIATRIC GENETICS

In the field of psychiatric genetics there are three classic approaches to studying depression or indeed any other complex disorder: family, twin, and adoption studies. The family study asks: Does depression run in families? Essentially this question implies that if genes are important in the etiology of a disorder, then relatives of depressed individuals would be more likely to suffer depression than would members of the population at large. The family study method, largely because of its ease of use, is one of the most widely used tools in psychiatric genetics. Unfortunately, it suffers from one serious drawback: it cannot definitely disentangle the genetic and environmental sources of familial transmission of depression. For that somewhat more complex task we need twin and adoption studies. In reviewing these studies, it is of advantage to conceptualize the causes of any complex *phenotype* (an observable trait or disease) as arising from three sources:

1. Genes.
2. Shared environment (also called common environment); both shared environment and genes contribute to familial similarity.
3. Nonshared environment, that is, environmental effects that tend to make family members different from each other.

Twin and adoption studies allow us to disentangle these effects, but because each method has its limitations, ideally we must look for a consistent pattern of *converging* evidence from the three types of investigation that would help confirm genetic and/or environmental contributions to the familial transmission of depression.

Family Studies

Family studies have contributed significantly to our current understanding of major depression. Although, as we have already noted, family studies cannot on their own establish that there is a genetic contribution to depression, they do offer a crucial first step toward dissecting the genetic basis of the disorder. For this reason, studies that focus on the family have made a crucial contribution to the epidemiological foundations of psychiatric genetics and to our improved understanding of depression. Family studies have provided an ideal opportunity to examine the interplay between social and genetic variables, integrating social and biological components within a single investigative study (McGuffin, Katz, & Bebbington, 1988). These studies are an important step in the process by which we clarify the etiology of this common disorder.

Evaluating Family Studies

Family studies set out to determine whether a disorder like depression is *familial*, that is, do the cases cluster in families? In genetic epidemiology a *case* is someone who has the disorder under investigation, in this instance depression, and a *proband* is a case that brings the disorder to the attention of the researchers. If we wish to show that depression runs in families, we need to demonstrate that the disorder occurs more frequently among relatives of "cases" who suffer from depression than among relatives of "controls" who do not have the disorder. If genes are involved in a disorder, we would predict that the risk of depression in relatives of probands would be greater than the risk to relatives of controls. We would, of course, always control for confounders such as age, sex, and class—factors that in themselves might influence the presence or absence of depression. Just studying the relatives of individuals who have depression will tell us little beyond simply outlining the rate of the disorder in a particular family. By using controls, however, we can tell if the case and control families differ from each other, and then draw more valid conclusions from our results by reducing important forms of bias.

In evaluating any family study we need to address two issues: how the individual family members were assessed and how the families themselves were initially selected. Family approaches to depression choose between two ways of assessing and evaluating family members: the *family history* and the *family study* methods. In employing these methods, researchers have tended to concentrate on first-degree relatives rather than on more extended families. *First-degree relatives* are parents, siblings, and offspring. These individuals share half their genes in common with the proband. The *family study method* determines diagnosis by interviewing all family members in person (Faraone, Tsuang, & Tsuang, 1999). This approach typically involves interviewing participants directly with a diagnostic instrument such as the Schedules for Clinical Assessment in Neuropsychiatry (SCAN; Wing et al., 1990), or the Schedule for Affective Disorder and Schizophrenia (SADS; Endicott & Spitzer, 1978; also see Nezu, Nezu, McClure, & Zwick, Chapter 3, this volume). The use of such semistructured interviews leads to a more accurate diagnosis and allows a more realistic appraisal of the rates of rigorously defined depression in the relatives of the cases compared with the rates of reliably defined depression in the relatives of the controls.

The *family history* method, on the other hand, relies on a more indirect approach. It uses indirect information determined by interviewing a single individual who reports on the presence or absence of symptomatology among different family members. There are both advantages and limitations associated with each type of family investigation. A major advantage of the family history method is that it is comparatively inexpensive: interviewing one family member about the entire family is less expensive and time-consuming than directly interviewing all the family members individually.

While the family history method is more financially accessible and requires less time, a disadvantage is that the method has consistently been shown to underestimate the true prevalence rates of many psychiatric disorders despite efforts to address this by standardizing data collection (Andreasen, Rice, Endicott, Reich, & Coryell, 1986, Orvaschel, Douglas Thompson, Belanger, Prusoff, & Kidd, 1982). This lack of sensitivity in detecting depression among family members is particularly true for the less severe forms of pathology, for example, where the threshold for "caseness" is set below admission to a hospital (Duggan, Sham, Minne, Lee, & Murray, 1998). We know that the family history method underestimates the true prevalance of a psychiatric disorder because some studies also used the family study method on the same subjects and found that the family history method failed to correctly diagnose many of those family members who were, in reality, unwell with the psychiatric disorder under investigation. Consequently, in looking at a family history paper, it is important to remember that the risk of depression to relatives is probably an underestimation.

In deciding between a family history method and a family study design we must take into account the quality of the data we are aiming for, together with the likely expense of data collection. The family history method, then, is valuable in the initial stages of an investigation when few data are available on the disorder. Once the family history approach detects familiality, however, the more rigorous family study approach is the preferred choice to catalogue the degree of familial transmission (Faraone et al., 1999).

The second important source of bias in family studies may be associated with the manner in which the families themselves were initially selected. This bias arises from problems of subject ascertainment depending on where our cases are drawn from. We can either select probands with depression directly from the general population or we can seek them out in places such as psychiatric clinics that are likely to have many cases with depressive illness. The major strength of the population-based study is that it allows generalization from a specific sample to the entire population. However, these population-based family studies can be difficult to carry out from a practical point of view, and can also be very costly. Clinic-based studies, on the other hand, are easier to carry out and are less expensive to implement. Many researchers do indeed recruit from treatment centers and hospitals, sources of large numbers of depressed patients. There is evidence, however, that a significant number of depressed individuals will never seek treatment and attend these centers. Consequently, these studies miss out on many relevant cases, which in turn can reduce the generalizability of the family study (Weissman et al., 1986). Furthermore, individuals with a family history of depression may be more likely to seek treatment at these centers than those without a family history, also tending to skew the results (Sullivan, Neale, & Kendler, 2000). Thus, population-based and clinic-based family studies have different strengths and weaknesses. We need to consider these factors when evaluating the results of these studies.

Despite these shortcomings, both family history and family study methods of investigating depression are highly consistent in finding higher rates of the disorder in relatives of depressed probands than in relatives of healthy controls or in the general population (McGuffin & Katz, 1986; Sullivan et al., 2000). In assessing or attributing risk, many studies find it best to express the risk of developing depression as a *relative risk,* that is, the risk of developing a disorder in one group relative to the risk of developing the same disorder in a comparison group. While in most studies the relative risk among the first-degree family members of depressives, compared with comparison groups, has been around three (Sullivan et al., 2000), a recent study using a rather strict interpretation of the *International Classification of Diseases* (ICD-10) criteria found that the lifetime prevalence of depression was almost 10 times as high in the siblings of depressed probands as in the siblings of never-depressed controls (Farmer, Owen, & McGuffin, 2000).

Clearly, then, family studies indicate that depression runs in families. Although these data support the idea that genes contribute to depression, they are far from definitive because a disorder can be familial for a variety of reasons. A disorder may run in families for nongenetic reasons, as family members typically share a common environment and a common culture. All factors that could conceivably contribute to the familial clustering of the illness need to be addressed. To disentangle these genetic and environmental contributions to depression we must now look at two further types of investigation: twin and adoption studies.

Twin Studies

Studying the rates of depression in monozygotic (MZ) and dizygotic (DZ) twins offers us what is essentially a natural experiment whereby the relative contributions of genes and environment can be assessed. MZ twins are genetically identical, while DZ twins, like full siblings, have on average 50% of their genes in common. If we make an "equal environments assumption" that the extent of environmental sharing is about the same for MZ and DZ pairs, then any greater similarity in MZ pairs over DZ pairs should reflect the effects of genes. We use *concordance rates* to describe this resemblance between twins when we are interested in discrete traits. A twin pair is concordant for an illness if both have the disorder. If, however, only one member of the twin is ill, then the pair is discordant for that illness. Thus, a *pairwise concordance rate* is the proportion of pairs who are concordant. In studies in which the sample is ascertained via affected index cases or probands, concordance rates are expressed *probandwise,* that is, as the proportion of co-twins who are affected. The two methods may give different results since the correct procedure for ascertainment of probands is to count each one as independent. Thus, some twin pairs, where both are independently ascertained to be probands, will be counted twice.

Evaluating Twin Studies

While studies on affectively ill twins do have many advantages over other approaches, they nevertheless have a number of potential shortcomings. The ability of twin studies to generate meaningful results may be compromised by a variety of factors. Sources of bias in twin studies include incomplete ascertainment of all available affected twins in a given population, with haphazardly collected twin samples leading to an overestimation of the number of MZ pairs. Still other sources of error in twin studies include psychiatric diagnostic misclassification and zygosity misclassification. Allegiance bias can affect the investigator who makes a nonindependent assessment of zygosity (MZ or DZ), leading to an overestimation of the proportion of MZ-concordant pairs. Thus, the ability of the twin method to provide meaningful results is inextricably linked to its ability to correctly determine zygosity, that is, whether a pair of twins is MZ or DZ. A substantial misclassification of MZ as DZ or visa versa would lead to meaningless results. The most precise laboratory methods of zygosity determination use DNA or other genetic markers, but these may be prohibitively costly for very large studies. Fortunately, questionnaire measures, particularly if supplemented by inspection of photographs by an experienced observer, can give over 95% agreement with laboratory-based testing (McGuffin et al., 1993).

The Equal-Environments Assumption

The critical *equal-environments assumption* posits that MZ and DZ twins are equally correlated in their exposure to environmental events of etiological relevance to major depression. This is open to criticism since, in some studies (e.g., McGuffin, Katz, Watkins, & Rutherford, 1996), MZ pairs have been found to be more alike, for example with regard to sharing friends or being dressed similarly as children. Nevertheless, such factors do not appear to be substantial and do not appear to contribute significantly to similarity for traits such as depression, or indeed for behavior generally. In fact, the assumption of equal environments in MZ and DZ twins has been found to be reasonable for most practical purposes (Plomin, DeFries, McClearn, & McGuffin, 2001; Kendler & Gardner, 1998).

Generalizability

Because there may be systematic biological or psychosocial differences between twins and *non-twins*, there are concerns that estimates of *heritability*, that is, the proportion of liability explained by genes, from twin studies may not generalize to non-twins. For example, conclusions about major depression from twins may not generalize to singletons if there are protective or risk factors specifically associated with being a twin. However, because twins are not more or less likely to develop a wide range of psychiatric conditions than is the general population, it is reasonable to assume that for psychiatric studies of depression the twin method is not compromised by significant differences between twins and non-twins (Faraone et al., 1999). Furthermore, while twins differ from singletons in a number of potentially important ways, it is critical to note that the incidence of treated major depression is similar in singletons, MZ twins, and DZ twins (Kendler, Pedersen, Farahmand, & Persson, 1996). It seems reasonable, then, in the case of depression, to generalize from twins to singletons.

There are two other potential complications, however, that must be considered. It may be the case that the risk of affective disorder to the proband's relatives varies with the severity of the depressive illness in the index twin. That is, there may be a higher risk to relatives of developing depression if the proband suffers from a more severe form of the disorder.

Severity of depression in the proband may influence the results of twin studies. Furthermore, the risk to relatives may also vary with the proband's age of onset for the disorder, perhaps again reflecting the severity of the disorder. Early onset of depression in the proband may be associated with higher rates of the disorder among his or her relatives, although this is not universally accepted (McGuffin, Katz, & Rutherford, 1991).

Evidence from Older Twin Studies

Unfortunately, some of the older twin studies, deferring to the older Kraepelinian model, did not distinguish between bipolar and unipolar depression. These studies examined twins with depression regardless of whether one of the pair had attracted a diagnosis of depression alone (unipolar depression) or a diagnosis of manic–depression (bipolar disorder) (Gershon, Bunney, Leckman, Van Eerdewegh, & De Bauche, 1976). In contrast, studies conducted during the last 3 decades have presented results separately for unipolar (UP) and bipolar (BP) illness, a major advance.

The older studies indicate a tendency for twin pairs concordant for affective illness to be concordant also for the subtypes BP and UP disorder, with a suggestion of stronger genetic influences in bipolar disorder (Zerbin-Rudin, 1979). Bipolar disorder, then, may be "more genetic" than is unipolar or major depression. However, even in genetically identical twins, homotypia can be incomplete, with a minority of probands showing one type of disorder and the co-twin the other. Older twin studies tend to indicate that UP and BP disorders may differ quantitatively but not necessarily qualitatively—that is, the two conditions may, in fact, overlap and share some genes in common.

Evidence from More Recent Twin Studies

McGuffin et al. (1991) studied twins who had been systematically ascertained via 84 MZ and 130 DZ probands. For a lifetime history of hospital-treated depression concordance rates were 68% for MZ twins and 43% for DZ twins. Using DSM-III diagnosis of any major lifetime affective disorder, the MZ and DZ concordance rates were 53% and 28%, respectively. Three older classical studies that did not use explicit diagnostic criteria gave broadly similar figures (Farmer, 1996). Model fitting assigned 51% of the variance to genetic factors and 31% to common environment. These newer studies, looking at more rigorously diagnosed unipolar depression, indicate a significant genetic contribution to depressive disorder.

Studies focusing on unipolar as distinct from bipolar disorder tend, singly, to find somewhat lower MZ concordances in unipolar disorder (McGuffin et al., 1991). Twin, family, and adoption studies confirm a genetic contribution to the etiology of depressive illness that is greater in bipolar than in unipolar disorder. Nevertheless, using formal biometric model fitting, results suggest that substantial additive genetic, as well as common environmental factors, are both needed to explain the transmission of unipolar illness. A substantial body of research documents the limited effect of common rearing, especially on measures of affect and disposition (McGue, Sharma, & Benson, 1996). *Vulnerability* or *susceptibility* is an individual's unobservable predisposition to develop a disorder. Research indicates that unipolar depression is a substantially heritable condition with vulnerability caused by multiple genes that confer a susceptibility to develop the disorder (Farmer, 1996).

Severity of the unipolar condition is a significant factor to be considered in this type of research, with more severe forms of depression differing perhaps in their etiology from milder disorders (Malhi, Moore, & McGuffin, 2000). Lyons et al. (1998) stratified the diagnosis of depression according to severity. They found that the best fitting biometric twin model for more severe depression contained only genetic and nonshared environmental factors. In contrast, a nongenetic model, containing only common family environment and nonshared environment, best explained *dysthymia* (a low-grade, chronic depression), as well as mild and moderate depression. The heritability of unipolar depression appears to be higher than was once thought, with estimates now in the region of 40 to 70% (Malhi et al., 2000). This is particularly true for more severe forms of depression; other less pronounced forms of depression, such as dysthymia and mild and moderate depression, are best explained by a nongenetic model (Malhi et al., 2000).

A study by Kendler, Neale, Kessler, Heath, & Eaves (1992) approached the issue from a different perspective. They looked at a population-based, volunteer sample of "normal" twins and assessed them for depression using standardized psychiatric interviews. Again, the correlations in liability for all definitions of depression were higher for MZ than for DZ twins. The results indicate heritability of around 40%.

Data on twins reared apart, where one has an affective disorder, are sparse (McGuffin, 1994). Where data on these rare twin pairs do exist, the majority of the twins tend to be concordant for affective disorder despite their different environments. Indeed, the rate is similar to the rate for pairs reared together (Bertelsen, 1985). Again, such findings are highly suggestive of a significant genetic component in the transmission of depression.

A recent review and meta-analysis of twin studies of major depression by Sullivan et al. (2000) suggested that despite the many differences across the twin studies, the fundamental genetic architecture of major depression appears homogenous across samples and across gender. More than 212,000 individuals were included in the review and all the studies used DSM-III-R criteria for major depression. A *meta-analysis* attempts to combine data across studies in an attempt to narrow the confidence interval on a parameter and so improve precision. Sullivan et al. found that the variance in liability to depression is mostly due to individual specific environmental effects (58–67%) and additive genetic effects (31–42%), with a negligible contribution by environmental effects shared by siblings (0–5%). Estimates were similar for subjects ascertained from community and clinical sources, although it should be noted that clinically ascertained samples have tended to suggest higher heritability, perhaps reflecting greater severity of the disorder (McGuffin et al., 1996). An interesting point is that the one analysis of clinical data where treatment was included as part of the diagnostic criteria suggested a common environmental effect, perhaps indicating that treatment seeking is partly influenced by family environment (McGuffin et al., 1991). Furthermore, it might be said that, in general, primary studies of the genetic epidemiology of major depression tend to suggest that similar genetic effects on liability to major depression operate in males and females (Sullivan et al., 2000).

It is not possible to prove that the results from twin studies are uncontaminated by all conceivable biases and violations of critical assumptions. However, given the available data, there is no reason at present to question the validity of the conclusions about major depression from twin studies (Sullivan et al., 2000). There is no conclusive evidence at present that these various potential limitations substantially detract from our current interpretation of twin study research. Results from twin studies, classical and new, drawn from clinical and general population sources and including twins reared apart, indicate a sizeable genetic contribution to unipolar depression. Data from twin studies can be applied in a liability threshold model that allows the variance contributed by genetic and environmental etiological factors to be estimated. Despite the differences in defining major depression, and differences in estimating lifetime prevalence rates, a variety of studies, employing different methodologies, all indicate a substantial genetic contribution to depressive illness, with severe depression very much characterized in terms of a major genetic contribution to its etiology.

Crucially, twin studies also provide the most solid evidence for what clinicians have known for years: the environment plays a substantial role in causing most types of mental illness, including depression. Heritability is a useful index of the relative importance of genes and environment in causing a disease. But high heritabilities do not mean that patients are fated to endure the inexorable effects of pathogenic genes. Genes are not destiny. By changing the biological, psychological, or social environment, effective treatments mitigate, cure, and eventually prevent disease.

Adoption Studies

Adoption studies provide yet another important method of disentangling the genetic and environmental components of the familial aggregation of a disorder such as depression. Children adopted at an early age have primarily a genetic relationship with their biological parents and a totally environmental relationship with their adoptive parents. If genes are responsible for the familial transmission of a disorder, then we should observe transmission of depression from parents to their natural children, but not from parents to adopted children.

Results of adoption studies on mood disorders are mixed. Only three adoption studies have been carried out in depression, and all of these had significant methodological problems, including small sample size and/or indirect methods of clinical diagnosis, such as sick leave registrations (Sullivan et al., 2000). The largest and most thorough of the three found evidence of a strong genetic effect, with an odds ratio of over seven for occurrence of depression in those biologically related versus those not biologically related to a depressed proband (Wender et al., 1986). Despite the methodological difficulties already alluded to, this can be taken as further evidence of a significant genetic contribution to depressive illness. The two other adoption studies addressing depression found little evidence for a genetic influence, but they relied on medical records rather than more robust methods (Plomin et al., 2001).

An adoption study that focused on adoptees with bipolar depression found stronger evidence of a genetic influence (Mendlewicz & Rainer, 1977). The rate of bipolar disorders in the biological parents of the bipolar adoptees was 7%, but it was 0% for the parents of control adoptees. While bipolar disorder is regarded as a more severe condition than unipolar depression, these figures nevertheless are consistent with a significant genetic contribution to mood disorders in general, and to depression in particular.

Evaluating Adoption Studies

Because of a number of methodological problems, we must view the results of adoption studies, like those of family and twin studies, with circumspection. The biggest difficulty with studies that focus on adoption is that adoptees and their families may not be representative of the population in general. Some mothers may become pregnant and give up their children because of factors related to a psychiatric condition, or because of associated maladaptive coping mechanisms, such as alcohol or substance abuse. Although not all adopted-away children have such parents, if the likelihood of having such a parent, with a significant genetic risk for depression, is greater for adoptees than for nonadoptees, then the results of adoption studies could be misleading.

Interpretation is further complicated by the fact that the adoption process itself is stressful for the adoptee and his or her family. Unfortunately, adoptees are indeed at greater risk for psychiatric disorder than are nonadoptees, and this further limits the generalizability of results of adoption studies, as the adoption procedure itself may be a risk factor for depression. Nevertheless, despite these reservations, the evidence for genetic influence on bipolar disorder from these studies is reasonably consistent, and the results suggest that more severe major depressive illness also shows a significant genetic influence.

MODELS OF TRANSMISSION

It is likely that depression is caused by more than one gene, and it is also likely that what is inherited is not a certainty, but a liability, or predisposition, toward depression (Farmer, 1996). *Liability* to depression describes an unobserved variable, resulting from a combination of genetic and environmental effects, that is assumed to be normally distributed (or that can be readily transformed to normality) in the population (Falconer, 1965). If an individual's liability at some point exceeds a particular threshold, then he or she will develop the disorder. Relatives of depressed patients have a mean liability that is elevated compared with the population mean; therefore, more of them lie beyond the threshold for developing depression. Knowing the proportion of affected individuals in the general population and the proportion of affected individuals in a particular class of relatives allows calculation of a correlation in liability (Falconer & McKay, 1996). If this is known for MZ and DZ twins, it is possible to estimate *heritability*. Heritability, in the broad sense, is the proportion of liability to a disorder accounted for by genetic effects. Biometric model fitting allows a formal comparison of hypotheses concerning whether, and to what extent, genetic and environmental factors contribute to liability to a disorder.

Heritability and Beyond

While there has been much speculation about possible involvement of major genes in bipoloar disorder (O'Rourke, McGuffin, & Reich, 1983), the detection of a major gene or genes in unipolar depression has generated less interest. Most of the attention of genetic model fitting has been directed toward estimating the size of genetic and nongenetic effects, and toward attempts to explain the interplay of genes and environment. Biometric model fitting allows a formal comparison of hypotheses concerning whether, and to what extent, genetic and environmental factors contribute to liability to a disorder. Applying a liability/threshold model to published twin data on affective disorder as a whole (unipolar and bipolar disorders combined), McGuffin and Katz (1986) estimated a heritability in excess of 80%, with a minimal contribution from shared environment. A subsequent biometric analysis of unipolar twin data indicated that additive genetic effects were essential in explaining the transmission of unipolar disorder (McGuffin et al., 1991). There is now consistent evidence from several other studies, all taking formal model-fitting approaches to twin data and using DSM-III or DSM-IV criteria, that depression is essentially a result of an interplay between nonfamily environmental effects and genes (Kendler, Neale, Kessler, Heath, & Eaves, 1993; McGuffin et al., 1996; Lyons et al., 1998).

Changes in Heritability with Age

There is evidence that the effects of genes on behavior do not remain the same throughout life but can change with age (Plomin et al., 2001). The influence of genes, then, is not constant and static. Thapar and McGuffin (1994) set out to assess the importance of genetic and environmental factors on depressive symptoms during childhood and adolescence in an epidemiological sample of twins. For the whole sample, the heritability of depressive scores was estimated at 79%. On splitting the sample, however, symptoms in children could be explained by shared environmental factors only, while symptoms in adolescents (ages 11–16 years) remained highly heritable. The results suggested that although depressive symptoms appear to be largely heritable, the relative impact of genetic and environmental factors varies with age.

Silberg et al. (1999) examined the possible causes of greater depressive symptomatology among adolescent girls by investigating the variation in the influence of genetic and environmental risk factors, and by comparing the trajectory of depressive symptoms among boys and girls from childhood to adolescence. Examining a population sample of juvenile twins, Silberg et al. found that boys and girls were quite similar in their level of depression before age 12, but that the rate for girls increased over that for boys thereafter. Examining the components of variance for depression, Silberg and her colleagues found increased heritability for pubescent girls. They also found that the long-term stability of depression in pubertal girls is best explained by latent genetic factors. This altering impact of genes on behavior throughout the life span will become an increasingly important consideration in the planning of future research.

Age of Onset

There is evidence from a number of studies (McGuffin et al., 1996; Harrington et al., 1997) that age of onset of the illness may distinguish highly familial from less familial forms of depression. Comparing early- versus late-onset depression, there is a tendency for early-onset depression to have a higher familial loading. However, Sullivan et al. (2000) point out that this tendency attains statistical significance in only three out of nine family or twin studies.

McGue and Christensen (1997) examined a sample of 406 same-sex Danish twin pairs 75 years of age and older. The heritability of depression symptomatology was relatively constant over the age ranges sampled, and their analysis revealed that depression symptomatology is moderately heritable even in late life. Interestingly, their estimates were similar in magnitude to heritability estimates for depression symptomatology in young adult and middle-aged samples.

In contrast, Maier et al. (1991) observed from family studies that the rate of depression among the relatives of depressed probands is significantly lower when the proband has an age of onset after, as compared with before, 60 years. They suggest that genetic factors have less of an influence on depression among older adults than among individuals at other stages of the life span. They propose low familial transmission of late-onset clinical depression. All of this suggests that the influence a person's genetic makeup has on a disorder such as depression may not be static and fixed throughout his or her life but, developmentally, may exert a varying influence. This is an important consideration when considering the complex interaction of genes and the environment.

GENE–ENVIRONMENT INTERPLAY

The relationship between environmental and familial factors in the etiology of depression is more complex than originally thought (Farmer, 1996). For example, in the past we embraced the classic reactive versus endogenous depression dichotomy. This division implied that the rate of depression among the relatives of "endogenous" probands would be higher than among the relatives of patients with "reactive depression," because endogenous depression was believed to be somehow "more genetic". Endogenous depression was regarded as being somehow unrelated to environmental events. Reactive depression, in contrast, was regarded as stress-related, more "environmental," and less severe (Tsuang & Faraone,

1994). Initially at least, some evidence appeared to support the assumption of a difference between what was seen as two distinct forms of depressive disorder (Pollitt, 1972; Stenstedt, 1966). However, with the development of more sophisticated methods of measuring adversity and stress, it was found that depression was, in fact, no more common in the relatives of endogenous probands than among the relatives of those whose depression appeared to be a reaction to adverse life events (McGuffin et al., 1988). The endogenous–reactive dichotomy did not hold true. Indeed a "neurotic" pattern of symptoms in probands can be associated with a higher rate of illness in relatives (McGuffin, Katz, & Bebbington, 1987). Although a subsequent twin study did find a suggestion of a stronger genetic effect where the proband had an endogenous pattern of symptoms (McGuffin et al., 1996) there is no compelling evidence that endogenous symptoms "breed true" or that the division is a valid one.

A related issue is whether depression can be considered to be etiologically heterogeneous consisting of pure genetic and nongenetic forms? Andrew, McGuffin, and Katz (1998) applied a twin-family history analysis to DSM-IV major depression in order to examine this question. They found no difference in the lifetime prevalence of major depression among siblings or parents of MZ and DZ twins concordant or discordant for the disorder. If depression consisted of nongenetic and genetic forms, one would predict that discordance in twins would often result from the affected member of the pair having a nongenetic form of the disorder. One would then expect to find lower rates of major depression in the relatives of discordant as compared with concordant pairs. Andrew et al.'s (1998) failure to find such a difference suggests that, at least in their narrowly defined sample of hospital-treated probands, there is homogeneity with respect to a genetic contribution to major depression. It is not useful, then, to separate major depression simply into genetic and nongenetic forms in terms of etiology.

We know that genes confer a liability, not a certainty, and it is also well established that life events are of importance in the etiology of depression. Brown and Harris (1978) showed that adverse life events that carry a threat have a strong association with the onset of depression (see also Monroe and Hadjyannakis, Chapter 13, this volume). However, there have been few systematic attempts to study both environmental adversity and genetic factors at the same time, in the same sample.

Significantly, studies that attempt to investigate familial liability along with adversity often find that the environmental measure is contaminated by genetic factors. The tendency to experience or report life events appears to be influenced by shared family environment. Familial factors may be influencing the liability to major depression *indirectly* by predisposing the individual to a more adverse environment (Kendler, 1998). Part of the association between depression and adverse life events may be due to the fact that both show familial aggregation (McGuffin et al., 1988). Event-associated depression may be something that occurs in hazard-prone individuals or threat-perceiving persons, rather than simply in stress-susceptible individuals.

A twin-study design that used bivariate genetic model fitting to examine 270 twin pairs, ages 8–17 years, demonstrated that some depressive symptoms and some life events share a common genetic influence (Thapar, Harold, & McGuffin, 1998). The study looked at the extent to which genetic and environmental factors mediate between life events and depressive symptoms. Thapar et al. concluded that at least part of the association between life events and depressive symptoms is mediated by familial factors that include both genes and shared environment. Genes may contribute to both the tendency to experience certain life events and the tendency to experience depression.

As we noted above, it is possible that event-associated depression is something that occurs in hazard-prone, not just stress-susceptible, individuals. Some life events are influenced by genetic factors. There is evidence that the genetic factors operating in depression and in the predisposition to life events are positively correlated (Thapar et al., 1998). It appears that the association between life events and depression may be mediated via a common set of genes. The reaction to life events may indeed be genetically influenced (Farmer, 1996). That said, the bulk of the evidence suggests that the association between life events and depression remains, to some extent at least, causal (Kendler, Karkowski, & Prescott, 1999).

Importantly, Silberg et al. (1999) also concluded that there is a common genetic factor that influences both risk for depression and for experiencing negative life events. While there are substantial genetic effects specific to depression, part of the genetic risk for depression is attributable to a genetic predisposition to experiencing particular stressful life events. This may be one aspect of the cause of the complex association between life events and depression. There is a growing literature demonstrating genetic control over exposure to the environment (Kendler & Eaves, 1986). Overall, Silberg and her colleagues (1999) indicate something that is also suggested by the results of other research: there are notable genetic influences on both depression and life events, with the influence of genes not stable over time but, in fact, with a developmentally related increase in genetic variance for certain life events.

Social Support

Social aspects of the environment obviously affect depression, and a number of attempts have been made to identify them. Wade and Kendler (2000), for example, showed that inadequate social support is associated with major depression. Using interview data from female twin pairs from a population-based registry study, these investigators found that risk for depression in the previous year was directly associated with problems in relative and spouse relationships. However, the relationship between depression and social support again is complex, and it may be that (1) low social support increases the risk for depression; (2) depression in the proband decreases social support; and/or (3) both variables reflect a common genetic liability.

Social support is often viewed as an environmental provision independent of the characteristics brought to the situation by the individual. Of course, it may also be an individual difference variable and an environmental provision. Furthermore, the capacity to establish and maintain supportive relationships is influenced by genetic factors (Henderson, 1998). The association seen between major depression and social support could be because both are affected by a common set of temperamental traits, which are in turn genetically influenced. Kendler and Karkowski-Shuman (1997) showed this mechanism to be at work in the association between stressful life events and major depression.

Wade and Kendler (2000) emphasize that the results of their research favor the hypothesis that an association between spouse support and major depression is partly causal and partly the result of genetic factors that predispose both to major depression and to the elicitation of low levels of support from a spouse. They found that decreased social support may be a risk factor for depression, that it may be influenced by depressed mood, and that it may share genetic risk factors with major depression. Thus, the relationship between the dimensions of social support and the risk for depression is complex and may be due to at least three distinct mechanisms. First, low levels of social support from intimate others can increase risk for major depression. Second, the experience of major depression can itself change levels of social support. Third, a set of genetic factors may exist that increase the risk both for major depression and for low levels of social support. Wade and Kendler warn against assuming that the association between social support and depression is purely causal and due solely to low social support increasing the risk for depressive illness. Genes may, in fact, reduce an individual's capacity to elicit stable and caring support from social relationships, a case of genetic influence on the nature of our exposure to certain elements of our environment.

Gender Differences

Most studies suggest that the heritability of depression is similar in men and women (McGuffin et al., 1996; Sullivan et al., 2000). This, however, may not be the case, especially when community-based samples employing a broader definition of disorder are used. For example, Bierut et al. (1999) found that in women, the simplest model to fit the data implicated genetic factors and also environmental factors unique to the individual in the development of depression, with heritability estimates ranging from 36 to 44%. In contrast, depression in men was only modestly familial, and genetic factors in this study accounted for a significantly greater proportion of the liability to develop DSM-III-R depression in women compared with men. The results suggested that for both men and women, individual environmental experiences play a large role in the development of depression, with major depressive disorder more heritable in women than in men.

MOLECULAR GENETICS

Finding the Genes: Mapping and Positional Cloning

All of the data discussed so far are consistent with the view that major depression is a complex disorder, with environmental and genetic influences important in its etiology, and that the condition has moderate to high heritability. This being the case, can we locate and identify the actual genes that are responsible for the disorder? The process by which we do this is known as *positional cloning*. The general underlying idea behind positional cloning is outlined in Figure 7.1. A chromosomal region containing a gene that confers susceptibility to depression is identified by linkage mapping (or by linkage disequilibrium mapping where the marker and the susceptibility locus are very closely linked). Using a variety of methods, the region is then narrowed down until the gene itself is identified. Subsequently the mutations (or variations) that confer susceptibility to the disease are identified. The distribution, level of expression, and functions of the gene products can then be studied. The whole process of positional cloning carries with it the possibility of incremental benefits for clini-

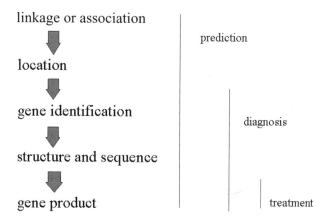

FIGURE 7.1. Positional cloning.

cal practice in the forms of predictive testing, refined diagnosis, and eventually the development of targeted specific treatments. It has provided major advances in knowledge about rare single gene neuropsychiatric disorders including Huntington disease and early-onset familial Alzheimer's disease. The burning issue is whether this approach is feasible in common complex disorders such as depression that may involve multiple genes.

Linkage analysis refers to a statistical gene hunting method that traces patterns of heredity based on the tendency of two alleles at different loci on the same chromosome to be inherited together. Studies attempting to detect linkage have become increasingly feasible even in complex diseases, with dramatic improvements over the past decade in refining the map of the human genome, the 23 pairs of chromosomes. By the late 1990s, a dense map of thousands of DNA markers of a type called *short sequence tandem repeats,* or microsatellites, had been published; currently, an international consortium is producing a map consisting of hundreds of thousands of markers of the latest generation, a type called *single nucleotide polymorphisms* (SNPs). DNA markers enable the possibility of "tagging" a trait or disorder within families in which multiple members are affected. A trait that appears to be coinherited with a particular marker at a level greater than chance is likely to be contributed to by a gene lying close to the marker on the same chromosome.

Unfortunately, conventional linkage analysis requires several assumptions: that there are major gene effects to be detected; that there is some way of ensuring genetic heterogeneity; and that the mode of transmission of the disorder is known. These are potentially hazardous assumptions in common complex traits. Nevertheless, a focus on large, multiply-affected, pedigrees with early onset has enabled these problems to be overcome in some complex disorders such as Alzheimer's disease and breast cancer. To date, this has not been the case with other psychiatric disorders such as schizophrenia or manic–depression, where a bewildering and apparently contradictory array of positive linkage study results has been reported (Riley & McGuffin, 2000; Craddock & Jones, 2000). Linkage studies have only just begun in depression, and so far there are no clearly positive findings (Mahli et al., 2000).

An alternative approach to detecting susceptibility genes for depression is sib-pair analysis. This has been successful in identifying susceptibility loci for disorders such as type I diabetes, and the approach is currently being applied in a range of common disorders. The main drawback is that susceptibility loci of very small effect (e.g., conferring a relative risk of less than 2) may require large samples of sib-pairs (in the region of 600–800) for these genes to be detected (Risch & Merikangas, 1996). Because in a disorder such as depression the relative risk in a sibling is less than 10, it could be that if several additive genes are involved, none will individually have a relative risk of more than about 2. Therefore, although collecting 800 sib-pairs is feasible (and indeed is underway in studies of depression in several centers), it is worth considering other approaches that might be complementary to linkage and that have greater power to detect small effects.

Allelic association is the main such approach. Classically, this is carried out as a case–control study in which the frequency of a marker allele is compared in the two groups. There are two main causes of allelic association. The first is linkage disequilibrium (LD), whereby the marker and the susceptibility locus are so closely linked that their relationship is preserved over many generations of recombination. The second is when the marker itself confers susceptibility to the disorder; for example, the marker is a functional variant in a gene encoding a protein involved in the pathogenesis of the disorder. Unfortunately, there is also a "nuisance" cause of allelic association, which occurs when there has been a recent admixture of populations where the component subpopulations have different frequencies of susceptibility to disease and different frequency of marker alleles, a situation known as *stratification.* Although stratification can be overcome by careful matching of cases and controls on ethnicity, new approaches have been put forward which, in effect, derive the controls from family members. For example, the transmission disequilibrium test (TDT; Spielman, McGinnis, & Ewens, 1993) examines affected individuals where the parents have also been genotyped and where at least one parent is heterozygous for the marker allele being tested. There is then a simple comparison cross-tabulating whether the marker allele versus the alternative ("nontest") allele is transmitted or nontransmitted to the affected individuals.

The advantage of mapping genes using LD is that it can detect very small effects, as little as 1% of variance in liability to the disorder (Plomin, Owen, & McGuffin, 1994). The disadvantage is that because LD only takes place over very short distances, several thousand markers would be required to complete a genome search for susceptibility loci. For this reason, most allelic association studies to date have concentrated on so-called candidate genes, hoping to detect variations that themselves confer a susceptibility or that are so close as to be in LD with such variants. However, new methods are now being developed, for example, that are based on DNA pooling (Daniels et al., 1998), or that examine SNPs on microarrays that allow very high throughput genotyping. These methods should allow close scrutiny of "regions of interest" identified by linkage and even whole genome scans for LD to be completed for common psychiatric diseases such as depression within the foreseeable future.

Candidate Genes

In the meantime, molecular genetic studies of depression have been restricted mainly to studies of *candidate genes,* that is, genes that encode for proteins that have a plausible chance of being involved in the causes of depressed mood. Candidate genes for major depression (and anxiety disorders) have, in the main, been suggested by the molecular mechanisms implicated in the action of therapeutic drugs and the putative pathophysiology for these disorders. Of particular interest are genes associated with neurotransmitter systems. Many of the association studies associated with these phenotypes have focused on the serotonergic system and in particular the serotonin transporter gene located on chromosome 17 (17q11.1-17q12). Many antidepressant and anxiolytic drugs, such as tricyclic antidepressants and the newer serotonin selective reuptake inhibitors, influence the transporter facilitated uptake of serotonin. Indeed, several polymorphisms of the serotonin transporter (SERT) gene have been described.

A 44 bp insertion/deletion polymorphism in the transcriptional control region of the gene has been described; the short version of this promoter polymorphism has been shown to be associated with decreased transcriptional efficiency, resulting in reduced serotonin transporter expression. Since the publication of a report of associations between this genetic variant and personality traits that are likely to be relevant to vulnerablility to depression (Lesch et al., 1996), various studies have explored this association further. Although Katsuragi et al. (1999) replicated the finding in a Japanese sample, several other investigations have failed to do so (reviewed by Malhi et al., 2000). O'Hara et al. (1998) described a tendency for the shorter variant of this polymorphism to be more frequent in patients diagnosed with an anxiety disorder using DSM-IV criteria. Associations of this polymorphism with affective disorders have also been described (Collier et al., 1996). Similar associations have been shown for both unipolar and bipolar subtypes separately (Furlong et al., 1998), although this, too, has not been replicated (O'Hara et al., 1998).

A further variable number tandem repeat polymorphism, in the second intron of the serotonin transporter gene, has also been described (Lesch et al., 1994). Several variants of this polymorphism have been found to be associated with affective disorder (Collier et al.,

1996; Rees et al., 1997). In particular, an association of the 9-copy variant with unipolar depression has been reported (Ogilvie et al., 1996). However, this has not been replicated in independent studies (Kunugi et al., 1997). Gelernter, Cubells, Kidd, Pakstis, and Kidd (1999) investigated the range of allele frequency variation for both the promoter and second intron polymorphisms of the serotonin transporter gene in seven different populations and found significant global variation. Linkage disequilibrium varied among the populations, suggesting a large potential for population stratification in association studies employing population controls. Taken as a whole, therefore, the various association findings suggest that polymorphic variation at this gene results in some phenotypic effect, but it is unclear at present what phenotypic construct best captures this (Gelernter, Kranzler, Coccaro, Siever, & New, 1998).

Other candidate gene association studies in depression and anxiety have investigated the dopamine receptor genes, the tryosine hydroxylase gene related to the gamma-aminobutryic acid system, and the catechol-O-methyltransferase gene (Malhi et al., 2000). The main limitation of candidate gene approaches is that they are dependent on disease pathophysiology. However, a likely prospect for the future is the convergence of positional and candidate gene approaches brought about by the final stage of the Human Genome Project. That is, regions of interest will be identified by linkage, refined by LD, and finally potential candidates will be identified by searches of computer databases containing complete information on all of the genes in that region, a process that has been called positional cloning in silico.

A further approach to be mentioned, as it may facilitate gene mapping in the future, is the use of animal models (Owen, Cardno, & O'Donovan, 2000). Rodent emotionality may be a reasonable homologue for human neuroticism (Flint, 1997). Other examples of psychiatric disorders for which plausible animal models currently exist include depression, substance abuse, and hyperactivity (Owen et al., 2000). Animal models for human psychiatric disorders might emerge by generating large numbers of new mouse phenotypes, many of which will carry disorders that model human genetic disease.

THE LIKELY FUTURE IMPACT OF GENETICS ON CLINICAL PRACTICE

There are three main challenges that face psychiatric genetics in the future: the creation of new technologies for gene finding; the diagnostic and therapeutic use of "depression genes" that will someday be discovered; and the ethical, legal, and social implications of knowing who is, and who is not, at genetic risk for clinical depression.

Common diseases with complex patterns of genetic transmission account for a high proportion of medical illnesses in human populations. Gaining some understanding of the genetic basis of these disorders, including depression, is one of the foremost challenges of human genetics in the next decade. We can expect major contributions from the technological innovations of the Human Genome Project. This project is an immense collaborative effort producing and refining the tools and technologies needed to discover the genes that cause mental illness and other common disorders. Recent scientific and technological advances should enable many more susceptibility alleles to be discovered. Advances include progress in completing the human physical gene map and genome sequence. Other strategies include the development of very high throughput genotyping, sequencing, and differential gene display systems (Gershon, 2000). Further key statistical developments can be expected in the conceptualization and analysis of oligogenic inheritance. These statistical and technological advances can be expected to greatly improve our conceptual understanding of the genetic basis of depressive illness.

Potential Applications

Once susceptibility mutations are identified, the potential applications of this knowledge will include diagnostic tests of vulnerability, a new understanding of the biology of susceptibility, and the tailoring and targeting of treatments based on genotypes.

With increased knowledge, a new psychiatric genetic nosology would seek to classify depressed and other patients into categories that correspond to distinct genetic entities. Psychiatric genetics need not forever rely on diagnostic constructs created for other purposes. Overcoming measurement error will be one of the main challenges facing psychiatric genetics in the coming years.

Once susceptibility mutations for depression are discovered, the focus of research will shift from gene detection to the biological role of these genes in the illness, and then on to developing treatments based on these findings. The genetic contribution to cognitive differences, personality, and preferences (including sexual preference) might then be explored with resultant controversy. The ethical implications are, of course, significant. The new knowledge itself will be a challenge and will require genetic counseling to change and perhaps move toward becoming a much more complex form of intervention.

Clinical Uses of Genetic Testing

Our knowledge of the molecular genetics of depressive illness is too rudimentary at present for use in genetic counseling. It is, however, possible to provide approximate empirical risks on the basis of existing data (Scourfield & McGuffin, 1999), and it may be possible to refine such risk estimates considerably by using DNA tests in relatives of affected individuals. However, risk prediction in complex diseases is always going to be probabilistic and is never likely to be useful for screening at a population level.

Genetic testing in the future may be of value to patients and clinicians in helping to optimize treatment choices by testing genes that are found to influence treatment responsiveness or susceptibility to side effects. This will lead to greater individualization of treatment. There is already preliminary evidence that genotypes can be used to predict treatment response in other disorders such as schizophrenia (Arranz et al., 2000). The discovery of genes involved in the susceptibility to unipolar depression has major potential to lead on to the discovery of novel targets for new drug development. This area of pharmacogenomics is seen by leading figures in the pharmaceutical industry as likely to become the most exciting and potentially productive area in pharmacology in the 21st century (Roses, 2000).

Neurobiology

Considerable evidence indicates that, regardless of the initial triggers, the final common pathway of depression involves biochemical changes in the brain. It is these changes that ultimately give rise to the deep sadness and the other salient characteristics of depression. Disturbed functioning of serotonin or noradrenaline contributes to depression in many (perhaps all) individuals. Dysregulation of brain circuits that control the activities of certain *hormones* have also been implicated in depression. The strongest case has been made for the dysregulation of the hypothalamic–pituitary–adrenal (HPA) axis, the system that manages our response to stress. Chronic activation of the axis may lay the groundwork for illness and depression. The finding of HPA axis hyperactivity is the most replicated in biological psychiatry.

Nemeroff (1998) has proposed that aberrations in the corticotrophin releasing factor producing neurones of the hypothalmus and elsewhere bear most of the responsibility for

HPA axis hyperactivity and the emergence of depressive symptoms. Postmortum brain tissue studies have revealed a marked exaggeration in the expression of the corticotropin releasing factor (CRF) gene (resulting in elevated CRF synthesis) in depressed patients as compared with controls. Neurobiologists do not yet know how the genetic, monoamine, and hormonal findings fit together, but it is possible that certain genes may lower the threshold for depression in susceptible individuals. This genetic feature may directly or indirectly diminish monoamine levels or increase the reactivity of the HPA axis to stress. The genetically determined threshold may be pushed even lower by adversity and stress. Abuse or neglect in childhood may chronically boost the output of, and responsiveness to, CRF, and therefore increase the individual's lifelong vulnerability to depression.

More work on the neurobiology of depression in the future is clearly indicated, together with attempts to integrate this neurobiology with the genetic basis of affective disorder. The advances achieved so far are clearly being translated into ideas for new medications with significant implications for diagnosis and treatment. Blockers of CRF receptors may have antidepressant properties. Activators of specific serotonin receptors may potentially exert powerful antidepressant effects, without unnecessarily stimulating serotonin receptors on neurones that play no direct part in depression. Increased knowledge of the genetic basis of depression is likely to greatly enhance our understanding of the neurobiology of this common disorder, with far-reaching implications for the development of new forms of treatment and management.

FUTURE DIRECTIONS

In the future, genetic research will move beyond estimating heritabilities or simply demonstrating that genetic factors are important in the etiology of psychiatric disorders such as depression. The questions *whether* or *how much* genetic factors affect psychological disorders represent important first steps in understanding why some individuals develop a disorder such as depressive illness while others do not. These, however, are initial, preliminary steps. We have moved on from these questions, and we have already begun to ask how genes exert their effect and what are the mechanisms by which genes give rise to a disorder such as depression. What are the biological pathways between genes and behavior? How do genes and the environment interact and correlate? The future will see genetics moving beyond merely documenting genetic influence. Large-scale collaborative research projects that focus on important and more complex issues are already underway (Plomin et al., 2001).

A question concerning psychiatric genetics that will be increasingly addressed in the future is whether genetic and environmental components of variance change during development. Do the effects of genes alter during development? We know from work in general cognitive ability that although shared family environment is important in childhood, its influence becomes negligible after adolescence. Genetic influences, therefore, can alter and become increasingly important throughout the life span. The influence of a person's genetic makeup on a disorder such as depression may not be static and fixed throughout his or her life but, developmentally, may exert a varying influence on the phenotype. In the future, developmental genetic analysis will consider change, as well as continuity, throughout the individual's lifetime.

Interesting discoveries await us, not just regarding developmental changes, but concerning the environmental mechanisms that impact on depressive disorders. Genetically sensitive designs will tell us much more about the role of the environment in the development of psychopathology and about the interaction between nature and nurture. Genetic research in the past has told us much about the role of the environment in disorders such as depression, and we can expect that it will continue to do so in the future.

Another intriguing question increasingly demanding the attention of psychiatric geneticists will be the question of comorbidity (see Lewinsohn & Essau, Chapter 23, this volume). Why in the field of psychopathology do so many disorders coexist? In the future, multivariate genetic research will investigate this question and may confirm that a genetic overlap between disorders, such as depression and anxiety, accounts for much of this comorbidity. Multivariate genetic analysis has the advantage of focusing on the covariance between traits, rather than on the variance of each trait considered in isolation.

Thus, psychiatric genetics is moving away from questions concerning how *much* a disorder such as depression is genetically determined to the question of *how* it is genetically influenced. Molecular genetic research will increasingly address heritable components of disorders throughout the human life span as they alter and interact with the environment (Plomin et al., 2001). The results of this research are likely to have a significant impact in terms of prediction, diagnosis, treatment, and prevention of depressive disorder.

The practical implications of this work are enormous. As the technology becomes increasingly less expensive, genotyping will become more available in clinical practice. This will allow prediction of treatment response and the individual tailoring of treatments to take into account both susceptibility to drug side effects and the likely therapeutic efficacy of particular medication. It may even allow preventative strategies, pharmacological and cognitive, to be implemented before the disorder has caused significant impairment.

CONCLUSIONS

The heritability for milder forms of depression is 20–45% (Kendler et al., 1992). Severe depression ascertained through hospital treated cases, however, probably has a much higher heritability (McGuffin et al., 1996). It seems probable that much of the genetic liability for milder depressive conditions and anxiety disorders is the same, and may be mediated, in part, through personality traits such as neuroticism (Kendler et al., 1993). It also appears that at least part of the genetic component involves a susceptibility to environmental stressors, the frequency of which itself is influenced in part by genetic factors (Foley, Neale, & Kendler, 1996).

Progress in psychiatric genetics has been inhibited to date because, despite reasonable reliability, current systems for psychiatric classification are of uncertain biological validity. Furthermore, genetic research has not been able to elucidate a specific causal pathophysiology involved in mood disorders. But if susceptibility genes can be identified, and if this leads to an improved understanding of how genes work and what they actually do to bring about depression, it would help enormously in understanding the basic biological causal processes at work in the disorder. It is worth remembering that the pathway of knowledge will span several quite different scientific domains and will demand collaboration and an integration of perspectives.

Genetic dissection of depressive illness is continuing. While understanding of the mechanisms of familial components that contribute to affective disorders has improved substantially at a epidemiological level, our understanding of genomic determinants is still impeded by the complex pattern of expression of the phenotype (Maier et al., 1994). Despite these significant difficulties, however, it is likely that over the next few years susceptibility genes for depression will be discovered. This will have a major impact on our understanding of the disease pathophysiology. This knowledge will also provide important opportunities for investigation of the interaction of genetic and environmental factors that are involved in the pathogenesis of depression. Although this is likely to lead to major improvements in treatment and patient care, it is also likely to raise important and fundamental ethical issues regarding the prevention and treatment of this common and debilitating condition.

REFERENCES

Andreasen, N. C., Rice, J., Endicott. J., Reich, T., & Coryell, W. (1986). The family history approach to diagnosis. *Archives of General Psychiatry, 43,* 421–429.

Andrew, M., McGuffin, P., & Katz, R. (1998). Genetic and non-genetic subtypes of major depressive disorder. *British Journal of Psychiatry, 173,* 523–526.

Arranz, M. J., Munro, J., Birkett, J., Bolonna, A., Mancama, D., Sodhi, M., Lesch, K. P., Meyer, J. F., Sham, P., Collier, D. A., Murray, R. M., & Kerwin, R. W. (2000). Pharmacogenetic prediction of clozapine response. *Lancet, 355*(9215), 1615–1616.

Beirut, L. J., Heath, A. C., Bucholz, K., Dinwiddle, S., Madden, P., Strathay, D., Dunne, M. P., & Martin, N. (1999). Major depressive disorder in a community based sample: Are there different genetic and environmental contributions for men and women? *Archives of General Psychiatry, 56*(60), 557–563.

Bertelsen, A. (1985). Controversies and consistencies in psychiatric genetics. *Acta Psychiatrica Scandinavica, 319*(Suppl.), 61–75.

Brown, G. W., & Harris, T. (1978). *The social origins of depression: A study of psychiatric disorder in women.* London: Tavistock.

Collier, D. A., Stober, G., Li, T., Heils, A., Catalano, M., Di Bella, D., Arranz, M. J., Murry, R. M., Vallada, H. P., Bengel, D., Muller, C. R., Roberts, G. W., Smeraldi, E., Kirov, G., Sham, P., & Lesch, K. P. (1996). A novel functional polymorphism within the promoter of the serotonin transporter gene: Possible role in the susceptibility to affective disorder. *Molecular Psychiatry, 2,* 224–226.

Craddock, N., & Jones, I. (1999). Genetics of bipolar disorder. *Journal of Medical Genetics, 36*(8), 585–594.

Daniels, J., Holmans, P., Williams, N., Turic, D., McGuffin, P., Plomin, R., & Owen, M. J. (1998). A simple method for analyzing microsatellite allele image patterns generated from DNA pools and its application to allelic association studies. *American Journal of Human Genetics, 62,* 1189–1197.

Duggan, C., Sham, P., Minne, C., Lee, A., & Murray, R. (1998). Does the method of data collection affect the reporting of depression in the relatives of depressed probands? *Journal of Affective Disorders, 47,* 151–158.

Endicott, J., & Spitzer, R. L. (1978). A diagnostic interview: The Schedule for Affective Disorders and Schizophrenia. *Archives of General Psychiatry, 35,* 837–844.

Falconer, D. S. (1965). The inheritance of liability to certain diseases, estimated from the incidence among relatives. *Annals of Human Genetics, 29,* 51–76.

Falconer, D. S., & Mackay, T. F. (1996). *Introduction to quantitative genetics* (4th ed.). London: Longman, Harlow.

Faraone, S. V., Tsuang, M. T., & Tsuang, D. W. (1999). *Genetics of mental disorders: A guide for students, clinicians, and researchers.* New York: Guilford Press.

Farmer, A. (1996). The genetics of depressive disorders. *International Review of Psychiatry, 8,* 369–372.

Farmer, A. E., Owen, M. J., & McGuffin, P. (2000). Bioethics and genetic research in psychiatry [editorial]. *British Journal of Psychiatry, 176,* 105–108.

Flint, J. (1997). Freeze! *Nature Genetics, 17,* 250–251.

Foley, D. L., Neale, M., & Kendler, K. (1996). A longitudinal study of stressful life events. *Psychiatric Medicine, 26,* 1239–1252.

Furlong, R. A., Ho, L., Walsh, C., Rubinsztein, J. S., Jain, S., Paykel, E. S., Easton, D. F., & Rubinsztein, D. C. (1998). Analysis and meta-analysis of two serotonin transporter gene polymorphisms in bipolar and unipolar affective disorders. *American Journal of Medical Genetics, 81,* 58–63.

Gelernter, J., Cubells, J. F., Kidd, J. R., Pakstis, A. J., & Kidd, K. K. (1999). Population studies of polymorphisms of the serotonin transporter protein gene. *American Journal of Medical Genetics, 88,* 61–66.

Gelernter, J., Kranzler, H., Coccaro, E. F., Siever, L. J., & New, A. S. (1998). Serotonin transporter protein gene polymorphism and personality measures in African American and European American subjects. *American Journal of Psychiatry, 155,* 1332–1338.

Gershon, E. S. (2000). Bipolar illness and schizophrenia as oligogenic diseases: Implications for the future. *Biological Psychiatry, 47*(3), 240–244.

Gershon, E., Bunney, W. E., Leckman, J., Van Eerdewegh, M., & De Bauche, B. A. (1976). The inheritance of affective disorders: A review of data and hypotheses. *Behavior Genetics, 6,* 227–261.

Harrington, R., Rutter, M., Weissman, M., Fudge, H., Groothues, C., Bredenkamp, D., Pickles, A., Rende, R., & Wickramratne, P. (1997). Psychiatric disorders in the relatives of depressed probands. *Journal of Affective Disorders, 42,* 9–22.

Henderson, A. (1998). Social support: Its present significance for psychiatric epidemiology. In B. P. Dohrenwend (Ed.), *Adversity, stress and psychopathology* (pp. 390–397). New York: Oxford University Press.

Katsuragi, S., Kunugi, H., Sano, A., Tsutsumi, T., Isowaga, K., Nanko, S., & Akiyoshi, J. (1999). Association between serotonin transporter gene polymorphism and anxiety-related traits. *Biological Psychiatry, 45,* 368–370.

Kendler, K. (1993). Twin studies of psychiatric illness. *Archives of General Psychiatry, 50*(11), 905–915.

Kendler, K. (1998). Major depression and the environment: A psychiatric genetic perspective. *Pharmacopsychiatry, 31,* 5–9.

Kendler, K., & Eaves, L. (1986). Models for the joint effect of genotype and environment on liability to psychiatric illness. *American Journal of Psychiatry, 143,* 279–289.

Kendler, K., & Gardner, C. O. (1998). Twin studies of adult psychiatric and substance dependence disorders. *Psychological Medicine, 28*(3), 625–633.

Kendler, K. S., Karkowski, L. M., & Prescott, C. A. (1999). Causal relationship between stressful life events and the onset of major depression. *Amercia Journal of Psychiatry, 156,* 837–841.

Kendler, K., & Karkowski-Shuman, L. (1997). Stressful life events and genetic liability to major depression. *Psychological Medicine, 27,* 539–547.

Kendler, K., Neale, M., Kessler, R., Heath, A., & Eaves, L. (1992). Major depression and generalized anxiety disorder. *Archives of General Psychiatry, 49,* 716–722.

Kendler, K., Neale, M., Kessler, R., Heath, A., & Eaves, L. (1993). A twin study of recent life events and difficulties. *Archives of General Psychiatry, 50,* 863–870.

Kendler, K. S., Pedersen, N. L., Farahmand, B., & Persson, P. G. (1996). The treated incidence of psychotic and affective illness in twins compared to the general population expectation: A study in the Swedish twin and psychiatric registries. *Psychological Medicine, 26,* 1135–1144.

Kunugi, H., Hattori, M., Kato, T., Tatsumi, M., Sakai, T., Sasaki, T., Hirose, T., & Nanko, S. (1997). Serotonin transporter gene polymorphisms: Ethnic difference and possible association with bipolar affective disorder. *Molecular Psychiatry, 2,* 457–462.

Lesch, K. P., Balling, U., Gross, J., Strauss, K., Wolozin, B. L., Murphy, D. L., & Riederer, P. (1994). Organisation of the human serotonin transporter gene. *Journal of Neural Transmission. General Section, 95,* 157–162.

Lesch, K. P., Bengel, D., Heils, A., Sabol, S. Z., Greenberg, B. D., Petri, S., Benjamin, J., Muller, C. R., Hamer, D. H., & Murphy, D. L. (1996). Association of anxiety-related traits with a polymorphism in the serotonin transporter gene regulatory region. *Science, 274,* 1527–1531.

Lyons, M. J., Eisen, S. A., Goldberg, J., True, W., Lin, N., Meyer, J. M., Toomey, R., Faraone, S. V., Merla-Ramos, M., & Tsuang, M. T. (1998). A registry-based twin study of depression in men. *Archives of General Psychiatry, 5,* 468–472.

Maier, W., Lichermann, D., & Merikangas, K. (1994). Epidemiology and genetics of affective disorders: Recent developments. In H. Hippius & C. Stefanis (Eds.), *Research in mood disorders.* Goettingen, Germany: Hogrefe & Huber.

Maier, W., Lichtermann, D., Minges, J., Heun, R., Hallmayer, J., & Klinger, T. (1991). Unipolar depression in the aged: Determinents of familial aggregation. *Journal of Affective Disorders, 23,* 53–61.

Malhi, G. S., Moore, J., & McGuffin, P. (2000). The genetics of major depressive disorder. *Current Psychiatry Reports, 2,* 165–169.

McGue, M., & Christensen, K. (1997). Genetic and environmental contributions to depression symptomatology: Evidence from Danish twins 75 years of age. *Journal of Abnormal Psychology, 106*(3), 439–448.

McGue, M., Sharma, A., & Benson, P. (1996). Parent and sibling influences on adolescent alcohol use and misuse: Evidence from a U.S. adoption cohort. *Journal of Studies on Alcohol, 57*(1), 8–18.

McGuffin, P. (1994). Genetics. In E. S. Paykel & R. Jenkins (Eds.), *Prevention in psychiatry.* London: Gaskell Press.

McGuffin, P. (1996). Genetic aspects of mental illness. In A. Kuper & J. Kuper (Eds.), *The social science encyclopedia* (pp. 332–333). London: Routledge.

McGuffin, P., & Katz, R. (1986). Nature, nurture and affective disorders. In J. W. K. Deakin (Ed.), *The biology of depression* (pp. 26–51). London: Gaskell Press.

McGuffin, P., Katz, R., & Bebbington, P. (1987). Hazard, heredity, and depression: A family study. *Journal of Psychiatric Research, 21*(4), 365–375.

McGuffin, P., Katz, R., & Bebbington, P. (1988). The Camberwell Collaborative Depression: Study 3. Depression and adversity in the relatives of depressed probands. *British Journal of Psychiatry, 152,* 775–782.

McGuffin, P., Katz, R., & Rutherford, J. (1991). Nature, nurture and depression: A twin study. *Psychological Medicine, 21,* 329–335.

McGuffin, P., Katz, R., Rutherford, J., Watkins, S., Farmer, A. E., & Gottesman, I. (1993). Twin studies as vital indicators of phenotypes in molecular genetic research. In T. Bouchard & P. Poppin (Eds.), *Twins as tools of behavioural genetics* (pp. 224–256). Chichester, UK: Wiley.

McGuffin, P., Katz, R., Watkins, S., & Rutherford, J. (1996). A hospital-based twin register of heritability of DSM-IV unipolar depression. *Archives of General Psychiatry, 53,* 129–136.

Mendlewicz, J., & Rainer, J. D. (1977). Adoption study supporting genetic transmission in manic-depressive illness. *Nature, 268*(5618), 327–329.

Murray, C. J. L., & Lopez, A. D. (1996). Evidence-based health policy: Lessons from the Global Burden of Disease Study. *Science, 274,* 740–743.

Nemeroff, C. B. (1998, June). The neurobiology of depression. *Scientific American,* pp. 28–35.

Ogilvie, A. D., Battersby, S., Bubb, V. J., Fink, G., Harmar, A. J., Goodwin, G. M., & Smith, C. A. D. (1996). Polymorphism in serotonin transporter gene associated with susceptibility to major depression. *Lancet, 347,* 731–733.

Ohara, K., Nagai, M., Tsukamoto, T., Tani, K., Suzuki, Y., & Ohara, K. (1998). Functional polymorphism in the serotonin transporter promoter at the SLC6A4 locus and mood disorders. *Biological Psychiatry, 44,* 550–554.

O'Rourke, D. H., McGuffin, P., & Reich, T. (1983). Genetic analysis of manic-depressive illness. *American Journal of Physical Anthropology, 62,* 51–59.

Orvaschel, H., Douglas Thompson, W., Belanger, A., Prusoff, B. A., & Kidd, K. K. (1982). Comparison of the family history method to direct interview. *Journal of Affective Disorders, 4,* 49–59.

Owen, M. J., Cardno, A. G., & O'Donovan, M. C. (2000). Psychiatric genetics: Back to the future. *Molecular Psychiatry, 5*(1), 22–31.

Plomin, R., DeFries, J. C., McClearn, G. E., & McGuffin, P. (2001). *Behavioral genetics* (4th ed.). New York: Worth.

Plomin, R., Owen, M. J., & McGuffin, P. (1994). The genetic basis of complex human behaviours. *Science, 264,* 1733–1739.

Pollitt, C. (1972). The relationship between genetic and precipitating factors in depressive illness. *British Journal of Psychiatry, 121,* 67–70.

Rees, M., Norton, N., Jones, I., McCandless, F., Scourfield, J., Holmans, P., Moorhead, S., Feldman, E., Sadler, S., Cole, T., Redman, K., Farmer, A., McGuffin, P., Owen, M., & Craddock, N. (1997). Association studies of bipolar disorder at the human serotonin transporter gene (hSERT; 5HTT). *Molecular Psychiatry, 2,* 398–402.

Riley, B. P., & McGuffin, P. (2000). Linkage and associated studies of schizophrenia. *American Journal of Medical Genetics, 97,* 23–44.

Risch, N., & Merikangas, K. (1996). The future of genetic studies of complex human disease. *Science, 273,* 1516–1517.

Roses, A. D. (2000). Pharmacogenetics and the practice of medicine. *Nature, 405*(6788), 857–865.

Rutter, M. (1997). Implications of genetic research for child psychiatry. *Canadian Journal of Psychiatry, 42*(6), 569–576.

Scourfield, J., & McGuffin, P. (1999). Familial risks and genetic counselling for common psychiatric disorders. *Advances in Psychiatric Treatment, 5,* 39–45.

Silberg, J., Pickles, A., Rutter, M., Hewitt, J., Simonoff, E., Maes, H., Carbonneau, R., Murrelle, L., Foley, D., & Eaves, L. (1999). The influence of genetic factors and life stress on depression among adolescent girls. *Archives of General Psychiatry, 56,* 225–232.

Spielman, R. S., McGinnis, R. E., & Ewens, W. J. (1993). Transmission test for linkage disequilibrium: The insulin gene region and insulin dependent diabetes mellitus. *American Journal of Human Genetics, 52,* 506–516.

Stenstedt, A. (1966). Genetics of neurotic depression. *Acta Psychiatrica Scandinavica, 42*(4), 392–409.

Sullivan, P., Neale, M., & Kendler, K. (2000). General epidemiology of major depression: Review and meta-analysis. *American Journal of Psychiatry, 157,* 1552–1562.

Thapar, A., Harold, G., & McGuffin, P. (1998). Life events and depressive symptoms in childhood: Shared genes or shared adversity? A research note. *Journal of Child Psychology and Psychiatry, 39*(8), 1153–1158.

Thapar, A., & McGuffin, P. (1994). A twin study of depressive symptoms in childhood. *British Journal of Psychiatry, 165,* 259–265.

Tsuang, M. T., & Faraone, S. V. (1994). The genetic epidemiology of schizophrenia. *Comprehensive Therapy, 20*(2), 130–135.

Tsuang, M. T., & Farone, S. V. (1996). The inheritance of mood disorders. In L. L. Hall (Ed.), *Genetics and mental illness: Evolving issues for research and society* (pp. 79–109). New York: Plenum Press.

Wade, T., & Kendler, K. (2000). The relationship between social support and major depression. *Journal of Nervous and Mental Disease, 188,* 251–258.

Weissman, M. M., Merikangas, K. R., John, K., Wickramaratne, P., Prusoff, B. A., & Kidd, K. K. (1986). Family-genetic studies of psychiatric disorders. *Acta Psychiatrica Scandinavica, 43,* 1104–1115.

Wender, P. H., Kety, S. S., Rosenthal, D., Schulsinger, F., Ortmann, J., & Lunde, I. (1986). Psychiatric disorders in the biological and adoptive families of adopted individuals with affective disorders. *Archives of General Psychiatry, 43,* 923–929.

Wing, J. K., Babor, T., Brugha, T., Burke, J., Cooper, J. E., Giel, R., Jablenski, A., Regier, D., & Sartorius, N. (1990). SCAN: Schedules for Clinical Assessment in Neuropsychiatry. *Archives of General Psychiatry, 47*(6), 589–593.

Zerbin-Rudin, E. (1979). Genetics of affective disorders. In M. Schou & E. Stromgren (Eds.), *Origin, prevention and treatment of affective disorders* (pp. 185–197). London: Academic Press.

8

Biological Aspects of Depression

Michael E. Thase, Ripu Jindal, and Robert H. Howland

There have been speculations about the biological basis of depressive disorders since antiquity (Jackson, 1986). Indeed, the term currently used to describe one of the most severe forms of depression, *melancholia*, reflects the ancient theory that depression was caused by an excessive amount of black bile. In the broadest sense, all modern formulations of depression must incorporate biological factors because biology is the study of life processes. Thus, putting aside metaphysical and spiritual perspectives for the moment, all disturbances of human cognition, affects, and behavior have biological underpinnings.

Our group has reviewed the evidence pertaining to a wide range of neurochemical, neuroendocrine, neurophysiological, and structural correlates of depression (e.g., Thase, Frank, & Kupfer, 1985; Thase & Howland, 1995). In this chapter, we emphasize research published since 1994 and focus on a conceptual model that posits that many aspects of depression can be understood in terms of dysregulation of central nervous system (CNS) responses to stress. *Dysregulation* refers to both a longer duration and a greater intensity of CNS stress responses that are normally transient and adaptive. We examine the impact of various mediating and moderating factors, including genetics, age, sex, and developmental history. We also consider relationships between neurobiological findings and the clinical phenomenology, longitudinal course, and treatment of the depressive disorders. Notable new developments include research on the intracellular processes that link receptors and second messengers to gene activity and the process of *neurogenesis*, the brain's capacity to create new neurons.

BACKGROUND

The methodology to study brain function in depression began to be developed in the 1950s. In relatively short order, converging lines of evidence pointed to the likelihood of dysfunction of CNS systems subserved by two key neurotransmitters: the catecholamine norepinephrine (NE) and the indoleamine serotonin (also known as 5-hydroxytryptamine, or 5-HT). Both these monoamines were found to regulate vital bodily functions that often are disturbed during depression (e.g., energy, sleep, appetite, libido, and psychomotor behavior). Moreover, the first effective pharmacological treatments, the tricyclic antidepressants (TCAs) and monoamine oxidase inhibitors (MAOIs), were shown to have effects that enhanced NE and/or 5-HT neurotransmission.

In the earliest monoamine theories, depression was proposed to be caused by a deficit of 5-HT or NE activity, whereas mania resulted from increased NE activity, perhaps in the context of diminished 5-HT (Bunney & Davis, 1965; Glassman, 1969; Schildkraut, 1965). Subsequently, evidence of diminished activity of a third monoamine, dopamine, was integrated into biological models of depression (Korf & van Praag, 1971). Several decades of vigorous research subsequently disconfirmed the most simplistic models, but yielded substantial evidence of disturbed monoamine function in subgroups of people with depressive or bipolar disorders (Maes & Meltzer, 1995; Schatzberg & Schildkraut, 1995; Willner, 1995). Perhaps even more importantly, this research revealed the staggering complexity of integrated CNS response systems. Examples of such complexity included the identification of dozens of additional peptide and amino acid neurotransmitters, recognition that neurons could express receptors for several different neurotransmitters (thus enabling direct "cross-talk" between various neuronal systems), and elucidation of intracellular mechanisms of gene transduction (Duman, Heninger, & Nestler, 1997; Nemeroff, 1998).

Several findings from the initial wave of neurobiological studies of mood disorders have had enduring relevance. First, a subgroup of depressed patients was found to excrete low urinary levels of the NE metabolite 3-methoxy-4-hydroxyphenylglycol (MHPG) (Ressler & Nemeroff, 1999; Schatzberg & Schildkraut, 1995). Because approximately 30–40% of urinary MHPG is derived from the brain, this finding indicated that depressed patients may indeed manifest some diminution of central NE function. Low urinary MHPG also was linked to the bipolar subtype of depression, to psychomotor retardation, and to a relatively favorable response to TCAs and the related tetracyclic compound maprotiline (Schatzberg & Schildkraut, 1995). Because these medications directly affect NE neurotransmission by inhibition of cell membrane-bound reuptake transporters, the potential functional significance of low urinary MHPG was underscored. However, it was also clearly established that most depressions are not characterized by systemic reductions in NE activity. In fact, more severely depressed patients were found to manifest multiple signs of excessive peripheral NE activity.

The second important finding was that a minority of depressed patients had low cerebrospinal fluid (CSF) levels of the 5-HT metabolite 5-hydroxyindoleacetic acid (5-HIAA) (Maes & Meltzer, 1995). This abnormality, which is indicative of decreased 5-HT neurotransmission, has been linked to increased risk of completed suicide, potentially lethal suicide attempts, and other violent, life-threatening behaviors (Maes & Meltzer, 1995; Mann, Brent, & Arango, 2001). The ability of medications that enhance 5-HT function to treat depression further stimulated research. Low CSF 5-HIAA was not found, however, to predict favorable response to antidepressants with strong effects on 5-HT systems, such as the TCA clomipramine or the more recently introduced selective serotonin reuptake inhibitors (SSRIs; e.g., fluoxetine or sertraline) (Maes & Meltzer, 1995). Moreover, low CSF 5-HIAA was also not found to be specific to depression. As we discuss later in this chapter, low CSF 5-HIAAA may be a more enduring, trait-like phenomenon that is associated with impulsivity, aggressivity, and violent behavior. Research now focuses on the broader role of 5-HT neurotransmission as a modulator of CNS stress response systems.

A third finding pertains to the stress-responsive glucocorticoid hormone cortisol. Cortisol is released by the adrenal cortex in response to a wide variety of physical and psychosocial stresses. Perceived stress and adrenal gland activity are linked by a cascade of neuropeptides extending from the cerebral cortex and hypothalamus to the pituitary. In health, the cortical–hypo–thalamic–pituitary–adrenocortical axis is tightly regulated. Plasma cortisol levels follow a well-characterized daily variation, ranging from highest in the morning to lowest at about the time of sleep onset. Both elevated cortisol levels and blunting of the diurnal secretion pattern have been observed in virtually all body fluids of depressed people, including plasma, urine, saliva, and CSF specimens (Holsboer, 1995; Thase & Howland, 1995). Such hypercortisolism, which is typically evident in 40–60% of study groups of depressed people, has been associated with older age, psychosis, greater global severity, weight loss, insomnia, and suicidality (Thase & Howland, 1995). Moreover, hypercortisolism tends to coaggregate with various measures of NE and 5-HT dysfunction, representing a convergent pathway of dysregulated CNS responses (Holsboer, 1995; Maes & Meltzer, 1995; Schatzberg & Schildkraut, 1995).

The fourth critical finding involves alterations in brain activity during sleep, as originally measured by all-night electroencephalographic (EEG) or polysomnographic (PSG) recordings. These changes were especially intriguing because studies of routine waking EEG rhythms gradually revealed no differences between depressed people and normal controls (Thase et al., 1985). Although more precise methods of structural and functional neuroimaging have now largely replaced the waking EEG as a research tool, PSG studies have continued relevance as a means to examine the rhythmic shifts between restful, deep sleep and psychologically charged periods of rapid eye movement (REM) sleep. Deep sleep is characterized by slow, high-amplitude desynchronized waves, known as delta or slow waves. Slow wave sleep (SWS) is characterized by low activity of monoamine systems and increased intracellular protein synthesis. REM sleep, in contrast, involves high-frequency, low-amplitude brain waves, coupled with hypotonia of skeletal muscles and darting, rapid eye movements. The first REM sleep period thereafter occurs after 60–90 minutes of sleep and normally recurs at 90-minute intervals throughout the night, with each interval lasting from 5 to 30 minutes. Most studies of depressed adults have confirmed the presence of decreased SWS, increased intensity of REM sleep, and/or reduced latency to the onset of the first REM sleep period (Thase et al., 1985); between 40% and 80% of patient groups manifest all three abnormalities (Thase, Kupfer, et al., 1997). Interestingly, however, none of the changes is specific to, or diagnostic for, depression (Benca, Obermeyer, Thisted, & Gillin, 1992).

ABNORMALITIES OF NEUROBIOLOGICAL RESPONSE SYSTEMS

Although the early monoamine hypotheses formulated by Schildkraut (1965), Bunney and Davis (1965), and Glassman (1969) have undergone much revision, understanding the function of norepinephrine (NE), serotonin (5-HT), and dopamine (DA) remains critical to the study of the pathophysiology of mood disorders.

Noradrenergic Systems

Almost all the NE cell bodies in the brain are located in a single nucleus, the locus ceruleus (LC), located in the rostral pons. Noradrenergic neurons project from the LC to the thalamus, hypothalamus, limbic system, basal ganglia, and cerebral cortex (see Figure 8.1) (Kandel, Schwarz, & Jessell, 1991; Kingsley, 2000). Such diffuse distribution reflects the broad role of NE in initiating and maintaining limbic and cortical arousal, as well as modulating other neural systems. For example, noradrenergic projections to the amygdala and hippocampus have been implicated in behavioral sensitization to stress (Ferry, Roozendaal, & McGaugh, 1999). Stimulation of the medial forebrain bundle, another major NE pathway

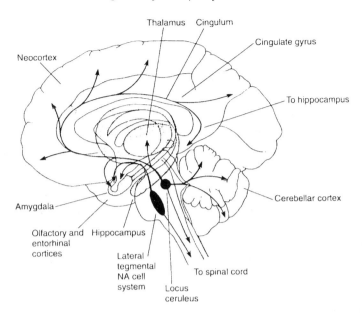

FIGURE 8.1. A lateral view of the brain demonstrates the course of the major noradrenergic pathways emanating from the locus ceruleus and from the lateral brain stem tegmentum. From Kandel, Schwartz, and Jessell (1991). Copyright 1991 by Springer-Verlag GmbH & Co, KG. Reprinted by permission.

in the brain, enhances attention and increases levels of goal-directed or reward-seeking behavior (Aston-Jones, Rajkowski, & Cohen, 1999).

Perception of novel or threatening stimuli is relayed from the cerebral cortex to the LC via the thalamus and hypothalamus and from the periphery via the nucleus prepositus hypoglossi. These inputs can provoke an almost immediate increase in NE activity. Cognitive processes affecting perception thus can amplify or dampen NE cellular responses to internal or external stimuli. In addition, activation from fibers projecting from the nucleus paragigantocellularis (probably using a small, excitatory neurotransmitter such as glutamate), and release of the hypothalamic neuropeptide corticotropin-releasing hormone (CRH) can "turn on" the LC (Nestler, Alreja, & Aghajanian, 1999). The peripheral component of response to stress is triggered by the LC via the sympathoadrenal pathway. Norepinephrine is released into the bloodstream from endochromafin cells in the medulla of the adrenal glands. It is probably not a coincidence that the principal effectors of peripheral stress response, NE and cortisol, are released from glands that are located only a few centimeters apart, deep in the abdomen. The peripherally arousing effects of the sympathoadrenal response are largely mediated by cells expressing the α_1 and β-type of NE receptors.

The activity of NE neurons is regulated in part by the autoinhibitory effects of α_2 receptors. Thus, neuronal release of NE immediately begins to decrease the sensitivity of LC neurons to repeated firing. It is now known that α_2 receptors also are located on serotoninergic cell bodies and stimulation of these heteroceptors activates inhibitory 5-HT neurons. A sustained increase in LC firing (i.e., in response to persistent stress) also causes the number of α_1 and β receptors to decrease, a process known as down-regulation or desensitization. Together, α_2 autoinhibition, α_1 and β receptor downregulation, and activation of colocalized inhibitory 5-HT tracts constitute the counterregulatory forces that promote homeostasis in the face of sustained threat (i.e., NE-mediated arousal). However, if the stress is unresolvable, the stores of NE available for release will become depleted as demand or turnover eventually will exceed synthetic capacity. When this occurs, there will be diminished inhibitory α_2 and 5-HT input to the LC. Homeostasis of NE neurotransmission thus may become dysregulated, resulting in increased firing of the LC but inefficient signal transduction. Over time, the net effect is that ascending central NE neurotransmission will decrease (reflected in lower urinary excretion of MHPG), whereas peripheral output from the adrenal medulla may remain high.

The behavioral consequences of sustained stress on NE systems include decreased exploratory and consummatory behavior, a state described in experimental paradigms as learned helplessness (Maier & Seligman, 1976). Although not synonymous with depression in humans, "learned helplessness" can be viewed as an analogous state of CNS "exhaustion" associated with reductions of monoamine levels in the CNS and elevated glucocorticoid activity (Weiss & Kilts, 1998). It is the contextual and representational (i.e., verbal, cognitive, or attributional) correlates of such exhaustion that helps to define the clinical state of depression in humans. For example, subjective descriptors of constructs such as entrapment, powerlessness, hopelessness, or personal responsibility (guilt) may distinguish depression in humans from the more artificially induced states of learned helplessness observed in animal studies (Gilbert, 1992).

Although there is no doubt that NE systems are disturbed, studies using contemporary research methods have not clarified whether NE dysfunction in depression is a primary or secondary abnormality (Anand et al., 2000; Ressler & Nemeroff, 1999). To date, no evidence of involvement of specific genes that code for NE receptors or relevant enzymes has emerged. The most consistently replicated abnormalities of NE function, namely, a subgroup of patients with lower urinary MHPG excretion, a partly overlapping subgroup of patients with elevated peripheral NE metabolites, and patients who manifest a blunted response to α_1 agonists, could simply reflect the consequences of sustained activation of the LC (Anand et al., 2000; Ressler & Nemeroff, 1999).

A variety of antidepressant interventions decrease the turnover of NE, as well as the firing rate of LC neurons (Ressler & Nemeroff, 1999). Studies of NE-active antidepressants have yielded evidence of enhanced functional efficiency, as reflected by normalization of pineal function or blood pressure responses to orthostatic challenge (Golden, Markey, Risby, Cowdry, & Potter, 1998; Ressler & Nemeroff, 1999). Enhanced NE function also has been demonstrated in studies of serotonin-selective medications, indicating that a direct effect of NE neurotransmission is not necessary to "correct" LC dysregulation (Miller, Ekstrom, Mason, Lydiard, & Golden, 2001; Ressler & Nemeroff, 1999). Despite such common effects, administration of an analogue of the NE precursor tyrosine (α-methyl-paratyrosine), which inhibits the synthetic enzyme tyrosine hydroxylase, has been shown to reverse the effects of norepinephrine reuptake inhibitors (NRI) but not of SSRIs (Miller, Delgado, Salomon, Heninger, & Charney, 1996). Moreover, additive effects on rapidity and magnitude of β-receptor downregulation have been observed when an SSRI and an NRI are simultaneously administered to animals (Baron et al., 1988). Together, these data suggest that antidepressant interventions that target both NE and 5-HT systems may have greater or broader effects than interventions that target only one of these systems (Thase, Entsuah, & Rudolph, 2001).

Serotoninergic Systems in Depression

Most of the serotonin (5-HT) in the brain is synthesized in clusters of cell bodies in the pons known as the dorsal raphé nuclei. From the dorsal brain stem, these 5-HT neurons project to the cerebral cortex, hypothalamus, thalamus, basal ganglia, septum, and hippocampus

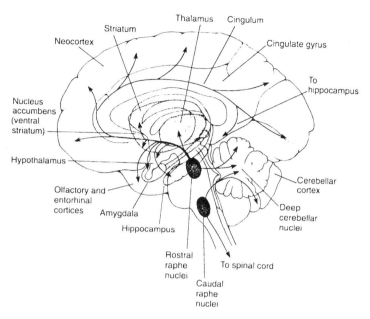

Thalamus Cingulum
Striatum
Neocortex Cingulate gyrus

To hippocampus

Nucleus accumbens (ventral striatum)

Hypothalamus

Cerebellar cortex

Olfactory and entorhinal cortices
Amygdala

Deep cerebellar nuclei

Hippocampus

Rostral raphe nuclei
To spinal cord

Caudal raphe nuclei

FIGURE 8.2. A lateral view of the brain demonstrates the course of the major serotonergic pathways. Although the raphe nuclei form a fairly continuous collection of cell groups throughout the brain stem, they are graphically illustrated here as two groups, one rostral and one caudal. From Kandel, Schwartz, and Jessell (1991). Copyright 1991 by Springer-Verlag GmbH & Co, KG. Reprinted by permission.

(see Figure 8.2) (Kandel et al., 1991; Kingsley, 2000). Serotonin pathways are largely colocalized with NE pathways and generally have tonic and inhibitory effects that counterbalance NE activity. For example, much evidence indicates that 5-HT input to the thalamus is an important facilitator of appetite (Thase & Howland, 1995). Serotoninergic neurons projecting to the suprachiasmatic nucleus (SCN) of the anterior hypothalamus help to regulate circadian rhythms (e.g., sleep–wake cycles, body temperature, and hypothalamic–pituitary–adrenocortical axis function) (Bunney & Bunney, 2000; Duncan, 1996). An intact 5-HT system also is needed to modulate the 90-minute infraradian cycle of alternating periods of REM and nonREM sleep (Duncan, 1996). Tonic 5-HT neurotransmission is necessary for affiliative behavior (Insel & Winslow, 1998), and for the expression of goal-directed motor and consummatory behaviors that are primarily mediated by NE and DA. In the wild, animals with lower basal 5-HT levels (as measured by CSF 5-HIAA levels) are more impulsive, have more scars from fighting, and generally have lower rankings on social dominance hierarchies than do animals with higher basal levels of 5-HT (Higley, Mehlman, Higley, et al., 1996; Higley, Mehlman, Poland, et al., 1996). Conversely, a rise in social dominance is accompanied by an increase in CSF 5-HIAA (Mehlman et al., 1995), and treatment with SSRIs decreases impulsive aggression (Fairbanks, Melega, Jorgensen, Kaplan, & Mcguire, 2001). As noted previously, there is ample documentation from studies of humans that low 5-HIAA is associated with suicide and other violent behaviors (Mann et al., 2001).

The basal or tonic level of 5-HT neurotransmission in primates is relatively stable, but does increase reliably in the fall (Higley, Mehlman, Higley, et al., 1996; Zajicek et al., 2000); it is also partly under genetic control (Higley, Mehlman, Higley, et al., 1996). Such heritability could be mediated by allelic variation in the genes that code for the serotonin transporter, the enzymes involved in synthesis or degradation, or any number of the sub-types of 5-HT receptors (Mann et al., 2001). Studies investigating specific genes are under-way throughout the world and, although results are inconsistent, multiple genes appear to be implicated (Mann et al., 2001).

Regardless of heritable risk factors, chronic stress will down-regulate 5-HT$_{1A}$ receptors, eventually depleting 5-HT stores (López, Liberzon, Vázquez, Young, & Watson, 1999; Weiss & Kilts, 1998). In animal models of depression, this state is associated with weight loss, decreased sleep, and decreased exploratory behavior. With respect to brain function, increased release of CRH, glutamate, and NE (i.e., dysregulation of multiple arousing inputs) can result from diminished inhibitory 5-HT activity (Weiss & Kilts, 1998).

Available evidence from studies using receptor imaging techniques suggests that dys-function of 5-HT$_{1A}$ receptors is clearly implicated in depression (Drevets et al., 1999; Staley Malison, & Innis, 1998), although in animal models the 5-HT$_{1B}$ receptor is more closely linked to trait-like patterns of aggressivity (Fairbanks et al., 2001). Reduced numbers of 5-HT uptake transporters also have been demonstrated in blood platelets and in postmortem studies (see review by Maes & Meltzer, 1995).

The integrity of 5-HT neurotransmission also can be compromised by dietary manipu-lation, specifically by eliminating the 5-HT precursor tryptophan from the food source. In studies of depressed people, acute response to SSRI antidepressants is reversed rapidly by tryptophan depletion whereas NRI response is unaffected (Delgado et al., 1991; Moore et al., 2000). A brief period of tryptophan depletion does not, however, worsen untreated de-pression and does not provoke frank depressive symptoms in healthy controls (Moore et al., 2000). Mild depressive symptoms have been observed following tryptophan depletion in unaffected relatives of people with bipolar disorder (Quintin et al., 2001). Studies of more sustained periods of tryptophan depletion have not yet been completed, although experi-ments are underway.

Dopaminergic Systems in Depression

There are four principal DA pathways in the brain (see Figure 8.3) (Kandel et al., 1991; Kingsley, 2000). The tuberoinfundibular system projects from cell bodies in the hypothala-mus to the pituitary and inhibits secretion of the hormone prolactin. The nigrostriatral sys-tem, which helps to regulate psychomotor activity, originates from cell bodies in the sub-stantia nigra and projects to the basal ganglia. The mesolimbic pathway begins with cell bodies located in the ventral tegmentum and projects to the nucleus accumbens, amygdala, hippocampus, medial dorsal nucleus of the thalamus, and cingulate gyrus. The mesolimbic DA pathway modulates emotional expression and goal-directed or consummatory behav-ior. The mesocortical DA pathway, which projects from the ventral tegmentum or-bitofrontal and prefrontal cerebral cortex, subserves motivation, initiation of goal-directed tasks, and "executive" cognitive processes. Decreased DA activity has obvious implications in the motoric, hedonic, and cognitive symptoms of depression (Willner, 1995). Moreover, DA activity is potentiated by stimulation of nicotine receptors (a subtype of receptors for acetylcholine), which may help to explain the high prevalence of tobacco consumption among depressed people (Glassman, 1993). A selective increase in DA activity in mesocorti-cal regions, perhaps induced by elevated cortisol levels, also may be implicated in develop-ment of hallucinations and delusions, which affect about 10% of the most severely de-pressed patients (Schatzberg & Rothschild, 1992).

As with the other monoamines, chronic stress reduces DA levels and results in behav-ioral changes suggestive of depression (Willner, 1995). For example, in an animal model of depression, chronic mild stress reduces the reinforcing effects of low concentrations of su-

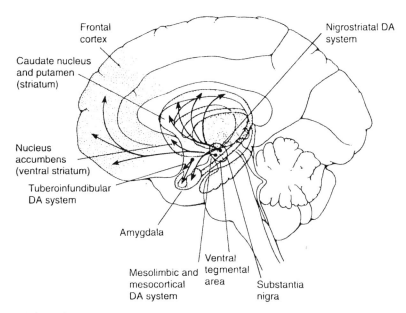

FIGURE 8.3. A lateral view of the brain demonstrates the course of the four major dopaminergic tracts. From Kandel, Schwartz, and Jessell (1991). Copyright 1991 by Springer-Verlag GmbH & Co, KG. Reprinted by permission.

crose solution. Dopaminergic neurotransmission also is partly dependent on the integrity of 5-HT systems (Sasaki-Adams & Kelley, 2001), providing another example of how dysfunction in one system can provoke secondary changes in the others. Although none of the currently available antidepressants is strongly pro-dopaminergic, studies utilizing TCAs, SSRIs, NRIs, and MAOIs have found that treatment can reverse or prevent the DA dysfunction caused by chronic stress (Cuadra, Zurita, Gioino, & Molina, 2001; Willner, 1997).

Stress, Monoamines, and the Hypothalamic–Pituitary–Adrenocortical Axis

The foregoing discussion has focused on the changes in monoamine function that link depression to a broader pattern of effects associated with the brain's responses to sustained, unresolvable stress. No discussion of stress responses is complete, however, without review of the hypothalamic–pituitary–adrenocortical (HPA) axis.

Elevated HPA activity is the hallmark of mammalian stress responses. As discussed previously, the HPA axis is partly under the control of phasic NE (activating) and tonic 5-HT (inhibitory) neurotransmission. This axis has three levels of organization and modulation (see Figure 8.4). In the hypothalamus, the neuropeptide CRH is released in response to activating NE, cholinergic, and glutaminergic inputs, typically in response to the perception of stress or threat. CRH then triggers release of adrenocorticotropic hormone (ACTH), which travels from the pituitary gland via the bloodstream to the cortex of the adrenal glands, where glucocorticoids are synthesized. Once stimulated by ACTH, glucocorticoid hormones are released into the blood stream.

Cortisol is the principal glucocorticoid hormone of humans. The cellular effects of cortisol are triggered by intracellular glucocorticoid receptors (GR), which migrate between the cell membrane and cell nuclei (Holsboer, 2000). The release of cortisol into the bloodstream thus leads to rapid changes in the gene activity of cells expressing GRs, which in-

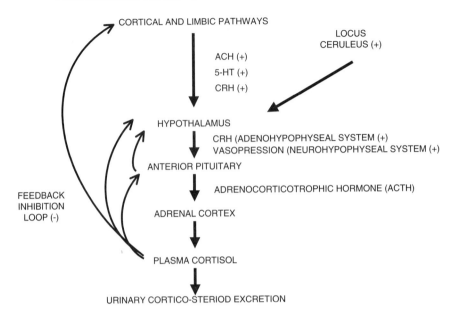

FIGURE 8.4. Schematic illustration of the hypothalamic–pituitary–adrenocortical axis, highlighting sites for feedback inhibition and potential sources of dysregulation. From Thase and Howland (1995). Copyright 1995 by The Guilford Press. Reprinted by permission.

clude anti-inflammatory effects on immune function and insulin-antagonist effects on glucose and lipid metabolism. Overall, these acute changes appear to facilitate short-term survival in response to overwhelming or life-threatening circumstances. Such benefits are time-limited, however, and negative compensatory (allostatic) changes will begin to accumulate if the axis remains overly active for prolonged periods (McEwen, 2000). Such allostatic changes can include increased risks of hypertension, obesity, heart disease, and (possibly) autoimmune diseases.

The HPA axis, like the NE and 5-HT components of stress response, is regulated by a redundant, multileveled system of inhibitory control. This type of negative feedback inhibition occurs at the levels of the hypothalamus, pituitary, and adrenal cortex, as well as that of the hippocampus. As acute stresses pass or resolve, the elevated plasma cortisol levels of healthy humans will normalize within a matter of minutes or hours.

Sustained hypercortisolism thus can result from increased CRH drive (from the hypothalamus or above), increased secretion of ACTH (secreted, for example, by a pituitary tumor), dysfunctional GRs, unrestrained noradrenergic stimulation from the locus ceruleus, and/or the failure of one or more mechanisms of feedback inhibition (Holsboer, 1995; Thase & Howland, 1995). It is now known that the neurons containing CRH are diffusely located throughout the cerebral cortex, with particularly high concentrations within the thalamus, amygdala, and other components of the limbic system. Studies measuring CRH synthesis demonstrate that these brain regions "light up" immediately following exposure to stress (Holsboer, 1995). Further, because CRH activates the locus ceruleus, which in turn further stimulates the thalamus, hypothalamus, and amygdala, sustained stress can provoke a "reverberating circuit" or a positive feedback loop. Closely regulated systems are invariably destabilized by such a state of affairs. The role of CRH as a destabilizing factor in both the onset and persistence of depressive disorders has thus gained increasing relevance (Holsboer, 2000; Nemeroff, 1998).

There is evidence that sustained hypercortisolism can impair the integrity of HPA feedback inhibition (Bremner, 1999). For example, prolonged ACTH drive can cause adrenal hypertrophy, which results in increased synthesis and release of cortisol. The cells expressing GRs in the hippocampus are also sensitive to very high concentrations of cortisol and will eventually begin to dehydrate and subsequently die (apostosis) (Sapolsky, 1996). As discussed later, this may be the mechanism underlying observations of cortical atrophy in chronic or recurrent depressions (Sheline, Sanghavi, Mintun, & Gado, 1999). Hippocampal cell death in response to sustained hypercortisolism appears to be most likely early in development and in old age. Exposure to various forms of stress early in life has been shown to compromise the regulation of HPA activity for a lifetime (Bremner, 1999; Coplan et al., 2001). In animal models of early trauma, even brief periods of maternal separation can result in long-standing changes in stress responses (Coplan et al., 2001). Fortunately, this effect can be partly mitigated by competent maternal behavior. Stress in later life appears to accelerate the slow decline in the integrity of HPA axis regulation that normally accompanies aging. This age-dependent change has been shown to result from death of cells containing GRs in the hippocampus. Importantly, treatments that effectively reduce hypercortisolism have also been shown to at least partly reverse hippocampal atrophy (Bremner, 1999; Starkman et al., 1999).

Like stress itself, hypercortisolism is not unique to depression. A significant minority of people with acute schizophrenia, mania, posttraumatic stress disorder, and other distressing mental disorders will manifest one or more signs of hypercortisolism. Across mental disorders, intensity of dysphoric arousal increases the likelihood of hypercortisolism (Thase & Howland, 1995). Abnormalities of HPA regulation also commonly occur in advanced Alzheimer's disease, presumably due to acceleration of hippocampal cell death. Nevertheless, dysregulation of HPA activity plays an important role in the pathophysiology of depression, and ultimately may prove to be a key factor in the differential therapeutics of mood disorders (Holsboer, 2000; Nemeroff, 1998).

Antidepressants, Monoamine Receptors, and Intracellular Mechanisms

Although it was known by the mid–1960s that TCAs and MAOIs enhance NE and 5-HT neurotransmission, several puzzling discrepancies indicated that the mechanisms underlying antidepressant response were not simply due to monoamine agonist effects. For example, increased NE or 5-HT levels were available in the synaptic cleft within hours of administration of NE or 5-HT reuptake inhibitors, yet antidepressant responses took weeks to emerge (Duman et al., 1997; Shelton, 2000). By contrast, some NE agonists, as exemplified by cocaine, were shown to have rapid mood-elevating properties but no sustained antidepressant effects. The MAOIs, which increase synaptic monoamine levels by inhibiting intracellular degradation of NE, 5-HT, and DA, similarly were associated with a time course of antidepressant effects that typically lagged at least several weeks behind the biochemical effects. Subsequently, other compounds that did not have clear-cut monoamine agonist effects, such as mianserin and mirtazapine, also were identified to be effective antidepressants.

It is now clear that the synaptic effects of the TCAs, MAOIs, and newer antidepressants only serve to initiate a sequence or cascade of effects that culminate within cell nuclei, at the level of gene activity (Duman et al., 1997; Shelton, 2000). Specifically, the minute "signal" of cellular electrical activity and the mechanics of receptor occupancy must be transduced into a series of molecular reactions that activate or inhibit the activity of selected genes. A schematic illustrating the intracellular signal transduction cascade is presented in Figure 8.5. The antidepressant medication initiates an effect at 5-HT or NE receptors, either diffusely (as is the case for the reuptake inhibitors and MAOIs), or selec-

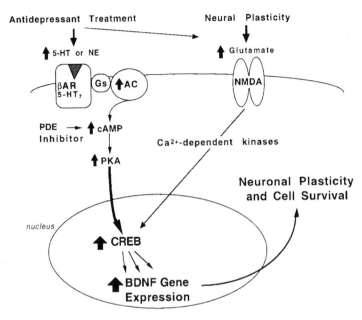

FIGURE 8.5. Influence of antidepressant treatment on the cyclic adenosine monophosphate (cAMP)-<u>c</u>AMP <u>r</u>esponse <u>e</u>lement-<u>b</u>inding protein (CREB) cascade. Antidepressant treatment increases synaptic levels of norepinephrine (NE) and serotonin (5-HT) via blocking the reuptake or breakdown of these monoamines. This results in activation of intracellular signal transduction cascades, one of which is the cAMP-CREB cascade. Chronic antidepressant treatment increases G_s coupling to adenylyl cyclase (AC), particulate levels of cAMP-dependent protein kinase (PKA), and CREB. CREB can also be phosphoylated by Ca^{2+}-dependent protein kinases, which can be activated by the phosphatidylinositol pathway (not shown) or by glutamate ionotropic receptors (e. g., N-methyl-D-aspartate [NMDA]). Glutamate receptors and Ca^{2+}-dependent protein kinases are also involved in neural plasticity. One gene target of antidepressant treatment and the cAMP-CREB cascade is brain-derived neurotrophic factor (BDNF), which contributes to the cellular processes underlying neuronal plasticity and cell survival. BAR, β-adrenergic receptor; PDE, phosphodiesterase. From Duman, Malberg, Nakagawa, and D'Sa (2000). Copyright 2000 by the Society of Biological Psychiatry. Reprinted by permission of Elsevier Science.

tively at specific receptor subtypes (e.g., the 5-HT_2 blocking antidepressants trazodone, nefazodone, mianserin, and mirtazapine). Receptor binding activates membrane-bound g-proteins and enzymes such as phospholipase C (PLC) and adelylate cyclase (AC). These enzymes catalyze the formation of the so-called second messengers (which actually are at least the third step in the sequence), such as cyclic adenomonophosphate (cAMP) and diacylglycerol. The second messengers, in turn, activate intracellular enzymes protein kinases A and C (PKA and PKC, respectively), which phosphorylate the gene transcription factor CREB (<u>c</u>AMP <u>r</u>esponse <u>e</u>lement <u>b</u>inding protein). CREB appears to be the first common step shared by antidepressants that selectively modulate NE or 5-HT neurotransmission (Shelton, 2000).

Phosphorylated CREB regulates the activity of a number of genes related to stress responses, including the genes that code for CRH, GRs, brain-derived neutrophic factor (BDNF), and the BDNF receptor (Duman et al., 1997; Shelton, 2000). BDNF is receiving increasing attention because it has been shown to reverse or inhibit stress-induced apoptosis. It has now been shown that various interventions with antidepressant effects can increase BDNF levels, including electrically induced seizures, TCAs, MAOIs, and various newer antidepressants (Duman et al., 1997; Madsen et al., 2000). At least some antidepressants also bind directly to GR (Barden, 1996; Holsboer, 2000), which may represent an additional or synergistic mechanism of action.

Other Neurotransmitter Disturbances

Neuron fibers containing acetylcholine (ACH) are distributed diffusely throughout the cerebral cortex, and interact extensively with monoamine and glucocorticoid systems (Kingsley, 2000). At the most general level, ACH neurons have alerting or activating acute effects on brain systems, as reflected by increased release of ACTH and cortisol, increased nocturnal awakenings, and increased firing of LC neurons (Janowsky & Overstreet, 1995). The two principal subtypes of ACH receptors are called nicotinic and muscarinic receptors. Although muscarinic receptors have received the most attention, the interaction between DA and nicotinic neurotransmission also is significant (Glassman, 1993; Stolerman & Reavill, 1989).

Drugs that have agonist and antagonist effects on ACH have modest, opposing effects on depressive symptoms (Janowsky & Overstreet, 1995). Behavioral changes following administration of an ACH agonist include lethargy, anergia, and psychomotor retardation in normal subjects and, among patients, exacerbation of depression. ACH agonist drugs also have weak and transient antimanic effects (Janowsky & Overstreet, 1995). ACH antagonists also have some mood-elevating effects, although the anticholinergic effects of the TCAs appear to be completely unrelated to therapeutic efficacy (Thase et al., 1985).

There is evidence from studies of animals and humans that heightened muscarinic ACH receptor sensitivity can mimic some of the neurobiological changes associated with depression (Janowsky & Overstreet, 1995). For example, a strain of mice bred to be supersensitive to cholinergic effects shows heightened vulnerability to development of learned helplessness (Overstreet, 1993). Similarly, some remitted patients with recurrent mood disorders, as well as their never-ill first-degree relatives, manifest a trait-like supersensitivity to cholinergic agonists (Sitaram, Dubé, Keshavan, Davies, & Reynal, 1987). A specific gene accounting for such supersensitivity has not yet been identified, however, and changes indicative of cholinergic supersensitivity can be induced by attenuating adrenergic activity (Schittecatte et al., 1992).

Gamma-aminobutyric acid (GABA) has inhibitory effects on NE and DA pathways. GABA receptors are densely localized in the thalamus and ascending mesocortical and mesolimbic systems (Kingsley, 2000; Paul, 1995). GABA is released in a calcium (Ca^{+2}) dependent fashion from interneurons in the cortex, brain stem, and spinal cord and dampens the activity of excitatory neural circuits. There are two principal subtypes of GABA receptors, referred to as A and B (Paul, 1995). Benzodiazepines and barbiturates attach to $GABA_A$ receptors, which serve to "gate" the control of membrane chloride (Cl^-) ion channels. This results in localized hyperpolarization of neurons, which decreases their responsivity to excitatory neurotransmitters. $GABA_B$ receptors are indirectly coupled to membrane potassium (K^+) channels via a G-protein and have uncertain relevance to mood disorders (Kingsley, 2000; Paul, 1995).

Chronic stress can reduce or deplete GABA levels in these regions of the brain, perhaps reflecting, yet again, an example of an excessive demand outstripping the capacity for synthesis (Weiss & Kilts, 1998). Reduction of GABA in depression has been observed in plasma and CSF specimens (Petty, 1995). Conversely, GABAergic medications have weak antidepressant and anxiolytic effects (Petty, 1995). The greatest contemporary therapeutic applications of GABAergic medications in psychiatry have been demonstration of the sedative and anxiolytic effects of benzodiazepines and $GABA_A$ selective agonists (Paul, 1995) and the antimanic effects of divalproex (Bowden et al., 1994).

The excitatory amino acid glutamate is one of the most widely distributed neurotransmitters in the CNS (Kingsley, 2000). Glutamate binds to the N-methyl-D-aspartate (NMDA) receptor and, in excess, can have neurotoxic effects. Importantly, the hippocampus and amygdala have high concentrations of NMDA receptors (Mathew et al., 2001). It is thus likely that glutamate contributes to the progressive, deleterious neurocognitive effects of chronic stress, mania, and severe recurrent depressions (Mathew et al., 2001). There is also some evidence that drugs that antagonize NMDA receptors may have antidepressant effects (Anand et al., 2000).

Glycine is the major inhibitory amino acid in the brain stem and forebrain (Kingsley, 2000). Glycine receptors share some structural overlap with GABA$_A$ receptors and have a similar effect on membrane Cl$^-$ channels. It is not yet certain if glycine receptor agonists will have therapeutic effects (Paul, 1995).

Abnormalities of Hormonal Regulatory Systems

Hypothalamic–Pituitary–Adrenocortical Axis Dysregulation

About 20–40% of depressed outpatients and 60–80% of depressed inpatients manifest one or more signs of increased cortisol secretion. Hypercortisolism is one of the best-documented biological findings that distinguish between milder major depressive episodes and the more restrictive subtypes (i.e., melancholia or endogenous depression) (Holsboer, 1995; Thase & Howland, 1995). This distinction, which is more continuous than categorical, probably results from the converging effects of age, recurrence, and episode severity. In any case, hypercortisolism is associated with memory impairments and decrements in abstraction and complex problem solving (Belanoff, Gross, Yager, & Schatzberg, 2001).

A variety of methods are used to study HPA activity, including excretion of urinary free cortisol, continuous intravenous sampling of plasma cortisol levels, and measurement of cortisol levels in saliva. The integrity of feedback inhibition of the HPA axis is most often tested by measurement of plasma cortisol levels before and after administration of dexamethasone, a potent synthetic glucocorticoid. Normally, a single test dose of 0.5 or 1 mg of dexamethasone will suppress pituitary ACTH and glucocorticoid secretion for 24 hours. Impaired feedback inhibition results in nonsuppression of cortisol secretion the following morning or, more commonly, "escape" from suppression later that day (i.e., at 4:00 P.M. or 11:00 P.M.). In the absence of confounding factors (e.g., fever or medications that induce the liver enzymes that metabolize dexamethasone), nonsuppression could result from increased CRH drive, diminished effects of inhibitory hippocampal glucocorticoid receptors, or both factors simultaneously. The dexamethasone suppression test is sometimes paired with an infusion of CRH, which challenges the integrity of the HPA axis at several levels of regulation, to yield more sensitive test results (Holsboer, 1995). Various measures of cortisol hypersecretion are imperfectly correlated with dexamethasone suppression test results (i.e., about 60–80% concordance) (Thase & Howland, 1995).

Hypercortisolism has important therapeutic implications. Patients with increased HPA activity are less responsive to placebo interventions (Ribeiro, Tandon, Grunhaus, & Greden, 1993) and may also be less likely to benefit from psychosocial treatments (Thase, Dubé, et al., 1996). Although hypercortisolism does not predict favorable response to ECT or pharmacotherapy (Ribeiro et al., 1993), computation of the ratio of responders to active and placebo therapies does suggest that patients manifesting hypercortisolism gain relatively greater benefit from somatic therapies (Thase & Howland, 1995). This may indicate that interventions with more direct cellular effects may be needed to control the dysregulated HPA activity of a subgroup of depressed patients.

Effective treatment typically normalizes hypercortisolism and, when the abnormality is persistent, it is associated with a high risk of relapse (Holsboer, 1995; Ribeiro et al., 1993). This is presumed to reflect continued increased CRH "drive" and/or faulty GR function (Holsboer, 2000). Dexamethasone or the cortisol synthesis inhibitor ketoconazole are sometimes used to suppress the HPA axis of hypercortisolemic patients who have not responded to standard treatments (Belanoff et al., 2001). Development of safer, more selective CRH or GR antagonists is an area of considerable therapeutic promise (Holsboer, 2000; Nemeroff, 1998).

Thyroid Axis Dysregulation

About 5–10% of people evaluated for depression are found to have previously undetected or subclinical thyroid dysfunction, as reflected by elevated plasma thyroid-stimulating hormone (TSH) levels or an exaggerated TSH response to an infusion of the hypothalamic neuropeptide thyroid releasing hormone (TRH) (Holsboer, 1995; Thase & Howland, 1995). Such occult hypothyroidism is often associated with elevated antithyroid antibody levels, and is more common among women and patients who have been treated with lithium (Thase & Howland, 1995). Depressed patients with subclinical hypothyroidism usually require hormone replacement therapy to ensure optimal response to treatment (Kirkegaard & Faber, 1998).

Another 20–40% of depressed patients manifest a different type of abnormality, namely, a blunted TSH response to TRH. This abnormal response would normally indicate hyperthyroidism, yet, in depression, it usually occurs in the context of normal thyroid function studies (Mason, Garbutt, & Prange, 1995). Neurons utilizing TRH as a neurotransmitter are located in the paraventricular nucleus of the hypothalamus and (like CRH) are diffusely distributed throughout the cerebral cortex. A blunted TSH response is presumed to result from down-regulation of pituitary responsiveness because of sustained elevation of TRH "drive" (Holsboer, 1995). Thus, increased TRH activity may represent another component of the brain's homeostatic response to sustained dysphoric arousal. Although not as well studied as various abnormalities of the HPA axis, there is evidence that a blunted TSH response does not rapidly reverse with effective treatment and may predict heightened vulnerability to subsequent relapse (Kirkegaard & Faber, 1998). Low normal indices of peripheral thyroid function similarly have been associated with poorer response to antidepressants (Cole et al., 2002; Gorman & Hatterer, 1994) and greater risk of relapse (Joffe & Marriott, 2000).

Growth Hormone

Growth hormone (GH) is secreted by cells in the anterior pituitary. GH release is stimulated by the hypothalamic (arcuate nucleus) neuropeptide growth hormone-releasing factor (GHRF), as well as (via α_2 receptors) NE (Holsboer, 1995). GH secretion is principally inhibited by somatostatin, another hypothalamic (paraventricular nucleus) neuropeptide, and CRH. GH secretion normally follows a 24-hour circadian rhythm, with higher levels between 2300 hours and 0200 hours (i.e., the first few hours of sleep). The nocturnal rise in GH secretion is normally coincident with the initial 60–90 minutes of sleep and thus typically occurs during the SWS (i.e., before the first REM period).

The most consistent disturbance of GH secretion in depression involves blunted release following sleep onset or in response to various provocative challenges, including hypoglycemia, the selective α_2 agonist clonidine, or a variety of antidepressants with noradrenergic effects (Holsboer, 1995; Thase & Howland, 1995). Blunted GH release has been documented in childhood-onset depression (Dahl et al., 2000) and appears to be state-independent or trait-like. Blunted GH release is linked temporally by two PSG findings, decreased SWS and reduced REM sleep latency, which also are viewed as persistent markers of depressive vulnerability.

Somatostatin

Significant concentrations of this inhibitory hypothalamic neuropeptide also are found in the amygdala, hippocampus, nucleus accumbens, prefrontal cortex, and LC (Plotsky, Owens, & Nemeroff, 1995). In addition to inhibition of GH release, somatostatin can "dampen" the effects of CRH, ACTH, and TSH. Somatostatin levels have been reported to be decreased in depression, so any resulting dysfunction would tend to disinhibit the HPA and HPT axes (Holsboer, 1995). There is some evidence that decreased CSF somatistatin levels normalize following successful treatment (Plotsky et al., 1995).

Prolactin

Prolactin is one of the pituitary hormones most closely involved in regulation of mammalian reproduction, including nursing and menstruation (Kingsley, 2000). Prolactin release from the pituitary is stimulated by 5-HT and inhibited by DA. One consequence of the latter effect is that medications that potently block D_2 receptors, such as most of the older antipsychotics, increase circulating prolactin levels. Most studies have not found significant abnormalities of basal or circadian prolactin secretion in depression, although a blunted prolactin response to various 5-HT agonists has been reported (Maes & Meltzer, 1995; Mann et al., 2001). This abnormality appears to be associated with decreased 5-HT_{1A} function (Maes & Meltzer, 1995). Blunted prolactin responsivity is less likely among premenopausal women, which suggests that estrogen may have an attenuating effect on 5-HT_{1A} dysfunction (Parry & Haynes, 2000).

Alterations of Sleep Neurophysiology

As noted earlier, people prone to depression often experience a premature loss of SWS and an early onset of the first period of rapid eye movement (REM) (Benca et al., 1992; Thase & Howland, 1995). These abnormalities are significantly correlated, largely because 30–40 minutes of deep, restful SWS normally preceed the onset of the first REM period. Results of family and twin studies indicate that SWS propensity is partly under genetic control (see Ehlers, Frank, & Kupfer, 1988). Consistent with the "behavior" of heritable traits, reduced REM latency and decreased SWS may both precede the onset of a depressive episode and persist following recovery (Kupfer & Ehlers, 1989; Thase, Fasiczka, Berman, Simons, & Reynolds, 1998).

The amount of SWS also decreases across the decades of healthy aging; this decline is accompanied by an increase in the number of nocturnal awakenings and a decrease in total sleep time. Increasing depressive symptom severity similarly is associated with decreased sleep efficiency and more wakefulness. Thus, with respect to both the depth and the quality of sleep, the effects of depression appear to mimic those of normal aging, perhaps one to two decades prematurely. The paired, deleterious effects of aging and recurrent depressive episodes on inhibitory CNS systems, particularly those mediated by 5-HT or GABA, may account for this progression (Thase & Howland, 1995).

Severity of depressive episodes also is associated with an increase in the intensity of phasic REM sleep (i.e., the frequency and amplitude of eye movements). The temporal pattern of such increased phasic REM also tends to be shifted into the first several REM periods. In contrast to reduced REM latency, these abnormalities appear to be state-dependent because they usually normalize following remission. Increased "phasic" REM sleep typically co-occurs with other state-dependent biological abnormalities, including poor sleep maintenance, hypercortisolemia, elevated peripheral levels of NE metabolites, and increased nocturnal body temperature (Kupfer & Ehlers, 1989; Thase & Howland, 1995). Of note, phasic REM sleep is more pronounced in recurrent depression (as compared to a single lifetime episode), even when the effects of age and symptom severity are taken into account (Jindal et al., in press; Thase et al., 1995).

The neurochemical processes mediating sleep are fairly well characterized. The propensity to sleep follows a circadian rhythm that is marked by a nocturnal rise in the hormone melatonin and by low levels of ACTH and cortisol. Melatonin, which is released from the pineal gland following the onset of darkness and in response to β-adrenergic stimulation, increases sleep propensity and may enhance the amount and duration of SWS. The sleep–wake circadian rhythm is "paced" by the suprachiasmatic nucleus of the hypothalamus. The strength of this effect has been called "process C," which is contrasted to the homeostatic propensity to sleep, or sleep "debt," which is referred to as "process S" (Wirz-Justice, 1995). Optimal sleep thus occurs when the accumulating sleep debt coincides with the circadian propensity to sleep. It is assumed that neuropeptides will subsequently be identified to take the place of these hypothetical processes.

The desynchronization of EEG rhythms following sleep onset partly reflects decreased activity of the LC and increased inhibitory GABA activity. Serotoninergic neurons projecting from the dorsal raphe nuclei tonically inhibit the onset of REM sleep. This effect appears to be mediated by stimulation of 5-HT_{1A} receptors. Serotoninergic projections to the thalamus and prefrontal cortex also help to "gate" against alerting inputs (Horne, 1992). This effect appears to be mediated by 5-HT_2 receptors. Near the end of each 90-minute cycle, 5-HT neurons cease firing, which "releases" the pontine cholinergic neurons that initiate REM sleep.

The sleep disturbances of depression thus could result from dysregulation of 5-HT, NE, and/or ACH neurotransmission (Duncan, 1996; Thase & Howland, 1995). Increased glucocorticoid activity can further impair sleep. For example, nocturnal awakenings and increased phasic REM sleep are caused by injections of CRH and are associated with elevated nocturnal cortisol levels (Thase & Howland, 1995). Conversely, experimentally disrupted sleep increases glucocorticoid levels. Dysregulation of sleep and HPA activity therefore represent a physiologic example of deleterious "positive" feedback.

The combination of reduced REM latency, increased REM density, and decreased sleep maintenance identifies about 40% of depressed outpatients and 80% of depressed inpatients; only about 10% of age- and sex-matched normal controls manifest this pattern of disturbances (Thase, Kupfer, et al., 1997). As was the case with hypercortisolism, an abnormal EEG sleep profile has been associated with reduced responsivity to psychotherapy (Thase, Simons, & Reynolds, 1996; Thase, Buysse, et al., 1997) and, hence, may indicate a preferential need for pharmacotherapy. Although such findings might justify the use of PSG studies as diagnostic tests, the procedures are frankly too inconvenient and expensive to be used in everyday practice. Moreover, like dexamethasone nonsuppression, abnormal sleep profiles are relatively common in other psychiatric disorders, including schizophrenia, alcoholism (even months after detoxification), and borderline personality disorder (Benca et al., 1992).

The sleep profiles of a majority of younger depressed outpatients are remarkably normal, especially if the patient complains of excessive sleepiness or hypersomnia (Thase, Kupfer, et al., 1997). A high prevalence of "false negative" test results probably reflects both the heterogeneity of major depressive disorder and the age-dependent nature of the sleep changes associated with depression (Thase & Howland, 1995). The sleep disturbances associated with depression also emerge at a somewhat later age among depressed women (as compared with men) (Reynolds et al., 1990), likely reflecting a beneficial interaction between 5-HT function and estrogen.

Hypersomnolence is *not* a prototypic mammalian response to stress. Oversleeping is relatively more common among younger depressed adults, particularly among women and people with either recurrent winter depressions or bipolar disorder (Thase & Howland, 1995). If the changes in sleep associated with depression are the result of a slowly progressive impairment of central inhibitory systems, then hypersomnolence may be viewed as an allostatic adaptation (Thase, 1998). For example, if the capacity to sleep deeply is beginning to become disrupted, then a large increase in total sleep time would provide a small increase in SWS time (i.e., 60 minutes of sleep might yield 6 additional minutes of SWS). Each additional 90 minutes of sleep also will result in an additional period of REM sleep. This could have adaptive consequences because REM sleep normally subserves consolidation of waking memories and related affects (Kramer, 1993). A rigorous test of this hypothesis will require longitudinal evaluation of the integrity of inhibitory CNS systems and PSG profiles among age- and sex-matched groups selected for either hypersomnolence or insomnia.

Pharmacotherapy with TCAs, MAOIs, and SSRIs delays the onset of REM sleep and suppresses phasic REM sleep (Sharpley & Cowen, 1995; Thase & Kupfer, 1987). REM suppression is mediated by stimulation of postsynaptic 5-HT$_{1A}$ receptors, as well as by less well-characterized effects of NE neurotransmission. Nonpharmacological deprivation of REM sleep (implemented by EEG monitored awakenings) also has been shown to have bona fide antidepressant effects. Several novel antidepressants, including nefazodone and bupropion, do not suppress REM sleep (Nofzinger et al., 1995; Rush et al., 1998), however, which indicates that REM suppression is not mechanistically necessary to treat depression.

Antidepressants have diverse effects on the ability to fall asleep and stay asleep. Antihistaminic effects of some TCAs and mirtazapine, which are largely unrelated to antidepressant effects, convey rapid, albeit nonspecific sedative actions (Thase, 1998). Therapy with monoamine reuptake inhibitors, the SSRIs, and the selectively noradrenergic TCAs (i.e., desipramine and nortriptyline) may actually increase nocturnal awakenings, although most successfully treated patients complain less of insomnia. The several antidepressants that block 5-HT$_2$ receptors (e.g., trazodone, nefazodone, and mirtazapine) also convey slower emerging improvements in sleep maintenance (Rush et al., 1998; Thase, 1998). To date, however, no antidepressant has been identified that produces large and sustained increases in slow wave sleep.

Is Depression a Disorder of Circadian Rhythms?

Sleep disturbances, increased cortisol secretion, blunted nocturnal growth hormone secretion, and elevated nocturnal body temperature all reflect abnormalities of circadian biological rhythms (Wirz-Justice, 1995). These changes were originally proposed to represent a phase advance of the sleep–wake cycle, although subsequent studies suggest that circadian rhythm disturbances associated with severe depression are better viewed as a disorganization of functions rather than a phase advance (Howland & Thase, 1999). In essence, heightened LC activity, increased levels of CRH and cortisol, and decreased inhibitory 5-HT or GABA control "overpower" the more subtle regulation of circadian rhythms. It also has been noted that changes in the lives of depressed people disturb circadian rhythms by affecting social zeitgebers ("time givers") such as meal times, periods of companionship, and exercise (Ehlers et al., 1988). There is, however, evidence of a circadian phase delay in recurrent winter depression (Wirz-Justice, 1995), which is responsive to manipulations of the photoperiod via exposure to bright white light (phototherapy) or dawn simulation (Avery et al., 2001).

Immunological Disturbances

Depressive disorders are associated with several immunological abnormalities, including decreased lymphocyte proliferation in response to mitogens and other forms of impaired cellular immunity (Thase & Howland, 1995). These lymphocytes produce neuromodulators such as CRH and cytokine peptides known as interleukins (Petito, Repetto, & Hartemink, 2001). There appears to be an association between immune dysfunction and clinical severity, which is probably mediated by both sleep deprivation and hypercortisolism (Thase & Howland, 1995). Moreover, the cytokine interleukin–1 appears to activate the genes for synthesis of CRH and GRs (Petito et al., 2001).

Studies of Brain Structures in Depressive Disorders

Computed tomography (CT) and magnetic resonance imaging (MRI) scans provide sensitive and noninvasive methods to visualize brain structures, including cortical and subcortical tracts, as well as tumors and white matter lesions. One well-replicated abnormality observed in patients with mood disorders is an increased frequency of small hyperintensities in subcortical and periventricular regions (Sheline, 2000; Soares & Mann, 1997). These hyperintensities appear to reflect both neurodegenerative effects of recurrent affective episodes and, especially among those with onset of depression in later life, cerebrovascular disease (Alexopoulous et al., 1997; Krishnan, Hays, & Blazer, 1997).

A modification of MRI technology is increasingly being used to study dynamic brain functions. These studies using functional MRI (fMRI) have great potential because they involve essentially no radiation exposure and can track changes in brain nuclei activity across seconds in response to various provocations or shifts in affects (Whalen et al., 1998). Recently, Sheline et al. (2001) observed increased activation of the left amygdala in depression in response to fearful faces. This abnormality was overcorrected by successful pharmacotherapy (i.e., lower activation than seen among normals). (See Davidson, Pizzagalli, & Nitschke, Chapter 9, this volume, for a detailed discussion of findings obtained using fMRI with depressed individuals.)

Another technical modification, magnetic resonance spectroscopy, has been used to study brain phosphorus metabolism in affective disorders. These studies focus on phosphorus metabolites because they reflect metabolic activity of cell-membrane-bound second messengers such as cAMP, cGMP, and phosphatidylinositol. An asymmetrical abnormality of phosphorus metabolism has been observed in the frontal lobes of patients with bipolar disorder compared to normal controls (Deicken, Fein, & Weiner, 1995; Kato et al., 1995), as well as the left frontal lobe and basal ganglia of depressed patients (Kato et al., 1995).

Cerebral Metabolic Studies in Depressive Disorders

Positron emission tomography (PET) scanning is currently the most widely used method for visualizing brain metabolism during rest and various states of activation. As blood glucose is the principal source of neuronal energy, changes in cerebral blood flow reflects changes in the activity of relevant neural circuits in the regions visualized by PET. Experimentally provoked emotional arousal in healthy controls has been shown to increase cerebral blood flow (CBF) to the thalamus and medial prefrontal cortex (Lane, Reiman, Ahern, Schwartz, & Davidson, 1997; Liotti et al., 2000; Mayberg et al., 1997). More specific activation associated with induced sadness is seen in the left amygdala, with deactivation of the dorsal parahippocampal gyrus (Mayberg et al., 1999).

The most widely replicated PET finding in severe depression is decreased blood flow and reduced glucose metabolism in the anterior (i.e., prefrontal/frontal) cerebral cortex, which is generally more pronounced on the left side (Drevets, 2000). This abnormality has been observed in both unipolar and bipolar depressions, as well as in depression that is co-morbid with obsessive–compulsive disorder (Baxter et al., 1989). There is also a reversal of hypofrontality following shifts from depression into hypomania, such that there are greater left hemisphere reductions in depression and greater right hemisphere reductions in mania (Ketter et al., 1994). Other studies have observed reductions of cerebral blood flow and/or metabolism in the dopaminergically enervated tracts of the mesocortical and mesolimbic systems in depression (Ho et al., 1996).

There is evidence that antidepressants and perhaps psychotherapy at least partially normalize some of these deficits (Brody et al., 2001; Drevets, 2000; Martin, Martin, Rai, Richardson, & Royall, 2001). Moreover, the effects of pharmacotherapy may not be confined to reversal of state-dependent abnormalities, but may also include enhancement of compensatory neural circuits (Mayberg et al., 2000).

In addition to a global reduction of anterior cerebral metabolism, increased glucose metabolism has been observed in several limbic regions (Drevets, 2000). Nofzinger and colleagues (2000) found that waking limbic hypermetabolism was particularly evident among patients with nocturnal PSG disturbances. The strongest evidence of limbic hypermetabolism has been observed in studies of patients with a family history of severe, recurrent depression (Drevets, 2000). Among this high-risk group, limbic hypermetabolism is suppressed by effective pharmacotherapy, but appears to reemerge when patients are restudied off medication (Drevets, 2000). Consistent with a trait-like abnormality, Bremner et al. (1997) found that tryptophan depletion of recently remitted, antidepressant-treated subjects provoked increased amygdalar activity. If truly state-independent, such amygdalar hypermetabolism could represent the emotional "amplifier" that helps to distort the signal of relatively minor stressors in vulnerable people. Studies of never-ill, but high-risk subjects (i.e., first-degree relatives of affected probands) will be needed to clarify this relationship.

SUMMARY AND FUTURE DIRECTIONS

Major depressive disorder is associated with a wide range of neurobiological disturbances. When viewed as either "traits" or "states," some order begins to emerge to this diverse constellation of disturbances. These abnormalities tend to coaggregate among older and more severely symptomatic patients, particularly those who experience recurrent depressive episodes. This clinical profile matches the classic prototype of endogenous depression or melancholia, although it must be recognized that the "typical" or average depressed outpatient (at the beginning of the 21st century) does not manifest the full melancholic syndrome (Thase & Friedman, 1999). The state-dependent abnormalities of depression include elevated peripheral levels of NE metabolites, increased phasic REM sleep, poor sleep maintenance, hypercortisolism, impaired cellular immunity, decreased cerebral blood flow and glucose metabolism within anterior cortical structures, and increased blood flow and glucose metabolism in paralimbic regions.

When considered together, these state-dependent abnormalities of depression appear to reflect the brain's response to sustained stress. Depressive episodes characterized by these abnormalities tend to be longer, more disabling, may be less likely to respond to supportive or specific psychotherapeutic interventions, and more likely to relapse without effective treatment. Although some depressed patients with abnormal sleep, HPA, or PET findings are responsive to psychosocial interventions (Brody et al., 2001; Martin et al., 2001; Thase,

Simons, & Reynolds, 1996; Thase, Buysse, et al., 1997), it appears that clinical remission may be facilitated by interventions that dampen more directly pathologic circuits or activate compensatory circuits. Conversely, it is possible that the impairments in concentration, abstraction, and executive decision making that accompany severe depression may compromise response to psychotherapy. We propose that this is precisely why the best evidence of additive effects for psychotherapy–pharmacotherapy combinations has been observed in studies of patients with recurrent (Thase, Greenhouse, et al., 1997), chronic (Keller et al., 2000), or late-life (Reynolds et al., 1999) depressive disorders.

The trait-like abnormalities associated with depression, which include decreased SWS, reduced REM latency, blunted nocturnal growth hormone response, and various other indicators of decreased 5-HT neurotransmission, do not appear to have clear-cut therapeutic implications beyond the implication of greater vulnerability to recurrent episodes of illness. These abnormalities are associated with an early age of onset, however, and might someday be used to target at-risk individuals for early intervention. The heritability of these abnormalities has been established by family studies and other at-risk paradigms. To date, however, no specific genes that mediate such increased risk have been identified.

Two of the more heritable forms of mood disorders, early-onset recurrent depression and bipolar depression, are often nonmelancholic in initial clinical presentations. Both of these forms of mood disorder are characterized by a greater likelihood of reverse neurovegetative symptoms. In these disorders, symptom expression may be shaped by the developmental trajectory of functional inhibitory response systems (i.e., 5-HT and GABA neurotransmission and GR-mediated feedback inhibition), thus resulting in compensatory adaptations such as overeating and oversleeping. Given that estrogen enhances these inhibitory responses, it is not surprising that reverse neurovegetative features are most common among depressed premenopausal women.

Stress, aging, and the accumulating consequences of recurrent depressive episodes are inextricably connected. In young adulthood, a stressful life event more often than not is implicated in the onset or worsening of the first depressive episode (Kendler et al., 2000). This process may be accelerated by genetic vulnerability (Drevets, 2000; Kendler, Karkowski, & Prescott, 1999) or a history of early trauma (Weiss, Longhurst, & Mazure, 1999). In midlife, the association between life stress and onset of depressive episodes begins to weaken (Kendler, Thornton, & Gardner, 2001). At the same time, the prevalence of state-dependent neurobiologic abnormalities begins to increase. Later in life, the diseases of aging that damage brain function heighten vulnerability to depression and compromise treatment responses. The late-onset form of depression associated with periventricular hyperintensities illustrates that even subtle vascular changes can increase the risk of mood disorder.

Although many aspects of the neurobiology of depression remain poorly understood, the experience of depression is one of the most understandable of the mental disorders, because virtually all humans have experienced sadness or grief. Moreover, in the modern world, few are immune to thoughts of powerlessness or incompetence that may emerge during protracted, stressful difficulties. We share with other mammals a well-regulated set of CNS responses to stress that have evolved over tens of millions of years. In this context, the 50,000 or so year reign of *Homo sapiens* is just a brief moment. The massive changes in how humans live and relate to each other that have occurred over the past several hundred years have occurred in a nanosecond of evolutionary time. Fortunately, the technology to investigate the exquisite interplay between perceived stress, subjective well-being, and the activity of brain systems, cells, and the genes that shape adaptation and maladaptation is rapidly advancing. Understanding the brain mechanisms that predispose to, sustain, and reverse depression represents our best hope to relieve the misery of those who suffer from this common yet devastating condition.

REFERENCES

Alexopoulos, G. S., Meyers, B. S., Young, R. C., Campbell, S., Silbersweig, D., & Charlson, M. (1997). "Vascular depression" hypothesis. *Archives of General Psychiatry, 54,* 915–922.

Anand, A., Charney, D. S., Oren, D. A., Berman, R. M., Hu, X. S., Cappiello, A., & Krystal, J. H. (2000). Attenuation of the neuropsychiatric effects of ketamine with lamotrigine: Support for hyperglutamatergic effects of N-methyl-D-aspartate receptor antagonists. *Archives General Psychiatry, 57,* 270–276.

Aston-Jones, G., Rajkowski, J., & Cohen, J. (1999). Role of locus coeruleus in attention and behavioral flexibility. *Biological Psychiatry, 46*(9), 1309–1320.

Avery, D. H., Eder, D. N., Bolte, M. A., Hellekson, C. J., Dunner, D. L., Vitiello, M. V., & Prinz, P. N. (2001). Dawn stimulation and bright light in the treatment of SAD: A controlled study. *Biological Psychiatry, 50*(3), 205–216.

Barden, N. (1996). Modulation of glucocorticoid receptor gene expression by antidepressant drugs. *Pharmacopsychiatry, 29,* 12–22.

Baron, B. M., Ogden, A., Siegel, B. W., Stegeman, J., Ursillo, R. C., &. Dudley, M. W. (1988). Rapid down regulation of -adrenoceptors by co-administration of desipramine and fluoxetine. *European Journal of Pharmacology, 154,* 125–134.

Baxter, L. R., Schwartz, J. M., Phelps, M. E., Mazziotta, J. C., Guze, B. H., Selin, C. E., Gerner, R. H., & Sumida, R. M. (1989). Reduction of prefrontal cortex glucose metabolism common to three types of depression. *Archives of General Psychiatry, 46,* 243–250.

Belanoff, J. K., Gross, K., Yager, A., & Schatzberg, A. F. (2001). Corticosteroids and cognition. *Journal of Psychiatric Research, 35,* 127–145.

Benca, R. M., Obermeyer, W. H., Thisted, R. A., & Gillin, J. C. (1992). Sleep and psychiatric disorders: A meta-analysis. *Archives of General Psychiatry, 4,* 651–668.

Bowden, C. L., Brugger, A. M., Swann, A. C., Calabrese, J. R., Janicak, P. G., Petty, F., Dilsaver, S. C., Davis, J. M., Rush, A. J., Small, J. G., Garza-Trevino, E. S., Risch, S. C., Goodnick, P. J., Morris, D. D. & Depakote Mania Study Group. (1994). Efficacy of divalproex vs lithium and placebo in the treatment of mania. *Journal of the American Medical Association, 271,* 918–924.

Bremner, J. D. (1999). Does stress damage the brain? *Biological Psychiatry, 45*(7), 797–805.

Bremner, J. D., Innis, R. B., Salomon, R. M., Staib, L. H., Ng, C. K., Miller, H. L., Bronen, R. A., Krystal, J. H., Duncan, J., Rich, D., Price, L. H., Malison, R., Dey, H., Soufer, R., & Charney, D. S. (1997). Positron emission tomography measurement of cerebral metabolic correlates of tryptophan depletion-induced depressive relapse. *Archives of General Psychiatry, 54,* 364–374.

Brody, A. L., Saxena, S., Stoessel, P., Gillies, L. A., Fairbanks, L. A., Alborzian, S., Phelps, M. E., Huang, S. C., Wu, H. M., Ho, M. L., Ho, M. K., Au, S. C., Maidment, K., & Baxter, J. R., Jr. (2001). Regional brain metabolic changes in patients with major depression treated with either paroxetine or interpersonal therapy: Preliminary findings. *Archives of General Psychiatry, 58,* 631–640.

Bunney, W. E., & Bunney, B. G. (2000). Molecular clock genes in man and lower animals: Possible implications for circadian abnormalities in depression. *Neurospychopharmacology, 22*(4), 335–345.

Bunney, W. E., Jr., & Davis, J. M. (1965). Norepinephrine and depressive reactions: A review. *Archives of General Psychiatry, 13,* 483–494.

Cole, D. P., Thase, M. E., Mallinger, A. G., Soares, J. C., Luther, J. F., Kupfer, D. J., & Frank E. (2002). Slower treatment response in bipolar depression predicted by lower pretreatment thyroid function. *American Journal of Psychiatry, 159*(1), 116–121.

Coplan, J. D., Smith, E. L. P., Altemus, M., Scharf, B. A., Owens, M. J., Nemeroff, C. B., Gorman, J. M., & Rosenblum, L. A. (2001). Variable foraging demand rearing: Sustained elevations in cisternal cerebrospinal fluid corticotropin-releasing factor concentrations in adult primates. *Biological Psychiatry, 50*(3), 200–204.

Cuadra, G., Zurita, A., Gioino, G., & Molina, V. (2001). Influence of different antidepressant drugs on the effect of chronic variable stress on restraint-induced dopamine release in frontal cortex. *Neuropsychopharmacology, 25*(3), 384–394.

Dahl, R. E., Birmaher, B., Williamson, D. E., Dorn, L., Perel, J., Kaufman, J., Brent, D. A., Axelson, D. A., & Ryan, N. D. (2000). Low growth hormone response to growth hormone-releasing hormone in child depression. *Biological Psychiatry, 48*(10), 981–988.

Deicken, R. F., Fein, G., & Weiner, M. W. (1995). Abnormal frontal lobe phosphorous metabolism in bipolar disorder. *American Journal of Psychiatry, 152*(6), 915–918.

Delgado, P. L., Price, L. H., Miller, H. L., Salomon, R. M., Licinio, J., Krystal, J. H., Heninger, G. R., & Charney, D. S. (1991). Rapid serotonin depletion as a provocative challenge test for patients with major depression: Relevance to antidepressant action and the neurobiology of depression. *Psychopharmacology Bulletin, 27,* 321–330.

Drevets, W. C. (2000). Functional anatomical abnormalities in limbic and prefrontal cortical structures in major depression. *Progress in Brain Research, 126,* 413–431.

Drevets, W. C., Frank, E., Price, J. C., Kupfer, D. J., Holt, D., Greer, P. J., Huang, Y., Gautier, C., & Mathis, C. (1999). PET imaging of serotonin 1A receptor binding in depression. *Biological Psychiatry, 46*(10), 1375–1338.

Duman, S., Heninger, G. R., & Nestler, E. J. (1997). A molecular and cellular theory of depression. *Archives of General Psychiatry, 54,* 597–606.

Duman, R. S., Malberg, J., Nakagawa, S., & D'Sa, C. (2000). Neuronal plasticity and survival in mood disorders. *Biological Psychiatry, 48*(8), 732–739.

Duncan, W. C., Jr. (1996). Circadian rhythms and the pharmacology of affective illness. *Pharmacology Therapy, 71*(3), 253–312.

Ehlers, C. L., Frank, E., & Kupfer, D. J. (1988). Social zeitgebers and biological rhythms: A unified approach to understanding the etiology of depression. *Archives of General Psychiatry, 45,* 948–952.

Fairbanks, L. A., Melega, W. P., Jorgensen, M. J., Kaplan, J. R., & Mcguire, M. T. (2001). Social impulsivity inversely associated with CSF 5-HIAA and fluoxetine exposure in vervet monkeys. *Neuropsychopharmacology, 24*(4), 370–378.

Ferry, B., Roozendaal, B., & McGaugh, J. L. (1999). Role of norepinephrine in mediating stress hormone regulation of long-term memory storage: A critical involvement of the amygdala. *Biological Psychiatry, 46*(9), 1140–1152.

Gilbert, P. (1992). *Depression: The evolution of powerlessness.* Hove, UK: Erlbaum.

Glassman, A. H. (1969). Indoleamines and affective disorders. *Psychosomatic Medicine, 31,* 107–114.

Glassman, A. H. (1993). Cigarette smoking: Implications for psychiatric illness. *American Journal Psychiatry, 150*(4), 546–553.

Golden, R. N., Markey, S. P., Risby, E. D., Cowdry, R. W., & Potter, W. Z. (1998). Antidepressants reduce whole-body norepinephrine turnover while enhancing 6-hydroxymelatonin output. *Archives of General Psychiatry, 45,* 150–154.

Gorman, J. M., & Hatterer, J. A. (1994). The role of thyroid hormone in refractory depression. In W. A. Nolen, J. Zohar, S. P. Roose, & J. D. Amsterdam (Eds.), *Refractory depression: Current strategies and future directions* (pp. 121–128). New York: Wiley.

Higley, J. D., Mehlman, P. T., Higley, S. B., Fernald, B., Vickers, J., Lindell, S. G., Taub, D. M., Suomi, S. J., & Linnoila, M. (1996). Excessive mortality in young free-ranging male nonhuman primates with low cerebrospinal fluid 5-hydroxyindoleacetic acid concentrations. *Archives of General Psychiatry, 53,* 537–543.

Higley, J. D., Mehlman, P. T., Poland, R. E., Taub, D. M., Vickers, J., Suomi, S. J., & Linnoila, M. (1996). CSF testosterone and 5-HIAA correlate with different types of aggressive behaviors. *Biological Psychiatry, 40*(11), 1067–1082.

Ho, A. P., Gillin, J. C., Buchsbaum, M. S., Wu, J. C., Abel, L., & Bunney, W. E. (1996). Brain glucose metabolism during non-rapid eye movement sleep in major depression. *Archives of General Psychiatry, 53,* 645–652.

Holsboer, F. (1995). Neuroendocrinology of mood disorders. In F. E. Bloom & D. J. Kupfer (Eds.), *Psychopharmacology: The fourth generation of progress* (pp. 957–969). New York: Raven Press.

Holsboer, F. (2000). The corticosteroid receptor hypothesis of depression. *Neuropsychopharmacology, 23*(5), 477–501.

Horne, J. (1992). Human slow-wave sleep and the cerebral cortex. *Journal of Sleep Research, 1*(2), 122–124.

Howland, R. H., & Thase, M. E. (1999). Affective disorders: Biological aspects. In T. Millon, P. Blaney, & R. Davis (Eds.), *Oxford textbook of psychopathology* (pp. 166–202). Oxford, UK: Oxford University Press.

Insel, T. R., & Winslow, J. T. (1998). Serotonin and neuropeptides in affiliative behaviors. *Biological Psychiatry, 44*(3), 207–219.

Jackson, S. W. (1986). *Melancholia and depression from Hippocratic times to modern times*. New Haven, CT: Yale University Press.

Janowsky, D. S., & Overstreet, D. H. (1995). The role of acetylcholine mechanisms in mood disorders. In F. E. Bloom & D. J. Kupfer (Eds.), *Psychopharmacology: The fourth generation of progress* (pp. 945–956). New York: Raven Press.

Jindal, R. D., Thase, M. E., Fasiczka, A. L., Friedman, E. S., Buysse, D. J., Frank, E., & Kupfer, D. J. (in press). Electroencephalographic sleep profiles in single episode and recurrent unipolar forms of major depression: II. Comparison during remission. *Biological Psychiatry*.

Joffe, R. T., & Marriott M. (2000). Thyroid hormone levels and recurrence of major depression. *American Journal of Psychiatry, 157*(10), 1689–1691.

Kandel, E. R., Schwarz, J. H., & Jessell, T. M. (1991). *Principles of neural science* (3rd ed). New York: Elsevier Press.

Kato, T., Shioiri, T., Murashita, J., Hamakawa, H., Takahashi, Y., Inubushi, T., & Takahashi, S. (1995). Lateralized abnormality of high energy phosphate metabolism in the frontal lobes of patients with bipolar disorder detected by phase-encoded ^{31}P-MRS. *Psychological Medicine, 25*, 557–566.

Keller, M. B., McCullough, J. P., Klein, D. N., Arnow, B., Dunner, D. L., Gelenberg, A. J., Markowitz, J. C., Nemeroff, C. B., Russell, J. M., Thase, M. E., Trivedi, M. H., & Zajecka, J. (2000). A comparison of nefazodone, the cognitive behavioral-analysis system of psychotherapy, and their combination for the treatment of chronic depression. *New England Journal of Medicine, 342*(20), 1462–1470.

Kendler, K. S., Karkowski, L. M., & Prescott, C. A. (1999). Causal relationship between stressful life events and the onset of major depression. *American Journal of Psychiatry, 156*(6), 837–841.

Kendler, K. S., Thornton, L. M., & Gardner, C. O. (2000). Stressful life events and previous episodes in the etiology of major depression in women: An evaluation of the "kindling" hypothesis. *American Journal of Psychiatry, 157*(8), 1243–1251.

Kendler, K. S., Thornton, L. M., & Gardner, C. O. (2001). Genetic risk, number of previous depressive episodes, and stressful life events in predicting onset of major depression. *American Journal of Psychiatry, 158*(4), 582–586.

Ketter, T. A., George, M. S., Ring, H. A., Pazzaglia, P., Marangell, L., Kimbrell, T. A., & Post, R. M. (1994). Primary mood disorders: Structural and resting functional studies. *Psychiatric Annals, 24*(12), 637–642.

Kingsley, R. E. (2000). *Concise text of neuroscience* (2nd. ed.). Philadelphia: Lippincott Williams & Wilkins.

Kirkegaard, C., & Faber, J. (1998). The role of thyroid hormones in depression. *European Journal of Endocrinology, 138*(1), 1–9.

Korf, J., & van Praag, H. M. (1971). Retarded depressions and the dopamine metabolism. *Psychopharmacologia, 19*(2), 199–203.

Kramer, M. (1993). The selective mood regulatory function of dreaming: An update and revision. In A. R. Moffitt, M. Kramer, & R. F. Hoffman (Eds.), *The function of dreaming* (pp. 139–195). Albany: State University of New York Press.

Krishnan, K. R. R., Hays, J. C., & Blazer, D. G. (1997). MRI-defined vascular depression. *American Journal of Psychiatry, 154*(4), 497–501.

Kupfer, D. J., & Ehlers, C. L. (1989). Two roads to rapid eye movement latency. *Archives of General Psychiatry, 46*, 945–948.

Lane, R. D., Reiman, E. M., Ahern, G. L., Schwartz, G. E., & Davidson, R. J. (1997). Neuroanatomical correlates of happiness, sadness, and disgust. *American Journal of Psychiatry, 154*(7), 926–933.

Liotti, M., Mayberg, H. S., Brannan, S. K., McGinnis, S., Jerabek, P., & Fox, P. T. (2000). Differential limbic–cortical correlates of sadness and anxiety in healthy subjects: Implications for affective disorders. *Biological Psychiatry, 48,* 30–42.

López, J. F., Liberzon, I., Vázquez, D. M., Young, E. A., & Watson, S. J. (1999). Serotonin 1A receptor messenger RNA regulation in the hippocampus after acute stress. *Biological Psychiatry, 45*(7), 934–937.

Madsen, T. M., Treschow, A., Bengzon, J., Bolwig, T. G., Lindvall, O., & Tigström, A. (2000). Increased neurogenesis in a model of electroconvulsive therapy. *Biological Psychiatry, 47*(12), 1043–1049.

Maes, M., & Meltzer, H. Y. (1995). The serotonin hypothesis of major depression. In F. E. Bloom & D. J. Kupfer (Eds.), *Psychopharmacology: The fourth generation of progress* (pp. 933–944). New York: Raven Press.

Maier, S. F., & Seligman, M. E. P. (1976). Learned helplessness: Theory and evidence. *Journal of Experimental Psychology, 105,* 3–46.

Mann, J. J., Brent, D. A., & Arango, V. (2001) The neurobiology and genetics of suicide and attempted suicide: A focus on the serotonergic system. *Neurospychopharmacology, 24*(5), 467–477.

Martin, S. D., Martin, E., Rai, S. S., Richardson, M. A., & Royall, R. (2001). Brain blood flow changes in depressed patients treated with interpersonal psychotherapy or venlafaxine hydrochloride: Preliminary findings. *Archives of General Psychiatry, 58,* 641–648.

Mason, G. A., Garbutt, J. C., & Prange, A. J., Jr. (1995). Thyrotropin-releasing hormone: Focus on basic neurobiology. In F. E. Bloom & D. J. Kupfer (Eds.), *Psychopharmacology: The fourth generation of progress* (pp. 493–503). New York: Raven Press.

Mathew, S. J., Coplan, J. D., Smith, E. L. P., Schloepp, D. D., Rosenblum, L. A., & Gorman, J. M. (2001). Glutamate–hypothalamic–pituitary–adrenal axis interactions: Implications for mood and anxiety disorders. *CNS Spectrums, 6*(7), 555–564.

Mayberg, H. S., Brannan, S. K., Mahurin, R. K., Jerabek, P. A., Brickman, J. S., Tekell, J. L., Silva, J. A., McGinnis, S., Glass, T. G., Martin, C. C., & Fox, P. T. (1997). Cingulate function in depression: A potential predictor of treatment response. *Clinical Neuroscience and Neuropathology, 8*(4), 1057–1061.

Mayberg, H. S., Brannan, S. K., Tekell, J. L., Silva, J. A., Mahurin, R. K., McGinnis, S., & Jerabek, P. A. (2000). Regional metabolic effects of fluoxetine in major depression: Serial changes and relationship to clinical response. *Biological Psychiatry, 48*(8), 830–843.

Mayberg, H. S., Liotti, M., Brannan, S. K., McGinnis, S., Mahurin, R. K., Jerabek, P. A., Silva, J. A., Tekell, J. L., Martin, C. C., Lancaster, J. L.,, & Fox, P. T. (1999). Reciprocal limbic–cortical function and negative mood: Converging PET findings in depression and normal sadness. *American Journal of Psychiatry, 156*(5), 675–682.

McEwen, B. S. (2000). Allostasis and allostatic load: Implications for neuropsychopharmacology. *Neuropsychopharmacology, 22*(2), 108–124.

Mehlman, P. T., Higley, J. D., Faucher, I., Lilly, A. A., Taub, D. M., Vickers, J., Suomi, S. J., & Linnoila, M. (1995). Correlation of CSF 5-HIAA concentration with sociality and the timing of emigration in free-ranging primates. *American Journal of Psychiatry, 152*(6), 907–913.

Miller, H. L., Delgado, P. L., Salomon, R. M., Heninger, G. R., & Charney D. S. (1996). Effects of α-methyl-para-tyrosine (ampt) in drug-free depressed patients. *Neuropsychopharmacology, 14*(3), 151–157.

Miller, H. L., Ekstrom, R. D., Mason, G. A., Lydiard, R. B., & Golden, R. N. (2001). Noradrenergic function and clinical outcome in antidepressant pharmacotherapy. *Neuropsychopharmacology, 24*(6), 617–623.

Moore, P., Landolt, H.-P., Seifritz, E., Clark, C., Bhatti, T., Kelso, J., Rapaport, M., & Gillin, J. C. (2000). Clinical and physiological consequences of rapid tryptophan depletion. *Neuropsychopharmacology, 23*(6), 601–622.

Nemeroff, C. B. (1998). Psychopharmacology of affective disorders in the 21st century. *Biological Psychiatry, 44*(7), 517–525.

Nestler, E. J., Alreja, M., & Aghajanian, G. K. (1999). Molecular control of locus coeruleus neuro-transmission. *Biological Psychiatry, 46*(9), 1131–1139.

Nofzinger, E. A., Fasiczka, A., Berman, S., & Thase, M. E. (2000). Bupropion SR reduces periodic limb movements associated with arousals from sleep in depressed patients with periodic limb movement disorder. *Journal of Clinical Psychiatry, 61*(11), 858–862.

Nofzinger, E. A., Reynolds, C. F., III, Thase, M. E., Frank, E., Jennings, J. R., Fasiczka, A. L., Sullivan, L. R., & Kupfer, D. J. (1995). REM sleep enhancement by bupropion in depressed men. *American Journal of Psychiatry, 152*, 274–276.

Overstreet, D. H. (1993). The Flinders sensitive line rats: A genetic animal model of depression. *Neuroscience and Biobehavioral Reviews, 17*(1), 51–68.

Parry, B. L., & Haynes, P. (2000). Mood disorders and the reproductive cycle. *Journal of Gender Specific Medicine, 3*(5), 53–58.

Paul, S. M. (1995). GABA and glycine. In F. E. Bloom & D. J. Kupfer (Eds.), *Psychopharmacology: The fourth generation of progress* (pp. 87–94). New York: Raven Press.

Petito, J. M., Repetto, M. J., & Hartemink, D. A. (2001). Brain-immune interactions in neuropsychiatry: Highlights of the basic science and relevance to pathogenic factors and epiphenomena. *CNS Spectrums, 6*(5), 383–391.

Petty, F. (1995). GABA and mood disorders: A brief review and hypothesis. *Journal of Affective Disorders, 34*(4), 275–281.

Plotsky, P. M., Owens, M. J., & Nemeroff, C. B. (1995). Neuropeptide alterations in mood disorders. In F. E. Bloom & D. J. Kupfer (Eds.), *Psychopharmacology: The fourth generation of progress* (pp. 971–981). New York: Raven Press.

Quintin, P., Benkelfat, C., Launay, J. M., Arnulf, I., Pointereau-Bellenger, A., Barbault, S., Alvarez, J. C., Varoquaux, O., Perez-Diaz, F., Jouvent, R., & Leboyer, M. (2001). Clinical and neurochemical effect of acute tryptophan depletion in unaffected relatives of patients with bipolar affective disorder. *Biological Psychiatry, 50*(3), 184–190.

Ressler, K. J., & Nemeroff, C. B. (1999). Role of norepinephrine in the pathophysiology and treatment of mood disorders. *Biological Psychiatry, 46*(9), 1219–1233.

Reynolds, C. F., III, Frank, E., Perel, J. M., Imber, S. D., Cornes, C., Miller, M. D., Mazumdar, S., Houck, P. R., Dew, M. A., Stack, J. A., Pollock, B. G., & Kupfer, D. J. (1999). Nortriptyline and interpersonal psychotherapy as maintenance therapies for recurrent major depression: A randomized controlled trial in patients older than 59 years. *Journal of the American Medical Association, 281*(1), 39–45.

Reynolds, C. F. III, Kupfer, D. J., Thase, M. E., Frank, E., Jarrett, D. B., Coble, P. A., Hoch, C. C., Buysse, D. J., Simons, A. D., & Houck, P. R. (1990). Sleep, gender, and depression: An analysis of gender effects on the electroencephalographic sleep of 302 depressed outpatients. *Biological Psychiatry, 28*, 673–684.

Ribeiro, S. C. M., Tandon, R., Grunhaus, L., & Greden, J. F. (1993). The DST as a predictor of outcome in depression: A meta-analysis. *American Journal of Psychiatry, 150*(11), 1618–1629.

Rush, A. J., Armitage, R., Gillin, J. C., Yonkers, K. A., Winokur, A., Moldofsky, H., Vogel, G. W., Kaplita, S. B., Fleming, J. B., Montplasir, J., Erman, M. K., Albala, B. J., & McQuade, R. D. (1998). Comparative effects of nefazodone and fluoxetine on sleep in outpatients with major depressive disorder. *Biological Psychiatry, 44*(1), 3–14.

Sapolsky, R. M. (1996). Why stress is bad for your brain. *Science, 273*, 749–750.

Sasaki-Adams, D. M., & Kelley, A. E. (2001). Serotonin–dopamine interactions in the control of conditioned reinforcement and motor behavior. *Neuropsychopharmacology, 25*(3), 440–452.

Schatzberg, A. F., & Rothschild, A. J. (1992). Psychotic (delusional) major depression: Should it be included as a distinct syndrome in DSM-IV? *American Journal of Psychiatry, 149*(6), 733–745.

Schatzberg, A. F., & Schildkraut, J. J. (1995). Recent studies on norepinephrine systems in mood disorders. In F. E. Bloom & D. J. Kupfer (Eds.), *Psychopharmacology: The fourth generation of progress* (pp. 911–920). New York: Raven Press.

Schildkraut, J. J. (1965). The catecholamine hypothesis of affective disorder: A review of supporting evidence. *American Journal of Psychiatry, 122*, 509–522.

Schittecatte, M., Charles, G., Machowski, R., Garcia-Valentin, J., Mendlewicz, J., & Wilmotte, J.

(1992). Reduced clonidine rapid eye movement sleep suppression in patients with primary major affective illness. *Archives of General Psychiatry, 49*, 637–642.

Sharpley, A., & Cowen, P. (1995). Effect of pharmacologic treatment on the sleep of depressed patients. *Biological Psychaitry, 37*(2), 85–98.

Sheline, Y. I. (2000). 3D MRI studies of neuroanatomic changes in unipolar major depression: The role of stress and medical comorbidity. *Biological Psychiatry, 48*(8), 793–800.

Sheline, Y. I., Barch, D. M., Donnelly, J. M., Ollinger, J. M., Snyder, A. Z., & Mintun, M. A. (2001). Increased amygdala response to masked emotional faces in depressed subjects resolves with antidepressant treatment: An fMRI study. *Biological Psychiatry, 50*(9), 651–658.

Sheline, Y. I., Sanghavi, M., Mintun, M. A., & Gado, M. H. (1999). Depression duration but not age predicts hippocampal volume loss in medically healthy women with recurrent major depression. *Journal of Neuroscience, 19*(12), 5034–5043.

Shelton, R. C. (2000). Cellular mechanisms in the vulnerability to depression and response to antidepressants. *Psychiatric Clinics of North America, 23*, 713–729.

Sitaram, N., Dubé, S., Keshavan, M., Davies, M., & Reynal, P. (1987). The association of supersensitive cholinergic REM-induction and affective illness within pedigrees. *Biological Psychiatry, 21*(4), 487–497.

Soares, J. C., & Mann, J. J. (1997). The anatomy of mood disorders: Review of structural neuroimaging studies. *Biological Psychiatry, 41*(1), 86–106.

Staley, J. K., Malison, R. T., & Innis, R. B. (1998). Imaging of the serotonergic system: Interactions of neuroanatomical and functional abnormalities of depression. *Biological Psychiatry, 44*(7), 534–549.

Starkman, M. N., Giordani, B., Gebarski, S. S., Berent, S., Schork, M. A., & Schteingart, D. E. (1999). Decrease in cortisol reverses human hippocampal atrophy following treatment of Cushing's disease. *Biological Psychiatry, 46*(12), 1595–1602.

Stolerman, I. P., & Reavill, C. (1989). Primary cholinergic and indirect dopaminergic mediation of behavioural effects of nicotine. *Progress in Brain Research, 79*, 227–237.

Thase, M. E. (1998). Depression, sleep, and antidepressants. *Journal of Clinical Psychiatry, 59*(Suppl. 4), 55–65.

Thase, M. E., Buysse, D. J., Frank, E., Cherry, C. R., Cornes, C. L., Mallinger, A. G., & Kupfer, D. J. (1997). Which depressed patients will respond to interpersonal psychotherapy?: The role of abnormal electroencephalographic sleep profiles. *American Journal of Psychiatry, 154*, 502–509.

Thase, M. E., Dubé, S., Bowler, K., Howland, R. H., Myers, J. E., Friedman, E., & Jarrett, D. B. (1996). Hypothalamic–pituitary–adrenocortical activity and response to cognitive behavior therapy in unmedicated, hospitalized depressed patients. *American Journal of Psychiatry, 153*(7), 886–891.

Thase, M. E., Entsuah, A. R., & Rudolph, R. L. (2001). Remission rates during treatment with venlafaxine or selective serotonin reuptake inhibitors. *British Journal of Psychiatry, 178*(3), 234–241.

Thase, M. E., Fasiczka, A. L., Berman, S. R., Simons, A. D., & Reynolds, C. F., III. (1998). Electroencephalographic sleep profiles before and after cognitive behavior therapy of depression. *Archives of General Psychiatry, 55*, 138–144.

Thase, M. E., Frank E., & Kupfer, D. J. (1985). Biological processes of major depression. In E. E. Beckham & W. R. Leber (Eds.), *Handbook of depression: Treatment, assessment, and research* (pp. 816–913). Homewood, IL: Dorsey Press.

Thase, M. E., & Friedman, E. S. (1999). Is psychotherapy, alone, an effective treatment for melancholia and other severe depressive states? *Journal of Affective Disorders, 54*, 1–19.

Thase, M. E., Greenhouse, J. B., Frank, E., Reynolds, C. F., III, Pilkonis, P. A., Hurley, K., Grochocinski, V., & Kupfer, D. J. (1997). Treatment of major depression with psychotherapy or psychotherapy–pharmacotherapy combinations. *Archives of General Psychiatry, 54*, 1009–1015.

Thase, M. E., & Howland, R. H. (1995). Biological processes in depression: An updated review and integration. In E. E. Beckham & W. R. Leber (Eds.), *Handbook of depression* (2nd ed., pp. 213–279). New York: Guilford Press.

Thase, M. E., & Kupfer, D. J. (1987). Current status of EEG sleep in the assessment and treatment of depression. In G. D. Burrows & J. S. Werry (Eds.), *Advances in human psychopharmacology* (Vol. 4, pp. 93–148). Greenwich, CT: JAI Press.

Thase, M. E., Kupfer, D. J., Buysse, D. J., Frank, E., Simons, A. D., McEachran, A. B., Rashid, K. F., & Grochocinski, V. J. (1995). Electroencephalographic sleep profiles in single-episode and recurrent unipolar forms of major depression: 1. Comparison during acute depressive states. *Biological Psychiatry, 38,* 506–515.

Thase, M. E., Kupfer, D. J., Fasiczka, A. L., Buysse, D. J., Simons, A. D., & Frank, E. (1997). Identifying an abnormal electroencephalographic sleep profile to characterize major depressive disorder. *Biological Psychiatry, 41,* 964–973.

Thase, M. E., Simons, A. D., & Reynolds, C. F., III. (1996). Abnormal electroencephalographic sleep profiles in major depression: Association with response to cognitive behavior therapy. *Archives of General Psychiatry, 53,* 99–108.

Weiss, E. L., Longhurst, J. G., & Mazure, C. G. (1999). Childhood sexual abuse as a risk factor for depression in women: Psychosocial and neurobiological correlates. *American Journal of Psychiatry, 156*(6), 816–828.

Weiss, J. M., & Kilts, C. D. (1998). Animal models of depression and schizophrenia. In A. F. Schatzberg & C. B. Nemeroff (Eds.), *Textbook of psychopharmacology* (2nd ed., pp. 89–131). Washington, DC: American Psychiatric Press.

Whalen, P. J., Rauch, S. L., Etcoff, N. L., McInerney, S. C., Lee, M. B., & Jenike, M. A. (1998). Masked presentations of emotional facial expressions modulate amygdala activity without explicit knowledge. *Journal of Neuroscience, 18*(1), 411–418.

Willner, P. (1995). Dopaminergic mechanisms in depression and mania. In F. E. Bloom & D. J. Kupfer (Eds.), *Psychopharmacology: The fourth generation of progress* (pp. 921–931). New York: Raven Press.

Willner, P. (1997). The mesolimbic dopamine system as a target for rapid antidepressant action. *International Clinical Psychopharmacology, 12*(Suppl. 3), S7-S14.

Wirz-Justice, A. (1995). Biological rhythms in mood disorders. In F. E. Bloom & D. J. Kupfer (Eds.), *Psychopharmacology: The fourth generation of progress* (pp. 999–1017). New York: Raven Press.

Zajicek, K. B., Price, C. S., Shoaf, S. E., Mehlman, P. T., Suomi, S. J., Linnoila, M., & Highley, J. D. (2000). Seasonal variation in CSF 5-HIAA concentrations in male rhesus monkeys. *Neuropsychopharmacology, 22*(3), 240–250.

9

The Representation and Regulation of Emotion in Depression
Perspectives from Affective Neuroscience

Richard J. Davidson, Diego Pizzagalli, and Jack B. Nitschke

Affective neuroscience is the subdiscipline that examines the underlying neural bases of mood and emotion. The application of this body of theory and data to the understanding of affective disorders is helping to generate a new understanding of the brain circuitry underlying these disorders. Moreover, parsing the heterogeneity of these disorders on the basis of known circuits in the brain is providing a novel and potentially very fruitful approach to subtyping that does not rely on the descriptive nosology of psychiatric diagnosis, but rather is based on a more objective characterization of the specific affective deficits in patients with mood disorders. At a more general level, this approach is helping to bridge the chasm between the literature that focuses on normal emotion and the literature that focuses on the disorders of emotion. Historically, these research traditions emerged independently and have had little to do with one another. However, affective neuroscience has helped to integrate these approaches into a more unified project that focuses on understanding individual differences in affective style, its constituent components, and its neural bases (e.g., Davidson, 2000; Davidson, Jackson, & Kalin, 2000a).

Affective neuroscience takes as its overall aim a project that is similar to that pursued by its cognate discipline, cognitive neuroscience, though focused instead on affective processes. The decomposition of cognitive processes into more elementary constituents that can then be studied in neural terms has been remarkably successful. We no longer query subjects about the contents of their cognitive processes because many of the processes so central to important aspects of cognitive function are opaque to consciousness. Instead, contemporary cognitive scientists and neuroscientists have developed laboratory tasks to interrogate and reveal more elementary cognitive functions. These more elementary processes can then be studied using imaging methods in humans, lesion methods in animals, and human patients with focal brain damage. Affective neuroscience approaches emotion using the same strategy. Global constructs of emotion are giving way to more specific and elementary constituents that can be examined with objective laboratory measures. For example, our laboratory has been developing methods to probe the chronometry of affect using both neuroimaging and peripheral startle measures. These measures allow us to examine an anticipatory period prior to the delivery of an emotional stimulus, a recovery period following the delivery of an emotional stimulus, and other related parameters that can be assessed objectively and that reveal systematic individual differences (see Davidson, 2000). Though it is still tempting and often important to obtain measures of subjects' conscious experience of the contents of their emotional states and traits, these self-reports no longer constitute the sole source of information about emotion.

Because there are recent reviews of the basic literature on the circuitry underlying emotion and emotion regulation (e.g., Davidson & Irwin, 1999; Davidson et al., 2000a; Davidson, Putnam, & Larson, 2000d; Rolls, 1999), these data will not be systematically reviewed in this chapter. Moreover, because two recent reviews cover much of the literature prior to the past 3 years (Davidson, Abercrombie, Nitschke, & Putnam, 1999; Drevets, 1998), we emphasize studies that have been published since that time. We wish to underscore at the outset that one of the crucial issues that plagues research in this area is the heterogeneity of depression. From an examination of the inconsistencies across studies, it is apparent that traditional methods for parsing heterogeneity based upon descriptive phenomenology are not yielding clean separation of underlying neural circuitry. For example, the melancholic versus nonmelancholic distinction does not systematically reveal differences in neural correlates (see below). Recommendations for moving beyond phenomenology will be provided throughout this chapter.

We have three broad goals for this chapter:

1. To review the functional role of the prefrontal cortices, anterior cingulate, hippocampus, and amygdala in affect and emotion regulation (see Figure 9.1 for a depiction of these structures and their locations);
2. To review the functional and structural abnormalities that have been found in these regions in depression;
3. Based on the first and second goals above, (a) to advance hypotheses about symptom clusters that may arise as a consequence of dysfunctions in specific regions; and (b) to offer suggestions for different ways of parsing the heterogeneity of depression in ways that reflect more directly the circuitry of emotion and emotion regulation in the brain.

THE EMOTIONAL CIRCUITRY OF THE BRAIN AND ITS DYSFUNCTION IN DEPRESSION

Prefrontal Cortex

The Role of the Prefrontal Cortex in Emotion and Emotion Regulation

Abnormalities in activation of prefrontal regions in depression have been reported more frequently than for any other brain region, mostly in the direction of decreased bilateral or predominantly left-sided activation (Davidson et al., 1999; George, Ketter, & Post, 1994). Miller and Cohen (2001) have recently outlined a comprehensive theory of prefrontal function based on nonhuman primate anatomical and neurophysiological studies, human neuroimaging findings, and computational modeling. The core feature of their model holds that the prefrontal cortex (PFC) maintains the representation of goals and the means to achieve them. Particularly in situations that are ambiguous, the PFC sends bias signals to other areas of the brain to facilitate the expression of task-appropriate responses in the face of

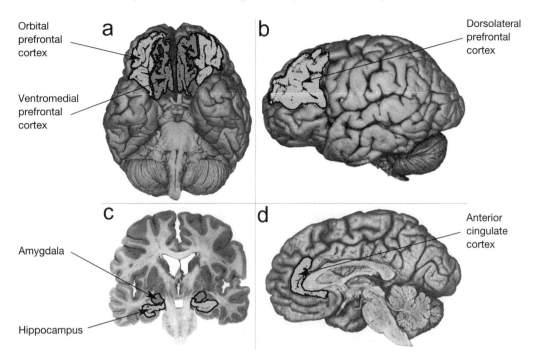

FIGURE 9.1. Key brain regions involved in affect and mood disorders. (a) Orbital prefrontal cortex and the ventromedial prefrontal cortex. (b) Dorsolateral prefrontal cortex. (c) Hippocampus and amygdala. (d) Anterior cingulate cortex.

competition with potentially stronger alternatives. In the affective domain, we often confront situations in which the arousal of emotion is inconsistent with other goals that have already been instantiated. For example, the availability of an immediate reward offers a potent response alternative that may not be in the best service of the overall goals of the person. In such a case, the PFC is required to produce a bias signal to other brain regions that guides behavior toward the acquisition of a more adaptive goal, which in this case would entail delay of gratification. Affect-guided planning and anticipation that involves the experience of emotion associated with an anticipated choice is the hallmark of adaptive, emotion-based decision making that has repeatedly been found to become impaired in patients with lesions of ventromedial PFC (Damasio, 1994). The instantiation of affect-guided anticipation is most often accomplished in situations that are heavily laden with competition from potentially stronger alternatives. In such cases in particular, we would expect PFC activation to occur.

Our laboratory has contributed extensively to the literature on asymmetries in PFC function associated with approach- and withdrawal-related emotion and mood (e.g., Davidson & Irwin, 1999; Davidson et al., 2000a). In this context, we suggest that left-sided PFC regions are particularly involved in approach-related, appetitive goals. The instantiation of such goals, particularly in the face of strong alternative responses, requires left-sided PFC activation. In contrast, right-sided PFC regions are hypothesized to be particularly important in the maintenance of goals that require behavioral inhibition and withdrawal in situations that involve strong alternative response options to approach. The prototype of such a process has recently been captured in several neuroimaging studies that involve variants of a go/no go task in which a dominant response set is established to respond quickly except on those trials in which a cue to inhibit the response is presented. Two recent studies using event-related functional magnetic resonance imaging (fMRI) have found a lateralized focus of activation in the right lateral PFC (inferior frontal sulcus) to cues that signaled response inhibition that were presented in the context of other stimuli toward which a strong approach set was established (Garavan, Rose, & Stein, 1999; Konishi et al., 1999).

Depressed individuals with hypoactivation in certain regions of the PFC may be deficient in the instantiation of goal-directed behavior and in the overriding of more automatic responses that may involve the perseveration of negative affect and dysfunctional attitudes. Such deficits would be expected to be unmasked in situations where decision making is ambiguous and where the maintenance of goal-directed behavior is required in the face of potentially strong alternative responses. As we argue below, when the strong alternative responses involve affect, which they often do, the ventromedial PFC is particularly implicated.

Results from recent neuroimaging and electrophysiological studies suggest that the orbital and ventral frontal cortex in particular may be especially important for the representation of rewards and punishments, and that different sectors within this cortex may emphasize reward versus punishment (Kawasaki et al., 2001; O'Doherty, Kringelbach, Rolls, Hornak, & Andrews, 2001). In particular, a left-sided medial region of the orbitofrontal cortex (OFC) appears particularly responsive to rewards, while a lateral right-sided region appears particularly responsive to punishments (O'Doherty et al., 2001). Differential responsivity to rewards versus punishments has been found behaviorally in two studies in our laboratory (Henriques, Glowacki, & Davidson, 1994; Henriques & Davidson, 2000). In particular, while normal individuals exhibited systematic modification of response bias to monetary reward, depressed patients failed to show such changes but did show response bias shifts in response to monetary punishment. On the basis of these behavioral findings, we would predict that left medial OFC would be hyporesponsive to manipulations of reward in such patients, while right lateral OFC to punishment would either be normal or perhaps accentuated.

Role of the Prefrontal Cortex in Depression

Consistent with prior literature, recent reports have documented decreased activation in both dorsolateral and dorsomedial prefrontal cortex as well as the pregenual region of the anterior cingulate gyrus in depressed patients (see Drevets, 1998, for a comprehensive review of this literature). The reduction in activation in this latter region, particularly on the left side, appears to be at least partially a function of a reduction in the volume of gray matter as revealed by MRI-derived morphometric measures (Drevets et al., 1997). Consistent with the notion that the metabolic reduction found in this region is at least partially a function of the volume reduction, Drevets et al. (1997) have reported that remission of symptoms associated with successful treatment is not accompanied by a normalization of activation in this area.

This general decrease in dorsolateral PFC and in the pregenual region of the anterior cingulate cortex (ACC) tends to be accompanied by an increase in other regions of the PFC, particularly in the ventrolateral and orbital (lateral and medial). Treatment studies have found that activation in dorsolateral PFC, particularly on the left side, increases following successful antidepressant treatment (Kennedy et al., 2001). Less consistent are findings for ventrolateral and orbital PFC regions: whereas some studies have found increases in these regions (Kennedy et al., 2001), others have reported decreases (e.g., Brody et al., 1999; Mayberg et al., 1999).

As suggested above, recent reports of anatomical differences between depressed patients and normal controls in the PFC are of critical import to any claims made about functional differences between these two groups of individuals. Consistent with earlier work conducted by Coffey et al. (1993), who found depressed inpatients to have frontal lobe volumes that were 7% smaller than those of nonpsychiatric controls, Drevets et al. (1997) reported that unipolar and bipolar depressives with a family history of mood disorders showed a 48% and a 39% reduction in subgenual PFC volume, respectively. In a postmortem study by the same group (Öngür, Drevets, & Price, 1998b), glial cell number was significantly reduced in subgenual PFC in both unipolar (24%) and bipolar patients (41%) with a family history of major depressive disorder. No significant effects were observed for nonfamilial major depressive disorder (MDD) or bipolar disorder (BD). Rajkowska (2000) has further examined alterations in neuronal and glial histopathology in postmortem brains of patients who suffered from mood disorders. She and her colleagues found that left prefrontal cortices (no other brain areas were examined) of subjects with MDD had decreases in cortical thickness, neuronal size, and neuronal and glial densities in upper cortical layers (II–IV) of left rostral OFC; decreases in neuronal size and glial densities in lower cortical layers (V–VI); and decreases in neuronal and glial size and density in supra- and infragranular layers. Of note, they found a 12–15% reduction of cortical thickness in the lateral OFC. Furthermore, they argued that the 22–37% reduction in density of large neurons and 6–27% increase of small neurons in the rostral OFC and dorsolateral PFC (DLPFC) may implicate cell atrophy rather than cell loss as the mechanism for the reduced cortical volume seen in depression. Similar results were observed in the left DLPFC of bipolar patients. These brains were characterized by a 16–22% reduction in neuronal density in layer III, a 17–30% reduction in pyramidal cell density in layers III and V, and a 19% reduction in glial density in sublayer IIIc. The fact that these anatomical differences in patients with mood disorders might account for some of the functional differences as noted by Drevets et al. (1997) does not in itself provide any direct measure of causal influence. Longitudinal studies of patients at risk for mood disorders are needed to ascertain whether these structural differences are present prior to the onset of a depressive episode. Heritable factors can be examined by studying monozygotic twins discordant for mood disorders to ascertain whether the anatomical abnormalities are found in the affected twin only.

The common observation in electroencephalographic (EEG) studies of an altered pattern of asymmetric activation in anterior scalp regions in the direction of reduced left relative to right activation in depressed or dysphoric individuals has also been replicated several times in recent years (Bell, Schwartz, Hardin, Baldwin, & Kline, 1998, Bruder et al., 1997; Debener et al., 2000; Gotlib, Ranganath, & Rosenfeld, 1998; Pauli, Wiedemann, & Nickola, 1999; though see Reid, Duke, & Allen, 1998, for complications, and Davidson, 1998, for a rejoinder). In an important extension of the work on electrophysiological asymmetries, Bruder and his colleagues (Bruder et al., 2001) examined whether brain electrical asymmetry measures acquired during a pretreatment period predicted response to treatment with selective serotonin reuptake inhibitors (SSRIs). They found that among women in particular, the treatment responders had significantly less relative right-sided activation compared with the nonresponders, though this effect was present in both anterior and posterior scalp regions. Based upon the role of right prefrontal regions in components of negative affect (Davidson, 2000) and right posterior regions in arousal and anxiety (Heller & Nitschke, 1998), these findings imply that those subjects with global right activation who would be expected to have symptoms of negative affect and anxious arousal are least likely to show improvements with SSRI treatment.

Anterior Cingulate Cortex

The Role of the Anterior Cingulate Cortex in Emotion and Emotion Regulation

Several theorists have proposed that the ACC acts as a bridge between attention and emotion (Devinsky, Morrell, & Vogt, 1995; Ebert & Ebmeier, 1996; Mayberg, 1997; Vogt, Nimchinsky, Vogt, & Hof, 1995). In their recent review, Thayer and Lane (2000) described the ACC as "a point of integration for visceral, attentional, and affective information that is critical for self-regulation and adaptability" (p. 211). In light of its anatomical connections (see below), the ACC appears well equipped for assessing and responding to the behavioral significance of external stimuli. Critical roles of the ACC in selective attention (i.e., prioritizing incoming information), affect, and specific characteristic mammalian social behaviors have been described (Devinsky et al., 1995; Vogt, Finch, & Olson, 1992). However, in order to fully understand the role of the ACC in psychopathology, affective states, and emotional processing, it seems mandatory to recognize that the ACC is far from being a functionally homogeneous region, and at least two subdivisions can be discerned (Devinsky et al., 1995; Vogt et al., 1992, 1995). The first, referred to as the "affect subdivision," encompasses rostral and ventral areas of the ACC (Brodmann's areas 25, 32, 33, and rostral Brodmann's area 24). The second, referred to as the "cognitive subdivision," involves dorsal regions of the ACC (caudal Brodmann's area 24' and 32', cingulate motor area). The affect subdivision possesses extensive connections with limbic and paralimbic regions, such as the amygdala, nucleus accumbens, OFC, periaqueductal grey, anterior insula, and autonomic brainstem motor nuclei, and is assumed to be involved in regulating visceral and autonomic responses to stressful behavioral and emotional events, emotional expression, and social behavior. Because of its strong connections with the lateral hypothalamus, the subgenual ACC (Brodmann's area 25) is considered the most important autonomic region within the frontal region (Öngür, An, & Price, 1998a).

Conversely, the cognitive subdivision is intimately connected with the DLPFC (Brodmann's area 46/9), posterior cingulate, parietal cortex (Brodmann's area 7), supplementary motor area, and spinal cord, and plays an important role in response selection and processing of cognitively demanding information. In functional neuroimaging studies, evidence is emerging suggesting a functional differentiation between ventral (affective) and dorsal (cognitive) ACC subdivisions (Bush et al., 1998; Bush, Luu, & Posner, 2000; Whalen et al., 1998a).

From a functional perspective, activation of the cognitive subdivision of the ACC has been reported during interference between competing information (Pardo, Pardo, Janer, & Raichle, 1990), visual attention (Nobre et al., 1997), monitoring of cognitive (Carter, Botvinick, & Mendels, 2000; MacDonald, Cohen, Stenger, & Carter, 2000) and reward-related (Rogers et al., 1999) conflicts, task difficulty (Paus et al., 1997), and increased risk-associated outcome uncertainty (Critchley, Mathias, & Dolan, 2001), among other experimental manipulations. A common denominator among these experimental conditions is that they all required modulation of attention or executive functions and monitoring of competition (Bush et al., 2000). The role of the ACC in conflict monitoring has been especially emphasized by Cohen and colleagues (Carter, Botvinick, & Cohen, 1999; Carter et al., 2000; Miller & Cohen, 2001). These authors proposed that the ACC may serve an evaluative function, reflecting the degree of response conflict elicited by a given task. Conflict occurs when two or more possible task-related decisions compete or interfere with each other. According to the *competition monitoring hypothesis,* the cognitive subdivision of the ACC monitors conflicts or crosstalk between brain regions. If a signal of competition emerges, this output signals the need for controlled processing. The DLPFC (Brodmann's area 9) is assumed to be critical for this form of controlled processing, in that it represents and maintains task demands necessary for such control and inhibits (e.g., Garavan et al., 1999) or increases neural activity in brain regions implicated in the competition. Thus, dorsal ACC activation leading to a call for further processing by other brain regions may represent a mechanism for effortful control. From a functional perspective, activation of the affective subdivision of the ACC has been reported during various emotional states and manipulations (for reviews, see Reiman, 1997; Bush et al., 2000). Collectively, recent findings suggest that the affective subdivision of the ACC is critically involved in conscious experience of affect, and possibly of uncertainty, conflict, and expectancy violation arising from affectively and motivationally salient situations (see below).

In light of the many types of experimental manipulations that have been found to activate the ACC, is there a common denominator underlying activation of the rostral/ventral ACC in such disparate experimental conditions, such as pain, classical conditioning, transient mood, activation of primary drive states, Stroop task, and perceiving facial expressions, among others? A possible answer to this question is that the affective subdivision of the ACC may be critical for assessing the presence of possible conflicts between the current functional state of the organism and incoming information with potentially relevant motivational and emotional consequences. This suggestion is based on the observation that the affective subdivision of the ACC is involved in behaviors characterized by monitoring and evaluation of performance, internal states, and presence of reward or punishment, which often require change in behavior. Extant evidence suggests that ACC activation may be present when effortful emotional regulation is required in situations where behavior is failing to achieve a desired outcome or when affect is elicited in contexts that are not normative, which includes most laboratory situations (Bush et al., 2000; Ochsner & Barrett, 2001). Relatedly, it is not surprising that the ACC is one of the most consistently activated regions in patients with different anxiety disorders, such as obsessive–compulsive disorder (OCD; Breiter et al., 1996; Rauch, Savage, Alpert, Fischman, & Jenike, 1997), simple phobia (Rauch et al., 1995), and posttraumatic stress disorder (PTSD; Rauch et al., 1996; Shin et al., 1997), in which conflicts between response tendencies and environments are prominent. Interestingly, psychosurgical lesioning of the ACC has been used as a treatment for mood and anxiety disorders (e.g., Baer et al., 1995; see Binder & Iskandar, 2000, for review), possibly because of a reduction of conflict monitoring and uncertainty that otherwise characterize these psychiatric conditions.

The Role of the Anterior Cingulate Cortex in Depression

In major depression, decreased ACC activation relative to controls has been reported repeatedly. In single photon emission computed tomography (SPECT) studies, decreased regional cerebral blood flow (rCBF) in the left (Curran, Tucker, Kutas, & Posner, 1993; Mayberg, Lewis, Regenold, & Wagner, 1994) or right (Ito et al., 1996) ACC has been found in medicated depressed unipolar patients compared to controls. Decreased ACC activation has been recently replicated with positron emission tomography (PET) (Bench et al., 1992; Drevets et al., 1997; George et al., 1997; Kumar et al., 1993) and fMRI (Beauregard et al., 1998) techniques. Interestingly, the region of the ACC found to be hypoactive in major depression (dorsal ACC: dorsal region of Brodmann's area 32 and Brodmann's areas 24′, 32′) appears to be different from the region found to be hyperactive in eventual treatment responders (ventral and rostral ACC, including pregenual Brodmann's areas 24, 32). Whereas the state of being depressed is associated with reduced dorsal ACC activity (see above), remission has been characterized by increased activity in the same region (Bench, Frackowiak, & Dolan, 1995; Buchsbaum et al., 1997; Mayberg et al., 1999). Based on the functional neuroimaging and animal literature reviewed above, it is conceivable to postulate that (1) hypoactivation in dorsal regions of the ACC (Brodmann's areas 24', 32') may be associated with impaired modulation of attention or executive functions and impaired monitoring of competition among various response options; (2) hypoactivation in ventral regions of the ACC may be associated with blunted conscious experience of affect, hypoarousal, anhedonia, reduced coping potential in situations characterized by uncertainty, conflict, and expectancy violation between the environment and one's affective state; and (3) hyperactivation in ventral regions of the ACC may be associated with increased attentional and behavioral responses to anxiety-provoking situations, especially in depressed subjects showing comorbidity with anxiety. Such hyperactivation may cause attentional and affective stereotypies. While future studies will need to test these assumptions more explicitly, recent findings are consistent with some of them. For example, in a recent PET study, Brody et al. (2001) found that reduction of anxiety/somatization symptoms was associated with decreased glucose metabolism in the ventral ACC. Conversely, improvement in psychomotor retardation symptoms was associated with increased activation in the dorsal ACC.

The interplay between the affective and cognitive subdivision of the ACC is currently unknown. From a theoretical perspective, several authors have suggested that the affective subdivision of the ACC may integrate salient affective and cognitive information (such as that derived from environmental stimuli or task demands), and subsequently modulate attentional processes within the cognitive subdivision accordingly (Mega, Cummings, Salloway, & Malloy, 1997; Mayberg, 1997; Mayberg et al., 1999; Pizzagalli et al., 2001). In agreement with this hypothesis, dorsal anterior and posterior cingulate pathways devoted to attentional processes and amygdalar pathways devoted to affective processing converge within Brodmann's area 24 (Mega et al., 1997). These mechanisms may be especially important for understanding the repeatedly demonstrated finding that increased pretreatment activity in the rostral ACC (Brodmann's area 24a/b) is associated with eventual better treatment response (Mayberg et al., 1997; Ebert, Feistel, & Barocka, 1991; Pizzagalli et al., 2001; Wu et al., 1992, 1999). In an influential paper, Mayberg and colleagues (1997) reported that unipolar depressed patients who responded to treatment after 6 weeks showed higher pretreatment glucose metabolism in rostral region of the ACC that compared to both nonresponders and nonpsychiatric comparison subjects. Recently, we (Pizzagalli et al., 2001) replicated this finding with EEG source localization techniques and demonstrated that even among those patients who responded to treatment, the magnitude of treatment response was predicted by baseline levels of activation in the same region of the ACC as identified by Mayberg et al. (1997). In addition, we suggested that hyperactivation of the rostral ACC in depression might reflect an increased sensitivity to affective conflict such that the disparity between one's current mood and the responses expected in a particular context activates this region of the ACC, which then in turn issues a call for further processing to help resolve the conflict. This call for further processing is hypothesized to aid the treatment response.

One of the major outputs from the ACC is a projection to the PFC. This pathway may be the route through which the ACC issues a call to the PFC for further processing to address a conflict that has been detected. Thus, abnormalities in PFC function in depression may arise as a consequence of the failure of the normal signals from the ACC, may be intrinsic to the PFC, or both. It is also possible, and even likely, that there are different subtypes of depression that may involve primary dysfunction in one or another part of the circuitry that we review in this chapter. It is important to underscore the possibility that there may exist a primary ACC-based depression subtype and a primary PFC-based depression subtype. These subtypes might not conform to the phenomenological and descriptive nosologies that are currently prevalent in the psychiatric literature.

Hippocampus

The Role of the Hippocampus in Emotion and Emotion Regulation

The hippocampus is critically involved in episodic, declarative, contextual, and spatial learning and in memory (Fanselow, 2000; Squire & Knowlton, 2000). In addition, the hippocampus is also importantly involved in the regulation of adrenocorticotropic hormone secretion (Jacobson & Sapolsky, 1991). With respect to conditioning, in recent years rodent studies have convincingly shown that the hippocampus plays a key role in the formation, storage, and consolidation of contextual fear conditioning (see Fanselow, 2000, for a review). In this form of hippocampal-dependent Pavlovian conditioning, fear (e.g., expressed in increased freezing) is acquired to places or contexts (e.g., a specific cage) previously associated with aversive events (e.g., shock). This fact has important implications for our understanding of the abnormalities in affective function that may arise as a consequence of hippocampal dysfunction.

In functional neuroimaging studies, hippocampal/parahippocampal activation has been reported during perception of several negatively valenced stimuli and/or experiencing of negatively valenced affective states, such as trace conditioning (Büchel, Dolan, Armony, & Friston, 1999), perception of aversive complex stimuli (Lane, Fink, Chau, & Dolan, 1997), threat-related words (Isenberg et al., 1999), increasing music dissonance (Blood, Zatorre, Bermudez, & Evans, 1999), tinnitus-like aversive auditory stimulation (Mirz, Gjedde, Sodkilde-Jrgensen, & Pedersen, 2000), vocal expressions of fear (Phillips et al., 1998), aversive taste (Zald, Lee, Fluegel, & Pardo, 1998), anticipatory anxiety (Javanmard et al., 1999), procaine-induced affect (Ketter et al., 1996; Servan-Schreiber, Perlstein, Cohen, & Mintun, 1997), and monetary penalties (Elliott & Dolan, 1999). However, it seems that valence is not the critical variable for evoking hippocampal activation. Indeed, hippocampal activation has been also reported during experimental manipulation of positive affect, such as reevoking pleasant affective autobiographical memories (Fink et al., 1996), increases in winning in a game-like task (Zalla et al., 2000), and perception of a loved person (Bartels & Zeki, 2000). Also, hippocampal activation has been found to be correlated with long-term recognition memory for pleasant films (Hamann, Ely, Grafton, & Kilts, 1999).

In reconciling these findings, we suggest that most of the experimental manipulations leading to hippocampal activation contain contextual cues. That is, we assume that they involve the consolidation of a memory for an integrated representation of a context similar to that associated with the presented stimulus (Fanselow, 2000). This is clearly the case during Pavlovian and trace conditioning, for instance, but it is also true during presentation of both positively and negatively valenced visual, olfactory, and auditory cues that may induce reevocation and consolidation of contextual information associated with similar situations in the past (e.g., Nader, Shafe, & Le Doux, 2000). Although in humans the mechanisms underlying contextual conditioning are still unclear, it is possible that plasticity in functional connectivity between the hippocampus and regions crucially involved in decoding the behavioral significance of incoming information, such as the amygdala and the pulvinar, may critically contribute to contextual learning (Morris, Friston, & Dolan, 1997; Morris, Ohman, & Dolan, 1999), even when the information is presented below the level of conscious awareness (Morris et al., 1999). As recently reviewed by Davis and Whalen (2001), animal studies clearly suggest that the amygdala exerts a modulatory influence on hippocampal-dependent memory systems, possibly through direct projections from the basolateral nucleus of the amygdala. Consistent with this view, stimulation of the amygdala causes LTP induction in the dentate gyrus of the hippocampus (Ikegaya, Abe, Saito, & Nishiyama, 1995a). Conversely, lesions to (Ikegaya, Saito, & Abe, 1994) or local anesthetics within (Ikegaya, Saito, & Abe, 1995b) the basolateral nucleus of the amygdala attenuate long-term potentiation in the dentate gyrus. Although drawing conclusions from these rodent studies to humans is speculative at this stage, it is intriguing that most of the human neuroimaging studies reporting hippocampal activation during aversive affective manipulations have also found amygdalar activation (Büchel et al., 1999; Isenberg et al., 1999; Ketter et al., 1996; Mirz et al., 2000; Servan-Schreiber et al., 1997; Zald et al., 1998). In the future, neuroimaging studies should directly test the interplay between the hippocampus and the amygdala in these processes and in fear-related learning and memory, especially in light of recent animal data suggesting an interplay between these regions in modulating extinction of conditioned fear (Corcoran & Maren, 2001).

The Role of the Hippocampus in Depression

In their recent review, Davidson et al. (2000a) noted that various forms of psychopathology involving disorders of affect could be characterized as disorders in context regulation of affect. That is, patients with mood and anxiety disorders often display normative affective responses but in inappropriate contexts. Given the preclinical and functional neuroimaging literature reviewed above, one may hypothesize that patients showing inappropriate context regulation of affect may be characterized by hippocampal dysfunction. Consistent with this conjecture, recent morphometric studies using MRI indeed reported hippocampal atrophy in patients with major depression (Sheline, Wang, Gado, Csernansky, & Vannier, 1996; Sheline, Sanghavi, Mintun, & Gado, 1999; Bremner et al., 2000; Shah, Ebmeier, Glabus, & Goodwin, 1998; von Gunten, Fox, Cipolotti, & Ron, 2000; Steffens et al., 2000; Mervaala et al., 2000; but see Vakili et al., 2000; Ashtari et al., 1999), bipolar disorder (Noga, Vladar, & Torrey, 2001), PTSD (Bremner et al., 1995, 1997a; Stein, Koverola, Hanna, Torchia, & McClarty, 1997), and borderline personality disorder (Driessen et al., 2000) (for reviews, see Sapolsky, 2000; Sheline, 2000). Where hippocampal volume reductions in depression have been found, the magnitude of reduction ranges from 8 to 19%. Recently, functional hippocampal abnormalities in major depression have also been reported at baseline using PET measures of glucose metabolism (Saxena et al., 2001). Whether hippocampal dysfunction precedes or follows onset of depressive symptomatology is still unknown.

In depression, inconsistencies across studies may be explained by several methodological considerations. First, as pointed out by Sheline (2000), studies reporting positive findings generally used MRI with higher spatial resolution (~0.5–2 mm) compared to those reporting negative findings (~3–10 mm). Second, it seems that age, severity of depression, and, most significantly, duration of recurrent depression may be important moderator variables. Indeed, studies reporting negative findings either studied younger cohorts (e.g., Vakili et al., 2000: 38 ± 10 years vs. Sheline et al., 1996: 69 ± 10 years; von Gunten et al., 2000: 58 ± 9 years; Steffens et al., 2000: 72 ± 8 years) or less severe and less chronic cohorts (Ashtari et al., 1999, vs. Sheline et al., 1996; Shah et al., 1998; Bremner et al., 2000). In a recent study (Rusch, Abercrombie, Oakes, Schaefer, & Davidson, 2001), we also failed to find hippocampal atrophy in a relatively young subject sample (33.2 ± 9.5 years) with moderate depression severity. Notably, in normal early adulthood (18–42 years), decreased bilateral hippocampal volume has been reported with increasing age in male but not female healthy subjects (Pruessner, Collins, Pruessner, & Evans, 2001). Finally, in females, initial evidence suggests that total lifetime duration of depression, rather than age, is associated with hippocampal atrophy (Sheline et al., 1999), inviting the possibility that hippocampal atrophy may be a *symptom* rather than a *cause* of depression. Future studies should carefully assess the relative contribution of these possible modulatory variables in the hippocampal pathophysiology and examine hippocampal changes longitudinally in individuals at risk for mood disorders.

Structurally, the hippocampal changes may arise due to neuronal loss through chronic hypercortisolemia, glial cell loss, stress-induced reduction in neurotrophic factors, or stress-induced reduction in neurogenesis, but the precise mechanisms are not completely known (Sheline, 2000). In depression, the hypothesis of an association between sustained, stress-related elevations of cortisol and hippocampal damage has received considerable attention. This hypothesis is based on the observation that the pathophysiology of depression involves dysfunction in negative feedback of the hypothalamic–pituitary–adrenal (HPA) axis (see Pariante & Miller, 2001, for a review), which results in increased levels of cortisol during depressive episodes (e.g., Carroll, Curtis, & Mendels, 1976). Higher levels of cortisol may, in turn, lead to neuronal damage in the hippocampus, since this region possesses high levels of glucocorticoid receptors (Reul & De Kloet, 1986) and glucocorticoids are neurotoxic (Sapolsky, Krey, & McEwan, 1986). Since the hippocampus is involved in negative feedback control of cortisol (Jacobson & Sapolsky, 1991), hippocampal dysfunction may result in reduction of the inhibitory regulation of the HPA axis, which could then lead to hypercortisolemia. Consistent with this view, chronic exposure to increased glucocorticoid concentrations has been shown to lower the threshold for hippocampal neuronal degeneration in animals (Gold, Goodwin, & Chrousos, 1988; Sapolsky, Uno, Roberts, & Finch, 1990; McEwen, 1998) and humans (Lupien et al., 1998). At least in nonhuman primates, this association is qualified by the observation that chronically elevated cortisol concentrations in the absence of chronic "psychosocial" stress do not produce hippocampal neuronal loss (Leverenz et al., 1999). Conversely, naturalistic, chronic psychosocial stress has been shown to induce structural changes in hippocampal neurons of subordinate animals (Magarinos, McEwen, Flugge, & Fuchs, 1996). In depression, hippocampal volume loss has been shown to be associated with lifetime duration of depression (Sheline et al., 1999), consistent with the assumption that long-term exposure to high cortisol levels may lead to hippocampal atrophy. However, this conjecture has not been verified empirically in humans.

Although intriguing, these findings cannot inform us about the causality between hippocampal dysfunction, elevated levels of cortisol and, most importantly, inappropriate context regulation of affect in depression. Unfortunately, none of the structural neuroimaging studies in depression investigating hippocampal volume were prospective and took into account cortisol data in an effort to unravel the causal link between cortisol output and hippocampal dysfunction.

The possibility of plasticity in the hippocampus deserves particular comment. In rodents, recent studies have shown hippocampal neurogenesis as a consequence of antidepressant pharmacological treatment (Chen, Rajkowska, Du, Seraji-Bozorgzad, & Manji, 2000; Malberg, Eisch, Nestler, & Duman, 2000), electroconvulsive shock (Madhav, Pei, Grahame-Smith, & Zetterstrom, 2000) and, most intriguingly, as a consequence of positive handling, learning and exposure to an enriched environment (Kempermann, Kuhn, & Gage, 1997; see Gould, Tanapat, Rydel, & Hastings, 2000, for review). In humans, neurogenesis in the adult human hippocampus has also been reported (Eriksson et al., 1998). Further, in patients with Cushing's disease, who are characterized by very high levels of cortisol, increases in hippocampal volume were significantly associated with magnitude cortisol decrease produced by microadrenomectomy (Starkman et al., 1999). As a corpus, these animal and human data clearly suggest that plasticity in the human hippocampus is possible (for reviews, see Duman, Malberg, Nakagawa, & D'Sa, 2000; Jacobs, Praag, & Gage, 2000; Gould et al., 2000), a finding that suggests that structural and functional changes in the hippocampus of depressed patients may be reversible.

In summary, preclinical and clinical studies converge in suggesting an association between major depression and hippocampal dysfunction. Future studies should (1) assess whether hippocampal atrophy precedes or follows onset of depression; (2) assess the causal relation between hypercortisolemia and hippocampal volume reduction; (3) directly test a putative link between inappropriate context-dependent affective responding and hippocampal atrophy; and (4) assess putative treatment-mediated plastic changes in the hippocampus.

Amygdala

The Role of the Amygdala in Emotion and Emotion Regulation

Although a link between amygdala activity and negative affect has been a prevalent view in the literature, particularly when examined in response to exteroceptive aversive stimuli (e.g., LeDoux, 2000), recent findings from invasive animal, human lesion, and functional neuroimaging studies are converging on a broader view that regards the role of the amygdala in negative affect as a special case of its more general role in directing attention to affectively salient stimuli and issuing a call for further processing of stimuli that have major significance for the individual. Extant evidence is consistent with the argument that the amygdala is critical for recruiting and coordinating cortical arousal and vigilant attention for optimizing sensory and perceptual processing of stimuli associated with underdetermined contingencies, such as novel, "surprising," or "ambiguous" stimuli (e.g., Davis & Whalen, 2001; Holland & Gallagher, 1999; Whalen, 1998). Most stimuli in this class may be conceptualized as having an aversive valence since we tend to have a negativity bias in the face of uncertainty (Taylor, 1991).

The Role of the Amygdala in Depression

In major depression, structural and functional abnormalities in the amygdala have been reported. Structurally, several recent studies reported an association between enlargement of amygdala volume and depression. This association has been found in depressed patients with bipolar disorders (Altshuler, Bartzokis, Grieder, Curran, & Mintz, 1998; Strakowski et al., 1999) as well as with temporal lobe epilepsy (TLE; Tebartz van Elst, Woermann, Lemieux, & Trimble, 1999; Tebartz van Elst, Woermann, Lemieux, & Trimble, 2000). In a recent study, Mervaala et al. (2000) observed significant asymmetry in amygdalar volumes (right smaller than left) in patients with MDD but not in controls. In patients with TLE and dysthymia, left amygdala volume was positively correlated with depression severity, as assessed with the Beck Depression Inventory (Tebartz van Elst et al., 1999). Although these findings depict a relation between increased amygdalar volume and depression, it is important to stress that (1) the casual relations between the two entities are still unknown; and (2) some inconsistencies among studies are present. Indeed, some studies reported either decreased bilateral volume in the amygdala core nuclei (Sheline et al., 1998) or null findings (Ashtari et al., 1999; Coffey et al., 1993; Pantel et al., 1997). Although the reasons are still unclear, it is interesting to note that two null findings were found in geriatric depression (Ashtari et al., 1999; Pantel et al., 1997).

Functionally, abnormal elevations of resting rCBF or glucose metabolism in the amygdala have been reported in depression during both wakefulness (Drevets et al., 1992) and sleep (Ho et al., 1996; Nofzinger et al., 1999). In a PET study, Ho et al. (1996) reported increased absolute cerebral glucose metabolism in several brain regions, particularly the amygdala (+44%), in 10 unmedicated men with unipolar depression during non-REM sleep period. Further, in his recent review, Drevets (2001) reports data from five consecutive studies, in which increased amygdalar rCBF or glucose metabolism has been consistently replicated in depressives with familial MDD or melancholic features. In a postmortem study, serotonin 5-HT$_2$ receptor density was significantly increased in the amygdala of depressive patients who committed suicide (Hrdina, Demeter, Vu, Sotonyi, & Palkovits, 1993). Abnormally increased amygdalar activation has also been recently reported in bipolar depression (Ketter et al., 2001) and anxiety disorders, which often show a high degree of comorbidity with depression (Birbaumer et al., 1998; Liberzon et al., 1999; Rauch et al., 1996, 2000; Schneider et al., 1999; Semple et al., 2000; Shin et al., 1997). Further establishing a link between depression and amygdalar activation, two studies have reported a positive correlation between amygdalar activation and depression severity or dispositional negative affect in patients with MDD (Drevets et al., 1992; Abercrombie et al., 1998). After pharmacologically induced remission from depression, amygdalar activation has been observed to decrease to normative values (Drevets, 2001). In familial pure depressive disease, however, increased (left) amygdalar activation may persist during the remitted phases (Drevets et al., 1992), suggesting that at least in some subtypes of depression amygdalar dysfunction may be trait-like. Interestingly, patients with remitted MDD showing symptom relapse as a consequence of serotonin depletion showed increased amygdalar activation prior to the depletion compared to those who did not relapse (Bremner et al., 1997b). Finally, in one of the first fMRI studies using an activation paradigm, Yurgelun-Todd et al. (2000) reported higher left amygdalar activation for bipolar patients than controls in response to fearful faces.

In light of the pivotal role of the amygdala in recruiting and coordinating vigilant behavior toward stimuli with underdetermined contingencies, hyperactivation of the amygdala in major depression may bias initial evaluation of and response to incoming information. Although still speculative, this mechanism may rely on norepinephrine which is (1) oftentimes abnormally elevated in depression (e.g., Veith et al., 1994); (2) involved in amygdala-mediated emotional learning (Ferry, Roozendaal, & McGaugh, 1999); and (3) affected by glucocorticoid secretion, which is often elevated in MDD (e.g., Carroll et al., 1976). Thus, these findings may explain cognitive biases toward aversive or emotionally arousing information observed in depression.

Increased amygdalar activation in depression may also represent a possible biological substrate for anxiety, which is often comorbid with depression. In this respect, elevated levels of glucocorticoid hormones—which characterize at least some subgroups of patients with depression—may be especially relevant, since elevated glucocorticoid hormones have been shown to be associated with increased corticotropin-releasing hormone (CRH) in the amygdala. Increased CRH availability may increase anxiety, fear, and expectation of adversity (Schulkin, 1994).

In light of evidence suggesting a link between amygdalar activation, on the one hand, and memory consolidation and acquisition of long-term declarative knowledge about emotionally salient information, on the other hand, the observations of dysfunctionally increased amygdalar activation in major depression is intriguing. As recently pointed out by Drevets (2001), tonically increased amygdalar activation during depressive episodes may favor the emergence of rumination based on increased availability of emotionally negative memories. Although still untested, it is possible that these aberrant processes may rely on dysfunctional interactions between the amygdala, the PFC, and the ACC. Notably, structural abnormalities have been reported in territories of the PFC intimately connected with the ACC (Drevets et al., 1997; Öngür et al., 1998b). ACC dysfunction, in particular, may lead to a decreased capability of monitoring potential conflict between memory-based ruminative processes and sensory information coming from the environment.

SUMMARY AND FUTURE DIRECTIONS

This chapter reviewed circuitry that underlies the representation and regulation of emotion. It is this circuitry that exhibits different kinds of abnormalities in depression. Different territories of the PFC, the ACC, the hippocampus, and the amygdala were considered. These structures are all interconnected in regionally specific ways and exhibit bidirectional feedback. Abnormalities in the morphometry and functioning of each of these structures have been reported in depression. Because longitudinal studies that involve the measurement of brain structure and function in at-risk individuals have not yet been performed, we cannot specify at the present point in time which of the abnormalities may be primary in the sense of occurring first, and which may be secondary to dysfunctions initially occurring in another brain region. For example, PFC abnormalities may arise as a consequence of ACC abnormalities or may be independent. In addition, a paucity of work has examined functional and/or structural connectivity among these regions. Some of the abnormalities in depression may arise as a consequence of impaired connectivity, either functional, structural, or both. Future research should include measures of both functional (e.g., Cordes et al., 2000) and structural connectivity. The latter can be beautifully measured with diffusion tensor imaging (Le Bihan et al., 2001).

In the course of this review, we have drawn on the animal and human literature on basic processes in emotion and emotion regulation to help interpret the abnormalities that have been reported in depression and to highlight the kinds of studies that have not yet been performed but are important to conduct. The findings on the basic processes in animals and normal humans provide the foundation for a model of the major components in affect representation and regulation. The input to affect representation can be either a sensory stimulus or a memory. Most sensory stimuli are relayed through the thalamus and from there they can take a short route to the amygdala (LeDoux, 2000) and/or go up to the cortex. From both association cortex and from subcortical regions including the amygdala, information is relayed to different zones of the PFC. The PFC plays a crucial role in the representation of goals. In the presence of ambiguous situations, the PFC sends bias signals to other brain regions to facilitate the expression of task-appropriate responses in the face of competition with potentially stronger alternatives. We argued that in the affective domain, the PFC implements affect-guided anticipatory processes. Left-sided PFC regions are particularly involved in approach-related appetitive goals, while right-sided PFC regions are involved in the maintenance of goals that require behavioral inhibition. Abnormalities in PFC function would be expected to compromise goal instantiation in patients with depression. Left-sided hypoactivation would result in deficits specifically in pregoal attainment forms of positive affect, while right-sided hyperactivation would result in excessive behavioral inhibition and anticipatory anxiety. Hypoactivation in regions of the PFC with which the amygdala is interconnected may result in a decrease in the regulatory influence on the amygdala and a prolonged time course of amygdala activation in response to challenge. This might be expressed phenomenologically as perseveration of negative affect and rumination.

The ACC is critically involved in conflict monitoring and is activated whenever an individual is confronted with a challenge that involves conflict among two or more response options. According to an influential theory of ACC function (Carter et al., 1999), the ACC monitors the conflicts or cross-talk among brain regions. When such conflict is detected, the ACC issues a call for further processing to the PFC that then adjudicates among the various response options and guides behavior toward a goal. The ACC is very frequently activated in neuroimaging studies of human emotion (see Bush et al., 2000, for review), in part because when emotion is elicited in the laboratory it produces response conflict. There is the general expectation to behave in an unemotional fashion since subjects are participating in a scientific experiment, yet there are responses that are pulled by the emotional challenge, such as certain patterns of facial expression. This is commonly reported by subjects and is associated with ACC activation.

There is sometimes a conflict between an individual's mood state and the behavior that is expected of the individual in a particular social or role context. For example, among depressed individuals, their dispositional mood state may predispose them to set few goals and engage in little intentional action, yet the demands of their environments may include expectations to behave and act in specific ways. In an individual with normal levels of ACC activation, the signal from the ACC would issue a call to other brain regions, the PFC being the most important, to resolve the conflict and engage in the appropriate goal-directed behavior. However, in an individual with abnormally low levels of ACC activation, the conflict between her dispositional mood state and the expectations of her context would not be effectively monitored, and thus the usual call for further processing would not be issued. The data on ACC function in depression most consistently reveal a pattern of decreased activation in certain regions of the ACC. Interestingly, as we noted above, those depressed patients with greater activation in the ventral ACC before antidepressant treatment are the ones most likely to show the largest treatment response. In normal individuals, activation of the affective subdivision of the ACC may also be associated phenomonologically with the "will to change."

The hippocampus appears to play an important role in encoding context. Lesions to the hippocampus in animals impair context conditioning. In addition, this structure has a high density of glucocorticoid receptors. Elevated levels of cortisol in animal models have been found to produce hippocampal cell death. In humans, various stress-related disorders, including depression, have been found to be associated with hippocampal atrophy. Whether such hippocampal volume differences are a cause or a consequence of the depression cannot be answered from extant data. However, to the extent that hippocampal dysfunction is present, we would expect that such individuals would show abnormalities in the context-appropriate modulation of emotional behavior. This type of abnormality would be expressed as the display of normal emotion in inappropriate contexts. Thus, the persistence of sadness in situations that would ordinarily engender happiness could in part arise as a consequence of a hippocampally dependent problem in the context modulation of emotional responses. We have shown such effects in rhesus monkeys (see Davidson et al., 2000a, for a review), though they have not yet been studied in depressed patients. The extensive connections between the hippocampus and the PFC would presumably provide the requisite anatomical substrate for conveying the contextual information to the PFC to regulate emotional behavior in a context-appropriate fashion. The connections between the hippocampus and the PFC are another potential target of dysfunction in depression. It is possible that a certain subtype of individual exists wherein contextual encoding is intact and PFC-implemented goal-directed behavior is intact but context fails to adequately guide and reprioritize goals. In such cases, the functional and/or anatomical connectivity between the hippocampus and PFC might be a prime candidate for dysfunction. As noted above, the tools are now available to examine both types of connectivity using noninvasive measures.

The amygdala has long been viewed as a key site for both the perception of cues that signal threat and the production of behavioral and autonomic responses associated with aversive responding. As we noted above, current evidence suggests that the amygdala's role in negative affect may be a special case of its more general role in directing attention and resources to affectively salient stimuli and issuing a call for further processing of stimuli that have potentially major significance for the individual. As with other parts of the circuit we have addressed, there are extensive connections between the amygdala and each of the other structures we have considered. The amygdala receives input from a wide range of cortical zones and has even more extensive projections back to cortex, enabling the biasing of cortical processing as a function of the early evaluation of a stimulus as affectively salient. Also like the other components of the circuit we have described, there are individual differences in amygdala activation at baseline (Schaefer et al., 2000), as well as in response to challenge (see Davidson & Irwin, 1999, for review). Moreover, as we have delineated above, it is likely that regions of the PFC play an important role in modulating activation in the amygdala and thus influencing the time course of amygdala-driven negative affective responding. In light of the associations that have been reported between individual differences in amygdala activation and affect measures, it is likely that when it occurs, hyperactivation of the amygdala in depression is associated more with the fear-like and anxiety components of the symptoms than with the sad mood and anhedonia. In our own work, we have found that amygdala activation predicts dispositional negative affect in depressed patients but is unrelated to variations in positive affect (Abercrombie et al., 1998). Excessive activation of the amygdala in depressed patients may also be associated with hypervigilance, particularly toward threat-related cues, which further exacerbates some of the symptoms of depression.

There are several types of studies that critically need to be performed in light of the extant evidence reviewed in this chapter. First, studies are needed that relate specific abnormalities in particular brain regions to objective laboratory tasks that are neurally inspired and designed to capture the particular kinds of processing that are hypothesized to be implemented in those brain regions. Relatively few studies of that kind have been conducted. Most studies on depressed patients that examine relations between individual differences in neural activity and behavioral phenomena almost always relate such neural variation to symptom measures that are either self-report or interview-based indices. In the future, it will be important to complement the phenomenological description with laboratory measures that are explicitly designed to highlight the processes implemented in different parts of the circuit that we described.

Such future studies should include measures of both functional and structural connectivity to complement the activation measures. It is clear that interactions among the various components of the circuitry we describe are likely to play a crucial role in determining behavioral output. Moreover, it is possible that connectional abnormalities may exist in the absence of abnormalities in specific structures. This possibility underscores the real necessity of including measures of connectivity in future research.

As noted in several places in this review, longitudinal studies of at-risk samples with the types of imaging measures that are featured in this review are crucial. We do not know if any of the abnormalities discussed above, both of a structural and a functional variety, precede the onset of the disorder, co-occur with the onset of the disorder, or follow by some time the expression of the disorder. It is likely that the timing of the abnormalities in relation to the clinical course of the disorder varies for different parts of the circuitry. The data reviewed earlier showing a relation between the number of cumulative days depressed over the course of the lifetime and hippocampal volume suggests that this abnormality may follow the expression of the disorder and represent a consequence rather than a primary cause of the disorder. However, before such a conclusion is accepted, it is important to conduct the requisite longitudinal studies to begin to disentangle these complex causal factors.

Finally, we regard the evidence presented in this review as offering strong support for the view that depression refers to a heterogeneous group of disorders. It is possible that depression-spectrum disorders can be produced by abnormalities in many different parts of the circuitry reviewed. The specific subtype, symptom profile, and affective abnormalities should vary systematically with the location and nature of the abnormality. It is likely that some of the heterogeneity that might be produced by deficits in particular components of the circuitry reviewed will not map precisely onto the diagnostic categories we have inherited from descriptive psychiatry. A major challenge for the future will be to build a more neurobiologically plausible scheme for parsing the heterogeneity of depression based on the location and nature of the abnormality in the circuitry featured in this review. We believe that this ambitious effort will lead to considerably more consistent findings at the biological level and will also enable us to more rigorously characterize different endophenotypes that could then be exploited for genetic studies.

ACKNOWLEDGMENTS

We wish to thank Alexander J. Shackman and William Irwin for invaluable comments, and Andrew M. Hendrick, Kathryn A. Horras, Megan Zuelsdorff, and Jenna Topolovich for skilled and dedicated assistance in the preparation of the manuscript. This work was supported by NIMH Grant Nos. MH40747, P50-MH52354, MH43454, and P50-MH61083, and by NIMH Research Scientist Award No. K05-MH00875 to Richard J. Davidson. Diego Pizzagalli was supported by grants from the Swiss National Research Foundation (No. 81ZH-52864) and "Holderbank"-Stiftung zur Förderung der Wissenschaftlichen Fortbildung. Jack B. Nitschke was supported by NIMH Training Grant No. T32-MH18931. Portions of this chapter are adapted from Davidson, Pizzagalli, Nitschke, and Putnam (2002). Copyright 2002 by *Annual Review of Psychology*. Adapted by permission.

REFERENCES.

Abercrombie, H. C., Schaefer, S. M., Larson, C. L., Oakes, T. R., Holden, J. E., Perlman, S. B., Krahn, D. D., Benca, R. M., & Davidson, R. J. (1998). Metabolic rate in the right amygdala predicts negative affect in depressed patients. *NeuroReport, 9,* 3301–3307.

Altshuler, L. L., Bartzokis, G., Grieder, T., Curran, J., & Mintz, J. (1998). Amygdala enlargement in bipolar disorder and hippocampal reduction in schizophrenia: An MRI study demonstrating neuroanatomic specificity. *Archives of General Psychiatry, 55,* 663–664.

Ashtari, M., Greenwald, B. S., Kramer-Ginsberg, E., Hu, J., Wu, H., Patel, M., Aupperle, P., & Pollack, S. (1999). Hippocampal/amygdala volumes in geriatric depression. *Psychological Medicine, 29,* 629–638.

Baer, L., Rauch, S. L., Ballantine, H. T. J., Martuza, R., Cosgrove, R., Cassem, E., Giriunas, I., Manzo, P. A., Dimino, C., & Jenike, M. A. (1995). Cingulotomy for intractable obsessive–compulsive disorder: Prospective long-term follow-up of 18 patients. *Archives of General Psychiatry, 52,* 384–392.

Bartels, A., & Zeki, S. (2000). The neural basis of romantic love. *NeuroReport, 11,* 3829–3834.

Beauregard, M., Leroux, J. M., Bergman, S., Arzoumanian, Y., Beaudoin, G., Bourgouin, P., & Stip, E. (1998). The functional neuroanatomy of major depression: An fMRI study using an emotional activation paradigm. *NeuroReport, 9,* 3253–3258.

Bell, I. R., Schwartz, G. E., Hardin, E. E., Baldwin, C. M., & Kline, J. P. (1998). Differential resting quantitative electroencephalographic alpha patterns in women with environmental chemical intolerance, depressives, and normals. *Biological Psychiatry, 43,* 376–388.

Bench, C. J., Frackowiak, R. S., & Dolan, R. J. (1995). Changes in regional cerebral blood flow on recovery from depression. *Psychological Medicine, 25,* 247–251.

Bench, C. J., Friston, K. J., Brown, R. G., Scott, L. C., Frackowiak, S. J., & Dolan, R. J. (1992). The anatomy of melancholia-focal abnormalities of cerebral blood flow in major depression. *Psychological Medicine, 22,* 607–615.

Binder, D. K., & Iskandar, B. J. (2000). Modern neurosurgery for psychiatric disorders. *Neurosurgery, 47,* 9–21.

Birbaumer, N., Grodd, W., Diedrich, O., Klose, U., Erb, E., Lotze, M., Schneider, F., Weiss, U., & Flor, H. (1998). fMRI reveals amygdala activation to human faces in social phobics. *NeuroReport, 9,* 1223–1226.

Blood, A. J., Zatorre, R. J., Bermudez, P., & Evans, A. C. (1999). Emotional responses to pleasant and unpleasant music correlate with activity in paralimbic brain regions. *Nature Neuroscience, 2,* 382–387.

Breiter, H. C., Rauch, S. L., Kwong, K. K., Baker, J. R., Weisskoff, R. M., Kennedy, D. N., Kendrick, A. D., Davis, T. L., Jiang, A., Cohen, M. S., Stern, C. E., Belliveau, J. W., Baer, L., O'Sullivan, R. L., Savage, C. R., Jenike, M. A., & Rosen, B. R. (1996). Functional magnetic resonance imaging of symptom provocation in obsessive–compulsive disorder. *Archives of General Psychiatry, 53,* 595–606.

Bremner, J. D., Innis, R. B., Salomon, R. M., Staib, L. H., Ng, C. K., Miller, H. L., Bronen, R. A., Krystal, J. H., Duncan, J., Rich, D., Price, L. H., Malison, R., Dey, H., Soufer, R., & Charney, D. S. (1997b). Positron emission tomography measurement of cerebral metabolic correlates of tryptophan depletion-induced depressive relapse. *Archives of General Psychiatry, 54,* 364–374.

Bremner, J. D., Narayan, M., Anderson, E. R., Staib, L. H., Miller, H. L., & Charney, D. S. (2000). Hippocampal volume reduction in major depression. *American Journal of Psychiatry, 157,* 115–118.

Bremner, J. D., Randall, P., Scott, T. M., Bronen, R. A., Seibyl, J. P., Southwick, S. M., Delaney, R. C., McCarthy, G., Charney, D. S., & Innis, R. B. (1995). MRI-based measurement of hippocampal volume in patients with combat-related posttraumatic stress disorder. *American Journal of Psychiatry, 152,* 972–981.

Bremner, J. D., Randall, P., Vermetten, E., Staib, L. H., Bronen, R. A., Mazure, C., Capelli, S., McCarthy, G., Innis, R. B., & Charney, D. S. (1997a). Magnetic resonance imaging-based measurement of hippocampal volume in posttraumatic stress disorder related to childhood physical and sexual abuse: A preliminary report. *Biological Psychiatry, 41,* 23–32.

Brody, A. L., Saxena, S., Mandelkern, M. A., Fairbanks, L. A., Ho, M. L., & Baxter, L. R., Jr. (2001). Brain metabolic changes associated with symptom factor improvement in major depressive disorder. *Biological Psychiatry, 50,* 171–178.

Brody, A. L., Saxena, S., Silverman, D. H., Alborzian, S., Fairbanks, L. A., Phelps, M. E., Huang, S. C., Wu, H. M., Maidment, K., & Baxter, L. R., Jr. (1999). Brain metabolic changes in major depressive disorder from pre- to post-treatment with paroxetine. *Psychiatry Research, 91,* 127–139.

Bruder, G. E., Stewart, J. W., Mercier, M. A., Agosti, V., Leite, P., Donovan, S., & Quitkin, F. M. (1997). Outcome of cognitive-behavioral therapy for depression: Relation to hemispheric dominance for verbal processing. *Journal of Abnormal Psychology, 106,* 138–144.

Bruder, G. E., Stewart, J. W., Tenke, C. E., McGrath, P. J., Leite, P., Bhattacharya, N., & Quitkin, F. M. (2001). Electroencephalographic and perceptual asymmetry differences between responders and nonresponders to an SSRI antidepressant. *Biological Psychiatry, 49,* 416–425.

Büchel, C., Dolan, R., Armony, J. L., & Friston, K. J. (1999). Amygdala–hippocampal involvement in human aversive trace conditioning revealed through event-related functional magnetic resonance imaging. *Journal of Neuroscience, 19,* 10869–10876.

Buchsbaum, M. S., Wu, J., Siegel, B. V., Hackett, E., Trenary, M., Abel, L., & Reynolds, C. (1997). Effect of sertraline on regional metabolic rate in patients with affective disorder. *Biological Psychiatry, 41,* 15–22.

Bush, G., Luu, P., & Posner, M. I. (2000). Cognitive and emotional influences in anterior cingulate cortex. *Trends in Cognitive Sciences, 4,* 215–222.

Bush, G., Whalen, P. J., Rosen, B. R., Jenike, M. A., McInerney, S. C., & Rauch, S. L. (1998). The counting Stroop: An interference task specialized for functional neuroimaging–validation study with functional MRI. *Human Brain Mapping, 6,* 270–282.

Carroll, B. J., Curtis, G. C., & Mendels, J. (1976). Cerebrospinal fluid and plasma free cortisol concentrations in depression. *Psychological Medicine, 6,* 235–244.

Carter, C. S., Botvinick, M. M., & Cohen, J. D. (1999). The contribution of the anterior cingulate cortex to executive processes in cognition. *Review of Neuroscience, 10,* 49–57.

Carter, C. S., Macdonald, A. M., Botvinick, M., Ross, L. L., Stenger, V. A., Noll, D., & Cohen, J. D. (2000). Parsing executive processes: Strategic vs. evaluative functions of the anterior cingulate cortex. *Proceedings of the National Academy of Sciences USA, 97,* 1944–1948.

Chen, G., Rajkowska, G., Du, F., Seraji-Bozorgzad, N., & Manji, H. K. (2000). Enhancement of hippocampal neurogenesis by lithium. *Journal of Neurochemistry, 75,* 1729–1734.

Coffey, C. E., Wilkinson, W. E., Weiner, R. D., Parashos, I. A., Djang, W. T., Webb, M. C., Figiel, G. S., & Spritzer, C. E. (1993). Quantitative cerebral anatomy in depression: A controlled magnetic resonance imaging study. *Archives of General Psychiatry, 50,* 7–16.

Corcoran, K. A., & Maren, S. (2001). Hippocampal inactivation disrupts contextual retrieval of fear memory after extinction. *Journal of Neuroscience, 21,* 1720–1726.

Cordes, D., Haughton, V. M., Arfanakis, K., Wendt, G., Turski, P. A., Moritz, C. H., Quigley, M. A., & Meyerand, M. E. (2000). Mapping functionally related regions of brain with functional connectivity MR imaging. *American Journal of Neuroradiology, 21,* 1636–1644.

Critchley, H. D., Mathias, C. J., & Dolan, R. J. (2001). Neural activity in the human brain relating to uncertainty and arousal during anticipation. *Neuron, 29,* 537–545.

Curran, T., Tucker, D. M., Kutas, M., & Posner, M. I. (1993). Topography of the N400: Brain electrical activity reflecting semantic expectancy. *Electroencephalography and Clinical Neurophysiology, 88,* 188–209.

Damasio, A. R. (1994). *Descartes' error: Emotion, reason, and the human brain.* New York: Avon Books.

Davidson, R. J. (1998). Anterior electrophysiological asymmetries, emotion and depression: Conceptual and metholological conundrums. *Psychophysiology, 35,* 607–614.

Davidson, R. J. (2000). Affective style, psychopathology and resilience: Brain mechanisms and plasticity. *American Psychologist, 55,* 1193–1214.

Davidson, R. J., Abercrombie, H. C., Nitschke, J. B., & Putnam, K. M. (1999). Regional brain function, emotion and disorders of emotion. *Current Opinion in Neurobiology, 9,* 228–234.

Davidson, R. J., & Irwin W. (1999). The functional neuroanatomy of emotion and affective style. *Trends in Cognitive Sciences, 3,* 11–21.

Davidson, R. J., Jackson, D. C., & Kalin, N. H. (2000a). Emotion, plasticity, context and regulation. *Psychological Bulletin, 126,* 890–906.

Davidson, R. J., Jackson, D. C., & Larson, C. L. (2000b). Human electroencephalography. In J. T. Cacioppo, G. G. Bernston, & L. G. Tassinary (Eds.), *Principles of psychophysiology* (2nd ed., pp. 27–52). New York: Cambridge University Press.

Davidson, R. J., Marshall, J. R., Tomarken, A. J., & Henriques, J. B. (2000c). While a phobic waits: Regional brain electrical and autonomic activity in social phobics during anticipation of public speaking. *Biological Psychiatry, 47,* 85–95.

Davidson, R. J., Pizzagalli, D., Nitschke, J. B., & Putnam, K. M. (2002). Depression: Perspectives from affective neuroscience. *Annual Review of Psychology, 53,* 545–574.

Davidson, R. J., Putnam, K. M., & Larson, C. L. (2000d). Dysfunction in the neural circuitry of emotion regulation: A possible prelude to violence. *Science, 289,* 591–594.

Davis, M., & Whalen, P. J. (2001). The amygdala: Vigilance and emotion. *Molecular Psychiatry, 6,* 13–34.

Debener, S., Beauducel, A., Nessler, D., Brocke, B., Heilemann, H., & Kayser, J. (2000). Is resting anterior EEG alpha asymmetry a trait marker for depression?: Findings for healthy adults and clinically depressed patients. *Neuropsychobiology, 41,* 31–37.

Denton, D., Shade, R., Zamarippa, F., Egan, G., Blair-West, J., McKinley, M., Lancaster, J., & Fox, P. (1999). Neuroimaging of genesis and satiation of thirst and an interoceptor-driven theory of origins of primary consciousness. *Proceedings of the National Academy of Sciences USA, 96,* 5304–5309.

Devinsky, O., Morrell, M. J., & Vogt, B. A. (1995). Contributions of anterior cingulate cortex to behaviour. *Brain, 118,* 279–306.

Drevets, W. C. (1998). Functional neuroimaging studies of depression: The anatomy of melancholia. *Annual Review of Medicine, 49,* 341–361.

Drevets, W. C. (2001). Neuroimaging and neuropathological studies of depression: Implications for the cognitive–emotional features of mood disorders. *Current Opinion in Neurobiology, 11,* 240–249.

Drevets, W. C., Price, J. L., Simpson, J. R. J., Todd, R. D., Reich, T., Vannier, M., & Raichle, M. E. (1997). Subgenual prefrontal cortex abnormalities in mood disorders. *Nature, 386,* 824–827.

Drevets, W. C., Videen, T. O., Price, J. L., Preskorn, S. H., Carmichael, S. T., & Raichle, M. E. (1992). A functional anatomical study of unipolar depression. *Journal of Neuroscience, 12,* 3628–3641.

Driessen, M., Herrmann, J., Stahl, K., Zwaan, M., Meier, S., Hill, A., Osterheider, M., & Petersen, D. (2000). Magnetic resonance imaging volumes of the hippocampus and the amygdala in women with borderline personality disorder and early traumatization. *Archives of General Psychiatry, 57,* 1115–1122.

Duman, R. S., Malberg, J., Nakagawa, S., & D'Sa, C. (2000). Neuronal plasticity and survival in mood disorders. *Biological Psychiatry, 48,* 732–739.

Ebert, D., & Ebmeier, K. P. (1996). The role of the cingulate gyrus in depression: From functional anatomy to neurochemistry. *Biological Psychiatry, 39,* 1044–1050.

Ebert, D., Feistel, H., & Barocka, A. (1991). Effects of sleep deprivation on the limbic system and the frontal lobes in affective disorders: A study with Tc–99m-HMPAO SPECT. *Psychiatry Research, 40,* 247–251.

Elliott, R., & Dolan, R. J. (1999). Differential neural responses during performance of matching and nonmatching to sample tasks at two delay intervals. *Journal of Neuroscience, 19,* 5066–5073.

Eriksson, P. S., Perfilieva, E., Bjork-Eriksson, T., Alborn, A., Nordborg, C., Peterson, D. A., & Gage, F. H. (1998). Neurogenesis in the adult human hippocampus. *Nature Medicine, 4,* 1313–1317.

Fanselow, M. S. (2000). Contextual fear, gestalt memories, and the hippocampus. *Behavioural Brain Research, 110,* 73–81.

Ferry, B., Roozendaal, B., & McGaugh, J. L. (1999). Role of norepinephrine in mediating stress hormone regulation of long-term memory storage: A critical involvement of the amygdala. *Biological Psychiatry, 46,* 1140–1152.

Fink, G. R., Markowitsch, H. J., Reinkemeier, M., Bruckbauer, T., Kessler, J., & Heiss, W. (1996). Cerebral representation of one's own past: Neural networks involved in autobiographical memory. *Journal of Neuroscience, 16,* 4275–4282.

Fredrikson, M., Furmark, T., Olsson, M. T., Fischer, H., Andersson, J., & Langstrom, B. (1998). Functional neuroanatomical correlates of electrodermal activity: A positron emission tomographic study. *Psychophysiology, 35,* 179–185.

Garavan, H., Ross, R. H., & Stein, E. A. (1999). Right hemispheric dominance of inhibitory control: An event-related functional MRI study. *Proceedings of the National Academy of Sciences USA, 96,* 8301–8306.

George, M. S., Ketter, T. A., Parekh, P. I., Rosinsky, N., Ring, H. A., Pazzaglia, P. J., Marangell, L. B., Callahan, A. M., & Post, R. M. (1997). Blunted left cingulate activation in mood disorder subjects during a response interference task (the Stroop). *Journal of Neuropsychiatry and Clinical Neuroscience, 9,* 55–63.

George, M. S., Ketter, K. A., & Post, R. M. (1994). Prefrontal cortex dysfunction in clinical depression. *Depression, 2,* 59–72.

Gold, P. W., Goodwin, F. K., & Chrousos, G. P. (1988). Clinical and biochemical manifestations of depression: Relation to the neurobiology of stress. *New England Journal of Medicine, 314,* 348–353.

Gotlib, I. H., Ranganath, C., & Rosenfeld, P. J. (1998). Frontal EEG alpha asymmetry, depression and cognitive functioning. *Cognition and Emotion, 12,* 449–478.

Gould, E., Tanapat, P., Rydel, T., & Hastings, N. (2000). Regulation of hippocampal neurogenesis in adulthood. *Biological Psychiatry, 48,* 715–720.

Hamann, S. B., Ely, T. D., Grafton, S. T., & Kilts, C. D. (1999). Amygdala activity related to enhanced memory for pleasant and aversive stimuli. *Nature Neuroscience, 2,* 289–293.

Heller, W., & Nitschke, J. B. (1998). The puzzle of regional brain activity in depression and anxiety: The importance of subtypes and comorbidity. *Cognition and Emotion, 12,* 421–447.

Henriques, J. B., & Davidson, R. J. (2000). Decreased responsiveness to reward in depression. *Cognition and Emotion, 15,* 711–724.

Henriques, J. B., Glowacki, J. M., & Davidson, R. J. (1994). Reward fails to alter response bias in depression. *Journal of Abnormal Psychology, 103,* 460–466.

Ho, A. P., Gillin, J. C., Buchsbaum, M. S., Wu, J. C., Abel, L., & Bunney, W. E., Jr. (1996). Brain glucose metabolism during non-rapid eye movement sleep in major depression: A positron emission tomography study. *Archives of General Psychiatry, 53,* 645–652.

Holland, P. C., & Gallagher, M. (1999). Amygdala circuitry in attentional and representational processes. *Trends in Cognitive Sciences, 3,* 65–73.

Hrdina, P. D., Demeter, E., Vu, T. B., Sotonyi, P., & Palkovits, M. (1993). 5-HT uptake sites and 5-HT2 receptors in brain of antidepressant-free suicide victims/depressives: Increase in 5-HT2 sites in cortex and amygdala. *Brain Research, 614,* 37–44.

Ikegaya, Y., Abe, K., Saito, H., & Nishiyama, N. (1995a). Medial amygdala enhances synaptic transmission and synaptic plasticity in the dentate gyrus of rats in vivo. *Journal of Neurophysiology, 74,* 2201–2203.

Ikegaya, Y., Saito, H., & Abe, K. (1994). Attenuated hippocampal long-term potentiation in basolateral amygdala-lesioned rats. *Brain Research, 656,* 157–164.

Ikegaya, Y., Saito, H., & Abe, K. (1995b). Requirement of basolateral amygdala neuron activity for the induction of long-term potentiation in the dentate gyrus in vivo. *Brain Research, 671,* 351–354.

Isenberg, N., Silbergsweig, D., Engelien, A., Emmerich, S., Malavade, K., Beattie, B., & Leon, A. C. (1999). Linguistic threat activates the human amygdala. *Proceedings of the National Academy of Sciences USA, 96,* 10456–10459.

Ito, H., Kawashima, R., Awata, S., Ono, S., Sato, K., Goto, R., Koyama, M., Sato, M., & Fukuda, H. (1996). Hypoperfusion in the limbic system and prefrontal cortex in depression: SPECT with anatomic standardization technique. *Journal of Nuclear Medicine, 37,* 410–414.

Jacobs, B. L., Praag, H., & Gage, F. H. (2000). Adult brain neurogenesis and psychiatry: A novel theory of depression. *Molecular Psychiatry, 5,* 262–269.

Jacobson, L., & Sapolsky, R. M. (1991). The role of the hippocampus in feedback regulation of the hypothalamic–pituitary–adrenocortical axis. *Endocrinology Review, 12,* 118–134.

Javanmard, M., Shlik, J., Kennedy, S. H., Vaccarino, F. J., Houle, S., & Bradwejn, J. (1999). Neuroanatomic correlates of CCK-4-induced panic attacks in healthy humans: A comparison of two time points. *Biological Psychiatry, 45,* 872–882.

Kawasaki, H., Adolphs, R., Kaufman, O., Damasio, H., Damasio, A. R., Granner, M., Bakken, H., Hori, T., & Howard, M. A., III. (2001). Single-neuron responses to emotional visual stimuli recorded in human ventral prefrontal cortex. *Nature Neuroscience, 4,* 15–16.

Kempermann, G., Kuhn, H. G., & Gage, F. H. (1997). More hippocampal neurons in adult mice living in an enriched environment. *Nature, 386,* 493–495.

Kennedy, S. H., Evans, K. R., Kruger, S., Mayberg, H. S., Meyer, J. H., McCann, S., Arifuzzman, A. I., Houle, S., & Vaccarino, F.J. (2001). Changes in regional brain glucose metabolism measured with positron emission tomography after paroxetine treatment of major depression. *American Journal of Psychiatry, 158,* 899–905.

Ketter, T. A., Andreason, P. J., George, M. S., Lee, C., Gill, D. S., Parekh, P. I., Willis, M. W., Herscovitch, P., & Post, R. M. (1996). Anterior paralimbic mediation of procaine-induced emotional and psychosensory experiences. *Archives of General Psychiatry, 53,* 59–69.

Ketter, T. A., Kimbrell, T. A., George, M. S., Dunn, R. T., Speer, A. M., Benson, B. E., Willis, M. W., Danielson, A., Frye, M. A., Herscovitch, P., & Post, R. M. (2001). Effects of mood and subtype on cerebral glucose metabolism in treatment-resistant bipolar disorder. *Biological Psychiatry, 49,* 97–109.

Konishi, S., Nakajima, K., Uchida, I., Kikyo, H., Kameyama, M., & Miyashita, Y. (1999). Common inhibitory mechanism in human inferior prefrontal cortex revealed by event-related functional MRI. *Brain, 122,* 981–991.

Kumar, A., Newberg, A., Alavi, A., Berlin, J., Smith, R., & Reivich M. (1993). Regional glucose metabolism in late-life depression and Alzheimer disease: A preliminary positron emission tomography study. *Proceedings of the National Academy of Sciences USA, 90,* 7019–7023.

Lane, R. D., Fink, G. R., Chau, P. M., & Dolan, R. J. (1997). Neural activation during selective attention to subjective emotional responses. *NeuroReport, 8*, 3969–3972.

Le Bihan, D., Mangin, J. F., Poupon, C., Clark, C. A., Pappata, S., Molko, N., & Chabriat, H. (2001). Diffusion tensor imaging: Concepts and applications. *Journal of Magnetic Resonance Imaging, 13*, 534–546.

LeDoux, J. E. (2000). Emotion circuits in the brain. *Annual Review of Neuroscience, 23*, 155–184.

Leverenz, J. B., Wilkinson, C. W., Wamble, M., Corbin, S., Grabber, J. E., Raskind, M. A., & Peskind, E. R. (1999). Effect of chronic high-dose exogenous cortisol on hippocampal neuronal number in aged nonhuman primates. *Journal of Neuroscience, 19*, 2356–2361.

Liberzon, I., Taylor, S. F., Amdur, R., Jung, T. D., Chamberlain, K. R., Minoshima, S., Koeppe, R. A., & Fig, L. M. (1999). Brain activation in PTSD in response to trauma-related stimuli. *Biological Psychiatry, 45*, 817–826.

Lupien, S. J., de Leon, M., de Santi, S., Convit, A., Tarshish, C., Nair, N. P., Thakur, M., McEwen, B. S., Hauger, R. L., & Meaney, M. J. (1998). Cortisol levels during human aging predict hippocampal atrophy and memory deficits. *Nature Neuroscience, 1*, 69–73.

MacDonald, A. W., Cohen, J. D., Stenger, V. A., & Carter, C. S. (2000). Dissociating the role of the dorsolateral prefrontal and anterior cingulate cortex in cognitive control. *Science, 288*, 1835–1838.

Madhav, T. R., Pei, Q., Grahame-Smith, D. G., & Zetterstrom, T. S. (2000). Repeated electroconvulsive shock promotes the sprouting of serotonergic axons in the lesioned rat hippocampus. *Neuroscience, 97*, 677–683.

Magarinos, A. M., McEwen, B. S. Flugge, G., & Fuchs, E. (1996). Chronic psychosocial stress causes apical dendritic atrophy of hippocampal CA3 pyramidal neurons in subordinate tree shrews. *Journal of Neuroscience, 16*, 3534–3540.

Malberg, J. E., Eisch, A. J., Nestler, E. J., & Duman, R. S. (2000). Chronic antidepressant treatment increases neurogenesis in adult rat hippocampus. *Journal of Neuroscience, 20*, 9104–9110.

Mayberg, H. S. (1997). Limbic–cortical dysregulation: A proposed model of depression. *Journal of Neuropsychiatry and Clinical Neuroscience, 9*, 471–481.

Mayberg, H. S., Brannan, S. K., Mahurin, R. K., Jerabek, P. A., Brickman, J. S., Tekell, J. L., Silva, J. A., McGinnis, S., Glass, T. G., Martin, C. C., & Fox, P. T. (1997). Cingulate function in depression: A potential predictor of treatment response. *NeuroReport, 8*, 1057–1061.

Mayberg, H. S., Lewis, P. L., Regenold, W., & Wagner, H. N. (1994). Paralimbic hypoperfusion in unipolar depression. *Journal of Nuclear Medicine, 35*, 929–934.

Mayberg, H. S., Liotti, M., Brannan, S. K., McGinnis, S., Mahurin, R. K., Jerabek, P. A., Silva, J. A., Tekell, J. L., Martin, C. C., Lancaster, J. L., & Fox, P. T. (1999). Reciprocal limbic–cortical function and negative mood: Converging PET findings in depression and normal sadness. *American Journal of Psychiatry, 156*, 675–682.

McEwen, B. S. (1998). Protective and damaging effects of stress mediators. *New England Journal of Medicine, 338*, 171–179.

Mega, M. S., Cummings, J. L., Salloway, S., & Malloy, P. (1997). The limbic system: An anatomic, phylogenetic, and clinical perspective. *Journal of Neuropsychiatry and Clinical Neuroscience, 9*, 315–330.

Mervaala, E., Föhr, J., Könönen, M., Valkonen-Korhonen, M., Vainio, P., Partanen, K., Partanen, J., Tiihonen, J., Viinamäki, H., Karjalainen, A.-K., & Lehtonen, J. (2000). Quantitative MRI of the hippocampus and amygdala in severe depression. *Psychological Medicine, 30*, 117–125.

Miller, E. K., & Cohen, J. D. (2001). An integrative theory of prefrontal cortex function. *Annual Review of Neuroscience, 24*, 167–202.

Mirz, F., Gjedde, A., Sodkilde-Jrgensen, H., & Pedersen, C. B. (2000). Functional brain imaging of tinnitus-like perception induced by aversive auditory stimuli. *NeuroReport, 11*, 633–637.

Morris, J. S., Friston, K. J., & Dolan, R. J. (1997). Neural responses to salient visual stimuli. *Proceedings of the Royal Society of London, 264*, 769–775.

Morris, J. S., Ohman, A., & Dolan, R. J. (1999). A subcoritcal pathway to the right amygdala mediating "unseen" fear. *Proceedings of the National Academy of Sciences USA, 96*, 1680–1685.

Nader, K., Schafe, G. E., & Le Doux, J. E. (2000). Fear memories require protein synthesis in the amygdala for reconsolidation after retrieval. *Nature, 406,* 722–726.

Nobre, A. C., Sebestyen, G. N., Gitelman, D. R., Mesulam, M. M., Frackowiak, R. S., & Frith, C. D. (1997). Functional localization of the system for visuospatial attention using positron emission tomography. *Brain, 120,* 515–533.

Nofzinger, E. A., Nichols, T. E., Meltzer, C. C., Price, J., Steppe, D. A., Miewald, J. M., Kupfer, D. J., & Moore, R. Y. (1999). Changes in forebrain function from waking to REM sleep in depression: Preliminary analyses of [18F]FDG PET studies. *Psychiatry Research, 91,* 59–78.

Noga, J. T., Vladar, K., & Torrey, E. F. (2001). A volumetric magnetic resonance imaging study of monozygotic twins discordant for bipolar disorder. *Psychiatry Research: Neuroimaging, 106,* 25–34.

Ochsner, K. N., & Barrett, L. F. (2001). A multiprocess perspective on the neuroscience of emotion. In T. J. Mayne & G. A. Bonanno (Eds.), *Emotions: Current issues and future directions* (pp. 38–81). New York: Guilford Press.

O'Doherty, J., Kringelbach, M. L., Rolls, E. T., Hornak, J., & Andrews, C. (2001). Abstract reward and punishment representations in the human orbitofrontal cortex. *Nature Neuroscience, 4,* 95–102.

Öngür, D., An, X., & Price, J. L. (1988a). Prefrontal cortical projections to the hypothalamus in macaque monkeys. *Journal of Comparative Neurology, 401,* 480–505.

Öngür, D., Drevets, W. C., & Price, J. L. (1998b). Glial reduction in the subgenual prefrontal cortex in mood disorders. *Proceedings of the National Academy of Sciences USA, 95,* 13290–13295.

Pantel, J., Schroder, J., Essig, M., Popp, D., Dech, H., Knopp, M. V., Schad, L. R., Eysenbach, K., Backenstrass, M., & Friedlinger, M. (1997). Quantitative magnetic resonance imaging in geriatric depression and primary degenerative dementia. *Journal of Affective Disorders, 42,* 69–83.

Pardo, J. V., Pardo, P. J., Janer, K. W., & Raichle, M. E. (1990). The anterior cingulate cortex mediates processing selection in the Stroop attentional conflict paradigm. *Proceedings of the National Academy of Sciences USA, 87,* 256–259.

Pariante, C. M., & Miller, A. H. (2001). Glucocorticoid receptors in major depression: Relevance to pathophysiology and treatment. *Biological Psychiatry, 49,* 391–404.

Pauli, P., Wiedemann, G., & Nickola, M. (1999). Pain sensitivity, cerebral laterality, and negative affect. *Pain, 80,* 359–364.

Paus, T., Zatorre, R. J., Hofle, N., Caramanos, Z., Gotman, J., Petrides, M., & Evans, A. C. (1997). Time-related changes in neural systems underlying attention and arousal during the performance of an auditory vigilance task. *Journal of Cognitive Neuroscience, 9,* 392–408.

Phillips, M. L., Young, A. W., Scott, S. K., Calder, A. J., Andrew, C., Giampietro, V., Williams, S. C., Bullmore, E. T., Brammer, M., & Gray, J. A. (1998). Neural responses to facial and vocal expressions of fear and disgust. *Proceedings of the Royal Society of London, 265,* 1809–1817.

Pizzagalli, D., Pascual-Marqui, R. D., Nitschke, J. B., Oakes, T. R., Larson, C. L., Abercrombie, H. C., Schaefer, S. M., Koger, J. V., Benca, R. M., & Davidson, R. J. (2001). Anterior cingulate activity as a predictor of degree of treatment response in major depression: Evidence from brain electrical tomography analysis. *American Journal of Psychiatry, 158,* 405–415.

Pruessner, J. C., Collins, D. L., Pruessner, M., & Evans, A. C. (2001). Age and gender predict volume decline in the anterior and posterior hippocampus in early adulthood. *Journal of Neuroscience, 21,* 194–200.

Rajkowska, G. (2000). Postmortem studies in mood disorders indicate altered numbers of neurons and glial cells. *Biological Psychiatry, 48,* 766–777.

Rauch, S. L., Savage, C. R., Alpert, N. M., Fischman, A. J., & Jenike, M. A. (1997). A study of three disorders using positron emission tomography and symptom provocation. *Biological Psychiatry, 42,* 446–452.

Rauch, S. L., Savage, C. R., Alpert, N. M., Miguel, E. C., Baer, L., Breiter, H. C., Fischman, A. J., Manzo, P. A., Moretti, C., & Jenike, M. A. (1995). A positron emission tomographic study of simple phobic symptom provocation. *Archives of General Psychiatry, 52,* 20–28.

Rauch, S. L., van der Kolk, B. A., Fisler, R. E., Alpert, N. M., Orr, S. P., Savage, C. R., Fischman, A. J., Jenike, M. A., & Pitman, R. K. (1996). A symptom provocation study of posttraumatic stress disorder using positron emission tomography and script-driven imagery. *Archives of General Psychiatry, 53,* 380–387.

Rauch, S. L., Whalen, P. J., Shin, L. M., McInerney, S. C., Macklin, M. L., Lasko, N. B., Orr, S. P., & Pitman, R. K. (2000). Exaggerated amygdala response to masked facial stimuli in posttraumatic stress disorder: A functional MRI study. *Biological Psychiatry, 47,* 769–776.

Reid, S. A., Duke, L. M., & Allen, J. J. B. (1998). Resting frontal electroencephalographic asymmetry in depression: What are the mediating factors? *Psychophysiology, 35,* 389–404.

Reiman, E. M. (1997). The application of positron emission tomography to the study of normal and pathologic emotions. *Journal of Clinical Psychiatry, 58,* 4–12.

Reul, J. M., & De Kloet, E. R. (1986). Anatomical resolution of two types of corticosterone receptor sites in rat brain with in vitro autoradiography and computerized image analysis. *Journal of Steroid Biochemistry and Molecular Biology, 24,* 269–272.

Rogers, R. D., Owen, A. M., Middleton, H. C., Williams, E. J., Pickens, J., Sahakian, B. J., & Robbins, T. W. (1999). Choosing between small, likely rewards and large, unlikely rewards activates inferior and orbital prefrontal cortex. *Journal of Neuroscience, 20,* 9029–9038.

Rolls, E. T. (1999). The functions of the orbitofrontal cortex. *Neurocase, 5,* 301–312.

Rusch, B. D., Abercrombie, H. C., Oakes, T. R., Schaefer, S. M., & Davidson, R. J. (2001). Hippocampal morphometry in depressed patients and control subjects: Relations to anxiety symptoms. *Biological Psychiatry, 50,* 960–964.

Sapolsky, R. M. (2000). Glucocorticoids and hippocampal atrophy in neuropsychiatric disorders. *Archives of General Psychiatry, 57,* 925–935.

Sapolsky, R. M., Krey L. C., & McEwan, B. S. (1986). The neuroendocrinology of stress and aging: The glucocorticoid cascade hypothesis. *Endocrine Review, 7,* 284–301.

Sapolsky, R. M., Uno, H., Rebert, C. S., & Finch, C. E. (1990). Hippocampal damage associated with prolonged glucocorticoid exposure in primates. *Journal of Neuroscience, 10,* 2897–2902.

Saxena, S., Brody, A. L., Ho, M. L., Alborzian, S., Ho, M. K., Maidment, K., Huang, S. C., Wu, H., Au, S. C., & Baxter, L. R., Jr. (2001). Cerebral metabolism in major depression and obsessive–compulsive disorder occuring separately and concurrently. *Biological Psychiatry, 50,* 159–170.

Schaefer, S. M., Abercrombie, H. C., Lindgren, K. A., Larson, C. L., Ward, R. T., Oakes, T. R., Holden, J. E., Perlman, S. B., Turski, P. A., & Davidson, R. J. (2000). Six-month test–retest reliability of MRI-defined PET measures of regional cerebral glucose metabolic rate in selected subcortical structures. *Human Brain Mapping, 10,* 1–9.

Schneider, F., Weiss, U., Kessler, C., Muller-Gartner, H. W., Posse, S., Salloum, J. B., Grodd, W., Himmelmann, F., Gaebel, W., & Birbaumer, N. (1999). Subcortical correlates of differential classical conditioning of aversive emotional reactions in social phobia. *Biological Psychiatry, 45,* 863–871.

Schulkin, J. (1994). Melancholic depression and the hormones of adversity: A role for the amygdala. *Current Directions in Psychological Science, 3,* 41–44.

Semple, W. E., Goyer, P. F., McCormick, R., Donovan, B., Muzic, R. F. J., Rugle, L., McCutcheon, K., Lewis, C., Liebling, D., Kowaliw, S., Vapenik, K., Semple, M. A., Flener, C. R., & Schulz, S. C. (2000). Higher brain blood flow at amygdala and lower frontal cortex blood flow in PTSD patients with comorbid cocaine and alcohol abuse compared with normals. *Psychiatry, 63,* 65–74.

Servan-Schreiber, D., Perlstein, W. M., Cohen, J. D., & Mintun, M. (1998). Selective pharmacological activation of limbic structures in human volunteers: A positron emission tomography study. *Journal of Neuropsychiatry and Clinical Neuroscience, 10,* 148–159.

Shah, P. J., Ebmeier, K. P., Glabus, M. F., & Goodwin, G. M. (1998). Cortical grey matter reductions associated with treatment-resistant chronic unipolar depression: Controlled magnetic resonance imaging study. *British Journal of Psychiatry, 172,* 527–532.

Sheline, Y. I. (2000). 3D MRI studies of neuroanatomic changes in unipolar major depression: The role of stress and medical comorbidity. *Biological Psychiatry, 48,* 791–800.

Sheline, Y. I., Gado, M. H., & Price, J. L. (1998). Amygdala core nuclei volumes are decreased in recurrent major depression. *NeuroReport, 9,* 2023–2028.

Sheline, Y. I., Sanghavi, M., Mintun, M. A., & Gado, M. H. (1999). Depression duration but not age predicts hippocampal volume loss in medically healthy women with recurrent major depression. *Journal of Neuroscience, 19,* 5034–5043.

Sheline, Y. I., Wang, P. W., Gado, M. H., Csernansky, J. G., & Vannier, M. W. (1996). Hippocampal atrophy in recurrent major depression. *Proceedings of the National Academy of Sciences USA, 93,* 3908–3913.

Shin, L. M., Kosslyn, S. M., McNally, R. J., Alpert, N. M., Thompson, W. L., Rauch, S. L., Macklin, M. L., & Pitman, R. K. (1997). Visual imagery and perception in posttraumatic stress disorder. A positron emission tomographic investigation. *Archives of General Psychiatry, 54,* 233–241.

Squire, L. R., & Knowlton, B. J. (2000). The medial temporal lobe, the hippocampus, and the memory systems of the brain. In M. S. Gazzaniga (Ed.), *The new cognitive neurosciences* (pp. 765–779). Cambridge, MA: MIT Press.

Starkman, M. N., Giordani, B., Gebarski, S. S., Berent, S., Schork, M. A., & Schteingart, D. E. (1999). Decrease in cortisol reverses human hippocampal atrophy following treatment of Cushing's disease. *Biological Psychiatry, 46,* 1595–1602.

Steffens, D. C., Byrum, C. E., McQuoid, D. R., Greenberg, D. L., Payne, M. E., Blitchington, T. F., MacFall, J. R., & Krishnan, K. R. (2000). Hippocampal volume in geriatric depression. *Biological Psychiatry, 48,* 301–309.

Stein, M. B., Koverola, C., Hanna, C., Torchia, M. G., & McClarty, B. (1997). Hippocampal volume in women victimized by childhood sexual abuse. *Psychological Medicine, 27,* 951–959.

Strakowski, S. M., DelBello, M. P., Sax, K. W., Zimmerman, M. E., Shear, P. K., Hawkins, J. M., & Larson, E. R. (1999). Brain magnetic resonance imaging of structural abnormalities in bipolar disorder. *Archives of General Psychiatry, 56,* 254–260.

Talairach, J., & Tournoux, P. (1988). *Co-planar stereotaxic atlas of the human brain.* Stuttgart: Thieme.

Taylor, S. E. (1991). Asymmetrical effects of positive and negative events: The mobilization–minimization hypothesis. *Psychological Bulletin, 110,* 67–85.

Teasdale, J. D., Howard, R. J., Cox, S. G., Ha, Y., Brammer, M. J., Williams, S. C., & Checkley, S. A. (1999). Functional MRI study of the cognitive generation of affect. *American Journal of Psychiatry, 156,* 209–215.

Tebartz van Elst, L., Woermann, F. G., Lemieux, L., & Trimble, M. R. (1999). Amygdala enlargement in dysthymia: A volumetric study of patients with temporal lobe epilepsy. *Biological Psychiatry, 46,* 1614–1623.

Tebartz van Elst, L., Woermann, F., Lemieux, L., & Trimble, M. R. (2000). Increased amygdala volumes in female and depressed humans: A quantitative magnetic resonance imaging study. *Neuroscience Letters, 281,* 103–106.

Thayer, J. F., & Lane, R. D. (2000). A model of neurovisceral integration in emotion regulation and dysregulation. *Journal of Affective Disorders, 61,* 201–216.

Vakili, K., Pillay, S. S., Lafer, B., Fava, M., Renshaw, P. F., & Bonello-& Cintron, C. M. (2000). Hippocampal volume in primary unipolar major depression: A magnetic resonance imaging study. *Biological Psychiatry, 47,* 1087–1090.

Veith, R. C., Lewis, N., Linares, O. A., Barnes, R. F., Raskind, M. A., Villacres, E. C., Murburg, M. M., Ashleigh, E. A., Castillo, S., & Peskind, E. R. (1994). Sympathetic nervous system activity in major depression: Basal and desipramine-induced alterations in plasma norepinephrine kinetics. *Archives of General Psychiatry, 51,* 411–422.

Vogt, B. A., Finch, D. M., & Olson, C. R. (1992). Functional heterogeneity in cingulate cortex: The anterior executive and posterior evaluative regions. *Cerebral Cortex, 2,* 435–443.

Vogt, B. A., Nimchinsky, E. A., Vogt, L. J., & Hof, P. R. (1995). Human cingulate cortex: Surface features, flat maps, and cytoarchitecture. *Journal of Comparative Neurology, 359,* 490–506.

von Gunten, A., Fox, N. C., Cipolotti, L., & Ron, M. A. (2000). A volumetric study of hippocampus and amygdala in depressed patients with subjective memory problems. *Journal of Neuropsychiatry and Clinical Neuroscience, 12,* 493–498.

Whalen, P. J. (1998). Fear, vigilance, and ambiguity: Initial neuroimaging studies of the human amygdala. *Current Directions in Psychological Science, 7,* 177–188.

Whalen, P. J., Bush, G., McNally, R. J., Wilhelm, S., McInerney, S. C., Jenike, M. A., & Rauch, S. L. (1988). The emotional Stroop paradigm: A functional magnetic resonance imaging probe of the anterior cingulate affective division. *Biological Psychiatry, 44,* 1219–1228.

Williams, L. M., Brammer, M. J., Skerrett, D., Lagopolous, J., Rennie, C., Kozek, K., Olivieri, G., Peduto, T., & Gordon, E. (2000). The neural correlates of orienting: An integration of fMRI and skin conductance orienting. *NeuroReport, 11,* 3011–3015.

Wu, J., Buschbaum, M. S., Gillin, J. C., Tang, C., Cadwell, S., Wiegland, M., Najafi, A., Klein, E., Hazen, K., & Bunney, W. E. (1999). Prediction of antidepressant effects of sleep deprivation by metabolic rates in the ventral anterior cingulate and medical prefrontal cortex. *American Journal of Psychiatry, 156,* 1149–1158.

Wu, J. C., Gillin, J. C., Buchsbaum, M. S., Hershey, T., Johnson, J. C., & Bunney, W. E. (1992). Effect of sleep deprivation on brain metabolism of depressed patients. *American Journal of Psychiatry, 149,* 538–543.

Yurgelun-Todd, D. A., Gruber, S. A., Kanayama, G., Killgore, D. S., Baird, A. A., & Young, A. D. (2000). fMRI during affect discrimination in bipolar affective disorder. *Bipolar Disorders, 2,* 237–248.

Zald, D. H., Lee, J. T., Fluegel, K. W., & Pardo, J. V. (1998). Aversive gustatory stimulation activates limbic circuits in humans. *Brain, 121,* 1143–1154.

Zalla, T., Koechlin, E., Pietrini, P., Basso, G., Aquino, P., Sirigu, A., & Grafman, J. (2000). Differential amygdala responses to winning and losing: A functional magnetic resonance imaging study in humans. *European Journal of Neuroscience, 12,* 1764–1770.

10

Depression and Early Adverse Experiences

Sherryl H. Goodman

For decades, researchers and clinicians seeking the keys to understanding depression have considered early adverse experiences as having potentially great etiological significance. Links have been drawn between depression, in both children and adults, and exposure to prenatal stress, inadequate parenting, abuse and neglect, early trauma, and loss of a parent. Each of these events could hold potentially vital clues to etiological mechanisms and identification of groups at risk for the development of depression. The purpose of this chapter is to examine knowledge about associations between early experiences and depression from a developmental psychopathology perspective. The advantages of this perspective include the opportunity to take into account both normal and abnormal processes and alternative developmental pathways (Cicchetti & Sroufe, 2000).

A developmental psychopathology perspective begins with a consideration of developmental processes. At a minimum, therefore, it is important to know the timing of exposure to an adverse experience. Timing is important for at least two reasons. First, it is informative in terms of children's stage-salient needs, which might be disrupted as a result of the adverse experiences. Second, consideration of timing allows one to take into account the potential advantage of developmental accomplishments that children might have achieved prior to any disruption associated with the adverse experiences. This chapter is organized around developmental course, beginning with prenatal experiences and then considering experiences during infancy and early childhood.

Further, developmental psychopathology offers a wealth of constructs and models from many related disciplines for helping to understand the role of early experience in the emergence of depression. Thus, this chapter also considers several conceptual models that have been proposed to explain the role of early experiences in the development of depression. Among these are biological systems (stress-related neurobiology, brain development, and psychophysiology), the attachment system, cognitive diathesis models, and emotional expression and regulation.

In addition, a developmental psychopathology perspective works toward models that integrate multiple, transactional influences and that consider the concepts of pathways, *multifinality* (the same risk factors being associated with different outcomes), and *equifinality* (the multiple pathways by which individuals can develop a particular outcome, in this case depression) (Cicchetti & Rogosch, 1996). Therefore, each of these models will be considered not only alone but also as parts of integrative models, including diathesis–stress, vulnerability, and transactional models. In the concluding sections of this chapter, some of the alternative developmental pathways are delineated. Finally, future directions for research are suggested.

EXPERIENCES DURING FETAL DEVELOPMENT: MATERNAL STRESS AND DEPRESSION

Studies of both animals and humans have revealed that mothers' stress during pregnancy contributes to risk for the development of a range of behavioral disturbances in the offspring, some of which might be associated with depression. Rhesus monkeys who are mildly stressed during pregnancy produce offspring with lower birthweight, poorer neuromotor maturation, and delayed cognitive development, and who engage in less exploration of novel stimuli as infants (Schneider, 1992). As juveniles, they demonstrate abnormal social behavior and greater hypothalamic–pituitary–adrenal (HPA) activity (elevated cortisol) at baseline and even more so in response to stress (Clarke & Schneider, 1993; Clarke, Wittwer, Abbott, & Schneider, 1994). The effects are stronger if the mothers were stressed early, rather than in mid- to late pregnancy (Schneider, Roughton, Koehler, & Lubach, 1999). Similarly, the offspring of rats who had been stressed during pregnancy had lower birthweight, less vocalization during isolation in a novel environment, less exploration of novel environments, suppressed immune function, and persistent hyperactivity of their HPA axis (Kay, Tarcic, Poltyrev, & Weinstock, 1998; Poltyrev, Keshet, Kay, & Weinstock, 1996; Williams, Hennessy, & Davis, 1998; see review by Graham, Heim, Goodman, Miller, & Nemeroff, 1999).

These early outcomes that have been associated with fetal exposure to stress could contribute to the later development of depression in many ways. For example, elevated cortisol is likely to be revealed in infancy as dysregulation of affect and behavior, which, if persistent, might leave children vulnerable to stress-induced depression. Similarly, the abnormal social behavior may emerge as tendencies toward behavioral inhibition, such that children fail to acquire adequate social relationships and competencies that would protect them against the later development of depression. Each of these possible pathways from early outcomes to the later emergence of depression is discussed later in this chapter in terms of conceptual models to explain the role of early experiences in the development of depression.

Studies linking adverse experiences during fetal development with depression are not limited to animal research. In a longitudinal study of a large sample of humans, O'Connor, Heron, Golding, the ALSPAC Study Team, Beveridge, and Glover (in press) found that mothers who had high self-reported anxiety, particularly late in pregnancy (32 weeks gestation), were significantly more likely to report that their children's level of emotional problems exceeded a cutoff of two standard deviations above the mean at age 4 years. These findings remained significant even after controlling for sociodemographic risk, obstetrical and antenatal risks (birthweight, smoking, and alcohol intake), and levels of anxiety and depression at 8 weeks postpartum. While important in demonstrating a significant association between prenatal stress and adverse outcome, this set of findings does not identify the primary mechanisms that account for these outcomes.

Researchers from several different theoretical perspectives have examined the fetal environment in order to identify possible mechanisms of abnormal fetal development that could place human infants at risk for the later development of depression. Among the aspects of fetal environment that have been considered are (1) neuroendocrine abnormalities, (2) reduced blood flow to the fetus, (3) poor health behaviors, and (4) the mother's use of antidepressant medications.

Possible Mechanisms

Neuroendocrine Abnormalities

Because the fetus's first transactions with the mother occur at gestational days 13–14, when *in utero* blood flow is established, fetal exposure to the neuroendocrine correlates of the mother's stress or depression begins early and could potentially influence all aspects of fetal development. Knowledge of the neurobiology of depression leads to a concern for individuals who, as fetuses, might be exposed to corticotropin-releasing factor (CRF) hypersecretion. As reviewed by Graham et al. (1999), CRF is the prime regulator of the endocrine stress response. Evidence has been building for its role in coordinating the behavioral, immunological, and autonomic responses to stress. As such, the anticipated consequences for individuals exposed to CRF hypersecretion during fetal development include abnormal stress reactivity, abnormal behavioral and affective functioning, and abnormal EEG patterns. Moreover, each of these aspects of functioning is known to be disrupted in adult depression (Davidson & Fox, 1988; Gotlib, Ranganath, & Rosenfeld, 1998; see Davidson, Pizzagalli, & Nitschke, Chapter 9, this volume, and Gotlib & Hammen, 1992, for reviews of this research).

In children exposed to CRF hypersecretion as fetuses, these indices of abnormal functioning may represent markers of risk for depression, especially for the later emergence of stress-induced depression. Fetal exposure to high levels of cortisol could result in changes in HPA axis functioning that may not be reversible (Graham et al., 1999; Henry, Kabbaj, Simon, Le Moal, & Maccari, 1994) and are likely to be reflected in dysregulation of affect and behavior in infants. The latter are likely to then become part of a transactional system with the childrearing environment, which further contributes to risk for the development of depression.

Cortisol and corticotropin-releasing hormone (CRH) concentrations in plasma or urine are among the primary indices of HPA axis activity. Consequently, it has been important to know whether neuroendocrine correlates of stress or depression in pregnant women are circulated to the fetus. Researchers have found that stress and depression during pregnancy are associated with increased levels in the women of plasma and urinary cortisol, beta-endorphins, CRH, catecholamines, epinephrine, and norepinephrine (Emory, Hatch, Blackmore, & Strock, 1993; Field, 1998; Handley, Dunn, Waldron, & Baker, 1980; Smith et al., 1990). Among these hormones, only cortisol has been found to cross the placenta to the fetus; at 20–36 weeks of pregnancy, maternal levels of cortisol accounted for 50% of the variance in the fetus's levels of cortisol (Glover, Teixeira, Gitau, & Fisk, 1998).

Reduced Blood Flow to the Fetus

The second aspect of fetal development that might contribute to risk for the later development of depression is reduced blood flow to the fetus. Glover (1997; Glover et al., 1998) found maternal trait anxiety to be associated with impaired uterine blood flow in nonsmoking, healthy women in the third trimester of pregnancy. Reduced uterine blood flow, in turn, was associated with lower birthweight or prematurity of the babies. These infants may come into the world being more difficult to care for, thus adding stress to an already anxious mother, and may be more likely to have an elevated stress response, both of which would increase vulnerability to depression.

Mother's Poor Health Behaviors

Third, fetuses may be at risk for the later development of depression because of the mother's inadequate health care and health risk behaviors during pregnancy. Depression during pregnancy has been associated with less frequent and less adequate prenatal care, more unhealthy eating and sleeping patterns, and more smoking. Although these maternal behaviors have most often been associated with risk for externalizing disorders in the offspring (Milberger, Biederman, Faraone, Chen, & Jones, 1996), they could also contribute to the risk for depression through their association with other risk factors such as premature birth and inadequate parenting of the infant.

Mother's Use of Antidepressant Medications

Fourth, the subset of fetuses whose mothers are clinically depressed during pregnancy may also be exposed *in utero* to antidepressant medications. The two dominant medications prescribed for treatment of major depression, tricyclic antidepressants and fluoxetine, cross the placental barrier. Yet researchers have found no discernible adverse effects on social, cognitive, or behavioral functioning in children from infancy through age 7 years that could not be accounted for by the greater severity of depression among women who need continued medication throughout pregnancy (see review by Goodman & Gotlib, 1999). Thus, prenatal exposure to antidepressant medications is unlikely to contribute to risk for the later development of depression.

In sum, adverse experiences during fetal development, including exposure to neuroendocrine abnormalities, reduced bloodflow, and the mother's poor health behaviors, but not the mother's use of antidepressant medications, may precipitate a set of events that contribute to the later emergence of depression. Among the mechanisms that have been considered are an altered stress response system, a higher sensory threshold, and a more difficult infant who stresses the mother–infant relationship (Abrams, Field, Scafidi, & Prodromidis, 1995; Glover et al., 1998; Zuckerman, Bauchner, Parker, & Cabral, 1990). As will be discussed later with regard to integrative models, each of these mechanisms is likely to contribute to transactional processes, any number of which could result in depression.

EXPERIENCES DURING INFANCY AND EARLY CHILDHOOD

The predominant aspect of early life experiences of infants and young children that has been associated with risk for depression is inadequate parenting, including the extreme of abuse. Inadequate parenting exposes children to maladaptive models of social skills and affective expression, stresses infants if they experience inappropriate stimulation and inadequate arousal modulation, and, more broadly, interferes with healthy development to the extent that parents fail to provide for infants' and young children's stage-salient needs. Thus, infants and young children who experience inadequate parenting may develop inadequate emotion regulation and interpersonal skills and a dysfunctional stress response. This pattern may predispose children to the later development of depression.

As reviewed by Graham et al. (1999), there is some evidence of elevated cortisol in response to physical stressors such as physical illness or surgical procedures in neonates, suggesting the capacity of humans to respond to stress from very early in life. These findings underscore the importance of studies of stressors in infancy in that high levels of stress hormones could potentially damage still-developing neurons, engendering vulnerability to future stressors.

Animal models have yielded helpful information on the effects of early life stressors, in terms of both correlations with neurobiological alterations and behavioral consequences. Maternal separation in rats in the first few weeks of life has been reliably associated with both HPA axis alterations and behavioral changes that mimic adult depression (Levine, Haltmeyer, & Karas, 1967; Pihoker, Owens, Kuhn, Schanberg, & Nemeroff, 1993). Moreover, the alterations in HPA axis response to stress persist into adulthood in these early stressed rats (Ladd, Owens, & Nemeroff, 1996). In fact, the most recent studies suggest that an important mechanism of these changes may be associated changes in maternal care when the pups are returned (Ladd et al., 2000). Studies of nonhuman primates separated from their mothers have produced similar findings (e.g., Byrne & Suomi, 1999). Thus, the animal models provide strong support for a model of early loss or separation or alterations in maternal care disrupting the development of sensitive neurobiological systems, leaving the organism vulnerable to psychopathology.

Unresponsive or Neglectful Parenting

Both Tronick and Gianino's (1986) mutual regulation model and Field's (1985) psychobiological attunement model describe a mother who is inattentive and emotionally unresponsive, failing to respond to her infant's needs for help with behavioral or affective regulation, and, ultimately, contributing to the infant's difficulty in developing arousal modulation. In both models, the infant becomes agitated in attempts to elicit responses from the mother, then withdraws and begins to show signs of depression. Findings consistent with these models come from studies of infants whose mothers were instructed to simulate depression as well as studies of infants with depressed mothers.

When nondepressed mothers were instructed to respond to their infant's positive affect displays with a still face, their infants responded with sober expressions and were found to avert their gaze from their mother (Cohn & Elmore, 1988; Cohn & Tronick, 1983). In face-to-face interactions between depressed mothers and their infants, depressed mothers have been observed to display less positive affect, more frequent expressions of sadness, and fewer expressions of interest than well mothers (Pickens & Field, 1993). The infants with depressed mothers, in turn, engaged in more gaze and head aversion, consistent with the idea that the infants were using self-regulatory behaviors to minimize the negative affect associated with maternal unresponsiveness. Lyons-Ruth, Lyubchik, Wolfe, and Bronfman (2002) found that infants whose mothers related to them in a fearful and withdrawn manner, in contrast to intrusive mothers (described in the next section), were more likely to develop disorganized secure attachment styles with signs of apprehension and dysphoria. Weinberg and Tronick (1998) found that boys were particularly vulnerable to a withdrawn maternal interaction style, which they speculated may be associated with boys' greater need for regulatory support. In a longitudinal study, Field (2002) found that infants whose depressed mothers had been withdrawn, compared to intrusive (see the next section), showed less adaptive interactive behavior and lower Bayley Mental Scale scores. Persistent exchanges with a sad and unresponsive caregiver thus disrupt infants' early affect development, failing to provide infants with the help they need to learn to manage arousal and socializing depression-like affective expressions. Moreover, from a social learning theory perspective (Bandura, 1977), infants and young children who experience low levels of contingent responsiveness to their initiatives may fail to learn healthy patterns of self-reward and adaptive attributional styles. The latter consideration is expanded in the later section on Parenting That Increases Vulnerability to Depression.

Intrusive, Harsh, or Coercive Parenting

Inadequate parenting may also be characterized as intrusive, harsh, or coercive. Researchers have revealed that maternal depression is associated not only with a withdrawn, unresponsive pattern of interaction with their infants, but also with a pattern of hostile-intrusive overstimulation (Cohn, Matias, Tronick, Lyons-Ruth, & Connell, 1986; Field, Healy, Goldstein, & Guthertz, 1990). This subset of mothers has been observed to overstimulate, to be physically intrusive (e.g., by poking and jabbing their infants), to interfere with the infants' exploratory activities, and to show hostile and irritable affect (Cohn et al., 1986; Lyons-Ruth, Zoll, Connell, & Grunebaum, 1986; Malphurs et al., 1996).

Maternal hostility and intrusiveness is associated with infant avoidance and fussiness. Intrusive or hostile mothers interfere with their infants' autonomous functioning (Egeland, Pianta, & O'Brian, 1993). Cohn et al. (1986) observed that infants interacting with their intrusive mothers protested less than 5% of the time and spent 55% of the time avoiding their mothers. Field et al. (1990) noted a high frequency of fussing in infants interacting with their intrusive mothers. One study has shown that girls may be more vulnerable than boys to intrusive mothering (Weinberg & Tronick, 1998). Each of these behavioral reactions could contribute to risk for depression, especially in terms of the infants' contribution to transactional patterns.

Regardless of depression status, parents who engage in coercive and controlling parenting, particularly if it is a persistent quality of early parenting, might contribute to children's developing a sense of helplessness and a tendency to view themselves as having little control over outcomes (Racusin & Kaslow, 1991). Each of these sets of beliefs, and their associated behavior patterns, increases children's vulnerability to depression. Some support for these contentions comes from studies in which parents of clinically depressed children were found to use more coercion and were observed to be more controlling and less democratic compared to parents of nondepressed children (Amanat & Butler, 1984; Dadds, Sanders, Morrison, & Rebgetz, 1992).

Inconsistent Parenting

Some mothers, perhaps a distinct subgroup of depressed mothers, display inconsistencies in parenting their infants. Lyons-Ruth et al. (2002) theorized that these women's own ambivalence about attachment would lead them to engage in contradictory caregiving strategies with their infants. The infants, in turn, may develop disorganized insecure attachment styles and hostile/punitive behavior. From a transactional perspective, it will be important to follow groups of infants reared by mothers who engage in these different patterns of inadequate parenting in order to determine whether these patterns are associated with the development of different emotional or behavioral problems in the children.

Abusive Parenting

Physical or sexual abuse or neglect of a child by a parent represents the extreme of inadequate parenting and adverse early life experiences. Thus, it is no surprise that infants or toddlers who have been maltreated have high rates of disorganized attachment, negative views of themselves, and lower cortisol reactivity (Barnett, Ganiban, & Cicchetti, 1999; Erickson,

Egeland, & Pianta, 1989; Hart, Gunnar, & Cicchetti, 1995). Infants and toddlers are the most frequently reported victims of physical abuse, which may reflect a tendency of individuals to be more likely to report suspected abuse of younger children, who are perceived as more vulnerable (Gelles, 1998). On the other hand, violence-prone parents may view infants' and toddlers' needs for protection from danger as justification for abuse (Crittenden, 1998).

Parents who abuse their children also may be depressed or abusing drugs or alcohol (Gelles, 1998). Other factors associated with abuse, such as high levels of stress in the family, social isolation, being single and young, being in an abusive partner relationship, and having low income also contribute to the likelihood of an accumulation of early adverse experiences. Both Gelles (1998) and Belsky (1993) have developed models that describe the multiple adverse influences that converge in families where parents abuse their children. Maternal depression and abuse may have independent effects on depression, with the combination being associated with higher levels of depression in the children (Kinard, 1995).

Although the consequences of abuse in young children are wide-ranging, of particular concern with regard to risk for depression are findings that the children are likely to have lower self-esteem, difficulty relating to peers, insecure attachment relationships, dysfunctional attributions, social-cognitive biases (being hypervigilant to cues of danger), and neuroendocrine abnormalities (see review by Crittenden, 1998). Each of these processes has been associated with later emergence of depression. Samples of 7- to 12-year-old children from abusive homes, who may also have been abused at younger ages, have shown high rates of depression, even relative to children from neglectful homes (Kaufman, 1991; Toth, Manly, & Cicchetti, 1992).

Also important to consider is that the stressful context of the lives of many abuse victims likely contributes to the negative cascade of outcomes. Many of the correlates of abuse are risk factors for depression in offspring in their own right. According to Crittenden (1998), many of the consequences of abuse can be attributed to the context of neglect and psychological maltreatment.

Recently, Heim et al. (2000) reported that a small group of adult women who had been sexually or physically abused as children showed persistent, hyperactive HPA axis responses to stress relative to women with no history of childhood abuse. This pattern was strongest among the women who had been abused and had a current major depression. In sum, abuse leaves children with behavioral, cognitive, emotional, and neuroendocrine vulnerabilities to depression.

Loss of Parent

The early experience of loss, particularly a parent's death, and the associated grief has long been considered a severe stressor that may place children at risk for depression. Death of a loved one may occur as a function of illness, disaster, or even more extreme events such as homicide or suicide. Other losses may occur as a function of parents' separation or divorce. As reviewed by Pfeffer (1996), children's psychological responses will vary as a function of the characteristics of the loss experience. Important variables are the extent to which the loss is associated with changes and ongoing disruptions in children's environment and routine, children's age and sex, and other family characteristics such as the availability of supportive others. As Tennant, Beggington, and Hurry (1980) note in their review, the evidence linking parental death in childhood with later depressive disorders is inconsistent at best, once experimental and control samples are carefully matched. Although there is no doubt that loss of one's parent early in life can contribute to a risk for depression, the risk is likely to be limited to those who experience further risks surrounding and following the loss.

International conflicts are a particular form of disaster that have left orphaned many children, some of whom are raised in sparse, institutional orphanages and others of whom are adopted either early or later in childhood. Several groups of researchers saw the opportunity to learn about maternal deprivation by studying different groups of these children, most recently from Romania. Gunnar and colleagues studied Romanian orphans who had been adopted either prior to 4 months of age or later (Gunnar, 2000; Gunnar, Bruce, & Grotevant, 2000). Whereas the early adopted children were not significantly different behaviorally from matched controls, the later adopted children showed behavioral deficits, blunted circadian rhythm during day care at 3–4 years of age and elevated cortisol levels even 6–7 years later. O'Connor, Rutter, and the English and Romanian Adoptees Study Team (2000) reported on a related finding, in which the duration of deprivation, in terms of time spent in the orphanage, was related to severity of attachment disorder behaviors. Rutter et al. (1999) reported on multiple outcomes that followed the same pattern. The best predictor of positive outcome at age 4 in Romanian orphans adopted into the United Kingdom was having been adopted when younger. In sum, extremes of early deprivation might be overcome if adopted early. Those adopted even after 8 months of age show adverse behavioral and neuroendocrine abnormalities, suggesting vulnerability to stress-induced depression.

Parenting That Increases Vulnerability to Depression

In addition to the extreme family circumstances already described, a number of other aspects of family functioning have also been hypothesized to be associated with the later emergence of depression. Abnormal family functioning may contribute to children developing patterns of coping, beliefs, and interpersonal styles that leave them vulnerable to depression. For example, according to social learning theory (Bandura, 1977), children whose parents set overly stringent criteria for reward and consequently reward their children at low rates may internalize those standards and contingencies for reinforcement (Cole & Rehm, 1986). These children would then engage in low rates of self-reward and high rates of self-criticism, may selectively attend to negative feedback, and be more likely to blame themselves for negative outcomes and less likely to take credit for positive outcomes (Nolen-Hoeksema, Girgus, & Seligman, 1992; Rehm & Carter, 1990). Consistent with cognitive-behavioral models of depression, each of these processes has been associated with increased risk for depression.

Similarly, parents' level of emotional overinvolvement with their children may increase risk for depression. Emotional overinvolvement, along with criticism and hostility, is frequently studied in relation to the construct of *expressed emotion*, which refers to the emotional aspects of family members' communication patterns (Hooley, 1998; Hooley & Gotlib, 2000). In one study of children who became depressed, mothers of children with a gradual onset of depression were found to have high levels of emotional overinvolvement, in contrast to mothers of children with an acute onset of their depression episode (Asarnow, Ben-Meir, & Goldstein, 1987).

Another set of family process that might increase risk for depression involves interparental conflict. Several processes might be implicated in linking exposure to conflict and depression in children, particularly if the conflict is intense, aggressive, and unresolved and children are exposed repeatedly and at early ages (Davies & Cummings, 1994). Children may feel threatened and overwhelmed, have heightened emotional arousal (increased heart rate and elevated cortisol), have difficulty regulating their emotions (inability to suppress vagal tone), may develop depressotypic attributional styles, and may withdraw as a way of coping with their own level of distress (Davies & Cummings, 1994; Grych & Fincham, 1990; Katz & Gottman, 1995). Difficulty regulating emotions and focusing attention in stressful situations, along with these cognitive patterns, increase vulnerability to depression (Gottman, Katz, & Hooven, 1997; Ingoldsby, Shaw, Owens, & Winslow, 1999).

Poor family functioning itself is unlikely to be sufficiently stressful to trigger depression. Rather, it is likely to function as part of an integrative model in which biological, psychological, and interpersonal components contribute. Overall, too few prospective studies have been conducted to be able to draw conclusions on this risk factor, either alone or in combination with other risks.

CONCEPTUAL MODELS TO EXPLAIN THE ROLE OF EARLY EXPERIENCES

Biological Systems

Neuroendocrine: Stress Hormones

As reviewed by Graham et al. (1999), the HPA system coordinates the behavioral, immunological, endocrinological, and autonomic responses to stress. In adults, dysregulation of the HPA system is related to major depression and posttraumatic stress disorder (PTSD). Cortisol is the primary steroid hormone produced by the HPA system in humans (corticosterone in rodents) in response to stress. By the age of 3 months, human infants have adult-equivalent levels of cortisol, and thus are capable of responding to stress.

Brief elevations of cortisol levels are considered to be adaptive. Individuals may experience enhanced ability to manage the stressor, both physiologically and behaviorally. In contrast, prolonged hyperactivity of the HPA axis, with persistently elevated cortisol levels, has been associated with negative effects on physiological and behavioral systems. In particular, early life stress is likely to predispose children to at least transient if not permanent alterations in the CRF system, interfering with their ability to respond adaptively to later stressors. Consistent with this model, cortisol hypersecretion has been reported in prepubertal depressed children (Weller & Weller, 1988), and less cortisol reactivity was found in 47- to 75-month-old children who had been maltreated (Hart et al., 1996). In rats, chronic early life stress has been shown to result in dysregulation of the HPA system and in attenuated emotionality in adulthood. Thus, neuroendocrine abnormalities resulting from early exposure to stress hold promise for elucidating some of the mechanisms for the emergence of depression in association with early life stress.

Nervous System: Vagal Tone

Vagal tone is a measure of nervous system variability that has been associated with individual differences in expression and regulation of emotion. Vagal tone is measured as heart rate variability. Lower levels of vagal tone may reflect infants' efforts to cope with inadequate environmental support (Porges, Doussard-Roosevelt, & Maiti, 1994). For example, Field, Pickens, Fox, Nawrocki, and Gonzalez (1995) found lower vagal tone in 3- to 6-month-old infants of depressed mothers. Moreover, whereas infants with nondepressed mothers showed a developmental increase in vagal tone between 3 and 6 months, infants with depressed mothers did not. Among 6-month-olds, lower vagal tone was correlated with fewer vocalizations and facial expressions during interactions. Field (2002) interpreted her findings to suggest that, compared to infants with nondepressed mothers, infants with depressed mothers experienced different contextual demands if their mothers are less expressive and responsive. The failure to show the developmental increase in vagal tone may reflect cumulative effects of agitated states in trying to elicit responses from their mothers. A tendency toward lower vagal tone could also be inherited or a function of *in utero* environmental-based physiological differences in neural regulation.

Regardless of the origins, lower vagal tone is associated with poorer emotion regulation abilities and less expression of positive affect. Among infants of nondepressed mothers or unselected samples, lower vagal tone is associated with poorer abilities to self-soothe, fewer expressions of joy and interest, and less exploration of novel stimuli (Pickens & Field, 1993; Porges et al., 1994). Each of these deficits could serve as vulnerabilities in a transactional model of pathways to depression.

Frontal Lobe Development

Postnatal brains undergo significant continued development. Of particular concern with regard to potential influence on depression are the rapid development during the first year of life of the frontal lobes, the interhemispheric connections, and the neurotransmitter systems that mediate emotional behavior (Chugani, 1994). Each of these structures or systems is related to the experience and regulation of affect. Evidence is increasing that quality of caregiving relates to the manner in which these systems develop. Specifically, Field and her colleagues' (Field, Fox, Pickens, & Nawrocki, 1995) studies of infants in the first few months of life and Dawson and her colleagues' (Dawson et al., 1999) studies of 11- to 18-month-old children showed links between inadequate parenting and abnormal development of the frontal lobe. These abnormalities were reflected in hemispheric asymmetries as measured by EEG. Infants with depressed mothers exhibited atypical patterns of frontal EEG asymmetry: compared to infants of nondepressed mothers, infants of depressed mothers exhibited reduced left frontal brain activity during playful interactions with their mothers.

In studies of unselected infants and adults, right-brain activation is associated with the experience of the negative emotions of sadness and distress, whereas activation of the left frontal region is associated with positive emotions of joy and interest (Davidson & Fox, 1982). In addition, the atypical pattern exhibited by children with depressed mothers has been found to be predictive of an infants' vulnerability to experience negative affect (Davidson & Fox, 1989), and thus may be a marker of current or chronic depressed mood state (Field et al., 1995). In depressed adults, reduced left frontal activity was not only present during episodes but persisted into remission (Davidson, Schaffer, & Saron, 1985; Henriques & Davidson, 1990). Thus, early experience with a depressed mother may lead to abnormal brain functions that are specifically associated with vulnerability to depressive mood states.

Inherited Vulnerabilities

Genetics undoubtedly plays a role in explaining the risk for depression in association with early experience. Indeed, efforts to understand the contribution of genetics to the link between early experience and the later emergence of depression may help to explain the notion of heritability of depression. Several possible roles of genetics have been considered. Children may inherit a tendency to experience negative affect (Plomin et al., 1993). Genetics may explain some portion of individual differences in the brain asymmetries described above. Evidence also supports a role of heritability in the tendency to experience negative events (Plomin, 1994). The ways in which genes and adverse early environments might work together to increase risk for depression will be discussed later in this chapter.

Attachment System

Theories of attachment and accumulating empirical evidence support a strong case for the idea that disturbances in the attachment relationship as a function of early adverse experiences contribute to vulnerability to the development of depression (Cummings & Cicchetti, 1990). With insecure attachment, children are likely to experience negative feelings about themselves and others and to be particularly sensitive to loss. The emotional unavailability or unresponsiveness of a depressed mother or the experience of maltreatment or loss could increase infants' risk for both insecure attachment and depression. Insecure attachment could mediate the association between maternal depression, maltreating caregivers, and other early adversities and the development of child depression or, alternatively, serve as an added risk factor (Cummings & Cicchetti, 1990).

Support for the association between maternal depression and insecure attachments in infants is strong but not unequivocal (Dawson, Klinger, Panagiotides, Spieker, & Frey, 1992; Radke-Yarrow, 1998; Teti, Gelfand, Messinger, & Isabella, 1995; Zahn-Waxler, Chapman, & Cummings, 1984). It may be only infants of the most severely and chronically depressed women (Cohn & Campbell, 1992) and those with bipolar, rather than unipolar depression, who are likely to develop insecure attachment (DeMulder & Radke-Yarrow, 1991).

Consistent support has emerged for the association between physical abuse of infants by their caregivers and insecure attachment. A higher percentage of maltreated infants are classified as insecure compared to nonmaltreated infants (Cicchetti & Barnett, 1991; Crittendon, 1988). The most common classification is "disorganized" (Carlson, Cicchetti, Barnett, & Braunwald, 1989).

In sum, the findings from at least the most severely depressed mothers and from infants who experienced maltreatment are consistent with a role of disturbed attachment as a mechanism to explain the association between early adverse experiences and the later development of depression. Children who experience these adversities early in life may develop insecure attachment relationships. These insecure attachments, with their associated internalized negative views of the self and the world, serve to organize how children perceive and behave in interpersonal relationships and thus are carried forward in development beyond the early adversities. Children may become increasingly unable to deal with challenges and subsequent difficulties may precipitate depression.

Cognitive Vulnerabilities and the Self System

Early adverse experiences may also be linked to later depression through the mechanism of depressotypic cognitions. Early childhood, beginning in the second year of life, is a critical period for the construction of the sense of self and self in relation to others and the world (Brooks-Gunn & Lewis, 1979). As with secure attachment, a healthy sense of oneself is facilitated by warm, responsive parenting. The early adverse experiences discussed in this chapter are associated with cognitive distortions such as a sense of oneself as unlovable, as unworthy of others' positive interest, and as unlikely to get one's needs met. Children may develop a sense of hopelessness and helplessness and may be deficient in administering self-reinforcements. For example, depressed mothers expose their children to more self-criticism as well as criticism of the child (Radke-Yarrow, Belmont, Nottelmann, & Bottomly, 1990). Children who experience other aspects of inadequate parenting or other early life traumas may develop distorted views of themselves and the world. The children may set high, unrealistic standards for themselves, leading to negative self-views. Pessimistic explanatory styles and negative self-concepts prospectively predict depression (Hammen, 1988; Peterson & Seligman, 1984). Kovacs, Akiskal, Gatsonis, and Parrone (1994) described cognitive characteristics such as self-deprecation and negative self-esteem as one of two prominent features of dysthymia in children, along with mood features.

Affect: Emotional Expression and Regulation

Another model to explain the association between early adverse experiences and the later emergence of depression is that the early stressors are associated with deficits and delays in emotional expression or regulation. Affective dysregulation is a predominant feature of dysthymia in children, including a persistent gloomy mood as well as irritability and anger (Kovacs et al., 1994). Caregivers play an essential role in the socialization of their children's emotions. Thus, particular concerns are raised about children with depressed mothers. Infants have been observed to imitate their depressed mothers' negative affect (Field, 1994). Moreover, depressed mothers less often reinforce their infants' positive affect with displays of interest, thus discouraging the infants' expression of positive affect (Pickens & Field, 1993). Similar connections can be drawn between the other aspects of early adverse experiences described here and affective dysregulation. Moreover, Garber, Braafladt, and Zeman (1991) provided strong support for the role of abnormalities in the regulation of sad affect in the development of depression in children.

Integrative Models

Clearly, the emergence of depression is not solely (directly or inevitably) determined by any childhood experience in a main effects type model. Thus, we are challenged to develop and test integrative models that take into account the likely complexities. Two models that were proposed in the past are now considered too simplistic: the early experience model and the main effects model. Three other models have offered promise for explaining findings and generating testable hypotheses, each building upon the other: stress–diathesis models, vulnerability models, and transactional models. Each of these will be introduced in turn, with suggestions for their role in models of early adverse experience and risk for depression.

Stress–Diathesis Models

As reviewed by Monroe and Simon (1991), stress–diathesis models explain that a vulnerability manifests itself only in the context of stress or, more broadly, maladaptive environments. Thus, this model tries to correct for the oversimplification of early experience models by proposing the conditions under which a vulnerability, or *diathesis,* would or would not lead to disorder. In this way of thinking, the stress is a moderator variable. The model has been proposed as a way to explain why some people with the diathesis develop the disorder whereas others do not, and why some people remain disorder-free until a certain point in time and then the disorder emerges.

Although originally developed to explain the development of schizophrenia in individuals with genetic predisposition, several variations on stress–diathesis models could be developed for the issues discussed in this chapter. As reviewed here, there is strong support from the empirical findings for suggesting that children who experience early adverse experiences develop one or more diatheses for depression, including a dysregulated HPA system, lower vagal tone, reduced left frontal EEG activation, insecure attachment, dysfunctional cognitions, and deficits and delays in emotional expression or regulation. Children who acquire one or more of these diatheses would be expected to be more sensitive to the effects of additional stressors relative to their less vulnerable counterparts. Longitudinal studies would be required to test these predictions from the model.

To be more usefully applied to the issues with regard to early adversity and risk for depression, many aspects of the stress–diathesis model need further elaboration and testing. For example, it would be important to note whether the moderating processes operate similarly over the course of development. It is not clear whether children would remain vulnerable to depression equally over the course of their development or if they might, for example, accomplish some developmental tasks that would reduce the potential triggering mechanism of later occurring stressors. Support for consideration of different developmental processes comes from Hammen's (1992) analysis of longitudinal data. She found that for young children, adverse experiences alone predict depression. In contrast, for older children, the addition of negative attributional style added to the prediction of depression. Thus, although a stress–diathesis model adds to our understanding of associations between early adverse experiences and the development of depression, it also leaves unexplained many of the complexities of causal pathways, processes, and multiple determinants of outcome that a transactional model promises to encompass.

Vulnerability Models

In vulnerability models, individuals inherit or acquire deficits or dysfunctions or abnormalities that increase their likelihood of developing psychopathology. With regard to the topic of this chapter, the vulnerability acquired as a function of the early adverse experience is a liability, but not a singular, linear cause of depression, either concurrently or later in development. For example, children with the pattern of frontal EEG abnormalities described here will be likely to experience a predominance of negative emotions. The children may engage the environment less actively or less positively. Similarly, children who acquire cognitive vulnerabilities may selectively attend to, or be more sensitive to, negative aspects of their environment. Thus, children's developmental course will be influenced by these traits or tendencies.

The extent to which a vulnerability is expressed is likely to be influenced by other factors that contribute to adverse outcomes, that is, other risk factors, as well as by factors that contribute to positive outcomes, that is, resilience or protective factors. More complex models are needed to clarify these processes. In addition, transactional processes likely play a role in that others will interact with the child in ways that are evoked by the child's affective, interpersonal, and cognitive styles. Thus, early adverse experiences should be considered liabilities that cannot, alone, predict ensuing patterns of developmental processes. Transactional models help to clarify those processes.

Transactional Models

Goodman and Gotlib (1999) asserted the need for a developmentally sensitive, transactional, integrated model to best understand risk for depression in a special population: children with depressed parents. The case for such a model is even stronger with the emphasis on early adverse experience. For example, considering biological and psychosocial models in an integrative manner, especially within a transactional model, offers great potential for understanding the role of early adverse experience in the emergence of depression.

In early stages of development, children must develop mechanisms to regulate affect, arousal, and attention; develop secure attachment relationships; and develop a differentiated sense of self and self in relation to others—any aberration of which could propel a child onto a pathway to depression (Cicchetti & Toth, 1998). Inherent in children accomplishing all of these developmental challenges are not only the socioemotional environment, that is, good quality parenting, but also the still maturing brain and neuroendocrine mechanisms.

As reviewed, evidence is accumulating for the impact of caregiving on neurobiological growth and particularly the mechanisms that relate to affect and emotional behavior (Dawson et al., 1992).

The transactional model not only integrates the multiple potential pathogenic processes, but also takes into account the continuous processes of child and environment mutually influencing each other (Sameroff, 1975). Environmental characteristics will influence the child's course of development and the child's characteristics will influence the nature of the environment. Over time these processes may be adaptive or maladaptive, or may vary from one to the other. Thus, both vulnerabilities and stress–diatheses considerations are taken into account. In addition, developmental processes are given serious consideration, including accounting for influences that may be stage-specific and adaptive or "self-righting" influences inherent in growth and development (Cicchetti & Rogosch, 1997).

The transactional model provides a theoretical context within which one can ask questions that promise to help explain the alternative courses of development of children who are exposed early to adverse experiences. In the final two sections of this chapter, ideas are presented for some of the influences on alternative pathways and suggestions are made for research that promises to further knowledge of the roles of early adverse experiences on the development of depression.

ALTERNATIVE DEVELOPMENTAL PATHWAYS

Multiple alternative pathways connect early experiences with the later emergence of depression and other outcomes. Even within the limited time frame of early childhood, a broad range of experiences may set children on one or another pathway to depression. The particular experience may relate to the relative degree of involvement of cognitive, socioemotional, representational, or biological domains in the depression that emerges (Cicchetti & Toth, 1998). Evidence from the few longitudinal studies of depression in children and adults suggests both that many pathways lead to depression and that children with early adverse experiences have a range of outcomes.

Some of the alternative pathways reflect the tremendous differences in the nature of any of the adverse experiences described in this chapter. That is, there is no single characterization of abuse, loss, a depressed mother, and so forth. Each of these situations is associated with a set of experiences that will vary for individual children. Moreover, as mentioned earlier, the timing of the experience will influence the developmental course. Further, the transactional processes that unfold over time add even more variation in alternative pathways. Innumerable alternative pathways could be described. A few examples are presented here. Most important is to consider the advantages of process-oriented research that will help to elucidate the patterns of adaptation and maladaptation that may unfold over time (Cicchetti & Sroufe, 2000).

As described earlier, depressed mothers might be characterized as predominantly withdrawn or as hostile/intrusive. Field (2002) provided converging evidence suggesting widely diverging pathways for the infants of those two groups of mothers. As fetuses, infants of mothers who were classified as withdrawn (based on interactions with their 3-month-old infants) had lower activity levels, and the fetuses of intrusive mothers had higher activity levels than did the fetuses of nondepressed mothers. As newborns, those with withdrawn mothers had lower Brazelton orientation and motor scores and lower levels of the neurotransmitter dopamine. As reviewed by Field (2002), low dopamine levels are associated with depressed behavior in children and rats. Field also found support for a hypothesis that these different interactive patterns would expose children differentially to approach and withdrawal emotions, and thus be associated with different frontal activation EEG patterns and, later, with different behavioral outcomes. Three-month-old infants whose mothers had been withdrawn had greater relative right frontal EEG activation, a pattern associated with withdrawal emotions (Fox & Davidson, 1986). In contrast, infants whose mothers had been intrusive had greater relative left frontal EEG activation, a pattern associated with approach emotions. Thus, infants with withdrawn mothers may be more vulnerable to depression as a function of developing a withdrawn style themselves, and of having a lower capacity to experience pleasure. Infants with intrusive mothers, on the other hand, may be more vulnerable to depression in response to stress, given their patterns of experience. Each of these tendencies would, of course, be expressed differently depending on the ongoing interactive style of the mother and others with whom the child relates, and on other later experiences of the child. Overall, Field's findings epitomize the convergence of multiple biological systems, maternal interactive style, and infant characteristics that contribute to pathways to depression. Further research is needed along these lines, especially taking into account interactive processes that unfold over time.

Just as depressed mothers cannot be characterized in a single way, neither can parents who abuse their young children or the children who have been abused. Crittenden (1998) describes one group of children who have been abused who, as early as during toddlerhood, respond by being exceedingly compliant, vigilantly attentive to parents' cues, quiet and withdrawn, and displaying false positive affect. While these behaviors may be adaptive in the immediate context, they are likely to be maladaptive in other contexts and could contribute to risk for depression. Another pattern described by Crittenden was that of abused infants who became increasingly distressed and angry over the course of development. As toddlers, they were angry and aggressive, demanding, negative, and noncompliant, possibly as a strategy to get parents' attention. These children may be less likely to develop depression, at least in the short term, and more likely to emerge with externalizing disorders, or they may be more resilient to the negative influences in the family. Helpful further research would explore the interplay over time of processes such as the child's tendencies, which may reflect the early adverse experiences, and the qualities of the interpersonal environment.

FUTURE DIRECTIONS

Considering the role of early experience in the emergence of depression within an integrative, transactional model raises many important areas requiring further study. A few examples will be mentioned here. One area that has received some attention is the role of attachment relationships in stress reactivity. As children approach their first birthday and attachment behaviors become increasingly focused on one or two individuals (Ainsworth, Blehar, Waters, & Wall, 1978), parents have the potential to help modulate stress reactivity. Support for this contention comes from Gunnar and others who have shown that security of mother–child attachment is associated with the mother's ability to inhibit cortisol increases among toddlers when the toddlers are exposed to stressors, including brief separations, inoculations, and strange events (Gunnar, Brodersen, Nachmias, Buss, & Rigatuso, 1996; Hertsgaard, Gunnar, Erickson, & Nachmias, 1995; Spangler & Grossman, 1993). More research is needed to determine the specific cognitive and social processes that are effective in helping children to dampen their HPA reactions to stressors and how those processes might change with development.

For example, toddlers with secure attachments may have already developed beliefs about their experiences that help them to regulate their emotion. Researchers might explore children's narrative representations using the story-stem completion tasks, which have been useful in revealing young children's representations of relationships (Bretherton & Munholland, 1999). Recently, Toth, Cicchetti, Macfie, Rogosch, and Maughan (2000) measured the extent of conflictual representations from such narratives in preschool-age children who had been maltreated and found those narratives to partially mediate the association between child maltreatment and externalizing behavior problems.

Also needing further study is whether this purported supportive role of parents, as a function of the attachment relationship, changes as children develop. In particular, teachers and peers may take on some of this capacity as children move into spending more of their time in school and peer settings. Qualities of the environments in which children spend their time might also be worth exploring, in that they may vary in degree of stressfulness and supports that are available.

At the same time, it will be important to stay open to serendipitous findings, which, if replicated, may suggest modifications to our theoretical models. For example, Dawson et al. (1992) reported the surprising finding that securely attached infants of mothers with high levels of depression, compared to securely attached infants of nondepressed mothers, showed reduced left frontal activation when exposed to neutral or positive emotions. This pattern, typical of findings with depressed adults, was not found for insecurely attached infants (most of whom were classified as avoidant) of depressed mothers. If replicated with a larger sample, the findings fail to support the idea that insecure attachment mediates the association between maternal depression and adverse outcomes in the children. Instead, as suggested by Dawson et al., children who have avoidant relationships with their depressed mothers may in fact be protected in that they are less likely to model their mothers compared to those who have secure attachment relationships.

Along different lines, researchers might also benefit from borrowing the behavior genetics notion of active/evocative gene by environment interaction. Silberg and Rutter (2002) expanded on this idea for the situation of children with depressed parents. As applied to the situation of early adverse experiences, the vulnerabilities acquired as a function of the early adverse experiences might be considered the equivalent of an active/evocative gene. That is, children's abnormal stress reactivity, relative right frontal EEG activation, lower vagal tone, cognitive vulnerabilities, and so forth, might be expressed in ways that evoke particular reactions from others. Infants and young children with these characteristics might be less responsive, expressive, and attentive. Others might find these children to be particularly challenging and might react with harshness or withdrawal. It will be important for researchers to examine the extent to which children's biological and cognitive vulnerabilities are expressed in behavioral tendencies that, in turn, influence the patterns of parent–child interaction that emerge over children's early years of development.

Another formulation needing further study is that children with these biological and cognitive vulnerabilities may be particularly sensitive to environmental stressors. Children with one or more of these vulnerabilities would be expected to show more problems in response to stress than children with fewer of the vulnerabilities. As an example, Dettling, Gunnar, and Donzella (1999) found that being in day care was associated with a disruption of the circadian rhythm for cortisol in contrast to being at home and that child characteristics like shyness and poor self-control were related to increases in cortisol over the course of the day in day care, but not at home. Longitudinal studies would further explicate these pathways and the ways in which the unfolding transactional processes may contribute to risk for depression.

Finally, although not the emphasis of this chapter, the ideas presented here have important implications for interventions. For example, research that furthers our understanding of the neurobiology of the stress response could lead to the development of both biological and behavioral interventions. An important first step will be to establish the extent of contribution of any of the aspects of the fetal environment to the later emergence of depression. If a significant role is found, such individuals could be studied for other signs of vulnerability. For example, for those who are identified early as having abnormal stress responses, the goal would be to decrease individuals' vulnerability to develop depression, including increasing environmental supports. This is only one of many implications for preventive and therapeutic interventions that could be developed from the research exploring associations between early adverse experiences and depression.

ACKNOWLEDGMENTS

This work was partially funded by an Emory University Research Committee Grant and by Silvio O. Conti Center for the Neurobiology of Mental Disease NIH Grant No. MH58922.

REFERENCES

Abrams, S. M., Field, T., Scafidi, F., & Prodromidis, M. (1995). Newborns of depressed mothers. *Infant Mental Health Journal, 16,* 233–239.

Ainsworth, M. S., Blehar, M. C., Waters, E., & Wall, S. (1978). *Patterns of attachment: A psychological study of the strange situation.* Hillsdale, NJ: Erlbaum.

Amanat, E., & Butler, C. (1984). Oppressive behaviors in the families of depressed children. *Family Therapy, 11,* 65–75.

Asarnow, J. R., Ben-Meir, S. L., & Goldstein, M. J. (1987). Coping factors in childhood depressive and schizophrenia-spectrum disorders: A preliminary report. In K. Hahlweg & M. J. Goldstein (Eds.), *Understanding major mental disorder: The contribution of family interaction research* (pp. 123–138). New York: Family Process Press.

Bandura, A. (1977). *Social learning theory.* Englewood Cliffs, NJ: Prentice-Hall.

Barnett, D., Ganiban, J., & Cicchetti, D. (1999). Maltreatment, negative expressivity, and the development of Type D attachments from 12- to 24-months of age. *Monographs of the Society for Research in* Child Development, 64(3), 97–118.

Belsky, J. (1993). Etiology of child maltreatment: A developmental–ecological analysis. *Psychological Bulletin, 114,* 413–434.

Bretherton, I., & Munholland, K. A. (1999). Internal working models in attachment relationships: A construct revisited. In J. Cassidy & P. Shaver (Eds.), *Handbook of attachment: Theory, research, and clinical applications* (pp. 89–111). New York: Guilford Press.

Brooks-Gunn, J., & Lewis, M. (1979). Why "mama" and "papa"?: The development of social labels. *Child Development, 50,* 1203–1206.

Byrne, G., & Suomi, S. J. (1999). Social separation in infant *Cebus appella:* Patterns of behavioral and cortisol response. *International Journal of Developmental Neuroscience, 17,* 265–274.

Carlson, V., Cicchetti, D., Barnett, D., & Braunwald, K. (1989). Disorganized/disoriented attachment relationships in maltreated infants. *Developmental Psychology, 25,* 382–393.

Chugani, H. T. (1994). Development of regional brain glucose metabolism in relation to behavior and placticity. In G. Dawson & K. W. Fischer (Eds.), *Human behavior and the developing brain* (pp. 153–175). New York: Guilford Press.

Cicchetti, D., & Barnett, D. (1991). Attachment organization in maltreated preschoolers. *Development and Psychopathology, 3,* 397–411.

Cicchetti, D., & Rogosch, F. A. (1996). Equifinality and multifinality in developmental psychopathology. *Development and Psychopathology, 8,* 597–600.

Cicchetti, D., & Rogosch, F. A. (1997). The role of self-organization in the promotion of resilience in maltreated children. *Development and Psychopathology, 9,* 799–817.

Cicchetti, D., & Sroufe, L. A. (2000). The past as prologue to the future: The times, they've been a-changin'. *Development and Psychopathology, 12,* 255–264.

Cicchetti, D., & Toth, S. L. (1998). The development of depression in children and adolescents. *American Psychologist, 53,* 221–241.

Clarke, A. S., & Schneider, M. L. (1993). Prenatal stress has long-term effects on behavioral repsonses to stress in juvenile rhesus monkeys. *Development Psychobiology, 26,* 296–304.

Clarke, A. S., Wittwer, D. J., Abbott, D. H., & Schneider, M. L. (1994). Long-term effects of prenatal stress on HPA axis activity in juvenile rhesus monkeys. *Development Psychobiology, 27,* 256–269.

Cohn, J. F., & Campbell, S. (1992). Influence of maternal depression on infant affect regulation. In D. Cicetti & S. L. Toth (Eds.), *Rochester Symposium on Developmental Psychopathology: Vol. 4. Developmental perspectives on depression* (pp. 103–130). Rochester, NY: University of Rochester Press.

Cohn, J. F., & Elmore, M. (1988). Effect of contingent changes in mothers' affective expression on the organization of behavior in 3-month-old infants. *Infant Behavior and Development, 11,* 493–505.

Cohn, J. F., Matias, R., Tronick, E. Z., Lyons-Ruth, K., & Connell, D. (1986). Face-to-face interactions, spontaneous and structured, of mothers with depressive symptoms. *New Directions for Child Development, 34,* 31–46.

Cohn, J. F., & Tronick, E. Z. (1983). Three-month-old infants' reaction to simulated maternal depression. *Child Development, 54,* 185–193.

Cole, D. A., & Rehm, L. P. (1986). Family interaction patterns and childhood depression. *Journal of Abnormal Child Psychology, 14,* 297–314.

Crittendon, P. M. (1988). Relationships at risk. In J. Belsky & T. Nesworski (Eds.), *Clinical implications of attachment theory* (pp. 136–174). Hillsdale, NJ: Erlbaum.

Crittenden, P. M. (1998). Dangerous behavior and dangerous contexts: A 35-year perspective on research on the developmental effects of child physical abuse. In P. K. Trickett & C. J. Schellenbach (Eds.), *Violence against children in the family and the community* (pp. 11–38). Washington, DC: American Psychological Association Press.

Cummings, E. M., & Cicchetti, D. (1990). Toward a transactional model of relations between attachment and depression. In M. T. Greenberg, D. Cicchetti, & E. M. Cummings (Eds.), *Attachment in the preschool years: Theory, research, and intervention* (pp. 339–372). Chicago: University of Chicago Press.

Dadds, M. R., Sanders, M. R., Morrison, M., & Rebgetz, M. (1992). Childhood depression and conduct disorder: II. An analysis of family interaction patterns in the home. *Journal of Abnormal Psychology, 101,* 505–513.

Davidson, R. J., & Fox, N. A. (1982). Asymmetrical brain activity discriminates between positive versus negative affective stimuli in human infants. *Science, 218,* 1235–1237.

Davidson, R. J., & Fox, N. A. (1988). Cerebral asymmetry and emotion: Development and individual differences. In D. L. Molfese & S. J. Segalowitz (Eds.), *Brain lateralization in children: Developmental implications* (pp. 191–206). New York: Guilford Press.

Davidson, R. J., & Fox, N. A. (1989). Frontal brain asymmetry predicts infants' response to maternal separation. *Journal of Abnormal Psychology, 98,* 127–131.

Davidson, R. J., Schaffer, C. E., & Saron, C. (1985). Effects of lateralized stimulus presentations on the self-report of emotion and EEG asymmetry in depressed and non-depressed subjects. *Psychophysiology, 22,* 353–364.

Davies, P. T., & Cummings, E. M. (1994). Marital conflict and child adjustment: An emotional security hypothesis. *Psychological Bulletin, 116,* 387–411.

Dawson, G., Frey, K., Self, J., Panagiotides, H., Hessl, D., Yamada, E., & Rinaldi, J. (1999). Frontal brain electrical activity in infants of depressed and nondepressed mothers: Relation to variations in infant behavior. *Development and Psychopathology, 11,* 589–605.

Dawson, G., Klinger, L. G., Panagiotides, H., Spieker, S., & Frey, K. (1992). Infants of mothers with depressive symptoms: Electroencephalographic and behavioral findings related to attachment status. *Development and Psychopathology, 4,* 67–80.

DeMulder, E. K., & Radke-Yarrow, M. (1991). Attachment with affectively ill and well mothers: Concurrent behavioral correlates. *Development and Psychopathology, 3,* 227–242.

Dettling, A. C., Gunnar, M. R., & Donzella, B. (1999). Cortisol levels of young children in full-day childcare centers: Relations with age and temperament. *Psychoneuroendocrinology, 24,* 519–536.

Egeland, B., Pianta, R., & O'Brian, M. (1993). Maternal intrusiveness in infancy and child maladaptation in early school years. *Development and Psychopathology, 5,* 359–370.

Emory, E., Hatch, M., Blackmore, C., & Strock, B. (1993). *Psychophysiologic responses to stress during pregnancy.* Atlanta, GA: Centers for Disease Control and Prevention, Division of Reproductive Health.

Erikson, M., Egeland, B., & Pianta, R. (1989). The effects of maltreatment on the development of young children. In D. Cicchetti & V. Carlson (Eds.), *Child maltreatment: Theory and research on the causes and consequences of child abuse and neglect* (pp. 647–684). New York: Cambridge University Press.

Field, T. (1985). Attachment as psychological attunement: Being on the same wavelength. In M. Reite & T. Field (Eds.), *Psychobiology of attachment* (pp. 415–454). New York: Academic Press.

Field, T. (1994). The effects of mother's physical and emotional unavailability on emotion regulation. In N. A. Fox (Ed.), The development of emotion regulation: Biological and behavioral considerations. *Monographs of the Society for Research in Child Development, 59*(2–3, Serial No. 240), 208–227.

Field, T. M. (1998, April 2–5). *Depressed mothers and their newborns.* Paper presented at the 11th Biennial Conference on Infant Studies, Atlanta, GA.

Field, T. (2002). Maternal depression effects can be transmitted prenatally. In S. H. Goodman & I. H. Gotlib (Eds.), *Children of depressed parents: Mechanisms of risk and implications for treatment* (pp. 59–88). Washington, DC: American Psychological Association Press.

Field, T., Fox, N. A., Pickens, J., & Nawrocki, T. (1995). Relative right frontal EEG activation in 3- to 6-month-old infants of "depressed" mothers. *Developmental Psychology, 31,* 358–363.

Field, T., Healy, B., Goldstein, S., & Guthertz, M. (1990). Behavior–state matching and synchrony in mother–infant interactions of nondepressed versus depressed dyads. *Developmental Psychology, 26,* 7–14.

Field, T., Pickens, J., Fox, N. A., Nawrocki, T., & Gonzalez, J. (1995). Vagal tone in infants of depressed mothers. *Development and Psychopathology, 7,* 227–231.

Fox, N. A., & Davidson, R. J. (1986). Psychophysiological measures of emotion: New directions in developmental research. In C. E. Izard & P. B. Read (Eds.), *Measuring emotions in infants and children. Vol. 2: Cambridge studies in social and emotional development* (pp. 13–47). New York: Cambridge University Press.

Garber, J., Braafladt, N., & Zeman, J. (1991). The regulation of sad affect: An information-processing perspective. In J. Garber & K. A. Dodge (Eds.), *The development of emotion regulation and dysregulation* (pp. 208–240). New York: Cambridge University Press.

Gelles, R. J. (1998). The youngest victims: Violence toward children. In R. K. Berger (Ed.), *Issues in intimate violence* (pp. 5–24). Thousand Oaks, CA: Sage.

Glover, V. (1997). Maternal stress or anxiety in pregnancy and emotional development of the child. *British Journal of Psychiatry, 171,* 105–106.

Glover, V., Teixeira, J., Gitau, R., & Fisk, N. (1998, April 2–5). *Links between antenatal maternal anxiety and the fetus.* Paper presented at the 11th Biennial Conference on Infant Studies, Atlanta, GA.

Goodman, S. H., & Gotlib, I. H. (1999). Risk for psychopathology in the children of depressed parents: A developmental approach to the understanding of mechanisms. *Psychological Review, 106,* 458–490.

Gotlib, I. H., & Hammen, C. L. (1992). *Psychological aspects of depression: Toward a cognitive-interpersonal integration.* Chichester, UK: Wiley.

Gotlib, I. H., Ranganath, C., & Rosenfeld, J. P. (1998). Frontal EEG alpha asymmetry, depression, and cognitive functioning. *Cognition and Emotion, 12,* 449–478.

Gottman, J., Katz, L., & Hooven, C. (1997). *Meta-emotion: How families communicate emotionally.* Mahwah, NJ: Erlbaum.

Graham, Y. P., Heim, C., Goodman, S. H., Miller, A. H., & Nemeroff, C. B. (1999). The effects of neonatal stress on brain development: Implications for psychopathology. *Development and Psychopathology, 11,* 545–565.

Grych, J., & Fincham, F. (1990). Marital conflict and children's adjustment: A cognitive-contextual framework. *Psychological Bulletin, 108,* 267–290.

Gunnar, M. (2000). The effects of adversity on neuro-behavioral development. In C. A. Nelson (Ed.), *Early adversity and the development of stress reactivity and regulation* (Vol. 31, pp. 163–200). Hillsdale, NJ: Erlbaum.

Gunnar, M., Brodersen, L., Nachmias, M., Buss, K., & Rigatuso, J. (1996). Stress reactivity and attachment security. *Developmental Psychobiology, 29*(3), 191–204.

Gunnar, M. R., Bruce, J., & Grotevant, H. D. (2000). International adoption of institutionally reared children: Research and policy. *Development and Psychopathology, 12,* 677–693.

Hammen, C. (1988). Self cognitions, stressful events, and the prediction of depression in children of depressed mothers. *Journal of Abnormal Child Psychology, 16,* 347–360.

Hammen, C. (1992). Cognitive, life stress, and interpersonal approaches to a developmental psychopathology model of depression. *Development and Psychopathology, 4,* 189–206.

Handley, S. L., Dunn, T. L., Waldron, G., & Baker, J. M. (1980). Tryptophan, cortisol and puerperal mood. *British Journal of Psychiatry, 136,* 498–508.

Hart, J., Gunnar, M., & Cicchetti, D. (1995). Salivary cortisol in maltreated children: Evidence of relations between neuroendocrine activity and social competence. *Development and Psychopathology, 7,* 11–26.

Hart, J., Gunnar, M., & Cicchetti, D. (1996). Altered neuroendocrine activity in maltreated children related to symptoms of depression. *Development and Psychopathology, 8,* 201–214.

Heim, C., Newport, J., Heit, S., Graham, Y., Wilcox, M., Bonsall, R., Miller, A., & Nemeroff, C. (2000). Pituitary–adrenal and autonomic responses to stress in women after sexual and physical abuse in childhood. *Journal of the American Medical Association, 284,* 592–597.

Henriques, J. B., & Davidson, R. J. (1990). Regional brain electrical asymmetries discriminate between previously depressed subjects and healthy controls. *Journal of Abnormal Psychology, 99,* 22–31.

Henry, C., Kabbaj, M., Simon, H., Le Moal, M., & Maccari, S. (1994). Prenatal stress increases the hypothalamo–pituitary–adrenal axis response in young and adult rats. *Journal of Neuroendocrinology, 6,* 341–345.

Hertsgaard, L., Gunnar, M., Erickson, M., & Nachmias, M. (1995). Adrenocortical responses to the strange situation in infants with disorganized/disoriented attachment relationships. *Child Development, 66,* 1100–1106.

Hooley, J. M. (1998). Expressed emotion and psychiatric illness: From empirical data to clinical practice. *Behavior Therapy, 29,* 631–646.

Hooley, J. M., & Gotlib, I. H. (2000). A diathesis–stress conceptualization of expressed emotion and clinical outcome. *Journal of Applied and Preventive Psychology, 9,* 135–151.

Ingoldsby, E. M., Shaw, D. W., Owens, E. B., & Winslow, E. B. (1999). A longitudinal study of interparental conflict, emotional and behavioral reactivity, and preschoolers' adjustment problems among low-income families. *Journal of Abnormal Child Psychology, 27,* 343–356.

Katz, L., & Gottman, J. (1995). Vagal tone protects children from marital conflict. *Development and Psychopathology, 7,* 83–92.

Kay, G., Tarcic, N., Poltyrev, T., & Weinstock, M. (1998). Prenatal stress depresses immune function in rats. *Physiology and Behavior, 63,* 397–402.

Kaufman, J. (1991). Depressive disorders in maltreated children. *Journal of the American Academy of Child and Adolescent Psychiatry, 30,* 257–265.

Kinard, E. M. (1995). Mother and teacher assessments of behavior problems in abused children. *Journal of the American Academy of Child and Adolescent Psychiatry, 34,* 1043–1053.

Kovacs, M., Akiskal, H. S., Gatsonis, C., & Parrone, P. L. (1994). Childhood-onset dysthymic disorder: Clinical features and prospective naturalistic outcome. *Archives of General Psychiatry, 51,* 365–374.

Ladd, C., Huot, R. L., Thrivikraman, K. V., Nemeroff, C. B., Meaney, M. M., & Plotsky, P. M. (2000). Long-term behavioral and neuroendocrine adaptations to early adverse experiences. In E.

Mayer & C. Saper (Eds.), *Progress in brain research: The biological basis for mind–body interactions* (Vol. 122, pp. 79–101). Amsterdam, The Netherlands: Elsevier.

Ladd, C., Owens, M., & Nemeroff, C. (1996). Persistent changes in corticotropin-releasing factor neuronal systems induced by maternal deprivation. *Endocrinology, 137,* 1212–1218.

Levine, S., Haltmeyer, G., & Karas, G. (1967). Physiological and behavioral effects of infantile stimulation. *Physiology and Behavior, 2,* 55–63.

Lyons-Ruth, K., Lyubchik, A., Wolfe, R., & Bronfman, E. (2002). Parental depression and child attachment: Hostile and helpless profiles of parent and child behavior among families at risk. In S. H. Goodman & I. H. Gotlib (Eds.), *Children of depressed parents: Alternative pathways to risk for psychopathology* (pp. 89–120). Washington, DC: American Psychological Association Press.

Lyons-Ruth, K., Zoll, D. L., Connell, D., & Grunebaum, H. Y. (1986). The depressed mother and her one-year-old infant: Environment, interaction, attachment and infant development. In E. Tronick & T. Field (Eds.), *Maternal depression and infant disturbance* (pp. 61–82). New York: Jossey-Bass.

Malphurs, J., Larrain, C. M., Field, T., Pickens, J., Pelaez-Noqueras, M., Yando, R., & Bendell, D. (1996). Altering withdrawn and intrusive interaction behaviors of depressed mothers. *Infant Mental Health Journal, 17,* 152–160.

Milberger, S., Beiderman, J., Faraone, S. V., Chen, L., & Jones, J. (1996). Is maternal smoking during pregnancy a risk factor for attention deficit hyperactivity disorder in children? *American Journal of Psychiatry, 153,* 1138–1142.

Monroe, S. M., & Simons, A. D. (1991). Diathesis–stress theories in the context of life-stress research: Implications for depressive disorders. *Psychological Bulletin, 110,* 406–425.

Nolen-Hoeksema, S., Girgus, J. S., & Seligman, M. E. (1992). Predictors and consequences of childhood depressive symptoms: A 5-year longitudinal study. *Journal of Abnormal Psychology, 101,* 405–422.

O'Connor, T. G., Heron, J., Golding, J., the ALSPAC Study Team, Beveridge, M., & Glover, V. (in press). Maternal antenatal anxiety predicts behavioural problems in early childhood.

O'Connor, T. G., Rutter, M., & English and Romanian Adoptees Study Team, England. (2000). Attachment disorder behavior following early severe deprivation: Extension and longitudinal follow-up. *Journal of the American Academy of Child and Adolescent Psychiatry, 39,* 703–712.

Peterson, C., & Seligman, M. (1984). Causal explanations as a risk factor for depression: Theory and evidence. *Psychological Review, 91,* 347–374.

Pfeffer, C. R. (1996). *Severe stress and mental disturbance in children.* Washington, DC: American Psychiatric Press.

Pickens, J., & Field, T. (1993). Facial expressivity in infants of "depressed" mothers. *Developmental Psychology, 29,* 986–988.

Pihoker, C., Owens, M., Kuhn, C., Schanberg, S., & Nemeroff, C. (1993). Maternal separation in neonatal rats elicits activation of the hypothalamic–pituitary–adrenocortical axis: A putative role for corticotropin-releasing factor. *Psychoneuroendocrinology, 7,* 485–493.

Plomin, R. (1994). *Genetics and experience: The interplay between nature and nurture.* Thousand Oaks, CA: Sage.

Plomin, R., Emde, R. N., Braungart, J. M., Campos, J., Corley, R., Fulker, D. W., Kagan, J., Reznick, J. S., Robinson, J., Zahn-Waxler, C., & DeFries, J. C. (1993). Genetic change and continuity from fourteen to twenty months: The MacArthur Longitudinal Twin Study. *Child Development, 64,* 1354–1376.

Poltyrev, T., Keshet, G. I., Kay, G., & Weinstock, M. (1996). Role of experimental conditions in determining differences in exploratory behavior of prenatally stressed rats. *Developmental Psychobiology, 29,* 453–462.

Porges, S. W., Doussard-Roosevelt, J. A., & Maiti, A. K. (1994). Vagal tone and the physiological regulation of emotion. In N. A. Fox (Ed.), Emotion regulation: Behavioral and biological considerations. *Monographs of the Society for Research in Child Development, 59*(2–3), 167–186.

Racusin, G. R., & Kaslow, N. J. (1991). Assessment and treatment of childhood depression. In P. A. Keller & S. R. Hyman (Eds.), *Innovations in clinical practice: A sourcebook* (Vol. 10, pp. 223–243). Sarasota, FL: Professional Resource Exchange.

Radke-Yarrow, M. (1998). *Children of depressed mothers: From early childhood to maturity.* New York: Cambridge University Press.

Radke-Yarrow, M., Belmont, B., Nottelmann, E., & Bottomly, L. (1990). Young children's self-conceptions: Origins in the natural discourse of depressed and normal mothers and their children. In D. Cicchetti & M. Beeghly (Eds.), *The self in transition* (pp. 345–361). Chicago: University of Chicago Press.

Radke-Yarrow, M., Cummings, E. M., Kuczynski, L., & Chapman, J. (1985). Patterns of attachment in two- and three-year-olds in normal families and families with parental depression. *Child Development, 56,* 884–893.

Rehm, L. P., & Carter, A. S. (1990). Cognitive components of depression. In M. Lewis & S. M. Miller (Eds.), *Handbook of developmental psychopathology: Perspectives in developmental psychology* (pp. 341–351). New York: Plenum Press.

Rutter, M., Andersen-Wood, L., Beckett, C., Bredenkamp, D., Castle, J., Dunn, J., Ehrich, K., Groothues, C., Harborne, A., Hay, D., Jewett, J., Keaveney, L., Kreppner, J., Messer, J., O'Connor, T., Quinton, D., & White, A. (1999). Developmental catch-up, and deficit following adoption after severe global early privation. In S. J. Ceci & W. M. Williams (Eds.), *The nature–nurture debate: The essential readings. Essential readings in developmental psychology* (pp. 107–133). Malden, MA: Blackwell.

Sameroff, A. J. (1975). Transactional models in early social relations. *Human Development, 18,* 65–79.

Schneider, M. L. (1992). Prenatal stress exposure alters postnatal behavioral expressions under conditions of novelty challenge in rhesus monkey infants. *Developmental Psychobiology, 25,* 529–540.

Schneider, M. L., Roughton, E. C., Koehler, A. J., & Lubach, G. R. (1999). Growth and development following prenatal stress exposure in primates: An examination of ontogenetic vulnerability. *Child Development, 70,* 263–274.

Silberg, J. & Rutter, M. (2002). Nature–nurture interplay in the risks associated with parental depression. In S. H. Goodman & I. H. Gotlib (Eds.), *Children of depressed parents: Mechanisms of risk and implications for treatment* (pp. 13–36). Washington, DC: American Psychological Association Press.

Smith, R., Cubis, J., Brinsmead, M., Lewin, T., Singh, B., Owens, P., Eng-Cheng, C., Hall, C., Adler, R., Lovelock, M., Hurt, D., Rowley, M., & Nolan, M. (1990). Mood changes, obstetric experience and alterations in plasma cortisol, beta-endorphin and corticotrophin-releasing hormone during pregnancy and the puerperium. *Journal of Psychosomatic Research, 34,* 53–69.

Spangler, G., & Grossmann, K. E. (1993). Biobehavioral organization in securely and insecurely attached infants. *Child Development, 64,* 1439–1450.

Tennant, C., Bebbington, P. E., & Hurry, J. (1980). Parental death in childhood and risk of adult depressive disorders: A review. *Psychological Medicine, 10,* 289–299.

Teti, D. M., Gelfand, D. M., Messinger, D. S., & Isabella, R. (1995). Maternal depression and the quality of early attachment: An examination of infants, preschoolers, and their mothers. *Developmental Psychology, 31,* 364–376.

Toth, S. L., Cicchetti, D., Macfie, J., Rogosch, F. A., & Maughan, A. (2000). Narrative representations of moral-affiliative and conflictual themes and behavioral problems in maltreated preschoolers. *Journal of Clinical Child Psychology, 29,* 307–318.

Toth, S. L., Manly, J. T., & Cicchetti, D. (1992). Child maltreatment and vulnerability to depression. *Development and Psychopathology, 4,* 97–112.

Tronick, E. Z., & Gianino, A. F. (1986). The transmission of maternal disturbance to the infant. In E. Z. Tronick & T. Field (Eds.), *Maternal depression and infant disturbance* (pp. 5–12). San Francisco: Jossey-Bass.

Weinberg, M. K., & Tronick, E. Z. (1998). The impact of maternal psychiatric illness on infant development. *Journal of Clinical Psychiatry, 59,* 53–61.

Weller, E. B., & Weller, R. A. (1988). Neuroendocrine changes in affectively ill children and adolescents. *Psychiatric Clinics of North America, 6,* 41–54.

Williams, M. T., Hennessy, M. B., & Davis, H. N. (1998). Stress during pregnancy alters rat offspring morphology and ultrasonic vocalizations. *Physiology and Behavior, 63,* 337–343.

Zahn-Waxler, C., Chapman, M., & Cummings, E. M. (1984). Cognitive and social development in infants and toddlers with a bipolar parent. *Child Psychiatry and Human Development, 15,* 75–85.

Zuckerman, B. S., Bauchner, H., Parker, S., & Cabral, H. (1990). Maternal depressive symptoms during pregnancy and newborn irritability. *Developmental and Behavioral Pediatrics, 11,* 190–194.

11

Cognitive Vulnerability–Stress Models of Depression in a Self-Regulatory and Psychobiological Context

Lyn Y. Abramson, Lauren B. Alloy, Benjamin L. Hankin,
Gerald J. Haeffel, Donal G. MacCoon, and Brandon E. Gibb

Although depression has long been recognized as an important form of psychopathology, experimental psychopathologists neglected this disorder until the 1970s. At that time, research on depression burgeoned within clinical psychology, and many investigators began to emphasize cognitive processes in the etiology, maintenance, and treatment of depression.

Two developments at the University of Pennsylvania in the late 1960s and early 1970s galvanized this cognitive approach to depression. Coming from a clinical perspective, Aaron Beck (1967), a psychiatrist, had abandoned the psychoanalytic account of depression and had begun to develop a cognitive theory that emphasized the negative "automatic thoughts" that seemed to trigger depressive symptoms among his patients. At the same time, Martin Seligman (1975), an experimental psychologist, had begun to formulate his theory of learned helplessness and depression, based on laboratory research about the deleterious effects of uncontrollable, aversive events. Similar to Beck, Seligman emphasized that maladaptive cognitions such as pervasive expectancies of no control over events could precipitate depressive symptoms. These two cognitive theories ignited a veritable explosion of research on depression.

Although it is difficult to reconstruct the forces that fueled cognitive approaches to depression, Dykman and Abramson (1990) listed a few whose impact appears likely. First, the rise of information-processing approaches in general (e.g., Neisser, 1967) and the study of social cognition in particular (e.g., Nisbett & Ross, 1980) provided a basic science foundation for a cognitive approach to depression. Second, basic researchers (e.g., Lazarus, 1966) demonstrated that cognitive processes mediate emotional reactions, with the specific contents of thought (e.g., threat and danger) producing specific emotional reactions (e.g., anxiety). Third, many researchers had become disenchanted with the psychoanalytic approach to depression, in part because it seemed untestable. In contrast, the cognitive theories of Beck and Seligman were particularly appealing because of their scientific testability. Finally, many psychologists had begun to question the adequacy of purely behavioral accounts of various psychological phenomena (e.g., language acquisition; Chomsky, 1959).

In this chapter we present two cognitive theories of depression: the hopelessness theory (Abramson, Metalsky, & Alloy, 1989), a successor of Seligman's original helplessness theory of depression, and Beck's theory (Beck, 1967, 1987; Clark, Beck, & Alford, 1999). After evaluating the empirical status of these theories, we ask how well they can explain the "big facts" of depression. In addition, we elaborate the comparison of their respective conceptualization and assessment of cognitive vulnerability. We show that despite conceptual similarities, the cognitive vulnerability factors for depression hypothesized by the two theories are not identical. Then we use a self-regulatory perspective to elaborate the relation between cognitive vulnerability and rumination. Finally, in discussing future directions for research in this area, we embed the cognitive theories in a broader psychobiological context.

TWO COGNITIVE THEORIES OF DEPRESSION: HOPELESSNESS THEORY AND BECK'S THEORY

Overview of the Theories

Why are some people vulnerable to depression whereas others never seem to become depressed at all? According to the hopelessness theory and Beck's theory, the meaning or interpretation that people give to their experiences importantly influences whether they will become depressed and whether they will suffer repeated, severe, or long-duration episodes of depression. Indeed, the demonstrated efficacy of cognitive therapy for depression underscores the powerful clinical implications of a cognitive approach to depression.

Hopelessness Theory

According to the hopelessness theory (Abramson et al., 1989), the expectation that highly desired outcomes will not occur or that highly aversive outcomes will occur and that one cannot change this situation—hopelessness—is a proximal sufficient cause of depressive symptoms, specifically the hypothesized syndrome of "hopelessness depression" (HD). Symptoms of HD are hypothesized to include sadness, retarded initiation of voluntary responses, suicidality, low energy, apathy, psychomotor retardation, sleep disturbance, poor concentration, and mood-exacerbated negative cognitions.

How does a person become hopeless and, in turn, develop the symptoms of HD? As presented graphically in Figure 11.1, negative life events (or the nonoccurrence of desired positive life events) are "occasion setters" for people to become hopeless. However, the relation between negative life events and depression is imperfect; not all people become depressed when confronted with negative life events. According to hopelessness theory, three kinds of inferences that people may make when confronted with negative events contribute to the development of hopelessness and, in turn, depressive symptoms: causal attributions, inferred consequences, and inferred characteristics about the self. In brief, hopelessness and, in turn, depressive symptoms are likely to occur when negative life events are (1) attributed to stable (i.e., likely to persist over time) and global (i.e., likely to affect many areas of life) causes and viewed as important; (2) viewed as likely to lead

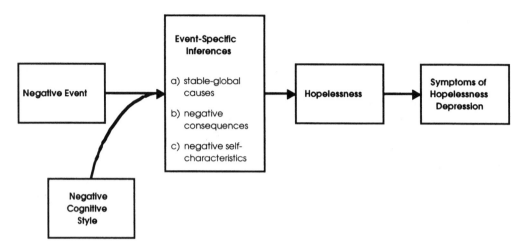

FIGURE 11.1. Causal chain in the hopelessness theory.

to other negative consequences; and (3) construed as implying that the person is unworthy or deficient. (When the causal attribution for a negative event is internal, stable, and global, hopelessness will be accompanied by lowered self-esteem and dependency as well as the other symptoms of HD.)

For example, suppose a student fails a test. According to the theory, the student should be likely to become depressed if she believes that the failure (1) was due to her low intelligence; (2) will prevent her from getting into medical school; and (3) means that she is worthless. In contrast, another student who fails the same test will be protected from becoming depressed if he believes that the failure (1) was due to not studying hard enough; (2) will motivate him to do especially well on the next test; and (3) has no implications for his self-worth.

In the hopelessness theory, informational cues in the situation (e.g., consensus, consistency, and distinctiveness information; Kelley, 1967), as well as individual differences in cognitive style, influence the content of people's inferences about cause, consequence, and self when negative life events occur. Individuals who exhibit a general style to attribute negative events to stable and global causes, to infer that current negative events will lead to further negative consequences, and to infer that the occurrence of negative events means that they are deficient or unworthy, should be more likely to make these depressogenic inferences about a given negative event than should individuals who do not exhibit this cognitive style. However, in the absence of negative life events, people exhibiting the depressogenic inferential style should be no more likely to develop hopelessness and, in turn, depressive symptoms than people not exhibiting this style. This aspect of the theory is a cognitive vulnerability–stress component: negative cognitive styles are the cognitive vulnerability and negative life events are the stress. A cognitive vulnerability in a particular content domain (e.g., for interpersonal events) provides "specific vulnerability" when a person is confronted with negative events in that same domain (e.g., social rejection).

Additional environmental factors also have been hypothesized to moderate the cognitive vulnerability–stress interaction. Much evidence indicates that social support buffers against depression when people experience stressful events (Barnett & Gotlib, 1988; Monroe & Hadjiyannakis, Chapter 13, this volume). Material, emotional, and informational support from others may buffer against depression by preventing the development of hopelessness. In particular, other people may provide "adaptive inferential feedback" that promotes benign, rather than depressogenic, inferences about the causes, consequences, and meaning of negative events (Panzarella, Alloy, & Whitehouse, 2002).

Beck's Theory

Beck's cognitive theory of depression has been interpreted in several different ways (e.g., Abramson & Alloy, 1990; Abramson et al., 1989; Haaga, Dyck, & Ernst, 1991). However, in all accounts, the etiological hypotheses of Beck's (1967, 1987; Clark et al., 1999) theory are conceptually similar to those of the hopelessness theory. As Figure 11.2 shows, in Beck's theory, maladaptive self-schemata containing dysfunctional attitudes involving themes of loss, inadequacy, failure, and worthlessness constitute the cognitive vulnerability for depression. Such dysfunctional attitudes often involve the theme that one's happiness and worth depend on being perfect or on other people's approval. Examples of dysfunctional attitudes include "If I fail partly, it is as bad as being a complete failure" or "I am nothing if a person I love doesn't love me." When these hypothesized depressogenic self-schemata are activated by the occurrence of negative life events (the stress), they generate specific negative cognitions (automatic thoughts) that take the form of overly pessimistic views of oneself, one's world, and one's future (the *negative cognitive triad*) that, in turn, lead to sadness and the other symptoms of depression. In the absence of activation by negative events, however, the depressogenic self-schemata remain latent, less accessible to awareness, and do not directly lead to negative automatic thoughts or depressive mood and symptoms (Haaga et al., 1991). Beck (1987) has hypothesized that his cognitive vulnerability–stress model applies to only some forms of depression, particularly nonendogenous, unipolar depressions.

In Beck's (1983, 1987) theory, individual differences in the value people place on different kinds of experiences influence whether or not particular negative events will activate the cognitive vulnerability (depressogenic self-schemata) for depression. People who value social relationships, intimacy, and acceptance from others are high in "sociotropy" and are likely to become depressed when they experience social rejection or interpersonal losses. In contrast, people who are high in "autonomy" and value independence, freedom, and achievement will be more likely to become depressed when they experience failures or threats to their personal control.

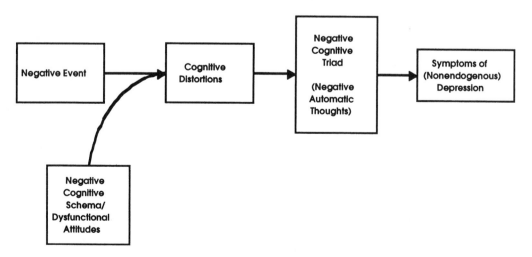

FIGURE 11.2. Causal chain in Beck's theory.

Comparison of the Hopelessness Theory and Beck Theory: Similarities and Differences

Although differing in some specifics, the hopelessness and Beck theories share many important features. At the most basic level, both theories emphasize the role of cognition in the origins and maintenance of depression. In addition, both theories contain a cognitive vulnerability hypothesis in which negative cognitive patterns increase people's vulnerability to depression when they experience negative life events in congruent or highly valued content domains. Moreover, both theories also propose a mediating sequence of negative inferences that influence whether or not negative events will lead to depressive symptoms. Finally, both theories recognize the heterogeneity of depression and either explicitly (hopelessness theory) or implicitly (Beck's theory) propose the existence of a cognitively mediated subtype of depression. This subtype may not map neatly on to any currently diagnosed category of depression. Instead, the hypothesized subtype may cut across currently diagnosed categories of clinical depression, or even some anxiety or personality disorders, and may be found in subsyndromal form in nonclinical populations as well. Of course, the possibility exists that this "subtype" may not be a bona fide subtype with characteristic cause, symptoms, course, treatment, and prevention. Instead, the etiological chains featured in the hopelessness and Beck theories may be two of many pathways to a final common outcome of depressive symptoms.

Despite their similarities, there is one striking difference between the hopelessness and Beck theories. To understand this difference, it is useful to distinguish between cognitive *processes* and cognitive *products* (Ingram, Miranda, & Segal, 1998). Cognitive processes involve the operations of the cognitive system such as informational encoding, retrieval, and attentional allocation. Cognitive products are the end result of the cognitive system's information-processing operations and consist of the cognitions and thoughts that the individual experiences. Inferences about cause, consequences, and self, as featured in the hopelessness theory, are examples of cognitive products. According to hopelessness theory, depressive and nondepressive cognition differ in content (e.g., stable, global vs. unstable, specific causal attributions for negative events) but not in process. In contrast, Beck's (1967) original theory emphasized that depressive and nondepressive cognition differs not only in content but also in process. Beck (1987) suggested that the inference process is "schema-driven" among depressives and "data-driven" among nondepressives. Thus, although both Abramson et al. (1989) and Beck (1967, 1987) emphasized that depressed people's inferences are negative, Beck further proposed that depressed people's inferences are unwarranted given current information. Specifically, Beck suggested that depressed individuals ignore positive situational information and are unduly influenced by current negative situational information in making their negative inferences. Nondepressed individuals, in contrast, appropriately utilize current information in making inferences. In short, Beck's (1967, 1987) original theory emphasized that depressive cognition is distorted whereas hopelessness theory is silent on the distortion issue.

Empirical Evaluation of the Theories

There are five central predictions from hopelessness theory and Beck's theory. First, both theories posit an interaction between cognitive vulnerability and stress that culminates in depressive symptoms. That is, cognitive vulnerability is hypothesized to moderate the effects of a negative life event on depression. When faced with a negative life event, individuals who exhibit cognitive vulnerability are hypothesized to be at higher risk for developing depression than are individuals who do not exhibit cognitive vulnerability. Second, both theories include mediating links (e.g., hopelessness, negative cognitive triad) between the occurrence of a negative life event and the formation of depressive symptoms. For example, in the hopelessness theory, when cognitively vulnerable individuals encounter a negative life event, they are hypothesized to make depressogenic inferences about the event's cause, consequences, and implications for their self-concept. According to the hopelessness theory, these depressogenic inferences contribute to hopelessness, which in turn contributes to depression. Third, both theories posit causal chains that culminate in a particular subtype of depression (e.g., HD). Fourth, both theories hypothesize that a "match" in a particular domain (e.g., interpersonal or achievement) between the cognitive vulnerability and the negative event increases the likelihood of the development of depressive symptoms relative to a domain "mismatch." Finally, Beck's original theory emphasizes that depressive cognition is distorted; hopelessness theory is silent on this issue.

Research Designs for Testing the Etiological Hypotheses of the Cognitive Theories

What is the most powerful way to test the etiological hypotheses of the cognitive theories of depression? One research design that has figured prominently in testing the cognitive vulnerability hypotheses featured in Beck's theory and hopelessness theory is the *remitted* depression paradigm (see Ingram & Siegle, Chapter 4, this volume, and Just, Abramson, & Alloy, 2001, for reviews). In this design, the cognitive patterns of depressed individuals are examined during the depressed state as well as later, when the depression has remitted. The key assumption underlying the remitted design is that if negative cognitive patterns provide vulnerability for depression, they must be trait-like and persist beyond the remission of a current episode. According to this logic, any cognitive pattern not exhibited by previously depressed individuals cannot qualify as a vulnerability for depression. However, recent researchers have challenged the theoretical fidelity of remitted depression studies, as they are typically conducted, as potent tests of the cognitive theories (e.g., Just et al., 2001; Persons & Miranda, 1992). In particular, Just et al. (2001) argued that the conclusions based on the typical remitted depression studies are not justified because they are based on an erroneous assumption—namely, that cognitive vulnerability should be an immutable trait (see also Ingram et al., 1998). Making an analogy to the immune system and biological vulnerability, Just et al. (2001) showed that a factor need not be immutable to qualify as a vulnerability factor. If the remitted depression design is not adequate for testing the etiological hypotheses of the cognitive theories, what is?

A more powerful strategy for testing the cognitive vulnerability and other etiological hypotheses of the cognitive theories of depression is the behavioral *high-risk design* (e.g., Depue et al., 1981). As with the genetic high-risk paradigm, the behavioral high-risk design involves studying participants who do not currently have the disorder of interest but who are hypothesized to be at high or low risk for developing it. In contrast to the genetic high-risk paradigm, however, individuals in the behavioral high-risk study are selected on the basis of hypothesized psychological, rather than genetic, vulnerability or invulnerability to the disorder. Thus, to test the cognitive vulnerability hypothesis of depression, one would select currently nondepressed people who are at high versus low risk for depression based on the presence versus absence of the hypothesized depressogenic cognitive patterns. One would then compare these cognitively high- and low-risk groups on their likelihood of exhibiting depression both in the past (retrospective version of the design) and in the future (prospective version of the design). The prospective version of the design is superior to the retrospective version because the cognitive "vulnerability" that is assessed in the latter might actually be a *scar* of a prior depressive episode (Rohde, Lewinsohn, & Seeley, 1991) rather than a *causal* factor in that prior episode (Gotlib & Abramson, 1999).

Etiological Hypotheses Featured in Hopelessness Theory

Many cross-sectional studies have established that cognitive vulnerability (typically attributional style and dysfunctional attitudes) is associated positively with depression in adults (Sweeney, Anderson, & Bailey, 1986; Haaga et al., 1991) and in children/adolescents (Gladstone & Kaslow, 1995; Joiner & Wagner, 1995). However, such cross-sectional studies do not provide strong tests of the cognitive vulnerability hypothesis because they cannot distinguish between the possibility that the cognitive vulnerability came first and contributed to the occurrence of depression as hypothesized in the cognitive theories and the alternative possibility that cognitive vulnerability does not contribute to depression and, instead, is a correlate or consequence of depression. Prospective behavioral high-risk studies are needed to establish temporal precedence. The prospective studies described below used a variant of a behavioral high-risk design (conceptualizing cognitive vulnerability as a continuous factor) to test the etiological hypotheses of the hopelessness theory for the development of depressive symptoms.

Recent prospective studies with children (Hilsman & Garber, 1995; Nolen-Hoeksema, Girgus, & Seligman, 1992; Robinson, Garber, & Hilsman, 1995), adolescents (Hankin, Abramson, & Siler, 2001), and adults (Alloy & Clements, 1998; Alloy, Just, & Panzarella, 1997; Hankin, Abramson, Miller, & Haeffel, 2002; Metalsky, Halberstadt, & Abramson, 1987; Metalsky & Joiner, 1992; Metalsky, Joiner, Hardin, & Abramson, 1993; Reilly-Harrington, Alloy, Fresco, & Whitehouse, 1999) consistently have found that individuals who exhibit the hypothesized cognitive vulnerability featured in the hopelessness theory are more likely to develop depressive moods and/or depressive symptoms when they experience negative life events than are individuals who do not show this vulnerability. The few studies examining whether hopelessness mediates the relation between the cognitive vulnerability × stress interaction and increases in depression have provided partial support in adolescents (Hankin et al., 2001) and adults (Alloy & Clements, 1998; Metalsky & Joiner, 1992). Further work is needed to more fully test the hopelessness-as-mediator hypothesis of the hopelessness theory.

Work has only just begun to test the specific vulnerability or domain-match hypothesis of hopelessness theory. Supporting this hypothesis, in their academic midterm study Metalsky et al. (1987) reported that attributional vulnerability in the academic, but not the interpersonal, domain interacted with receipt of a low grade to predict sustained increases in depressed mood. Also consistent with the domain-match hypothesis, Joiner and Rudd (1995) found that negative attributional style for interpersonal events interacted with severe interpersonal disruptions to predict increases in suicidal ideation.

Hopelessness Depression Subtype Hypothesis

Preliminary evidence supports the HD subtype hypothesis. Five prospective studies have demonstrated that the cognitive vulnerability × stress interaction featured in hopelessness theory predicts changes in HD symptoms (Alloy & Clements, 1998; Alloy, Just, & Panzarella, 1997; Hankin et al., 2001, 2002; Metalsky & Joiner, 1997). Moreover, using structural equation modeling in clinical and nonclinical samples, Joiner et al. (2001) found support for the HD symptom cluster as a cohesive and distinct syndrome that stood out statistically even from closely related depressive symptoms.

Etiological Hypotheses and Nonendogenous Subtype Hypothesis Featured in Beck's Theory

Testing Beck's theory, recent prospective studies have found that the cognitive vulnerability × stress interaction (more specifically, dysfunctional attitudes × negative events) predicts increases in depressive symptoms over time (Brown, Hammen, Craske, & Wickens, 1995; Dykman & Johll, 1998; Hankin et al., 2002; Joiner, Metalsky, Lew, & Klocek, 1999; Klocek, Oliver, & Ross, 1997; Kwon & Oei, 1992). Regarding the mediational component, two prospective studies found that depression-specific negative thoughts mediated the association between the cognitive vulnerability × stress interaction and subsequent changes in depression (Joiner et al., 1999; Kwon & Oei, 1992). A number of studies have examined whether a domain match in Beck's theory (sociotropy/interpersonal and autonomy/achievement) is associated with depression. However, many of these studies have been cross-sectional and have produced inconsistent findings (see Coyne & Whiffen, 1995, for a critical review). Although a number of studies found that sociotropic individuals are particularly likely to become depressed following negative interpersonal events, some studies found that these individuals also become depressed following negative achievement events. Support is even less strong for the prediction that autonomous individuals are particularly likely to become depressed following negative achievement, but not interpersonal, events. The one study to date (Gibb et al., 2001) testing whether the cognitive vulnerability–stress and mediational components in Beck's theory lead to the hypothesized nonendogenous subtype found support for this formulation.

The Cognitive Vulnerability to Depression Project

The Cognitive Vulnerability to Depression (CVD) Project is a collaborative, two-site (Temple University and the University of Wisconsin) study that used both a retrospective and prospective behavioral high-risk design to test the cognitive vulnerability and other etiological hypotheses of hopelessness and Beck's theories of depression for both depressive symptoms and clinically significant depressive episodes. In the CVD Project, first-year college students at either high or low cognitive risk for depression who were nondepressed and had no other current Axis I psychopathology at the outset of the study were followed for 2.5 years with self-report and structured interview assessments every 6 weeks. The participants then were followed for an additional 3 years, with assessments occurring every 4 months.

Because the cognitively high-risk (HR) participants were required to score in the highest quartile on measures of the cognitive vulnerabilities featured in both the hopelessness theory (Cognitive Style Questionnaire [CSQ]; Abramson, Metalsky, & Alloy, 2000) and Beck's theory (expanded Dysfunctional Attitude Scale [DAS]; Weissman & Beck, 1978), and the cognitively low-risk (LR) participants were required to score in the lowest quartile on both of these measures, the CVD Project provides a broad test of a "generic" or "pooled" cognitive vulnerability hypothesis. A strength of this study is that the two sites permit a built-in assessment of generalizability of results.

The initial findings of the CVD Project provided direct and compelling support for the cognitive theories of depression. With their retrospective behavioral high-risk design, Alloy et al. (2000) found that, consistent with the cognitive vulnerability hypothesis, the HR group showed greater lifetime prevalence of DSM-III-R/RDC major depressive disorder, RDC minor depressive disorder, and HD than did the LR group (see also Alloy, Lipman, & Abramson, 1992, for similar findings). Moreover, the prospective results (Abramson et al., 1999; Alloy, Abramson, et al., 1999) also were consistent with the cognitive vulnerability hypothesis. Among participants with no prior history of depression, HR participants showed a greater likelihood than LR participants of a *first onset* of DSM-III-R/RDC major depressive disorder, RDC minor depressive disorder, and HD during the initial 2.5 year prospective follow-up. These findings provide especially important support for the cognitive vulnerability hypothesis because they are based on a truly prospective test, uncontaminated by prior history of depression.

What about those participants who, though nondepressed at the outset of the CVD Project, did have a prior history of clinically significant depression? This subsample allows a test of whether the cognitive vulnerability hypothesis holds for recurrences of depression, which is particularly important given that depression often is recurrent (Belsher & Costello, 1988; see Boland & Keller, Chapter 2, this volume, for a review of this literature). Consistent with the cognitive vulnerability hypothesis, HR participants with a past history of clinically significant depression were more likely than LR participants with previous depression to develop recurrences of depressive episodes during the follow-up.

Finally, HR participants also were more likely than LR participants to exhibit suicidality, on a continuum from suicidal ideation to suicidal behavior, during the initial prospective follow-up (Abramson et al., 1998). Fortunately, no participants died by suicide.

These findings provide the first demonstration that the hypothesized cognitive vulnerabilities do indeed confer risk for both first onsets and recurrences of full-blown, clinically significant depressive disorders, the hypothesized subtype of HD, and suicidality. These results refute the criticism that the cognitive theories of depression apply only to mild depression. Moreover, the results also provide support for the hypothesis that the specific subtype of HD exists in nature and conforms to theoretical description. Complementing findings from the prospective portion of the CVD Project, Hankin et al. (2002) found that cognitive vulnerability (both negative cognitive styles from hopelessness theory and dysfunctional attitudes from Beck's theory) interacted with negative life events occurring over a 2-year prospective interval to predict onsets of clinically significant depressive episodes.

Recently, Lewinsohn, Joiner, and Rohde (2001) reported that both dysfunctional attitudes (at the level of a statistical trend) and attributional styles interacted with stress to predict major depressive disorder (MDD) among adolescents over a 1-year interval. Interestingly, the form of the interaction between cognitive vulnerability and stress differed for attributional styles and dysfunctional attitudes. Specifically, attributional style had its largest effect on depression under lower levels of stress, whereas it had little impact on depression under higher levels of stress. This result for attributional style is intriguing because it supports the *titration* model of vulnerability–stress relations featured in the original statement of the hopelessness theory (Abramson et al., 1989; Abramson, Alloy, & Hogan, 1997; see also Monroe & Simons, 1991). According to the titration model of the cognitive vulnerability–stress interaction, lower "doses" of stress are sufficient to trigger depression in cognitively vulnerable individuals, whereas higher doses of stress are required to precipitate depression in nonvulnerable individuals. At lower levels of stress, only cognitively vulnerable individuals may become depressed, whereas at very high levels of stress both cognitively vulnerable and nonvulnerable individuals alike may become depressed. In contrast to the titration model, it typically has been assumed that the vulnerability–stress model featured in both hopelessness theory and Beck's theory is a *synergistic* interaction in which only cognitively vulnerable individuals who experience a high level of stress develop depression. Lewinsohn et al.'s (2001) results for dysfunctional attitudes, as well as the results of the prior studies reviewed above, conform to this synergistic interaction model. However, Lewinsohn et al. (2001) acknowledged limitations in their assessment of attributional styles and stress that preclude definitive conclusions from their study about the relations of attributional style versus dysfunctional attitudes with stress in precipitating depression among adolescents. An exciting direction for future research is to specify more precisely how cognitive vulnerability and stress combine to produce depression.

Summary of Empirical Tests of the Etiological Hypotheses in the Hopelessness and Beck Theories

Results of prior studies using methods less adequate than the behavioral high-risk design (e.g., remitted depression design) to test the etiological hypotheses of the cognitive theories of depression have been equivocal (see Barnett & Gotlib, 1988, and Just et al., 2001, for reviews). In contrast, the more recent studies reviewed above using or approximating a behavioral high-risk design have obtained considerable support for the etiological hypotheses of these theories. Indeed, we are especially excited by the findings from the CVD Project demonstrating that the hypothesized cognitive vulnerabilities confer risk for full-blown clinically significant depressive disorders. Although this newer work is very promising, future studies are needed to test more fully the role of cognition in the etiology of depression. Future work should target evaluations of the relations between cognitive vulnerability and stress in predicting clinically significant depression, the hypothesized mediating links, and the specific vulnerability hypothesis. Finally, it will be important to further explore whether HD actually is a bona fide subtype of depression.

Beck's Cognitive Distortion Hypothesis

In contrast to Beck's (1967, 1987) original characterization of "depressive cognitive distortion" and "nondepressive accuracy," research has demonstrated pervasive optimistic biases among nondepressed people and a "depressive realism effect" in which depressed individuals actually are more accurate than nondepressed individuals (see Alloy, Albright, Abramson, & Dykman, 1990, for a review). For example, nondepressed individuals often exhibit an "illusion of control" in which they believe that they control outcomes over which they objectively have no control, whereas depressed individuals seem less susceptible to this illusion (e.g., Alloy et al., 1990). Research on optimistic biases among "normal" people suggests that in formulating theories of depressive cognition, clinical researchers may have been wrong in assuming accuracy as the baseline of normal cognitive functioning. Consistent with Coyne and Gotlib's (1983) conceptual analysis, laboratory work has demonstrated that *both* depressed and nondepressed people show cognitive biases and illusions that are consistent with their preconceived beliefs or schemata (Dykman, Abramson, Alloy, & Hartlage, 1989; Gotlib, McLachlan, & Katz, 1988; McCabe & Gotlib, 1995). Thus, although work on depressive realism and nondepressive optimistic illusions has not established that depressed people always are more accurate than nondepressed people, these studies nevertheless have posed an important challenge to Beck's original portrayal of depressed people as either impervious to information in their environments or hopelessly biased by pervasive negative schemata and of nondepressed people as completely data-driven and free of the influence of biasing schemata (Gotlib & Abramson, 1999). In response to this work, modifications of Beck's theory have been proposed that emphasize differences in the content, rather than in the process, of depressive and nondepressive cognition (e.g., Dykman et al., 1989; Haack, Metalsky, Dykman, & Abramson, 1996; Haaga & Beck, 1995; Hollon & Garber, 1988).

How Well Can the Cognitive Theories Explain the "Big Facts" of Depression?

Descriptive research has produced some big, undisputed facts about depression. We consider seven of these facts and evaluate how well the cognitive theories can explain them.

First, depression is *recurrent* (Belsher & Costello, 1988; Boland & Keller, Chapter 2, this volume). One plausible explanation for this finding is that some individuals are especially depression-prone and likely to experience multiple episodes of depression. This possibility is consistent with the cognitive vulnerability hypothesis and the findings from the CVD Project that negative cognitive styles/dysfunctional attitudes provide vulnerability to both first onsets and recurrences of depression. Of interest and consistent with Teasdale's (1988) differential activation hypothesis, Lewinsohn, Allen, Seeley, and Gotlib (1999) reported that dysphoria, in combination with dysfunctional attitudes, was a stronger predictor of recurrence than of first onset of depression. These results, combined with those from the CVD Project, suggest that the processes underlying first onsets and recurrences are not completely identical, although cognitive vulnerability contributes importantly to both first onsets and recurrences.

Second, *life events* play a role in the development of depression (Brown & Harris, 1989; Monroe & Hadjiyannakis, Chapter 13, this volume). This fact is incorporated directly into the cognitive vulnerability–stress component of the cognitive theories (i.e., life events moderate the role of cognitive vulnerability).

Third, depression can be lethal as it clearly increases risk for *suicide* (e.g., Davila & Daley, 2000). Research has suggested that hopelessness is the key factor contributing to suicide among depressed individuals (e.g., Minkoff, Bergman, Beck, & Beck, 1973). Drawing on this work, Abramson et al. (1989) hypothesized that suicidality, on a continuum from suicidal ideation to completed suicide, is a core symptom of HD. Consistent with this hypothesis, Abramson et al. (1998) reported results from the CVD Project indicating that cognitively vulnerable individuals were more likely to show suicidality, mediated by hopelessness, over the prospective follow-up than were cognitively nonvulnerable individuals.

Fourth, depression is a *common* disorder (Kessler et al., 1994). This fact suggests that typical, as opposed to rare, factors cause depression. Negative life events, featured in the causal chains of the cognitive theories, are, unfortunately, all too common. Furthermore, as we described above, depressed individuals do not appear to exhibit rare or aberrant cognitive processes. Instead, depressed and nondepressed people likely rely on much the same cognitive processes but differ mainly in cognitive content (e.g., Dykman et al., 1989).

Fifth, the rates of depression *surge* during middle to late *adolescence* (Hankin et al., 1998). A rise in negative life events, the stressor in the cognitive vulnerability × stress interaction depicted in the cognitive theories, has been observed throughout adolescence, and this developmental trajectory parallels the increase in depression rates (Ge, Lorenz, Conger, Elder, & Simons, 1994). Furthermore, cognitive vulnerability appears to have developed and been consolidated by late childhood (Nolen-Hoeksema et al., 1992; Turner & Cole, 1994), and thus has become accessible for the cognitive vulnerability × stress interaction. Finally, the mediating link of hopelessness is within cognitive capability and available for participation in the causal chain culminating in depression by early adolescence (e.g., Kazdin, French, Unis, Esveldt-Dawson, & Sherick, 1983; Hankin et al., 2001). Thus, the cognitive theories can explain the surge in depression among adolescence through a rise in negative events that can interact with consolidated cognitive vulnerability which, in turn, can contribute to hopelessness and thereby eventuate in depression.

Sixth, *gender differences* in depression exist among adults, with twice as many women as men experiencing depression (Nolen-Hoeksema, Chapter 21, this volume). Consistent with this gender difference in depression, women show elevations on two of the factors featured in the causal chain of hopelessness theory: negative life events, especially in the interpersonal domain (see Hankin & Abramson, 2001, for a review) and negative cognitive styles (Angell et al., 1999; Hankin & Abramson, 2002). Holding everything else equal, then, women should be at greater risk than men for the depressogenic cognitive vulnerability × stress interaction, and therefore for depression. Surprisingly, men actually exhibit *greater* dysfunctional attitudes, the cognitive vulnerability featured in Beck's theory, than do women (e.g., Angell et al., 1999; Gotlib, 1984; Haeffel et al., 2002). It is surprising that opposite patterns of gender differences are found on measures of cognitive vulnerability for the two cognitive theories. However, as we argue below, a growing body of empirical work indicates that the cognitive vulnerabilities defined in Beck's theory and in hopelessness theory, respectively, represent somewhat distinct constructs. Indeed, negative cognitive styles, as defined in hopelessness theory, may be more generally maladaptive whereas some "dysfunctional" attitudes such as perfectionism may be adaptive when paired with other characteristics such as high ability and/or high self-efficacy but maladaptive when paired with low ability and/or low self-efficacy. Perhaps males show elevations on the more "adaptive" dysfunctional attitudes. Future work is necessary to determine why men's elevations on dysfunctional attitudes do not appear to put them at heightened risk for depression.

Finally, depression long has been viewed as *heterogeneous* with multiple *causes*. The cognitive theories recognize this heterogeneity by postulating hypothesized depressive subtypes.

In showing that the cognitive theories can explain, or at least are consistent with, these big facts about depression, we don't mean to imply that other theories cannot also explain these facts. We simply are suggesting that the cognitive theories meet this explanatory requirement.

ADDITIONAL CONSIDERATIONS IN THE CONCEPTUALIZATION AND ASSESSMENT OF COGNITIVE VULNERABILITY

Cognitive vulnerability is a core construct in the cognitive theories of depression that provides the mechanism by which, given the same negative life event, some individuals become depressed whereas others do not. This construct, more so than any other in the theories, has captured research attention. Indeed, despite the fact that Abramson et al.'s (1989) theory is termed the hopelessness theory and features hopelessness as a proximal sufficient cause of depressive symptoms, far more work testing the theory has examined predictions about cognitive vulnerability than about hopelessness. Perhaps researchers have focused on cognitive vulnerability because it addresses the intuition of both clinical scientists and laypeople that some individuals seem to be highly susceptible to depression, whereas others appear to be highly resistant, even under the most dire circumstances.

A Comparison of the Cognitive Vulnerability Construct in Beck's Theory and Hopelessness Theory

Up to this point, we have focused largely on the similarities of the cognitive vulnerabilities featured in hopelessness theory and Beck's theory. Despite these conceptual similarities, however, the two theories' respective hypothesized cognitive vulnerability factors to depression are not identical. For Beck, cognitive vulnerability consists of negative schemata containing dysfunctional attitudes. According to Beck, Rush, Shaw, and Emery (1979), dysfunctional attitudes differ from more adaptive attitudes in that the former are inappropriate, rigid, and excessive. Beck (1976) provided examples of dysfunctional attitudes hypothesized to provide vulnerability to depression (pp. 255–256): "In order to be happy, I have to be successful in whatever I undertake," "If I make a mistake, it means that I am inept," and "My value as a person depends on what others think of me." As these examples illustrate, dysfunctional attitudes often are expressed in absolute and extreme terms.

Indeed, Beck et al. (1979) described dysfunctional attitudes as often incorporating phrases such as "should," "have to," and "must." Additionally, Beck contended that many dysfunctional attitudes have an "*if, then*" contingency as in one of the examples above. These rigid, extreme, and idealized standards (i.e., dysfunctional attitudes) often involve themes regarding approval and love from others, performance, perfectionistic standards, and self-worth.

In the hopelessness theory (Abramson et al., 1989), cognitive vulnerability is defined as the tendency to make negative inferences about the causes, consequences, and self-implications of a negative life event. Some of the dysfunctional attitudes in Beck's theory clearly overlap with the negative inferential tendencies featured in hopelessness theory. For example, the dysfunctional attitude "If I make a mistake, it means that I am inept" is an instance of making a negative inference about the self (I'm inept) given the occurrence of a negative life event (making a mistake). Given this overlap, it is not surprising that positive correlations between the CSQ and the DAS routinely are obtained (e.g., Haeffel et al., 2002). However, other aspects of dysfunctional attitudes, such as their focus on an individual's rigid and extreme rules for happiness, have no apparent counterpart in the hopelessness theory.

Consistent with these theoretical distinctions, a growing body of empirical evidence indicates that the cognitive vulnerabilities defined in Beck's theory and hopelessness theory, respectively, represent *distinct* constructs. Cross-sectional studies investigating the factor structures of measures of dysfunctional attitudes and attributional style have found that they load on two distinct factors labeled Self-Regard and Attributional Generality, respectively (e.g., Joiner & Rudd, 1996). In addition, Spangler, Simons, Monroe, and Thase (1997) reported that depressed patients with a cognitive vulnerability–stress match, according to Beck's theory, were largely distinct from patients with a cognitive vulnerability–stress match according to hopelessness theory. Moreover, Hollon, DeRubeis, and Evans (1996) reported that attributional styles significantly mediated the relapse prevention effect of cognitive therapy whereas dysfunctional attitudes did not. Similarly, Alloy, Reilly-Harrington, et al. (1999) found that attributional styles interacted with life events to prospectively predict both depressed and hypomanic symptoms, whereas dysfunctional attitudes did not. Furthermore, using an unselected sample of college students to begin to "unpack" the generic cognitive vulnerability of the CVD Project (Alloy & Abramson, 1999), Haeffel et al. (2002) reported that negative cognitive styles, but not dysfunctional attitudes, uniquely predicted lifetime history of clinically significant depression and anxiety comorbid with depression. Preliminary investigations of a link between cognitive and biological vulnerability to depression have revealed yet another difference: the depressogenic attributional style was related to hemispheric asymmetry (Davidson, Abramson, Tomarken, & Wheeler, 1991), whereas dysfunctional attitudes were not (Gotlib, Ranganath, & Rosenfeld, 1998). Finally, *opposite* patterns of gender differences are found for the two cognitive vulnerabilities. High school and college females exhibit more negative cognitive styles than do their male counterparts (Angell et al., 1999; Hankin & Abramson, 2002). In contrast, college males exhibit higher levels of dysfunctional attitudes than do college females (Angell et al., 1999; Gotlib, 1984; Haeffel et al., 2002). Thus, although overlapping, the vulnerability factors featured in Beck's theory and hopelessness theory are distinct in important ways. We caution, however, that the empirical differences between the two vulnerabilites might reflect measurement, as opposed to true conceptual, differences. While the intent of both the CSQ and the DAS is to identify cognitively vulnerable people, the creators of these two questionnaires have adopted different measurement approaches.

There are two noteworthy differences between the CSQ and the DAS. First, the CSQ provides the participant with hypothetical situations that serve as references from which questions are to be answered whereas the DAS does not. Some researchers contend that priming is required for adequate measurement of cognitive vulnerability (Persons & Miranda, 1992; see Just et al., 2001, for further discussion). The CSQ is unique in that it provides a "built-in" event priming mechanism (Hollon, 1992). For each hypothetical situation, participants are asked to vividly imagine the situation happening to them (i.e., they prime themselves) and make inferences about its cause, consequences, and self-concept implications. The DAS does not provide this built-in priming mechanism, but rather asks participants to make ratings about statements without a contextual situation upon which to rely.

The second major difference between the CSQ and the DAS is the level of self-awareness needed by participants to complete the questionnaire accurately. The CSQ, compared to the DAS, requires a much lower level of self-awareness on the part of the participant. The CSQ simply asks questions about the cause, consequence, and self-concept implications of specific events and does not directly inquire whether or not the participant "thinks" he or she has a negative cognitive style. In essence, participants provide a "cognitive sample" on the CSQ that is thought to reveal their general cognitive style. Conversely, the DAS *does* require the participant to possess a relatively high level of self-awareness. The DAS directly asks participants to make global judgments about themselves. For example, an item on the DAS reads, "My value as a person depends greatly on what others think of me." To rate accurately how much he or she agrees or disagrees with this statement, the participant must have insight into his or her own concept of self-worth. Moreover, as this example illustrates, items composing the DAS are very general statements (unlike the specific events on the CSQ). Answering questions about general beliefs, rather than specific events, requires a greater degree of self-awareness on the part of the participant. Indeed, Beck et al. (1979) stated that dysfunctional attitudes are "not articulated by the patient without considerable introspection" (p. 247).

These two differences in measurement may explain some of the obtained empirical differences between the cognitive vulnerabilities featured in Beck's theory and in the hopelessness theory. However, even with equal accuracy of measurement, dysfunctional attitudes and negative cognitive styles, although overlapping, seem to be somewhat distinct constructs. Indeed, we speculate that negative cognitive styles may be more generally maladaptive, whereas some "dysfunctional" attitudes such as perfectionism may be adaptive when paired with other characteristics such as high ability and/or high self-efficacy but maladaptive when paired with low ability and/or low self-efficacy (see also Gibb, Zhu, Alloy, & Abramson, in press).

An important future task will be to compare the CSQ and the DAS to other operationalizations of cognitive vulnerability. In this regard, Alloy, Abramson, Murray, Whitehouse, and Hogan (1997) reported that cognitively HR participants in the CVD project exhibited negative biases on self-referent information-processing tasks. The recent debate in social psychology about implicit (automatic, overlearned, and nonconscious) versus explicit (more controlled, conscious) attitudes (see Bosson, Swann, & Pennebaker, 2000) has a parallel in work on cognition and depression. Relying on "network" theories of cognition, some investigators have developed implicit measures of depressive self-schemata such as the "emotional" Stroop task (e.g., Gotlib & McCann, 1984). In contrast, both the CSQ and the DAS can be construed as more explicit measures. Currently, little direct evidence exists that the implicit measures of cognitive vulnerability prospectively predict the development of clinically significant depression. In contrast, the CVD results demonstrate that a more explicit measure (i.e., pooled CSQ and DAS) of cognitive vulnerability prospectively predicts both first onsets and recurrences of clinically significant depression in a behavioral high-risk design. We are excited about the possibility of developing implicit measures of negative cognitive styles and dysfunctional attitudes to see if they predict as well in a behavioral high-risk design as do the current explicit measures of these constructs.

THE RELATION BETWEEN COGNITIVE VULNERABILITY AND RUMINATION: INSIGHTS FROM A SELF-REGULATORY PERSPECTIVE

In parallel with work on the hopelessness theory and Beck's theory, investigators have demonstrated that rumination also plays an important role in many aspects of depression. Work by Martin and Tesser (1996) and Nolen-Hoeksema (1991) suggests that rumination represents a process of perseverative attention directed to specific (often internal) content. For example, in depression, attention may be focused on an individual's negative affect and the causes and consequences of their depressed mood (Nolen-Hoeksema, 1991). The tendency to ruminate is associated with vulnerability to depressed mood (Nolen-Hoeksema & Morrow, 1991), onsets of depressive episodes (Just & Alloy, 1997), longer (Nolen-Hoeksemsa, Morrow, & Fredrickson, 1993) and more severe (Nolen-Hoeksema, Parker, & Larson, 1994) episodes of depression, gender differences in vulnerability to depression (Nolen-Hoeksema, Larson, & Grayson, 1999), and various symptoms of depression (Gotlib, Roberts, & Gilboa, 1996).

What is the relation between cognitive vulnerability, as defined in hopelessness theory and Beck's theory, and rumination? Although little has been done to integrate these constructs (but see Alloy et al., 2000, and Spasojevic & Alloy, 2001, for exceptions), we take a self-regulatory perspective and suggest that cognitive vulnerability, by its very nature, should lead to rumination. Thus, we argue that cognitively vulnerable individuals should be at especially high risk for engaging in rumination. To make this case, we present a four-part argument that describes rumination as a particular type of self-regulatory problem.

The Four-Part Argument

Attention Increases Salience and Influence

Attention increases the salience and influence of whatever content is the subject of focus (see also Williams, Watts, MacLeod, & Matthews, 1997). For example, self-focus increases the intensity of whatever affective state is most salient at the time (Ingram, 1990). When attention is focused on the self, people are more responsive to whatever mood state has been induced, regardless of whether that mood state was positive or negative (Scheier & Carver, 1977). From this perspective, attention is a "spotlight" that selects the "subject" that will influence behavior and mood at a given moment.

Discrepancies Initiate a Self-Regulatory Shift of Attention

Self-regulatory theories converge on the conclusion that a negative event, or "discrepancy," initiates a shift of attention to evaluation of the current situation. For example, Gray (1994) has posited a behavioral inhibition system (BIS) that responds to punishment cues and negative events (as well as unexpected events) by initiating a self-regulatory process that involves the interruption or inhibition of ongoing behavior to "check out" or evaluate the undesired or unexpected situation. Thus, the individual switches attention to addressing the current discrepancy. Similarly, Carver and Scheier (1998) specified that a self-regulatory cycle begins with attention directed internally (e.g., self-focus), allowing individuals to compare their current versus their desired state (e.g., goal) and to initiate behavior to reduce any discrepancy (see also Higgins, 1987).

So far, so good. Self-regulatory theories emphasize that when confronted with a negative event, it is adaptive for people to switch their attention to the problem (presumably to try to remedy it). Of course, as Figures 11.1 and 11.2 show, in the cognitive theories of depression, the occurrence of a negative event is the first step in the causal chain culminating in depression. The self-regulatory theories suggest that at this point, people, cognitively vulnerable and nonvulnerable alike, shift their attention to an evaluation of the unfortunate situation. Consistent with the self-regulatory perspective, the cognitive theories of depression emphasize that when confronted with a negative event, individuals make inferences about the cause, consequences, and implications for self-concept of the event (part of the "checking" process). Recall the example presented earlier in the chapter of the two students who failed the test. According to the self-regulatory perspective, upon discovering the failing grade, both students will begin self-regulation by shifting attention to consideration of the "discrepancy" between the desired grade and the actual "F." This attentional switch to negative cognitive content (i.e., a grade of "F") is likely to produce initial negative affect in *both* students regardless of their respective levels of cognitive vulnerability. Consistent with this prediction, the academic midterm studies (e.g., Metalsky et al., 1987, 1993) have shown that both cognitively vulnerable and cognitively nonvulnerable students experience initial depressive affect after receiving a low grade. Thus, it appears that the crucial difference between cognitively vulnerable and nonvulnerable individuals lies in what happens after the initial self-regulatory step.

Cognitively Vulnerable Individuals Have Difficulty Disengaging Their Attention from This Evaluation ("Sticky Attention")

Drawing on work by self-regulation theorists (e.g., Carver & Scheier, 1998; Pyszczynski & Greenberg, 1987), we contend that cognitively vulnerable individuals find it more difficult to disengage from this "checking" process (i.e., focusing attention on the discrepancy), once initiated, than do nonvulnerable individuals. Cognitively vulnerable individuals become stuck in the self-regulatory cycle and perseverate in this checking. This self-regulatory perseveration (Pyszczynski & Greenberg, 1987) constitutes rumination.

Why do cognitively vulnerable individuals persist in a ruminative checking process whereas nonvulnerable individuals disengage? There are three hypothesized way to disengage from rumination: (1) resume progress toward the goal (i.e., a solution for resolving the discrepancy, remedying the problem, or overcoming the obstacle, etc., is found); (2) relinquish desire for the goal (Pyszczynski & Greenberg, 1987); or (3) distract attention away from the discrepancy or problem (Carver & Scheier, 1998; Martin & Tesser, 1996; Nolen-Hoeksema, 1987). We suggest that cognitively vulnerable individuals have difficulty passing through any of these three exits.

1. *Resume progress toward a goal (i.e., a solution is found).* Cognitively vulnerable individuals are not likely to find a solution to their discrepancy or problem. Indeed, their stable and global attributions encourage the perception that problems cannot be solved. In our example of the student who attributed her failing grade to low intelligence, there is no easy solution for doing better in the future. A problem without a solution is described by Mandler (1972) as helplessness, one consequence of which is "the repetitive circling through of previous behavior patterns" (p. 260). If we view attention as a kind of cognitive behavior, then this is a good description of rumination. Moreover, the globality of the student's attribution suggests that other negative events will befall her outside of school and thus suggests new discrepancies about which to ruminate. The inferred negative consequence that the failing grade will prevent her from getting into medical school suggests an even more major discrepancy to ponder.

In contrast, unstable and specific attributions for negative events suggest reasonable solutions. For the other student in the example who attributed the same failing grade to not studying hard enough, the solution is to study harder. He can exit from the self-regulatory cycle and move on to preparing for the next test. Moreover, because he did not infer that negative consequences will result from the failing grade, he does not have any additional negative events to "check out."

2. *Relinquish desire for the goal.* We suggest that cognitively vulnerable individuals are also less likely than are nonvulnerable individuals to relinquish desire for the goal, even when a solution appears impossible or unlikely. Thus, cognitively vulnerable individuals may be stuck wanting something they are convinced they cannot have (Pyszczynski & Greenberg, 1987).

Both hopelessness theory and Beck's theory are compatible with this point of view. First, the stable, global causal attributions featured in hopelessness theory are likely to increase the importance of negative outcomes by *linking* (see Martin & Tesser, 1996) the current negative situation to other, more important goals. Following Carver and Scheier (1998), we suggest that goals and behaviors are structured hierarchically. For example, at the top of a student's hierarchy is a globalized sense of idealized self, who she really wants to be. At the next subordinate level in the hierarchy are guiding principles that specify the qualities required to achieve her idealized self, such as intelligence. The type of behaviors needed to be intelligent are embodied at the next level down in the hierarchy and might include achieving good test grades. Our first student attributed her failing grade to low intelligence, a stable, global attribution that links her lower order behavior (failing the test) to her higher order goal of being intelligent. Given the hierarchical organization of goals, being intelligent is more important to her than the test itself. Indeed, one might argue that the student's failure is important to the extent that it is linked to her higher order goals (e.g., being intelligent). It is easy to see that the same logic applies for this student's negative inferences about consequences ("The low grade will prevent me from getting into medical school") and self ("I'm worthless") linking to higher order goals.

According to Carver and Scheier (1998), higher order goals such as these (being intelligent and worthy, getting into medical school) are much harder to relinquish because doing so necessitates a reorganization of one's value system. In contrast, the inferences of the cognitively nonvulnerable person do not have such negative implications for higher order goals. Thus, cognitively vulnerable individuals may be less likely than cognitively nonvulnerable individuals to relinquish their currently thwarted goal because it is vital to their self-concept.

Linking also is related to the perfectionism and rigid standards embodied in Beck's concept of cognitive vulnerability. Items on the DAS such as "If I don't set the highest standards for myself, I am likely to end up a second-rate person" reveal evidence of linking lower to higher order goals. If a person *must* achieve a certain standard (rigidity) and must achieve it perfectly, it is unlikely that the person will achieve it (unless he or she is exceptionally competent) or relinquish desire for it.

3. *Distraction.* Distraction involves shifting attention to content unrelated to the current discrepancy—thinking about something else. Distraction can be construed as the *temporary* relinquishing of a goal. As we argued above, cognitively vulnerable individuals should have difficulty relinquishing a goal, even temporarily.

Although distraction is only a temporary solution because it does nothing to directly relieve the conditions that led to rumination in the first place, it may be viewed as a form of problem solving, either strategic or automatic. Such a solution will be especially difficult to implement for a cognitively vulnerable individual, whose attention already is strongly focused on an important, threatened goal in his or her hierarchy. As already suggested, the more important the goal of current focus, the more difficult it should be to move attention elsewhere. The student who believed that low intelligence caused her to fail the exam, that she never will get into medical school, and that she is worthless would seem to have an especially hard time becoming *engrossed* in a new goal or activity (a requirement for effective distraction). Distraction can also take the form of overt behavior (e.g., exercising). However, the hopelessness engendered by cognitive vulnerability likely suggests that such behaviors will not reduce negative feelings or lead to positive outcomes. Moreover, the response initiation deficits hypothesized to result from hopelessness (Abramson et al., 1989) should decrease the hopeless person's likelihood of initiating voluntary distracting behaviors.

In summary, discrepancy checking may be a relatively universal self-regulatory response following a negative life event. However, cognitively nonvulnerable individuals may quickly disengage their attention from their discrepancy by finding a solution, relinquishing their current thwarted goal, or distracting themselves. In contrast, these exits may be blocked for cognitively vulnerable individuals, such that they get "stuck" ruminating about a goal they can neither attain nor relinquish. In short, following a negative event, the cognitively vulnerable individual is left with the spotlight of attention fixed on relatively negative content (e.g., expectations of hopelessness, stable and global attributions for negative events, anticipated future negative events, negative views of the self; see also Teasdale, 1988). In turn, this attentional spotlighting of negative content allows it to strongly influence affect and behavior (see below). Whereas cognitively vulnerable and nonvulnerable individuals alike may experience initial negative affect when first encountering a negative event/discrepancy, the nonvulnerable are protected from the development of more severe or prolonged depression whereas the vulnerable are not (see also Teasdale, 1988). Consistent with this hypothesis, in the academic midterm studies (e.g., Metalsky et al., 1987, 1993) cognitively vulnerable students experienced persistent depressive mood for several days after receiving a low grade whereas nonvulnerable students recovered more quickly.

Increased Activation of Negative Content and Resulting Symptoms

The inability to disengage attention from negative cognitive content is a plausible mechanism underlying several symptoms of HD. Most obviously, rumination should increase negative affect because it provides a constant reminder of just how bad things appear to be. Difficulty in disengaging attention from a discrepancy and its associates also may account for the poor concentration characteristic of many depressed individuals (Pyszczynski & Greenberg, 1987). Simply put, if attention is directed to task-irrelevant cues (e.g., negative content related to the discrepancy, failure, or negative event), it is not available to activate and enhance task-relevant cues. In addition, rumination may contribute to insomnia, another hypothesized symptom of HD, by interfering with the calm state associated with falling asleep. Finally, rumination may increase the risk of suicidality, a core symptom of HD. A person not focused currently on negative cognitions is unlikely to be suicidal. Providing clinical support for the intuitive notion that suicide is related to focusing attention on negative thoughts, one common intervention in preventing suicide is to remind the suicidal individual of reasons to live.

Summary

Our integration of self-regulatory perspectives with hopelessness theory and Beck's theory highlights the important association between cognitive vulnerability and rumination. Namely, a negative event causes an interruption of ongoing behavior and calls for a shift of attention to monitor the discrepancy between the actual event and the desired event. A person is ruminating when his or her attention is "stuck" on this discrepancy and its associates. The three exits from rumination are less available to the cognitively vulnerable individual than to the nonvulnerable individual. For the cognitively vulnerable person, attention continues to activate discrepancies and other negative content, a process that may account for some of the symptoms composing HD. Thus, the negative cognitive content associated with cognitive vulnerability helps instigate the process of rumination, which in turn contributes to depressive symptoms.

Empirically supporting this view, both stress-reactive (Alloy et al., 2000) and mood-related (Spasojevic & Alloy, 2001) rumination have been found to be positively related to cognitive vulnerability. Furthermore, in the CVD Project, rumination was found to mediate the association between cognitive vulnerability and the prospective development of episodes of major depressive disorder, suggesting that rumination is a proximal mechanism through which cognitive vulnerability contributes to depression (Spasojevic & Alloy, 2001).

FUTURE DIRECTIONS: PLACING THE COGNITIVE THEORIES OF DEPRESSION IN A PSYCHOBIOLOGICAL CONTEXT

We close by suggesting an important future direction for the cognitive theories of depression. Given the empirical support for these theories and the success of cognitive therapy for depression, it is critical to integrate the cognitive approach with other successful approaches to depression. Much important work has been conducted demonstrating the fruitfulness of integrating cognitive and interpersonal approaches to depression (e.g., Gotlib & Hammen, 1992; Haines, Metalsky, Cardamone, & Joiner, 1999). However, little has been done to integrate the cognitive perspective with powerful biological approaches to depression and, more generally, with major advances in understanding the psychobiology of motivation. Below we speculate about how we may move toward placing the cognitive theories of depression in a psychobiological context.

Over the past 25 years, experimental psychologists have made major advances in understanding the motivational bases of behavior. Coming from diverse perspectives including animal learning and behavioral pharmacology (e.g., Gray, 1994), the neural substrates of emotion (e.g., Davidson, 1994; Davidson, Pizzagalli, & Nitschke, Chapter 9, this volume), personality (e.g., Cloninger, 1987), and psychopathology (e.g., Depue & Iacono, 1989), investigators have converged on the conclusion that two (sometimes more) fundamental psychobiological systems are critical in regulating behavior. One of these systems regulates approach behavior to attain rewards and goals, which the other regulates withdrawal and/or inhibition of behavior in response to threat and punishment. The former variously has been called the Behavioral Approach System (BAS; Gray, 1994), Behavioral Activation System (BAS; Cloninger, 1987; Fowles, 1980), and the Behavioral Facilitation System (BFS; Depue & Iacono, 1989). We will call this system the BAS. The latter system typically is called the Behavioral Inhibition System (BIS; Gray, 1994), although Davidson (1994) has referred to it as a withdrawal system. We will term this system the BIS.

In its regulation of approach behavior to attain rewards and goals, the BAS is sensitive to signals of reward, nonpunishment, and escape from punishment. These signals can be external (e.g., environmental events such as the presence of an attractive goal object) or internal (e.g, expectations of goal attainment). Activation of the BAS by these signals causes the person to begin (or to increase) movement toward goals. Activation of the BAS is hypothesized to be associated with hope, elation, and happiness (e.g., Carver & White, 1994).

In contrast, in its regulation of withdrawal and/or inhibition of behavior in response to threat or punishment, the BIS is sensitive to signals of punishment and nonreward (e.g., failure). Again, as with the BAS, the signals activating the BIS can be external environmental events or internal cognitions. Activation of the BIS inhibits behavior that may lead to negative or painful outcomes in response to signals of punishment, nonreward, and failure. Activation of the BIS is hypothesized to be associated with negative affect such as anxiety (e.g., Carver & White, 1994). Investigators have suggested that BAS and BIS stand in reciprocal relation to each other. As one becomes active, the other becomes inactive (e.g., Fowles, 1993).

Within this psychobiological motivational perspective, depression is viewed as associated with the activation of aversive motivation (increased BIS; e.g., Fowles, 1993) and/or a disruption or "shutdown" of appetitive motivation (decreased BAS; Davidson, 1994; Fowles, 1993), with the greater emphasis being on the latter. Indeed, examination of the hypothesized symptoms of HD reveals that some (e.g., brooding, difficulty in concentration, insomnia) appear to reflect an active BIS, whereas other symptoms (e.g., retarded initiation of voluntary responses, lack of energy, apathy) likely reflect an inactive BAS.

It is useful to examine, from a BIS/BAS perspective, the hypothesized causal pathways that culminate in depression in the cognitive theories. The causal chain starts with the occurrence of a negative event, as in our example of the student failing a test. The receipt of the failing grade should activate the BIS, which entails the interruption or inhibition of ongoing behavior as the student "evaluates" the failing grade (e.g., makes inferences about the grade's cause, likely consequences, and self-concept implications). As we argued above, initial negative affect should occur at this point in the causal chain. However, if the student is cognitively nonvulnerable, he or she will make inferences that facilitate exit from this self-regulatory process (and the associated negative affect), and he or she will resume progress toward goals. This resumption of goal-seeking activity should be reflected in deactivation of the BIS and reactivation of the BAS. Thus, the cognitively nonvulnerable student is protected from a large-scale deactivation of the BAS. In contrast, the cognitively vulnerable student makes inferences (e.g., I failed the test because I'm stupid) that lead to hopelessness about achieving important current and future goals and, in turn, the symptoms of HD. Fowles (1993) has argued that as expectancies move in the direction of hopelessness, appetitive motivation (e.g., BAS) will decrease. From this perspective, then, hopelessness and the associated symptoms of HD together may represent the cognitive, affective, and behavioral manifestations of an inactive BAS (and possibly of a relatively more active BIS).

Although much important work has been conducted on cognitive and biological vulnerability to depression, these two lines of research have proceeded in relative isolation from each other (Gotlib & Abramson, 1999). However, placing the cognitive theories in a psychobiological motivational context facilitates their integration with powerful biological theories of depression. Enabling such an integration, recent research (Harmon-Jones & Allen, 1997; Sutton & Davidson, 1997) has begun to elucidate the neural circuitry involved in implementing the approach and inhibition/withdrawal systems. Specifically, the BAS, as measured by Carver and White's (1994) BIS/BAS scale, is associated with increased left frontal cortical activity during resting baseline (Harmon-Jones & Allen, 1997; Sutton & Davidson, 1997). Relating depression to frontal cortical activity, Davidson and colleagues (see Davidson, 1994) have demonstrated that depressed individuals exhibit greater relative right-sided frontal activation (i.e., lesser relative left-sided frontal activation) of their cerebral hemispheres than do nondepressed individuals. In Davidson's scheme, this pattern is consistent with withdrawal from the environment (active BIS) and decreased approach behavior (inactive BAS). These cerebral activation differences appear to be, at least in part, state-independent. Asymptomatic remitted depressed individuals exhibit greater relative right-sided frontal activation than never-depressed individuals (e.g., Gotlib et al., 1998;

Henriques & Davidson, 1990). Based on these and other findings, Davidson and colleagues (e.g., Davidson, 1994) and Gotlib et al. (1998) have suggested that relative right frontal hemispheric activation may represent a vulnerability to depression.

What is the nature of the relationship between cognitive vulnerability to depression and biological vulnerability to this disorder as indexed by patterns of cerebral asymmetry? To the extent that hopelessness, the expectation to which cognitively vulnerable individuals are hypothesized to be predisposed, may be particularly powerful in signaling a shutdown of approach motivation (inactive BAS), we suggest that cognitively vulnerable individuals may be characterized by relative right-sided frontal activation of their cerebral hemispheres, the biological vulnerability featured in Davidson's theory. Consistent with this hypothesis, Davidson et al. (1991) reported that attributionally vulnerable college students exhibited relative right frontal hemispheric activation. In contrast, Gotlib et al. (1998) failed to obtain a relationship between cognitive vulnerability as measured by DAS scores and hemispheric asymmetry. Consistent with our earlier comments, dysfunctional attitudes, as currently conceptualized and operationalized in the DAS, may include some adaptive components such as perfectionism. It is intriguing to consider the possibility that individuals characterized by the combination of perfectionism and high self-efficacy (e.g., Arnold Schwarzenegger!) may show relatively high approach motivation and low withdrawal motivation (relative left frontal hemispheric activation), the pattern opposite to the biological vulnerability to depression featured in Davidson's theory. The presence of such individuals might have diluted the relationship between DAS scores and cerebral asymmetry in Gotlib et al.'s study.

Future research that "unpacks" the cognitive vulnerability featured in Beck's theory and that utilizes various measures of cognitive vulnerability (e.g., explicit vs. implicit) will facilitate the empirical comparison of biological and cognitive vulnerability. Davidson et al.'s (1991) results provide preliminary evidence that attributional vulnerability and right frontal hemispheric asymmetry may share a common biocognitive process that increases people's risk for depression. We speculate that those cognitive styles that predispose an individual to hopelessness and to a generalized loss of self-efficacy should be especially likely to be related to biological vulnerabilities associated with "shutdowns" of the behavioral approach system. Integrating the cognitive and biological theories of depression promises to be an exciting and important direction for future theory and research.

ACKNOWLEDGMENTS

The research reviewed in this chapter was supported by National Institute of Mental Health Grant Nos. MH 43866 and MH 52662 to Lyn Y. Abramson and Nos. MH 48216 and MH 52617 to Lauren B. Alloy.

REFERENCES

Abramson, L. Y., & Alloy, L. B. (1990). Search for the "negative cognition" subtype of depression. In C. D. McCann & N. S. Endler (Eds.), *Depression: New directions in theory, research, and practice* (pp. 77–109). Toronto: Wall & Thompson.

Abramson, L. Y., Alloy, L. B., & Hogan, M. E. (1997). Cognitive/personality subtypes of depression: Theories in search of disorders. *Cognitive Therapy and Research, 21,* 247–265.

Abramson, L. Y., Alloy, L. B., Hogan, M. E., Whitehouse, W. G., Cornette, M., Akhavan, S., & Chiara, A. (1998). Suicidality and cognitive vulnerability to depression among college students: A prospective study. *Journal of Adolescence, 21,* 157–171.

Abramson, L. Y., Alloy, L. B., Hogan, M. E., Whitehouse, W. G., Donovan, P., Rose, D., Panzarella, C., & Raniere, D. (1999). Cognitive vulnerability to depression: Theory and evidence. *Journal of Cognitive Psychotherapy: An International Quarterly, 13,* 5–20.

Abramson, L. Y., Metalsky, G. I., & Alloy, L. B. (1989). Hopelessness depression: A theory-based subtype of depression. *Psychological Review, 96,* 358–372.

Abramson,L. Y., Metalsky,G. I., & Alloy, L. B. (2002). *The Cognitive Style Questionnaire: A measure of the vulnerability featured in the hopelessness theory of depression.* Manuscript in preparation, University of Wisconsin–Madison.

Alloy, L. B., & Abramson, L. Y. (1999). The Temple–Wisconsin Cognitive Vulnerability to Depression (CVD) Project: Conceptual background, design, and methods. *Journal of Cognitive Psychotherapy: An International Quarterly, 13,* 227–262.

Alloy, L. B., Abramson, L. Y., Hogan, M. E., Whitehouse, W. G., Rose, D. T., Robinson, M. S., Kim, R. S., & Lapkin, J. B. (2000). The Temple–Wisconsin Cognitive Vulnerability to Depression (CVD) Project: Lifetime history of Axis I psychopathology in individuals at high and low cognitive risk for depression. *Journal of Abnormal Psychology, 109,* 403–418.

Alloy, L. B., Abramson, L. Y., Murray, L. A., Whitehouse, W. G., & Hogan, M. E. (1997). Self-referent information-processing in individuals at high and low cognitive risk for depression. *Cognition and Emotion, 11,* 539–568.

Alloy, L. B., Abramson, L. Y., Whitehouse, W. G., Hogan, M. E., Tashman, N., Steinberg, D., Rose, D. T., & Donovan, P. (1999). Depressogenic cognitive styles: Predictive validity, information processing and personality characteristics, and developmental origins. *Behaviour Research and Therapy, 37,* 503–531.

Alloy, L. B., Albright, J. S., Abramson, L. Y., & Dykman, B. M. (1990). Depressive realism and nondepressive optimistic illusions: The role of the self. In R. E. Ingram (Ed.), *Contemporary psychological approaches to depression: Treatment, research, and theory* (pp. 71–86). New York: Plenum Press.

Alloy, L. B., & Clements, C. M. (1998). Hopelessness theory of depression: Tests of the symptom component. *Cognitive Therapy and Research, 22,* 303–335.

Alloy, L. B., Just, N., & Panzarella, C. (1997). Attributional style, daily life events, and hopelessness depression: Subtype validation by prospective variability and specificity of symptoms. *Cognitive Therapy and Research, 21,* 321–344.

Alloy, L. B., Lipman, A., & Abramson, L. Y. (1992). Attributional style as a vulnerability factor for depression: Validation by past history of mood disorders. *Cognitive Therapy and Research, 16,* 391–407.

Alloy, L. B., Reilly-Harrington, N., Fresco, D., Whitehouse, W. G., & Zechmeister, J. S. (1999). Cognitive styles and life events in subsyndromal unipolar and bipolar disorders: Stability and prospective prediction of depressive and hypomanic mood swings. *Journal of Cognitive Psychotherapy: An International Quarterly, 13,* 21–40.

Angell, K. E., Abramson, L. Y., Alloy, L. B., Hankin, B. L., Hogan, M. E., Whitehouse, W. G., & Hyde, J. S. (1999, November). *Gender differences in dysphoria and etiological factors: Ethnic variations.* Paper presented at the meeting of the Association for Advancement of Behavior Therapy, Toronto, Canada.

Barnett, P. A., & Gotlib, I. H. (1988). Psychosocial functioning and depression: Distinguishing among antecedents, concomitants, and consequences. *Psychological Bulletin, 104,* 97–126.

Beck, A. T. (1967). *Depression: Clinical, experimental, and theoretical aspects.* New York: Harper & Row.

Beck, A. T. (1976). *Cognitive therapy and the emotional disorders.* New York: International Universities Press.

Beck, A. T. (1987). Cognitive models of depression. *Journal of Cognitive Psychotherapy: An International Quarterly, 1,* 5–37.

Beck, A. T., Rush, A. J., Shaw, B. F., & Emery, G. (1979). *Cognitive therapy of depression.* New York: Guilford Press.

Belsher, G., & Costello, C. G. (1988). Relapse after recovery from unipolar depression: A critical review. *Psychological Bulletin, 104,* 84–96.

Bosson, J. K., Swann, W. B., & Pennebaker, J. W. (2000). Stalking the perfect measure of implicit self-esteem: The blind men and the elephant revisited. *Journal of Personality and Social Psychology, 79*, 631–643.

Brown, G. P., Hammen, C. L., Craske, M. G., & Wickens, T. D. (1995). Dimensions of dysfunctional attitudes as vulnerabilities to depressive symptoms. *Journal of Abnormal Psychology, 104,* 431–435.

Brown, G. W. & Harris, T. O. (Eds.). (1989). *Life events and illness.* New York: Guilford Press.

Carver, C. S., & Scheier, M. F. (1998). *On the self-regulation of behavior.* New York: Cambridge University Press.

Carver, C. S., & White, T. L. (1994). Behavioral inhibition, behavioral activation, and affective responses to impending reward and punishment: The BIS/BAS scales. *Journal of Personality and Social Psychology, 67,* 319–333.

Chomsky, N. (1959). Review of *Verbal Behavior,* by B. F. Skinner. *Language, 35,* 26–58.

Clark, D. A., Beck, A. T., & Alford, B. A. (1999). *Scientific foundations of cognitive theory and therapy of depression.* New York: Wiley.

Cloninger, C. R. (1987). A systematic method of clinical description and classification of personality variants: A proposal. *Archives of General Psychiatry, 44,* 573–588.

Coyne, J. C., & Gotlib, I. H. (1983). The role of cognition in depression: A critical appraisal. *Psychological Bulletin, 94,* 472–505.

Coyne, J. C., & Whiffen, V. E. (1995). Issues in personality as diathesis for depression: The case of sociotropy–dependency and autonomy–self-criticism. *Psychological Bulletin, 118,* 358–378.

Davidson, R. J. (1994). Asymmetric brain function, affective style, and psychopathology: The role of early experience and plasticity. *Development and Psychopathology, 6,* 741–758.

Davidson, R. J., Abramson, L. Y., Tomarken, A. J., & Wheeler, R. E. (1991). *Asymmetrical anterior temporal brain activity predicts beliefs about the causes of negative life events.* Manuscript in preparation, University of Wisconsin–Madison.

Davila, J., & Daley, S. E. (2000). Studying interpersonal factors in suicide: Perspectives from depression research. In T. Joiner & M. O. Rudd (Eds.), *Suicide science: Expanding the boundaries* (pp. 175–200). Boston: Kluwer Academic.

Depue, R. A., & Iacono, W. G. (1989). Neurobehavioral aspects of affective disorders. *Annual Review of Psychology, 40,* 457–492.

Depue, R. A., Slater, J., Wolfstetter-Kausch, H., Klein, D., Goplerud, E., & Farr, D. (1981). A behavioral paradigm for identifying persons at risk for bipolar depressive disorder: A conceptual framework and five validation studies [Monograph]. *Journal of Abnormal Psychology, 90,* 381–437.

Dykman, B. M., & Abramson, L. Y. (1990). Contributions of basic research to the cognitive theories of depression. *Personality and Social Psychology Bulletin, 16,* 42–57.

Dykman, B. M., Abramson, L. Y., Alloy, L. B., & Hartlage, S. (1989). Processing of ambiguous feedback among depressed and nondepressed college students: Schematic biases and their implications for depressive realism. *Journal of Personality and Social Psychology, 56,* 431–445.

Dykman, B. M., & Johll, M. (1998). Dysfunctional attitudes and vulnerability to depressive symptoms: A 14-week longitudinal study. *Cognitive Therapy and Research, 22,* 337–352.

Fowles, D. C. (1980). The three arousal model: Implications of Gray's two-factor learning theory for heart rate, electrodermal activity, and psychopathy. *Psychophysiology, 17,* 87–104.

Fowles, D. C. (1993). Behavioral variables in psychopathology: A psychobiological perspective. In P. B. Sutker & H. E. Adams (Eds.), *Comprehensive handbook of psychopathology* (2nd ed., pp. 57–82). New York: Plenum Press.

Ge, X., Lorenz, F. O., Conger, R. D., Elder, G. H., & Simons, R. L. (1994). Trajectories of stressful life events and depressive symptoms during adolescence. *Developmental Psychology, 30,* 467–483.

Gibb, B. E., Alloy, L. B., Abramson, L. Y., Rose, D. T., Whitehouse, W. G., Donovan, P., Hogan, M. E., Cronholm, J., & Tierney, S. (2001). History of childhood maltreatment, depressogenic cognitive style, and episodes of depression in adulthood. *Cognitive Therapy and Research, 25,* 425–446.

Gibb, B. E., Zhu, L., Alloy, L. B., & Abramson, L. Y. (in press). Cognitive styles and academic achievement in university students: A longitudinal investigation. *Cognitive Therapy and Research*.

Gladstone, T. R., & Kaslow, N. J. (1995). Depression and attributions in children and adolescents: A meta-analytic review. *Journal of Abnormal Child Psychology, 23,* 597–606.

Gotlib, I. H. (1984). Depression and general psychopathology in university students. *Journal of Abnormal Psychology, 93,* 19–30.

Gotlib, I. H., & Abramson, L. Y. (1999). Attributional theories of emotion. In T. Dalgleish & M. Power (Eds.), *Handbook of cognition and emotion* (pp. 613–636). Chichester, UK: Wiley.

Gotlib, I. H., & Hammen, C. L. (1992). *Psychological aspects of depression: Toward a cognitive–interpersonal integration*. New York: Wiley.

Gotlib, I. H., & McCann, C. D. (1984) Construct accessibility and depression: An examination of cognitive and affective factors. *Journal of Personality and Social Psychology, 47,* 427–439.

Gotlib, I. H., McLachlan, A. L., & Katz, A. N. (1988). Biases in visual attention in depressed and nondepressed individuals. *Cognition and Emotion, 2,* 185–200.

Gotlib, I. H., Ranganath, C., & Rosenfeld, J. P. (1998). Frontal EEG alpha asymmetry, depression, and cognitive functioning. *Cognition and Emotion, 12,* 449–478.

Gotlib, I. H., Roberts, J. E., & Gilboa, E. (1996). Cognitive interference in depression. In I. G. Sarason, G. R. Pierce, & B. R. Sarason (Eds.), *Cognitive interference: Theories, methods, and findings* (pp. 347–378). Mahwah, NJ: Erlbaum.

Gray, J. A. (1994). Three fundamental emotions systems. In P. Ekman, & R. J. Davidson (Eds.), *The nature of emotion: Fundamental questions* (pp. 243–247). New York: Oxford University Press.

Haack, L. J., Metalsky, G. I., Dykman, B. M., & Abramson, L. Y. (1996). Use of current situational information and causal inference: Do dysphoric individuals make "unwarranted" causal inferences? *Cognitive Therapy and Research, 20,* 309–331.

Haaga, D. A. F., & Beck, A. T. (1995). Perspectives on depressive realism: Implications for cognitive theory of depression. *Behaviour Research and Therapy, 33,* 41–48.

Haaga, D. A. F., Dyck, M. J., & Ernst, D. (1991). Empirical status of cognitive theory of depression. *Psychological Bulletin, 110,* 215–236.

Haeffel, G. J., Abramson, L. Y., Voelz, Z. R., Metalsky, G. I., Halberstadt, L., Dykman, B. M., Donovan, P., Hogan, M. E., & Hankin, B. L. (2002). *Cognitive vulnerability to depression and lifetime history of Axis I psychopathology: A comparison of negative cognitive styles (CSQ) and dysfunctional attitudes (DAS)*. Manuscript submitted for publication.

Haines, B. A., Metalsky, G. I., Cardamone, A. L., & Joiner, T. (1999). Interpersonal and cognitive pathways into the origins of attributional style: A developmental perspective. In T. Joiner & J. C. Coyne (Eds.), *The interactional nature of depression* (pp. 65–92). Washington, DC: American Psychiatric Association Press.

Hankin, B. L., & Abramson, L. Y. (2001). Development of gender differences in depression: An elaborated cognitive vulnerability–transactional stress theory. *Psychological Bulletin, 127,* 773–796.

Hankin, B. L., & Abramson, L. Y. (2002). *Measuring cognitive vulnerability to depression in adolescence: Reliability, validity, and gender differences*. Manuscript in preparation, University of Wisconsin–Madison.

Hankin, B. L., Abramson, L. Y, Miller, N., & Haeffel, G. J. (2002). *A 2-year prospective test of cognitive theories of depression: Predicting depressive symptoms and episodes*. Manuscript submitted for publication.

Hankin, B. L., Abramson, L. Y., Moffitt, T. E., Silva, P., McGee, R., & Angell, K. E. (1998). Development of depression from preadolescence to young adulthood: Emerging gender differences in a 10-year longitudinal study. *Journal of Abnormal Psychology, 107,* 128–140.

Hankin, B. L., Abramson, L. Y., & Siler, M. (2001). A prospective test of the hopelessness theory of depression in adolescence. *Cognitive Therapy and Research, 25,* 607–632.

Harmon-Jones, E., & Allen, J. J. B. (1997). Behavioral activation sensitivity and resting frontal EEG asymmetry: Covariation of putative indicators related to risk for mood disorders. *Journal of Abnormal Psychology, 106,* 159–163.

Henriques, J. B., & Davidson, R. J. (1990). Regional brain electrical asymmetries discriminate between previously depressed and healthy control subjects. *Journal of Abnormal Psychology, 99,* 22–31.

Higgins, E. T. (1987). Self-discrepancy: A theory relating self and affect. *Psychological Review, 94,* 319–340.

Hilsman, R., & Garber, J. (1995). A test of the cognitive diathesis–stress model of depression in children: Academic stressors, attributional style, perceived competence, and control. *Journal of Personality and Social Psychology, 69,* 370–380.

Hollon, S. D. (1992). Cognitive models of depression from a psychobiological perspective. *Psychological Inquiry, 3,* 250–253.

Hollon, S. D., DeRubeis, R. J., & Evans, M. D. (1996). Cognitive therapy in the treatment and prevention of depression. In P. M. Salkovskis (Ed.), *Frontiers of cognitive therapy* (pp. 293–317). New York: Guilford Press.

Hollon, S. D., & Garber, J. (1988). Cognitive therapy. In L. Y. Abramson (Ed.), *Social cognition and clinical psychology: A synthesis* (pp. 204–253). New York: Guilford Press.

Ingram, R. E. (1990). Self-focused attention in clinical disorders: Review and a conceptual model. *Psychological Bulletin, 107,* 156–176.

Ingram, R. E., Miranda, J., & Segal, Z. V. (1998). *Cognitive vulnerability to depression.* New York: Guilford Press.

Joiner, T. E., Metalsky, G. I., Lew, A., & Klocek, J. (1999). Testing the causal mediation component of Beck's theory of depression: Evidence for specific mediation. *Cognitive Therapy and Research, 23,* 401–412.

Joiner, T. E., & Rudd, M. D. (1995). Negative attributional style for interpersonal events and the occurrence of severe interpersonal disruptions as predictors of self-reported suicidal ideation. *Suicide and Life-Threatening Behavior, 25,* 297–304.

Joiner, T. E., & Rudd, M. D. (1996). Toward a categorization of depression-related psychological constructs. *Cognitive Therapy and Research, 20,* 51–68.

Joiner, T. E., Steer, R. A., Abramson, L. Y., Alloy, L. B., Metalsky, G. I., & Schmidt, N. B. (2001). Hopelessness depression as a distinct dimension of depressive symptoms among clinical and nonclinical samples. *Behaviour Research and Therapy, 39,* 523–536.

Joiner, T. E., & Wagner, K. D. (1995). Attributional style and depression in children and adolescents: A meta-analytic review. *Clinical Psychology Review, 8,* 777–798.

Just, N., Abramson, L. Y., & Alloy, L. B. (2001). Remitted depression studies as tests of the cognitive vulnerability hypotheses of depression onset: A critique and conceptual analysis. *Clinical Psychology Review, 21,* 63–83.

Just, N., & Alloy, L. B. (1997). The response styles theory of depression: Tests and an extension of the theory. *Journal of Abnormal Psychology, 106,* 221–229.

Kazdin, A. E., French, N. H., Unis, A. S., Esveldt-Dawson, K., & Sherick, R. B. (1983). Hopelessness, depression, and suicidal intent among psychiatrically disturbed inpatient children. *Journal of Consulting and Clinical Psychology, 54,* 241–245.

Kelley, H. H. (1967). Attribution theory in social psychology. In D. Levine (Ed.), *Nebraska Symposium on Motivation* (Vol. 15, pp. 192–238). Lincoln: University of Nebraska Press.

Kessler, R. C., McGonagle, K. A., Zhao, S., Nelson, C. B., Hughes, M., Eshleman, S., Wittchen, H. U., & Kendler, K. S. (1994). Lifetime and 12-month prevalence of DSM-III-R psychiatric disorders in the United States: Results from the National Comorbidity Survey. *Archives of General Psychiatry, 51,* 8–19.

Klocek, J. W., Oliver, J. M., & Ross, M. J. (1997). The role of dysfunctional attitudes, negative life events, and social support in the prediction of depressive dysphoria: A prospective longitudinal study. *Social Behaviour and Personality, 25,* 123–136.

Kwon, S. M., & Oei, T. P. (1992). Differential causal roles of dysfunctional attitudes and automatic thoughts in depression. *Cognitive Therapy and Research, 16,* 309–328.

Lazarus, R. S. (1966). *Psychological stress and the coping process.* New York: McGraw-Hill.

Lewinsohn, P. M., Allen, N. B., Seeley, J. R., & Gotlib, I. H. (1999). First onset versus recurrence of depression: Differential processes of psychosocial risk. *Journal of Abnormal Psychology, 108,* 483–489.

Lewinsohn, P. M., Joiner, T. E., & Rohde, P. (2001). Evaluation of cognitive diathesis–stress models in predicting major depressive disorder in adolescents. *Journal of Abnormal Psychology, 110,* 203–215.

Mandler, G. (1972). Helplessness: Theory and research in anxiety. In C. D. Spielberger (Ed.), *Anxiety: Current trends in theory and research* (Vol. II, pp. 359–378). New York: Academic Press.

Martin, L. L., & Tesser, A. (1996). Some ruminative thoughts. In R. S. Wyer, Jr. (Ed.), *Ruminative thoughts* (pp. 1–47). Mahwah, NJ: Erlbaum.

McCabe, S. B., & Gotlib, I. H. (1995). Selective attention and clinical depression: Performance on a deployment-of-attention task. *Journal of Abnormal Psychology, 104,* 241–245.

Metalsky, G. I., Halberstadt, L. J., & Abramson, L. Y. (1987). Vulnerability to depressive mood reactions: Toward a more powerful test of the diathesis–stress and causal mediation components of the reformulated theory of depression. *Journal of Personality and Social Psychology, 52,* 386–393.

Metalsky, G. I., & Joiner, T. E. (1992). Vulnerability to depressive symptomatology: A prospective test of the diathesis–stress and causal mediation components of the hopelessness theory of depression. *Journal of Personality and Social Psychology, 63,* 667–675.

Metalsky, G. I., & Joiner, T. E. (1997). The Hopelessness Depression Symptom Questionnaire. *Cognitive Therapy and Research, 21,* 359–384.

Metalsky, G. I., Joiner, T. E., Hardin, T. S., & Abramson, L. Y. (1993). Depressive reactions to failure in a naturalistic setting: A test of the hopelessness and self-esteem theories of depression. *Journal of Abnormal Psychology, 102,* 101–109.

Minkoff, K., Bergman, E., Beck, A. T., & Beck, R. (1973). Hopelessness, depression, and attempted suicide. *American Journal of Psychiatry, 130,* 455–459.

Monroe, S. M., & Simons, A. D. (1991). Diathesis–stress theories in the context of life stress research: Implications for the depressive disorders. *Psychological Bulletin, 110,* 406–425.

Neisser, U. (1967). *Cognitive psychology.* East Norwalk, CT: Appleton-Century-Crofts.

Nisbett, R. E., & Ross, L. (1980). *Human inference: Strategies and shortcomings of social judgment.* Englewood Cliffs, NJ: Prentice-Hall.

Nolen-Hoeksema, S. (1987). Sex differences in unipolar depression: Evidence and theory. *Psychological Bulletin, 101,* 259–282.

Nolen-Hoeksema, S. (1990). *Sex differences in depression.* Stanford, CA: Stanford University Press.

Nolen-Hoeksema, S. (1991). Responses to depression and their effects on the duration of depressive episodes. *Journal of Abnormal Psychology, 100,* 569–582.

Nolen-Hoeksema, S., Girgus, J. S., & Seligman, M. E. P. (1992). Predictors and consequences of childhood depressive symptoms: A 5-year longitudinal study. *Journal of Abnormal Psychology, 101,* 405–422.

Nolen-Hoeksema, S., Larson, J., & Grayson, C. (1999). Explaining the gender differences in depressive symptoms. *Journal of Personality and Social Psychology, 77,* 1061–1072.

Nolen-Hoeksema, S., & Morrow, J. (1991). A prospective study of depression and posttraumatic stress symptoms after a natural disaster: The 1989 Loma Prieta earthquake. *Journal of Personality and Social Psychology, 61,* 115–121.

Nolen-Hoeksema, S., Morrow, J., & Fredrickson, B. L. (1993). Response styles and the duration of episodes of depressed mood. *Journal of Abnormal Psychology, 102,* 20–28.

Nolen-Hoeksema, S., Parker, L. E., & Larson, J. (1994). Ruminative coping with depressed mood following loss. *Journal of Personality and Social Psychology, 67,* 92–104.

Panzarella, C., Alloy, L. B., & Whitehouse, W. G. (2002). *Expanded hopelessness theory of depression: On the mechanisms by which social support protects against depression.* Manuscript submitted for publication.

Persons, J. B., & Miranda, J. (1992). Cognitive theories of vulnerability to depression: Reconciling negative evidence. *Cognitive Therapy and Research, 16,* 485–502.

Pyszczynski, T., & Greenberg, J. (1987). Self-regulatory perseveration and the depressive self-focusing style: A self-awareness theory of reactive depression. *Psychological Bulletin, 102,* 122–138.

Reilly-Harrington, N., Alloy, L. B., Fresco, D. M., & Whitehouse, W. G. (1999). Cognitive styles and life events interact to predict bipolar and unipolar symptomatology. *Journal of Abnormal Psychology, 108,* 567–578.

Robinson, N. S., Garber, J., & Hilsman, R. (1995). Cognitions and stress: Direct and moderating effects on depressive versus externalizing symptoms during the junior high transition. *Journal of Abnormal Psychology, 104,* 453–463.

Rohde, P., Lewinsohn, P. M., & Seeley, J. R. (1991). Are people changed by the experience of having an episode of depression?: A further test of the scar hypothesis. *Journal of Abnormal Psychology, 99,* 264–271.

Scheier, M. F., & Carver, C. S. (1977). Self-focused attention and the experience of emotion: Attraction, repulsion, elation, and depression. *Journal of Personality and Social Psychology, 35,* 625–636.

Seligman, M. E. P. (1975). *Helplessness: On depression, development, and death.* New York: Freeman.

Spangler, D. L., Simons, A. D., Monroe, S. M., & Thase, M. E. (1997). Comparison of cognitive models of depression: Relationships betweeen cognitive constructs and cognitive diathesis–stress match. *Journal of Abnormal Psychology, 106,* 395–403.

Spasojevic, J., & Alloy, L. B. (2001). Rumination as a common mechanism relating depressive risk factors to depression. *Emotion, 1,* 25–37.

Sutton, S. K., & Davidson, R. J. (1997). Prefrontal brain asymmetry: A biological substrate of the behavioral approach and inhibition systems. *Psychological Science, 8,* 204–210.

Sweeney, P. D., Anderson, K., & Bailey, S. (1986). Attributional style in depression: A meta-analytic review. *Journal of Personality and Social Psychology, 50,* 974–991.

Teasdale, J. D. (1988). Cognitive vulnerability to persistent depression. *Cognition and Emotion, 2,* 247–274.

Turner, J. E., Jr., & Cole, D. A. (1994). Developmental differences in cognitive diatheses for child depression. *Journal of Abnormal Child Psychology, 22,* 15–32.

Weissman, A., & Beck, A. T. (1978). *Development and validation of the Dysfunctional Attitude Scale: A preliminary investigation.* Paper presented at the annual meeting of the American Educational Research Association, Toronto, Canada.

Williams, J. M. G., Watts, F. N., MacLeod, C., & Matthews, A. (1997). *Cognitive psychology and emotional disorders* (2nd ed.). New York: Wiley.

12

Depression in Its Interpersonal Context

Thomas E. Joiner, Jr.

We are a gregarious species, and it is thus unsurprising that interpersonal analyses have long been a feature of intellectual discourse. For example, from Plato to Rousseau and beyond, political philosophers have emphasized the importance of accounting for—and perhaps even taking advantage of—the powerful influence of the interpersonal context on human affairs. For Plato's philosopher-ruler, for example, interpersonal relations and processes are to be confidently managed and engineered so that the state and thus the individual will be well. It is interesting to note the confident and efficacious tone of these writings, particularly because they stand in contrast to later views of clinical interpersonal phenomena.

Clinical views of interpersonal processes have often not shared this confidence, seeing them as mysterious, annoying, and recalcitrant. Consider a sampling regarding depressed people:

Their complaints are really "plaints" in the legal sense of the word. . . . [E]verything derogatory that they say of themselves at bottom relates to someone else. . . . [T]hey give a great deal of trouble, perpetually taking offence and behaving as if they had been treated with great injustice. (Freud, 1917/1951, p. 247)

The physician tends to shun such persons since they threaten not only his need for professional gratification but, even worse, may affect his own spirits by contagion. (Berblinger, 1970, in a statement that foreshadows later work on "depression contagion," cited in Akiskal, 1983, p. 12).

We wish to insist on the important and little realized fact that the depressed person . . . is always truly aggressive toward others through the very medium of the manifestations of his depression. His suffering is an accusation. His sense of incurableness is a reproach. His demands are perhaps humbling, but devastating. His depression is tyrannical. He wallows in suffering, whilst trying to enmesh his object in it as well. (Nacht & Racamier, 1961, p. 671)

Akiskal (1983) provides similar examples, although not in the same exasperated tone. He refers to the belief in some clinical circles that depressed patients believe in "an aristocracy of suffering," and notes some anecdotes from his clinic in which depressed patients made statements like "I was born depressed" and "I've been unhappy since conception" (p. 12).

Quite a litany. One wonders whether the clinicians might have benefited from the efficacious and analytical approach of the philosophers. Perhaps it is possible, in light of recent work on the interpersonal aspects of depression, to partly achieve this, such that depressotypic interpersonal behavior is demystified and loses the distress and frustration evident in the words of the clinicians. An understanding of the characteristics, motivations, and consequences of depressotypic interpersonal behavior may be a step toward the middle ground. To this end, the goal of this chapter is to survey work examining interpersonal functioning in depression. First, interpersonal characteristics and features of depressed people are summarized. Second, the role of interpersonal factors in etiology is discussed. Third, the interpersonal motivations and consequences of depressotypic interpersonal behaviors are summarized, with a focus on two lines of work that have revealed particular promise. Finally, an interpersonal model of depression chronicity is discussed, one that incorporates much of the material on the interpersonal characteristics, causes, and consequences of depression.

INTERPERSONAL–BEHAVIORAL CHARACTERISTICS OF DEPRESSED PEOPLE

Social Skills and Depression

There is considerable consensus that depression is associated with social skills problems (see Segrin, 2001, which informed several sections below, for a thorough review). People with depression consistently evaluate their own social skills more negatively than do nondepressed people (e.g., Lewinsohn, Mischel, Chaplin, & Barton, 1980; Segrin & Dillard, 1992; Youngren & Lewinsohn, 1980). This result applies to depressed children as well as to depressed adults (e.g., Perez, Pettit, David, Kistner, & Joiner, 2001).

It is not particularly surprising that depressed people evaluate their social skills negatively. But are their negative views of their social skills simply a function of a negative self-evaluation bias (Gotlib, 1983), or do others also rate their social skills negatively? Among others, Dykman, Horowitz, Abramson, and Usher (1991) found that depressed people's negative self-views of their social skills are based, at least in part, on actual performance deficits (this too applies to children; see Perez et al., 2001). When observers or conversational partners rate depressed people's social skills, a common finding is that depressed people's skills are rated as lower than those of nondepressed controls (Lewinsohn et al., 1980; Segrin, 1992), although this has not always been the case (Gotlib & Meltzer, 1987). Segrin's (1990) meta-analysis concluded that depressed-nondepressed differences on partner or observer ratings of social skills are real, but not as strong as depressed-nondepressed differences on self-reported social skills.

Therefore, it appears that depressed persons' self-ratings of their social skills contain at least some accuracy: the negative self-ratings do correspond to skills problems as assessed by observer ratings (e.g., Segrin, 1990). However, depressed-nondepressed differences on self-ratings usually exceed depressed-nondepressed differences on observer ratings, such that depressed people may view their social skills more negatively than others do. This pattern of findings is consistent with a tradition of work that suggests that misperceptions of one's own characteristics typify mental illness. In the case of depressed people, the misperception is in the negative direction; interestingly, it has been shown that misperceptions in the positive direction (i.e., peoples' self-evaluations exceed others' evaluations) also may be characteristic of psychopathology, especially personality disorders (e.g., narcissistic personality disorders) and disruptive behavior disorders (e.g., conduct disorder; Asendorpf & Ostendorf, 1998; Colvin, Block, & Funder, 1995; Perez et al., 2001). Also of interest, the result that depressed people may overestimate the negative quality of their social skills is at odds with the concept of depressive realism (i.e., that those with depression-related symptoms are actually less biased in their perceptions of self than others, that they are "sadder but wiser"; Alloy & Abramson, 1979). Perhaps it is not surprising that self-denigration is associated with more depression-related symptomatology, in that the connection between negative perceptual and cognitive distortions and psychopathological symptoms pervades nosological schemes (e.g., the DSM), and also forms the foundation for cognitive theory and therapies (e.g., Beck, Rush, Shaw, & Emery, 1979) for several syndromes, including depression.

Communication Behaviors and Depression

A related line of research has examined the communication behaviors of depressed versus nondepressed people. For example, compared to nondepressed people, depressed people speak more slowly and with less volume and voice modulation; depressed people have longer pauses in their speech patterns and take longer to respond when someone else addresses them (e.g., Talavera, Saiz-Ruiz, & Garcia-Toro, 1994; Teasdale, Fogarty, & Williams, 1980; Youngren & Lewinsohn, 1980). Because factors like voice modulation, rate of speech, and verbal responses account for the animated and appealing qualities of speech, it is not surprising that the voices of depressed people are perceived negatively by others (e.g., Tolkmitt, Helfrich, Standke, & Scherer, 1982).

In addition to the *quality* of speech, investigators have also examined the *content* of speech in depression. In studies of married couples with a depressed member, themes involving dysphoric feelings and negative self-evaluation were likely to emerge in their conversations (e.g., Hautzinger, Linden, & Hoffman, 1982). Angry exchanges and less cooperation have also been noted in marital interaction studies involving depressed people. It has been found that depressed people may be at their most expressive with their spouses when they are discussing negative issues (e.g., Hinchliffe, Vaughan, Hooper, & Roberts, 1977). Similar findings have been obtained among other types of dyads, including college student friendships, strangers paired together in the laboratory, telephone conversations between friends, and therapist–patient dyads (e.g., Belsher & Costello, 1991; Coyne, 1976a; Gotlib & Robinson, 1982; Weissman & Klerman, 1993).

However, there is some evidence that negativity in social interactions is particularly likely to emerge between depressed people and intimate relationship partners, as opposed to strangers or nonintimate acquaintances. For example, Segrin and Flora (1998) studied depressed and nondepressed students discussing "events of the day" with either a friend or a stranger. They reported that depressed students tended to withhold negative verbal content when talking with strangers, but were more likely to disclose negative topics when talking with a friend.

The finding by Segrin and Flora (1998) qualifies the more general result that depressed people are more likely than others to engage in negative self-disclosures. Jacobson and Anderson (1982), for example, found that depressed participants were more likely than nondepressed participants to emit unsolicited negative self-disclosures. The study by Segrin and Flora (1998) suggests that this problem may be particularly acute in relationships between depressed people and intimate others.

Marital and Parental Relationships and Depression

In this context, it is not surprising that depression and disruptions in marital relationships have been shown to be robustly associated (e.g., Beach & O'Leary, 1993). Interestingly, changes in depressive symptoms correspond to changes in marital functioning—that is, as depressive symptoms wax and wane, the quality of marital relationships falls and rises. The relationship between depressive symptoms and marital quality appears to be bidirectional, in that one leads to the other, and vice versa. There is some evidence that the direction from depression to marital problems is more pronounced for depressed men and their wives, whereas the direction from marital problems to depression is more pronounced for depressed women and their husbands (Fincham, Beach, Harold, & Osborne, 1997). Another potential explanation for the association between depression and marital problems is that depressed people may marry earlier—and perhaps more hastily—than others, perhaps in an effort to solve ongoing depression-related problems (Gotlib, Lewinsohn, & Seeley, 1998). It would not be surprising if such efforts frequently backfired.

Hinchcliffe and her colleagues have documented some specific problems that arise between depressed people and their marital partners (e.g., Hinchcliffe, Hooper, Roberts, & Vaughn, 1975; Hinchcliffe et al., 1977). For example, depressed people may be excessively self-focused and thus may not be as able as nondepressed people to respond sensitively to the perspective and feelings of their spouses. Other documented interpersonal problems that occur between depressed people and their spouses are similar to those that have been observed between depressed people and others generally, such as self-denigration, poor problem-solving communications, anger and hostility, and intimacy problems (Basco, Prager, Pite, Tamir, & Stephens, 1992).

Just as relationship problems have been documented as both antecedents and consequences of depression among marital dyads, they have been shown to operate similarly among parent–child dyads. The findings on the interpersonal–behavioral characteristics of depressed people in relationships generally (e.g., withdrawal, anger, poor problem solving) appear to also apply to depressed parents in relationship to their children. It has been repeatedly shown that the children of depressed parents are at increased risk for depression themselves (as well as for other behavioral and emotional disturbances). There is little doubt that this association stems, in part, from genetic and neurobiological sources, which parents and children share (especially depressed mothers and children *in utero*). Additional likely sources include shared family stressors, including marital disputes, and parental underinvolvement (see Goodman & Gotlib, 1999, for a thorough review of this literature). Although much of this literature has focused on depressed mothers and their children, there is evidence that many of the same problems occur between depressed fathers and their children (e.g., Phares & Compas, 1992).

Similar to the evidence that depressed people may marry earlier and more hastily than others (Gotlib et al., 1998), perhaps in an attempt to solve ongoing problems, it is possible that depressed women may become pregnant earlier than others, perhaps in an attempt to solve depression-related problems, including low intimacy. In fact, consistent with this possibility, Wagner, Berenson, Harding, and Joiner (1998) reported that initially pessimistic teenagers reported low depression while pregnant (perhaps because of the belief that connection to the baby and the baby's father would solve ongoing problems), but reported high depression postpartum (perhaps because, in addition to the usual physiological and psychological challenges of childbirth, the idea that motherhood would solve ongoing problems was not confirmed).

Basic Behavioral Features of Depression

Some of depressed people's interpersonal difficulties may stem from basic differences between depressed and nondepressed people on such factors as facial expressions, eye contact, posture, gesturing, and so forth. There is evidence to suggest that the facial expressions of depressed people are more animated than those of other people when expressing sadness; otherwise, depressed people's facial expressions are generally less animated than others' (Schwartz, Fair, Salt, Mandel, & Klerman, 1976a, 1976b). This result is reminiscent of that mentioned earlier in which depressed people are at their most expressive when discussing negative issues with their spouses. In addition to less animation (except when sad), depressed people's facial expressions have been characterized as including a corrugated brow, squinting or closed eyes, and a turned-down mouth (e.g., Greden, 1986). Interestingly, these features have been shown to improve with successful treatment (Ellgring, 1986).

Several studies have demonstrated that depressed people engage in less eye contact than do nondepressed people (e.g., Kazdin, Sherick, Esveldt-Dawson, & Rancurello, 1985; Segrin, 1992; Youngren & Lewinsohn, 1980). Interestingly, Segrin (1992) showed that this phenomenon is even more pronounced in naturalistic situations where eye contact is measured with unobtrusive measurement techniques, as opposed to more standard laboratory situations, which may be less ecologically valid and in which measurement may be more obtrusive. This result parallels the finding described earlier regarding the tendency for depressotypic interpersonal behavior to be intensified in more intimate relationships.

Similar findings have emerged with regard to posture and nonverbal gestures. For example, depressed individuals may hold their head in a downward position more than nondepressed persons, and may engage in more self-touching (e.g., rubbing, scratching—possible indicators of distress and discomfort) than nondepressed people (e.g., Ranelli & Miller, 1981).

Depressed people have also been found to engage in less head-nodding than others (an affirmative gesture that others find rewarding; Troisi & Moles, 1999). Here, as before, this finding appears stronger when depressed people are interacting with intimate than with nonintimate others (Hale, Jansen, Bouhuys, & Jenner, 1997). Kazdin et al. (1985) found that depressed children may not use illustrators (speech-accompanying gestures) as much as nondepressed children do. Interestingly, as with facial expressions, it appears that as the symptoms of depression remit, the tendency to use illustrators increases (e.g., Ekman & Friesen, 1972).

Summary

To summarize, depressed people, compared to their nondepressed counterparts, have been characterized as lower in self-rated and actual social skills, as more negative in speech quality and content, as more likely to have less animated facial expressions (except when sad), as exhibiting less eye contact, and as demonstrating less nonverbal gesturing showing interest in others. The effects of these characteristics, including on marital and parental relationships, is likely to be negative. While these interpersonal variables appear to be concomitants of depression, what is the evidence that interpersonal variables are related to vulnerability to depression in the first place?

INTERPERSONAL RISK FACTORS FOR DEPRESSION

Generally speaking, work on interpersonal vulnerability to depression falls into three nonexclusive categories: (1) impaired social skills as a risk factor, (2) excessive interpersonal dependency as a risk factor, and (3) excessive interpersonal inhibition as a risk factor. Each of these areas is briefly summarized in turn.

Social Skill Impairment as a Risk Factor for Depression

Although there is some support in the literature for the view that social skills problems are an antecedent of depression, it appears that the majority of this evidence does not support this view. On the positive side of the ledger, studies by Wierzbicki and McCabe (e.g., 1988) found that social skill deficits at one point and time were predictive of depressive symptoms assessed 2 months later. However, other studies have failed to find this effect; importantly, the negative studies have several strong methodological features, including structured clinical interviews for mood disorders among large samples (e.g., Lewinsohn et al., 1994) and longer time frames (e.g., Segrin, 1996). Thus, evidence for the main effect of social skills problems on later depression is relatively weak.

Nonetheless, this leaves open the possibility that social skills deficits operate as a risk factor for depression *only under certain circumstances,* such as in the presence of negative life events. Although this possibility has not yet received abundant research attention, Segrin and colleagues have provided evidence in support of this view. For example, in a study of college freshmen who had moved a long distance from home to attend college (conceived as a stressful experience), Segrin and Flora (2000) found that social skills problems assessed during the senior year of high school predicted depressive symptoms at the end of the first college semester. From this perspective, social skills problems comprise a diathesis that leads to depression only when it is activated by stress.

There is emerging evidence that a particular instance of impaired social skills, termed *negative feedback seeking,* may also serve as a risk factor for depression. Negative feedback seeking is defined as the tendency to actively solicit criticism and other negative interpersonal feedback from others, and derives from self-verification theory (Swann, 1990). This theory argues that the need to attain self-consistent and self-verifying information is powerful enough that it may override the pain of seeking and receiving negative feedback. Thus, for people with negative self-views, including depressed people, negative feedback is sought even at the expense of the pain it may cause.

Because it may seem counterintuitive, it is sometimes questioned whether people actively seek feedback that is negative and painful. In a convincing series of studies, Swann and colleagues have shown that people with low self-esteem are indeed attracted to negative feedback, even when they are simultaneously presented with choices for neutral and positive feedback. In an application of the theory to bulimic symptoms, Joiner (1999a) showed that women with bulimic symptoms sought negative feedback about appearance, weight, and body shape, even though clinical descriptions of bulimia (and reports of bulimic patients themselves) indicate that such feedback would be painful and upsetting indeed.

In an application of the theory specifically to depression, Swann and colleagues (Swann, Wenzlaff, Krull, & Pelham, 1992; Swann, Wenzlaff, & Tafarodi, 1992) proposed that depressed people elicit interpersonal rejection because they gravitate to persons who evaluate them negatively (a form of negative feedback seeking). Consistent with this view, these researchers found that, compared to nondepressed students, depressed students sought more negative feedback from others and were more rejected by others. Giesler, Josephs, and Swann (1996) examined self-verification theory among clinically depressed participants and reported that, when presented with a choice between negative and positive feedback, 82% of clinically depressed adults chose unfavorable over favorable feedback, compared to 64% of nondepressed, low self-esteem participants and 25% of nondepressed, high self-esteem participants. Joiner, Katz, and Lew (1997) extended this work to children and adolescents, and found that depressed youth psychiatric inpatients expressed more interest in negative feedback than did nondepressed youth psychiatric inpatients.

Negative feedback seeking may also represent an antecedent of depression. Joiner (1995) found that requests for negative feedback, if honored (i.e., negative feedback provided), predisposed people to future depressive reactions. This finding, like the diathesis–stress results on social skills by Segrin and Flora (2000), suggests that negative feedback seeking not only characterizes depressed people, but, at least under certain conditions, may render people vulnerable to future onset of depression.

Interpersonal Inhibition as a Risk Factor for Depression

Although the possibility has not received enough empirical attention, there is at least some reason to suspect that interpersonal inhibition (e.g., avoidance, withdrawal, shyness) represents a risk factor for depression. There is little doubt that depression is associated with low assertiveness, social withdrawal, avoidance, and shyness. Ball, Otto, Pollack, and Rosenbaum (1994) found that lack of assertiveness was a predictor of major depression, even beyond the variance accounted for by a very strong clinical predictor: past history of depression. Pini, Cassano, Simonini, and Savino (1997) found that social phobia—an avoidance-related syndrome—was highly associated with depression versus closely related conditions, such as bipolar disorder. Similarly, Alpert, Uebelacker, McLean, and Nierenberg (1997) reported that avoidant personality disorder was strongly associated with depression, and, further, found that depressed people with avoidant pathology were more likely than other depressed people to report an early age of depression onset—a mark of depression chronicity. Various reports have also demonstrated that shyness is associated with depression (Alfano, Joiner, Perry, & Metalsky, 1994; Anderson & Harvey, 1988), as well as with many of its symptoms (e.g., low self-esteem; Cheek & Buss, 1981; Jones, Cavert, Snider, & Bruce, 1986), and correlates (e.g., negative cognitive style; Alfano et al., 1994; loneliness; Jones et al., 1986). Parker, Hadzi-Pavlovic, Brodaty, and Boyce (1992) reported that absence of childhood shyness predicted better outcome (e.g., longer remission, fewer relapses) among depressed adults.

In addition, there is some evidence that shyness and withdrawal serve as vulnerability factors for future depression. VanValkenberg, Winokur, Lowry, Behar, and Van Velkenberg (1983) found a retrospectively reported premorbid personality profile, which included shyness, in depressed women. Nystrom and Lindegard (1975) reported that a number of traits, including shyness, may serve as predisposing factors to depression. Joiner (1997) found that shy undergraduates were prone to increases in depression symptoms in the absence, but not in the presence, of social support, as a function of increases in loneliness. Among children, Boivin, Hymel, and Burkowski (1995) reported that social withdrawal was a risk factor for the subsequent occurrence of depressive symptoms.

In this context, it is interesting to note that Price, Sloman, Gardner, Gilbert, and Rohde (1994) have argued from an evolutionary–psychological perspective that depression may represent an evolved form of a primordial "involuntary subordinate strategy," which arose as a means to cope with social competition and conflict, particularly losses therein. These authors contend that the primary function of depression is to facilitate *withdrawal* in threatening interpersonal conflict situations, so that people can "cut their losses," "live to fight another day," and, relatedly, communicate a "no threat" signal to others. Consistent with this model, Shively, Laber-Laird, and Anton (1997) reported that manipulation of social status among female cynomolgus monkeys, such that previously dominant animals became subordinate, produced behavioral and hormonal depressive reactions (e.g., fearful scanning of the environment, hypersecretion of cortisol). Notably, a key behavioral feature of newly subordinate animals was decreased social affiliation (cf. interpersonal avoidance).

From a conceptual standpoint, it stands to reason that interpersonal inhibition and avoidance may lead to future depression because they involve diminution of social reinforcement and social support. As Lewinsohn (e.g., Lewinsohn, 1974), Rehm (e.g., 1977), and others have persuasively argued, lack of positive reinforcement is involved in maintaining depression; low social support, too, maintains depression (Joiner, 1997; Roos & Cohen, 1987) and predicts depression chronicity (Brugha, Bebbington, MacCarthy, & Stuart, 1990; Lara, Leader, & Klein, 1997).

Excessive Interpersonal Dependency as a Risk Factor for Depression

There is a reasonably well-established empirical tradition, especially in psychiatry and personality psychology, identifying *interpersonal dependency* as a risk factor for depression (Blatt, Quinlan, Chevron, McDonald, & Zuroff, 1982; Hirschfeld, Klerman, Clayton, & Keller, 1983; Kendler, Neale, Kessler, Heath, & Eaves, 1993). In this regard, a relevant line of thought regarding interpersonal vulnerability has emerged from within the cognitive approach. Beck's (1983) notion of sociotropy (cf. Arieti & Bemporad's [1980] notion of the dominant-other orientation, and Blatt's [1974] concept of anaclitic depression) indicates that excessive need for and doubt of interpersonal attachment (e.g., acceptance, support, guidance, admiration; see Beck, 1983, p. 272) leads to behaviors (e.g., obsequiousness) that cause and maintain depression. Beck (1983) proposed that autonomy—a pronounced need for control, achievement, and independence—may also represent a depression risk. Interestingly, although the empirical literature is not uniform (see Coyne & Whiffen, 1995), the weight of the evidence indicates that sociotropy is a stronger risk factor for depression than is autonomy (e.g., Allen, de L. Horne, & Trinder, 1996; Enns & Cox, 1997). Robins, Block, and Peselow (1989) found that sociotropy was strongly related to depressotypic clinical features, particularly those aspects that involve interpersonal sensitivity (e.g., response to caregivers, lability of mood; see also Robins & Luten, 1991; Peselow, Robins, Sanfilipo, Block, & Fieve, 1992). Similarly, Hammen et al. (1995) reported that interpersonal attachment cognitions combined with interpersonal stress to predict depression and other symptoms. Mazure, Bruce, Maciejewski, and Jacobs (2000) reported that sociotropy was significantly related to onset of major depression.

The results of other studies examining the general personality construct of interpersonal dependency also support its role in contributing to the development of depression. For example, using a daily experiences methodology, Stader and Hokanson (1998) found that feelings of dependency preceded, by one day, the onset of periods of relatively intense depression. Fichman, Koestner, and Zuroff (1997) showed that children high in dependency were more prone than other children to experience depressive symptoms in the context of going to "sleepaway" camp. Self-criticism, a construct related to autonomy, did not predict depressive reactions among the "sleepaway" camp children. Alnaes and Torgersen (1997) reported that dependency predicted relapse of major depression among psychiatric outpatient adults. VanValkenberg et al. (1983) found that a premorbid personality profile, including demandingness and neediness (cf. dependency), characterized depressed people.

Recently, Joiner, Metalsky, and colleagues have argued that a specific facet of interpersonal dependency, termed *excessive reassurance seeking*, may represent a vulnerability factor for future depression. Similar to sociotropy, excessive reassurance seeking is defined as the tendency to repeatedly seek assurance from others concerning one's worth and lovability, regardless of whether such assurance has already been provided. The concept stems from Coyne's (1976b) work, which proposed that depression-prone people may excessively seek reassurance in response to negative affect or a negative life event. Although others may provide reassurance, depression-prone people doubt its sincerity, and are again compelled to seek reassurance. A repetitive pattern is thus established, in which increasing demands for reassurance are made, inducing frustration, irritation, even depression in others, and increasing the likelihood that others will reject depression-prone people. The ensuing interpersonal disruption increases risk for the onset of depression.

In empirical tests of this perspective, Joiner and Metalsky (2001) reported that, among clinically diagnosed participants, those diagnosed with depression attained higher scores on a measure of excessive reassurance seeking compared to those diagnosed with other disorders. Interestingly, this pattern of findings did not apply to other interpersonal variables, suggesting that there is specificity to the link between excessive reassurance seeking and depression. This series of studies also showed that adults who develop future depressive symptoms (compared to those who remain symptom-free) obtained elevated reassurance seeking scores at baseline, when all participants were symptom-free, but did not obtain elevated scores on other interpersonal variables. Furthermore, in two separate studies within the series, excessive reassurance seeking predicted future depressive reactions to stress in both the interpersonal and the achievement domains. Additional studies have supported this view as well (Joiner, 1999b; Joiner, Metalsky, Gencoz, & Gencoz, 2001; Joiner & Schmidt, 1998; Potthoff, Holahan, & Joiner, 1995).

INTERPERSONAL CONSEQUENCES OF DEPRESSION

Given that depression may be associated with negative feedback seeking, impaired social skills, interpersonal avoidance, and excessive reassurance seeking *premorbidly,* and given that current symptoms are clearly associated with social skills problems, negative verbal and nonverbal parameters, and so forth, it is not surprising that the personal relationships of depressed people are affected. In fact, the relationships of depressed people are characterized by such dimensions as rejection, dissatisfaction, low intimacy, and decreased activity and involvement (e.g., Gotlib & Lee, 1989; Joiner, Alfano, & Metalsky, 1992, 1993).

Depression is clearly associated with problems in marital interactions and relationships (Beach, Sandeen, & O'Leary, 1990). As noted earlier, dysphoric feelings and negative self-evaluation were likely to emerge in conversations between married partners with a depressed member (e.g., Hautzinger et al., 1982), and anger and low cooperation have been noted in such marriages as well. Depressed spouses may be less likely to reciprocate their partner's positive behaviors with positive behaviors of their own (Johnson & Jacob, 2000). It is possible that these negative relationship patterns are maintained because depressive behaviors may inhibit the hostile and irritable behaviors of the spouse.

Evidence is also accumulating that interpersonal problems extend to the parent–child as well as the marital relationship. In general, this literature demonstrates that such problems as hostility, negativity, lack of positive reciprocation, and so forth, occur between parents and children much as they do between spouses (e.g., Hammen, Adrian, Gordon, & Jaenicke, 1987). As noted earlier, the children of depressed parents appear to be at heightened risk for depression themselves, both in childhood and in adulthood, perhaps partly as a consequence of disrupted parent–child relations (see Downey & Coyne, 1990, for a review).

In addition to relationship problems, there is some evidence that one interpersonal consequence of depression is *contagious depression,* the spread of depressive symptoms from one person to another. Recall Berblinger's (1970) statement, mentioned earlier, about depressed people, that "the physician tends to shun such persons since they threaten not only his need for professional gratification but, even worse, may affect his own spirits by contagion." It is clear that spouses who live with a depressed person often experience high levels of depression themselves (e.g., Benazon & Coyne, 2000; Coyne et al., 1987). In a meta-analysis on contagion of depressive symptoms and mood from 36 studies ($N = 4,952$), Joiner and Katz (1999) reached the following conclusions: (1) there was substantial support for the view that depressive symptoms and mood are contagious, but the phenomenon was most pronounced in studies of depressive symptoms (vs. depressive mood); (2) contagion of depressive mood depended upon methodological approach, with strongest to weakest results in the following order: transcript studies, audio/videotape studies, studies using actual strangers, studies using actual friends/acquaintances, and confederate studies; (3) contagion of depressed mood/symptoms held across combinations of target × respondent gender; and (4) there was some tentative evidence that contagion was specific to depressive versus other symptoms and moods.

In a study specifically designed to address contagion of depressive symptoms, Joiner (1994) demonstrated that the roommates of depressed college students tended to experience increased depressive symptoms themselves over the course of a few weeks. Shared negative life stress was ruled out as an explanation of the finding. This effect was particularly pronounced among roommate dyads in which there were high levels of reassurance seeking, a finding consistent with the view that excessive reassurance seeking may serve as an "interpersonal vehicle" that carries the distress and desperation of depressive symptoms from one person to another.

In fact, this same line of reasoning appears to apply to interpersonal rejection (just as it may apply to contagion of depressive symptoms). Specifically, Joiner, Metalsky and colleagues have found that those with depressive symptoms do *not* elicit interpersonal rejection *unless* they are *also* excessive in reassurance seeking (Joiner et al., 1992, 1993; Joiner & Metalsky, 1995; Joiner, 1999b). This line of work has also found that those with depressive symptoms and who engage in multiple depressotypic interpersonal behaviors (e.g., excessive reassurance seeking and negative feedback seeking) are especially likely to disaffect others (e.g., Joiner & Metalsky, 1995). Notably, in these studies, neither depression nor depressotypic interpersonal behavior was *individually* related to indices of interpersonal rejection, but their combination was.

An interesting question thus emerges: Why is neither depression nor, for example, reassurance seeking, sufficient in themselves to induce rejection from others? It may be that, without the urgency and desperation associated with depressive symptoms, reassurance seeking alone may be relatively tolerable to others (Joiner et al., 1992, 1993). Furthermore, without the interpersonal mobility afforded by persistent reassurance seeking, depression may be relatively tolerable to others (i.e., others tolerate depression unless it is persistently "taken to them"). Indeed, in some studies depressed *low* reassurance seekers have been *positively* appraised, perhaps because they are viewed as self-sufficient in the face of hardship (Joiner et al., 1992).

AN INTEGRATIVE INTERPERSONAL FRAMEWORK
FOR THE STUDY OF DEPRESSION AND ITS CHRONICITY

Two important features of depression are that it persists and that it recurs. The average length of major depressive episodes is approximately 8 months in adults (Shapiro & Keller, 1981), and is similar in children (Kovacs, Obrosky, Gatsonis, & Richards, 1997). Mean length of dysthymic episodes may be as much as 30 *years* in adults (Shelton, Davidson, Yonkers, & Koran, 1997); the corresponding figure for children is 4 years (Kovacs et al.,

1997). High proportions of people who previously experienced depression will experience it again; Emslie, Rush, Weinberg, and Guillon (1997) found that 61% of depressed children experienced recurrence of depression within 2 years, and similar 2-year relapse rates have been reported among adults (Belsher & Costello, 1988; Bothwell & Scott, 1997). In studies with long-term follow-ups (e.g., of 10 years or more), Coryell and Winokur (1992) reported that, on average, 70% of people with one depressive episode subsequently experienced at least one more. In the DSM-IV Mood Disorders Field Trial (Keller et al., 1995), the most frequent course among several hundred patients with current major depression was "recurrent, with antecedent dysthymia, without full interepisode recovery." Indeed, it is quite common for subclinical depressive symptoms to persist in the wake of a remitted depressive episode (Judd et al., 2000), and it has been shown that these subclinical symptoms cause considerable distress and impairment (Hays, Wells, Sherbourne, Rogers, & Spritzer, 1995), including heightened risk for future episodes (Judd et al., 2000). Depression is thus persistent within acute episodes, and recurrent across substantial portions of people's lives. Chronicity is a feature of depression about which a useful explanatory model should have something to say.

Joiner (2000) argued that interpersonal self-propagatory processes were involved in generating and maintaining depression, and may thus partly explain the chronicity of depression. Joiner defines a self-propagatory process as a complex of psychological and behavioral factors, that (1) represents depression-related, initiated, and active behaviors that (2) serve to prolong or exacerbate existing symptoms or to induce the recurrence of past symptoms.

The general logic of this perspective is that several depression-related mechanisms actively produce an array of interpersonal and other problems; these problems, in turn, are strong predictors of lengthened and/or future depression. The framework borrows heavily from Hammen and colleagues' (e.g., Hammen, 1991) work on *stress generation* (contributing to the occurrence of one's own negative interpersonal events). Stress generation is viewed as a higher order concept that may subsume several specific mechanisms for the generation of stress and the propagation of depression. Several of these specific mechanisms have been mentioned already (e.g., negative feedback seeking, excessive reassurance seeking, interpersonal avoidance). Each of these mechanisms was claimed to propagate depression through diminution of social reinforcement and social support.

For example, excessive reassurance seeking is an active and motivated behavior on the part of the depressed person, in keeping with the definition for a self-propagatory process. It has been well established that interpersonal dependency in general (Blatt et al., 1982), and excessive reassurance seeking in particular (Joiner & Schmidt, 1998), are common concomitants of depression. Moreover, excessive reassurance seeking is involved in the generation of interpersonal stress (e.g., rejection—Potthoff et al., 1995; and "contagious" depression—Coyne et al., 1987; Joiner, 1994). As described earlier, there is evidence that excessive reassurance seeking is implicated in the development of depression itself (e.g., Joiner & Metalsky, 2001). Overall, then, excessive reassurance seeking, interpersonal stress, and depression are all reciprocally involved, with one often leading to the other in serial fashion. In this light, the chronicity of depression is a consequence of this serial, unfolding process in people's lives. Similar arguments can be made for such variables as negative feedback seeking and interpersonal avoidance.

Borrowing from the work of Sacco (1999), Joiner (2000) noted an additional process that deserves mention and future research, namely, *blame maintenance,* defined as the development of negatively tinged and autonomous person perceptions of the depressed person in the minds of others. Once these perceptions are developed, they take on an independent and autonomous quality, in that they selectively guide attention to confirm themselves.

Once crystallized, these perceptions of negative behaviors are more difficult to change than representations of positive behaviors (Rothbart & Park, 1986).

Importantly, negative person perceptions can be viewed as an antecedent of blaming and otherwise negative communications from others to the depressed person. It has been documented that these negative communications, in turn, predict various forms of depression and its chronicity (Hooley & Teasdale, 1999). Ironically, due to the press of self-verification needs, depressed patients may actively solicit these negative communications; even if they do not, they may be forthcoming nonetheless because of the influence of blame maintenance processes.

FUTURE DIRECTIONS

Depression, depressotypic interpersonal behaviors (e.g., social skills problems, negative verbal and nonverbal behaviors, excessive reassurance seeking, negative feedback seeking, etc.), interpersonal rejection (along with other types of stress), and contagious depression comprise intertwining threads that together make up the fabric of the depressive social environment. Each of these categories of variables may act as vulnerability factors for the others. Each class may serve as an entree into a circular and self-amplifying pathway featuring the others.

A more textured understanding of the threads of this pathway, and how they relate to noninterpersonal risk factors for depression, represents a major avenue for future research from an interpersonal perspective. Importantly, it is not claimed here that interpersonal factors account for most aspects of depression. Additional factors are clearly at play, including noninterpersonal, stable vulnerability factors, that maintain risk over time (actually, factors such as negative feedback seeking, excessive reassurance seeking, and interpersonal conflict avoidance may have stable qualities, as shyness clearly does; see Kagan, Resnick, & Snidman, 1988). Examples of persistent vulnerabilities may include genetic and neurobiological risk factors, as well as cognitive style risk factors (Abramson, Metalsky, & Alloy, 1989; Beck, 1983; Goodman & Gotlib, 1999; Nolen-Hoeksema, 1991). The interplay of interpersonal and noninterpersonal risks for depression is an understudied question: Do these factors interact with one another to amplify risk? Does an interpersonal factor lead to depression *because* it exacerbates underlying cognitive or neurobiological variables, or vice versa?

As one example, Nolen-Hoeksema and colleagues (e.g., Nolen-Hoeksema, Morrow, & Fredrickson, 1993) have proposed that a ruminative response style represents a stable vulnerability to depression (see Nolen-Hoeksema, Chapter 21, this volume). Specifically, they have argued that the duration of depressive symptoms is influenced by the manner in which individuals respond to their own symptoms. Ruminative response styles include persistent attention to one's negative emotions; this attention is focused on one's symptoms, as well as on the causes, meanings, and consequences of those symptoms. According to this view, ruminative responses inhibit constructive, goal-directed activity geared toward problem solving and symptom relief. Nolen-Hoeksema and colleagues have shown that depressed people tend to display ruminative response styles, and that such styles lengthen the duration of depressive symptoms (e.g., Nolen-Hoeksema et al., 1993).

Although speculative, one possibility for an integration of interpersonal with cognitive views is that rumination drives such behaviors as excessive reassurance seeking and negative feedback seeking. With respect to reassurance seeking, it is the case that dysphoric ideation and mood fuels excessive reassurance seeking (Joiner et al., 1999). Because rumination may sustain negative ideation and dysphoric mood, it could also drive reassurance seeking. Reassurance seeking, in turn, has been shown to lead to such outcomes as increased depression, interpersonal rejection, and "depression contagion." Similarly, because rumination may maintain focus on feelings of inadequacy or social incompetence, it may induce negative feedback seeking and interpersonal avoidance.

A related direction for future research involves the simultaneous empirical scrutiny of the several interpersonal characteristics and processes summarized here. Although there is reason to believe that each of these variables is associated with depression in substantive ways, a large-scale project clearly documenting involvement in clinical depression would prove illuminating. This same project would also allow comparison of the relative explanatory power of each process in light of the others. Especially if conducted longitudinally, this same project could delineate some particulars of the self-propagatory processes described by Joiner (2000), including their interplay with one another. For example, it is possible that interpersonal avoidance may focus the effects of excessive reassurance seeking and negative feedback seeking on just one or two relationships, thus breaking those relationships and leaving the person bereft of depression-buffering social support.

Another research direction involves the tailoring of psychotherapeutic approaches, based on findings from an interpersonal perspective. Interestingly, on the surface, interpersonal psychotherapy (IPT) for depression (Klerman, Weissman, Rounsaville, & Chevron, 1984) seems to flow naturally from viewing depression in its interpersonal context (and crucially, the treatment seems effective; see, e.g., Weissman & Klerman, 1993; Weissman & Markowitz, Chapter 17, this volume). There is clear compatibility, but nonetheless real discontinuity, between basic research on the interpersonal aspects of depression, on the one hand, and the development and application of IPT on the other hand. Specifically, the emphasis of IPT, on the interpersonal domains of grief, role transitions, role disputes, and social skills does not rely heavily and specifically on the detailed research on, for example, verbal and nonverbal behaviors, or on excessive reassurance seeking and negative feedback seeking. This is less a criticism of IPT (which has proved its merit) than an underscoring of an area for future work that could significantly refine and improve IPT.

Other therapies could be improved as well. Specifically, it is suggested that, within the structure of other empirically validated depression psychotherapies (e.g., cognitive therapy), the following issues be emphasized and examined in future clinical research:

1. *Low self-esteem/social status:* because low self-perceived social status is a painful symptom in itself, because it may serve as a vulnerability factor for increased depression (Arieti & Bemporad, 1980; Butler, Hokanson, & Flynn, 1994), because it fuels both negative feedback seeking and excessive reassurance seeking (Joiner, Katz, & Lew, 1999; Swann, Wenzlaff, et al., 1992), and because it impairs the ability to remedy chronic stressors (Hammen, 1991).
2. *Coping skills:* to develop alternative ways of meeting needs for consolation and confirmation, and to enhance ways of confronting and remedying stressors.
3. *Didactics,* with both depressed patients and significant others, to inform them of depression-related interpersonal processes, and to develop ways to obviate their potentially pernicious effects. Development of written or videotaped materials discussing, for example, excessive reassurance seeking, negative feedback seeking, their motivations, and their consequences, seems quite feasible.

Without knowledge of the characteristics, motivations, and consequences of depressotypic interpersonal behavior, depression and its social vicissitudes would seem bewildering. Considered in this light, the frustrated reactions of many theoreticians and clinicians to depressed patients, highlighted at the beginning of the chapter, become understandable. With knowledge from an interpersonal perspective, they become remediable.

REFERENCES

Abramson, L. Y., Metalsky, G. I., & Alloy, L. B. (1989). Hopelessness depression: A theory-based subtype of depression. *Psychological Review, 96,* 358–372.

Akiskal, H. S. (1983). Dysthymic disorder: Psychopathology of proposed chronic depressive subtypes. *American Journal of Psychiatry, 140,* 11–20.

Alfano, M. S., Joiner, T. E., Jr., Perry, M., & Metalsky, G. I. (1994). Attributional style: A mediator of the shyness–depression relationship? *Journal of Research in Personality, 28,* 287–300.

Allen, N. B., de L. Horne, D. J., & Trinder, J. (1996). Sociotropy, autonomy, and dysphoric emotional responses to specific classes of stress: A psychophysiological evaluation. *Journal of Abnormal Psychology, 105,* 25–33.

Alloy, L. B., & Abramson, L Y. (1979). Judgment of contingency in depressed and nondepressed students: Sadder but wiser? *Journal of Experimental Psychology: General, 108,* 441–485.

Alnaes, R., & Torgersen, S. (1997). Personality and personality disorders predict development and relapses of major depression. *Acta Psychiatrica Scandinavica, 95,* 336–342.

Alpert, J. E., Uebelacker, L. A., McLean, N. E., & Nierenberg, A. A. (1997). Social phobia, avoidant personality disorder and atypical depression: Co-occurrence and clinical implications. *Psychological Medicine, 27,* 627–633.

Anderson, C. A., & Harvey, R. J. (1988). Discriminating between problems in living: An examination of measures of depression, loneliness, shyness, and social anxiety. *Journal of Social and Clinical Psychology, 6,* 482–491.

Arieti, S., & Bemporad, J. (1980). The psychological organization of depression. *American Journal of Psychiatry, 137,* 1360–1365.

Asendorpf, J. B., & Ostendorf, F. (1998). Is self-enhancement healthy? Conceptual, psychometric, and empirical analysis. *Journal of Personality amd Social Psychology, 74,* 955–966.

Ball, S. G., Otto, M. W., Pollack, M. H. . & Rosenbaum, J. F. (1994). Predicting prospective episodes of depression in patients with panic disorder: A longitudinal study. *Journal of Consulting and Clinical Psychology, 62,* 359–365.

Basco, M. R., Prager, K. J., Pite, J. M., Tamir, L. M., & Stephens. (1992). Communication and intimacy in the marriages of depressed patients. *Journal of Family Psychology, 6,* 184–194.

Beach, S. R., & O'Leary, K. D. (1993). Dysphoria and marital discord: Are dysphoric individuals at risk for marital maladjustment? *Journal of Marital and Family Therapy, 19,* 355–368.

Beach, S. R. H., Sandeen, E. E., & O'Leary, K. D. (1990). *Depression in marriage: A model for etiology and treatment.* New York: Guilford Press.

Beck, A. T. (1983). Cognitive therapy of depression: New perspectives. In P. Clayton & J. E. Barret (Eds.), *Treatment of depression: Old controversies and new approaches* (pp. 265–290). New York: Raven Press.

Beck, A. T., Rush, A. J., Shaw, B., & Emery, G. (1979). *Cognitive therapy of depression.* New York: Guilford Press.

Belsher, G., & Costello, C. G. (1988). Relapse after recovery from unipolar depression: A critical review. *Psychological Bulletin, 104,* 84–96.

Belsher, G., & Costello, C. G. (1991). Do confidants of depressed women provide less social support than confidants of nondepressed women? *Journal of Abnormal Psychology, 100,* 516–525.

Benazon, N. R., & Coyne, J. C. (2000). Living with a depressed spouse. *Journal of Family Psychology, 14,* 70–79.

Blatt, S. J. (1974). Levels of object representation in anaclitic and introjective depression. *Psychoanalytic Study of the Child, 29,* 7–157.

Blatt, S., Quinlan, D., Chevron, E., McDonald, C., & Zuroff, D. (1982). Dependency and self criticism: Psychological dimensions of depression. *Journal of Consulting and Clinical Psychology, 50,* 113–124.

Boivin, M., Hymel, S., & Burkowski, W. M. (1995). The roles of social withdrawal, peer rejection, and victimization by peers in predicting loneliness and depressed mood in childhood. *Development and Psychopathology, 7,* 765–785.

Bothwell, R., & Scott, J. (1997). The influence of cognitive variables on recovery in depressed inpatients. *Journal of Affective Disorders, 43,* 207–212.

Brugha, T. S., Bebbington, P. E., MacCarthy, B., & Stuart, E. (1990). Gender, social support, and recovery from depressive disorders: A prospective clinical study. *Psychological Medicine, 20,* 147–156.

Butler, A. C., Hokanson, J. E., & Flynn, H. A. (1994). A comparison of self-esteem lability and low trait self-esteem in vulnerability factors for depression. *Journal of Personality and Social Psychology, 66,* 166–177.

Cheek, J. M., & Buss, A. H. (1981). Shyness and sociability. *Journal of Personality and Social Psychology, 41,* 330–339.

Colvin, C. R., Block, J., & Funder, D. C. (1995). Overly positive self-evaluations and personality: Negative implications for mental health. *Journal of Personality and Social Psychology, 68,* 1152–1162.

Coryell, W., & Winokur, G. (1992). Course and outcome. In E. Paykel (Ed.), *Handbook of affective disorders* (pp. 89–108). New York: Guilford Press.

Coyne, J. C. (1976a). Depression and the response of others. *Journal of Abnormal Psychology, 85,* 186–193.

Coyne, J. C. (1976b). Toward an interactional description of depression. *Psychiatry, 39,* 28–40.

Coyne, J. C., Kessler, R. C., Tal, M., Turnbull, J., Wortman, C. B., & Creden, J. F. (1987). Living with a depressed person. *Journal of Consulting and Clinical Psychology, 55,* 347–352.

Coyne, J. C., & Whiffen, V. E. (1995). Issues in personality as diathesis for depression: The case of sociotropy/dependency and autonomy/self-criticism. *Psychological Bulletin, 118,* 358–378.

Downey, G., & Coyne, J. C. (1990). Children of depressed parents: An integrative review. *Psychological Bulletin, 108,* 50–76.

Dykman, B. M., Horowitz, L. M., Abramson, L. Y., & Usher, M. (1991). Schematic and situational determinants of depressed and nondepressed students' interpretation of feedback. *Journal of Abnormal Psychology, 100,* 45–55.

Ekman, P., & Friesen, W. V. (1972). Hand movements. *Journal of Communication, 22,* 353–374.

Ellgring, H. (1986). Nonverbal expression of psychological studies in psychiatric patients. *European Archives of Psychiatry and Neurological Sciences, 236,* 31–34.

Emslie, G., Rush, A. J., Weinberg, W. A., & Guillon, C. M. (1997). Recurrence of major depressive disorder in hospitalized children and adolescents. *Journal of the American Academy of Child and Adolescent Psychiatry, 36,* 785–792.

Enns, M. W., & Cox, B. J. (1997). Personality dimensions and depression: Review and commentary. *Canadian Journal of Psychiatry, 42,* 274–284.

Fichman, L., Koestner, R., & Zuroff, D. C. (1997). Dependency and distress at summer camp. *Journal of Youth and Adolescence, 26,* 217–232.

Fincham, F. D., Beach, S. R. H., Harold, G. T., & Osborne, L. N. (1997). Marital satisfaction and depression: Different causal relationships for men and women? *Psychological Science, 8,* 351–357.

Freud, S. (1951). Mourning and melancholia. In J. Strachey (Ed. and Trans.), *The standard edition of the complete psychological works of Sigmund Freud* (Vol. 14, pp. 237–260). London: Hogarth Press. (Original work published 1917)

Giesler, R. B., Josephs, R. A., & Swann, W. B. (1996). Self-verification in clinical depression: The desire for negative evaluation. *Journal of Abnormal Psychology, 105,* 358–368.

Goodman, S. H., & Gotlib, I. H. (1999). Risk for psychopathology in the children of depressed mothers: A developmental model for understanding mechanisms of transmission. *Psychological Review, 106,* 458–490.

Gotlib, I. H. (1983). Perception and recall of interpersonal feedback: Negative bias in depression. *Cognitive Therapy and Research, 7,* 399–412.

Gotlib, I. H., & Lee, C. M. (1989). The social functioning of depressed patients: A longitudinal assessment. *Journal of Social and Clinical Psychology, 8,* 223–237.

Gotlib, I. H., Lewinsohn, P. M., & Seeley, J. R. (1998). Consequences of depression during adolescence: Marital status and marital functioning in early adulthood. *Journal of Abnormal Psychology, 107,* 686–690.

Gotlib, I. H., & Meltzer, S. J. (1987). Depression and the perception of social skill in dyadic interaction. *Cognitive Therapy and Research, 11,* 41–54.

Gotlib, I. H., & Robinson, L. A. (1982). Response to depressed individuals: Discrepancies between self-report and observer-rated behavior. *Journal of Abnormal Psychology, 91,* 231–240.

Greden, J. F. (1986). Facial electromyography in depression: Subgroup differences. *Archives of General Psychiatry, 43,* 269–274.

Hale, W. W. III, Jansen, J. H. C., Bouhuys, A. L., & Jenner, J. A. (1997). Non-verbal behavioral interactions of depressed patients with partners and strangers: The role of behavioral social support and involvement in depression persistence. *Journal of Affective Disorders, 44,* 111–122.

Hammen, C. (1991). Generation of stress in the course of unipolar depression. *Journal of Abnormal Psychology, 100,* 555–561.

Hammen, C. L., Adrian, C., Gordon, D., & Jaenicke, C. (1987). Children of depressed mothers: Maternal strain and symptom predictors of dysfunction. *Journal of Abnormal Psychology, 96,* 190–198.

Hammen, C. L., Burge, D., Daley, S. E., Davila, J., Paley, B., & Rudolph, K. D. (1995). Interpersonal attachment cognitions and prediction of symptomatic responses to interpersonal stress. *Journal of Abnormal Psychology, 104,* 436–443.

Hammen, C., Davila, J., Brown, G., Ellicott, A., & Gitlin, M. (1992). Psychiatric history and stress: Predictors of severity of unipolar depression. *Journal of Abnormal Psychology, 101,* 45–52.

Hautzinger, M., Linden, M., & Hoffman, N. (1982). Distressed couples with and without a depressed partner: An analysis of their verbal interaction. *Journal of Behavior Therapy and Experimental Psychiatry, 13,* 307–314.

Hays, R. D., Wells, K. B., Sherbourne, C. D., Rogers, W., & Spritzer, K. (1995). Functioning and well-being outcomes of patients with depression compared with chronic general medical illnesses. *Archives of General Psychiatry, 52,* 11–19.

Hinchliffe, M., Hooper, D., Roberts, F. J., & Vaughn, P. W. (1975). A study of the interaction between depressed patients and their spouses. *British Journal of Psychiatry, 126,* 164–172.

Hinchliffe, M. K., Vaughan, P. W. Hooper, D., & Roberts, F. J. (1977). The melancholy marriage: An inquiry into the interaction of depression: II. Expressiveness. *British Journal of Medical Psychology, 50,* 125–142.

Hirschfeld, R. M. A., Klerman, G. L., Clayton, P. J., & Keller, M. B. (1983). Personality and depression: Empirical findings. *Archives of General Psychiatry, 40,* 993–998.

Hooley, J. M., & Teasdale, J. D. (1989). Predictors of relapse in unipolar depressives: Expressed emotion, marital distress, and perceived criticism. *Journal of Abnormal Psychology, 98,* 229–235.

Jacobson, N. S., & Anderson, E. (1982). Interpersonal skill deficits and depression in college students: A sequential analysis of the timing of self-disclosure. *Behavior Therapy, 13,* 271–282.

Johnson, S. L., & Jacob, T. (2000). Sequential interactions in the marital communication of depressed men and women. *Journal of Consulting and Clinical Psychology, 68,* 4–12.

Joiner, T. E., Jr. (1994). Contagious depression: Existence, specificity to depressed symptoms, and the role of reassurance-seeking. *Journal of Personality and Social Psychology, 67,* 287–296.

Joiner, T. E., Jr. (1995). The price of soliciting and receiving negative feedback: Self-verification theory as a vulnerability to depression theory. *Journal of Abnormal Psychology, 104,* 364–372.

Joiner, T. E., Jr. (1997). Shyness and low social support as interactive diatheses, and loneliness as mediator: Testing an interpersonal-personality view of depression. *Journal of Abnormal Psychology, 106,* 386–394.

Joiner, T. E., Jr. (1999a). Self-verification and bulimic symptoms: Do bulimic women play a role in perpetuating their own dissatisfaction and symptoms? *International Journal of Eating Disorders, 26,* 145–151.

Joiner, T. E., Jr. (1999b). A test of interpersonal theory of depression among youth psychiatric inpatients. *Journal of Abnormal Child Psychology, 27,* 75–84.

Joiner, T. E., Jr. (2000). Depression's vicious scree: Self-propagatory and erosive factors in depression chronicity. *Clinical Psychology: Science and Practice, 7,* 203–218.

Joiner, T. E., Jr., Alfano, M. S., & Metalsky, G. I. (1992). When depression breeds contempt: Reassurance-seeking, self-esteem, and rejection of depressed college students by their roommates. *Journal of Abnormal Psychology, 101,* 165–173.

Joiner, T. E., Jr., Alfano, M. S., & Metalsky, G. I. (1993). Caught in the crossfire: Depression, self-consistency, self-enhancement, and the response of others. *Journal of Social and Clinical Psychology, 12,* 113–134.

Joiner, T. E., Jr., & Katz, J. (1999). Contagion of depressive symptoms and mood: Meta-analytic review and explanations from cognitive, behavioral, and interpersonal viewpoints. *Clinical Psychology: Science and Practice, 6,* 149–164.

Joiner, T. E., Jr., Katz, J., & Lew, A. (1997). Self-verification and depression in youth psychiatric inpatients. *Journal of Abnormal Psychology, 106,* 608–618.

Joiner, T. E., Jr., Katz, J., & Lew, A. (1999). Harbingers of depressotypic reassurance-seeking: Negative life events, increased anxiety, and decreased self-esteem. *Personality and Social Psychology Bulletin, 25,* 646–653.

Joiner, T. E., Jr., & Metalsky, G. I. (1995). A prospective test of an integrative interpersonal theory of depression: A naturalistic study of college roommates. *Journal of Personality and Social Psychology, 69,* 778–788.

Joiner, T. E., Jr., & Metalsky, G. I. (2001). Excessive reassurance-seeking: Delineating a risk factor involved in the development of depressive symptoms. *Psychological Science, 12,* 371–378.

Joiner, T., Metalsky, G., Gencoz, F., & Gencoz, T. (2001). The relative specificity of excessive reassurance-seeking to depression in clinical samples of adults and youth. *Journal of Psychopathology and Behavioral Assessment, 23,* 35–42.

Joiner, T. E., Jr., & Schmidt, N. B. (1998). Excessive reassurance-seeking predicts depressive but not anxious reactions to acute stress. *Journal of Abnormal Psychology, 107,* 533–537.

Jones, W. H., Cavert, C. W., Snider, R. L., & Bruce, T. (1986). Relational stress: An analysis of situations and events associated with loneliness. In S. Duck & D. Perlman (Eds.), *Understanding personal relationships: An interdisciplinary approach* (pp. 221–242). Thousand Oaks, CA: Sage Publications.

Judd, L. L., Paulus, M. J., Schettler, P. J., Akiskal, H. S., Endicott, J., Leon, A. C., Maser, J. D., Mueller, T., Solomon, D. A., & Keller, M. B. (2000). Does incomplete recovery from first lifetime major depressive episode herald a chronic course of illness? *American Journal of Psychiatry, 157,* 1501–1504.

Kagan, J., Resnick, J. S., & Snidman, N. (1988). Biological bases of childhood shyness. *Science, 240,* 167–171.

Kazdin, A. E., Sherick, R. B., Esveldt-Dawson, K., & Rancurello, M. D. (1985). Nonverbal behavior and childhood depression. *Journal of the American Academy of Child Psychiatry, 24,* 303–309.

Keller, M. B., Klein, D. N., Hirschfeld, R. M. A., Kocsis, J. H., McCullough, J. P., Miller, I., First, M. B., Holzer, C. P., Keitner, G. I., Marin, D., & Shea, T. (1995). Results of the DSM-IV mood disorders field trial. *American Journal of Psychiatry, 152,* 843–849.

Kendler, K. S., Neale, M. C., Kessler, R. C., Heath, A. C., & Eaves, L. J. (1993). A longitudinal twin study of personality and major depression in women. *Archives of General Psychiatry, 50,* 853–862.

Klerman, G. L., Weissman, M. M., Rounsaville, B. J., & Chevron, E. S. (1984). *Interpersonal therapy for depression.* New York: Basic Books.

Kovacs, M., Obrosky, S., Gatsonis, C., & Richards, C. (1997). First-episode major depressive and dysthymic disorder in childhood: Clinical and sociodemographic factors in recovery. *Journal of the American Academy of Child and Adolescent Psychiatry, 36,* 777–784.

Lara, M. E., Leader, J., & Klein, D. N. (1997). The association between social support and course of depression: Is it confounded with personality? *Journal of Abnormal Psychology, 106,* 478–482.

Lewinsohn, P. M. (1974). A behavioral approach to depression. In R. J. Friedman & M. M. Katz (Eds.), *The psychology of depression: Contemporary theory and research* (pp. 54–77). Washington, DC: Winston-Wiley.

Lewinsohn, P. M., Mischel, W., Chaplin, W., & Barton, R. (1980). Social competence and depression: The role of illusory self-perceptions. *Journal of Abnormal Psychology, 89,* 203–212.

Lewinsohn, P. M., Roberts, R. E., Seeley, J. R., Rohde, P., Gotlib, I. H., & Hops, H. (1994). Adolescent psychopathology: II. Psychosocial risk factors for depression. *Journal of Abnormal Psychology, 103,* 302–315.

Marcus, D. K., & Nardone, M. E. (1992). Depression and interpersonal rejection. *Clinical Psychology Review, 12,* 433–449.

Mazure, C. M., Bruce, M. L., Maciejewski, P. K., & Jacobs, S. C. (2000). Adverse life events and cognitive-personality characteristics in the prediction of major depression and antidepressant response. *American Journal of Psychiatry, 157,* 896–903.

Nacht, S., & Racamier, P. C. (1961). The depressive states. *Psyche, 14,* 651–677.

Nolen-Hoeksema, S. (1991). Responses to depression and their effects on the duration of depressive episodes. *Journal of Abnormal Psychology, 100,* 569–582.

Nolen-Hoeksema, S., Morrow, J., & Fredrickson, B. L. (1993). Response styles and the duration of episodes of depressed mood. *Journal of Abnormal Psychology, 102,* 20–28.

Nystrom, S., & Lindegard, B. (1975). Depression: Predisposing factors. *Acta Psychiatrica Scandinavica, 51,* 77–87.

Parker, G., Hadzi-Pavlovic, D., Brodaty, H., & Boyce, P. (1992). Predicting the course of melancholic and nonmelancholic depression: A naturalistic comparison study. *Journal of Nervous and Mental Disease, 180,* 693–702.

Perez, M., Pettit, J. W., David, C. F., Kistner, J. A., & Joiner, T. (2001). The interpersonal consequences of inflated self-esteem in an inpatient youth psychiatric sample. *Journal of Consulting and Clinical Psychology, 69,* 712–716.

Peselow, E. D., Robins, C. J., Sanfilipo, M. P., Block, P., & Fieve, R. R. (1992). Sociotropy and autonomy: Relationship to antidepressant drug treatment response and endogenous–nonendogenous dichotomy. *Journal of Abnormal Psychology, 101,* 479–486.

Phares, V., & Compas, B. E. (1992). The role of fathers in child and adolescent psychopathology: Make room for daddy. *Psychological Bulletin, 111,* 387–412.

Pini, S., Cassano, G. B., Simonini, E., & Savino, M. (1997). Prevalence of anxiety disorders comorbidity in bipolar depression, unipolar depression, and dysthymia. *Journal of Affective Disorders, 42,* 145–153.

Potthoff, J. G., Holahan, C. J., & Joiner, T. E., Jr. (1995). Reassurance-seeking, stress generation, and depressive symptoms: An integrative model. *Journal of Personality and Social Psychology, 68,* 664–670.

Price, J., Sloman, L., Gardner, R., Jr., Gilbert, P., & Rohde, P. (1994). The social competition hypothesis of depression. *British Journal of Psychiatry, 164,* 309–315.

Ranelli, C. J., & Miller, R. E. (1981). Behavioral predictors of amitriptyline response in depression. *American Journal of Psychiatry, 138,* 30–34.

Rehm, L. P. (1977). Self-control model of depression. *Behavior Therapy, 8,* 787–804.

Robins, C. J., Block, P., & Peselow, E. D. (1989). Relations of sociotropic and autonomous personality characteristics to specific symptoms in depressed patients. *Journal of Abnormal Psychology, 98,* 86–88.

Robins, C. J., & Luten, A. G. (1991). Sociotropy and autonomy: Differential patterns of clinical presentation in unipolar depression. *Journal of Abnormal Psychology, 98,* 86–88.

Roos, P. E., & Cohen, L. H. (1987). Sex roles and social support as moderators of life stress adjustment. *Journal of Personality and Social Psychology, 52,* 576–585.

Rothbart, M., & Park, B. (1986). On the confirmability and disconfirmability of trait concepts. *Journal of Personality and Social Psychology, 50,* 131–142.

Sacco, W. P. (1999). A social-cognitive model of interpersonal processes in depression. In T. Joiner & J. C. Coyne (Eds.), *The interactional nature of depression* (pp. 329–362). Washington, DC: American Psychological Association Press.

Schwartz, G. E., Fair, P. L., Salt, P., Mandel, M. R., & Klerman, G. (1976a). Facial muscle patterning to affective imagery in depressed and nondepressed subjects. *Science, 192,* 489–491.

Schwartz, G. E., Fair, P. L., Salt, P., Mandel, M. R., & Klerman, G. (1976b). Facial expression and imagery in depression: An electromyographic study. *Psychosomatic Medicine, 38,* 337–347.

Segrin, C. (1990). A meta-analytic review of social skill deficits in depression. *Communication Monographs, 57,* 292–308.

Segrin, C. (1992). Specifying the nature of social skill deficits associated with depression. *Human Communication Research, 19,* 89–123.

Segrin, C. (1996). The relationship between social skills deficits and psychosocial problems: A test of a vulnerability model. *Communication Research, 23,* 425–450.

Segrin, C. (2001). *Interpersonal processes in psychological problems.* New York: Guilford Press.

Segrin, C., & Dillard, J. P. (1992). The interactional theory of depression: A meta-analysis of the research literature. *Journal of Social and Clinical Psychology, 11,* 43–70.

Segrin, C., & Flora, J. (1998). Depression and verbal behavior in conversations with friends and strangers. *Journal of Language and Social Psychology, 17,* 492–503.

Segrin, C., & Flora, J. (2000). Poor social skills are a vulnerability factor in the development of psychosocial problems. *Human Communication Research, 26,* 489–514.

Shapiro, R. W., & Keller, M. B. (1981). Initial 6-month follow-up of patients with major depressive disorder. *Journal of Affective Disorders, 3,* 205–220.

Shelton, R. C., Davidson, J., Yonkers, K. A., & Koran, L. (1997). The undertreatment of dysthymia. *Journal of Clinical Psychiatry, 58,* 59–65.

Shively, C. A., Laber-Laird, K., & Anton, R. F. (1997). Behavior and physiology of social stress and depression in female cynomolgus monkeys. *Biological Psychiatry, 41,* 871–882.

Stader, S. R., & Hokanson, J. E. (1998). Psychosocial antecedents of depressive symptoms: An evaluation using daily experiences methodology. *Journal of Abnormal Psychology, 107,* 17–26.

Swann, W. B., Jr. (1990). To be known or to be adored: The interplay of self-enhancement and self-verification. In E. T. Higgins & R. M. Sorrentino (Eds.), *Handbook of motivation and cognition* (Vol. 2, 408–448). New York: Guilford Press.

Swann, W. B., Jr., Stein-Seroussi, A., & Giesler, R. B. (1992). Why people self-verify. *Journal of Personality and Social Psychology, 62,* 392–401.

Swann, W. B., Wenzlaff, R. M., Krull, D. S., & Pelham, B. W. (1992). Allure of negative feedback: Self-verification strivings among depressed persons. *Journal of Abnormal Psychology, 101,* 293–305.

Swann, W. B., Jr., Wenzlaff, R. M., & Tafarodi, R. W. (1992). Depression and the search for negative evaluations: More evidence of the role of self-verification strivings. *Journal of Abnormal Psychology, 101,* 314–317.

Talavera, J. A., Saiz-Ruiz, J., & Garcia-Toro, M. (1994). Quantitative measurement of depression through speech analysis. *European Psychiatry, 9,* 185–193.

Teasdale, J. D., Fogarty, S. J., & Williams, J. M. (1980). Speech rate as a measure of short-term variation in depression. *British Journal of Social and Clinical Psychology, 19,* 271–278.

Tolkmitt, F., Helfrich, H., Standke, R., & Scherer, K. R. (1982). Vocal indicators of psychiatric treatment effects in depressives and schizophrenics. *Journal of Communication Disorders, 15,* 209–222.

Troisi, A., & Moles, A. (1999). Gender differences in depression: An ethological study of nonverbal behavior during interviews. *Journal of Psychiatric Research, 33,* 243–250.

VanValkenberg, C., Winokur, G., Lowry, M., Behar, D., & VanValkenberg, D. (1983). Depression occurring in chronically anxious patients. *Comprehensive Psychiatry, 24,* 285–289.

Wagner, K. D., Berenson, A., Harding, O., & Joiner, T. E., Jr. (1998). Attributional style and depression in pregnant teenagers. *American Journal of Psychiatry, 155,* 1227–1233.

Weissman, M., & Klerman, G. (Eds.). (1993). *New applications of interpersonal psychotherapy.* Washington, DC: American Psychiatric Press.

Wierzbicki, M., & McCabe, M. (1988). Social skills and subsequent depressive symptomatology in children. *Journal of Clinical Child Psychology, 17,* 203–208.

Youngren, M. A., & Lewinsohn, P. M. (1980). The functional relation between depression and problematic interpersonal behavior. *Journal of Abnormal Psychology, 89,* 333–341.

13

The Social Environment and Depression
Focusing on Severe Life Stress

Scott M. Monroe and Katholiki Hadjiyannakis

The social environment has long been thought to play an integral role in depression. Theorists, clinicians, depressed persons, and others witnessing the personal miseries and social ravages of depression often assume people become depressed at least in part due to problems in their lives. Many believe that these troubled social circumstances penetrate to the core of the depressive experience. It follows from this perspective that gaining insight into the problems of the social realm could yield important clues to the causes, and possibly the cures, of depression. Guided by scientific inquiry, research has sharpened the focus on the social environment and its implications for depression. Much has been learned over the past few decades, and the apparent simplicity of the original ideas has given way to more sophisticated thinking about the social environment and depression (Brown & Harris, 1989; Cronkite & Moos, 1995; Hammen, 1991, 2001; Monroe & Simons, 1991).

The development of more complex, multivariate models of the social environment and depression represents a promising extension of recent research. Yet the expansion of concepts and the intricacies of ideas involved raise many questions and present several challenges. Most generally, how might the multifaceted ideas about the social environment be most meaningfully framed and investigated? How might these ideas be integrated with other concepts and levels of analysis in depression research (e.g., biological, cognitive)? How well do the ideas and data from different perspectives on the social environment and depression come together into a coherent picture? How might apparently conflicting ideas and information be productively reconciled?

The objectives for the present chapter are to characterize the literature on the relationship between the social environment and depression, providing a general overview of the conceptual, methodological, and empirical state of present knowledge. We initially review findings from diverse domains and evaluate the information to narrow the scope of inquiry, with the subsequent goal of developing a more focused and defined working agenda for research. We suggest that life stress represents the most promising nexus between the social environment and depression. To focus matters further, we argue that major, severe life events provide an especially fruitful focal point for theory and for developing research guidelines. Finally, we address the main issues and inconsistencies in the literature and point toward promising directions for future research and theory.

PRELIMINARY CONSIDERATIONS AND CLARIFICATION

Both the "social environment" and "depression" are terms that harbor many meanings. We find it helpful initially to delimit and specify what is to be considered within the broad scope of these expressions. First, it is useful to ask what about the social environment might be most relevant for depression. For instance, at the broadest level the social environment might reflect cultural variation or differences in socioeconomic status (SES); at a more circumscribed level, the social environment might reflect individual differences in major life events or chronic difficulties; at the most individual level, the social environment might reflect ongoing person–environment transactions and daily hassles. It is of use to narrow this range of considerations to the most promising, based on the existing empirical information. Second, it is useful to ask what aspects of depression might be influenced by the social environment. Although most thinking is naturally anchored in ideas about the etiology and onset of depression, it is important to explicitly differentiate separate aspects of depression (Monroe & McQuaid, 1994). For example, do social factors contribute to the onset of depression, to distinctions between different types of depression, or to the clinical course of depression? By first working through these general considerations, we may subsequently focus attention on the most promising leads for developing a differentiated understanding of the many roles social factors may play in depression.

What Is It about the Social Environment That Is Important for Depression?

Speculation about the qualities of people's lives that are psychologically noxious and contribute to depression has been wide-ranging. A challenge for investigators is how to limit and focus the scope of inquiry. The social environment captures an extremely extensive array of interesting, and often intuitively appealing, possibilities. The domains of consideration range from the very broad and enduring (e.g., cultural factors, SES), through to the more individual (life events), to the small-scale and frequent, if not constant and chronic (e.g., ongoing emotional transactions between person and environment). What sources of evidence may serve as guidelines to condense these diverse socioenvironmental forces and to bring the respective research literatures into focus?

Two areas of study are relevant for narrowing the conceptual scope and operational agenda: SES and behavior-genetic studies of depression. Considering each in relation to the other is helpful to establish strong evidence for the role of the social environment in depression, and, more importantly, to guide inquiry toward more specific underlying processes. It is from this dual vantage point that the particular and pivotal role of severe life stress becomes most apparent.

One of the most consistent findings in research on psychopathology is the relationship between SES and the incidence of psychological disorders. Research on SES and screening scale scores of depressive symptoms has consistently demonstrated an inverse linear association, with lower SES correlating with higher depressive symptomatology. Findings for SES and major depression appear to be more complex, possibly varying by gender, geography, ethnicity, and diagnostic interview procedures (cf. American Psychiatric Association, 2000;

Regier et al., 1993). However, combined with the studies on SES and depressive symptoms, there is a large body of evidence strongly suggesting an inverse relationship between SES and depression (see Kohn, Dohrenwend, & Mirotznik, 1998).

Dohrenwend and colleagues have developed a creative line of quasi-experimental research directed toward disentangling possible explanations for the association between SES and specific forms of psychopathology. This work further supports pursuing the implications of social factors in the etiology of depression. The findings point persuasively toward the role of social causation in depression for women (Dohrenwend et al., 1992; Dohrenwend, 2000; Johnson, Cohen, Dohrenwend, Link, & Brook, 1999). Other avenues of recent research also indicate that the daily stress associated with disadvantaged economic status is important for depression (Ross, 2000).

Overall, the SES literature establishes the association between broad indices of social privation and psychopathology in general, depression in particular. The literature on SES provides strong support for the general premise that there is something about social class and economic status that predispose an individual to depression. A favored interpretation is that low SES leads to adversity and life stress—the particular stressful circumstances and events the individual faces—which in turn serve as the proximal mechanisms via which SES vulnerability translates into individual risk (Dohrenwend, 2000). Nonetheless, not all individuals in low social classes become depressed, and individuals within more privileged positions in society do become depressed. Other factors, discussed next, must be considered.

The second line of evidence that supports the role of the social environment in depression comes from the extensive and consistent literature on the behavior genetics of mood disorders. Family, twin, and, to a certain extent, adoption studies suggest heritability for mood disorders (Nurnberger & Gershon, 1992; Sanders, Detera-Wadleigh, & Gershon, 1999). Since the heritability estimates are generally only moderate, this research simultaneously underscores the importance of nongenetic factors in the genesis of depression. Thus, genetic investigations indirectly support the environment (in the most general, nongenetic sense) for modeling depression. While such an "argument by subtraction" (Dohrenwend, 1998) may not be wholly satisfying for specifying the meaning of the environmental input, it provides the broad parameters within which theorizing must be entertained. In particular, this literature is useful to further delimit thinking about environmental factors. Specifically, behavior genetic studies generally indicate that the nonshared environment, as opposed to the shared environment, is most strongly related to depression (Sullivan, Neale, & Kendler, 2000). It is again the unique experiences of the individual—the personal failures and defeats, losses and idiosyncratic adversities—that are the suspected agents of blame and distinguish who will, from who will not, develop depression.[1]

It is intriguing to speculate how one might integrate findings from these two literatures. From the broad social perspective, we have macrolevel social factors (SES), more specific processes implicated by quasi-experimental designs (social causation), and finally proximal and specific variation of individual experiences (life stress). This social cascade of forces may be one process via which depression arises. Social influences, however, are uninformed and silent about genetic influences. From the genetics literature, there are strong implications that the nonshared environment is pivotal for predicting disorder (in addition to genes). Overall, these two lines of research—the behavior genetic and the SES and psychopathology—can be seen as complementary and converging on the utility of focusing on life circumstances unique to the individual. Put somewhat differently, between-subjects analyses involving SES and within-groups analyses involving heritable characteristics together point to the importance of the unique environments of the individual for developing depression. These distal forms of susceptibility (i.e., SES, genetics) may "play out" through their association with individual circumstances and experiences. The variability in personal adversity and life stress may be a nodal point linking social and genetic risk to the production of pathology.

What Aspects of Depression Might Be Influenced by the Social Environment?

At first glance, this question may seem mundane or unnecessary. Most attention addresses the core question of depression onset. Many believe that social factors contribute to, if not cause, depression.

A comprehensive account of the role environmental factors play in depression requires attention to broader issues involving the construct of depression and its dynamic nature over time. Over the past several years it has become apparent that the influence of life stress may not be confined to issues of onset and etiology. Indeed, awareness of this matter can cast old questions in a new light, and can raise novel questions about the nature of depression and its association with life experiences. There are two major themes within this topic that we will address. First and most obvious is the question of social factors in the origins of depression. Guided by our reasoning about the converging information from the SES and behavior genetic research literatures, we focus our efforts on life stress and the onset of depression. Second and less obvious, but equally important for clinical and theoretical reasons, is the role of life stress for the course of depression once begun. Attention to these matters expands the focus of inquiry and the research agenda along several lines, and also holds considerable promise for bettering understanding of depression and its treatment.

LIFE STRESS AND DEPRESSION: RESEARCH ISSUES AND EMPIRICAL FINDINGS

One of the most compelling findings in research on depression is the consistent relationship between depression and prior life stress (Mazure, 1998). Despite a general consensus about this association, the precise implications are not entirely clear (Kessler, 1997). Several concerns suggest alternative explanations for the relationship between life stress and depression. On the one hand, some special and intriguing challenges are posed when trying to operationalize ideas such as life stress. How these challenges have been handled has important implications for evaluating the reported findings. On the other hand, the twin questions posed previously are germane once again: What is it about life stress that may be important for depression, and what aspects of depression are influenced by life stress?

Conceptualization and Measurement of Life Stress

It is commonly assumed that psychological stress is an especially modern problem, or at least a problem that has become more widespread and virulent with advances in civilization. A brief glimpse back into time, however, places this mode of thought into a more informed and guarded perspective. Over 100 years ago, Sir Clifford Allbutt (1895), Regius Professor of Medicine at Cambridge University, wrote:

> To turn now . . . to nervous disability, to hysteria . . . to the frightfulness, the melancholy, the unrest due to living at a high pressure, the world of the railway, the pelting of telegrams, the strife of business . . . surely, at any rate, these maladies or the causes of these maladies are more rife than they were in the days of our fathers? (p. 217)

Attributing illnesses of unknown origins to stress, adversity, and negative emotions is a recurrent theme in the history of attempts to explain disease and mental disorder. Before an organic etiology was discovered, many physical diseases were thought to be caused by the amorphous sweep of socioenvironmental factors. Such was the case, for example, of viewpoints about the origins of general paresis (tertiary syphilis):

> Civilization favors general paresis through the demands which it makes on physical and mental powers, competition, reckless and feverish pursuit of wealth and social position, overstudy, overwork, unhygenic modes of life, the massing of people in large cities, the indulgence in tea, coffee, tobacco, stimulants, and social and sexual excesses, and artificial modes of life. (Kellogg, 1897, p. 657)

The history of medicine and psychopathology is replete with examples of such ill-conceived ideas, and should give one pause when invoking psychosocial factors as causes of depression or other disorders of unknown origin (Sontag, 1978).

It is against this psychological backdrop of potential bias that modern research on life stress must be examined and evaluated. Psychological stressors represent a popular explanation for unwanted emotional and physical states. As a result of their intuitive appeal, they can possess unwarranted explanatory power that overshadows their scientific utility. The challenge is to translate the potentially productive ideas about psychological stressors into more precise concepts, definitions, and operational procedures, thereby providing an appropriate empirical platform for scientific inquiry (Monroe, 2000).

Self-Report Checklist Procedures

Research on life stress burgeoned in the late 1960s and 1970s as a result of methodological innovations in the measurement of life events. The development of the Schedule of Recent Experiences (SRE) by Holmes and Rahe (1967) introduced the idea of measuring individual differences in exposure to life stress, with the potential of doing so in a standard and objective manner. The SRE was a brief 43-item self-report checklist of common life events "empirically observed to occur just prior to the time of onset of disease" (Holmes, 1979, p. 46).

Expediency, however, tended to outweigh rigor in the early development of this method for research on stress and illness. Serious deficiencies in the self-report checklist approach were recognized, such as confounding between life events and symptoms of depression (e.g., trouble with boss, sexual difficulties, change in sleeping habits, change in eating habits) and confounding between life events as consequences (not causes) of depression (e.g., divorce, marital separation, fired at work, change in recreation, etc.). Despite early recognition of these serious limitations (Brown & Harris, 1978; Monroe, 1982; Paykel, 1983), as well as mounting empirical evidence underscoring extensive problems with self-report life event checklists (Dohrenwend, Link, Kern, Shrout, & Markowitz, 1990; McQuaid, Monroe, Roberts, & Johnson, 1992; McQuaid, Monroe, Roberts, Kupfer, & Frank, 2000), the ease of use of self-report methods has resulted in an extensive literature on life stress and its consequences for disease in general, depression in particular (cf. Duggal et al., 2000).

Investigator-Based Methods

Fortunately, other investigators embraced the promise of such ideas and developed the procedures along more scientifically sound lines (Brown & Harris, 1978; Dohrenwend, Raphael, Schwartz, Stueve, & Skodol, 1993; Hammen, 1991; Paykel, 1983). Probably the most elaborate system for assessing, defining, and rating life stress has been developed over the past three decades by George Brown and Tirril Harris. The Life Events and Difficulties

Schedule (LEDS) incorporates explicit rules and operational criteria for defining events and for distinguishing between complex constellations of events and life circumstances (Brown & Harris, 1978, 1989). In general, the LEDS system provides a standardized methodology for categorizing whether or not a particular event (or chronic stressor) meets threshold criteria for inclusion, and if it does, the system also provides case exemplars depicting weights for rating specific dimensions. In a creative additional step in the process, the biographical context of the person is taken into account in a systematic manner, to provide more sensitive "contextual" ratings in accord with the unique biographical circumstances of the individual's life. The purpose of the contextual ratings is to approximate the likely subjective experience of the person, without incurring the myriad methodological liabilities of subjective self-report procedures. Importantly, the interview-based information is presented in a separate meeting to raters, who are kept blind to the subjective reactions of the particular subject (to avoid confounding of reaction with possible depression status). Overall, the approach is "investigator-based" in the sense that the responsibilities for measurement are largely under the control of the investigator, beginning with the range of information inquired about through the decisions about what "counts" and how it should be rated.

Other investigators have developed or adapted stress assessment procedures that are consonant with the LEDS philosophy and incorporate many of the same methodological advantages (Dohrenwend et al., 1993; Hammen, 1995; Wethington, Brown, & Kessler, 1995). Most importantly, these investigator-based approaches have been found to be much more psychometrically sound and yield more robust and powerful predictors of depression onset and course (Brown & Harris, 1989; Mazure, 1998; McQuaid et al., 1992, 2000; Monroe & Simons, 1991).

Life Stress and the Onset of Depression

The bulk of thinking and empirical effort in research on social factors and depression has been on matters involving life stress and the origins of a depressive episode. On the surface, the question appears reasonably straightforward: Does life stress predict depression? And, on the surface, at least, the empirical literature generally provides a qualified but consistently supportive answer of "yes" to the question. These findings represent some of the strongest and most promising information available for discovering important clues about the etiology of depression, yet a number of intriguing and thorny questions remain.

Beginning with the life event checklist approaches in the 1960s and continuing with more methodologically sophisticated interview-based procedures (Brown & Harris, 1978; Paykel, 1983), the relationship between heightened life stress and depression has been amply documented (Monroe & Depue, 1991). Recently, Mazure (1998) reviewed over 20 studies (including case–control and community-based designs), and concluded that the consistency and strength of the associations provides "compelling evidence for an association between adverse life experience and subsequent major depression" (p. 291). Further, the association appears not to be simply a generic stress effect: "occurrences that are defined as *undesirable, major* life events are likely to be associated with depressive onset" (p. 294, emphasis in original). Similarly, in another recent review of this literature, Kessler (1997) came to a comparable conclusion: "There is a consistently documented association between exposure to major stressful life events and subsequent onset of episodes of major depression" (p. 193).

Interestingly, Kessler (1997) takes the refinement of life stress prediction further, suggesting that life stress associations are "generally stronger when 'contextual' measures are used rather than simple life event checklists" (p. 193). In this regard, a review of nine studies specifically using the LEDS methodology is especially informative. Across these studies, a particular class of contextually rated life events termed "severe events" has been found consistently to predict the onset of depression (Brown & Harris, 1989). These types of events represent highly aversive experiences, generally involving serious threats to core relationships or occupation, sometimes involving severe economic or health problems (Brown & Harris, 1989; Monroe & McQuaid, 1994). The samples for these studies have included women from working-class homes, inner-city environments, rural settings, and general medical practice; in all, approximately 2,000 women between the ages of 18 and 65 have been studied.

Severe major life events are likely to be of special importance for depression onset. In particular, it appears that the presence or absence of a severe event carries the most weight for predicting an episode of depression. More minor forms of stress, albeit frequent and undesirable, have not been consistently found to be significant predictors of depression once these major forms of adversity are taken into account (Brown & Harris, 1989; Monroe & Simons, 1991; Stueve, Dohrenwend, & Skodol, 1998). This strongly implies specificity of environmental stress in terms of severity and possible qualities of stressors for depression onset. In other words, particular classes of environmental challenges might be uniquely pertinent for precipitating the psychobiological response pattern of depression.[2] Further elucidating the nature and qualities of such stressors could enhance the prediction of depression onset based on life stress (e.g., Brown, Harris, & Hepworth, 1995). Additional research along these lines could also begin to inform theory about why such a link between particular forms of stress and affective states might exist, providing a conceptual basis for developing a taxonomy of life stress (Nesse, 2000).

Life Stress and the Clinical Characteristics of Depression

One major issue facing depression researchers in general is how to explain the great heterogeneity in phenotypic presentation of depression. Why do depressed people exhibit such different combinations of signs and symptoms? Clearly, a full account of depression must be capable of explaining such variability across depressed persons. In pursuing the implications of life stress for an episode of depression, several lines of research have attempted to explain individual differences in depressive symptoms as a result of stress. The major approaches can be categorized into (1) studies of symptom severity and symptom profiles; and (2) studies of depressive subtypes (Monroe & Depue, 1991).

Life Stress, Symptom Severity, and Symptom Profiles

Depressed people with severe life stress have been found to have greater depressive symptomatology compared to depressed people without such stress (e.g., Dolan, Calloway, Fonagy, De Souza, & Wakeling, 1985; Hammen, Davila, Brown, Ellicott, & Gitlin, 1992; Monroe, Kupfer, & Frank, 1992; Monroe, Thase, & Simmons, 1992). Interestingly, some evidence indicates that these effects are primarily attributable to preonset severe events; postonset events have not correlated as strongly (e.g., Monroe, Harkness, Simons, & Thase, 2001). Since the preonset events are more removed in time relative to the postonset events, it suggests that the effect reflects matters of etiologic relevance (as opposed to simply a nonspecific stress effect on symptoms).

Yet little research or thought has pursued the lead of why life stress might predict symptom severity in depressed people. Are individuals with prior stress elevated "across the board" for all depressive symptoms? Are the associations primarily with particular classes of symptoms (e.g., cognitive-affective vs. somatic), or with more specific, individual symptoms (e.g., worthlessness, suicidality)? Existing research suggests stress–severity associations often hold for depressive symptoms assessed with the Beck Depression Inventory (BDI; Beck, Steer, & Garbin, 1988), but not for depressive symptoms assessed with the Hamilton Rating Scale for Depression (HRSD; Hamilton, 1960). These findings indirectly support the idea that stress is linked to particular classes of symptoms (e.g., Monroe, Kupfer, & Frank, 1992; Monroe, Thase, & Simmons, 1992). Due to the different loadings of cognitive (BDI) versus somatic (HRSD) symptoms on the two instruments, these findings suggest some degree of symptom specificity. Alternatively, method variance may account for the differences found between the self-report BDI and the interview-based HRSD (Monroe et al., 2001).

A small number of studies have addressed the relationship between life stress and symptoms of depression. However, few studies have provided direct tests of the association between life stress and specific symptoms of depression. In a recent report, Monroe et al. (2001) found life stress to be associated principally with cognitive-affective symptoms, not somatic symptoms. There also was a strong and consistent association across different assessment methods between severe events and suicidal ideation in particular. Finally, once again the associations in this study held specifically for severe events occurring prior to onset, not for severe events occurring after onset.

Overall, the literature bearing upon the issue of life stress and the symptoms of depression is sparse. Yet the relevant studies performed suggest pursuing further the idea that life stress is associated with more severe, and possibly different types, of symptoms. This line of study, and its implications for a stress-related form of depression, are pursued next.

Life Stress and Subtypes of Depression

Studies of stress and symptom severity and symptom profiles suggest that there are distinct subtypes of depression distinguished by the presence or absence of life stress. Yet findings from these studies are only indirect indicators, and could reflect other stress influences that are not necessarily indicative of a specific etiology or subtype of the disorder (e.g., stress may influence phenotypic expression—specific symptoms—rather than the substantive nature of the disorder; Monroe, 1990). Theories about subtypes of depression commonly posit that life stress holds a special position in the scheme of such classifications, a tradition of thought that has a long and plentiful history in writings on depression.

Many of the earliest accounts of depression refer to a syndrome of "sadness without reason" (Klibansky, Panofsky, & Saxl, 1979; Monroe & Depue, 1991). Kraepelin (1921) and others suggested that some forms of depression "may be to an astonishing degree largely *independent of external influences*" (p. 181, emphasis in original). Others, addressing similar concepts, invoke terms such as "'excessive depression,' 'unjustified depression,' and 'depression disproportionate to causative factors'"(Jackson, 1986, p. 316). All of these observations reflect the central idea that social circumstances cannot fully explain the onset of some forms of depression. As a result of these observations and writings, it is often assumed that an "endogenous" subtype of depression exists that is biologically based, arising autonomously of environmental circumstances. This viewpoint also suggests that other forms of depression arise from adverse social circumstances—as perhaps understandable responses to hardship and adversity—indicating a nonendogenous, or reactive, form of depression (Jackson, 1986).

The general distinction between stress-related (psychogenic) and biologically based (endogenous) subtypes of depression has stimulated a variety of related classification schemes and distinctions. Such dichotomies as "endogenous–reactive," "neurotic–psychotic," and "endogenous–neurotic" have been proposed and investigated. Many other terms loosely reflect one or the other of the two hypothesized etiologic distinctions (e.g., *situational, sec-*

ondary, and *nonendogenous* for the stress-based concept; *melancholic, retarded,* and *vital* for the biologically based concept). Unfortunately, adding to the confusion, such terms have been used to describe differences between depressed persons in their presenting symptomatic and syndromal features, irrespective of social versus biological assumptions about cause. For instance, people exhibiting psychomotor retardation, unreactive mood, and pervasive anhedonia have been considered to represent an endogenous or melancholic subtype of the disorder (Rush & Weissenburger, 1994). Overall, despite the appeal of such typologies, inconsistency and confusion in their usage have hampered progress (Hammen, 2001; Katschnig, Pakesch, & Egger-Zeidner, 1986; Monroe & Depue, 1991).

Despite definitional difficulties, attempts to validate such subtype distinctions based on the presence or absence of life stress have been numerous over many decades. The debates have been extensive and often contentious (Mapother, 1926; Monroe & Depue, 1991). Several reviews of the literature from the past 20 years have suggested that life stress appears to be more common prior to the onset of almost any depressive subtype based on symptomatic differences (relative to the rate for nondepressed populations; Mazure, 1998). Yet these studies also indicate that there is perhaps a weak relationship between life events and a particular symptom pattern or depressive subtype (Mazure, 1998; Katschnig et al., 1986; Monroe & Depue, 1991; Paykel & Cooper, 1992). Part of the inconsistencies across studies can be ascribed to the lack of standardization for defining stress and for defining the endogenous and nonendogenous forms of depression (see Katschnig et al., 1986). Also, there are promising leads suggesting that the relationship of life stress to subtypes depends on whether or not the depressive episode is a first onset or a recurrence. For example, patients who suffer a recurrence of depression and present with an endogenous symptom pattern have been found to report fewer severe events relative to first-onset patients, recurrence patients with nonendogenous symptoms, and community controls (Brown et al., 1995; Frank, Anderson, Reynolds, Ritenour, & Kupfer, 1994). Further work on these leads, as well as more work on leads incorporating other factors that may help distinguish groups (Parker et al., 1999), might help clarify the possible importance of such distinctions.

Given the history of interest in this matter, and the centrality of such concepts to depression, one might think contemporary clinical science would provide a more satisfying explanation. Why some forms of depression appear to "arise out of the blue," while others appear to originate, at least in part, out of psychosocial adversity, remains a vexing challenge with potentially productive yields for depression researchers (Monroe & Depue, 1991).

Life Stress and the Clinical Course of Depression

A number of studies have begun to examine the association between life stress and the course of a depressive episode. In several respects, this area of study is not as straightforward as research on life stress and depression onset, yet it possesses great potential for yielding findings of clinical significance and theoretical relevance.

Whereas research on life stress and the onset of depression has essentially one focal point for prediction (i.e., onset of depression), research on life stress and the clinical course of depression has many possible points of interest over time (e.g., remission, relapse, recurrence). And whereas the timing of life stress vis-à-vis onset is fixed by the nature of the question (i.e., stress precedes onset), there are important questions about the clinical course of a depressive episode involving stress at any point in time, pre- or postonset. The implications of stress effects on the course of disorder differ, however, as a function of their timing with respect to onset. For example, when life stress prior to onset predicts a differential course, there are obvious clinical implications, yet such findings are also of theoretical relevance. If stress-related depressions display a different course—for example, higher or faster rate of remission, less likelihood of relapse or later recurrence—it also lends support to the construct validity of a stress-related subtype. When stress occurs after onset and influences the course of disorder, the clinical implications remain relevant, but the theoretical implications are less meaningful.

Research on life stress and the clinical course of depression, however, has not been as extensive as research on life stress and depression onset. This is due to the overall lack of attention devoted to clinical course issues, as well as to the diffusion of the existing attention across the different components that comprise the topic (i.e., remission, relapse, recurrence). Variations in design (e.g., definitions of the relevant outcomes such as remission, relapse, recurrence), populations (community depressives, patients in different forms of treatment), and methods (self-report checklists and investigator-based stress assessments) further render the absolute number of studies within any topic area small. Yet such research holds considerable promise for uncovering important clinical and conceptual matters.

Remission

With regard to remission, two related considerations are most readily apparent: the timing of recovery and the absolute likelihood of recovery. Do stress-related depressions remit more or less quickly than nonstress-related depressions? Do stress-related depressions have a better or worse likelihood of recovery?

While a few studies have addressed these issues, once again the variability in methods and the heterogeneity of depressed populations complicate the interpretive picture. The major concerns are the timing of life stress (preonset vs. postonset), the nature of life stress (severe life events vs. other indices of stress), the population of depressed people studied (first onset, recurrences, severity, age), and the presence or nature of treatment (natural course, psychotherapy, pharmacotherapy) (Monroe & McQuaid, 1994). In terms of events prior to onset and time to recovery, inconsistent findings have been reported. In some instances, a more rapid resolution of depression has been reported (e.g., Kendler, Walters, & Kessler, 1997; Parker & Blignault, 1985), whereas others have reported a slower response time to remission in relation to preonset stress (Karp et al., 1993). In terms of life events following onset, there are data suggesting that recovery is delayed considerably when stressors occur during treatment (e.g., Monroe, Roberts, Kupfer, & Frank, 1996). Again, however, caution is warranted owing to the diversity of methods, definitions, designs, and populations employed.

Research on life stress and the *likelihood of recovery* from depression has been somewhat more plentiful. A review of 14 studies by Paykel and Cooper (1992) concluded that life events that occur at onset are weakly associated with better outcomes, whereas life events that occur concurrently with treatment are associated with poorer outcomes. In a more recent review, Mazure (1998) reached somewhat different conclusions: the evidence for events occurring before treatment predicting treatment course was viewed as not consistent, whereas findings for concurrent events again were found to predict a more consistent adverse effect. Some of the discrepancies in this literature again may be due to difference in methods and populations studied. For example, prior life stress might forecast a lower likelihood of recovery for people with severe forms of depression (e.g., recurrent depression) compared to those with less severe forms of the disorder (e.g., first onset) (Monroe et al., 1996; Zimmerman, Pfohl, Coryell, & Stangl, 1987). Overall, the question of preonset events and clinical course remains unclear, whereas there is more consistency in the adverse effects of concurrent stressors on recovery.

Relapse and Recurrence

Once a depressed person recovers, is life stress of relevance for the relapsing back into depression or, at a much later point in time, incurring a new episode? Too little work has focused on these topics with regard to preonset life events to form tentative conclusions (cf. Monroe et al., 1996). However, postonset life events appear to create a greater likelihood of relapse. The consistency in measures of stress, interim treatments, and definitions of relapse, though, indicate the need for further work on this clinically important topic (Belsher & Costello, 1988; Monroe & Depue, 1991).

With regard to life stress and recurrence, the basic question is identical to the question of life stress and depression onset, only the "onset" is for people with at least one prior lifetime episode (and a suitably lengthy interval since remission from the previous episode; see Frank et al., 1991). An important additional question is whether or not the same combination of etiologic factors is involved in a recurrence as in an initial episode. For example, in reviewing studies for both unipolar and bipolar disorders, Post (1992) found life events to be more common prior to first episodes of depression compared to recurrences (see also Monroe & Depue, 1991). Some recent work, as well, indicates the possibility that the role of life stress may change over time with recurrences of disorder (Daley, Hammen, & Rao, 2000; Kendler, Thornton, & Gardner, 2000). Overall, the topic of recurrence is becoming increasingly timely and important for life stress research, a point upon which we will expand in the next section.

UNRESOLVED ISSUES AND RESEARCH IMPLICATIONS

Research has supported the belief that life stress represents an important consideration for the onset of a depressive episode. Moreover, life stress can forecast the clinical course of depression. The domain of life stress has been narrowed, focusing inquiry upon major, acute life events. There is little coherence, however, once we move past these consistent but general associations. Part of the problem, we suspect, is due to the great plausibility of stress as an explanatory rationale: the face validity provides a premature sense of conceptual closure, undermining the search for more substantive underlying explanations and mechanisms.

There are several intriguing leads, however, that may be discerned when we adopt the viewpoint that severe life events represent an especially important focus for depression. The different leads develop the implications of major life events for depression along different lines, depending upon the particular mechanisms via which stress is inferred to be related to depression. We focus on three major issues that are especially timely and promising: (1) methodological concerns and considerations; (2) subtypes, typologies, and dimensions of depression; and (3) the long-term, or lifetime, clinical course of depression.

Methodological Concerns and Considerations

Despite the mounting evidence for the importance of severe events—or because of it—remaining concerns about the methods used to define and measure life stress in general, and severe life events in particular, need to be taken quite seriously. We address these concerns next.

Accuracy of Reporting

Questions have been raised regarding the accuracy of reporting life events and the possible biases involved with investigator-based methods. For instance, retrospective accounts of life stress might be influenced by "differential recall accuracy or differential willingness to disclose and discuss stressful experiences among currently (at the time of interview) depressed versus nondepressed respondents in such a way that created the appearance that life events cause depression" (Kessler, 1997, pp. 193–194). However, the degree to which semistructured interviews provide salient and sufficiently detailed probes and cues for recall mitigates this potential problem. Further, the degree of disruption entailed by a severe life event argues against it being readily "forgotten." Reliability studies, too, support the premise that severe events are reliably reported, perhaps up to 10 years retrospectively (Neilson, Brown, & Marmot, 1989).

The sensitive nature of some life events, though, could compromise disclosure. This might be especially problematic if assurances about confidentiality and a trusting rapport are not well established. Underreporting of sensitive material also would be undetected with conventional psychometric methods. Studies attempting to independently corroborate the life stress histories of people may be of some value to help lessen concerns about this matter (e.g., Kessler, 1997; Nazroo, Edwards, & Brown, 1997), although again there may be serious limitations owing to the likelihood that others may not be informed about or aware of the life events, particularly if they are of a sensitive nature.

Contamination and Contextual Ratings

There is a more subtle concern about investigator-based methods, too, that deserves additional scrutiny and attention. With the awareness of depression onset, it is possible that information about the context of life events could become biased, either by the respondent's more detailed reporting or by the interviewer's more intensive probing and/or relaying of information to "blind" raters. In either case, ratings of the person's biographical context could be contaminated in subtle ways, and the resulting contextual ratings of events directly influenced in a manner so as to spuriously increase severity ratings (Kessler, 1997).

Interestingly, there is little research on the degree to which contextual ratings enhance prediction beyond basic investigator-based event definitions. Does the activity of tailoring event ratings in accord with the biographical circumstances of the individual improve prediction beyond ratings from less sensitive, yet still standardized procedures? (Note that issues of interviewing, probing, employing rules, and operational criteria for defining and rating events are maintained; just the added contextual raising or lowering of the final rating is questioned.) Research using interview-based methods and definitional rules and operational criteria, but less extensive reliance upon contextual ratings than the LEDS system, has reported strong associations between severe events and depression onset (e.g., Shrout et al., 1989). These latter data suggest that the supportive findings in the literature cannot be ascribed solely to this possible methodological artifact of biographical context contamination. The question hinges, in part, upon how many life events cross the definitional threshold to qualify as severe or not as a function of contextual input, and represents an important line of research to be developed.

Conceptual Concerns about Contextual Ratings

Conceptually, concerns have been raised about the contextual rating system. It has been contended that these procedures confound information about life event severity with information about stress modifiers (Kessler, 1997). For example, economic circumstances and social support form part of the context for rating; it is argued that these different facets of the social environment should be studied separately for their unique and interactive importance with life stress in depression (Kessler, 1997; Mazure, 1998; Tennant, Bebbington, &

Hurry, 1981). This concern again stems from questions about the contextual layer of information derived from such methods as the LEDS. But in this instance, the concern is with the plausibility of alternative predictors of potential importance, as opposed to spurious associations. Again, there is little empirical information on the incremental utility afforded by contextual ratings beyond the more normative ratings that might be adapted within the LEDS or other investigator-based systems. Existing work on the topic suggests that such forms of contamination are not common (Brown & Harris, 1986). If the contextual ratings prove superior, then further analyses attempting to disaggregate the component features of suspected importance would be warranted (e.g., SES, social support). If the contextual ratings do not prove superior, such results provide intriguing leads for abbreviating the LEDS and for rebutting criticisms based on the contextual premises.

Finally, from a slightly different conceptual perspective, we do not view the conceptual criticisms of the contextual rating procedure as necessarily problematic. Our stance is that severe events represent one of the best available predictors for episode onset and clinical course of depression in the current literature. From this perspective, severe events are a critical focal point for future inquiry. Perhaps severe events might be considered a "marker" for depression vulnerability, rather than a "maker" of the disorder. Viewed in this manner, the underlying nature of the marker itself is not as important at the current stage of development as is its utility for pointing toward additional phenomena of theoretical relevance (see also Brown & Harris, 1986). Once the relations between the marker and other risk factors are more firmly delineated, we will be in a better position to examine the nature of the marker, its correlates, and ultimate implications for etiology.

Subtypes, Multifactorial Models, and Dimensions of Depression

Despite a consensus that life stress holds important clues for understanding depression, there has been surprisingly little penetrating or sustained discussion about the meaning of the matter. In this section, we outline three theoretical alternatives that can explain the current empirical picture and provide a rudimentary framework for guiding research.

A starting point for these ideas begins with the recognition that not all people with depression report prior severe events, nor do all people who experience severe events go on to develop depression. More precisely, it is estimated that approximately 50% or more of depressed patients have experienced recent stress, as have over 80% of community depressives (compared to approximately 24% for nondepressed samples; Mazure, 1998, Table 1). Between 20% to 50% of persons experiencing life stress succumb to depression (Brown & Harris, 1989; Monroe & Simons, 1991). Thus, additional factors must be entertained to explain why some people become depressed under stress while others do not, and why some depressed persons have not experienced recent severe stressors. The most obvious alternatives are that (1) there is a subtype of depression that is uniquely stress-related; (2) stress is but one factor in a larger model of depression; and (3) stress and depression may be associated in a dimensional manner.

Life Stress and Depression Subtypes

Although a subtype of stress-related depression has received at best modest support, creative approaches to the matter may still unveil a form of depression that is largely, if not uniquely, linked to life stress. Stepping back and viewing the cognate literatures, such optimism is bolstered by findings indicating that (1) a substantial proportion of (but not all) depressed people experience severe stress relative to nondepressed controls; (2) severe stress predicts the clinical course of depressed persons; and (3) severe stress predicts greater levels of depressive symptoms, specificity of symptoms, and possibly symptom profiles. While one can debate the details of research within any one of these three literatures, the emerging picture that is reasonably consistent within each of these areas, along with the general picture across the literatures, is that severe stress is especially important for a large proportion of depressed persons. These multiple sources establish the broad contours of information that support the construct validity of a stress-related subtype of depressive disorder.

One possible obstacle in the way of detecting a distinctive stress-induced subtype of depression is the great heterogeneity of the signs, symptoms, and presentations of major depression. Different people diagnosed with major depression often display considerably different permutations of the requisite criterial features—indeed stretching the boundaries of the syndrome concept. While it is reasonable to think that distinctive presentations of depression might imply differences in etiology or subtype, variability in presenting features conceivably may be the result of stress effects that are independent of etiology. Awareness of such possibilities may be required to explain individual differences in depressive features and syndromes.

There are several potential explanations for the variability in presenting signs and symptoms of major depression. With respect to psychosocial factors, early loss experiences by separation or death may predict neurotic versus psychotic depressive features (Brown & Harris, 1978). Personality characteristics, too, have been implicated to explain variability in symptomatic expression of depression (Hirschfeld & Shea, 1992). Another intriguing possibility derives from the idea that the phenotype of depression changes over the course of repeated episodes. As noted previously, rates of severe life events may be comparable for patients diagnosed on symptomatic criteria as endogenous and nonendogenous for a first episode. However, for recurrences of depression, severe events may be more importantly related to subsequent nonendogenous presentations of depression (Brown et al., 1995; Frank et al., 1994). Further work along such lines could prove of considerable value in delineating differences in symptoms in relation to the presence or absence of life stress.

Finally, an overlooked advantage of a life stress perspective on validation of depressive subtypes is the potential for more rigorously isolating a subtype of depression that is entirely independent of psychosocial considerations. The classic endogenous depression has been recognized throughout recorded time both for its stark presentation and for the seemingly paradoxical and complete inability of psychosocial considerations to account for the disorder. Indeed, depressions that "arise out of the blue" appear to do so in the lives of people who are not only stress-free, but often leading advantaged and apparently attractive existences. We wonder if cases of stress-independent depression are often overlooked, masked by the apparent ubiquitousness of stress in most people's lives and the utility of stress as a "catch-all" explanation for disorder and disease. With rigorous assessments of life stress and more precise definitions of particular stressors (e.g., severe events), the possibility of detecting a subtype of disorder independent of life circumstances should be pursued more vigorously.

Diathesis–Stress Theories and Multifactorial Models

Recent theorists have adopted diathesis–stress perspectives on depression (Abramson, Metalsky, & Alloy, 1989; Monroe & Simons, 1991; Zuckermann, 1999). Within this conceptual scheme, life stress is an important component in the etiology of depression (or subtype of depression), but *requires* other vulnerability factors (diatheses) to explain onset conditions. The occurrence of stress activates, or interacts with, the underlying diathesis, transforming predisposition into manifest depression. Returning to the theme of severe events as an important marker in depression vulnerability, we pose the questions: What other forms of vulnerability do severe events mark? What additional susceptibilities are required to allow severe stress to eventuate in depression?

There are a variety of ways in which research on the implications of severe stress for vulnerability factors in depression might proceed. Initially, a better understanding of how severe stress is related to other vulnerability factors is required to provide a more informed approach to predict onset. For example, how are severe events related to cognitive vulnerability or genetic liability? Patient samples, although limited for some research purposes, represent a useful starting point for testing severe stress associations with vulnerability and for testing predictions afforded by such models in relation to other validating considerations (e.g., clinical characteristics, clinical course, and outcome). Since patient samples typically report approximately 50% incidence of recent severe stress (Mazure, 1998), the implications of severe stress for cognitive functioning and possible subtypes of depression are well worth pursuing. The approximate 50% prevalence provides an optimal level of variability for severe stress to probe associations with other vulnerability factors and to delineate potentially useful implications. Once the nature of severe stress, other risk parameters, and their interactions are better modeled and validated (possibly indexing a depression subtype), the groundwork will be laid for targeting vulnerable individuals and prospectively studying the process of depression onset and course in relation to life stress.

It is intriguing to point out that two very different predictions are tenable for life stress and diatheses based upon the existing literature. On the one hand, traditional diathesis–stress theory posits an *ipsative,* or inverse, relationship: the greater the allotment of one factor, the less of the other is required (Abramson et al., 1989; Ingram & Price, 2001; Monroe & Simons, 1991; Zubin & Spring, 1977). It is the sum of the two factors (or more, by extension to multifactorial models) that is critical—not the relative loading of either. Thus, severe stress might require relatively little cognitive vulnerability, while lesser degrees of stress necessitate a higher level of cognitive vulnerability to bring about depression. This perspective can parsimoniously account for many diverse findings in the research literature. For instance, the twin concerns about not all people with severe stress developing depression and not all depressed people reporting recent life stress are readily explained within this perspective.

On the other hand, if there is something of particular etiologic importance about severe life events, a different prediction scheme is also tenable. Recognizing again that not all people with severe stress succumb to depression, other factors are required to explain why some people break down and others do not. Within this conceptualization, severe life events should be associated with one (or more) additional vulnerability indices in a "permissive" manner. As opposed to the ipsative model, severe stress is associated with *heightened* cognitive vulnerability or greater genetic predisposition from this perspective. For instance, in a study of life stress and genetic liability to depression, Kendler et al. (1995) found that the likelihood of depression onset was greatest for women with heightened genetic liability *and* a recent major life event.

There are two noteworthy added implications of this perspective on diathesis–stress interactions. First, this viewpoint implicitly specifies that the class of major depression is heterogeneous. Since not all people with major depression have prior severe life events, alternative etiologic arrangements need to be entertained for such contrasting conditions. Second, this perspective readily incorporates many popular concepts as moderators of stress impact in the genesis of depression. Thus, social support (or lack thereof), coping efficacy, personality attributes, and so on all are easily integrated into the framework.

Clearly, these contrasting models are but two that can be proposed. We could extrapolate to three or more subtypes of depression, each with different arrangements of vulnerability factors and their interrelations. The two models proposed, though, provide a reasonable starting point for thinking and research. Once more is learned about how severe stress "goes with" other indicators of risk, we will be in a better position to debate the relative merits of each perspective, and to extend such thinking to other theoretically consonant, if not parsimonious, frameworks for inquiry.

These ideas and models of depression depend upon a conceptualization of major depression as one or more distinct categories of disorder. Life stress perspectives may be uniquely useful, however, for promoting thinking and research on the boundaries and dimensions of depression. We turn to these neglected matters next.

Life Stress and Dimensional Models of Depression

Models of psychopathology based upon categorical assumptions of the disorder possess many virtues. They simplify questions about the target dependent variable, and possess a number of important clinical and practical benefits. In terms of the history of medicine, too, a categorical perspective has been extraordinarily productive in revealing the nature of many diseases and thereby alleviating sundry scourges of humankind (Gordon, 1993). With such virtues and victories in its favor, it is easy to understand why categorical approaches continue to dominate conceptual systems in psychopathology.

Alternatively, dimensional models of psychopathology have had their advocates, particularly for depression (Lewis, 1934, 1971). Recently, there has been a resurgence of questioning the utility of a categorical approach and promoting dimensional models of disorder (Ruscio & Ruscio, 2000; Widiger & Clark, 2000). The ongoing debates between these two viewpoints have stimulated thought and controversy, but little research resolving the matter (Coyne, 1994; Vredenburg, Flett, & Krames, 1993; Flett, Vredenburg, & Krames, 1997). Might ideas about social factors and depression be capable of breaking the stalemate and moving research along more productive lines?

Perhaps there is a basic problem in how person–environment transactions currently are viewed in relation to psychopathology that prejudices thinking in subtle ways against dimensional perspectives. From DSM-III through DSM-IV-TR, the criteria for mental disorders require that "this syndrome or pattern must not be merely an expectable and culturally sanctioned response to a particular event . . ." (American Psychiatric Association, 2000, p. xxi). But what *is* an expectable response to an event? And why would an expectable response to an event—if the response meets the requisite criteria and impairment qualifications—be dismissed on such a basis, then rendered entirely inconsequential by the adverb "merely"?

Perhaps insight into these matters has been blinded once again by the overvalued explanatory power of life stress. Comments and attitudes such as those in the DSM make it appear that clinical science possesses firm knowledge about the human reaction norm to the vicissitudes of life, that for a given situation *X* normal responses are *Y,* abnormal responses are *Z.* While the argument has apparent plausibility at the extremes (e.g., depression emerging under completely tranquil circumstance or under extreme duress), many people—and more likely most people with depression—have social worlds filled with dilemmas and hardships that exist in a gray area of suspected determination, for which the "expectable" responses are simply not known (or are so varied as to render the notion of "expectable" meaningless). By directly addressing the issue conceptually and empirically, we might develop (1) better ways of thinking about adversity, emotion, depression, and psychopathology; and (2) an empirical basis for delineating the expectable response range to diverse socioenvironmental challenges.

Taking seriously the lead that severe events represent unique challenge conditions predisposing to depression, some interesting possibilities follow. If depression represents a psychobiologic response to a particular class of environmental challenges (i.e., severe events), probing the meaning of this relationship raises some intriguing ideas. One avenue to pursue is that the specificity of severe event effects might be broken down further in terms of the qualities of the stressors. For instance, recent findings suggest that particular types of severe events are especially potent in eliciting depression, potentially a subtype of depression (e.g., humiliation or entrapment events; Brown et al., 1995). And if people do tend to succumb to situations with relatively specific psychological meanings, what might such associations between organism and environmental challenge signify? While tradition-al thinking is based upon a "breakdown" model with a discrete, dichotomous outcome of "depression" or "no depression," consideration of a more finely tuned fit between chal-lenge and response suggests a more graded reaction potential as a function of varying de-grees of challenge (Weiner, 1992). In other words, depression may not simply be a gener-ic breakdown under stress, but a more complex mixture of adaptation and maladaptation to psychologically meaningful and specific environmental challenges (Nesse, 2000). The association between stress and depression may not be a binary/categorical one in terms of independent and dependent variables, but rather a graded, perhaps dose–response form (Kessler, 1997). If so, one might anticipate a linear association between severity of envi-ronmental challenge and severity of depression, a dimensional portrayal of stress–depres-sion associations.

At first glance, such speculation appears to contradict a central premise of our discus-sion: there is something about severe events that might lead to important insights about de-pression. But again, by focusing on events as a marker of importance, novel directions for thinking and research may come to light—directions that may ultimately reveal the limita-tions of the life stress story. For example, one could argue that the findings for severe events are an artifact of categorical systems for defining depression, that by arbitrarily constrain-ing the information to two categories of outcome (depressed/nondepressed) particular levels of adversity are overemphasized. Could it be that the "average" response range to a severe event is simply sufficient to place many people over the threshold for current definitions of major depression? Perhaps people with events that fall just below the definitional threshold for a severe event also fall just below the definitional threshold for major depression. In this regard, it is extremely pertinent to point out that there has been little systematic study of people with severe life stress who do not meet full criteria for major depression; existing in-formation suggests that these people do not escape unscathed, that they suffer, too—possibly considerably—from milder forms of the disorder (Brown, 1991; see also Gotlib, Lewinsohn, & Seeley, 1995). Perhaps if investigator-based systems of measuring life stress adopt dimensional measures of depression in nonpatient samples, a more continuous asso-ciation between severity of depressive conditions and severity of life conditions would be revealed.

Why would an expectable response to adversity be summarily dismissed as "merely," suggesting that it does not merit full consideration as a syndrome, a mental disorder? In addressing this point, we hesitantly shift from matters of science to considering matters of values in the recognition and remediation of human suffering. What forms of misery are sanctioned by a society? Which groups of the dysphoric and debilitated are accorded so-cial legitimacy, allowed to be "ill" and not held accountable or blamed for their incapac-ity? From this vantage point, a categorical approach to defining psychopathology lends a shorthand legitimacy to depression: it is consonant with a medical (legitimate) viewpoint and, importantly, provides an appearance of clearly demarcating the normal from the ab-normal. A dimensional approach is less desirable in this regard: who is deserving is diffi-cult to discern from the undeserving, and there is no "natural" reference point or cultur-al sanctioning to guide decision making. When and where depression shades into demoralization, where and when syndromes merge into expressions of the miseries of everyday life, are at best arbitrary and clearly indeterminate at present (if at all). It is the frank inability of clinical science to address the question of "an expectable response" to diverse forms of adversity that belies the great gap in understanding of so-called normal responses and the limits of normal functioning. Without such a knowledge base, discussions and definitions of the abnormal, demarcating the boundaries of the pathological, possess an inevitable arbitrary aspect, for they are grounded in society's values as well as in current science (Wakefield, 1992).

Classification systems and diagnoses are the tools society uses for many purposes. One most apparent use is to advance knowledge. Another less apparent use is to arbitrate the social legitimacy of disorder, dysfunction, and impairment. The latter is also an important function. And great strides have been made in recent decades to overcome the stigma attached to mental problems and to recognize depression as an authentic disorder that is not "all in one's head" or simply a matter of deficient character and willpower. In such a context, though, it is very delicate to address social adversity as an integral element in the symptoms of depression, to suggest that the boundaries of depression may not be so clearcut, and to propose that some forms of depression may exist along a continuum that is perhaps in part related to social conditions. While life stress research holds promise to make many contributions at different layers of analysis to an understanding of the construct of depression, there are these subtle background considerations—where ideas and values merge—that may undermine the research agenda.

Overall, our intent is not to argue the validity of these ideas about dimensional models of depression beyond establishing their potential utility. It is quite conceivable that the dimensional issues play into the previously discussed problem of subtypes of depression, yielding even more complex frameworks that incorporate distinct categorical subtypes and dimensional typologies (Kendell, 1976). In all likelihood, the class of depression as currently accepted will turn out to be a complex and cumbersome patchwork of categorical and dimensional subgroup distinctions, with different, yet possibly overlapping, etiologic factors and arrangements. Finding solutions to the riddle of depression may depend as much upon intelligent and creative probing of the definitional and boundary considerations, with such tools as life stress, as upon seeking answers within the currently accepted boundaries of the phenotype.

The Lifetime Course and Recurrence of Depression

Attention to the long-term course of depression has moved from the periphery to the center of research and clinical interest over the past 2 decades. Belsher and Costello (1988) were among the first to provide scholarly insights into the problem of recurrence of depression over the life course of an afflicted individual. These authors concluded that about 50% of patients suffer another episode of depression within 2 years following successful treatment. Since then, estimates of long-term morbidity have steadily risen. Most recently, DSM-IV-TR (American Psychiatric Association, 2000) reports that "at least 60% of individuals with Major Depressive Disorder, Single Episode, can be expected to have a second episode. Individuals who have had two episodes have a 70% chance of having a third, and individuals who have had three episodes have a 90% chance of having a fourth" (p. 372).

Current figures from the Epidemiologic Catchment Area (ECA) Study help to frame this issue with respect to research involving life stress. Of the ECA respondents with an episode of depression in the prior year, 91% reported a previous history of depression (Kessler, 1997). Extrapolating to patient samples, it seems reasonable to assume that the high prevalence of prior depression would be at least comparable. This "implies that studies of the relationship between stressful life events and depression in adult samples should explicitly recognize that they are, in effect, studying recurrence of depression" (Kessler, 1997, p. 206). What are the implications of such estimates and inferences for understanding the role of life stress for the onset of depression?

We address two considerations. First, might the role of stress differ depending upon the person's history of depression? Second, are people who have already incurred a depressive episode more likely to lead stressful lives, to generate the very problems they must endure (Hammen, 1991)? Importantly, we try to reconcile the implications of these two ideas with respect to each other and with respect to the existing research. As we shall see, there are some tensions between concepts, and between concepts and data, that help point toward important avenues for future work.

Life Stress and the Recurrence of Depression

Kraepelin observed that one of his patients became depressed "after the death first of her husband, next of her dog, and then of her dove" (1921, p. 179). More recently, Post (1992; Post & Weiss, 1999) has provided a conceptual structure for such observations. The relationship of stress to subsequent episodes of depression is hypothesized to change over time with repeated recurrences, such that progressively less severe levels of stress are required to bring about onset; eventually, after many episodes, recurrences may become autonomous of psychosocial origins. These intriguing ideas are derived from animal laboratory work on electrophysiological kindling and behavioral sensitization, paradigms that demonstrate the plausibility of transitions from precipitated episodes to episodes of autonomous, or endogenous, origins (Post, 1992).

The idea that severe stress is more common in early episodes of depression finds support from many studies of life stress and depression (Post, 1992). However, there is some ambiguity about the implications for conceptualizing life stress within this important viewpoint. Does stress become *more* or *less* relevant in the initiation of progressive recurrences? On the one hand, it can be reasoned that stress effects becomes progressively less important over time, with autonomous/endogenous features predominating. On the other hand, viewed from the perspective of stress sensitization, life stress becomes *more* important. That is, since minor amounts of stress can begin to bring about a recurrence of depression, these frequent and common forms of stress will vastly increase the probability of recurrence onset. In other words, high and infrequent levels of severe stress may be a critical "rate-limiting" step in the production of early depressions, whereas more low and common levels of stress may remain crucial and dominant components for recurrence (see Hlastala et al., 2000, for similar reasoning with regard to bipolar disorder). Theoretically, it is cumbersome to posit an abrupt, all-or-none shift to autonomous biogenetic mechanisms, rather than a progressive transfer of influence from one domain to the other.

Fortunately, there are some fairly straightforward empirical implications of the two positions that can be readily tested. For example, if severe stress is essential for the onset of early episodes, it seems only probable from the "sensitization" point of view that severe stress would be all the *more* effective for bringing about recurrence in a sensitized system. Thus, while proportionately fewer people with many episodes of depression will have experienced severe events before the onset of recurrence (because severe events are less common than more minor stressors, which may become capable of bringing on recurrences), those people who do incur such stress should have a very high likelihood of breakdown. Put differently, people with a history of many depressions who have the misfortune to incur a severe event should have a higher likelihood of recurrence than people with no or few prior episodes of depression who incur a severe event.

There is also some tension between these ideas about mechanisms for life stress and depression recurrence and the epidemiologic information on life stress and recurrence of depression. If depression researchers are indeed largely studying recurrence, as suggested by Kessler (1997), why are severe events the strongest predictor of episode onset? If 91% of depressed persons in the community have a prior episode of the disorder, how do we account for 80% reporting a recent severe life event (Mazure, 1998)? Why is there relatively little firm evidence indicating that more minor degrees of stress can initiate depression? If stress becomes progressively less important in the lifetime course of depression and recurrence, relatively low proportions of people should report both severe events and prior depression history, and minor forms of stress would yield stronger associations with depression. Different aspects of these ideas have begun to be studied (Hammen, Henry, & Daly, 2000; Kendler, Thornton, & Gardner, 2000), and the relationships may be moderated by other factors (such as genetic liability; see Kendler et al., 2001), yet there is much work to be done on this important issue. Future studies, too, may benefit from simultaneous consideration of a related matter, addressed next.

Stress Generation and Recurrence

From a different vantage point, it has been proposed that people with depression begin to engender stress in their lives, potentially promoting the circumstances needed to precipitate recurrences of the disorder. The "stress generation" hypothesis, formulated by Hammen (1991), proposes that formerly depressed persons "generate stressful conditions and events, which in turn cause additional symptomatology" (p. 555). There are a number of reasons this vicious cycle might begin and perpetuate, including maladaptive personality characteristics and the social consequences of depression (Monroe & Simons, 1991). There is mounting evidence supporting the basic premise that formerly depressed people are at higher risk for incurring new stress over time (Hammen, 1991; Rudolph et al., 2000; Harkness, Monroe, Simons, & Thase, 1999).

Related literatures, too, suggest the importance of this idea and provide a context for conceptualizing the issues. There are several reports suggesting that both depression and the propensity to experience life events are familial and/or genetic (Kendler, Karkowski, & Prescott, 1999; McGuffin, Katz, & Bebbington, 1988). One interpretation of this literature is that some effects of life stress may be noncausal. However, there is substantial complementary evidence indicating severe events that are independent of the person's behavior, and consequently not "generated" by him or her, also strongly predict episodes of depression (Kendler et al., 1999; Shrout et al., 1989). Consequently, the processes over time via which vulnerability interacts with social circumstances take on added layers of complexity (Hammen, 1992; Monroe & Simons, 1991).

An important question for the stress generation theory is whether or not formerly depressed people generate the specific forms of stress suspected to bring about episodes of depression. It is at this juncture that articulating the "stress generation hypothesis" with the "stress sensitization hypothesis" represents a logical conceptual and empirical development. For example, if people are progressively stress-sensitized with repeated depressions, the potential power of the stress generation premise would be amplified considerably in the predictive scheme for recurrence. Alternatively, if episodes become more autonomous over time, then the stress generation hypothesis will have less formative importance for the recurrence of depression. Finally, if stress sensitization does not progress with repeated episodes, the stress generation hypothesis would benefit from studies demonstrating that such processes hold for the types of events currently found most important for episode onset: severe life events.

FUTURE DIRECTIONS

We have attempted to provide a general framework for considering the social environment in depression, to outline how different associations reflect upon the construct of depression, and to focus on what we view as promising empirical reference points for guiding future inquiry. There is little doubt that social circumstances and depression are intertwined, likely in many ways, over time. While all forms of association are important to document, only some are likely to lead to a better understanding of the nature of depression (Barnett & Gotlib, 1988). By selectively attending to major life events as the critical link between diverse features of the social environment and depression, we highlight inconsistencies in theory and research, provide novel hypotheses, and open up alternative modes of thinking about the associations between life stress, other vulnerability factors, and depression.

Targeting the specific reference point of severe events and working through the implications necessarily limits consideration of other factors of potential importance from the social environment in relation to depression. Our approach was not meant to minimize the contribution of other factors, but rather to clarify the issues involving life stress to allow for a more informed integration with other factors and levels of analysis. There are many additional features of people's social worlds that merit attention in relation to depression. Consideration of these features will help build more comprehensive models of social factors in depression. For example, the importance of social relationships and social support have long been suspected to moderate stress-related vulnerability to depression (Brown & Harris, 1978; Harris, Brown, & Robinson, 1999). More recently, the contribution of early adversity and abuse as a risk factor for depression, possibly interacting with life stress, has come to light (Bifulco, Brown, Moran, Ball, & Campbell, 1998; Hammen et al., 2000). The domain of stress also might be broadened for understanding depression, such as the role of chronic stressors (Brown & Harris, 1978; Kessler, 1997). Probing the generality of existing findings in relation to depression in men, too, represents another important arena, since the vast majority of research on life stress and depression has focused upon women. Finally, research on the mechanisms and processes via which stress may contribute to depression is another important avenue for inquiry. Developing each area of investigation individually, as well as interactively with the other risk elements, represents promising, yet as we have seen quite demanding and complex, lines of study for future research (Brown & Harris, 1989; Dohrenwend, 1998; Hammen, 2001; Mazure, 1998).

There is a potential hazard, however, in developing such lines of work too far in modeling the causes of depression, when the very nature of the disorder remains in doubt. Is depression a unitary disorder in terms of etiology and presentation, a heterogeneous group of disorders, or an amalgamation of dimensional problems and discrete disorders? Ultimately, it may not be useful to model depression—holding questions about the construct constant—with different predictors and their interrelations. To the degree that different samples comprise potentially different subspecies of depression, the emerging literature will be disjointed and incoherent. Depression investigators have a very difficult task facing them: not only do they have to consider what predicts and causes depression, they also have to consider what depression "is." This dilemma of simultaneously "working both ends of the street" is inherent to the process of construct validation, yet is infrequently viewed this way in the depression literature. It is in this spirit that we consider a focus on relatively specific and promising predictors of depression such as severe life events to be of particular value to inform us about the causes and nature of depression.

NOTES

1. It may at first glance appear that these two literatures are at odds in their implications for understanding the role of environmental contributions to depression. For example, differences in adversity associated with variation in SES constitute a "shared environment" factor, and, as just reviewed, the shared environment is not generally found to be a strong predictor in the behavior genetic literature. The major issue here is that differences in risk factors *within* populations provide a different perspective than risk factors *between* populations. As Brown (1996) has noted, the "lack of a shared environment effect does not necessarily mean that there is no overall effect in terms of the population as a whole" (p. 396). The mean level of disorder in a population may be substantially influenced by shared environmental factors, while the variation of disorder within the population may not be systematically associated with shared environmental factors. Restricted ranges for the environmental factors could in part account for such effects (e.g., behavior genetic studies may employ relatively homogeneous samples with relatively little social adversity) (for other explanations of such findings, see Brown, 1996; also Stoolmiller, 1999).

2. These reviews emphasize the main effects of life stress. Other avenues of inquiry have addressed the possibility that more minor forms of life stress may interact with high levels of vulnerability to produce depression. For instance, more minor levels of stressful life events may match particular personality styles of vulnerability (e.g., sociotryopy/autonomy; Hammen et al., 1995; Segal, Shaw, Vella, & Katz, 1992).

REFERENCES

Abramson, L. Y., Metalsky, G. I., & Alloy, L. B. (1989). Hopelessness depression: A theory-based subtype of depression. *Psychological Review, 96,* 358–372.

Allbutt, C. (1895). Nervous diseases and modern life. *Contemporary Review, 67,* 217.

American Psychiatric Association. (2000). *Diagnostic and statistical manual of mental disorders* (4th ed., text rev.). Washington, DC: Author.

Barnett, P. A., & Gotlib, I. H. (1988). Psychosocial functioning and depression: Distinguishing among antecedents, concomitants, and consequences. *Psychological Bulletin, 104,* 97–126.

Beck, A. T., Steer, R. A., & Garbin, M. G. (1988). Psychometric properties of the Beck Depression Inventory: Twenty-five years of evaluation. *Clinical Psychology Review, 8,* 77–100.

Belsher, G., & Costello, C. G. (1988). Relapse after recovery from unipolar depression: A critical review. *Psychological Bulletin, 104,* 84–96.

Bifulco, A., Brown, G. W., Moran, P., Ball, C., & Campbell, C. (1998). Predicting depresion in women: The role of past and present vulnerability. *Psychological Medicine, 28,* 39–50.

Brown, G. W. (1991). Aetiology of depression: Something of the future? In P. E. Bebbington (Ed.), *Social psychiatry: Theory, methodology, and practice* (pp. 35–63). New Brunswick, NJ: Transaction.

Brown, G. W. (1996). Genetics of depression: A social science perspective. *International Review of Psychiatry, 8,* 387–401.

Brown, G. W., & Harris, T. O. (1978). *Social origins of depression: A study of psychiatric disorder in women.* New York: Free Press.

Brown, G. W., & Harris, T. O. (Eds.). (1989). *Life events and illness.* New York: Guilford Press.

Brown, G. W., Harris, T. O., & Hepworth, C. (1995). Loss, humiliation and entrapment among women developing depression: A patient and non-patient comparison. *Psychological Medicine, 25,* 7–21.

Coyne, J. C. (1994). Self-reported distress: Analog or ersatz depression? *Psychological Bulletin, 116,* 29–45.

Cronkite, R. C., & Moos, R. H. (1995). Life context, coping processes, and depression. In E. E. Beckham & W. R. Leber (Eds.), *Handbook of depression* (2nd ed., pp. 569–587). New York: Guilford Press.

Daley, S. E., Hammen, C., & Rao, U. (2000). Predictors of first onset and recurrence of major depression in young women during the 5 years following high school graduation. *Journal of Abnormal Psychology, 109*, 525–533.

Dohrenwend, B. P. (1998). Adversity, stress, and psychopathology. New York: Oxford University Press.

Dohrenwend, B. P. (2000). The role of adversity and stress in psychopathology: Some evidence and its implications for theory and research. *Journal of Health and Social Behavior, 41*, 1–19.

Dohrenwend, B. P., Levav, I., Shrout, P. E., Schwartz, S., Naveh, G., Link, B. G., Skodol, A. E., & Steuve, A. (1992). Socioeconomic status and psychiatric disorders: The causation–selection issue. *Science, 255*, 946–952.

Dohrenwend, B. P., Levav, I., Shrout, P. E., Schwartz, S., Naveh, G., Link, B. G., Skodol, A. E., & Steuve, A. (1998). Ethnicity, socioeconomic status, and psychiatric disorders: A test of the social causation–social selection issue. In B. Dohrenwend (Ed.), *Adversity, stress, and psychopathology* (pp. 285–318). New York: Oxford University Press.

Dohrenwend, B. P., Link, B. G., Kern, R., Shrout, P. E., & Markowitz, J. (1990). Measuring life events: The problem of variability within event categories. *Stress Medicine, 6*, 179–187.

Dohrenwend, B.P., Raphael, K. G., Schwartz, S., Stueve, A., & Skodol, A. (1993). The Structured Event Probe and Narrative Rating method for measuring stressful life events. In L. Goldberger & S. Breznitz (Eds.), *Handbook of stress: Theoretical and clinical aspects* (pp. 174–199). New York: Free Press.

Dolan, R. J., Calloway, S. P., Fonagy, P., De Souza, F. V. A., & Wakeling, A. (1985). Life events, depression and hypothalamic–pituitary–adrenal axis function. *British Journal of Psychiatry, 147*, 429–433.

Duggal, S., Malkoff-Schwartz, S., Birmaher, B., Anderson, B. P., Matty, M. K., Houck, P. R., Bailey-Orr, M., Williamson, D. E., & Frank, E. (2000). Assessment of life stress in adolescents: Self-report versus interview methods. *Journal of the American Academy of Child and Adolescent Psychiatry, 39*, 445–452.

Flett, G. L., Vredenburg, K., & Krames, L. (1997). The continuity of depression in clinical and non-clinical samples. *Psychological Bulletin, 121*, 395–416.

Frank, E., Anderson, B., Reynolds, C. F., Ritenour, A., & Kupfer, D. J. (1994). Life events and the research diagnostic criteria endogenous subtype: A confirmation of the distinction using the Bedford College methods. *Archives of General Psychiatry, 51*, 519–524.

Frank, E., Prien, R. F., Jarrett, R. B., Keller, M. B., Kupfer, D. J., Lavori, P. W., Rush, J., & Weissman, M. (1991). Conceptualization and rationale for consensus definitions of terms in major depressive disorder. *Archives of General Psychiatry, 48*, 851–855.

Gordon, R. (1993). *The alarming history of medicine: Amusing anecdotes from Hippocrates to heart transplants.* New York: St. Martin's Press.

Gotlib, I. H., Lewinsohn, P. M., & Seeley, J. R. (1995). Symptoms versus a diagnosis of depression: Differences in psychosocial functioning. *Journal of Consulting and Clinical Psychology, 63*, 90–100.

Hamilton, M. (1960). A rating scale for depression. *Journal of Neurology, Neurosurgery, and Psychiatry, 23*, 56–62.

Hammen, C. (1991). Generation of stress in the course of unipolar depression. *Journal of Abnormal Psychology, 100*, 555–561.

Hammen, C. (1992). Life events and depression: The plot thickens. *American Journal of Community Psychology, 20*, 179–193.

Hammen, C. (1995). The social context of risk for depression. In K. D. Craig & K. S. Dobson (Eds.), *Anxiety and depression in adults and children* (pp. 82–96). Thousand Oaks, CA: Sage.

Hammen, C. (2001). Vulnerability to depression in adulthood. In R. E. Ingram & J. M. Price (Eds.), *Vulnerability to psychopathology: Risk across the lifespan* (pp. 226–257). New York: Guilford Press.

Hammen, C., Burge, D., Daley, S., Davila, J., Paley, B., & Rudolph, D. (1995). Interpersonal attachment cognitions and prediction of symptomatic response to interpersonal stress. *Journal of Abnormal Psychology, 104*, 436–443.

Hammen, C., Davila, J., Brown, G., Ellicott, A., & Gitlin, M. (1992). Psychiatric history and stress: Predictors of severity of unipolar depression. *Journal of Abnormal Psychology, 101,* 45–52.

Hammen, C., Henry, R., & Daley, S. E. (2000). Depression and sensitization to stressors among young women as a function of childhood adversity. *Journal of Consulting and Clinical Psychology, 68,* 782–787.

Harkness, K. L., Monroe, S. M., Simons, A. D., & Thase, M. (1999). The generation of life events in recurrent and non-recurrent depression. *Psychological Medicine, 29,* 135–144.

Harris, T., Brown, G. W., & Robinson, R. (1999). Befriending as an intervention for chronic depression among women in an inner city: I. Randomized controlled trial. *British Journal of Psychiatry, 174,* 219–224.

Hirschfeld, R. M. A., & Shea, M. T. (1992). Personality. In E. S. Paykel (Ed.), *Handbook of affective disorders* (2nd ed., pp. 185–194). New York: Guilford Press.

Hlastala, S. A., Frank, E., Kowalski, J., Sherrill, J. T., Tu, X. M., Anderson, B., & Kupfer, D. J. (2000). Stressful life events, bipolar disorder, and the "kindling model." *Journal of Abnormal Psychology, 109,* 777–786.

Holmes, T. H. (1979). Development and application of a quantitative measure of life change magnitude. In J. E. Barrett, R. M. Rose, & G. L. Klerman (Eds.), *Stress and mental disorder* (pp. 37–53). New York: Raven Press.

Holmes, T. H., & Rahe, R. H. (1967). The Social Readjustment Rating Scale. *Journal of Psychosomatic Research, 11,* 213–218.

Ingram, R. E., & Price, J. M. (2001). The role of vulnerability in understanding psychopathology. In R. E. Ingram & J. M. Price (Eds.), *Vulnerability to psychopathology: Risk across the lifespan* (pp. 3–19). New York: Guilford Press.

Jackson, S. W. (1986). *Melancholia and depression.* New Haven, CT: Yale University Press.

Johnson, J. G., Cohen, P., Dohrenwend, B. P., Link, B. G., & Brook, J. S. (1999). A longitudinal investigation of social causation and social selection processes involved in the association between socioeconomic status and psychiatric disorders. *Journal of Abnormal Psychology, 108,* 490–499.

Karp, J. F., Frank, E., Anderson, B., George, C. J., Reynolds, C. F. I., Mazumdar, S., & Kupfer, D. J. (1993). Time to remission in late-life depression: Analysis of effects of demographic, treatment, and life-events measures. *Depression, 1,* 250–256.

Katschnig, H., Pakesch, G., & Egger-Zeidner, E. (1986). Life stress and depressive subtypes: A review of present diagnostic criteria and recent research results. In H. Katschnig (Ed.), *Life events and psychiatric disorders: Controversial issues* (pp. 201–245). Cambridge, UK: Cambridge University Press.

Kellogg, T. H. (1897). *A textbook of mental diseases.* New York: Wood.

Kendell, R. E. (1976). The classification of depressions: A review of contemporary confusion. *British Journal of Psychiatry, 129,* 15–28.

Kendler, K. S., Karkowski, L. M., & Prescott, C. A. (1999). Causal relationship between stressful life events and the onset of major depression. *American Journal of Psychiatry, 156,* 837–848.

Kendler, K. S., Kessler, R. C., Walters, E. E., MacLean, C. J., Sham, P. C., Neale, M. C., Heath, A. C., & Eaves, L. J. (1995). Stressful life events, genetic liability and onset of an episode of major depression in women. *American Journal of Psychiatry, 152,* 833–842.

Kendler, K. S., Thornton, L. M., & Gardner, C. O. (2000). Stressful life events and previous episodes in the etiology of major depression in women: An evaluation of the "kindling" hypothesis. *American Journal of Psychiatry, 157,* 1243–1251.

Kendler, K. S., Thornton, L. M., & Gardner, C. O. (2001). Genetic risk, number of previous depressive episodes, and stressful life events in predicting onset of major depression. *American Journal of Psychiatry, 158,* 582–586.

Kendler, K. S., Walters, E. E., & Kessler, R. C. (1997). The prediction of length of major depressive episodes: Results from an epidemiological sample of female twins. *Psychological Medicine, 27,* 107–117.

Kessler, R. C. (1997). The effects of stressful life events on depression. *Annual Review of Psychology, 48,* 191–214.

Klibansky, R., Panofsky, E., & Saxl, F. (1979). *Saturn and melancholy: Studies in natural philosophy, religion and art*. Nendeln, Liechtenstein: Kraus Reprint.

Kohn, R., Dohrenwend, B. P., & Mirotznik, J. (1998). Epidemiological findings on selected psychiatric disorders in the general population. In B. Dohrenwend (Ed.), *Adversity, stress, and psychopathology* (pp. 235–284). New York: Oxford University Press.

Kraepelin, E. (1921). *Manic–depressive insanity and paranoia*. Edinburgh, UK: E. & S. Livingstone.

Lewis, A. J. (1934). Melancholia: A historical review. *Journal of Mental Science, 80*, 1–42.

Lewis, A. J. (1971). Endogenous and exogenous: A useful dichotomy? *Psychological Medicine, 1*, 191–196.

Mapother, E. (1926). Discussion on manic–depressive psychosis. *British Medical Journal, 2*, 872–879.

Mazure, C. M. (1998). Life stressors as risk factors in depression. *Clinical Psychology, Science and Practice, 5*, 291–313.

McGuffin, P., Katz, R., & Bebbington, P. (1988). The Camberwell Collaborative Depression Study: III. Depression and adversity in the relatives of depressed probands. *British Journal of Psychiatry, 153*, 775–782.

McQuaid, J. R., Monroe, S. M., Roberts, J. E., & Johnson, S. L. (1992). Toward the standardization of life stress assessment: Definitional discrepancies and inconsistencies in methods. *Stress Medicine, 8*, 47–56.

McQuaid, J. R., Monroe, S. M., Roberts, J. E., Kupfer, D. J., & Frank, E. (2000). A comparison of two life stress assessment approaches: Prospective prediction of treatment outcome in recurrent depression. *Journal of Abnormal Psychology, 109*, 787–791.

Monroe, S. M. (1982). Life events assessment: Current practices, emerging trends. *Clinical Psychology Review, 2*, 435–453.

Monroe, S. M. (1990). Psychosocial factors in anxiety and depression. In J. D. Maser & R. C. Cloninger (Eds.), *Comorbidity of mood and anxiety disorders* (pp. 463–497). Washington, DC: American Psychiatric Press.

Monroe, S. M. (2000). Psychological stressors: Overview. In G. Fink (Ed.), *Encyclopedia of stress* (pp. 287–294). New York: Academic Press.

Monroe, S. M., & Depue, R. A. (1991). Life stress and depression. In J. Becker & A. Kleinman (Eds.), *Psychosocial aspects of depression* (pp. 101–130). New York: Erlbaum.

Monroe, S. M., Harkness, K. L., Simons, A. D., & Thase, M. E. (2001). Life stress and the symptoms of major depression. *Journal of Nervous and Mental Disease, 189*, 168–175.

Monroe, S. M., Kupfer, D. J., & Frank, E. F. (1992). Life stress and treatment course of recurrent depression: I. Response during index episode. *Journal of Consulting and Clinical Psychology, 60*, 718–724.

Monroe, S. M., & McQuaid, J. R. (1994). Measuring life stress and assessing its impact on mental health. In W. R. Avison & I. H. Gotlib (Eds.), *Stress and mental health: Contemporary issues and prospects for the future* (pp. 43–73). New York: Plenum Press.

Monroe, S. M., Roberts, J. E., Kupfer, D. J., & Frank, E. (1996). Life stress and treatment course of recurrent depression: II. Postrecovery associations with attrition, symptom course, and recurrence over 3 years. *Journal of Abnormal Psychology, 105*, 313–328.

Monroe, S. M., & Simons, A. D. (1991). Diathesis stress in the context of life stress research: Implications for the depressive disorders. *Psychological Bulletin, 110*, 406–425.

Monroe, S. M., Thase, M. E., & Simons, A. D. (1992). Social factors and the psychobiology of depression: Relations between life stress and rapid eye movement sleep latency. *Journal of Abnormal Psychology, 101*, 528–537.

Nazroo, J. Y., Edwards, A. C., & Brown, G. W. (1997). Gender differences in the onset of depression following a shared life event: A study of couples. *Psychological Medicine, 27*, 9–19.

Neilson, E., Brown, G. W., & Marmot, M. (1989). Myocardial infarction. In G. W. Brown & T. O. Harris (Eds.), *Life events and illness* (pp. 313–342). New York: Guilford Press.

Nesse, R. M. (2000). Is depression an adaptation? *Archives of General Psychiatry, 57*, 14–20.

Nurnberger, J. I., Jr., & Gershon, E. S. (1992). Genetics. In E. S. Paykel (Ed.), *Handbook of affective disorders* (2nd ed., pp. 131–148). New York: Guilford Press.

Parker, G., & Blignault, I. (1985). Psychosocial predictors of outcome in subjects with untreated depressive disorder. *Journal of Affective Disorders, 8*, 73–81.

Parker, G., Roy, K., Wilhelm, K., Mitchell, P., Austin, M. P., Hadzi-Pavlovic, D., & Little, C. (1999). Sub-grouping non-melancholic depression from manifest clinical features. *Journal of Affective Disorders, 53,* 1–13.

Paykel, E. S. (1983). Methodological aspects of life events research. *Journal of Psychosomatic Research, 27,* 341–352.

Paykel, E. S., & Cooper, Z. (1992). Life events and social stress. In E. S. Paykel (Ed.), *Handbook of affective disorders* (2nd ed., pp. 149–170). New York: Guilford Press.

Post, R. (1992). Transduction of psychosocial stress into the neurobiology of recurrent affective disorder. *American Journal of Psychiatry, 149,* 999–1010.

Post, R. M., & Weiss, S. R. B. (1999). Neurobiological models of recurrence in mood disorders. In D. S. Charney, E. J. Nestler, & B. S. Bunney (Eds.), *Neurobiology of mental illness* (pp. 365–384). New York: Oxford University Press.

Regier, D. A., Farmer, M. E., Rae, D. S., Myers, J. K., Kramer, M., Robins, L. N., George, L. K., Karno, M., & Locke, B. Z. (1993). One-month prevalence of mental disorders in the United States and sociodemographic characteristics: The Epidemiologic Catchment Area program. *Acta Psychiatrica Scandinavica, 88,* 35–47.

Ross, C. E. (2000). Neighborhood disadvantage and adult depression. *Journal of Health and Social Behavior, 41,* 177–187.

Rudolph, K. D., Hammen, C., Burge, D., Lindberg, N., Herzberg, D., & Daley, S. E. (2000). Toward an interpersonal life-stress model of depression: The developmental context of stress generation. *Development and Psychopathology, 12,* 215–234.

Ruscio, J., & Ruscio, A. M. (2000). Informing the continuity controversy: A taxometric analysis of depression. *Journal of Abnormal Psychology, 109,* 473–487.

Rush, A. J., & Weissenburger, J. E. (1994). Melancholic symptom features and DSM-IV. *American Journal of Psychiatry, 151,* 489–498.

Sanders, A. R., Detera-Wadleigh, S. D., & Gershon, E. S. (1999). Molecular genetics of mood disorders. In D. S. Charney, E. J. Nestler, & B. S. Bunney (Eds.), *Neurobiology of mental illness* (pp. 299–316). New York: Oxford University Press.

Segal, Z. V., Shaw, B. F., Vella, D. D., & Katz, R. (1992). Cognitive and life stress predictors of relapse in remitted unipolar depressed patients: Test of the congruency hypothesis. *Journal of Abnormal Psychology, 101,* 26–36.

Shrout, P. E., Link, B. G., Dohrenwend, B. P., Skodol, A. E., Steuve, A., & Mirotzhik, J. (1989). Characterizing life events as risk factors for depression: The role of fateful loss events. *Journal of Abnormal Psychology, 98,* 460–467.

Sontag, S. (1978). *Illness as metaphor.* Toronto: McGraw-Hill Ryerson.

Stoolmiller, M. (1999). Implications of the restricted range of family environments for estimates of heritability and nonshared environments in behavior-genetic adoption studies. *Psychological Bulletin, 125,* 392–409.

Stueve, A., Dohrenwend, B. P., & Skodol, A. E. (1998). Relationships between stressful life events and episodes of major depression and nonaffective psychotic disorders: Selected results from a New York risk factor study. In B. P. Dohrenwend (Ed.), *Adversity, stress, and psychopathology* (pp. 341–357). New York: Oxford University Press.

Sullivan, P. F., Neale, M. C., & Kendler, K. S. (2000). Genetic epidemiology of major depression: Review and meta-analysis. *American Journal of Psychiatry, 157,* 1552–1562.

Tennant, C., Bebbington, P., & Hurry, J. (1981). The role of life events in depressive illness: Is there a substantial causal relation? *Psychological Medicine, 11,* 379–389.

Vredenburg, K., Flett, G. L., & Krames, L. (1993). Analogue versus clinical depression: A critical reappraisal. *Psychological Bulletin, 113,* 327–344.

Wakefield, J. C. (1992). The concept of mental disorder: On the boundary between biological facts and social values. *American Psychologist, 47,* 373–388.

Weiner, H. W. (1992). *Perturbing the organism: The biology of stressful experience.* Chicago: University of Chicago Press.

Wethington, E., Brown, G. W., & Kessler, R. C. (1995). Interview measurement of stressful life events. In S. Cohen, & R. C. Kessler (Eds.), *Measuring stress: A guide for health and social scientists* (pp. 59–79). New York: Oxford University Press.

Widiger, T. A., & Clark, L. A. (2000). Toward DSM-V and the classification of psychopathology. *Psychological Bulletin, 126,* 946–963.

Zimmerman, M., Pfohl, B., Coryell, W., & Stangl, D. (1987). The prognostic validity of DSM-III Axis IV in depressed inpatients. *American Journal of Psychiatry, 144,* 102–106.

Zubin, J., & Spring, B. (1977). Vulnerability: A new view of schizophrenia. *Journal of Abnormal Psychology, 86,* 103–126.

Zuckerman, M. (1999). *Vulnerability to psychopathology: A biosocial model.* Washington, DC: American Psychological Association Press.

PART III

PREVENTION AND TREATMENT
OF DEPRESSION

In recent years there have been significant developments in interventions for depression. This part includes six chapters that review the methods and evidence for the effectiveness of both prevention and treatment efforts. Muñoz, Le, Clarke, and Jaycox (Chapter 14) discuss prevention, its importance, and the diverse ways in which investigators have attempted to head off the development of depression or to reduce its impact in adults and children. Among typical treatments, pharmacotherapy is the most widely disseminated approach; in this context, both standard and innovative approaches to acute, continuation, and maintenance treatment are discussed by Gitlin (Chapter 15). Two of the most effective and well-validated psychotherapies are discussed by authors who have contributed to their development and empirical evaluation. Cognitive-behavioral treatment is presented and reviewed by Hollon, Haman, and Brown (Chapter 16), and interpersonal psychotherapy is discussed by Weissman and Markowitz (Chapter 17). Increasingly, marital and family interventions are being utilized in the treatment of depression, especially given the interpersonal context in which this disorder often occurs. Beach and Jones (Chapter 18) discuss various approaches to this form of intervention. Finally, Kaslow, McClure, and Connell (Chapter 19) review the unique issues and treatment methods applied to the treatment of depression in children and adolescents.

14

Preventing the Onset of Major Depression

Ricardo F. Muñoz, Huynh-Nhu Le, Gregory Clarke, and Lisa Jaycox

Depression is a major public health problem. In the United States, 17% of adults experience at least one episode of major depression during their lives (Kessler et al., 1994). The prevalence of major depression has been increasing since World War II in many countries. There is evidence that with each generation depression begins earlier and earlier (Klerman & Weissman, 1989). The World Health Organization reports that (1) major depression is the number one cause of disability in the world; and (2) in terms of the burden of disease in the world, taking into account both disability and mortality, major depression was the fourth most important disorder in 1990, and will become the second most important by the year 2020 (Murray & Lopez, 1996). When there is an epidemic of this type, treatment is not enough. It is necessary to dedicate a substantial portion of our resources to prevention. George Albee has said it well:

> John Gordon, a professor of epidemiology at Harvard in the late fifties, sat me down and said: "No mass disorder afflicting humankind has ever been brought under control or eliminated by attempts at treating the afflicted individual nor by training large numbers of therapists." . . . One does not get rid of mass plagues afflicting humankind, including the plague of mental and emotional disorders, by attempts at treating the individual. (1985, p. 213)

Most mental health resources are currently dedicated to treatment. However, in the case of major depression, there are many serious limits to treatment. It reaches very few: of those meeting criteria for major depression in the United States, only 22% of non-Hispanic whites, and even fewer (11%) Mexican Americans, receive mental health treatment (Hough et al., 1987). It is effective in only about two-thirds of those who adhere to treatment as directed (most do not) (Depression Guideline Panel, 1993a). Even if treatment is effective, the chances of the recurrence of a major depressive episode are 50% after one episode, 70% after two episodes, and 90% after three episodes (Depression Guideline Panel, 1993b; Judd, 1997). Therefore, preventing new episodes of major depression is essential. The ideal would be to prevent the first episode.

343

DELINEATING THE SCOPE OF PREVENTIVE INTERVENTIONS: THE INSTITUTE OF MEDICINE REPORT ON PREVENTING MENTAL DISORDERS

The Institute of Medicine (IOM) Report on Preventing Mental Disorders (Mrazek & Haggerty, 1994) was a spirited call for increased research on preventive interventions. Eschewing the traditional, three-level public health definitions (primary, secondary, or tertiary prevention), the IOM Committee proposed a more categorical definition: *Prevention* refers to interventions occurring *before the onset* of the disorder, and designed to prevent the occurrence of the disorder. *Treatment* refers to interventions occurring after the onset of the disorder, to bring a quick end to the clinical episode. Treatment can be provided after early case-finding outreach efforts or as traditional treatment services, in which patients bring themselves in, or are brought into treatment, once they are afflicted by the disorder. *Maintenance* refers to interventions that occur after the acute episode has abated, in order to prevent relapse, recurrence, or disability in a patient who has received treatment.

Within prevention, three sublevels were defined:

Universal preventive interventions are targeted at entire communities regardless of risk. An example is the San Francisco Mood Survey Project (Muñoz, Glish, Soo-Hoo, & Robertson, 1982), an intervention delivered through television, and thus potentially available to all individuals in the community. The outcome was a significant reduction in depressive symptoms in those individuals who initially scored at high levels and who watched the segments. However, this study did not address the question of whether major depressive episodes were prevented.

Selective preventive interventions are targeted at high-risk groups within a community, chosen by demographic characteristics rather than individual risk profiles. An example is the San Francisco Depression Prevention Research Project (Muñoz et al., 1995), which targeted low-income, minority, primary care patients. This study measured both depressive symptoms and major depressive episodes, and thus could detect reduction in incidence. Results showed significant reduction in symptoms, but not in episodes.

Indicated preventive interventions are targeted at individuals with early signs or symptoms but who do not meet criteria for major depressive episodes. An example is the Coping with Stress Course (Clarke et al., 1995), which targeted high school students who did not meet criteria for major depressive episodes, but scored high on a self-report measure of depressive mood, the Center for Epidemiologic Studies Depression Scale (the CES-D). Results demonstrated a significant reduction in onset of major depressive episodes.

In this chapter, we refer to prevention of major depression using the IOM definition, that is, interventions intended to prevent the onset of new episodes of major depression. Thus, we exclude studies that select participants because they meet criteria for major depression at the start of the study. Because the field is not yet advanced enough to provide a large number of such randomized control trials, we also mention studies that attempt to reduce symptoms, as long as participants were not recruited for the study because they were already "cases." Subclinical depressive symptoms can have a substantial impact on functioning (Wells et al., 1989) and thus can be an important target for preventive interventions.

SPECIAL ISSUES INVOLVED IN PREVENTION RESEARCH

All participants in treatment trials meet diagnostic criteria for the disorder being treated. They have generally sought help, either having volunteered for treatment trials or having come into a mental health treatment center, and are thus fairly motivated for treatment. Participants in prevention trials, by definition, have not developed the disorder to be prevented. Thus, outreach to them is an essential component of prevention research. It is crucial to provide people with a convincing rationale for attending the intervention, using the methods taught, and allowing researchers to interview them. This generally requires added attention to issues of recruitment and retention. Some minority groups heavily underutilize treatment services (Hough et al., 1987). Therefore, it is particularly important to provide preventive services that will be accessible and acceptable to them.

The life-cycle approach to prevention encourages us to turn our attention to milestones in the life of individuals. There are many stages in life in which well-tailored interventions might be particularly effective. Prevention professionals recommend providing services as early as possible in the life cycle. Depression research has generally focused more on adults, and only recently has begun to focus on younger populations. Therefore, we have organized our review of the literature into three areas: adulthood, the school years, and the beginning of life.

STEPS IN PREVENTION RESEARCH

Five steps are involved in prevention research (Muñoz & Ying, 1993):

1. *Identifying the target: What do you want to prevent?* At this stage in the development of preventive interventions, the primary target of our efforts should be preventing the onset of major depressive episodes. The first episode of major depression often sets in motion a recurrent course. Therefore, our eventual goal should be preventing the first episode.

2. *Choosing a theory to guide the intervention: What mechanisms are involved?* Prevention intervention research is particularly useful for testing theories about healthy development and the course of psychopathology. Well-designed prevention studies test whether the high-risk groups indeed differ from low-risk groups in the targeted risk factors, whether these factors are modifiable by the intervention, and whether these changes are related to improved mood regulation and the reduction in major depressive episodes (Muñoz et al., 1995).

3. *Identifying high-risk groups: For whom is the intervention most appropriate?* From a public health perspective, it is important to identify those groups that are at highest risk in order to use limited resources wisely. From a research perspective, it is crucial to select groups at high imminent risk for major depressive episodes (Miranda, Muñoz, & Shumway, 1990). High incidence (i.e., a high number of new episodes) is required for adequate statistical power. For example, if the expected incidence in the group being studied is 20% in one year, a sample size of 156 per each of two conditions will be needed to detect a 50% reduction in incidence with power of .80 (alpha = .05, one-tailed). If the expected incidence is 10%, a sample size of 342 per condition would be needed to detect a similar effect size. To make preventive trials feasible, we must identify subgroups at very high imminent risk.

4. *Designing the intervention: How do you propose to prevent the target condition?* Intervention protocols specify the methods by which the high risk factors are to be modified. Detailed descriptions of both content and process are important. *Content* refers to the specific information being communicated to the participants. *Process* refers to the ways in which this information is conveyed, such as in individual or group format, via written materials, the phone, television, or the Internet (Christensen, Miller, & Muñoz, 1978). The same information may be differentially effective for groups of different educational levels, age, gender, or ethnicity.

5. *Designing the study: How will you measure the effects of the intervention?* Prevention trials should utilize state-of-the-science clinical research methods. These include ran-

dom assignment to conditions, the use of control or comparison groups, sample sizes that provide sufficient statistical power, intervention protocols that allow replication, assessment of treatment adherence, use of reliable and valid assessment instruments, reporting of attrition and attempts to reduce such to the minimum possible, assessment of mediators, multiple measures of outcome, and assessment of possible negative effects (Gillham, Shatté, & Freres, 2000; Muñoz, Mrazek, & Haggerty, 1996).

PREVENTING DEPRESSION IN ADULTHOOD

We now address three stages in the life cycle: adulthood, the school years, and the beginning of life. We begin with adulthood because the first depression prevention trials were with adults, and have gradually moved to younger groups. Studies limited to reducing depressive symptoms will be considered preliminary studies. Randomized depression prevention trials are those that explicitly test differences in incidence of major depressive episodes.

Preliminary Work toward Prevention

Strategies to prevent depression have often come from what we already know about the treatment of depression. We have much evidence that learning skills to regulate our mood states, including among patients who are already suffering from an episode of major depression, not only produces improvement similar to that of antidepressants, but also reduces the likelihood of relapse and recurrence (Fava, Rafanelli, Grandi, Conti, & Belluardo, 1998; Paykel et al., 1999; Teasdale et al., 2000). Why wait until someone is suffering from clinical depression to teach them these methods? The idea is logical. But is it practical? If we do not want to wait until the person is sufficiently depressed to have to come to a psychologist, a psychiatrist, or another mental health professional, how do we reach him or her ahead of time?

Studies Focusing on Symptom Levels

A number of studies have attempted to reduce symptoms of depression in a variety of nonclinical populations. The San Francisco Mood Survey Study examined the effects of presenting self-control mood management methods (Lewinsohn, Muñoz, Youngren, & Zeiss, 1978, 1986) via television (Muñoz et al., 1982). Video segments describing these methods were presented daily as part of the noon, 6 P.M., and 11 P.M. news programs, for 2 consecutive weeks. Watching the segments was related to a significant reduction in depressive symptoms for those who had initially high depressive levels. The Life Satisfaction Course focused on individuals 55 and older. Using a nonrandomized pre–post design, the investigators found that a group cognitive-behavioral intervention reduced depressive symptoms (Breckenridge, Zeiss, & Thompson, 1987). Raphael (1977) randomly assigned 64 widows considered to be "at risk" to either an experimental condition consisting of home visits by a psychiatrist in which issues related to the grief process were addressed, or a usual care control condition, with no visits. The author reported significant differences in overall "good" or "bad" emotional health outcomes. Most interestingly, four of the women in the control condition required hospitalization for depression during the follow-up period versus none in the intervention group. Stress management training focused on women on public assistance has shown positive effects (i.e., improvement in depressive symptoms) in two studies, one with Caucasians, and one with African Americans (Tableman, 1987, 1989).

The Hispanic Social Network Study recruited Mexican women 35 to 55 years of age at high risk for depression. They were provided with two interventions, involving indigenous Hispanic natural helpers who either provided one-on-one contacts or led educational peer groups. No overall prevention effect was found, but the investigators reported preventing exacerbation of symptoms in women originally scoring low on depression (Vega, Valle, Kolody, & Hough, 1987). Price and colleagues (e.g., Vinokur, Price, & Schul, 1995) have analyzed the effects of a job-seeking intervention on both reemployment rates and depressive symptoms. Individuals classified as "high risk" according to baseline depression, financial strain, and assertiveness showed significantly greater rates of reemployment and lower depression symptom scores.

An interesting hybrid of prevention and treatment interventions is the Coping with Depression (CWD) Course developed by Lewinsohn and colleagues (Brown & Lewinsohn, 1984; Lewinsohn, Hoberman, & Clarke, 1989). The course is advertised in newspapers, on radio, and on television and has minimal exclusion criteria. Although it is an intervention open to the community as a whole, 80% of the participants met criteria for clinical depression. The CWD course produces consistent reductions in depressive symptoms, with continued improvement effects evident at least up to 6-month follow-ups. A meta-analysis of 20 studies using the course indicates that it is effective in ameliorating depressive symptoms in both preventive and treatment interventions (Cuijpers, 1998).

Randomized Trials Designed to Prevent Major Depressive Episodes

Table 14.1 presents details of the four currently existing randomized trials. Two focused on adults are described here. The San Francisco Depression Prevention Research Project, conducted from 1983 to 1986, was the first randomized control prevention trial intended to test whether an intervention could prevent new clinical episodes of major depression (Muñoz & Ying, 1993; Muñoz, Ying, Armas, Chan, & Gurza, 1987). Participants were 150 English- and Spanish-speaking, predominantly minority, primary care patients, without any psychiatric disorder. Those in the intervention condition received the Depression Prevention Course (Muñoz, 1984, 1998a), consisting of eight 2-hour sessions presented in a small-group format. The course's cognitive-behavioral self-control approaches are based on social learning theory (Bandura, 1977), as applied to depression by Lewinsohn (Lewinsohn et al., 1978, 1986). Of the 150 randomized participants, 139 were contacted at 1 year. Of these, six met DSM criteria for major depression during the last year: four in the control group, and two in the experimental condition (both dropped out early from the intervention). Although in the desired direction, the low incidence does not allow sufficient power to test whether the rate of new cases was significantly reduced. Depressive symptoms measured by the Beck Depression Inventory, but not the CES-D, were significantly lower after intervention when compared with the control condition. There was also evidence of mediation of cognitive-behavioral variables on the reduction in symptoms (Muñoz et al., 1995).

Seligman, Schulman, DeRubeis, and Hollon (1999) conducted a randomized control prevention trial focusing on college freshmen. The intervention tested was the Apex Project (Gillham et al., 1991), which includes cognitive restructuring and problem-solving components. Participants were 231 Ivy League college students chosen because they scored in the most pessimistic quartile on a measure of explanatory style. At 3-year follow-up, 11% of controls and 13% of the prevention group participants had experienced definite episodes of major depression, a nonsignificant difference. The investigators reported a significantly lower rate of moderate generalized anxiety in the prevention group. No effects were found for academic achievement, but significant effects were found for health factors, such as fewer symptoms of physical illness and fewer visits to the student health center (Gillham et al., 2000). There were significant reductions in both depressive and anxiety symptoms, and evi-

TABLE 14.1. Randomized Trials Designed to Test Reduction of Onset of Major Depressive Episodes

Study	Depression Prevention Research Project (Muñoz et al., 1987; Muñoz & Ying, 1993; Muñoz et al., 1995)	Clarke et al., 1995	Apex Project (Seligman et al., 1999)	Clarke et al., 2001
Participants	150 Spanish- and English-speaking adult public-sector primary care patients	150 high school students with elevated depression symptoms	231 college freshmen	94 adolescent offspring of depressed parents
Condition assignment	Random (78 Control, 72 Exp)	Random (74 Control, 76 Exp)	Random (124 Control, 109 Exp)	Random (49 Control, 45 Exp)
Intervention	8 weekly 2-hour group sessions teaching cognitive-behavioral self-control methods	15 hour-long group sessions teaching cognitive restructuring skills	8 weekly 2-hour group sessions teaching cognitive-behavioral skills; 6 individual meetings	15 hour-long group sessions teaching cognitive restructuring skills
Manual	Depression Prevention Course	Coping with Stress Course	Apex Project Manual for Group Leaders	Coping with Stress Course (modified)
Control/comparison condition	No intervention and 40-minute videotape version of CBT methods	Usual care (very little)	No intervention; assessments only	HMO usual care
Assessment intervals	Pre, post, 6-, and 12-month follow-ups	Pre, post, 6-, 12-month follow-ups	Pre, post, 6-, 12-, 18-, 24-, 30-, 36-month follow-ups; plus 36 monthly symptom ratings	Pre, post, 12-, 24-month follow-ups
Assessment instruments: Incidence	Diagnostic Interview Schedule	KSADS, LIFE	SCID, LIFE	KSADS, LIFE
Assessment instruments: Other	Depression: BDI, CES-D; other: CES, PAS, PBI, SAQ, SPQ	Depression: CES-D, Hamilton Depression; other: GAF	Depression: BDI, Hamilton Depression; anxiety: BAI, Hamilton Anxiety	Depression: CES-D, Hamilton Depression; other: CBCL, GAF
Findings: Incidence	MDE incidence at 12-month follow-up: Control: 4/72 (5.5%); Exp: 2/67 (3.0%); n.s.	Total depression[a] incidence at 12-month follow-up: Control: 25.7%; Exp: 14.5% ($p < .05$)	MDE incidence (3 years): Control: 13/119 (10.9%); Exp: 14/106 (13.2%); n.s.	MDE incidence at 12-month follow-up: Control: 28.8%; Exp: 9.3% ($p < .005$)
Depressive symptoms	BDI: Significant; CES-D: n.s.	CES-D: n.s.	BDI, BAI: significant; Hamilton Depression: n.s.; Hamilton Anxiety: n.s.	CES-D: Significant
Other findings	Significant changes in cognitions, pleasant activities, social activities. These changes were related to reductions in depressive symptoms.	GAF: n.s.	Significant changes in explanatory style, hopelessness, dysfunctional attitudes. These changes mediated the depression symptoms prevention in experimental group.	GAF: Significant CBCL: n.s.

[a]Includes major depressive episodes and dysthymia.

dence that changes in explanatory style, dysfunctional attitudes, and hopelessness partially mediated changes in depressive symptoms.

Preventive interventions for adults have promise, but have not yet yielded significant reduction in incidence of major depressive episodes. The key to improved outcomes will be the combination of identifying groups with higher incidence and increasing the potency of the preventive interventions. However, we must ask ourselves whether intervening earlier might be preferable. The next section focuses on interventions for children in school.

INTERVENTIONS DURING THE SCHOOL YEARS

Epidemiological studies indicate a point prevalence of between 0.4% and 2.5% for depressive disorders among prepubertal children (Birmaher et al., 1996), with most recent estimates hovering around 2% (American Academy of Child and Adolescent Psychiatry, 1998). However, the number of children who are experiencing distress in the form of depressive symptoms is much larger, and even a few symptoms of depression are associated with psychosocial impairment and multiple comorbidities.

Depression rates begin to rise in early adolescence, at about age 12 or 13 (reviewed by Birmaher et al., 1996), especially for girls, suggesting that late childhood or early adolescence is a particularly fruitful period in which to mount preventive efforts. Older adolescents report rates of depression close to those seen in adults, with an estimated point prevalence between 3% to 8% and annual incidence between 3% and 11% (Lewinsohn, Hops, Roberts, Seeley, & Andrews, 1993; Weissman, Fendrich, Warner, & Wickramaratne, 1992). By age 18, as many as 20% of all adolescents will have experienced at least one episode of unipolar depression (Lewinsohn et al., 1993). An episode of depression in childhood or adolescence significantly increases the risk of repeated depressive episodes later in life (Garber, Kriss, Koch, & Lindholm, 1988; Lewinsohn, Rohde, Klein, & Seeley, 1999; Pine, Cohen, Gurley, Brook, & Ma, 1998). The school years are an important period in which to attempt prevention and treatment.

Preventing Depression in Adolescence

Nonrandomized Trials Focusing on Symptoms

Klein, Greist, Bass, and Lohr (1987) developed an interactive, educational computer "Wellness" program to provide information about a range of health problems, including depression. A quasi-experimental study compared outcomes when this program was implemented in the health clinic of one high school relative to students in another control school. There were no effects of the intervention on self-reported depression scores nor on global severity.

Randomized Trials Focusing on Symptoms

Two linked but separate studies attempted to reduce self-reported depression symptoms in an unselected sample of high school students (Clarke, Hawkins, Murphy, & Sheeber, 1993). In the first trial, 9th- and 10th-grade health classes were randomly assigned to receive a three-session prevention curriculum or the usual health class curriculum, which did not address depression. The three-session program covered the causes, signs, and treatments for depression, but provided no direct training in skills to cope with depression. There were no enduring preventive effects for boys, girls, or for youth with high baseline depression scores. The second study added behavioral activation training (Hoberman & Lewinsohn,

1985), which increased the program length from three to five sessions. Despite the intervention revisions, no program effects were noted for any group.

Another universal, school-based, depression symptom prevention study was the Penn State Adolescent Study (Petersen, Leffert, Graham, Alwin, & Ding, 1997). Students enrolled in three middle schools were randomized to either a control condition or to receive a 16-session, psychoeducational program that covered problem solving, assertiveness, relaxation, friendship skills, and cognitive restructuring. Significant short-term program effects were found for coping and self-reported internalizing problem behaviors, but not for self-reported or clinician-rated depression. However, intervention girls reported much less depression at postintervention than girls in the control condition, while intervention boys reported worsening depression compared to boys in the control group.

Hains and Ellmann (1994) examined the effectiveness of a school-based, "stress-inoculation" prevention program addressing multiple targets, including depression symptoms. Participants were divided into high and low emotional arousal subgroups. Although the authors conclude that significant short-term depression symptom reduction was obtained for the high arousal youth, the study is difficult to interpret for several reasons, including a small sample (11 intervention youth and 10 control youth).

A series of reports by Beardslee and colleagues (Beardslee et al., 1993; Beardslee, Salt, et al., 1997; Beardslee, Wright, Salt, & Drezner, 1997) compared two versions of family-directed interventions to address offspring (ages 8 to 15) risk of depression in parents being treated for depression. Both manualized interventions provided psychoeducational information about depression, encouraged discussions about depression and its impact on the family, and directed parents to reinforce resilient capacities in their children. One version was delivered in two brief group lectures ($N = 18$ families). The other version was delivered to individual families ($N = 19$) in six to 10 sessions by study staff (social workers or psychologists) trained in the intervention. The clinician-based intervention was significantly superior to the lecture in patient satisfaction (Beardslee et al., 1993), parent-rated program benefit (Beardslee, Salt, et al., 1997), greater child understanding of parental affective disorder, and better child adaptive functioning (Beardslee, Wright, et al., 1997). There were no differences for parent report or child report of child psychopathology, family relations, and child-reported self-worth. Mood disorder episode data were described, but no outcome results were reported.

Randomized Prevention Trials with Adolescents

Two randomized trials for adolescents are noted in Table 14.1 and described below.

INDICATED PREVENTION IN YOUTH WITH ELEVATED SUBDIAGNOSTIC DEPRESSION SYMPTOMS

This investigation (Clarke et al., 1995) was linked to the two universal prevention trials described above (Clarke et al., 1993). A total of 1,652 youth were administered a self-report depression scale (the CES-D) while receiving the universal prevention health class curriculums, or in the control classrooms. Youth above the 75th percentile on the CES-D ("Demoralized") were invited to take part in this subsequent, indicated prevention study. Consenting youth with current affective diagnoses were referred to nonexperimental services. The remaining Demoralized adolescents were randomly assigned to either a 15-session cognitive group prevention intervention ($N = 76$), or to a "usual care" control condition ($N = 74$). The prevention program (Clarke & Lewinsohn, 1995) focused on teaching adolescents to identify and challenge irrational or highly negative thoughts (see Clarke, 2000, for details). Prevention subjects, compared to controls, reported significantly lower total incidence of depressive disorder over the follow-up period (14.5% vs. 25.7%, respectively).

INDICATED PREVENTION IN YOUTH WITH DEPRESSED PARENTS

Another indicated prevention study has recently been completed with adolescent offspring of depressed parents (Clarke et al., 2001). Index parents were recruited from HMO-enrolled adults being treated for depression who had offspring ages 13 to 18. Youth were classified into one of three mutually exclusive depression severity groups: (1) a Depressed group with current diagnoses of either major depressive disorder and/or dysthymia; (2) a Demoralized group with subdiagnostic depressive symptoms, or with a past episode of major depression; or (3) a Resilient group with no current or past depressive symptoms or disorder. The Demoralized youth were the focus of the indicated prevention study. Demoralized youth were randomized to either usual HMO care ($N = 49$) or usual care plus a 15-session group prevention program using cognitive therapy methods ($N = 45$). Adolescents in the experimental group program were taught to identify negative thinking patterns and to generate more realistic and positive counterthoughts. Significant prevention effects were found for self-reported depressive symptoms as well as for global functioning. Survival analysis of total incident major depressive episodes indicated a significant advantage for the experimental condition (9.3% cumulative major depression incidence) compared to the usual care control condition (28.8%) at the median 14-month follow-up.

Preventing Depression during the Grammar School Years

Prevention work for school-aged children is still in the preliminary stages. To date, there have been no universal or selected prevention studies published that focus on prevention of depressive disorders. Instead, preliminary work falls into the "indicated" category, where studies have focused on high-risk populations and assessed changes in depressive symptoms.

Early work on the impact of depression interventions for children focused on relieving depressive symptoms rather than a diagnosed depressive disorder. These early studies did not generally follow children over enough time to gauge prevention effects, nor did they attempt to assess the presence or absence of depressive disorders at any of the follow-ups. Nonetheless, they are important because of their impact on subsyndromal depression (see Asarnow, Jaycox, & Thompson, 2001, for a review). In four of six studies that provided data on the impact of CBT, these techniques were found to be superior in reducing depressive symptoms, as compared to no treatment or wait-list controls (Kahn, Kehle, Jenson, & Clark, 1990; Reynolds & Coats, 1986; Stark, Reynolds, & Kaslow, 1987; Weisz, Thurber, Sweeney, Proffitt, & LeGagnoux, 1997). However, the CBT techniques usually did not differ from the nonspecific controls, such as relaxation training. Two studies did not support the efficacy of CBT: Liddle and Spence (1990) found no differences between those children treated with a social competence enhancement therapy, attention control, and no treatment control; Marcotte and Baron (1993) found no difference between those 14- to 17-year-olds receiving rational-emotive therapy and no treatment controls. Thus, the impact of CBT in this age group appears to be modest.

Three other studies sought to prevent depressive symptoms, but also did not assess depression disorder status among participants. A study of a school-based intervention explicitly sought to prevent depressive symptoms among children at risk for depression by virtue of subthreshold depressive symptoms or a high degree of family conflict at home (Jaycox, Reivich, Gillham, & Seligman, 1994). This study randomized schools to CBT or wait-list control conditions, and assessed matched no-treatment controls from a neighboring school district. The intervention was broad, incorporating cognitive therapy, social problem solving, peer group entry skills, and emotion control. Immediately after treatment, the 69 treated children showed lower levels of depressive symptoms and better classroom behavior compared to 73 children in the wait-list and no-treatment conditions (Jaycox et al., 1994). Moreover, the treated children continued to report fewer depressive symptoms at a 2-year follow-up assessment, with the number of treated children who reported symptoms of depression in the moderate to severe range reduced by half (Gillham, Reivich, Jaycox, & Seligman, 1995).

King and Kirschenbaum (1990) selected children at risk for general adjustment problems, and conducted a program of social skills training and consultation with parents and teachers. Children were randomized to social skills training and parent/teacher consultation, or parent/teacher consultation only, within two rural elementary schools. Children in both groups improved in their competencies and decreased problematic behaviors over time, but children who received the more comprehensive intervention also decreased depressed mood.

Death of a parent is also thought to predispose children to increased depression, anxiety, and social withdrawal (Gersten, Beals, & Kallgren, 1991). Sandler and colleagues (Sandler, West, Baca, & Pillow, 1992) conducted a randomized trial with 7- to 17-year-olds who had lost a parent. The intervention included a three-session grief workshop attended by multiple families, followed by a 13-session program (six parent-only sessions, six family sessions, and a termination session). The intervention focused on parental demoralization and warmth, planning stable positive events, and coping with negative stress events. Children who underwent the intervention were compared to a delayed-treatment control group. Results showed improvement on some of the mediators as a function of the treatment, as well as parent reports of decreased depressive symptoms, conduct problems, and overall problems in older children. There were no intervention effects on children's self-reported depressive symptoms, or for younger children.

Preventing Depression during the Prenatal Period and the Early Childhood Years

Many sequelae of maternal depression and other risk factors are already present long before school starts. Ideally, one would begin prevention efforts before birth, or even before conception. We now turn to work that focuses on the beginning of life.

Incidence and Prevalence of Major Depression in the Preschool Years

The incidence of major depression for children younger than age 6 is not known (Luby, 2000). It is challenging to assess this incidence for at least two reasons. First, it is uncertain whether symptoms that resemble depression are actually due to depression or are merely developmentally transient and normative difficulties. Second, given that infants are dependent on their primary caregivers, it is uncertain to what degree the depression is due to the maladaptive early parent–child relationship or resides within the individual child.

To understand the development of emotion dysregulation processes during early childhood, investigators have studied infants and children of depressed parents (although the majority of these studies focus on mothers; for an overview, see Shafii & Shafii, 1992). Compared to nondepressed controls, depressed mothers perceive themselves to be less competent parents, show more maladaptive parenting, and are less consistent and often either under- or overstimulating in their interactions with their infants (e.g., Field, 1995; Teti & Gelfand, 1991). Their infants, in turn, react to their parent's depression with their own "depressive" symptomatology (e.g., loss of weight, weepy and withdrawn behavior) (Luby, 2000). Moreover, children of depressed parents are at an increased risk of becoming depressed themselves in their lifetime (Beardslee, Versage, & Gladstone, 1998; Downey & Coyne, 1990). In early childhood, the focus of prevention of depression should begin with mothers-to-be who are at risk for developing depression during pregnancy and the early postpartum period. If maternal depression is untreated during this time, it may interfere with parenting, impair mother–child interactions, and subsequently increase the risk of the child's development of pathology.

Preliminary Work toward Prevention of Depression

To date, no study has focused exclusively on preventing depression by targeting infants, mothers, or their relationship. However, there are a few large-scale programs that focus on preventing Preliminary work toward prevention of depression a variety of negative outcomes that affect the health of infants and children, such as child abuse, neglect, and low birthweight (Hardy & Street, 1989; Olds, Henderson, Chamberlin, & Tatelbaum, 1986) or promote better parent–child relationships from birth (Tsiantis, Smith, Dragonas, & Cox, 2000). Of these trials, some have included mood measures to assess for depressive symptomatology among mothers and thus investigate whether the intervention can decrease their negative mood symptoms, thereby also ameliorating their children's mood symptoms. We will review two examples of preventive interventions that are exemplary and may help to inform future research.

Olds and colleagues (e.g., Olds et al., 1986; Olds et al., 1998) evaluated the effect of prenatal and early childhood home-visitation programs by public health nurses. These were designed to prevent preterm delivery and low birthweight for the prenatal phase, and child maltreatment, injuries, developmental delays, and behavioral problems for the postpartum phase. The target sample included 400 young low-income predominantly European American women, of whom 324 mothers and their children were followed for 15 years after their child's birth. Participants were randomly assigned to one of four treatment conditions (treatment 1 = sensory and developmental screening for child at 12 and 24 months; treatment 2 = screening in treatment 1 and free transportation for prenatal and well-child care; treatment 3 = services in treatments 1 and 2 and home-nurse visitation during pregnancy; treatment 4 = services in treatments 1, 2, and 3, and home-visitation until the child was 2 years old). Relative to individuals in treatments 1 and 2, individuals in treatments 3 and 4 had improved health-related behaviors; improved pregnancy outcomes; decreased criminal behaviors; rates of child abuse and neglect, and substance use; increased economic self-sufficiency; and improved abilities in infant caregiving. These findings suggest that such a program can have long-term public health and socioeconomic benefits. However, this intervention did not produce reductions in maternal depression scores, in part because the research team did not specifically target depression.

The EU/WHO Programme promoted health in early childhood by including primary health care workers (PHCWs) in the provision of educational services. The goal was to help parents understand and promote healthy psychosocial development during the first 2 years of the child's life (Tsiantis et al., 2000). The study evaluated whether PHCWs trained in issues relevant to children's psychosocial development had improved outcomes compared to PHCWs who were not given additional training. The study took place in Cyprus, Greece, the Federal Republic of Yugoslavia, and Portugal. Mothers' scores on the Edinburgh Postnatal Depression Scale (Cox, Holden, & Sagovsky, 1987), a measure of postpartum depressive symptomatology, did not differ between the two groups, except for the Greek sample, where Greek intervention mothers had significantly lower depressive scores compared to the control group. Intervention mothers in all countries were more likely to express positive feelings about the baby, less likely to express negative feelings about their role as mothers, and less likely to identify areas of difficulty with their baby.

The research on preventing depression during early childhood is still in its early stages. It will be important for future research to identify the modifiable characteristics during the pre- and postpartum period that may predispose women to develop postpartum depression and intervene to reduce these characteristics (Murray, 1992; Spinelli, 1999). One strategy has been to target women who have had a history of major depression or are at risk for a major depressive episode, and provide them with interventions to prevent its recurrence. This strategy is being used in a research project in progress. The "*Mamás y Bebés*/Mothers and Babies: Mood and Health Project" (Muñoz, Le, Ghosh Ippen, & Lieberman, 2000) has two goals: (1) identify a group at high risk for developing a major depressive episode (Le & Muñoz, 2000), and (2) develop and evaluate a prevention trial protocol designed to improve mood regulation and increase maternal self-efficacy. The Depression Prevention Course (Muñoz, 1984; Muñoz, 1998a) has been adapted for use with pregnant young women ("The Mothers and Babies Course," Muñoz et al., 2001). In addition to the original information about how to use thoughts, activity, and contacts with other people to maintain a healthy mood state, the investigators include information related to pregnancy, parenting, and child development. They are testing whether this intervention would reduce the incidence of major depressive episodes in the control relative to the experimental group. Currently, the investigators are pilot testing the intervention in preparation for a full-scale randomized controlled trial.

FUTURE DIRECTIONS

Depression prevention studies focused on prevention or reduction of depressive symptoms in individuals who do not meet criteria for major depressive episodes at entry into the study have generally shown positive effects. The next logical step is outcome studies designed to test whether major depressive episodes can be prevented. There are currently only four completed randomized control prevention trials for major depressive episodes (see Table 14.1). The field needs to implement a new generation of depression prevention trials with improved designs.

A first step would be to develop standards for the identification of participants at high imminent risk and standardized measurement and analysis of new episodes of major depression. To provide a reasonable test of whether rates of onset of major depressive episodes can be reduced, preventive randomized control trials (RCTs) need to include a sufficiently long follow-up period (at least 1 year). Prevention studies should test specific, well-defined interventions, so that either positive or negative outcomes inform the field about the intervention's impact. Brown and Liao (1999) discuss design issues for prerandomization, intervention, and postintervention, focusing on different examples of prevention research as a primary strategy to prevent mental health problems. Ideally, the preventive intervention should address healthy development as well as prevention of psychopathology (Muñoz, 1998b). Studies should explicitly measure effects on collateral public health problems, such as smoking, other substance abuse, unplanned pregnancies, marital problems, school performance, job performance, and physical health. Prevention studies should consciously target varied specific populations, including ethnically diverse populations and specific age groups. We must avoid the weakness of the treatment outcome literature, which has few studies that test efficacy of depression treatment with ethnic minority groups. In addition, we must address differences in developmental stage: the literature is sorely lacking in the area of preventing of depression among the very young and the elderly. Given that depression is highly comorbid, prevention studies should also be designed to evaluate effects on disorders in addition to depression. For example, one of the strengths of Seligman et al.'s (1999) study was its focus on both depression and anxiety. Prevention studies are more likely to reach their intended audiences if they involve collaboration with community settings, such as the home, schools, health systems, religious networks, and so on.

Preventive interventions need to be adapted for implementation with innovative methods, not just delivery by licensed professionals. For example, an intervention provided via television or the Internet can reach many more people per year than face-to-face interventions by doctoral-level professionals. Given the need to reach larger groups with preventive interventions, we will need to develop and test interventions in which the usual ratio of professionals to consumers is significantly smaller. Otherwise, we will have the same shortage of personnel to provide preventive interventions as we do now in terms of providing treatment.

Developing methods to prevent the onset of major depression is the next great challenge for the mental health field. The World Health Organization has identified unipolar major depression as the number one cause of disability worldwide (Murray & Lopez, 1996). The Institute of Medicine has determined that major depression is the best bet for the first mental disorder that we will be able to prevent (Mrazek & Haggerty, 1994). It is time to start the journey toward a world without depression (Muñoz, 2001).

ACKNOWLEDGMENTS

We gratefully acknowledge support from the University of California Office of the President Committee on Latino Research for the University of California, San Francisco/San Francisco General Hospital Latino Mental Health Research Program, Drs. Cloyce Duncan and Gwendolyn Evans for their generous support of the Mothers and Babies Project, and the National Institute of Mental Health (Grant Nos. MH 37992 and MH 596056) for support of the Depression Prevention Research Project and the Mothers and Babies Intervention Development Project (Ricardo F. Muñoz, Principal Investigator). Huynh-Nhu Le's work was supported by the Health Psychology Program, Department of Psychiatry, at the University of California, San Francisco, funded by the National Institute of Mental Health. We also gratefully acknowledge Sonia Gálvez for assistance in preparation of this chapter.

REFERENCES

Albee, G. (1985). The argument for primary prevention. *Journal of Primary Prevention, 5,* 213–219.

American Academy of Child and Adolescent Psychiatry. (1998). Practice parameters for the assessment and treatment of children and adolescents with depressive disorders. *Journal of the American Academy of Child and Adolescent Psychiatry, 37*(10, Suppl.), 4–26.

Asarnow, J., Jaycox, L. H., & Thompson, M. (2001). Depression in youth: Psychosocial interventions. *Journal of Child Clinical Psychology, 30,* 33–47.

Bandura, A. (1977). *Social learning theory.* Englewood Cliffs, NJ: Prentice-Hall.

Beardslee, W. R., Salt, P., Porterfield, K., Rothberg, P. C., Van, D. V., Swatling, S., Hoke, L., Moilanen, D. L., & Wheelock, I. (1993). Comparison of preventive interventions for families with parental affective disorder. *Journal of the American Academy of Child and Adolescent Psychiatry, 32,* 254–263.

Beardslee, W. R., Salt, P., Versage, E. M., Gladstone, T. R., Wright, E. J., & Rothberg, P. C. (1997). Sustained change in parents receiving preventive interventions for families with depression. *American Journal of Psychiatry, 154,* 510–515.

Beardslee, W. R., Versage, E. M., & Gladstone, T. R. G. (1998). Children of affectively ill parents: A review of the past 10 years. *Journal of the American Academy of Child and Adolescent Psychiatry, 37*(11), 1134–1141.

Beardslee, W. R., Wright, E. J., Salt, P., & Drezner, K. (1997). Examination of children's responses to two preventive intervention strategies over time. *Journal of the American Academy of Child and Adolescent Psychiatry, 36*(2), 196–204.

Birmaher, B., Ryan, N. D., Williamson, D. E., Brent, D. A., Kaufman, J., Dahl, R. E., Perel, J., & Nelson, B. (1996). Childhood and adolescent depression: A review of the past 10 years, Part 1. *Journal of the American Academy of Child and Adolescent Psychiatry, 35*(11), 1427–1439.

Breckenridge, J. S., Zeiss, A. M., & Thompson, L. W. (1987). The Life Satisfaction Course: An intervention for the elderly. In R. F. Muñoz (Ed.), *Depression prevention: Research directions* (pp. 185–196). Washington, DC: Hemisphere.

Brown, C. H., & Liao, J. (1999). Principles for designing randomized preventive trials in mental health: An emerging developmental epidemiology paradigm. *American Journal of Community Psychology, 27*(5), 673–710.

Brown, R., & Lewinsohn, P. M. (1984). A psychoeducational approach to the treatment of depression: Comparison of group, individual, and minimal contact procedures. *Journal of Consulting and Clinical Psychology, 52*, 774–783.

Christensen, A., Miller, W. R., & Muñoz, R. F. (1978). Paraprofessionals, partners, peers, paraphernalia, and print: Expanding mental health service delivery. *Professional Psychology, 9*, 249–270.

Clarke, G. N. (2000). Prevention of depression in at-risk samples of adolescents. In C. A. Essau & F. Petermann (Eds.), *Depressive disorders in children and adolescents: Epidemiology, risk factors, and treatment* (13th ed., pp. 341–360). Northvale, NJ: Aronson.

Clarke, G. N., Hawkins, W., Murphy, M., & Sheeber, L. B. (1993). School-based primary prevention of depressive symptomatology in adolescents: Findings from two studies. *Journal of Adolescent Research, 8*, 183–204.

Clarke, G. N., Hawkins, W., Murphy, M., Sheeber, L. B., Lewinsohn, P. M., & Seeley, J. R. (1995). Targeted prevention of unipolar depressive disorder in an at-risk sample of high school adolescents: A randomized trial of a group cognitive intervention. *Journal of the American Academy of Child and Adolescent Psychiatry, 34*, 312–321.

Clarke, G. N., Hornbrook, M. C., Lynch, F. L., Polen, M., Gale, J., Beardslee, W. R., O'Connor, E., & Seeley, J. R. (2001). A randomized trial of a group cognitive intervention for preventing depression in adolescent offspring of depressed parents. *Archives of General Psychiatry, 58*, 1127–1134.

Clarke, G. N., & Lewinsohn, P. M. (1995). *Instructor's manual for the Adolescent Coping with Stress Course.* Unpublished manuscript, Center for Health Research, Portland, OR.

Cox, J. L., Holden, J. M., & Sagovsky, R. (1987). Detection of postnatal depression: Development of the Edinburgh Postnatal Depression Scale. *British Journal of Psychiatry, 150*, 782–786.

Cuijpers, P. (1998). A psychoeducational approach to the treatment of depression: A meta-analysis of Lewinsohn's "Coping with Depression course." *Behavior Therapy, 29*, 521–533.

Depression Guideline Panel. (1993a). *Depression in primary care: Vol. 2. Treatment of major depression* (Clinical Practice Guideline No. 5, AHCPR Publication No. 93-0551). Rockville, MD: Department of Health and Human Services, Public Health Service, Agency for Health Care Policy and Research.

Depression Guideline Panel. (1993b). *Depression in primary care: Detection, diagnosis and treatment: Quick reference guide for clinicians* (Clinical Practice Guideline No. 5, AHCPR Publication No. 93-0552). Rockville, MD: Department of Health and Human Services, Public Health Service, Agency for Health Care Policy and Research.

Derogatis, L. R., Lipman, R. S., & Covi, L. (1973). SCL-90: An outpatient psychiatric rating scale. Preliminary report. *Psychopharmacology Bulletin, 9*, 13–28.

Downey, G., & Coyne, J. C. (1990). Children of depressed parents: An integrative review. *Psychological Bulletin, 108*(1), 50–76.

Fava, G. A., Rafanelli, C., Grandi, S., Conti, S., & Belluardo, P. (1998). Prevention of recurrent depression with cognitive behavioral therapy: Preliminary findings. *Archives of General Psychiatry, 55*(9), 816–820.

Field, T. (1995). Infants of depressed mothers. *Infant Behavior and Development, 18,*1–13.

Garber, J., Kriss, M. R., Koch, M., & Lindholm, L. (1988). Recurrent depression in adolescents: A follow-up study. *Journal of the American Child Adolescent Psychiatry, 27,* 49–54.

Gersten, J., Beals, J., & Kallgren, K. (1991). Epidemiological and preventive interventions: Parental death in childhood as a case example. *American Journal of Community Psychology, 19,* 481–500.

Gillham, J., Jaycox, L., Reivich, K., Hollon, S. D., Freeman, A., DeRubeis, R. J., & Seligman, M. E. P. (1991). *The Apex Project manual for group leaders.* Unpublished manuscript.

Gillham, J. E., Reivich, K. J., Jaycox, L. H., & Seligman, M. E. P. (1995). Prevention of depressive symptoms in schoolchildren: Two-year follow-up. *Psychological Science, 6*(6), 343–351.

Gillham, J. E., Shatté, A. J., & Freres, D. R. (2000). Preventing depression: A review of cognitive-behavioral and family interventions. *Applied and Preventive Psychology, 9*(2), 63–88.

Hains, A. A., & Ellmann, S. W. (1994). Stress inoculation training as a preventative intervention for high school youths. *Journal of Cognitive Psychotherapy, 8*(3), 219–232.

Hardy, J. B., & Street, R. (1989). Family support and parenting education in the home: An effective extension of clinic-based preventive health care services for poor children. *Journal of Paediatrics, 115*(6), 927–931.

Hoberman, H. M., & Lewinsohn, P. M. (1985). The behavioral treatment of depression. In E. E. Beckham & W. R. Leber (Eds.), *Handbook of depression: Treatment, assessment, and research* (pp. 39–81). Homewood, IL: Dorsey Press.

Hough, R. L., Landsverk, J. A., Karno, M., Burnam, M. A., Timbers, D. M., Escobar, J. I., & Regier, D. A. (1987). Utilization of health and mental health services by Los Angeles Mexican-Americans and Non-Hispanic Whites. *Archives of General Psychiatry, 44*(8), 702–709.

Jaycox, L. H., Reivich, K. J., Gillham, J. E., & Seligman, M. E. P. (1994). Prevention of depressive symptoms in school children. *Behavioral Research and Therapy, 32,* 801–816.

Judd, L. L. (1997). The clinical course of unipolar major depressive disorders. *Archives of General Psychiatry, 54,* 989–991.

Kahn, J. S., Kehle, T. J., Jenson, W. R., & Clark, E. (1990). Comparison of cognitive-behavioral, relaxation, and self-modeling interventions for depression among middle-school students. *School Psychology Review, 19,* 196–211.

Kessler, R. C., McGonagle, K. A., Shanyang, Z., Nelson, C. B., Hughes, M., Eshleman, S., Wittchen, H. U., & Kendler, K. S. (1994). Lifetime and 12-month prevalence of DSM-III-R psychiatric disorders in the United States: Results from the National Comorbidity Survey. *Archives of General Psychiatry, 51*(1), 8–19.

King, C. A., & Kirschenbaum, D.S. (1990). An experimental evaluation of a school-based program for children at-risk: Wisconsin Early Intervention. *Journal of Community Psychology, 18,* 167–177.

Klein, M. H., Greist, J. H., Bass, S. M., & Lohr, M. J. (1987). Autonomy and self-control: Key concepts for the prevention of depression in adolescents. In R. F. Muñoz (Ed.), *Depression prevention: Research directions* (pp. 103–123). Washington, DC: Hemisphere.

Klerman, G. L., & Weissman, M. M. (1989). Increasing rates of depression. *Journal of the American Medical Association, 261,* 2229–2235.

Le, H. N., & Muñoz, R. F. (2000). [The Depression Risk Study]. Unpublished raw data.

Lewinsohn, P. M., Hoberman, H. M., & Clarke, G. N. (1989). The Coping with Depression Course: Review and future directions. *Canadian Journal of Behavioral Science, 21,* 471–493.

Lewinsohn, P. M., Hops, H., Roberts, R. E., Seeley, J. R., & Andrews, J. A. (1993). Adolescent psychopathology: I. Prevalence and incidence of depression and other DSM-III-R disorders in high school students. *Journal of Abnormal Psychology, 102,* 133–144.

Lewinsohn, P. M., Muñoz, R. F., Youngren, M. A., & Zeiss, A. M. (1978). *Control your depression.* Englewood Cliffs, NJ: Prentice-Hall.

Lewinsohn, P. M., Muñoz, R. F., Youngren, M. A., & Zeiss, A. M. (1986). *Control your depression* (rev. ed.). New York: Prentice-Hall.

Lewinsohn, P. M., Rohde, P., Klein, D. N., & Seeley, J. R. (1999). Natural course of adolescent major depressive disorder: I. Continuity into young adulthood. *Journal of the American Academy of Child and Adolescent Psychiatry, 38,* 56–63.

Liddle, B., & Spence, S. H. (1990). Cognitive-behaviour therapy with depressed primary school children: A cautionary note. *Behavioural Psychotherapy, 18,* 85–102.

Luby, J. L. (2000). Depression. In C. H. Zeanah, Jr. (Ed.), *Handbook of infant mental health* (2nd ed., pp. 382–396). New York: Guilford Press.

Marcotte, D., & Baron, P. (1993). The efficacy of a school-based rational–emotive intervention strategy with depressive adolescents. *Canadian Journal of Counselling, 27*(2), 77–92.

Miranda, J., Muñoz, R. F., & Shumway, M. (1990). Depression prevention research: The need for screening scales that truly predict. In C. Attkisson & J. M. Zich (Eds.), *Depression in primary care: Screening and detection* (pp. 232–250). New York: Routledge.

Mrazek, P., & Haggerty, R. (1994). *Reducing risks for mental disorders: Frontiers for preventive intervention research.* Washington, DC: National Academy Press.

Muñoz, R. F. (1984). *The Depression Prevention Course.* Unpublished manuscript, University of California, San Francisco.

Muñoz, R. F. (1998a). *The Depression Prevention Course* (rev. ed.). Unpublished manuscript, University of California, San Francisco.

Muñoz, R. F. (1998b). Preventing major depression by promoting emotion regulation: A conceptual framework and some practical tools. *International Journal of Mental Health Promotion* (Inaugural Issue, September), 23–40.

Muñoz, R. F. (2001). On the road to a world without depression. *Journal of Primary Prevention, 21,* 325–338.

Muñoz, R. F., Glish, M., Soo-Hoo, T., & Robertson, J. L. (1982). The San Francisco Mood Survey Project: Preliminary work toward the prevention of depression. *American Journal of Community Psychology, 10*(3), 317–329.

Muñoz, R. F., Le, H. N., Ghosh Ippen, C., & Lieberman, A. F. (2000). [Mothers and Babies: Mood and Health Project]. Unpublished raw data.

Muñoz, R. F., Le, H. N., Ghosh Ippen, C., Lieberman, A. F., Diaz, M. A., & La Plante, L. (2001). *The Mothers and Babies Course: A reality management approach.* Unpublished manuscript, University of California–San Francisco.

Muñoz, R. F., Mrazek, P. J., & Haggerty, R. J. (1996). Institute of Medicine Report on Prevention of Mental Disorders: Summary and commentary. *American Psychologist, 51*(11), 1116–1122.

Muñoz, R. F., & Ying, Y. (1993). *The prevention of depression: Research and practice.* Baltimore: Johns Hopkins University Press.

Muñoz, R. F., Ying, Y. W., Armas, R., Chan, F., & Gurza, R. (1987). The San Francisco Depression Prevention Research Project: A randomized trial with medical outpatients. In R. F. Muñoz (Ed.), *Depression prevention: Research directions* (pp. 199–215). Washington, DC: Hemisphere.

Muñoz, R. F., Ying, Y. W., Bernal, G., Pérez-Stable, E. J., Sorensen, J. L., Hargreaves, W. A., Miranda, J., & Miller, L. S. (1995). Prevention of depression with primary care patients: A randomized controlled trial. *American Journal of Community Psychology, 23*(2), 199–222.

Murray, J. (1992). Prevention and the identification of high risk groups. *International Review of Psychiatry, 4*(3–4), 281–286.

Murray, C. J. L., & Lopez, A. D. (1996). *The global burden of disease: Summary.* Cambridge, MA: Harvard University Press.

Olds, D., Henderson, C. R., Jr., Chamberlin, R., & Tatelbaum, R. (1986). Preventing child abuse and neglect: A randomized trial of nurse home visitation. *Paediatrics, 78*(1), 65–78.

Olds, D., Henderson, C. R., Jr., Cole, R., Eckenrode, J., Kitzman, H., Luckey, D., Pettitt, L., Sidora, K., Morris, P., & Powers, J. (1998). Long-term effects of nurse home visitation on children's criminal and antisocial behavior: 15-year follow-up of a randomized controlled trial. *Journal of the American Medical Association, 280*(14), 1238–1244.

Paykel, E. S., Scott, J., Teasdale, J. D., Johnson, A. L., Garland, A., Moore, R., Jenaway, A., Cornwall, P. L., Hayhurst, H., Abbott, R., & Pope, M. (1999). Prevention of relapse in residual depression by cognitive therapy: A controlled trial. *Archives of General Psychiatry, 56,* 829–835.

Petersen, A. C., Leffert, N., Graham, B., Alwin, J., & Ding, S. (1997). Promoting mental health during the transition into adolescence. In J. Schulenberg, J. Maggs, & K. Hurrelmann (Eds.), *Health risks and developmental transitions during adolescence* (18th ed., pp. 471–497). New York: Cambridge University Press.

Pine, D. S., Cohen, P., Gurley, D., Brook, J., & Ma, Y. (1998). The risk for early-adulthood anxiety and depressive disorders in adolescents with anxiety and depressive disorders. *Archives of General Psychiatry, 55,* 56–64.

Raphael, B. (1977). Preventive intervention with the recently bereaved. *Archives of General Psychiatry, 34,* 1450–1454.

Reynolds, W. M., & Coats, K. I. (1986). A comparison of cognitive-behavioral therapy and relaxation training for the treatment of depression in adolescents. *Journal of Consulting and Clinical Psychology, 54*(5), 653–660.

Sandler, I. N., West, S. G., Baca, L., & Pillow, D. R. (1992). Linking empirically based theory and evaluation: The Family Bereavement Program. *American Journal of Community Psychology, 20*(4), 491–521.

Seligman, M. E. P., Schulman, P., DeRubeis, R. J., & Hollon, S. D. (1999). The prevention of depression and anxiety. *Prevention and Treatment, 2,* Article 8. Retrieved December 17, 2001, from http://journals. apa.org/prevention/volume2/pre0020008a.html

Shafii, M., & Shafii, S. L. (1992). Clinical manifestations and developmental psychopathology of depression. In M. Shafii & S. L. Shafii (Eds.), *Clinical guide to depression in children and adolescents* (pp. 3–42). Washington, DC: American Psychiatric Press.

Spinelli, M. G. (1999). Prevention of postpartum mood disorders. In L. J. Miller (Ed.), *Postpartum mood disorders* (pp. 217–235). Washington, DC: American Psychiatric Press.

Stark, K. D., Reynolds, W. M., & Kaslow, N. J. (1987). A comparison of the relative efficacy of self-control therapy and a behavioral problem-solving therapy for depression in children. *Journal of Abnormal Child Psychology, 15*(1), 91–113.

Tableman, B. (1987). Stress management training: An approach to the prevention of depression in low-income populations. In R. F. Muñoz (Ed.), *Depression prevention: Research directions* (pp. 171–184). Washington, DC: Hemisphere.

Tableman, B. (1989). Stress management training for low income women. *Prevention in Human Services, 6*(2), 259–284.

Teasdale, J. D., Segal, Z. V., Williams, J. M. G., Ridgeway, V. A., Soulsby, J. M., & Lau, M. A. (2000). Prevention of relapse/recurrence in major depression by mindfulness-based cognitive therapy. *Journal of Consulting and Clinical Psychology, 68*(4), 615–623.

Teti, D., & Gelfand, D. M. (1991). Behavioral competence among mothers of infants in the first year: The mediational role of maternal self-efficacy. *Child Development, 62,* 918–929.

Tsiantis, J., Smith, M., Dragonas, T., & Cox, A. (2000). Early mental health promotion in children through primary health care services: A multi-centre implementation. *International Journal of Mental Health Promotion, 2*(3), 5–17.

Vega, W. A., Valle, R., Kolody, B., & Hough, R. (1987). The Hispanic Social Network Prevention Intervention Study: A community-based randomized trial. In R. F. Muñoz (Ed.), *Depression prevention: Research directions* (pp. 217–231). Washington, DC: Hemisphere.

Vinokur, A. D., Price, R. H., & Schul, Y. (1995). Impact of the JOBS intervention on unemployed workers varying in risk for depression. *American Journal of Community Psychology, 23*(1), 39–74.

Weissman, M. M., Fendrich, M., Warner, V., & Wickramaratne, P. (1992). Incidence of psychiatric disorder in offspring at high and low risk for depression. *Journal of the American Academy of Child and Adolescent Psychiatry, 31,* 640–648.

Weisz, J., Thurber, C., Sweeney, L., Proffitt, V., & LeGagnoux, G. (1997). Brief treatment of mild to moderate child depression using primary and secondary control enhancement training. *Journal of Consulting and Clinical Psychology, 65,* 703–707.

Wells, K. B., Stewart, A., Hays, R. D., Burnam, M. A., Rogers, W., Daniels, M., Berry, S., Greenfield, S., & Ware, J. (1989). The functioning and well-being of depressed patients: Results from the Medical Outcomes Study. *Journal of the American Medical Association, 262,* 914–919.

15

Pharmacological Treatment of Depression

Michael J. Gitlin

Antidepressants as a class have been available for over 40 years. Although insulin shock and then electroconvulsive therapy (ECT) had been used from the early 1940s onward, these were hardly mainstream therapies. In the late 1950s, studies following two serendipitous discoveries demonstrated the efficacy of imipramine, the first tricyclic antidepressant, and iproniazid, the first monoamine oxidase (MAO) inhibitor, as effective antidepressant medications. From that time until 1987 the pharmacotherapy of depression evolved slowly since all antidepressants released during this time were very similar to the two initial agents. In 1987, the first agent of the second generation of antidepressants, fluoxetine (Prozac), was released. Within a brief period of time, clinicians and patients alike realized that the new agents "felt" different from the older agents. Their side effect profiles differed, compliance rates were higher, and their efficacy in a wider spectrum of disorders was apparent.

Without question, the explosive growth of antidepressant prescriptions with the new generation of antidepressants has been among the dominant themes of psychological/psychiatric treatment over the last two decades. As one example, in 1999, three of the 12 most prescribed medications of any type in the United States were antidepressants (Drugtopics.com, 2000). This acceleration of prescriptions has, not surprisingly, induced a variety of responses, including both thoughtless acceptance ("Let's put Prozac in the drinking water") and equally biased vehement criticism, exemplified by the number of available books warning of the dire dangers of antidepressants. These polarized opinions have obscured both the knowledge gained and the knowledge gaps in antidepressant therapies. In this chapter, a middle-ground approach is presented. I review the phases of treatment for depression with antidepressants, the choices of available agents, the advantages and disadvantages of the antidepressant classes and agents, the choices for treating resistant patients, the use of antidepressants for special populations, and continuation and maintenance treatments. I conclude with a summary of some of the critical current clinical research questions in the area.

PHASES OF PHARMACOTHERAPY OF DEPRESSION

Antidepressants can be prescribed for any one of three goals or phases of treatment, described as acute, continuation, and maintenance treatment. The goal of *acute treatment* is to alleviate the symptoms of an active depression. The goal of *continuation treatment* is to prevent a relapse into the same episode for which treatment was begun. By definition, continuation treatment begins at the time of remission from the acute depressive episode. The reasons for the longer length of time—typically measured in months not weeks—needed for continuation treatment (as opposed to acute treatment) are unknown. This may reflect simply protecting a patient from relapse until spontaneous remission might have occurred without treatment. Another possibility is that, as with other disorders in medicine, clinical remission precedes biological remission. Longer time may be needed for the therapeutic effects of antidepressants on brain function (see Thase, Jindal, and Howland, Chapter 8, this volume) to become more permanent. *Maintenance therapy* is considered to begin when the goal is to prevent future recurrences of depressive episodes (or to prevent a recurrence of depressive symptoms following the successful treatment of a chronic depression). Given the recent data on the natural history of depression (see Chapter 2, this volume), consideration of maintenance treatment with antidepressants should be commonly discussed with patients.

These phases of treatment follow naturally from one to another. This chapter will focus intensively on acute treatment, following which both the data and current clinical practice on continuation and maintenance treatment will be presented.

ACUTE PHARMACOLOGICAL TREATMENT OF DEPRESSION

Currently Available Agents

Table 15.1 shows the 24 antidepressants available at the end of 2001, divided into pharmacological classes, with typical dose ranges. Table 15.2 lists the antidepressants by their side effect profiles. No classification scheme is either consistent or comprehensive, with each class being defined by different unifying characteristics. The tricyclic antidepressants share a similar chemical structure and a relatively similar side effect profile, but differ in their neurotransmitter effects. Selective serotonin reuptake inhibitors (SSRIs) vary widely in chemical structure but share similar neurotransmitter effects and side effect profiles. Similarly, MAO inhibitors share both biological effects and side effect profiles. The other agents, listed as novel agents, are each dissimilar from each other and from other classes. Conceptually, each novel agent should be listed as a separate class of antidepressants containing only one currently available medication.

The dissimilarity among antidepressant classes highlights the difficulty of establishing a universal mechanism of action of antidepressants (covered in greater detail by Boland and Keller, Chapter 2, this volume). All currently available antidepressants alter the function of either central nervous system serotonin or norepinephrine or both. Yet explaining antidepressant efficacy by their effects on these neurotransmitters is naïve and likely to be incorrect. As an example, tricyclics and SSRIs block the reuptake of norephinephrine and/or serotonin into the presynaptic neuron, thereby allowing more of the neurotransmitter to be available to the postsynaptic neuron. This effect is relatively immediate after a first antidepressant dose, yet patients do not improve for many weeks thereafter. The temporal dissociation of a biological effect from a clinical effect implies that another set of biological effects may be more relevant. Thus, a second set of hypotheses has examined the "downstream"

TABLE 15.1. Antidepressants

Name (trade name)	Typical starting dose	Usual dosage range (mg daily)
Selective serotonin reuptake inhibitors		
Citalopram (Celexa)	10–20	20–60
Fluoxetine (Prozac)	10–20	10–80
Fluvoxamine (Luvox)	25–50	100–300
Paroxetine (Paxil)	10–20	20–60
Sertraline (Zoloft)	25–50	50–200
Novel antidepressants		
Bupropion (Wellbutrin)	100–150	300–450
Mirtazapine (Remeron)	15–30	15–60
Nefazodone (Serzone)	50	400–600
Trazodone[a] (Desyrel)	50	150–400
Venlafaxine (Effexor)	37.5–75	150–300
Tricyclics and related compounds		
Amitriptyline (Elavil, Endep)	25–50	100–300
Amoxapine (Asendin)	50–100	150–400
Clomipramine (Anafranil)	25–50	100–250
Desipramine (Norpramin, Pertofrane)	25–50	100–300
Doxepin (Sinequan, Adapin)	25–50	100–300
Imipramine (Tofranil)	25–50	100–300
Maprotiline (Ludiomil)	25–50	100–225
Nortriptyline (Aventyl, Pamelor)	10–25	50–150
Protriptyline (Vivactil)	10	15–60
Trimipramine (Surmontil)	25–50	100–300
Monoamine oxidase inhibitors (MAOIs)		
Isocarboxazid (Marplan)	10–20	30–60
Phenelzine (Nardil)	15–30	30–90
Selegiline (Eldepryl)	10	20–60
Tranylcypromine (Parnate)	10–20	30–60

[a]Rarely used as antidepressant; prescribed more in low dose as hypnotic.

TABLE 15.2. Common Side Effects of Antidepressants

Name (trade name)	Sedation	Stimulation	Postural hypotension	Anticholinergic	Other side effects
Selective serotonin reuptake inhibitors					
Citalopram (Celexa)	+	+	0	0–(+)	Sexual
Fluoxetine (Prozac)	0–+	+++	0	0–(+)	Sexual
Fluvoxamine (Luvox)	+	+	0	0–(+)	Sexual
Paroxetine (Paxil)	+	+	0	+	Sexual, weight gain
Sertraline (Zoloft)	0–+	++	0	0–(+)	Sexual
Novel antidepressants					
Bupropion (Wellbutrin)	0	++	0	0	
Mirtazapine (Remeron)	+++	0	0	0	Weight gain
Nefazodone (Serzone)	+++	0	++	0	
Trazodone (Desyrel)	+++	0	+++	0	
Venlafaxine (Effexor)	+	+	0	0	Dose-related hypertension
Tricyclics and related compounds					
Amitriptyline (Elavil, Endep)	+++	0	+++	+++	
Amoxapine (Asendin)	+	0	++	+	
Clomipramine (Anafranil)	+++	0	+++	+++	
Desipramine (Norpramin, Pertofrane)	+	+	++	+	
Doxepin (Sinequan, Adapin)	+++	0	++	++	
Imipramine (Tofranil)	++	+	+++	++	
Maprotiline (Ludiomil)	++	+	+	+	
Nortriptyline (Aventyl, Pamelor)	++	0	+	+	
Protriptyline (Vivactil)	+	+	++	+++	
Trimipramine (Surmontil)	+++	0	++	+++	
Monoamine oxidase inhibitors					
Isocarboxazid (Marplan)	++	+	+++	+	Weight gain, insomnia, sexual
Phenelzine (Nardil)	++	+	+++	+	Weight gain, insomnia, sexual
Selegiline (Eldepryl)	+	+	++	+	
Tranylcypromine (Parnate)	+	+	+++	+	Insomnia, sexual

effects of antidepressants, that is, the effects beyond the cell surface receptor sites. Current areas of investigation are the intracellular second messenger systems and more specific effects on intracellular protein synthesis (Duman, Heninger, & Nestler, 1997). For now, it would be reasonable to conclude that antidepressants enhance the function of monoamines, which then sets in motion a series of intracellular changes that mediate the clinical response.

Selective Serotonin Reuptake Inhibitors

The antidepressants in this class dominate the treatment of depression in the United States. Their popularity reflects their relatively benign side effect profile, their ease of administration (once daily dosing for all agents at all doses), and the fact that their initial dose is close to the therapeutic dose, thereby making careful slow-dose titration unnecessary. Although all SSRIs strongly block the presynaptic reuptake of serotonin, which increases its availability to the postsynaptic neuron, thereby enhancing serotonergic function, the individual agents are not biologically identical, merely similar. As examples, citalopram (Celexa) is the most selective of the SSRIs, fluoxetine the least selective; sertraline (Zoloft) additionally blocks the reuptake of dopamine (albeit weakly). The clinical significance of these differences is unclear. Some experts hypothesize that these biological differences may explain the clinical observation that one individual patient may respond better to one SSRI than another, but no data bear on this question.

All SSRIs share a relatively similar side effect profile (see Table 15.2). The common side effects potentially seen with all SSRIs are nausea, activation (insomnia, nervousness), sedation, and sexual side effects (Gitlin & Suri, 1999). Nausea and activation effects are seen maximally in the beginning of treatment and diminish over the first few days to weeks of treatment. In contrast, tolerance does not typically develop to sedation and sexual side effects, making these more problematic side effects in the long term. In general, rates of nausea and sexual side effects are relatively similar across individual SSRI agents. Rates of sedation and activation, however, differ. Fluoxetine and sertraline are most commonly associated with activation effects, while paroxetine and fluvoxamine are more likely to cause sedation.

Another difference between the individual SSRI antidepressants is their capacity to alter the metabolism of other medications through the P450 system, the group of hepatic (liver) enzymes that metabolize foods, toxins, and medications (Nemeroff, DeVane, & Pollock, 1996). Because the P450 system is composed of many different enzymes, each of which metabolize different medications, and each SSRI has a different profile of P450 effects, simple generalizations are impossible. With healthy patients on no other medications (thereby precluding drug–drug interactions), these effects are irrelevant. For medically complicated depressed persons who may be on many other medications, the possibility of interactions may be important. Although interindividual variability is large, fluoxetine, paroxetine, and fluvoxamine have greater potential for P450 interactions than do citalopram and sertraline.

Bupropion (Wellbutrin) and Bupropion SR

Released in 1989, bupropion is a novel agent with effects on norepinephrine and dopamine and no serotonergic effects (Ascher et al., 1995). Its side effect profile follows from its known biological effects. It is a stimulating antidepressant whose most common side effects are insomnia, anxiety, tremor, and headache. It is never sedating, is associated with very few sexual side effects, and causes no weight gain. Safety concerns and the need for multiple doses within a day are the major drawbacks for bupropion. The major safety concern is bupropion's propensity to cause seizures at a slightly higher rate than the other new antidepressants (0.4% at high dose vs. 0.2% for the SSRIs) (Davidson, 1989). Unfortunately, the obligatory warnings in the *Physician's Desk Reference* (PDR) (2001) and in the package insert sound rather alarming and have frightened some clinicians and patients alike. Because of the concern that peak blood levels may increase seizure risk, bupropion is recommended to be prescribed in a divided dose regimen, up to three times daily with a full dose of 450 mg, making compliance more problematic. Bupropion is contraindicated in patients with seizure disorders or active eating disorders such as bulimia nervosa or anorexia nervosa (which lower the seizure threshold via electrolyte abnormalities). In 1996, bupropion SR (sustained release), which allows for twice daily dosing (up to 200 mg twice daily) was released. The risk of seizure with bupropion SR is comparable to the SSRIs up to 300 mg daily but is unknown at higher doses, thereby alleviating only some of the problems associated with bupropion IR (immediate release).

Venlafaxine (Effexor) and Venlafaxine XR

First released in 1994, venlafaxine is another novel agent, different from all others in its biological activities. At low–moderate dose (up to 125 mg or so), venlafaxine is an SSRI with strong, selective effects on serotonin. As the dose is increased beyond that level, reuptake blockade of norepinephrine begins, giving venlafaxine a dual effect (Harvey, Rudolph, & Preskorn, 2000). Some studies indicate that, especially at higher doses, venlafaxine may show greater efficacy than the SSRIs, especially for more severely depressed individuals. The side effect profile of venlafaxine is almost identical to that of the SSRIs. As venlafaxine doses increase, a dose-related hypertension may emerge, affecting up to 9% of treated patients at high dose (Thase, 1998). Therefore, at daily doses of 150 mg or above, blood pressure monitoring is required. Because venlafaxine was associated with high rates of nausea, and because it was usually given twice daily due to its short half-life, in 1997 venlafaxine XR (extended release) was released and has since become the more commonly prescribed brand of venlafaxine. It is administered once daily and is associated with far less nausea than the immediate release brand.

Nefazodone (Serzone)

Nefazodone has a unique biological profile in that it only weakly blocks the reuptake of serotonin, has weak noradrenergic activity, and strongly blocks the serotonin–2 receptor (Taylor et al., 1995). It is unclear how this translates into antidepressant activity. Nefazodone can be highly sedating, thereby making its use preferable in anxious, agitated, insomniac patients. Other side effects less commonly seen with its use are nausea, dizziness, and dry mouth. Nefazodone strongly inhibits one of the P450 enzymes, requiring some care when used in combination with other medications. Studies over the last few years have demonstrated that nefazodone's full antidepressant efficacy is seen at higher doses (400–600 mg) than originally thought. Many patients have difficulty achieving these doses because of the sedation. Advantages of nefazodone are the lack of sexual side effects and lack of weight gain associated with its use.

Mirtazapine (Remeron)

Least frequently prescribed among the new generation of antidepressants, mirtazapine's presumed mechanism of antidepressant activity is complex, with presynaptic noradrenergic blocking (thereby enhancing noradrenergic function) and secondary enhancement of sero-tonergic activity (Gorman, 1999). It has a relatively simple dosing structure with once daily nighttime administration of 15–60 mg. The major problems associated with mirtazapine's use are its common side effects of sedation and weight gain. These same effects may, in con-trast, be helpful to depressed patients with anorexia, agitation, and insomnia.

Tricyclics

As the oldest class of antidepressants, the tricyclics, so designated because of their three ringed structure, are still prescribed for depression but rarely as first-line agents. (Tricylic agents are, however, still prescribed first line for the treatment of chronic pain, since they are more effective than the newer antidepressants for this indication.) These changes in pre-scribing practices reflect the relative side effect profiles of the tricyclics versus the newer agents, not their efficacy. No newer antidepressant has shown greater efficacy than the tri-cylics, which are still frequently used as the reference drugs in evaluating new agents. Ad-vantages of the tricyclics include their long track record of efficacy; once daily dosing for all agents; relative inexpensive cost because they are available in generic preparations; and the ability to measure their concentration in blood which, for some agents, correlates with effi-cacy and potential toxicity (Perry, Zeilmann, & Arndt, 1994). (In contrast, levels of SSRI antidepressants are available but do not correlate with either efficacy or side effects.) The disadvantages of tricyclics include the need to gradually increase the dose to full effect, a process that may take weeks; a substantial side effect profile, including dry mouth, blurry vision, constipation, urinary hesitation, dizziness upon standing up, sedation, weight gain, and others; greater likelihood of exacerbating a number of coexisting medical disorders; and high lethality in overdose. Tricyclic antidepressants are especially difficult and poten-tially dangerous medications in the presence of cardiac disease since agents of this antide-pressant class alter cardiac conduction and may either cause or exacerbate cardiac ar-rhthymias (Roose & Spatz, 1999).

Despite sharing many basic similarities, individual tricyclic agents differ in both biolog-ical effects and side effects. Biologically, some tricyclics such as desipramine are relatively selective in their effects on norepinephrine, while others are more mixed in their effects. Clomipramine (Anafranil) differs from all other tricyclics in its powerful serotonergic prop-erties, akin to the SSRIs, which allows it to be used as a first-line agent to treat obsessive–compulsive disorder. In side effects profiles, desipramine, nortriptyline, and imipramine are much less sedating than are amitriptyline, clomipramine, and doxepin.

Monoamine Oxidase Inhibitors

In general, MAO inhibitors have been relegated to third- or fourth-line antidepressants, de-spite their unique utility for a subset of depressed patients. Their disfavor among clinicians and patients is due partly to their side effect profile but more because their use requires strict dietary restrictions without which severe, potentially life-threatening hypertensive re-actions may occur. Because of these dangers, only responsible compliant patients should take MAO inhibitors. Although early studies seemed to indicate that MAO inhibitors were not as effective as the tricyclics for severe, classic depression, this observation was due to the low, inadequate doses used in these studies. In later studies, using higher doses, the MAO inhibitors proved to be equivalently effective to other antidepressant classes. (Davis, Wang, & Janicak, 1993).

The dietary restrictions are predicated on the need to avoid certain amines in foods, es-pecially tyramine, which can raise blood pressure to dangerous levels in the presence of an

MAO inhibitor. The mechanism by which MAO inhibitors cause hypertension in association with certain foods has been well elucidated. In the absence of MAO inhibitors, ingested tyramine is metabolized by the enzyme MAO, which exists in both the lining of the intestinal tract and in the liver. Additionally, tyramine releases norepinephrine intracellularly. The amount of norepinephrine available is decreased in the presence of an MAO inhibitor. Both of the mechanisms independently contribute to the food-related hypertension. By far, aged cheeses are the most dangerous foods for patients taking MAO inhibitors and should be strictly forbidden. Any competent psychopharmacologist will have a written list of proscribed foods to be given to any patient taking an MAO inhibitor (Gardner, Shulman, Walker, & Tailor, 1996).

By somewhat different mechanisms, certain medications are also contraindicated for use with an MAO inhibitor. Most important among these are over-the-counter cold preparations containing pseudoephedrine, certain opiates such as meperidine (Demerol), and all strongly serotonergic antidepressants, such as the SSRIs and venlafaxine. The combination of a strongly serotonergic agent with an MAO inhibitor will provoke a serotonin syndrome, a potentially fatal syndrome characterized by fever, muscle rigidity, low blood pressure, and mental status changes.

MAO inhibitors are also characterized by nondangerous but problematic side effects that further limit their acceptance by patients and which severely decrease compliance with their use. These include postural dizziness, weight gain (especially with phenelzine), insomnia, daytime fatigue, and sexual dysfunction.

Rational Selection of an Antidepressant

Table 15.3 shows the factors used by skillful clinicians to choose a specific antidepressant. As can be seen, issues relating to compliance, side effect profile, and ease of administration (i.e., once daily dosing vs. multiple doses required), dominate the decision. Thus, non-SSRIs such as bupropion, nefazodone, or mirtazapine would be reasonable first-line agents for patients for whom sexual side effects would be psychologically most distressing. Experienced clinicians use the differences among antidepressants of sedation/activation to benefit patients by typically prescribing activating agents to lethargic, psychomotor-retarded, depressed patients and sedating agents to more anxious, agitated, insomnic individuals. Safety/medical considerations are especially relevant in the gradual shift away from the tricyclics and MAO inhibitors toward the newer antidepressants, which are generally medically safer. Among the newer agents, the only safety considerations are the relative P450 effects (described in the SSRI section above) and the seizure concerns with bupropion for those with preexisting seizure disorders and eating disorder patients. Depressive subtypes are those that may predict response to one class of antidepressant more than another, such as atypical depression (see below).

Among the secondary factors that determine choice of medications, no consistent data

TABLE 15.3. Considerations in Choosing a Specific Antidepressant

Primary	Secondary
• Side effect profile	• Neurotransmitter specificity
• Ease of administration	• Family history of response
• History of past response	• Blood level considerations
• Safety/medical issues	• Cost
• Depressive subtype (e.g., atypical depression)	

have shown that depressions can be subtyped by neurotransmitter effects—that is, clinicians cannot categorize a patient as having a serotonergic versus a noradrenergic depression. Although family history of response is a commonsense approach to choosing a specific antidepressant, data supporting this approach are remarkably sparse (Duffy, Grof, Robertson, & Alda, 2000). Blood levels, as noted above, are useful only in monitoring some of the tricyclic agents. Cost continues to be a factor for those patients without medical insurance that reimburses for medications. All newer agents are relatively expensive compared to generic tricylics.

Although in double-blind studies of unselected patients with major depression, no single antidepressant is more or less effective than the others, the following depressive subtypes may predict differential responses and/or require different approaches:

- Depression with psychotic features.
- Depression with atypical features.
- Seasonal (winter) depression.
- Severe/melancholic depression.

Psychotic depression (DSM-IV-TR major depression with psychotic features) has been shown in a number of studies to respond less well to antidepressants than to an antidepressant plus an antipsychotic or to ECT. Some recent studies have indicated that SSRIs may be beneficial for psychotic depressions (Wheeler Vega, Mortimer, & Tyson, 2000). Current recommendations allow for single agent treatment or antidepressant plus antipsychotic for milder psychotic depression; combination treatment or ECT should be used first line in the more severe cases.

Atypical depression (DSM-IV-TR depression with atypical features) responds preferentially to MAO inhibitors versus tricyclics, although both are significantly more effective than placebo (Liebowitz et al., 1988). Although some studies using either post hoc analyses or small sample sizes also found SSRIs to be effective, a recent controlled study found fluoxetine to be equivalently effective to imipramine for atypical depression with response rates lower than those found in other studies with MAO inhibitors (McGrath et al., 2000). However, given the differential side effect profiles, SSRIs are typically prescribed first for those with atypical depression. Additionally, many clinicians have observed (without consistent supporting data) that depressed patients with marked irritability and/or rejection sensitivity but without meeting full criteria for atypical depression respond very well to SSRIs.

Seasonal (winter) depression, which typically emerges between October and December, and spontaneously remits in the late winter or early spring, responds to light therapy as well as to antidepressants. Lights used to treat winter depression are full frequency, similar to indoor grow lights or to sunlight. With high intensity (6,000–10,000 lux) light boxes used for 30 minutes daily, usually in the morning, remission rates within 2–4 weeks are seen in 50–60% of patients (Eastman, Young, Fogg, Liu, & Meaden, 1998). Side effects seen with light therapy are typically mild and include headaches and eye or vision problems (Kogan & Guilford, 1998).

Whether more severe depressed patients respond better to non-SSRIs than to SSRIs is a source of some controversy. In a diverse group of studies, markers for severity have included hospitalization, melancholic subtype, or higher Hamilton depression scores (usually 25 or higher). A number of individual studies have found greater efficacy for tricyclics, venlafaxine, and mirtazapine in severely depressed patients (Thase, 2000). Many other studies have found no difference (Hirschfeld, 1999).

In an attempt to systematize treatment of depression, treatment algorithms have recently been developed using a consensus approach of clinical experts in the area (Crismon et al., 1999). The effect of these algorithms on clinical practice has yet to be established. These algorithms systematize the factors noted in choosing an agent (discussed above) and the options for treatment-resistant depression (described below). They are generally useful for less sophisticated clinicians since experts in the area integrate the subtle factors unique to each individual patient in deciding a specific treatment course.

General Principles of Pharmacotherapy of Depression

Response rates to a single antidepressant are generally considered to be 60–70%, compared to a placebo response rate of 30% (Klein, Gittelman-Klein, Quitkin, & Rifkin, 1980). These figures are somewhat inflated compared to what might be seen in clinical practice since they exclude those who fail to complete the trial (typically estimated as 10–15% even with the newer agents). In research studies, response is usually defined as a 50% or more decrease in the Hamilton Rating Scale for Depression (HRSD) and a Clinical Global Improvement score of 1 or 2 (which equate to "very much improved" or "much improved"); in some studies, an additional requirement for response is a lowering of the HRSD score to less than a predetermined score, typically 10. However, 65% is the response rate, not the remission rate. Many antidepressant responders are substantially better but still show many residual depressive signs and symptoms. In one recent study, even among those classified as complete responders (with HRSD scores less than 7), residual symptomatology was common (Nierenberg et al., 1999).

Full responses to antidepressants generally require 4–6 weeks, although additional benefit may accrue over 8–12 weeks (Gelenberg & Chesen, 2000). Partial responses are seen much earlier in treatment, often within the first week. Sometimes, early responses reflect therapeutic side effects, with improvement in anxiety and insomnia in association with a sedating antidepressant, or, conversely, improvement in energy due to a stimulating agent. These effects are generally considered to be distinct from a true antidepressant effect. At other times, a genuine partial improvement occurs within the first week. Rarely do patients show no response for 5 weeks and a sudden and complete response in the sixth week. Consistent with this, a partial response at 2–4 weeks of treatment is a relatively robust predictor of a full antidepressant effect at 6 weeks (Nierenberg et al., 2000).

Treatment-Resistant Depression

With antidepressant response rates of 65% at best, and with many of those called responders still suffering from residual symptoms, approaches to the 35–40% nonresponders and those with partial responses have been described in many books, book chapters, data-based studies, and review articles (Fava, 2000a). Unfortunately, the field still lacks a data-based approach to antidepressant treatment failures since the vast majority of studies in this area typically describe a pharmacotherapeutic approach compared to a placebo condition. Studies evaluating comparative approaches to treatment-resistant depression are rare, and no consensus approach exists.

For the purposes of this discussion, it will be assumed that, in cases of treatment failure, a diagnostic review has been undertaken (Keller, 1990). Most important among these would be to confirm that the patient actually has an Axis I depressive disorder, not dysphoric mood based solely on a personality disorder or another psychiatric disorder associated with depressive mood. Comorbid medical and psychiatric disorders (including comorbid drug/alcohol abuse) may also predict a negative antidepressant response and should be vigorously treated when present. The presence of severe psychosocial factors has been reported to be associated with a poorer antidepressant response. Finally, noncompliance should always be considered with antidepressant treatment failure.

Pharmacological options for treatment resistance have been conceptually divided into optimization, switching, augmentation, or combination (Price, 1990). *Optimization* refers to continuing to prescribe the original antidepressant but at higher dose or for a longer trial (such as for 10–12 weeks). On the basis of research studies, no specific doses define an adequate trial for any of the newer antidepressants. Typical maximal doses are listed in Table 15.1, but a small number of patients may require higher daily doses. *Switching* to another antidepressant is a self-evident option. *Augmentation* is defined as adding a second agent which is itself not an antidepressant but which might augment the effect of the original medication. In *combination* treatment, a second agent, which itself is an antidepressant, is added.

The relative merits of switching within an antidepressant class versus across classes is still unknown. Practically, the usual clinical question is whether to switch to a second SSRI if a depressed patient has failed an adequate trial of the first SSRI versus switching to an agent from a different class, such as bupropion, venlafaxine or others. (*Failure to respond* must be distinguished from *inability to tolerate* the first agent, in which case most clinicians would continue to pursue other agents within the same class.) Noncontrolled studies suggest response rates of approximately 50% for treatment with a second SSRI after failure with a first SSRI (Fava, 2000b). However, all studies examining this question are flawed, and none compare switching within the SSRI class to switching to an antidepressant from another class. Some experienced clinicians prescribe a second SSRI before switching to a different class, while others switch antidepressant classes after only one failed SSRI trial. Only rarely will a clinician prescribe a third SSRI if a patient has failed two prior agents.

Once a full trial (i.e., an adequate dose for an adequate period of time) has been achieved, the clinical question is whether to switch to another antidepressant or to add another agent, whether an adjunctive agent or another antidepressant. Although there has been a tradition of switching antidepressants in the case of nonresponse and adding a second agent when a patient is a partial responder, there are no data that bear on this issue. Therefore, actual prescribing practices are dictated by local customs and individual practitioner experiences and treatment philosophies.

Options for adding a second agent are listed in Table 15.4. Lithium is the most well-studied agent with nine double-blind studies published, with seven showing efficacy compared to placebo (Bauer & Dopfmer, 1999). Response typically occurs within 2 weeks and at doses that tend to be lower than those used in treating bipolar disorder. Despite the strength of the research evidence, many clinicians feel negatively toward adjunctive lithium both because of a poorer observed response than is seen in published studies and because of the lack of patient acceptance due to side effects and the need for blood tests with lithium use.

TABLE 15.4. Adjunctive/Combination Strategies for Treatment-Resistant Depression

First line	Second line	Other
Lithium	Buspirone	Electroconvulsive therapy (ECT)
T$_3$	Pindolol	
Combination of two antidepressants[a]	Atypical neuroleptic	
Stimulant	Anticonvulsants	

[a]Except for a strongly serotonergic antidepressant plus MAO inhibitor.

T$_3$ (triiodothyronine, marketed as Cytomel), a thyroid hormone, has been tested in five double-blind studies as an adjunctive antidepressant treatment, with positive response seen in some but not all studies (Aronson, Offman, Joffe, & Naylor, 1996). Its mechanism of action is not well understood but it is unlikely that it is simply supplementing thyroid hormone to patients who are hypothyroid (low thyroid) since pretreatment thyroid function does not predict T$_3$ response. Consistent with this, T$_3$ may be more effective than T$_4$, the other active thyroid hormone (Joffe & Singer, 1990). Prescribing T$_3$ as an adjunctive agent is simple, with doses relatively low compared to when it is prescribed for overt thyroid disease. T$_3$ is associated with few side effects. Despite its simplicity, clinicians tend to use other adjunctive approaches before T$_3$ because of a general clinical sense that it is not effective often enough.

Adjunctive stimulants such as methylphenidate (Ritalin), *d*-amphetamine (Dexedrine), and, more recently, modafinil (Provigil), are popular choices as adjunctive agents. Unfortunately, clinical studies with adjunctive stimulants are rare and no double-blind study has examined the issue (Masand, Anand, & Tanquary, 1998). Nonetheless, stimulants are often prescribed as the first adjunctive treatment. When stimulants work as adjunctive agents, they do so within a few days at most, which adds to their popularity.

Combining two antidepressants is the last of the first-line treatments for refractory depression. Almost always, the second agent prescribed is from a different class than is the first antidepressant. Thus, combining fluoxetine and paroxetine makes little sense; combining an SSRI with bupropion or mirtazapine is more common and is theoretically more reasonable. Open case series and case reports attest to the popularity of combination treatment. However, only one random assignment controlled treatment trial has demonstrated greater efficacy of combination treatment (desipramine plus fluoxetine) compared to either drug given alone (Nelson, 2000).

Second-line treatments for treatment refractory depression are also listed in Table 15.4. Buspirone (Buspar) is an antianxiety agent that enhances serotonin. As with other approaches, open studies tend to be positive, while the one double-blind study showed no difference in response rates when buspirone or placebo were added to the regimen of depressed patients who had failed to respond to an SSRI (Landén, Björling, Agren, & Fahlén, 1998). Pindolol (Visken) is a beta blocker which, in contrast to other medications of the class, also increases serotonergic function. It has shown inconsistent positive results in augmenting antidepressants (Fava, 2000a). The less common approaches, such as atypical antipsychotics (such as risperidone [Risperdal] or olanzapine [Zyprexa]) and anticonvulsants, have been studied only in small case series.

Studies comparing any of these approaches are few. In one study, lithium and T$_3$ were both significantly more effective as augmenting agents of a tricyclic compared to placebo and equivalently effective to each other (Joffe, Singer, Levitt, & MacDonald, 1993). In a more recent study, nonresponders or partial responders to fluoxetine 20 mg were randomly assigned in a double-blind fashion to increased fluoxetine dose (optimization), adjunctive desipramine, or adjunctive lithium (Fava, Alpert, Nierenberg, Worthington, & Rosenbaum, 2000). Response rates for the three groups ranged between 27 and 38% with no significant differences between the approaches. Partial responders were more likely to respond than were nonresponders.

In the area of augmentation/combination approaches to treatment-resistant depression, actual clinical practices do not necessarily follow the research literature. Whereas lithium and T$_3$ are the best documented treatments, surveys indicate that the most commonly used approaches among expert clinicians are combinations (especially SSRIs and bupropion) and adjunctive stimulants (Fava, Mischoulon, & Rosenbaum, 1998).

Electroconvulsive Therapy

Although it is not, of course, a pharmacotherapy but rather a somatic treatment, ECT is the most important approach for treatment-resistant depression. Although it still retains a reputation in many parts of the country as a barbaric and dangerous treatment, the modern use of ECT is remarkably safe and effective. ECT is rarely used as a first-line treatment for depression. Typically, it is recommended for patients who have failed multiple antidepressant therapies, especially if the depression is severe, associated with significant suicidal ideation and/or functional impairment. ECT may be the treatment of choice for depression with psychotic features (Wheeler Vega, et al., 2000).

The major side effects of ECT are cognitive (American Psychiatric Association, 1990). Patients can expect to have post-ECT confusion, especially after the later treatments. Anterograde and retrograde memory deficits are common and are maximal for the time close to the ECT. Memory improves over many weeks, typically, but not always to normal levels (with the exception of the time around the ECT itself), although the evaluation of memory in ECT patients is confounded by the cognitive disturbances associated with the depression. A few patients complain of long-term cognitive disturbances.

ECT is given as a series of treatments, usually 2–3 times weekly, for a total of six to 12 treatments (American Psychiatric Association, 1990). It may be given to inpatients or outpatients. Safety is ensured by the use of short-acting anesthesia, a muscle relaxant (to prevent the broken bones of the past) and, in the better settings, EEG monitoring. Technical considerations primarily include whether to use bilateral or unilateral placement (i.e., passing the electrical current through both hemispheres of the brain vs. the nondominant hemisphere only) and the dose of electricity used. Bilateral placement and higher voltage are both associated with greater cognitive side effects but may be more effective for some patients. Recent data have suggested that high-voltage, unilateral ECT may be the best compromise to achieve efficacy with fewer cognitive side effects (Sackeim et al., 2000).

TREATING SPECIAL POPULATIONS

Three populations of depressed patients warrant separate discussions because of the unique considerations associated with their treatment. They are patients with bipolar depression, with dysthymic disorder and chronic major depression, and with depression during pregnancy and the postpartum period.

Bipolar Depression

Bipolar depression is the depression associated with patients who have had one or more manias or hypomanias. Compared to major depression, for which there are hundreds of double-blind treatment studies, bipolar depression has, until recently, been relatively ignored as a topic of clinical research. This presumably reflects the concerns about inducing manic or hypomanic episodes by the antidepressant and the difficulty in managing these episodes within a clinical research study.

Conceptually, in contrast to treating major depression, deciding how best to treat bipolar depression requires considerations of safety as well as efficacy—that is, will the antidepressant provoke mania/hypomania or induce rapid cycling between depression and mania (a notoriously treatment-resistant phase of bipolar disorder)? All antidepressant treatments (including ECT) have the capacity to provoke manic switches in some individuals. (Although some patients with unipolar/major depression will become manic *de novo* with antidepressants, the risk is relatively small. These individuals are usually presumed to have latent bipolar disorder that simply did not express itself until provoked by the antidepressant.) Studies published in the pre-SSRI era demonstrated the capacity of the tricyclic antidepressants to cause mania and/or induce rapid cycling relatively commonly, leading to a notion of avoiding antidepressants in bipolar patients whenever possible. A difficulty in quantifying this risk is the natural course of bipolar disorder in which many patients will become manic after a depression regardless of whether antidepressants are prescribed. Despite this caveat, one retrospective review estimated that antidepressants provoked manias in 35% of treatment-resistant patients and a more rapid cycling pattern in 26% (Altshuler et al., 1995). Because of these concerns, many bipolar depressed patients are initially treated with manipulations of mood stabilizers such as lithium, valproate (Depakote), or lamotrigine (Lamictal) since these medications presumably do not cause pharmacological manias/hypomanias (Calabrese et al., 1999).

But recent studies using the newer antidepressants—SSRIs and the novel agents—seem to indicate a relatively larger measure of safety compared to the tricyclics, although this conclusion must be considered tentative because of the paucity of controlled studies. Among the few studies in the area, bupropion was associated with fewer switches into mania compared to desipramine (Sachs et al., 1994). In a naturalistic study, SSRIs were associated with fewer emergent manic states compared to tricyclics (Peet, 1994). In an earlier study, switch rates with tricyclic and MAO inhibitor antidepressants were similar, but the tricyclics were associated with more severe and sudden switches (Himmelhoch, Thase, Mallinger, & Houck, 1991). No study has shown a difference in pharmacological switch rates between any of the newer antidepressants. Recent data have also suggested that bipolar II patients (those with milder manias, hypomanias) can be treated with serotonergic antidepressants with seemingly low rates of pharmacological switches (Amsterdam, 1998; Amsterdam et al., 1999).

Despite the difference in switch rates across antidepressant classes, most studies seem to indicate similar rates of antidepressant efficacy. The exception was a study in which tranylcypromine, an MAO inhibitor, was more effective than imipramine, a tricyclic, in treating bipolar depressives with prominent anergic features, such as psychomotor retardation and lethargy (Himmelhoch et al., 1991).

Dysthymic Disorder and Chronic Depressions

Increasingly, dysthymic disorder is being viewed as simply a mild chronic depression, and not a distinct and separate disorder from major depression (except, of course, in DSM-IV-TR). Therefore, dysthymic disorder should be treated in a manner indistinguishable from that of major depression. Consistent with this notion, many, but not all, of the relatively few pharmacotherapy studies in this area have combined chronic major depression, dysthymic disorder, and double depression in their inclusion criteria. Response rates to antidepressants of chronic major depression versus double depression versus dysthymia are comparable (DeLima, Hotoph, & Wessely, 1999). A diverse range of antidepressants has been found to be superior to placebo in the treatment of chronic depression, with no single agent more consistently effective than any other, similar to classic major depression. As expected from the acute depression studies, two large studies comparing an SSRI to a tricyclic have found similar efficacy but difference in tolerability, with tricyclic-treated patients showing higher dropout rates (Keller et al., 1998; Thase et al., 1996). A recent study demonstrated a robust effect of nefazodone in treating chronic depression (Keller et al., 2000). These studies also suggest that antidepressant response rates with chronic depression are generally similar to those seen in acute depression studies, although direct comparison studies are limited.

Other than establishing a cohort of studies examining the efficacy of antidepressants for chronic depressive disorders, the importance of this growing literature is to demonstrate that patients who have been depressed for decades (in one study, the average duration of dysthymia was 30 years; Thase et al., 1996) are still capable of robust antidepressant responses. Therefore, chronicity should never preclude a thorough set of antidepressant trials.

Depression during Pregnancy or the Postpartum Period

Since the mean age of onset of depression and the age at which women are most likely to become pregnant coincide, the problem of how to manage depression and antidepressants in preparation for, during, and following pregnancy is a critical issue in psychopharmacology. A full discussion of these issues is beyond the scope of this chapter; interested readers are referred elsewhere for more in-depth discussions (Altshuler et al., 1996; Wisner, Gelenberg, Leonard, Zarin, & Frank, 1999).

The central concern in considering the use of antidepressants during pregnancy are their potential effects on fetal and then infant development. The three main areas of potential concern are physical teratogenicity, neonatal toxicity, and behavioral teratogenicity. These terms refer respectively to physical malformations present at birth, reversible abnormalities present at birth that are due to the active presence of the medication and are typically reversible, and longer term abnormalities such as cognitive effects, activity levels, and propensity for development of psychiatric disorders later in life. All conclusions in this area must be tempered by two methodological considerations: (1) the lack of controlled studies in this area, which are ethically impossible; (2) maternal anxiety, distress, and depression during pregnancy itself may affect some aspects of neonatal development (Wisner et al., 1999).

Tricyclic antidepressants show no association with fetal malformations (Altshuler et al., 1996). For the SSRIs, the most data are available for fluoxetine, the oldest of the SSRIs, and citalopram, which has been available in Europe for many years. Overall, neither fluoxetine nor citalopram seem to be associated with major fetal malformations (Ericson, Källén, & Wiholm, 1999; Wisner et al., 1999). Preliminary data for the other SSRIs are similarly reassuring. One study (Chambers, Johnson, Dick, Felix, & Jones, 1996), but not others, found a higher rate of minor physical anomalies associated with fluoxetine exposure *in utero*. Insufficient data are available about the potential teratogenicity of the other new antidepressants. MAO inhibitors are generally avoided during pregnancy because of blood pressure concerns and the results of animal studies (Altshuler et al., 1996).

Neonatal side effects have been inconsistently described after exposure to SSRIs and tricyclic antidepressants (Wisner et al., 1999; Chambers et al., 1996). When present, neonatal side effects from antidepressants are similar to those seen with adult patients and do not appear to pose long-term health risks.

Data on behavioral teratogenicity are exceedingly sparse since studies in this area require long-term follow-up. Thus far, no evidence of cognitive, temperamental, or behavioral developmental abnormalities have been demonstrated in children exposed *in utero* to tricyclic antidepressants or SSRIs (Nulman et al., 1997). Data on development into adolescence and young adulthood do not exist.

Overall, these preliminary data suggest the safety of the tricyclic antidepressants and the SSRIs in treating depression in pregnant women. The decision on how best to manage the depression for any individual woman is, of course, best made through discussion between the prescribing physician, the pregnant woman (preferably seen in anticipation of pregnancy), the father (if present), and the therapist. In these discussions, the potential and, in many cases, the unknown risk of treating must be balanced against the risk of not treating with the potential for depression during pregnancy. Possible decisions include withdrawing the antidepressant before conception, discontinuing the antidepressant when pregnancy is confirmed, avoiding medication during the first trimester, or continuing the medication throughout the pregnancy. The severity of the depression, its recurrent nature, whether the woman has previously been able to withdraw from antidepressants without depressive relapse for some time, and the availability and efficacy of psychotherapeutic intervention are all important factors to weigh in the decision.

Whether to breast-feed is another issue for depressed women on antidepressants (Wisner, Perel, & Findling, 1996; Austin & Mitchell, 1998). The context of this decision is the high risk of postpartum depression in women with a prior history of depression (O'Hara, 1995). Although definitive studies are lacking, preliminary evidence suggests that prophylactic antidepressants may prevent the development of postpartum depression (Wisner & Wheeler, 1994).

In contrast to the ingestion of medications during pregnancy, infant and maternal exposure to antidepressants can, of course, be separated after birth. All psychotropic medications are secreted in breast milk in variable amounts. Plasma levels of the antidepressant of the infant are usually extremely low or undetectable by current assay techniques, indicating little risk for harm. However, a few case reports suggest that an occasional breast-feeding neonate either accumulates relatively higher amounts of medications or is unusually susceptible to side effects and may show negative effects. Effects of long-term exposure to antidepressants from breast-feeding are unknown.

CONTINUATION TREATMENT

The goal of continuation treatment is, as noted above, to prevent a relapse soon after improvement from the acute depressive episode. Clinically, continuation treatment begins when patient and clinician agree that the former is conclusively better and further changes in medications to control symptoms are not needed. Continuation treatment with antidepressants using the acute treatment dose is associated with reduced relapse rates compared to switching to placebo (Prien & Kupfer, 1986). Only two studies have specifically examined the optimal length of continuation period. In one study, in which patients were treated with a tricyclic antidepressant, a continuation period of 16–20 weeks (4–5 months), during which time patients were euthymic, was associated with a low relapse rate if the antidepressant was withdrawn thereafter (Prien & Kupfer, 1986). In the more recent study, 6 months of continuation therapy (following 12 weeks of acute therapy, somewhat longer than is typical) resulted in significantly fewer relapses compared to those switched to placebo (Reimherr et al., 1998). A longer time of continuation therapy was not more effective than placebo in preventing relapse. Therefore, the usual recommendations for 4–9 months of continuation treatment fit the available data.

If long-term maintenance treatment is clinically unnecessary (see next section), and the antidepressant is to be discontinued, common sense dictates that it be tapered rather than stopped suddenly. Should depressive symptoms return during tapering, they are typically milder and treatment can be more easily reinstated compared to a full sudden recurrence, which is more likely to occur if the antidepressant is precipitously stopped. Additionally, discontinuation/withdrawal symptoms may be seen with a variety of antidepressants and will also be avoided with medication tapering. The only reasonable exception to these recommendations would be fluoxetine, which, because of its long half-life, is essentially self-tapering. The optimal time period for medication tapering after continuation therapy is unstudied, but a reasonable time period is 4–8 weeks.

MAINTENANCE TREATMENT

Since, in the majority of patients, depression is either a recurrent or a chronic disorder (see Boland & Keller, Chapter 2, this volume), long-term preventive treatment should be commonly considered. Factors to be used in deciding which depressed individuals are appropriate candidates for maintenance therapy are based more on common sense than on hard data. They include the number of depressive episodes over a lifetime, the frequency of depressive episodes, the severity of the depressions (including both symptom severity and functional consequences), the responsiveness of episodes to prior treatments, the speed with which episodes have emerged, and insight into emerging depressive symptoms (Gitlin, 1996). Some agencies have provided reports with more concrete guidelines for maintenance treatment—for example, two episodes plus either a first-degree relative with a major mood disorder or age of onset before 20, and so forth. These recommendations seem simply to substitute rigid rules for good judgment. Knowing the natural course of depression and engaging the patient in a thoughtful discussion is likely to be a superior strategy.

Many patients are concerned about potential long-term side effects of antidepressants on bodily organs such as liver, kidney, and especially brain. Although definitive studies do not exist, there is no evidence whatsoever that antidepressants as a class (available for over 40 years) or SSRIs in particular (available for almost 15 years), are associated with any long-term negative effects on organ function or physiology. It is also important to remind patients that untreated depression may have long-term medical consequences. As with the decision about antidepressants and pregnancy, the potential risks of treating must always be balanced against the risks of not treating.

Because of the length of time needed for proper study of maintenance treatment, no truly long-term studies have examined the efficacy of antidepressants in preventing depressive recurrences. The best maintenance treatment study examined the effects of imipramine, interpersonal psychotherapy (IPT), and their combination as maintenance treatments over a 3-year period in patients who had had at least two prior depressive episodes with the most recent episode no more than 2.5 years earlier, and who had been successfully treated with imipramine and IPT in acute and continuation therapy during the current episode (Frank et al., 1990). Imipramine was highly effective in preventing depressive recurrences compared to IPT or placebo. In this study, although IPT was more effective than placebo, it did not add to imipramine's efficacy. Limiting the generalizability of this study was the highly recurrent nature of the depressions for subjects included in the study and the relatively low frequency of psychotherapy. Nonetheless, imipramine's efficacy as a maintenance treatment was robust.

In a follow-up of this study, 20 depressed patients who had survived the 3 years on imipramine without relapse were randomly assigned to either continuing the medication or switching to placebo for 2 additional years (Kupfer et al., 1992). Even within this small sample, the recurrence rate was significantly higher among those switched to placebo. These 5-year data are the longest maintenance treatment data available.

Other shorter (typically 1–2 years) maintenance treatment trials with SSRIs, MAO inhibitors, and other antidepressant classes show similar results: that maintenance treatment is significantly more effective than placebo in preventing depressive relapses (Blacker, 1996). Additionally, although uncommonly used in the United States, lithium has been demonstrated to be an effective preventive antidepressant therapy (Souza & Goodwin, 1991).

Few studies have addressed the question of optimal antidepressant doses in maintenance treatment. In the long-term imipramine study, the mean daily dose was 216 mg and the 2-year recurrence rate was 20% (Frank et al., 1990). This contrasts with an earlier study in which the mean imipramine dose was 137 mg and the 2-year recurrence rate was 50% (Prien et al., 1984). (Placebo responses were similar in the two studies.) In another study by the same group, patients randomized to a full antidepressant dose survived longer without a relapse compared to those randomized to a half dose (Frank et al., 1993). Based on these two observations, the current consensus is that patients in maintenance treatment should remain on their acute treatment doses. The only exception to this would be a patient for whom the side effects are sufficiently distressing that adherence to treatment is jeopardized.

The efficacy of antidepressants as maintenance treatment for chronic depressions has also been shown in two recent studies examining a tricyclic and an SSRI, respectively (Kocsis et al., 1996; Keller et al., 1998). In both studies, after successful acute and continuation treatment, the antidepressant was associated with significantly lower recurrence rates compared to placebo over 2 years and 1.5 years, respectively. What is striking in these two studies is the percentage of depressed patients randomized to placebo after effective acute and continuation treatment (totaling approximately 6 months in each study) who did not show depressive recurrences after antidepressant discontinuation. Survival rates for the patients (who had been depressed for a mean of over 20 years prior to treatment) switched to placebo as a maintenance treatment were 48% and 50%, respectively, using reemergence of clinically significant depressive symptoms as the criterion. Thus, sustained response to a relatively brief period of antidepressant use was maintained after medication withdrawal in a substantial number of patients despite the chronicity of the depressive disorder.

A final area of inquiry concerns proper continuation/maintenance treatment for patients who successfully responded to ECT. It has long been known that without prophylactic antidepressant treatment after successful ECT, relapse rates are very high. More recent studies, however, have indicated that relapse rates are still high despite preventive antidepressant therapies, especially with those patients who had not responded to antidepressants prior to ECT (as opposed to those given ECT because of psychotic features or clinical urgency) (Sackeim et al., 1990). Many patients are therefore treated with combination treatment—for example, with an antidepressant plus lithium—in order to prevent relapse following acute ECT. Another option that is commonly considered is maintenance ECT in which the frequency of ECT is gradually reduced to once monthly treatments. Case series suggest the efficacy of this approach but no controlled studies are available (Schwarz, Loewenstein, & Isenberg, 1995).

FUTURE DIRECTIONS

Although antidepressants are consistently effective and the newer agents are safer and better tolerated than the older agents, the pharmacotherapy of depression still leaves much to be desired. As a first goal, it must be acknowledged that no antidepressant has been shown to be more effective than imipramine, the first agent released over 40 years ago. Partly, this reflects the tendency for pharmaceutical firms to synthesize and then test as new medications those that are similar to the currently effective agents (typically, but not exclusively, those that enhance norepinephrine or serotonin function or both.) This leads to refining of efficacy but not to greater efficacy.

Two examples of novel approaches to depression are the antiglucocorticoid agents and medications (still in development) that directly alter intracellular mechanisms thought to be related to both the pathophysiology of depression and the effects of currently available antidepressants. Antiglucocorticoid medications diminish hypothalamic–pituitary–adrenal axis function. Since glucocorticoids (such as cortisol) are excessive in severe depression, and excessive glucocorticoid function is associated with depressive symptoms (as in Cushing's disease), decreasing cortisol activity is a theoretically legitimate approach to treating depression. Preliminary data in this area, however, are conflicting (Wolkowitz & Reus, 1999). Increasing knowledge about the intracellular components of depressed states and the effects of currently available antidepressants on intracellular function lead to a different set of novel therapeutic approaches. These include the development of agents that stimulate the effect of intracellular protein kinases, or that inhibit cyclic adenosine $3'$, $5'$-monophosphate (AMP) breakdown, which would then lead to enhanced function of the transcription factor cAMP response element-binding protein (CREB) and neurotrophic factors such as brain-derived neurotrophic factor (BDNF). With a shift to new biological mechanisms of efficacy, hopefully we will also have agents that are more effective than currently available antidepressants (Duman et al., 1997).

For a second goal, we must more systematically evaluate potential treatment approaches for the 35–40% of patients who do not respond to single agent pharmacotherapy. Table 15.4 lists a number of current strategies, but the database supporting their efficacy is slim except for adjunctive lithium. Furthermore, less than a handful of studies have examined the relative efficacy of these approaches, which would allow clinicians to thoughtfully choose among the available alternatives. Future studies must systematically compare various treatment approaches for treatment of nonresponsive patients and develop predictors of these responses.

A corollary of this question reflects the theoretical underpinnings of many of these adjunctive strategies. Many academic psychopharmacologists recommend a neurotransmitter-based algorithm of treatment, adding dopaminergic agents to augment serotonergic antidepressants, or combining medications for their specific neurotransmitter effects. Although theoretically satisfying, data supporting this approach are lacking. It would be exceedingly helpful if clinicians could depend on theoretical considerations supporting clinical decisions, an approach that is not possible today.

Our recognition of chronically depressed individuals—those with dysthymic disorder or chronic major depression—is recent. Therefore, even though there is a beginning literature as reviewed above, we need more studies examining issues on long-term antidepressant therapies such as predicting which patients need lifetime treatment.

Among the depressive subtypes, bipolar depression has been ignored the most by clinical research. The field needs an entire body of data in this area. Some studies are currently ongoing and will hopefully be followed by others in order to ascertain both relative efficacies and, even more importantly, relative polarity switch rates across antidepressant classes.

Even beyond these goals of greater efficacy and greater capacity to predict antidepressant response, there are a series of practical questions that have been heretofore left unaddressed in the clinical research literature (Klein, 1993). Even though these questions are vitally important to clinicians, they are treated as far less important by the two most important funding sources of psychopharmacological research, governmental agencies such as the National Institute of Mental Health and the pharmaceutical firms. The former is primarily interested in more fundamental hypothesis-driven studies, while the latter focuses on demonstrating the efficacy of one particular drug. The practical questions that need to be addressed are myriad and include issues such as clinical predictors of antidepressant responses; the use of antidepressants in special populations such as pregnant women and those with comorbid disorders such as substance abuse; how best to raise doses; the development of treatments designed to minimize side effects; optimal doses during maintenance treatment; and how best to taper and discontinue antidepressants. Practical management of side effects, for which there is an astonishing paucity of systematic data, is a particularly critical issue given the relationship between side effect burden and noncompliance. Without attention to these exceedingly practical issues, the utility of the more sophisticated areas of research is limited, since the advances will not properly reach the legions of depressed patients whose current treatments are either inadequate or subjectively burdensome.

REFERENCES

Altshuler, L. L, Cohen, L., Szuba, M. P., Burt, V. K., Gitlin, M., & Mintz, J. (1996). Pharmacologic management of psychiatric illness during pregnancy: Dilemmas and guidelines. *American Journal of Psychiatry, 153*(5), 592–606.

Altshuler, L. L., Post, R. M., Leverich, G. S., Mikalauskas, K., Rosoff, A., & Ackerman, L. (1995). Antidepressant-induced mania and cycle acceleration: A controversy revisited. *American Journal of Psychiatry, 152*(8), 1130–1138.

American Psychiatric Association. (1990). *The practice of electroconvulsive therapy: Recommendations for treatment, training, and privileging: A task force report.* Washington, DC: American Psychiatric Press.

Amsterdam, J. D. (1998). Efficacy and safety of venlafaxine in the treatment of bipolar II major depressive episode. *Journal of Clinical Psychopharmacology, 18*(5), 414–417.

Amsterdam, J. D., Garcia-España, F., Fawcett, J., Quitkin, F. M., Reimherr, F. W., Rosenbaum, J. F., Schweizer, E., & Beasley, C. (1998). Efficacy and safety of fluoxetine in treating bipolar II major depressive episode. *Journal of Clinical Psychopharmacology, 18*(6), 435–440.

Aronson, R., Offman, H. J., Joffe, R. T., & Naylor, C. D. (1996). Triiodothyronine augmentation in the treatment of refractory depression. *Archives of General Psychiatry, 53,* 842–848.

Asher, J. A., Cole, G. O., Colin, J. N., Feighner, J. P., Ferris, R. M., Fibiger, H. C., Golden, R. N., Martin, P., Potter, W. Z., Richelson, E., & Sulser, F. (1995). Bupropion: A review of its mechanisms of antidepressant activity. *Journal of Clinical Psychiatry, 56,* 395–401.

Austin, M. P., & Mitchell, P. B. (1998). Use of psychotropic medications in breast-feeding women: Acute and prophylactic treatment. *Australian and New Zealand Journal of Psychiatry, 32,* 778–784.

Bauer, M., & Döpfmer, S. (1999). Lithium augmentation in treatment-resistant depression: Meta-analysis of placebo-controlled studies. *Journal of Clinical Psychopharmacology, 19*(5), 427–434.

Blacker, D. (1996). Maintenance treatment of major depression: A review of the literature. *Harvard Review of Psychiatry, 4,* 1–9.

Calabrese, J. R., Bowden, C. L., Sachs, G. S., Ascher, J. A., Monaghan, E., & Rudd, G. D. (1999). A double-blind placebo-controlled study of lamotrigine monotherapy in outpatients with bipolar I depression. *Journal of Clinical Psychiatry, 60*(2), 79–88.

Chambers, C. D., Johnson, K. A., Dick, L. N., Felix, R. J., & Jones, K. L. (1996). Birth outcomes in pregnant women taking fluoxetine. *New England Journal of Medicine, 335,* 1010–1015.

Crismon, M. L., Trivedi, M., Pigott, T., Rush, A. J., Hirschfeld, M. A., Kahn, D. A., DeBattista, C., Nelson, J. C., Nierenberg, A. A., Saceim, H. A., Thase, M. E., & the Texas Consensus Conference Panel on Medication Treatment of Major Depressive Disorder. (1999). The Texas Medication Algorithm Project: Report of the Texas Consensus Conference Panel on Medication Treatment of Major Depressive Disorder. *Journal of Clinical Psychiatry, 60*(3), 142–156.

Davidson, J. R. T. (1989). Seizures and bupropion: A review. *Journal of Clinical Psychiatry, 50,* 256–261.

Davis, J. M., Wang, Z., & Janicak, P. G. (1993). A quantitative analysis of clinical drug trials for the treatment of affective disorders. *Psychopharmacological Bulletin, 29,* 175–181.

De Lima, M. S., Hotoph, M., & Wessely, S. (1999). The efficacy of drug treatments for dysthymia: A systematic review and meta-analysis. *Psychological Medicine, 29,* 1273–1289.

Drugtopics.com [Website of Medical Economics, Inc., Montvale, NJ]. (2000).

Duffy, A., Grof, P., Robertson, C., & Alda, M. (2000). The implications of genetic studies of major mood disorders for clinical practice. *Journal of Clinical Psychiatry, 61*(9), 630–637.

Duman, R. S., Heninger, G. R., & Nestler, E. J. (1997). A molecular and cellular theory of depression. *Archives of General Psychiatry, 54,* 597–606.

Eastman, C. I., Young, M. A., Fogg, L. F., Liu, L., & Meaden, P. M. (1998). Bright light treatment of winter depression: A placebo-controlled trial. *Archives of General Psychiatry, 55,* 883–889.

Ericson, A., Källén, B., & Wiholm, B. E. (1999). Delivery outcome after the use of antidepressants in early pregnancy. European *Journal of Clinical Pharmacology, 55,* 503–508.

Fava, M. (2000a). New approaches to the treatment of refractory depression. *Journal of Clinical Psychiatry, 61*(Suppl. 1), 26–32.

Fava, M. (2000b). Management of nonresponse and intolerance: Switching strategies. *Journal of Clinical Psychiatry, 61*(Suppl. 2), 10–12.

Fava, M., Alpert, J. E., Nierenberg, A. A., Worthington, J. J., & Rosenbaum, J. F. (2000, May 13–18). Double-blind study of high-dose fluoxetine versus lithium or desipramine augmentation of fluoxetine in partial and nonresponders to fluoxetine. In *Syllabus of American Psychiatric Association 2000 Annual Meeting,* Chicago, IL (pp. 35–36).

Fava, M., Mischoulon, D., & Rosenbaum, J. (1998). Augmentation strategies for failed SSRI treatment. *American Society of Clinical Psychopharmacology Progress Notes, 9,* 7.

Frank, E., Kupfer, D. J., Perel, J. M., Cornes, C., Jarrett, D. B., Mallinger, A. G., Thase, M. E., McEachran, A. B., & Grochocinski, V. J. (1990). Three-year outcomes for maintenance therapies in recurrent depression. *Archives of General Psychiatry, 47,* 1093–1099.

Frank, E., Kupfer, D. J., Perel, J. M., Cornes, C., Mallinger, A. G., Thase, M. E., McEachran, A. B., & Grochocinski, V. J. (1993). Comparison of full-dose versus half-dose pharmacotherapy in the maintenance treatment of recurrent depression. *Journal of Affective Disorders, 27,* 139–145.

Gardner, D. M., Shulman, K. I., Walker, S. E., & Tailor, S. A. N. (1996). The making of a user friendly MAOI diet. *Journal of Clinical Psychiatry, 57*(3), 99–104.

Gelenberg, A. J., & Chesen, C. L. (2000). How fast are antidepressants? *Journal of Clinical Psychiatry, 61*(10), 712–721.

Gitlin, M. J. (1996). *The psychotherapist's guide to psychopharmacology* (2nd ed.). New York: Free Press.

Gitlin, M. J., & Suri, R. (1999). Management of side effects of SSRIs and newer antidepressants. In R. Balon (Ed.), *Practical management of the side effects of psychotropic drugs* (pp. 85–118). New York: Basel.

Gorman, J. M. (1999). Mirtazapine: Clinical overview. *Journal of Clinical Psychiatry, 60*(Suppl. 17), 9–13.

Harvey, A. T., Rudolph, R. L., & Preskorn, S. H. (2000). Evidence of the dual mechanisms of action of venlafaxine. *Archives of General Psychiatry, 57,* 503–509.

Himmelhoch, J. M., Thase, M. E., Mallinger, A. G., & Houck, P. (1991). Tranylcypromine versus imipramine in anergic bipolar depression. *American Journal of Psychiatry, 148,* 910–916.

Hirschfeld, R. M. A. (1999). Efficacy of SSRIs and newer antidepressants in severe depression: Comparison with TCAs. *Journal of Clinical Psychiatry, 60*(5), 326–335.

Joffe, R. T., & Singer, W. (1990). A comparison of tri-iodothyronine and thyroxine in the potentiation of tricyclic antidepressants. *Psychiatry Research, 32,* 241–251.

Joffe, R. T., Singer, W., Levitt, A. J., & MacDonald, C. (1993). A placebo-controlled comparison of lithium and tri-iodothyronine augmentation in tricyclic antidepressants in unipolar refractory depression. *Archives of General Psychiatry, 50,* 387–393.

Keller, M. B. (1990). Diagnostic and course of illness variables pertinent to refractory depression. In A. Tasman, S. Goldfinger, & C. Kaufmann (Eds.), *Review of psychiatry* (Vol. 9, pp. 10–32). Washington, DC: American Psychiatric Press.

Keller, M. B., Gelenberg, A. J., Hirschfeld, R. M. A., Rush, A. J., Thase, M. E., Kocsis, J. H., Markowitz, J. C., Fawcett, J. A., Koran, L. M., Klein, D. M., Russell, J. M., Kornstein, S. G., McCullough, J. P., Davis, S. M., & Harrison, W. M. (1998). The treatment of chronic depression: Part 2. A double-blind, randomized trial of sertraline and imipramine. *Journal of Clinical Psychiatry, 59*(11), 598–606.

Keller, M. B., McCullough, J. P., Klein, D. N., Arnow, B., Dunner, D. L., Gelenberg, A. J., Markowitz, J. C., Nemeroff, C. B., Russell, J. M., Thase, M. E., Trivedi, M. H., & Zajecka, J. (2000). Nefazodone, psychotherapy, and their combination for the treatment of chronic depression: A comparison of nefazodone, the cognitive behavioral-analysis system of psychotherapy, and their combination for the treatment of chronic depression. *New England Journal of Medicine, 342,* 1462–1470.

Klein, D. F. (1993). Clinical psychopharmacologic practice: The need for developing a research base. *Archives of General Psychiatry, 50,* 491–494.

Klein, D. F., Gittelman-Klein, R., Quitkin, F. M., & Rifkin, A. (1980). *Diagnosis and drug treatment of psychiatric disorders.* Baltimore: Williams & Wilkins.

Kocsis, J. H., Friedman, R. A., Markowitz, J. C., Leon, A. C., Miller, N. L., Gniwesch, L., & Parides, M. (1996). Maintenance therapy for chronic depression: A controlled clinical trial of desipramine. *Archives of General Psychiatry, 53,* 769–774.

Kogan, A. O., & Guilford, P. M. (1998). Side effects of short-term 10,000-lux light therapy. *American Journal of Psychiatry, 155*(2), 293–294.

Kupfer, D. J., Frank, E., Perel, J. M., Cornes, C., Mallinger, A. G., Thase, M. E., McEachran, A. B., & Grochocinski, V. J. (1992). Five-year outcome for maintenance therapies in recurrent depression. *Archives of General Psychiatry, 49,* 769–773.

Landén, M., Björling, G., Ågren, H., & Fahlén, T. (1998). A randomized, double-blind placebo-controlled trial of buspirone in combination with an SSRI in patients with treatment-refractory depression. *Journal of Clinical Psychiatry, 59,* 664–668.

Liebowitz, M. R., Quitkin, F. M., Stewart, J. W., McGrath, P. J., Harrison, W. M., Markowitz, J. S., Rabkin, J. G., Trichina, E., Goetz, D. M., & Klein, D. F. (1988). Antidepressant specificity in atypical depression. *Archives of General Psychiatry, 45,* 129–137.

Masand, P. S., Anand, V. S., & Tanquary, J. F. (1998). Psycho-stimulant augmentation of second-generation antidepressants: A case series. *Depression and Anxiety, 7,* 89–91.

McGrath, P. J., Stewart, J. W., Janal, M. N., Petkova, E., Quitkin, F. M., & Klein, D. F. (2000). A placebo-controlled study of fluoxetine versus imipramine in the acute treatment of atypical depression. *American Journal of Psychiatry, 157*(3), 344–350.

Nelson, J. C. (2000). Augmentation strategies in depression. *Journal of Clinical Psychiatry, 61*(Suppl. 2), 13–19.

Nemeroff, C. B., DeVane, C. L., & Pollock, B. G. (1996). Newer antidepressants and the cytochrome P450 system. *American Journal of Psychiatry, 153*(3), 311–320.

Nierenberg, A. A., Farabaugh, A. H., Alpert, J. E., Gordon, J., Worthington, J. J., Rosenbaum, J. F., & Fava, M. (2000). Timing of onset of antidepressant response with fluoxetine treatment. *American Journal of Psychiatry, 157*(9), 1423–1428.

Nierenberg, A. A., Keefe, B. R., Leslie, V. C., Alpert, J. E., Pava, J. A., Worthington, J. J., Rosenbaum, J. F., & Fava, M. (1999). Residual symptoms in depressed patients who respond acutely to fluoxetine. *Journal of Clinical Psychiatry, 60*(4), 221–225.

Nulman, I., Rovet, J., Stewart, D. E., Wolpin, J., Gardner, H. A., Theis, J. G. W., Kulin, N., & Koren, G. (1997). Neurodevelopment of children exposed in utero to antidepressant drugs. *New England Journal of Medicine, 336*(4), 258–262.

O'Hara, M. (1995). *Postpartum depression: Causes and consequences.* New York: Springer-Verlag.

Peet, M. (1994). Induction of mania with selective serotonin re-uptake inhibitors and tricyclic antidepressants. *British Journal of Psychiatry, 194,* 549–550.

Perry, P. J., Zeilmann, C., & Arndt, S. (1994). Tricyclic antidepressant concentrations in plasma: An estimate of their sensitivity and specificity as a predictor of response. *Journal of Clinical Psychopharmacology, 14,* 230–240.

Physician's Desk Reference. (2001). Montvale, NJ: Medical Economics.

Price, L. H. (1990). Pharmacological strategies in refractory depression. In A. Tasman, S. Goldfinger, & C. Kaufmann (Eds.), *Review of psychiatry* (Vol. 9, pp. 116–131). Washington, DC: American Psychiatric Press.

Prien, R. F., & Kupfer, D. J. (1986). Continuation drug therapy for major depressive episodes: How long should it be maintained? *American Journal of Psychiatry, 143*(1), 18–23.

Prien, R. F., Kupfer, D. J., Mansky, P. A., Small, J. G., Tuason, U. B., Voss, C. B., & Johnson, W. E. (1984). Drug therapy in the prevention of recurrences in unipolar and bipolar affective disorders: A report of the NIMH Collaborative Study Group comparing lithium carbonate, imipramine and a lithium carbonate–imipramine combination. *Archives of General Psychiatry, 41,* 1096–1104.

Reimherr, F. W., Amsterdam, J. D., Quitkin, F. M., Rosenbaum, J. F., Fava, M. F., Zajecka, J., Beasley, C. M., Michelson, D., Roback, P., & Sundell, K. (1998). Optimal length of continuation therapy in depression: A prospective assessment during long-term fluoxetine treatment. *American Journal of Psychiatry, 155*(9), 1247–1253.

Roose, S. P., & Spatz, E. (1999). Treating depression in patients with ischemic heart disease. *Drug Safety, 20*, 459–465.

Sachs, G. S., Lafer, B., Stoll, A. L., Banov, M., Thibault, A. B., Tohen, M., & Rosenbaum, J. F. (1994). A double-blind trial of bupropion versus desipramine for bipolar depression. *Journal of Clinical Psychiatry, 55*(9), 391–393.

Sackeim, H. A., Prudic, J., Devanand, D. P., Decina, P., Kerr, B., & Malitz, S. (1990). The impact of medication resistance and continuation pharmacotherapy on relapse following response to electroconvulsive therapy in major depression. *Journal of Clinical Psychopharmacology, 10*, 96–104.

Sackeim, H. A., Prudic, J., Devanand, D. P., Nobler, M. S., Lisanby, S. H., Peyser, S., Fitzsimons, L., Moody, B. J., & Clark, J. (2000). A prospective, randomized, double-blind comparison of bilateral and right unilateral electroconvulsive therapy at different stimulus intensities. *Archives of General Psychiatry, 57*, 425–434.

Schwarz, T., Lowenstein, J., & Isenberg, K. E. (1995). Maintenance ECT: Indications and outcome. *Convulsive Therapy, 11*, 14–23.

Souza, F. G. M., & Goodwin, G. M. (1991). Lithium treatment and prophylaxis in unipolar depression: A meta-analysis. *British Journal of Psychiatry, 158*, 666–675.

Taylor, D. P., Carter, R. B., Eison, A. S., Mullins, U. L., Smith, H. L., Torrente, J. R., Wright, R. N., & Yocca, F. D. (1995). Pharmacology and neurochemistry of nefazodone, a novel antidepressant drug. *Journal of Clinical Psychiatry, 56*(Suppl. 6), 3–11.

Thase, M. E. (1998). Effects of venlafaxine on blood pressure: A meta-analysis of original data from 3744 depressed patients. *Journal of Clinical Psychiatry, 59*(10), 502–508.

Thase, M. E. (2000). Treatment of severe depression. *Journal of Clinical Psychiatry, 61*(Suppl. 1), 17–25.

Thase, M. E., Fava, M., Halbreich, U., Koscis, J. H., Koran, L., Davidson, J., Rosenbaum, J., & Harrison, W. (1996). A placebo-controlled, randomized clinical trial comparing sertraline and imipramine for the treatment of dysthymia. *Archives of General Psychiatry, 53*, 777–784.

Wheeler Vega, J. A., Mortimer, A. M., & Tyson, P. J. (2000). Somatic treatment of psychotic depression: Review and recommendations for practice. *Journal of Clinical Psychopharmacology, 20*(5), 504–519.

Wisner, K. L., Gelenberg, A. J., Leonard, H., Zarin, D., & Frank, E. (1999). Pharmacologic treatment of depression during pregnancy. *Journal of the American Medical Association, 282*(13), 1264–1269.

Wisner, K. L., Perel, J. M., & Findling, R. L. (1996). Antidepressant treatment during breast-feeding. *American Journal of Psychiatry, 153*(9), 1132–1137.

Wisner, K. L., & Wheeler, S. B. (1994). Prevention of recurrent postpartum major depression. *Hospital and Community Psychiatry, 45*(12), 1191–1196.

Wolkowitz, O. M., & Reus, V. I. (1999). Treatment of depression with antiglucocorticoid drugs. *Psychosomatic Medicine, 61*, 698–711.

16

Cognitive-Behavioral Treatment of Depression

Steven D. Hollon, Kirsten L. Haman, and Laurel L. Brown

The cognitive-behavioral therapies have emerged as some of the most effective psychosocial treatments for depression. Along with interpersonal psychotherapy, these approaches have been shown to be effective in the reduction of acute distress and compare favorably to medications among all but the most severely depressed patients (American Psychiatric Association, 2000). Moreover, there are indications that they may possess an enduring effect that protects patients against subsequent relapse or recurrence after treatment termination (Hollon & Shelton, 2001). Finally, there are even indications that they can prevent the initial onset of first episodes or the emergence of symptoms in persons at risk who have never been depressed (Gillham, Shatte, & Freres, 2000).

This chapter focuses on the nature and efficacy of the various cognitive and behavioral interventions. These include not only cognitive therapy and related cognitive-behavioral interventions, but also more traditional behavioral interventions and recent efforts to integrate each within a more interpersonal context. These approaches often overlap in their underlying conceptualizations and actual procedures of operation, but they also often differ in matters of both theory and practice. Whether these differences really matter remains to be seen, but they may have implications for both the nature of the patients treated and the ease with which the respective interventions can be disseminated to the larger clinical community. All have been generally successful, particularly with less severely depressed patients, and there are indications that their range is being extended in recent years to patients with more chronic and comorbid conditions (Hollon, 2000).

COGNITIVE THERAPY AND THE COGNITIVE-BEHAVIORAL INTERVENTIONS

Cognitive therapy is one of the earliest and best established of the cognitive-behavioral interventions (Hollon & Beck, 1994). Although it differs in some respects from the other cognitive-behavioral interventions, the similarities far outweigh the differences, and we will use this approach to illustrate the major themes relevant to all these approaches. Cognitive therapy is based on the notion that the way a person interprets life experiences influences how he or she feels about those events and what he or she tries to do to cope with them behaviorally (Beck, 1991). According to cognitive theory, people who are prone to depression are unduly negative in their perceptions of themselves, their worlds, and their futures. These three realms are known as the *negative cognitive triad*. Moreover, they are seen as being susceptible to a host of information-processing distortions—for example, arbitrary inference or selective abstraction—that makes it difficult for them to benefit from positive experience or be open to corrective information. Their thinking is seen as being dominated by negative cognitive schemata, organized knowledge systems that contain both core beliefs and underlying assumptions and that dictate the operation of biases in information processing. These schemata often function as "silent" propensities that are activated by negative life events; for patients with more chronic distress, the schemata may be continuously activated.

The Nature of Cognitive Therapy

Cognitive therapy is predicated on the notion that teaching patients to recognize and examine their negative beliefs and information-processing proclivities can produce relief from their distress and enable them to cope more effectively with life's challenges (Beck, Rush, Shaw, & Emery, 1979). Put more simply, thoughts affect feelings and behaviors, and changing those thoughts changes feelings and behaviors. The primary role of the therapist is to educate patients in the use of various techniques that allow them to examine their thoughts and modify maladaptive beliefs and behaviors. One of the ultimate goals of therapy is to help the client learn to use these tools independently. Such skills are not only important for symptom relief, but may also minimize the chances of future recurrence of symptoms. For a more in-depth description of the cognitive theory, see Alford and Beck (1997) and Clark, Beck, and Alford (1999).

A successful course of cognitive therapy accomplishes its goals through a structured, collaborative process that includes three distinct but interrelated components. Exploration, examination, and experimentation are all designed to help the patient replace maladaptive negative thoughts with more adaptive beliefs. The first component consists of a thorough *exploration* of the patient's dysfunctional beliefs, or, more generally, the patient's personal meaning system. A careful *examination* of that well-articulated belief system comprises the second component of the therapy process. In this process, evidence speaking for and against the belief is reviewed, alternative explanations or interpretations are considered, and the actual consequences that might ensue if the belief were true are considered and put in a realistic perspective. Finally, active *experimentation,* designed specifically to "test" the validity of the maladaptive belief system, makes up the third component of the therapeutic endeavor. It is important to note that these three components are not simply incorporated into the course of therapy in a linear fashion. For instance, experimentation, in the form of activity monitoring, is often effectively used in early sessions as a means of both promoting symptom relief and gathering empirical data. Later in the course of therapy, other forms of experimentation are used to challenge faulty core beliefs.

The Structure of Cognitive Therapy within and across Sessions

Therapy sessions begin with the therapist and patient collaboratively forming an agenda for that session. The process of working together to form an agenda accomplishes several goals in and of itself. First, the patient and therapist can most efficiently utilize their time together by prioritizing matters of importance, noting specific issues that may either be addressed within the session or held for future sessions. Early in therapy, agenda items focus on assessing the patient's perceptions of his or her problematic areas, expectations for therapy, and concrete goals. Second, the collaborative process and the predictability of the structure help the patient develop a sense of empowerment and self-control.

Once areas of functional difficulty are delineated, a series of gentle, thoughtful questions are used to help bring to light the dysfunctional thoughts and beliefs that may be driving the patient's distress and maladaptive behaviors. This process of exploring maladaptive automatic thoughts and the underlying core beliefs that lie behind them, referred to as "Socratic questioning," is critical to successful cognitive therapy. By its very nature, it avoids being confrontational, since the goal is to discover whether certain thoughts and beliefs are not serving the patient well, not to expose them as "faulty thinkers." A failure to fully understand the patient's personal meaning system could hinder progress. In particular, it is often important to "follow the affect." To the extent that the theory is correct, than any strong affect should be associated with thoughts and beliefs that make the reaction sensible. If the therapist cannot sit back and imagine feeling what the patient feels if he or she believed what the patient believes, then there is still more to the meaning system that needs to be explored.

From the first session, assignments are collaboratively generated for the patient to complete between sessions. These assignments, which can be written or behavioral, often incorporate the experimental component of the therapeutic process. They allow for the testing of negative beliefs and predictions and for the gathering of evidence necessary for cognitive change.

As therapy continues, the therapist and the patient collaboratively work to examine whether the patient's interpretations of events and beliefs about him- or herself, the world, and the future are accurate and/or adaptive. Progress is regularly and systematically assessed in terms of concrete behavioral outcomes. As the therapist's understanding of the patient's worldview and personal aspirations expands, and beliefs are successfully examined, goals may be revisited. New techniques are introduced throughout therapy, but all serve to address the same concept: the testing of negative expectations and interpretations. For a complete session-by-session description of the process of therapy, see J. Beck (1995).

Cognitive therapy emphasizes the links between thought, mood, and behavior. As a result, many effective techniques incorporate behavioral interventions in the service of testing specific automatic negative thoughts and underlying beliefs or assumptions. For example, a depressed patient often feels overwhelmed and unable to cope with life's demands. In fact, the patient may indeed be facing serious demands in a number of different areas: friction in relationships, financial difficulties, or insufficient work productivity. Such a patient may be encouraged to make a list of what he or she needs to do and then to break large tasks into their smallest constituent steps.

The patient is then encouraged to run an experiment to see if he or she can get things done by focusing on accomplishing just one small step at a time. Patients often find after doing this graded task assignment that they more easily complete the larger tasks they set for themselves because now they are less likely to be overwhelmed by their own negative thinking. This experience of success is used to disconfirm their negative expectation and to question their underlying belief in their own incompetence.

Use of the various techniques depends on the patient's goals and symptoms. Some techniques, like the graded task assignment described above, or a detailed schedule of activities to complete across a given period of time (activity schedule), are particularly useful early in therapy. Such concrete behavioral assignments allow patients to learn the observational and problem-solving skills that they will use throughout therapy. They also help clients learn and practice skills that lead to success and motivate them to continue to take an active approach to problem solving and the pursuit of goals.

Other techniques emphasize the cognitive aspect. For instance, patients typically are taught to ask themselves a series of questions in order to ascertain their negative beliefs:

1. "What is the evidence for and against my belief?"
2. "What are alternative ways of viewing the situation?"
3. "What are the implications for my life if my belief is true?"

The Dysfunctional Thought Record is a formalized way for the patient to identify, evaluate, and respond to negative automatic thoughts in a written format. The Dysfunctional Thought Record is introduced early in therapy and used throughout the process. Additional techniques include teaching problem-solving and decision-making skills, the development of flash cards with important phrases as patient self-reminders, and the in-session employment of role play to practice or work through real-life interactions.

The Course of Cognitive Therapy

Cognitive therapy is designed to be an efficient, structured, short-term form of treatment. For patients with uncomplicated depressions—that is, for people who have an essentially adaptive view of themselves, the world, and the future when they are not depressed—that might mean a treatment length of four to 14 sessions (J. Beck, 1995). On the other hand, for individuals with a lengthy history of rigid dysfunctional beliefs, treatment may need to last longer. For these patients, the inaccurate beliefs and related maladaptive behaviors are deeply entrenched because the individual has had little experience questioning those beliefs and behaviors. As a result, more exploration and examination of the faulty belief system, and more experimentation designed to modify those beliefs, is required. Thus, regardless of the persistence of depressive symptoms, it is the particular set of maladaptive or dysfunctional beliefs held that is the primary target of the cognitive-behavioral approach to treatment.

In recent years, cognitive therapy has evolved with respect to its approach to the treatment of long-standing symptoms and personality disorders (Beck, Freeman, & Associates, 1990). The process of providing a cognitive conceptualization was always the central organizing principle of the approach. Earlier efforts with episodically depressed patients focused more exclusively on applying cognitive and behavioral techniques to the resolution of negative thoughts and maladaptive behaviors in response to life difficulties "in the here-and-now." Attention to the earlier life events and childhood antecedents that contributed to the development of these underlying schemata was reserved for later sessions, after the patient was largely free of symptoms. In a similar fashion, attention was paid to the therapeutic relationship only when problems arose in the working alliance.

Over the last two decades, it has become clear that patients with histories of chronic depression or depressions superimposed on long-standing character disorders have no other way of thinking of themselves and often need help to construct completely new schemata to guide their thinking and behavior. For these patients, Beck uses the metaphor of a "three-legged stool" to describe his approach to the implementation of cognitive therapy. According to this metaphor, the therapist not only explores the thoughts and feelings that surround some current life concern. He or she also explores the historical antecedents that gave rise to the beliefs that underlie those thoughts and feelings and the way those beliefs manifest themselves in the therapeutic relationship.

This process seems to help the patient with long-standing maladaptive beliefs recognize that much of his or her distress stems from these beliefs (and not just from events). Moreover, it further helps the patient to recognize that these beliefs were often acquired early in life before he or she developed the capacity to make the kinds of reasoned judgments that came with greater maturity. Dealing with the manifestations of these beliefs and attitudes in the therapeutic relationship provides an opportunity for the patient to try out new behaviors in a somewhat safer interpersonal context. Although many of these strategies are reminiscent of more dynamic therapies, the therapist always moves the discussion back to just how these beliefs can be tested in current life situations and makes no effort made to explore unconscious sexual or aggressive drives.

IS COGNITIVE-BEHAVIOR THERAPY EFFECTIVE IN THE TREATMENT OF DEPRESSION?

Cognitive therapy and the related cognitive-behavioral interventions have been among the most extensively tested psychosocial treatments for depression, having been studied in over 80 controlled trials (American Psychiatric Association, 2000). These approaches have typically been found to be superior to minimal treatment controls and at least as effective as alternative types of treatment (Gaffan, Tsaousis, & Kemp-Wheeler, 1995). Specific comparisons to other psychosocial interventions in fully clinical populations have been few, but there are indications that they might be superior to more traditional dynamic-eclectic interventions (Svartberg & Stiles, 1991). In a recent review, the cognitive-behavior therapy was one of the few psychosocial interventions to meet criteria as an empirically supported intervention for the treatment of depression (DeRubeis & Crits-Christoph, 1998).

Questions still remain about the efficacy of the cognitive-behavioral approaches relative to medications. Two early studies suggested that they might be superior to drugs, but each was flawed in key respects (Meterissian & Bradwejn, 1989). In the first, Rush and colleagues found that depressed outpatients showed greater response to 12 weeks of cognitive therapy than they did to imipramine pharmacotherapy (Rush, Beck, Kovacs, & Hollon, 1977). However, drug dosages were low by current standards and medication withdrawal was begun at least 2 weeks before the end of active treatment. In the second study, Blackburn and colleagues found cognitive therapy (alone or in combination with medications) superior to medications alone in a general practice setting (Blackburn, Bishop, Glen, Whalley, & Christie, 1981). However, medication dosages were not controlled and the rate of response was so low (14%) as to raise questions about the adequacy with which pharmacotherapy was implemented.

Studies that have done a better job of providing adequate drug treatment have suggested that cognitive therapy is roughly comparable to medications in initial efficacy. For example, Blackburn and colleagues found cognitive therapy to be about as effective as medications (and combined treatment somewhat better still) when drug treatment was provided by experienced research psychiatrists (Blackburn et al., 1981). Murphy and colleagues found no differences between cognitive therapy and nortriptyline (either alone or in combination) in a study that used blood levels to monitor medication doses (Murphy, Simons, Wetzel, & Lustman, 1984). Similarly, our group found cognitive therapy to be about as effective as medications (either alone or in combination) in a study that went to great lengths to ensure that drug treatment was implemented in an adequate fashion (Hollon et al., 1992).

To date, the National Institute of Mental Health (NIMH) Treatment of Depression Collaborative Research Project (TDCRP) is the only study to suggest that drugs might be more effective than cognitive therapy in the treatment of depressed outpatients (Elkin et al., 1989). Although in that study there were no differences between the different treatment conditions among less severely depressed patients, both imipramine and interpersonal psychotherapy were superior to pill-placebo in the treatment of more severely depressed outpatients. However, cognitive therapy was not (Elkin et al., 1995). Given the size of this study and the fact that it was the first placebo-controlled trial in the literature, the TDCRP has had a major impact on consensus in the field. As a consequence, a number of treatment guidelines recommend that cognitive therapy not be used without medications in the treatment of more severely depressed patients (American Psychiatric Association, 2000; Depression Guideline Panel, 1993).

However, there were problems with the TDCRP. In particular, there were differences among the sites with respect to their prior experience with cognitive therapy that mirrored the efficacy of the approach (Jacobson & Hollon, 1996a). At the two sites with less prior experience with the modality, cognitive therapy did no better than pill-placebo, whereas at a third site with greater prior experience in the approach cognitive therapy did as well as medications (Jacobson & Hollon, 1996b). This suggests that the TDCRP may have failed to implement cognitive therapy in an adequate fashion at each of its sites, just as some of the earlier comparative trials may have failed to implement drug treatment adequately.

DeRubeis and colleagues have recently conducted a mega-analysis on data from the TDCRP and several other studies (DeRubeis, Gelfand, Tang, & Simmons, 1999). They found that cognitive therapy was as effective as medications in the treatment of more severely depressed patients, with the TDCRP being the sole exception. Another recent mega-analysis came to a different conclusion, suggesting that psychotherapy alone (including cognitive therapy) was less effective than medications in the treatment of more severely depressed patients (Thase et al., 1997). However, the only studies included in that latter mega-analysis were drawn from a single site and included data from the TDCRP, in which the implementation of cognitive therapy was suspect.

It seems likely that the TDCRP will turn out to be an anomaly in the literature. Since it was published, two additional studies have failed to find differences between drugs and cognitive therapy. The first was conducted in a sample of outpatients with recurrent depression (Blackburn & Moore, 1997) and the second in a mixed sample of in- and outpatients with nonendogenous depression (Hautzinger, de Jong-Meyer, Trieber, & Rudolf, 1996). However, neither trial was placebo-controlled, leaving open questions in the minds of some about whether medication treatment was adequately implemented and whether the patients sampled were truly drug-responsive (Klein, 1996). In that regard, Jarrett and colleagues recently published the results of a placebo-controlled trial that found cognitive therapy as effective as a monoamine oxidase inhibitor, with both superior to a pill-placebo control in the treatment of atypical depression (depression characterized by reversed vegetative symptoms, mood reactivity, and rejection sensitivity) (Jarrett et al., 1999). Similarly, our group has recently completed a controlled trial in collaboration with colleagues at the University of Pennsylvania, in which we found cognitive therapy comparable to drugs in the treatment of more severely depressed outpatients, with each superior to a pill-placebo control. There are several other placebo-controlled trials currently underway. What they will show remains to be seen, but it is clear that the issue should be resolved through further experimentation.

WHO RESPONDS TO COGNITIVE-BEHAVIOR THERAPY?

Closely related to the issue of patient severity is the notion that patients with endogenous depressions respond less well to cognitive-behavior therapy than they do to medications. Traditionally, the word *endogenous* described depressions that were characterized by melancholic symptomatology and were hypothesized to result from more internal, biological causes; these depressions were assumed to best respond to medications. By and large, there has been little empirical support for this notion in the studies already described (Blackburn et al., 1981; Hollon et al., 1992; Kovacs, Rush, Beck, & Hollon, 1981; Murphy et al., 1984). Thase and colleagues found that over 80% of a sample of endogenous inpatients showed a full response to a brief course of cognitive therapy in the absence of medications (Thase, Bowler, & Harden, 1991). Even the TDCRP failed to find that endogenous status predicted differential response (Sotsky et al., 1991).

Nonetheless, it would be premature to conclude that certain types of patients don't respond better to one type of treatment than another. Such indices would be prescriptive; patient characteristics that predict which patients benefit most from a certain treatment could be used to select the best treatment for a given individual. For a variety of reasons, it is simply more difficult to detect an interaction between patient characteristics and treatment type (moderation) than it is to detect a main effect for treatment (Smith & Sechrest, 1991). The appropriate designs are more complex, prescriptive indices need to be carefully assessed, and larger samples are required to generate comparable power. Few of the existing studies would meet any, let alone all, of these requirements.

There are indications that men are both more likely to show endogenous depressions and respond better to tricyclic antidepressants, whereas women are more likely to show atypical patterns and respond better to specific serotonin reuptake inhibitors, at least until they go through menopause (Kornstein et al., 2000). It remains unclear whether gender or subtype is the critical determinant or whether the mechanisms involved are specific to medication response, but these findings do highlight the fact that we still know too little to conclude that some depressions are biological in nature and require medications, whereas others are not and do not. Thase and colleagues have found evidence that women do less well than men in cognitive therapy if they are more severely depressed (Thase et al., 1994). Pooling these findings with data from other studies conducted at their site led them to suggest that more severely depressed women might do better still in interpersonal psychotherapy (Thase, Frank, Kornstein, & Yonkers, 2000). However, the initial data were purely prognostic in nature (i.e., treatment was held constant while individual differences were allowed to vary) and the latter comparison did not involve experimental controls, so these findings need to be interpreted with considerable caution.

Thase and colleagues also found that a number of biological abnormalities, including sleep disorders and hypothalamic–pituitary–adrenal axis activity, predicted poor response to cognitive therapy, independent of severity (Thase, Dube, et al., 1996; Thase, Simons, & Reynolds, 1996). However, as mentioned above, their designs were purely prognostic and do not necessarily indicate that such patients should not be treated with cognitive therapy. Those studies that have examined such biological indices in the context of a truly prescriptive design in which such patients are randomly assigned to different treatment conditions typically have found little evidence of differential response as a function of treatment (Corbishley et al., 1990; McKnight, Nelson-Gray, & Barnhill, 1992). In those studies, biological abnormalities typically predict poor response regardless of treatment modality.

A recent treatment guideline suggested that cognitive therapy may be superior to other interventions in the treatment of patients with underlying personality disorders (American Psychiatric Association, 2000). However, this statement appears to be based upon a misreading of conclusions drawn from the TDCRP. In an earlier report, Shea and colleagues noted that patients with personality disorders did worse than patients without personality disorders when treated with drugs or with interpersonal psychotherapy, but not with cognitive therapy (Shea et al., 1990). However, the lack of difference within cognitive therapy was more a function of the relatively poor response of patients without personality disorders, not any superior response on the part of patients with personality disorders in cognitive therapy (see Table 2 on page 715). The American Psychiatric Association guideline also cites a study by Patience and colleagues in support of this notion, but there is nothing in that report to support that assertion (Patience, McGuire, Scott, & Freeman, 1995). Hardy and colleagues reported that differences between patients with and without Cluster C disorders were more likely to be significant at the end of treatment for patients treated with dynamic psychotherapy than for patients treated with cognitive therapy (Hardy et al., 1995). However, the magnitude of change reported for each type of patient was quite comparable within the respective modalities. Thus, there currently is little empirical support for the notion that cognitive therapy is more effective than other interventions at treating the personality disorders that sometimes underlie depression. Whether such evidence will emerge when more recent schema-focused modifications are finally tested remains to be seen, but the current indications are based largely on a misreading of the existing literature.

One recent study (based on a reanalysis of the data from the TDCRP) suggested that patients who engage in avoidance behaviors in relationships do better in cognitive therapy than in interpersonal psychotherapy and that patients with a more obsessive style show the opposite pattern of response (Barber & Muenz, 1996). This study is particularly noteworthy since it represents a nice model for how to go about looking for prescriptive indices. If replicated, its findings could serve as a basis for matching patients to treatments. Moreover, it suggests once again that perceived similarity of problem and intervention is a treacherous basis for matching patients to treatments (Rude & Rehm, 1991). Patients with problems with avoidance might have been expected to do better in interpersonal psychotherapy, with its focus on relationships and the exploration of affect, whereas patients with an obsessive style might have been expected to prefer cognitive therapy, with its emphasis on using a rational approach to problem resolution. Contrary to expectations, each type of patient did better in the kind of treatment that seemed more poorly matched to their particular personality style. This is reminiscent of earlier findings from the TDCRP that suggested that patients with greater evidence of cognitive distortions did less well in cognitive therapy and that patients with greater interpersonal problems did less well in interpersonal psychotherapy (Sotsky et al., 1991). Whether this pattern will replicate in other studies remains to be seen, but it does suggest once again why it is so important to subject clinical lore to empirical scrutiny.

There is a long-standing notion that depression is related to two different sets of personality styles, sometimes labeled "sociotropy versus autonomy" (Beck, 1983) or "social dependency versus self-criticism" (Blatt, Quinlan, Chevron, McDonald, & Zuroff, 1982). *Sociotropy* (or social dependence) refers to an investment in positive interaction with others and is marked by a passive style and a strong desire to be loved and cared for by other people. *Autonomy* (or self-criticism) refers to an investment in preserving one's independence and a sense of competence and is marked by an active style in which the individual seeks to attain meaningful goals. People who are highly sociotropic are presumed to be placed at risk for depression when they suffer loss in the interpersonal domain and to exhibit clinical features like grief and loneliness. Conversely, people who are highly autonomous are presumed to be placed at risk when they are thwarted in the achievement domain and to respond with a sense of pessimism and withdrawal. In terms of clinical theory, people who are sociotropic are likely to have underlying core beliefs regarding unlovability, whereas people who are autonomous are likely to have core beliefs regarding incompetence (J. Beck, 1995).

There is evidence to support the notion of differential risk (Hammen, Ellicott, Gitlin, & Jamison, 1989) and differential expression (Robins & Luten, 1991). People with sociotropic styles are more likely to become grief-stricken and turn to others when they encounter interpersonal loss, and people with autonomous styles are more likely to become pessimistic and withdraw when their achievement goals are frustrated. Moreover, sociotropy has been linked to reactive or atypical depression, which tends to be more common in women, whereas autonomy has been linked to endogenous depression, which tends to be more common in men (Peselow, Robins, Sanfilipo, Block, & Fieve, 1992). Whether these personality distinctions account for more (or a different portion) of the variance in treatment response than gender or subtype remains to be seen, but they clearly play an important role in guiding the actual practice of cognitive therapy.

DOES COGNITIVE THERAPY HAVE AN ENDURING EFFECT?

There is evidence that cognitive therapy may have an enduring effect that reduces subsequent risk for relapse or recurrence following successful treatment (Hollon, Shelton, & Loosen, 1991). *Relapse* is defined as the return of symptoms associated with the treated episode, while *recurrence* describes the onset of a wholly new episode (Frank et al., 1991). Similarly, *remission* is defined as the point at which symptoms first go away, whereas *recovery* is defined as the point at which the underlying episode has actually run its course. By convention, patients are believed to be at increased risk for symptoms returning (relapse) between the time they first get better (remit) and the time it takes for the underlying episode to run its course (recover). Following that point (typically presumed to occur about 6–9 months following remission), any renewed symptoms are presumed to reflect the onset of a wholly new episode (recurrence).

~ Several studies have shown that patients treated to remission with cognitive therapy are less likely to relapse following treatment termination than patients treated to remission with medications (Blackburn, Eunson, & Bishop, 1986; Evans et al., 1992; Kovacs et al., 1981; Simons, Murphy, Levine, & Wetzel, 1986). In these studies, the amount of protection afforded by prior exposure to cognitive therapy is about as great as that afforded by keeping patients on medications in the drug continuation literature (Prien & Kupfer, 1986). In fact, the one study that included a continuation medication condition found that prior exposure to cognitive therapy was at least as effective in preventing subsequent relapse (Evans et al., 1992). This is a finding that we appear to have replicated in our recent collaboration with the University of Pennsylvania. In that more recent trial, patients treated to remission with cognitive therapy were no more likely to relapse following treatment termination than patients continued on medications, with relapse rates considerably lower for both groups than for patients withdrawn onto pill-placebo. To date, the only study that did not find evidence of an enduring effect for cognitive therapy was the NIMH TDCRP, and such differences as were apparent did favor prior cognitive therapy (Shea et al., 1992).

Klein (1996) has argued that these findings could be an artifact of differential attrition. If high-risk patients are more likely to need medication and low-risk patients are less able to tolerate side effects, then acute treatment could act like a "differential sieve" that leads to a disproportionate number of high-risk patients among the medication responders. However, a recent trial suggests that this effect may be more than just an artifact. In that study, Paykel and colleagues provided a brief course of cognitive therapy to patients who had not fully remitted on medications (Paykel et al., 1999). The addition of cognitive therapy reduced both residual symptoms and risk for subsequent relapse relative to continuation medications alone. The fact that medications were continued throughout makes it less likely that the enduring effect associated with cognitive therapy was just an artifact of differential attrition.

Although the research described above indicates a possible effect for cognitive therapy in preventing relapse back into symptoms after remission, prevention of relapse is not necessarily the same thing as prevention of recurrence. Patients treated to remission with medications are about three times more likely to have symptoms return if the medications are withdrawn within 6–12 months of remission (the expected life of the untreated episode) then if they are continued to the point of recovery (Hollon, Evans, & DeRubeis, 1990). Thus, to assess the impact of therapy on recurrence, studies have to follow patients past the point of recovery. With the possible exception of the study by Paykel and colleagues just described, only one study suggesting an enduring effect for cognitive therapy has kept patients on medications long enough to see if that effect extends to the prevention of recurrence. In that study, Fava and colleagues first treated a sample of patients with recurrent depression to remission with medications (Fava, Rafanelli, Grandi, Conti, & Belluardo, 1998). All patients were then kept on medications during an extended continuation phase, with cognitive therapy added for half. Once patients had met criteria for recovery, they were withdrawn from all treatment (drugs and cognitive therapy) and followed over a subsequent 36-month interval to monitor the onset of new episodes (recurrence). Exposure to cognitive therapy not only reduced residual symptoms during the continuation phase, it also reduced risk for recurrence following treatment termination.

Thus, there is evidence that cognitive therapy not only has an enduring effect, but that this effect may well extend to the prevention of recurrence. Moreover, this effect is robust regardless of whether cognitive therapy is provided alone or in combination with medications, and whether it is introduced while the patient is still acutely symptomatic or after drugs have been used to reduce acute distress. There are even indications that cognitive therapy can be used to prevent the onset of symptoms of depression and anxiety in people at risk who are not currently depressed (Seligman, Schulman, DeRubeis, & Hollon, 1999).

It is intriguing that the studies suggesting an enduring effect for cognitive therapy have had so little impact on the field (Hollon, 1996). Although these findings are sometimes cited in recent treatment guidelines, that is usually done in a relatively perfunctory way (see, e.g., American Psychiatric Association, 2000, p. 36). Instead, these guidelines typically focus on studies that suggest that extending treatment into the continuation or maintenance phase can prevent relapse or recurrence, respectively (Fava, Grandi, Zielezny, Canestrari, & Morphy, 1994; Fava, Grandi, Zielezny, Rafanelli, & Canestrari, 1996; Jarrett et al., 1998). While these studies are important and deserve to be highlighted, they do not speak directly to the presence of an enduring effect based on learning. Given the growing consensus in the medical community that depression is a chronic recurrent disorder that requires indefinite medication, this omission is conspicuous by its absence (Hollon & Shelton, 2001).

HOW DOES COGNITIVE THERAPY WORK?

It also remains unclear precisely how cognitive therapy produces these effects, but early studies suggest that it may work (at least in part) through processes and mechanisms specified by theory. For example, in a pair of studies, DeRubeis and colleagues have found that the extent to which therapists utilized concrete behavioral and cognitive change strategies in early sessions predicted subsequent change in depression (DeRubeis & Feeley, 1990; Feeley, DeRubeis, & Gelfand, 1999). On the other hand, the quality of the helping alliance (a nonspecific aspect of the therapeutic relationship) was more a consequence than a cause of such change. This suggests that it may not be necessary to wait to build the relationship before trying to produce change; rather, adhering to the model may itself produce change, and that in turn appears to build a sense of trust and collaboration.

Similarly, cognitive theory suggests that disconfirming negative expectations may be the most efficient way of reducing existing distress, but that changing underlying explanatory style or self-concept may be more central to the prevention of future episodes (Abramson, Metalsky, & Alloy, 1989; Hollon & Garber, 1980). Several of the early studies that examined change in beliefs over time found that patients who were treated with drugs alone were just as likely to become more hopeful as patients treated to remission with cognitive therapy. However, the pattern of change in the two modalities appears to be different, in that change in expectations appears to drive change in depression in cognitive therapy, whereas change in depression appears to drive change in expectations in drug treatment (DeRubeis et al., 1990). This suggests that disconfirming negative expectations may play an important role as a causal mediator in cognitive therapy. Taken along with the findings just described regarding treatment process, it further suggests that encouraging the patients to use their own behaviors to test the accuracy of their beliefs may be close to the essence of the approach.

At the same time, our own work suggests that changes in core beliefs and information-processing proclivities may be more central to the prevention of subsequent relapse and recurrence. For example, in an earlier trial, we found that changes in explanatory style were specific to cognitive therapy and predictive of subsequent relapse following treatment termination (Hollon et al., 1990). Whereas change in expectations was nonspecific and occurred earlier in treatment, change in explanatory style occurred only in cognitive therapy and happened later in the course of therapy, well after the bulk of the change in depression. This suggests that change in these underlying proclivities is not necessary for initial symptom reduction, but may be central to the prevention of subsequent symptom return. Similar changes in information-processing proclivities appeared to mediate the preventive effects observed in our study with a nonclinical sample at risk (Seligman et al., 1999). These are the same processes targeted by theory and shown in longitudinal designs to confer risk. The fact that we get differential change (drugs do little to reduce these underlying diatheses) suggests strong convergence across different types of evidence regarding possible mediation. It remains unclear whether patients are changed in some way that redresses underlying vulnerabilities or if they merely develop compensatory skills, but it clear that risk is reduced (Barber & DeRubeis, 1989).

DOES ADDING MEDICATION ENHANCE RESPONSE?

Although widely used in clinical practice, it is not clear that adding drugs necessarily enhances the effects of an effective psychotherapy. There are indications that at least some patients who fail to respond to cognitive therapy will respond to medications (Stewart, Mercier, Agosti, Guardino, & Quitkin, 1993), but, as we have seen, the same can be said for patients who fail to show a complete response to medications (Paykel et al., 1999). Most practice guidelines call for adding either drugs or psychotherapy to the other if symptomatic relief is not achieved within a matter of 6–8 weeks (American Psychiatric Association, 2000; Depression Guideline Panel, 1993). This is a recommendation that we wholly endorse (Hollon & Shelton, 2001).

Several studies have suggested that adding cognitive behavior therapy to standard treatment involving medications tends to enhance response in severely depressed inpatient samples (Bowers, 1990; de Jong-Meyer, Hautzinger, Rudolf, & Strauss, 1996; Miller, Norman, Keitner, Bishop, & Dow, 1989). Conversely, there are indications that combined treatment may be more effective than psychotherapy alone with more severely depressed outpatients, but those data come from a single site and are heavily influenced by findings from the TDCRP (Thase et al., 1997). However, in those studies in which cognitive therapy has performed as well as medications alone combined treatment rarely has exceeded the efficacy of either single modality (Hollon et al., 1991). This is why most practice guidelines recommend that combined treatment be reserved for more complex or comorbid patients or patients who have shown less than full response to either single modality (American Psychiatric Association, 2000; Depression Guideline Panel, 1993).

Nonetheless, combined treatment often shows a modest advantage over either single modality that falls short of statistical significance unless aggregated across multiple trials (Conte, Plutchik, Wild, & Karasu, 1986). Moreover, combined treatment typically retains any advantages associated with either single modality (such as more rapid response for drugs or more enduring change for cognitive therapy) and it also provides a hedge against the possibility that either single modality is less than adequately implemented (Hollon & Fawcett, 1995).

A recent trial by Keller and colleagues is likely to lead to a renewed interest in combined treatment. In that study, the combination of drugs and a novel cognitive-behavioral treatment targeted at interpersonal change was considerably more effective than either single modality alone in a sample of patients with chronic depression (Keller et al., 2000). Drugs worked more rapidly over the first several weeks of treatment, whereas patients started showing greater response to the psychotherapy in the later stages. Patients who received both drugs and psychotherapy showed both rapid early change and subsequent continued improvement such that they achieved an overall response rate considerably greater than that obtained for either single modality.

The specific psychosocial intervention, a cognitive-behavioral analysis system for psychotherapy (CBASP), was designed specifically for working with patients with long-standing affective distress. Those patients are presumed to suffer from arrested emotional development that prevents them from learning from experience (McCullough, 2000). It represents an amalgamation of cognitive, behavioral, and interpersonal strategies designed to motivate chronically depressed persons to change and help them develop needed problem-solving and relationship skills. Although its underlying theoretical rationale is rich and complex, its actual operational procedures are relatively straightforward and concrete; patients are trained to apply a simple algorithm in problematic interpersonal situations to guide their choice of specific behaviors most likely to help them get what they want. It remains to be seen whether this approach will live up to its initial promise, but it has proven to be particularly attractive to therapists trained in more traditional approaches and has already generated considerable enthusiasm in the field.

MORE PURELY BEHAVIORAL INTERVENTIONS

There also exist a number of related interventions that are considered to be more purely behavioral, like problem solving, training in self-control, skills training, and contingency management. Although cognitive and behavioral approaches can be differentiated theoretically, they are often combined in actual clinical practice and a precise taxonomy is sometimes hard to maintain. Certainly, problem-solving therapy and training in self-control have important cognitive elements, as can skills training (depending on how it is done), whereas contingency management is typically conducted in accordance with a more purely behavioral conceptualization. Although they have not been tested as extensively as cognitive therapy, each generally has fared well in controlled trials (American Psychiatric Association, 2000).

For example, problem-solving therapy is predicated on the notion that deficits in coping skills contribute to the onset and maintenance of depression (D'Zurilla & Nezu, 1982). It seeks to teach patients how to define life problems in ways that facilitate finding a solution, and helps them generate and choose between a number of possible alternatives. Problem-solving therapy has been found to be superior to minimal treatment and nonspecific controls in a pair of studies with symptomatic community volunteers (Nezu, 1986; Nezu & Perri, 1989). More recently, investigators in England have found a brief version of problem-solving therapy to be comparable to drugs and superior to placebo in the treatment of depression in a general practice sample (Mynors-Wallis, Gath, Lloyd-Thomas, & Tomlinson, 1995). These studies suggest that problem-solving approaches may have considerable merit, although they typically have been incorporated into larger treatment packages rather than used as the sole means of intervention in their own right.

Self-control therapy involves teaching patients to monitor and evaluate their own actions more positively and to reward themselves when they meet reasonable standards of behavior (Rehm, 1977). Although typically classified as a behavioral intervention because it draws so heavily on reinforcement theory, it clearly contains some cognitive elements in terms of the attention devoted to the standards that patients use for self-evaluation. Self-control therapy has been evaluated in a number of controlled trials, most involving less severely depressed community volunteers. In these studies, it typically has been found to be superior to minimal treatment controls and comparable to other treatment interventions (Fuchs & Rehm, 1977; Kornblith, Rehm, O'Hara, & Lamparski, 1983; Rabin, Kaslow, Rehm, 1984; Rehm, Fuchs, Roth, Kornblith, & Romano, 1979; Rehm, Kornblith, O'Hara, Lamparski, Romano, & Volkin, 1981; Rude, 1986). Studies in fully clinical populations have been few, but generally supportive. For example, Roth and colleagues found that adding drugs did little to enhance the efficacy of self-control therapy alone in an outpatient sample (Roth, Bielski, Jones, Parker, & Osborn, 1982). Similarly, van den Hout and colleagues found that the addition of self-control therapy enhanced response relative to usual care in a day-treatment sample (van den Hout, Arntz, & Kunkels, 1995).

More purely behavioral interventions based on operant theory typically also have done well in controlled trials, although once again they have not been extensively tested. Hersen and colleagues found no differences between social skills training (combined with either drugs or pill-placebo) versus drugs alone or a brief dynamic psychotherapy in a sample of depressed female outpatients (Hersen, Bellack, Himmelhoch, & Thase, 1984). McLean and Hakstian (1979) found a modest advantage for a behavioral intervention based on contingency management relative to either medications alone or a brief dynamic psychotherapy in the treatment of depressed outpatients. O'Leary and Beach (1990) found that behavioral marital therapy was as effective as cognitive therapy and superior to a wait-list control with respect to the treatment of depression in couples with marital distress. Similarly, Jacobson and colleagues found that behavioral marital therapy was as effective as cognitive therapy in reducing depression for women with marital distress, but less effective than cognitive therapy for women without such marital problems (Jacobson, Dobson, Fruzetti, Schmaling, & Salusky, 1991).

This latter work has led to a line of research that may prove to revitalize interest in more purely behavioral interventions. Work in this area had stagnated somewhat before publication of a recent component analysis by Jacobson and colleagues, in which the behavioral activation component of cognitive therapy produced as much change as the full treatment package (Jacobson et al., 1996). Moreover, there were no differences in subsequent rates of relapse following treatment termination (Gortner, Gollan, Dobson, & Jacobson, 1998). These findings were so unexpected that Jacobson and colleagues developed a more comprehensive version of the approach based on a contextual analysis (Jacobson, Martell, & Dimidjian, 2001). This approach largely ignores the role of thinking in the service of focusing on specific behaviors and their consequences in problematic situations (which are often interpersonal in nature). In particular, patients are encouraged to act proactively instead of engaging in avoidance behaviors. This is a strategy that is similar in many respects to the one that forms the core of the cognitive-behavioral analysis system for psychotherapy (CBASP) that was previously described (McCullough, 2000). Jacobson's approach is currently being compared to both drugs and cognitive therapy in a placebo-controlled trial designed to evaluate both acute response and subsequent relapse prevention. Although this trial is still in progress, initial findings look quite promising. Behavioral activation is considerably easier to apply and lends itself more readily to dissemination than either cognitive therapy or more traditional psychotherapeutic approaches. If these early findings hold, it may go a long way to reviving interest in more purely behavioral interventions (Hollon, 2000).

FUTURE DIRECTIONS

Despite all that has been learned in recent years, there is clearly much that we still need to know. Although the cognitive-behavioral interventions are clearly effective in the treatment of depression, it is still not clear precisely which patients respond best to which interventions. There are recurring suggestions that certain types of patients may do better on medications and that the same may prove true for other types of psychosocial treatments. However, these "indications" are hard to pin down and sometimes seem more firmly entrenched in clinical lore than they are in the empirical data. Nonetheless, it is easier to determine whether something works on average than it is to determine the best treatment for a particular type of patient. Clearly, more work needs to be done in this regard.

Even more critically, it remains to be seen whether the enduring effect produced by cognitive therapy extends to the prevention of recurrence. That cognitive therapy has an enduring effect seems to be clear, but this effect would be more interesting theoretically and more important pragmatically if it worked to prevent the onset of wholly new episodes. As effective as medications are (and they *are* remarkably safe and effective), there is no evidence that they do anything to reduce subsequent risk once their use is discontinued (Hollon, 1996). Because depression tends to be a chronic episodic disorder, any treatment that can reduce subsequent risk would be a real boon to the field, both in terms of the reduction of human misery and the savings in costs to society. Clearly, more work is needed to determine whether cognitive-behavioral interventions really reduce risk for subsequent episodes (recurrence).

Closely related is the notion of primary prevention. Not only do the cognitive-behavioral interventions appear to have an enduring effect, there also is reason to believe that they may have a preventive effect in persons at risk who have yet to have their first episode. Throughout the history of medical science, the major advances in terms of public health have occurred more as a consequence of prevention than of treatment and it appears that we stand on the verge of being able to prevent the initial occurrence of depression (Hollon, DeRubeis, & Seligman, 1992). Much of this work will need to take place outside of traditional service delivery settings, most likely in schools and in general practice settings. Nonetheless, it is clear that the technology already exists to both detect persons at risk and to provide them with strategies and tools that can protect them against subsequent risk (Gillham et al., 2000).

Much of this progress has occurred in conjunction with a growing understanding of the basic processes that underlie the nature and expression of depression. Depression is a disorder that is clearly affected by biological, psychological, and sociological factors and important advances in treatment both draw upon and feed back to advances in basic research (Muñoz, Hollon, McGrath, Rehm, & Vandenbos, 1994). The cognitive-behavioral interventions in particular have benefited from advances in understanding of basic cognitive processes and our growing understanding of information processing (Hollon & Garber, 1990). The development of interpersonal psychotherapy clearly has been informed by advances in basic attachment theory, and the development of new drug therapies clearly has benefited from and contributed to the growth in knowledge about the basic neurological processes underlying affective distress (Shelton, Hollon, Purdon, & Loosen, 1991). The direct links between basic and applied research rarely are clear, but they are there and they are important.

In this regard, there are several questions that seem particularly important. For example, depression often involves disruptions in social bonds, yet drugs and cognitive-behavior therapy are among its most effective interventions (along with interpersonal psychotherapy). Similarly, biological processes often trigger affective distress and both genes and environmental events appear to confer risk for subsequent distress. Maladaptive beliefs and attitudes appear to be acquired through either route and further amplify risk for those who are so predisposed. Nonetheless, we still have little clear understanding how these various processes relate to one another or exactly how our treatments work when they do indeed work. The brain is an organ designed to mediate interaction with the environment and there is reason to think that it should be capable of responding to external contingencies within the constraints set by biology. Clearly, more needs to be done to explore the ways in which cognitive and interpersonal processes interface with basic biology in determining the nature and expression of depression.

CONCLUSIONS

The cognitive-behavioral interventions are clearly effective in the treatment of depression and may have enduring effects that prevent subsequent risk. They appear to work by teaching patients to identify and test their negative beliefs and information-processing strategies, and may provide a set of strategies that patients can use to relieve their own distress. It remains unclear exactly who best benefits from these approaches, although work in this regard is underway, but it does appear that they can be extended to patients with more severe and chronic depressions.

Recent studies further suggest that simpler and more concrete behavioral interventions may prove to be effective with many patients with affective distress, including those with chronic depression. To the extent that this is true, it may facilitate the dissemination of these approaches to the clinical practice community, which is increasingly coming to rely on less extensively trained practitioners and shorter treatment intervals. Combined with indications that the cognitive-behavioral interventions may have enduring effects that can be used to prevent the onset of both initial and subsequent episodes, these findings should create real enthusiasm for these approaches in the field.

ACKNOWLEDGMENTS

Preparation of this chapter was supported by a research grant from the National Institute of Mental Health (No. MH55875) to Steven D. Hollon, as well as by an independent scientist award (No. K02-MH01697).

REFERENCES

Abramson, L. Y., Metalsky, G. I., & Alloy, L. B. (1989). Hopelessness depression: A theory-based subtype of depression. A metatheoretical analysis with implications for psychopathology research. *Psychological Review, 96,* 358–372.

Alford, B. A., & Beck, A. T. (1997). *The integrative power of cognitive therapy*. New York: Guilford Press.

American Psychiatric Association. (2000). Practice guideline for the treatment of patients with major depressive disorder (revision). *American Journal of Psychiatry, 157* (Suppl. 4), 1–45.

Barber, J. P., & DeRubeis, R. J. (1989). On second thought: Where the action is in cognitive therapy for depression. *Cognitive Therapy and Research, 13,* 441–457.

Barber, J. P., & Muenz, L. R. (1996). The role of avoidance and obsessiveness in matching patients to cognitive and interpersonal psychotherapy: Empirical findings from the Treatment for Depression Collaborative Research Program. *Journal of Consulting and Clinical Psychology, 64,* 951–958.

Beck, A. T. (1983). Cognitive therapy of depression: New perspectives. In P. J. Clayton & J. E. Barrett (Eds.), *Treatment of depression: Old controversies and new approaches* (pp. 265–290). New York: Raven Press.

Beck, A. T. (1991). Cognitive therapy: A 30-year retrospective. *American Psychologist, 46,* 368–375.

Beck, A. T., Freeman, A., & Associates (1990). *Cognitive therapy of personality disorders*. New York: Guilford Press.

Beck, A. T., Rush, A. J., Shaw, B. F., & Emery, G. (1979). *Cognitive therapy of depression*. New York: Guilford Press.

Beck, J. (1995). *Cognitive therapy: Basics and beyond*. New York: Guilford Press.

Blackburn, I. M., Bishop, S., Glen, A. I. M., Whalley, L. J., & Christie, J. E. (1981). The efficacy of cognitive therapy in depression: A treatment trial using cognitive therapy and pharmacotherapy, each alone and in combination. *British Journal of Psychiatry, 139,* 181–189.

Blackburn, I. M., Eunson, K. M., & Bishop, S. (1986). A two-year naturalistic follow-up of depressed patients treated with cognitive therapy, pharmacotherapy and a combination of both. *Journal of Affective Disorders, 10,* 67–75.

Blackburn, I. M., & Moore, R. G. (1997). Controlled acute and follow-up trial of cognitive therapy and pharmacotherapy in outpatients with recurrent depression. *British Journal of Psychiatry, 171,* 328–334.

Blatt, S. J., Quinlan, D. M., Chevron, E. S., McDonald, C., & Zuroff, D. (1982). Dependency and self-criticism: Psychological dimensions of depression. *Journal of Consulting and Clinical Psychology, 50,* 123–124.

Bowers, W. A. (1990). Treatment of depressed in-patients: Cognitive therapy plus medication, relaxation plus medication, and medication alone. *British Journal of Psychiatry, 156,* 73–78.

Clark, D. A., & Beck, A. T., with Alford, B. A. (1999). *Cognitive theory and therapy of depression*. New York: Wiley.

Conte, H. R., Plutchik, R., Wild, K. V., & Karasu, T. B. (1986). Combined psychotherapy and pharmacotherapy for depression. *Archives of General Psychiatry, 43,* 471–479.

Corbishley, M., Beutler, L., Quan, S., Bamford, C., Meredith, K., & Scogin, F. (1990). Rapid eye movement density and latency and dexamethasone suppression as predictors of treatment response in depressed older adults. *Current Therapeutic Research, 47,* 846–859.

de Jong-Meyer, R., Hautzinger, M., Rudolf, G. A., & Strauss, W. (1996). The effectiveness of antidepressants and cognitive behaviour therapy in patients with endogenous depression: Results of analyses of variance on main and secondary outcome measures [in German]. *Zeitschrift fur Klinische Psychologie. Forschung und Praxis, 25,* 93–109.

Depression Guideline Panel. (1993). *Depression in primary care: Vol. 2. Treatment of major depression* (Clinical Practice Guideline No. 5, AHCPR Publication No. 93-0551). Rockville, MD: Department of Health and Human Services, Public Health Service, Agency for Health Care Policy and Research.

DeRubeis, R. J., & Crits-Christoph, P. (1998). Empirically supported individual and group psychological treatments for adult mental disorders. *Journal of Consulting and Clinical Psychology, 66,* 37–52.

DeRubeis, R. J., Evans, M. D., Hollon, S. D., Garvey, M. J., Grove, W. M., & Tuason, V. B. (1990). How does cognitive therapy work? Cognitive change and symptom change in cognitive therapy and pharmacotherapy for depression. *Journal of Consulting and Clinical Psychology, 58,* 862–869.

DeRubeis, R. J., & Feeley, M. (1990). Determinants of change in cognitive therapy for depression. *Cognitive Therapy and Research, 14,* 469–482.

DeRubeis, R. J., Gelfand, L. A., Tang, T. Z., & Simons, A. D. (1999). Medication versus cognitive behavior therapy for severely depressed outpatients: Mega-analysis of four randomized comparisons. *American Journal of Psychiatry, 156,* 1007–1013.

D'Zurilla, T. J., & Nezu, A. (1982). Social problem solving in adults. In P. C. Kendall (Ed.), *Advances in cognitive-behavioral research and therapy* (Vol. 1, pp. 202–274). New York: Academic Press.

Elkin, I., Gibbons, R. D., Shea, T., Sotsky, S. M., Watkins, J. T., Pilkonis, P. A., & Hedeker, D. (1995). Initial severity and differential treatment outcome in the National Institute of Mental Health Treatment of Depression Collaborative Research Program. *Journal of Consulting and Clinical Psychology, 63,* 841–847.

Elkin, I., Shea, M. T., Watkins, J. T., Imber, S. D., Sotsky, S. M., Collins, J. F., Glass, D. R., Pilkonis, P. A., Leber, W. R., Docherty, J. P., Fiester, S. J., & Parloff, M. B. (1989). National Institute of Mental Health Treatment of Depression Collaborative Research Program: General effectiveness of treatments. *Archives of General Psychiatry, 46,* 971–982.

Evans, M. D., Hollon, S. D., DeRubeis, R. J., Piasecki, J., Grove, W. M., Garvey, M. J., & Tuason, V. B. (1992). Differential relapse following cognitive therapy and pharmacotherapy for depression. *Archives of General Psychiatry, 49,* 802–808.

Fava, G. A., Grandi, S., Zielezny, M., Canestrari, R., & Morphy, M. A. (1994). Cognitive behavioral treatment of residual symptoms in primary major depressive disorder. *American Journal of Psychiatry, 151,* 1295–1299.

Fava, G. A., Grandi, S., Zielezny, M., Rafanelli, C., & Canestrari, R. (1996). Four-year outcome for cognitive behavioral treatment of residual symptoms in major depression. *American Journal of Psychiatry, 153,* 945–947.

Fava, G. A., Rafanelli, C., Grandi, S., Conti, S., & Belluardo, P. (1998). Prevention of recurrent depression with cognitive behavioral therapy. *Archives of General Psychiatry, 55,* 816–820.

Feeley, M., DeRubeis, R. J., & Gelfand, L. A. (1999). The temporal relation of adherence and alliance to symptom change in cognitive therapy for depression. *Journal of Consulting and Clinical Psychology, 67,* 578–582.

Frank, E., Prien, R. F., Jarrett, R. B., Keller, M. B., Kupfer, D. J., Lavori, P. W., Rush, A. J., & Weissman, M. M. (1991). Conceptualization and rationale for consensus definitions of terms in major depressive disorder: Remission, recovery, relapse, and recurrence. *Archives of General Psychiatry, 48,* 851–855.

Fuchs, C. Z., & Rehm, L. P. (1977). A self-control behavior therapy program for depression. *Journal of Consulting and Clinical Psychology, 45,* 206–215.

Gaffan, E. A., Tsaousis, I., & Kemp-Wheeler, S. M. (1995). Researcher alliance and meta-analysis: The case of cognitive therapy for depression. *Journal of Consulting and Clinical Psychology, 63,* 966–980.

Gillham, J. E., Shatte, A. J., & Freres, D. R. (2000). Preventing depression: A review of cognitive-behavioral and family interventions. *Applied and Preventive Psychology, 9,* 63–88.

Gortner, E. T., Gollan, J. K., Dobson, K. S., & Jacobson, N. S. (1998). Cognitive-behavioral treatment for depression: Relapse prevention. *Journal of Consulting and Clinical Psychology, 66,* 377–384.

Hammen, C., Ellicott, A., Gitlin, M., & Jamison, K. R. (1989). Sociotropy/autonomy and vulnerability to specific life events in patients with unipolar depression and bipolar disorders. *Journal of Abnormal Psychology, 98,* 154–160.

Hardy, G. E., Barkham, M., Shapiro, D. A., Stiles, W. B., Rees, A., & Reynolds, S. (1995). Impact of Cluster C personality disorders on outcomes of contrasting brief psychotherapies for depression. *Journal of Consulting and Clinical Psychology, 63,* 997–1004.

Hautzinger, M., de Jong-Meyer, R., Treiber, R., & Rudolf, G. A. (1996). The efficacy of cognitive behaviour therapy and pharmacotherapy, alone or in combination, in nonendogenous unipolar depression [in German]. *Zeitschrift fur Klinische Psychologie. Forschung und Praxis, 25,* 130–145.

Hersen, M., Bellack, A. S., Himmelhoch, J. M., & Thase, M. E. (1984). Effects of social skill training, amitriptyline, and psychotherapy in unipolar depressed women. *Behavior Therapy, 15,* 21–40.

Hollon, S. D. (1996). The efficacy and effectiveness of psychotherapy relative to medications. *American Psychologist, 51,* 1025–1030.

Hollon, S. D. (2000). Do cognitive change strategies matter in cognitive therapy? *Prevention and Treatment, 3,* Article 25. Available on the World Wide Web at: http:// journals. apa. org/prevention/volume3/pre0030025c. html

Hollon, S. D., & Beck, A. T. (1994). Cognitive and cognitive-behavioral therapies. In A. E. Bergin & S. L. Garfield (Eds.), *Handbook of psychotherapy and behavior change* (4th ed., pp. 428–466). New York: Wiley.

Hollon, S. D., DeRubeis, R. J., Evans, M. D., Wiemer, M. J., Garvey, M. J., Grove, W. M., & Tuason, V. B. (1992). Cognitive therapy and pharmacotherapy for depression: Singly and in combination. *Archives of General Psychiatry, 49,* 774–781.

Hollon, S. D., DeRubeis, R. J., & Seligman, M. E. P. (1992). Cognitive therapy and the prevention of depression. *Applied and Preventive Psychology, 1,* 89–95.

Hollon, S. D., Evans, M. D., & DeRubeis, R. J. (1990). Cognitive mediation of relapse prevention following treatment for depression: Implications of differential risk. In R. E. Ingram (Ed.), *Psychological aspects of depression* (pp. 114–136). New York: Plenum Press.

Hollon, S. D., & Fawcett, J. (1995). Combined medication and psychotherapy. In G. O. Gabbard (Ed.), *Treatments of psychiatric disorders* (2nd ed., pp. 1221–1236). Washington, DC: American Psychiatric Press.

Hollon, S. D., & Garber, J. (1980). A cognitive-expectancy theory of therapy helplessness and depression. In J. Garber & M. E. P. Seligman (Eds.), *Human helplessness: Theory and applications* (pp. 173–195). New York: Academic Press.

Hollon, S. D., & Garber, J. (1990). Cognitive therapy of depression: A social–cognitive perspective. *Personality and Social Psychology Bulletin, 16,* 58–73.

Hollon, S. D., & Shelton, R. C. (2001). Treatment guidelines for major depressive disorder. *Behavior Therapy, 32,* 235–258.

Hollon, S. D., Shelton, R. C., & Loosen, P. T. (1991). Cognitive therapy versus pharmacotherapy for depression. *Journal of Consulting and Clinical Psychology, 59,* 88–99.

Jacobson, N. S., Dobson, K., Fruzzetti, A. E., Schmaling, K. B., & Salusky, S. (1991). Marital therapy as a treatment for depression. *Journal of Consulting and Clinical Psychology, 59,* 547–557.

Jacobson, N. S., Dobson, K. S., Truax, P. A., Addis, M. E., Koerner, K., Gollan, J. K., Gortner, E., & Prince, S. E. (1996). A component analysis of cognitive-behavior treatment for depression. *Journal of Consulting and Clinical Psychology, 64,* 295–304.

Jacobson, N. S., & Hollon, S. D. (1996a). Cognitive-behavior therapy versus pharmacotherapy: Now that the jury's returned its verdict, its time to present the rest of the evidence. *Journal of Consulting and Clinical Psychology, 64,* 74–80.

Jacobson, N. S., & Hollon, S. D. (1996b). Prospects for future comparisons between drugs and psychotherapy: Lessons from the CBT-versus-pharmacotherapy exchange. *Journal of Consulting and Clinical Psychology, 64,* 104–108.

Jacobson, N. S., Martell, C., & Dimidjian, S. (2001). Behavioral activation treatment for depression: Returning to contextual roots. *Clinical Psychology: Science and practice, 8,* 255–270.

Jarrett, R. B., Basco, M. R., Riser, R., Ramanan, J., Marwill, M., & Rush, A. J. (1998). Is there a role for continuation phase cognitive therapy for depressed outpatients? *Journal of Consulting and Clinical Psychology, 66,* 1036–1040.

Jarrett, R. B., Schaffer, M., McIntire, D., Witt-Browder, A., Kraft, D., & Risser, R. C. (1999). Treatment of atypical depression with cognitive therapy or phenelzine: A double-blind, placebo-controlled trial. *Archives of General Psychiatry, 56,* 431–437.

Keller, M. B., McCullough, J. P., Klein, D. N., Arnow, B., Dunner, D. L., Gelenberg, A. J., Markowitz, J. C., Nemeroff, C. B., Russell, J. M., Thase, M. E., Trivedi, M. H., & Zajecka, J. (2000). A comparison of nefazodone, the cognitive behavioral-analysis system of psychotherapy, and their combination for the treatment of chronic depression. *New England Journal of Medicine, 342,* 1462–1470.

Klein, D. F. (1996). Preventing hung juries about therapy studies. *Journal of Consulting and Clinical Psychology, 64,* 81–87.

Kornblith, S. J., Rehm, L. P., O'Hara, M. W., & Lamparski, D. M. (1983). The contribution of self-reinforcement training and behavioral assignments to the efficacy of self-control therapy for depression. *Cognitive Therapy and Research, 7,* 499–527.

Kornstein, S. G., Schatzberg, A. F., Thase, M. E., Yonkers, K. A., McCullough, J. P., Keitner, G. I., Gelenberg, A. J., Davis, S. M., Harrison, W. M., & Keller, M. B. (2000). Gender differences in treatment response to sertraline versus imipramine in chronic depression. *American Journal of Psychiatry, 157,* 1445–1452.

Kovacs, M., Rush, A. J., Beck, A. T., & Hollon, S. D. (1981). Depressed outpatients treated with cognitive therapy or pharmacotherapy. *Archives of General Psychiatry, 38,* 33–39.

McCullough, J. P. (2000). *Treatment for chronic depression: Cognitive behavioral analysis system for psychotherapy (CBASP).* New York: Guilford Press.

McKnight, D. L., Nelson-Gray, R. O., & Barnhill, J. (1992). Dexamethasone suppression test and response to cognitive therapy and antidepressant medication. *Behavior Therapy, 23,* 99–111.

McLean, P. D., & Hakstian, A. R. (1979). Clinical depression: Comparative efficacy of outpatient treatments. *Journal of Consulting and Clinical Psychology , 47,* 818–836.

Meterissian, G. B., & Bradwejn, J. (1989). Comparative studies on the efficacy of psychotherapy, pharmacotherapy, and their combination in depression: Was adequate pharmacotherapy provided? *Journal of Clinical Psychopharmacology, 9,* 334–339.

Miller, I. W., Norman, W. H., Keitner, G. I., Bishop, S., & Dow, M. G. (1989). Cognitive-behavioural treatment of depressed inpatients. *Behavior Therapy, 20,* 25–47.

Muñoz, R. F., Hollon, S. D., McGrath, E., Rehm, L. P., & Vandenbos, G. R. (1994). On the AHCPR Depression in Primary Care Guidelines: Further considerations for practioners. *American Psychologist, 49,* 42–61.

Murphy, G. E., Simons, A. D., Wetzel, R. D., & Lustman, P. J. (1984). Cognitive therapy and pharmacotherapy, singly and together, in the treatment of depression. *Archives of General Psychiatry, 41,* 33–41.

Mynors-Wallis, L. M., Gath, D. H., Lloyd-Thomas, A. R., & Tomlinson, D. (1995). Randomised controlled trial comparing problem solving treatment with amitriptyline and placebo for major depression in primary care. *British Medical Journal, 310,* 441–445.

Nezu, A. M. (1986). Efficacy of a social problem-solving therapy approach for unipolar depression. *Journal of Consulting and Clinical Psychology, 54,* 196–202.

Nezu, A. M., & Perri, M. G. (1989). Social problem-solving therapy for unipolar depression: An initial dismantling investigation. *Journal of Consulting and Clinical Psychology, 57,* 408–413.

O'Leary, K. D., & Beach, S. R. H. (1990). Marital therapy: A viable treatment for depression and marital discord. *American Journal of Psychiatry, 147,* 183–186.

Patience, D. A., McGuire, R. J., Scott, A. J., & Freeman, C. P. (1995). The Edinburgh Primary Care Depression Study: Personality disorders and outcome. *British Journal of Psychiatry, 167,* 324–330.

Paykel, E. S., Scott, J., Teasdale, J. D., Johnson, A. L., Garland, A., Moore, R., Jenaway, A., Cornwall, P. L., Hayhurst, H., Abbott, R., & Pope, M. (1999). Prevention of relapse in residual depression by cognitive therapy. *Archives of General Psychiatry, 56,* 829–835.

Peselow, E. D., Robins, C. J., Sanfilipo, M. P., Block, P., & Fieve, R. R. (1992). Sociotropy and autonomy: Relationship to antidepressant drug treatment response and endogenous–nonendogenous dichotomy. *Journal of Abnormal Psychology, 101,* 479–486.

Prien, R. F., & Kupfer, D. J. (1986). Continuation drug therapy for major depressive episodes: How long should it be maintained? *American Journal of Psychiatry, 143,* 18–23.

Rabin, A. S., Kaslow, N. J., & Rehm, L. P. (1984). Changes in symptoms of depression during course of therapy. *Cognitive Therapy and Research, 8,* 479–488.

Rehm, L. P. (1977). A self-control model of depression. *Behavior Therapy, 8,* 787–804.

Rehm, L. P., Fuchs, C. Z., Roth, D. M., Kornblith, S. J., & Romano, J. M. (1979). A comparison of self-control and assertion skills treatments of depression. *Behavior Therapy, 10,* 429–442.

Rehm, L. P., Kornblith, S. J., O'Hara, M. W., Lamparski, D. M., Romano, J. M., & Volkin, J. (1981). An evaluation of major components in a self-control behavior therapy program for depression. *Behavior Modification, 5,* 459–490.

Robins, C. J., & Luten, A. G. (1991). Sociotropy and autonomy: Differential patterns of clinical presentation in unipolar depression. *Journal of Abnormal Psychology, 100,* 74–77.

Roth, D., Bielshi, R., Jones, M., Parker, W., & Osborn, G. (1982). A comparison of self-control therapy and combined self-control therapy and antidepressant medication in the treatment of depression. *Behavior Therapy, 13,* 133–144.

Rude, S. S. (1986). Relative benefits of assertion or cognitive self-control treatment for depression as a function of proficiency in each domain. *Journal of Consulting and Clinical Psychology, 54,* 390–394.

Rude, S. S., & Rehm, L. P. (1991). Response to treatments for depression: The role of initial status on targeted cognitive and behavioral skills. *Clinical Psychology Review, 11,* 493–514.

Rush, A. J., Beck, A. T., Kovacs, M., & Hollon, S. D. (1977). Comparative efficacy of cognitive therapy and pharmacotherapy in the treatment of depressed outpatients. *Cognitive Therapy and Research, 1,* 17–38.

Seligman, M. E. P., Schulman, P., DeRubeis, R. J., & Hollon, S. D. (1999). Primary prevention of depression and anxiety with cognitive therapy. *Prevention and Treatment, 2,* Article 8. Available on the World Wide Web at: http://journals. apa. org/prevention/volume2/pre002008a. html

Shea, M. T., Elkin, I., Imber, S. D., Sotsky, S. M., Watkins, J. T., Collins, J. F., Pilkonis, P. A., Beckham, E., Glass, D. R., Dolan, R. T., & Parloff, M. B. (1992). Course of depressive symptoms over follow-up: Findings from the National Institute of Mental Health Treatment of Depression Collaborative Research Program. *Archives of General Psychiatry, 49,* 782–787.

Shea, M. T., Pilkonis, P. A., Beckham, E., Collins, J. F., Elkin, I., Sotsky, S. M., & Docherty, J. P. (1990). Personality disorders and treatment outcome in the NIMH Treatment of Depression Collaborative Research Program. *American Journal of Psychiatry, 147,* 711–718.

Shelton, R. C., Hollon, S. D., Purdon, S. E., & Loosen, P. T. (1991). Biological and psychological aspects of depression. *Behavior Therapy, 22,* 201–228.

Simons, A. D., Murphy, G. E., Levine, J. E., & Wetzel, R. D. (1986). Cognitive therapy and pharmacotherapy for depression: Sustained improvement over one year. *Archives of General Psychiatry, 43,* 43–49.

Smith, B., & Sechrest, L. (1991). Treatment of aptitude × treatment interactions. *Journal of Consulting and Clinical Psychology, 59,* 233–244.

Sotsky, S. M., Glass, D. R., Shea, M. T., Pilkonis, P. A., Collins, J. F., Elkin, I., Watkins, J. T., Imber, S. D., Leber, W. R., Moyer, J., & Oliveri, M. E. (1991). Patient predictors of response to psychotherapy and pharmacotherapy: Findings in the NIMH Treatment of Depression Collaborative Research Program. *American Journal of Psychiatry, 148,* 997–1008.

Stewart, J. W., Mercier, M. A., Agosti, V., Guardino, M., & Quitkin, F. M. (1993). Imipramine is effective after unsuccessful cognitive therapy: Sequential use of cognitive therapy and imipramine in depressed outpatients. *Journal of Clinical Psychopharmacology, 13,* 114–119.

Svartberg, M., & Stiles, T. C. (1991). Comparative effects of short-term psychodynamic psychotherapy: A meta-analysis. *Journal of Consulting and Clinical Psychology, 59,* 704–714.

Thase, M. E., Bowler, K., & Harden, T. (1991). Cognitive behavior therapy of endogenous depression: Part 2. Preliminary findings in 16 unmedicated inpatients. *Behavior Therapy, 22,* 469–477.

Thase, M. E., Dube, S., Bowler, K., Howland, R. H., Myers, J. E., Friedman, E., & Jarrett, D. B. (1996). Hypothalamic–pituitary–adrenocortical activity and response to cognitive behavior therapy in unmedicated, hospitalized depressed patients. *American Journal of Psychiatry, 153,* 886–891.

Thase, M. E., Frank, E., Kornstein, S., & Yonkers, K. A. (2000). Gender differences in response to treatments of depression. In E. Frank (Ed.), *Gender and Its Effects on Psychopathology* (pp. 103–129). Washington, DC: American Psychiatric Press.

Thase, M. E., Greenhouse, J. B., Frank, E., Reynolds, C. F., Pilkonis, P. A., Hurley, K., Grochocinski, V., & Kupfer, D. J. (1997). Treatment of major depression with psychotherapy–pharmacotherapy combinations. *Archives of General Psychiatry, 54,* 1009–1015.

Thase, M. E., Reynolds, C. F., Frank, E., Simons, A. D., McGeary, J., Fasiczka, A. L., Garamoni, G. G., Jennings, J. R., & Kupfer, D. J. (1994). Do depressed men and women respond similarly to cognitive behavior therapy? *American Journal of Psychiatry, 151,* 500–505.

Thase, M. E., Simons, A. D., & Reynolds, C. F. (1996). Abnormal electroencephalographic sleep pro-
files in major depression: Association with response to cognitive behavior therapy. *Archives of General Psychiatry, 53,* 99–108.

Van den Hout, J. H., Arntz, A., & Kunkels, F. H. (1995). Efficacy of a self-control therapy program
in a psychiatric day-treatment center. *Acta Psychiatrica Scandinavica, 92,* 25–29.

17

Interpersonal Psychotherapy for Depression

Myrna M. Weissman and John C. Markowitz

Interpersonal psychotherapy (IPT), a time-limited treatment for adult outpatients with major depression, was originally developed by the late Gerald L. Klerman, Myrna M. Weissman, and collaborators in the 1970s. It was defined in a manual, and tested in randomized clinical trials (Klerman, Weissman, Rounsaville, & Chevron, 1984). The manual was recently updated (Weissman, Markowitz, & Klerman, 2000). Evidence for efficacy in research trials for patients with major depressive disorder led to its modification for adolescent and geriatric depressed patients; for bipolar and dysthymic patients; for depressed HIV-positive, depressed pregnant patients, and depressed primary care patients. IPT has also been adapted for use as a maintenance treatment in couples and group formats, as a telephone intervention, and in a patient self-help guide. IPT has also been modified and tested for nonmood disorders, although the current chapter focuses on mood disorders.

Begun as a research intervention, IPT has only lately been disseminated among clinicians and in residency training programs. There have been increasing requests for training in IPT following the publication of efficacy data, the promulgation of practice guidelines that embrace IPT among antidepressant treatments, and its endorsement by *Consumers Reports* (1995; Seligman, 1995). Managed care and economic pressures have also aroused growing interest in defined, time-limited, evidenced-based treatments like IPT.

In 1993, practice guidelines appeared for mental health professionals (Karasu et al., 1993) and primary care practitioners (Depression Guideline Panel, 1993). These guidelines differ considerably in their scope, audience, and the level of scientific basis required for treatment recommendation. Neither set of guidelines claimed to define the standard of care for individual patients. Each discussed IPT as an acute and maintenance treatment for depression, used alone and in combination with medication.

American Psychiatric Association practice guidelines for adults with major depression cited IPT among the few recommended psychotherapies. The guidelines did not require efficacy data from controlled clinical trials as criteria for inclusion. IPT is described as useful for patients in the "midst of recent conflicts with significant others and for those having difficulty adjusting to an altered career or social role or other life transition" (Karasu et al., 1993, p. 6). Although many patients do present with such recent life changes, the empirical support for IPT—some of which is documented below—makes these appear as minimal, conservative indications.

Primary care guidelines for depression comprise four volumes (Depression Guideline Panels, 1993). Both the physician and patient guides list IPT, cognitive-behavioral therapy (CBT), behavioral therapy, brief dynamic therapy, and marital therapy as treatments for depression. IPT is recommended as an acute treatment for nonpsychotic depression, to remove symptoms, prevent relapse and recurrence, correct causal psychological problems with secondary symptom resolution, and correct secondary consequences of depression. The guidelines state that medication alone may suffice to prevent relapse or recurrence, and to maintain remitted patients with recurrent depression (Frank et al., 1990; Frank, Kupfer, Wagner, McEachran, & Cornes, 1991). These guidelines describe IPT, CBT, and behavioral treatments as "effective in most cases of mild-to-moderate depression" (Depression Guideline Panel, 1993, Vol. 2, p. 12) but indications "for continuation phase psychotherapy are unclear" (Depression Guideline Panel, 1993, Vol. 2, p. 18) even though "two studies are suggestive that continuation psychotherapy may reduce the relapse rate" (Depression Guideline Panel, 1993, Vol. 2, p. 18). The Patient Guidelines list behavioral therapy, CBT, and IPT as the "most well-studied [*sic*] for their effectiveness in reducing symptoms of major depressive disorder" (Depression Guideline Panel, 1993, Vol 4, p. 23).

IPT has been translated into Italian, German, Japanese, and Spanish and is being used in non-English-speaking countries. Descriptions of IPT have appeared in Spanish (Puig, 1995) and Dutch journals (Blom, Hoencamp, & Zwaan, 1996). An International Society for Interpersonal Psychotherapy was formed at the American Psychiatric Association annual meeting held in May 2000 in Chicago; it is led by S. Stuart, MD, of the University of Iowa, and M. Robertson, MD, of Sydney, Australia.

This chapter describes the concepts and techniques of IPT; its adaptations and efficacy data for depressive disorders; issues in training; concerns; and future directions. (For a complete description of the IPT method, see Klerman et al., 1984; Weissman, Markowitz, & Klerman, 2000; for the patient guide, see Weissman, 1995; for the group adaptation, see Wilfley, MacKenzie, Welch, Ayres, & Weissman, 2000; for the adaptation for depressed adolescents, see Mufson, Moreau, & Weissman, 1993; for the adaptation for dysthymic disorder, see Markowitz, 1998.)

BACKGROUND

IPT is based on interpersonal theory stemming from the post–World War II work of Adolph Meyer, Harry Stack Sullivan (1953), and later John Bowlby and others (see Klerman et al., 1984, for a review). The general principle derived from these theories is that life events occurring after the early formative years influence psychopathology. IPT uses this principle in nonetiological fashion. It does not presume to discern the cause of a depressive episode, but pragmatically uses the connection between current life events and the onset of the symptoms to help the patient understand and deal with his or her episode of illness. IPT is further based on psychosocial and life events research on depression, which has bolstered these theories by demonstrating the relationships between depression and grief (complicated bereavement), role disputes (e.g., bad marriages), role transitions (and meaningful life changes), and interpersonal deficits.

CONDUCTING INTERPERSONAL PSYCHOTHERAPY

In IPT, depression is defined as a *medical illness,* a treatable condition that is not the patient's fault. This definition of depression tends to displace the guilt of the depressed patient from the patient him- or herself to the illness, making the symptoms ego-dystonic and discrete. It also provides the hope of response to treatment. The therapist uses DSM-IV-TR (American Psychiatric Association, 2000) to make a diagnosis and rating scales such as the Hamilton Rating Scale for Depression (HRSD; Hamilton, 1960) or the Beck Depression Inventory (BDI, Beck, 1978) to assess and explain the symptoms that comprise the depressive syndrome. This helps the patient recognize that he or she is dealing with a common malady with a set of predictable symptoms—not the personal failing or weakness that the depressed patient often believes to be the problem. To implement this approach, IPT therapists formally give depressed patients the "sick role" (Parsons, 1951), excusing them from what their illness prevents them from doing, but also obliging them to work as patients in order to ultimately recover the healthy role they have lost.

The overall strategy of IPT is that by solving an interpersonal problem—for example, dealing with complicated bereavement, a role dispute or transition, or an interpersonal deficit—the patient will both improve his or her life situation and simultaneously relieve the symptoms of the depressive episode. This coupled formula has been validated by the randomized controlled trials in which IPT has been tested, and hence can be offered with confidence and optimism. This optimistic approach, while hardly specific to IPT, very likely provides part of its power in remoralizing the patient.

IPT is an eclectic therapy, using techniques developed in various psychotherapies. For example, IPT employs a medical model of depressive illness consistent with pharmacotherapy; shares role playing and a "here-and-now" focus with cognitive therapy; and addresses interpersonal issues in a manner familiar to marital therapists. It is not its specific techniques but rather its overall strategies that make it a unique and coherent approach. Although IPT overlaps to some degree with psychodynamic psychotherapies, it also differs from them in significant ways: in its focus on the present, not the past, and on real life change; in its medical model; and in its avoidance of the transference and of genetic and dream interpretations (Markowitz, Svartberg, & Swartz, 1998). While it shares with cognitive-behavioral therapy a focus on a syndromal constellation (e.g., major depression), attention to the "here and now," and techniques like role playing, IPT is considerably less structured, requires no explicit homework, and uses interpersonal problem areas as the major focus. Each of the four IPT interpersonal problem areas has discrete, if to some degree overlapping, goals for the therapist and the patient to pursue.

The techniques of IPT aid the patient's pursuit of these interpersonal goals. The therapist repeatedly helps the patient to link life events to mood and symptoms. These techniques including an *opening question* that leads the patient to provide an interval history of mood and events; *communication analysis,* a re-creation of recent, effectively charged life circumstances; an *exploration of the patient's wishes and options,* to achieve those wishes in particular interpersonal situations; *decision analysis,* to help the patient decide which options to employ; and *role playing,* to help patients rehearse tactics for real life.

IPT deals with current rather than past interpersonal relationships, focusing on the patient's immediate social context. The IPT therapist attempts to intervene in symptom formation and social dysfunction associated with depression rather than addressing enduring aspects of personality. Personality is difficult to accurately assess during an episode of an Axis I disorder such as depression.

Phases of Treatment

As an acute treatment, IPT has three phases. The *first phase,* usually one to three sessions, includes diagnostic evaluation and psychiatric history and sets the framework for the treatment. The therapist reviews symptoms, diagnoses the patient as depressed by standard criteria (American Psychiatric Association, 2000), and gives the patient the sick role (Parsons, 1951). The sick role may excuse the patient from overwhelming social obligations, but requires the patient to work in treatment to recover full function. The psychiatric history includes the "interpersonal inventory," a review of the patient's current social functioning and close relationships, their patterns and mutual expectations. (The interpersonal inventory is careful, interpersonally focused anamnesis, not a semistructured interview.) Changes in relationships proximal to the onset of symptoms are elucidated: for example, death of a loved one, children leaving home, worsening marital strife, or isolation from a confidant. This review provides a framework for understanding the social and interpersonal context of the onset of depressive symptoms and defines the focus of treatment.

Having assessed the need for medication based on symptom severity, past history and response to treatment, and patient preference, the therapist educates the patient about depression by explicitly discussing the diagnosis, including the constellation of symptoms that define major depression, and what the patient might expect from treatment. The therapist next links the depressive syndrome to the patient's interpersonal situation in a formulation (Markowitz & Swartz, 1997) that uses as a framework one of four interpersonal problem areas: (1) grief, (2) interpersonal role disputes, (3) role transitions, or (4) interpersonal deficits. If the patient explicitly accepts this formulation as a focus for subsequent treatment, therapy enters the middle phase.

In the *middle phase,* the therapist pursues strategies specific to the chosen interpersonal problem area. For *grief,* defined as complicated bereavement following the death of a loved one, the therapist facilitates the catharsis of mourning and gradually helps the patient to find new activities and relationships to compensate for the loss. *Role disputes* are conflicts with a significant other: a spouse or other family members, coworker, or close friend. The therapist helps the patient explore the relationship, the nature of the dispute, whether it has reached an impasse, and available options to resolve it. If these fail, therapist and patient may conclude that the relationship has reached an impasse and consider ways to change the impasse or to end the relationship. *Role transition* includes change in life status—for example, beginning or ending a relationship or career, moving, promotion, retirement, graduation, or diagnosis of a medical illness. The patient learns to deal with the change by mourning the loss of the old role while recognizing positive and negative aspects of the new role he or she is assuming, and taking steps to gain mastery over the new role. *Interpersonal deficits,* the residual fourth IPT problem area, defines the patient as lacking social skills, including having problems in initiating or sustaining relationships, and helps the patient to develop new relationships and skills. Some patients who might seem to fall into the interpersonal deficits category may in fact suffer from dysthymic disorder, for which separate strategies have been developed (Markowitz, 1998).

IPT sessions address present "here-and-now" problems rather than childhood or developmental issues. Sessions open with the question: "How have things been since we last met?" This focuses the patient on recent interpersonal events and recent mood, which the therapist helps the patient to link. Therapists take an active, nonneutral, supportive, and hopeful stance to counter the depressed patient's pessimism. They elicit and emphasize the options that exist for change in the patient's life, options that the depression may have kept the patient from seeing or exploring fully. Moreover, therapists stress the need for patients to test these options in order to improve their lives and simultaneously treat their depressive episodes.

The *final phase* of IPT, occupying the last few of the 12–16 weeks of treatment or last months in case of maintenance treatment, supports the patient's newly regained sense of independence and competence by recognizing and consolidating therapeutic gains. The therapist also helps the patient to anticipate and develop ways of identifying and countering depressive symptoms should they arise in the future. Compared to psychodynamic psychotherapy, IPT deemphasizes termination: it is a graduation from successful treatment. The sadness of parting is distinguished from depressive feelings. If the patient has not improved, the therapist emphasizes that it is the treatment that has failed, not the patient, and stresses the existence of alternative effective treatment options. The conduct of IPT is fully described, with case examples, in Weissman et al. (2000).

USES OF INTERPERSONAL PSYCHOTHERAPY IN DEPRESSION: EFFICACY AND ADAPTATIONS

Acute Treatment of Major Depression

IPT was first tested as an acute antidepressant treatment in a four-cell, 16-week randomized trial comparing IPT, amitriptyline (AMI), their combination, and a nonscheduled control treatment for 81 outpatients with major depression (DiMascio et al., 1979; Weissman et al., 1979). Although AMI alleviated symptoms more quickly, no significant difference appeared between IPT and AMI in symptom reduction at the end of treatment. Each active treatment more efficaciously reduced symptoms than did the nonscheduled control group, and combined AMI-IPT was more efficacious than either of the active monotherapies. Patients with psychotic depression did poorly on IPT alone. Naturalistic follow-up at 1 year found that many patients sustained benefits from the brief IPT intervention, and that IPT patients developed significantly better psychosocial functioning whether or not they received medication. This effect on social function was not found for AMI alone, nor had it been evident for IPT at the end of the 16-week trial (Weissman, Klerman, Prusoff, Sholomskas, & Padian, 1981).

The multisite National Institute of Mental Health Treatment of Depression Collaborative Research Program (NIMH TDCRP) (Elkin et al., 1989) is the most ambitious acute treatment study to date. Investigators randomly assigned 250 outpatients with major depression to 16 weeks of IPT, CBT, or either imipramine (IMI) or placebo plus clinical management. Most subjects completed at least 15 weeks or 12 treatment sessions. Patients with milder depression—having a 17-item HRSD score of 19 or less—improved equally in all four treatments. Among more severely depressed patients, IMI worked fastest and was most consistently superior to placebo. IPT was comparable to IMI on several outcome measures, including the HRSD, and superior to placebo for the more severely depressed patients. CBT was not superior to placebo for this group.

Klein and Ross (1993) reanalyzed the NIMH TDCRP data using the Johnson–Neyman technique. This yielded an ordering for treatment efficacy with "medication superior to psychotherapy, [and] the psychotherapies somewhat superior to placebo . . . particularly among the symptomatic and impaired patients" (Klein & Ross, 1993, p. 241). The authors found "CBT relatively inferior to IPT for patients with BDI scores greater than approximately 30, generally considered the boundary between moderate and severe depression" (p.

247). The reanalysis is consistent with the report of Elkin et al. (1989), but sharpens differences among treatments.

In an 18-month naturalistic follow-up study of TDCRP subjects, Shea et al. (1992) found no significant difference in recovery among remitters (defined by the presence of minimal or no symptoms following the end of treatment, sustained during follow-up) among the four treatment groups. Thirty percent of CBT, 26% of IPT, 19% of imipramine, and 20% of placebo subjects who had acutely remitted remained in remission during that time span. Among remitters at the end of the 16 weeks, relapse over the 18-month follow-up was 36% for CBT, 33% for IPT, 50% for imipramine, and 33% for placebo. The authors concluded that 16 weeks of specific treatments were insufficient to achieve full and lasting recovery for many patients.

Hoencamp (personal communication, 1996) and colleagues in the Hague are undertaking a study of IPT versus nefazodone, alone and in combination, for acute treatment of major depression.

Maintenance Treatment

IPT was first developed and tested for an 8-month, six-cell trial (Klerman, DiMascio, Weissman, Prusoff, & Paykel, 1974; Paykel, DiMascio, Haskell, & Prusoff, 1975). Today this study would be considered a continuation rather than a maintenance treatment, as the concept of long-term antidepressant treatment has lengthened. Acutely depressed outpatient women ($N = 150$) who responded ($\geq 50\%$ symptom reduction rated by a clinical interviewer) to a 4- to 6-week acute phase of AMI were randomly assigned to receive 8 months of treatment with weekly IPT alone, AMI alone, combined IPT-AMI, IPT-placebo alone, or no pill. Randomization to IPT or a low-contact psychotherapy condition occurred at entry into the continuation phase, whereas randomization to medication, placebo, or no pill occurred at the end of the second month of continuation. Maintenance pharmacotherapy was found to prevent relapse and symptom exacerbation, whereas IPT improved social functioning (Weissman, Klerman, Paykel, Prusoff, & Hanson, 1974). The effects of IPT on social functioning were not apparent for 6–8 months. No negative treatment interactions were found, and combined psychotherapy–pharmacotherapy had the best outcome.

The longest maintenance trial of psychotherapy for prophylaxis of depression, by Frank et al. (1990, 1991), studied 128 outpatients with multiply and rapidly recurrent depression. Patients were initially treated with combined high dose (> 200 mg/day) imipramine and weekly IPT. For responders, medication remained at high dosage while IPT was tapered to a monthly frequency during a 4-month continuation phase. Patients who remained in remission were then randomly assigned to 3 years of either: (1) ongoing high-dose imipramine plus clinical management; (2) high-dose imipramine plus monthly IPT; (3) monthly IPT alone; (4) monthly IPT plus placebo; or (5) placebo plus clinical management. The investigators found high-dose imipramine to be the most effective treatment, whereas most patients on placebo relapsed, mainly in the first few months. Once-a-month IPT, while less effective than medication, was statistically and clinically superior to the placebo condition in this high-risk patient population.

Women of childbearing age are the modal patients with depression. The finding of an 82-week survival time without recurrence with IPT alone is an impressive duration, sufficient to protect many women with recurrent depression through pregnancy and nursing without medication. Further study is required to determine the efficacy of IPT relative to newer medications (e.g., selective serotonin reuptake inhibitors), and the efficacy of more-frequent-than-monthly doses of maintenance IPT. A study of differing doses of maintenance IPT for depressed patients is underway in Pittsburgh.

Geriatric Depressed Patients

IPT was first used with geriatric depressed patients as an addition to a 6-week pharmacotherapy trial in order to enhance compliance and to provide some treatment for the placebo control group (Rothblum, Sholomskos, Berry, & Prusoff, 1982; Sholomskas, Chevron, Prusoff, & Berry, 1983). The investigators noted that grief and role transition specific to life changes were the prime focus of treatment, and suggested modifying IPT with more flexible duration of sessions, greater use of practical advice and support (e.g., arranging transportation, calling the physician), and the recognition that major role changes may be impractical and detrimental (e.g., divorce at age 75).

A 6-week clinical trial compared standard IPT to nortriptyline in 30 geriatric depressed patients. Results showed some advantages for IPT, largely due to medication side effects that produced higher attrition in the medication group (Sloane, Stapes, & Schneider, 1985).

A 3-year maintenance study for geriatric patients with recurrent depression in Pittsburgh (Reynolds et al., 1999) used a similar design to the Frank et al. (1990) study. The IPT manual was modified to allow more flexible length of sessions, as some elderly patients may not tolerate 50-minute sessions. The authors found that older patients need to address early life relationships in their psychotherapy, a distinction from the typical "here-and-now" focus of IPT. Like Sholomskas et al. (1983), they felt that therapists needed to help patients solve practical problems and to acknowledge that some problems may not be amenable to resolutions, such as existential late life issues or lifelong psychopathology (Rothblum et al., 1982). Elderly depressed patients whose sleep quality normalized by early continuation phase had an 80% chance of remaining well during the first year of maintenance treatment. The response rate was similar for patients receiving nortriptyline or IPT.

Reynolds and colleagues (1999) included acutely treated 187 geriatric patients (60 years and older) with recurrent major depression using the combination of IPT and nortriptyline. The 107 who remitted and then reached recovery after continuation therapy were randomly assigned to one of four 3-year maintenance conditions: (1) medication clinic with nortriptyline alone, with steady-state nortriptyline plasma levels maintained in a therapeutic window of 80–120 ng/ml.; (2) medication clinic with placebo; (3) monthly maintenance IPT with placebo; or (4) monthly IPT-Maintenance Treatment (IPT-M) plus nortriptyline. Recurrence rates were 43% for nortriptyline alone, 90% for placebo, 64% for IPT with placebo, and 20% for combined treatment. Each monotherapy was statistically superior to placebo, whereas combined therapy showed superiority to IPT alone and trend for superiority over medication alone. Patients in their seventies were more likely to suffer recurrence and to do so more quickly than patients in their sixties. This study replicates the basic maintenance findings of Frank and colleagues (Frank, 1991a; Frank et al., 1990, 1991), with the difference that combined treatment had advantages over pharmacotherapy alone for the geriatric population.

The comparison of high-dose tricyclic antidepressants to low-dose IPT-M, in both the Frank and the Reynolds study, is easy to misinterpret. Had the tricyclics been lowered comparably to the psychotherapy dosage, recurrence in the medication groups might well have been greater. Yet as there were no precedents for this research, the choice of a monthly dosing interval for IPT-M was reasonable, and indeed showed some benefit. This research raises the issue of dose-finding studies for psychotherapy: What might biweekly IPT-M do?

Depressed Adolescents

Mufson et al. (1993) modified IPT to incorporate adolescent developmental issues (IPT-A), adding as a fifth problem area the single-parent family, an interpersonal situation found frequently among their adolescent treatment population. Mufson and colleagues conducted an open feasibility and follow- up trial, and then a controlled 12-week clinical trial comparing IPT-A and clinical monitoring in 48 clinic-referred adolescents, ages 12 to 18, who met DSM-III-R criteria for major depressive disorder. Patients were seen biweekly by a blind independent evaluator to assess symptomatology, social functioning, and social problem-solving skills. Thirty-two of the 48 patients completed the protocol (21 IPT-A, 11 control).

Patients who received IPT-A reported significantly greater improvement of depressive symptoms and overall social functioning, including functioning with friends and problem-solving skills. In the intent-to-treat sample, 75% of IPT-A patients met the criterion for recovery (HRSD score ≤ 6), compared to 46% of control patients. The findings support the feasibility, patient acceptance, and efficacy of 12 weeks of IPT-A with acutely depressed adolescents in reducing depressive symptomatology and improving social functioning and interpersonal problem-solving skills (Mufson, Weissman, Moreau, & Garfinkel, 1999). Mufson will be testing IPT-A in a large-scale effectiveness study in school-based clinics and is also piloting it in a group format for depressed adolescents.

Depressed HIV-Positive Patients

Markowitz, Klerman, Perry, Clougherty, and Mayers (1992) modified IPT for depressed HIV patients (IPT-HIV), emphasizing common issues among this population including concern about illness and death, grief, and role transitions. In a pilot open trial, 21 of the 24 depressed patients responded with symptom reduction. A 16-week study randomized 101 subjects to IPT-HIV, CBT, supportive psychotherapy (SP), and IMI plus SP (Markowitz et al., 1998). Echoing the results of the more severely depressed subjects in the TDCRP study (Elkin et al., 1989), all treatments were associated with some symptom reduction, but IPT and IMI produced symptomatic and functional improvement significantly greater than the other two psychotherapies.

Depressed Primary Care Patients

Schulberg and colleagues compared IPT to pharmacotherapy for depressed ambulatory medical patients in a primary care setting (Schulberg & Scott, 1991; Schulberg, Scott, Madonia, & Imber, 1993). The IPT manual was not modified, but IPT conformed with practices of the primary care center—for example, nurses took vital signs before each session. If a patient was medically hospitalized, IPT was continued in the hospital when possible.

Patients with current major depression ($N = 276$) were randomly assigned to IPT, nortriptyline, or primary care physicians' usual care. They were seen weekly for 16 weeks and monthly thereafter for 4 months in IPT (Schulberg et al., 1996). Depressive severity declined more rapidly with either nortriptyline or IPT than in usual care. Among treatment completers, approximately 70% receiving nortriptyline or IPT, but only 20% in usual care, were judged recovered at 8 months. Brown, Schulberg, Madonia, Shear, and Houck (1996) found that patients with a lifetime history of comorbid panic disorder, compared to major depression alone, had poorer response regardless of treatment. These pilot findings on comorbid panic disorder are corroborated by those reported by Frank, Shear, and colleagues (2000).

Conjoint Interpersonal Psychotherapy for Depressed Patients with Marital Disputes

Marital conflict, separation, and divorce have been associated with onset and course of depressive episodes (Rounsaville, Weissman, Prusoff, & Herceg-Baron, 1979). Individual psychotherapy for depressed patients in marital disputes may lead to premature rupture of some marriages (Gurman & Kniskern, 1978). For these reasons, a manual was developed for conjoint therapy of depressed patients with marital disputes (IPT-CM) (Klerman & Weissman, 1993). IPT-CM focuses on the current marital dispute and includes the spouse in all sessions. Eighteen patients with major depression linked to the onset or exacerbation of marital disputes were randomly assigned to 16 weeks of either individual IPT or IPT-CM. Although patients in both treatments showed similar reduction in depressive symptoms, patients receiving IPT-CM had significantly better marital adjustment, greater marital affection, and better sexual relations than did IPT-alone patients (Foley, Rounsaville, Weissman, Sholomskas, & Chevron, 1989). These pilot findings require replication with a larger sample and other control groups.

Antepartum/Postpartum Depression

Spinelli at Columbia University is using IPT to treat women with antepartum depression. Examination of this role transition addresses the depressed pregnant woman's self-evaluation as a parent, the physiological changes of pregnancy, and altered relationships with the spouse or significant other and with other children. Spinelli has added "complicated pregnancy" as a fifth interpersonal problem area. Timing and duration of sessions shift in response to bedrest, delivery, obstetrical complications, and child care. Young children may be brought to sessions and breast-fed by postpartum mothers. Telephone sessions and hospital visits are sometimes necessary (Spinelli, 1997). A controlled clinical trial is comparing IPT to a didactic parent education group in depressed pregnant women over 16 weeks of acute treatment and 6 monthly follow-up sessions is underway.

Stuart and O'Hara (1995) compared IPT to a waiting-list control in 120 women with postpartum depression. The acute treatment trial lasted 12 weeks, with an 18-month follow-up. They assessed both the mothers' symptom states and their interactions with their infants. Preliminary results indicate the superiority of IPT: 44% of the IPT group, but only 14% of the waiting-list group, remitted on the BDI (Stuart, O'Hara, & Blehar, 1998). Sixty percent of IPT patients, versus 16% of controls, showed a greater than 50% reduction on the BDI. Women receiving IPT also showed significant improvement in measures of social adjustment relative to the control group.

Dysthymic Disorder

In a modification of IPT for dysthymic disorder (IPT-D), patients are encouraged to reconceptualize what they had seen as their lifelong character flaws as ego-dystonic, chronic mood-dependent symptoms—that is, as a chronic but treatable "state" rather than an immutable "trait." Therapy itself was defined as an iatrogenic role transition from believing oneself flawed in personality to recognizing and treating the mood disorder. Open treatment in 16 weekly IPT sessions yielded a reduction in depressive symptoms among dysthymic patients with lifelong chronicity. Markowitz (1994, 1998) treated a total of 17 pilot subjects: none worsened, and 11 remitted. Medication benefits roughly half of dysthymic patients (Kocsis et al., 1988; Thase et al., 1996), but nonresponders may need psychotherapy, and even medication responders may benefit from combined treatment (Markowitz, 1994). Based on these pilot results, a comparative study of 16 weeks of IPT-D alone, supportive psychotherapy (SP); sertraline plus clinical management, as well as a combined IPT/sertraline cell, is underway at Weill Medical College of Cornell University.

Browne, Steiner, and others at McMaster University in Hamilton, Ontario, Canada, treated more than 700 dysthymic patients in the community with either 12 sessions of standard IPT, sertraline, or their combination for 4 months. Patients were then followed up over 2 years. Results have not yet been published, but preliminary findings have been presented at several conferences (e.g., World Psychiatric Association, Jerusalem, Israel, 1997). Based on a 40% reduction of the Montgomery–Asberg Depression Rating Scale (MADRS) score at 1 year follow-up, 51% of IPT-alone subjects improved, significantly fewer than the 63% for sertraline and 62% for combined treatment. Yet in the follow-up phase IPT was associated with significant economic savings in direct use of health care and social services; thus combined treatment was as efficacious as but less expensive than sertraline alone.

Bipolar Disorder

Frank and colleagues in Pittsburgh are assessing the benefits for bipolar patients of adjunctive IPT modified by social Zeitgeber theory—behavioral scheduling of daily and sleep patterns (Ehlers, Frank, & Kupfer, 1988; Malkoff et al., 2000)—as maintenance treatment of lithium-stabilized bipolar patients. Comparing IPSRT (interpersonal social rhythms therapy) to medication alone (Frank, 1991b; Frank, Swartz, & Kupfer, 2000), the 3-year maintenance treatment study will initially include biweekly psychotherapy visits, tapering to monthly sessions in the final 2 years.

Their preliminary report comparing IPSRT as adjunctive treatment to conventional medication-clinic treatment found comparable changes in symptomatology in the two groups over the 52-week treatment period. Ultimately, more than 50 patients will be studied in each condition. The first 18 patients assigned to IPSRT did show significantly greater stability of daily routines as treatment proceeded. Patients assigned to the medication-clinic condition ($N = 20$) showed essentially no change in social rhythms as measured by SRM. The authors conclude that IPSRT influenced lifestyle regularity in patients with bipolar disorder, possibly providing protection against future episodes.

Subsyndromally Depressed Hospitalized Elderly Patients

Mossey, Knott, Higgins, and Talerico (1996), noting that depressive symptoms that did not reach criteria for major depression nonetheless impeded recovery of hospitalized elderly patients, conducted a 10-session trial of a modification of IPT to be administered by nonpsychiatric nurses called interpersonal counseling (IPC) for elderly hospitalized medical patients with depressive symptoms. Patients were seen for 10 1-hour sessions with flexibility of scheduling from once weekly to a timetable that accommodated the patient's medical status. Seventy-six hospitalized patients over age 60, who did not meet criteria for major depression but had depressive symptoms on two consecutive assessments, were randomly assigned to receive either IPC administered by clinical nurse specialists or usual care (UC). Researchers also followed a nondepressed, untreated control group. Patients found IPC feasible and tolerable. Assessment after 3 months showed nonsignificantly greater reduction in depressive symptoms and greater improvement on all outcome variables for IPC relative to UC, whereas controls had a slight symptomatic worsening. Rehospitalization in the IPC and nondepressed control groups was virtually identical (11–15%), and significantly less than the subsyndromally depressed group receiving UC (50%). At 6 months, differences between IPC and UC groups were statistically significant for reduction of depressive symptoms and self-rated health, but not for physical or social functioning. The investigators felt that 10 sessions were insufficient for some patients, and that a maintenance phase might have been useful. The clinical nurse specialists were considered acceptable therapists.

Interpersonal Psychotherapy by Telephone

Because many patients avoid or have difficulty reaching an office for face-to-face treatment, IPC is being tested as a telephone treatment.

Another pilot feasibility trial underway compares IPT by telephone to no treatment in 30 patients with recurrent major depression who have not received regular treatment (Miller & Weissman, 2002).

Interpersonal Psychotherapy Patient Guide

Weissman (1995) developed a user-friendly IPT patient guide with accompanying worksheets designed for depressed readers who want to learn about or are receiving IPT. It explains the treatment in simple language. Worksheets can be used to facilitate sessions or to monitor problem areas after treatment. Testing to determine whether the patient book facilitates treatment has not been done.

Summary of Interpersonal Psychotherapy Effects

In summary, IPT has demonstrated its utility as an acute and maintenance monotherapy and as part of combined treatment for major depressive disorder. It also appears to have utility for a variety of other mood syndromes, although the evidence for these is more limited. Combined treatment is probably best reserved for severely or chronically ill patients (Rush & Thase, 1999). How best to combine time-limited psychotherapy with pharmacotherapy—for which patients, in what sequence, and so on—requires ongoing research.

Studies such as the TDCRP, which compared IPT and CBT, have suggested factors that might predict better outcome with either IPT or CBT. Sotsky and colleagues (1991) found that depressed patients with a low baseline level of social dysfunction responded well to IPT, whereas those with severe social deficits (probably equivalent to the "interpersonal deficits" problem area) responded less well. Patients with greater symptom severity and difficulty in concentrating responded poorly to CBT. Initial severity of major depression and of impaired functioning predicted superior response to IPT and to imipramine. Imipramine also worked most efficaciously for patients with difficulty functioning at work, likely reflecting its faster onset of action. Patients with atypical depression responded better to either IPT or CBT than to imipramine or placebo (Shea, Elkin, & Sotsky, 1999). Barber and Muenz (1996), looking only at subjects who completed treatment, found that IPT was more efficacious than CBT for patients with obsessive personality disorder, whereas CBT fared better for avoidant personality disorder. Biological factors such as abnormal sleep profiles on EEG predicted significantly poorer response to IPT than for patients with undisturbed sleep parameters (Thase et al., 1997). Also, the adherence of psychotherapists to a focused IPT approach may enhance outcome (Frank et al., 1991). The replication and further elaboration of these predictive factors should be targets of future research.

TRAINING

Until recently, IPT practitioners were few, and almost exclusively limited to therapists in research studies. In response to requests, IPT training is now increasingly included in professional workshops and conferences, with training courses conducted at university centers in Canada, the United Kingdom, elsewhere in Europe, Asia, and New Zealand.

Training workshops for mental health professionals from a variety of disciplines have been held by Markowitz at Weill Cornell Medical School, New York; by Stuart at the University of Iowa; and by Gillies in Toronto, Canada. IPT is taught in a still small but growing number of psychiatric residency training programs in the United States (Markowitz, 1995) and has been included in family practice and primary care training (Gillies, personal communication, 1996).

Although the principles of IPT are straightforward, training requires more than reading the manual (Weissman, Rounsaville, & Chevron, 1982; Rounsaville, O'Malley, Foley, & Weissman, 1988). Candidates should have a graduate clinical degree (MD, PhD, MSW, RN), several years of experience conducting psychotherapy, and clinical familiarity with the diagnosis they plan to treat. IPT training programs are designed to help experienced therapists refocus their treatment by learning new techniques, not to teach novices psychotherapy. The training used in the TDCRP (Elkin et al., 1989) has become a model for subsequent research studies. This included a brief didactic phase, reviewing the manual, and a longer practicum during which the therapist treats two or three patients under close supervision monitored by videotapes of the sessions (Chevron & Rounsaville, 1983). Rounsaville, Chevron, Weissman, Prusoff, and Frank (1986) found that psychotherapists who performed well on a first supervised IPT case often did not require further intensive supervision, and that experienced therapists committed to the approach required less supervision (Rounsaville et al., 1988). Some clinicians have taught themselves IPT using the IPT manual (Klerman et al., 1984) and peer supervision. For research certification, we continue to recommend at least two or three successfully treated cases with hour-for-hour supervision of taped sessions (Markowitz, 2001).

Even for experienced therapists, training programs in IPT are still not widely available; the U.S. Surgeon General's recent report noted this lack (Satcher, 1999). Psychiatry residency programs still focus on long-term psychodynamic psychotherapy. Psychology training programs focus on cognitive and behavioral psychotherapy although even here the lack of training in time-limited treatment has been noted (Sanderson & Woody, 1995; Weissman & Sanderson, 2001) Finally, social work training programs do not include training in time-limited psychotherapies. Psychiatric residency and other mental health care treatment training programs should include clinical instruction in the time-limited psychotherapies described in manuals, in addition to providing exposure to long-term psychotherapy. To our knowledge, no accepted model psychotherapy curriculum is available.

The educational process for IPT in clinical practice requires further study. For example, what educational level and experience are required to learn IPT? Does an experienced therapist require supervision? Would reading the manual suffice?

CONCERNS

The recent success of IPT and other brief psychotherapies is, in part, a reflection of the restrictions on reimbursement for long-term psychotherapy in the new health care scene. This success of brief treatments raises concerns about increasing limitations of coverage, about training, efficacy studies, and erosion of patient confidentiality.

Limitations of Coverage

Although IPT is time-limited, some patients may need treatment over longer periods of time. Major depression, for which IPT was first developed, fits the model of a chronic illness in that it is often recurrent. Treatment therefore needs to be available when these episodes occur and possibly to prevent future episodes. For many unipolar or bipolar patients, IPT may need to be available during periods of stress and symptom reemergence.

The relationship of psychotherapy to somatic therapies, and the need to retain flexible treatment choices, are well illustrated by the case of women of childbearing age who are at high risk for depression. Although some recent studies indicate no long-term effects on offspring from several antidepressant medications taken during pregnancy, many pregnant women refrain from their use. Psychotherapy is an alternative to medication during pregnancy. Although considerable evidence supports the efficacy of antidepressant medication, in the few studies where psychotherapy has been included, medication and time-limited psychotherapy have had equal efficacy in reducing depressive symptoms. Medications have a faster and more consistent onset of action than psychotherapy. In the Frank et al. (1990) study, which included patients who had severe recurrent depression, IPT alone, delivered once monthly, prevented recurrence in nearly 70% of patients over a 36-week period. If these results can be generalized to depression in pregnant women—most of whom would have lower risk than the high-risk subjects recruited for the Pittsburgh study—psychotherapy could provide an effective alternative to antidepressant medication during gestation.

Insurance policies and health care benefits that restrict access to psychotherapy may thus jeopardize the health of some women who require antidepressant treatment during pregnancy and postpartum and who do not want to take medication. Managed care demands for efficiency will focus most heavily on psychotherapy, which most managed care organizations tend to exclude from the benefit package, or, at most, to limit the benefit to only a few sessions. This exclusion is reflected in the recent Agency for Health Care Policy in Research (AHCPR) guidelines that recommend psychotherapy only when depression is mild to moderate, nonpsychotic, nonchronic and not highly recurrent.

Training

Training a skilled therapist in the techniques of IPT differs from training a novice to do psychotherapy. Training experienced psychotherapists is relatively easy. If psychotherapy training is devalued or eliminated, we will be training IPT therapists who do not have a general background in psychotherapy. Inexperienced therapists often adhere closely to the manual but end up lecturing patients. If basic psychotherapy training is truncated, manualized psychotherapies may not work well in the hands of such therapists.

Efficacy Studies

There are far fewer efficacy studies of psychotherapy than of pharmacotherapy, in large part because there is no equivalent of the pharmaceutical industry to support efficacy studies in psychotherapy. A typical drug before it gets to market goes through four phases and then undergoes postmarketing surveillance. These studies ascertain doses, feasibility, side effects, interactions, and efficacy. Researchers who are skilled to do Phase 1 studies (e.g., chemists) are not the same people who are skilled to do Phase 4 studies (clinicians). A similar model is applicable to but not practiced for psychotherapy. Most psychotherapy trials begin prematurely, without a series of open trials to determine optimal dose, specificity, or even what diagnostic subgroups might benefit from the intervention. The absence of these data can be used as a rationale for eliminating the treatment. In the face of diminishing resources for this type of research, it is unlikely that this situation will change.

Cost Offset

The spread of managed care has created a strong financial incentive to limit treatment (Schowalter, 1995). The managed care assessment of a patient's clinical outcome tends to focus on short-term treatment costs. Their focus in considering cost offset or treatment efficiency is in eliminating days spent in hospital and reducing suicidal risk. These are not necessarily the major outcomes for psychotherapy, nor outcomes that fully reflect the morbidity of illness. The assessment of psychotherapy or pharmacotherapy outcomes should be broadened to include issues such as impact of a parent's depression on their offspring over time. In depression it has been well documented that the offspring of depressed parents are themselves at high risk for developing depression as well as behavioral, school, and health problems. Treatment cost offset studies need to have a long-term view, which includes assessment of the impact of the illness on the immediate family and other aspects of social functioning.

Confidentiality

Patients and therapists have been quick to discover that, in the new health care system, they must waive the confidentiality of their doctor–patient relationships to obtain treatment approval. Unlike traditional insurance plans, where a brief medical record summary may have been sent for review, patients now find their problems explained in detail over the phone to a case coordinator who is often not trained in mental health. The therapist is forced to bargain for more therapeutic time. The coordinator then determines if there is an emergency. A physician or other mental health professional, seeking approval of further sessions for continuation of patient care, often must reveal very private details of the patient's illness to assure the screener or manager that the patient is sufficiently ill to warrant further treatment. Disclosure about the patient's private life will be far more detailed than what has been done in the past in traditional insurance plans and inherently undercuts patient trust. Confidentiality is an issue whether the patient is receiving pharmacotherapy or psychotherapy. However, in the latter, more detailed information on personal issues is revealed.

FUTURE DIRECTIONS

What do we see as the future of IPT or other brief psychotherapies? There will be increasing interest by managed care companies, increasing manualization, decreasing coverage, and increasing treatment provision by persons of decreasing education and training. Treatment may be done by telephone or perhaps computer and, under these circumstances, may show decreased efficacy. More research is needed to determined the efficacy of IPT with particular depressive subtypes, its efficacy relative to other psychotherapies (e.g., CBT) and pharmacotherapy for particular populations, and especially the timing and sequencing of IPT with antidepressant pharmacotherapy. Unusually for a psychotherapy, research on IPT has focused almost exclusively on outcome. Now that the efficacy of IPT has been established for major depression, process research may be helpful to examine which interventions explain its potency.

In summary, IPT is a time-limited psychotherapy that was first developed for adult ambulatory patients with major depression. Its efficacy is well established in controlled clinical trials for acute and maintenance treatment for adults and geriatric patients with major depression.

It is partially established for adolescent depression; depressed HIV-positive patients; depressed patients in primary care; conjoint treatment for depressed patients with marital disputes; and dysthymic patients. Trials are ongoing for depressed ante-and postpartum patients and for patients with bipolar disorder and for use over the telephone. There is a gap between the interest in and demonstrated efficacy of IPT and the mechanism for training.

ACKNOWLEDGMENTS

A portion of this material appeared in Weissman and Markowitz (1994). Copyright 1994 by American Medical Association. Reprinted by permission.

REFERENCES

American Psychiatric Association. (2000). *Diagnostic and statistical manual of mental disorders* (4th ed., text rev.) Washington, DC: Author.

Barber, J. P., & Muenz, L. R. (1996). The role of avoidance and obsessiveness in matching patients to cognitive and interpersonal psychotherapy: Empirical findings from the Treatment for Depression Collaborative Research Program. *Journal of Consulting and Clinical Psychology, 64*, 951–958.

Beck, A. T. (1978). *Depression inventory*. Philadelphia: Center for Cognitive Therapy.

Blom, M. B. J., Hoencamp, E., & Zwaan, T. (1996). Interpersoonlijke psychotherapie voor depressie: Een pilot-onderzoek [in Dutch]. *Tijdschrift voor Psychiatrie, 38*, 398–402.

Brown, C., Schulberg, H. C., Madonia, M. J., Shear, M. K., & Houck, P. R. (1996). Treatment outcomes for primary care patients with major depression and lifetime anxiety disorders. *American Journal of Psychiatry, 153*(10), 1293–1300.

Chevron, E. S., & Rounsavillle, B. J. (1983). Evaluating the clinical skills of psychotherapists: A comparison of techniques. *Archives of General Psychiatry, 40*, 1129–1132.

Consumer Reports. (1995, November). p. 739.

Depression Guideline Panel. (1993). *Clinical practice guideline: Depression in primary care.* (Vols. 1–4). (AHCPR Publications No. 93-0550-0553). Rockville, MD: U.S. Department of Health and Human Services, Agency for Health Care Policy and Research.

DiMascio, A., Weissman, M. M., Prusoff, B. A., Neu, C., Zwilling, M., & Klerman, G. L. (1979). Differential symptom reduction by drugs and psychotherapy in acute depression. *Archives of General Psychiatry, 36*, 1450–1456.

Ehlers, C. L., Frank, E., & Kupfer, D. J. (1988). Social zeitgebers and biological rhythms: A unified approach to understanding the etiology of depression. *Archives of General Psychiatry, 45*, 948–952.

Elkin, I., Shea, M. T., Watkins, J. T., Imber, S. D., Sotsky, S. M., Collins, J. F., Glass, D. R., Pilkonis, P. A., Leber, W. R., Docherty, J. P., Fiester, S. J., & Parloff, M. B. (1989). National Institute of Mental Health Treatment of Depression Collaborative Research Program: General effectiveness of treatments. *Archives of General Psychiatry, 46*, 971–982.

Foley, S. H., Rounsaville, B. J., Weissman, M. M., Sholomskas, D., & Chevron, E. (1989). Individual versus conjoint interpersonal psychotherapy for depressed patients with marital disputes. *International Journal of Family Psychiatry, 10*(1–2), 29–42.

Frank, E. (1991a). Interpersonal psychotherapy as a maintenance treatment for patients with recurrent depression. *Psychotherapy, 28*, 259–266.

Frank, E. (1991b, March). *Biological rhythms and bipolar disorder.* Paper presented at the annual meeting of the American Psychosomatic Society, Santa Fe, NM.

Frank, E., Kupfer, D. J., Perel, J. M., Cornes, C., Jarrett, D. B., Mallinger, A. G., Thase, M. E., McEachran, A. B., & Grochocinski, V. J. (1990). Three-year outcomes for maintenance therapies in recurrent depression. *Archives of General Psychiatry, 47*, 1093–1099.

Frank, E., Kupfer, D. J., Wagner, E. F., McEachran, A. B., & Cornes C. (1991). Efficacy of interpersonal psychotherapy as a maintenance treatment of recurrent depression. *Archives of General Psychiatry, 48*, 1053–1059.

Frank, E., Shear, M. K., Rucci, P., Cyanowski, J. M., Endicott, J., Fagiolini, A., Grochocinski, V. J., Houck, P., Kupfer, D. J., Maser, J. D., & Cassano, G. B. (2000). Influence of panic–agoraphobic spectrum symptoms on treatment response in patients with recurrent major depression. *American Journal of Psychiatry, 157*, 1101–1107.

Frank, E., Swartz, H. A., & Kupfer, D. J. (2000). Interpersonal and social rhythm therapy: Managing the chaos of bipolar disorder. *Biological Psychiatry, 48*, 593–604.

Gurman, A. S., & Kniskern, D. P. (1978). Research on marital and family therapy: Progress, perspective, and prospect. In S. B. Garfield & A. B. Bergen (Eds.), *Handbook of psychotherapy and behavior change* (pp. 817–902). New York: Wiley.

Hamilton, M. (1960). A rating scale for depression. *Journal of Neurology, Neurosurgery, and Psychiatry, 25,* 56–62.

Karasu, T. B., Docherty, J. P., Gelenberg, A., Kupfer, D. J., Merriam, A. E., & Shadoan, R. (1993). Practice guideline for major depressive disorder in adults. *American Journal of Psychiatry, 150*(Suppl.), 1–26.

Klein, D. F., & Ross, D. C. (1993). Reanalysis of the National Institute of Mental Health Treatment of Depression Collaborative Research Program General Effectiveness Report. *Neuropsychopharmacology, 8,* 241–251.

Klerman, G. L., DiMascio, A., Weissman, M. M., Prusoff, B. A., & Paykel, E. S. (1974). Treatment of depression by drugs and psychotherapy. *American Journal of Psychiatry, 131,* 186–191.

Klerman, G. L., & Weissman, M. M. (1993). *New applications of interpersonal psychotherapy.* Washington, DC: American Psychiatric Press.

Klerman, G. L., Weissman, M. M., Rounsaville, B. J., & Chevron, E. S. (1984). *Interpersonal psychotherapy of depression.* New York: Basic Books.

Kocsis, J. H., Frances, A. J., Voss, C., Mann, J. J., Mason, B. J., & Sweeney, J. (1988). Imipramine treatment for chronic depression. *Archives of General Psychiatry, 45,* 253–257.

Malkoff-Schwartz, S., Frank, E., Anderson, B. P., Hlastala, S. A., Luther, J. F., Sherrill, J. T., Houck, P. R., & Kupfer, D. J. (2000). Social rhythm disruption and stressful life events in the onset of bipolar and unipolar episodes. *Psychological Medicine, 30,* 1005–1016.

Markowitz, J. C. (1994). Psychotherapy of dysthymia. *American Journal of Psychiatry, 151,* 1114–1121.

Markowitz, J. C. (1995). Teaching interpersonal psychotherapy to psychiatric residents. *Academic Psychiatry, 19,* 167–173.

Markowitz, J. C. (1998). *Interpersonal psychotherapy for dysthymic disorder.* Washington, DC: American Psychiatric Press.

Markowitz, J. C. (2001). Learning the new psychotherapies. In M. M. Weissman (Ed), *Treatment of Depression: Bridging the 21st Century* (pp. 281–300). Washington, DC: American Psychiatric Press.

Markowitz, J. C., Klerman, G. L., Perry, S. W., Clougherty, K. F., & Mayers, A. (1992). Interpersonal therapy of depressed HIV–seropositive patients. *Hospital and Community Psychiatry, 43,* 885–890.

Markowitz, J. C., Kocsis, J. H., Fishman, B., Spielman, L. A., Jacobsberg, L. B., Frances, A. J., Klerman, G. L., & Perry, S. W. (1998). Treatment of HIV-positive patients with depressive symptoms. *Archives of General Psychiatry, 55,* 452–457.

Markowitz, J. C., Svartberg, M., & Swartz, H. A. (1998) Is IPT time-limited psychodynamic psychotherapy? *Journal of Psychotherapy Practice and Research, 7,* 185–195.

Markowitz, J. C., & Swartz, H. A. (1997). Case formulation in interpersonal psychotherapy of depression. In T. D. Eels (Ed.), *Handbook of psychotherapy case formulation* (pp. 192–222). New York: Guilford Press.

Miller, L., & Weissman, M. M. (2002). *Interpersonal psychotherapy delivered over the telephone for depression: A pilot study.* Manuscript submitted for publication.

Mossey, J. M., Knott, K. A., Higgins, M., & Talerico, K. (1996). Effectiveness of a psychosocial intervention, interpersonal counseling, for subdysthymic depression in medically ill elderly. *Journal of Gerontology, 51A*(4), M172–M178.

Mufson, L., Moreau, D., Weissman, M. M., & Klerman, G. L. (1993). *Interpersonal psychotherapy for depressed adolescents.* New York: Guilford Press.

Mufson, L., Weissman, M. M., Moreau, D., & Garfinkel, R. (1999). Efficacy of interpersonal psychotherapy for depressed adolescents. *Archives of General Psychiatry, 56,* 573–579.

Parsons, T. (1951). Illness and the role of the physician: A sociological perspective. *American Journal of Orthopsychiatry, 21,* 452–460.

Paykel, E. S., DiMascio, A., Haskell, D., & Prusoff, B. A. (1975). Effects of maintenance amitriptyline and psychotherapy on symptoms of depression. *Psychological Medicine, 5,* 67–77.

Puig, J. S. (1995). Psicoterapia interpersonal (1). *Rev Psiquiatría Fac Med Barna, 22*(4), 91–99.

Reynolds, C. F., III, Frank, E., Perel, J. M., Imber, S. D., Cornes, C., Miller, M. D., Mazumdar, P. R., Houck, P. R., Dew, M. A., Stack, J. A., Pollock, B. G., & Kupfer, D. J. (1999). Nortriptyline and interpersonal psychotherapy as maintenance therapies for recurrent major depression: A randomized controlled trial in patients older than fifty-nine years. *Journal of the American Medical Association, 281,* 39–45.

Rothblum, E. D., Sholomskas, A. J., Berry, C., & Prusoff, B. A. (1982). Issues in clinical trials with the depressed elderly. *Journal of the American Geriatric Society, 30,* 694–699.

Rounsaville, B. J., Chevron, E. S., Weissman, M. M., Prusoff, B. A., & Frank, E. (1986). Training therapists to perform interpersonal psychotherapy in clinical trials. *Comprehensive Psychiatry, 27,* 364–371.

Rounsaville, B. J., O'Malley, S. S., Foley, S. H., & Weissman, M. M. (1988). The role of manual-guided training in the conduct and efficacy of interpersonal psychotherapy for depression. *Journal of Consulting and Clinical Psychology, 56,* 681–688.

Rounsaville, B. J., Weissman, M. M., Prusoff, B. A., & Herceg-Baron, R. L. (1979). Marital disputes and treatment outcome in depressed women. *Comprehensive Psychiatry, 20,* 483–490.

Rush, A. J., & Thase, M. E. (1999). Psychotherapies for depressive disorders: A review. In M. Maj & N. Sartorius (Eds.), *Depressive disorders* (pp. 161–206). Chichester, UK: Wiley.

Sanderson, W. C., & Woody, S. (1995). Manuals for empirically validated treatments: A project of the Task Force on Psychological Interventions. *Clinical Psychologist, 48,* 7–11.

Satcher, D. (1999). *Surgeon general's reference: Mental health. A report of the surgeon general.* Rockville, MD: U.S. Department of Health and Human Services.

Schulberg, H. C., Block, M. R., Madonia, M. J., Scott, C. P., Rodriguez, E., Imber, S. D., Perel, J., Love, J., Houck, P. R., & Coulehan, J. L. (1996). Treating major depression in primary care practice. *Archives of General Psychiatry, 53*(10), 913–919.

Schulberg, H. C., & Scott, C. P. (1991), Depression in primary care: Treating depression with interpersonal psychotherapy. In C. S. Austad & W. H. Berman (Eds.), *Psychotherapy in managed health care: The optimal use of time and resources* (pp.153–170). Washington, DC: American Psychological Association.

Schulberg, H. C., Scott, C. P., Madonia, M. J., & Imber, S. D. (1993). Applications of interpersonal psychotherapy to depression in primary care practice. In G. L. Klerman & M. M. Weissman (Eds.), *New applications of interpersonal psychotherapy* (pp. 265–291). Washington, DC: American Psychiatric Press.

Seligman, M. E. P. (1995). The effectiveness of psychotherapy: The *Consumer Reports* study. *American Psychologist, 12,* 965–974.

Shea, M. T., Elkin, I., Imber, S. D., Sotsky, S. M., Watkins, J. T., Collins, J. F., Pilkonis, P. A., Beckham, E., Glass, D. R., Dolan, R. T., & Parloff, M. B. (1992). Course of depressive symptoms over follow-up: Findings from the National Institute of Mental Health Treatment for Depression Collaborative Research Program. *Archives of General Psychiatry, 49,* 782–787.

Shea, M. T., Elkin, I., & Sotsky, S. M. (1999). Patient characteristics associated with successful treatment: Outcome findings from the NIMH Treatment of Depression Collaborative Research Program. In D. S. Janowsky (Ed.), *Psychotherapy indications and outcomes* (pp. 71–90). Washington, DC: American Psychiatric Press.

Sholomskas, A. J., Chevron, E. S., Prusoff, B. A., & Berry, C. (1983). Short-term interpersonal therapy (IPT) with the depressed elderly: Case reports and discussion. *American Journal of Psychotherapy, 36,* 552–566.

Showalter, J. E. (1995). Managed care: Income to outcome. *Journal of American Academy of Child and Adolescent Psychiatry, 34*(9), 1123.

Sloane, R. B., Stapes, F. R., & Schneider, L. S. (1985). Interpersonal therapy versus nortriptyline for depression in the elderly. In G. D. Burrows, T. R. Norman, & L. Dennerstein (Eds.), *Clinical and pharmacological studies in psychiatric disorders* (pp. 344–346). London: Libbey.

Sotsky, S. M., Glass, D. R., Shea, M. T., Pilkonis, P. A., Collins, J. F., Elkin, I., Watkins, J. T., Imber, S. D., Leber, W. R., Moyer, J., & Oliveri, M. E. (1991). Patient predictors of response to psychotherapy and pharmacotherapy: Findings in the NIMH Treatment of Depression Collaborative Research Program. *American Journal of Psychiatry, 148,* 997–1008.

Spinelli, M. (1997). *Manual of interpersonal psychotherapy for antepartum depressed women (IPT-P)*. Available through Dr. Spinelli, Columbia University College of Physicians and Surgeons, New York, NY.

Stuart, S., & O'Hara, M. W. (1995). IPT for postpartum depression. *Journal of Psychotherapy Practice and Research, 4,* 18–29.

Stuart, S., O'Hara, M. W., & Blehar, M. C. (1998). Mental disorders associated with childbearing: Report of the biennial meeting of The Marce Society. *Psychopharmacological Bulletin, 34,* 333–338.

Sullivan, H. S. (Ed.). (1953). *The interpersonal theory of psychiatry.* New York: Norton.

Thase, M. E., Buysse, D. J., Frank, E., Cherry, C. R., Cornes, C. L., Mallinger, A. G., & Kupfer, D. J. (1997). Which depressed patients will respond to interpersonal psychotherapy?: The role of abnormal EEG profiles. *American Journal of Psychiatry, 154,* 502–509.

Thase, M. E., Fava, M., Halbreich, U., Kocsis, J. H., Koran, L., Davidson, J., Rosenbaum, J., & Harrison, W. (1996). A placebo-controlled, randomized clinical trial comparing sertraline and imipramine for the treatment of dysthymia. *Archives of General Psychiatry, 53,* 777–784.

Weissman, M. M. (1995). *Mastering depression: A patient guide to interpersonal psychotherapy.* Albany, NY: Graywind Publications. Currently available through The Psychological Corporation, Order Service Center, P. O. Box 839954, San Antonio, TX 78283–3954, Tel 1–800–228–0752, Fax 1–800–232–1223.

Weissman, M. M., Klerman, G. L., Paykel, E. S., Prusoff, B. A., & Hanson, B. (1974). Treatment effects on the social adjustment of depressed patients. *Archives of General Psychiatry, 30,* 771–778.

Weissman, M. M., Klerman, G. L., Prusoff, B. A., Sholomskas, D., & Padian, N. (1981). Depressed outpatients: Results one year after treatment with drugs and/or interpersonal psychotherapy. *Archives of General Psychiatry, 38,* 52–55.

Weissman, M. M., & Markowitz, J. C. (1994). Interpersonal psychotherapy. *Archives of General Psychiatry, 51,* 599–606.

Weissman, M. M., Markowitz, J. C., & Klerman, G. L. (2000). *Comprehensive guide to interpersonal psychotherapy.* New York: Basic Books.

Weissman, M. M., Prusoff, B. A., DiMascio, A., Neu, C., Goklaney, M., & Klerman, G. L. (1979). The efficacy of drugs and psychotherapy in the treatment of acute depressive episodes. *American Journal of Psychiatry, 136,* 555–558.

Weissman, M. M., Rounsaville, B. J., & Chevron, E. S. (1982). Training psychotherapists to participate in psychotherapy outcome studies: Identifying and dealing with the research requirement. *American Journal of Psychiatry, 139,* 1442–1446.

Weissman, M. M., & Sanderson, W. C. (2001, October). Promises and problems in modern psychotherapy: The need for increased training in evidence-based treatments. Paper presented at the Josiah Macy Jr. Foundation Conference, Toronto, Canada.

Wilfley, D. E., MacKenzie, R. K., Welch, R. R., Ayres, V. E., & Weissman, M. M. (2000). *Interpersonal psychotherapy for group.* New York: Basic Books.

18

Marital and Family Therapy
for Depression in Adults

Steven R. H. Beach and Deborah J. Jones

Depression is a common psychiatric disturbance. Each year, more than 100 million people worldwide develop clinically recognizable depression. Moreover, it is estimated that between 8 and 18% of the general population will experience at least one clinically significant episode of depression during the course of their lifetime (Boyd & Weissman, 1981; Karno et al., 1987). For a significant portion of these individuals, depression will result in a suicide, with some estimates suggesting that 15% of depressed individuals will commit suicide (Hirschfeld & Goodwin, 1988). Given its incidence and prevalence across the life span, depression is a major social problem with tremendous social, familial, and economic costs. At the same time, depressed individuals often report problems with family relationships. Concerns about family relationships are prominent for many depressed persons. This has led to suggestions that depressed persons may often benefit from marital or family approaches to treatment, and has spawned several approaches to intervention. Given the scope of the problem, this is a suggestion that deserves close scrutiny.

Are marital and family interventions useful for persons suffering from depression? Some argue that the rhetoric in favor of marital and family intervention has begun to outstrip the data (e.g., Coyne & Benazon, 2001). In this chapter, however, we briefly lay out the argument in favor of the use of marital and family therapy in the treatment of depression, and respond to several areas of concern. We begin by presenting the evidence that the close relationships of depressed persons, and particularly their marital and parenting relationships, are often in need of repair. In addition, we discuss stress-generation theory as a framework for understanding the connection between problems in close relationships and depression. Second, we review the evidence that there are established and efficacious interventions for repair of marital and parental relationship difficulties. Third, we examine data regarding the efficacy of marital and parent training for depressed individuals and assess whether these interventions are appropriate and useful for depressed persons. We conclude that there is reason to offer treatment for marital or parenting relationship difficulties to many depressed adults, that efficacious treatments are available for these problems, and that the available interventions appear applicable to a depressed population.

After making the case in favor of marital and parenting interventions for depressed persons, we examine possible guidelines for choosing marital or parenting interventions for depression. First, we discuss predictors of response to treatment and suggest guidelines for application of marital and parenting interventions that may maximize "efficacy." Second, we examine the possibility that marital partners and other family members may often refuse to participate in treatment, rendering these approaches "ineffective" despite their apparent "efficacy," and we suggest guidelines to enhance "effectiveness."

In the final section of the chapter we discuss future directions for research and highlight the importance of basic research in the development of new forms of marital and family interventions. We conclude that marital and family therapies should stay closely tied to an empirical foundation. We examine the implications of recurrent depression and suggest the potential value of including a greater focus on the needs of the partner, and broadening intervention to deal with individual diatheses as well as reduction of relationship stress as ways of broadening the applicability of marital and family interventions. We suggest as well that new targets of intervention are likely to be highlighted within the framework provided by stress-generation theory. As this occurs and new targets of intervention are identified, it should be possible to enhance current marital and parenting interventions by better tailoring interventions to fit the needs of particular depressed individuals. It is this type of theory-guided integrative treatment that seems most likely to result in incremental enhancement of efficacy of marital and family treatments for depression. We also examine the need for additional studies of efficacy to establish marital and parenting interventions as efficacious treatments for depression.

THE CASE FOR MARITAL AND PARENTING INTERVENTIONS FOR DEPRESSION

There Is a Link between Marital and Family Relationships and Depression

How strong is the link between marital distress and depression? In a quantitative and exhaustive review of the marital literature, Whisman (2001) found that, across 26 cross-sectional studies, marital quality was negatively associated with depressive symptomatology for both women ($r = -.42$) and men ($r = -.37$), indicating a significant, albeit small, gender difference. Across 10 studies using diagnosed patient populations, Whisman (2001) found that the magnitude of the association was somewhat stronger for both women and men ($r = -.66$). The average dyadic adjustment scale (DAS) score for the diagnosed population was 93.7 ($SD = 25.2$), indicating that the average depressed individual is also maritally distressed (DAS cutoff = 97). Thus, marital relationships are often (but not always) distressed among depressed men and women. (See also Whiffen & Johnson, 1998, for a review of the postpartum literature).

There Is a Link between Parenting and Depression

What is the nature of the link between parenting behavior and depression? It has long been noted clinically that depressed patients report considerable distress and difficulty in their parenting relationships (e.g., Weissman & Paykel, 1974) and some have attributed depressed mothers' level of dysphoria, at least in part, to her belief that she is an inadequate parent (Teti & Gelfand, 1991). Supplementing clinical observation and patient self-report is a large body of direct observation documenting problems in parenting behavior. In a recent review of 46 observational studies of the parenting behavior of depressed women, Lovejoy, Gracyk, O'Hare, and Neuman (2000) found evidence supporting Goodman and Brumley's (1990) hypothesis that depressed mothers would display more withdrawn behavior, with an overall average correlation between depression and withdrawn behavior of .14. They also found support for Forehand, Lautenschlager, Faust, and Graziano's (1986) hypothesis that depressed mothers would display more negative parenting behavior, with an overall average correlation between depression and negative parenting behavior of .22, with a stronger effect for those in a current depressive episode than for those with only a history of depression. As with marital relationships, there is reason to believe that many, but not all, depressed persons experience difficulty in the area of parenting.

There Is a Causal Model Relating Family Problems and Depression

But what is the nature of the longitudinal relationship between depression and relationship difficulties? At the broadest level, possible causal relationships between family difficulties and depression include an effect of marital or family difficulties on depression, an effect of depression on marital or family difficulties, and a bidirectional pattern of causation. It is also possible that the nature of the relationship might change across different types of relationships as a function of the number of episodes of depression experienced, as a function of age, or as a function of other personal or symptom characteristics. The potential complexity of the relationships is somewhat overwhelming relative to currently available analytic strategies (Beach, Davey, & Fincham, 1999), yet some generalizations can be made based on available evidence. In addition, a model is available to guide further investigation and to help draw implications for clinical intervention.

What generalizations can be drawn regarding the link between family relationships and depression? In the marital area, many theorists have adopted some variant of Hammen's (1991) stress-generation theory to guide their theorizing about the link between marital discord and depression. Stress-generation theory suggests a bidirectional pattern of causation between family relationships and depression. It is posited that depressed individuals can generate stress in their interpersonal environments in a variety of ways, but this interpersonal stress can also exacerbate depressive symptoms. Illustrating the vicious cycle between depressive symptoms and marital difficulties, Davila, Bradbury, Cohan, and Tochluk, (1997) found that persons with more symptoms of depression were more negative in their supportive behavior toward the spouse and in their expectations regarding partner support. These negative behaviors and expectations, in turn, were related to greater marital stress. Finally, closing the loop, level of marital stress predicted subsequent depressive symptoms (controlling for earlier symptoms). Likewise, in his review of self-propagating processes in depression, Joiner (2000) highlights the propensity for depressed persons to seek negative feedback, to engage in excessive reassurance seeking, to avoid conflict and so withdraw, and to elicit changes in the partner's view of them. In each case, the behavior resulting from the individual's depression carries the potential to generate increased interpersonal stress or to shift the response of others in a negative direction. Joiner suggests that increased interpersonal negativity, in turn, helps maintain depressive symptoms.

Recent research also provides illustrations of the way in which stressful marital or family events can precipitate or exacerbate depressive symptoms among the vulnerable and so initiate the stress-generation process. For example, Cano and O'Leary (2000) found that humiliating events such as partner infidelity and threats of marital dissolution resulted in a sixfold increase in diagnosis of depression, and that this increased risk remained after controlling for family and personal history of depression. Further, Whisman and Bruce (1999) found that marital dissatisfaction increased risk of subsequent diagnosis of depression by

2.7-fold in a large, representative community sample; again, the increased risk remained significant after controlling for demographic variables and personal history of depression. As these studies suggest, marital distress and specific types of marital events may be sufficiently potent to precipitate a depressive episode. Thus, in the marital area, the broad outlines of the reciprocal relationship between depression and marital difficulties are already coming into focus .

In the area of parenting relationships, the reciprocal relationships between depression, parenting behavior, and parenting stress are also clear in broad brush. The data reviewed above, for example, suggest that parental depression is associated with a shift toward more lax, detached, inconsistent, and ineffective child management (see also Cummings & Davies, 1999, for a model and review), and problematic parenting practices in turn increase child deviance (e.g., Conger, Patterson, & Ge, 1995). As a consequence, depressed parents perceive their children as having more problems, their children actually do have more problems on average, and relationships between depressed parents and their children are more distressed. Recent research suggests that strained parent–child relationships may also predict maintenance of depressive symptoms (Jones, Beach, & Forehand, 2001). Jones et al. (2001) examined family stress generation among intact community families with adolescent children, and found that mothers' depressive symptoms generated perceived stress in both marital and mother–adolescent relationships 1 year later. In turn, greater mother-reported family relationship stress was related to greater exacerbation of her depressive symptoms. It appears, therefore, that parenting behavior is another area in which stress-generation may connect depression and family relationships.

Is Everyone at Equal Risk?

Are all persons equally reactive or vulnerable to negative interpersonal events? A large literature suggests that this is not the case. Personality variables (Davila, 2001), interpersonal sensitivities (Joiner, 2000), individual differences in biological vulnerability (Gold, Goodwin, & Chrousos, 1988), various negative childhood experiences (Kessler & Magee, 1993; Hammen, Henry, & Daley, 2000), and other individual difference variables have been linked to differential vulnerability to depression, differential vulnerability to stress, and differential vulnerability to recurrence. This literature suggests that everyone does not start with an equal chance of responding to negative interpersonal events with depression. In particular, it may be that some individuals are more sensitive to particular types of interpersonal problems and so may have a lower threshold for a depressive response (e.g., Hammen et al., 2000).

WHICH FAMILY INTERVENTIONS SHOULD BE USED TO INTERRUPT THE STRESS-GENERATION PROCESS?

What are the implications of stress-generation theory for family interventions with depressed persons? If depressive symptoms are maintained by a vicious cycle in which symptoms lead to stress-generating processes, which in turn help maintain symptoms, it should be useful to treat the stress-generating processes using efficacious interventions. Marital relationships and parenting relationships may provide excellent points of therapeutic intervention with depressed persons if (1) the stress-generating behaviors in each domain are amenable to change, (2) depressed persons can make the necessary changes in response to treatment, and (3) these changes can be maintained over time. Even if intervention in these domains did not produce rapid reduction in depressive symptoms, these are areas in need of attention by many depressed persons and appear to be implicated in the maintenance of depressive episodes via stress-generation processes. In fact, a growing body of literature suggests that failure to address marital and family issues in therapy for depression may interfere with the recovery process and increase the risk for relapse (cf. Hooley & Gotlib, 2000). Accordingly, the stress-generation perspective suggests that the marital and parenting relationships may be particularly useful targets of intervention for depressed individuals. An intervention for a vicious cycle requires the application of some efficacious method for interrupting the cycle. Once the vicious cycle is interrupted, more beneficial feedback processes may be set in motion, perhaps without additional direct therapeutic intervention. Marital and parenting interventions therefore seem to be appropriate and promising starting points for family intervention with depressed adults.

There Are Well-Established Interventions for Marital Discord and Parenting Difficulties

Are there effective interventions for marital discord and for parenting difficulties? For both marital discord and for parenting behavior there are already well-specified approaches that have been shown to be efficacious and that are easily accessible to clinicians. With regard to marital problems, several approaches to marital therapy have been found to be efficacious, including behavioral marital therapy, cognitive-behavioral marital therapy, emotion-focused therapy, and insight-oriented marital therapy (see Baucom, Shoam, Mueser, Daiuto, & Stickle, 1998, for a comprehensive review). Behavioral marital therapy, in particular, is an efficacious and specific treatment for marital discord that has been successfully applied cross-culturally (Hahlweg & Markman, 1988), is well specified, and is widely available for clinical application on a broad scale (e.g., Markman, Stanley, & Blumberg, 1994). Likewise, parent management training (Patterson, 1982; Patterson, Reid, & Dishion, 1992) is an efficacious intervention for a range of child behavior problems including conduct disorder (Kazdin, 1998), and has been elaborated and applied to a range of child behavior problems (McMahon, Forehand, Griest, & Wells, 1981; Sanders & Dadds, 1993; Taylor & Biglan, 1998). Accordingly, there is substantial reason to expect that depressed persons could be helped to enhance their functioning in these areas and so interrupt stress-generation processes triggered by an ongoing depressive episode. If so, one might expect benefit both with regard to greater relationship satisfaction and with regard to decreased symptoms over time.

Goals and Basic Elements of Major Treatment Approaches

Behavioral Marital Therapy

Behavioral marital therapy (BMT) is typically a relatively brief approach to treatment that focuses on changing problem behavior through skill building . The therapist using BMT for depression adopts a combination of social learning, behavioral exchange, and cognitive techniques across three phases of treatment. First, the therapist will focus on identifying and rapidly eliminating extreme stressors within the relationship, as well as reestablishing positive exchanges through homework assignments that pinpoint behaviors associated with marital satisfaction (e.g., identifying and engaging in mutually pleasant activities). When successfully implemented, this stage of therapy will often produce a substantial elevation in mood for the depressed patient and increased expressions of positive feelings by both partners. This initial boost in morale and positive feelings provides the foundation for the couple to confront the second phase of therapy: restructuring the marital relationship.

The second phase of therapy is focused on the way the spouses communicate, solve problems, and interact on a daily basis. This phase of therapy provides the couple with a more supportive pattern of problem resolution; it systematically increases the support value of the relationship in the areas of acceptance of emotional expression, actual and perceived coping assistance, perceived spousal dependability, and couple intimacy. During this phase of therapy, there will typically be further decreases in the stress previously associated with coercive patterns of exchange within the couple. Relationship cohesion and self-esteem support are likely to receive some additional attention during this phase of therapy, but they will typically be less a focus of attention than during the first phase. When successfully implemented, this phase of therapy leaves the couple better integrated and better able to handle difficulties they may encounter in the future.

The third phase of therapy has as its focus preparing the couple for termination, which requires the therapist to take a less directive stance. In this final phase of therapy, the therapist is interested primarily in helping the client identify likely high-risk situations that may produce either relapse of depressive symptoms or a return to marital dissatisfaction. Vulnerabilities for further problems and warning signs are reviewed. The therapist prepares the couple to expect, and be accepting of, transitory symptoms of both depression and marital difficulties. Appropriate ways of coping with both are reviewed. During the final phase, the therapist helps the couple attribute their gains in therapy to their caring and love for one another.

In recent years, BMT has undergone some changes in an effort to enhance the efficacy of marital therapy with couples who were less responsive to traditional approaches. Many of these changes are reflected in integrative couples therapy (ICT; Jacobson & Christensen, 1996). Couples with lower levels of commitment, who were older, emotionally disengaged, or had relatively divergent goals for the relationship were less likely to compromise, accommodate, and collaborate—all of which were required for success with traditional BMT. Rather than relying entirely on change strategies in which one of the partners accommodates to the requests of the other, ICT integrates strategies for fostering both acceptance and change.

Interpersonal Psychotherapy–Conjoint Marital Therapy

Interpersonal psychotherapy for the treatment of depression (IPT; Klerman, Weissman, Rounsaville, & Chevron, 1984) is an individually based approach developed in the 1970s that aims to help the depressed individual understand and negotiate his or her interpersonal context that is associated with the onset and maintenance of his or her depressive symptoms. The treatment addresses four major interpersonal difficulties: grief, role disputes, role transitions, and interpersonal deficits.

More recently, IPT was modified to involve the spouse of the patient in the treatment process, in what is called conjoint marital therapy (CM). This approach, IPT-CM, incorporates some aspects of marital therapy into the IPT framework, with a focus on incorporating techniques that enhance couple communication (Foley, Rounsaville, Weissman, Sholomskas, & Chevron, 1989). Accordingly, the two major goals of IPT-CM are to facilitate the remission of the identified patient's depressive symptoms and to resolve marital disputes by renegotiating roles. Similar to other marital therapy approaches, IPT-CM progresses in three phases: initial, intermediate, and termination.

The initial phase of IPT-CM focuses on obtaining a history of the depressive symptoms from the patient, and the spouse, educating the couple about depression and its correlates, obtaining a history of the marital relationship, and identifying treatment goals. The intermediate phase focuses on renegotiating marital roles. The couple's level of relationship functioning is assessed in the areas of communication, intimacy, boundary management, leadership, and attainment of socially appropriate goals. A feature that may distinguish IPT-CM from other marital approaches is the focus on the individual problems of the identified patient. The IPT-CM therapist is careful to distinguish between the individual problems of each spouse and the conjoint problems of their marriage. Accordingly, the therapist shifts between focusing on the individual problems of each partner and the couple's issues as a couple. Consistent with BMT, the termination phase involves reviewing the couple's progress, identifying potential obstacles, and evaluating possible solutions using IPT-CM techniques.

Well-Established Marital Therapy Approaches Work When Applied to Depressed Persons

Do these approaches work when applied to depressed patients? Given the reciprocal link between marital discord and depression, a number of clinicians and researchers have suggested that marital interventions are indicated in the treatment of depression. Several studies have examined well-specified approaches and have examined their efficacy in reducing symptoms of depression and in enhancing marital satisfaction. Three trials compared a standard couple therapy, behavioral marital therapy, to individual therapy (Beach & O'Leary, 1992; Emanuels-Zuurveen & Emmelkamp, 1996; Jacobson, Dobson, Fruzzetti, Schmaling, & Salusky, 1991). Two clinical trials involved adaptation of individual therapies for depression to a couples format (Emanuels-Zuurveen & Emmelkamp, 1997; Foley et al., 1989). There has been one trial of a cognitive couple therapy (Teichman, Bar-El, Shor, Sirota, & Elizur, 1995) and one trial comparing marital therapy to antidepressant medication (Leff et al., 2000), but these did not examine change in marital satisfaction. Because stress-generation theory suggests the value of modifying the stress-generation process as a way of influencing symptoms of depression, we examine first those studies that assessed change in marital satisfaction.

Three studies compared behavioral marital therapy to individual therapy with similar results. First, Jacobson et al. (1991) randomly assigned 60 married, depressed women to either BMT, individual CT, or a treatment combining BMT and CT. Couples were not selected for the presence of marital discord and so could be divided into those who were more and less maritally distressed. Next, Beach and O'Leary (1992) randomly assigned 45 couples in which the wife was depressed to one of three conditions: (1) conjoint BMT, (2) individual CT, or (3) a 15-week waiting-list condition. To be included in the study, both partners had to score in the discordant range of the DAS and report ongoing marital discord. Finally, Emanuels-Zuurveen and Emmelkamp (1996) assigned 27 depressed outpatients to either individual cognitive-behavioral therapy or communication-focused marital therapy. As in Foley et al. (1989), the sample for this study included both depressed husbands ($N = 13$) and depressed wives ($N = 14$). Consistent across the three studies, BMT and individual CT yielded equivalent outcomes when the dependent variable was depressive symptoms and a better outcome in marital therapy than in individual therapy when the dependent variable was marital functioning. In addition, marital therapy was found to be significantly better than wait-list control (Beach & O'Leary, 1992)

Foley and colleagues (1989) was the first to empirically test an individual therapy for depression adapted for couples format. In their study, 18 depressed outpatients were randomly assigned to either individual interpersonal psychotherapy (IPT) or a newly developed, couple-format version of IPT. Consistent with the findings of the studies comparing behavioral marital therapy with an individual approach, Foley et al. (1989) found that participants in both treatments exhibited a significant reduction in depressive symptoms, but found no significant differences between treatment groups in amount of reduction in depressive symptoms. Both interventions also produced equal enhancement of general interpersonal functioning. However, participants receiving couple IPT reported marginally higher marital satisfaction scores on the Locke–Wallace Short Marital Adjustment Test and scored significantly higher on one subscale of the DAS at session 16.

In a separate study of a modified individual treatment for depression, Emanuels-Zuurveen and Emmelkamp (1997) involved spouses in the treatment of depression in the absence of marital discord. Spouse-aided cognitive therapy, as developed by Emanuels-Zuurveen and Emmelkamp (1997), was similar to individual CT, except that the spouse attended all sessions and worked with the depressed individual to develop strategies to cope with the depression. The authors reported that in their trial of couples who were not dissatisfied with their marital relationships, spouse-aided CT was equally, but not more, effective than individual therapy in treating depression. Neither treatment had an effect on marital dissatisfaction.

Two of the studies reviewed above indicate that the effect of marital therapy on level of symptoms of depression is mediated by changes in marital adjustment. Beach and O'Leary (1992) found that posttherapy marital satisfaction fully accounted for the effect of marital therapy on depression. Likewise, Jacobson et al. (1991) found that changes in marital adjustment and depression covaried for depressed individuals who received marital therapy, but not for those who received CT. Therefore, it appears that marital therapy influences depressive symptomatology either by enhancing marital satisfaction or else by producing changes in the marital environment associated with enhanced satisfaction. CT appears to work through a different mechanism of change (i.e., cognitive change; see Whisman, 1993).

Two additional studies have examined conjoint therapy in the treatment of marital therapy, but did not assess change in level of marital satisfaction. Cognitive marital therapy (CMT) was developed by Teichman and colleagues (1995) as a couple therapy for depression with the aim of addressing "dysfunctional reciprocities" that exist in marital relationships, such as overprotection on the part of the spouse, hostility, or ambivalence. Teichman et al. (1995) compared CMT to CT and a no-treatment control group in a sample of 45 married depressed individuals. CMT was superior to CT and no-treatment at posttherapy assessment. However, in contrast to the research reviewed above by Jacobson et al. (1991) and Beach and O'Leary (1992), Teichman et al. (1995) did not find individual CT to be superior to a control group at posttherapy assessment. Further clouding the interpretation of the superiority of CMT to CT, at 6-month follow-up there were no significant differences between the two active treatment groups. Also, because Teichman and colleagues did not measure marital satisfaction, it is not possible to tell whether CMT was successful in enhancing the marital relationships of the participants. Nonetheless, it is possible to conclude that CMT was superior to no-treatment in reducing depressive symptomatology in a depressed sample.

Leff et al. (2000) conducted a randomized control trial of antidepressants ($N = 37$) versus couple therapy ($N = 40$) in the treatment and maintenance of major depression. The authors reported that depression improved as a function of therapy in both groups (but only on the Hamilton Rating Scale for Depression). At the same time, participants in the couple therapy condition demonstrated a significant advantage, both posttreatment and at a 2-year follow-up (but only on the BDI). Moreover, attrition rates were significantly greater for the antidepressant group (56.8%) relative to the couple therapy group (15%). Because the authors did not find evidence of a significant interaction between treatment and time of assessment for either index of depressive symptoms (i.e., no evidence of differential change pre–post by condition), the study provides only marginal support for the efficacy of marital therapy. This weakness of the findings is especially noteworthy given that one might have expected end-point analysis (the only analysis of outcome reported), which penalizes the condition with higher dropout rates, to favor marital therapy.

Only the Beach and O'Leary (1992) study is a controlled study of BMT for depression.

Only the Teichman study is a controlled study of CMT for depression. The other studies reviewed above demonstrate equivalence of marital interventions and individual interventions for depression, but they do not have sufficient sample sizes to satisfy current reviewer requirements for concluding that treatments are equivalent ($N = 25$ to 30 per condition; Chambless & Hollon, 1998). The Leff et al. (2000) study has sufficient power in its comparison of marital therapy and pharmacotherapy, but demonstrated an effect of treatment on only one outcome measure, rendering the demonstration of equivalence ambiguous. Accordingly, unless one treats different types of marital therapy as functionally equivalent, and uses a meta-analytic approach to combine samples, there are not sufficient data to argue that marital therapy has been shown to be an efficacious treatment for depression. Nonetheless, cast within a stress-generation framework, the studies are sufficient to suggest several important conclusions. First, it is clear that efficacious forms for marital therapy can be safely and usefully applied to a depressed population. *Furthermore, BMT emerges as a specific and efficacious treatment for marital discord,* even when the marital discord is occurring in the context of depression. That is, BMT has been shown in three independent studies to produce significant change in marital distress in a discordant and depressed population, and in each case it has outperformed a control group and/or an alternative intervention. Because the marital relationship appears to be an important context for stress generation, successful intervention of this sort can be viewed as particularly promising and provides a strong rationale for recommending marital intervention, where appropriate, with depressed patients. Given the promising effects on reduction of depressive symptoms, it is important that work continue to establish as well that marital therapy may be an efficacious treatment for depression, and to clearly specify the conditions under which it may serve as a treatment for depression in its own right.

Well-Established Approaches to Parent Training Work for Depressed Patients

Given the prominence of parent–child disputes among the concerns of depressed parents (Weissman & Paykel, 1974), it seems likely that parent training could also be an important point of intervention with depressed patients. Intervention programs designed to enhance parenting skills and ultimately parenting efficacy may reduce depressed mothers' depressive symptomatology, as well as enhance child and family adjustment. Surprisingly, there have been relatively few efforts to examine the efficacy of parent training for parental depressive symptoms, and only one study has examined the efficacy of parent training by itself in relieving depression among parents diagnosed with depression.

In an early suggestive attempt to examine the effect of parent training on depressive symptoms, Forehand, Wells, and Griest (1980) examined the effects of a parent-training program in a sample of 15 clinic-referred children and their mothers. The program involved teaching parents to use social reinforcement and time-out. The clinic-referred families were compared to non-clinic-referred mother–child dyads ($N = 15$) pre- and posttreatment on measures of child adjustment, parent adjustment, home observation, and consumer satisfaction. Of relevance to our discussion of family therapies for depression, Forehand and colleagues (1980) reported that parents of clinic children were significantly more depressed pretreatment, but not posttreatment, than nonclinic mothers. Furthermore, the mothers in the clinic-referred, but not the nonclinic group, evidenced a significant reduction in depressive symptoms from pre- to posttreatment (see also Dadds & McHugh, 1992, and Webster-Stratton, 1994, for other demonstrations with depressive symptoms).

One reason that parent training might have been underinvestigated as an intervention for parents with a diagnosis of depression is that depressed parents seem to do somewhat less well in parent training than do other parents. For example, depressed mothers have greater difficulty learning parenting skills (e.g., Dumas, Gibson, & Albin, 1989) and are more prone to drop out of treatment prematurely (e.g., McMahon et al., 1981). Accordingly, one obstacle to the use of parent training may be providing it in a way that allows it to be successful with a depressed population.

In a direct test of the value of parent training for clinically depressed mothers, Sanders and McFarland (2000) compared two forms of behavioral family intervention to examine the effect of a parent-training intervention (behavioral family intervention [BFI]) with that of a combination CT–parent-training intervention (cognitive-behavioral family intervention [CBFI]). Forty-seven families in which the mother met diagnostic criteria for major depression and in which at least one child met diagnostic criteria for either conduct disorder or oppositional–defiant disorder were randomly assigned to one of two conditions. Those assigned to the traditional BFI ($N = 24$, with 19 completing treatment) received instruction, role playing, feedback, and coaching in the use of social learning principles. Those assigned to the CBFI condition ($N = 23$, with 20 completing treatment) received cognitive interventions integrated into each treatment session that were designed to increase personally reinforcing family activities, identify and interrupt dysfunctional child-related cognitions and automatic thoughts, and increase relaxation. In each case, therapy was provided individually once a week and was accompanied by two home visits each week. There were 12 sessions with either one or both parents present, with treatment completed over a 3- to 5-month time period.

Of importance for the current review, both parenting interventions produced substantial reduction in depressive symptoms and negative cognitions, and there was no interaction of condition with time of assessment. There was also significant improvement in child behavior problems in both conditions. Significantly more mothers in the CBFI condition (72%) than in the BFI condition (35%) were nondepressed at follow-up, however, suggesting a superior effect for CBFI with regard to maternal depression at follow-up. Accordingly, it appears that a highly structured and comprehensive version of parent training can benefit parents who are depressed, but some direct attention to cognitive symptoms of depression may enhance longer term effects on depression.

Another combination approach was attempted by Gelfand, Teti, Seiner, and Jameson (1996). They evaluated a multicomponent program in which registered nurses visited depressed mothers of infants at their homes to assess mothers' parenting skills, enhance mothers' self-confidence, and reinforce mothers' existing parenting techniques. Depressed mothers ($N = 73$) were referred by their clinicians and carried a diagnosis of major depression. Nondepressed control mothers ($N = 38$) were recruited from the community and matched on social and demographic variables. Depressed mothers were either assigned to the intervention group ($N = 37$) or the usual mental health care group (i.e., ongoing treatment with referral source). The intervention group involved assessment of mothers' needs and the development of individualized programs including modeling warm interactions with the infants, offering mild suggestions, and building self-confidence by appropriately reinforcing parenting skills. Nurses visited mothers and infants 25 times in 3-week intervals over a period of 6–12 months, then phased out home visits over four final visits. Gelfand and colleagues (1996) reported that there were no significant differences on Beck Depression Inventory scores (BDI) between the depressed intervention ($M = 22.51$, $SD = 11.24$) and depressed control ($M = 22.06$, $SD = 10.36$) groups at the start of the study. However, the intervention group demonstrated significantly greater improvement in depressive symptoms (posttherapy $M = 13.86$, $SD = 9.51$) than those in usual care (posttherapy $M = 20.06$, $SD = 12.35$). Once again, this program suggests that parent training may be a useful point of intervention to break into a stress-generation process for some depressed individuals.

Unless one combines data from studies of parent training for parents of infants and parent training for parents of children 3–9, the available research is not sufficient to show that parent training, by itself, is an efficacious intervention for major depression among parents dealing with problematic children. However, the research does suggest that parent training, itself an efficacious form of therapy for child management problems, can be provided to depressed persons in a safe and efficacious manner and may have beneficial effects both with regard to child outcomes and with regard to parental depression. As the Sanders and McFarland (2000) study suggests, it will be useful to consider ways to enhance parent training to make it easier to consume for depressed parents and perhaps to enhance its long-term effects on depressive symptoms. Combinations with various elements of CT may be useful in this regard.

TOWARD TREATMENT GUIDELINES

Predictors of Therapeutic Response

Should we expect marital and parenting interventions to be useful for all depressed persons so long as they are married or have children? Predictors of response to marital therapy suggest decision rules that may enhance outcome of marital therapy for depression. BMT appears to work best when the marital problems are salient to the depressed spouse (Beach & O'Leary, 1992) or when the depressed person believes that his or her marital difficulties have caused his or her current episode of depression (O'Leary, Risso, & Beach, 1990). Likewise, although severity of depressive symptoms may influence the ease of treatment, moderate to severe depression does not appear to preclude the use of marital therapy as an adjunctive intervention strategy (Beach, 1996). It seems, therefore, that BMT can be a safe and effective alternative to individual therapy for depression. Likewise, although it is in need of direct examination, it seems likely that marital therapy could prove a useful adjunctive treatment to medication (cf. Friedman, 1975). Similar conclusions are likely to hold for IPT-CM. Although predictors of response to treatment have not been examined empirically for IPT-CM, it is consistent with IPT to choose as targets those problem areas that are salient to the patient and that may be related to the maintenance of the current depressive episode (Weissman, Markowitz, & Klerman, 2000).

Although the research is less well developed in the case of parent training as an intervention for the depressed, one might hypothesize similar patterns will emerge as additional work accumulates. If so, one would expect to find better response to parent training when the child's behavior problems are salient and seen as a serious problem, or alternatively when the child's problem behavior is viewed as a major source of dysphoria and agitation. This suggests the value of parent training when the child carries a diagnosis such as conduct disorder or when the depressed adult is at a key transition that might render the parent relationship more salient—for example, the birth of a child. An advantage of parent training relative to marital therapy is that it may lend itself more easily to combination with CT (e.g., Sanders & McFarland, 2000) because parent training is often conducted with only the depressed person in attendance. However, the apparent success of a cognitive marital therapy in the Teichman et al. (1995) study suggests the potential to deal with individual or cognitive vulnerabilities in a couple context (see also EFT for a possible model in this regard; Greenberg & Johnson, 1988). Parent training may also be easier for some depressed parents to accept than an offer of marital therapy. Accordingly, it may be a better point of entry into the stress-generation process for some depressed patients.

Effectiveness

A major barrier to the use of marital and parenting interventions in the treatment of adult depression is the possibility that other family members will sabotage the therapy or render it ineffective by refusing to participate or by actively undermining the process of therapy. This might appear in randomized trials as refusal to be assigned to marital or parenting interventions, or as premature discontinuation of treatment. This may be conceptualized as a threat to the "effectiveness" of these interventions. That is, just as an efficacious medication may prove to be ineffective if its side effects are sufficiently unpalatable, marital and parenting interventions could prove to be ineffective if they led to negative reactions from other family members (or if depressed persons believe they will elicit such reactions).

Currently there is equivocal evidence regarding the degree to which refusal to participate represents a threat to the effectiveness of marital therapy for depression. On the one hand, an effectiveness study of marital therapy for depression conducted 25 years ago in a primary care setting failed when it proved impossible to enlist enough husbands to participate (McLean & Miles, 1975). On the other hand, the Leff et al. (2000) study reviewed above found much greater acceptance of marital therapy than CT, and their marital therapy condition produced a significantly lower dropout rate than did their medication condition. One interpretation of these widely varying results is that the acceptability of marital therapy as an intervention for depressed patients varies widely depending on subcultural characteristics. Perhaps marital therapy may now be more acceptable to a broad range of potential clients than it was 25 years ago (or perhaps it is more acceptable in England than in the Midwestern United States). Alternatively, one might suspect that consumer response is powerfully influenced by factors such as the enthusiasm of the referrer, the perception that the intervention is stigmatizing (or would be if others knew), the perceived burden of the intervention, and the perceived likelihood of the intervention proving helpful, among other factors. If so, one response to discrepant assessments of "effectiveness" might be to examine more closely the factors that help make "efficacious" interventions effective. Therefore, an important focus of research on marital and parenting interventions for depressed persons will be to examine consumer response to referrals for such treatments. Research that closely monitors the issues that render referral for family treatment more and less acceptable to depressed persons and their families seems particularly timely (for a discussion of general issues and directions in the relationship between efficacy and effectiveness research, see Nathan, Stuart, & Dolan, 2000).

With regard to parent training, we might suppose the acceptability and so the effectiveness would be greater and the limitations fewer. Parent training does not require the active participation of both parents (although it is desirable), and there may be fewer self-esteem challenges or perceived sources of embarrassment in enrolling in parent training than enrolling in marital therapy. Also, parent training is commonly presented with great confidence by referring agents and is rarely seen as implying anything negative about the parents despite the fact that change in the parent's behavior is the primary focus of the intervention. However, as with marital therapy, one might expect little benefit unless depressed patients identify their relationships with their children as difficult and a source of strain and emotional turmoil. If parent training should prove to be a generally "safer" and more acceptable recommendation than marital therapy for many depressed patients, it may prove useful in some cases to recommend parent training as a first step when both parent training and marital therapy seem indicated.

FUTURE DIRECTIONS

Efficacy and Effectiveness Research

No specific marital therapy or parent training program can be designated efficacious for the alleviation of depression. Accordingly, it would seem reasonable to set as one priority establishing at that least one form of marital therapy and one form of parent training that are efficacious treatments for depression in their own right. This would require either one additional controlled investigation of the behavioral intervention in each case, or one larger scale investigation in which the therapy was compared with an alternative treatment know to be efficacious.

Attention to Vulnerability and Interpersonal Stress

Although there is a growing literature suggesting good outcome following marital therapy and parent training, there is considerable room for improvement in outcomes. One approach to enhancing the efficacy of these approaches would be to combine family therapy with individual therapies and/or antidepressant medications as a way of addressing individual vulnerabilities and interpersonal stressors together. There has been only one published attempt (Jacobson et al., 1991) to combine a well-specified marital therapy with individual therapy in the treatment of depression. Jacobson and colleagues (1991) combined BMT with CT and compared the efficacy of the combined approach with each of the component treatments. Contrary to the authors' hypotheses, however, the combined group was similar to CT in the treatment of depression in dissatisfied couples, and similar or slightly worse in treating depression in the nondistressed couples. In terms of marital satisfaction, the combined treatment did not work as well as BMT with the dissatisfied couples, but only the combined treatment yielded statistically significant improvement in level of satisfaction reported by the satisfied couples. These results are not very supportive of the hope that individual and family interventions can be combined to produce an enhanced approach.

In an attempt to explain why the combination treatment failed to yield better outcomes than each of the component treatments, Jacobson and colleagues proposed that in delivering the same number of meetings across the three groups, the combined treatment offered a "suboptimal dosage" of each of its component treatments. Additionally, Beach, Whisman, and O'Leary (1994) suggested that husbands may have felt relatively uninvolved in the combination treatment because they were typically included only after individual treatment had already been initiated. Building on these hypotheses, Whisman and Uebelacker (1999) suggested that Jacobson and colleagues' combined treatment may have been less efficacious than expected because the authors merely *combined* rather than *integrated* the two component techniques. An integrated treatment would be one " in which the component treatments are blended together into a "unified whole" rather than "joined two by two," as with Jacobson and colleagues' combined approach. This idea is given additional force by Teichman et al.'s (1995) apparent success in combining elements of CT and marital therapy and by Sanders and McFarland's successful attempt to combine elements of CT and parent training. Likewise, insight-oriented marital therapy (Snyder & Wills, 1989), emotion-focused marital therapy (Greenberg & Johnson, 1988), and integrative couples therapy (Jacobson & Christensen, 1996) offer interesting and apparently successful models for integrating a focus on individual vulnerabilities with a focus on marital interaction. Thus, there is some basis for optimism that an integrative intervention targeting both individual vulnerabilities and marital interaction could work.

Combination with Pharmacotherapy

Attrition rates for outpatient clinical trials of psychotropic medications are 30–40 % (Thase & Kupfer, 1997), and family conflicts are associated with poorer outcome to antidepressant trials (e.g., Rounsaville, Sholomskas, & Prusoff, 1980; Rounsaville, Weissman, Prusoff, &

Herceg-Baron, 1979). Possibly stress-generation processes within the family may be implicated as an impediment to successful medication management. If so, marital and parenting interventions might be seen as an avenue for increasing the effectiveness of antidepressant medication while decreasing stress within the family. Alternatively, one might suggest that antidepressant medications are a method for dealing with individual vulnerability to depression, whereas family intervention provides a method for dealing with the stress-generation processes that are common in depression and may set the stage for greater difficulty with depressive symptoms. If so, one might hypothesize that relapse and recurrence rates might be improved when efficacious family interventions are combined with antidepressant medication. Because no adequate trial of this hypothesis has been reported in the literature, this is an important area for future investigation.

Dealing with Recurrent Depression

Because most episodes of depression are recurrences and are likely to be followed by recurrences, marital and parenting interventions may be of limited value if their goal is merely to bring to an end a particular episode. What if the couple is not prepared for subsequent relapses and recurrences? If most episodes of depression in both mental health and primary practice settings are recurrences (Coyne, Pepper, & Flynn, 1999), and if many of the first episodes will have recurrences, clinicians need to consider subsequent episodes likely as they advise the couple or the depressed parent about the future. In addressing this issue for marital therapy, Coyne and Benazon (2001) suggest that it may be desirable to provide greater attention to the spouse and the spouse's potential sense of burden. This might involve helping the nondepressed partner do more to look after his or her own needs and to develop the skills of tolerance and patience that seemed called for if one is to live with recurrent depression. Alternatively, one might suggest a focus on "acceptance" and "joining with the partner" to help the nondepressed partner feel a greater sense of alliance with the depressed partner (see Cordova & Gee, 2001, for a discussion of ICT for depression). Likewise, one might suggest a greater focus on accessing and exploring the primary emotional responses that may be triggered by a partner's depression (Greenberg & Johnson, 1988). In common across these suggestions is an additional component in marital therapy for depression to help couples handle the longer term struggle with a difficult chronic problem, not just the short-term problems of a particular episode. In the context of parent-training interventions, this might take the form of additional efforts to involve the nondepressed partner in planning together for recurrences of depression. If so, parent training for depression might often evolve into some form of marital therapy for depression.

Identification of Health Benefits

It is interesting to hypothesize that attention to family concerns may constitute an important part of "health maintenance" for depressed persons, even when they are already receiving an individual psychotherapy or antidepressant medication. From the perspective of stress-generation theory, it is of interest whether or not successful individual approaches to the treatment of depression also alleviate the stress-generation process, and whether or not the stress-generation processes are linked to negative health outcomes other than depression. The outcome literature reviewed above suggests that individual therapies may not usually address significant sources of interpersonal distress. Likewise, a growing literature provides evidence for multiple mechanisms by which family relationships influence various health indices in addition to depressive symptomatology. In laboratory studies, marital discord has been linked to compromised immune functioning (e.g., Kiecolt-Glaser et al., 1988; Miller, Dopp, Myers, Stevens, & Fahey, 1999), disadvantageous endocrine system changes (e.g,. Malarkey, Kiecolt-Glaser, Pearl, & Glaser, 1994), and increases in blood pressure (Ewart, Taylor, Kraemer, & Agras, 1991). Accordingly, the stress-generation model lends itself to linking family intervention with the broader domain of general health outcomes, and provides a useful rationale for addressing family relationship problems among persons receiving individual or pharmacological interventions for depression.

Attention to the Disadvantaged and to Alternative Family Forms

Some work has suggested that the families most in need of treatment for depression either do not have access to or fail to seek mental health services (Sarason, 1974). Socially and economically disadvantaged families may be less likely to self-refer and typically do not do as well in treatment compared with middle-class populations (Dumas, 1986; Webster-Stratton, 1985). Many disadvantaged families fail to access services, and those who do tend to see the service as coercive and intrusive rather than as beneficial (Wahler, 1980). Efforts to offer family treatments for depression to disadvantaged groups, therefore, will likely involve special planning. One way to reach disadvantaged families may involve routine screenings by health care professionals trusted by the family members, such as family practice physicians or social workers (but see Coyne, Thompson, Palmer, Kagee, & Maunsell, 2000, for an argument against routine screening in the absence of adequate follow-up). Alternatively, information about family intervention services may be provided in a nonthreatening manner at nontreatment points of contact, such as community health care clinics, family practitioners, and day care centers, or through public service announcements. An additional challenge to widespread dissemination of efficacious interventions for marital and parenting difficulties, however, is that they must be low cost, easily accessible, and available on a continuing basis. This suggests that an important challenge for the future research is that of packaging efficacious interventions and developing delivery systems that can meet the expanding needs of a depressed population.

Family interventions for depression must also begin to consider alternative family forms (Johnson & Lebow, 2000). For example, the adaptation of family therapy to different ethnic and cultural contexts is imperative in order to ensure "effectiveness" in an increasingly diverse population. The special needs of gay and lesbian couples, or the specific needs of those who are remarried or part of stepfamilies, remains largely unexamined in the empirical literature, limiting the generalizability of current efficacy research. Issues of ethnicity, class, and culture are likely to influence the expectations that depressed individuals have for family relationships, and consequently their perceptions of the success of family intervention for depression. It will be necessary for marital and family therapists to consider how social, cultural, and economic factors may influence the link between depression and family distress and then to tailor family approaches to treatment to meet the needs of the depressed client and the family members. Issues such as racism, changing gender roles, multiple family forms, and same-sex relationships merit attention in the empirical literature and must be recognized as potentially influential variables that may impact the effectiveness of disseminating family approaches for depression to at-risk groups.

CONCLUSIONS: THE FUTURE OF FAMILY THERAPY FOR DEPRESSION

We have come far in the study of effective ways to intervene with the families of depressed patients. Although the current level of success should not be oversold (Coyne & Benazon,

2001), it is clear that a solid conceptual foundation is being constructed to guide and support family interventions with depressed patients. A large and robust literature indicates that marital and parenting relationships are often problematic for depressed persons. From the perspective of stress-generation theory, difficulties in the area of marital and parenting relationships, and the likelihood that they will continue even after individual pharmacological treatment, is troubling. At the same time, there is good evidence that these problematic relationships can be repaired. So it seems appropriate to recommend an efficacious, targeted intervention to effect that repair.

Stress-generation theory suggests that targeted, efficacious interventions have the potential to break the vicious cycles that may serve to maintain depression. If so, interventions that include attention to problematic family relationships may decrease future distress and decrease the risk for or severity of future episodes. This promise, however, awaits a conclusive demonstration. Likewise, it has not yet been shown conclusively that marital and parenting interventions provide efficacious and specific treatment for depression. However, available evidence is promising and continuing efforts to document the conditions under which marital and parenting interventions are efficacious in relieving an episode of depression seems warranted. In the meantime, both marital and parenting interventions can claim to be efficacious interventions for important sources of stress generation in depression.

Stress-generation theory also highlights the potential for particular areas of individual vulnerability to lead to problematic interpersonal processes. As the connection between particular areas of individual vulnerability and interpersonal stress generation is more clearly mapped, it may be possible to develop integrated approaches that combine attention to both individual sensitivities and problematic interpersonal relations. In particular, stress-generation theory lends itself to increasingly refined models and corresponding refinement of intervention. Stress-generation theory also provides an excellent "neutral" framework within which researchers of various backgrounds and orientations can share information and innovative suggestions (cf. Beach & Fincham, 2000). As we keep marital and family interventions for depression tightly focused on their empirical foundation, it may be increasingly useful to adopt stress-generation theory as a useful way of summarizing the many empirical findings into a single comprehensive set that can guide intervention.

REFERENCES

Baucom, D. H., Shoam, V., Mueser, K. T., Daiuto, A., & Stickle, T. R. (1998). Empirically supported couple and family interventions for marital distress and adult mental health problems. *Journal of Consulting and Clinical Psychology, 66,* 53–88.

Beach, S. R. H. (1996). Marital therapy in the treatment of depression. In C. Mundt, M. J. Goldstein, K. Hahlweg, & P. Fiedler (Eds.), *Interpersonal factors in the origin and course of affective disorders* (pp. 341–361). London: Gaskell.

Beach, S. R. H., Davey, A., & Fincham, F. D. (1999). The time has come to talk of many things: A commentary on Kurdek (1998) and the emerging field of marital processes in depression. *Journal of Family Psychology, 13,* 663–668.

Beach, S. R. H., & Fincham, F. D. (2000). Marital therapy and social psychology: Will we choose explicit partnership or cryptomnesia? In G. Fletcher & M. Clark (Eds.), *Blackwell handbook of social psychology: Interpersonal processes* (pp. 558–586). Oxford, UK: Blackwell.

Beach, S. R. H., & O'Leary, K. D. (1992). Treating depression in the context of marital discord: Outcome and predictors of response for marital therapy versus cognitive therapy. *Behavior Therapy, 23,* 507–258.

Beach, S. R. H., Whisman, M., & O'Leary, K. D. (1994). Marital therapy for depression: Theoretical foundation, current status, and future directions. *Behavior Therapy, 25,* 345–372.

Boyd, J. H., & Weissman, M. M. (1981). Epidemiology of affective disorders. *Archives of General Psychiatry, 38,* 1039–1046.

Cano, A., & O'Leary, K.D. (2000). Infidelity and separations precipitate major depressive episodes and symptoms of nonspecific depression and anxiety. *Journal of Consulting and Clinical Psychology, 68,* 774–781.

Chambless, D. L., & Hollon, S. D. (1998). Defining empirically supported therapies. *Journal of Consulting and Clinical Psychology, 66,* 7–18.

Conger, R., Patterson, G., & Ge, X. (1995). It takes two to replicate: A mediational model of the impact of parents' stress on adolescent adjustment. *Child Development, 66,* 80–97.

Cordova, J., & Gee, C. B. (2001). Couple therapy for depression: Using healthy relationships to treat depression. In S. R. H. Beach (Ed.), *Marital and family processes in depression: A scientific fourndation for intervention* (pp. 185–203). Washington, DC: American Psychological Association.

Coyne, J. C., & Benazon, N. R. (2001). Coming to terms with the nature of depression in marital research and treatment. In S. R. H. Beach (Ed.), *Marital and family processes in depression* (pp 25–43). Washington, DC: American Psychological Association.

Coyne, J. C., Pepper, C. M., & Flynn, H. (1999). Significance of prior episodes of depression in two patient populations. *Journal of Consulting and Clinical Psychology, 67,* 76–81.

Coyne, J. C., Thompson, R., Palmer, S. C., Kagee, A., & Maunsell, E. (2000). Should we screen for depression?: Caveats and potential pitfalls. *Applied and Preventive Psychology, 9,* 101–122.

Cummings, E. M., & Davies, P. T. (1999). Depressed parents and family functioning: Interpersonal effects and children's functioning and development. In T. Joiner & J. C. Coyne (Eds.), *Recent advances in interpersonal approaches to depression* (pp. 299–327). Washington, DC: American Psychological Association.

Dadds, M. R., & McHugh, T. A. (1992). Social support and treatment outcome in behavioral family therapy for child conduct problems. *Journal of Consulting and Clinical Psychology, 60,* 252–259.

Davila, J. (2001). Paths to unhappiness: The overlapping courses of depression and romantic dysfunction. In S. Beach (Ed.), *Marital and family processes in depression* (pp. 71–87). Washington, DC: American Psychological Association Press.

Davila, J., Bradbury, T. N., Cohan, C. L., & Tochluk, S. (1997). Marital functioning and depressive symptoms: Evidence for a stress generation model. *Journal of Personality and Social Psychology, 73,* 849–861.

Dumas, J. E. (1986). Parental perception and treatment outcome in families of aggressive children: A causal model. *Behavior Therapy, 17,* 420–432.

Dumas, J. E., Gibson, J. A., & Albin, J. B. (1989). Behavioral correlates of maternal depressive symptomatology in conduct-disorder children. *Journal of Consulting and Clinical Psychology, 57,* 516–521.

Emanuels-Zuurveen, L., & Emmelkamp, P. M. (1996). Individual behavioral-cognitive therapy vs. marital therapy for depression in maritally distressed couples. *British Journal of Psychiatry, 169,* 181–188.

Emanuels-Zuurveen, L., & Emmelkamp, P. M. (1997). Spouse-aided therapy with depressed patients. *Behavior Modification, 21,* 62–77.

Ewart, C. K., Taylor, C.B., Kraemer, H. C., & Agras, W. S. (1991). High blood pressure and marital discord: Not being nasty matters more than being nice. *Health Psychology, 10,* 155–163.

Foley, S. H., Rounsaville, B. J., Weissman, M. M., Sholomskas, D., & Chevron, E. (1989). Individual versus conjoint interpersonal psychotherapy for depressed patients with marital disputes. *International Journal of Family Psychiatry, 10,* 29–42.

Forehand, R., Lautenschlager, G. J., Faust, J., & Graziano, W. G. (1986). Parent perceptions and parent–child interactions in clinic-referred children: A preliminary investigation of the effects of maternal depressive moods. *Behavior Research and Therapy, 24,* 73–75.

Forehand, R. L., & McMahon, R. J. (1981). Helping the noncompliant child: A clinician's guide to parent training. New York: Guilford Press.

Forehand, R., Wells, K.C., & Griest, D.L. (1980). An examination of the social validity of a parent training program. *Behavior Therapy, 11,* 488–502.

Friedman, A. S. (1975). Interaction of drug therapy with marital therapy in depressive patients. *Archives of General Psychiatry, 32,* 619–637.

Gelfand, D. M., Teti, D. M., Seiner, S. A., & Jameson, P. B. (1996). Helping mother fight depression:

Evaluation of a home-based intervention for depressed mothers and their infants. *Journal of Clinical Child Psychology, 24,* 406–422.

Gold, P. W., Goodwin, F. K., & Chrousos, G. P. (1988). Clinical and biochemical manifestations of depression: Relation to the neurobiology of stress. *New England Journal of Medicine, 319,* 348–419.

Goodman, S. H., & Brumley, H. E. (1990). Schizophrenic and depressed mothers: Relational deficits in parenting. *Developmental Psychology, 26,* 31–39.

Greenberg, L. S., & Johnson, S. M. (1988). *Emotionally focused therapy for couples.* New York: Guilford Press.

Hahlweg, K., & Markman, H. J. (1988). Effectiveness of behavioral marital therapy: Empirical status of behavioral techniques in preventing and alleviating marital distress. *Journal of Consulting and Clinical Psychology, 56,* 440–447.

Hammen, C. (1991). *Depression runs in families: The social context of risk and resilience in children of depressed mothers.* New York: Springer-Verlag.

Hammen, C., Henry, R., & Daley, S. E. (2000). Depression and sensitization to stressors among young women as a function of childhood adversity. *Journal of Consulting and Clinical Psychology, 68,* 782–787.

Hirschfeld, R. M. A., & Goodwin, F. K. (1988). Mood disorders. In J. A. Talbott, R. E. Hales, & S. C. Yudofsky (Eds.), *Textbook of psychiatry* (pp. 403–441). Washington, DC: American Psychiatric Press.

Hooley, J. M., & Gotlib, I. H. (2000). A diathesis–stress conceptualization of expressed emotion and clinical outcome. *Applied and Preventive Psychology, 9,* 135–152.

Jacobson, N. S., & Christensen, A. (1996). *Integrative couple therapy: Promoting acceptance and change.* New York: Norton.

Jacobson, N. S., Dobson, K., Fruzzetti, A. E., Schmaling, K. B., & Salusky, S. (1991). Marital therapy as a treatment for depression. *Journal of Consulting and Clinical Psychology, 59,* 547–557.

Johnson, S., & Lebow, J. (2000). The coming of age of couple therapy: A decade of review. *Journal of Marriage and Family Counseling, 26,* 23–38.

Joiner, T. E. (2000). Depression's vicious scree: Self-propogating and erosive processes in depression chronicity. *Clinical Psychology: Science and Practice, 7,* 203–218.

Jones, D. J., Beach, S. R. H., & Forehand, R. (2001). Stress generation in intact community families: Depressive symptoms, perceived family relationship stress, and implications for adolescent adjustment. *Journal of Social and Personal Relationships, 18,* 443–462.

Karno, M., Hough, R.L., Burnam, A., Escobar, J., Timbers, D. M., Santana, F., & Boyd, J. H. (1987). Lifetime prevalence of specific psychiatric disorders among Mexican Americans in Los Angeles and non-Hispanic whites in Los Angeles. *Archives of General Psychiatry, 44,* 695–701.

Kazdin, A. E. (1998). Psychosocial treatments for conduct disorder in children. In P. E. Nathan & J. M. Gormon (Eds.), *Treatments that work* (pp. 65–89). New York: Oxford University Press.

Kessler, R. C., & Magee, W. J. (1993). Childhood adversities and adult depression: Basic patterns of association in a U.S. national survey. *Psychological Medicine, 23,* 679–690.

Kiecolt-Glaser, J. K., Kennedy, S., Malkoff, S., Fisher, L., Speicher, C. E., & Glaser, R. (1988). Marital discord and immunity in males. *Psychosomatic Medicine, 50,* 213–229.

Klerman, G. L., Weissman, M. M., Rounsaville, B. J., & Chevron, E. S. (1984). *Interpersonal psychotherapy of depression.* New York: Basic Books.

Leff, J., Vearnals, S., Brewin, C. R., Wolff, G., Alexander, B., Asen, E., Dayson, D., Jones, E., Chisholm, D., & Everitt, B. (2000). The London Depression Intervention Trial. *British Journal of Psychiatry, 177,* 95–100.

Lovejoy, M. C., Gracyk, P. A., O'Hare, E., & Neuman, G. (2000). Maternal depression and parenting behavior: A meta-analytic review. *Clinical Psychology Review, 20,* 561–592.

Malarkey, W. B., Kiecolt-Glaser, J. K., Pearl, D., & Glaser, R. (1994). Hostile behavior during marital conflict alters pituitary and adrenal hormones. *Psychosomatic Medicine, 56,* 41–51.

Markman, H., Stanley, S., & Blumberg, S. I. (1994). *Fighting for your marriage.* San Francisco: Jossey-Bass.

McLean, P. D., & Miles, J. E. (1975). Training family physicians in psychosocial care: An analysis of a program failure. *Journal of Medical Education, 50,* 900–902.

McMahon, R. J., Forehand, R., Griest, D. L., & Wells, K. C. (1981). Who drops out of therapy during parent training? *Behavioral Counseling Quarterly, 1,* 79–85.

Miller, G. E., Dopp, J. M., Myers, H., Stevens, S. Y., & Fahey, J. L. (1999). Psychosocial predictors of natural killer cell mobilization during marital conflict. *Health Psychology, 18,* 262–271.

Nathan, P. E., Stuart, S. P., & Dolan, S. L. (2000). Research on psychotherapy efficacy and effectiveness: Between Scylla and Charybdis? *Psychological Bulletin, 126,* 964–981.

O'Leary, K. D., Risso, L., & Beach, S. R. H. (1990). Beliefs about the marital discord/depression link: Implications for outcome and treatment matching. *Behavior Therapy, 21,* 413–422.

Patterson, G. R. (1982). *Coercive family processes.* Eugene, OR: Castilia.

Patterson, G. R., Reid, J. B., & Dishion, T. J. (1992). *Antisocial boys.* Eugene, OR: Castilia.

Rounsaville, B. J., Sholomskas, D., & Prusoff, B. A. (1980). Chronic mood disorders in depressed outpatients: Diagnosis and response to pharmocotherapy. *Journal of Affective Disorders, 2,* 73–88.

Rounsaville, B. J., Weissman, M. M., Prusoff, B. A., & Herceg-Baron, R. L. (1979). Marital disputes and treatment outcome in depressed women. *Comprehensive Pyschiatry, 20,* 483–490.

Sanders, M. R., & Dadds, M. R. (1993). *Behavioral family intervention.* Needham Heights, MA: Allyn & Bacon.

Sanders, M. R., & McFarland, M. (2000). Treatment of depressed mothers with disruptive children: A controlled evaluation of cognitive behavioral family intervention. *Behavior Therapy, 31,* 89–112.

Sarason, S. B. (1974). *The psychological sense of community: Prospects for community psychology.* Cambridge, MA: Brookline.

Snyder, D., & Wills, R. (1989). Behavioral versus insight oriented marital therapy: Effects on individual and interspousal functioning. *Journal of Consulting and Clinical Psychology, 57,* 39–46.

Taylor, T. K., & Biglan, A. (1998). Behavior family interventions for improving child-rearing: A review of the literature for clinicians and policy makers. *Clinical Child and Family Psychology Review, 1,* 41–60

Teichman, Y., Bar-El, Z., Shor, H., Sirota, P., & Elizur, A. (1995). A comparison of two modalities of cognitive therapy (individual and marital) in treating depression. *Psychiatry, 58,* 136–148.

Teti, D. M., & Gelfand, D. M. (1991). Behavioral competence among mothers of infants in the first year: The mediational role of maternal self-efficacy. *Child Development, 62,* 918–929.

Thase, M. E., & Kupfer, D. J. (1997). Recent developments in the pharmocotherapy of mood disorders. *Journal of Consulting and Clinical Psychology, 64,* 646–659.

Wahler, R. G. (1980). The insular mother: Her problems in parent–child treatment. *Journal of Applied Behavior Analysis, 13*(2), 207–219.

Webster-Stratton, C. (1985). Predictors of treatment outcome in parent training for conduct disordered children. *Behavior Therapy, 16,* 223–243.

Webster-Stratton, C. (1994). Advancing video tape parent training: A comparison study. *Journal of Consulting and Clinical Psychology, 62,* 583–593.

Weissman, M. M., Markowitz, J. C., & Klerman, G. L. (2000). *Comprehensive guide to interpersonal psychotherapy.* New York: Basic Books.

Weissman, M. M., & Paykel, E. S. (1974). *The depressed woman: A study of social relationships.* Chicago: University of Chicago Press.

Whiffen, V. E., & Johnson, S. M. (1998). An attachment theory framework for the treatment of childbearing depression. *Clinical Psychology: Science and Practice, 5,* 478–493.

Whisman, M. A. (2001). The association between depression and marital dissatisfaction. In S. R. H. Beach (Ed.), *Marital and family processes in depression: A scientific foundation for clinical practice* (pp. 3–24). Washington, DC: American Psychological Association.

Whisman, M. A. (1993). Mediators and moderators of change in cognitive therapy of depression. *Psychological Bulletin, 114,* 248–265.

Whisman, M. A., & Bruce, M. L. (1999). Marital distress and incidence of major depressive episode in a community sample. *Journal of Abnormal Psychology, 108,* 674–678.

Whisman, M. A., & Uebelacker, L. A. (1999). Integrating couple therapy with individual therapies and antidepressant medications in the treatment of depression. *Clinical Psychology: Science and Practice, 6*(4), 415–429.

19

Treatment of Depression in Children and Adolescents

Nadine J. Kaslow, Erin B. McClure, and Arin M. Connell

In recent years, increased attention has been paid to evidence-based psychosocial and pharmacological interventions for depressed youth. The need to highlight what we know about treatment is underscored by the fact that most depressed youth do not receive treatment (Keller, Lavori, Beardslee, Wunder, & Ryan, 1991). However, as knowledge about treatments for youth depression has increased, the rate of treatment appears to have improved (Hamilton & Bridge, 1999). Although depression among youth is treated more often, it is not clear that standard practice is effective at alleviating depressive symptoms or preventing recurrence. In addition, there is a bias toward the use of medication and extremely brief psychosocial interventions. This chapter reviews psychosocial and pharmacological treatments for depression in infancy through adolescence, uses the criteria for determining empirically supported treatments set forth by the Society of Clinical Psychology (Division 12) of the American Psychological Association (Chambless et al., 1998) to provide information about whether interventions are ready for wide dissemination, summarizes strengths and weaknesses of the research, and suggests future directions for study.

PSYCHOSOCIAL TREATMENTS FOR INFANTS AND TODDLERS

Although depression may occur in infants and toddlers, the myriad challenges associated with the assessment and diagnosis of depression in these youngsters has hindered the conduct of treatment outcome studies (Lous, De Wit, De Bruyn, Riksen-Walraven, & Rost, 2000). Therefore, it is not surprising that there is a dearth of empirical examination of treatment efficacy and effectiveness studies in this area. Several researchers, however, have examined interventions for high-risk infants and toddlers whose mothers are depressed.

Field, Grizzle, Scafidi, and Schanberg (1996) found that relative to an attention control, massage therapy reduced crying, salivary cortisol, and alertness in 1- to 3-month-olds with depressed, disadvantaged, teen mothers. Posttreatment, massaged infants slept more than controls. Six weeks later, they had gained more weight; improved more on emotionality, sociability, and soothability ratings; and their stress-hormone levels had decreased more. In a second study, massage attenuated right frontal EEG asymmetry (depression marker) in 25 1-month-olds of depressed mothers; lack of a control condition limits interpretation (Jones, Field, & Davalos, 1998).

Lyons-Ruth, Connell, Grunebaum, and Botein (1990) found effects on children's cognitive functioning following a home-visit intervention for depressed, disadvantaged mothers. Thirty-one mothers of babies ranging in age from newborn to 9-months-old participated in a 9- to 18-month home-visit intervention designed to provide mothers with a supportive relationship, increase access to community services, model and reinforce appropriate mother–infant interactions, and decrease feelings of social isolation. Mothers in the home-visit group were compared to an untreated group of 10 high-risk mothers, and to 35 community controls. Children of treated mothers showed more improvement on the Bayley Mental Development Index (MDI) than children of untreated depressed mothers, and were twice as likely to be classified as securely attached after treatment. However, other researchers have not found that treatments for postpartum depressed women have had a positive effect on their infants' cognitive development (Cooper & Murray, 1997; Gelfand, Teti, Seiner, & Jameson, 1996).

Cicchetti, Rogosch, and Toth (2000) examined toddler–parent psychotherapy (TPP), an attachment-oriented treatment based on the work of Fraiberg (Fraiberg, Adelson, & Shapiro, 1975), on the cognitive development of toddlers of depressed mothers. TPP provides mothers with a corrective emotional experience, helps them alter internalized attachment representations, and ultimately fosters improved mother–child interactions. In Cicchetti and colleagues' (2000) investigation, depressed mothers and their 20-month-olds were assigned to either TPP ($N = 43$) or nonintervention control groups ($N = 53$). Both groups were compared to a nondepressed control group ($N = 61$). Mothers in the TPP condition attended an average of 46 sessions. Although at 20 months, no differences were found in children's Bayley MDI scores across groups, at 3-year follow-up, children of untreated depressed mothers scored lower on a cognitive measure (WPPSI-R) than children in the depressed-TPP or nondepressed control groups. Children in the latter two groups did not differ from one another. These data suggest that improving mother–child interactions fosters the cognitive development of at-risk children.

In sum, two studies link massage therapy with decreased depressive symptoms and more adaptive development for infants of depressed mothers. However, further research that includes control conditions and long-term follow-up is needed. Home visitation may also help high-risk infants of depressed mothers. However, long-term follow-up data are needed before a more complete evaluation of such programs is possible. While TPP appears potentially efficacious for toddlers at risk for depression, the intervention length may be cumbersome for stressed families, as highlighted by the relatively high attrition rate ($\approx 33\%$). Further, although all three treatments are related to positive outcomes in infants and children at high risk for developing depression, there is no treatment efficacy data regarding very young children showing signs of depression.

PSYCHOSOCIAL TREATMENTS FOR CHILDREN

Psychosocial treatments for depression during middle childhood (8- to 12-year-olds) have been examined in 10 studies (or series of studies). This growing literature has focused almost exclusively on cognitive-behavioral therapy (CBT). Studies vary in terms of sample (e.g., school, clinic), assessment procedures (e.g., symptom ratings, diagnostic interviews), comparison groups (e.g., wait-list, placebo, or nonspecific interventions, alternative treatments), and length of follow-up. Table 19.1 provides sample descriptions, treatment conditions, and outcomes.

In the earliest study, Butler, Meizitis, Friedman, and Cole (1980) examined small-group role play, cognitive restructuring, attention-placebo, and wait-list control groups for students identified by self- and teacher reports of depressive symptoms. In the role-playing treatment, role plays and homework assignments sensitized children to their own and others' thoughts and feelings, and taught social and problem-solving skills. Children in the cognitive restructuring group learned listening skills, the relation between thoughts and feelings, and how to challenge irrational or self-deprecating automatic thoughts. The role-playing group showed the most positive results after 10 weeks, with improved depressive symptoms, self-esteem, cognitive distortions, and locus of control. Cognitive restructuring group members only reported improved depressive symptoms and self-esteem. However, as posttreatment group differences were only found in self-reported depression and locus of control, and no specific between-groups comparisons were conducted, the relative efficacy of these two treatments is unclear.

Stark, Reynolds, and Kaslow (1987) compared self-control and behavioral problem-solving interventions to a wait-list control group for students with depressive symptoms. Both 5-week active treatments consisted of 12 small-group sessions, with didactic presentations, in-therapy activities, and homework. Whereas the self-control therapy taught self-monitoring, self-evaluation, and self-reinforcement, the behavioral problem-solving therapy taught self-monitoring, pleasant events scheduling, and problem solving. Although the treatments overlapped, self-control therapy was more structured, emphasized cognitive events and attributions more, and taught a wider array of skills. Children in both active conditions showed reduced depression at posttest and 8-week follow-up, while youth in the control condition showed little improvement. At follow-up, the self-control group was rated as less depressed than the behavioral problem-solving group on structured interview; self-report depression measures showed no between-group differences.

These results led to a study comparing a revised CBT to a nonspecific therapy control condition (Stark, Brookman, & Frazier, 1990; Stark, Rouse, & Livingston, 1991). Children with elevated levels of depressive symptoms were recruited using a multiple-gate screening procedure and randomly assigned to one of two treatment conditions that consisted of 24–26 small-group sessions over 3½ months and monthly in-home family meetings. The CBT consisted of training in self-control, assertiveness, social skills, cognitive restructuring, problem solving, and relaxation skills. During family sessions, parents learned to support their children as they practiced new skills. In the nondirective control condition, empathic group leaders taught about causes of depression, strategies to decrease symptoms, and an expectation for improvement. Family sessions focused on improving communication and increasing family engagement in pleasant activities. Children in both treatments showed reductions in self-reported depressive symptoms at posttreatment and 7-month follow-up. At posttreatment, children in the CBT group showed greater symptom reductions during a structured interview and fewer depressive cognitions than children in the control group. Differences did not remain at follow-up, perhaps due to attrition.

Rehm and Sharp (1996) investigated Stark's (Stark et al., 1990) treatment program with children nominated by school personnel. Sessions were conducted as described above, with parent meetings poorly attended. Results showed minimal changes following treatment. However, among children who met diagnostic criteria for depression, decreases in depression were found, as were improvements in social skills and attributional style. Thus, Stark et al.'s (1990) school-based treatment program appears to help children with depressive symptoms and disorders.

TABLE 19.1. Psychosocial Treatment Outcome: Child Studies

Authors	Sample	Treatments	Results	Follow-up
Butler, Miezitis, Friedman, & Cole (1980)	56 fifth to sixth graders with elevated depressive symptoms; no data on ethnicity.	(A) Role play (B) Cognitive restructuring (C) Attention-placebo (D) Wait-list control	Children in (A) showed most improvement, followed by children in (B).	None reported.
Stark, Reynolds, & Kaslow (1987)	29 fourth to fifth graders with elevated depressive symptoms; no data on ethnicity.	(A) Self-control (B) Behavioral problem solving (C) Wait-list control	Children in (A) and (B) showed significant reductions in depression.	Results maintained at 8-week follow-up.
Stark, Rouse, & Livingston (1991)	24 fourth to sixth graders with elevated depressive symptoms; no data on ethnicity.	(A) Cognitive-behavioral treatment with monthly home meetings (B) Nondirective counseling	Children in (A) showed greatest reductions in depressive symptoms, though children in (B) also showed significant reductions.	7-month follow-up showed maintenance of improvements, but no significant differences between children in (A) and (B).
Rehm & Sharp (1996)	60 fourth to fifth graders exhibiting symptoms of depression; 36% Caucasian, 21% African American, 26% Hispanic, 15% Asian, 2% other ethnic minority.	Cognitive-behavioral treatment with monthly home meetings	Significant improvements in subset of children who met diagnostic criteria for depression.	None reported.
Kahn, Kehle, Jenson, & Clark (1990)	68 sixth to eighth graders with elevated depressive symptoms; no data on ethnicity.	(A) Cognitive-behavioral treatment (B) Relaxation training (C) Self-modeling (D) Wait-list control	Children in (A), (B), and (C) showed significant reductions in depressive symptoms.	1-month follow-up: Children in (A) and (B) maintained gains; children in (C) did not.
Liddle & Spence (1990)	31 Australian third to sixth graders with elevated depressive symptoms; no data on ethnicity.	(A) Social competence training (B) Attention-placebo (C) No-treatment control	Children in (A), (B), and (C) showed equivalent reductions in depression.	Improvements maintained at 3-month follow-up.

Study	Sample	Conditions	Results	Follow-up
Weisz, Thurber, Sweeney, Proffitt, & Legagnoux (1997)	48 third to sixth graders with elevated depressive symptoms; 63% Caucasian, 37% ethnic minority.	(A) Cognitive-behavioral treatment (primary and secondary control enhancement training) (B) No-treatment control	Children in (A) showed significant reductions in depressive symptoms.	Effects maintained at 9-month follow-up.
Jaycox, Reivich, Gillham, & Seligman (1994); Gillham, Reivich, Jaycox, & Seligman (1995)	143 "at-risk" 10- to 13-year-olds, selected based on elevated depressive symptoms and/or parental conflict scores; 83% Caucasian, 11% African American, 6% other ethnic minority.	(A) Cognitive training (B) Social problem solving (C) Combined group (D) Wait-list control (E) No-treatment control	Children in (A), (B), and (C) showed significant reductions in depressive symptoms.	Effects maintained at 6-month follow-up. At 2-year follow-up, effects of prevention program grew larger.
Fristad, Arnett, & Gavazzy (1998)	35 8- to 11-year-olds with mood disorder diagnoses; 89% Caucasian, 11% ethnic minority.	Multifamily psychoeducation group		None reported.
Harrington et al. (1998)	162 lower-class British 10- to 16-year-olds with recent suicide attempts; no data on ethnicity.	(A) Home-based family intervention (B) Routine care	(A) Only greater parental satisfaction with treatment.	At 6 months; no additional benefits.
Vostanis, Feehan, Grattan, & Bickerton (1996)	56 8- to 17-year-old outpatients with diagnoses of depression; 88% Caucasian, 12% ethnic minority.	(A) Cognitive-behavioral treatment (B) Nonfocused control intervention	Children in both (A) and (B) showed significant reductions in depression.	Improvements for children in both (A) and (B) generally maintained at 9-month and 2-year follow-up, though high relapse rate noted.

Kahn, Kehle, Jenson, and Clark (1990) compared three active treatments to a wait-list control group for students with elevated levels of depressive symptoms on both self-report and structured diagnostic interview. The CBT adapted the Coping with Depression Adolescent Version (CWD-A) course (Clarke & Lewinsohn, 1984), which teaches self-monitoring, self-reinforcement, cognitive restructuring, and social skills. The relaxation treatment taught children how anxiogenic situations, stress, and depression relate, and trained children to use relaxation techniques. Both treatments consisted of 12 small-group sessions held over 6–8 weeks. The control treatment, a self-modeling intervention, consisted of two brief weekly individual sessions for 6–8 weeks. Children watched brief videotapes of themselves behaving in a manner inconsistent with depression (i.e, interacting appropriately, or talking prosocially about pleasant events). Results supported the effectiveness of the CBT and relaxation groups, as children in both groups reported greater decreases in depressive symptoms than those in the control group. Most children in both active treatment groups moved into the nonclinical range on depression measures, and maintained these gains at 1-month follow-up. Although most children in the self-modeling group also showed reduced depressive symptoms at posttreatment, they did not generally maintain their gains.

In contrast to the above-noted studies, Liddle and Spence (1990) found little evidence that a cognitive-behaviorally oriented social competence training (SCT) intervention was superior to no treatment or attention-placebo. Based on self-reported depressive symptoms, schoolchildren were randomly assigned to a condition. Children in the SCT group attended eight weekly group sessions that taught social and interpersonal problem-solving and cognitive-restructuring techniques. Children in the attention-placebo group took part in a drama-training program. All groups showed comparable declines in depressive symptoms and maintained these improvements at 3-month follow-up. Results may have been obscured by the small sample size, the heterogeneity of problems displayed by children in the SCT group, or the relatively short treatment duration.

However, short duration need not preclude a treatment from demonstrating efficacy (Weisz, Thurber, Sweeney, Proffitt, & LeGagnoux, 1997). Schoolchildren with mild-to-moderate levels of depressive symptoms were assigned randomly to a no-treatment control condition or to an 8-week primary and secondary control enhancement (PASCET) program. Children in this CBT oriented program learned to enhance rewards and decrease punishments through primary (modifying their objective environments) and secondary (modifying their thoughts and attributions to objective conditions) control skills. The PASCET program yielded greater reductions in depression than the control condition; reductions were maintained at a 9-month follow-up.

As part of a 5-year prospective study, Jaycox, Reivich, Gillham, and Seligman (1994) assigned students "at risk" for depression based on elevated levels of depressive symptoms and perceived parental conflict to cognitive training, social problem solving, combined treatment, wait-list, and no treatment. After 12 weekly small group sessions, children in all three active groups showed reductions in depressive symptoms that were maintained at 6-month and 2-year follow-ups (Gillham, Reivich, Jaycox, & Seligman, 1995). Two-year follow-up analyses indicated that changes in participants' explanatory styles mediated the program's "prevention" effect.

While the above studies have largely targeted children, Fristad and colleagues have examined a psychoeducational program for families. Their Multifamily Psychoeducation Group (MFPG) program is based on evidence that families of depressed children often display high levels of expressed emotion (criticism, hostility, emotional overinvolvement), which has been linked to negative outcomes (Fristad, Arnett, & Gavazzi, 1998). The MFPG program, an adjunct to other treatments, consists of six sessions that inform families about their children's disorders, available treatments, healthy responses to their children's problems, and systems and procedures for securing help for their children. The program also focuses on improving family communication and problem solving. Preliminary uncontrolled studies demonstrated that the MFPG intervention increased parental knowledge about mood disorders and parent-reported improvements in family interaction quality (Fristad, Arnett, & Gavazzi, 1998; Fristad, Gavazzi, & Soldano, 1998). In a controlled study, families in the MFPG program showed increased parental knowledge of mood disorders and reports of family interaction, more child reports of parental support, and greater access to mental health services relative to families in a wait-list control group. Such results demonstrate that MFPG helps families of children with mood disorders. It remains to be examined, however, if improved family functioning translates into reduction in children's depressive symptoms beyond that due to standard treatment.

While the aforementioned studies have focused on children under age 13, several studies have examined treatments for children and adolescents combined. Harrington and colleagues (1998) compared a brief home-based family intervention to routine care alone for suicide attempters, most of whom met criteria for depression. The five-session family intervention focused on improving communication and problem solving, and teaching about adolescent issues and their impact on family functioning. Analyses with depressed and nondepressed children showed only that suicidal ideation decreased more for nondepressed children in the family intervention than for nondepressed children in the treatment-as-usual group. The finding of no specific benefits of the family intervention program for depressed youth may indicate that the intervention was too brief to address long-standing or severe family problems.

Vostanis and colleagues (Vostanis, Feehan, Grattan, & Bickerton, 1996b) randomly assigned children and adolescent outpatients diagnosed as depressed to a nine-session CBT or a nonfocused control intervention, in which they reviewed their mental state and social activities. Postintervention, 9-month, and 2-year follow-up data revealed comparable improvements in the two groups (Vostanis, Feehan, & Grattan, 1998; Vostanis, Feehan, Grattan, & Bickerton, 1996a). There also was a substantial risk of relapse; nearly half the children in both groups experienced significant depressive symptoms at 9-month follow-up. For both groups, continued use of mental health services after the trial predicted maintenance of treatment gains. Although CBT was not superior to the control condition, the continued treatment of many children in both groups following the study hinders examination of long-term benefits specific to this intervention.

PSYCHOSOCIAL TREATMENT FOR ADOLESCENTS

Table 19.2 depicts the various therapeutic approaches for depressed teenagers.

Cognitive-Behavioral Therapy

Most studies have focused on CBT, with promising early results. A meta-analysis of the six outcome studies published from 1970 to 1997 that compared CBT versus a control group indicated a significant overall effect size ($d = -1.02$) for posttest difference scores among depressed teenagers, suggesting that CBT may be more effective than control conditions for youth depression (Reinecke, Ryan, & DuBois, 1998). Notably, given the recurrent nature of depressive disorders, treatment gains for the CBT group were maintained at follow-up ($d = -0.61$).

In the first published controlled study, Reynolds and Coats (1986) compared CBT self-control therapy, relaxation training, and a wait-list control for high school students with

TABLE 19.2. Psychosocial Treatment Outcome: Adolescent Studies

Authors	Sample	Treatments	Results	Follow-up
Cognitive-behavioral therapy				
Reynolds & Coats (1986)	30 ninth to twelfth graders (63% female) with elevated depressive symptoms; 100% European American.	(A) CBT (B) Relaxation training (C) Wait-list control	(A) and (B) improved more than (C); no differences between (A) and (B).	None reported.
Lewinsohn, Clarke, Hops, & Andrews (1990)	59 ninth to twelfth graders (61% female) with diagnoses of depression; no data on ethnicity.	(A) CBT (CWD-A) (B) CBT (CWD-A) + parent sessions (C) Wait-list control	(A) and (B) showed significant reductions in depression.	Results maintained at 24-month follow-up.
Clarke, Rohde, Lewinsohn, Hops, & Seeley (1999)	96 14- to 18-year-olds (70.8% female) with diagnoses of depression; no data on ethnicity.	(A) CBT (CWD-A) (B) CBT (CWD-A) + parent sessions (C) Wait-list control At end of treatment, unrecovered adolescents assigned to: (D) Booster session (E) Assessment only	(A) and (B) showed significant reductions in depression.	At 12-month follow-up 100% in (D) recovered versus 50% in (E); at 24-month follow-up recovery comparable across (D) and (E).
Fine, Forth, Gilbert, & Haley (1991)	66 13- to 17-year-olds with diagnoses of MDD or dysthymia; no data reported on gender or ethnicity.	(A) Social skills group (B) Therapeutic support group	(B) showed greater reductions in depression and self-concept than (A).	At 9-month follow-up, no group differences. Therapeutic support effects maintained, social skills effects increased.

448

Interpersonal psychotherapy

Study	Sample	Treatment conditions	Findings	Follow-up
Mufson, Moreau, Weissman, Wickmaratne, Martin, & Samoilov (1994)	14 12- to 18-year-olds (86% female) with diagnoses of depression; 79% Hispanic, 21% African American.	Interpersonal therapy for adolescents (IPT-A)	Completers ($N = 11$) showed significant reductions in depression and improved social and global functioning.	Results maintained at 12-month follow-up.
Mufson, Weissman, Moreau, & Garfinkel (1999)	48 12- to 18-year-olds (73% female) with diagnoses of major depressive disorder; 71% Hispanic, 29% other.	(A) IPT-A (B) Clinical monitoring control	(A) showed greater reductions in depression and more improvement in social and global functioning than (B).	None reported.
Rosselo & Bernal (1999)	71 13- to 18-year-olds (54% female) with diagnoses of depression; 100% Puerto Rican.	(A) IPT-A (B) CBT (C) Wait-list control	(A) and (B) improved more than (C); (A) showed greatest improvement in social functioning and self-esteem.	No significant differences between (A) and (B) at 3-month follow-up.

Family therapy

Study	Sample	Treatment conditions	Findings	Follow-up
Brent et al. (1997)	107 13- to 18-year-olds (76% female) with major depressive disorder; 83% European American, 17% other ethnicity.	(A) Systemic behavior family therapy (SBFT) (B) CBT (C) Nondirective supportive treatment (NST)	(B) improved more than (C); (A) not significantly different from (B) or (C).	No significant differences among groups at 24-month follow-up.
Brent, Poling, McCain, & Baugher (1993)	Parents of 34 13- to 18-year-olds (64.7% female) with diagnosed mood disorders; 88.2% European American, 17.8% other ethnicity.	Family psychoeducation program	Parents' knowledge about causes, course, and treatment of depression increased.	None reported.

self-reported depressive symptoms. CBT group members were taught self-control skills, provided information about depression, and completed and reviewed homework assignments applying the session material. Relaxation group members learned the relation between stress and depression, basic relaxation exercises, and ways to generalize their new relaxation skills. They also were assigned homework. The controls were assigned to one of the two active groups, but did not start treatment until 10 weeks after the beginning of the trial. Teens randomly assigned to the 10-session CBT or relaxation groups reported less depression and anxiety and better academic self-concept than did controls at postintervention and 5-week follow-up. The two active treatments did not differ in their effects on depressive symptoms.

In 1990, Lewinsohn, Clarke, Hops, and Andrews (1990) initiated a comprehensive research program examining CBT for nonreferred, depressed adolescents. High school students with depression diagnoses were randomly assigned to one of the two active treatments or a wait-list control. In the first active condition, a CBT group for adolescents based on the Coping with Depression (CWD) course for adults, teens completed 14 experientially oriented sessions aimed at decreasing depressive symptoms, anxiety, and depressogenic cognitions; increasing participation in pleasant activities; enhancing social and conflict resolution skills, and preventing relapse. The second active condition incorporated CWD-A plus seven parent group sessions designed to educate about the CWD-A course; teach communication, negotiation, and problem-solving skills; and help parents reinforce adolescents' newly acquired skills. During two sessions, parents and adolescents met together to practice skills. Adolescents in both active treatments showed greater reductions in self-reported depressive symptoms and cognitions, and increases in participation in pleasant activities, than did controls. Whereas just over half the members of each active treatment group still met diagnostic criteria for a depressive disorder at posttreatment, 95% of the controls continued to meet criteria. At 6-month and 2-year follow-ups, youth in both active groups had maintained their improvement. Control participants were not examined at follow-up, because they were offered active treatment following the postintervention assessment.

Clarke, Rohde, Lewinsohn, Hops, and Seeley (1999) replicated Lewinsohn and colleagues' study (Lewinsohn et al., 1990), using a community sample. They also found lower levels of depressive symptoms in the active treatment groups immediately after acute treatment. Youth who remained depressed after acute treatment were randomly assigned to either a booster session group or to one of two assessment-only groups. Booster session group members attended 1–2 sessions designed to help them apply skills learned during acute treatment. All five participants who completed booster sessions were recovered at 12-month follow-up. In contrast, fewer assessment group members had recovered. Long-term recovery rates were comparable across groups; by 24-month follow-up, all but one adolescent had recovered.

Three studies that examined features of CWD-A revealed that group cohesiveness predicted recovery posttreatment (Lewinsohn, Clarke, & Rohde, 1994), and parent involvement in treatment best predicted depressive symptoms scores after acute treatment (Clarke et al., 1992). Equivocal findings were obtained for initial depression level (Clarke et al., 1992; Rohde, Lewinsohn, & Seeley, 1994). In light of these mixed findings, more research is needed to evaluate the relative efficacy of the CWD-A course for teens with varying levels of depression.

In one of the few studies to tease CBT elements apart, Fine, Forth, Gilbert, and Haley (1991) compared the efficacy of five-session social skills training and therapeutic support groups for adolescents with depression diagnoses. Contrary to predictions, the support group improved more than the social skills group in depression and self-concept at posttreatment. At 9-month follow-up, however, no differences remained; the social skills group continued to improve after therapy, perhaps through use of their new skills, and those in the support group maintained their gains.

Interpersonal Therapy

A growing literature has examined interpersonal psychotherapy (IPT) for depressed teens. Like CBT, IPT treats depressive symptoms in a problem focused, time-limited manner, with attention to engagement in social and recreational activities, problem solving, self-monitoring, and improvement of interpersonal relationships (Fombonne, 1998; Stark, Laurent, Livingston, Boswell, & Swearer, 1999). Unlike CBT, IPT addresses interpersonal conflicts, deficits, and themes rather than changing cognitive patterns (Moreau, Mufson, Weissman, & Klerman, 1991; Stark et al., 1999). Because IPT was designed originally for adults, Moreau and colleagues (1991) adapted it to focus on issues of concern to teens (IPT-A) (e.g., separating from parents, negotiating relationships).

Mufson and coworkers (1994) conducted the first open clinical trial of IPT-A with clinically depressed adolescents. After 12 individual therapy sessions supplemented with phone contacts, treatment completers no longer met criteria for depressive disorders and reported decreased depressive symptoms and improved social adjustment and global functioning. At 12-month follow-up, most adolescents maintained their gains (Mufson & Fairbanks, 1996). Mufson, Weissman, Moreau, and Garfinkel (1999) conducted a controlled clinical trial comparing IPT-A to clinical monitoring for clinically referred, depressed adolescents. After treatment, more members of the IPT-A group than of the clinical monitoring group were recovered. Further, IPT-A adolescents demonstrated better global and interpersonal functioning.

Clearly, IPT, like CBT, holds promise, at least relative to relaxation or clinical monitoring. Little research, however, has examined the two in tandem, which will be necessary to establish which treatments work best for which adolescents. Rossello and Bernal (1996) compared IPT-A, CBT, and wait-list control conditions for clinic-referred, depressed Puerto Rican adolescents. After 12 sessions, both active treatment groups reported fewer depressive symptoms than did controls. Social adaptation and self-esteem did not differ between adolescents who received IPT-A and CBT. However, only the IPT-A group showed increased self-esteem and social adaptation relative to controls. These findings merit replication in larger samples if they are to be generalized.

Family Therapy

In the first clinical trial of a family-oriented treatment, Brent and colleagues (1997) compared systemic behavior family therapy (SBFT) to CBT and nondirective supportive therapy (NST) in a mixed clinically referred and community sample of adolescents. SBFT comprised two treatment phases. In the first phase, consistent with functional family therapy, the therapist helped the family clarify and reframe the presenting problems to increase treatment engagement and understanding of dysfunctional patterns. In the second phase, based on a problem-solving model, the focus shifted to changing dysfunctional patterns of interaction via improved communication and problem solving. Adolescents in the CBT condition attended individual sessions and learned about collaborative empiricism, the cognitive model, ways to modify maladaptive cognitions, and strategies to enhance their problem solving, affect regulation, and social skills. NST participants received support, empathy, and assistance with identifying and expressing feelings. All participants received family psychoeducation about depression and its treatment.

Results suggested that SBFT might be less effective than CBT, at least in the short term. After a 12- to 16-session active treatment phase, 17% of CBT participants, 32.3% of SBFT teens, and 42.4% of the NST group met criteria for major depressive disorder (MDD). Rates of MDD in the SBFT group did not differ from those of the other groups. Thus, although two-thirds of the SBFT group no longer met criteria for MDD, benefits were less pervasive than those associated with CBT. Further, differences between SBFT and CBT remained significant when teen characteristics associated with poor outcome after acute treatment were covaried (Brent et al., 1998).

A focus on recovery rates may obscure the benefits of SBFT. SBFT, designed to bring about systemic as well as individual change, may have a slower and subtler effect on depressive symptoms than CBT. Thus, although treatment response was faster and remission rates were higher in the CBT than in the SBFT group (Brent et al., 1997), 83.7% of all participants were in remission 2 years posttreatment (Birmaher et al., 2000). Participant characteristics better predicted long-term remission and recovery than did treatment condition; 2-year remission and recovery rates did not differ among the three groups. Youth in each condition most likely to recover by the end of treatment were less depressed at baseline; reported less parent–child conflict, hopelessness, and cognitive distortions; and were more rapid responders (Birmaher et al., 2000; Renaud et al., 1998). Brent, Kolko, Birmaher, Baugher, and Bridge (1999) also found that approximately half of the participants, evenly distributed across groups, received additional services, largely during the 2-year follow-up. Those who obtained additional treatment reported more or worse depressive symptoms and comorbid dysthymia than did participants who sought no extra services, and were slower to recover.

Researchers have also examined family psychoeducation. Brent, Poling, McKain, and Baugher (1993) administered a 2-hour psychoeducational session to parents of depressed adolescents. After the session, parents demonstrated increased knowledge about the etiology, course, and treatment of depression. Brent and coworkers (1993) did not report if the intervention affected adolescents' depression levels.

PSYCHOPHARMACOLOGICAL TREATMENTS FOR DEPRESSED CHILDREN AND ADOLESCENTS

Table 19.3 provides sample descriptions, treatment conditions, and outcomes for efficacy studies of tricyclic antidepressants (TCAs), nontricyclic antidepressants, and the newer selective serotonin reuptake inhibitors (SSRIs). Since the tricyclic antidepressants are not being used very often and have generally not been found to be effective, they will not be detailed in Table 19.3.

Tricyclic Antidepressants

Of the antidepressant medications currently available, the TCAs (nortriptyline [Pamelor, Aventyl], amitriptyline [Elavil], desipramine [Norpramin, Perdofrane], and imipramine [Tofranil]) have been the most thoroughly studied. Unfortunately, there is little evidence that TCAs alleviate depression in youth. In a review, Sommers-Flanagan and Sommers-Flanagan (1996) reported that no double-blind placebo-controlled studies had shown significant effects of TCAs over placebo. However, small samples and placebo effects may have limited power to detect effects. Cardiac monitoring during treatment has been recommended due to concerns that TCA use increases risk for adverse cardiac effects (Mezzacappa, Steingard, Kindlon, Saul, & Earls, 1998).

TABLE 19.3. Pharmacological Treatment Outcome Studies

Authors	Sample	Treatments	Results	Follow-up
Simeon, Dinicola, Ferguson, & Copping (1990)	40 13- to 18-year-olds with depression diagnosis; no data on ethnicity reported.	(A) Fluoxetine (B) Placebo	No significant group differences.	No significant group differences at 24 month follow-up.
Emslie et al. (1997)	96 7–17 year olds (50% female) with major depressive disorder; 79% European American, 21% other ethnicity.	(A) Fluoxetine (B) Placebo	(A) improved more than (B) on clinician-rated depression and global functioning; no group differences on self-ratings of depression.	None reported.
Boulos, Kutcher, Gardner, & Young (1992)	15 16- to 24-year-olds (53% female) with mood disorders; no data on ethnicity reported.	Fluoxetine	Improvement in depression in 64% of sample and in global functioning in 73% of sample.	None reported.
Colle, Belair, DiFeo, Weiss, & LaRoche (1994)	9 15- to 18-year-olds (89% female) with major depressive disorder; no data on ethnicity reported.	Fluoxetine	88% of sample "very much" or "much" improved.	None reported.
Ghaziuddin, Naylor, & King (1994/1995)	6 15- to 18-year-olds (67% female) with major depressive disorder; no data on ethnicity reported.	Fluoxetine	Significant improvement in depression.	None reported.
Riggs, Mikulich, Coffman, & Crowley (1997)	8 14- to 18-year-old males with major depressive disorder, conduct disorder, and substance dependence; no data on ethnicity reported.	Fluoxetine	Significant improvement in depression and global functioning.	None reported.
Waslick et al. (1999)	19 12- to 18-year-olds (68.4% female) with major depressive disorder or dysthymia; 47% Hispanic, 53% other ethnicity.	Fluoxetine	Improvement in 73% of sample.	None reported.
Rey-Sánchez & Gutiérrez-Casares (1997)	45 preadolescents (49% female) with major depressive disorder; no data regarding ethnicity reported.	Paroxetine	100% remission at 8 months.	None reported.
Masi, Marcheschi, & Pfanner (1997)	7 14- to 18-year-olds (14% female) with major depressive disorder; no data regarding ethnicity reported.	Paroxetine	Improvement in clinician-rated depression for 86% of sample.	None reported.

(continued)

453

TABLE 19.3. *Continued*

Authors	Sample	Treatments	Results	Follow-up
Nobile, Bellotti, Marino, Molteni, & Battaglia (2000)	9 10- to 18-year-olds year (29% female) with dysthymia; no data regarding ethnicity reported.	Paroxetine	Improvement in depression and global functioning in 71% of sample.	None reported.
McConville et al. (1996)	13 12- to 18-year-olds (77% female) with major depressive disorder; no data regarding ethnicity reported.	Sertraline	Significant improvement in depression and clinician-rated global functioning.	None reported.
Ambrosini et al. (1999)	53 12- to 19-year-olds (51% female) with major depressive disorder; 79% European American, 8% African American, 13% other ethnicity.	Sertraline	Improvement in depression and global functioning in 55% of sample.	4-week continuation phase led to continued improvement; no follow-up reported.
Apter et al. (1994)	6 13- to 18-year-olds (83% female) with major depressive disorder and varied comorbid disorders; no data regarding ethnicity reported.	Fluvoxamine	Significant improvement in depression.	None reported.
Rabe-Jablonska (2000)	21 adolescents (mean age 15 ± 1 years; 62% female) with dysthymia; no data regarding ethnicity reported.	Fluvoxamine	Significant improvement in depression in 44% of sample.	None reported.
Mandoki, Tapia, Tapia, Sumner, & Parker (1997)	33 8- to 18-year-olds (24% female) with major depressive disorder; no data regarding ethnicity reported.	(A) Venlafaxine (B) Placebo	No significant between-group differences.	None reported.

Because little evidence indicates that TCAs alone are effective, researchers have augmented them with other mood-regulating compounds. Despite evidence that lithium supplementation leads to improvement (Ryan et al., 1988), this is not true for TCA nonresponders (Strober, Freeman, Rigali, Schmidt, & Diamond, 1992). A review of monoamine oxidase inhibitors (MAOIs) used to amplify TCAs found only that MAOI augmentation was safe for adolescent use (Ryan et al., 1988). No comments about efficacy were possible, as potentially biased treators measured improvement.

Selective Serotonin Reuptake Inhibitors and Nontricyclic Antidepressants

Since the early 1990s, researchers have directed attention toward the SSRIs (e.g., fluoxetine, paroxetine, fluvoxamine, sertraline) and other nontricyclic antidepressants (e.g., venlafaxine, bupropion, and nefazodone). These medications have fewer side effects and are less toxic than TCAs in overdose, and hold promise for treatment of multiple disorders (Emslie, Walkup, Pliszka, & Ernst, 1999). Despite their advantages, SSRIs and other nontricyclic antidepressants have yet to be thoroughly studied in youth and a variety of side effects have been associated with their use. Although open trials have yielded optimistic findings, double-blind, placebo-controlled trials of SSRIs indicate that they may not be more effective than TCAs.

Fluoxetine (Prozac)

Of the SSRIs, fluoxetine has received the most research attention. Most open trials have yielded positive findings; 52–88% of youth, typically adolescents with MDD, improve on fluoxetine after poor response to TCAs (Boulos, Kutcher, Gardner, & Young, 1992; Ghaziuddin, Naylor, & King, 1994–1995) or failed psychosocial treatment (Colle, Belair, DiFeo, Weiss, & LaRoche, 1994; Waslick et al., 1999). Similarly high improvement rates were evident in adolescent substance abusers in residential treatment (Riggs, Mikulich, Coffman, & Crowley, 1997). After 7–18 weeks of treatment, most participants reported fewer depressive symptoms and demonstrated improved global functioning.

Double-blind, placebo-controlled studies have produced mixed results. In the first study, Simeon and coworkers (Simeon, Dinicola, Ferguson, & Copping, 1990) found that by week 3 of eight, MDD adolescents in both the fluoxetine and placebo groups had improved on clinician and self-ratings of depression and global functioning. No between-group differences, however, were evident at posttreatment or at 24-month follow-up. At follow-up, individuals who had not responded initially to fluoxetine functioned more poorly. Emslie and colleagues (1997) conducted a larger double-blind, placebo-controlled study of adolescents with MDD. After 8 weeks, clinician, but not self-report, ratings of global status and depressive symptoms revealed more improvements for youth randomly assigned to the fluoxetine group than to the placebo group.

Paroxetine (Paxil)

Paroxetine also appears safe for use with youth (Findling et al., 1999). In an open trial examining paroxetine's efficacy for child MDD, Rey-Sánchez and Gutiérrez-Casares (1997) found evidence of clinical response within 1 month. All children achieved remission by 8 months, with brief benzodiazepine augmentation for those with comorbid anxiety or insomnia. In a second open-label trial for adolescents with MDD and mild intellectual disability, clinician ratings of depressive symptoms decreased after 9 weeks (Masi, Marcheschi, & Pfanner, 1997). Nobile, Bellotti, Marino, Molteni, and Battaglia (2000) obtained similar results in their open-label study of dysthymic youth. After 3 months, depressive symptoms decreased by half and global functioning improved in 71% of participants.

Sertraline (Zoloft)

Sertraline has been evaluated in two open-label trials. McConville and colleagues (1996) used sertraline to treat inpatient teens with MDD and comorbid diagnoses for 12 weeks. During treatment, both self-report and clinician ratings of depressive symptoms decreased. Over half of the adolescents, however, experienced at least one adverse side effect. Ambrosini and coworkers (1999) examined the effects of sertraline on depressive symptoms in adolescents with moderate-to-severe MDD during a 10-week open-label trial. Results indicated improvement after treatment on self-report measures of depressive symptoms and clinician ratings of global functioning. About half of the adolescents continued treatment for 12 weeks after the trial; all maintained or increased their gains during this phase.

Fluvoxamine (Luvox)

Apter and colleagues (1994) administered fluvoxamine along with psychosocial treatment to hospitalized adolescents with treatment-resistant or comorbid MDD. Self-reported depressive symptoms decreased in all participants, but only two-thirds improved in global functioning. More recently, in an open trial, Rabe-Jablonska (2000) treated 21 dysthymic, adolescent outpatients with fluvoxamine. After 26 weeks, 44% of participants showed at least a 50% decrease in depressive symptoms; however, approximately one-third relapsed.

Venlafaxine (Effexor)

One double-blind, placebo-controlled study examined venlafaxine for child and adolescent MDD. Mandoki, Tapia, Tapia, Sumner, and Parker (1997) randomly assigned participants to 6-week-long venlafaxine/psychotherapy or placebo/psychotherapy groups. Both groups showed comparable improvement. Several side effects were evident, but mild.

EMPIRICALLY SUPPORTED TREATMENTS FOR DEPRESSION

This section summarizes the literature in light of the criteria for empirically supported treatments, highlighting interventions that have demonstrated efficacy and are ready for widespread dissemination. The criteria of Chambless and colleagues (1996), used by Kaslow and Thompson (1998) to review the psychosocial treatment literature on youth depression, are employed. To be deemed "well-established," a treatment must meet the following criteria:

1. In at least two between-group studies it must either be superior to pill, psychological placebo, or another treatment, or be equivalent to already established treatment. Alternatively, a large series of single-case design studies can demonstrates effects of treatment.
2. Experiments must be conducted in accordance with a treatment manual, sample characteristics must be detailed, and at least two different research teams must demonstrate intervention effects.

For an intervention to be deemed "probably efficacious," two experiments must meet all of the criteria for "well-established" except for the requirement that effects be shown by two or more independent research teams. In reviewing the psychosocial literature in light of these criteria, Kaslow and Thompson (1998) found that no treatments were well-established, although CBT treatments for children (Stark et al., 1991) and adolescents (Lewinsohn, Clarke, Rohde, Hops, & Seeley, 1996) met probably efficacious criteria. For children, the status of the literature has not changed, as shown in Table 19.4. The one CBT approach for adolescents that meets probably efficacious criteria is Lewinsohn and colleagues' CBT-A (Lewinsohn et al., 1990) (see Table 19.4). Both of the CBT programs need only to be implemented successfully by a second research team to attain well-established standing. In contrast, two independent research groups have replicated IPT-A (Moreau et al., 1991), making it the only treatment for adolescent depression that meets well-established criteria.

Aside from the three treatments that qualify as probably efficacious or well-established, no other interventions have adequate support to be recommended for use in clinical practice. In general, more independent efforts to replicate treatment effects are needed. No treatments targeting depressive symptoms in infants and toddlers have been empirically examined, and little evidence indicates that psychopharmacological therapies are efficacious for youth.

SUMMARY AND FUTURE DIRECTIONS

Group CBT interventions reduce depressive symptoms in school and community samples of children. There has been little effort, however, to examine widely used treatment approaches beyond CBT, such as psychodynamic, family, or interpersonal therapies, or to study treatments of clinically depressed children. Further, little is known about long-term outcomes of children treated with CBT. Only one study followed children up to 2 years posttreatment; most studies include brief or no follow-up. As relapse is common, examining long-term outcomes is critical. For depressed adolescents, in contrast, short-term CBT, IPT, and SBFT are all promising. Each confers different benefits; thus, research matching treatment and participant characteristics is an important next step. IPT may be best for teens whose depression is associated with disrupted relationships. SBFT may be preferable when family behavior patterns support the maintenance of depression or when multiple family members are depressed. CBT may be useful for youth who manifest depressive cognitions and associated behaviors.

To permit such research, researchers must design large, multicenter studies that include at least two of these treatments (e.g., National Institute of Mental Health [NIMH] studies on the Treatment of Adolescent Depression [TADS] and the Treatment of Resistant Depression in Adolescents [TORDIA]). Studies that examine common combined treatment approaches (e.g., psychosocial and medication), such as those underway comparing CBT and IPT-A, as well as specific components of treatment, also need to be conducted. Further, the efficacy of varied treatments must be evaluated across different age groups. Such research will be especially useful for specific subgroups, such as those with resistant depression (James, 1999), comorbid disorders (Birmaher et al., 1996), or suicidal ideation (Rotheram-Borus, Piancentini, Miller, Graae, & Castro-Blanco, 1994).

The impact of comorbid diagnoses on outcome also warrants attention. In the only study to consider comorbidity on outcome in youth, comorbid anxiety predicted poor outcome for adolescents at the end of treatment (Brent et al., 1998). Several case studies suggest that individual CBT may be effective for depression combined with varied concomitant difficulties, including school refusal (Rollings, King, Tonge, Heyne, & Young, 1998) and trauma (Runyon & Orvaschel, 1999). As research progresses, it will also be important to consider the impact of common comorbid problems in the treatment of large samples of depressed youth.

TABLE 19.4. Well-Established and Probably Efficacious Treatments

Population and treatment approach	Authors	I	II	III	IV	Well-established	V	VI	Probably efficacious
Child									
CBT	Butler, Miezitis, Friedman, & Cole (1980)	N	Y	Y	N	N	N	N	N
	Stark, Reynolds, & Kaslow (1987)	N	Y	Y	N	N	N	N	Y[a]
	Stark, Rouse, & Livingston (1991)	Y	Y	Y	N	N	Y	Y	Y[a]
	Rehm & Sharp (1996)	Y	Y	Y	N	N	N	Y	Y[a]
	Kahn, Kehle, Jenson, & Clark (1990)	N	N	Limited	N	N	N	N	N
	Liddle & Spence (1990)	N	N	Limited	N	N	N	N	N
	Weisz, Thurber, Sweeney, Proffitt, & Legagnoux (1997)	N	Y	Y	Y	N	N	N	N
	Jaycox, Reivich, Gillham, & Seligman (1994); Gillham, Reivich, Jaycox, & Seligman (1995)	N	Y	Y	Y	N	N	N	N
	Vostanis et al. (1996)	N	Y	Y	N	N	N	N	N
Psychoeducation (multifamily psychoeducation group)	Fristad, Arnett, & Gavazzi (1998)	N	Y	Y	N	N	N	N	N
Home-based family intervention	Harrington et al. (1998)	N	Y	Y	N	N	N	N	N
Adolescent									
CBT	Reynolds & Coats (1986)	Y	N	Y	N	N	N	N	N
	Lewinsohn, Clarke, Hops, & Andrews (1990)	Y	Y	Y	N	N	Y	Y	Y[b]
	Clarke, Rohde, Lewinsohn, Hops, & Seeley (1999)	Y	Y	Y	N	N	Y	Y	Y[b]
Social skills versus therapeutic support groups	Fine, Forth, Gilbert, & Haley (1991)	N	N	Y	N	N	N	N	N
IPT	Mufson, Moreau, Weissman, Wickmaratne, Martin, & Samoilov (1994)	*	Y	Y	N	Y[c]	N	N	
	Mufson, Weissman, Moreau, & Garfinkel (1999)	Y	Y	Y	Y	Y[c]	Y	Y	
	Rosselo & Bernal (1999)	Y	Y	Y	Y	Y[c]	Y	Y	
Systemic family behavior therapy (SBFT), CBT, and nondirective supportive therapy (NST)	Brent et al. (1997)	Y	Y[†]	Y	N	N	Y[†]	Y	Y
Psychoeducation	Brent, Poling, McCain, & Baugher (1993)	N	Y	Y	N	N	N	N	N

Note. Y, meets criterion; N, does not meet criterion; Limited, meets criterion to a limited degree. Criteria are as follows. *For well-established treatment:* I. In at least two between-group studies, one of the following: (a) superior to pill, psychological placebo, or another treatment; (b) equivalent to already established treatment. II. Experiments conducted in accordance with treatment manual. III. Sample characteristics detailed. IV. At least two different research teams must demonstrate intervention effects. *For probably efficacious treatment:* Either V. Two experiments that treatment is more effective than wait-list control, or VI. One or more experiments meet all criteria for well-established treatment except for being shown by two or more research teams. Studies with the same superscript letters used the same treatment manuals.

*Criterion I not applicable; study used a within-participants design.

†CBT superior to NST; no significant differences between CBT and SBFT or NST and SBFT.

It is critical for researchers to consider sex and ethnicity in treatment studies. No protocols have been designed with gender in mind; it is therefore unclear whether particular treatment components are more critical to success with youth of either sex. At least one gender-specific study, evaluating family treatment for depressed African American girls with an abuse history, is underway (Griffith, Zucker, Bliss, Foster, & Kaslow, 2001). Much more research examining psychosocial and pharmacological therapies for youth of either sex is warranted. More research is also needed to determine how well interventions cross cultural boundaries. Researchers have just begun to examine CBT and IPT for more diverse populations, and findings suggest that the treatments may generalize to members of other cultural groups (Rossello & Bernal, 1999). Further study is needed, however, in traditionally underserved populations such as African American, Asian American, Latino, and Native American youth.

Studies of medication treatment for depressed youth have yielded less promising findings than has psychosocial research. Researchers have failed to find significant effects of either TCAs or SSRIs for treatment of depression in most well-controlled studies. Because most studies used small samples, it is unclear whether findings reflect actual inefficacy or lack of statistical power. To resolve this question, future researchers must recruit larger samples and report effect sizes.

Notably, however, a few studies of medication treatment have yielded positive findings. For example, fluoxetine has been shown in two well-controlled studies (Emslie et al., 1997; Simeon et al., 1990) to improve clinician ratings of functioning in depressed youth. Comparable decreases in self-reported depression were absent, raising questions about adequate blinding of clinicians to treatment condition. Possibly, though, subjective perceptions of improvement may emerge more slowly than does observable change in depressed youth, and further study of fluoxetine's effects, using both self- and observer ratings, is needed.

Further, it behooves researchers to conduct double-blind, placebo-controlled trials using a wider range of medications, particularly SSRIs and other nontricyclic antidepressants. Implementation of a placebo washout phase is important (Malone & Simpson, 1998). Because use of convenience samples composed of youth with varying comorbid diagnoses may prevent clear conclusions about medication efficacy, use of "pure" diagnostic samples has been recommended (Sommers-Flanagan & Sommers-Flanagan, 1996). Given that comorbidity is common, however, especially among the severely depressed (Birmaher et al., 1996), it may be difficult and ecologically invalid to exclude those with comorbid diagnoses.

Despite the lack of consistent empirical evidence supporting the efficacy of medication, clinicians routinely issue prescriptions, especially for SSRIs, to depressed youth. To systematize existing practice, Hughes and colleagues (1999) developed an algorithm to guide medical treatment of youth MDD. According to this algorithm, when medication is warranted, SSRIs should serve as first line treatments. If symptoms respond inadequately or if excessive side effects are present, switching SSRIs and then, if effects are still inadequate, augmentation with lithium or buspirone is recommended. For youth who still respond poorly, the third stage involves switching to another class of antidepressant (e.g., TCAs). When symptoms still resist treatment, the algorithm recommends combining antidepressants across classes or augmenting treatment with lithium if augmentation has not already been tried. The final stages of treatment for resistant depression involve use of MAOIs and electroconvulsive therapy, which has been evaluated in several studies (Bertagnoli & Borchardt, 1990; Moise & Petrides, 1996; Walter & Rey, 1997). For youth with comorbid diagnoses, variations aimed at relieving a wider range of symptoms are recommended. Finally, although not discussed in the algorithm, there is some evidence that light therapy is effective for seasonal affective disorder (Swedo et al., 1997).

Few investigators have examined psychopharmacological or psychosocial treatments informed by a developmental perspective. Rather, researchers have downwardly extended psychosocial treatment strategies that work with adults or have prescribed medications that have been developed and tested only for adult use. Treatment strategies formulated within a developmental framework may be more effective than strategies examined thus far.

REFERENCES

Ambrosini, P., Wagner, K. D., Biederman, J., Glick, I., Tan, C., Elia, J., Hebeler, J. R., Rabinovich, H., Lock, J., & Geller, D. (1999). Multicenter open-label stertraline study in adolescent outpatients with major depression. *Journal of the American Academy of Child and Adolescent Psychiatry, 38,* 566–572.

Apter, A., Ratzoni, G., King, R. A., Wiezman, A., Iancu, I., Binder, M., & Riddle, M. A. (1994). Fluvoxamine open-label treatment of adolescent inpatients with obsessive–compulsive disorder or depression. *Journal of the American Academy of Child and Adolescent Psychiatry, 33,* 342–348.

Bertagnoli, M. W., & Borchardt, C. M. (1990). A review of ECT for children and adolescents. *Journal of the American Academy of Child and Adolescent Psychiatry, 29,* 302–307.

Birmaher, B., Brent, D. A., Kolko, D., Baugher, M., Bridge, J., Holder, D., Iyengar, S., & Ulloa, R. E. (2000). Clinical outcome after short-term psychotherapy for adolescents with major depressive disorder. *Archives of General Psychiatry, 57,* 29–36.

Birmaher, B., Ryan, N. D., Williamson, D. E., Brent, D. A., Kaufman, J., Dahl, R. E., Perel, J., & Nelson, B. (1996). Childhood and adolescent depression: A review of the past 10 years, Part 1. *Journal of the American Academy of Child and Adolescent Psychiatry, 35,* 1427–1439.

Boulos, C., Kutcher, S., Gardner, D., & Young, E. (1992). An open naturalistic trial of fluoxetine in adolescents and young adults with treatment resistant major depression. *Journal of Child and Adolescent Psychopharmacology, 2,* 103–111.

Brent, D. A., Holder, D., Kolko, D., Birmaher, B., Baugher, M., Roth, C., Iyengar, S., & Johnson, B. (1997). A clinical psychotherapy trial for adolescent depression comparing cognitive, family, and supportive therapy. *Archives of General Psychiatry, 54,* 877–885.

Brent, D. A., Kolko, D., Birmaher, B., Baugher, M., & Bridge, J. (1999). A clinical trial for adolescent depression: Predictors of additional treatment in the acute and follow-up phases of the trial. *Journal of the American Academy of Child and Adolescent Psychiatry, 38,* 263–269.

Brent, D. A., Kolko, D. J., Birmaher, B., Baugher, M., Bridge, J., Roth, C., & Holder, D. (1998). Predictors of treatment efficacy in a clinical trial of three psychosocial treatments for adolescent depression. *Journal of the American Academy of Child and Adolescent Psychiatry, 37,* 906–914.

Brent, D. A., Poling, K., McKain, B., & Baugher, M. (1993). A psychoeducational program for families of affectively ill children and adolescents. *Journal of the American Academy of Child and Adolescent Psychiatry, 32,* 770–774.

Butler, L., Miezitis, S., Friedman, R., & Cole, E. (1980). The effect of two school-based intervention programs on depressive symptoms in preadolescents. *American Education Research Journal, 17,* 111–119.

Chambless, D. L., Baker, M. J., Baucom, D. H., Beutler, L. E., Calhoun, K. S., Crits-Christoph, P., Daiuto, A., DeRubeis, R., Detweiler, J., Haaga, D. A. F., Johnson, S. B., McCurry, S., Mueser, K. T., Pope, K. S., Sanderson, W. C., Shoham, V., Stickle, T., Williams, D. A., & Woody, S. R. (1998). Update on empirically validated therapies, Part 2. *Clinical Psychologist, 51,* 3–16.

Chambless, D. L., Sanderson, W., Shoham, V., Johnson, S., Pope, K., Crits-Cristoph, P., Baker, M., Johnson, B., Woody, S., Sue, S., Beutler, L., Williams, D., & McCurry, S. (1996). An update on empirically validated therapies. *Clinical Psychologist, 49,* 5–18.

Cicchetti, D., Rogosch, F. A., & Toth, S. L. (2000). The efficacy of toddler–parent psychotherapy for fostering cognitive development in offspring of depressed mothers. *Journal of Abnormal Child Psychology, 28,* 135–148.

Clarke, G., Hops, H., Lewinsohn, P. M., Andrews, J., Seeley, J. R., & Williams, J. (1992). Cognitive-behavioral group treatment of adolescent depression: Prediction of outcome. *Behavior Therapy, 23,* 341–352.

Clarke, G., & Lewinsohn, P. M. (1984). *The Coping with Depression Course Adolescent Version: A psychoeducational intervention for unipolar depression in high school students.* Eugene, OR: Oregon Research Institute.

Clarke, G., Rohde, P., Lewinsohn, P., Hops, H., & Seeley, J. (1999). Cognitive-behavioral treatment of adolescent depression: Efficacy of acute group treatment and booster sessions. *Journal of the American Academy of Child and Adolescent Psychiatry, 38,* 272–279.

Colle, L. M., Belair, J. F., DiFeo, M., Weiss, J., & LaRoche, C. (1994). Extended open-label fluoxetine treatment of adolescents with major depression. *Journal of Child and Adolescent Psychopharmacology, 4,* 225–232.

Cooper, P. J., & Murray, L. (1997). The impact of psychological treatments of postpartum depression on maternal mood and infant development. In L. Murray & P. J. Cooper (Eds.), *Postpartum depression and child development* (pp. 201–220). New York: Guilford Press.

Emslie, G. J., Rush, A. J., Weinberg, W. A., Kowatch, R. A., Hughes, C. W., Carmody, T., & Rintelmann, J. (1997). A double-blind, randomized, placebo-controlled trial of fluoxetine in children and adolescents with depression. *Archives of General Psychiatry, 54,* 1031–1037.

Emslie, G. J., Walkup, J. T., Pliszka, S. R., & Ernst, M. (1999). Nontricyclic antidepressants: Current trends in children and adolescents. *Journal of the American Academy of Child and Adolescent Psychiatry, 38,* 517–528.

Field, T., Grizzle, N., Scafidi, F., & Schanberg, S. (1996). Massage and relaxation therapies' effects on depressed adolescent mothers. *Adolescence, 31,* 904–911.

Findling, R. L., Reed, M. D., Myers, C., O'Riordan, M. A., Fiala, S., Branicky, L., Waldorf, B., & Blumer, J. L. (1999). Paroxetine pharmacokinetics in depressed children and adolescents. *Journal of the American Academy of Child and Adolescent Psychiatry, 38,* 952–959.

Fine, S., Forth, A., Gilbert, M., & Haley, G. (1991). Group therapy for adolescent depressive disorder: A comparison of social skills and therapeutic support. *Journal of the American Academy of Child and Adolescent Psychiatry, 30,* 79–85.

Fombonne, E. (1998). Interpersonal psychotherapy for adolescent depression. *Child Psychology and Psychiatry Review, 3,* 169–175.

Fraiberg, S., Adelson, E., & Shapiro, V. (1975). Ghosts in the nursery: A psychoanalytic approach to the problem of impaired infant–mother relationships. *Journal of the American Academy of Child Psychiatry, 14,* 387–422.

Fristad, M. A., Arnett, M. M., & Gavazzi, S. M. (1998). The impact of psychoeducational workshops on families of mood-disordered children. *Family Therapy, 25,* 151–159.

Fristad, M. A., Gavazzi, S. M., & Soldano, K. W. (1998). Multi-family psychoeducation groups for childhood mood disorders: A program description and preliminary efficacy data. *Contemporary Family Therapy, 20,* 385–402.

Gelfand, D., Teti, D., Seiner, S., & Jameson, P. (1996). Helping mothers fight depression: Evaluation of a home-based intervention program for depressed mothers and their infants. *Journal of Clinical Child Psychology, 25,* 406–422.

Ghaziuddin, N., Naylor, M. W., & King, C. A. (1994–1995). Fluoxetine in tricyclic refractory depression in adolescents. *Depression, 2,* 287–291.

Gillham, J., Reivich, K., Jaycox, L., & Seligman, M. E. P. (1995). Prevention of depressive symptoms in school children: Two year follow-up. *Psychological Science, 6,* 343–351.

Griffith, J., Zucker, M., Bliss, M., Foster, J., & Kaslow, N. (2001). Family interventions for depressed African American adolescent females. *Innovations in Clinical Practice, 19,* 159–173.

Hamilton, J. D., & Bridge, J. (1999). Outcome at 6 months for 50 adolescents with major depression treated in a health maintenance organization. *Journal of the American Academy of Child and Adolescent Psychiatry, 37,* 35–39.

Harrington, R., Kerfoot, M., Dyer, E., McNiven, F., Gill, J., Harrington, V., Woodham, A., & Byford, S. (1998). Randomized trial of a home-based family intervention for children who have deliberately poisoned themselves. *Journal of the American Academy of Child and Adolescent Psychiatry, 37,* 512–518.

Hughes, C. W., Emslie, G. J., Crismon, M. L., Wagner, K. D., Birmaher, B., Geller, B., Pliszka, S. R., Ryan, N. D., Strober, M., Trivedi, M. H., Toprac, M. G., Sedillo, A., Llana, M. E., Lopez, M.,

Rush, A. J., & Texas Consensus Conference Panel on Medication Treatment of Childhood Major Depressive Disorder. (1999). Texas Children's Medication Algorithm Project: Report of the Texas Consensus Conference Panel on medication treatment of childhood major depressive disorder. *Journal of the American Academy of Child and Adolescent Psychiatry, 38,* 1442–1454.

James, A. (1999). Resistant depression in childhood and adolescence. *Clinical Child Psychology and Psychiatry, 4,* 483–491.

Jaycox, L., Reivich, K., Gillham, J., & Seligman, M. E. P. (1994). Prevention of depressive symptoms in school children. *Behavioral Research and Therapy, 32,* 801–816.

Jones, N., Field, T., & Davalos, M. (1998). Massage therapy attenuates right frontal EEG asymmetry in one-month old infants of depressed mothers. *Infant Behavior and Development, 21,* 527–530.

Kahn, J., Kehle, T., Jenson, W., & Clark, E. (1990). Comparison of cognitive behavioral, relaxation, and self-modeling interventions for depression among middle-school students. *School Psychology Review, 19,* 196–211.

Kaslow, N. J., & Thompson, M. P. (1998). Applying the criteria for empirically supported treatments to studies of psychosocial interventions for child and adolescent depression. *Journal of Clinical Child Psychology, 27,* 146–155.

Keller, M. B., Lavori, P. W., Beardslee, W. R., Wunder, J., & Ryan, N. (1991). Depression in children and adolescents: New data on "undertreatment" and a literature review on the efficacy of available treatments. *Journal of Affective Disorders, 21,* 163–171.

Lewinsohn, P. M., Clarke, G., Hops, H., & Andrews, J. (1990). Cognitive-behavioral treatment for depressed adolescents. *Behavior Therapy, 21,* 385–401.

Lewinsohn, P. M., Clarke, G. N., & Rohde, P. (1994). Psychological approaches to the treatment of depression in adolescents. In W. M. Reynolds & H. F. Johnston (Eds.), *Handbook of depression in children and adolescents* (pp. 309–344). New York: Plenum Press.

Lewinsohn, P. M., Clarke, G., Rohde, P., Hops, H., & Seeley, J. (1996). A course in coping: A cognitive-behavioral approach to the treatment of adolescent depression. In E. D. Hibbs & P. S. Jensen (Eds.), *Psychosocial treatments for child and adolescent disorders: Empirically based strategies for clinical practice* (pp. 109–135). Washington, DC: American Psychological Association.

Liddle, B., & Spence, S. (1990). Cognitive behavior therapy with depressed primary school children: A cautionary note. *Behavioural Psychotherapy, 18,* 85–102.

Lous, A. M., De Wit, C. A. M., De Bruyn, E. E. J., Riksen-Walraven, J. M., & Rost, H. (2000). Depression and play in early childhood: Play behavior of depressed and nondepressed 3- to 6-year-olds in various play situations. *Journal of Emotional and Behavioral Disorders, 8,* 249–260.

Lyons-Ruth, K., Connell, D., Grunebaum, H., & Botein, S. (1990). Infants at social risk: Maternal depression and family support services as mediators of infant development and security of attachment. *Child Development, 61,* 85–98.

Malone, R. P., & Simpson, G. M. (1998). Use of placebos in clinical trials involving children and adolescents. *Psychiatric Services, 49,* 1413–1417.

Mandoki, M. W., Tapia, M. R., Tapia, M. A., Sumner, G. S., & Parker, J. L. (1997). Venlafaxine in the treatment of children and adolescents with major depression. *Psychopharmacology Bulletin, 33,* 149–154.

Masi, G., Marcheschi, M., & Pfanner, P. (1997). Paroxetine in depressed adolescents with intellectual disability: An open-label study. *Journal of Intellectual Disability Research, 41,* 268–272.

McConville, B. J., Minnery, K. L., Sorter, M. T., West, S. A., Friedman, L. M., & Christian, K. (1996). An open study of the effects of sertraline on adolescent major depression. *Journal of Child and Adolescent Psychopharmacology, 6,* 41–51.

Mezzacappa, E., Steingard, R., Kindlon, D., Saul, J., & Earls, F. (1998). Tricyclic antidepressants and cardiac autonomic control in children and adolescents. *Journal of the American Academy of Child and Adolescent Psychiatry, 37,* 52–59.

Moise, F. N., & Petrides, G. (1996). Case study: Electroconvulsive therapy in adolescents. *Journal of the American Academy of Child and Adolescent Psychiatry, 35,* 312–318.

Moreau, D., Mufson, L., Weissman, M. M., & Klerman, G. L. (1991). Interpersonal psychotherapy for adolescent depression: Description of modification and preliminary application. *American Academy of Child and Adolescent Psychiatry, 30,* 642–651.

Mufson, L., & Fairbanks, J. (1996). Interpersonal psychotherapy for depressed adolescents: A one-year naturalistic follow-up study. *Journal of the American Academy of Child and Adolescent Psychiatry, 35,* 1145–1155.

Mufson, L., Moreau, D., Weissman, M., Wickramaratne, P., Martin, J., & Samoilov, A. (1994). Modification of interpersonal psychotherapy with depressed adolescents (IPT-A): Phase I and II studies. *Journal of the American Academy of Child and Adolescent Psychiatry, 33,* 695–705.

Mufson, L., Weissman, M. M., Moreau, D., & Garfinkel, R. (1999). Efficacy of interpersonal psychotherapy for depressed adolescents. *Archives of General Psychiatry, 56,* 573–579.

Nobile, M., Bellotti, B., Marino, C., Molteni, M., & Battaglia, M. (2000). An open trial of paroxetine in the treatment of children and adolescents diagnosed with dysthymia. *Journal of Child and Adolescent Psychopharmacology, 10,* 103–109.

Rabe-Jablonska, J. (2000). Therapeutic effects and tolerability of fluvoxamine treatment in adolescents with dysthymia. *Journal of Child and Adolescent Psychopharmacology, 10,* 9–18.

Rehm, L. P., & Sharp, R. N. (1996). Strategies for childhood depression. In M. A. Reinecke, F. M. Dattilio, & A. Freeman (Eds.), *Cognitive therapy with children and adolescents: A casebook for clinical practice* (pp. 103–123). New York: Guilford Press.

Reinecke, M. A., Ryan, N. E., & DuBois, D. L. (1998). Cognitive behavioral therapy of depression and depressive symptoms during adolescence: A review and meta-analysis. *Journal of the American Academy of Child and Adolescent Psychiatry, 37,* 26–34.

Renaud, J., Brent, D., Baugher, M., Birmaher, D., Kolko, D., & Bridge, J. (1998). Rapid response to psychosocial treatment for adolescent depression: A two year follow-up. *Journal of the American Academy of Child and Adolescent Psychiatry, 37,* 1184–1190.

Reynolds, W., & Coats, K. (1986). A comparison of cognitive-behavioral therapy and relaxation training for the treatment of depression in adolescents. *Journal of Consulting and Clinical Psychology, 54,* 653–660.

Rey-Sánchez, F., & Gutiérrez-Casares, J. R. (1997). Paroxetine in children with major depressive disorder: An open trial. *Journal of the American Academy of Child and Adolescent Psychiatry, 36,* 1443–1447.

Riggs, P. D., Mikulich, S. K., Coffman, L. M., & Crowley, T. J. (1997). Fluoxetine in drug-dependent delinquents with major depression: An open-trial. *Journal of Child and Adolescent Psychopharmacology, 7,* 87–95.

Rohde, P., Lewinsohn, P. M., & Seeley, J. R. (1994). Response of depressed adolescents to cognitive-behavioral treatment: Do differences in initial severity clarify the comparison of treatments? *Journal of Consulting and Clinical Psychology, 62,* 851–854.

Rollings, S., King, N., Tonge, B., Heyne, D., & Young, D. (1998). Cognitive behavioral intervention with a depressed adolescent experiencing school attendance difficulties. *Behavior Change, 15,* 87–97.

Rossello, J., & Bernal, G. (1996). Adapting cognitive-behavioral and interpersonal treatments for depressed Puerto Rican adolescents. In E. D. Hibbs & P. Jensen (Eds.), *Psychosocial treatments for child and adolescent disorders* (pp. 157–185). Washington, DC: American Psychological Association.

Rossello, J., & Bernal, G. (1999). The efficacy of cognitive-behavioral and interpersonal treatments for depression in Puerto Rican adolescents. *Journal of Consulting and Clinical Psychology, 67,* 734–745.

Rotheram-Borus, M. J., Piancentini, J., Miller, S., Graae, F., & Castro-Blanco, D. (1994). Brief cognitive behavioral treatment for adolescent suicide attempters and their families. *Journal of the American Academy of Child and Adolescent Psychiatry, 33,* 508–517.

Runyon, M., & Orvaschel, H. (1999). Cognitive behavioral treatment for adolescent depression complicated by childhood trauma: Case illustration. *Clinical Child Psychology and Psychiatry, 4,* 493–504.

Ryan, N. D., Puig-Antich, J., Rabinovich, H., Fried, J., Ambrosini, P., Meyer, V., Torres, D., Dachille, S., & Mazzie, D. (1988). MAOIs in adolescent major depression unresponsive to tricyclic antidepressants. *Journal of the American Academy of Child and Adolescent Psychiatry, 27,* 755–758.

Simeon, J. G., Dinicola, V. F., Ferguson, H. B., & Copping, W. (1990). Adolescent depression: A placebo-controlled fluoxetine study and follow-up. *Progress in Neuropsychopharmacology:* Biological Psychiatry, 14, 791–795.

Sommers-Flanagan, J., & Sommers-Flanagan, R. (1996). Efficacy of antidepressant medication with depressed youth: What psychologists should know. *Professional Psychology: Research and Practice, 27,* 145–153.

Stark, K. D., Brookman, C. S., & Frazier, R. (1990). A comprehensive school-based treatment program for depressed children. *School Psychology Quarterly, 5,* 111–140.

Stark, K. D., Laurent, J., Livingston, R., Boswell, J., & Swearer, S. (1999). Implications of research for the treatment of depressive disorders during childhood. *Applied and Preventive Psychology, 8,* 79–102.

Stark, K. D., Reynolds, W. M., & Kaslow, N. J. (1987). A comparison of the relative efficacy of self-control therapy and behavior problem-solving therapy for depression in children. *Journal of Abnormal Child Psychology, 15,* 91–113.

Stark, K. D., Rouse, L., & Livingston, R. (1991). Treatment of depression during childhood and adolescence: Cognitive behavioral procedures for the individual and family. In P. Kendall (Ed.), *Child and adolescent therapy* (pp. 165–206). New York: Guilford Press.

Strober, M., Freeman, R., Rigali, J., Schmidt, S., & Diamond, R. (1992). The pharmacotherapy of depressive illness in adolescence: II. Effects of lithium augmentation in nonresponders to imipramine. *Journal of the American Academy of Child and Adolescent Psychiatry, 31,* 16–20.

Swedo, S. E., Allen, A. J., Glod, C. A., Clark, C. H., Teicher, M., Richter, D., Hoffman, C., Hamburger, S., Dow, S., Brown, C., & Rosenthal, N. (1997). A controlled trial of light therapy for the treatment of pediatric seasonal affective disorder. *Journal of the American Academy of Child and Adolescent Psychiatry, 36,* 816–821.

Vostanis, P., Feehan, C., & Grattan, E. (1998). Two-year outcome of children treated for depression. *European Child and Adolescent Psychiatry, 7,* 12–18.

Vostanis, P., Feehan, C., Grattan, E., & Bickerton, W. (1996a). A randomized controlled outpatient trial of cognitive behavioral treatment for children and adolescents with depression: 9-month follow-up. *Journal of Affective Disorders, 40,* 105–116.

Vostanis, P., Feehan, C., Grattan, E., & Bickerton, W. (1996b). Treatment for children and adolescents with depression: Lessons from a controlled trial. *Clinical Child Psychology and Psychiatry, 1,* 199–212.

Walter, G., & Rey, J. M. (1997). An epidemiological study of the use of ECT in adolescents. *Journal of the American Academy of Child and Adolescent Psychiatry, 36,* 809–815.

Waslick, B. D., Walsh, B. T., Greenhill, L. L., Eilenberg, M., Capasso, L., & Lieber, D. (1999). Open-trial of fluoxetine in children and adolescents with dysthymic disorder or double depression. *Journal of Affective Disorders, 56,* 227–236.

Weisz, J., Thurber, C., Sweeney, L., Proffitt, V., & LeGagnoux, G. (1997). Brief treatment of mild to moderate child depression using primary and secondary control enhancement training. *Journal of Consulting and Clinical Psychology, 65,* 703–707.

PART IV

DEPRESSION IN
SPECIFIC POPULATIONS

While depressive disorders occur in all cultural, demographic, and age groups, their mani-festations, meanings, treatments, and possible causes may differ importantly from one pop-ulation to another. The six chapters in this part detail the considerations about the experi-ence of depression in particular groups. Tsai and Chentsova-Dutton (Chapter 20) discuss a growing body of research on cultural differences in the expression and experience of depres-sion. The well-known gender differences in the experience of depression, reviewed by Nolen-Hoeksema (Chapter 21), continue to challenge simple unitary explanations of this disorder. Depression in children, addressed by Garber and Horowitz (Chapter 22), and de-pression in adolescents, discussed by Lewinsohn and Essau (Chapter 23), are presented as separate chapters in recognition of both the unique features of these groups and the enormous body of recent research on these topics. Powers, Thompson, Futterman, and Gallagher-Thompson (Chapter 24) review the experience of depression in later life, a topic of increasing social concern. Finally, although suicide is not uniquely associated with de-pressive disorders, Stolberg, Clark, and Bongar (Chapter 25) address the relatively common experience of suicidality in depressed individuals and discuss its management.

20

Understanding Depression across Cultures

Jeanne L. Tsai and Yulia Chentsova-Dutton

Depression is neither a simple "reflection" in personal experience of psychophysiological processes nor a culturally constituted phenomenon free of physiological constraints. Depression is of such interest to anthropologists and psychiatrists alike because it provides a prime opportunity for exploration of the interaction of culture and biology.
—KLEINMAN AND GOOD (1985, p. 31)

Since the 1960s and 1970s, clinical scientists and practitioners alike have been interested in understanding how culture influences the constellation of symptoms that comprise depression, as defined by Western diagnostic classification systems. Although social scientists agree that the core feelings of emptiness, loss, and helplessness associated with depression are universally experienced (Shweder, 1985), there is much debate about whether the other aspects of depression are too. Moreover, it is unclear whether the personal and social implications of these symptoms are the same across cultures. By revealing the aspects of our moods that are similar across cultures and those that are shaped by our cultural environments, cross-cultural studies of depression have much to contribute to our understanding of human function and dysfunction. This understanding is critical if we are to develop interventions that are effective in treating depression across different cultural contexts.

Studying depression across cultures, however, is fraught with many obstacles. The most challenging of obstacles may be the fact that the very definition of depression is imbued with Western cultural assumptions. Scholars have identified at least three ways in which modern conceptions of depression have been influenced by Western culture. First, current views of depression are shaped by Western culture's emphasis on positive emotions and feeling good about the self. As argued by Lutz (1985), depressed mood, loss of interest in pleasurable activities, and decreases in self-esteem are only viewed as abnormal in cultures that assume that having positive emotions and feeling good about oneself is a normal and healthy way of being. Second, conceptions of depression are influenced by the Western view of the individual. Lewis-Fernandez and Kleinman (1994) argue that because Western cultures view individuals as independent, self-contained, and autonomous, depressive symptoms are attributed to internal disturbances. In cultures that view individuals as interdependent, connected with others, and defined by the social context (e.g., Japan, China; Markus & Kitayama, 1991), these same symptoms may be attributed to interpersonal disturbances. Moreover, in these cultures, more relational symptoms of depression, such as social withdrawal or failure to maintain interpersonal obligations, may be more salient and exact a greater toll on daily functioning than other depressive symptoms.

Finally, current views of depression are based on Western assumptions about the mind and body (Lewis-Fernandez & Kleinman, 1994). In Western cultures, depression (and other forms of mental illness) has been characterized as stemming from either mental *or* biological disturbances. Historically, depression was depicted as a mental disorder best treated by psychological means, such as psychotherapy. Over the last few decades, however, new evidence for the neurobiological bases of depression has emerged, and now depression has become primarily viewed as a biological disorder best treated by medical means, such as antidepressants (Kramer, 1994). In contrast, many non-Western cultures do not view the mind and body as separate and distinct entities. Instead, the mind and body are seen as intimately related and mutually constitutive, as illustrated by non-Western treatments of illness such as acupuncture and traditional Chinese medicine.

How, then, does one study cultural variation in a disorder whose very definition may be culturally constructed (Schieffelin, 1985)? Researchers have approached this challenge in one of two ways. The ethnographic approach (typically employed by anthropologists) assumes that even if members of a particular culture experience the symptoms defined by Western culture as depression, the meanings and implications of these symptoms may vary considerably across cultures. Proponents of the ethnographic approach focus on the structures, norms, and values that determine the meaning of these depressive symptoms within a particular cultural context and compare them to those of Western culture. Most of the work that falls under this approach is based on ethnographic interviews and behavioral observations.

The biomedical approach (typically employed by psychologists and psychiatrists) assumes that regardless of the cultural context, the disorder exists if individuals report having the symptoms associated with depression. To date, the bulk of the research employing a biomedical approach focuses on the prevalence rates of depression in various nations. Variations in prevalence rates of depression are typically attributed to cultural factors, in a somewhat post-hoc fashion. Most of this work is based on survey data or data gleaned from structured diagnostic interviews. For example, several studies have found that rates of depression are generally lower in Asian cultures than in Western cultures, which may be due to different perceptions of mental illness in these cultures (Bland, 1997; Hwu, Chang, Yeh, Chang, & Yeh, 1996; Sato & Takeichi, 1993; Simon, VonKorff, Picvinelli, Fullerton, & Ormel, 1999).

In this chapter, we present research findings from both approaches; however, because most research falls under the biomedical approach, we spend more time reviewing this type of research. We highlight consistent themes that emerge from the literature and then propose other ways of studying depression across cultures that we believe will advance our current knowledge base. We end with a discussion of specific topics that require further study. But first, we define what we mean by *culture*.

DEFINING CULTURE

According to Kroeber and Kluckhohn (1952):

> Culture consists of patterns, explicit and implicit, of and for behavior acquired and transmitted by symbols, constituting the distinctive achievement of human groups, and including their embodiments in artifacts; the essential core of culture consists of traditional (i.e., historically derived and selected) ideas and especially their attached values; culture systems may, on the one hand, be considered as products of action, and on the other, as conditioning elements of further action. (p. 181)

Clearly, culture is complex and multifaceted. Ethnographic and biomedical researchers have operationalized culture in different ways. Because ethnographic studies focus on cultural meaning systems, practices, and structures, they are explicit about the specific facets of culture that they are examining. Biomedical approaches, however, tend to assume that national differences are cultural ones. Often it is only after finding differences in specific aspects of depression that cultural values, beliefs, or structures are recruited to explain the variation. As a result, biomedical approaches tend to be less clear than ethnographic approaches about which aspects of culture they are focusing on. Regardless of which approach they fall under, however, most studies fail to demonstrate direct links between the specific cultural factors and the specific aspects of depression under investigation. In order to understand comprehensively how culture influences depression, we must measure culture in more specific and systematic ways than we have in the past.

ETHNOGRAPHIC APPROACHES TO UNDERSTANDING DEPRESSION

In trying to understand depression across cultures, proponents of the ethnographic approach typically develop an in-depth understanding of the culture and, based on that understanding, then examine whether conceptions of depression in that culture are similar to those of Western culture. Ethnographic accounts suggest that while the feelings of emptiness, learned helplessness, even "soul loss" as described by Shweder (1985) may exist across cultures, other aspects of depression may not (see Schieffelin's work among the Kaluli of Papua New Guinea, 1985; Obeyesekere's study of Buddhists in Sri Lanka, 1985; Kleinman's work among the mainland Chinese, 1986; Good, Del Vecchio, and Moradi's studies in Iran, 1985). To illustrate the ethnographic approach to understanding depression across cultures, we provide descriptions of two accounts that suggest that the personal and social meanings of depression differ in cultures where there is a greater emphasis on social reciprocity and where there are more mechanisms of reparation for social transgressions than in Western cultures.

Depression among the Kaluli of New Guinea

According to Schieffelin (1985), emotions for the Kaluli of New Guinea are expressed in order to influence others:

> When the Kaluli feel strongly about something, they are not usually ones to hide their feelings. Rage, grief, dismay, embarrassment, fear, and compassion may be openly and often dramatically expressed. The expression of affect is in part aimed at influencing others, whether by intimidation (e.g., with anger) or by evoking their compassion and support (e.g., with grieving). (p. 109)

These expressions of emotion are used to ensure social reciprocity, which is highly scripted in Kaluli cultures and embedded in social interaction styles, rituals, and ceremonies. That is, Kaluli culture provides clear scripts for how one should behave in order to get what one wants or deserves. Schieffelin argues that because cultural structures exist to enable Kaluli to recover any losses that incur, they rarely experience depression. In fact, during the 3 years he spent studying the Kaluli, Scheffielin was able to identify only one case of depression, which involved a woman who was unhappy in her marriage and who, due to her particular circumstances, had no outlet to express her grief. Notably, Schefflielin observes that this particular woman reported physical complaints that resembled the somatic symptoms of depression.

Pena in Highland Ecuador

Tousignant and Maldonaldo (1989) provide another example of a culture for which they believe that the meanings of depressive symptoms differ from those of Western culture. They studied the experience of *pena*, which means sadness or suffering, in highland Ecuador. In its severe form, individuals with *pena* have crying spells, poor concentration, anhedonia, social withdrawal, poor personal hygiene, sleep and appetite disturbances, gastrointestinal complaints, and heart pain. Like depression, *pena* is also often experienced in response to personal loss. However, Tousignant and Maldonaldo argue that unlike depression, *pena* is an "appeal, implicitly or explicitly expressed, for payment of an incurred loss" (p. 900). That is, *pena* provides an opportunity for others to restore equity and ensure social reciprocity among individuals. An injured party in a conflict may signal distress by withdrawing from others and displaying symptoms characteristic of *pena*. In turn, the party's social circle may attempt to remedy the situation by sharing feelings with the sufferer and by reintegrating him or her into the social network. Thus, although *pena* looks like sadness and, in its more severe forms, depression, Tousignant and Maldonaldo (1989) argue that its personal and social implications differ from those of depression in Western cultures.

In summary, although expressions of loss and grief can be found in both Kaluli and Ecuadorian cultures, Schieffelin (1985) and Tousignant and Maldonaldo (1989) argue that the meaning of these expressions differs from that of depression in Western culture. While contributing to our understanding of depression across cultures, ethnographic studies such as these have a number of limitations. Because of their in-depth nature, most ethnographic studies are based on a small number of participants, limiting the generalizability of the research findings. Moreover, although the researchers have firsthand knowledge about the cultures that they are studying, it is unclear to what extent their observations are influenced by their own cultural biases. Finally, because most of these studies are not comparative (i.e., do not include direct comparisons of data collected in more than one culture), it is unclear whether the meaning and consequences of depressive symptoms differ as drastically across cultures as these accounts suggest. Thus, other researchers have assumed a different approach to studying cultural influences on depression.

BIOMEDICAL APPROACHES TO UNDERSTANDING
DEPRESSION ACROSS CULTURES

In stark contrast to the ethnographic approach, the biomedical approach assumes that if the symptoms associated with depression exist, then the disorder can be identified, diagnosed, and understood. These studies tend to consider culture as separate from and secondary to the disorder. For example, culture is used to explain national differences in the prevalence rates of depression. In an attempt to examine how culture might influence the symptoms of depression, researchers assuming the biomedical approach have also compared the basic elements (or factors) that comprise depression across cultures. We review findings from these studies next.

Different Rates of Depression across Cultures

Many epidemiological studies have found that the prevalence rate of depression varies considerably across national (and presumably, cultural) lines. For example, the Epidemiologic Catchment Area Study (United States), the Edmonton Survey of Psychiatric Disorders (Canada), the Christchurch Survey (New Zealand), the Zurich Cohort Study of Young Adults (Switzerland), the Munich Follow-Up Study (Germany), the French Study of Psychiatric Disorders (France), the Florence Community Survey of Mood Disorders (Italy), the Beirut War Events and Depression Study (Lebanon), the Taiwan Psychiatric Epidemiology Project (Taiwan), the Korean Epidemiological Study of Mental Disorders, and the Epidemiological Study of Puerto Rico document different lifetime prevalence rates for major depression by nation, ranging from 1.5% in Taiwan to 19% in Lebanon, based on the diagnostic criteria of the third edition of the *Diagnostic and Statistical Manual of Mental Disorders* (DSM-III) (Merikangas et al., 1996; Weissman et al., 1993; Weissman et al., 1996). Figure 20.1 illustrates the tremendous variation in prevalence rates of depression across various nations, based on data obtained from Bland (1997), Kessler et al. (1994), Szadoczky, Papp, Vitrai, Rihmer, and Fueredi (1998), and Weissman et al. (1996).

Notably, the prevalence rate of depression for the United States is lower in the Epidemiologic Catchment Area Study (ECA) conducted in 1980–1984 (Weissman, Bruce, Leaf, Florio, & Holzer, 1991) than in the National Comorbidity Study (NCS), conducted in 1990–1992 (Kessler et al., 1994). These differences may be due to the subtle methodological differences between the two studies: the NCS included a larger and a more representative sample, used DSM-IV diagnostic criteria rather than those of the DSM-III, and probed more comprehensively for signs of depression than did the ECA (Kessler et al., 1994). However, it is also possible that rates of depression increased from the early 1980s to the early 1990s.

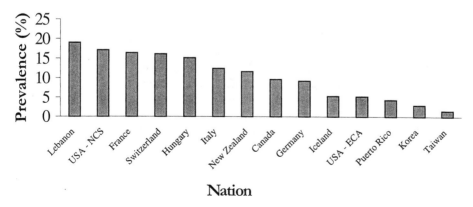

FIGURE 20.1. DSM-III/III-R lifetime prevalence of major depression by nation. Prevalence rates were obtained from Bland (1997), Kessler et al. (1994), Szadoczky, Papp, Vitrai, Rihmer, and Fueredi (1998), and Weissman et al. (1996). USA–NCS, United States according to the National Comorbidity Study; USA–ECA, United States according to the Epidemiologic Catchment Area Study.

Because the assessment instruments used to diagnose depression in the above studies varied across the studies, it is possible that the different prevalence rates that were found were due to the different methods of assessing depression rather than to culture. Therefore, in 1991, the World Health Organization (WHO) compared the prevalence of mental disorders in the primary care clinics of 14 countries on five continents (Simon, VonKorff, et al., 1999) using the Composite International Diagnostic Interview—Primary Care Version (CIDI-PHC) (Wittchen et al., 1991). Once again, the prevalence rate of major depression showed considerable variation across nations, ranging from 1.5% in Nagasaki, Japan, to 27.3% in Santiago, Chile, based on DSM-IV criteria.

One notable pattern that has emerged from the epidemiological literature is that depression appears to be less prevalent in Asian (e.g., Japan, China, Taiwan) than in Western cultures (United States, Canada, New Zealand, Germany, The Netherlands) (Bland, 1997; Hwu et al., 1996; Sato & Takeichi, 1993; Simon, VonKorff, et al., 1999). For example, the WHO study reported that the prevalence of depression in primary care settings was 1.5% in Japan and 2.4% in China, whereas the prevalence rates for Western countries, such as the United Kingdom or the United States, were significantly higher (17.1% and 6.4%, respectively; Simon, VonKorff, et al., 1999). This pattern has been found in different age groups, including college student and geriatric samples (Chen, Copeland, & Wei, 1999; Crittenden, Fugita, Bae, Lamug, & Lin, 1992). As mentioned earlier, these differences have been attributed to cultural variation in the conception of mental illness (with Western cultures viewing emotional problems as separate from physical complaints more than Asian cultures), to differences in the amount of stigma attached to mental illness (with Asian cultures stigmatizing emotional problems more than Western cultures), and to different levels of available social and familial support (with Asian participants having more social support than their Western peers). Differences among specific Asian groups, however, have also been found. For example, a study of self-reported symptoms of depression in college students (Crittenden et al., 1992) demonstrated that Korean students had the greatest proportion (32%) of individuals who reported high levels of depression, followed by Filipino and American students (17% and 15%, respectively), and finally, by Taiwanese students (11%). According to the authors, the greater rates of depression among the Korean students compared to their Filipino and Taiwanese peers reflect their more self-effacing and pessimistic styles, as well as their greater tendency to support "taking in and absorbing psychic insults" (Crittenden et al., 1992).

In addition to epidemiological studies on cross-cultural differences in rates of depression, an increasing amount of research examines rates of depression among cultural and ethnic minorities living in host countries such as Europe, the United States, Canada, and Australia (Beiser, Cargo, & Woodbury, 1994; Lin et al., 1992; Roberts, Roberts, & Chen, 1997; Ying, 1988; Kuo, 1984). For example, several studies suggest that prevalence rates of depression differ among ethnic groups within the United States. Both the National Comorbidity Survey (Kessler, 1994) and the Epidemiologic Catchment Area Study (Weissman et al., 1991) have reported that lifetime prevalence rates of affective disorders are lower for African Americans as compared to European Americans, with the rates for Hispanics falling between the two.

Epidemiological studies conducted in the United States have not included sufficiently large samples of Asian Americans or Native Americans to be able to draw conclusions about the national prevalence of depression in these groups. However, smaller community studies of depression have been conducted. A study of the prevalence of depression in a Native American primary care clinic sample (Wilson, Civic, & Glass, 1995) reported a prevalence rate of depression that was comparable to that of European American samples from the WHO study (Simon, VonKorff, et al., 1999). However, other studies have found that

Native American youth have higher levels of depressive symptoms (Manson, Ackerson, Dick, Baron, & Fleming, 1990) and rates of suicide (Sigurdson, Staley, Matas, Hildahl, & Squair, 1994) than non-Native American samples.

Studies with Asian Americans suggest that their rates of depression are equal to or greater than those of European Americans (Kuo, 1984; Ying, 1988). For example, Korean Americans had higher prevalence rates of depression (Lin et al., 1992) than their European American counterparts (Weissman et al., 1993). Foreign-born Asians also tend to report more symptoms of depression than do American-born Asians (Kuo, 1984), suggesting that Asian Americans' higher rates of depression may be due to the stresses they endure as immigrants and minorities in the United States.

Why do the prevalence rates of depression vary across national and ethnic lines? Although we have already mentioned a few possible explanations, others have been proposed. These include cultural differences in the use of diagnostic labels, the occurrence of specific symptoms, the existence of alternative forms of illness, and the experience of environmental stressors. We discuss each explanation and its supporting evidence below.

Use of Diagnostic Labels

Differences in prevalence rates may be due to the differential use of diagnostic labels among psychologists, psychiatrists, and other health care providers across cultures. Cultural conceptions of mental illness and health may influence whether or not specific behaviors are viewed as abnormal by both laypeople and physicians. Data from a study conducted by the WHO demonstrate that the probability of recognition of depression by a primary care clinician varies substantially across cultures (Simon, Goldberg, Tiemens, & Ustun, 1999). In this study, patients were independently assessed by the study interviewers and by a group of primary care clinicians. Primary care clinicians assigned psychiatric and medical diagnoses to each patient. A case of depression was deemed "unrecognized" when the study interviewer, but not the primary care clinician, assigned a diagnosis of depression. In Turkey, Greece, Nigeria, Japan and China, only 20% or less of depressed cases were recognized and treated. This is in contrast to the United Kingdom, France, Chile, United States, and Italy, where 50% or more of the depressed cases were recognized. Because recognition rates vary for countries with comparable base rates of depression, it is unlikely that they are the cause of these differences in recognition rates.

Although the use of standardized interviews and diagnostic systems should reduce subjectivity in assigning psychiatric diagnoses, cultural bias appears to exist even when these standardized instruments are used. For example, Katz, LeBars, Itil, Prilipko, and DeGiralamo (1994) asked psychiatrists from 14 countries to view a videotaped recording of a patient hospitalized for depression during an interview. The interview consisted of a brief mental status examination and a set of performance tasks (e.g., copying designs). Psychiatrists were asked to rate the expressive behavior and symptoms of the patient. Psychiatrists agreed about the presence and intensity of depressed mood, about the behavioral and somatic symptoms expressed, and about the patient's facial expressions, but they disagreed about the patient's rate of speech and energy level, as well as her cognitive and sexual symptoms. In a similar study, videotaped standardized interviews with psychiatric patients were rated by researchers from China, Korea, and Japan (Nakane et al., 1988). Even though the raters used identical assessment instruments and were all from Asian cultures, substantial diagnostic differences emerged in this study as well. Specifically, Japanese raters tended to diagnose patients as having affective disorders, whereas Chinese raters tended to diagnose the same individuals as having anxiety disorders. Korean raters tended to diagnose both affective disorders and anxiety disorders equally. The authors suggest that the Japanese raters may have diagnosed affective disorders more than their Chinese counterparts because historically, Japanese psychiatric practice has been more influenced by Western psychiatry than Chinese psychiatric practice (Nakane et al., 1988). These findings suggest that culture may influence how mental health providers view similar depressive symptoms, or how they use diagnostic criteria, which may result in different prevalence rates of depression across cultures. Future studies are needed to determine whether or not this is the case.

Specific Symptoms of Depression

National differences in prevalence rates of depression may also reflect cultural differences in the occurrence of specific depressive symptoms. For example, when accepted diagnostic criteria for a disorder include symptoms that occur more or less frequently in a particular cultural context (in comparison to the cultural contexts in which the diagnostic criteria were normed), cultural differences in the prevalence rates of the disorder may arise. Weissman et al. (1996) reviewed data from 10 epidemiological studies from around the world (United States, Canada, Puerto Rico, France, Germany, Italy, Lebanon, Taiwan, Korea, and New Zealand) and found that insomnia, loss of energy, difficulty concentrating, and thoughts of death and suicide were reported by the majority of depressed individuals in all of the countries sampled. On the other hand, other symptoms, such as poor appetite, feelings of worthlessness or guilt, and slowed thinking were not common at all sites. For instance, poor appetite was a common symptom in non-Western countries (Lebanon, Korea, and Taiwan), but not in Western countries. Thus, specific symptoms may vary in their ability to differentiate between cases and noncases of depression across cultures.

Another demonstration of cultural differences in the extent to which specific symptoms differentiate between depressed and nondepressed cases is provided by the 1991 WHO study, in which Goldberg, Oldehinkel, and Ormel (1998) compared patients' responses to the General Health Questionnaire (GHQ; Goldberg, 1972) across study sites. The GHQ is a self-report instrument of psychological distress and maladaptive behavior that has been used to screen for psychiatric disorders in primary care and community settings. This scale has good reliability and validity, and has been translated into many languages. Goldberg and colleagues found that most GHQ items (which correspond to the individual symptoms of depression) did not function in the same way across cultures. For example, "lost concentration" and "enjoy activities" discriminated between depressed and nondepressed groups for some cultures, but not for others. Only a few items functioned similarly across cultures. For example, feelings of depression tended to have low specificity (i.e., were unable to identify individuals who were not depressed) and high sensitivity (i.e., were able to identify individuals who were depressed) across cultures, and feelings of worthlessness and loss of confidence tended to have high specificity (were able to detect individuals who were not depressed) and low sensitivity (were unable to detect individuals who were depressed) across cultures.

The occurrence of a specific symptom may depend on how salient it is to members of that particular culture. For example, Pang (1995) used semistructured interviews to study the experience of depression in elderly Korean immigrants. Pang found that many depressed immigrants did not report feeling depressed; instead, they explained and communicated their distress in terms of loneliness, family dynamics, or somatic complaints. In another study, Jenkins (1997) asked European American and Latino (mostly Puerto Rican) individuals with major depression and schizophrenia to describe their life situations. Almost half of all subjects from both cultural groups failed to mention their illness in describing their lives, focusing instead on emotional distress, restricted activities, significant life events, accomplishments, and relationships. However, European Americans were more likely to describe their lives in terms of mental and physical illness than Latinos, and Latinos were more likely to use the culturally acceptable term of *nervios* (Jenkins & Cofresi, 1998). Koss-Chioino (1999) also found that depressed Puerto Rican women also reported visions of spirits, prolonged and uncontrollable crying, and headaches, none of which are included in the DSM diagnostic criteria.

Nonwestern cultures (e.g., Taiwanese, Korean, Phillipino, Arab, Turkish, Japanese) appear to emphasize the somatic symptoms of depression. Somatic symptoms may be more salient to members of non-Western cultures than to members of Western cultures because of beliefs about the integration of body and mind, of a lack of emphasis on emotional expression, and/or of a stigma attached to mental illness. For example, depressed inpatients and outpatients (Ebert & Martus, 1994; Hamdi, Amin, & Abou-Saleh, 1997) in the United Arab Emirates and Turkey were more likely to describe their depression in terms of somatic concerns (such as psychomotor retardation, somatic anxiety, and hypochondriasis) as compared to depressed individuals from Western cultures. Another study comparing depressed African Americans and European Americans found that despite comparable levels of cognitive and affective symptoms of depression, African Americans reported more somatic symptoms (Brown, Schulberg, & Madonia, 1996). In contrast, depressed Westerners were more likely to report symptoms such as suicidal ideation and feelings of guilt. Similarly, Waza, Graham, Zyzanski, and Inoue (1999) reviewed medical charts of patients in Japanese and American primary care clinics who had received new diagnoses of depression. They found that depressed Japanese patients were more likely to present with exclusively physical symptoms, whereas American patients were more likely to present with exclusively psychological ones. Interestingly, according to a WHO study (Simon, Goldberg, et al., 1999), depressed patients across cultures differed in their tendency to reveal somatic rather than emotional distress to their primary care providers. For example, in Turkey and Greece, nearly all depressed participants reported only physical symptoms as the reason for seeking a doctor. Moreover, somatization occurred more frequently in walk-in primary care centers that did not facilitate an ongoing relationship between patients and health care providers than those that did. Thus, in some cases, somatic presentation may reflect the quality of relationship between medical doctors and their patients.

Alternative Forms of Depressive Illness

Rates of depression may be lower in cultures where there exist alternative explanations for depressive symptoms. That is, depressive symptoms may co-occur with other symptoms that are part of another form of illness. The DSM-IV refers to disorders that have some depressive symptoms but that have other defining features as "culture-bound syndromes." Examples include *hwa-byung* in Korea (Lin et al., 1992), *sinking heart* among the Punjabi Sikhs (Krause, 1989), *pena* in Ecuador (Tousignant & Maldonaldo, 1989), *khoucherang* in Cambodia (D'Avanzo & Barab, 1998), *neurasthenia* or *somatization* in China (Grauer, 1984; Kleinman, 1982), and *wacinko syndrome* among the Sioux (Shore & Manson, 1981). For example, *hwa-byung* (Lin et al., 1992) is defined by constricted and oppressed sensations in the chest, and *sinking heart* (Krause, 1989) by irregular movement and shrinking sensation in the heart. Despite these unique features, some scholars have suggested that these culture-bound syndromes are essentially subtle variants of depression (Mumford, 1996). For instance, Lin et al. (1992) found that Korean subjects with *hwa-byung* were more likely to meet criteria for current and past major depression and had higher levels of depressive symptoms than those without the disorder. The agreement was not perfect, however, with only a half of self-defined *hwa-byung* sufferers actually meeting criteria for major depression. Similarly, Beiser et al. (1994) administered measures of depression, anxiety, somatization, and culture-bound syndromes to 1,348 Southeast Asian refugees and 319 Canadians and found that for both groups, reported symptoms were best described in terms of depression.

Does the existence of "culture-bound" syndromes affect the prevalence rate of depression? To address the question of whether lower prevalence rates of depression are related to the greater prevalence of *somatization*, the WHO examined the prevalence of both disorders in different primary care centers across the world (Simon, VonKorff, et al., 1999). Researchers defined *somatization* as the presentation of unexplained medical symptoms or denial of psychological symptoms of depression (to distinguish it from the mere reporting of somatic symptoms). They found that rates of somatization were similar across cultures. Moreover, when the ratio of somatic symptoms to psychological symptoms of depression was examined, it became apparent that this ratio did not vary with culture. For example, even though patients in Nagasaki, Japan, reported few overall symptoms compared to patients in Santiago, Chile, the ratio of somatic to psychological symptoms did not differ for the two groups. These findings cast doubt on theories that *somatization* can account for cross-cultural differences in the prevalence of depression. Future studies should assess whether the same can be said for other culture-bound syndromes.

Environmental Stressors

Urbanization and Westernization have been hypothesized to have a negative effect on mental health in general and levels of depression in particular (Freeman, 1988). A study conducted in the United States found that urban samples were more depressed than rural samples (Blazer et al., 1985). However, a study conducted in Indonesia found that psychological symptoms were primarily associated with poverty and that inhabitants of villages in the process of urbanization with improved standards of living and increased socioeconomic development reported fewer psychological symptoms (Bahar, Henderson, & Mackinnon, 1992). Similarly, in Taiwan, rates of depression were twice as high in rural communities as compared to urban communities (Cheng, 1989). Thus, urbanization may serve as a proxy for poverty in certain countries. For example, in the United States, urban populations may be poorer than rural and suburban population, whereas in other cultures the reverse may be true. Poverty has been shown to be associated with depression (Murphy et al., 1991; Patel, Araya, de Lima, Ludermir, & Todd, 1999). In fact, some differences in levels of depression between ethnic groups may be entirely due to differences in socioeconomic status. For example, one study found that African Americans had higher levels of depression than European Americans; however, these differences disappeared when the researchers controlled for group differences in socioeconomic status (Comstock & Helsing, 1979).

In summary, an enormous literature has documented and attempted to explain the substantial variation in prevalence rates of depression across cultures. Clearly, there is evidence that the use of diagnostic labels, the salience/occurrence of specific symptoms, and the existence of alternative forms of illness and of environmental stressors have some influence. Future research is needed to examine how these factors interact with each other and to assess the degree to which they influence prevalence rates of depression.

Different Conceptions of Depressive Symptoms across Cultures

Although the bulk of biomedical studies on depression across cultures has focused on prevalence rates of depression, another body of research examines whether culture influences the basic elements or factors that comprise depression by examining the relationships among different depressive symptoms. To achieve this, researchers typically employ factor analytic techniques. For example, studies of British patients (Goldberg & Hillier, 1979; Goldberg, Rickels, Downing, & Hesbacher, 1976; Huppert, Walters, Day, & Elliott, 1989) found that the factor structure of the GHQ was comprised of four or six (one primary-order and five second-order) factors, including depression, anxiety, insomnia, social dysfunction, somatic symptoms, and diminished coping capacity. Most of the studies validating the GHQ among non-Western populations, such as adolescents (Shek, 1993) and parents of mentally handicapped children (Shek & Tsang, 1995) in Hong Kong, Japanese students (Takeuchi & Kitamura, 1991), and Turkish immigrants in Australia (Stuart, Klimidis, Minas, & Tuncer, 1993), find comparable factor structures, suggesting that in these cultures the basic elements that comprise depression are similar. Other studies with different cultural groups (Mexican general practice patients, middle-aged and elderly Japanese), however, have reported more factors (Medina-Mora et al., 1983; Ohta, Kawasaki, Araki, Mine, & Honda, 1995). For example, Ohta and colleagues (1995) found that depressive symptoms were described by eight factors (depression, anxiety and tension, anergia, interpersonal dysfunction, difficulty in coping, insomnia, anhedonia, and social avoidance) in a sample of middle-aged and elderly Japanese. This finding suggests that for these groups, the underlying elements of depression may differ.

Another widely used self-report measure of depression is the Center for Epidemiological Studies—Depression Scale (CES-D) (Radloff, 1977). Radloff (1977) found that in European American community samples, depressive symptoms were organized into four factors: depressed affect, positive affect, somatic and retarded activity, and interpersonal problems. Studies conducted with members of non-Western cultures and ethnic minorities, however, reveal different factors. For example, a study of older community samples from several Asian countries, including Indonesia, North Korea, Myanmar, Sri Lanka, and Thailand, found that the four-factor structure described above, with an additional general factor of depression, applied well to Indonesia and Thailand, but not to Korea, Sri Lanka, and Myanmar (Mackinnon, McCallum, Andrews, & Anderson, 1998). Interestingly, for all the samples, the depression and somatic factors were highly correlated (.92–.98), which is consistent with prevailing beliefs that emotions in many Asian cultures are situated in the body, as demonstrated by traditional Chinese medicine and Ayurvedic medicine. These systems of medicine view problems as psychobiological rather than purely psychological and expect emotional distress to be expressed through bodily complaints (Barnes, 1998). Thus, syndromes similar to depression are attributed to deficiencies in the functioning of bodily organs, such as kidney, heart, or spleen (Ots, 1990) or the imbalance of elements or humours in the body (Krause, 1989). Thus, it is possible that depression is comprised of three factors (e.g., positive affect, interpersonal problems, and a factor combining the depression and somatic factors) for samples from Korea, Sri Lanka, and Myanmar rather than four, as found for European Americans. Beliefs about the integration of mind and body also exist in many Native American cultures; therefore, it is not surprising that a factor combining affective and somatic symptoms of depression has been found for Native American boarding school students (Dick, Beals, Keane, & Manson, 1994) and Native American adults (Somervell et al., 1993) as well.

Studies conducted with immigrant groups in the United States also support claims that cultural differences in the factor structure of depression may reflect cultural differences in conceptions of emotion and mental health. As immigrants become more acculturated to American culture, their conceptions of depression begin to resemble those of American culture. For example, several studies have found that whereas a two-factor structure (i.e., depression and well-being) best fits CES-D data obtained from older Latino immigrants, CES-D data obtained from younger Latino immigrants best fit a three- or four-factor structure

(Golding & Aneshensel, 1989; Guernaccia, Angel, & Lowe Worobey, 1989; Miller, Markides & Black, 1997; Stroup-Benham, Lawrence, & Treviño, 1992). In one study comparing the CES-D factor structure for Mexican American and Puerto Rican women (Stroup-Benham et al., 1992), two- and three-factor solutions fit recent immigrant' responses best, whereas four-factor solutions were more appropriate for Hispanics born in the United States.

Research focusing on Asian and Asian American samples report similar findings. Groups that are less oriented to American culture are less likely to produce the European American four-factor structure. A study of mostly foreign-born monocultural Chinese American adults living in Chinatown, San Francisco, revealed a three-factor structure (Ying, 1988), with depressed and somatic factors combined. On the other hand, a five-factor solution with depression, interpersonal, positive affect, and two somatic factors was obtained for a sample of bicultural Chinese American college students (Ying, Lee, Tsai, Yeh, & Huang, 2000).

Cultural differences have emerged in the order of extraction of different factors, suggesting that the most significant elements of depression also vary across cultures. For example, social dysfunction emerged as a first factor for the GHQ–60 among Japanese students (Takeuchi & Kitamura, 1991) and Spanish adults (Vazquez-Barquero, Williams, Diez-Manrique, Lequerica, & Arenal, 1988), whereas it was one of the last factors that was extracted for Chinese and British samples (Huppert et al., 1989; Shek, 1993). This pattern of extraction may indicate that the social dimension is relatively more important in the experience of distress for Japanese and Spanish adults than for Chinese students or for a British community sample. Somatic symptoms comprised the first extracted factor for a sample of Mexican patients (Medina-Mora et al., 1983) and Chinese students (Chan, 1985), suggesting that the somatic aspects of depression may be more significant for these groups than the affective and interpersonal ones.

In summary, researchers employing the biomedical approach have also explored the influence of culture on conceptions of depression, as manifested by the factor structure of different symptoms of depression. Findings from these studies suggest that although the symptoms may be the same across cultures, how they relate to each other and what elements they represent may differ. One major criticism of this work is that the types of elements that can be found depend on what symptoms are assessed. Thus, some elements of depression or depression-like disorders in different cultures may not be represented well by Western diagnostic instruments. Future studies should include other symptoms and then test the equivalence of various factor structures across cultural groups.

OTHER APPROACHES TO STUDYING DEPRESSION ACROSS CULTURES

Both ethnographic and biomedical approaches to studying depression have taught us important lessons about the role culture plays in this disorder. Each approach, however, has important limitations. While ethnographic studies capture the depth of meaning of symptoms associated with depression, they preclude extensive comparison across cultures. Biomedical studies, however, often gloss over important differences in the meanings of depressive symptoms by defining a priori what depression is. Moreover, both approaches tend to rely on self-report data, and neither approach explicitly links cultural variables to depressive symptoms. Both clinicians and scientists recognize the importance of developing new approaches to studying psychopathology across cultures that address these limitations. For example, Ritsher, Ryder, Karasz, and Castille (2002) argue that qualitative and quantitative methods of data collection should be combined in the study of psychopathology across cultures. In this next section, we discuss other approaches that address these limitations and that promise to reveal more about the influence of culture on depression.

Measuring Culture by Integrating Interview and Questionnaire Methods

Although a plethora of studies have focused on how culture influences different aspects of depression, few studies have clearly defined or measured culture. Neither ethnographic nor epidemiological studies demonstrate that cultural variables (e.g., values, ideas, practices) are causally linked to different conceptions of illness. By integrating interview and questionnaire methods, researchers can identify the specific aspects of a given culture that are hypothetically influencing depression (e.g., religious beliefs, conceptions of illness, engagement in rituals, orientation to social relationships, locus of control), measure these variables in their samples, and then examine whether a relationship between those variables and depression actually exists. For example, ethnographers have found that cultures differ in whether their members view life events as internally or externally caused, as dispositional or situational, or as event-specific or global, which in turn may influence their susceptibility to depression. According to the hopelessness theory of depression (Abramson, Metalsky, & Alloy, 1989), individuals who tend to attribute negative events to internal, stable, and global causes may be at increased risk for depression (Fazio & Palm, 1998; Tripp, Catano, & Sullivan, 1997). However, in certain cultures, these attribution styles may be more normative than in European American culture, and therefore members of these cultures may be more susceptible to depressive feelings. For example, one study (Anderson, 1999) compared the attributional styles of Chinese and American students and found that Chinese students used more maladaptive attributions in imagined and scripted situations than American students. That is, they tended to attribute failures rather than successes to their internal abilities and traits. Chinese students in this study also reported higher levels of depression than American students, suggesting that their attributional styles made them more susceptible to depression. Because this study examined levels of depressive symptoms only, we do not know whether cultural differences in attribution styles result in different rates of clinical depression. We should also note that the magnitude of the correlation between attributional styles and levels of depression has been found to vary cross-culturally as well. Sakamoto and Kambara (1998) found that the depressive consequences of attributing negative events to internal, stable, and global causes are less for Japanese students compared to Western subjects. Despite these caveats, the studies illustrate how one might measure a specific cultural factor and then examine its relationship to depression.

Studies that directly measure cultural variables may also reveal which variables are not related to depression. Having an external locus of control, or believing that life events are out of one's personal control, is thought to be a risk factor for depression (Benassi, Sweeney, & Dufour, 1988; Neff & Hoppe, 1993; Rotter, 1966). For example, Mirowsky and Ross (1984) found that among Mexican Americans and Mexicans, being fatalistic (i.e., having an external locus of control) was predictive of higher levels of depression. However, cross-cultural studies have demonstrated that the association between external locus of control (or fatalism) and depression is not universal. While having an external locus of control was positively correlated with levels of depression for American and Turkish college students, it was not for Nigerian or Filipino college students (Akande & Lester, 1994; Lester, Castromayor, & Icli, 1991). Similarly, Sastry and Ross (1998) found that although having personal control was related to lower levels of depression across cultural groups, the magnitude of the correlation was weaker for Asian Americans and South Koreans, Indians, Chinese, and Japanese than for non-Asians living in the United States and living abroad. Thus, by measuring cultural variables directly, we can test specific hypotheses about the relationships between specific cultural variables and depression.

Focusing on Emotional, Cognitive, and Social Functioning

Surprisingly few studies have examined whether individuals diagnosed with depression, or a disorder comparable to depression, show the same types of impairments in emotional, cognitive, and social functioning across cultures. By examining deficits in psychological functioning, researchers can transcend the diagnostic challenges that accompany studying depression across cultures to assess whether the effects of the disorders, however defined, are the same. For instance, depression impairs the perception of emotional cues: depressed individuals are less able to detect positive and negative emotional words than nondepressed individuals (Wexler et al., 1994). Depression also influences the behavioral and physiological aspects of emotional responding. In terms of expressive behavior, depressed individuals express less happiness while imagining happy events (Berenbaum, 1992; Schwartz, Fair, Salt, Mandel, & Klerman, 1976) and during clinical interviews (Ekman, Matsumoto, & Friesen, 1997; Ellgrip, 1989). However, depressed individuals also demonstrate more contempt, anger, and disgust than nondepressed individuals while imagining disgusting events (Berenbaum, 1992) and during clinical interviews (Ekman et al., 1997). Surprisingly, depressed and nondepressed individuals do not differ in their facial expressions of sadness when imagining sad events (Schwartz et al., 1976). Other studies have found differences between depressed and nondepressed individuals in their physiological responses during challenging tasks (e.g., mental arithmetic). Depressed individuals demonstrate faster heart rates and smaller skin conductance responses compared to nondepressed individuals (Dawson, Schell, & Catania, 1977; Zeiner, 1975). These studies and others (Davidson, 1998) collectively demonstrate that depression influences the physiological and behavioral components of emotion. Future studies should examine whether the individuals with somatization, hwabyung, or other disorders thought to be similar to depression show similar deficits to determine whether the disorders are the same along these lines.

Using Physiological and Behavioral Measures

Most studies of depression across cultures rely primarily on the self-reports of the patients themselves, or on the relatively unsystematic observations of others. While valuable, self-report data are susceptible to numerous biases, including self-presentation biases, unreliability, and contextual demands. Because of these biases, researchers have made inferences about the meaning of these self-reports that may or may not be justified. As described above, depression affects not only subjective emotional experience, but physiological functioning and interpersonal behavior as well. Moreover, differences among different subtypes of depression may be clarified using these procedures. For example, Lader and Wing (1969) found pulse rate differences between agitated and retarded depressed patients. Given existing physiological measurement techniques and microanalytic behavioral coding systems (e.g., Facial Action Coding System, Specific Affect System), the field is well equipped to move beyond self-report when assessing depression across cultures. It is possible that physiologically, depression looks quite similar across cultures, but that behaviorally, it looks quite different.

For instance, we conducted a study that examined the effects of depression on the emotional responses of Spanish-speaking Latinas to sad and amusing film clips, using physiological, behavioral, and self-report measures (Tsai, Pole, Levenson, & Muñoz, 2002). In terms of physiological responding, depressed Latinas demonstrated lower levels of skin conductance activity than did their nondepressed peers. Interestingly, this finding was consistent with a body of literature on depression in Anglo-American samples, which suggests that depressed individuals have lower levels of skin conductance response than nondepressed individuals (Dawson et al., 1977; Donat & McCollough, 1983; Greenfield, Katz, Alexander, & Roessler, 1963; Iacono et al., 1983; Lader & Wing, 1969; McCarron, 1973; Noble & Lader, 1971; Zuckerman, Persky, & Curtis, 1968). Thus, there may be a universal, physiological substrate of depression. Depressed Latinas also reported feeling more anger and contempt during both film clips and showed fewer unfelt smiles during the amusing film clip compared to their nondepressed peers. These findings were somewhat inconsistent with the literature on the effects of depression on Anglo-American groups (Berenbaum & Oltmanns, 1992), suggesting that the effects of depression on subjective emotional experience and behavior may differ across cultures. Thus, studies that employ physiological and behavioral measures will considerably advance our knowledge about the effects of depression on different levels of functioning and how these effects vary by culture.

FUTURE DIRECTIONS

In this chapter, we have reviewed ethnographic and biomedical approaches to understanding depression across cultures. Despite their different theoretical and methodological approaches, both have demonstrated the various ways in which culture may influence depression—from concepts of depression and illness, to diagnosis, to the meaning of depressive symptoms. On the one hand, it is sobering to realize how little we know about depression across cultures. On the other hand, we are encouraged by current techniques that may significantly advance our knowledge base. Perhaps by using different approaches, we can move beyond simply measuring depression and instead examine more comprehensively how culture influences other aspects of depression, such as its relationship to other disorders, the course of depression, the protective and risk factors associated with depression, and the treatment of depression and related disorders. We discuss each of these topics in detail.

How Does Culture Influence the Comorbidity of Depression with Other Disorders?

Research focusing on depression tends to conceptualize it as a phenomenon that is distinct and separate from other forms of psychopathology. This assumption may not be true. Instead, depression may be more appropriately viewed as one possible expression of psychological distress. Existing literature suggests that the degree of comorbidity of depression with other disorders differs substantially across cultures (Merikangas et al., 1996). For example, the odds ratio for the association of depression with an anxiety disorder is 2.7 in Switzerland, but 14.9 in Puerto Rico. These differences indicate that "pure" depression may be an exception rather than the norm across cultures. Studies of comorbidity of mental disorders (Krueger, 1999) have revealed that depression functions as one of the indicators of a higher order internalizing factor. Other indicators include other mood (such as dysthymia) and anxiety (such as phobias and generalized anxiety disorder) diagnoses. Thus, the pursuit of studying depression across cultures in isolation from other internalizing disorders may be of limited value. Future research should examine the comorbidity of depression with other disorders across cultures.

Is the Course of Depression and Depression-Like Disorders Similar across Cultures?

Much remains to be learned about the impact of cultural variables on the course and outcome of depression. Does depression remit faster in some cultural contexts than in others?

What aspects of the culture facilitate or hinder this process? Very few studies have attempted to answer this question. The World Health Organization Collaborative Study examined cases of depression in Canada, Iran, Japan, and Switzerland and followed them 10 years later (Thornicroft & Sartorius, 1993). With the exception of social dysfunction, outcome and course variables differed significantly by site. Japan had the highest proportion of cases with poor clinical and social outcomes, whereas Canada had the highest proportion of cases with poor course, characterized by longer duration of depressive episodes and fewer remissions. However, these comparisons did not control for differences in severity of depression at baseline or availability of treatment, and therefore should be interpreted cautiously. Ormel et al. (1994) found that psychiatric diagnoses were associated with increased disability across cultures, although the degree of occupational and physical disability associated with psychiatric diagnoses varied across centers. Another study of course and outcome of acute affective disorder in rural and urban clinics in India (Brown et al., 1998) reported that 100% of depressed participants experienced brief recovery period (defined as at least 1 month free of any symptoms) during the year after the initial assessment. A substantial number of patients (71%) sustained recovery at 1-year follow-up, a considerably greater percentage than that of the United States (28–52%; from Picinelli & Wilkinson, 1994). It is unclear, however, what aspects of Indian culture are responsible for this finding. Moreover, the evaluations in the Indian study were performed by the treating psychiatrists, which may have influenced the results. Clearly, future work assessing the specific aspects of culture that may be responsible for these differences must be conducted. Furthermore, the use of physiological and behavioral techniques may also provide more objective assessments of improvement than standard instruments.

Are the Factors that Place Individuals at Risk for Depression Similar across Cultures?

After decades of intensive research, a number of risk factors for depression have been described for Western samples: being female, experiencing negative and stressful life events, being physically ill, lacking education, having financial difficulties, not working, and lacking social support. To what extent, if any, do these factors also place members of other cultures at risk for depression or depression-like states? A number of studies have identified the same risk factors for non-Western cultures (Chen et al., 1999; Hwu et al., 1996; Madianos & Stefanis, 1992; Patel et al., 1999), although much more work is needed. For example, some studies that investigated the risk factors for depression among European and African Americans found that, for both groups, gender, marital status, and socioeconomic status (Jones-Webb & Snowden, 1993) and dissatisfaction with personal relationships (Rodriguez, Allen, Fronglio, & Chandra, 1999) were associated with depression. Similarly, the positive link between interpersonal sensitivity (appraising interpersonal situations as threatening, needing approval, being timid, and having separation anxiety) and depression that has been documented for Western samples (Boyce et al., 1992) has also been replicated for a sample of Japanese hospital workers (Sakado et al., 1999). However, other factors, such as being widowed or unemployed, were less predictive of depression among African Americans as compared to European Americans, and while higher income has been shown to be a protective factor against depression, this association is stronger for African Americans than for European Americans (Cockerham, 1990).

Another way in which culture may influence vulnerability to depression is via perceptions of the self. Self-discrepancy theory (Higgins, 1989) purports that the greater the discrepancy between how one would like to be ("ideal self") and how one is ("actual self"), the more susceptible one is to depression. This theory is consistent with Western cultural values that place a premium on having a positive image about oneself. Heine and Lehman (1999), however, found that the relationship between depression and discrepancies between ideal and actual selves is stronger for European Canadians than for Japanese, with a bicultural Asian Canadian sample falling in between the two groups. Thus, actual–ideal self-discrepancy may be less of a risk factor for depression for Asian than for European cultural groups, perhaps because Asian cultures place less emphasis on promoting the self than do Western cultures. In fact, Cheung (1997) found that the discrepancy between actual and *undesirable* selves predicted levels of depression among Hong Kong adolescents better than did the discrepancy between actual and ideal selves. Moreover, for these adolescents, discrepancy in identity based on social roles, rather than on individual characteristics, predicted levels of depression. This finding is consistent with reports that Asians are more interdependent than Westerners, that is, they base their identities more on relationships with others (Markus & Kitayama, 1991). Thus, the above findings suggest that some of the factors that place individuals at increased risk for depression in the United States do not function in the same way in other cultural contexts.

In addition, research should focus on the factors that protect individuals from depression. For example, Vega and colleagues (1998) found that Mexicans living in Mexico had lower rates of depression than did Mexican-born immigrants living in the United States or American-born Mexicans living in the United States. The authors suggest that Mexicans living in Mexico have stronger support networks, and that this social structure protects individuals from experiencing depression. Similarly, Obeyeskere (1985) suggests that Buddhist philosophical beliefs also protect one from depression or paralyzing feelings of loss and emptiness.

How Does Culture Influence the Effectiveness of Treatments for Depression?

Culture has been thought to influence all aspects of the treatment process, ranging from the utilization of mental health services to beliefs about the therapist–client relationship, to the effectiveness of particular psychotherapeutic as well as psychopharmacological interventions. Although an enormous literature exists regarding the influence of culture on the treatment of depression, this literature is comprised primarily of case studies (e.g., Cheung & Lin, 1997; Eisenbruch, 1983; Ruiz, 1998) and clinical guidelines (Sue & Sue, 1999; Pederson, Draguns, Lonner, & Trimble, 1996). Few empirical studies have actually been conducted on the effects of culture on various aspects of the treatment process.

What are the ways in which common treatments for depression are imbued with Western values and assumptions? Toukmanian and Brouwers (1998) argue that despite the conceptual and technical differences between psychodynamic, cognitive-behavioral, and humanistic-existential psychotherapies, "all are formulated from the basic premise that problems reside within the individual, that change is an internal process, and that the responsibility for bringing about this change rests primarily with the individual" (p. 113). Thus, Western psychotherapeutic treatments may be less effective with individuals whose cultures place less emphasis on internal processes and who do not view the individual as the basic unit of experience than those that do. For example, interventions that emphasize personal agency may be ineffective for cultural groups that view behavior as externally influenced (Kaiser, Katz, & Shaw, 1998). In addition, many Western treatments are based on the notion that disclosing one's feelings alleviates distress and is a necessary ingredient for change. However, in many Asian cultures, disclosing one's distressing experiences may result in great shame rather than great relief (Toukmanian & Brouwers, 1998).

Of the empirical studies of cultural influences on the treatment of depression, the bulk of the literature has focused on cultural and ethnic differences in the utilization of mental health services. For example, Sue, Fujino, Hu, Takeuchi, and Zane (1991) found that within the United States, ethnic groups vary in their utilization of mainstream mental health services. Specifically, Asian Americans are less likely to go to psychiatric and community mental health clinics compared to their European American counterparts and only do so as a last resort. This finding is consistent with reports that mainland Chinese are more likely to go to medical health centers for psychological and emotional problems than they are to go to mental health services (Kleinman, 1986). Moreover, over 60% of Asian Americans who actually seek services do not return after the first session. Ethnic differences in the use of mainstream mental health services may reflect the Western orientation of such services as well as the emphasis on Western conceptions of depression in these settings. Takeuchi, Sue, and Yeh (1995) found that in Los Angeles, Asian American, African American, and Mexican American clients were more likely to remain in mental health programs if those programs were oriented toward their cultural heritage. Moreover, members of non-Western cultural groups often use other services (e.g., traditional healers) to address psychological and emotional concerns. Even among individuals who attend mainstream mental health services, a significant percentage of patients are concurrently receiving some form of complementary and alternative care, particularly those with depressive symptoms (Knaudt, Connor, Weisler, Churchill, & Davidson, 1999; Unuetzer et al., 2000).

To address possible differences in values, beliefs, traditions, and expectations between the Western clinician and the non-Western client, a number of clinicians have proposed ways of adjusting Western treatments for depression. For example, Randall (1994) discusses ways of adjusting traditional cognitive-behavioral techniques for use with disadvantaged African American women. Even psychopharmacological treatments have had to be adjusted for use with non-Western clients. For example, Hispanic patients require less antidepressant medication and report more side effects at lower dosages than do their white counterparts (Marcos & Cancro, 1982; Mendoza, Smith, Poland, Lin, & Strickland, 1991). Despite the plethora of recommendations regarding the adjustment of Western therapies for the treatment of non-Western groups, few studies have actually empirically examined whether these cultural adjustments improve the effectiveness of various treatments of depression. Clearly, this research is needed.

Almost no cross-cultural studies have compared the effectiveness of Western treatments of depression with those that may be more indigenous to a particular culture. However, a number of researchers are beginning to explore non-Western treatments and their effects on depression in Western populations. For example, Allen, Schnyer, and Hitt (1998) found that acupuncture provided symptom relief to depressed women, compared to waitlist controls. Similarly, Roeschke et al. (2000) found that depressed patients taking mianserin (a tetracyclic antidepressant) who also received acupuncture improved more than patients who received placebo acupuncture and those who did not receive any acupuncture. Future studies should compare the characteristics of Western and non-Western treatments for depression to assess their similarities and differences and to determine how these similarities and differences influence treatment effectiveness across cultural contexts.

REFERENCES

Abramson, L. Y., Metalsky, G. I., & Alloy, L. B. (1989). Hopelessness depression: A theory-based subtype of depression. *Psychological Review, 96,* 358–372.

Akande, A., & Lester, D. (1994). Suicidal preoccupation, depression and locus of control in Nigerians and Americans. *Personality and Individual Differences, 16*(6), 979.

Allen, J. B., Schnyer, R. N., & Hitt, S. K. (1998). The efficacy of acupuncture in the treatment of major depression in women. *Psychological Science, 9*(5), 397–401.

Anderson, C. A. (1999). Attributional style, depression, and loneliness: A cross-cultural comparison of American and Chinese students. *Personality and Social Psychology Bulletin, 25*(4), 482–499.

Bahar, E., Henderson, A. S., & Mackinnon, A. J. (1992). An epidemiological study of mental health and socioeconomic conditions in Sumatra, Indonesia. *Acta Psychiatrica Scandinavica, 85*(4), 257–263.

Barnes, L. L. (1998). The psychologizing of Chinese healing practices in the United States. *Culture, Medicine and Psychiatry, 22*(4), 413–443.

Beiser, M., Cargo, M., & Woodbury, M. A. (1994). A comparison of psychiatric disorder in different cultures: Depressive typologies in Southeast Asian refugees and resident Canadians. *International Journal of Methods in Psychiatric Research, 4*, 157–172.

Benassi, V. A., Sweeney, P. D., & Dufour, C. L. (1988). Is there a relation between locus of control orientation and depression? *Journal of Abnormal Psychology, 97*(3), 357–367.

Berenbaum, H. (1992). Posed facial expressions of emotion in schizophrenia and depression. *Psychological Medicine, 22*, 929–937.

Berenbaum, H., & Oltmanns, T. F. (1992). Emotional experience and expression in schizophrenia and depression. *Journal of Abnormal Psychology, 101*, 37–44.

Bland, R. C. (1997). Epidemiology of affective disorders: A review. *Canadian Journal of Psychology, 42*, 367–377.

Blashfield, R. K. (1984). *The classification of psychopathology: Neo-Kraepelinian and quantitative approach.* New York: Plenum Press.

Blazer, D., George, L. K., Landerman, R., Pennybacker, M., Melville, M. L., Woodbury, M., Manton, K. G., Jordan, K., & Locke, B. (1985). Psychiatric disorders: A rural/urban comparison. *Archives of General Psychiatry, 42*(7), 651–656.

Boyce, P., Hickie, I., Parker, G., Mitchell, P., Wilhelm, K., & Brodaty, H. (1992). Interpersonal sensitivity and the one-year outcome of a depressive episode. *Australian and New Zealand Journal of Psychiatry, 26*(2), 156–161.

Brown, A. S., Varma, V. K., Malhotra, S., Jilona, R. C., Conover, S. A., & Susser, E. S. (1998). Course of acute affective disorders in a developing country setting. *Journal of Nervous and Mental Disease, 186*(4), 207–213.

Brown, C., Schulberg, H. C., & Madonia, M. J. (1996). Clinical presentations of major depression by African-Americans and whites in primary medical care practice. *Journal of Affective Disorders, 41*(3), 181–191.

Chan, D. W. (1985). The Chinese version of the General Health Questionnaire: Does language make a difference? *Psychological Medicine, 15*, 147–155.

Chen, R., Copeland, J. R., & Wei, L. (1999). A meta-analysis of epidemiological studies in depression of older people in the People's Republic of China. *International Journal of Geriatric Psychiatry, 14*, 821–830.

Cheng, T. A. (1989). Urbanization and minor psychiatric morbidity: A community study in Taiwan. *Social Psychiatry and Psychiatric Epidemiology, 24*(6), 309–316.

Cheung, F., & Lin, K. M. (1997). Neurasthenia, depression and somatoform disorder in a Chinese-Vietnamese woman migrant. *Culture, Medicine and Psychiatry, 21*, 247–258.

Cheung, S. K. (1997). Self-discrepancy and depressive experiences among Chinese early adolescents: Significance of identity and the undesirable self. *International Journal of Psychology, 32*(5), 347–359.

Cockerham, W. C. (1990). A test of the relationship between race, socioeconomic status, and psychological distress. *Social Science and Medicine, 31*(12), 1321–1326.

Comstock, G. W., & Helsing, K. J. (1976). Symptoms of depression in two communities. *Psychological Medicine, 6*(4), 551–563.

Crittenden, K. S., Fugita, S. S., Bae, H., Lamug, C. B., & Lin, C. (1992). A cross-cultural study of self-report depressive symptoms among college students. *Journal of Cross-Cultural Psychology, 23*(2), 163–178.

D'Avanzo, C. E., & Barab, S. A. (1998). Depression and anxiety among Cambodian refugee women in France and the United States. *Issues in Mental Health Nursing, 19*, 541–556.

Davidson, R. (1998). Anterior electrophysiological asymmetries, emotion, and depression: Conceptual and methodological conundrums. *Psychophysiology, 35,* 607–614.

Dawson, M. E., Schell, A., & Catania, J. (1977). Autonomic correlates of depression and clinical improvement following electroconvulsive shock therapy. *Psychophysiology, 14,* 569–578.

Dick, R. W., Beals, J., Keane, E. M., & Manson, S. M. (1994). Factorial structure of the CES-D among American Indian adolescents. *Journal of Adolescence, 17,* 73–79.

Donat, D. C., & McCullough, J. P. (1983). Psychophysiological discriminants of depression at rest and in response to stress. *Journal of Clinical Psychology, 39,* 315–320.

Ebert, D., & Martus, P. (1994). Somatization as a core symptom of melancholic type depression: Evidence from a cross-cultural study. *Journal of Affective Disorders, 32,* 253–256.

Eisenbruch, M. (1983). "Wind illness" or somatic depression?: A case study in psychiatric anthropology. *British Journal of Psychiatry, 143,* 323–326.

Ekman, P., Matsumoto, D., & Friesen, W. (1997). Facial expressions in affective disorders. In P. Ekman & E. Rosenberg (Eds.), *What the face reveals.* New York: Oxford University Press.

Ellgrip, H. (1989). *Nonverbal communication in depression.* New York: Cambridge University Press.

Fazio, N. M., & Palm, L. J. (1998). Attributional style, depression, and grade point averages of college students. *Psychological Reports, 83*(1), 159–162.

Freeman, H. L. (1988). Psychiatric aspects of environmental stress. *International Journal of Mental Health, 17*(3), 13–23.

Goldberg, D. P. (1972). *The detection of psychiatric illness by questionnaire.* Oxford, UK: Oxford University Press.

Goldberg, D. P., & Hillier, V. F. (1979). A scaled version of the General Health Questionnaire. *Psychological Medicine, 9,* 139–145.

Goldberg, D. P., Oldehinkel, T., & Ormel, J. (1998). Why GHQ threshold varies from one place to another. *Psychological Medicine, 28,* 915–921.

Goldberg, D. P., Rickels, K., Downing, R., & Hesbacher, P. (1976). A comparison of two psychiatric screening tests. *British Journal of Psychiatry, 129,* 61–67.

Golding, J. M., & Aneshensel, C. S. (1989). Factor structure of the Center for Epidemiological Studies Depression Scale among Mexican Americans and non-Hispanic whites. *Journal of Consulting and Clinical Psychology, 1*(3), 163–168.

Good, B. J., Del Vecchio, M., & Moradi, R. (1985). Interpretation of Iranian depressive illness and dysphoria. In A. Kleinman & B. Good (Eds.). *Culture and depression: Studies in the anthropology and cross-cultural psychiatry of affect and disorder* (pp. 369–428). Berkeley and Los Angeles: University of California Press.

Grauer, H. (1984). Geriatric depression in the West and the Far East. *Psychiatric Journal of the University of Ottawa, 9*(3), 118–120.

Greenfield, N. S., Katz, D., Alexander, A. A., & Roessler, R. (1963). The relationship between physiological and psychological responsivity: Depression and galvanic skin response. *Journal of Nervous and Mental Disease, 136,* 535–539.

Guernaccia, P. J., Angel, R., & Lowe Worobey, J. (1989). The factor structure of the CES-D in the Hispanic Health and Nutrition Examination Survey: The influences of ethnicity, gender and language. *Social Science and Medicine, 29*(1), 85–94.

Hamdi, E., Amin, Y., & Abou-Saleh, M. T. (1997). Performance of the Hamilton Depression Rating Scale in depressed patients in the United Arab Emirates. *Acta Psychiatrica Scandinavica, 96,* 416–423.

Heine, S. J., & Lehman, D. R. (1999). Culture, self-discrepancies, and self-satisfaction. *Personality and Social Psychology Bulletin, 25*(8), 915–925.

Higgins, E. T. (1989). Self-discrepancy theory: What patterns of self-beliefs cause people to suffer? In L. Berkowitz (Ed.), *Advances in experimental social psychology* (Vol. 22, pp. 93–136). San Diego: Academic Press.

Huppert, F. A., Walters, D. E., Day, N. E., & Elliott, B. J. (1989). The factor structure of the General Health Questionnaire (GHQ–30): A reliability study on 6,317 community residents. *British Journal of Psychiatry, 155,* 178–185.

Hwu, H.-G., Chang, I -H., Yeh, E.-K., Chang, C.-J., & Yeh, L.-L. (1996). Major depressive disorder in Taiwan defined by the Chinese Diagnostic Interview Schedule. *Journal of Nervous and Mental Disease, 184*(8), 497–502.

Iacono, W. G., Lykken, D., Peloquin, L., Lumry, A., Valentine, R. H., & Tuason, V. (1983). Electrodermal activity in euthymic unipolar and bipolar affective disorders: A possible marker for depression. *Archives of General Psychiatry, 40,* 557–565.

Jenkins, J. H. (1997). Subjective experience of persistent schizophrenia and depression among U.S. Latinos and Euro-Americans. *British Journal of Psychiatry, 171,* 20–25.

Jenkins, J. H., & Cofresi, N. (1998). The sociosomatic course of depression and trauma: A cultural analysis of suffering and resilience in the life of a Puerto Rican woman. *Psychosomatic Medicine, 60,* 439–447.

Jones-Webb, R. J., & Snowden, L. R. (1993). Symptoms of depression among blacks and whites. *American Journal of Public Health, 83*(2), 240–244.

Kaiser, A. S., Katz, R., & Shaw, B. F. (1998). Cultural issues in the management of depression. In S. S. Kazarian & D. R. Evans (Eds.), *Cultural clinical psychology: Theory, research, and practice* (pp. 177–214). New York: Oxford University Press.

Katz, M. M., LeBars, P., Itil, T. M., Prilipko, L., & DeGiralamo, G. (1994). A cross-national case study of depression: Video analysis of symptoms and expressive behavior by clinicians from fourteen national settings. *Integrative Psychiatry, 10*(2), 85–89.

Kessler, R. C., McGonagle, K. A., Zhao, S., Nelson, C. B., Hughes, M., Eshleman, S., Wittchen, H.-U., & Kendler, K. S. (1994). Lifetime and 12-month prevalence of DSM-III-R psychiatric disorders in the United States. *Archives of General Psychiatry, 51,* 8–14.

Kleinman, A. (1982). Neurasthenia and depression: A study of somatization and culture in China. *Culture, Medicine and Psychiatry, 6*(2), 117–190.

Kleinman, A. (1986). *Social origins of distress and disease: Depression, neurasthenia, and pain in modern China.* New Haven, CT: Yale University Press.

Kleinman, A., & Good, B. (Eds.). (1985). *Culture and depression: Studies in the anthropology and cross-cultural psychiatry of affect and disorder.* Berkeley and Los Angeles: University of California Press.

Knaudt, P. R., Connor, K. M., Weisler, R. H., Churchill, L., & Davidson, J. (1999). Alternative therapy use by psychiatric outpatients. *Journal of Nervous and Mental Disease, 187,* 692–695.

Koss-Chioino, J. D. (1999). Depression among Puerto Rican women: Culture, etiology and diagnosis. *Hispanic Journal of Behavioral Sciences, 21*(3), 330–350.

Kramer, P. D. (1994). *Listening to Prozac.* New York: Penguin Books.

Krause, I. B. (1989). Sinking heart: A Punjabi communication of distress. *Social Science and Medicine, 29*(4), 563–575.

Kroeber, A. L., & Kluckhohn, C. (1952). Culture: A critical review of concepts and definitions. *Papers: Peabody Museum of Archaeology and Ethnology, Harvard University, 47*(1), viii, 223.

Krueger, R. F. (1999). The structure of common mental disorders. *Archives of General Psychiatry, 56,* 921–926.

Kuo, W. H. (1984). Prevalence of depression among Asian-Americans. *Journal of Nervous and Mental Disease, 172*(8), 449–457.

Lader, M. H., & Wing, L. (1969). Physiological measures in agitated and retarded depressed patients. *Journal of Psychiatric Research, 7,* 89–100.

Lester, D., Castromayor, I. J., & Icli, T. (1991). Locus of control, depression, and suicidal ideation among American, Philippine, and Turkish students. *Journal of Social Psychology, 131*(3), 447–449.

Lewis-Fernandez, R., & Kleinman, A. (1994). Culture, personality and psychopathology. *Journal of Abnormal Psychology, 103*(1), 67–71.

Lin, K.-M., Lau, J. K., Yamamoto, J., Zheng, Y.-P., Kim, H.-S., Cho, K.-H., & Nakasaki, G. (1992). Hwa-byung: A community study of Korean Americans. *Journal of Nervous and Mental Disease, 180*(6), 386–391.

Lin, T.-Y., Chu, H. M., Rin, H., Hsu, C., Yeh, E. K., & Chen, C. (1989). Effects of social change on mental disorders in Taiwan: Observations based on a 15-year follow-up survey of general populations in three communities. *Acta Psychiatrica Scandinavica, 79*(348), 11–33.

Lutz, C. A. (1985). Depression and the translation of emotional worlds. In A. Kleinman & B. Good (Eds.), *Culture and depression: Studies in the anthropology and cross-cultural psychiatry of affect and disorder* (pp. 63–100). Berkeley and Los Angeles: University of California Press.

Mackinnon, A., McCallum, J., Andrews, G., & Anderson, I. (1998). The Center for Epidemiological Studies Depression Scale in older community samples in Indonesia, North Korea, Myanmar, Sri Lanka, and Thailand. *Journal of Gerontology: Psychological Sciences, 53B*(6), P343–352.

Madianos, M. G., & Stefanis, C. N. (1992). Changes in the prevalence of symptoms of depression and depression across Greece. *Social Psychiatry and Psychiatric Epidemiology, 27,* 211–219.

Manson, S., Ackerson, L. M., Dick, R. W., Baron, A. E., & Fleming, C. M. (1990). Depressive symptoms among American Indian adolescents: Psychometric characteristics of the Center for Epidemiologic Studies Depression Scale (CES-D). *Psychological Assessment, 2*(3), 231–237.

Marcos, L. R., & Cancro, R. (1982). Pharmacotherapy of Hispanic depressed patients: Clinical observations. *American Journal of Psychotherapy, 36,* 505–512.

Markus, H. R., & Kitayama, S. (1991). Culture and the self: Implications for cognition, emotion, and motivation. *Psychological Review, 98*(2), 224–253.

McCarron, L. T. (1973). Psychophysiological discriminants of reactive depression. *Psychophysiology, 10,* 223–229.

Medina-Mora, M. E., Padilla, G. P., Campillo-Serrano, C., Mas, C. C., Ezban, M., Caraveo, J., & Corona, J. (1983). The factor structure of the GHQ: A scaled version for a hospital's general practice service in Mexico. *Psychological Medicine, 13,* 355–361.

Mendoza, R., Smith, M. W., Poland, R. E., Lin, K., & Stickland, T. L. (1991). Ethnic psychopharmacology: The Hispanic and Native American perspective. *Psychopharmacology Bulletin, 27*(4), 449–461.

Merikangas, K. R., Angst, J., Eaton, W., Canino, G., Rubio-Stipec, M., Wacker, H., Wittchen, H.-U., Andrade, L., Essau, C., Whitaker, A., Kraemer, H., Robins, L. N., & Kupfer, D. J. (1996). Comorbidity and boundaries of affective disorders with anxiety disorders and substance misuse: Results of international task force. *British Journal of Psychiatry, 30,* 58–67.

Miller, T. Q., Markides, K. S., & Black, S. A. (1997). The factor structure of the CES-D in two surveys of elderly Mexican-Americans. *Journal of Gerontology, 52B*(5), S259–269.

Mirowsky, J., & Ross, C. E. (1984). Mexican culture and its emotional contradictions. *Journal of Health and Social Behavior, 25*(1), 2–13.

Mumford, D. B. (1996). The "Dhat syndrome": A culturally determined symptom of depression? *Acta Psychiatrica Scandanavica, 94,* 163–167.

Murphy, J. M., Olivier, D. C., Monson, R. R., Sobol, A. M., Federman, E. B., & Leighton, A. H. (1991). Depression and anxiety in relation to social status: A prospective epidemiologic study. *Archives of General Psychiatry, 48*(3), 223–229.

Nakane, Y., Ohta, Y., Uchino, J., Takada, K., Yan, H. Q., Wang, X. D., Min, S. K., & Lee, H. Y. (1988). Comparative study of affective disorders in three Asian countries: Differences in diagnostic classification. *Acta Psychiatrica Scandinavica, 78,* 698–705.

Neff, J. A., & Hoppe, S. K. (1993). Race/ethnicity, acculturation, and psychological distress: Fatalism and religiosity as cultural resources. *Journal of Community Psychology, 21,* 3–20.

Noble, P., & Lader, M. (1971). The symptomatic correlates of the skin conductance changes in depression. *Journal of Psychiatric Research, 9,* 61–69.

Obeyesekere, G. (1985). Depression, Buddhism, and the work of culture in Sri Lanka. In A. Kleinman & B. Good (Eds.), *Culture and depression: Studies in the anthropology and cross-cultural psychiatry of affect and disorder* (pp. 134–152). Berkeley and Los Angeles: University of California Press.

Ohta, Y., Kawasaki, N., Araki, K., Mine, M., & Honda, S. (1995). The factor structure of the General Health Questionnaire (GHQ-30) in Japanese middle-aged and elderly residents. *International Journal of Social Psychiatry, 41*(4), 268–275.

Ormel, J., VonKorff, M., Ustun, T. B., Pini, S., Korten, A., & Oldehinkel, T. (1994). Common mental disorders and disability across cultures. *Journal of the American Medical Association, 272*(22), 1741–1748.

Ots, T. (1990). The angry liver, the anxious heart and the melancholy spleen: The phenomenology of perceptions in Chinese culture. *Culture, Medicine and Psychiatry, 14*(1), 21–58.

Pang, K. Y. (1995). A cross-cultural understanding of depression among elderly Korean immigrants: Prevalence, symptoms and diagnosis. *Clinical Gerontologist, 15*(4), 3–20.

Patel, V., Araya, R., de Lima, M., Ludermir, A., & Todd, C. (1999). Women, poverty and common mental disorders in four restructuring societies. *Social Science and Medicine, 49,* 1461–1471.

Pedersen, P. B., Draguns, J. G., Lonner, W. J., & Trimble, J. E. (1996). *Counseling across cultures.* Thousand Oaks, CA: Sage.

Piccinelli, M., & Wilkinson, G. (1994). Outcome of depression in psychiatric settings. *British Journal of Psychiatry, 164,* 297–304.

Radloff, L. (1977). The CES-D Scale: A self report depression scale for research in the general population. *Applied Psychological Measurement, 1,* 385–401.

Randall, E. J. (1994). Cultural relativism in cognitive therapy with disadvantaged African American women. *Journal of Cognitive Psychotherapy: An International Quarterly, 8,* 195–207.

Ritsher, J. E. B., Ryder, A., Karasz, A., & Castille, D. (2002). *Methodological issues in the study of psychopathology across cultures.* Manuscript under review.

Roberts, R. E., Roberts, C. R., & Chen, Y. R. (1997). Ethnocultural differences in prevalence of adolescent depression. *American Journal of Community Psychology, 25*(1), 95–110.

Rodriguez, E., Allen, J. A., Fronglio, E. A., & Chandra, P. (1999). Unemployment, depression and health: A look at the African-American community. *Journal of Epidemiology and Community Health, 53*(6), 335–342.

Roeschke, J., Wolf, Ch., Mueller, M. J., Wagner, P., Mann, K., Groezinger, M., & Bech, S. (2000). The benefit from whole body acupuncture in major depression. *Journal of Affective Disorders, 57,* 73–81.

Rotter, J. B. (1966). Generalized expectancies for internal vs. external control of reinforcement. *Psychological Monographs, 80,* 1–28.

Ruiz, P. (1998). The role of culture in psychiatric care. *American Journal of Psychiatry, 155,* 1763–1765.

Sakado, K., Sato, T., Uehara, T., Sakado, M., Kuwabara, H., & Someya, T. (1999). The association between the high interpersonal sensitivity type of personality and a lifetime history of depression in a sample of employed Japanese adults. *Psychological Medicine, 29,* 1243–1248.

Sakamoto, S., & Kambara, M. (1998). A longitudinal study of the relationship between attributional style, life events, and depression in Japanese undergraduates. *Journal of Social Psychology, 138*(2), 229–240.

Sastry, J., & Ross, C. E. (1998). Asian ethnicity and the sense of personal control. Social Psychology Quarterly, 61(2), 101–120.

Sato, T., & Takeichi, M. (1993). Lifetime prevalence of specific psychiatric disorders in a general medicine clinic. *General Hospital Psychiatry, 15,* 224–233.

Schieffelin, E. L. (1985). Cultural analysis of depressive affect: An example from New Guinea. In A. Kleinman & B. Good (Eds.), *Culture and depression: Studies in the anthropology and cross-cultural psychiatry of affect and disorder* (pp. 102–133). Berkeley and Los Angeles: University of California Press.

Schwartz, G. E., Fair, P. L., Salt, P., Mandel, M. R., & Klerman, G. L. (1976). Facial expression and imagery in depression: An electromyographic study. *Psychosomatic Medicine, 38*(5), 337–347.

Shek, D. T., & Tsang, S. K. (1995). Reliability and factor structure of the Chinese GHQ-30 for parents with preschool mentally handicapped children. *Journal of Clinical Psychology, 51*(2), 227–235.

Shek, T. L. (1993). Factor structure of the Chinese version of the General Health Questionnaire (GHQ-30): A confirmatory factor analysis. *Journal of Clinical Psychology, 49*(5), 678–684.

Shore, J. H., & Manson, S. M. (1981). Cross-cultural studies of depression among American Indians and Alaska Natives. *White Cloud Journal, 2*(2), 5–12.

Shweder, R. (1985). Menstrual pollution, soul loss, and the comparative study of emotions. In A. Kleinman & B. Good (Eds.), *Culture and depression: Studies in the anthropology and cross-cultural psychiatry of affect and disorder* (pp. 134–152). Berkeley and Los Angeles: University of California Press.

Sigurdson, E., Staley, D., Matas, M., Hildahl, K., & Squair, K. (1994). A five year review of youth suicide in Manitoba. *Canadian Journal of Psychiatry, 39*(8), 397–403.

Simon, G. E., Goldberg, D., Tiemens, B. G., & Ustun, T. B. (1999). Outcomes of recognized and unrecognized depression in an international primary care study. *General Hospital Psychiatry, 21,* 97–105.

Simon, G. E., VonKorff, M., Picvinelli, M., Fullerton, C., & Ormel, J. (1999). An international study of the relation between somatic symptoms and depression. *New England Journal of Medicine, 18,* 1329–1335.

Somervell, P. D., Beals, J., Kinzie, J. D., Boehnlein, J., Leung, P., & Manson, S. M. (1992). Use of the CES-D in an American Indian village. *Culture, Medicine and Psychiatry, 16*(4), 503–517.

Stroup-Benham, C. A., Lawrence, R. H., & Treviño, F. M. (1992). CES-D factor structure among Mexican American and Puerto Rican women from single- and couple-headed households. *Hispanic Journal of Behavioral Sciences, 14*(3), 310–326.

Stuart, G. W., Klimidis, S., Minas, I. H., & Tuncer, C. (1993). The factor structure of the Turkish version of the General Health Questionnaire. *International Journal of Social Psychiatry, 39*(4), 274–284.

Sue, D. W., & Sue, D. (1999). *Counseling the culturally different: Theory and practice.* New York: Wiley.

Sue, S., Fujino, D., Hu, L., Takeuchi, D. T., & Zane, N. W. (1991). Community mental health services for ethnic minority groups: A test of the cultural responsiveness hypothesis. *Journal of Consulting and Clinical Psychology, 59,* 533–540.

Szadoczky, E., Papp, Z., Vitrai, J., Rihmer, Z., & Fueredi, J. (1998). The prevalence of major depressive and bipolar disorders in Hungary: Results from a national epidemiologic survey. *Journal of Affective Disorders, 50*(2–3), 153–162.

Takeuchi, D. T., Sue, S., & Yeh, M. (1995). Return rates and outcomes from ethnicity-specific mental health programs in Los Angeles. *American Journal of Public Health, 85,* 638–643.

Takeuchi, M., & Kitamura, T. (1991). The factor structure of the General Health Questionnaire in a Japanese high school and university student sample. *International Journal of Social Psychiatry, 37*(2), 99–106.

Thornicroft, G., & Sartorius, N. (1993). The course and outcome of depression in different cultures: 10-year follow-up of the WHO collaborative study on the assessment of depressive disorders. *Psychological Medicine, 23,* 1023–1032.

Toukmanian, S. G., & Brouwers, M. C. (1998). Cultural aspects of self-disclosure and psychotherapy. In S. S. Kazarian & D. R. Evans (Eds.), *Cultural clinical psychology: Theory, research, and practice* (pp. 106–124). New York: Oxford University Press.

Tousignant, M., & Maldonaldo, M. (1989). Sadness, depression and social reciprocity in highland Ecuador. *Social Science and Medicine, 28*(9), 899–904.

Tripp, D. A., Catano, V., & Sullivan, M. J. (1997). The contributions of attributional style, expectancies, depression, and self-esteem in a cognition-based depression model. *Canadian Journal of Behavioral Sciences, 29*(2), 101–111.

Tsai, J. L., Pole, N., Levenson, R. W., & Muñoz, R. F. (2002). *The effects of depression on the emotional responses of Spanish-speaking Latinas.* Manuscript under review.

Unuetzer, J., Klap, R., Sturm, R., Young, A., Marmon, T., Shatkin, J., & Wells, K. B. (2000). Mental disorders and the use of alternative medicine: Results from a national survey. *American Journal of Psychiatry, 157,* 1851–1857.

Vazquez-Barquero, J. L., Williams, P., Diez-Manrique, J. F., Lequerica, J., & Arenal, A. (1988). The factor structure of the GHQ–60 in a community sample. *Psychological Medicine, 18,* 211–218.

Vega, W. A., Kolody, B., Aguilar-Gaxiola, S., Aldrete, E., Catalano, R., & Caraveo-Anduaga, J. (1998). Lifetime prevalence of DSM-III-R psychiatric disorders among urban and rural Mexican-Americans in California. *Archives of General Psychiatry, 55*(9), 771–778.

Waza, K., Graham, A. V., Zyzanski, S. J., & Inoue, K. (1999). Comparison of symptoms in Japanese and American depressed primary care patients. *Family Practice, 16*(5), 528–533.

Weissman, M. M., Bland, R., Canino, G. J., Faravelli, C., Greenwald, S., Hwu, H.-G., Joyce, P. R., Karam, E. G., Lee, C.-K., Lellouch, J., Lépine, J.-P., Newman, S. C., Rubio-Stipec, M., Wells, J.

E., Wickramaratne, P. J., Wittchen, H.-U., & Yeh, E.-K. (1996). Cross-national epidemiology of major depression and bipolar disorder. *Journal of the American Medical Association, 24*(31), 293–299.

Weissman, M. M., Bland, R., Joyce, P. R., Newman, S., Wells, J. E., & Wittchen, H.-U. (1993). Sex differences in rates of depression: Cross-national perspectives. *Journals of Affective Disorders, 29*, 77–84.

Weissman, M. M., Bruce, M. L., Leaf, P. J., Florio, L. P., & Holzer, C. (1991). Affective disorders. In L. N. Robins & D. A. Regier (Eds.), *Psychiatric disorders in America: The Epidemiologic Catchment Area Study* (pp. 53–80). New York: Free Press.

Wexler, B. E., Levenson, L., Warrenburg, S., & Price, L. (1994). Decreased perceptual sensitivity to emotion-evoking stimuli in depression. *Psychiatry Research, 51*, 127–138.

Wilson, C., Civic, D., & Glass, D. (1995). Prevalence and correlates of depressive syndromes among adults visiting an Indian primary care clinic. *American Indian and Alaska Native Mental Health Research, 6*(2), 1–12.

Wittchen, H.-U., Robins, L. N., Cottler, L. B., Sartorius, N., Burke, J. D., & Regier, D. (1991). Cross-cultural feasibility, reliability and sources of variance of the Composite International Diagnostic Interview (CIDI). *British Journal of Psychiatry, 159*, 645–653.

Ying, Y.-W. (1988). Depressive symptomatology among Chinese-Americans as measured by the CES-D. *Journal of Clinical Psychology, 44*(5), 739–746.

Ying, Y.-W., Lee, P. A., Tsai, J. L., Yeh, Y.-Y., & Huang, J. S. (2000). The conception of depression in Chinese American college students. *Cultural Diversity and Ethnic Minority Psychology, 6*(2), 183–195.

Zeiner, A. R. (1975). Psychophysiology of depression. *Biological Psychology Bulletin, 4*, 91–102.

Zuckerman, M., Persky, H., & Curtis, G. C. (1968). Relationships among anxiety, depression, hostility, and autonomic variables. *Journal of Nervous and Mental Disease, 146*, 481–487.

21

Gender Differences in Depression

Susan Nolen-Hoeksema

Unipolar depression is a relatively common psychiatric problem, but it is even more common among women than among men (Nolen-Hoeksema, 1987, 1990). Most large epidemiological studies of community samples in the United States find that about twice as many women as men meet the criteria for major depression or dysthymic disorder (Eaton et al., 1997; Keller, & Shapiro, 1981; Kessler, McGonagle, Swartz, Blazer, & Nelson, 1993). For example, the National Comorbidity Study found a lifetime prevalence for major depressive disorder of 21.3% for women and 12.7% for men (Kessler et al., 1993). Women also tend to score higher than men on measures of subclinical depressive symptoms (see Nolen-Hoeksema, 1987, 1990). The absolute prevalence of depression varies substantially across cultures and nations, but the gender difference in depression remains significant across most demographic and cultural groups (Weissman et al., 1996).

In this chapter, I first review the epidemiology of gender differences in depression in more detail. Then I describe the most prominent explanations for this difference, including biological, psychological, and social explanations. Finally, I present a model integrating the best-supported explanations.

THE EPIDEMIOLOGY OF THE GENDER DIFFERENCE IN DEPRESSION

Epidemiological studies of children often find no gender difference in depression, or find that boys are somewhat more prone to depression than girls (Angold, Erkanli, Loeber, & Costello, 1996; Nolen-Hoeksema & Girgus, 1994). At about age 12 or 13 years, however, girls' rates of depression begin to increase sharply, whereas boys' rates remain stable or increase much less (Twenge & Nolen-Hoeksema, in press). By late adolescence, girls are twice as likely as boys to be diagnosed with unipolar depression, and they score significantly higher on continuous measures of depressive symptoms (Nolen-Hoeksema & Girgus, 1994). The absolute prevalence of diagnosable depression varies across the adult age span, but the gender difference remains significant (Eaton et al., 1997; Keller & Shapiro, 1981; Kessler et al., 1993).

It is important to note that most studies of the emergence of gender differences in depression in early adolescence have focused primarily on European American samples. The few published studies with substantial samples of ethnic minority adolescents raise some doubts that a gender difference in depression emerges in early adolescence in these samples (Hayward, Gotlib, Schraedley, & Litt, 1999). Among adults, however, the gender difference in depression is as large among African American and Latino samples as among European American samples (Blazer, Kessler, McGonagle, & Swartz, 1994). This suggests that the emergence of a gender difference in depression in African Americans and Latinos occurs at a later developmental period than the emergence in European Americans.

The observed greater prevalence of depression among women compared to men could be due to women having a greater number of first onsets, longer depressive episodes, a greater recurrence of depression than men, or all of these. In fact, data from three large epidemiological studies conducted in the United States suggest that the adult gender difference is primarily due to a greater number of first onsets of depression in women than men, and not to gender differences in the duration or recurrence of depression (Eaton et al., 1997; Keller & Shapiro, 1981; Kessler et al., 1993). As we will see, most of the theories of why women are more prone to depression than men imply that women should have longer and more recurrent depressions than men, as well as more first onsets.

BIOLOGICAL EXPLANATIONS

The fact that, among adults, women are more prone to depression than men across many nations and cultures suggests that biological factors play a role in the gender difference in depression. Most biological explanations have focused on the effects of gonadal hormones, especially estrogen and progesterone, on women's moods. Recently, several studies have investigated whether women may carry a greater genetic vulnerability to depression than men. Finally, a recent trend in the research is a focus on gender differences in biological reactivity to stress, and the contribution of these gender differences to women's greater vulnerability to depression.

Hormonal Explanations

Hormones have long been thought to play a role in women's depressions because some women experience new onsets of depression, or significant exacerbation of existing depressions, during periods when levels of their gonadal hormones are undergoing substantial change, specifically puberty, the premenstrual phase of the menstrual cycle, the postpartum period, and menopause. The literature on hormones and moods among women is vast (for detailed reviews see Seeman, 1997; Steiner, 1992; Steiner & Dunn, 1996). I will summarize the major trends in the literatures on each of the periods of the life cycle during which women are thought to be especially prone to depression.

Puberty

As noted earlier, the gender difference in depression does not emerge until early adolescence. Some investigators have suggested that the activation of gonadal hormone systems in puberty plays a role in the increase in rates of depression in girls. The evidence that hormonal changes play a direct role in the emergence of gender differences in depression in early adolescence is inconsistent. In a report on 1,073 U.S. children 9 to 13 years of age, depression levels in girls rose significantly in midpuberty, whereas boys' depression levels did not (Angold,

Costello, & Worthman, 1998). In analyses of hormonal data from only the girls in this study, testosterone and estradiol levels better accounted for increases in depressive symptoms in the girls than did pubertal stage or age (Angold, Costello, Erkanli, & Worthman, 1999).

Several other studies have found no relationship between pubertal stage or hormonal levels and mood in girls or boys going through puberty (see Buchanan, Eccles, & Becker, 1992). For example, in a study of 103 girls 10 to 14 years of age, Brooks-Gunn and Warren (1989) found no association between depressive symptom levels and any of five different hormones. In an analysis of follow-up data on 72 of these girls, Paikoff, Brooks-Gunn, and Warren (1991) found a positive linear relation between levels of estradiol and one self-report measure of depressive symptoms, but estradiol levels were not significantly correlated with maternal reports of the girls' depressive symptom levels or with a second self-report measure of depressive symptoms. Susman and colleagues (Susman, Nottelmann, Inoff-Germain, Dorn, & Chrousos, 1987; Susman, Dorn, & Chrousos, 1991) found no significant relation between estradiol levels (or levels of several other hormones) and depressive symptoms in either early adolescent girls or boys.

The normal hormonal changes of puberty may only trigger depression in girls with a genetic vulnerability to the disorder. There are multiple, complex relationships between gonadal hormones and the neurotransmitters that regulate mood, including serotonin. In genetically vulnerable girls, normal hormonal cycling, which begins in puberty, may trigger dysregulation of neurotransmitter systems, leading to increases in depressive symptoms. If this is correct, we would not expect to see consistent relationships between hormone levels and mood in nonselected community samples of girls. Instead, it would only be among genetically vulnerable girls that an association between hormones and mood should be apparent.

Several studies have found that the *timing* of puberty (compared to a girl's or boy's peers), rather than a specific stage of puberty, is associated with risk for several types of psychopathology. Girls who go through the peak pubertal changes (e.g., menarche, weight gain, development of secondary sex characteristics) several months before their female peer group are more likely than girls who mature around the same time as their peer group to show depression, anxiety disorders, eating disorders, substance abuse, and delinquent symptoms (Caspi & Moffitt, 1991; Graber, Lewinsohn, Seeley, & Brooks-Gunn, 1997; Hayward, Killen, Wilson, & Hammer, 1997). Late-maturing girls have not shown a consistent pattern of difficulty compared to on-time-maturing girls, although one study found that they had higher rates of major depression than on-time girls (Graber et al., 1997). For boys, both early- and late-maturing boys begin to drink alcohol earlier than their peers, and late-maturing boys may be more likely to develop an alcohol abuse problem in young adulthood (Andersson & Magnusson, 1990; Graber et al., 1997). It is important to note that these patterns have been consistently found for white youngsters, but not for African American youngsters (Michael, 1996).

The reasons for these differences in the impact of pubertal timing on white girls' and boys' vulnerabilities are not entirely clear, but several investigators have suggested that the meanings associated with pubertal changes are very different for boys and girls (see Brooks-Gunn, 1988). Girls are much more likely than boys to dislike the physical changes that accompany puberty, particularly the weight gain in fat and the loss of the long, lithe, prepubescent look that is idealized in modern fashions (Dornbusch et al., 1984; Simmons, Blyth, Van Cleave, & Bush, 1979; Tobin-Richards, Boxer, & Petersen, 1983). Girls who reach menarche considerably earlier than their peers are particularly dissatisfied and unhappy with their bodies (Rierdan & Koff, 1991). In turn, several studies have shown that the more negative body image in girls is associated with increased levels of depressive symptoms in girls compared to boys (Allgood-Merten, Lewinsohn, & Hops, 1990).

A number of researchers have suggested that girls are especially likely to experience depression during puberty if they face difficult events at the same time their bodies are undergoing the changes of puberty (Angold & Rutter, 1992; Brooks-Gunn & Warren, 1989; Simmons & Blyth, 1987). Studies of several kinds of difficult events have found support for this hypothesis (Petersen, Sarigiani, & Kennedy, 1991; Simmons & Blyth, 1987). For example, Petersen and colleagues (1991) found that girls who moved from elementary to junior high school within 6 months of undergoing the peak time of pubertal change had significantly more depressive symptoms at the time and were still at higher levels of depressive symptoms in 12 grade. In this study, the synchronicity of peak pubertal growth and school change was not associated with depressive symptoms in boys, however. This may be because boys like their pubertal changes and so are less reactive to stressful events than similarly situated girls or because peak pubertal change coincided with the change from elementary to junior high school relatively infrequently in boys.

The Premenstrual Phase of the Menstrual Cycle

The Diagnostic and Statistical Manual, fourth edition (DSM-IV-TR; American Psychiatric Association, 2000), defines premenstrual dysphoric disorder (PMDD) as the presence, during most menstrual cycles in the last year, of five or more symptoms representing a significant mood disturbance, which emerge during the last week of the luteal phase of the menstrual cycle, and begin to remit a few days after the onset of menses. Although many women report that they have mild-to-moderate physical symptoms (e.g., bloating and breast tenderness) during the premenstrual phase of the menstrual cycle, many fewer women (probably between 3 and 8%) have symptoms that meet the criteria for PMDD (Angst, 1999).

Evidence that PMDD is heritable (Chang, Holroyd, & Chau, 1995) and that premenstrual complaints can be eliminated with suppression of ovarian activity (Schmidt, Nieman, Danaceau, Adams, & Rubinow, 1998) or surgical menopause (Casper & Hearn 1990) suggests that the disorder has biological roots. For years, investigators searched for hormonal imbalances in women with PMDD, with few consistent positive findings (Steiner & Born, 2000). The current consensus in the field is that normal hormonal fluctuations trigger biochemical events within the central nervous system and other target tissues that unleash premenstrual symptoms in vulnerable women (Rubinow & Schmidt, 1995). In particular, serotonin systems may be dysregulated by normal hormonal changes in vulnerable women, leading to changes in their moods. Recent studies suggest that the selective serotonin reuptake inhibitors are effective in treating premenstrual symptoms, even when the drugs are taken only around the premenstrual phase (Steiner & Born, 2000).

The Postpartum Period

Approximately 10–15% of women experience a depressive episode severe enough to qualify for a diagnosis of major depression in the first few weeks after giving birth (O'Hara & Swain, 1996). Many more women, perhaps the majority of women, experience the postpartum blues in the first few weeks after giving birth. Symptoms of the postpartum blues include dysphoria, mood lability, crying, anxiety, insomnia, poor appetite, and irritability. Although annoying and sometimes confusing, these symptoms are usually not debilitating and typically subside within 2–3 weeks postpartum.

Major depression with postpartum onset can be very debilitating and, if not treated, can linger for months or more (O'Hara & Swain, 1996). Because the onset of major depression during postpartum coincides with large changes in levels of estrogen, progesterone, and several other hormones, these changes have been thought to play a causal role (Steiner,

1998). Only a handful of studies have attempted to measure these changes, especially in gonadal hormones and prolactin. To date, the results do not seem to correlate strongly with changes in mood and are mostly disappointing and inconsistent.

Family history studies show that women with postpartum depression often have a family history of depression (Steiner & Tam, 1999). These women also tend to have a personal history of depression prior to becoming pregnant, or are depressed during pregnancy (O'Hara & Swain, 1996). Thus, it may be primarily women who carry some underlying vulnerability to depression who tend to develop postpartum depressions. Indeed, when unselected community samples of postpartum women are compared to matched groups of nonpostpartum women, differences often are not found in the prevalence of major depression (O'Hara & Swain, 1996), suggesting that postpartum changes in hormones do not induce major depression in women in the general population.

Further evidence that postpartum depressions are not a distinct type of depressive disorder comes from a study by Whiffen and Gotlib (1993). They found that women in a postpartum depression did not differ from women in a nonpostpartum depression in past psychiatric history, in the course of the episode, or in the psychosocial variables covarying with the episode (i.e., negative interpersonal relations, stress, and poor coping). The only major difference between the two groups was that the postpartum depressions were milder in severity than were the nonpostpartum depressions.

Menopause

During menopause, estrogen levels decline gradually. Symptoms associated with this decline include hot flashes, night sweats, and vaginal dryness. Although menopause previously was considered a time of increased vulnerability to depression for women, studies of women in the general population do not support this assumption (Matthews, 1992; Matthews et al., 1990).

Summary

The available data suggest that the normal hormonal changes associated with puberty, the menstrual cycle, the postpartum period, and menopause do not induce significant depressive symptoms or disorders in women in the general population. In women with a genetic or other type of vulnerability to depression, however, these hormonal changes may trigger episodes of depression or exacerbate existing episodes, perhaps by dysregulating neurotransmitter systems.

Genetic Factors

Family history studies clearly show that depression runs in families, particularly among female members (MacKinnon, Jamison, & DePaulo, 1997). Some twin studies of major depression suggest that genetics play a heavier role in this disorder for women than for men (Bierut et al., 1999; Jacobson & Rowe, 1999; Silberg et al., 1999). Other twin studies, however, have found no gender difference in the heritability of depression (Eaves et al., 1997; Kendler & Prescott, 1999; Rutter, Silberg, O'Connor, & Simonoff, 1999). Even in one study showing gender differences in the heritability of depression, these differences were found when DSM-III-R criteria for depression were used, but not when DSM-IV criteria for depression were used (Bierut et al., 1999). Much more research is needed before conclusions can be drawn about the contributions of genetic factors to the gender difference in depression.

Biological Stress Reactivity

Recently, investigators have suggested that women are more likely than men to have a dys-regulated response to stress, which makes them more likely to develop depression in re-sponse to stress (Weiss, Longhurst, & Mazure, 1999). The hypothalamic–pituitary–adrenal (HPA) axis plays a major role in regulating stress responses. People with major depressive disorder often show elevated cortisol responses to stress, indicating dysregulation of the HPA response. Women may be more likely to have a dysregulated HPA response because they are more likely to have suffered traumatic events, which are known to contribute to HPA dysregulation (Heim et al., 2000). In addition, ovarian hormones modulate HPA axis regulation (Young & Korzun, 1999). Some women may have depressions during periods of rapid change in levels of ovarian hormones (i.e., the postpartum period, premenstrual peri-od, menopause, and puberty) because hormonal changes trigger dysregulation of the stress response, making these women more vulnerable to depression, particularly when they are confronted with stress. Currently, the evidence that women are more prone to HPA axis dysregulation is thin, but this is likely to be a focus of future research.

Summary of Biological Explanations

For years, the major biological explanation for women's greater vulnerability to depression compared to men has been that normal fluctuations in ovarian hormones cause many women to become depressed. The bulk of the evidence does not support this view. Some women do become depressed during periods of hormonal change, including puberty, the premenstrual period, the postpartum period, and menopause. These women are a minority, however, who probably carry some type of underlying vulnerability, perhaps a genetic vul-nerability, to depression. In women in the general population, normal hormonal changes are not consistently associated with significant mood changes. There also has not been con-sistent evidence that women are more genetically vulnerable to depression than men.

Gender differences in biological reactivity to stress may play a role in women' greater rates of depression. These differences may be tied to differences in women's and men's his-tories of traumatic events, discussed later in this chapter.

PSYCHOLOGICAL EXPLANATIONS

As with the biological explanations, psychological explanations for the gender difference in depression have evolved over the last few decades. Early psychoanalytic explanations attrib-uted women's excess vulnerability to depression to masochism and psychological dependen-cy (Deutsch, 1944). In the 1960s and 1970s, women were said to be more vulnerable to de-pression because they suffered low self-esteem and tended to make self-defeating attributions (Dweck & Gilliard, 1975; Radloff, 1975). New perspectives on gender role de-velopment introduced by authors such as Gilligan (1982) led to theories that girls were si-lenced during their adolescent years as they were socialized to play subservient roles to male partners and to focus their attention solely on becoming a good wife and mother (Chevron, Quinlan, & Blatt, 1978; Jack, 1991; Helgeson, 1994; Hill & Lynch, 1983). Across several decades, a theme in the psychological literature is that women are less assertive than men and more prone to helplessness, and both contribute to their higher rates of depression (see Radloff, 1975; Nolen-Hoeksema, 1990).

A review of the literatures on all these psychological variables is beyond the scope of this chapter (see Nolen-Hoeksema, 1987, 1990, and Nolen-Hoeksema & Girgus, 1994, for more detailed reviews). Instead, I focus here on two psychological variables that have been studied extensively in the last several years in relation to the gender difference in depression: interpersonal orientation and rumination.

Interpersonal Orientation

One of the most consistent psychological differences between women and men is in interpersonal orientation (Feingold, 1994). Women are more likely than men to feel strong emotional ties with a wide range of people in their lives, to see their roles vis à vis others (e.g., as daughter, wife/partner, mother) as central to their self-concepts, to care what others think of them, and to be emotionally affected by events in the lives of other people.

An interpersonal orientation may increase vulnerability to depression by several mechanisms. First, having many people to whom you feel emotionally close may increase the chance that tragedy will befall one of these people and have a negative emotional impact on one's own well-being, a hypothesis that Kessler and colleagues term "the cost of caring" (Kessler, McLeod, & Wethington, 1985). Examining evidence from five epidemiological studies, Kessler and McLeod (1984) found that women reported a greater number of negative events occurring to people in their social network than did men, presumably because this network was larger for women than for men. In this study, and several others (e.g., Leadbeater, Blatt, & Quinlan, 1995), women also reported that these social network events had a greater impact on their well-being than did men. This suggests that it is not just a greater exposure to negative events that comes with broad social networks, but that women experience more emotional pain than do men when such events occur.

Jack (1991) and Helgeson (1994) both argue that some women cross a line from an interpersonal orientation to an excessive concern about their relationships with others, which leads them to silence their own wants and needs in favor of maintaining a positive emotional tone in the relationships, and to feel too responsible for the quality of the relationship. This leads these females to have less power and obtain less benefit from relationships. In recent studies using measures to tap "feeling too responsible for relationships" or "unmitigated communion," women or adolescent girls have scored higher on such measures than men or adolescent boys, and high scores on these measures have been correlated with depression (Helgeson & Fritz, 1996).

Thus, women may be more likely than men to overvalue relationships as sources of self-worth, which interpersonal theories of depression have identified as a risk factor for depression (e.g., Barnett & Gotlib, 1988; Joiner & Coyne, 1998). Women who do overvalue relationships may seek reassurance from others to an extent that is excessive and annoys them (Joiner, Metalsky, Katz, & Beach, 1999). This can lead to rejection by others, or at least conflict in relationships, which then only feeds a woman's worries about the status of her relationships.

Rumination

Rumination is the tendency to focus on one's symptoms of distress, and the possible causes and consequences of these symptoms, in a repetitive and passive manner rather than in an active, problem-solving manner (Nolen-Hoeksema, 2000). When people ruminate, they have thoughts such as: "Why am I so unmotivated? I just can't get going. I'm never going to get my work done feeling this way." Although some rumination may be a natural response to distress and depression, there are stable individual differences in the tendency to ruminate (Nolen-Hoeksema & Davis, 1999). People who ruminate a great deal in response to their sad or depressed moods have longer periods of depressive symptoms and are more likely to be diagnosed with major depressive disorder (Nolen-Hoeksema, 2000). The effects of rumination on depression over time remain significant even after controlling for baseline levels of depression.

Women are more likely than men to ruminate in response to sad, depressed, or anxious moods (Nolen-Hoeksema & Jackson, 2001; Nolen-Hoeksema, Larson, & Grayson, 1999). The gender difference in rumination is found both in self-report survey and interview studies, and in laboratory studies in which women's and men's responses to sad moods are observed (Butler & Nolen-Hoeksema, 1994). In turn, when gender differences in rumination are statistically controlled, the gender difference in depression becomes nonsignificant, suggesting that rumination helps to account for the gender difference in depression (Nolen-Hoeksema et al., 1999).

How does rumination contribute to depression? Laboratory studies show that when people ruminate in response to a depressed mood, their memories of their past, their interpretations of the present, and their expectations for the future become more negative and distorted (Lyubomirsky & Nolen-Hoeksema, 1995; Lyubomirsky, Caldwell, & Nolen-Hoeksema, 1998). Thus, ruminators become increasingly negative and hopeless in their thinking, and show many of the cognitive errors described by Beck (1987) as contributing to depression. Moreover, the quality of solutions ruminators generate to solve their problems is lowered, and they are less confident about implementing these solutions (Lyubomirsky & Nolen-Hoeksema, 1995; Ward, Lyubomirsky, Sousa, & Nolen-Hoeksema, 2000). Thus, they are less likely to take positive action on their environment to overcome other factors contributing to their depression.

Summary of Psychological Explanations

Two psychological variables that have been shown to contribute to the gender difference in depression in recent research are interpersonal orientation and rumination. Women are more interpersonally oriented than men, and this may lead them to sacrifice their own wants and needs excessively to maintain positive relationships with others, which in turn may contribute to depression. Women's care and concern for others may also make them more vulnerable to depressive reactions to negative events in the lives of others.

Women are also more prone than men to engage in rumination when sad, blue, or anxious, and this appears to contribute to their higher rates of depression. Rumination enhances negative thinking and interferences with good problem solving and motivation, making it more difficult for individuals to overcome problems that may be associated with their depression.

SOCIAL EXPLANATIONS

The social explanations for women's greater rates of depression compared to men's have focused on negative events and conditions that result from women's social roles and status relative to men. Although no gender differences are often found on general life events or hassles surveys, when investigators have examined specific events or chronic hassles that are linked to women's social roles, they often find large differences (Kessler & McLeod, 1984).

Traumatic Events

The traumatic events most consistently linked to women's high rates of depression are physical and sexual abuse (see Weiss et al., 1999, for a review). One study estimated that one woman in three globally has been beaten, coerced into sex, or otherwise abused in her life-time (Heise, Ellsburg, & Gottemuller, 1999). Men are the victims of sexual and physical abuse as well, but women represent 85% of the victims of nonfatal intimate assaults that occur in the United States each year (Kilpatrick, Edmunds, & Seymour, 1992).

Estimates of the prevalence of different forms of abuse vary widely depending on definitions of abuse and assessment methods. Large nationally representative studies of rape suggest that about 13–15% of women are the victims of completed rape at sometime in their lives (Kilpatrick et al., 1992; Kilpatrick & Saunders, 1996; Koss, Gidycz, & Wisniewski, 1987; Tjaden & Thoennes, 1998). Most sexual assaults against women occur first during childhood and adolescence. The National Violence Against Women Survey found that 54 percent of the women reporting rape reported having first been victimized before the age of 18 (Tjaden & Thoennes, 1998). Cutler and Nolen-Hoeksema (1991) reviewed the most methodologically sound studies including both male and female participants, and found rates of childhood sexual assault between 7 and 19% for females and between 3 and 7% for males. Regarding physical abuse, studies suggest between 10 and 15% of women in the United States are abused by their intimate partners each year, and 4% sustain assaults serious enough to produce injury (Tjaden & Thoenes, 1998; Straus & Gelles, 1990).

Sexual and physical assault have been linked both retrospectively and prospectively to depression and posttraumatic stress disorder. For example, the National Women's Study (Saunders, Kilpatrick, Hanson, Resnick, & Walker, 1999) found that women who had been the victims of completed rape in childhood had a lifetime prevalence of depression of 52%, compared to 27% in nonvictimized women. Similarly, the Epidemiological Catchment Area Study found that rape during childhood or adulthood increased a woman's risk of depression by 2.4 (Burnam et al., 1988). A meta-analysis of 18 studies of depression and intimate violence found that the mean prevalence rate of depression among battered women was 48% (Golding, 1999).

Childhood sexual assault appears to be an especially potent predictor of depression, both during childhood and continuing into adulthood (Whiffen & Clark, 1997). Cutler and Nolen-Hoeksema (1991) estimated that as much as 35% of the gender difference in adult depression could be accounted for by the higher incidence of assault of girls relative to boys. Similar calculations have not been done with regard to other forms of abuse, but given the much higher rates of abuse of females compared to males, and the strong relation between a history of abuse and depression, different forms of abuse, taken together, may account for a substantial amount of the difference in rates of depression between women and men.

Chronic Negative Events

Women's social status relative to men's also leads them to experience certain chronic negative events that may contribute to their higher rates of depression, including poverty, sexual harassment, and lack of equity and affirmation in close relationships.

Poverty

Women are significantly more likely than men to have incomes below the poverty line, and high levels of depressive symptoms are common among people with low incomes, particularly among mothers with young children (e.g., Belle, Longfellow, & Makosky, 1982). Adults in poverty are twice as likely as nonpoor adults to experience new episodes of major depression (Bruce, Takeuchi, & Leaf, 1991), and rates of major depression in low-income mothers are about twice as high as in the general population of women (Bassuk, Buckner, Perloff, & Bassuk, 1998; Brown & Moran, 1997).

Sexual Harassment

The U.S. Equal Employment Opportunity Commission defines sexual harassment as "unwelcome sexual advances, requests for sexual favors, and other verbal or physical conduct of a sexual nature" that are either a condition or employment or that create an intimidating or hostile work environment (Gutek & Done, 2001). Studies of random samples suggest that between 35 and 50% of women, compared to 9 to 35% of men, have been sexually harassed at some point in their working lives, with higher estimates being found in male-dominated work settings (Gutek, 1985). The most common form of sexual harassment is sexist or sexual comments (see Fitzgerald, Swan, & Magley, 1997). Sexual coercion in community samples is much more rare, involving 1–3% of women in many samples (Barak, Pitterman, & Yitzhaki, 1995; Firtzgerald et al., 1997). Allegations that result in court cases usually involve much more severe behaviors.

Experiences of sexual harassment are associated with both elevated depressive symptoms and an increased risk of major depression (Dansky & Kilpatrick, 1997; Fitzgerald et al., 1997). Women who have been sexually harassed also show higher levels of posttraumatic stress symptoms and disorders (Dansky & Kilpatrick, 1997). Unfortunately, most of the research on the impact of sexual harassment on mental health has been conducted exclusively with samples of women (Gutek & Done, 2001). Thus, we do not know to what extent sexual harassment experiences contribute to the gender difference in depression. This is an important target for future research.

Inequities in Heterosexual Relationships

In intimate heterosexual relationships, some women face inequities in the distribution of power over important decisions that must be made, such as the decision to move to a new city, or decisions about how to spend the family's income (Nolen-Hoeksema et al., 1999). Even when they voice their opinions, women may feel that their opinions are not taken seriously, or that their viewpoints on important issues are not respected and affirmed by their partners. Nolen-Hoeksema and colleagues (1999) grouped inequities in workload and in heterosexual relationships under a variable labeled "chronic strain," and showed that chronic strain predicted increases in depression over time and partially mediated the gender difference in depression. Depression also contributed to more chronic strain over time, probably because it was associated with reductions in mastery and effective problem solving.

Summary of Social Explanations

The social explanations for women's increased vulnerability to depression attribute this vulnerability to acute and chronic stressors that women experience more often than men, due to the fact that women have less social power and status than men. The evidence that the higher rates of sexual and physical abuse of women compared to men contribute to the gender difference in depression is strong. Women's more frequent experiences of poverty, sexual harassment, and inequities in close relationships also may contribute to their higher rates of depression compared to men, although these factors warrant more research.

AN INTEGRATIVE MODEL

Although each of the factors discussed in this chapter could independently contribute to women's higher rates of depression compared to men, these factors likely interact in complex ways to produce depression in women. The major stressors that are more common in women's lives than men's, particularly early abuse experiences, could contribute to a greater biological reactivity to stress in women compared to men. Studies of survivors of child sexual abuse show that, even as adults, they have a more poorly regulated biological response to stress, as measured by cortisol levels, adrenocorticotropic hormone levels, and cardiac measures, compared to people who did not suffer child sexual abuse (Heim et al., 2000; Zahn-Waxler, 2000). In turn, this greater biological reactivity is associated with a greater adult prevalence of major depression. Moreover, women who have more poorly regulated biological responses to stress will find it more difficult to engage in efficacious behavioral responses to new stressors, raising the likelihood that they will experience chronic and frequent stressors.

The stresses in women's lives could also contribute to a greater psychological reactivity to stress. For example, people who have a history of sexual abuse are more likely to engage in rumination, perhaps because they remain hypervigilant for new threats (Nolen-Hoeksema, 1998). In addition, women who face chronic stressors because of inequities in their heterosexual relationships become more ruminative over time (Nolen-Hoeksema et al., 1999). In turn, rumination impairs problem solving, increasing the likelihood of new stressors.

Depression has its own effects on stressors and biological and psychological stress reactivity. Hammen (1991) has shown that depressed women are more likely than nondepressed women to report stressful events to which they had contributed, especially interpersonal conflicts and other interpersonal events. For example, depressed women have lower quality interactions and communications with their children, even though they may fervently desire to be good mothers. The problems these women show in parenting may be a direct result of their symptoms of depression, such as irritability, apathy, and poor concentration. The children of depressed mothers are often themselves distressed, oppositional, and critical, and trigger or exacerbate irritability and criticality in their mothers (Hammen, Burge, & Adrian, 1991).

Depression is also often associated with dysfunctional marital or romantic relationships (see Downey & Coyne, 1990; Gotlib & Beach, 1995), some of which are a consequence of depression. Depression elicits discomfort and rejection from others (Joiner & Coyne, 1999). In addition, depressed women often marry men with psychopathology (Hammen, Rudoph, Weisz, Rao, & Burge, 1999). Even in their teenage years, depressed adolescent women have more stressful romantic relationships, including more experiences of physical and psychological coercion in romantic relationships, and are more likely to pair with adolescent mates with symptoms of personality disorder (Rao, Hammen, & Daley, 1999). Thus, depression may contribute to poor interpersonal skills and choices, increasing a woman's vulnerability to interpersonal stressors.

Depression may also increase the tendency to ruminate by activitating and strengthening associative networks of negative cognitions (Teasdale, 1988). With each new depressive episode, these networks are more interconnected and more easily primed, increasing the probability of rumination.

Finally, depression may increase biological reactivity to stress by sensitizing the neurotransmitter and neuroendocrine systems linked to depression (Post, 1992; Post & Weiss, 1995). In turn, this lowers the threshold for new depressive episodes, so that increasingly milder stressors can trigger new episodes.

The complex interrelationships among stress, stress reactivity, and depression call for comprehensive interventions that address the variety of problems a depressed woman might face in overcoming her depression and preventing new depressions. Simply relieving her depressive symptoms, for example, through medication, is unlikely to break the negative interpersonal and cognitive cycles that maintain depression and keep a woman at risk for new episodes of depression.

FUTURE DIRECTIONS

A number of the risk factors for depression identified in this chapter require further research before conclusions can be drawn about their contributions to the gender difference in depression. First, although the new research on possible gender differences in biological stress reactivity is interesting, much more research is needed, incorporating both female and male participants, to determine whether such gender differences do exist and, if they do, the extent to which they explain the gender difference in depression. Second, the long history of theory on women's interpersonal orientation as a contributor to their vulnerability to depression, and recent evidence favoring these theories, makes this an important target for future research. This research should use both longitudinal and experimental designs to try to establish the predictive and causal relationships between excessive interpersonal orientation and depression. Third, some of the social factors hypothesized to contribute to women's vulnerability to depression, particularly sexual harassment, poverty, and inequities in close relationships, should be studied in designs that allow researchers to determine the magnitude of the contribution these factors make to the gender difference in depression.

Fourth, a critical focus for new research is the emergence of gender differences in depression in adolescence. Many questions remain to be answered. What is the time course for the emergence of this gender difference in different ethnic and cultural groups, and why does the time course seem to differ across these groups? Is it only girls who have preadolescent risk factors for depression who become depressed in adolescence, or do many girls with no preexisting risk factors develop depression in adolescence? What are the critical biological, psychological, and social factors that contribute to the increase in depression in girls in adolescence? How do these variables interact with one another over time? All of the risk factors for depression discussed in this chapter may show increases in prevalence in early adolescence, or may interact with the many changes of adolescence, leading girls to be more vulnerable to depression. For example, a genetic vulnerability to depression, or more broadly to neurotransmitter or HPA axis dysregulation, may be triggered by the hormonal changes of puberty in girls. A heightened interpersonal orientation or a tendency to ruminate may interact with changes at puberty, such as the beginning of heterosexual dating, to contribute to depression in some girls. Some social risk factors for depression in girls, especially sexual abuse, are likely to increase in prevalence at puberty. Understanding the emergence of gender differences in depression in adolescence will be crucial to the design of effective prevention and intervention programs for adolescent girls.

Finally, the evidence that women suffer more first onsets of depression, but not longer or more recurrent depressions, has largely been ignored by researchers of the gender differences in depression. Yet most of the theories of why women are more vulnerable to depression than men imply that they should have longer and more recurrent depressions, as well as more first onsets. If this set of epidemiological trends continues to be supported by future research, it will be important to understand why this pattern of results is found.

This simplest explanation for this pattern of results may be that once depression is triggered, its course and likelihood of recurrence are determined by endogenous neurophysiological factors that do not vary by sex. Instead, what varies by sex may be the frequency or likelihood of triggers of an initial episode. An alternative explanation is that women may carry protective factors that keep them from experiencing longer and more recurrent depressions than men. For example, Nolen-Hoeksema (2000) found that women are more likely than men to use "positive emotions strategies" (cf. Folkman & Moskowitz, 2000)— purposeful activities to lift their moods, such as recalling a positive interaction with a friend or looking at a beautiful scene in nature—to lift sad and blue moods. In turn, the more people used positive emotions strategies, the less likely they were to remain depressed over an extended period of time. Women's use of positive emotion strategies may compensate for their greater exposure to depression-maintaining factors, leading them to have shorter depressions than might otherwise be expected.

What is clear from the existing literature on the gender differences in depression is that no single factor is likely to explain these differences. Instead, the differences may be overdetermined by a confluence of social, psychological, and biological differences between women and men.

REFERENCES

Allgood-Merten, B., Lewinsohn, P. M., & Hops, H. (1990). Sex differences and adolescent depression. *Journal of Abnormal Psychology, 99,* 55–63.

American Psychiatric Association. (2000). *Diagnostic and statistical manual of mental disorders* (4th ed., text rev.). Washington, DC: Author.

Andersson, T., & Magnusson, D. (1990). Biological maturation in adolescence and the development of drinking habits and alcohol abuse among young males: A prospective longitudinal study. *Journal of Youth and Adolescence, 19,* 33–41.

Angold, A., Costello, E. J., Erkanli, A., & Worthman, C. M (1999). Pubertal changes in hormones of adolescent girls. *Psychological Medicine, 29,* 1043–1053.

Angold, A., Costello, E. J., & Worthman, C. M. (1998). Puberty and depression: The roles of age, pubertal status and pubertal timing. *Psychological Medicine, 28,* 51–61.

Angold, A., Erkanli, A., Loeber, R., & Costello, E. J. (1996). Disappearing depression in a population sample of boys. *Journal of Emotional and Behavioral Disorders, 4,* 95–104.

Angold, A., & Rutter, M. (1992). Effects of age and pubertal status on depression in a large clinical sample. *Developmental Psychopathology, 4,* 5–28.

Angst, J. (1999). Perimenstrual symptoms in the community: Prevalence, stability, comorbidity. *European Neuropsychopharmacology, 9* (Suppl. 5), S144.

Barak, A., Pitterman, Y., & Yitzhaki, R. (1995). An empirical test of the role of power differential in originating sexual harassment. *Basic and Applied Social Psychology, 17,* 497–518.

Barnett, P. A., & Gotlib, I. H. (1988). Psychosocial functioning and depression: Distinguishing among antecedents, concomitants, and consequences. *Psychological Bulletin, 104,* 97–126.

Bassuk, E., Buckner, J., Perloff, J., & Bassuk, S. (1998). Prevalence of mental health and substance use disorders among homeless and low-income housed mothers. *American Journal of Psychiatry, 155,* 1561–1564.

Beck, A. T. (1987). Cognitive models of depression. *Journal of Cognitive Psychotherapy: An International Quarterly, 1,* 5–37.

Belle, D., Longfellow, C., & Makosky, V. (1982). Stress, depression and the mother–child relationship: Report of a field study. *International Journal of Sociology of the Family, 12,* 251–263.

Bierut, L. J., Heath, A. C., Bucholz, K. K., Dinwiddie, S. H., Madden, P. A. F., Statham, D. J., Dunne, M. P., & Martin, N. G. (1999). Major depressive disorder in a community-based twin sample: Are there different genetic and environmental contributions for men and women? *Archives of General Psychiatry, 57,* 557–563.

Blazer, D. G., Kessler, R. C., McGonagle, K. A., & Swartz, M. S. (1994). The prevalence and distribution of major depression in a national community sample: The National Comorbidity Survey. *American Journal of Psychiatry, 151,* 979–986.

Brooks-Gunn, J. (1988). Antecedents and consequences of variations in girls' maturational timing. *Journal of Adolescent Health Care, 9,* 365–373.

Brooks-Gunn, J., & Warren, M. P. (1989). Biological and social contributions to negative affect in young adolescent girls. *Child Development, 60,* 40–55.

Brown, G., & Moran, P. (1997). Single mothers, poverty and depression. *Psychological Medicine, 27,* 21–33.

Bruce, M. L., Takeuchi, D., & Leaf, P. (1991). Poverty and psychiatric status. *Archives of General Psychiatry, 48,* 470–474.

Buchanan, C. M., Eccles, J. S., & Becker, J. B. (1992). Are adolescents the victims of raging hormones?: Evidence for activational effects of hormones on moods and behavior at adolescence. *Psychological Bulletin, 111,* 62–107.

Burnam, M. A., Stein, J. A., Golding, J. M., Siegel, J. M., Sorensen, S. B., Forsythe, A. B., & Telles, C. A. (1988). Sexual assault and mental disorders in a community population. *Journal of Consulting and Clinical Psychology, 56,* 843–850.

Butler, L. D., & Nolen-Hoeksema, S. (1994). Gender differences in responses to a depressed mood in a college sample. *Sex Roles, 30,* 331–346.

Casper, R. F., & Hearn, M. T. (1990). The effect of hysterectomy and bilateral oophorectomy in women with severe premenstrual syndrome. *American Journal of Obstetrics and Gynecology, 162,* 105–109.

Caspi, A., & Moffitt, T. (1991). Individual differences are accentuated during periods of social change: The sample case of girls at puberty. *Journal of Personality and Social Psychology, 61,* 157–168.

Chang, A. M., Holroyd, E., & Chau, J. P. C. (1995). Premenstrual syndrome in employed Chinese women in Hong Kong. *Health Care for Women International, 16,* 551.

Chevron, E. S., Quinlan, D. M., & Blatt, S. H. (1978). Sex roles and gender differences in the expression of depression. *Journal of Abnormal Psychology, 87,* 680–683.

Cutler, S. E., & Nolen-Hoeksema, S. (1991). Accounting for sex differences in depression through female victimization: Childhood sexual abuse. *Sex Roles, 24,* 425–438.

Dansky, B. S., & Kilpatrick, D. G. (1997). Effects of sexual harassment. In W. O'Donohue (Ed.), *Sexual harassment: Theory, research, treatment* (pp. 152–174). Boston: Allyn & Bacon.

Deutsch, H. (1944). *The psychology of women.* New York: Grune & Stratton.

Dornbusch, S. M., Carlsmith, J. M., Duncan, P. D., Gross, R. T., Martin, J. A., Ritter, P. L., & Siegel-Gorelick, B. (1984). Sexual maturation, social class, and the desire to be thin among adolescent females. *Developmental and Behavioral Pediatrics, 5,* 308–314.

Downey, G., & Coyne, J. C. (1990). Children of depressed parents: An integrative review. *Psychological Bulletin, 108,* 50–76.

Dweck, C. S., & Gilliard, D. (1975). Expectancy statements as determinants of reactions to failure: Sex differences in persistence and expectancy change. *Journal of Personality and Social Psychology, 32,* 1077–1084.

Eaton, W., Anthony, J., Gallo, J., Cai, G., Tien, A., Romanoski, A., Lyketsos, C., & Chen, L. (1997). Natural history of Diagnostic Interview Schedule/ DSM-IV major depression. *Archives of General Psychiatry, 54,* 993–999.

Eaves, L. J., Silberg, J. L., Meyer, J. M., Maes, H. H., Simonoff, E., Pickles, A., Rutter, M., Neale, M. C., Reynolds, C. A., Erikson, M. T., Heath, A. C., Loeber, R., Truett, K. R., & Hewitt, J. K. (1997). Genetics and developmental psychopathology: 2. The main effects of genes and environment on behavioral problems in the Virginia Twin Study of Adolescent Behavioral Development. *Journal of Child Psychology and Psychiatry, 38,* 965–980.

Feingold, A. (1994). Gender differences in personality: A meta-analysis. *Psychological Bulletin, 116,* 429–456.

Fitzgerald, L. F., Swan, S., & Magley, V. J. (1997). But was it really sexual harassment?: Legal, behavioral, and psychological definitions of the workplace victimization of women. In W. O'Donohue (Ed.), *Sexual harassment: Theory, research, treatment* (pp. 5–28). Boston: Allyn & Bacon.

Folkman, S., & Moskowitz, J. T. (2000). Positive affect and the other side of coping. *American Psychologist, 55,* 647–654.

Gilligan, C. (1982). *In a different voice: Psychological theory and women's development.* Cambridge, MA: Harvard University Press.

Golding, J. M. (1999). Intimate partner violence as a risk factor for mental disorders: A meta-analysis. *Journal of Family Violence, 14,* 99–132.

Gotlib, I., & Beach, S. (1995). A marital/family discord model of depression: Implications for therapeutic intervention. In N. S. Jacobson & A. S. Gurman (Eds.), *Clinical handbook of couple therapy* (pp. 411–436). New York: Guilford Press.

Graber, J. A., Lewinsohn, P. M., Seeley, J. R., & Brooks-Gunn, J. (1997). Is psychopathology associated with the timing of pubertal development? *Journal of the American Academy of Child Adolescent Psychiatry, 36,* 1768–1776.

Gutek, B. A. (1985). *Sex and the workplace.* San Francisco: Jossey-Bass.

Gutek, B. A., & Done, R. (2001). Sexual harassment. In R. K. Unger (Ed.), *Handbook of the psychology of women and gender* (pp. 367–387). New York: Wiley.

Hammen, C. L. (1991) *Depression runs in families: The social context of risk and resilience in children of depressed mothers.* New York: Springer-Verlag.

Hammen, C., Burge, D., & Adrian, C. (1991). Timing of mother and child depression in a longitudinal study of children at risk. *Journal of Consulting and Clinical Psychology, 59,* 341–345.

Hammen, C., Rudolph, K., Weisz, J., Rao, U., & Burge, D. (1999). The context of depression in clinic-referred youth: Neglected areas in treatment. *Journal of the American Academy of Child and Adolescent Psychiatry, 38,* 64–71.

Hayward, C., Gotlib, I. H., Schraedley, P. K., & Litt, I. F. (1999). Ethnic differences in the association between pubertal status and symptoms of depression in adolescent girls. *Journal of Adolescent Health, 25,* 143–149.

Hayward, C., Killen, J. D., Wilson, D. M., & Hammer, L. D. (1997). Psychiatric risk associated with early puberty in adolescent girls. *Journal of the American Academy of Child and Adolescent, 36,* 255–262.

Heim, C., Newport, J., Heit, S., Graham, Y., Wilcox, M., Bonsall, R., Miller, A., & Nemeroff, C. (2000). Pituitary–adrenal and autonomic responses to stress in women after sexual and physical abuse in childhood. *Journal of the American Medical Association, 284,* 592–596.

Heise, L., Ellsberg, M., & Gottenmuller, M. (1999, December). Ending violence against women. *Population Reports* (Series L, No. 11), 1–43. Baltimore: Johns Hopkins University School of Public Health, Population Information Program.

Helgeson, V. (1994). Relation of agency and communion to well-being: Evidence and potential explanations. *Psychological Bulletin, 116,* 412–428.

Helgeson, V., & Fritz, H. (1996). Implications of communion and unmitigated communion for adolescent adjustment to Type I diabetes. *Women's Health: Research on Gender, Behavior, and Policy, 2,* 169–194.

Hill, J. P., & Lynch, M. E. (1983). The intensification of gender-related role expectations during early adolescence. In J. Brooks-Gunn & A. C. Petersen (Eds.), *Girls at puberty* (pp. 201–228). New York: Plenium Press.

Jack, D. C. (1991). *Silencing the self: Women and depression.* New York: HarperPerennial.

Jacobson, K. C., & Rowe, D. C. (1999). Genetic and environmental influences on the relationships between family connectedness, school connectedness, and adolescent depressed mood: Sex differences. *Developmental Psychology, 35,* 926–939.

Joiner, T., & Coyne, J. C. (1999). *The interactional nature of depression: Advances in interpersonal approaches.* Washington, DC: American Psychological Association.

Joiner, T., Metalsky, G., Katz, J., & Beach, S. R. (1999). Depression and excessive reassurance-seeking. *Psychological Inquiry, 10,* 269–278.

Keller, M., & Shapiro, R. (1981). Major depressive disorder: Initial results from a one-year prospective naturalistic follow-up study. *Journal of Nervous Mental Disorders, 169,* 761–768.

Kendler, K. S., & Prescott, C. A. (1999). A population based twin study of lifetime major depression in men and women. *Archives of General Psychiatry, 56,* 39–44.

Kessler, R. C., McGonagle, K. A., Swartz, M., Blazer, D. G., & Nelson, C. B. (1993). Sex and depression in the National Comorbidity Survey: I. Lifetime prevalence, chronicity, and recurrence. *Journal of Affective Disorders, 29,* 85–96.

Kessler, R. C., & McLeod, J. D. (1984). Sex differences in vulnerability to undesirable life events. *American Sociological Review, 49*, 620–631.

Kessler, R. C., McLeod, J. D., & Wethington, E. (1985). The costs of caring: A perspective on the relationship between sex and psychological distress. In I. G. Sarason & B. R. Sarason (Eds.), *Social support: Theory, research and applications* (pp. 491–506). Dordrecht, The Netherlands: Martinus Nijhoff.

Kilpatrick, D. G., Edmunds, C., & Seymour, A. (1992). *Rape in America: A report to the nation.* Charleston, SC: Medical University of South Carolina, National Victims Center and the Crime Victims Research and Treatment Center.

Kilpatrick, D. G., & Saunders, B. E. (1996). *Prevalence and consequences of child victimization: Results from the National Survey of Adolescents.* Washington, DC: U.S. Department of Justice, Office of Justice Programs, National Institute of Justice.

Koss, M. P., Gidycz, C. A., & Wisniewski, N. (1987). The scope of rape: Incidence and prevalence of sexual aggression and victimization in a national sample of higher education students. *Journal of Consulting and Clinical Psychology, 55*, 162–170.

Leadbeater, B. J., Blatt, S. J., & Quinlan, D. M. (1995). Gender-linked vulnerabilities to depressive symptoms, stress, and problem behaviors in adolescents. *Journal of Research on Adolescence, 5*, 1–29.

Lyubomirsky, S., Caldwell, N. D., & Nolen-Hoeksema, S. (1998). Effects of ruminative and distracting responses to depressed mood on retrieval of autobiographical memories. *Journal of Personality and Social Psychology, 75*, 166–177.

Lyubomirsky, S., & Nolen-Hoeksema, S. (1995). Effects of self-focused rumination on negative thinking and interpersonal problem-solving. *Journal of Personality and Social Psychology, 69*, 176–190.

MacKinnon, D., Jamison, K. R., & DePaulo, J. R. (1997). Genetics of manic depressive illness. *Annual Review of Neuroscience, 20*, 355–373.

Matthews, K. A. (1992). Myths and realities of the menopause. *Psychosomatic Medicine, 54*, 1–9.

Matthews, K. A., Wing, R., Lewis, H., Meilahn, E., Kelsey, S., Costello, E., & Caggiula, A. (1990). Influences of natural menopause on psychological characteristics and symptoms of middle-aged healthy women. *Journal of Consulting and Clinical Psychology, 58*, 345–351.

Michael, A. (1996, March). *Pubertal maturation: Relations to adolescent mental health in two ethnic groups.* Poster presented at the sixth biennial meeting of the Society for Research in Adolescence, Boston.

Nolen-Hoeksema, S. (1987). Sex differences in unipolar depression: Evidence and theory. *Psychological Bulletin, 101*, 259–282.

Nolen-Hoeksema, S. (1990). *Sex differences in depression.* Stanford, CA: Stanford University Press.

Nolen-Hoeksema, S. (1998, August). *Contributors to the gender difference in rumination.* Paper presented at the annual meeting of the American Psychological Association, San Francisco.

Nolen-Hoeksema, S. (2000). The role of rumination in depressive disorders and mixed anxiety/depressive symptoms. *Journal of Abnormal Psychology, 109*, 504–511.

Nolen-Hoeksema, S., & Davis, C. G. (1999). "Thanks for sharing that": Ruminators and their social support networks. *Journal of Personality and Social Psychology, 77*, 801–814.

Nolen-Hoeksema, S., & Girgus, J. S. (1994). The emergence of gender differences in depression in adolescence. *Psychological Bulletin, 115*, 424–443.

Nolen-Hoeksema, S., & Jackson, B. (2001). Mediators of the gender difference in rumination. *Psychology of Women Quarterly, 25*, 37–47.

Nolen-Hoeksema, S., Larson, J., & Grayson, C. (1999). Explaining the gender difference in depression. *Journal of Personality and Social Psychology, 77*, 1061–1072.

O'Hara, M. W., & Swain, A. M. (1996). Rates and risk of postpartum depression: A meta-analysis. *International Review of Psychiatry, 8*, 37–54.

Paikoff, R. L., Brooks-Gunn, J., & Warren, M. P. (1991). Effects of girls' hormonal status on depressive and aggressive symptoms over the course of one year. *Journal of Youth and Adolescence, 20*, 191–215.

Petersen, A. C., Sarigiani, P. A., & Kennedy, R. E. (1991). Adolescent depression: Why more girls? *Journal of Youth and Adolescence, 20,* 247–271.

Post, R. M. (1992). Transduction of psychosocial stress into the neurobiology of recurrent affective disorder. *American Journal of Psychiatry, 149,* 999–1010.

Post, R. M., & Weiss, S. R. B. (1995). The neurobiology of treatment-resistant mood disorders. In F. E. Bloom & D. J. Kupfer (Eds.), *Psychopharmacology: The fourth generation of progress* (pp. 1155–1170). New York: Raven Press.

Radloff, L. S. (1975). Sex differences in depression: The effects of occupational and marital status. *Sex Roles, 1,* 249–265.

Rao, U., Hammen, C., & Daley, S. (1999). Continuity of depression during the transition to adulthood: A 5-year longitudinal study of young women. *Journal of the American Academy of Child and Adolescent Psychiatry, 38,* 908–915.

Rierdan, J., & Koff, E. (1991). Depressive symptomatology among very early maturing girls. *Journal of Youth and Adolescence, 20,* 415–425.

Rubinow, D. R., & Schmidt, P. J. (1995). The treatment of premenstrual syndrome: Forward into the past. *New England Journal of Medicine, 332,* 1574–1575.

Rutter, M., Silberg, J., O'Connor, T., & Simonoff, E. (1999). Genetics and child psychiatry: II. Empirical research findings. *Journals of Child Psychology and Psychiatry, 40,* 19–55.

Saunders, B. E., Kilpatrick, D. G., Hanson, R. F., Resnick, H. S., & Walker, M. E. (1999). Prevalence, case characteristics, and long-term psychological correlates of child rape among women: A national survey. *Child Maltreatment, 4,* 607–613.

Schmidt, P. J., Nieman, L. K., Danaceau, M. A., Adams, L. F., & Rubinow, D. R. (1998). Differential behavioral effects of gonadal steroids in women with and in those without premenstrual syndrome. *New England Journal of Medicine, 338,* 209–216.

Seeman, M. V. (1997). Psychopathology in women and men: Focus on female hormones. *American Journal of Psychiatry, 154,* 1641–1647.

Silberg, J., Pickles, A., Rutter, M., Hewitt, J., Simonoff, E., Maes, H., Carbonneau, R., Murrelle, L., Foley, D., & Eaves, L. (1999). The influence of genetic factors and life stress on depression among adolescent girls. *Archives of General Psychiatry, 56,* 225–232.

Simmons, R. G., & Blyth, D. A. (1987). *Moving into adolescence: The impact of pubertal change and school context.* New York: Aldine de Gruyter.

Simmons, R. G., Blyth, D. A., Van Cleave, E. F., & Bush, D. M. (1979). Entry into early adolescence: The impact of school structure, puberty, and early dating on self-esteem. *American Sociological Review, 44,* 948–967.

Steiner, M. (1992). Female-specific mood disorders. *Clinical Obstetric Gynecology, 35,* 599–611.

Steiner, M. (1998). Perinatal mood disorders: Position paper. *Psychopharmacology Bulletin, 34,* 301–306.

Steiner, M., & Born, L. (2000). Advances in the treatment of premenstrual dysphoria. *CNS Drugs, 13,* 286–304.

Steiner, M., & Dunn, E. (1996). The psychobiology of female-specific mood disorders. *Infertility and Reproductive Medical Clinics of North America, 7,* 297–313.

Steiner, M., & Tam, W. Y. K. (1999). Postpartum depression in relation to other psychiatric disorders. In L. Miller (Ed.), *Postpartum mood disorders* (pp. 47–63). Washington, DC: American Psychiatric Press.

Straus, M. A., & Gelles, R. J. (1990). *Physical violence in American families: Risk factors and adaptation to violence in 8,145 families.* New Brunswick, NJ: Transaction Books.

Susman, E. J., Dorn, L. D., & Chrousos, G. P. (1991). Negative affect and hormone levels in young adolescents: Concurrent and predictive perspectives. *Journal of Youth and Adolescence, 20,* 167–190.

Susman, E. J., Nottelmann, E. D., Inoff-Germain, G. E., Dorn, L. D., & Chrousos, G. P. (1987). Hormonal influences on aspects of psychological development during adolescence. *Journal of Adolescent Health Care, 8,* 492–504.

Teasdale, J. (1988). Cognitive vulnerability to persistent depression. *Cognition and Emotion, 2,* 247–274.

Tjaden, P., & Thoennes, N. (1998). *Prevalence, incidence and consequence of violence against women: Findings from the National Violence Against Women Survey. Research in brief.* Washington, DC: U.S. Department of Justice, National Institute of Justice.

Tobin-Richards, M., Boxer, A., & Petersen, A. C. (1983). The psychological significance of pubertal change: Sex differences in perception of self during early adolescence. In J. Brooks-Gunn & A. C. Petersen (Eds.), *Girls at puberty: Biological and psychosocial perspectives* (pp. 127–154), New York: Plenum Press.

Twenge, J., & Nolen-Hoeksema, S. (in press). Age, gender, race, SES, and birth cohort differences on the Children's Depression Inventory: A meta-analysis. *Journal of Abnormal Psychology.*

Ward, A., Lyubomirsky, S., Sousa, L., & Nolen-Hoeksema, S. (2000). *Can't quite commit: Ruminators and uncertainty.* Manuscript submitted for publication.

Weiss, E. L., Longhurst, J. G., & Mazure, C. M. (1999). Childhood sexual abuse as a risk factor for depression in women: Psychosocial and neurobiological correlates. *American Journal of Psychiatry, 156,* 816–828.

Weissman, M. M., Bland, R. C., Canino, G. J., Faravelli, C., Greenwald, S., Hwu, H.-G., Joyce, P. R., Karam, E. G., Lee, C.-K., Lellouch, J., Lepine, J.-P., Newman, S. C., Rubio-Stipc, M., Wells, E., Wickramaratne, P. J., Wittchen, H.-U., & Yeh, E.-K. (1996). Cross-national epidemiology of major depression and bipolar disorder. *Journal of the American Medical Association, 276,* 293–299.

Whiffen, V. E., & Clark, S. E. (1997). Does victimization account for sex differences in depressive symptoms? *British Journal of Clinical Psychology, 36,* 185–193.

Whiffen, V. E., & Gotlib, I. H. (1993). Comparison of postpartum and nonpostpartum depression: Clinical presentation, psychiatric history, and psychosocial functioning. *Journal of Consulting and Clinical Psychology, 61,* 485–494.

Young, E., & Korszun, A. (1999). Women, stress, and depression: Sex differences in hypothalamic–pituitary–adrenal axis regulation. In E. Leibenluft (Ed.), *Gender differences in mood and anxiety disorders: From bench to bedside* (pp. 31–52). Washington, DC: American Psychiatric Press.

Zahn-Waxler, C. (2000). The development of empathy, guilt, and internalization of distress: Implications for gender differences in internalizing and externalizing problems. In R. Davidson (Ed.), *Anxiety, depression, and emotion: Wisconsin Symposium on Emotion* (Vol. 1, pp. 222–265). Oxford, UK: Oxford University Press.

22

Depression in Children

Judy Garber and Jason L. Horowitz

Do children experience depression? The answer to this question is quite complex, and depends on the definition of depression and the age of the child. Depression can be defined as a symptom, a syndrome, and a nosological disorder. The single symptom of sadness or depressed affect is a subjective state experienced by most individuals at various points in their lives, and by itself is not necessarily pathological. The syndrome of depression is comprised of more than an isolated dysphoric mood, and occurs in combination with other symptoms to form a symptom complex, or syndrome. When this clinical syndrome is characterized by a particular symptom picture with a specifiable course, outcome, treatment response, and etiological correlates, then it is considered a distinct nosological disorder.

Children as young as infants have been observed to experience sadness as well as several other symptoms of depressive syndrome including irritability, sleep and eating problems, and fatigue. The precise developmental level at which the other symptoms of depressive disorder emerge (e.g., anhedonia, psychomotor changes, low self-worth, guilt, concentration problems, hopelessness, and suicidality) is less clear. Moreover, the extent to which manifestations of depressive symptoms in very young children have continuity with adolescent- and adult-onset mood disorders is still a matter of debate. Nevertheless, there is now general consensus among clinicians and researchers that children can and do experience depressive symptoms and can be diagnosed with depressive disorders. The present chapter reviews the prevalence, phenomenology, course and outcome, comorbidity, and etiology of depressive disorders in children prior to adolescence. Several excellent recent reviews of child and adolescent depression are available (e.g., Birmaher et al., 1996a; Birmaher, Ryan, Williamson, Brent, & Kaufman, 1996b; Milling, 2001). The topics of bipolar depression and treatment are not addressed here because they are covered more extensively in other chapters in this book. Finally, we primarily focus on children, that is, infants, preschoolers, and preadolescents, although we discuss some findings with adolescents when relevant for comparisons with younger children or when studies included children ranging from childhood through adolescence.

PREVALENCE

Major depressive disorder (MDD) is very rare in young children and less common during childhood, with rates not reaching those of adulthood until middle adolescence (Fleming & Offord, 1990). Few large-scale epidemiological studies have examined the prevalence of mood disorders in very young children. Point prevalence rates of MDD in a sample of 1,000 preschool children were found to be about 1% (Kashani & Carlson, 1987).

In their review of epidemiological studies of depressive disorders, Fleming and Offord (1990) included four studies of children aged 12 or younger and concluded that the prevalence rates ranged from .03% to 2.5%. In two studies, MDD was more frequently identified by children than by parents. Since the Fleming and Offord (1990) review, several additional epidemiological studies have reported similar findings. Puura et al. (1997) assessed depressive diagnoses with self-report questionnaires and structured interviews with 8- to 9-year-old children and found prevalence rates of .48% for MDD and .06% for dysthymic disorder (DD). Cohen et al. (1993) reported a prevalence rate of 2% for MDD in children ages 10 to 13 years old based on interviews with parents and children. Polaino-Lorente and Domenech (1993) found in children ages 8 to 11 years old prevalence rates of .6% for MDD and 3% for DD using information from clinicians, teacher rating scales, and peer nominations. The rates were higher (1.8% for MDD, 6.4% for DD) when diagnoses were based on children's self-report questionnaires. Finally, in the Great Smokey Mountain Study of children aged 9, 11, and 13 years old, Costello, Angold, Burns, Erkanli, et al. (1996) reported 3-month prevalence rates based on interviews with both parents and children to be .03% for MDD, .13% for DD, and 1.45% for "depression not otherwise specified." Thus, the rates of diagnosed depressive disorders in preadolescents appears to be relatively low, although the rates tend to be higher for children's compared to parents' report about the children's depression.

The commonly found 2-to-1 female-to-male sex ratio in adults (Weissman & Olfson, 1995) has not been reported consistently in children. In preadolescents, the rate of MDD has been found to be about equal in girls and boys (Angold & Rutter, 1992; Fleming, Offord, & Boyle, 1989), and in some cases higher among boys (Anderson, Williams, McGee, & Silva, 1987; Costello, Angold, Burns, Stangl, et al., 1996). Ryan et al. (1987) reported that 62% of their depressed prepubertal patients were boys. In contrast, Polaino-Lorente and Domenech (1993) found that among children ages 8 to 11 years old the prevalence of DD (but not MDD) was greater in girls than boys.

Thus, the prevalence of diagnosable mood disorders has not really been assessed in infants, has been found to be quite rare in preschool-age children, and is about 3% in preadolescents. The rates tend to be higher based on child self-report compared to others' report. Finally, the 2-to-1 female-to-male ratio of depression is not apparent prior to adolescence.

PHENOMENOLOGY

The existence of depression in infants is still a matter of dispute. Spitz and Wolf (1946; Spitz, 1945) were the first to propose that infants could become depressed, and Trad (1987) has continued to argue that depression in infants exists. Core symptoms of depression that have been observed in infants include withdrawal, sad face, apathy, irritability, eating disturbances, abnormal stranger reactions, fussiness, and tantrums (Bowlby, 1980; Spitz & Wolf, 1946; Trad, 1994). This configuration of symptoms has been considered by some to be a form of depression.

Failure to thrive (FTT), a condition associated with undernutrition in infants, has several similarities to depression. The criterion for diagnosis of FTT is having a weight below the 3rd percentile on Gairdner–Pearson growth charts or body weight that decreases over two major centiles (97%, 90%, 50%, 10%, 3%). Infants with FTT also tend to show psychomotor delay, iron deficiency in their diet, behavioral difficulties, and feeding difficulties that suggest early oral motor dysfunction (Raynor & Rudolf, 1996). Ordinarily no organic disease can account for these symptoms. The main known risk factors for FTT are environmental, particularly poverty, parental psychopathology, maternal isolation, poor parent–child interactions, family dysfunction, and inadequate parental knowledge—all of which also are associated with depression in children (Frank & Drotar, 1994; Raynor & Rudolf, 1996). In addition, characteristics of the child such as low appetite, inadequate feeding skills, and being shy and undemanding can be maladaptive in feeding situations and thereby contribute to FTT (Wright & Birks, 2000). A noninteractive tendency by infants can lead to less responsiveness from parents, which then can contribute to FTT (Frank & Drotar, 1994). As this in turn can lead to greater withdrawal by the infant, a vicious cycle of maladaptive parent–child interactions can be created. Thus, failure to thrive in babies may be one form of depression in infants. More information is needed, however, about the extent to which such infant manifestations of distress share other similarities with childhood and adult mood disorders. For example, do infants with failure to thrive or other depression-like syndromes continue to experience depressive disorders later in life? Do they have similar correlates with regard to family history, neurobiological dysregulation, or psychosocial stress?

For children from preschool through adolescence, the criteria outlined in the *Diagnostic and Statistical Manual of Mental Disorders* (DSM-IV; American Psychiatric Association, 1994) are used to define depressive disorders similarly regardless of developmental level. Two minor variations in DSM-IV are that for children and adolescents, irritability is considered a manifestation of dysphoric mood, and the duration of dysthymia is 1 rather than 2 years. Thus, according to DSM-IV few real developmental differences exist in the symptoms of major depression or dysthymia.

Developmental psychopathologists (Carlson & Garber, 1986; Cicchetti & Schneider-Rosen, 1984), however, have suggested that manifestations of depression might depend on an individual's level of cognitive, social, and physiological development, and therefore the symptoms of depression might not be isomorphic across the life span. The broad criteria that define depression in adults may "need to be translated into age-appropriate guidelines for children, sensitive to developmental changes in the children's experience and expression of depression" (Cicchetti & Schneider-Rosen, 1984, p. 7). Although a core set of depressive symptoms might exist that are common across all ages, other symptoms might be uniquely associated with the syndrome at different developmental levels.

Weiss and Garber (2002) suggested two ways in which there could be developmental differences in depressive symptoms. First, children and adults might differ in how they express particular symptoms, although the basic symptoms would be similar regardless of age. For example, dysphoric mood might be manifest by excessive crying in very young children, nonverbal sadness in school-age children, and irritability in adolescents, but the core mood symptom is essentially the same across these age-specific expressions. Second, the symptoms that comprise the syndrome could differ developmentally. That is, different combinations of symptoms would define the syndrome in children versus adults. This could be because a certain level of cognitive or physiological maturation might be necessary for some depressive symptoms to occur and young children might not yet be developmentally capable of experiencing such symptoms.

The primary implication of this with respect to the phenomenology of depression across development is that some symptoms might be less likely than others to comprise the syndrome at different ages. This would appear as differences between depressed children and depressed adults in the rates of particular depressive symptoms and in the symptom structure of the syndrome. In a meta-analysis of 11 empirical studies that compared the rates of depressive symptoms in different age groups, Weiss and Garber (2002) found developmental effects for 18 of the 29 (62%) core and associated depressive symptoms, although these effects were not consistent across studies. Thus, there were developmental differences in the rates at which at least some depressive symptoms were endorsed.

Weiss and Garber (2002) also reviewed five studies that had compared the structure of depression at different age levels. Two of these studies found a similar factor structure across ages, two found developmental differences, and one found mixed results. Thus, contrary to current views in the literature (e.g., Ryan et al., 1987), the evidence does not support the conclusion that there are no developmental differences in the rates of depressive symptoms or that there are differences in the structure of depressive syndrome across development. Indeed, Goodyer (1996) asserted that "the suggestion that the clinical presentation of major depression varies with age is far from resolved and more developmentally sensitive studies are required" (p. 407).

COURSE AND OUTCOME

In general, the duration of episodes of clinically diagnosed depression in children (Kovacs, Feinberg, Crouse-Novak, Paulauskas, & Finkelstein, 1984a; Kovacs et al., 1984b) has been found to be similar to those reported in adults (Coryell et al., 1994). Kovacs and colleagues (1984a, 1984b) reported that in 8- to 13-year-old children, major depressive disorder tended to be acute, had a mean length of episode of about 32 weeks, a median length of episode of 9 months, and the maximal recovery rate of 92% of the sample was reached at about 18 months from onset. For dysthymia, eventually 91% recovered, although this took almost 9 years. The median episode length for dysthymia was 4 years.

Early-onset depressions tend to recur, and younger age of onset significantly predicts relapse (e.g., Keller, Lavori, Lewis, & Klerman, 1983). Kovacs et al. (1984b) found that the cumulative probability of a recurrent episode of major depression was .72 over 5 years from the onset of the disorder. In a 9-year follow-up of these same children, Kovacs (1996a) reported that 80% of children with dysthymia and 50% of children with MDD had subsequent bouts of depression. Moreover, 15% of those with MDD and 13% of those with dysthymia developed a bipolar disorder (Kovacs, 1996a). Asarnow et al. (1988) reported that 45% of their sample of depressed inpatients were rehospitalized within 2 years, McCauley et al. (1993) reported a 25% relapse rate within 1 year and 54% within 3 years, and Emslie et al. (1997a) found that 47.2% of their inpatients ages 8 to 17 years old had a recurrence within 1 year and 69.4% had one by 2 years from the offset of the index episode. Thus, a prior history of a depressive disorder is a significant risk factor for subsequent depressive episodes.

Evidence of continuity from childhood to adult depression is mixed. "Catch-up" longitudinal studies (e.g., Harrington, Fudge, Rutter, Pickles, & Hill, 1990) show that individuals who were depressed as children and adolescents tended to have recurrent episodes of depression as adults. Moreover, depressed children were more likely to have subsequent episodes of depression than were those who had had other psychiatric disorders (Harrington et al., 1990). In contrast, Weissman et al. (1999) reported no significant differences in the rates of depressive disorders between individuals with and without histories of prepubertal-onset depression. One important characteristic of the study by Weissman et al.

(1999) was that the groups differed with regard to gender; the depressed group was 62% male, whereas the normal controls were only 47% male. Thus, it is possible that prepubertal onset of depression in males is less recurrent and is more likely associated with subsequent alcohol abuse/dependence.

Harrington et al. (1990) reported that children with prepubertal onset of depression were at significantly lower risk of having major depression as adults than were postpubertal patients. These results are in contrast to the finding that early-onset mood disorders are considered a more severe and recurrent form of the disorder that are associated with increased familial loading of depression (e.g., Weissman, Warner, Wickramaratne, & Prusoff, 1988) and with increased risk of relapse (Keller et al., 1983). The finding by Weissman et al. (1999) of significantly higher rates of MDD in first-degree relatives of children with prepubertal onset depressions that recurred compared to those that did not recur may help to explain these discrepant findings. Thus, family history of mood disorders may be related to the likelihood of recurrence of prepubertal onset depressions.

Finally, stability of depressive symptoms in children and adolescents also has been found (Garrison, Jackson, Marsteller, McKeown, & Addy, 1990; Verhulst & van der Ende, 1992). Approximately one-third of those with elevated levels of self-reported depressive symptoms continue to report high levels of depression from 6 to 24 months later, although evidence also exists of change in depressive symptoms over time (Garrison et al., 1990). Parents' reports of children's anxious/depressive symptoms on the Child Behavior Checklist also have been found to be stable over 6 years (Verhulst & van der Ende, 1992). Thus, depressive symptoms tend to be quite stable over time, although some individuals do show change as well. The issues of continuity, stability, and change in depressive symptoms and disorders in children with different age of onsets from infancy through adulthood should be the focus of further study. Moreover, identification of factors that are associated with variability in episode length, recurrence, and relapse also needs to be investigated further.

COMORBIDITY

Estimates of the rate of comorbidity for children with depression range from 53% (Angold & Costello, 1993) to between 80 and 95% (Kovacs, 1996b). Comorbidity affects risk for recurrent depression, duration of depressive episodes, suicide attempts and behaviors, utilization of mental health services, and functional outcomes (Birmaher et al., 1996a; Hammen & Compas, 1994). Dysthymia has the highest rate of comorbidity; 30% of children with MDD had underlying dysthymia and 70% of early-onset dysthymia patients had a superimposed MDD (Kovacs, 1994). Children with such "double depression" have more severe and longer depressive episodes, a higher rate of other comorbid disorders, more suicidality, and worse social impairment. Less comorbidity (50–60%) has been found to be associated with adjustment disorders with depressed mood than with either dysthymia or MDD (Kovacs, Gatsonis, Paulauskas, & Richards, 1989).

Common comorbid diagnoses with dysthymia are anxiety disorders, conduct disorder, ADHD, and enuresis or encopresis; dysthymia has a 15% rate of comorbidity with two or more other disorders (Kovacs, 1994). Disruptive disorders often are comorbid with MDD, with estimates ranging from 10–80% (Anderson et al., 1987; Hammen & Compas, 1994). Estimates of the comorbidity of MDD with anxiety range from 30–75% (Hammen & Compas, 1994; Kovacs et al., 1989). Comorbidity of depressive and anxiety disorders is so high that some have challenged the discriminant validity of the two diagnoses (Achenbach, 1991; Patterson, Greising, Hyland, & Burger, 1994). Others have suggested that anxiety and depression share a single underlying process referred to as "negative affectivity" (Watson & Clark, 1984).

There is some evidence that anxiety precedes depression in children. Kovacs et al. (1989) reported that in a sample of depressed children comorbid with anxiety, two-thirds had anxiety before depression. However, longitudinal studies have not yet examined the extent to which diagnosis of anxiety disorders are followed by diagnoses of depressive disorders in children. With regard to the relation between anxious and depressive symptoms, Cole, Peeke, Martin, Truglio, and Seroczynski (1998) found in a group of 330 elementary school children that self- and parent-reported anxiety symptoms predicted depressive symptoms at follow-ups conducted from 6 months to 3 years later. The converse, however, was not true. That is, depressive symptoms in children did not predict anxious symptoms.

Other studies using dimensional measures also have shown high levels of covariation between depression and other syndromes. Self-report measures of anxiety and depression have been found to correlate between .60 and .80 (Brady & Kendall, 1992). Correlations between aggressive and depressive symptoms have ranged from .40 to .73 after controlling for shared method variance in reports of children, parents, and peers (Garber, Quiggle, Panak, & Dodge, 1991).

Thus, comorbidity between depression and other internalizing and externalizing problems in children is very common. This raises questions about whether depression in children is a distinct clinical entity that can be differentiated from other forms of psychopathology, and whether the current nomenclature needs to be adjusted to more accurately reflect such covariation among syndromes. Other questions needing to be explored are: (1) To what extent does the covariation of depression with other syndromes change with development? (2) What processes explain such developmental changes? and (3) What mechanisms account for comorbidity between depression and other particular forms of psychopathology (e.g., anxiety, aggression)?

ETIOLOGY

A comprehensive review of etiological theories and the evidence supporting them is beyond the scope of this chapter. Rather, we briefly describe the leading theories of depression and review the relevant evidence in children. Much research on the etiology of depression in children has been based on the downward extension of theories originally developed to explain depression in adults. If depression is essentially the same across development, then similar causal processes should underlie the disorder at any age. Therefore, it would not make sense to have different theories of childhood and adult depression. Rather, theories of depression would need to consider developmental variation in the characteristics of depression (e.g., epidemiology, phenomenology, course), and account for these differences. On the other hand, if child and adult depression are different, then different theories might be appropriate. Similar to juvenile- and adult-onset types of diabetes, which share some commonalities but also have important differences with regard to course, correlates, and treatment, if there are distinct child- and adult-onset types of depression, then different theories would be needed to explain them.

Cole's (1991) competency-based model of childhood depression proposes that evaluations of competence by important others (e.g., peers, teachers) predict self-perceived competence and depressive symptoms. This model has found some support when tested with children (Cole, 1991; Cole & Turner, 1993) and might explain depression across the life span, although it would need to be appropriately modified and investigated with older age groups.

The converse situation has been more typical. That is, most models of depression have been proposed to explain depression in adults. The validity of these models with regard to depression in children has been the focus of research over the last two decades. Although many theories of depression have been proposed, we highlight here those for which there is the most empirical support: genes, neurobiology, stressful life events, negative cognitions, and interpersonal relationships, as well as the interactions among these factors.

Genes

Family, twin, and adoption studies have yielded varying results regarding genetic contributions to individual differences in depression (Blehar, Weissman, Gershon, & Hirschfeld, 1988). Family studies of depressive disorders have shown that children of depressed parents are approximately three times more likely to experience a depressive episode (Beardslee, Versage, & Gladstone, 1998), are at increased risk of experiencing early-onset depressions (Weissman et al., 1987), and have longer depressive episode lengths compared to children of nondepressed parents (Warner, Weissman, Fendrich, Wickramaratne, & Moreau, 1992). In addition, the risk of having a depressive episode is higher in relatives of depressed children than in relatives of psychiatric and normal controls (Kovacs, Devlin, Pollock, Richards, & Mukerji, 1997).

However, family studies confound genetic and shared environmental effects. Familial depression also could be due to psychosocial factors such as maladaptive parenting styles, marital dysfunction, and stress, which also are associated with parental psychopathology (Goodman & Gotlib, 1999). Children exposed to these conditions early in development might be especially vulnerable to developing mood disorders. That is, childhood-onset depressions in particular may be associated with more severe environmental stressors or traumas (Nolen-Hoeksema, Girgus, & Seligman, 1992; Post, 1992).

Twin studies with children have yielded heritability estimates comparable to those found in adults (McGuffin, Katz, Watkins, & Rutherford, 1996). Evidence from twin studies indicates that genes account for approximately 30–50% of the variance in child-reported depression. Nonshared environmental factors have been found to play a moderate role in both child (.59 for girls, .70 for boys) and parent report (.35 for mothers, .40 for fathers) of children's depression (Eaves et al., 1997). Genetic and environmental influences on individual differences in depression, however, differ as a function of the informant (Eaves et al., 1997; Wierzbicki, 1987) and age (Eley, Deater-Deckard, Fombonne, Fulker, & Plomin, 1998; Thaper & McGuffin, 1994). Heritability estimates tend to be larger for parent compared to child report of children's depression. Early-onset (i.e., < 20 years old) depressions have been found to be associated with greater risk for depression in family members (Weissman et al., 1986, 1988). Alternatively, childhood depression has been associated with greater environmental contributions (Thaper & McGuffin, 1994). It is unclear whether earlier onset depression is due to greater genetic influences or factors within the shared environment of families with a depressed proband (Rutter et al., 1990). Moreover, age-related changes in heritability estimates can result from different gene effects at different ages, the same genes impacting the phenotypical expression of a trait at different ages, or environmental influences that vary with development (Plomin, 1990).

Adoption designs traditionally have been able to directly disentangle shared and nonshared environmental effects. Whereas adopted children share an environment but not their genes with their adoptive family, they share their genes but not their environment with their biological relatives. Using an offspring design combined with a sibling design, Eley et al. (1998) assessed the variance accounted for by genetic and environmental factors in child- and parent-reported depression. Neither the sibling nor the parent–offspring correlations showed a significant genetic effect. There was evidence of some shared environmental effects, although these were greater for parents' reports, indicating possible inflation due to method bias in the relation between mothers' report of their own and their children's symptoms. The results also suggested a substantial role for nonshared environmental effects.

Thus, findings from twin and adoption studies of childhood depression differ. Whereas twin studies suggest a moderate role for genetic influences on individual differences in depression, adoption studies typically have reported negligible genetic effects. Twin studies report nonsignificant effects of shared environment, whereas adoption studies suggest a small but significant effect of shared environment. Both designs provide evidence of moderate-to-large nonshared environmental influences. Plomin (1990) has suggested that differences in findings for twin and adoption studies are due to the larger heritability estimates for nonadditive effects shared by monozygotic twins compared to dyzogotic twins, parents and offspring, or siblings.

Finally, heritability of depression may vary as a function of symptom heterogeneity and severity. In adults, environmental factors tend to make a greater contribution to mild depression, whereas genes play a larger role in more severe cases (Rutter et al., 1990). In children, studies that have evaluated differences in genetic and environmental effects have reported mixed results. In two such studies (Eley, 1997; Rende, Plomin, Reiss, & Hetherington; 1993), child report on the CDI (Kovacs, 1981) was used to establish groups of varying severity. In a sample of 9- to 18-year-olds, Rende et al. (1993) found smaller genetic effects and significant shared environment effects in children with greater severity of symptoms. In contrast, Eley (1997) found in a sample of 8- to 16-year-olds similar heritability estimates for severe groups but less influence of shared environmental factors. There were slight differences in age that may explain the conflicting results for environmental effects, suggesting that environmental factors may be more important as children get older. In addition, the cutoff points used to identify the groups fell within the mild-to-moderate range of depressive symptoms, (i.e., between 13 and 17 on the CDI). Thus, the contribution of genes and environment to depression at varying levels of chronicity and severity needs to be explored further in children.

In sum, behavioral genetic designs provide evidence of both genetic and environmental effects on childhood depression (Plomin, 1990). Estimates of heritability tend to be moderate and shared environment effects tend to be small. However, both tend to vary as a function of informant, age, and severity of depressive symptoms. Although vulnerability to depression clearly has a genetic component, it is not yet clear what is inherited that places an individual at greater risk. Genetic factors may contribute to neurobiological and/or cognitive vulnerabilities, which then interact with the environment to produce depressive symptoms. Nonshared environmental effects emerge as the largest environmental influence on individual differences in childhood depression (Plomin, 1990); this also is true for most forms of psychopathology, certain personality traits, and cognitive abilities (Plomin, 1990). Additional research is needed to illuminate the mechanisms through which genes influence individual differences in depression as well as their potentially complex interactions with environmental factors.

Neurobiology

Psychobiological studies of depression in children have focused primarily on dysregulation in neuroendocrine and neurochemical systems and in disturbances in sleep architecture (Dahl & Ryan, 1996; Emslie, Weinberg, Kennard, & Kowatch, 1994). In addition, a few studies have investigated functional and anatomical brain differences in depressed and high-risk children (Dawson, Frey, Panagiotides, Osterling, & Hessl, 1997; Field, Fox, Pickens, & Nawrocki, 1995).

Psychoneuroendocrinology

Dysregulation of the human stress response in the hypothalamic–pituitary–adrenal (HPA) axis has been found in depressed individuals. Hypothalamic peptides act on the pituitary-releasing hormones that control the release of cortisol from the adrenal glands. Cortisol prepares the body to deal with stress and provides inhibitory feedback to the hypothalamus to prevent excessive production.

Gunnar (1989) found that the HPA axis is active from birth. Large increases in cortisol levels during infancy are correlated with stress, although quiescence also is associated with cortisol elevation at times. Some neuroendocrine changes have been associated with depression-like symptoms in infants, such as prolonged crying, withdrawal, and eventual apathy in response to stress, particularly separation (Trad, 1994). In addition, there is tremendous variability in the magnitude of cortisol response to stress among infants.

HPA axis functioning typically has been assessed through downstream hormonal measures of cortisol and growth hormone at both baseline levels and in response to physiological challenge (Ryan & Dahl, 1993). Whereas most studies have not found differences in basal cortisol secretion between depressed and nondepressed children (e.g., Kutcher et al., 1991), a few have shown elevated cortisol secretion near sleep onset in suicidal and depressed inpatients (Dahl et al., 1991a). Goodyer et al. (1996) also found differences in evening cortisol secretion between patients with major depressive disorder and normal controls. In general, however, depressed and nondepressed children have not been found to differ on baseline cortisol levels (Ryan, 1998).

In contrast to baseline assessments, challenging a regulatory system allows observation of its functioning when stressed. Depressive abnormalities in the HPA axis response to physiological stress have been investigated with the dexamethasone suppression test (DST). Numerous studies with in- and outpatient groups of children and adolescents have found greater sensitivity in children than in adolescents (58% vs. 44%), and in inpatients compared to outpatients (61% vs. 29%), but greater specificity in adolescents; that is, comparisons with psychiatric controls were stronger in adolescent samples (85%) than in child samples (60%) (Dahl & Ryan, 1996; Ryan & Dahl, 1993). DST nonsuppression also has been associated with concurrent suicidal behavior (Pfeffer, Stokes, & Shindledecker, 1991) and a prior history of major depressive disorder (Klee & Garfinkel, 1984).

Thus, basal cortisol levels have not been reliably associated with depression in children, although evening hypersecretion has been found to be associated with greater severity of symptoms (Dahl et al., 1991a). DST nonsuppression distinguishes groups of depressed children from both psychiatric and normal controls, but results are variable and some studies have not found significant sensitivity (Dahl et al., 1992a). Developmental changes in the HPA axis may be responsible for the lack of consistent findings in children as opposed to the stronger findings reported in adults (Halbreich, Asnis, Zumoff, Nathan, & Shindledecker, 1984).

Most studies of HPA axis abnormalities have been cross-sectional comparisons of children with MDD versus other psychiatric diagnoses and normal controls. In a sample of children ages 8 through 16 years old, Goodyer, Herbert, and Altham (1998) found that the nighttime ratio of cortisol to dehydroepiandrosterone (DHEA), an adrenal hormone, was higher in children with MDD who had not remitted by the 9-month follow-up compared to depressed children who had remitted. The extent to which HPA axis dysregulation is a stable vulnerability marker in children needs to be examined further. In addition, prospective studies of HPA axis functioning in children who may be at risk for depression are needed to clarify the role that dysregulation in this system plays in onset of depression in children.

Research on growth hormone regulation in children also has been used to study HPA axis functioning. Growth hormone (GH) is normatively secreted by the pituitary gland and functions as a growth-promoting agent throughout the body. In children, it is mostly secreted during sleep (Ryan & Dahl, 1993). Some studies have found an increase in unstimulated GH secretion at night in depressed children (Puig-Antich et al., 1984a), whereas others have found blunted GH secretion throughout the day (Meyer et al., 1991). In response to pharmacologic challenges, which attempt to artificially stimulate the growth hormone system, depressed children typically show blunted GH secretion. Studies comparing children with MDD to normal controls have found a blunted GH response to stimulation with insulin-induced hypoglycemia, arginine, clonidine, and growth hormone releasing hormone (GHRH) (Meyer et al., 1991; Ryan et al., 1994). Jensen and Garfinkel (1990) reported a blunted GH response to L-dopa and clonidine in prepubertal boys compared to normal controls. Children with endogenous depressions have demonstrated a blunted response to hypoglycemic stimulation in comparison to nondepressed neurotic children (Puig-Antich et al., 1984b), and they continue to hyposecrete GH in response to the insulin tolerance test after remission (Puig-Antich et al., 1984c).

In addition, Birmaher et al. (1999) reported that offspring of depressed parents (high risk) who themselves had not yet had a depressive episode showed a blunted GH response to administration of GHRH, but no differences in baseline GH compared to children with no familial psychiatric history (low risk). Moreover, the high-risk group did not differ from currently depressed children in GH response. Thus, growth hormone system dysregulation may be a vulnerability marker for depression. These high-risk children need to be followed, however, in order to determine whether they eventually develop depressive disorders.

Neurotransmitters

A second important area of biological dysregulation among depressed patients is in their neurochemistry, with serotonin, norepinephrine, and acetylcholine particularly implicated in the pathophysiology of mood disorders (Gold, Goodwin, & Chrousos; 1988). In comparison to normal controls, depressed children demonstrate hyposecretion of melatonin (Cavallo, Holt, Hejazi, Richards, & Meyer, 1987), and a blunted cortisol response and increased prolactin response after administration of L–5-hydroxytryptophan (L-5HTP), primarily in girls (Ryan et al., 1992). Similar results have been found in never-depressed children with high familial loadings for depression (Birmaher et al., 1997), suggesting a serotonergic system marker for depression. Birmaher et al. (1997) assessed central serotonergic functioning in high-risk, currently depressed, and low-risk children, ages 6 through 12 years old, before and after administration of L-5HTP. Although the groups did not differ at baseline, in response to the pharmacologic challenge, both high-risk and currently depressed children showed a blunted cortisol response compared to normal controls, and high-risk and currently depressed girls secreted more prolactin than control girls. No group differences were evident with regard to growth hormone secretion after challenge.

Investigation into the effectiveness of SSRIs in reducing depressive symptoms in children also has implicated serotonergic system dysregulation in childhood depression (Emslie et al., 1997b). Thus, overall there is evidence of neurotransmitter involvement in child depression. Moreover, serotonergic system dysregulation may be a risk factor for depression since it has been found in both high-risk and currently depressed children.

Functional and Anatomical Brain Differences

Abnormal functioning of the prefrontal cortex–limbic–striatal regions in the brain as well as reduced prefrontal volume has been associated with adult depression (Powell & Miklowitz,

1994). This finding, however, has yet to be replicated with children. Resting frontal brain asymmetry also has been linked with depression in adults and appears to persist into remission (Tomarken & Keener, 1998). Tomarken and Keener (1998) proposed that the prefrontal cortex is linked to approach/withdrawal systems and that the relative left frontal hypoactivation associated with depression might result in a bias away from approach and in favor of withdrawal, which may represent a behavioral precursor to the anhedonia typical of depressed individuals.

In children, a few studies have found left frontal hypoactivation in infants of depressed mothers compared to infants of nondepressed mothers (Dawson et al., 1997; Jones, Field, Fox, Lundy, & Davalos, 1997). Tomarken, Simien, and Garber (1994) showed that offspring of depressed mothers demonstrated left frontal hypoactivation relative to a low-risk group, suggesting a possible vulnerability marker for depression that was independent of current mood state or prior depressive episodes. More studies of functional and anatomical brain differences need to be conducted with preadolescents, particularly those who are at increased risk for depression.

Sleep Architecture Abnormalities

Although children subjectively report sleep disturbance, electroencephalogram (EEG) results are less consistent in children than in adults (Ryan & Dahl, 1993). Depressed children show some sleep anomalies such as prolonged sleep latencies, reduced REM latencies, especially in more severely depressed children, and decreased sleep efficiency (Emslie, Rush, Weinberg, Rintelmann, & Roffwarg, 1990; Dahl et al., 1991b). Several studies, however, have failed to find differences between depressed and nondepressed children in EEG sleep patterns (Dahl & Ryan, 1996). The absence of consistent patterns of sleep abnormalities in depressed youth has been attributed to the role of maturational changes. Dahl and Ryan (1996) suggested that the sleep of young children is difficult to disrupt because they are such deep sleepers. As children get older, however, this protective aspect of sleep begins to decrease. It may not be until adolescence or adulthood that the sleep disturbances associated with depression become evident.

In summary, the neurobiological literature in children is variable, although not inconsistent with adult findings. Depressed children show some neuroendocrine and neurochemical dysregulation, particularly in response to challenge. There also is some evidence of functional and anatomical brain differences in depressed children compared to normal controls and in offspring of depressed mothers. Sleep disturbances, although experientially common in depressed children, have not been consistently found in sleep studies of depressed children, possibly due to maturational factors (Dahl & Ryan, 1996). More longitudinal studies are needed that follow children with neurobiological abnormalities to determine if they subsequently develop mood disorders.

Stressful Life Events

Stress plays a prominent role in most theories of depression, and a clear empirical link exists between stressful life events and depression in children (Compas, 1987). In infants, depressive symptoms most often have been associated with stressful life circumstances and often are responsive to changes in the environment (Moreau, 1996). One stressor that particularly has been linked with depression in infants is separation. Spitz and Wolf (1946) noted that a common feature in dysphoric infants is separation from the mother between the ages of 6 and 8 months. Separation in young children has been found to be associated with grief responses characterized by negative changes in sleep patterns, activity, heart rate, temperature, monoamine systems, immune function, and endocrine function (Kalin & Carnes, 1984). Spitz (1945) noted the phenomenon of *hospitalism*, referring to evidence that infants subjected to long hospital stays experienced a number of psychological difficulties. Longer and more frequent hospital stays and earlier age of entering the hospital were associated with more depressive symptoms in infants (Moreau, 1996).

In school-age children, cross-sectional studies using either life events checklists or interview methods consistently have shown that depressive symptoms and disorders are significantly associated with both minor and major undesirable life events in children, particularly cumulative or chronic stressors, and negative life events are more prevalent among depressed compared to nondepressed children (e.g., Compas, 1987; Goodyer, Herbert, Tamplin, & Altham, 2000). Cross-sectional studies, however, are not informative about the direction of the relation between stress and depression. Given the association between dependent stressors and depression (Williamson et al., 1998), it is possible that depression contributes to the occurrence of stressors. Depressed individuals have been found to generate many of the stressors they encounter, and these stressors then serve to exacerbate and maintain the depressive symptoms (e.g., Hammen, 1991). Therefore, both laboratory and prospective studies of stress have been used to examine issues of direction of effects.

Animal studies that manipulate stress in the laboratory have shown that antenatal stress impacts the developing physiology of the fetus and later physiological and behavioral outcomes in offspring of stressed rat and primate mothers. Henry, Kabbaj, Simon, Le Moal, and Maccari (1994) found that prenatally stressed rat pups had an elevated corticosterone response to novel environments and reduced corticosteroid receptors in the hippocampus, suggesting that prenatal stress may affect the neurobiological development of systems associated with depression in children (i.e., the HPA axis). Behaviorally, rat pups stressed *in utero* had greater distress and defensive behavior (e.g., Takahashi, Baker, & Kalin, 1990) and reduced environmental exploration when they were exposed to aversive or stressful conditions (Poltyrev, Keshet, Kay, & Weinstock, 1996).

Prepartum exposure to stress also may result in hyperresponsiveness to later stressors. Clarke and Schneider (1993; Schneider, 1992) randomly assigned pregnant rhesus monkeys to stress and control conditions. The prenatally stressed offspring were less likely than control offspring to play and explore the environment and more likely to engage in clinging, which is associated with distress in primates. In addition, the prenatally stressed monkeys had significantly higher levels of cortisol and tended to have higher ACTH levels when blood levels were taken while the monkeys were anesthetized. In stressful situations while awake, the prenatally stressed offspring had marginally higher levels of ACTH but did not differ significantly from control offspring on levels of cortisol. Clarke and Schneider (1993; Schneider, 1992) suggested that HPA axis functioning is implicated in the hyperresponsiveness of prenatally stressed rhesus monkeys to later environmental stressors.

Thus, animal models indicate that stress that occurs as early as conception can influence outcomes that have been associated with depression in humans. In human infants, stress during pregnancy is associated with negative outcomes for offspring (e.g., Ward, 1991). Although the mechanisms by which stress impacts the developing fetus are still unknown, Glover (1997) hypothesized that fetal neurophysiological development may be sensitive to the intrauterine hormonal environment, and neurophysiological vulnerability (e.g., HPA axis dysregulation) may make these offspring more sensitive to stress and thereby predispose them to depression as they mature.

Prospective studies in which stressors are assessed prior to the onset of symptoms can be informative about the temporal relation between stress and depression. Several prospective studies in children have shown that stress predicts depressive symptoms (Goodyer et al., 2000; Little & Garber, 2000; Nolen-Hoeksema et al., 1992). The relations tend to be stronger predicting children's self-reports compared to parents' reports of children's depressive symptoms (Compas, Howell, Phares, Williams, & Giunta, 1989).

Fewer studies have examined the contribution of negative life events to the first onset of depressive disorders in children. Stress has predicted the onset of depressive symptoms in previously asymptomatic adolescents (Aseltine, Gore, & Colton, 1994) and the onset of clinically significant depressive episodes, controlling for prior symptom levels in children and adolescents (Garber, Martin, & Keiley, 2001; Goodyer et al., 2000; McFarlane, Bellissimo, Norman, & Lange, 1994; Monroe, Rohde, Seeley, & Lewinsohn, 1999). Only three of these studies (Aseltine et al., 1994; Garber et al., 2001; Monroe et al., 1999), however, controlled for lifetime history of MDD to rule out the possibility that earlier depressive disorder contributed to onset.

Reports of stressful life events have been shown to increase for both boys and girls from childhood through adolescence with increases being greater for girls (Ge, Lorenz, Conger, Elder, & Simons, 1994), paralleling increases in rates of depression for boys and girls (Hankin et al., 1998). However, few studies have found that gender moderates the relation between stress and depression. Cohen, Burt, and Bjork, (1987) reported that negative events predicted depressive symptoms in girls who had experienced minimal positive events in the same time interval, and Ge et al. (1994) showed that growth of stressful life events predicted growth in depressive symptoms for girls but not for boys.

Although no one specific type of stressful event invariably leads to depression in children, events such as disappointments, loss, separation, or interpersonal conflict or rejection are particularly linked with depression (Goodyer et al., 2000; Monroe et al., 1999; Panak & Garber, 1992; Reinherz et al., 1989; Rueter, Scaramella, Wallace, & Conger, 1999). This is especially probable for individuals who tend to be more socially dependent or sociotropic. According to the specific vulnerability hypothesis (e.g., Beck, 1983), individuals whose self-esteem is derived from interpersonal relationships (sociotropy) are at increased risk for depression when they experience stressors within the social domain; in contrast, those who derive their self-worth from achievement-related goals are at greater risk for depression when they encounter failure. Studies investigating this specific vulnerability hypothesis in children have been supportive (Hammen & Goodman-Brown, 1990; Little & Garber, 2000). In a short-term prospective study, Little and Garber (2000) found that among boys who experienced negative social stressors, those who were high in interpersonal connectedness reported increases in depressive symptoms. For girls, level of social stressors and connectedness each directly and significantly predicted depressive symptoms.

Thus, prospective studies have found support for the contribution of stressful life events to increases in depressive symptoms and the onset of depressive disorders in children, although more such studies have been conducted with adolescents. When the stressors that occur fall into an individual's particular area of vulnerability, the likelihood of depression is even greater. Identifying individuals' specific areas of concern should improve our ability to predict who is most likely to become depressed and under what circumstances (Monroe & Roberts, 1990).

In summary, a clear link exists between stress and depression. But by what mechanisms does stress increase an individual's vulnerability to depression? Although stressors often precede mood disorders, not all individuals exposed to stressors become depressed. That is, there is not a perfect correspondence between exposure to negative life events and the onset of depressive symptoms or disorders. Rather, how individuals interpret and respond to events differentiates who does and does not become depressed. Much of the individual variability is due to differences in appraisals of the meaning of the events with regard to the self and future. Such appraisal processes are central to cognitive theories of depression.

Negative Cognitions

According to cognitive theories of depression (Abramson, Metalsky, & Alloy, 1989; Beck, 1967), depressed individuals have more negative beliefs about themselves and their future, and tend to make global, stable, and internal attributions for negative events. When confronted with stressful life events, individuals who have such cognitive tendencies will appraise the stressors and their consequences more negatively, and hence are more likely to become depressed than are individuals who do not have such cognitive styles. These are essentially cognitive diathesis–stress models because cognitions are presumed to contribute to the onset of depression primarily in the context of stressful life events.

Depressed children report the hypothesized depressogenic attributional style, negative expectations and hopelessness, cognitive distortions, and cognitive errors more than nondepressed children (Garber & Hilsman, 1992; Gladstone & Kaslow, 1995). Although such covariation between negative cognitions and current depression is consistent with there being a cognitive vulnerability, the alternative that cognitions are a concomitant or consequence of a depressive state cannot be ruled out from cross-sectional studies (Barnett & Gotlib, 1988). Negative cognitions could be the result of the underlying depressive process and hold no particular causal status. Depressions that are clearly caused by a biological process, such as Cushing's disease, have been found to be characterized by some of the same kinds of negative cognitions found in other depressions (Hollon, 1992). Thus, negative cognitions could simply be a symptom of the depressive disorder.

In addition, the experience of depression itself could lead to depressogenic cognitions. Nolen-Hoeksema et al. (1992) reported that children with relatively higher levels of depressive symptoms had more pessimistic explanatory styles over time than did their less depressed peers. Moreover, explanatory style became more pessimistic over time in children with higher levels of depressive symptoms, even after their level of depression declined. Nolen-Hoeksema et al. (1992) concluded that "a period of depression during childhood can lead to the development of a fixed and more pessimistic explanatory style, which remains with a child after his or her depression has begun to subside" (p. 418). Given the differences in the ages of the subjects studied in the Nolen-Hoeksema et al. versus adult studies that have not found such evidence (e,g,, Lewinsohn, Steinmetz, Larson, & Franklin, 1981), it is possible that the "scarring" effect of depression on cognitive style occurs earlier in development.

Cole and colleagues (e.g., Cole, Martin, Peeke, Seroczynski, & Hoffman, 1998; Hoffman, Cole, Martin, Tram, & Seroczynski, 2000) have conducted several longitudinal studies of the relation between children's perceptions of their competence in multiple domains and depressive symptoms. Children's underestimation of their competence relative to others' perceptions predicted children's depressive symptoms 6 months later, controlling for prior depressive symptoms. Prior depression, however, also predicted children's underestimation of competence. Thus, the relation between perceived competence and depressive symptoms in children appears to be bidirectional.

Some have argued that if cognitive style is a vulnerability to depression, then it should be a stable characteristic present both during and after depressive episodes (Barnett & Gotlib, 1988), whereas others have questioned this assertion (Just, Abramson, & Alloy, 2001). If negative cognitions are a stable characteristic of depression-vulnerable individuals, then persons whose depression has remitted should continue to report a more negative cognitive style than never-depressed individuals, although possibly not at the same level as those who are currently depressed. The few studies to examine this issue in children have not found cognitive differences between remitted and nondepressed individuals (Asarnow & Bates, 1988; McCauley, Mitchell, Burke, & Moss, 1988).

Taken together, these mixed findings have been used to argue against there being a stable cognitive vulnerability to depression (e.g., Segal & Dobson, 1992). Just et al. (2001), however, have noted several limitations of these kinds of "remission" studies, including that (1) treatment could have altered formerly depressed patients' cognitions; (2) the formerly depressed group might have been heterogeneous with regard to cognitive style; and (3) cognitive style might need to be activated to be assessed properly. Thus, the stability of the cognitive vulnerability needs to be studied further.

Whereas some prospective studies have found a significant predictive relation between cognitions and depression in children and adolescents (e.g., Hoffman et al., 2000) others have not (e.g., Goodyer et al., 2000). Abramson et al. (1989) argued that longitudinal results have been mixed because some studies have tested a "cognitive trait theory" in which only the relation between the cognitive variables and depression was assessed, rather than testing a "cognition-stress interaction theory" in which both the cognitive predisposition and negative life events were considered in interaction with one another. Whereas a cognitive-trait theory would predict that all individuals who have the depressogenic cognitive predisposition should become depressed, the cognitive diathesis–stress model improves predictability by suggesting that cognitively vulnerable individuals will become depressed when they are faced with important stressful events.

In addition, developmental theorists (Cole & Turner, 1993; Nolen-Hoeksema et al., 1992; Weisz, Southam-Gero, & McCarty, 2001) have suggested that negative cognitions emerge over time and that their relation with depression becomes stronger with development. For example, in a longitudinal study of children in grades 3 through 8, Nolen-Hoeksema et al. (1992) showed that attributional style alone and in conjunction with stress significantly predicted depressive symptoms in the older but not in the younger children. Similarly, in a cross-sectional comparison of children in grades 4, 6, and 8, Turner and Cole (1994) found that negative cognitions contributed to the prediction of depressive symptoms for the oldest children, but not for the two younger groups. Thus, the relation between the cognition-stress interaction and depressive symptoms appears to be increasing from middle childhood to early adolescence.

Prospective studies in children have found support for the cognitive diathesis–stress model of depression. Garber and colleagues (Hilsman & Garber, 1995; Panak & Garber, 1992; Robinson, Garber, & Hilsman, 1995) showed in three different short-term longitudinal studies using different stressors (grades, peer rejection, and school transition), and different time periods, that cognitions (attributions, self-worth) measured before the stressors occurred moderated the effect of the stressors on depressive symptoms in children. Among children who experienced high levels of stress, the relation between negative cognitions about the self or causes of events and depressive symptoms was stronger compared to those without such negative cognitions. Thus, explicit tests of the cognitive-stress interaction in children have been supportive of cognitive models of depression.

If negative cognitions contribute to the development of mood disorders, then "high-risk" offspring of depressed parents should be more likely to exhibit a cognitive vulnerability than children whose parents have not experienced mood disorders. Indeed, children of depressed mothers report significantly lower perceived self-worth and a more depressive attributional style than do children of well mothers (Garber & Robinson, 1997; Goodman, Adamson, Riniti, & Cole, 1994, Jaenicke et al., 1987). Garber and Robinson (1997) found that particularly offspring of mothers with more chronic histories of depression reported significantly more negative cognitions than did children of mothers with no history of psychiatric disorders. Even when children's current level of depressive symptoms was controlled, high- and low-risk children continued to differ with regard to their attributional style and perceived self-worth. Thus, children who are at risk for depression, but who have not yet experienced depression themselves, have been found to report a more negative cognitive style that might be a vulnerability to later depression.

In summary, correlational, predictive, and offspring studies have provided evidence that there is a cognitive style that may be a vulnerability to depressive symptoms and disorders in children. This cognitive style involves beliefs about the self and explanations about the causes of negative events. More adequate studies examining the stability of this cognitive vulnerability need to be conducted (Just et al., 2001). In addition, future studies need to examine further the extent to which this cognitive vulnerability develops over time (Cole & Turner, 1993), and whether or not it needs to be primed in children (Ingram, Miranda, & Segal, 1998).

Interpersonal Relationships

Interpersonal perspectives on depression emphasize the importance of the social environment and the development of secure attachments (Gotlib & Hammen, 1992; Joiner & Coyne, 1999). Vulnerability to depression presumably arises in early family environments in which the children's needs for security, comfort, and acceptance are not met. Bowlby (1980) argued that children with caretakers who are consistently accessible and supportive will develop cognitive representations, or "working models," of the self and others as positive and trustworthy. In contrast, caretakers who are unresponsive or inconsistent will produce insecure attachments, leading to working models that include abandonment, self-criticism, and excessive dependency. Such working models presumably increase individuals' vulnerability to depression, particularly when they are exposed to new interpersonal stressors.

Reviews of the literature on the relation between the family environment and depression (e.g., Beardslee et al., 1998; Burbach & Borduin, 1986; Downey & Coyne, 1990; Kaslow, Deering, & Racusin, 1994; McCauley & Myers, 1992) indicate that families of depressed individuals are characterized by problems with attachment, communication, conflict, and social support. Although few studies have tested Bowlby's attachment model directly in relation to depression, some have reported findings consistent with it. Insecure attachment has been linked with behavioral withdrawal in infants (Trad, 1994). Security in attachments helps infants cope with the environment, and a lack of such attachments may lead infants to seek protection by withdrawing from the environment altogether (Bowlby, 1980; Trad, 1994). Two-year-old children with secure attachments have been found to be more cooperative, persistent, and enthusiastic; to show more positive affect; and to function better overall than 2-year-olds with insecure attachments (Matas, Arend, & Sroufe, 1978).

The association between attachment and depression has not been well studied in school-age children. In adolescents, depression has been linked with less secure attachments to parents (Kenny, Moilanen, Lomax, & Brabeck, 1993; Kobak, Sudler, & Gamble, 1991). Moreover, adolescents undergoing stressful life events are more likely to become depressed if they had insecure attachments to their parents than adolescents with more secure attachments (e.g., Kobak et al., 1991).

Beyond attachment, other kinds of dysfunctional interpersonal patterns have been found to be associated with depression in children (Kaslow et al., 1994). Serious abuse and neglect are among the most significant risk factors for depressive symptoms in infants (Trad, 1994). Such maltreatment interferes with normal expressions of emotions and leads to avoidant or resistant attachments, especially if the mother is the perpetrator of the abuse (Lamb, Gaensbauer, Malkin, & Schultz, 1985). Maltreatment also leads to withdrawal behaviors in infants and self-esteem deficits later in childhood (Gaensbauer & Sands, 1979; Trad, 1987). The parent–infant relationship is inevitably worsened from such abuse, which in turn puts the infant in higher danger of being abused again (Trad, 1987).

Two main parenting dimensions particularly associated with depression in children are acceptance/rejection and control/autonomy, (e.g., Parker, Tupling, & Brown, 1979; Schwarz, Barton-Henry, & Pruzinsky, 1985). In retrospective studies, currently depressed adults recalled their parents as critical, rejecting, controlling, and intrusive (Gerlsma, Emmelkamp, & Arrindell, 1990; Parker, 1983). Currently depressed children have described their parents as authoritarian, controlling, rejecting, and unavailable (Amanat & Butler, 1984; Stein et al., 2000), and tend to perceive their families to be less cohesive and more conflictual than nondepressed youth (e.g., Stark, Humphrey, Crook, & Lewis, 1990; although see Asarnow, Carlson, & Guthrie, 1987, for contrary findings).

The association between child depression and dysfunctional family environments is not simply due to the negative reporting tendencies of depressed children. Mothers of depressed children similarly describe themselves as more rejecting, less communicative, and less affectionate than do mothers of both normal and psychiatric controls (Lefkowitz & Tesiny, 1984; Puig-Antich et al., 1985a). Moreover, in observations of mother–child interactions, mothers of depressed children have been described as being less rewarding (Cole & Rehm, 1986) and more dominant and controlling (Amanat & Butler, 1984) than mothers of nondepressed children. Thus, there appears to be convergence among children's, parents' and observers' reports that families of depressed children are characterized by considerable dysfunction.

Depressed children also have significant peer difficulties and social skills deficits (e.g., Altmann & Gotlib, 1988). Self-reported depression significantly correlates with teachers' reports of peer rejection in children (Rudolph, Hammen, & Burge, 1994). In laboratory studies, children with depressive symptoms were rated by their peers more negatively than were children without symptoms (Peterson, Mullins, & Ridley-Johnson, 1985).

Interpersonal difficulties appear to persist after depressive symptoms have remitted. Puig-Antich et al. (1985a) reported that currently depressed children were less communicative and more distant with family members. Although the mother–child relationship showed some improvement with symptom remission, even in the absence of depression, children continued to show interpersonal difficulties, particularly with siblings (Puig-Antich et al., 1985b). Moreover, social adversities such as persistent poor friendships, low involvement of fathers, stressful family environments, and lack of responsiveness to maternal discipline can contribute to the maintenance or relapse of depressive disorders in youth (e.g., Goodyer, Germany, Gowrusankur, & Altham, 1991; McCauley et al., 1993). In addition, negative attitudes by family members toward depressed children have been found to predict relapse (Asarnow, Goldstein, Tompson, & Guthrie, 1993).

Thus, depression in children is associated with high levels of interpersonal conflict and rejection from various members in their social domain including family, friends, and peers. It is likely that the link between interpersonal vulnerability and depression is bidirectional (Coyne, 1976; Gotlib & Hammen, 1992). Longitudinal studies examining the contribution of family dysfunction, parent–child conflict, peer difficulties, and interpersonal rejection to increases in and maintenance of depressive symptoms in children have shown both that social problems temporally precede depression, and that depression contributes to interpersonal difficulties. Family dysfunction in the form of perceived lack of family cohesion or parental attachment (Garrison et al., 1990), hostile child-rearing attitudes (Katainen, Raeikkoenen, Keskivaara, & Keltikangas-Jaervinen, 1999), and maternal criticism (Garber, 2002) significantly predicts increases in depressive symptoms or the onset of depressive disorders in children.

With regard to peer rejection, French, Conrad, and Turner (1995) noted that rejection by peers predicted higher levels of self-reported depressive symptoms among antisocial, but not among nonantisocial youth. Panak and Garber (1992) found that increases in peer-rated aggression predicted increases in self-reported depression through the mediator of increases in peer-rated rejection. Moreover, the relation between peer-rated rejection and self-reported depression was mediated by perceived rejection. Kistner, Balthazor, Risi, and Burton (1999) similarly found that perceived rejection predicted increases in depressive symptoms during middle childhood.

Barber (1996) showed that children's ratings of parents' psychologically controlling behavior predicted children's depressive symptoms, beyond the contribution of prior levels of depression. Children's prior depressive symptoms, however, also predicted children's ratings of their parents' behavior. Using observational data of parental warmth, hostility, and disciplinary skills, Ge, Best, Conger, and Simons (1996) reported that parental warmth predicted lower levels and maternal hostility predicted higher levels of internalizing symptoms in adolescents, controlling for prior internalizing symptoms. In this same sample, Rueter et al. (1999) found that escalating conflict between parents and adolescents predicted increases in adolescent internalizing symptoms. Increasing internalizing symptoms, in turn, increased the risk of onset of an internalizing disorders.

Thus, several studies have found a concurrent relation between family factors and depression in both children and adolescents. Few studies, however, have tested this relation prospectively in preadolescents. Given the lack of longitudinal research in this domain, it remains unclear whether family factors are a cause, correlate, or consequence, or are merely epiphenomena of childhood depression. A transactional perspective would suggest that child and parental behaviors likely influence each other in a reciprocal fashion. More prospective investigations of the dynamics of the family environment and child depression are needed.

Finally, relationships between depressed parents and their children also consistently have been found to be disrupted (Goodman & Gotlib, 1999). Depressed parents report more conflict and less coherence in their families (Billings & Moos, 1983), are less involved and less affectionate with their children, and experience poorer communication in parent–child relationships than nondepressed parents (Weissman, Paykel, Siegal, & Klerman, 1971). Moreover, depressed mothers tend to feel more hostile toward their children and less positive and competent about their parenting than do well mothers (Webster-Stratton & Hammond, 1988).

Observations of depressed mothers interacting with their children reveal that these mothers are more negative (Garber et al., 1991; Lovejoy, 1991), more controlling (Kochanska, Kuczynski, Radke-Yarrow, & Welsh, 1987), less responsive and affectively involved (Cohn & Tronick, 1989; Goodman & Brumley, 1990), and use less productive communications (Gordon et al., 1989). Depressed mothers spend less time talking to and touching their infants, and show more negative affect in their interactions with their infants, who themselves display less positive affect, less activity, and protest more often (Field, 1995). Also, parental depression can lead to disturbed attachment behavior and an inability on the part of the infant to regulate emotions, both of which can put the infant at greater risk for developing depression (Gaensbauer, Harmon, Cytryn, & McKnew, 1984). Offspring of depressed caregivers have been found to have more insecure attachments compared to offspring of well mothers (DeMulder & Radke-Yarrow, 1991; Teti, Gelfand, Messinger, & Isabella, 1995). Moreover, insecurely attached offspring of depressed mothers tend to have difficulties in their relationships with peers (Rubin, Booth, Zahn-Waxler, Cummings, & Wilkinson, 1991). Finally, negative reciprocal interaction patterns have been observed between depressed mothers and their children (Hammen, Burge, & Stansbury, 1990; Radke-Yarrow, 1998).

In summary, two important findings emerge regarding the link between interpersonal vulnerability and depression in children. First, families with a depressed member tend to be characterized by less support and more conflict, and such family dysfunction increases children's risk of developing depression. Second, depressed children are themselves more interpersonally difficult, which results in greater problems in their social network. Thus, the relation between child depression and interpersonal dysfunction is bidirectional. That is, family and peer environments clearly are important and sometimes stressful contexts in which children develop schemata about themselves and others, which then can serve as a vulnerability to depression. In addition, children's own reactions to these environments can exacerbate and perpetuate negative social exchanges, which furthers the interpersonal vicious cycle, thereby resulting in more rejection and depression (Coyne, 1976). Thus, a transactional model of mutual influence probably best characterizes the association between depressed individuals and their social environment.

CONCLUSIONS AND FUTURE DIRECTIONS

Evidence indicates that depressive symptoms and disorders are an important concern even during childhood. Although diagnosed mood disorders are relatively rare in young children, symptoms of depressive syndrome can be found from infancy through preadolescence. During middle childhood, depressive disorders can be diagnosed, but they are still not as prevalent as during adolescence. Although there are many similarities in the symptoms that comprise the syndrome of depression at all ages, there also are noteworthy differences in the phenomenology and structure of depressive syndrome in children versus adults. Nevertheless, when children do have a depressive episode, it tends to show a similar course and outcome as has been found in adults. Comorbidity of depression with other forms of psychopathology is the rule rather than the exception during childhood.

Several important issues remain with regard to depression in very young children. It is still not clear if infants and toddlers actually experience full depressive episodes. More epidemiological studies are needed to address the question of prevalence across childhood. Such studies should not only assess diagnoses, but also should measure a range of problems that could be age-appropriate manifestations of mood disorder symptoms in the very young. Whether such symptom patterns represent depressive disorders then would need to be determined by examining the continuity across time as well as their relation to theoretically derived etiological correlates (e.g., neurobiological dysregulation, stress).

Several other developmental questions also need to be addressed. With regard to epidemiology, what accounts for the increase in depressive disorders from pre- to postadolescence? What changes from childhood to adolescence, or what is protecting children? What accounts for the shift in the sex ratio around puberty? Are there ethnic and cultural differences in the rates of mood disorders in children, and, if so, why? With regard to phenomenology, what is the structure of depression in children and how does this differ from adolescents and adults? What accounts for the changes in the structure of depression over time? What are the normative changes in depressive symptoms (e.g., irritability, anhedonia, fatigue) and what is the relevance of these changes for understanding changes in the rates of these symptoms across childhood? What influences the course and outcome of depressive disorders across development? What sustains depressive symptoms, and why do they remit? Are early-onset depressions more or less severe, recurrent, and familial than late-onset depressions? Do the same processes that underlie first-onset mood disorders explain relapses and recurrences? Why is depression so comorbid with other psychopathology during childhood? Is depression the cause or consequence of other emotional and behavioral problems?

What are the best methods for assessing depressive symptoms at different ages and how should discrepancies across informants be resolved?

With regard to etiology, some evidence supports each of the biological and psychosocial models of depression in children. How can all of these theories be right? One way to deal with such etiological heterogeneity has been to suggest specific subtypes that map on to different causal processes (Abramson et al., 1989; Winokur, 1997). Winokur (1997) proposed that unipolar depression can be divided into endogenous, reactive, and emotionally unstable on the basis of differences on clinical, follow-up, personality, familial, and treatment variables.

Another approach has been to formulate integrated models of depression that include the additive or interactive effects of multiple vulnerability factors (e.g., Abramson et al., 1989; Akiskal & McKinney, 1975; Gotlib & Hammen, 1992). In an earlier integrated model, Akiskal and McKinney (1975) suggested that most distal causal processes such as stressors and low rates of positive reinforcement went through a common final neuroanatomical pathway. Diathesis–stress models highlight the interaction of person characteristics such as genetic or cognitive vulnerability with the experience of environmental stressors (Abramson et al., 1989; Beck, 1967; Kendler et al., 1995; Monroe & Simons, 1991). Interpersonal cognitive approaches (e.g., Gotlib & Hammen, 1992) suggest that individuals' cognitions about important social relationships can be a vulnerability to depression when negative interpersonal events occur. Negative cognitive schemata about the self and others are the result of earlier attachment and interpersonal difficulties. Ingram et al. (1998), on the other hand, emphasized that cognitive processes were the common final pathway through which all social as well as nonsocial information were processed and linked to depression.

It is likely that a broad biopsychosocial model of depression is needed that will incorporate most of the etiological processes discussed here (e.g., Gotlib & Hammen, 1992). Such a model would suggest that children are born with certain biological propensities and tendencies, such as high stress reactivity or an irritable temperament, that make them more vulnerable to the effects of negative life events or less able to obtain help from others to deal with them. As children grow they learn, in part, through interactions with important others, that they either are or are not capable of coping with the stressors of life and that others either can or cannot be counted on for support. They also learn through such interactions that they are worthy of others' love and support. Exposure to stressful life events can activate negative affective structures that connect with developing negative schemata about the self and others (Ingram et al., 1998). A cycle begins in which they develop some symptoms of depression (e.g., negative affect, low self-esteem, anhedonia) that then lead to their being exposed to further stressors such as interpersonal rejection and academic failures. Also, exposure to chronic or severe stressors can produce biological changes that further maintain or exacerbate the depressive symptoms. Over time, depressions might become more autonomous (Post, 1992), but, at least during childhood, depression likely is more closely linked with exposure to stress.

What needs to be done from here? First, future studies should examine multivariate etiological models. Such investigations should not simply examine the independent contribution of individual risk factors, but should test more complex moderator and mediation models that explore how these vulnerability factors synergistically combine to explain the onset of depression. Second, by testing such multivariate models, we will be better able to address questions of specificity. Just because a particular risk factor (e.g., stress) predicts more than one disorder (e.g., anxiety and depression), does not mean that the risk factor cannot be part of a more complex causal model (Garber & Hollon, 1991). It will only be possible to address the issue of specificity by comparing multivariate models rather than individual risk factors.

Third, the various research strategies described here should be combined. For example, studies should compare currently depressed, remitted, high-risk, and never-depressed children with regard to these multivariate models. In addition, these groups should be followed over time to address the question of temporal precedence in the relations among the hypothesized etiological variables and depression. Finally, experimental designs that randomly assign children from each of these groups (i.e., currently depressed, remitted, high-risk, never-depressed) to singular as well as multimodal interventions are needed to examine questions of change. In addition, more laboratory analogue studies that experimentally manipulate specific processes are needed to understand causal mechanisms.

One final fundamental question is whether depressive vulnerabilities are permanent characteristics of individuals and by what internal and external mechanisms are they turned on and off. That is, what biological, psychosocial, or environmental processes set off vulnerabilities to produce depressive symptoms and episodes of disorder, and conversely, how do we explain the remission of symptoms? Do vulnerable individuals no longer have the risk factor(s) or do they develop mechanisms for compensating for them?

ACKNOWLEDGMENTS

This work was supported in part by grants from the National Institute of Mental Health (No. R01-MH57822-01A1) and from the William T. Grant Foundation (No. 96173096).

REFERENCES

Abramson, L. Y., Metalsky, G. I., & Alloy, L. B. (1989). Hopelessness depression: A theory-based subtype of depression. *Psychological Review, 96,* 358–372.

Achenbach, T. M. (1991). The derivation of taxonomic constructs: A necessary stage in the development of developmental psychopathology. In D. Cicchetti & S. Toth (Eds.), *Rochester Symposium on Developmental Psychopathology: Models and integrations* (Vol. 3, pp. 43–74). Hillsdale, NJ: Erlbaum.

Akiskal, H. S., & McKinney, W. T. (1975). Overview of recent research in depression: Integration of ten conceptual models into a comprehensive clinical framework. *Archives of General Psychiatry, 32,* 285–305.

Altmann, E. O., & Gotlib, I. H. (1988). The social behavior of depressed children: An observational study. *Journal of Abnormal Child Psychology, 16,* 29–44.

Amanat, E., & Butler, C. (1984). Oppressive behaviors in the families of depressed children. *Family Therapy, 11,* 65–75.

American Psychiatric Association. (1994). *Diagnostic and statistical manual of mental disorders* (4th ed.). Washington, DC: Author.

Anderson, J. C., Williams, S., McGee, R., & Silva, P. (1987). DSM-III disorders in preadolescent children. *Archives of General Psychiatry, 44,* 69–76.

Angold, A., & Costello, E. J. (1993). Depressive comorbidity in children and adolescents: Empirical, theoretical, and methodological issues. *American Journal of Psychiatry, 150,* 1779–1791.

Angold, A., & Rutter, M. (1992). Effects of age and pubertal status on depression in a large clinical sample. *Development and Psychopathology, 4,* 5–28.

Asarnow, J. R., & Bates, S. (1988). Depression in child psychiatric inpatients: Cognitive and attributional patterns. *Journal of Abnormal Child Psychology, 16,* 601–615.

Asarnow, J. R., Carlson, G. A., & Guthrie, D. (1987). Coping strategies, self-perceptions, hopelessness, and perceived family environments in depressed and suicidal children. *Journal of Consulting and Clinical Psychology, 55,* 361–366.

Asarnow, J., Goldstein, M., Carlson, G., Perdue, S., Bats, S., & Keller, J. (1988). Childhood-onset depressive disorders: A follow-up study of rates of rehospitalization and out of home placement among child psychiatric inpatients. *Journal of Affective Disorders, 15,* 245–253.

Asarnow, J. R., Goldstein, M. J., Tompson, M., & Guthrie, D. (1993). One-year outcomes of depressive disorders in child psychiatric in-patients: Evaluation of the prognostic power of a brief measure of expressed emotion. *Journal of Child Psychology and Psychiatry, 34,* 129–137.

Aseltine, R., Gore, S., & Colton, M. E. (1994). Depression and the social developmental context of adolescence. *Journal of Personality and Social Psychology, 67,* 252–263.

Barber, B. K. (1996). Parental psychological control: Revisiting a neglected construct. *Child Development, 67,* 3296–3319.

Barnett, P. A., & Gotlib, I. H. (1988). Psychosocial functioning and depression: Distinguishing among antecedents, concomitants, and consequences. *Psychological Bulletin, 104,* 97–126.

Beardslee, W. R., Versage, E. M., & Gladstone, T. R. G. (1998). Children of affectively ill parents: A review of the past 10 years. *Journal of the American Academy of Child and Adolescent Psychiatry, 37,* 1134–1141.

Beck, A. T. (1967). *Depression: Clinical, experiential, and theoretical aspects.* New York: Harper & Row.

Beck, A. T. (1983). Cognitive therapy of depression: New perspectives. In P. J. Clayton & J. E. Barrett (Eds.), *Treatment of depression: Old controversies and new approaches* (pp. 265–290). New York: Raven Press.

Billings, A. G., & Moos, R. H. (1983). Comparisons of children of depressed and non-depressed parents: A social–environmental perspective. *Journal of Abnormal Child Psychology, 11,* 483–486.

Birmaher, B., Dahl, R. E., Williamson, D. E., Perel, J. M., Brent, D. A., Axelson, D. A., Kaufman, J., Dorn, L. D., Stull, S., Rao, U., & Ryan, N. D. (1999). *Growth hormone secretion in children and adolescents at high risk for major depressive disorder.* Paper presented at the Child and Adolescent Depression Consortium, Western Psychiatric Institute and Clinic, Pittsburgh, PA.

Birmaher, B., Kaufman, J., Brent, D. A., Dahl, R. E., Perel, J. M., Al-Shabbout, M., Nelson, B., Stull, S., Rao, U., Waterman, G. S., Williamson, D. E., & Ryan, N. D. (1997). Neuroendocrine response to 5-hydroxy-l-tryptophan in prepubertal children at high risk of major depressive disorder. *Archives of General Psychiatry, 54,* 1113–1119.

Birmaher, B., Ryan, N., & Williamson, D. (1996). Depression in children and adolescents: Clinical features and pathogenesis. In K. I. Shulman, D. Tohen, & S. Kutcher (Eds.), *Mood disorders across the life span* (pp. 51–99). New York: Wiley-Liss.

Birmaher, B., Ryan, N., Williamson, D., Brent, D., & Kaufman, J. (1996b). Childhood and adolescent depression: A review of the past 10 years, Part II. *Journal of the American Academy of Child and Adolescent Psychiatry, 35,* 1575–1583.

Birmaher, B., Ryan, N., Williamson, D., Brent, D., Kaufman, J., Dahl, R., Perel, J., & Nelson, B. (1996a). Childhood and adolescent depression: A review of the past 10 years, Part I. *Journal of the American Academy of Child and Adolescent Psychiatry, 35,* 1427–1439.

Blehar, M. C., Weissman, M. M., Gershon, E. S., & Hirschfeld, R. M. A. (1988). Family and genetic studies of affective disorders. *Archives of General Psychiatry, 45,* 289–292.

Bowlby, J. (1980). *Attachment and loss: Vol. 3. Loss, sadness, and depression.* New York: Basic Books.

Brady, E., & Kendall, P. (1992). Comorbidity of anxiety and depression in children and adolescents. *Psychological Bulletin, 111,* 244–255.

Burbach, D. J., & Borduin, C. M. (1986). Parent–child relations and the etiology of depression: A review of methods and findings. *Clinical Psychology Review, 6,* 133–153.

Carlson, G. A., & Garber, J. (1986). Developmental issues in the classification of depression in children. In M. Rutter, C. E. Izard, & P. B. Read (Eds.), *Depression in young people* (pp. 399–434). New York: Guilford Press.

Cavallo, A., Holt, K. G., Hejazi, M. S., Richards, G. E., & Meyer, W. J. (1987). Melatonin circadian rhythm in childhood depression. *Journal of the American Academy of Child and Adolescent Psychiatry, 26,* 395–399.

Cicchetti, D., & Schneider-Rosen, K. (Eds.). (1984). Toward a transactional model of childhood depression. *New Directions in Child Development, 26,* 5–28.

Clarke, A. S., & Schneider, M. L. (1993). Prenatal stress has long-term effects on behavioral responses to stress in juvenile rhesus monkeys. *Developmental Psychobiology, 26,* 293–304.

Cohen, L. H., Burt, C. E., & Bjork, J. P. (1987). Life stress and adjustment: Effects of life events experienced by young adolescents and their parents. *Developmental Psychology, 23,* 583–592.

Cohen, P., Cohen, J., Kasen, S., Velez, C. N., Hartmark, C., Johnson, J., Rojas, M., Brook, J., & Streuning, E. L. (1993). An epidemiological study of childhood disorders in late childhood and adolescence: I. Age and gender-specific prevalence. *Journal of Child Psychology, Psychiatry and Allied Health Disciplines, 34,* 851–867.

Cohn, J. F., & Tronick, E. Z. (1983). Three-month-old infants' reaction to simulated maternal depression. *Child Development, 54,* 185–193.

Cole, D. A. (1991). Preliminary support for a competency-based model of depression in children. *Journal of Abnormal Psychology, 100,* 181–190.

Cole, D. A., Martin, J. M., Peeke, L. G., Seroczynski, A. D., & Hoffman, K. (1998). Are cognitive errors of underestimation predictive or reflective of depressive symptoms in children?: A longitudinal study. *Journal of Abnormal Psychology, 107,* 481–496.

Cole, D. A., Peeke, L. G., Martin, J. M., Truglio, R., & Seroczynski, A. D. (1998). A longitudinal look at the relation between depression and anxiety in children and adolescents. *Journal of Consulting and Clinical Psychology, 66,* 451–460.

Cole, D. A., & Rehm, L. P. (1986). Family interaction patterns and childhood depression. *Journal of Abnormal Child Psychology, 14,* 297–314.

Cole, D. A., & Turner, J. E. (1993). Models of cognitive mediation and moderation in child depression. *Journal of Abnormal Psychology, 102,* 271–281.

Colleta, N. D. (1983). At risk for depression: A study of young mothers. *Journal of Genetic Psychology, 142,* 301–310.

Compas, B. E. (1987). Stress and life events during childhood and adolescence. *Clinical Psychology Review, 7,* 275–302.

Compas, B. E., Howell, D. C., Phares, V., Williams, R. A., & Giunta, C. T. (1989). Risk factors for emotional/behavioral problems in young adolescents: A prospective analysis of parent and adolescent stress and symptoms. *Journal of Consulting and Clinical Psychology, 57,* 732–740.

Coryell, W., Akiskal, H. S., Leon, A. C., Winokur, G., Maser, J. D., Mueller, T., & Keller, M. B. (1994). The time course of nonchronic major depressive disorder: Uniformity across episodes and samples. *Archives of General Psychiatry, 51,* 405–410.

Costello, E. J., Angold, A., Burns, B. J., Erkanli, A., Stangl, D. K., & Tweed, D. L. (1996). The Great Smoky Mountains Study of Youth: Functional impairment and serious emotional disturbance. *Archives of General Psychiatry, 53,* 1137–1143.

Costello, E. J., Angold, A., Burns, B. J., Stangl, D. K., Tweed, D. L., Erkanli, A., & Worthman, C. M. (1996). The Great Smoky Mountains Study of Youth: Goals, design, methods, and the prevalence of DSM-III-R disorders. *Archives of General Psychiatry, 53,* 1129–1136.

Coyne, J. C. (1976). Toward an interactional description of depression. *Psychiatry, 39,* 28–40.

Dahl, R. E., Kaufman, J., Ryan, N. D., Perel, J., Al-Shabbout, M., Birmaher, B., Nelson, B., & Puig-Antich, J. (1992). The dexamethosone suppression test in children and adolescents: A review and controlled study. *Biological Psychiatry, 32,* 109–126.

Dahl, R. E., & Ryan, N. D. (1996). The psychobiology of adolescent depression. In D. Cicchetti & S. L. Toth (Eds.), *Rochester Symposium on Developmental Psychopathology: Vol. 7. Adolescence: Opportunities and challenges* (pp. 197–232). Rochester, NY: Rochester University Press.

Dahl, R. E., Ryan, N. D., Birmaher, B., Al-Shabbout, M., Williamson, D. E., Neidig, M., Nelson, B. & Puig-Antich, J. (1991b). Electroencephalographic sleep measures in prepubertal depression. *Psychiatry Research, 38,* 201–214.

Dahl, R. E., Ryan, N. D., Puig-Antich, J., Nguyen, N. A., Al-Shabbout, M., Meyer, V. A., & Perel J. (1991a). 24-hour cortisol measures in adolescents with major depression: A controlled study. *Biological Psychiatry, 30,* 25–36.

Dawson, G., Frey, K., Panagiotides, H., Osterling, J., & Hessl, D. (1997). Infants of depressed mothers exhibit atypical frontal brain activity: A replication and extension of previous findings. *Journal of Child Psychology and Psychiatry, 38,* 179–186.

DeMulder, E. K., & Radke-Yarrow, M. (1991). Attachment with affectively ill and well mothers: Concurrent behavioral correlates. *Development and Psychopathology, 3,* 227–242.

Downey, G., & Coyne, J. C. (1990). Children of depressed parents: An integrative review. *Psychological Bulletin, 108,* 50–76.

Eaves, L. J., Silberg, J. L., Meyer, J. M., Maes, H. H., Simonoff, E., Pickles, A., Rutter, M., Neale, M. C., Reynolds, C. A., Erikson, M. T., Heath, A. C., Loeber, R., Truett, K. R., & Hewitt, J. K. (1997). Genetics and developmental psychopathology: 2. The main effects of genes and environment on behavioral problems in the Virginia Twin Study of Adolescent Behavioral Development. *Journal of Child Psychology and Psychiatry, 38,* 965–980.

Eley, T. C. (1997). Depressive symptoms in children and adolescents: Etiological links between normality and abnormality: A research note. *Journal of Child Psychology and Psychiatry, 38,* 861–865.

Eley, T. C., Deater-Deckard, K., Fombonne, E., Fulker, D. W., & Plomin, R. (1998). An adoption study of depressive symptoms in middle childhood. *Journal of Child Psychology and Psychiatry, 39,* 337–345.

Emslie, G. J., Rush, A. J., Weinberg, W. A., Gullion, C. M., Rintelmann, J., & Hughes, C. W. (1997). Recurrence of major depressive disorder in hospitalized children and adolescents. *Journal of the American Academy of Child and Adolescent Psychiatry, 36,* 785–792.

Emslie, G. J., Rush, A. J., Weinberg, W. A., Kowatch, R. A., Hughes, C. W., Carnody, T., & Rintelmann, J. W. (1997). A double-blind, randomized, placebo-controlled trial of fluoxetine in children and adolescents with depression. *Archives of General Psychiatry, 54,* 1031–1037.

Emslie, G. J., Rush, A. J., Weinberg, W. A., Rintelmann, J. W., & Roffwarg, H. P. (1990). Children with major depression show reduced rapid eye movement latencies. *Archives of General Psychiatry, 47,* 119–124.

Emslie, G. J., Weinberg, W. A., Kennard, B. D., & Kowatch, R. A. (1994). Neurobiological aspects of depression in children and adolescents. In W. M. Reynolds & H. E. Johnston (Eds.), *Handbook of depression in children and adolescents* (pp. 143–165). New York: Plenum Press.

Field, T. (1995). Presidential address: Infants of depressed mothers. *Infant Behavior and Development, 18,* 1–13.

Field, T., Fox, A., Pickens, J., & Nawrocki, T. (1995). Relative right frontal EEG activation in 3- to 6-month-old infants of "depressed" mothers. *Developmental Psychology, 31,* 358–363.

Fleming, J. E., & Offord, D. R. (1990). Epidemiology of childhood depressive disorders: A critical review. *Journal of the American Academy of Child and Adolescent Psychiatry, 29,* 571–580.

Fleming, J. E., Offord, D. R., & Boyle, M. H. (1989). Prevalence of childhood and adolescent depression in the community. *British Journal of Psychiatry, 155,* 647–654.

Frank, D. A., & Drotar, D. (1994). Failure to thrive. In R. M. Reece (Ed.), *Child abuse: Medical diagnosis and management* (pp. 298–324). Philadelphia: Lea & Febiger.

French, D. C., Conrad, J., & Turner, T. M. (1995). Adjustment of antisocial and nonantisocial rejected adolescents. *Development and Psychopathology, 7,* 857–874.

Gaensbauer, T. J., Harmon, R. J., Cytryn, L., & McKnew, D. (1984). Social and affective development in infants with a manic–depressive parent. *American Journal of Psychiatry, 141,* 223–229.

Gaensbauer, T. J., & Sands, K. (1979). Distorted affective communications in abused/neglected infants and their potential impact on caretakers. *Journal of the American Academy of Child Psychiatry, 18,* 236–250.

Garber, J. (2002, April). *Maternal criticism predicts the first onset of depression in adolescents.* Paper presented at the Society for Research on Adolescence, New Orleans.

Garber, J., & Hilsman, R. (1992). Cognitions, stress, and depression in children and adolescents. *Child and Adolescent Psychiatric Clinics of North America, 1,* 129–167.

Garber, J., & Hollon, S. D. (1991). What can specificity designs say about causality in psychopathology research? *Psychological Bulletin, 110,* 129–136.

Garber, J., Martin, N. C., & Keiley, M. K. (2001, February). *Psychosocial predictors of depression in adolescents.* Paper presented at the Banbury Conference on Child Depression: A Critical Review, Cold Springs Harbor, NY.

Garber, J., Quiggle, N. L., Panak, W. F., & Dodge, K. A. (1991). Depression and aggression in children: Comorbidity and social cognitive processes. In D. Cicchetti & S. Toth (Eds.), *The Rochester Symposium on Developmental Psychopathology: Vol. 2. Internalizing and externalizing expressions of dysfunction* (pp. 225–264), New York: Cambridge University Press.

Garber, J., & Robinson, N. S. (1997). Cognitive vulnerability in children at risk for depression. *Cognitions and Emotions, 11,* 619–635.

Garrison, C., Jackson, K., Marsteller, F., McKeown, R., & Addy, C. (1990). A longitudinal study of depressive symptomatology in young adolescents. *Journal of the American Academy of Child and Adolescent Psychiatry, 29,* 581–585.

Ge, X., Best, K. M., Conger, R. D., & Simons, R. L. (1996). Parenting behaviors and the occurrence and co-occurrence of adolescent depressive symptoms and conduct problems. *Developmental Psychology, 32,* 717–731.

Ge, X., Lorenz, F., Conger, R., Edler, C., & Simons, R. L. (1994). Trajectories of stressful life events and depressive symptoms during adolescence. *Developmental Psychology, 30,* 467–483.

Gerlsma, C., Emmelkamp, P. M. G., & Arrindell, W. A. (1990). Anxiety, depression, and perception of early parenting: A meta-analysis. *Clinical Psychology Review, 10,* 251–277.

Gladstone, T. R. G., & Kaslow, N. J. (1995). Depression and attributions in children and adolescents: A meta-analytic review. *Journal of Abnormal Child Psychology, 23,* 597–606.

Glover, V. (1997). Maternal stress or anxiety in pregnancy and emotional development of the child. *British Journal of Psychiatry, 171,* 105–106.

Gold, P. W., Goodwin, F. K., & Chrousos, G. P. (1988). Clinical and biochemical manifestations of depression: Relation to the neurobiology of stress. *New England Journal of Medicine, 319,* 348–353.

Goodman, S. H., Adamson, L. B., Riniti, J., & Cole, S. (1994). Mothers' expressed attitudes: Associations with maternal depression and children's self-esteem and psychopathology. *Journal of the American Academy of Child and Adolescent Psychiatry, 33,* 1265–1274.

Goodman, S. H., & Brumley, H. E. (1990). Schizophrenic and depressed mothers: Relational deficits in parenting. *Developmental Psychology, 26,* 31–39.

Goodman, S. H., & Gotlib, I. H. (1999). Risk for psychopathology in the children of depressed mothers: A developmental model for understanding mechanisms of transmission. *Psychological Review, 106,* 458–490.

Goodyer, I. M. (1996). Physical symptoms and depressive disorders in childhood and adolescence. *Journal of Psychosomatic Research, 41,* 405–408.

Goodyer, I. M., Germany, E., Gowrusankur, J., & Altham, P. M. E. (1991). Social influences on the course of anxious and depressive disorders in school-aged children. *British Journal of Psychiatry, 158,* 676–684.

Goodyer, I. M., Herbert, J., & Altham, P. M. E. (1998). Adrenal steroid secretion and major depression in 8- to 16-year-olds: III. Influence of cortisol/DHEA ration at presentation on subsequent rates of disappointing life events and persistent major depression. *Psychological Medicine, 28,* 265–273.

Goodyer, I. M., Herbert, J., Altham, P. M. E., Pearson, J., Secher, S. M., & Shiers, H. M. (1996). Adrenal secretion during major depression in 8- to 16-year-olds: I. Altered diurnal rhythms in salivary cortisol and dehydrepiandrosterone (DHEA) at presentation. *Psychological Medicine, 26,* 245–256.

Goodyer, I. M., Herbert, J., Tamplin, A., & Altham, P. M. E. (2000). Recent life events, cortisol, dehydroepiandrosterone and the onset of major depression in high-risk adolescents. *British Journal of Psychiatry, 177,* 499–504.

Gordon, D., Burge, D., Hammen, C., Adrian, C., Jaenicke, C., & Hiroto, D. (1989). Observations of interactions of depressed women with their children. *American Journal of Psychiatry, 146,* 50–55.

Gotlib, I. H., & Hammen, C. L. (1992). *Psychological aspects of depression: Toward a cognitive–interpersonal integration.* Chichester, UK: Wiley.

Gunnar, M. R. (1989). Studies of the human infant's adrenocortical response to potentially stressful events. *New Directions for Child Development, 45,* 3–18.

Halbreich, U., Asnis, G. M., Zumoff, B., Nathan, R. S., & Shindledecker, R. (1984). Effect of age and sex on cortisol secretion in depressives and normals. *Psychiatry Research, 13,* 221–229.

Hammen, C. L. (1991). The generation of stress in the course of unipolar depression. *Journal of Abnormal Psychology, 100*, 555–561.

Hammen, C. L., Burge, D., & Stansbury, K. (1990). Relationship of mother and child variables to child outcomes in a high-risk sample: A causal modeling analysis. *Developmental Psychology, 26*, 24–30.

Hammen, C. L., & Compas, B. E. (1994). Unmasking masked depression in children and adolescents: The problem of comorbidity. *Clinical Psychology Review, 14*, 585–603.

Hammen, C. L., & Goodman-Brown, T. (1990). Self-schemas and vulnerability to specific life stress in children at risk for depression. *Cognitive Therapy and Research, 14*, 215–227.

Hankin, B. L., Abramson, L. Y., Moffitt, T. E., Silva, P. A., McGee, R., & Angell, K. E. (1998). Development of depression from preadolescence to young adulthood: Emerging gender differences in a 10-year longitudinal study. *Journal of Abnormal Psychology, 107*, 128–140.

Harrington, R., Fudge, H., Rutter, M., Pickles, A., & Hill, J. (1990). Adult outcomes of childhood and adolescent depression. *Archives of General Psychiatry, 47*, 465–473.

Henry, C., Kabbaj, M., Simon, H., Le Moal, M., & Maccari, S. (1994). Prenatal stress increases the hypothalamo–pituitary–adrenal axis response in young and adult rats. *Journal of Neuroendocrinology, 6*, 341–345.

Hilsman, R., & Garber, J. (1995). A test of the cognitive diathesis–stress model of depression in children: Academic stressors, attributional style, perceived competence, and control. *Journal of Personality and Social Psychology, 69*, 370–380.

Hoffman, K. B., Cole, D. A., Martin, J. M., Tram, J., & Serocynski, A. D. (2000). Are the discrepancies between self- and others' appraisals of competence predictive or reflective of depressive symptoms in children and adolescents: A longitudinal study, Part II. *Journal of Abnormal Psychology, 109*, 651–662.

Hollon, S. D. (1992). Cognitive models of depression from a psychobiological perspective. *Psychological Inquiry, 3*, 250–253.

Ingram, R. E., Miranda, J., & Segal, Z. V. (1998). *Cognitive vulnerability to depression.* New York: Guilford Press.

Jaenicke, C., Hammen, C., Zupan, B., Hiroto, D., Gordon, D., Adrian, C., & Burge, D. (1987). Cognitive vulnerability in children at risk for depression. *Journal of Abnormal Child Psychology, 15*, 559–572.

Jensen, J. B., & Garfinkel, B. D. (1990). Growth hormone dysregulation in children with major depressive disorder. *Journal of the American Academy of Child and Adolescent Psychiatry, 29*, 295–301.

Joiner, T. E., & Coyne, J. C. (Eds.). (1999). *The interactional nature of depression: Advances in interpersonal approaches.* Washington, DC: American Psychological Association.

Jones, N. A., Field, T., Fox, N. A., Lundy, B., & Davalos, M. (1997). EEG activation in 1-month-old infants of depressed mothers. *Development and Psychopathology, 9*, 491–505.

Just, N., Abramson, L. Y., & Alloy, L. B. (2001). Remitted depression studies as tests of the cognitive vulnerability hypothesis of depression onset: A critique and conceptual analysis. *Clinical Psychology Review, 21*, 63–83.

Kalin, N. H., & Carnes, M. (1984). Biological correlates of attachment bond disruption in humans and nonhuman primates. *Neuropsychopharmacology and Biological Psychiatry, 8*, 459–469.

Kashani, J. H., & Carlson, G. A. (1987). Seriously depressed preschoolers. *American Journal of Psychiatry, 144*, 348–350.

Kaslow, N. J., Deering, C. G., & Racusin, G. R. (1994). Depressed children and their families. *Clinical Psychology Review, 14*, 39–59.

Katainen, S., Raeikkoenen, K., Keskivaara, P., & Keltikangas-Jaervinen, L. (1999). Maternal child-rearing attitudes and role satisfaction and children's temperament as antecedents of adolescent depressive tendencies: Follow-up study of 6- to 15-year-olds. *Journal of Youth and Adolescence, 28*, 139–163.

Kazdin, A. E., Esveldt-Dawson, K., Unis, A. S., & Rancurello, M. D. (1983). Child and parent evaluations of depression and aggression in psychiatric inpatient children. *Journal of Abnormal Child Psychology, 11*, 401–413.

Keller, M. B., Lavori, P. W., Lewis, C. E., & Klerman, G. L. (1983). Predictors of relapse in major depressive disorder. *Journal of the American Medical Association, 250*, 3299–3304.

Kendler, K. S., Kessler, R. C., Walters, E. E., MacLean, C., Neale, M. C., Heath, A. C., & Eaves, L. J. (1995). Stressful life events, genetic liability, and onset of an episode of major depression in women. *American Journal of Psychiatry, 152,* 833–842.

Kenny, M. E., Moilanen, D. L., Lomax, R., & Brabeck, M. M. (1993). Contributions of parental attachments to views of self and depressive symptoms among early adolescents. *Journal of Early Adolescence, 13,* 408–430.

Kistner, J., Balthazor, M., Risi, S., & Burton, C. (1999). Predicting dysphoria in adolescence from actual and perceived peer acceptance in childhood. *Journal of Clinical Child Psychology, 28,* 94–104.

Klee, S. H., & Garfinkel, B. D. (1984). Identification of depression in children and adolescents: The role of the dexamethasone suppression test. *Journal of the American Academy of Child Psychiatry, 23,* 410–415.

Kobak, R. R., Sudler, N., & Gamble, W. (1991). Attachment and depressive symptoms during adolescence: A developmental pathways analysis. *Development and Psychopathology, 3,* 461–474.

Kochanska, G., Kuczynski, L., Radke-Yarrow, M., & Welsh, J. D. (1987). Resolutions of control episodes between well and affectively ill mothers and their young children. *Journal of Abnormal Child Psychology, 15,* 441–456.

Kovacs, M. (1981). Rating scales to assess depression in school-aged children. *Acta Paedopsychiatrica, 46,* 305–315.

Kovacs, M. (1994). Childhood-onset dysthymic disorder: Clinical features and prospective naturalistic outcome. *Archives of General Psychology, 51,* 365–374.

Kovacs, M. (1996a). The course of childhood-onset depressive disorders. *Psychiatric Annals, 26,* 326–330.

Kovacs, M. (1996b). Presentation and course of major depressive disorder during childhood and later years of the life span. *Journal of the American Academy of Child and Adolescent Psychiatry, 35,* 705–715.

Kovacs, M., Devlin, B., Pollock, M., Richards, C., & Mukerji, P. (1997). A controlled family history study of childhood-onset depressive disorder. *Archives of General Psychiatry, 54,* 613–623.

Kovacs, M., Feinberg, T. L., Crouse-Novak, M. A., Paulauskas, S. L., & Finkelstein, R. (1984a). Depressive disorders in childhood: I. A longitudinal prospective study of characteristics and recovery. *Archives of General Psychiatry, 41,* 229–237.

Kovacs, M., Feinberg, T. L., Crouse-Novak, M., Paulauskas, S. L., Pollock, M., & Finkelstein, R. (1984b). Depressive disorders in childhood: II. A longitudinal study of the risk for a subsequent major depression. *Archives of General Psychiatry, 41,* 653–649.

Kovacs, M., Gatsonis, C., Paulauskas, S. L., & Richards, C. (1989). Depressive disorders in childhood: IV. A longitudinal study of comorbidity with and risk for anxiety disorders. *Archives of General Psychiatry, 46,* 776–782.

Kutcher, S., Malkin, D., Silverberg, J., Marton, P., Williamson, P., Malkin, A., Szalai, J., & Katic, M. (1991). Nocturnal cortisol, thyroid stimulating hormone, and growth hormone secretory profiles in depressed adolescents. *Journal of the American Academy of Child and Adolescent Psychiatry, 30,* 407–414.

Lamb, M. E., Gaensbauer, T. J., Malkin, C. M., & Schultz, L. A. (1985). The effects of child maltreatment on security of infant–adult attachment. *Infant Behavior and Development, 8,* 35–45.

Lefkowitz, M. M., & Tesiny, E. P. (1984). Rejection and depression: Prospective and contemporaneous analyses. *Developmental Psychology, 20,* 776–785.

Lewinsohn, P. M., Steinmetz, J. L., Larson, D. W., & Franklin, J. (1981). Depression related cognitions: Antecedent or consequence? *Journal of Abnormal Psychology, 91,* 213–219.

Little, S. A., & Garber, J. (2000). Interpersonal and achievement orientations and specific hassles predicting depressive and aggressive symptoms in children. *Cognitive Therapy and Research, 24,* 651–671.

Lovejoy, M. C. (1991). Maternal depression: Effects on social cognition and behavior in parent–child interactions. *Journal of Abnormal Child Psychology, 19,* 693–706.

Matas, L., Arend, R. A., & Sroufe, L. A. (1978). Continuity of adaptation in the second year: The relationship between quality of attachment and later competence. *Child Development, 49,* 547–556.

McCauley, E., Mitchell, J. R., Burke, P., & Moss, S. (1988). Cognitive attributes of depression in children and adolescents. *Journal of Consulting and Clinical Psychology, 56,* 903–908.

McCauley, E., & Myers, K. (1992). Family interactions of mood-disordered youth. *Child and Adolescent Psychiatric Clinics of North America, 1,* 111–127.

McCauley, E., Myers, K., Mitchell, J., Calderon, R., Schloredt, K., & Treder, R. (1993). Depression in young people: Initial presentation and clinical course. *Journal of the American Academy of Child and Adolescent Psychiatry, 32,* 714–722

McFarlane, A. H., Bellissimo, A., Norman, G. R., & Lange, P. (1994). Adolescent depression in a school-based community sample: Preliminary findings on contributing social factors. *Journal of Youth and Adolescence, 23,* 601–620.

McGuffin, P., Katz, R., Watkins, S., & Rutherford, J. (1996). A hospital-based twin registry study of the heritability of DSM-IV unipolar depression. *Archives of General Psychiatry, 53,* 129–136.

Meyer, W. J., Richards, G. E., Cavallo, A., Holt, K. G., Hejazi, M. S., Wigg, C., & Rose, R. M. (1991). Depression and growth hormone. *Journal of the American Academy of Child and Adolescent Psychiatry, 30,* 335.

Milling, L. S. (2001). Depression in preadolescents. In C. E. Walker & M. C. Roberts (Eds.). *Handbook of clinical child psychology* (3rd ed., pp. 373–392). New York: Wiley.

Monroe, S. M., & Roberts, J. R. (1990). Definitional and conceptual issues in the measurement of life stress: Problems, principles, procedures, progress. *Stress Medicine, 6,* 209–216.

Monroe, S. M., Rohde, P., Seeley, J. R., & Lewinsohn, P. M. (1999). Life events and depression in adolescence: Relationship loss as a prospective risk factor for first onset of major depressive disorder. *Journal of Abnormal Psychology, 108,* 606–614.

Monroe, S. M., & Simons, A. D. (1991). Diathesis–stress theories in the context of life stress research: Implications for the depressive disorders. *Psychological Bulletin, 110,* 406–425.

Moreau, D. (1996). Depression in the young. *Annals of the New York Academy of Sciences, 789,* 31–44.

Nolen-Hoeksema, S., Girgus, J. S., & Seligman, M. E. P. (1992). Predictors and consequences of childhood depressive symptoms: A 5-year longitudinal study. *Journal of Abnormal Psychology, 101,* 405–422.

Panak, W., & Garber, J. (1992). Role of aggression, rejection, and attributions in the prediction of depression in children. *Development and Psychopathology, 4,* 145–165.

Parker, G. (1983). Parental "affectionless control"' as an antecedent to adult depression: A risk factor delineated. *Archives of General Psychiatry, 40,* 956–960.

Parker, G., Tupling, H., & Brown, L. B. (1979). A parental bonding instrument. *British Journal of Medical Psychology, 52,* 1–10.

Patterson, M. L., Greising, L., Hyland, L. T., & Burger, G. K. (1994). Childhood depression, anxiety, and aggression: A reanalysis of Epkins and Meyers. *Journal of Personality Assessment, 69,* 607–613.

Peterson, L., Mullins, L. L., & Ridley-Johnson, R. (1985). Childhood depression: Peer reactions to depression and life stress. *Journal of Abnormal Child Psychology, 13,* 597–609.

Pfeffer, C. R., Stokes, P., & Shindledecker, R. (1991). Suicidal behavior and hypothalamic–pituitary–adrenocortical axis indices in child psychiatric inpatients. *Biological Psychiatry, 29,* 909–917.

Plomin, R. (1990). *Nature and nurture: An introduction to human behavioral genetics.* Pacific Grove, CA: Brooks/Cole.

Polaino-Lorente, A., & Domenech, E. (1993). Prevalence of childhood depression: Results of the first study in Spain. *Journal of Child Psychology, Psychiatry and Allied Health Disciplines, 34,* 1007–1017.

Poltyrev, T., Keshet, G. I., Kay, G., & Weinstock, M. (1996). Role of experimental conditions in determining differences in exploratory behavior of prenatally stressed rats. *Developmental Psychobiology, 29,* 453–462.

Post, R. M. (1992). Transduction of psychosocial stress into the neurobiology of recurrent affective disorder. *American Journal of Psychiatry, 149,* 999–1010.

Powell, K. B., & Miklowitz, D. J. (1994). Frontal lobe dysfunction in the affective disorders. *Clinical Psychology Review, 14,* 525–546.

Puig-Antich, J., Goetz, R., Davies, M., Tabrizi, M. A., Novacenko, H., Hanlon, C., Sachar, E. J., & Weitzman, E. D. (1984a). Growth hormone secretion in prepubertal children with major depression: IV. Sleep-related plasma concentrations in a drug-free, fully recovered clinical state. *Archives of General Psychiatry, 41,* 479–483.

Puig-Antich, J., Lukens, E., Davies, M., Goetz, D., Brennan-Quattrock, J., & Todak, G. (1985a). Psychosocial functioning in prepubertal major depressive disorders: I. Interpersonal relationships during the depressive episode. *Archives of General Psychiatry, 42,* 500–507.

Puig-Antich, J., Lukens, E., Davies, M., Goetz, D., Brennan-Quattrock, J., & Todak, G. (1985b). Psychosocial functioning in prepubertal depressive disorders: II. Interpersonal relationships after sustained recovery from affective episode. *Archives of General Psychiatry, 42,* 511–517.

Puig-Antich, J., Novacenko, H., Davies, M., Chambers, W. J., Tabrizi, M. A., Krawiec, V., Ambrosini, P. J., & Sachar, E. J. (1984b). Growth hormone secretion in prepubertal children with major depression: I. Final report on response to insulin-induced hypoglycemia during a depressive episode. *Archives of General Psychiatry, 41,* 455–460.

Puig-Antich, J., Novacenko, H., Davies, M., Tabrizi, M. A., Ambrosini, P. J., Goetz, R., Bianca, J., Goetz, D., & Sachar, E. J. (1984c). Growth hormone secretion in prepubertal children with major depression: III. Response to insulin-induced hypoglycemia after recovery from a depressive episode and in a drug-free state. *Archives of General Psychiatry, 41,* 471–475.

Puura, K., Tamminen, T., Almqvist, F., Kresanov, K., Kumpulainen, K., Moilanen, I., & Koivisto, A. M. (1997). Should depression in young school children be diagnosed with different criteria? *European Child and Adolescent Psychiatry, 6,* 12–19.

Radke-Yarrow, M. (1998). *Children of depressed mothers: From early childhood to maturity.* New York: Cambridge University Press.

Raynor, P., & Rudolf, M. C. J. (1996). What do we know about children who fail to thrive? *Child: Care, Health and Development, 22,* 241–250.

Reinherz, H. Z., Stewart-Berghauer, M. A., Pakiz, B., Frost, A. K., Moeykens, B. A., & Holmes, W. M. (1989). The relationship of early risk and current mediators to depressive symptomatology in adolescence. *Journal of the American Academy of Child and Adolescent Psychiatry, 28,* 942–947.

Rende, R. D., Plomin, R., Reiss, D., & Hetherington, E. M. (1993). Genetic and environmental influences on depressive symptomatology in adolescence: Individual differences and extreme scores. *Journal of Child Psychology and Psychiatry, 34,* 1387–1398.

Robinson, N. S., Garber, J., & Hilsman, R. (1995). Cognitions and stress: Direct and moderating effects on depressive versus externalizing symptoms during the junior high school transition. *Journal of Abnormal Psychology, 104,* 453–463.

Rubin, K., Booth, L., Zahn-Waxler, C., Cummings, E. M., & Wilkinson, M. (1991). Dyadic play behaviors of children of well and depressed mothers. *Development and Psychopathology, 3,* 243–251.

Rudolph, K. D., Hammen, C., & Burge, D. (1994). Interpersonal functioning and depressive symptoms in childhood: Addressing the issues of specificity and comorbidity. *Journal of Abnormal Child Psychology, 22,* 355–371.

Rueter, M. A., Scaramella, L., Wallace, L. E., & Conger, R. D. (1999). First onset of depressive or anxiety disorders predicted by the longitudinal course of internalizing symptoms and parent–adolescent disagreements. *Archives of General Psychiatry, 56,* 726–732.

Rutter, M., Macdonald, H., Le Couteur, A., Harrington, R., Bolton, P. & Bailey, A. (1990). Genetic factors in child psychiatric disorders: II. Empirical findings. *Journal of Child Psychology and Psychiatry, 31,* 39–83.

Ryan, N. D. (1998). Psychoneuroendocrinology of children and adolescents. *Psychiatric Clinics of North America, 21,* 435–441.

Ryan, N. D., Birmaher, B., Perel, J. M., Dahl, R. E., Meyer, V., Al-Shabbout, M., Iyengar, S., & Puig-Antich, J. (1992). Neuroendocrine response to L-5-hydroxytryptophan challenge in prepubertal major depression. *Archives of General Psychiatry, 49,* 843–851.

Ryan, N., & Dahl, R. (1993). The biology of depression in children and adolescents. In J. J. Mann &

D. J. Kupfer (Eds.), *Biology of depressive disorders, Part B: Subtypes of depression and comorbid disorders* (pp. 37–58). New York: Plenum Press.

Ryan, N. D., Dahl, R. E., Birmaher, B., Williamson, D. E., Iyengar, S., Nelson, B., Puig-Antich, J., & Perel, J. M. (1994). Stimulatory tests of growth hormone secretion in prepubertal major depression: Depressed versus normal children. *Journal of the American Academy of Child and Adolescent Psychiatry, 33,* 824–833.

Ryan, N. D., Puig-Antich, J., Ambrosini, P., Rabinovich, H., Robinson, D., Nelson, B., Iyengar, S., & Twomey, J. (1987). The clinical picture of major depression in children and adolescents. *Archives of General Psychiatry, 44,* 854–861.

Schneider, M. L. (1992). Prenatal stress exposure alters postnatal behavioral expression under conditions of novelty challenge in rhesus monkey infants. *Developmental Psychobiology, 25,* 529–540.

Schwarz, J. C., Barton-Henry, M. L., & Pruzinsky, T. (1985). Assessing child-rearing behaviors: A comparison of ratings made by mother, father, child, and siblings on the CRPBI. *Child Development, 56,* 462–479.

Segal, Z. V., & Dobson, K. S. (1992). Cognitive models of depression: Report from a Consensus Development Conference. *Psychological Inquiry, 3,* 214–224.

Spitz, R. A. (1945). Hospitalism: An inquiry into the genesis of psychiatric conditions in early childhood. *Psychoanalytic Study of the Child, 1,* 53–74.

Spitz, R. A., & Wolf, K. M. (1946). Anaclitic depression: An inquiry into the genesis of psychiatric conditions in childhood: II. *Psychoanalytic Study of the Child, 2,* 313–342.

Stark, K. D., Humphrey, L. L., Crook, K., & Lewis, K. (1990). Perceived family environments of depressed and anxious children: Child's and maternal figure's perspectives. *Journal of Abnormal Child Psychology, 18,* 527–547.

Stein, D., Williamson, D. E., Birmaher, B., Brent, D. A., Kaufman, J., Dahl, R. E., Perel, J. M., & Ryan, N. D. (2000). Parent–child bonding and family functioning in depressed children and children at high risk for future depression. *Journal of the American Academy of Child and Adolescent Psychiatry, 39,* 1387–1395.

Takahashi, L. K., Baker, E. W., & Kalin, N. H. (1990). Ontogeny of behavioral and hormonal responses to stress in prenatally stressed male rat pups. *Physiology and Behavior, 47,* 357–364.

Teti, D., Gelfand, D., Messinger, D., & Isabella, R. (1995). Maternal depression and the quality of early attachment: An examination of infants, preschoolers, and their mothers. *Developmental Psychology, 31,* 364–376.

Thaper, A., & McGuffin, P. (1994). A twin study of depressive symptoms in childhood. *British Journal of Psychiatry, 165,* 259–265.

Tomarken, A. J., & Keener, A. D. (1998). Frontal brain asymmetry and depression: A self-regulatory perspective. *Cognition and Emotion, 12,* 387–420.

Tomarken, A. J., Simien, C., & Garber, J. (1994). Resting frontal brain asymmetry discriminates adolescent children of depressed mothers from low risk controls. *Psychophysiology, 3,* S97–S98.

Trad, P. V. (1987). *Infant and childhood depression: Developmental factors.* New York: Wiley.

Trad, P. V. (1994). Depression in infants. In W. M. Reynolds & H. F. Johnston (Eds.), *Handbook of depression in children and adolescents* (pp. 401–426). New York: Plenum Press.

Turner, J. E., & Cole, D. A. (1994). Developmental differences in cognitive diatheses for child depression. *Journal of Abnormal Child Psychology, 22,* 15–32.

Verhulst, F. C., & van der Ende, J. (1992). Six-year developmental course of internalizing and externalizing problem behaviors. *Journal of the American Academy of Child and Adolescent Psychiatry, 31,* 924–931.

Ward, A. J. (1991). Prenatal stress and childhood psychopathology. *Child Psychiatry and Human Development, 22,* 97–110.

Warner, V., Weissman, M. M., Fendrich, M., Wickramaratne, P., & Moreau, D. (1992). The course of major depression in the offspring of depressed parents. *Archives of General Psychiatry, 49,* 795–801.

Watson, D., & Clark, L. A. (1984). Negative affectivity: The disposition to experience aversive emotional states. *Psychological Bulletin, 96,* 465–490.

Webster-Stratton, C., & Hammond, M. (1988). Maternal depression and its relation to life stress, perceptions of child behavior problems, parenting behaviors, and child conduct problems. *Journal of Abnormal Child Psychology, 16,* 299–315.

Weiss, B., & Garber, J. (2002). *Developmental differences in the phenomenology of depression.* Manuscript under review.

Weissman, M. M., Gammon, G. D., John, K., Merikangas, K. R., Prusoff, B. A., & Sholomskas, D. (1987). Children of depressed parents: Increased psychopathology and early onset of major depression. *Archives of General Psychiatry, 44,* 847–853.

Weissman, M. M., Merikangas, K. R., Wickramaratne, P., Kidd, K. K., Prusoff, B. A., Leckman, J. F., & Pauls, D. L. (1986). Understanding the clinical heterogeneity of major depression using family data. *Archives of General Psychiatry, 43,* 430–434.

Weissman, M. M., & Olfson, M. (1995). Depression in women: Implications for health care research. *Science, 269,* 799–801.

Weissman, M., Paykel, E., Siegel, R., & Klerman, G. (1971). The social role performance of depressed women: Comparisons with a normal group. *American Journal of Orthopsychiatry, 43,* 390–405.

Weissman, M. M., Warner, V., Wickramaratne, P., & Prusoff, B. A. (1988). Early-onset major depression in parents and their children. *Journal of Affective Disorders, 15,* 269–277.

Weissman, M. M., Wolk, S.,Wickramaratne, P., Goldstein, R. B., Adams, P., Greenwald, S., Ryan, N. D., Dahl, R. E., & Steinberg, D. (1999). Children with prepubertal-onset major depressive disorder and anxiety grown up. *Archives of General Psychiatry, 56,* 794–801.

Weisz, J. R., Southam-Gerow, M. A., & McCarty, C. A. (2001). Control-related beliefs and depressive symptoms in clinic-referred children and adolescents: Developmental differences and model specificity. *Journal of Abnormal Psychology, 110,* 97–109.

Wierzbicki, M. (1987). Similarity of monozygotic and dizygotic child twins in level and lability of subclinically depressed mood. *American Journal of Orthopsychiatry, 57,* 33–40.

Williamson, D. E., Birmaher, B., Frank, E., Anderson, B. P., Matty, M. K., & Kupfer, D. J. (1998). Nature of life events and difficulties in depressed adolescents. *Journal of the American Academy of Child and Adolescent Psychiatry, 37,* 1049–1057.

Winokur, G. (1997). All roads lead to depression: Clinically homogeneous, etiologically heterogeneous. *Journal of Affective Disorders, 45,* 97–108.

Wright, C., & Birks, E. (2000). Risk factors for failure to thrive: A population-based survey. *Child: Care, Health and Development, 26,* 5–16.

23

Depression in Adolescents

Peter M. Lewinsohn and Cecilia A. Essau

Since the introduction of DSM-III, the study of major depressive disorder (MDD) among adolescents has attracted much attention. Interest in studying depression in this age group has been spurred by recent findings (for review, see Essau & Petermann, 1999) among adults demonstrating that depression has an age of onset in adolescence for many.

PHENOMENOLOGY OF DEPRESSION

Phenomenology and Age

Even though there is consensus that with minor modifications the DSM criteria are applicable to adolescents, it is important to ask whether age and gender alter some of the manifestations of depression (Cicchetti, 1984; Weinberger, Rutman, Sullivan, Penick, & Dietz, 1973). Some differences have been reported between adolescents and adults and between girls and boys. However, the results of the Oregon Adolescent Depression Project (OADP; Lewinsohn, Pettit, Joiner, & Seeley, 2002) suggest that the pattern of depressive symptoms identified in depressed adolescents is generally similar to those reported by adults.

Phenomenology in Clinical and Community Samples

Because many adolescents with major depression do not receive treatment (e.g., Essau, 2000; Lewinsohn, Rohde, & Seeley, 1998b), clinical samples may represent a severe subset that is not representative of the typical depressed adolescent. Thus, it is important to compare the phenomenology of depression of adolescents diagnosed as "cases" in community-based samples with depressed adolescents from clinical settings. Roberts, Lewinsohn, and Seeley (1995) reported that with minor exceptions, the patterns of depressive symptoms in community cases were phenomenologically very similar to cases of major depression in treatment settings. Adolescents in treatment settings, however, reported more thoughts of death and/or suicide than adolescents in the OADP community sample. Symptoms related to weight/appetite disturbance and sleep difficulties were more common in the community than in the clinical cases. There were also small gender differences among depressed cases. Depressed girls, compared to depressed boys, had significantly higher scores on weight/appetite disturbance (77% vs. 58.5%) and worthlessness/guilt (82.5% vs. 67.5%). Lewinsohn et al. (2002) found no systematic differences in the relative rate of occurrence of specific symptoms across episodes in multiple episode adolescents.

EPIDEMIOLOGY OF DEPRESSION

Prevalence of Major Depressive Disorder

Several epidemiological studies have clearly documented depression as a prevalent disorder in adolescence (Table 23.1). Estimates of the lifetime prevalence of MDD in adolescence range from 15% to 20% (Lewinsohn, Rohde, Seeley, Klein, & Gotlib, 2000). Dysthymic

TABLE 23.1. Prevalence Rates (Lifetime, 1 Year, and 6 Months) of Major Depression in Adolescents

Authors (year)	Age (years)	Diagnostic instrument (diagnostic criteria)	Depressive disorder (%)		
			LT	1 year	6-months/PP
Deykin, Levy, and Wells (1987)	16–19	DIS (DSM-III)	6.8	—	—
Kashani et al. (1987)	14–16	DICA (DSM-III)	—	—	4.7
McGee and Williams (1988)	15	DISC (DSM-III)	1.9	—	1.2
Velez, Johnson, and Cohen (1989)	13–18	DISC (DSM-III-R)	—	—	3.7
Fleming, Offord, and Boyle (1989)	12–16	SDI (DSM-III)	—	—	9.8
Whitaker et al. (1990)	14–17	Clinical interview (DSM-III)	4.0	—	—
Lewinsohn, Hops, Roberts, Seeley, and Andrews (1993)	14–18	K-SADS-E (DSM-III-R)	18.4	—	2.9
Reinherz, Giaconia, Lefkowitz, Pakiz, and Frost (1993)	18	DIS-III-R (DSM-III-R)	9.4	—	6.0
Fergusson, Horwood, and Lynskey (1993)	15	DISC (DSM-III-R)	—	4.2	0.7
Cooper & Goodyer (1993)	11–16	DISC (DSM-III-R)	—	6.0	3.6
Feehan, McGee, Raja, and Williams (1994)	18	DIS-III-R (DSM-III-R)	—	16.7	—
Verhulst, Van Der Ende, Ferdinand, and Kasius (1997)	13–18	DISC (DSM-III-R)	—	—	3.6
Essau, Conradt, and Petermann (2000)	12–17	CAPI (DSM-IV)	17.9	—	—

Note. %, prevalence rates; LT, lifetime rate; 1 year, 1-year rates; 6 months, 6-month rates; PP, point prevalence; DIS, Diagnostic Interview Schedule; DISC, Diagnostic Interview Schedule for Children; DICA, Diagnostic Interview for Children and Adolescents; K-SADS-E, Schedule for Affective Disorders and Schizophrenia for School-Age Children (epidemiologic version); DIS-III-R, Diagnostic Interview Schedule, third revised edition; SDI, Survey Diagnostic Instrument; CAPI, Computerized Munich version of the Composite International Diagnostic Interview; —, not reported.

disorder has been the focus of less investigation in adolescence, due to the fact that only 10% of depressed adolescents experience dysthymia alone.

In community studies, between 20% and 30% of those who met criteria for MDD were severely affected (e.g., Essau, 2000; Lewinsohn, Rohde, & Seeley, 1998a). The prevalence rates for MDD obtained in adolescents are comparable to those reported in recent epidemiological studies of adult population (e.g., Kessler, McGonagle, Swartz, Blazer, & Nelson, 1993; see also Kessler, Chapter 1, this volume). In regard to *incidence* (number of new cases over a period of time), the distinction between first onset of MDD versus recurrence is important. *First incidence* refers to the percentage of the sample developing their first episode of MDD during the time period specified. In the OADP, the first incidence rate for MDD for 1 year was 7.1% for girls, 4.4% for boys, and 5.7% for total sample. *Recurrence* refers to the percentage of the sample who had a previous episode of MDD and developed another episode during the time period specified (1 year); the relapse rate for an interval of 1 year for girls was 21.1%, 9.1% for boys, and 17.9% for total.

In adolescent samples, the episode of MDD under examination is frequently the first lifetime episode (Kovacs, 1996). Different predictors have been found for first onset than for recurrence of MDD (Lewinsohn, Allen, Seeley, & Gotlib, 1999; Monroe, Rohde, Seeley, & Lewinsohn, 1999). Stressful life events, such as the breakup of a romantic relationship (Monroe et al., 1999) were more likely to be associated with the first episode of MDD than with recurrences, suggesting that major depressive episodes may become less dependent on life events as the number of depressive episodes increases over time.

Onset Age, Duration, and Time to Recurrence of Major Depressive Disorder

There are two ways to examine age at onset. The first is to assess incidence via survival analysis, that is, the proportion of individuals who develop an episode by a certain age. In the OADP study, the rates of depression onset in childhood are low, doubling from an annual incidence rate of 1% to 2% at age 13, and from 3% to 7% at age 15. Approximately 28% of adolescents have experienced a major depressive episode by the age of 19 (Lewinsohn et al., 1998a). Earlier onset was associated with being female, lower parental education, a history of nonaffective disorders, and a history of suicide attempt. The second way of examining age of onset is more direct, and simply involves assessing the mean onset age of MDD cases. In the OADP, the mean age at MDD onset was 14.9 years. For girls and boys the mean age of onset of MDD was 14.8 years (range, 5.0–18.9) and 15.3 (range, 6.0–18.7), respectively. The difference between boys and girls was not statistically significant. Thus, it seems that while girls are more likely to become depressed and consequently a survival curve will show them to become depressed earlier than boys, there is no difference in onset age between girls and boys who develop an episode of MDD.

Even in a community sample, MDD episodes were quite long-lasting. MDD episodes in the OADP sample had a mean duration of 26 weeks, with a range of 2 to 250 weeks (Lewinsohn, Rohde, & Seeley, 1994). The median duration of MDD episodes was 8.0 weeks, indicating a highly skewed distribution. A survival function analysis projected that 25% of the subjects would be recovered by 3 weeks, 50% by 8 weeks, and 75% by 24 weeks.

Of the 336 subjects who recovered from an episode of MDD, 40% relapsed into a second MDD episode after an interval of approximately 1 year (Lewinsohn, Rohde, & Seeley, 1994). The mean and median survival times between two MDD episodes were 73.8 months and 73.0 months, respectively. Longer lasting episodes were observed in those whose depression occurred early (before age 15), in those whose depression had been accompanied by suicidal ideation, and in those for whom treatment was sought. Shorter time to relapse was associated with prior suicidal ideation and attempt, and with later first onset age.

COMORBIDITY

Frequency and Pattern of Comorbidity

Comorbidity is the rule rather than the exception for depression (for review, see Nottelmann & Jensen, 1995). Comorbidity appears to be more common in children and adolescents than in adults (Lewinsohn, Rohde, Seeley, & Hops, 1991; Rohde, Lewinsohn, & Seeley, 1991). After reviewing six community studies, Angold and Costello (1993) concluded that the presence of depression in children and adolescents increased the probability for another disorder by at least 20 times. In the Bremen Adolescent Study (Essau, Conradt, & Petermann, 2000), 40.1% of the adolescents who met the diagnosis of any depressive disorders had one additional disorder, and 17.9% had at least two other disorders.

The most common comorbidity is with anxiety disorders; for most depressed cases with a comorbid anxiety disorder, the anxiety preceded the onset of depressive disorder (Reinherz et al., 1989; Rohde et al., 1991). Disruptive behavior (attention-deficit/hyperactivity, conduct, or oppositional defiant disorder) and substance abuse disorders also frequently co-occur with depression.

Impact of Comorbidity

The presence of comorbidity has been found to be associated with a greater number of past depression episodes (Rohde et al., 1991) and with more impairment and distress (Essau, 2000). In the OADP cohort, adolescents with pure MDD, compared to depressed adolescents with another mental disorder, were much more likely to have received treatment, to be rated as showing poor global functioning, to have elevated rate of suicide attempts, and to show evidence of academic problems (Lewinsohn, Rohde, & Seeley, 1994). There is an interesting interaction between comorbidity and gender, in that males who are only depressed had a very low probability of being in treatment. The presence of a comorbid disorder markedly increased the likelihood of treatment, especially if the boy had a substance use disorder. In girls, those with pure depression were more likely to receive treatment, whereas those who had a comorbid disruptive behavior disorder were less likely to receive treatment. The highest use of mental health services was observed in depressed adolescents who had comorbid substance use disorders.

Rohde, Clark, Lewinsohn, Seeley, and Kaufman (2001) recently examined the impact of lifetime psychiatric comorbidity of depression with another mental disorder on participation in, and benefit from, a cognitive-behavioral group treatment for depression in adolescents. Comorbidity was not associated with the participation measures. Comorbidity was unrelated to recovery from the depression within the follow-up period, but a comorbid substance abuse/dependence was associated with slower recovery from the depression. Participants with disruptive behavior disorders were more likely to experience depression recurrence posttreatment. Thus, while some outcomes were worse for some comorbidities, it appears that the presence of comorbidity is not a contraindication for the use of structured group cognitive-behavioral interventions for depressed adolescents. More research is needed on this important topic.

ASSESSMENT

The availability of age-appropriate assessment devices with good psychometric properties is important for the assessment of depression symptoms, their duration, severity, and onset age. Good assessment measures are also critical for assessing the psychosocial problems associated with depression, and for evaluating the effectiveness of treatment. A less well recognized function of assessment is "screening" in order to identify from a large population those who have an elevated probability of being or of becoming depressed. "Screener" tests like the Center for Epidemiologic Studies Depression Scale (CES-D; Radloff, 1977) are used as the first stage of the two-stage process (e.g., Garrison, Addy, Jackson, McKeown, & Waller, 1992) in which those who score above a prespecified cutoff are identified as putative cases to whom a more extensive diagnostic interview is administered. An example of use of the CES-D as the first screen in a clinical trial is a study by Clarke et al. (1995), in which this test was administered to a total school population. Putative cases were then given a diagnostic interview on the basis of which a definite diagnosis was established or ruled out. To be useful, a screener should provide a fast, economical, and valid way of partitioning the study population into presumed "well" (negative on screener) and presumed "ill" (positive on screener) groups. Another screening function may be to help medical clinicians to recognize depression in their patients. Because clinicians have difficulty in detecting depression in adults, it would be interesting to know how well pediatricians are able to recognize depression in their patients (Sartorius et al., 1990).

Diagnostic Interview Schedules

By using specific and well-defined symptoms and probe questions, detailed coding rules and diagnostic algorithms, diagnostic interview schedules imposes a rigorous structure on the diagnostic process. Probe questions evaluate the presence of specific symptoms, their duration, and associated impairment. Examples of diagnostic interview schedules are the Diagnostic Interview Schedule for Children (DISC; Costello, Edelbrock, & Costello, 1985; Piacentini et al., 1993; Schwab-Stone et al., 1993), the Diagnostic Interview for Children and Adolescents (DICA; (Herjanic & Reich, 1982), the Kiddie—Schedule for Affective Disorders and Schizophrenia (K-SADS; Puig-Antich, Blau, Marx, Greenhill, & Chambers, 1978), and the Child and Adolescent Psychiatric Assessment (CAPA; Angold et al., 1995). (For a review of these measures, see Bird & Gould, 1995; Nezu, Nezu, McClure, & Zwick, Chapter 3, this volume). The availability of diagnostic criteria as per the DSM and the availability of structured interview schedules has the advantage of reducing observer, information, and criterion variance and thus enhances interrater reliability and criterion validity. It is important to note, however, that adolescents were found to be unreliable in dating the onset of a symptom for recall periods longer than 3 months (Angold, Erklanis, Costello, & Rutter, 1996). About 31% of the subjects reported depressed mood that lasted longer than 1 year during one interview, and in another interview less than 1 year. This kind of inconsistency could mean that the youngster would be seen as meeting criteria diagnosis in one interview, but not in the other.

It is advantageous to collect data from multiple sources (e.g., parents, teacher). Unfortunately, agreement among informants on the frequency and severity of depression symptoms, especially for adolescents, has been low (Angold et al., 1987; Cantwell, Lewinsohn, Rohde, & Seeley, 1997). Although the reason for this low agreement is unclear, some hypotheses have been put forward (Reynolds, 1994). For example, concerns about self-presentation and evaluation by others are among the most common fears in adolescence; hence, they may want to present themselves to others in a socially desirable way, which would make them especially reluctant to reveal their depression to others. Parents and adolescents also may have different thresholds concerning what comprises a "problematic" behavior. A major challenge for research is how to combine discordant information from different sources. Authors differ in their view as to which information should be used. For research, the "best estimate" approach (Leckman, Sholomskas, Thompson, Belanger, & Weissman, 1982) involves having two experienced diagnosticians independently review the diagnostic information and then reach a consensus diagnosis.

Self-Report Questionnaires

The fact that many depressive symptoms reflect subjective feelings and self-perceptions lends credence to the use of self-report questionnaires for their assessment in this age group (Reynolds, 1994). Questionnaires have been used to assess the presence and severity of depressive symptoms and to monitor changes during the therapeutic process (Reynolds, 1994). Some examples of self-report questionnaires for the assessment of depression include the Depression Self-Rating Scale (Birleson, 1981), the Dimensions of Depression Profile for Children and Adolescents (Harter & Nowakowski, 1987), the Center for Epidemiological Studies Depression Scale (Radloff, 1991), the Beck Depression Inventory (Chiles, Miller, & Cox, 1980), the Reynolds Adolescent Depression Scale (Reynolds, 1987), the Children's Depression Inventory (Kovacs, 1985), and the Mood and Feelings Questionnaire (Angold et al., 1987). Detailed description and summaries of the psychometric properties of these instruments have been presented by several authors (e.g., Essau, Conrad, & Petermann, 1999; Nezu et al., Chapter 3, this volume; Reynolds, 1994).

Measures of Related Constructs

Numerous measures for assessing depression-related constructs, that is, psychosocial constructs that are likely to be influenced by the depression, have been developed and used with adolescents. The range of domains and measures is large and includes the Children's Attributional Style Questionnaire (e.g., Gladstone, Kaslow, Seeley, & Lewinsohn, 1997; Kaslow, Tanenbaum, & Seligman, 1978) and other measures of cognitive function like the Dysfunctional Attitudes Scale (Andrews, Lewinsohn, Hops, & Roberts, 1993; Weissman & Beck, 1978) and the Self-Perception Profile for Adolescents (Harter, 1985). The assessment of pleasant activities (MacPhillamy & Lewinsohn, 1982) and unpleasant activities (Lewinsohn, Mermelstein, Alexander, & MacPhillamy, 1985) may be important, as is the assessment of social competence, for example, with the Matson Evaluation of Social Skills with Youngsters (Matson, Rotatori, & Helsel, 1983). For the assessment of family environment there are instruments like the Issues Checklist (Robin & Weiss, 1980) and the Family Environment Scale (Moos, 1974).

Psychosocial Impairment

Depression is associated with impairment in psychosocial functioning. For example, in the Whitaker et al. (1990) study, depressed cases were the most impaired compared to those with other disorders. In the Bremen study, almost all those with depressive disorders (98%) were impaired during their worst depressive episode (Essau et al., 2000).

Due to lack of an acceptable "gold standard" for validating "depressive caseness," psychosocial impairment has been used as an external validator (i.e., definition of caseness restricted to those who manifest impairment) (e.g., Bird et al., 1988). The assessment of psychosocial impairment is also important in its own right. Examples of instruments to measure psychosocial impairment include the Children's Global Assessment Scale (CGAS; Shaffer et al., 1983), the Columbia Impairment Scale (CIS; Bird et al., 1993), and the Social Adjustment Inventory for Children and Adolescents (SAICA; John, Gammon, Prusoff, & Warner, 1987) (see Bird & Gould, 1995, for a review of these measures).

Psychosocial impairment may manifest itself in different areas of functioning, such as interpersonal performance with peers, family members, and other adults. Performance in school or at work and the ability to enjoy life and to make good use of leisure time are also important. Recognizing this diversity, the measure of social impairment used by Lewinsohn and his colleagues (Lewinsohn, Solomon, Seeley, & Zeiss, 2000) makes use of an aggregate measure that includes stressful life events and social support from family and friends, as well as measures of social interaction, life satisfaction, engagement in pleasant activities, self-esteem, social skills, coping skills, and cognitive functioning. The justification for the use of such an aggregate is that all these factors have been shown to be associated with clinical depression, and they are correlated with each other (Lewinsohn et al., 2000).

In a series of publications using the OADP data, Lewinsohn and colleagues have examined the impact of "subthreshold" depressive symptoms on psychosocial impairment. In one publication (Gotlib, Lewinsohn, & Seeley, 1995), adolescents with elevated levels of depressive symptoms (but not meeting criteria for diagnosis of depression) did not differ significantly from clinically depressed adolescents on most measures of psychosocial dysfunction, and they were significantly more impaired than normal controls. Recently, Lewinsohn et al. (2000) examined the clinical implication of subthreshold depressive symptoms, based on CES-D scores, in three community samples (adults, older adults, adolescents). The result showed significant psychosocial impairment in those adolescents with subsyndromal levels of depression. Furthermore, subthreshold depressive symptoms predicted future major depression and the development of substance use disorder in a subsequent 5-year period.

An important issue that does not appear to be completely resolved concerns whether depressed adolescents who do not have a comorbid disorder like substance abuse/dependence or a conduct disorder show impaired academic performance. In the OADP (Lewinsohn, Roberts, et al., 1994), currently depressed adolescents did not differ from controls on academic variables (parental dissatisfaction with grades, not completing homework or having repeated a grade, days missed school, or being late). The depressed adolescents also did not differ from controls on the measure of intelligence that was included in the OADP: the Shipley Hartford Vocabulary Test (Shipley, 1940).

The fact that impaired functioning is observed in depressed cases in various areas of functioning raises the question of whether these difficulties are causes, concomitants, or consequences of depression and/or of the comorbid conditions. The finding that depression is associated with impairment is important because adolescence is a crucial period of life in which various skills are acquired for adult life.

PSYCHOSOCIAL CORRELATES AND PSYCHOSOCIAL RISK FACTORS FOR ADOLESCENT DEPRESSION

Gender

In childhood, rates of MDD are approximately equal in females and males (Rutter, 1986), but in adolescence all studies report a female preponderance with rates of depressive disorders being two to three times higher in girls than in boys (Cohen et al., 1993; Essau, 2000; Lewinsohn, Hops, Roberts, Seeley, & Andrews, 1993; Reinherz, Giaconia, Pakiz, et al., 1993). The gender difference in the prevalence of MDD seems to arise between the ages of 12 and 14 (Cohen et al., 1993; Petersen, Sarigiani, & Kennedy, 1991). The female:male ratio in older adolescents is comparable to that found in adults.

The level of severity of depressive episodes may also be higher in females than in males (Reinherz, Giaconia, Lefkowitz, Pakiz, & Frost, 1993). In an as yet unpublished paper

(Lewinsohn et al., 2002), female adolescents were significantly more likely to experience recurrent episodes of depression. Of the 371 females who had experienced an episode of depression, 46.4% had a second episode and 66 (38.4%) of those had a third episode. By contrast, of the 193 males with one episode, only 26.9% had a second episode (52), and 13 of those (25.0%) had a third episode. Thus, while all formerly depressed adolescents are at elevated risk for recurrence, there is a greater effect for females.

Explanations for adolescent sex differences in rates of depression include divergent socialization practices concerning power and control, victimization (e.g., child sexual and physical abuse), management of feelings, sex-role orientation, and more negative body image (Allgood-Merten, Lewinsohn, & Hops, 1990). The hormonal changes experienced by girls at puberty have also been used to explain sex difference in depression. Another explanation is that girls experience more challenges than boys in early adolescence (Petersen et al., 1991), and that they are more affected than boys by stressful life events (Petersen et al., 1991). Others (Aro, 1994) have suggested that the coping-with-adversity styles of girls and boys may differ. Nolen-Hoeksema and colleagues (Nolen-Hoeksema, Morrow, & Fredrickson, 1993; Nolen-Hoeksema & Girgus, 1994) have suggested that women are more likely than are men to ruminate and focus on emotion when depressed; focusing on one's distress exacerbates the depression. Men are more likely to distract themselves with activities.

Age and the Impact of Puberty

There have been numerous studies examining the relationship between the onset of puberty and the prevalence of depression. In the Great Smoky Mountain Study (Angold, Costello, & Worthman, 1998) pubertal status turned out to be a better predictor of the emergence of female preponderance than did age. That is, girls were more likely than boys to be depressed after the transition to midpuberty (Tanner Stage III and above). By contrast, boys had higher rates of depression than girls before Tanner Stage III. In a representative cohort of adolescents, 5th through 8th grades, Hayward, Gotlib, Schraedley, and Litt (1999) found pubertal status predicted depressive symptoms in Caucasian, but not African American or Hispanic girls. These authors suggest that girls in these two ethnic group attach different meaning to weight-related bodily changes. That is, the consequence of increasing body fat during puberty is interpreted less negatively in African American than in Caucasian girls.

An interesting interaction was found in a study by Garber, Robinson, and Valentiner (1997). Early- and, to a lesser extent, late-maturing girls compared to girls with average pubertal onset time had significantly elevated rates of major depression. In boys, the rate of major depression did not differ as a function of pubertal onset.

Psychosocial Characteristics of Young Adults Who Have Experienced and Recovered from an Episode of Depression

It has been shown repeatedly that depression during adolescence is a powerful predictor of recurrence of depression during young adulthood, especially in females (Lewinsohn, Rohde, Klein, & Seeley, 1999). Adolescents with MDD also had a high rate of nonaffective disorders in young adulthood but did not differ from adolescents with nonaffective disorder.

Another publication coming out of the OADP (Lewinsohn, Rohde, Seeley, Klein, & Gotlib, in press) documents the extensiveness of the psychosocial impairments shown by young adults who have recovered from an adolescent depression. To wit, these formerly depressed young adults were less likely to have completed college, to more recently have been unemployed, to have a lower income level, to have higher rates of child bearing, to be smoking cigarettes, to have lower levels of social support from family and friends and smaller social networks, and to be experiencing some (i.e., subsyndromal) depressive symptoms, elevated stressful life events, low life satisfaction, low self-esteem, elevated mental health treatment, and poor physical health. It is important to note that the above-mentioned impairments were detectable even in participants who remained free of depression recurrence in young adulthood. Most of the psychosocial impairments were specific to adolescent depression, that is, not observed in the nonaffective controls.

Family/Genetic Factors

Children of depressed parents have up to six times higher rates of depression than do children of nondepressed mothers and they also have an earlier onset age (for reviews, see Essau & Merikangas, 1999; Gotlib & Goodman, 1999). In the Bremen Adolescent Study (Essau, 2000) more than half (54.6%) of the depressed cases had parent(s) with depression. A high proportion of these adolescents also reported the presence of other disorders in their parents, including alcohol (22.2%), drug (11.4%), and anxiety disorders (32.4%). Further analysis showed a strong association between mother's depression and depression in females. An important issue is specificity: Does a family history of depression impart a specific vulnerability for depression in the offspring, or is there an increased vulnerability for other (i.e., nonaffective) disorders as well? Klein, Lewinsohn, Seeley, and Rohde (2001) compared the prevalence of psychiatric disorders in the first-degree relatives of adolescents with a history of MDD with the relatives of adolescents with a history of nonmood disorders, and to the relatives of adolescents with no history of disorder through age 18. MDD and dysthymic disorders were significantly elevated in the relatives of adolescent probands with a history of MDD. Probands with a history of MDD also had significantly higher rates of alcohol abuse/dependence in family members. However, the increased rate of alcoholism appeared to be due to the comorbidity of MDD and alcohol abuse/dependence in the probands. By contrast, no significant increased rate of mood disorders was found in relatives of probands with anxiety, disruptive behavior, and substance use disorders.

Numerous factors may be involved in the transmission of depression from parents to their offspring (Goodman & Gotlib, 1999), including dysfunctional parent–child interactions, marital conflict, emotional unavailability of parents, and genetic factors. For example, maternal depression may lead to marital discord or to divorce, and the children may have been exposed to a great deal of interparental conflict (Fendrich, Warner, & Weissman, 1990; Kovacs et al., 1984). Parental depression may have an impact on children through depression-related parental behaviors such as emotional unavailability and cognitive dysfunction (Cummings & Davies, 1994). Communication within the family of depressed patients has also been described as impaired (Weissman, Paykel, & Klerman, 1972). In the Bremen Adolescent Study (Essau, 2000), depressed compared to nondepressed adolescents reported significant problems in communicating with their parents. It is important to be cautious about drawing conclusions about the direction of causation. Many of the above-mentioned studies are cross-sectional, and it is possible that some of the negative parental behaviors are secondary to depression in the adolescent.

Although most studies show depression to run in families (Hammen, 1991a), it is important to note that not all children of depressed parents have depression (Essau, 2000) and that the child's gender may moderate familial transmission. For example, in the study by Davies and Windle (1997), maternal depressive symptoms had a stronger impact on girls than on boys. Even though familial transmission of depression has been shown, it is important to note that this does not necessarily *prove* genetic transmission. A family history of depression may be correlated with a host of other risk factors, such as poverty, minority-group status (Sameroff & Seifer, 1991), marital discord, single-parent status, comorbid disorders, low levels of social support, and child abuse (Goodman, Brogan, Lynch, & Fielding, 1993; Goodman & Gotlib, 1999; Hammen, 1992).

Life Events

An important issue in the life event literature concerns the relative merits of the methods used to assess life events. Assessment strategies range from simple self-report checklists (e.g., Holmes & Rahe, 1967) to more detailed self-report questionnaires (Dohrenwend, Krasnoff, Askenasy, & Dohrenwend, 1978), to very elaborate interview procedures such as the Bedford College Life Event Schedule (LEDS; Brown, 1974).

Despite the methodological problems associated with the questionnaire checklist assessment approach, it has been the method of choice, especially when large samples are involved. Among the life events that have been examined are those that are commonly experienced in the natural life cycle (e.g., failure in academic tasks, interpersonal rejection, criticism, marriage, being laid off from work, starting a new job). Studies generally show that depressed adolescents report more negative life events prior to the onset of the depressive episode (e.g., Lewinsohn, Roberts, et al., 1994; Reinherz et al., 1989). In the Commonwealth Fund 1997 Adolescent Health Survey, the presence of many stressful life events was found to increase the likelihood of reporting high levels of depressive symptoms by three times (Schraedley, Gotlib, & Hayward, 1999). The data also showed stress level to be more strongly associated with depressive symptoms for girls than for boys.

Numerous studies have examined the impact of specific life events. Goodyer and Altham (1991) found that exposure to at least two exit events (e.g., death, divorce of parents) was significantly more frequently reported by depressed and anxious children than by children in the control group. There were no differences in the number of lifetime exits between anxious and depressed cases. Reinherz, Giaconia, Lefkowitz, et al. (1993) found that the death of a parent before age 15, pregnancy, and health problems that interfered with daily functioning were associated with depression in females. In males, it was the remarriage of a parent that was more influential. Monroe et al. (1999) found breakup of a relationship to be an important event for occurrence of the first episode of depression but not for recurrence.

Although stressful life events appear to be involved in the onset of depression in adolescence, the mechanism involved in this association is unclear. Goodyer, Cooper, Vize, and Ashby (1993) suggested that some families may be "life-event-prone" as a consequence of lifetime episodes of parental psychopathology. Hammen (1991b) suggested that depressed individuals may contribute to the occurrence of stress. Hammen, Rudolph, Weisz, Rao, and Burge (1999) proposed a diathesis–stress model, in which depression develops as a result of the interaction between personal vulnerability (i.e., cognitive propensity toward depression-inducing interpretations or appraisals of events) and external stress, and that exposure to the latter may activate this underlying cognitive predisposition.

Individual differences in how adolescents cope with negative life events may also be important. Coping with adversity, or a person's coping style, has been postulated to be a factor that mediates the relation between stress and depression (e.g., Dohrenwend & Dohrenwend, 1981). The assumption is that given the same level of stress, people who use more effective coping strategies will experience less disruption of their behavior and consequently will experience less distress. Consistent with this formulation, depressed adolescents have been reported to use less effective coping styles (e.g., becoming intoxicated, isolating themselves, or running away from home), whereas nondepressed adolescents used more effective alternatives (e.g., minimizing the importance of the events, engaging in problem-solving behavior) in dealing with the negative life events experienced (Adams & Adams, 1991; Essau,

2000). Also consistent with the above-mentioned formulation, depression has been found to be positively correlated with emotion-focused strategies (Compas, Malcarne, & Fondacaro, 1988) and cognitive avoidance (Holahan & Moos, 1991), and negatively with problem-focused coping (Compas et al., 1988).

Conceptually similar to "coping" are constructs such as competence (D'Zurilla, 1986), problem-solving ability (Nezu, 1987), hardiness (Kobasa, 1979), antidepressant behaviors (Rippere, 1976), and learned resourcefulness (Rosenbaum, 1980). All of these can be postulated to be important for the development and maintenance of depression in adolescents.

PSYCHOSOCIAL CHARACTERISTICS OF DEPRESSED ADOLESCENTS

Cognitive Factors

Depressed adolescents have been reported to have low self-esteem and negative body image (especially in girls), to be pessimistic, and to show evidence of the depressotypic attributional style (i.e., blame self for failures and attribute positive experiences to external sources) (Allgood-Merten et al., 1990; Harter, 1990; King, Naylor, Segal, Evans, & Shain, 1993; Lewinsohn, Roberts, et al., 1994; Reinherz et al., 1989; Renouf & Harter, 1990). In the Bremen Adolescent Study (Essau, 2000), depressed adolescents had significantly lower scores on perceived control as measured using the Perceived Control Scale (Weisz, Sweeney, Proffitt, & Carr, 1993), and on perceived competence as measured using the Self-Perception Profile for Adolescents (Harter, 1988), than did nondepressed controls.

Health Problems

In the OADP, Lewinsohn, Seeley, Hibbard, Rohde, and Sack (1996) found the combination of physical disease and disease-related functional impairment to predict future depression. Among adolescents who reported no reduced activity due to physical disease, 8.4% had subsequent MDD episodes compared to 15.1% of those with reduced activity.

MENTAL HEALTH SERVICES UTILIZATION

In a survey of treatments provided to depressed adolescents in the general community, Lewinsohn et al. (1998b) present information about treatment utilization. The outcome measures included type of treatment, type of provider, approximate number of sessions, mean age at first outpatient treatment, mean age at first inpatient treatment, and use of medications. Results showed 60.7% of the depressed adolescents receiving some form of mental health service. Inpatient treatment was rare for depressed adolescents. The use of medications (9.0%) was also relatively rare. Factors that were positively related to treatment utilization included depression severity, number of depressive episodes, history of a suicide attempt, academic problems, disruptive family structure, being female, and the presence of a comorbid nonaffective disorder. For 72.9% of those with comorbid disorders, compared to 49.5% of the "pure" cases of depression, treatment had been sought.

FUTURE DIRECTIONS

Although our knowledge about adolescent depression has increased over the last decade, we have much more to learn before we can assert that we fully understand its onset, course, and long-term consequences. Many of the existing studies are cross-sectional. Prospective–longitudinal studies are needed to clarify some of the crucial issues. Because many of these studies are still in progress, we will learn more about the antecedents for adolescent depression and the transition from adolescence into adulthood in the coming years. We end by pointing to issues that deserve more attention than they have received.

Studies are needed to clarify the meaning of comorbidity. What are the implications of comorbidity for taxonomy, etiology, prognosis, and treatment? More detailed information is needed about the temporal sequencing of comorbid disorders. Is the etiology of depression that is "primary," that is, occurs first, different from depression that is "secondary," that is, follows another disorder? Another understudied topic is the role of sleep disturbances in the etiology and maintenance of depression (e.g., Dahl et al., 1996). With the kinds of pressures being put on adolescents, sleep deprivation may be an important topic (e.g., Maayan et al., 1998). The kinds of efforts that make use of computer-administered telephone probes and that are proving useful for the detection of depression in adults, such as the PrimeD (Kobak et al., 1997), might be adapted for use with adolescents in primary care settings.

Several factors have been identified as risk factors for adolescent depression (e.g., family dysfunction; history of parental and personal psychopathology, especially comorbidity; multiple episodes; depressive cognitions; and social–personal factors such as excessive interpersonal dependence and negative life events). This knowledge is the critical point of departure for generating hypotheses about possible mechanisms. It is also needed in order to identify those at elevated risk so they can be targeted for prevention and intervention. In contrast to the number of studies on risk factors, very few studies have examined protective factors of depression—what factors protect high-risk adolescents against becoming depressed?

Several psychosocial models of depression have been developed in the context of adult depression. None have been modified to incorporate the developmental factors that may be uniquely important during adolescence. Several integrative models of depression (e.g., Cummings & Cicchetti, 1990; Gotlib & Hammen, 1992; Lewinsohn, Hoberman, Teri, & Hautzinger, 1985) have been proposed that recognize that the etiology of depression is multifactorial and that stress the interplay between early childhood experiences, genetic and biological factors, cognitive factors, and family–environmental and developmentally related factors. The link between each of these factors and the combined contribution of all of these factors in the development and maintenance of depression in adolescents needs to incorporated into the design of future studies. Based on recent research findings, we suggest that theoretical formulations of depression should incorporate three complexities that have emerged. First, there is a large gender difference in depression, and it is possible that the etiology of depression differs in males and females. Second, it is important to consider that etiological factors may be different for those whose depression is "primary" (depression-only disorder or depression precedes the other disorder) than for those whose depression is "secondary" (depression follows the other disorder). Third, there may be different etiological factors involved in first onsets than in recurrence episodes of depression (Lewinsohn et al., 1999; Monroe et al., 1999).

Future research must also be sensitive to the possibility that some of the psychosocial characteristics associated with depression may be *concomitants* that occur only during the episode, but do not exist before or after the episode, (i.e., they are state-dependent); some may be *scars*, psychosocial characteristics that are consequences or residual effects of an episode (i.e., they didn't exist before the episode); and some may be *antecedents*, risk factors that precede the occurrence of depression and that are probably most relevant to etiology. Finally, investigators should examine the question of whether the impact of some risk factors is sensitive to developmental periods—for example, parental separation with subsequent absence of father from the home may have different effects depending on the age and gender of the adolescent.

REFERENCES

Adams, A., & Adams, J. (1991). Life events, depression, and perceived problem solving alternatives in adolescents. *Journal of Child Psychology and Psychiatry, 32,* 811–820.

Allgood-Merten, B., Lewinsohn, P. M., & Hops, H. (1990). Sex differences and adolescent depression. *Journal of Abnormal Psychology, 99,* 55–63.

Andrews, J. A., Lewinsohn, P. M., Hops, H., & Roberts, R. E. (1993). Psychometric properties of scales for the measurement of psychosocial variables associated with depression in adolescence. *Psychological Reports, 73,* 1019–1046.

Angold, A., & Costello, E. J. (1993). Depressive comorbidity in children and adolescents: Empirical, theoretical, and methodological issues. *American Journal of Psychiatry, 150,* 1779–1791.

Angold, A., Costello, E. J., & Worthman, C. M. (1998). Puberty and depression: The roles of age, pubertal status and pubertal timing. *Psychological Medicine, 28,* 51–61.

Angold, A., Erklanis, A., Costello, E. J., & Rutter, M. (1996). Precision, reliability and accuracy in the dating of symptom onsets in child and adolescent psychopathology. *Journal of Child Psychology and Psychiatry, 37,* 657–664.

Angold, A., Prendergast, M., Cox, A., Rutter, M., Harrington, R., & Simonoff, E. (1995). The Child and Adolescent Psychiatric Assessment: CAPA. *Psychological Medicine, 25,* 739–754.

Angold, A., Weissman, M. M., John, K., Merikangas, K. R., Prusoff, B. A., Wickramaratne, P., Gammon, G. D., & Warner, V. (1987). Parent and child reports of depressive symptoms in children at low and high risk of depression. *Journal of Child Psychology and Psychiatry, 28,* 901–915.

Aro, H. M. (1994). Risk and protective factors in depression: A developmental perspective. *Acta Psychiatrica Scandinavica,* (Suppl. 377), 59–64.

Bird, H. R., Canino, G., Rubio-Stipec, M., Gould, M. S., Ribera, J., Sesman, M., Woodbury, M., Huertas-Goldman, S., Pagan, A., Sanchez-Lacay, A., & Moscoso, M. (1988). Estimates of the prevalence of childhood maladjustment in a community survey in Puerto Rico: The use of combined measures. *Archives of General Psychiatry, 45,* 1120–1126.

Bird, H. R., & Gould, M. S. (1995). The use of diagnostic instruments and global measures of functioning in child psychiatry epidemiological studies. In F. C. Verhulst & H. M. Koot (Eds.), *The epidemilology of child and adolescent psychopathology* (pp. 86–103). New York: Oxford University Press.

Bird, H. R., Shaffer, D., Fisher, P., Gould, M. S., Staghezza, B., Chen, J. Y., & Hoven, C. (1993). The Columbia Impairment Scale (CIS): Pilot findings on a measure of global impairment for children and adolescents. *International Journal of Methods in Psychiatric Reseach, 3,* 167–176.

Birleson, P. (1981). The validity of depressive disorders in childhood and the development of a self-rating scale: A research report. *Journal of Child Psychology and Psychiaty, 22,* 73–88.

Brown, G. W. (1974). Meaning, measurement, and stress of life events. In B. S. Dohrenwend & B. P. Dohrenwend (Eds.), *Stressful life events: Their nature and effects* (pp. 217–243). New York: Wiley-Interscience.

Cantwell, D. P., Lewinsohn, P. M., Rohde, P., & Seeley, J. R. (1997). Correspondence between adolescent report and parent report of psychiatric diagnostic data. *Journal of the American Academy of Child and Adolescent Psychiatry, 36,* 610–619.

Chiles, C. A., Miller, M. L., & Cox, G. B. (1980). Epidemiology of depressive symptomatology in adolescence. *Journal of the American Academy of Child and Adolescent Psychiatry, 23,* 91–98.

Cicchetti, D. (1984). The emergence of developmental psychopathology. *Child Development, 55,* 1–7.

Clarke, G. N., Hawkins, W., Murphy, M., Sheeber, L., Lewinsohn, P. M., & Seeley, J. R. (1995). Targeted prevention of unipolar depressive disorder in an at-risk sample of high school adolescents: A randomized trial of a group cognitive intervention. *Journal of the American Academy of Child and Adolescent Psychiatry, 34*(3), 312–321.

Cohen, P., Cohen, J., Kasen, S., Velez, C. N., Hartmark, C., Johnson, J., Rojas, M., Brook, J., & Streuning, E. L. (1993). An epidemiological study of disorders in late childhood and adolescence: I. Age- and gender-specific prevalence. *Journal of Child Psychology and Psychiatry, 34,* 851–867.

Compas, B. E., Malcarne, V. L., & Fondacaro, K. M. (1988). Coping with stressful events in older children and young adolescents. *Journal of Consulting and Clinical Psychology, 56,* 405–411.

Cooper, P. J., & Goodyer, I. (1993). A community study of depression in adolescent girls: I. Estimates of symptom and syndrome prevalence. *British Journal of Psychiatry, 163,* 369–374.

Costello, E. J., Edelbrock, C. S., & Costello, A. J. (1985). Validity of the NIMH Diagnostic Interview Schedule for Children: A comparison between psychiatric and pediatric referrals. *Journal of Abnormal Child Psychology, 13,* 579–595.

Cummings, E. M., & Cicchetti, D. (1990). Toward a transactional model of relations between attachment and depression. In M. Greenberg, D. Cicchetti, & E. M. Cummings (Eds.), *Attachment in the preschool years: Theory, research, and intervention* (pp. 339–372). Chicago: University of Chicago Press

Cummings, E. M., & Davies, P. T. (1994). Maternal depression and child development. *Journal of Child Psychology and Psychiatry, 35,* 73–112.

D'Zurilla, T. J. (1986). *Problem-solving therapy: A social competence approach to clinical intervention.* New York: Springer.

Dahl, R. E., Ryan, N. D., Matty, M. K., Birmaher, B., Al-Shabbout, M., Williamson, D. E., & Kupfer, D. J. (1996). Sleep onset abnormalities in depressed adolescents. *Biological Psychiatry, 39,* 400–410.

Davies, P. T., & Windle, M. (1997). Gender-specific pathways between maternal depressive symptoms, family discord, and adolescent adjustment. *Developmental Psychology, 33,* 657–668.

Deykin, E. Y., Levy, J. C., & Wells. V. (1987). Adolescent depression, alcohol and drug abuse. *American Journal of Public Health, 77*(2), 178–182.

Dohrenwend, B. P., & Dohrenwend, B. S. (1981). Socioenvironmental factors, stress, and psychopathology. *American Journal of Community Psychology, 9,* 128–164.

Dohrenwend, B. P., Krasnoff, L., Askenasy, A. R., & Dohrenwend, B. S. (1978). Exemplification of a method for scaling life events: The PERI Life Events Scale. *Journal of Health and Social Behavior, 19,* 205–229.

Essau, C. A. (2000). *Angst und Depression bei Jugendlichen: Habilitationschrift.* Bremen: University of Bremen, Germany.

Essau, C. A., Conradt, J., & Petermann, F. (1999). Frequency, comorbidity, and psychosocial impairment of social phobia and social fears in adolescents. *Behaviour Research and Therapy, 37,* 831–843.

Essau, C. A., Conradt, J., & Petermann, F. (2000). Frequency, comorbidity, and psychosocial impairment of depressive disorders in adolescents. *Journal of Adolescent Research, 15,* 470–481.

Essau, C. A., & Merikangas, K. R. (1999). Familial and genetic factors. In C. A. Essau & U. Petermann (Eds.), *Depressive disorders in children and adolescents* (pp. 261–285). Northvale, NJ: Jason Aronson.

Essau, C. A., & Petermann, F. (Eds.). (1999). *Depressive disorders in children and adolescents.* Northvale, NJ: Jason Aronson.

Feehan, M., McGee, R., Raja, S. M., & Williams, S. M. (1994). DSM-III-R disorders in New Zealand 18-year-olds. *Australian and New Zealand Journal of Psychiatry, 28,* 87–99.

Fendrich, M., Warner, V., & Weissman, M. M. (1990). Family risk factors, parental depression, and psychopathology in offspring. *Developmental Psychology, 26,* 40–50.

Fergusson, D. M., Horwood, L. J., & Lynskey, M. T. (1993). Prevalence and comorbidity of DSM-III-R diagnoses in a birth cohort of 15 year olds. *Journal of the American Academy of Child and Adolescent Psychiatry, 32,* 1127–1134.

Fleming, J. E., Offord, D. R., & Boyle, M. H. (1989). Prevalence of childhood and adolescent depression in the community: The Ontario Child Health Study. *British Journal of Psychiatry, 155,* 647–654.

Garber, J., Robinson, N. S., & Valentiner, D. (1997). The relation between parenting and adolescent depression: Self-worth as a mediator. *Journal of Adolescent Research, 12,* 12–33.

Garrison, C. Z., Addy, C. L., Jackson, K. L., McKeown, R. E., & Waller, J. L. (1992). Major depressive disorder and dysthymia in young adolescents. *American Journal of Epidemiology, 135,* 792–802.

Gladstone, T. R. G., Kaslow, N. J., Seeley, J. R., & Lewinsohn, P. M. (1997). Sex differences, attributional style and depressive symptoms among adolescents. *Journal of Abnormal Child Psychology, 25,* 297–305.

Goodman, S. H., Brogan, D., Lynch, M. E., & Fielding, B. (1993). Social and emotional competence in children of depressed mothers. *Child Development, 64,* 516–531.

Goodman, S. H., & Gotlib, I. H. (1999). Risk for psychopathology in the children of depressed mothers: A developmental model for understanding mechanisms of transmission. *Psychological Review, 106,* 485–490.

Goodyer, I. M., & Altham, P. M. E. (1991). Lifetime exit events and recent social and family adversities in anxious and depressed school-age children and adolescents: I. *Journal of Affective Disorders, 21,* 219–228.

Goodyer, I. M., Cooper, P. J., Vize, C. M., & Ashby, L. (1993). Depression in 11–16-year-old girls: The role of past parental psychopathology and exposure to recent life events. *Journal of Child Psychology and Psychiatry, 34,* 1103–1115.

Gotlib, I. H., & Goodman, S. H. (1999). Children of parents with depression. In W. K. Silverman & T. H. Ollendick (Eds.), *Developmental issues in the clinical treatment of children and adolescents* (pp. 415–432). New York: Allyn & Bacon.

Gotlib, I. H., & Hammen, C. L. (1992). *Psychological aspects of depression: Toward a cognitive–interpersonal integration.* Chichester, UK: Wiley.

Gotlib, I. H., Lewinsohn, P. M., & Seeley, J. R. (1995). Symptoms versus a diagnosis of depression: Differences in psychosocial functioning. *Journal of Consulting and Clinical Psychology, 63,* 90–100.

Hammen, C. (1991a). *Depression runs in families: The social context of risk and resilience in children of depressed mothers.* New York: Springer-Verlag.

Hammen, C. (1991b). Generation of stress in the course of unipolar depression. *Journal of Abnormal Psychology, 100,* 555–561.

Hammen, C. (1992). The family–environment context of depression: A perspective on children's risk. In D. Cicchetti & S. L. Toth (Eds.), *Rochester Symposium on Developmental Psychopathology: Vol. 4. Developmental perspectives on depression* (pp. 251–281). Rochester, NY: University of Rochester Press.

Hammen, C., Rudolph, K., Weisz, J., Rao, U., & Burge, D. (1999). The context of depression in clinic-referred youth: Neglected areas in treatment. *Journal of the American Academy of Child and Adolescent Psychiatry, 38,* 64–71.

Harter, S. (1985). *Manual for the Self-Perception Profile for Children.* Unpublished manuscript.

Harter, S. (1988). *Manual for the Self-Perception Profile.* Denver, CO: University of Denver Press.

Harter, S. (1990). Self and identity development. In S. S. Feldman & G. R. Elliott (Eds.), *At the threshold: The developing adolescent* (pp. 352–387). Cambridge, MA: Harvard University Press.

Harter, S., & Nowakowski, M. (1987). *Manual for the Dimensions of Depression Profile for Children and Adolescents.* Denver, CO: University of Denver Press.

Hayward, C., Gotlib, I.H., Schraedley, P.K., & Litt, I.F. (1999). Ethnic differences in the association between pubertal status and symptoms of depression in adolescent girls. *Journal of Adolescent Health, 25,* 143–149.

Herjanic, B., & Reich, W. (1982). Development of a structured psychiatric interview for children: Agreement between child and parent on individual symptoms. *Journal of Abnormal Psychology, 10,* 307–324.

Holahan, C. J., & Moos, R. H. (1991). Life stressors, personal and social resources, and depression: A 4-year structural model. *Journal of Abnormal Psychology, 100,* 31–38.

Holmes, T. H., & Rahe, R. H. (1967). The Social Readjustment Rating Scale. *Psychosomatic Medicine, 11,* 213–218.

John, K., Gammon, D., Prusoff, B. A., & Warner, V. (1987). The Social Adjustment Inventory for Children and Adolescents (SAICA): Testing of a new semistructured interview. *Journal of the American Academy of Child and Adolescent Psychiatry, 26,* 898–911.

Kashani, J. H., Carlson, G. A., Beck, N. C., Hoeper, E. W., Corcoran, C. M., McAllister, J. A., Fallahi, C., Rosensberg, T. K., & Reid, J. C. (1987). Depression, depressive symptoms, and depressed mood among a community sample of adolescents. *American Journal of Psychiatry, 144,* 931–934.

Kaslow, N., Tanenbaum, R. L., & Seligman, M. E. P. (1978). *The KASTAN: A children's attributional style questionnaire.* Unpublished manuscript.

Kessler, R. C., McGonagle, K. A., Swartz, M., Blazer, D. G., & Nelson, C. B. (1993). Sex and depression in the National Comorbidity Survey: I. Lifetime prevalence, chronicity, and recurrence. *Journal of Affective Disorders, 29,* 85–96.

King, C. A., Naylor, M. W., Segal, H. G., Evans, T., & Shain, B. N. (1993). Global self-worth, specific self-perceptions of competence, and depression in adolescents. *Journal of the American Academy of Child and Adolescent Psychiatry, 32,* 745–752.

Klein, D. N., Lewinsohn, P. M., Seeley, J. R., & Rohde, P. (2001). A family study of major depressive disorder in a community sample of adolescents. *Archives of General Psychiatry, 58,* 13–20.

Kobak, K. A., Taylor, L. H., Dottl, S. L., Greist, J. H., Jefferson, J. W., Burroughs, D., Mantle, J. M., Katzelnick, D. J., Norton, R., Henk, H. J., & Serlin, R. C. (1997). A computer-administered telephone interview to identify mental disorders. *Journal of the American Medical Association, 278,* 905–910.

Kobasa, S. C. (1979). Stressful life events, personality, and health: An inquiry into hardiness. *Journal of Personality and Social Psychology, 37,* 1–11.

Kovacs, M. (1985). The Children's Depression Inventory. *Psychopharmacology Bulletin, 21,* 995–998.

Kovacs, M. (1996). The course of childhood-onset depressive disorders. *Psychiatric Annals, 26,* 326–330.

Kovacs, M., Feinberg, T. L., Crouse-Novack, M. A. Paulauskas, S. L., Pollock, M., & Finkelstein, R. (1984). Depressive disorders in childhood: II. A longitudinal study of the risk for a subsequent major depression. *Archives of General Psychiatry, 41,* 643–649.

Leckman, J. F., Sholomskas, D., Thompson, D., Belanger, A., & Weissman, M. M. (1982). Best estimate of lifetime psychiatric diagnosis: A methodological study. *Archives of General Psychiatry, 39,* 879–883.

Lewinsohn, P. M., Allen, N. B., Seeley, J. R., & Gotlib, I. H. (1999). First onset versus recurrence of depression: Differential processes of psychosocial risk. *Journal of Abnormal Psychology, 108,* 483–489.

Lewinsohn, P. M., Hoberman, H., Teri, L., & Hautzinger, M. (1985). An integrative theory of depression. In S. Reiss & R. Bootzin (Eds.), *Theoretical issues in behavior therapy* (pp. 331–359). San Diego, CA: Academic Press.

Lewinsohn, P. M., Hops, H., Roberts, R. E., Seeley, J. R., & Andrews, J. A. (1993). Adolescent psychopathology: I. Prevalence and incidence of depression and other DSM-III-R disorders in high school students. *Journal of Abnormal Psychology, 102,* 133–144.

Lewinsohn, P. M., Mermelstein, R. M., Alexander, C., & MacPhillamy, D. (1985). The Unpleasant Events Schedule: A scale for the measurement of aversive events. *Journal of Clinical Psychology, 41,* 483–498.

Lewinsohn, P. M., Pettit, J., Joiner, T. E., Jr., & Seeley, J. R. (2002). *Phenomenology of adolescent depression.* Manuscript under review.

Lewinsohn, P. M., Roberts, R. E., Seeley, J. R., Rohde, P., Gotlib, I. H., & Hops, H. (1994). Adolescent psychopathology: II. Psychosocial risk factors for depression. *Journal of Abnormal Psychology, 103,* 302–315.

Lewinsohn, P. M., Rohde, P., Klein, D. N., & Seeley, J. R. (1999). Natural course of adolescent major depressive disorder: I. Continuity into young adulthood. *Journal of the American Academy of Child and Adolescent Psychiatry, 38,* 56–63.

Lewinsohn, P. M., Rohde, P., & Seeley, J. R. (1994). Psychosocial risk factors for future adolescent suicide attempts. *Journal of Consulting and Clinical Psychology, 62,* 297–305.

Lewinsohn, P. M., Rohde, P., & Seeley, J. R. (1998a). Major depressive disorder in older adolescents: Prevalence, risk factors, and clinical implications. *Clinical Psychology Review, 18,* 765–794.

Lewinsohn, P. M., Rohde, P., & Seeley, J. R. (1998b). Treatment of adolescent depression: Frequency of services and impact on functioning in young adulthood. *Depression and Anxiety, 7,* 47–52.

Lewinsohn, P. M., Rohde, P., Seeley, J. R., & Hops, H. (1991). Comorbidity of unipolar depression: I. Major depression with dysthymia. *Journal of Abnormal Psychology, 100,* 205–213.

Lewinsohn, P. M., Rohde, P., Seeley, J. R., Klein, D. N., & Gotlib, I. H. (2000). Natural course of adolescent major depressive disorder in a community sample: Predictors of recurrence in young adults. *American Journal of Psychiatry, 157,* 1584–1591.

Lewinsohn, P. M., Rohde, P., Seeley, J. R., Klein, D. N., & Gotlib, I. (in press). Psychosocial characteristics of young adults who have experienced and recovered from major depressive disorder during adolescence. *Journal of Abnormal Psychology.*

Lewinsohn, P. M., & Seeley, J. R. (1993). *Sex differences in depression: Importance of first episode.* Manuscript in preparation.

Lewinsohn, P. M., Seeley, J. R., Hibbard, J., Rohde, P., & Sack, W. H. (1996). Cross-sectional and prospective relationships between physical morbidity and depression in older adolescents. *Journal of the American Academy of Child and Adolescent Psychiatry, 35*(9), 1120–1129.

Lewinsohn, P. M., Solomon, A., Seeley, J. R., & Zeiss, A. (2000). Clinical implications of "subthreshold" depressive symptoms. *Journal of Abnormal Psychology, 109,* 345–351.

Maayan, L. A., Roby, G., Casey, B. J., Livnat, R., Kydland, E. T., Williamson, D. E., & Dahl, R. E. (1998). Sleep deprivation in adolescents: Effects on emotional and cognitive processing. *Journal of Sleep and Sleep Disorders Research, 21* (Suppl.), 251.

MacPhillamy, D. J., & Lewinsohn, P. M. (1982). The Pleasant Events Schedule: Studies on reliability, validity, and scale intercorrelations. *Journal of Consulting and Clinical Psychology, 50,* 363–380.

Matson, J. L., Rotatori, A. F., & Helsel, W. J. (1983). Development of a rating scale to measure social skills in children: The Matson Evaluation of Social Skills with Youngsters (MESSY). *Behaviour Research and Therapy, 21,* 335–340.

McGee, R., & Williams, S. (1988). A longitudinal study of depression in nine-year-old children. *Journal of the American Academy of Child and Adolescent Psychiatry, 27,* 342–348.

Monroe, S. M., Rohde, P., Seeley, J. R., & Lewinsohn, P. M. (1999). Life events and depression in adolescence: Relationship loss as a prospective risk factor for first onset of major depressive disorder. *Journal of Abnormal Psychology, 108,* 606–614.

Moos, R. H. (1974). *Family Environment Scale and preliminary manual.* Palo Alto, CA: Consulting Psychologists Press.

Nezu, A. M. (1987). A problem-solving formulation of depression: A literature review and proposal of a pluralistic model. *Clinical Psychology Review, 7,* 121–144.

Nolen-Hoeksema, S., & Girgus, J. S. (1994). The emergence of gender differences in depression during adolescence. *Psychological Bulletin, 115,* 424–443.

Nolen-Hoeksema, S., Morrow, J., & Fredrickson, B. L. (1993). Response styles and the duration of episodes of depressed mood. *Journal of Abnormal Psychology, 102,* 20–28.

Nottelmann, E. D., & Jensen, P. S. (1995). Comorbidity of disorders in children and adolescents. In T. H. Ollendick & R. J. Prinz (Eds.), *Advances in clinical child psychology* (pp. 109–155). New York: Plenum Press.

Petersen, A. C., Sarigiani, P. A., & Kennedy, R. E. (1991). Adolescent depression: Why more girls? *Journal of Youth and Adolescence, 20,* 247–271.

Piacentini, J., Shaffer, D., Fisher, P., Schwab-Stone, M., Davies, M., & Gioia, P. (1993). The Diagnostic Interview Schedule for Children—Revised Version (DISC-R): III. Concurrent criterion validity. *Journal of the American Academy of Child and Adolescent Psychiatry, 32,* 658–665.

Puig-Antich, J., Blau, S., Marx, N., Greenhill, L., & Chambers, W. (1978). Prepubertal major depressive disorders: A pilot study. *Journal of the American Academy of Child Psychiatry, 17,* 695–707.

Radloff, L. S. (1977). The CES-D Scale: A self-report depression scale for research in the general population. *Applied Psychological Measurement, 1,* 385–401.

Radloff, L. S. (1991). The use of the Center for Epidemiological Studies Depression Scale in adolescents and young adults. *Journal of Youth and Adolescence, 20,* 149–166.

Reinherz, H. Z., Giaconia, R. M., Lefkowitz, E. S., Pakiz, B., & Frost, A. K. (1993). Prevalence of psychiatric disorders in a community population of older adolescents. *Journal of the American Academy of Child and Adolescent Psychiatry, 32,* 369–377.

Reinherz, H. Z., Giaconia, R. M., Pakiz, B., Silverman, A. B., Frost, A. K., & Lefkowitz, E. S. (1993). Psychosocial risks for major depression in late adolescence: A longitudinal community study. *Journal of the American Academy of Child and Adolescent Psychiatry, 32,* 1155–1163.

Reinherz, H. Z., Stewart-Berghauer, G., Pakiz, B., Frost, A. K., Moeykens, B. A., & Holmes, W. M. (1989). The relationship of early risk and current mediators to depressive symptomatology in adolescence. *Journal of the American Academy of Child and Adolescent Psychiatry, 28,* 942–947.

Renouf, A. G., & Harter, S. (1990). Low self-worth and anger as components of the depressive experience in young adolescent. *Development and Psychopathology, 2,* 293–310.

Reynolds, W. M. (1987). Treatment of major depression in children and adolescents. In M. Hersen & C. G. Last (Eds.), *Child behavior therapy casebook.* New York: Plenum Press.

Reynolds, W. M. (1994). Depression in adolescents. In T. H. Ollendick & R. J. Prinz (Eds.), *Advances in clinical child psychology* (pp. 261–316). New York: Plenum Press.

Rippere, V. (1976). Scaling the seriousness of illness: A methodological study. *Journal of Psychosomatic Research, 20,* 567–573.

Roberts, R. E., Lewinsohn, P. M., & Seeley, J. R. (1995). Symptoms of DSM-III-R major depression in adolescence: Evidence from an epidemiological survey. *Journal of the American Academy of Child and Adolescent Psychiatry, 34,* 1608–1617.

Robin, A. L., & Weiss, J. G. (1980). Criterion-related validity of behavioral and self-report measures of problem-solving communication skills in distressed and nondistressed parent–adolescent dyads. *Behavioral Assessment, 2,* 339–352.

Rohde, P., Clarke, G. N., Lewinsohn, P. M., Seeley, J. R., & Kaufman, N. (2001). Impact of comorbidity on a cognitive-behavioral group treatment for adolescent depression. *Journal of the American Academy of Child and Adolescent Psychiatry, 40,* 795–802.

Rohde, P., Lewinsohn, P. M., & Seeley, J. R. (1991). Comorbidity of unipolar depression: II. Comorbidity with other mental disorders in adolescents and adults. *Journal of Abnormal Psychology, 100,* 214–222.

Rosenbaum, M. (1980). Individual differences in self-control behaviors and tolerance of painful stimulation. *Journal of Abnormal Psychology, 89,* 581–590.

Rutter, M. (1986). The developmental psychopathology of depression: Issues and perspectives. In M. Rutter, C. Izard, & P. Read (Eds.), *Depression in young people: Developmental and clinical perspectives* (pp. 3–30). New York: Guilford Press.

Sameroff, A. J., & Seifer, R. (1991). The transmission of incompetence: The offspring of mentally ill women. In M. Lewis & L. Rosenblum (Eds.), *The uncommon child* (pp. 259–280). New York: Plenum Press.

Sartorius, N., Goldberg, D., de Girolamo, G., Costa e Silva, J.A., Lecrubier, Y., & Wittchen, H.-U. (Eds.). (1990). *Psychological disorders in general medical settings.* Bern, Switzerland: Hogrefe & Huber.

Schraedley, P. K., Gotlib, I. H., & Hayward, C. (1999). Gender differences in correlates of depressive symptoms in adolescents. *Journal of Adolescent Health, 25,* 98–108.

Schwab-Stone, M., Fisher, P., Piacentini, J., Shaffer, D., Davies, M., & Briggs, M. (1993). The Diagnostic Interview Schedule of Children—Revised Version (DISC-R): II. Test–retest reliability. *Journal of the American Academy of Child and Adolescent Psychiatry, 32,* 651–657.

Shaffer, D., Gould, M. S., Brasic, J., Ambrosini, P., Fisher, P., Bird, H., & Aluwahlia, S. (1983). A Children's Global Assessment Scale (CGAS). *Archives of General Psychiatry, 40,* 1228–1231.

Shipley, W. C. (1940). A self-administering scale for measuring intellectual impairment and deterioration. *Journal of Psychology, 9,* 371–377.

Velez, C. N., Johnson, J., & Cohen, P. (1989). A longitudinal analysis of selected risk factors for childhood psychopathology. *Journal of the American Academy of Child and Adolescent Psychiatry, 28*(6), 861–864.

Verhulst, F. C., Van Der Ende, J., Ferdinand, R. F., & Kasius, M. C. (1997). The prevalence of DSM-III-R diagnoses in a national sample of Dutch adolescents. *Archives of General Psychiatry, 54,* 329–336.

Weinberg, W., Rutman, J., Sullivan, L., Penick, E., & Dietz, S. (1973). Depression in children referred to an educational diagnostic center: Diagnosis and treatment. *Journal of Pediatrics, 83,* 1065–1077.

Weissman, A. N., & Beck, A. T. (1978, November). *Development and validation of the Dysfunctional Attitude Scale.* Paper presented at the annual meeting of the Association for the Advancement of Behavior Therapy, Chicago.

Weissman, M. M., Paykel, E. S., & Klerman, G. L. (1972). The depressed woman as a mother. *Social Psychiatry, 7,* 98–108.

Weisz, J. R., Sweeney, L., Proffitt, V., & Carr, T. (1993). Control-related beliefs and self-reported depressive symptoms in late childhood. *Journal of Abnormal Psychology, 102,* 411–418.

Whitaker, A., Johnson, J., Shaffer, D., Rapoport, J. L., Kalikow, K., Walsh, B. T., Davies, M., Braiman, S., & Dolinsky, A. (1990). Uncommon troubles in young people: Prevalence estimates of selected psychiatric disorders in a nonreferred adolescent population. *Archives of General Psychiatry, 47,* 487–496.

24

Depression in Later Life
Epidemiology, Assessment, Impact, and Treatment

*David V. Powers, Larry Thompson,
Andrew Futterman, and Dolores Gallagher-Thompson*

The goal of this chapter is twofold: (1) to reinforce the importance of the diverse nature of depression in older adults; and (2) to review key advances in research on the epidemiology, assessment, impact, and treatment of late-life depression. A review of the current literature has led us to focus on five questions that we believe to be important for both researchers and clinicians:

1. How big is the issue of late-life depression?
2. Is depression the same for older adults as for younger adults?
3. How is depression assessed?
4. What is the health impact of depression?
5. How is depression treated and how well do the treatments work?

PREVALENCE: HOW BIG A PROBLEM IS LATE-LIFE DEPRESSION?

By all accounts, America is getting older. According to the U.S. Bureau of Census (1991), in 1970, the median age of the U.S. population was 28 years; by 1986, the median age had increased to 31.8 years. The number of people over 65 years of age has increased from 20 million people in 1970 to 29.4 million people in 1986. Proportionally, elders comprised 9% of the population in 1960; today, they comprise almost 13% of the population, and projections indicate that by 2010, elders will comprise over 15% of the population.

A recent report on mental health by the U.S. surgeon general estimates that the 1-year prevalence rate for any psychiatric disorder among adults aged 65 and over is 19.8% (U.S. Department of Health and Human Services, 1999). Among this growing elder population, mood disorders are second only to anxiety disorders in prevalence, with overall rates of 4.4% and 11.4%, respectively. Prevalence estimates vary broadly, however, depending on the definition, method of assessment, and particular sample utilized. For example, in the National Institute of Mental Health (NIMH)/National Institutes of Health (NIH) Epidemiologic Catchment Area (ECA) study (Myers et al., 1984; Regier et al., 1988), if one included as depression diagnoses for any disorder in which clinically significant depressive symptoms figure prominently (e.g., major depressive disorder [MDD], bereavement, dysthymia), prevalence rates double from 3% to 6% using the same sample (Myers et al., 1984). Furthermore, self-reported, questionaire-based ratings of depressive symptoms suggest higher prevalence rates, as high as 13–27% in community samples if subsyndromal depression (SSD) is considered (Judd, Rapaport, Paulus, & Brown, 1994).

In addition, prevalence estimates for subgroups of older adults may be different from those obtained from aggregate community samples. For example, throughout adulthood and old age, unipolar depression appears to be more prevalent in women than in men (Gallo, Royall, & Anthony, 1993; Nolen-Hoeksema, 1987, Chapter 21, this volume). In addition, data from two large and growing groups of older adults—physically ill older nursing home residents and outpatients—suggest prevalence estimates double or triple those typically obtained in the community (Katon & Sullivan, 1990; Rapp, Parisi, Walsh, & Wallace, 1988; Von Korff et al., 1987).

Among older adults living in residential care facilities, Parmelee, Katz, and Lawton (1992a; Parmelee, Lawton, & Katz, 1989) estimated the prevalence of MDD to be approximately 15% and for incidence rates to increase over the course of a year. If one includes SSD, then prevalence estimates of depression are typically above 20% (Blazer, 1991), and perhaps up to 35% among older primary care patients (Gurland, Cross, & Katz, 1996). Because the numbers of institutionalized and physically ill elders are growing rapidly (U.S. Bureau of Census, 1991), the numbers of depressed elders in these subgroups will likely increase as well. In sum, there is little question that depression in later life is a significant and growing problem. However, it is not clear that depression is more of a problem for older adults than it is for younger adults. As we see in the next section, methodological differences among studies (e.g., in terms of definition of depression, means of assessment, or sample selected) make answering this question difficult.

DEPRESSION ACROSS THE LIFESPAN: IS DEPRESSION THE SAME FOR YOUNGER ADULTS AND OLDER ADULTS?

In a series of studies, Newmann and colleagues demonstrated that qualitatively different clusters of symptoms may exist for younger and older adults. Factor analysis of self-reported depressive symptoms in community-dwelling older women (between ages 51 and 92) yielded two major factors that accounted for the variability in depressive symptoms: "depressive syndrome," characterized by most of the emotional and cognitive features of depression (e.g., sad mood and self-blame), and "depletion syndrome," characterized by loss of appetite, lack of interest, hopelessness, and thoughts of death (Newman, Engel, & Jensen, 1990). The depression syndrome is more common among younger adults and diminishes with age, whereas the depletion syndrome appears to be more common among older adults and increases with age, both longitudinally and cross-sectionally (Newmann, Engel, & Jensen, 1991a, 1991b). In addition, Newmann, Klein, Jensen, and Essex (1996) found that diagnostic and summary scale measures differentially assess the depressive and depletion syndromes in a similar sample. Test measures were found to underestimate depletion syndrome, although these measures generally inflated the extent to which depression was found in older adults. Thus, the measures we are using may underestimate depression in older adults by virtue of not measuring the most common subtype of geriatric depression.

Using a different statistical modeling technique and clinical ratings rather than self-report, Blazer and colleagues examined naturally occurring clusters of symptoms for depressive disorders in community-dwelling younger and older adults (Blazer et al., 1988, 1989). Similar to Newmann, they found multiple types of depression, and also found that different types were more frequent in different age groups. Depressive subtypes are apparent in clinical work with older adults. For example, in our own center, dementia family caregivers often do not meet full criteria for MDD but nevertheless report significant levels of depressive symptoms and related forms of psychological distress (Gallagher-Thompson et al., 2000). Taken together, these observations argue for continued research into age-related differences in the type and severity of depressive disorders, and perhaps examination of differential treatment strategies.

HOW IS DEPRESSION ASSESSED IN OLDER ADULTS?

There are many scales and protocols for measuring depression—Nezu, Ronan, Meadows, and McClure (2000) recently published a guide that reviews 52 different empirically based measures of depression—but the approach of each measure impacts the assessment of depression. Nezu, Nezu, McCure and Zwick (Chapter 3, this volume) have examined the important differences between assessing depression with dichotomous scales indicating whether depression is either present or absent, or on a continuum indicating degree of severity. We recommend a three-stage procedure for assessing geriatric depression that includes both types of measures in order to do the best possible job of evaluating the severity and symptom profile of depression in a particular older adult: screening, interview-based assessment, and individual goal setting.

First, older adults who demonstrate physical or emotional distress should be screened for depression. Unfortunately, many elders are not screened; consequently, their depression is not identified or treated (Rapp et al., 1988). Standard self-report measures of depression that are reliable and valid measures of depression in younger adults generally are also reliable and valid in older adults (Thompson, Futterman, & Gallagher, 1988). Three measures in particular are frequently used, and each is recommended for use with older adults: the Beck Depression Inventory (BDI; Beck, Ward, Mendelson, Mock, & Erbaugh, 1961), the Center for Epidemiologic Studies Depression Scale (CES-D; Radloff, 1977), and the Geriatric Depression Scale (GDS; Yesavage et al., 1983). The reliability and validity of these measures have been thoroughly examined in older adults (Herzog, Van Alstine, Usala, Hultsch, & Dixon, 1990; Stiles & McGarrahan, 1998; Thompson, Gallagher, & Breckenridge, 1987). The BDI has recently been revised (BDI-II; Beck, Steer, & Brown, 1996). Preliminary data are currently available from only one study examining differences between the BDI and BDI-II in elderly populations (Jefferson, Powers, & Pope, 2000), so the utility of the BDI-II for depression screening in older adults is not yet clear.

Positive screening should be followed by interview-based assessment. Two structured interviews, the DIS and the SADS, have been used extensively in both research and clinical practice to diagnose late-life depression according to the RDC and DSM-III criteria. The Structured Clinical Interview for the DSM-IV Axis I disorders (SCID; First, Gibbon, Spitzer, & Williams, 1995) has been used less frequently with older adults, but provides information necessary for diagnosing depression and related disorders in later life according to DSM-IV and other standard criteria. Structured interviews are time-consuming and require training to administer properly, but they provide detailed symptom profiles and invaluable information about a patient's history of previous depressive episodes.

The Hamilton Rating Scale for Depression (HRSD; Hamilton, 1967) is an interview-based measure that supposedly improves accuracy of symptom rating over that of self-report screening measures, yet requires less time than longer interviews such as the SADS. The HRSD has been used extensively in treatment studies with older adults (Reynolds et al., 1992). Symptom ratings on the HRSD are obtained via interview and summed together to obtain a severity measure. The HRSD appears to yield little incremental validity over standard screening measures in community-dwelling elders (Stukenberg, Dura, & Kiecolt-Glaser, 1990), but may improve sensitivity and specificity over standard screening measures for diagnosing MDD in elderly medical patients (Rapp, Smith, & Britt, 1990). Based on these two studies, we cautiously recommend the HRSD for use in elderly medical patients, particularly when screening and interview steps cannot both be completed due to cost or time constraints.

Regardless of the particular screening and interview measures used to make diagnoses, a third stage of assessment is usually necessary. This stage, oriented toward establishing specific treatment goals and baselines for individual patients, involves systematic assessment of particular medical, psychological, and social problems. In situations in which diagnosis is unimportant or unnecessary (e.g., in cases when the patient seeks treatment for particular functional problems), this stage is usually of most interest to both practitioner and patient. This stage is also particularly important because of variability found in depressive symptomatology experienced by older adults. Patients who present with "depressive syndrome" symptoms (Newmann, 1989) will likely have very different specific difficulties and goals than patients with "depletion syndrome" symptoms, for example. The best way to ensure that the treatment fits the particular needs of the patient is to outline specific target problems and set goals for treatment accordingly. This is especially critical at present, because no current assessment tools discriminate between subtypes of geriatric depression that studies are recognizing more consistently.

In our clinical trials of psychotherapy and pharmacotherapy for late-life depression, we have found it useful for both the patient and the therapist to monitor change in mood, engagement in pleasant activities, coping styles, and dysfunctional attitudes during the course of treatment (Dick, Gallagher-Thompson, & Thompson, 1997; Thompson et al., 1987). A host of geropsychiatric measures have been developed for use in monitoring treatment progress. Evaluating the reliability and validity of such measures is beyond the scope of this chapter. The interested reader is referred to *The Handbook of Assessment in Clinical Gerontology* (Lichtenberg, 1999) which provides comprehensive reviews of measures useful in geropsychological practice, with a chapter addressing the assessment of geriatric depression in particular (Edelstein, Kalish, Drozdick, & McKee, 1999).

WHAT IS THE HEALTH IMPACT OF LATE-LIFE DEPRESSION?

In this section, we review recent research on factors implicated in the development and impact of late-life depression. We conceptualize depression in later life as both the outcome and the cause of biological, behavioral, cognitive, and social changes (Lewinsohn, 1974; Murrell & Meeks, 1992). Historically, studies have examined depression as a dependent variable or an outcome of changes in other biological or psychosocial factors (*onset studies*). Recently, more studies have been completed that conceptualize depression as an independent variable that influences quality-of-life variables, such as health, cognition, and social functioning (*impact studies*). This section focuses on impact studies, a growing area of research in studies of geriatric depression, in order to highlight examples of this research. A complete review of this research is beyond the scope of this chapter; for a more comprehensive review of one of these domains, the interested reader is referred to *Physical Illness and Depression in Older Adults: A Handbook of Theory, Research, and Practice,* by Williamson, Shaffer, and Parmalee (2000).

A growing group of studies focuses on the impact, or consequences, of depression on health and functioning in older adults. These studies conceptualize depression as an independent variable with influences on health, cognition, behavior, and social relations, and typically use prospective or longitudinal designs.

Among the most well-documented consequences of depression across the life span is the increased risk of continued or recurrent episodes of depression and other negative health consequences (Keller, Shapiro, Lavori, & Wolfe, 1982; Lewinsohn, Zeiss, & Duncan, 1989; Phifer & Murrell, 1986). In general, depressed older adults are more vulnerable to illness and functional impairments following stress than are nondepressed older adults (see Williamson et al., 2000). For example, depression was found to predict 6-month mortality and functioning following a heart attack (Frasure-Smith, Lesparance, & Talijic, 1993), and the risk of death for stroke patients during a 10-year follow-up period was 3.4 times higher for depressed patients than for nondepressed patients in one study (Morris, Robinson, Andrzejewski, Samuels, & Price, 1993). Depression also predicts higher illness rates, functional impairments, and mortality among nursing home residents over a 1-year period (Parmelee, Katz, & Lawton, 1992b; Rovner et al., 1991), poorer health and functioning among bereaved elders over a 2.5-year period following loss (Gilewski, Farberow, Gallagher, & Thompson, 1991), and diminished immune functioning and social interaction among Alzheimer caregivers (Kiecolt-Glaser & Glaser, 1989). A wide variety of both animal and human studies suggest that stress and depression in later life cause changes in the central nervous system (see Sapolsky, 1992, for a review).

Data from some studies suggest that depressive episodes in late life may be either a risk factor for, or an early symptom of, Alzheimer's disease (AD). Wetherell, Gatz, Johansson, and Pedersen (1999) note that several case–control studies (e.g., Barclay, Kheyfets, Zemcov, Blass, & McDowell, 1985; Kokmen et al., 1991) have found a relationship between depression and subsequent AD onset. Wetherell et al. examined 65 older adult monozygotic and dizygotic twin pairs from the Swedish Adoption/Twin Study of Aging (Pedersen et al., 1991). They found that late-life depression and general psychiatric illness were associated with an increased risk for AD (risk ratios of 3.38 and 3.55 compared to controls, respectively). Whereas previous studies found a relationship between exposure to antidepressant medications or electroconvulsive therapy (ECT) and increased risk of AD, Wetherell et al. found no such relationship. They concluded that depression and other psychiatric illnesses may serve as prodromal signs of dementia in some cases, although they stated that it is unclear whether psychiatric illness is a risk factor or an early symptom of AD. This study confirmed findings of previous studies (Reding, Haycox, & Blass, 1985; Kokmen et al., 1991) while controlling for familial risk factors by using twins.

It is important to note, however, that negative health influences of depression are not consistently demonstrated among otherwise healthy, community-dwelling older adults. In addition, in two large surveys of community elders, 2-year mortality rates were not associated with diagnoses of depression or severity of depressive symptoms (Fredman et al., 1989; Thomas, Kelman, Kennedy, Ahn, & Yang, 1992). Taken together, these studies and those cited above suggest that depression may significantly affect the health status of some older adults but not others, and that late-life depression may be a result of dementia in other cases. These conflicting results may be explained by different types of depression resulting in differential effects (see Ingram & Siegle, Chapter 4, this volume). It may be of great benefit to older adults for researchers to begin to examine how different expressions of depression in older adults result in different health impacts, so that interventions can be better targeted to the specific needs of particular older adults. Clearly, much remains to be demonstrated regarding the nature, mechanism, and generalizability of the negative effects of depression on physiological functioning and health in later life.

In the next section, we examine recent studies relating age and treatment outcome. In particular, we review the effectiveness of existing psychotherapeutic and pharmacological treatments for late-life depression, and address the question of whether there are specific treatments that are effective for treating special groups of older adult depressives, such as those elders with cognitive impairment.

HOW IS DEPRESSION TREATED AMONG OLDER ADULTS, AND HOW WELL DO THE TREATMENTS WORK?

Treatments are typically grouped into two modalities: psychosocial and somatic. Because most controlled treatment studies of geriatric depression have focused on either psychotherapy or pharmacotherapy (or both in combination), we focus our review on these studies. The interested reader is referred to Salzman's (1998) excellent text, *Clinical Geriatric Psychopharmacology*, for a comprehensive overview of general issues pertaining to geriatric psychopharmacology, or to *Psychiatric Medications for Older Adults: The Concise Guide* (Salzman, 2001) for a brief, practical summary. In addition, due to limitations of space, we will not review controlled clinical outcome studies of ECT. ECT is often used effectively in the treatment of severe geriatric depression, but it is not recommended as an initial treatment for the majority of less severe forms of geriatric depression (Blazer, 1989). It remains a controversial form of treatment. The interested reader is referred to Kelly and Zisselman (2000) for a recent review of the efficacy of ECT in treating geriatric depression.

Effectiveness of Psychotherapy

A variety of forms of psychotherapy have been used to treat depressive disorder and depressive symptoms in older adults. These include psychodynamic psychotherapy, life review or reminiscence approaches, family therapy, psychoeducational approaches, and various cognitive-behavioral therapies. Several studies to date have compared two or more of these approaches to each other and/or to a no-treatment or placebo group (Breckenridge, Gallagher, Thompson, & Peterson, 1986; Scogin, Jamison, & Gochneaur, 1989).

Reviews of psychotherapy outcome studies suggest that psychotherapy modalities that are effective in the treatment of depression in younger adults may be equally effective in treating depression in older adults (Garfield, 1994; Teri, Curtis, Gallagher-Thompson, & Thompson, 1994). Meta-analyses of psychotherapy outcome studies provide additional support for this view. Smith, Glass, and Miller (1980) report a .00 correlation between age and outcome. After matching studies with young and old subjects for duration of treatment and initial levels of symptom severity, Dobson (1987) also reported nonsignificant correlations between age and amount of symptom improvement following cognitive therapy. Moreover, the efficacy of psychotherapy for depression in older adults appears to be roughly comparable to efficacy of psychotherapy for depression in younger adults according to effect-size estimates derived from various meta-analyses. Scogin and McElreath (1994) report a .78 effect size for psychotherapy with older adults, whereas Robinson, Berman, and Neimeyer (1990) report a .73 effect size for psychotherapy with adults of all ages.

The Division of Clinical Psychology of the American Psychological Association has recently developed criteria in order to classify different types of treatments as "well established" or "probably efficacious" for treating particular psychological disorders (Chambless et al., 1996). In general, a treatment can be considered *well established* if either two group-design studies by different investigators or nine single-case studies show a treatment to be superior to a placebo or equally powerful to an already established treatment. Treatments are considered to be *probably efficacious* if there are at least three single-case studies meeting the criteria for well-established treatments, or if two group-design studies show either an effect in comparison to wait-list control groups or meet the well-established criteria and are completed by a single group of investigators.

Using the Chambless et al. criteria, Gatz et al. (1998) examined the effectiveness of a variety of psychological treatments for particular psychological disorders experienced by older adults. Gatz et al. concluded that cognitive and cognitive-behavioral therapy (CBT) were *probably efficacious* treatments "for depressed community-dwelling residents who are intact, have minimal comorbid psychopathology, and are not suicidal" (p. 13). This is in contrast to the conclusion of Chambless et al. (1996) that cognitive therapy and CBT were *well-established*, empirically validated treatments for depression in older adults and in the general adult population. Gatz et al. state that they are being conservative in their conclusion due to limited sample sizes in studies and inconsistent effects shown in comparison to other treatments. Behavioral/problem-solving therapy was also found to be probably efficacious. Psychodynamic, brief psychodynamic, and interpersonal therapies were considered together. Psychodynamic therapies as a class were designated as probably efficacious for treatment of depression in older adults, although some variants such as interpersonal therapy (IPT) have been demonstrated to be well established in treating depression in the general adult population (see Weissman & Markowitz, Chapter 17, this volume). Life review and reminiscence therapies are categorized as probably efficacious, but Gatz et al. note that although these therapies show some impact on depressive symptoms "studies comparing life review to other treatments generally favor the alternative treatment" (p. 21), and gains may not be maintained.

The research literature appears somewhat mixed regarding the question of how to modify "standard" therapies for older adults. Many writers emphasize that modification should involve structural features (e.g., setting, length of session, or when and how to involve family members) rather than content or process features (Garfield, 1994). We have found that an awareness of changes in acuity of vision and hearing, as well as a knowledge of any changes in cognition, are obviously important in establishing an adequate context for treatment. Also, because all forms of psychotherapy involve learning of some kind, we have found that multimodal presentation of information can be very helpful. Suggestions for increasing the involvement of older adults in behavioral therapy and CBT are discussed further in Zeiss and Steffen (1996) and Gallagher-Thompson and Thompson (1996), respectively.

There is clearly a need for research on psychotherapy outcome and depression by a number of different investigators targeting a broader spectrum of older adults. A large proportion of the studies on psychotherapy for geriatric depression have been completed in relatively few research clinics; replication and extension by different investigators would offer stronger support for the effectiveness of the treatments studied so far, while perhaps introducing other useful treatments. Furthermore, first-generation research on treatment of depression in older adults has often excluded participants whose cases are complicated by health issues or dual psychiatric diagnoses. A large number of older adults present with depression associated with multiple health problems or concurrent psychiatric diagnoses such as dementia. It is important to know how well treatments will work in more complicated cases seen so commonly in nonresearch settings. To that end, recently completed therapist and client companion manuals for cognitive-behavioral treatment of late-life depression (Dick, Gallagher-Thompson, & Thompson, 1997; Dick, Gallagher-Thompson, Coon, Powers, & Thompson, 1997) include specific modifications for older adults based on the experiences we and our colleagues have had in working with complex cases in an outpatient clinic setting.

Studies are just beginning to report on the effectiveness of psychotherapeutic treatment of depression in demented older adults. Teri (1994) found that depression could be effectively treated in demented older adults when caregivers were trained to implement a behavioral treatment for depressed care recipients. Teri, Logsdon, Uomoto, and McCurry (1997) compared two behavioral treatments—one focused on increasing pleasant events and the other emphasizing caregiver problem solving—to a typical-care condition and a wait-list control group. Participants in both behavioral treatments showed significant improvement in comparison to participants in the other two groups, and the caregivers in the two behavioral conditions also benefited from treatment. The data from these studies seem to indicate that caregivers themselves benefit from interventions that train them to help improve the functional status of their care recipients. This observation should be given consideration in developing interventions specific to decreasing caregiver distress. Modifications of cognitive-behavioral therapy are also being suggested for treatment of depression in the chronically ill elderly (Rybarczyk et al., 1992) and poststroke depression patients (Hibbard, Grober, Wayne, & Aletta, 1990), as well as in demented patients (Teri & Gallagher-Thompson, 1991). Research on psychotherapeutic interventions for older adults with various cognitive or physical impairments should receive major attention over the next decade.

Effectiveness of Pharmacotherapy

Before reviewing the literature on pharmacotherapy for geriatric depression, we should mention an important point regarding interpretation of results. Different response rates obtained in different pharmacotherapy trials reflect the manner in which response is assessed, the way drugs are administered and monitored, and the duration of treatment, as well as the variability in efficacy of different medications. For example, response may be defined in terms of reduction in symptom severity (e.g., a drop in symptom severity of at least 50% on the HRSD) or as remission of symptoms (e.g., a maintained HRSD score less than 10). In earlier studies, medication dosage for treatment of geriatric depression was often fixed at predetermined levels thought to be clinically effective. Finally, pharmacological treatment studies of late-life depression vary in the duration and monitoring of treatment. Recent studies have extended treatment longer than earlier studies (e.g., Bondareff et al., 2000) and monitor blood plasma levels closely in order to maximize initial response (e.g., Finkel, Richter, & Clary, 1999).

The most significant development in pharmacotherapy for geriatric depression in the last 7 years has clearly been the proliferation in the use of selective serotonin reuptake inhibitors (SSRIs; e.g., fluoxetine, sertraline, paroxetine) as a first line of treatment for depression in older adults. The key issues in the use of any medications in older adult populations are effectiveness, side effect profile, and considerations in special populations. There is a tendency in the literature to draw and apply general conclusions across all older adults about the overall utility of one class of antidepressants over another, and the near exclusive use of SSRIs rather than tricyclic antidepressants (TCAs) would seem to further support this conclusion.

However, in a recent meta-analysis of 102 randomized controlled trials (Anderson, 2000), SSRIs were found to be comparable to TCAs in overall effectiveness in treating depression in the general population. Use of SSRIs resulted in lower discontinuation rates in the general adult population (27% vs. 31% for TCAs, $p < .01$), but even though older adults were more likely than younger adults to discontinue treatment (21% vs. 14.8%), there was a minimal, nonsignificant difference in dropout rate between SSRIs and TCAs within the older adult samples (21.3% vs. 22.4%, $p > .05$). These results were supported in a meta-analysis of treatment response and tolerability of treatment for depression specifically in older adults (Gerson, Belin, Kaufman, Mintz, & Jarvik, 1999). Gerson et al. found no differences in percentage of symptom reduction between TCAs (49.5%), SSRIs (49.8%), and other medications (e.g., monoamine oxidase inhibitors [MAOIs], bupropion; 47.3%), but each of these were significantly more effective than placebo. They also found no overall differences in tolerability (as measured by percentage of dropouts due to side effects) between SSRIs (17.3%) and TCAs (19.4%, $p > .05$) in older adults, contrary to common treatment recommendations that SSRIs are preferred over TCAs due to greater tolerability of SSRI side effects. The authors state that they are unable to reconcile "possible explanations for discrepancies between treatment recommendations and the data upon which they rest" (p. 19), except to note that SSRIs usually had a slightly lower but statistically insignificant percentage dropout rate due to side effects relative to TCAs.

Roose and Suthers (1998) reached a similar conclusion in a review paper examining antidepressant response in late-life depression, and noted that fluoxetine has a significantly more variable remission rate (21–50% in reviewed studies) compared to other SSRIs among older adults. In an earlier review, Newhouse (1996) also expressed concern about use of fluoxetine in the elderly because of the common side effect of weight loss (also noted by Finkel, Richter, Clary, & Batzar, 1999), but concluded that the side effect profile of SSRIs made them generally preferable to TCAs. The failure to consistently find differences in tolerability between TCAs and SSRIs in older adult populations (as found in general adult populations; Anderson, 2000) may be due to age-related differences, or it may be due to reduced statistical power to find the effect. The tendency to find a nonsignifcant trend favoring SSRIs suggests that the difference in tolerability is not large even if it does exist. It is possible that this is a case in which a clinically significant difference does not reach statistical significance, but the best conclusion based on the data at this point is that there is not an overall difference between SSRIs and TCAs in effectiveness or tolerability as reflected in severity of side effects.

It is important to note, however, that not all depressed older adults have the same treatment needs. Some trends regarding pharmacotherapy for depression in subgroups of older adults are now being examined. SSRIs are currently recommended over TCAs and MAOIs for treatment of depression in patients with heart disease (Glassman, Rodriguez, & Shapiro, 1998; Murray, 2000). In contrast, one double-blind study has been conducted to date comparing a TCA (nortriptylene) to an SSRI (fluoxetine) and placebo in treating post-stroke depression (Robinson et al., 2000). Nortriptylene was found to be more effective than either fluoxetine or placebo, which were not significantly different from each other. Early studies in demented populations are showing the effectiveness of both SSRIs and TCAs in treatment of depression (Katona, Hunter, & Bray, 1997; Taragano, Lyketsos, Mangone, Allegri, & Comesana-Diaz, 1997), but it is not clear which medication or class of medications is superior in this population.

In conclusion, TCAs and SSRIs appear to be equally effective for treating depression in older adults in general, but there is not sufficient evidence to conclude that one class of antidepressants is clearly preferable to another. Specific considerations as to which TCA or SSRI medication is preferable are likely best made on a case-by-case basis, with particular emphasis on how the side effect profile of a specific medication will impact a specific patient. This strategy may be particularly robust as new medications with unique mechanisms of action and side effect profiles, such as bupropion (Weihs et al., 2000), are continuing to emerge and to show effectiveness in older adult populations.

Comparative Effectiveness of Psychotherapy and Pharmacotherapy

Only a handful of studies have directly compared psychotherapy with pharmacotherapy for late-life depression. Sloane, Staples, and Schneider (1985) used a variant of psychodynamic treatment for depression (interpersonal therapy [IPT]; Klerman, Weissman, Rounsaville, & Chevron, 1984) to treat elderly depressives. In a randomized clinical trial, they found that IPT was as effective as nortriptyline at 6 and 16 weeks in obtaining initial remission of depressive symptoms, and was also associated with lower dropout rates.

Williams et al. (2000) recently compared the effectiveness of paroxetine, placebo, and a psychosocial treatment called problem-solving treatment—primary care (PST-PC), for treating dysthymia and minor depression in older adults. PST-PC was designed specifically for primary care settings. Patients were randomly assigned to one of the three conditions. Participants in the PST-PC condition received six sessions of therapy over the 11-week period of the study. Paroxetine was found to be significantly more effective in treating depressive symptoms as measured by the HRSD in comparison to both placebo and PST-PC. No differences in effectiveness were found between placebo and PST-PC, although the authors note that PST-PC participants improved more rapidly than placebo group participants in the later weeks of treatment. We would also note that six sessions is an unusually brief length of treatment for a psychosocial intervention, and the improvement seen in the later weeks of treatment may have been the beginning of a therapeutic dose effect.

Thompson and Gallagher-Thompson (1991) reported slightly different results in their comparison of psychotherapy with medication treatment. They found that results varied depending on the outcome measure considered when CBT was compared with desipramine (DMI) in the treatment of geriatric depression. RDC diagnosis suggested that CBT resulted in greater improvement than DMI. However, the severity of depression as measured by the BDI and the HRSD suggested that improvement due to treatment was comparable for both types of treatment. Other studies that have compared CBT (both in individual and group formats) with pharmacotherapy (e.g., Beutler et al., 1987; Jarvik, Mintz, Steuer, & Gerner, 1982) have also demonstrated that CBT is at least as effective as pharmacological treatments of late-life depression and more effective than a wait-list control condition.

Combining Psychotherapy with Pharmacotherapy

The National Institutes of Health Consensus Development Conference Consensus Statement (1991), *Diagnosis and Treatment of Depression in Late Life,* pointed to the special effectiveness of combination psychotherapy and pharmacotherapy in both acute and maintenance phases of treatment of late-life depression. Unfortunately, few studies of treatment for late-life depression have utilized a combination condition of both psychotherapy and pharmacotherapy.

Reynolds et al. (1992) examined the efficacy of nortriptyline and weekly sessions of IPT in combination, during initial and continuation phases of treatment for geriatric depression. Seventy-three outpatient elderly depressives (mean age of 67.5 years) were randomized to the combined treatment condition or placebo. Seventy-nine percent of completers responded fully (achieved HRSD < 10 for 3 consecutive weeks) and 6% had a partial response (HRSD score > 11 but < 14). These patients were then continued in combined treatment and stabilized (HRSD scores < 10) for an additional 16 weeks. Ten percent of these patients relapsed during this period, but were then restabilized for 16 weeks. At the conclusion of continuation therapy, the patients were then randomized in a double-blind manner to a maintanence condition of nortriptyline alone or to placebo. Of the 25 subjects assigned to placebo, six relapsed in the first 4–6 weeks of maintenance therapy; in contrast, none of those assigned to the nortriptyline-alone condition relapsed. In a similar study involving continuation treatment, Reynolds et al. (1989) examined differences in response between patients who had their first episode of major depression either before or after age 60. They found no difference in remission, recovery, or relapse rates, but early-onset patients took 5–6 weeks longer to achieve remission.

Thompson and Gallagher-Thompson (1991) also examined the efficacy of combined treatment in a randomized, clinical trial comparing DMI and CBT, each alone and in combination. Patients in the combined condition showed greater improvement than patients receiving only DMI, but there was no difference between the combined treatment and CBT alone. As noted above, while CBT patients showed slightly greater improvement than patients receiving DMI, this difference was not statistically significant.

Thompson and Gallagher-Thompson (1991) also included a therapy continuation phase in their study, in which patients receiving only DMI were crossed over to the combined condition after the initial phase. Patients receiving only CBT continued to do so during the continuation phase. Patients who had not remitted after initial treatment were continued on CBT or combination treatment. Patients who were remitted continued in therapy, but were seen less often. It is noteworthy that after approximately 4 months of continuation therapy, more than 90% of the patients in the combination condition had remitted (an increase of nearly 30% from the initial phase); a smaller increase (from 60 to 66%) was noted in the CBT continuation condition. Thompson, Coon, Gallagher-Thompson, Sommer, and Koin (2001) reanalyzed the data in the initial phase, taking into consideration the severity of depression and the DMI dose levels. They reported a three-way interaction of dose level, severity, and treatment condition, such that the combined treatment was clearly superior to both treatments alone in the more severely depressed patients who were taking larger doses of DMI. There were no differences between CBT and DMI administered alone.

Although differences in study design, treatment modality, and assessment strategy make comparing some findings of Reynolds et al. (1992) to Thompson et al. (2001) difficult, both studies clearly point to the effectiveness of combination treatment in both initial and continuation phases of treatment. Thompson and Gallagher-Thompson (1991) also suggest that CBT alone is effective in obtaining initial remission of symptoms for patients unable or unwilling to take antidepressant medication.

Maintaining Gains Following Psychotherapy and Pharmacotherapy

Obtaining initial remission of depressive symptoms is one goal of treatment, but not the only goal. As Reynolds (1992) noted, "Getting well is not enough, it is staying well that counts." In the early 1980s it was thought that prognosis for older adults following treatment for late-life depression was generally poor: as many as two-thirds of all treated older adult depressives had recurrent episodes of depression within 1–3 years of treatment (Murphy, 1983). Recent studies that have followed patients after successful treatment suggest that better long-term outcomes may now be expected. For example, Gallagher-Thompson, Hanley-Peterson, and Thompson (1990) reported that initial gains made by patients receiving three types of psychotherapy (reported in Thompson et al., 1987) generally appear to be "durable." Using the RDC criteria, roughly 58% of depressed elders receiving brief cognitive, behavioral, or psychodynamic therapy, respectively, remained depression-free (i.e., received no RDC diagnosis of depression) at the 12-month follow-up assessment, and over

70% remained depression-free for all treatment modalities at the 24-month follow-up without additional treatment. These rates compare favorably with published reports of sustained remission rates of 56–70% over a 1-year period for younger depressed patients who received psychotherapy (e.g., Simons, Murphy, Levine, & Wetzel, 1986). Further examination of the Gallagher-Thompson et al. follow-up data suggest that maintenance of gains made in psychotherapy is strongly associated with continued use of specific skills learned in therapy (Powers, Thompson, & Gallagher-Thompson, 2001). In addition, Judd et al. (1998) have shown that level of recovery from MDD predicts duration of recovery in unipolar depressive patients in the general adult population. Asymptomatic recovery also appears to be associated with prolonged delay in recurrence of depression in older adults treated for MDD with psychotherapy (Canter, Thompson, & Gallagher-Thompson, 2001).

With respect to pharmacotherapy, Georgotas, McCue, Cooper, Nagachandran, and Chang (1988) were the first to demonstrate the safety and efficacy of continued adequate antidepressant medication beyond initial remission of symptoms in order to prevent relapse (return of symptoms) and recurrence (appearance of a new episode). More than 68% of the responders who agreed to continue in maintenance treatment remained in remission at the conclusion of the continuation phase of treatment. The authors conclude that "both drugs were safe and effective in continuation therapy with a low risk of relapse" (p. 929). Georgotas, McCue, and Cooper (1989) then completed a randomized clinical trial of the efficacy of "maintenance therapy" of phenelzine or nortriptyline using the 43 subjects who had remained well during the continuation phase of treatment. Patients receiving phenelzine had a significantly higher success rate and lower recurrence rate at 1 year than did either nortriptyline or placebo group patients. Based on these findings, Georgotas et al. concluded that although both medications appear to be equally effective in the initial and stabilization phases of treatment, phenelzine may be more effective in maintaining gains over longer periods of time.

In a study of more severely depressed, inpatient older adults, Reynolds et al. (1989) reported somewhat better success with nortripyline maintenance therapy in elder inpatient depressives. More recently, Walters, Reynolds, Mulsat, and Pollack (1999) conducted an 18-month open trial continuation in which older adults already receiving either paroxetine or nortryptiline remained in continuation treatment 18 months following remission of their symptoms. Walters et al. found nortriptyline and paroxetine to be comparable in preventing relapse and recurrence, but noted that future randomized controlled trials are necessary.

The number of studies including long-term outcome data are increasing, but remain insufficient for both pharmacotherapy and psychotherapy. Gerson et al. (1999) point out that many older adults remain on psychotropic medications for periods much longer than the 8–12 weeks examined in typical antidepressant outcome trials, and noted that more long-term follow-up studies are urgently needed. Likewise, research such as that by Reynolds and colleagues (1989, 1999) is just beginning to clarify what constitutes appropriate "maintenance" for patients who are successfully treated with medication. It is not clear what consititutes appropriate maintenance for psychosocial interventions for depression, or what the ideal scheduling for such maintenance should be.

In summary, treatment studies strongly indicate that certain forms of psychosocial and pharmacological therapy, alone and in combination, can be very effective in treating geriatric depression. At the same time, much remains to be learned regarding which factors account for the efficacy of psychotherapy; the efficacy of combination therapy in initial, continuation, and maintenence phases of treatment; and the best "match" between types of depression and types of treatment. As in other areas of research, little or no data describes the efficacy of treatment for depression in the oldest old, or in other subgroups, such as those with dementia or severe medical comorbidities.

CONCLUSIONS SO FAR

We believe existing data support the following conclusions:

1. Recent studies suggest that older adults do not necessarily demonstrate depression more frequently than younger adults. Depending on the assessment approach and definition used (e.g., classification vs. test approaches), and sample assessed (e.g., community vs. institutionalized), different relationships between depression and aging are described.

2. The validity of existing criteria for geriatric depressive disorders (e.g., DSM-IV-TR [American Psychiatric Association, 2000] MDD) continues to be questioned. Existing data suggest that there are differences in the clinical presentation of depression in younger and older adults, and that the different presentations of depression in older adults are not fully assessed by current measures of depression. These differences, however, have not been fully recognized in outcome studies or treatment protocols.

3. Studies are beginning to address the *consequences* of late-life depression as well as its *antecedents*. Depression increases illness and mortality rates among elders experiencing physical illness but not generally in otherwise healthy community samples. Late-life depression may be a risk factor for developing Alzheimer's disease, although it is not clear whether depression is a causative factor or a prodromal symptom of Alzheimer's.

4. Finally, different forms of psychotherapy and pharmacotherapy, alone and in combination, can be effective in obtaining initial remission of depressive symptoms in later life, in maintaining gains, and in reducing the risk of relapse and recurrence. As in treatment outcome research involving younger depressed patients, no one treatment (psychotherapy or pharmacotherapy or specific type of either) emerges as the most efficacious for all depressed patients. Recently developed guidelines for empirically validated psychotherapeutic treatments highlight the need for more psychotherapy outcome studies from varying research groups and theoretical perspectives. Pharmacological and psychotherapeutic interventions with demented older adults are beginning to show promise in reducing depression in this population. Results from the studies that combine psychotherapy and pharmacotherapy suggest that combination treatment may yield high success rates. More comparative, controlled studies using different drugs and psychotherapy combinations in initial, continuation, and maintenance phases of treatment need to be conducted.

FUTURE DIRECTIONS

There are several directions in which geriatric depression research may progress over the next several years, some of which are based on the development of research to date, and some of which are related to new issues that are developing among older adults.

1. *Treatment outcome studies among nursing home residents.* Psychologists are increasingly treating depressed patients in nursing homes. These patients have a wide variety of health issues as well as cognitive impairment, and psychotherapy may be preferred over pharmacotherapy for many of these patients given the high number of medications nursing residents often must take for other health problems. Research on treatment of cognitively impaired patients is just beginning (Teri et al., 1997), and we expect to see large-scale randomized controlled outcome trials for cognitively impaired and physically impaired older adults within the next 6–8 years.

2. *Differential treatment for subtypes of geriatric depression.* As the differences in subtypes of geriatric depression continue to be examined, the differential effectiveness of partic-

ular treatment strategies will almost certainly become a topic of interest. For example, ideal treatment strategies for "depletion syndrome" and "depression syndrome" (Newman et al., 1990) will vary and be more complex than what is typically done in the brief treatment offered to most depressed outpatients. This will also require more detailed research into the "active ingredients" in different treatment approaches. It may be the case that particular techniques within different therapies vary in their effectiveness depending on the type of depression an older adult is experiencing.

3. *Cost effectiveness studies.* Geriatric depression results in increased "cost," both in terms of well-being and in terms of increased health care for other medical problems that occur more often among depressed older adults. Interest in reducing these costs will increase, particularly as the burden of caring for a growing elderly population affects federal government policy. Studies comparing the cost effectiveness of different treatments, particularly pharmacotherapy versus psychotherapy, may begin to proliferate as the financial burden of caring for depressed older adults increases.

4. *The relationship between depression and anxiety.* As anxiety begins to receive increased attention as the most prevalent mental health problem for older adults, further examination of the comorbidity of anxiety and depression and the consequences of that comorbidity will occur. The overlap between these two disorders is a critical issue in terms of both adequate assessment and appropriate treatment. This may first require increased research on geriatric anxiety alone, but as the literature on geriatric anxiety grows, examination of the interrelationship between anxiety and depression will be a logical progression for both fields.

5. *Consideration of cohort differences.* Two trends in demographics will result in new areas of research into geriatric depression. The first of these is the movement of the baby boomers into older adulthood. This will result in both expected and unexpected changes in the understanding and expression of geriatric depression. One potential change, for example, is that there may be an increase in acceptance of psychotherapeutic treatment for depression among older adult baby boomers. The cohort shift may also result in changes in the type of symptoms reported, with a decline in the frequency of reporting physical symptoms relative to psychological symptoms.

6. *Depression among the oldest old.* The second demographic trend that will significantly impact the direction of depression research is the dramatic growth of the age group known as the "oldest old," those over age 85. This age group is the fastest growing of all age groups as a percentage of the population, and our understanding of the symptom profile, assessment, and treatment issues in this age group will require significant attention. There are very few health issues that are viewed exactly the same for people who are 20 years apart in age at any point in the life span, and equating the difficulties and treatment needs for depressed 85-year-olds with those of 65-year-olds may be inappropriate. This may be particularly true given the cohort differences for the young old and the oldest old over the next 15 years.

7. *Diversity and depression.* It is our hope that research into issues of cultural diversity and geriatric depression will expand significantly. The growing numbers of non-Caucasian elderly in the United States will require examination of all of the domains discussed in this chapter in diverse populations. The issue of diversity and psychotherapeutic treatment for older adults has shown growth in the recent explosion of interest in this topic within the field of dementia caregiving (cf. Aranda & Knight, 1997; Gallagher-Thompson, Arean, et al., 2000; Larson & Imai, 1996; Valle, 1998). Clearly, the geriatric depression literature would benefit greatly from a similar expansion.

8. *The role of positive emotion and positive coping in reducing negative mood.* Interesting research has recently been reported by Folkman and Moskowitz (2000) on the

role of positive emotions and related positive coping strategies in facilitating adaptation to long-term caregiving (and to the eventual death of the partner) among HIV/AIDS caregivers. Although it is counterintuitive to believe that people experience positive emotions in the midst of significant acute or chronic stress, in a review on this topic Tedeschi, Park, and Calhoun (1998) highlighted the fact that there are positive aspects to stress (including reports of growth and personal transformation) that can no longer be ignored when inquiring about individuals' perceived well-being. This line of research has not yet been extended to work with depressed individuals. However, it seems appropriate to begin to investigate the role of positive emotions in mitigating against late-life depression, and/or in being a component of the therapy and treatment that are provided. Folkman and Moskowitz (2000) conclude their review with a series of compelling but unanswered questions, including one that is relevant here: namely, To what extent can positive coping strategies be taught to people? To this question we add, To what extent can individuals be taught to generate positive emotions while they are also regulating distress? These and similar lines of inquiry are worth serious consideration in future research on the topic of late-life depression and its treatment.

ACKNOWLEDGMENT

Many thanks to Livia Kelly for her extensive help in searching pertinent databases and combing the library for articles.

REFERENCES

American Psychiatric Association. (2000). *Diagnostic and statistical manual of mental disorders* (4th ed., text rev.). Washington, DC: Author.

Anderson, I. M. (2000). Selective serotonin reuptake inhibitors versus tricyclic antidepressants: A meta-analysis of efficacy and tolerability. *Journal of Affective Disorders, 58,* 19–36.

Aranda, M., & Knight, B. G. (1997). The influence of ethnicity and culture on the caregiver stress and coping process: A sociocultural review and analysis. *Gerontologist, 37,* 342–354.

Barclay, L. L., Kheyfets, S., Zemcov, A., Blass, J. P., & McDowell, F. H. (1985). Risk factors in Alzheimer's disease. In A. Fisher, I. Hanin, & C. Lachman (Eds.), *Alzheimer's and Parkinson's diseases.* New York: Plenum Press.

Barrett, J. E., Barrett, J. A., Oxman, T. E., & Gerber, P. D. (1988). The prevalence of psychiatric disorders in a primary care practice. *Archives of General Psychiatry, 45,* 1100–1106.

Beck, A. T., Steer, R. A., & Brown, G. K. (1996). *Manual for the BDI-II.* San Antonio, TX: Psychological Corporation.

Beck, A. T., Ward, C., Mendelson, M., Mock, J., & Erbaugh, J. (1961). An inventory for measuring depression. *Archives of General Psychiatry, 4,* 561–571.

Beutler, L. E., Scogin, F., Kirkish, P., Schretlen, D., Corbishley, A., Hamblin, D., Meredith, K., Potter, R., Bamford, C. R., & Levenson, A. I. (1987). Group cognitive therapy and alprazolam in the treatment of depression in older adults. *Journal of Consulting and Clinical Psychology, 55,* 450–556.

Blazer, D. G. (1989). Affective disorders in late life. In E. Busse & D. G. Blazer (Eds.), *Geriatric psychiatry* (pp. 369–402). Washington, DC: American Psychiatric Press.

Blazer, D. G. (1991). Epidemiology of depressive disorders in late life. In *Abstracts of the Consensus Development Conference on the Diagnosis and Treatment of Depression in Late Life* (p. 18). Washington, DC: National Institutes of Health.

Blazer, D. G., Swartz, M., Woodbury, M., Manton, K. G., Hughes, D., & George, L. K. (1988). Depressive symptoms and depressive diagnoses in a community population: Use of a new procedure for analysis of psychiatric classification. *Archives of General Psychiatry, 45,* 1078–1084.

Blazer, D. G., Woodbury, M., Hughes, D. C., George, L. K., Manton, K. G., Bachar, J. R., & Fowler, N. (1989). A statistical analysis of the classification of depression in a mixed community and clinical sample. *Journal of Affective Disorders, 16,* 11–20.

Bondareff, W., Alpert, M., Friedhoff, A. J., Richter, E. M., Clary, C. M., & Batzar, E. (2000). Comparison of sertraline and nortriptyline in the treatment of major depressive disorder in late life. *American Journal of Psychiatry, 157*(5), 729–736.

Breckenridge, J. N., Gallagher, D., Thompson, L. W., & Peterson, J. A. (1986). Characteristic depressive symptoms of bereaved elders. *Journal of Gerontology, 41,* 163–168.

Canter, S. K., Thompson, L. W., & Gallagher-Thompson, D. (2001). *Residual subthreshold depressive symptoms and relapse in elderly depressive patients.* Paper presented at the annual meeting of the American Psychological Association, San Francisco.

Chambless, D. L., Sanderson, W. C., Shoham, V., Johnson, S. B., Pope, K. S., Crits-Cristoph, P., Baker, M., Johnson, B., Woody, S. R., Sue, S., Beutler, L., Williams, D. A., & McCurry, S. (1996). An update on empirically validated therapies. *Clinical Psychologist, 49,* 5–18.

Dick, L. P., Gallagher-Thompson, D., Coon, D. W., Powers, D. V., & Thompson, L. W. (1997). *Cognitive-behavioral therapy for late-life depression: A client manual.* Palo Alto, CA: VA Palo Alto Health Care System.

Dick, L. P., Gallagher-Thompson, D., & Thompson, L. W. (1997). *Cognitive-behavioral therapy for late-life depression: A therapist manual.* Palo Alto, CA: VA Palo Alto Health Care System.

Dobson, K. S. (1987). A meta-analysis of the efficacy of cognitive therapy for depression. *Journal of Consulting and Clinical Psychology, 57,* 414–419.

Edelstein, B., Kalish, K. D., Drozdick, L. W., & McKee, D. R. (1999). Assessment of depression and bereavement in older adults. In P. A. Lichtenberg (Ed.), *Handbook of assessment in clinical gerontology* (pp. 11–58). New York: Wiley.

Finkel, S. I., Richter, E. M., & Clary, C. M. (1999). Comparative efficacy and safety of sertraline versus nortriptyline in major depression in patients 70 and over. *International Psychogeriatrics, 11,* 85–99.

Finkel, S. I., Richter, E. M., Clary, C. M., & Batzar, E. (1999). Comparative efficacy of sertraline vs. fluoxetine in patients age 70 or over with major depression. *American Journal of Geriatric Psychiatry, 7,* 221–227.

First, M. B., Gibbon, M., Spitzer, R. L., & Williams, J. B. W. (1995). *User's guide for the Structured Clinical Interview for DSM-IV Axis I disorders.* New York: Biometrics Research.

Folkman, S., & Moskowitz, J. T. (2000). Stress, positive emotion, and coping. *Current Directions in Psychological Science, 9*(4), 115–118.

Frasure-Smith, N., Lesperance, F., & Talijic, M. (1993). Depression following myocardial infarction: Impact on six-month survival. *Journal of the American Medical Association, 270,* 819–825.

Fredman, L., Schoenback, V. J., Kaplan, B. H., Blazer, D. G., James, S. A., Kleinbau, D. G., & Yankaska, B. (1989). The association between depressive symptoms and mortality among older participants in the Epidemiological Catchment Area–Piedmont Health Survey. *Journals of Gerontology: Social Sciences, 44,* S141–S144.

Gallagher, D., Breckenridge, J., Steinmetz, J., & Thompson, L. W. (1983). The Beck Depression Inventory and research diagnostic criteria: Congruence in an older population. *Journal of Consulting and Clinical Psychology, 51,* 945–946.

Gallagher-Thompson, D., Arean, P., Coon, D., Menendez, A., Takagi, K., Haley, W., Arguelles, T., Rubert, M., Loewenstein, D., & Szapocznik, J. (2000). Development and implementation of intervention strategies for culturally diverse caregiving populations. In R. Schulz (Ed.), *Handbook on dementia caregiving* (pp. 151–185). New York: Springer Press.

Gallagher-Thompson, D., Hanley-Peterson, P., & Thompson, L. W. (1990). Maintenance of gains versus relapse following brief psychotherapy for depression. *Journal of Consulting and Clinical Psychology, 58,* 371–374.

Gallagher-Thompson, D., Lovett, S., Rose, J., McKibbin, C., Coon, D., Futterman, A., & Thompson, L. W. (2000). Impact of psychoeducational interventions on distressed family caregivers. *Journal of Clinical Geropsychology, 6,* 91–110.

Gallagher-Thompson, D., & Thompson, L. W. (1996). Applying cognitive/behavioral therapy to the psychological problems of later life. In S. H. Zarit & B. G. Knight (Eds.), A guide to psychotherapy and aging (pp. 61–82). Washington, DC: American Psychological Assocation Press.

Gallo, J. J., Royall, D. R., & Anthony, J. C. (1993). Risk factors for the onset of depression in middle age and later life. *Social Psychiatry and Psychiatric Epidemiology, 28,* 101–108.

Garfield, S. L. (1994). Research on client variables in psychotherapy. In A. E. Bergin & S. L. Garfield (Eds.), *Handbook of psychotherapy and behavior change* (4th ed., 190–228). New York: Wiley.

Gatz, M., Fiske, A., Fox, L. S., Kaskie, B., Kasl-Godley, J. E., McCallum, T. J., & Wetherell, J. L. (1998). Empirically validated psychological treatments for older adults. *Journal of Mental Health and Aging, 4,* 9–46.

Georgotas, A., McCue, R. E., & Cooper, T. B. (1989). A placebo-controlled comparison of nortriptyline and phenelzine in maintenance therapy depressed patients. *Archives of General Psychiatry, 46,* 783–786.

Georgotas, A., McCue, R. E., Cooper, T. B., Nagachandran, N., & Chang, I. (1988). How effective and safe is continuation therapy in elderly depressed patients? *Archives of General Psychiatry, 45,* 929–932.

Gerson, S., Belin, T. R., Kaufman, A., Mintz, J., & Jarvik, L. (1999). Pharmacological and psychological treatments for depressed older patients: A meta-analysis and overview of recent findings. *Harvard Review of Psychiatry, 7,* 1–28.

Gilewski, M., Farberow, N., Gallagher, D., & Thompson, L. W. (1991). Interaction of depression and bereavement on mental health in the elderly. *Psychology and Aging, 6,* 67–75.

Glassman, A. H., Rodriguez, A. I., & Shapiro, P. A. (1998). The use of antidepressant drugs in patients with heart disease. *Journal of Clinical Psychiatry, 59*(Suppl. 10), 16–21.

Gurland, B. J. (1991). The impact of depression on the quality of life of the elderly. In *Abstracts of the Consensus Development Conference on the Diagnosis and Treatment of Depression in Late Life* (pp. 25–30). Washington, DC: National Institutes of Health.

Gurland, B. J., Cross, P. S., & Katz, S. (1996). Epidemiological perspectives on opportunities for treatment of depression. *Americal Journal of Geriatric Psychiatry, 4*(Suppl. 1), S7–S13.

Hamilton, M. (1967). Development of a rating scale for primary depressive illness. *British Journal of Social and Clinical Psychology, 6*(4), 278–296.

Herzog, C., Van Alstine, J., Usala, P. D., Hultsch, D. F., & Dixon, R. (1990). Measurement properties of the Center for Epidemiological Studies Depression Scale (CES-D) in older populations. *Psychological Assessment: A Journal of Consulting and Clinical Psychology, 2,* 64–72.

Hibbard, M., Grober, S., Wayne, G., & Aletta, E. (1990). Modification of cognitive psychotherapy for the treatment of post-stroke depression. *Behavior Therapist,* 15–17.

Jarvik, L. F., Mintz, J. M., Steur, J., & Gerner, R. (1982). Treating geriatric depression: A 26 week interim analysis. *Journal of the American Geriatrics Society, 30,* 713–717.

Jefferson, A. L., Powers, D. V., & Pope, M. (2000). A preliminary comparative analysis of the Geriatric Depression Scale and the Beck Depression Inventory–II in older women. *Clinical Geropsychology, 22,* 3–12.

Judd, L. L., Akiskal, H. S., Maser, J. D., Zeller, P. J., Endicott, J., Coryell, W., Paulus, M. P., Kunovac, J. L., Leon, A. C., Mueller, T. I., Rice, J. A., & Keller, M. B. (1998). Major depressive disorder: A prospective study of residual subthreshold depressive symptoms as predictor of rapid relapse. *Journal of Affective Disorders, 50,* 97–108.

Judd, L. L., Rapaport, M. H., Paulus, M. P., & Brown, J. L. (1994). Subsyndromal symptomatic depression: A new mood disorder. *Journal of Clinical Psychiatry, 55*(Suppl.), 18–28.

Katon, W., & Sullivan, M. D. (1990). Depression and chronic medical illness. *Journal of Clinical Psychiatry, 51,* 3–11.

Katona, C. L. E., Hunter, B. M., & Bray, J. (1998). A double-blind comparison of the efficacy and safety of paroxetine and imipramine in the treatment of depression with dementia. *International Journal of Geriatric Psychiatry, 13,* 100–108.

Keller, M. B., Shapiro, R. W., Lavori, P. W., & Wolfe, N. (1982). Recovery in major depressive disorder. *Archives of General Psychiatry, 39,* 905–910.

Kelly, K. G., & Zisselman, M. (2000). Update on electroconvulsive therapy (ECT) in older adults. *Journal of the American Geriatrics Society, 48,* 560–566.

Kiecolt-Glaser, J. K., & Glaser, R. (1989). Caregiving, mental health, and immune function. In E. Light & B. Lebowitz (Eds.), *Alzheimer's disease, treatment, and family stress: Directions for research* (pp. 245–266). Washington, DC: Department of Health and Human Services, National Institute of Mental Health.

Klerman, G. L., Weissman, M. M, Rounsaville, B. J., & Chevron, E. S. (1984). *Interpersonal psychotherapy of depression*. New York: Basic Books.

Kokmen, E., Beard, C. M., Chandra, V., Offord, K. P., Schoenberg, B. S., & Ballard, D. J. (1991). Clinical risk factors for Alzheimer's disease: A population-based, case–control study. *Neurology, 41,* 1393–1397.

Larson, E. B., & Imai, Y. (1996). An overview of dementia and ethnicity with special emphasis on the epidemiology of dementia. In G. Yeo & D. Gallagher-Thompson (Eds.), *Ethnicity and the dementias* (pp. 9–20). Washington, DC: Taylor & Francis.

Lewinsohn, P. M. (1974). A behavioral approach to depression. In R. J. Friedman & M. M. Katz (Eds.), *The psychology of depression: Contemporary theory and research*. Washington, DC: Winston-Wiley.

Lewinsohn, P. M., Zeiss, A. M., & Duncan, E. M. (1989). Probability of relapse after recovery from an episode of depression. *Journal of Abnormal Psychology, 98,* 107–116.

Lichtenberg, P. A. (Ed.). (1999). *The handbook of assessment in clinical gerontology*. New York: Wiley.

Loevinger, J. (1957). Objective tests as instruments of psychological theory. *Psychological Reports, 3,* 635–694.

Morris, P. L. P., Robinson, R. G., Andrzejewski, P., Samuels, J., & Price, T. R. (1993). Association of depression with 10-year poststroke mortality. *American Journal of Psychiatry, 150,* 124–129.

Murphy, E. (1983). The prognosis of depression in old age. *British Journal of Psychiatry, 142,* 111–119.

Murray, J. B. (2000). Cardiac disorders and antidepressant medications. *Journal of Psychology, 134,* 162–168.

Murrell, S. A., & Meeks, S. (1992). Depressive symptoms in older adults: Predispositions, resources, and life experiences. In K. W. Schaie & M. P. Lawton (Eds.), *Annual review of gerontology and geriatrics* (Vol. 11, pp. 261–286). New York: Springer.

Myers, J. K., Weissman, M. M., Tischler, G. L., Holzer, C. E., III, Leaf, P. J., Orvaschel, H., Anthony, J. C., Boyd, J. H., Burke, J. D., Kramer, M., & Stoltzman, R. (1984). Six-month prevalence of psychiatric disorders in three communities. *Archives of General Psychiatry, 41,* 959–967.

National Institutes of Health Consensus Development Conference Consensus Statement. (1991). *Diagnosis and treatment of depression in late life, 9*(3), 1–27.

Newhouse, P. (1996). Use of serotonin selective reuptake inhibitors in geriatric depression. *Journal of Clinical Psychiatry, 57*(Suppl. 5), 12–22.

Newmann, J. P. (1989). Aging and depression. *Psychology and Aging, 4,* 150–165.

Newmann, J. P., Engel, R. J., & Jensen, J. (1990). Depressive symptoms among older women. *Psychology and Aging, 5,* 101–118.

Newmann, J. P., Engel, R. J., & Jensen, J. (1991a). Age differences in depressive symptom experiences. *Journals of Gerontology: Psychological Sciences, 46,* 224–235.

Newmann, J. P., Engel, R. J., & Jensen, J. (1991b). Changes in depressive symptom experiences among older women. *Psychology and Aging, 6,* 212–222.

Newmann, J. P., Klein, M. H., Jensen, J. E., & Essex, M. J. (1996). Depressive symptom experiences among older women: A comparison of alternative measurement approaches. *Psychology and Aging, 11,* 112–126.

Nezu, A. M., Ronan, G. F., Meadows, E. A., & McClure, K. S. (2000). *Practitioner's guide to empirically based measures of depression*. New York: Kluwer Academic Press.

Nolen-Hoeksema, S. (1987). Sex differences in unipolar depression. *Psychological Bulletin, 101,* 259–282.

Parmelee, P. A., Katz, I. R., & Lawton, M. P. (1992a). Incidence of depression in long-term care settings. *Journals of Gerontology: Medical Sciences, 47,* M189–M196.

Parmelee, P. A., Katz, I. R., & Lawton, M. P. (1992b). Depression and mortality among institutionalized aged. *Journals of Gerontology: Psychological Sciences, 47,* 3–10.

Parmelee, P. A., Lawton, M. P., & Katz, I. R. (1989). Psychometric properties of the Geriatric Depression Scale among the institutionalized aged. *Psychological Assessment: A Journal of Consulting and Clinical Psychology, 1,* 331–338.

Pedersen, N. L., , McClearn, G. E., Plomin, R., Nesselroade, J. R., Berg, S., & DeFaire, U. (1991). The Swedish Adoption/Twin Study of Aging. *Acta Geneticae Medicae Gemellologiae, 40,* 7–20.

Phifer, J. F., & Murrell, S. A. (1986). Etiologic factors in the onset of depressive symptoms in older adults. *Journal of Abnormal Psychology, 95,* 282–291.

Powers, D. V., Thompson, L., & Gallagher-Thompson, D. (2001, August). *Continued use of psychotherapy skills benefits older adults post-treatment.* Poster presented at the 109th Annual Convention of the American Psychological Association, San Francisco, CA.

Radloff, L. (1977). The CES-D Scale: A self-report depression scale for research in the general population. *Applied Psychological Measurement, 1,* 385–401.

Rapp, S. R., Parisi, S. A., Walsh, D. A., & Wallace, C. E. (1988). Detecting depression in elderly medical inpatients. *Journal of Consulting and Clinical Psychology, 56,* 509–513.

Rapp, S. R., Smith, S. S., & Britt, M. (1990). Identifying comorbid depression in elderly medical patients: Use of the Extracted Hamilton Depression Rating Scale. *Psychological Assessment, 2,* 243–247.

Reding, M., Haycox, J., & Blass, J. (1985). Depression in patients referred to a dementia clinic: A three-year prospective study. *Archives of Neurology, 42,* 894–896.

Regier, D. A., Boyd, J. H., Burke, J. D., Rae, D. S., Myers, J. K., Kramer, M., Robins, L. N., George, L. K., Karno, M., & Locke, B. Z. (1988). One month prevalence of mental disorders in the United States. *Archives of General Psychiatry, 45,* 977–986.

Reynolds, C. F. (1992). Treatment of depression in special populations. *Journal of Clinical Psychiatry, 53*(Suppl.), 45–53.

Reynolds, C. F., Frank, E., Perel, J. M., Imber, S. D., Cornes, C., Morycz, R., Mazumdar, S., Miller, M., Pollock, B., Rifai, A. H., Stack, J. A., George, C. J., Houck, P. R., & Kupfer, D. J. (1992). Combined pharmacotherapy and psychotherapy in the acute and continuation treatment of elderly patients with recurrent major depression: A preliminary report. *American Journal of Psychiatry, 149,* 1687–1692.

Reynolds, C. F., Frank, E., Perel, J. M., Imber, S., Thornton, J., Morycz, R. K., Cornes, C., & Kupfer, D. (1989). Open trial maintenance pharmacotherapy in late life depression: Survival analysis. *Psychiatry Research, 27,* 225–231.

Reynolds, C. F., Perel, J. M., Frank, E., Cornes, C., Miller, M. D., Houck, P. R., Mazumdor, S., Stack, J. A., Pollock, B. G., Dew, M. A., & Kupfer, D. S. (1999). Three-year outcomes of maintenance nortriptylene treatment in late-life depression: A study of two fixed plasma levels. *American Journal of Psychiatry, 156*(8), 1177–1181.

Robins, L. N., Helzer, J. E., Croughan, J. L., & Ratliff, K. S. (1981). National Institute of Mental Health Diagnostic Interview Schedule. *Archives of General Psychiatry, 38,* 381–389.

Robinson, L., Berman, J., & Neimeyer, R. A. (1990). Psychotherapy for the treatment of depression: A comprehensive review of controlled outcome research. *Psychological Bulletin, 108,* 30–49.

Robinson, R. G., Schultz, S. K., Castillo, C., Kopel, T., Kosier, J. T., Newman, R. M., Curdue, K., Petracca, G., & Starkstein, S. E. (2000). Nortriptyline versus fluoxetine in the treatment of depression and in short-term recovery after stroke: A placebo-controlled, double blind study. *American Journal of Psychiatry, 157,* 351–359.

Roose, M. P., & Suthers, K. M. (1998). Antidepressant response in late-life depression. *Journal of Clinical Psychiatry, 59*(Suppl. 10), 4–8.

Rovner, B. W., German, P. S., Brant, L. J., Clark, R., Burton, L., & Folstein, M. F. (1991). Depression and mortality in nursing homes. *Journal of the American Medical Association, 265,* 993–996.

Rybarczyk, B., Gallagher-Thompson, D., Rodman, J., Zeiss, A., Gantz, F., & Yesavage, J. (1992). Applying cognitive-behavioral psychotherapy to the chronically ill elderly: Treatment issues and case illustration. *International Psychogeriatrics, 4*(1), 127–140.

Salzman, C. (1998). *Clinical geriatric psychopharmacology* (3rd ed.). Baltimore: Williams & Wilkins.

Salzman, C. (2001). *Psychiatric medications for older adults: The concise guide.* New York: Guilford Press.

Sapolsky, R. M. (1992). *Stress, the aging brain, and the mechanisms of neuron death.* Cambridge, MA: MIT Press.

Scogin, F., Jamison, C., & Gochneaur, K. (1989). Comparative efficacy of cognitive and behavioral bibliotherapy for mildly and moderately depressed older adults. *Journal of Consulting and Clinical Psychology, 57,* 403–407.

Scogin, F., & McElreath, L. (1994). Efficacy of psychosocial treatments for geriatric depression: A quantitative review. *Journal of Consulting and Clinical Psychology, 62,* 69–74.

Simons, A. D., Murphy, G. E., Levine, J. L., & Wetzel, R. D. (1986). Cognitive therapy and pharmacotherapy for depression: Sustained improvement over one year. *Archives of General Psychiatry, 43,* 43–48.

Sloane, R. B., Staples, F. R., & Schneider, L. S. (1985). Interpersonal therapy versus nortriptyline for depression in the elderly. In G. D. Burrows, T. R. Norman, & L. Dennerstein (Eds.), *Clinical and pharmacological studies in psychiatric disorders* (pp. 344–346). London: Libby.

Smith, M. L., Glass, G. V., & Miller, T. I. (1980). *The benefits of psychotherapy.* Baltimore: Johns Hopkins University Press.

Stiles, P. G., & McGarrahan, J. F. (1998). The Geriatric Depression Scale: A comprehensive review. *Journal of Clinical Geropsychology, 4,* 89–110.

Stukenberg, K. W., Dura, J. R., & Kiecolt-Glaser, J. K. (1990). Depression screening scale validation in an elderly, community-dwelling population. *Psychological Assessment, 2,* 134–138.

Taragano, F. E., Lyketsos, C. G., Mangone, C. A., Allegri, R. F., & Comesana-Diaz, E. (1997). A double-blind, randomized, fixed-dose trial of fluoxetine vs. amitryptiline in the treatment of major depression complicating Alzheimer's disease. *Psychosomatics, 38,* 246–252.

Tedeschi, R. G., Park, C. L., & Calhoun, L. G. (Eds.). (1998). *Posttraumatic growth.* Mahway, NJ: Erlbaum.

Teri, L. (1994). Behavioral treatment of depression in patients with dementia. *Alzheimer's Disease and Related Disorders, 8,* 66–74.

Teri, L., Curtis, J., Gallagher-Thompson, D., & Thompson, L. W. (1994). Cognitive-behavior therapy with depressed older adults. In L. Schneider, C. F. Reynolds, B. D. Lebowitz, & A. Friedhoff (Eds.), *Diagnosis and treatment of depression in late life: Results of the NIH Consensus Development Conference* (pp. 279–291). Washington, DC: American Psychiatric Association Press.

Teri, L., & Gallagher-Thompson, D. (1991). Cognitive-behavioral interventions for the treatment of depression in Alzheimer's patients. *Gerontologist, 31,* 413–416.

Teri, L., Logsdon, R. G., Uomoto, J., & McCurry, S. M. (1997). Behavioral treatment of depression in dementia patients: A controlled clinical trial. *Journals of Gerontology, 52B,* 159–166.

Thomas, C., Kelman, H. R., Kennedy, G. J., Ahn, C., & Yang, C. (1992). Depressive symptoms and mortality in elderly persons. *Journals of Gerontology: Social Sciences, 47,* S80–S87.

Thompson, L. W., Coon, D. W., Gallagher-Thompson, D., Sommer, B., & Koin, D. (2001, Summer). Comparison of desipramine and cognitive/behavioral therapy in the treatment of elderly outpatients with mild to moderate depression. *American Journal of Geriatric Psychiatry (Special Issue), 9*(3), 225–240.

Thompson, L. W., Futterman, A., & Gallagher, D. (1988). Assessment of late-life depression. *Psychopharmacological Bulletin, 24,* 577–586.

Thompson, L. W., Gallagher, D., & Breckenridge, J. S. (1987). Comparative effectiveness of psychotherapies for depressed elders. *Journal of Consulting and Clinical Psychology, 55,* 385–330.

Thompson, L. W., & Gallagher-Thompson, D. (1991, November). *Comparison of desimpramine and cognitive/behavioral therapy in the treatment of late-life depression: A progress report.* Paper presented at the annual meeting of the Gerontological Society of America, San Francisco.

U.S. Bureau of Census. (1991). Tables 13, 18. In *Statistical abstract of the United States* (111th ed.). Washington, DC: U.S. Government Printing Office.

U.S. Department of Health and Human Services. (1999). *Mental health: A report of the surgeon general.* Rockville, MD: U.S. Department of Health and Human Services, Substance Abuse and Mental Health Services Administration, Center for Mental Health Services, National Institutes of Health, National Institute of Mental Health.

Valle, R. (1998). *Caregiving across cultures.* Washington, DC: Taylor & Francis.

Von Korff, M., Shapiro, S., Burke, J. D., Teitlebaum, M., Skinner, E. A., German, P., Turner, R. W., Klein, L., & Burns, B. (1987). Anxiety and depression in a primary care clinic: Comparison of Diagnostic Interview Schedule, General Health Questionnaire, and practitioner assessments. *Archives of General Psychiatry, 44*, 152–156.

Walters, G., Reynolds, C. F., Mulsant, B. H., & Pollock, B. G. (1999). Continuation and maintenance pharmacotherapy in geriatric depression: An open-trial comparison of paroxetine and nortriptyline in patients older than 70 years. *Journal of Clinical Psychiatry, 60*(Suppl. 20), 21–25.

Weihs, K. L., Settle, E. C., Batey, S. R., Houser, T. L., Donahue, R. M. J., & Ascher, J. A. (2000). Bupropion sustained release versus paroxetine for the treatment of depression in the elderly. *Journal of Clinical Psychiatry, 61*, 196–202.

Wetherell, J. L., Gatz, M., Johansson, B., & Pedersen, N. L. (1999). History of depression and other psychiatric illness as risk factors for Alzheimer disease in a twin sample. *Alzheimer's Disease and Related Disorders, 13*, 47–52.

Williams, J. W., Barrett, J., Oxman, T., Frank, E., Katon, W., Sullivan, M., Cornell, J., & Sengupta, A., (2000). Treatment of dysthymia and minor depression in primary care: A randomized controlled trial in older adults. *Journal of the American Medical Association, 284*, 1519–1526.

Williamson, G. R., Shaffer, D. R., & Parmalee, P. R. (Eds.). (2000). *Physical illness and depression in older adults: A handbook of theory, research, and practice.* New York: Kluwer Academic/Plenum Publishers.

Yesavage, J. A., Brink, T. L., Rose, T. L., Lum, O., Huang, V., Addey, M., & Leirer, V. O. (1983). Development and validation of a geriatric depression scale. *Journal of Psychiatric Research, 17*, 31–49.

Zeiss, A. M., & Steffen, A. (1996). Behavioral and cognitive/behavioral treatments: An overview of social learning. In S. H. Zarit & B. G. Knight (Eds.), *A guide to psychotherapy and aging* (pp. 35–60). Washington, DC: American Psychological Association Press.

25

Epidemiology, Assessment, and Management of Suicide in Depressed Patients

Ronald A. Stolberg, David C. Clark, and Bruce Bongar

Suicide is the major life-threatening complication of depression that most mental health professionals must face (Schein, 1976), and it is the most common clinical emergency encountered in mental health practice (Beutler, Clarkin, & Bongar, 2000). In the course of a career, half of all psychiatrists and 20% of all psychologists, for example, lose a patient in treatment by suicide (Bongar, Lomax, & Marmatz, 1992). Greaney (1995) reported that the average practicing psychologist treats an average of five suicidal patients per month, and that one in three of these psychologists has lost a patient to suicide. While the base rate of suicide in the general population is low, suicide remains the eighth leading cause of death in the United States. The suicide rate for psychiatric patients is about three times higher than it is for nonpatients (Babigian & Odoroff, 1969). Black, Warrack, and Winokur (1985) found that nearly one-third of patients who went on to complete suicide had a present, diagnosable affective disorder (Beutler et al., 2000). The lifetime risk of suicide among patients who have an untreated depressive disorder is nearly 20% (Montano, 1994; Isometsä, Henrikson, Hillevi, Kuoppasalmi, & Lönnqvist, 1994; Guze & Robins, 1970; Miles, 1977). The increased risk of suicide that is associated with comorbid depression can be summarized by the observation that the base rate of suicide in the United States is 11.2 per 100,000 people (Hirschfeld & Russell, 1997), but it is estimated to be between 230 and 566 per 100,000 people among patients who are in a current episode of depression (Clark, Young, Scheftner, Fawcett, & Fogg, 1987; Fremouw, de Perczel, & Ellis, 1990). This represents a 50-fold increase over the population base rate (Beutler et al., 2000). Thus, it is sensible for mental health professionals to adopt the perspective of their medical/surgical colleagues who know that some of their patients will inevitably die in the course of treatment. To deny this simple truth is to mislead the patient, the patient's family, and the self about the incompleteness of current-day knowledge about suicide and the effectiveness of available treatments for suicidal risk, and to pretend that suicides should always be understood as treatment failures.

Several studies (Boyd, 1983; Evans & Farberow, 1988; Maris, 1981, 1989; Roy, 1986; Shneidman, 1989; Weissman, Klerman, Markowitz, & Ouelette, 1989) show that members of high-risk groups (e.g., depressed, schizophrenic, substance abusers, etc) are at greater risk for attempting suicide than are members of the general population (Frederick, 1978; Maris, 1981, 1989). Also, studies suggest that rates of completed suicide among the mentally ill (Asnis et al., 1993; Hirschfeld & Davidson, 1988; Maris, 1981; Pokorny, 1964; Roy, 1986; Simon, 1988) far exceed that of the population as a whole. However, estimates of rate of death by suicide due to psychiatric disorders can vary greatly across such factors as country of origin (Roy, 1986), regional differences within a single country (Peterson, Bongar, & Netsoki, 1989), and the diagnostic criteria used in selecting the sample. For example, estimates of the number of individuals with bipolar depression who die by suicide range from 15 to 55% (Goldring & Fieve, 1984).

Recognition of suicidal risk is easiest when the patient voluntarily consults with a mental health professional and complains about preoccupations with suicidal thoughts or wishes. But suicidal persons do not always seek professional help, nor do they always communicate their suicidal thoughts and behavior to a health professional. In the course of outpatient therapy, a patient in treatment for a different condition may develop new symptoms associated with a greater risk for death by suicide (e.g., a patient with a borderline personality disorder develops a superimposed major depressive episode, or a patient suffering from major depression begins to abuse alcohol). At this point, midstream in therapy, and perhaps unknown to the treating clinician, the patient may begin to entertain suicidal thoughts. The new development may go undetected unless the clinician recognizes significant changes in the patient and initiates a new assessment for suicide risk.

Furthermore, persons suffering with psychiatric symptoms do not usually seek care in a mental health setting. Two-thirds of persons meeting diagnostic criteria for a mental disorder never make any contact with mental health services (Myers et al., 1984). Almost half of all persons who die by suicide have never seen a mental health professional in their lifetime (Barraclough, Bunch, Nelson, & Sainsbury, 1974; Beskow, 1979; Hagnell & Rorsman, 1978, 1979). While the suicide risk of some who never access mental health services is detected and treated in (nonpsychiatric) medical care settings, the fact remains that a large number of persons with mental disorders and suicidal thoughts receive no evaluation or treatment whatsoever for those conditions.

Yet there is evidence that persons who commit suicide have often seen a primary care physician within a few weeks or months of their death (Barraclough et al., 1974; Seager & Flood, 1965; Vassilas & Morgan, 1993). Systematic reviews of these medical contacts show that imminently suicidal individuals rarely visit a physician to complain of psychiatric symptoms, depression, or suicidal impulses. The patient is more likely to visit the doctor's office with multiple, vague complaints of physical symptoms that have gone undiagnosed—symptoms often associated with major depression or alcoholism (Murphy, 1975). Thus, a patient complaining of insomnia and fatigue may present in the primary care medical setting and be treated symptomatically with sleeping pills without consideration of the value of screening for mental disorders. In this case, the larger context is ignored and the patient goes untreated for the underlying and more serious psychiatric problem—for example, major depression.

Focusing on isolated physical symptoms rather than suspecting an underlying mental disorder is not the only reason why patients at risk for suicide are not recognized or evaluated appropriately. In a group of 60 suicide victims who had recently been under the care of physicians, 80% were interpreted as having depressive symptoms in reaction to situations or life events of an adverse nature (Murphy, 1975). The presence of these symptoms were accepted as a natural reaction to an upsetting life situation, and consequently was not interpreted as symptomatic of a depressive illness. The mistake evident in retrospect was that the physicians recognized psychological symptoms but failed to identify or treat a documentable psychiatric illness—because of naive theories about "normal-range stress reactions."

The problem of recognizing suicide risk is not limited to the outpatient physician's office. Prevalence rates of mental illness in prisons range from 16 to 66%, depending upon the type of facility (Gibbs, 1982; Ogloff & Otto, 1989; Teplin, 1983). The suicide rate for persons in jail is estimated to be nine times higher than that of the general population (Hayes & Rowan, 1988). Ironically, two-thirds of prison suicides occur while the inmate is being held in isolation for protection and/or surveillance (Hayes & Kajdin, 1981). Another group at elevated risk for death by suicide is patients on psychiatric inpatient units. About 1,500 suicides occur on inpatient units every year—about 5% of all suicides (Crammer, 1984). This fact probably reflects a concentration of high-risk persons in time and place by virtue of the presence of a mental disorder, the presence of a disorder of severe proportions requiring hospitalization, the inability of experts to always know which subset of patients at risk for suicide are the most intent on killing themselves, and the inability of experts to always know when the suicide intent of a patient will peak.

Even when a mental health professional has an opportunity to interview the patient about suicidal thoughts and behaviors, the task of assessing suicide risk is complex. It is demonstrably impossible to predict individual cases of suicide on a consistent statistical basis because suicide is such a rare event in any population (Rosen, 1954; MacKinnan & Farberow, 1975; Murphy, 1984; Pokorny, 1983). The best a clinician can do is determine which groups of persons are at greater risk for completing suicide and which persons are more likely to make nonfatal attempts. In order to detect persons at elevated risk for suicide, a complete assessment of suicide risk should include a mental status examination, a thorough assessment of psychopathology, systematic inquiry about suicidal thoughts and behavior, and application of a risk-assessment formula tailored to the principal psychiatric diagnosis identified in the diagnostic interview.

EPIDEMIOLOGY

In the United States, suicide ranks eighth as a leading cause of death, claiming more than 30,000 lives each year (National Center for Health Statistics, 1998). The suicide rate is three times higher for men than for women, two times higher for whites than for nonwhites, and one and a half times higher for the elderly than for the young. Adolescent suicide rates have more than quadrupled since 1955, while suicide rates among the elderly (i.e., those 65 years and over) have decreased by a factor of three over a similar period. The elderly continue to evidence a higher suicide rate than do youthful or middle-aged persons, although now age-group differences in suicide rates are nowhere near as marked as they used to be between 1930 and 1950. In fact, today, a person's age does not provide much useful information about statistical risk for suicide.

Other demographic markers for increased suicide risk include marital status and parental status. Young women who have been widowed have the highest suicide rate of any marital status group (Kreitman, 1988), but death of a spouse does not help predict suicide risk much for other age groups. Parental status may contribute more directly to estimating suicide risk than marital status. Veevers (1973) first showed that being responsible for children under the age of 18 years is associated with a lower risk for death by suicide, which may be the underlying reason why those who are single, separated, and divorced are at elevated risk for suicide.

The demographic profiles of persons who die by suicide and of persons who make non-fatal attempts are more different than alike (Linehan, 1986). About 2.9% of adults have made a suicide attempt in their lifetime (Moscicki et al., 1988). Women are three to four times more likely to make suicide attempts than men. Persons aged 25 to 44 make more attempts than those who are younger or older. Persons who are separated or divorced have a rate of suicide attempts that is four times higher than persons in other marital status categories. There are no remarkable distinctions among rates of suicide attempts for whites, blacks, and Hispanics. Living conditions, income, educational level, social circumstances, and acute life upsets seem to play a more important role in influencing suicide *attempts* than influencing suicidal *deaths*. Finally, personality disorders appear to be more prevalent among persons—particularly males—who make nonfatal attempts than among those who die by suicide.

It is important to try to distinguish among those who are at imminent risk for death by suicide, those who may be at long-term risk for death by suicide, and those who are at risk for repeated nonfatal suicide attempts. While nonfatal suicidal behavior requires evaluation and prompt intervention, and while chronic suicide risk requires vigilant treatment, the primary task of the clinician is to focus attention and therapeutic efforts on those who are most likely to die by suicide in the near future, and to keep the patient alive until the suicidal crisis passes. In the office, the clinic, and the hospital alike, the clinician must have access to a suicide risk prediction formula tailored to identify groups of persons at risk for *death* by suicide in the *short*-term future—a formula representing the summation of his or her understanding of extant scientific knowledge and his or her clinical experience.

INQUIRING ABOUT SUICIDAL THOUGHTS AND BEHAVIOR

Because patients who exhibit psychopathology—particularly those who meet criteria for a major depressive disorder, alcoholism, drug abuse dependence, or schizophrenia—are at elevated risk for suicide attempts and death by suicide, explicit questions about morbid thoughts, suicidal thoughts, hopelessness, and suicidal behavior should be included in any assessment interview. By doing so, the clinician elicits examples of current symptoms and simultaneously alerts the patient to the idea that the interviewer will continue to be interested in hearing about morbid/suicidal thoughts if they continue, recur, or emerge *de novo*. It is important to fully explore the patient's range and depth of suicidal thoughts and behavior without interrupting to lecture, discourage, or prohibit. Premature interruptions only serve to disrupt the patient's train of thought, break empathic contact, and encourage minimization and denial of extant symptoms.

Inquiry about suicidal thoughts and behavior should always begin with the patient's description of his or her problem. By letting the patient provide an overview of the current problems in his or her own language, the interviewer has the opportunity to develop a conceptual overview of the problem and to structure inquiry for the remainder of the interview. By listening to the patient discuss current problems for 5 or 10 minutes at the beginning, the interviewer also has the opportunity to learn something about the patient's pace and style of talking.

After the patient's initial description of his or her problems, the interviewer should inquire about dysphoric affect. Has the patient felt sad, apathetic, anhedonic, irritable, or anxious? If any of these dysphoric states have been present, the interviewer should determine their frequency, intensity, and duration. Next, the interviewer should inquire about feelings of pessimism, hopelessness, or despair by linking the predominant dysphoric affect to a view of the future: "When a person feels as sad/empty/cranky as you have been feeling for the last several weeks, he or she sometimes become discouraged, or convinced that nothing will work out well. Have you been feeling discouraged?" The frequency, intensity, and duration of any feelings of hopelessness should be explored.

The interview should next progress to thoughts of death or suicide by linking the predominant dysphoric affect and the experience of hopelessness to suicidal thoughts: "When a person feels as sad/empty/cranky as you have for the last several weeks, and feels this discouraged, he or she may begin to think about dying or even killing him/herself. Have you?" (Endicott & Spitzer, 1978). This type of direct questioning will elicit the most complete information with the least discomfort or embarrassment. To conduct a thorough evaluation, the patient should be allowed to speak freely about all suicidal plans and ideas without interruption. Even if the patient answers "no" to questions regarding suicide, the possibility of the patient having suicidal thoughts or having engaged in suicidal behavior should not be totally discounted (Glassmire, Stolberg, Greene, & Bongar, 2001). Often a quick or firm negative response may be indicative of one of the following: the patient may be reluctant to admit to his or her suicidal thoughts, the patient may be trying to signal that he or she is not having suicidal thoughts *at this moment*, or the patient may be trying to demonstrate that such thoughts are not significant because he or she would never *act* on them. In these cases, the interviewer should explain to the patient that it is important to determine whether the patient has experienced any suicidal thoughts, however fleeting or unlikely, during the current episode of illness. Further probing may be necessary to elicit this information. In addition, the patient's relatives or intimate friends should routinely be interviewed about suicidal communications if suicidal thoughts are suspected but denied. Suicidal persons are most likely to share their suicidal thoughts or intentions with family members and intimates, but sometimes actively conceal their suicidal thoughts from an evaluator.

If the patient admits to having had thoughts of death or suicide, it is important to determine whether these thoughts were active or passive (e.g., "I wish I were dead" vs. "I feel like killing myself"). If the patient has had active thoughts of suicide, the interviewer should probe persistently for the specific methods of suicide that have occurred to the patient. It is best to inventory the methods considered in one fell swoop, to build an exhaustive list, because the last plan identified is sometimes the most clinically significant. After all the considered methods have been counted, we recommend that the interviewer ask how often the patient considered each plan, the degree to which each plan was rehearsed mentally, and the degree to which each plan was translated into behavior. Where a patient has engaged in a great deal of mental rehearsal for a suicide, and particularly where the patient has translated some component of the plan into overt behavior, concern about imminent suicide risk is greatest.

If the patient denies having thought of any specific method of suicide, it is important for the interviewer to ask the patient if he or she intends to act on any suicidal thoughts in the near future, and why or why not. The interviewer ought not hesitate to pose these types of questions to the patient. This type of probing is typically not interpreted by the patient as encouragement to attempt suicide.

A final area to explore with the suicidal patient is the question of whether or not he or she includes other persons in the morbid or suicidal thinking. In 3–4% of all suicides, someone else—usually a spouse, intimate, or family member—is murdered at the same time (Beskow, 1979; Dorpat & Ripley, 1960; Robins, Gassner, Kaye, Wilkinson, & Murphy, 1959). In 5% of all homicides the perpetrator commits suicide or makes a suicide attempt soon after the homicide (Rosenbaum, 1990; Wolfgang, 1958). About 20% of those who have killed a child later die by suicide or make a suicide attempt (Adelson, 1961; Rodenburg, 1971). Explicit questions about homicidal/suicidal thinking often help the patient understand that these should be understood as symptoms of a current illness, and can be addressed in the course of treatment.

If the patient has suicidal thoughts or the clinician believes the patient is at more than negligible risk for suicide, the clinician will need to consider the patient's access to various instruments of suicide. If means for suicide (e.g., guns, medications) can be easily obtained by the patient, it is important to remove them from the patient's environment. It is wise to include family members in this discussion in order to educate them about suicide risk and suicidal communications, to obtain complete information, and to recruit their assistance.

The final step of a thorough risk assessment interview includes questioning a member of the patient's family and/or a close friend. More often than not, patients who experience suicidal thoughts and wishes discuss these feelings with family members and/or intimates. Community-based psychological autopsy studies consistently show that more than 40% of patients who died by suicide had expressed their suicidal intentions clearly and specifically, and that another 30% had talked about death and dying, in the months preceding suicide (Barraclough et al., 1974; Beskow, 1979; Chynoweth, Tonge, & Armstrong, 1980; Dorpat & Ripley, 1960; Fowler, Rich, & Young, 1986; Hagnell & Rorsman, 1978, 1979, 1980; Rich, Fowler, Fogarty, & Young, 1988; Rich, Young, & Fowler, 1986; Robins, 1981; Robins, Gassner, et al., 1959; Robins, Murphy, Wilkinson, Gassner, & Kayes, 1959). Mental health professionals cannot always elicit the same suicidal communications from their patients. In one prospective study, more than 50% of depressed psychiatric inpatients who died by suicide denied suicidal ideation or admitted to only vague thoughts of suicide when examined by an experienced clinical interviewer (Fawcett, 1988). Unfortunately, the suicidal communications directed to family members and friends are usually not interpreted as serious threats or as serious intentions to commit suicide. Thus, it is vital that the clinician educate family members about this aspect of suicide risk and question them about the patient's morbid or suicidal thoughts.

All suicidal ideation and behavior must be taken seriously. While clinicians are prone to review the psychosocial circumstances that led up to an episode of suicidal behavior in order to gauge the patient's "true intent" and interpret the patient's primary motives, it is important to recognize that the clinical value of these kinds of formulations for predicting future behavior has never been demonstrated. For example, Litman (1964) observed that intention is often ambivalent in cases of suicide—a strong wish to die and a strong wish to live can exist side by side, making decisive action appear hesitating or inconclusive. Many suicidologists are not convinced that suicidal intent can be established systematically after a death has occurred (Jobes, Berman, & Josselson, 1986).

Borderline patients can be particularly taxing in this regard. When a patient has exhibited a pattern of resorting to suicidal threats frequently in therapy as a coping strategy (e.g., as one aspect of a histrionic character style in response to disappointments or frustrations inside or outside the therapy), the therapist may decide that the patient has "cried wolf" one time too many and begin to discount all subsequent suicidal behavior. This can be a fatal mistake. Unless a complete strategy and context for managing chronic parasuicidal behavior has been developed in the therapy, the next instance of self-injury may be reflexively but erroneously tagged as "manipulative," when this instance actually represents the first grave communication of suicide intent in a borderline patient who has just now developed a comorbid major depressive episode. The reader who is interested in promising strategies for psychotherapy with chronically parasuicidal patients is referred to the cognitive-behavioral techniques of Linehan (1993a, 1993b), who has published the favorable results of controlled trials of her techniques (Linehan, Armstrong, Suarez, Allmon, & Heard, 1991; Linehan, Heard, & Armstrong, 1993), and the psychodynamic techniques of Maltsberger (1986).

Although a history of suicide attempts is not in and of itself a reliable index of risk for completed suicide—because half of all persons who die by suicide have never made a previous attempt—it is important to question patients about each nonfatal attempt because these are associated both with a higher risk for suicide and with subsequent attempts (Buglass & Horton, 1974; Clark, Gibbons, Fawcett, & Scheftner, 1989; Kreitman & Casey, 1988; Morgan, Barton, Pottle, Pocock, & Burns-Cox, 1976). Long-term follow-up studies of persons who have made nonfatal suicide attempts indicate that 7–10% eventually die by suicide (Cullberg, Wasserman, & Stefansson, 1988; Ettlinger, 1964; Motto, 1965; Weiss & Scott, 1974), a risk five times greater than the 1.4% lifetime risk of suicide for the U.S. general population (National Center for Health Statistics, 1992). Yet 90–93% of all nonfatal attempters will not die by suicide.

THE IMPORTANCE OF ASSESSING PSYCHOPATHOLOGY

Numerous reports reaffirm and continue to support the importance of disturbances of mood in suicidal acts. Psychiatric disorder and suicidal risk are related, although the nature of the association is unclear (Beutler, Clarkin, & Bongar, 2000). Suicide almost always occurs in the presence of major psychopathology. Research findings suggest that people who commit suicide are likely to have suffered from one or more psychiatric disorders (Henriksson et al., 1993; Robins, Murphy, et al., 1959; Runeson, 1989). Findings from psychological autopsy studies and follow-up mortality studies consistently demonstrate the strong association between major psychopathology and suicide. Community-based psychological autopsy studies of a 100 or more suicides in the United States, the United Kingdom, Sweden, and Australia implicate a recent major mental disorder in 88–93% of cases of adult suicide (Barraclough et al., 1974; Beskow, 1979; Chynoweth et al., 1980; Clark & Fawcett, 1992; Dorpat & Ripley, 1960; Fowler et al., 1986; Robins, Gassner, et al., 1959). While the casual relation of psychiatric disorder and suicide cannot be extrapolated directly from these findings, the figures are sobering and certainly suggest that psychiatric disorder be considered a risk factor for suicide (Beutler et al., 2000). The diagnoses most often present in these suicide cases have been major depression (40–60% of cases), chronic alcoholism (20% of cases), and schizophrenia (10% of cases) (Cheng, 1995; Clark, 1992; Clayton, 1985; Isometsä et al., 1994; Keller, 1994; Murphy, 1977; Rihmer, Barsi, Arató, & Demeter, 1990). Persons suffering from major depression, alcoholism, or both constitute 57–86% of all suicide cases. Of these three diagnoses, depressive disorder has consistently been the most common indicator and the strongest predictor of suicide (Isometsä et al., 1994; Keller, 1994; Rihmer et al., 1990; Zweig & Hinrichsen, 1993).

Follow-up mortality studies also demonstrate the strong relation between psychiatric disorders and suicide. The lifetime risk of suicide for patients with major affective disorder is 15%; for patients with alcoholism 3–4%; and for patients with schizophrenia 10% (Allebeck, 1989; Black et al., 1985; Drake, Gates, & Whitaker, 1986; Martin, Cloninger, Guze, & Clayton, 1985; Miles, 1977; Murphy & Wetzel, 1990; Tsuang, Woolson, & Fleming, 1980) in long-term follow-up mortality studies. For this reason it is extremely important to assess systematically symptoms of psychopathology whenever a question of suicide risk arises.

When assessing psychopathology, it is important for the clinician to consider patients who meet criteria for any psychiatric diagnosis as being at high risk until a second-stage evaluation can further clarify the degree of risk. Clinicians should pay special attention to persons who meet criteria for major depression, alcoholism or drug use disorders, schizophrenia, and organic brain syndromes, because these disorders are known to be associated with death by suicide. The second-stage evaluation is characterized by systematic inquiry about suicidal thoughts and behavior, as well as systematic inquiry about symptoms and features specifically suggestive of elevated risk among patients with the indicated psychiatric diagnosis.

RISK ASSESSMENT TAILORED TO A SPECIFIC CLINICAL DIAGNOSIS

In an effort to define who is at risk for suicide in a more specific and precise fashion than what can be predicted from diagnosis alone, Clark and Fawcett (1992) advocate the formulation of diagnosis-specific suicide risk profiles. Despite the failure to find clear suicide profiles, Fawcett et al. (1990) point out that the correlation between suicide rate and affective states provides enough of a reason to implement preventive care. They suggest that factors such as a depressive disorder, alcohol abuse, anxiety, and other correlates constitute modifiable risk factors. Much of what constitutes treatment for suicidal risk relies on the use of clinical wisdom and experience to treat such patients.

Most "suicide risk prediction formulas" are based on studies of nonfatal suicide attempters, who can be interviewed following an attempt, and who are far more numerous than suicide completers. Most risk prediction formulas have some value for identifying nonfatal suicide attempters, repeated attempters, and attempters who make medically dangerous attempts—because these are the clinical populations to whom researchers have devoted most of their attention. But if those who die by suicide are different from nonfatal attempters in important ways, then empirical profiles of nonfatal attempters may have relatively little value for identifying persons at risk for death by suicide. At this early stage in the science of suicide risk prediction, we think it is far more empirically sound to approach the problems of predicting nonfatal attempts and predicting death by suicide as relatively independent; thus, we recommend that clinicians be reluctant to reduce "suicide risk" prediction to a single all-purpose formula.

Risk assessment formulations should also be tailored to the specific principal diagnosis implicated in the diagnostic interview (Clark, 1990). By keying the risk assessment to a single diagnostic grouping (where the patient qualifies for one and not several mental disorders), the clinician is guided to search for features that distinguish the target patient from others affected with the same illness. This follows from our impression that the risk factors for suicide in major depression are different than the risk factors for suicide in alcoholism or in schizophrenia. Inaccuracy and inefficiency would result if a single risk profile were used to gauge risk for all psychiatric patients.

Patients Who Meet Criteria for a Major Depression

Major depression is the psychiatric diagnosis most commonly associated with suicide (40–60% of cases) (Clayton, 1985; Murphy, 1986). In a prospective study of patients with major depressive disorder, Fawcett et al. (1990) found the following symptoms to be associated with death by suicide within 1 year: severe psychic anxiety, severe anhedonia, global insomnia, diminished concentration, indecision, sleep disturbances, acute overuse of alcohol, and panic attacks (62% of patients in the study who committed suicide within the first year of follow-up reported panic attacks concurrent with the index episode of depression). In the same study, a current episode of cycling affective illness, early lifetime course (i.e., one to three lifetime episodes of depression), and the absence of responsibility for children under the age of 18 years were other notable suicide risk factors.

Along these lines, Peruzzi and Bongar (1999) identified eight critical risk factors for suicide in patients with major depression. They found the medical seriousness of previous attempts, history of suicide attempts, acute suicidal ideation, severe hopelessness, attraction to death, family history of suicide, acute overuse of alcohol, and the experience of recent loss or separation were the most critical factors with these patients.

In the study by Fawcett et al. (1990), bipolar and schizoaffective patients did not have a higher risk of suicide than did other patients with affective disorder. Subtype of affective disorder (e.g., psychotic, endogenous, incapacitated, agitated, primary) was not useful for predicting suicide. Other characteristics that were not indicative of an elevated risk of death by suicide included family history of suicide or suicidal behavior, duration of the index episode of depression, life stress levels as rated by a clinician, and life stress levels as reported by the patient.

In another important study, Fawcett et al. (1987) analyzed data from a large-scale prospective study of patients with major affective disorders, and found that 25 patients (out of a total of 954) committed suicide; hopelessness, loss of pleasure or interest, and mood cycling during the index episode differentiated the suicide group from patients who did not commit suicide. These researchers noted that although suicide is a relatively frequent event in depressed patients, it still has a statistically low base rate, and therefore may be statistically unpredictable on an individual basis using cross-sectional measures.

Other researchers have reported similar findings with a similar iconoclastic favor. For example, in a 2- to 13-year follow-up mortality study of 1,593 psychiatric inpatients admitted with a major affective disorder, Black, Winokur, and Nasrallah (1988) also found no difference in suicide rates when comparing psychotic and nonpsychotic by unipolar, bipolar, or combined subtypes. These findings are consistent with results from other recent retrospective reports as well (e.g., Coryell & Tsuang, 1982).

Other investigators have linked delusional depressions with increased suicide risk, but their data may not support their conclusions. For example, Roose, Glassman, Walsh, Woodring, & Vital-Herne (1983) conducted a follow-up study of patients at a psychiatric hospital who had died while on the hospital census (i.e., as inpatients, on pass, or after eloping) over a 25-year period. They concluded that delusional patients with unipolar major depression were five times more likely to die by suicide than were their nondelusional counterparts. But their data had three major shortcomings: (1) they only identified suicides occurring on the hospital census, neglecting to consider suicides in the same cohort occurring outside the hospital during the same period; (2) they counted "probable" cases (i.e., no evidence that the belief was fixed and unamenable to reason) as "definite" cases in their analysis; and (3) their comparison group consisted of a much lower fraction of men than did the suicide group. For these reasons we believe their study was inconclusive.

In Fawcett et al.'s (1987) study, clinical variables traditionally associated with elevated suicide risk were not found to be useful in the short term. These investigators found that while acute suicidal ideation, history of suicide attempts, medical seriousness of prior attempts, and severe hopelessness were not associated with short-term risk for suicide, the same features were associated with death by suicide 1–5 years later.

Fawcett et al.'s (1987) finding that severe hopelessness has value for predicting suicide risk 1–5 years later, but not in the imminent 6–12 months, appears to run contrary to Beck's oft-replicated finding (Beck, Kovacs, & Weissman, 1979) that hopelessness is the single best clinical predictor of suicide in depressed patients. A methodological problem inherent in suicide research may resolve this contradiction. Most studies of demographic and psychological variables that might predict suicide in large retrospective studies have followed patients from a clinical event—for example, a hospital or clinic admission—to a follow-up point 10 or 20 years later. To amass a sufficient number of suicide cases for purposes of statistical analysis, suicides occurring 1 week, 1 month, 1 year, and 10 years after the index event are lumped together and all are considered equivalent. But, as Fawcett et al. (1990) have pointed out, the task of predicting suicide in the clinical situation necessarily focuses on *imminent* suicide risk—that is, risk over a period of days or weeks, not months or years. The Fawcett et al. (1987) findings suggest that hopelessness predicts long-term risk for suicide much better than it does short-term risk.

This profile of depressed patients at highest risk for suicide during the next 6–12 months may appear counterintuitive. Nevertheless, the central discrimination task in the Fawcett study mimics the real clinical situation better than many other studies. When a psychiatrist or staff on an inpatient unit have responsibility for a dozen patients with severe major depression, significant impairment in functioning, severe suicidal ideation, and a history of recent suicide attempts (i.e., all are "high risk"), how does he or she begin to identify the subset at greatest risk for imminent suicide? The features that effectively discriminate suicide risk within an extremely high-risk sample of depressed patients will certainly be different than the features that discriminate risk effectively in a military physical screening setting or in a primary medical care setting.

The clinician will find it helpful to consider this profile of depressed patients at highest risk for suicide during the next 6–12 months for two reasons: (1) the Fawcett study represents the only large published clinical study in which patients were assessed in a standardized and reliable fashion prior to their suicide, so the perspective is a prospective one and the assessment data are not contaminated by hindsight bias; and (2) many of the same findings have emerged in (retrospective) long-term follow-up mortality studies of patients with a diagnosis of major depression (e.g., Black, Winokur, & Nasrallah, 1987, 1988).

Patients Who Meet Criteria for Depression and Alcoholism

The lifetime risk of suicide for persons who have had a history of inpatient treatment for alcoholism is 3.4%, and for untreated alcoholics is 1.8% (Murphy & Wetzel, 1990). Alcoholism is implicated in about 25% of all suicides in the United States. For alcoholics who have not abused other drugs, the mean duration of time from the beginning of excessive drinking to completed suicide is 19 years. For those who have abused other drugs, the mean duration is much shorter. Only a third of alcoholics who die by suicide ever received inpatient psychiatric treatment.

Drinking in conjunction with episodes of depression appears to play a major role in the high incidence of suicide in alcoholic patients. Suicides in a psychiatric inpatient setting are less likely to involve alcoholism than major depression or schizophrenia, probably because alcohol is difficult to access while the patient is hospitalized, and because depressive episodes are more likely to be detected and treated by staff.

The experience of a current or recent interpersonal loss seems to play a role in precipitating suicide among alcoholic patients in a fourth of all cases. In a study of alcoholic patients (Murphy et al., 1979), those who died by suicide were likely to have suffered from a major depression and the effects of an interpersonal loss in the 6 months before death. The disruption of a close personal relationship as a risk factor for death by suicide appears to be specific to the diagnosis of alcoholism (Murphy et al., 1979; Murphy & Wetzel, 1990), and is not characteristic of any other psychiatric disorder.

In addition, Canapary (1999), in a survey of clinicians' practices, found a two-tier series of suicide risk factors within an alcoholic population. The first tier of risk factors that clinicians' examine includes the seriousness of previous attempts, past suicide attempts, and the communication of suicidal ideation; the second tier of risk factors includes feelings of hopelessness, a family history of suicide, and the current use of alcohol.

Drug abuse or dependence and imprisonment also places alcoholic patients at increased risk for suicide. For alcoholics who have been imprisoned, intoxication and a history of drug abuse or dependence at the time of admission to a holding cell, detention cell, jail, or prison puts the patient at an even greater suicide risk, particularly during the first 24 hours (Hayes & Kajdin, 1981; Hayes & Rowan, 1988).

Persons Who Meet Criteria for Depression and Schizophrenia

About 10% of persons diagnosed with schizophrenia will die by suicide in the course of a lifetime (Bleuler, 1978; Miles, 1977; Tsuang, 1978). Some evidence suggests that persons with atypical psychoses (e.g., schizoaffective disorder, schizophreniform disorder) have a parallel high lifetime risk (Buda, Tsuang, & Fleming, 1988).

The following factors are associated with elevated risk for death by suicide among schizophrenic patients: periods of depressed mood and hopelessness during periods of clinical improvement following relapse, particularly during the months following discharge from the hospital (Allebeck, 1989; Allebeck, Varla, Kristjansson, & Wistedt, 1987; Allebeck & Wistedt, 1986; Black, 1988; Drake et al., 1986; Harrow, Grinker, Silverstein, & Holzman, 1978; Roy, 1982, 1986; Westermeyer & Harrow, 1989); young age; short duration of time since onset of the illness; good premorbid history (i.e., good social and intellectual functioning prior to illness onset); frequent exacerbations and remissions of the illness; suicidal communications; and periods when florid psychosis is minimal or mild (Drake & Cotton, 1986; Drake, Gates, Cotton, & Whitaker, 1984; Roy, 1982; Wilkinson & Bacon, 1984).

Assessing Risk in the General Population

Because fewer than a third of persons who die by suicide are under the care of a mental health professional at the time of their death, and because almost half of all persons who die by suicide have never seen a mental health professional during the course of their life, mental health professionals are not provided with the opportunity to forestall the majority of deaths by suicide. Screening in the general population for mental disorders and suicidal ideation are important avenues for reducing the death toll from suicide.

When screening the general population for persons at high risk for suicide, it is most efficient to probe for suicidal behavior of all sorts (e.g., morbid thoughts, suicidal ideation, suicide attempts, hopelessness) and prevalence of the mental disorders associated with an increased risk for suicide (i.e., major depression, alcohol and drug abuse, and schizophrenia). Positive findings related to suicidal behavior or mental disorder should be a strong indication for clinical evaluation, including a thorough evaluation for suicide risk. In this regard, hopelessness has been particularly useful in the prediction of suicidal ideation, intent, and completion (Beck, Brown, Berchick, Stewart, & Steer, 1990; Beck, Steer, Beck, & Newman, 1993).

RISK MANAGEMENT AND DECIDING ON THE SETTING FOR THERAPY

Clinicians have a duty to take steps to prevent suicide in a patient if they can reasonably anticipate the danger (Beutler et al., 2000). "Therefore, the key issues in determining liability are whether the psychotherapist should have predicted that the patient was likely to attempt suicidal behavior, and whether the therapist did enough to protect the patient" (Stromberg et al., 1988, p. 467). In this regard, Pope (1986) stressed the importance of staying within one's area of competence and of knowing one's personal limits, observing "that working with suicidal patients can be demanding, draining, crisis filled activity. It is literally life or death work" (p. 19).

In addition to obtaining training, mental health professionals must become familiar with the legal standards involving rights to treatment and to refuse treatment, and with the rules regarding confidentiality, involuntary hospitalization, and so forth. There should be frequent consultation and ready access to facilities needed to implement appropriate precautions such as hospitals, emergency rooms, crisis intervention centers, and day treatment facilities.

From the standpoint of any potential malpractice action, the most crucial element in the formulation of clinical judgment is that the psychologist's professional behavior not significantly deviate from what is usual and customary for the care of patients with these particular signs and symptoms. That is to say, the psychologist will have demonstrated the behavior of a reasonable and prudent practitioner and will not have made any significant omissions in assessment, and will have taken appropriate precautions to minimize the risk of a patient suicide (Berman & Cohen-Sandler, 1982, 1983). The importance of thorough documentation cannot be overstated.

Once the degree of suicidal risk has been estimated, the clinician must decide what type of treatment would be most suitable for the patient. In cases of acute suicidal crisis, the clinician's goal is to modify those risk features that can be modified, hoping to achieve a substantial decrease in suicide risk over a short period of time. One risk feature that can usually be modified within a period of weeks is a supervening episode of major depression. Time and resource limitations dictate that the clinician must carefully decide which patients are at most acute risk and require more intensive interventions to prevent suicide, and which patients do not require immediate and aggressive intervention (e.g., hospitalization).

If the clinician finds the patient to be at high risk for suicide, the most appropriate place for treatment is on a psychiatric inpatient unit, and the patient should be hospitalized. Suicidal patients do not always agree with this decision, however, and sometimes oppose the clinician's recommendation of hospitalization. This example of "help negation" may represent nothing more than a particularly problematic symptom of the underlying psychiatric illness: the patient may have reached a state of utter hopelessness concerning treatment and may reject all attempts at help and therapy. In this situation, it is the clinician's responsibility to initiate involuntary hospitalization procedures insofar as state mental health codes allow.

After explaining what symptoms or behaviors lead him or her to be concerned about imminent suicide risk, a relatively nonthreatening way for the clinician to raise the topic of hospitalization and involve the patient in a mutual decision is to proceed by increments—for example, "Would you wait with me while I call the hospital to find out whether there are any beds available? It will be much easier to discuss what to do next if we know all our options." Most patients will agree to this invitation, and it seems to pave the way for them to agree to enter the hospital voluntarily.

It is generally useful to enlist the awareness, understanding, and help of the patient's family when the patient opposes a reasonable recommendation for voluntary hospitalization. If the family is reluctant or unwilling to support this recommendation, as is often the case, the clinician must act on his or her risk formulation and best clinical judgment. If the patient requires hospitalization, he or she should be committed despite patient or family opposition if state laws allow.

Without agreement from the patient or support from the family, committing the patient is a difficult process. Many state mental health codes and commitment laws will not allow a patient to be involuntarily committed unless he or she has threatened or attempted suicide. Unfortunately, most persons who commit suicide have not made a prior attempt before, and some will deny their suicidal intentions in order to thwart a hospitalization. The clinician acting against the wishes of the patient and the family may be subjected to the family's threats of legal retribution. The clinician is in far more legal jeopardy, however, if he or she fails to hospitalize or make every attempt to hospitalize the patient based on the available data, and the patient then commits suicide.

One of the first steps of treatment, regardless of whether the patient has been hospitalized, is that of alleviating acute anxiety or agitation. The high prevalence rates of panic attacks and the high levels of psychic anxiety reported in depressed patients who die by suicide (Fawcett et al., 1990) suggests the possibility that acute suicide risk can be reduced by alleviating extreme levels of anxiety and fearfulness. The anxiety symptoms of depressed patients, for example, are highly responsive to *brief* regimens of antianxiety medications in the context of a superordinate treatment plan to address the prevailing major depression (i.e., the initiation of short-term psychotherapy or antidepressant medication). However, neuroleptics, which will sedate without the likelihood of inducing akathisia (extreme restlessness or agitation), should be used in treating patients who do not respond to benzodiazepines and who may manifest anxiety as a part of depression with psychotic features. Neuroleptics can also be used safely to reduce impulsive, agitated, driven behavior until the patient can be moved to a safe place and treated for his or her suicidal crisis and underlying psychiatric illness. Electroconvulsive therapy (ECT) is another approach for managing patients with acute agitated psychosis associated with a major affective disorder and those who are so intent on suicide that it seems unwise to wait for the beginning of a response to antidepressant medication. However, supplementary medication may still be necessary because ECT is not entirely effective in terms of reducing anxiety immediately. ECT may also pose problems as a form of therapy because it requires the patient's informed consent at a time when the patient may not be competent to give such consent.

Although a hospital is preferable over the patient's home as a setting for therapy, the patient is not necessarily safe once hospitalized. The determined patient is capable of suicide by hanging or asphyxiation even on 15-minute "suicide precaution" checks. Such patients need constant one-to-one supervision. Adequate doses of the medications mentioned above should be used to control the acutely suicidal patient within the hospital until the patient is sufficiently recovered to participate in verbal and other forms of psychotherapy.

Because it is not uncommon for suicide to occur in the first 6 months following hospitalization, the clinician must remain extremely alert and watchful of the patient even after discharge from hospital. The current high cost of hospitalization often plays a role in pressing decisions to send patients home before they are fully stable. Discharge is also a signal to the patient that he or she will not be receiving constant supervision or attention from a physician and medical staff. The patient may experience a sense of abandonment at this abrupt change in level of care. Without close or frequent contact with a therapist, the mood fluctuations that are characteristic of recovery from depression may be misinterpreted by the patient as relapse. These misapprehensions, combined with a lack of support, may cause the patient to begin thinking once again of suicide as an option to end feelings of hopelessness and despair.

Long-term outpatient therapy is most suitable for patients who are chronically suicidal. Litman (1992) estimates that 20–25% of chronically suicidal patients will eventually die by suicide, but in any one year the suicide rate for these patients is only 1–3%. Chronically suicidal patients feel they lack adequate resources and optimism to overcome their problems and are often convinced that they will eventually die of suicide. The clinician must offer continual support, yet not to the point of feeling overwhelmed or isolated with the patient. Limits must be set with the suicidal patient who becomes demanding and intrusive. Responsibility for the patient should be shared with others, especially with the patient's family and friends, who spend longer periods of time with the patient. If the clinician ever feels he or she has lost the compassionate detachment necessary to treat the patient, the clinician should transfer the patient to another clinician. But these kinds of monumental clinical decisions must be made in awareness of the possibility that the chronically suicidal patient will experience the change as a devastating abandonment and as a spur to suicide (Maltsberger, 1974).

Regardless of the setting for treatment, the clinician working with the suicidal patient should bear in mind four considerations. First, persons who have a psychiatric disorder and who eventually die by suicide often do not recognize the psychological aspects of their disorder and concern themselves instead with physical symptoms. Thus, patients may have little insight into the circumstances of the mental disorder, may be overfocused on situational crises that "explain" current distress and morbid thoughts, and may actively oppose any psychiatric intervention.

Second, the clinician should not dismiss or minimize the possibility of elevated suicide risk in patients with major depression who are experiencing a specific, definable life stressor. In a long-term follow-up study, Fawcett et al. (1990) found that patients with "endogenous" or "melancholic" depression and patients with "situational" depression are equally likely to die by suicide.

Third, many persons in a severe and acute suicidal crisis become convinced of the logic and elegance of suicide as an option to end unbearable pain and irresolvable problems. For a subset of extremely suicidal patients, there is deep conviction and certainty in the decision to commit suicide, which may be evident to the evaluating clinician as elaborate rationalization, justification, or mystification. Verbal interventions are no longer effective for patients in this situation, and hospitalization should be considered.

Finally, patients who have become intensely preoccupied with suicide may also demonstrate unshakable pessimism about the potential value of any intervention on their behalf, and so may abandon, terminate, or reject any form of treatment proffered. The treating clinician must resist temptations to comply with the decision of the hopeless, despairing patient to terminate treatment prematurely.

When clinicians select assessment criteria and then implement an intervention strategy with suicidal patients, they may find that traditional theories of psychotherapy, and traditional psychiatric diagnostic categories, are of limited practical value in precisely assessing suicidal risk. As Beutler (1989) pointed out, "The descriptive dimensions embodied in the current diagnostic system bear little relationship to the selection of the mode or frequency of psychosocial interventions. . . . While it would be unthinkable in any practice of medicine for the mode of treatment to be independent of patient diagnosis, this is precisely the case in the assignment of psychotherapy modes and formats" (p. 272).

Finally, the psychologist must understand that the final decision regarding suicide risk is an intuitive judgment, that "we are obliged to accept that no matter how much information is gathered, sooner or later all the data must be weighed together and an intuitive estimate of risk recorded. That it is only an educated guess does not diminish its importance or its value as a consideration in management and treatment planning" (Motto, 1989, p. 2).

FUTURE DIRECTIONS

Valid quantification of suicide risk in patients with an affective disorder continues to elude both clinicians and research investigators. In this regard, there are several directions of study and research that have the potential to add significantly to the existing knowledge base in this field. Some of the potential directions for further research include determining what constitutes an adequate level of education and training, discipline by discipline, for clinical work with suicidal patients; developing more clinically meaningful psychometric instruments for assessing suicide risk; exploring the biology of suicide in the context of depressive illness; and extending studies of suicidal ideation and behavior to more fully encompass children, adolescents, and older adults.

Recent studies suggest that relatively few trainees, or interns, receive any formal instruction or training in the assessment or management of the suicidal patient (Kleespies, 1993). This finding is supported by the results of surveys of graduate programs in clinical psychology reported by Bongar and Harmatz (1989, 1991). In these studies, Bongar and Harmatz surveyed two groups of graduate training programs in psychology, the National Council of Schools of Professional Psychology (NCSPP) and the Council of University Directors of Clinical Psychology (CUDCP) programs, to assess how these programs were preparing the next generation of clinical psychologists to meet this common clinical emergency. Bongar and Harmatz (1989, 1991) found that only 40% of all graduate programs in clinical psychology offer formal training in the study of suicide. Participants in a separate study conducted with therapists who had recently lost a patient to suicide were asked whether their graduate school or internship program provided instruction in the epidemiology and understanding of suicide (Kleespies, 1990). Sixty-three percent responded yes, although they indicated that such training was minimal (e.g., one or two lectures at most).

In this context, Bongar (1993) has proposed an educational model with a number of major components: "quality education in suicidology, the training and availability of appropriate consultants, clinical teamwork, and the recognition by our training programs and clinical institutions that the time has come to routinely consider a consultative risk management approach for working with our suicidal patients" (p. 303).

Is there a single scale, instrument, or tool that alone yields accurate suicide assessment and prediction? Unfortunately, there is no such instrument (Maris, Berman, & Maltsberger, 1992). Currently, none of the major personality assessment instruments do particularly well by themselves in predicting suicide. However, well-designed studies could maximize the usefulness of these instruments in providing better information to the clinician concerning suicidal risk factors and in directing the treating therapist to instruments designed specifically to gather information about suicide. This combination of global and specific assessment instruments may provide the clearest picture available, but there is little in the existing literature that could be thought of as a guide to this approach. Instruments such as the MMPI-2 and the Rorschach are used routinely to aid in making a diagnosis of depression. When these measures also show elevated risk for patient self-harm, a suicide specific scale should be used in follow-up sessions.

A number of lines of evidence have led to the suggestions that biological determinants may play a role in the multidetermined act that is suicide (Maris et al., 1992). Studies have reported a bimodal distribution of levels of cerebrospinal fluid (CSF) levels of the serotonin metabolite 5-hydroxyindoleacetic acid (5-HIAA) in the lumbar CSF of depressed patients. Researchers report that significantly more of the depressed patients in the "low" CSF 5-HIAA group attempted suicide than in the "high" CSF 5-HIAA group (Asberg, Traskman, & Thoren, 1976). More recently, studies have investigated region specific alterations in suicide victims with major depression in G-protein synthesis (Stockmeier, 1997), and low serum total cholesterol (Partonen, Haukka, Taylor, & Lonnqvist, 1999). Strong familial associations have been found in both suicide and depression. It is hoped that studies such as these and similar research in the future will help clarify the biological factors that play such an important role in suicide attempts of patients diagnosed with affective disorders.

Late-life depression and suicidal behavior in the primary care setting is a significant public health concern. Although the prevalence of depression in this population is substantial, rates of detection and treatment are far from adequate (Pearson, Conwell, & Lyness, 1997). If more can be learned about the barriers to the recognition and treatment of late-life depression, as well as about what constitutes useful screening tools and treatments for the depressed elderly, innovative and collaborative models of care can be implemented. Similarly, despite the dramatic increase of depression and suicidal behavior in children, research within this field is limited. Because depression can manifest itself in children of all ages, factors that identify elevated risk of self-harm are essential for each age group from toddlers to school-age children, and prevention strategies need to be accessible to the child, and family, both at home and at school (Workman & Prior, 1997).

Depression is a common psychiatric disorder that can lead, in some cases, to suicide. Mental health professionals and colleagues in other specialties share two important responsibilities. First, they must reach out to depressed individuals and make it easier for them to have access to the health care system. And second, they must combine and integrate clinical and empirical literatures to maximize the effectiveness of their treatments.

REFERENCES

Adelson, L. (1961). Slaughter of the innocents: A study of forty-six homicides in which the victims were children. *New England Journal of Medicine, 264,* 1345–1349.

Allebeck, P. (1989). Schizophrenia: A life-shortening disease. *Schizophrenia Bulletin, 15,* 81–89.

Allebeck, P., Varla, A., Kristjansson, E., & Wistedt, B. (1987). Risk factors for suicide among patients with schizophrenia. *Acta Psychiatrica Scandinavica, 76,* 414–419.

Allebeck, P., & Wistedt, B. (1986). Mortality in schizophrenia: A ten-year follow-up based on the Stockholm County Inpatient Register. *Archives of General Psychiatry, 43,* 650–653.

Asberg, M., Traskman, L., & Thoren, P. (1976). 5-HIAA in the cerebrospinal fluid: A biochemical suicide predictor? *Archives of General Psychiatry, 33,* 1193–1197.

Asnis, G. M., Friedman, T. A., Sanderson, W. C., Kaplan, M. L., van Praag, H. M., & Harkavy-Friedman, J. M. (1993). Suicidal behaviors in adult psychiatric outpatients: I. Description and prevalence. *American Journal of Psychiatry, 150*(1), 108–112.

Babigian, H. M., & Odoroff, C. L. (1969). The mortality experience of a population with psychiatric illness. *American Journal of Psychiatry, 126,* 470–480.

Barraclough, B., Bunch, J., Nelson, B., & Sainsbury, P. (1974). A hundred cases of suicide: Clinical aspects. *British Journal of Psychiatry, 125,* 355–373.

Beck, A. T. (1987). Hopelessness as a predictor of eventual suicide. *Annals of the New York Academy of Sciences: Psychobiology of Suicidal Behavior, 487,* 90–96.

Beck, A. T., Brown, G., Berchick, R. J., Stewart, B. L., & Steer, R. A. (1990). Relation of hopelessness to ultimate suicide: A replication with psychiatric outpatients. *American Journal of Psychiatry, 147*(2), 190–195.

Beck, A. T., Kovacs, M., & Weisman, A. (1979). Assessment of suicidal intention: The scale for suicidal ideation. *Journal of Consulting and Clinical Psychology, 47,* 343–352.

Beck, A. T., Steer, R. A., Beck, J. S., & Newman, C. F. (1993). Hopelessness, depression, suicidal ideation, and clinical diagnosis of depression. *Suicide and Life-Threatening Behavior, 23,* 139–145.

Berman, A. L., & Cohen-Sandler, R. (1982). Suicide and the standard of care: Optimal vs. acceptable. *Suicide and Life-Threatening Behavior, 12*(2), 114–122.

Berman, A. L., & Cohen-Sandler, R. (1983). Suicide and malpractice: Expert testimony and the standard of care. *Professional Psychology: Research and Practice, 14*(1), 6–19.

Beskow, J. (1979). Suicide and mental disorder in Swedish men. *Acta Psychiatrica Scandinavica, 277*(Suppl.), 1–138.

Beutler, L. E. (1989). Differential treatment selection: The role of diagnosis in psychotherapy. *Psychotherapy, 26*(3), 271–281.

Beutler, L. E., Clarkin, J. F., & Bongar, B. (2000). *Guidelines for the systematic treatment of the depressed patient.* New York: Oxford University Press.

Black, D. W. (1988). Mortality in schizophrenia—the Iowa record-linkage study: A comparison with general population mortality. *Psychosomatics, 29,* 55–60.

Black, D. W., Warrack, G., & Winokur, G. (1985). The Iowa record-linkage study: I. Suicides and accidental deaths among psychiatric patients. *Archives of General Psychiatry, 42,* 71–75.

Black, D. W., Winokur, G., & Nasrallah, A. (1987). Suicide in subtypes of major affective disorder: A comparison with general population suicide mortality. *Archives of General Psychiatry, 44,* 878–880.

Black, D. W., Winokur, G., & Nasrallah, A. (1988). Effect of psychosis on suicide risk in 1,593 patients with unipolar and bipolar affective disorders. *Archives of General Psychiatry, 145,* 849–852.

Bleuler, M (1978). *The schizophrenic disorders: Long-term and family studies.* New Haven, CT: Yale University Press.

Bongar, B. (1993). Consultation and the suicidal patient. *Suicide and Life-Threatening Behavior, 23*(4), 299–306.

Bongar, B., & Harmatz, M. (1989). Graduate training in clinical psychology and the study of suicide. *Professional Psychology: Research and Practice, 20*(4), 209–213.

Bongar, B., & Harmatz, M. (1991). Clinical psychology graduate education in the study of suicide: Availability, resources, and importance. *Suicide and Life-Threatening Behavior, 21*(3), 231–244.

Bongar, B., Lomax, J. W., & Marmatz, M. (1992). Training and supervisory issues in the assessment and management of the suicidal patient. In B. Bongar (Ed.), *Suicide: Guidelines for assessment, management and treatment* (pp. 253–267). New York: Oxford University Press.

Boyd, J. (1983). The increasing rate of suicide by firearms. *New England Journal of Medicine, 308,* 872–898.

Breier, A., & Astrachan, B. M. (1984). Characterization of schizophrenic patients who commit suicide. *American Journal of Psychiatry, 141,* 206–209.

Buda, M., Tsuang, M. T., & Fleming, J. A. (1988). Causes of death in DSM-III schizophrenics and other psychotics (atypical group). *Archives of General Psychiatry, 45,* 283–285.

Buglass, C. D., & Horton, J. (1974). The repetition of parasuicide: A comparison of three cohorts. *British Journal of Psychiatry, 125,* 168–174.

Canapary, A. (1999). *Suicidal risk factors with an alcoholic population.* Unpublished doctoral dissertation, Pacific Graduate School of Psychology.

Cheng, A. T. A. (1995). Mental illness and suicide: A case–control study in Taiwan. *Archives of General Psychiatry, 52,* 594–603.

Chynoweth, R., Tonge, J. I., & Armstrong, J. (1980). Suicide in Brisbane: A retrospective psychosocial study. *Australia and New Zealand Journal of Psychiatry, 14,* 37–45.

Clark, D. C. (1990). Suicide risk assessment and prediction in the 1990s. *Crisis, 11,* 104–112.

Clark, D. C. (1992). "Rational" suicide and people with terminal conditions or disabilities. *Issues in Law and Medicine, 8*(2), 147–166.

Clark, D. C., & Fawcett, J. (1992). Review of empirical risk factors for evaluation of the suicidal patient. In B. Bongar (Ed.), *Suicide: Guidelines for assessment, management, and treatment* (pp. 16–48). New York: Oxford University Press.

Clark, D. C., Gibbons, R. D., Fawcett, J., & Scheftner, W. A. (1989). What is the mechanism by which suicide attempts predispose to later suicide attempts?: A mathematical model. *Journal of Abnormal Psychology, 98,* 42–49.

Clark, D. C., Young, M. A., Scheftner, W. A., Fawcett, J., & Fogg, L. (1987). A field test of Motto's Risk Estimator for Suicide. *American Journal of Psychiatry, 144*(7), 923–926.

Clayton, P. J. (1985). Suicide. *Psychiatric Clinics of North America, 8,* 203–214.

Coryell, W., & Tsuang, M. T. (1982). Primary unipolar depression and the prognostic importance of delusions. *Archives of General Psychiatry, 39,* 1181–1184.

Crammer, J. L. (1984). The special characteristics of suicide in hospital in-patients. *British Journal of Psychiatry, 145,* 460–476.

Cullberg, J., Wasserman, D., & Stefansson, C. G. (1988). Who commits suicide after a suicide attempt?: An 8 to 10 year follow-up in a suburban catchment area. *Acta Psychiatrica Scandinavica, 77,* 598–603.

Dorpat, T. L., & Ripley, H. S. (1960). A study of suicide in the Seattle area. *Comprehensive Psychiatry, 1,* 349–359.

Drake, R. E., & Cotton, P. G. (1986). Depression, hopelessness and suicide in chronic schizophrenia. *British Journal of Psychiatry, 148,* 554–559.

Drake, R. E., Gates, C., Cotton, P. G., & Whitaker, A. (1984). Suicide among schizophrenics: Who is at risk? *Journal of Nervous and Mental Disease, 172,* 613–617.

Drake, R. E., Gates, C., & Whitaker, A. (1986). Cotton PG: Suicide among schizophrenics: A review. *Comprehensive Psychiatry, 26,* 90–100.

Endicott, J., & Spitzer, R. L. (1978). A diagnostic interview: The Schedule for Affective Disorders and Schizophrenia. *Archives of General Psychiatry, 35,* 837–844.

Ettlinger, R. W. (1964). Suicides in a group of patients who had previously attempted suicide. *Acta Psychiatrica Scandinavica, 40,* 363–378.

Evans, G., & Farberow, N. L. (1988). *The encyclopedia of suicide.* New York: Facts on File.

Fawcett, J. (1988). Predictors of early suicide: Identification and appropriate intervention. *Journal of Clinical Psychiatry, 49*(Suppl.), 7–8.

Fawcett, J., Scheftner, W., Clark, D., Hedeker, D., Gibbons, R., & Coryell, W. (1987). Clinical predictors of suicide in patients with major affective disorders: A controlled prospective study. *American Journal of Psychiatry, 144*(1), 35–40.

Fawcett, J., Scheftner, W. A., Fogg, L., Clark, D. C, Young, M. A., Hedeker, D., & Gibbons, R. (1990). Time-related predictors of suicide in major depressive disorder. *American Journal of Psychiatry, 147,* 1189–1193.

Fowler, R. C., Rich, C. L., & Young, D. (1986). San Diego Suicide Study: II. Substance abuse in young cases. *Archives of General Psychiatry, 43,* 962–965.

Frederick, C. J. (1978). Current trends in suicidal behavior. *American Journal of Psychotherapy, 32*(2), 172–200.

Fremouw, W. J., de Perczel, M., & Ellis, T. E. (1990). *Suicide risk: Assessment and response guidelines.* New York: Pergamon Press.

Gibbs, J. J. (1982). Problems and priorities: Perceptions of jail custodians and social service providers. *Journal of Criminal Justice, 11,* 327–338.

Glassmire, D. M., Stolberg, R. A., Greene, R. L., & Bongar, B. (2001). The utility of MMPI-2 suicide items for assessing suicidal potential: Development of a suicidal potential scale. *Assessment, 8*(3), 281–290.

Goldring, N., & Fieve, R. R. (1984). Attempted suicide in manic–depressive disorder. *American Journal of Psychotherapy, 38*(3), 373–383.

Greaney, S. (1995). *Psychologists' behavior and attitudes when working with the nonhospitalized suicidal patient.* Unpublished doctoral dissertation, Pacific Graduate School of Psychology.

Guze, S. B., & Robins, E. (1970). Suicide and primary affective disorders. *British Journal of Psychiatry, 117,* 437–438.

Hagnell, O., & Rorsman, B. (1978). Suicide and endogenous depression with somatic symptoms in the Lundby study. *Neuropsychobiology, 4,* 180–187.

Hagnell, O., & Rorsman, B. (1979). Suicide in the Lundby study: A comparative investigation of clinical aspects. *Neuropsychobiology, 5,* 61–73.

Hagnell, O., & Rorsman, B. (1980). Suicide in the Lundby study: A controlled prospective investigation of stressful life events. *Neuropsychobiology, 6,* 319–332.

Harrow, M., Grinker, R. R., Silverstein, M., & Holzman, P. (1978). Is modern-day schizophrenic outcome still negative? *American Journal of Psychiatry, 135,* 1156–1162.

Hayes, L. M., & Kajdin, B. (1981). *And darkness closes in: National study of jail suicides.* Washington, DC: National Center for Institutions and Alternatives.

Hayes, L. M., & Rowan, J. R. (1988). *National study of jail suicides: Seven years later.* Alexandria, VA: National Center for Institutions and Alternatives.

Henriksson, M. M., Aro, H. M., Marttuner, M. S., Heikkinen, M. E., Isometsä, E. T., Kuoppasalm, K. I., & Lönnqvist, J. K. (1993). Mental disorders and comorbidity in suicide. *American Journal of Psychiatry, 150,* 935–940.

Hirschfeld, R. M. A., & Davidson, L. (1988). Risk factors for suicide. *Review of Psychiatry, 7,* 307–333.

Hirschfeld, R. M., & Russell, J. M. (1997). Assessment and treatment of suicidal patients. *New England Journal of Medicine, 337*(13), 910–915.

Isometsä, E. T., Henriksson, M. M., Hillevi, M. E., Kuoppasalmi, K. I., & Lönnqvist, J. K. (1994). Suicide in major depression. *American Journal of Psychiatry, 151,* 530–536.

Jobes, D. A., Berman, A. L., & Josselson, A. R. (1986). The impact of psychological autopsies on medical examiners' determination of manner of death. *Journal of Forensic Sciences, 31,* 177–189.

Keller, M. (1994). Depression: A long-term illness. *British Journal of Psychiatry, 165,* 9–15.

Kleespies, P. M. (1993). The stress of patient suicidal behavior: Implications for interns and training programs in psychology. *Professional Psychology: Research and Practice, 24*(4), 447–482.

Kreitman, N. (1988). Suicide, age, and marital status. *Psychological Medicine, 18,* 121–128.

Kreitman, N., & Casey, P. (1988). Repetition of parasuicide: An epidemiological and clinical study. *British Journal of Psychiatry, 153,* 792–800.

Linehan, M. M. (1986). Suicide people: One population or two? *Annals of the New York Academy of Sciences, 487,* 16–33.

Linehan, M. M. (1993a). *Cognitive-behavioral treatment of borderline personality disorder.* New York: Guilford Press.

Linehan, M. M. (1993b). *Skills training manual for treating borderline personality disorder.* New York: Guilford Press.

Linehan, M. M., Armstrong, H. E., Suarez, A., Allmon, D., & Heard, H. L. (1991). Cognitive-behavioral treatment of chronically parasuicidal borderline patients. *Archives of General Psychiatry, 48,* 1060–1064.

Linehan, M. M., Heard, H. E., & Armstrong, H. E. (1993). Naturalistic follow-up of a behavioral treatment for chronically suicidal borderline patients. *Archives of General Psychiatry, 50,* 971–974.

Litman, R. E. (1964). Immobilization response to suicidal behavior. *Archives of General Psychiatry, 11,* 282–285.

Litman, R. E. (1992). Predicting and preventing hospital and clinic suicides. In R. W. Maris, A. L. Berman, J. T. Maltsberger, & R. I. Yufit (Eds.), *Assessment and prediction of suicide* (pp. 448–466). New York: Guilford Press.

MacKinnon, D., & Farberow, N. (1975). An assessment of the utility of suicide prediction. *Suicide and Life-Threatening Behavior, 6,* 86–91.

Maltsberger, J. T. (1986). *Suicide risk: The formulation of clinical judgment.* New York: State University of New York Press.

Maltsberger, J. T., & Buie, D. H. (1974). Countertransference hate in the treatment of suicidal patients. *Archives of General Psychiatry, 30,* 625–633.

Maris, R. W. (1981). *Pathways to suicide: A survey of self-destructive behaviors.* Baltimore: Johns Hopkins University Press.

Maris, R. W. (1989). Preface: Strategies for studying suicide and suicidal behavior. *Suicide and Life-Threatening Behavior, 19*(1), ix–x.

Maris, R. W., Berman, A. L., & Maltsberger, J. T. (1992). Summary and conclusions: What have we learned about suicide assessment and prediction?. In R. W. Maris, A. L. Berman, J. T. Maltsberger, & R. I. Yufit (Eds.), *Assessment and prediction of suicide* (pp. 640–672). New York: Guilford Press.

Martin, R. L., Cloninger, C. R., Guze, S. B., & Clayton, P. J. (1985). Mortality in a follow-up of 500 psychiatric outpatients: I. Total mortality. *Archives of General Psychiatry, 42,* 47–54.

Miles, C. P. (1977). Conditions predisposing to suicide: A review. *Journal of Nervous and Mental Disease, 164,* 213–242.

Montano, C. B. (1994). Recognition and treatment of depression in a primary care setting. *Journal of Clinical Psychiatry, 55*(12), 18–34.

Morgan, H. G., Barton, J., Pottle, S., Pocock, H., & Burns-Cox, C. J. (1976). Deliberate self-harm: A follow-up study of 279 patients. *British Journal of Psychiatry, 128,* 361–368.

Moscicki, E. K., O'Carroll, P., Rae, D. S,. Locke, B. Z., Roy, A., & Regier, D. A. (1988). Suicide attempts in the Epidemiologic Catchment Area Study. *Yale Journal of Biology and Medicine, 61,* 259–268.

Motto, J. (1965). Suicide attempts: A longitudinal view. *Archives of General Psychiatry, 13,* 516–520.

Motto, J. A. (1989). Problems in suicide risk assessment. In D. G. Jacobs & H. N. Brown (Eds.), *Sui-*

cide: Understanding and responding: Harvard Medical School perspectives on suicide (pp. 129–142). Madison, CT: International Universities Press.

Murphy, G. E. (1975). The physician's responsibility for suicide: II. Errors of omission. Annals of Internal Medicine, 82, 305–309.

Murphy, G. E. (1977). Suicide and attempted suicide. Hospital Practice, 12(11), 73–81.

Murphy, G. E. (1984). The prediction of suicide: Why is it so difficult? American Journal of Psychotherapy, 38, 341–349.

Murphy, G. E. (1986). The physician's role in suicide prevention. In A. Roy (Ed.), Suicide (p. 175). Baltimore: Williams & Wilkins.

Murphy, G. E., Armstrong, J. W., Hermele, S. L., Fischer, J. R., & Clendenin, W. W. (1979). Suicide and alcoholism: Interpersonal loss confirmed as a predictor. Archives of General Psychiatry, 36, 65–69.

Murphy, G. E., & Wetzel, R. D. (1990). The lifetime risk of suicide in alcoholism. Archives of General Psychiatry, 47, 383–392.

Myers, J. K., Weissman, M. M., Tischler, G. L., Holzer, C. E., Leaf, P. J., Orvaschel, H., Anthony, J. C., Boyd, J. H., Burke, J. D., Kramer, M., & Stoltzman, R. (1984). Six-month prevalence of psychiatric disorders in three communities. Archives of General Psychiatry, 41, 959–967.

National Center for Health Statistics. (1998). Vital statistics of the United States, 1996: Vol. II. Mortality, Part A. Washington, DC: U.S. Government Printing Office.

Ogloff, J. R., & Otto, R. K. (1989). Mental health intervention in jails. In P. Keller & S. Heyman (Eds.), Innovations in clinical practice: A source book (Vol. 8, pp. 357–370) Sarasota, FL: Professional Resource Exchange.

Partonen, T., Haukka, J., Taylor, P. R., & Lonnqvist, J. (1999). Association of low serum total cholesterol with major depression and suicide. British Journal of Psychiatry, 175, 259–262.

Pearson, J. L., Conwell, Y., & Lyness, J. M. (1997). Late life suicide and depression in the primary care setting. New Directions for Mental Health Services, 76, 13–38.

Peruzzi, N., & Bongar, B. (1999). Assessing risk for completed suicide in patients with major depression: Psychologists' views of critical factors. Professional Psychology: Research and Practice, 30(6), 576–580.

Peterson, L. G., Bongar, B., & Netoski, M. (1989). Regional use of violent suicidal methods: An analysis of suicide in Houston, Texas. American Journal of Emergency Medicine, 7(2), 21–27.

Pokorny, A. D. (1964). A follow-up study of 618 suicidal patients. American Journal of Psychiatry, 122, 1109–1116.

Pokorny, A. D. (1983). Prediction of suicide in psychiatric patients: Report of a prospective study. Archives of General Psychiatry, 40, 249–257.

Pope, K (1986). Assessment and management of suicidal risks: Clinical and legal standards of care. Independent Practitioner, 1, 17–23.

Rich, C. L., Fowler, R. C., Fogarty, L. A., & Young, D. (1988). San Diego Suicide Study: III. Relationships between diagnoses and stressors. Archives of General Psychiatry, 45, 589–594.

Rich, C. L., Young, D., & Fowler, R. C. (1986). San Diego Suicide Study: I. Young vs. old subjects. Archives of General Psychiatry, 43, 577–582.

Rihmer, Z., Barsi, J., Arató, M., & Demeter, E. (1990). Suicide in subtypes of primary major depression. Journal of Affective Disorders, 18, 221–225.

Robins, E. (1981). The final months: A study of the lives of 134 persons who committed suicide. New York: Oxford University Press.

Robins, E. (1986). Completed suicide. In A. Roy (Ed.), Suicide (pp. 123–133). Baltimore: Williams & Wilkins.

Robins, E., Gassner, S., Kaye, J., Wilkinson, R. H., & Murphy, G. E. (1959). The communication of suicidal intent: A study of 134 consecutive cases of successful (completed) suicide. American Journal of Psychiatry, 115, 724–733.

Robins, E., Murphy, G. E., Wilkinson, R. H., Gassner, S., & Kayes, J. (1959). Some clinical considerations in the prevention of suicide based on a study of 134 successful suicides. American Journal of Public Health, 49, 888–899.

Rodenburg, M. (1971). Child murder by depressed parents. Canadian Psychiatric Association Journal, 16, 41–48.

Roose, S. P., Glassman, A. H., Walsh, B. T., Woodring, S., & Vital-Herne, J. (1983). Depression, delusions, and suicide. *American Journal of Psychiatry, 140,* 1159–1162.

Rosen, A. (1954). Detection of suicidal patients: An example of some limitations in the prediction of infrequent events. *Journal of Consulting and Clinical Psychology, 18,* 397–403.

Rosenbaum, M. (1990). The role of depression in couples involved in murder–suicide and homicide. *American Journal of Psychiatry, 147,* 1036–1039.

Roy, A. (1982). Suicide in chronic schizophrenia. *British Journal of Psychiatry, 141,* 171–177.

Roy, A. (1986). Suicide in schizophrenia. In A. Roy (Ed.), *Suicide* (pp. 97–112). Baltimore: Williams & Wilkins.

Runeson, B. (1989). Mental disorders in youth suicide: DSM-III-R Axis I and II. *Acta Psychiatrica Scandinavica, 79,* 490–497.

Schein, H. M. (1976). Obstacles in the education of psychiatric residents. *Omega, 7,* 75–82.

Seager, C. P., & Flood, R. A. (1965). Suicide in Briston. *British Journal of Psychiatry, 111,* 919–932.

Shnediman, E. S. (1989). Overview: A multidimensional approach to suicide. In D G. Jacobs & H. N. Brown (Eds.), *Suicide: Understanding and responding: Harvard Medical School perspectives on suicide* (pp. 1–30). Madison, CT: International Universities Press.

Simon, R. I. (1988). *Concise guide to clinical psychiatry and the law.* Washington, DC: American Psychiatric Press.

Stockmeier, C. A. (1997). Neurobiology of serotonin in depression and suicide. *Annals of the New York Academy of Sciences, 836,* 220–223.

Stromberg, C., Haggarty, D., Leibenluft, R., McMillian, M., Ishkin, B., Rubin, B., & Trilling, H. (1988). *The psychologist's legal handbook.* Washington, DC: Council for the National Register of Health Service Providers in Psychology.

Teplin, L. A. (1983). The criminalization of the mentally ill: Speculation in search of data. *Psychological Bulletin, 94,* 54–67.

Tsuang, M. T. (1978). Suicide in schizophrenics, manics, depressives, and surgical controls. *Archives of General Psychiatry, 35,* 153–154.

Tsuang, M. T., Woolson, R. F., & Fleming, J. A. (1980). Premature deaths in schizophrenic and affective disorders. *Archives of General Psychiatry, 37,* 979–983.

Vassilas, C. A., & Morgan, H. G. (1993). General practitioners' contact with victims of suicide. *British Medical Journal, 307,* 300–301.

Veevers, J. E. (1973). Parenthood and suicide: An examination of a neglected variable. *Social Sciences and Medicine, 7,* 135–144.

Weiss, J. M. A., & Scott, K. F. (1974). Suicide attempters ten years later. *Comprehensive Psychiatry, 15,* 165–171.

Weissman, M. M., Klerman, G. L., Markowitz, J. S., & Ouelette, R. (1989). Suicidal ideation and suicide attempts in panic disorder and attacks. *New England Journal of Medicine, 321,* 1209–1214.

Westermeyer, J. F., & Harrow, M. (1989). Early phases of schizophrenia and depression: Prediction of suicide. In R. Williams & J. T. Dalby (Eds.), *Depression in schizophrenics* (pp. 153–169). New York: Plenum Press.

Wilkinson, G., & Bacon, N. A. (1984). A clinical and epidemiological survey of parasuicide and suicide in Edinburgh schizophrenics. *Psychological Medicine, 14,* 899–912.

Wolfgang, M. E. (1958). An analysis of homicide–suicide. *Journal of Clinical and Experimental Psychopathology, 19,* 208–217.

Workman, C. G., & Prior, M. (1997). Depression and suicide in young children. *Issues in Comprehensive Pediatric Nursing, 20*(2), 125–132.

Zweig, R. A., & Hinrichsen, G. A. (1993). Factors associated with suicide attempts by depressed older adults. *American Journal of Psychiatry, 150*(11), 1687–1692.

26

Closing Comments and Promising Directions for the Next Decade

Constance L. Hammen and Ian H. Gotlib

The distinguished scholars who have contributed to this volume have presented the state of the art in their area of investigation. Each chapter is a strong, comprehensive, and analytic examination of a specific area of study in the field of depression. We are grateful for the authors' contributions, not only to this volume, but more broadly, to the field of depression. Without exception, their research and writings have augmented our understanding of this remarkably complex and important disorder. Our goal in this final chapter is to identify themes and issues that emerge across these diverse presentations. In each chapter the authors have proposed ambitious agendas for future research and have outlined a number of important issues stemming from unresolved questions. We are in the enviable position of being able to have the last word in this volume, and we have taken advantage of this position, admittedly permitting some of our own interests and perspectives to play a role in highlighting what we believe are important directions for research in depression over the coming decade.

DESCRIPTIVE ASPECTS OF DEPRESSION

As Kessler notes in Chapter 1, over the past decades we have witnessed a number of important trends in the epidemiology of depression. Two of the most significant are an increase in the rates of depression in the general population and a decrease in the age of onset of this disorder. Importantly, these trends are evident not only in the United States, but in other countries. In addition to documenting the parameters of these trends and making predictions of future changes based on these data, one of the most important tasks facing investigators studying depression is to elucidate the factors that underlie these and other epidemiological trends. Undertaking such an endeavor, of course, involves gathering and integrating findings from epidemiological, psychological, and biological approaches to the study of depression. This volume represents a step in this direction.

In this context, the data Kessler describes in his chapter underscore the importance of making finer distinctions in the assessments of "depression" than are typically made in epidemiological investigations. Two such distinctions, in particular, stand out as important foci for future research. The first is the distinction between syndromal and subsyndromal depression. Kessler reviews evidence indicating that subsyndromal depression, which appears to be increasing in adolescents, is a significant predictor of the subsequent onset of major depressive disorder. Subsyndromal depression, therefore, may represent a marker for risk for depression among adolescents. Indeed, Ingram and Siegle (Chapter 4) urge investigators to study subsyndromal depression as an important construct in it own right. The predictive utility of subsyndromal depression, combined with the increasing number of large-scale studies that are adopting a longitudinal perspective (see also Chapter 2 by Boland & Keller), points to the potential utility of gleaning data from epidemiological investigations to identify risk factors for depression and, in subsequent studies, to identify and intervene with those children and adolescents who are most likely to develop this disorder.

The second important distinction involves differentiating among diagnosed cases of depression. One dimension along which individuals who are diagnosed with major depression differ concerns the chronicity of their depression. Although these individuals are all experiencing clinically significant depression, they vary with respect to whether the current depressive episode is their first or a recurrence of depression. In this context, it is important to note that the results of recent research indicate that there are significant differences between individuals who are experiencing their first depressive episode and those who are experiencing a recurrence. Lewinsohn, Allen, Seeley, and Gotlib (1999), for example, found that first episodes of depression were predicted by different constructs than were recurrence episodes (see also Daley, Hammen, & Rao, 2000). And although there is as of yet little relevant research, it is also likely that the consequences and the probability of having further episodes of depression are different for individuals with first onsets of depression than for individuals who are experiencing a recurrence of this disorder.

A number of authors highlight the importance of examining the issue of the comorbidity of depression and other disorders, both psychological disturbances and medical disorders. Boland and Keller, for example, note that we know relatively little about the effects of psychological and medical comorbidity on the course and outcome of depression, and urge investigators to devote greater resources to examining this important question. Ingram and Siegle also express the need for further research delineating the impact of comorbidity as a potential methodological confound in studies of depression. We agree that studying the impact of comorbidity with depression of both medical and psychological disorders is an important direction for future research. Depression has one of the highest rates of comorbidity of any psychiatric disorder, and understanding how various kinds of comorbidity affect the course and outcome of depression is of paramount importance in understanding the development and impact of this disorder.

Finally, virtually all the authors in this part emphasize the importance of conducting broader and more integrative research on depression. Klein, Durbin, Shankman, and Santiago (Chapter 5), for example, recommend that investigators conduct comprehensive assessments of personality characteristics and of Axis II disorders in studies of depression in order to gain a better understanding of precursors of this disorder. Similarly, Nezu, Nezu, McClure, and Zwick (Chapter 3) point out that this integration should extend to the assessment of depression in culturally and ethnically diverse populations. And in systematically elucidating differences and similarities between unipolar and bipolar depression, Johnson and Kizer (Chapter 6) further underscore the need for more comprehensive assessments of unipolar and bipolar depressions in order to delineate more precisely commonalities between these two forms of depressive disorders. Combining findings from biological, psychological, and epidemiological studies will permit the generation of broader descriptions of depressive disorders, which will undoubtedly lead to advances in nosology. Such integrations also have the potential to lead to more detailed and exact descriptions of the effects of different treatments on various aspects of depressive functioning.

VULNERABILITY, RISK, AND MODELS OF DEPRESSION

There is now little question that, in many respects, depression is a heterogeneous disorder. This heterogeneity is evident not only in the phenomenology and presentation of depressive disorders, but also in formulations of their etiology, in investigations of the factors that place individuals at elevated risk for developing a depressive disorder, and in the broad range of personal and societal consequences of depression. Given this heterogeneity, it is not surprising that each of the chapters in this part on vulnerability, risk, and models of depression takes a different perspective in understanding the origins and consequences of depression.

Wallace, Schneider, and McGuffin (Chapter 7) describe the basic methodologies used to study the genetics of affective disorders, including family, twin, and adoption studies. They discuss the results of investigations using these approaches, and evaluate models of the genetic transmission of risk for depression. Importantly, Wallace et al. point out that the nature of the relation between environmental and familial factors in the onset of depression is proving to be more complex than was originally thought. They raise issues concerning how research examining genetic aspects of depression must be integrated with investigations of other biological and psychological aspects of this disorder. These authors also discuss implications of the Human Genome Project for research in depression, and assert that investigators will soon need to address issues involving gene–behavior mechanisms, that is, questions concerning *how* genes exert their effect on disorders such as depression. Indeed, we believe that as we gain knowledge through the Human Genome Project, questions concerning the influence of cognitive and behavioral factors on the expression of depression will become more, not less, important to address.

Thase, Jindal, and Howland (Chapter 8) and Davidson, Pizzagalli, and Nitschke (Chapter 9) also focus on biological factors that might influence the onset and course of depression. There is little question at this point that specific neurotransmitters, such as norepinephrine, serotonin, and dopamine, are involved in the course of depression. As Thase et al. point out, investigators are making considerable progress in delineating the state–trait nature of neurotransmitter deficiencies in depression, and are also elucidating the moderating effects of age and gender in helping us to understand the relation between depression and abnormalities in neurotransmitter functioning. With the recent methodological advances in the study of neurotransmitter research described by Thase, Jindal, and Howland, the coming decade promises to bring greater clarity to issues of how normal biological functioning and normative developmental processes are impaired or adversely affected in depressive disorders.

Adding to this clarity are findings emanating from research exploiting the extraordinary innovations that have occurred in brain imaging technology. Davidson et al. review the results of research with both animals and humans examining the role of the hippocampus, prefrontal cortex, anterior cingulate cortex, and amygdala in affective disorders. Based on differential patterns of activations in these areas in depressed and nondepressed individuals, Davidson and his colleagues present intriguing possibilities about the nature of emotion dysregulation in depression. Although we are still at an early stage in this area of research, it is clear that we are moving toward integrating structural and functional imaging in order to gain a more complete understanding of the connectivity among structures in the brain that play a role in regulating emotion. Delineating the relation between various structures and their function in the context of emotional processing in depression will also certainly be informative in helping to make distinctions among the major subtypes of this heterogeneous disorder. Indeed, the results of studies examining the brain structures and their functional activations in depression may provide the strongest foundation for an empirically derived typology of subtypes of this disorder.

The delineation of specific subtypes of depression is also evident in Chapter 11 by Abramson, Alloy, Hankin, Haeffel, MacCoon, and Gibb, in which the authors describe recent approaches to studying cognitive aspects of depression. The extension of assessments of cognitive functioning to different subtypes of depressed persons, as well as to individuals at different stages and with different histories of this disorder, represents an important direction taken by investigators in this area. In describing advances in the study of interpersonal processes in depression, Joiner (Chapter 12) notes important extensions of research in this area to an examination of processes involved in bringing about therapeutic change in depressed individuals. Clearly, integrating cognitive and interpersonal factors in this extension represents a critical goal for the further development and refinement of psychologically focused therapies for depression.

Both Goodman (Chapter 10) and Monroe and Hadjiyannakis (Chapter 13) also discuss interpersonal functioning in depression, but do so from different vantage points. Whereas Goodman focuses on the early experiences of individuals who, as adults, experience episodes of depression, Monroe and Hadjiyannakis describe in detail the stressful environments and situations that often appear to be implicated in the onset of these depressive episodes. Despite these different foci, the authors of both chapters emphasize the importance of social relationships in the onset and course of depression, and both underscore the significance of context in understanding the individual's social world. In fact, working toward a more precise and comprehensive assessment of the interpersonal context of depression promises to be a critical direction to be pursued in future work. A delineation, or nosology, of the social environments of depressed persons would clearly be an important foundation for refining our understanding of how both cognitive and interpersonal dysfunction might lead to the onset or influence the course of depression.

Finally, despite their distinct orientations and foci, virtually every chapter in this part discusses the importance of integrating data and methodologies from conceptually different areas of research in attempting to understand factors implicated in the onset and maintenance of depression. Abramson et al. specifically discuss an approach that integrates cognitive and biological aspects of depression. We would like to take this opportunity to reiterate this call for a more integrative flavor of future research. As the chapters in this part eloquently demonstrate, remarkable advances have been made in virtually every area of research in the depressive disorders. Much of this progress in each area, however, has been made without drawing on advances in other areas of research. One logical next step in this process, therefore, is for investigators working within each of these areas of investigation to broaden the scope of their studies to include assessments of other aspects of functioning in depressed persons. The fruits of this type of integration are evident in Abramson et al.'s description of the relation between cognitive attributional style and lateral hemispheric EEG asymmetry in individuals who may be particularly vulnerable to experiencing depression. Similarly, Monroe and Hadjiyannakis discuss the possible relation between early adversity and abuse as risk factors for depression, and the subsequent experience, or elicitation, of stressful life events in people who develop depressive episodes. There is little question that we can now make considerable progress through concerted efforts to integrate experimental methodologies from diverse research areas in studying factors involved in the onset and course of depression.

PREVENTION AND TREATMENT OF DEPRESSION

Accomplishments in the treatment of depression in just the past 10 years are impressive and evident. It is somehow reassuring that even though the etiology of depression is not yet established in any definitive way, a number of treatment options have been demonstrated to reduce acute depressive symptoms. This is truly a great success story, and its implications have had far-reaching consequences—in health policies, in public perceptions, and in the scientific and pharmacological arenas.

There is an odd paradox to this success, however. It could be said that we now exemplify the Peter Principle, and have succeeded to the level of our incompetence. Simply, and perhaps provocatively, put, many interventions can reduce symptoms, but the real issues concern the prevention of recurrences, chronicity, and impairment—outcomes for which we have been far less successful.

Pharmacotherapy

Gitlin's chapter on pharmacotherapy for adults (Chapter 15) highlights the pattern of evident success, on the one hand, and rather astonishing gaps in knowledge, on the other. He notes that much of the activity in the drug development field has involved virtual chemical imitation of effective agents whose mechanisms are poorly understood. However, there have been no real improvements over the original tricyclic, imipramine. Moreover, cited rates of improvement may be somewhat inflated due to treatment discontinuers (or as is increasingly recognized in psychotherapy studies, selection of highly homogenous and less complicated and comorbid study samples than is reflected in the larger population of depressed persons). There remains a group of treatment-refractory depressions for which pharmacotherapy involving augmentation by combinations of medications is an art rather than an evidence-based set of guidelines. Also, critical issues of determining duration of continuation treatment and, especially, of maintenance treatment for recurrent depression, have been largely neglected in research.

It is possible that treatment outcome studies indicating successful acute treatment have been less successful than meets the eye. An argument must be made for including a wider array of outcome measures that are not entirely tied to symptom reduction (or even more limited, to achieving outcomes defined as meeting diagnostic criteria). It has been increasingly noted that there may be a discontinuity between clinical improvement and functional improvement. Evaluation of outcomes solely by symptom status may ignore the remaining difficulties that depressed individuals—perhaps especially those with recurrent depressions—have in maintaining effective employment and stable marital, family, and social relationships. Also, investigators have begun to focus increasingly on the debilitating effects of subclinical symptoms, as noted in earlier remarks, suggesting that treatment success must be measured by elimination of symptoms, not just by their reduction below diagnosable levels.

There is a need for drug development based on theoretically important biological mechanisms of depression, rather than replications of already-effective drugs that are helpful for reasons that are not yet understood. Some of the developmental, genetic, and neuroscientific perspectives reviewed in this volume may provide starting hypotheses. There is also a need for greater understanding of why some individuals may respond better to one drug than to another. Matching of patient characteristics to specific treatments is, of course, a long-time goal in psychotherapy, but remains elusive.

Finally, we underscore Gitlin's call for greater research on medication practices for unique populations, including bipolar depression and childbearing women, and emphasize the additional work that is needed to study the effects of medications on populations of different ages and different ethnicities. Pharmacotherapy for another unique population, children and adolescents, is discussed extensively in the chapter by Kaslow and her colleagues (Chapter 19), who describe many gaps for further study.

Psychotherapies for Depression

Four chapters discuss the accumulating evidence of effective psychotherapies for treatment of depression. Hollon, Haman, and Brown (Chapter 16) describe the enormous success of cognitive-behavioral interventions since their inception in the 1970s. A series of randomized clinical trials has established the effectiveness of cognitive-behavioral therapy (CBT) in the acute treatment of depression, and recent work suggests that it succeeds as well as does pharmacotherapy, even with severely depressed patients. Importantly, CBT also appears to prevent relapse and, possibly, recurrence. Hollon and colleagues note that this finding has nonetheless failed to be fully appreciated in psychiatric practice guidelines.

Despite the apparent success of CBT in the psychotherapy field, however, Hollon and colleagues note important remaining issues: more data are needed on the effects of CBT on preventing recurrence, on how best to match patient or illness characteristics to treatments, and in the further study of the mechanisms by which CBT has its effects. In the latter regard, recent studies by the late Neil Jacobson and his colleagues (Jacobson et al., 1996) showing that behavioral activation may be a component that works as well as the full CBT "package" raise questions to pursue about understanding the key ingredients of successful psychotherapy.

Many of the same issues may be raised concerning interpersonal psychotherapy (IPT). In Chapter 17, Weissman and Markowitz present the rapidly accumulating research evidence regarding the effectiveness of this brief form of psychotherapy and its adaptations for different patient groups, such as depressed adolescents. In some ways, dissemination of IPT may prove to be more widespread than that of CBT, to the extent that its methods may be more consistent with traditional insight-oriented therapies and less dependent on learning the more complex skills of cognitive restructuring. So far, IPT compares well with medication treatments, but its potential for prevention of recurrences remains a crucial test. IPT goes to the heart of key interpersonal difficulties that are at the core of most depressive episodes, but, as in the case of CBT, understanding the mechanisms by which the positive effects of IPT are achieved is an important goal that remains to be pursued.

Beach and Jones (Chapter 18) review the literature on marital and family therapies for depression, noting that unlike CBT and IPT, there is no single, dominant version that is widely practiced and tested. Nevertheless, the importance of marital and child–family issues in depression onset and course certainly provides the impetus for further studies. Like the other treatments presented in this volume, the authors identify the need for more outcome research including recurrence, more comparisons among treatments including pharmacotherapy, and the need for matching treatments to patient needs and characteristics. Beach and Jones also specifically emphasize the need for family treatments to adapt not only to culturally and ethnically diverse populations, but also to increasingly prevalent alternative family forms.

Chapter 19 on treatment of child and adolescent depression by Kaslow, McClure, and Connell presents a comprehensive evaluation of both psychotherapy and pharmacotherapy for depression in youngsters. Kaslow and her colleagues note that studies of treatment of children have lagged considerably behind those of adults, prompting the need for further controlled trials of psychotherapies for these age groups. This is an especially important goal to the extent that early-onset depressions likely signal high risk for recurrent depression and other psychological disorders and dysfunctions. Despite the presumed urgency of early treatment, however, the authors note that there is relatively little evidence of effective individual treatments for clinically ill children. This is an especially challenging task, since depressed children typically live in highly distressed family circumstances with elevated rates of parental disorder (e.g., Hammen, Rudolph, Weisz, Rao, & Burge, 1999). Treatments for adolescents are better established, with reasonably strong empirical support for CBT, IPT, and systemic behavior family therapy (SBFT).

Pharmacotherapy for children and adolescents has traditionally represented another gap in the child treatment area: the downward extension of adult treatments that might not be suited for youngsters. Initially, standard tricyclic antidepressants were shown to be ineffective with children; more recently, a few controlled studies indicate that the selective serotonin reuptake inhibitors may be more useful. Nevertheless, most of these studies have not included appropriate controls, and age effects are unclear. There is much to be done to evaluate the effects of medications on prevention of recurrences and generalization to functional as well as clinical improvements.

With respect both to pharmacotherapy and psychotherapy, Kaslow and colleagues emphasize the need for further developmentally appropriate treatments. They also note, as we discuss further in a later section of this chapter, that it is important to explore gender differences more fully, and to consider the need to develop treatments that might be unique to the experiences of girls at risk for depression. Moreover, few of the studies have included, or analyzed for, cultural diversity.

Preventive Interventions

Muñoz, Le, Clarke, and Jaycox (Chapter 14) present a comprehensive examination of interventions for preventing major depressive episodes in adults, adolescents, and children. They note promising achievements, especially for adolescents at risk for depression, but also point out that studies of adults have generally been quite sparse and have not shown significant reductions in episodes, although other benefits may be evident. Muñoz and his colleagues call for more randomized control prevention trials and also emphasize the need for outcome measures that might reveal reductions in collateral problems such as health-related behaviors, unplanned pregnancies, marital difficulties, work performance, and comorbid psychological disorders.

Although it is difficult and expensive to mount prevention studies, we believe that we have achieved a state of knowledge about certain high-risk populations that is sufficient to justify considerably more preventive interventions. For example, children at risk due to parental depression appear to be an appropriate target; we hope that more studies currently underway or in development will prove fruitful in enhancing the adjustment of such youngsters. Obviously, further research that refines the potential mechanisms of risk will help to identify potential preventive intervention subjects earlier, and will permit the development of interventions that are focused on treating the mechanism (or providing effective compensatory skills). For instance, learning about factors associated with high risk in young adolescent women might help to target this population for early intervention.

Although Muñoz and his colleagues focus on preventing depression onset, prevention of recurrences of depression could also be an important focus, although not truly "preventive" in the Institute of Medicine's sense of the term. As discussed previously, depressive episodes are so common and arise so generally from multiple causal factors that a significant challenge in treatment (and prevention) is to promote a mild course of disorder with minimal relapse.

It is also worth noting in the context of prevention that even the simple act of spreading knowledge about depressive disorders may have a potentially large impact: knowledge and recognition may affect self-perception, and may facilitate appropriate treatment seeking or treatment seeking at an earlier stage of the disorder. Despite the advantages in our knowledge of depressive disorders, however, history has shown the difficulties in teaching primary care physicians to recognize and treat depression, and the expansion of this information to include physicians who might have contact with high-risk populations (e.g., obstetricians) is recognized as a considerable challenge. Nevertheless, as Hollon, Haman, and Brown note, and Muñoz and colleagues would surely concur, major advances in health have occurred more as a result of prevention than of treatment.

DEPRESSION IN SPECIFIC POPULATIONS

Gender and Cultural Differences in Depression

Depression is a disorder that occurs primarily in women, and therefore theories about its etiology must account for this reality. To date, however, as Nolen-Hoeksema points out in Chapter 21, there is as yet no established and empirically supported model that accounts for gender differences. Therefore, she suggests that research in the next decades should continue to actively pursue the various leads that have been developed to date: biological factors, including possible hormone-related differences in reactivity to stress; psychological factors that include the different interpersonal orientations of men and women (that might also be biologically mediated); and social factors that include women's greater exposure to stressful life events, often involving other people—as well as women's greater experiences with both chronic social adversity and major traumatic events such as sexual and physical victimization.

Nolen-Hoeksema's chapter also points out that the answer to the puzzle of gender differences will not be a simple model. It is likely to involve multiple, interacting factors. Moreover, she suggests that the factors that *cause* more women to be depressed might also be expected to produce more chronic or recurrent depression. Yet, to date, research on the course of depression has not revealed gender differences. Whether this conclusion will stand up to further investigation remains to be seen, but if it proves to be robust, the interesting paradox of greater risk for onset but not worse course may provide a stimulating issue to pursue.

Women not only may have unique risk factors for development of depression, but it is also likely that depression in their lives may have uniquely disadvantageous consequences. Depression obviously takes a toll on family life, and is strongly associated with adverse marital outcomes, possibly due to greater risk for marrying at younger ages and marrying partners who may themselves be maladjusted, as well as conflict that might be a direct consequence of depressive symptoms. Moreover, it is well established that children of depressed parents are at higher risk for depression and other disorders and consequent maladjustment. Since women are more typically the caretakers in our society, the impact of their disorders on children may be especially pronounced to the extent that depression has a negative impact on the quality of parent–child interactions. While both genders obviously experience impairment and disruption due to depression, the toll on family life might be especially debilitating for women whose mood episodes may be exquisitely sensitive to disordered relationships.

If women are more numerous among the depressed, and their depressions possibly more reciprocally linked to the welfare of their marriages and children, it is curious that relatively little work has been done to develop treatment programs tailored to the needs of women. As we previously noted, a few steps have been taken in this direction, but there is a major gap between the knowledge that has been amassed about the negative consequences of maternal depression on children and programs to prevent depressive outcomes in offspring of depressed parents. There has also been an enormous gap in what we know about the emergence of depression in high-risk groups, such as adolescent women, and girls and women who have been exposed to abuse and battery, and treatments or preventive interventions.

Even less is known about cultural differences in depression. Tsai and Chentsova-Dutton (Chapter 20) indicate that an encouraging start has been made to address the gaps, and interest and appropriate tools are more available. Indeed, the need for clarifications about depressive experiences in different cultures is more apparent than ever before, as the composition of communities changes and diversifies. Assumptions of Western thought about mental disorder have been found to be inadequate for much of the world's people. Practical public health issues of recognizing treatable depressive conditions, and tailoring existing treatments or developing new ones to be acceptable, meaningful, and effective for diverse groups are obvious pressing needs in our own society.

There is much to be gained scientifically, as well, as research increasingly tackles cultural issues in depression. As Tsai and Chentsova-Dutton indicate, different cultural expressions of mood disorders may challenge our diagnostic divisions and concepts of "comorbidity." Also variations in the apparent severity and outcomes associated with depressive disorders in different cultures can help shed light on the role of social factors as they trigger episodes and shape the course of disorder. There is even much to be learned about the construct of "self," often a central focus of models of the origin of depression. It will prove to be illuminating as well to test the generality of psychological models of depression involving interpersonal and cognitive variables to different cultures, and to study different cultures' common experiences of stressful life events and their meanings in the onset of depressive reactions. Although there is a general need for further study of diverse cultures and depression, it is well to be mindful that age and gender differences within cultures are also of great importance to study, as experience teaches us the perils of overgeneralization from gender-neutral, adult norms. Finally, cultural perspectives may intersect with historical issues and events. It will be of interest to see, for example, whether rates of depression increase in the United States in the aftermath of the September 11, 2001 terrorist attacks, or in other regions of the world devastated by war and conflict, severe downturns in economic stability, or widespread natural disasters.

Child, Adolescent, and Late-Life Depression

The consideration of depression in different age groups reminds us of truths that are often overlooked. Depressions may have different meanings, origins, courses, and consequences depending on developmental status. While there may be—and likely are—universal aspects of symptoms, etiological features, and pathophysiological mechanisms, the important differences serve to remind us of the heterogeneity and complexity of depression. Three chapters in this part, by Garber and Horowitz (Chapter 22), Lewinsohn and Essau (Chapter 23), and Powers, Thompson, Futterman, and Gallagher-Thompson (Chapter 24), echo several themes in their call for further research.

One theme concerns the meaning of depression onset at different ages, raising both definitional and etiological issues. It appears that the question of appropriate diagnostic criteria is not a closed one, DSM-IV notwithstanding. The Garber and Horowitz and Powers et al. chapters, in particular, discuss the problems of distinguishing symptoms of the depression syndrome in populations in which key developmental considerations may obscure the ready application of adult criteria for specific symptoms to the very young or the elderly. Moreover, all the chapters raise questions about whether the structure of the depression may vary with developmental stage, and indeed, suggest that there is need for greater knowledge about the developmentally normative experience of individual symptoms such as fatigue, sleep changes, anhedonia, irritability, and the like. Powers and colleagues raise the intriguing possibility of different etiological subtypes among late-life depressions, and this issue could be applied to the other groups as well. The Powers et al. chapter also poses the challenging issue of need for study of a potentially "new" developmental group: the oldest old, individuals over the age of 85.

Questions about the meaning of depression also include the persistent puzzle of comorbidity. Garber and Horowitz note the near-universality of comorbidity in childhood depression, and they, as well as Lewinsohn and Essau, call for further studies of three unresolved issues raised by comorbidity: the high likelihood that anxiety disorders predict depressive disorders (an issue also noted by Powers and colleagues with respect to late-life depression); the question of whether there might be developmental issues in the expression of syndromes (perhaps from more diffuse to more crystallized); and whether there are different diagnostic and etiological implications for different comorbid sequences. Lewinsohn and Essau call for studies of possible "primary" versus "secondary" depressions, reviving a term that fell into disfavor for its ambiguous applications, but which flags a significant conceptual issue.

The primary–secondary issue is, perhaps, of pressing importance, as evidence is emerging of possible distinctions between children who have a pure or "primary" depressive disorder (perhaps with a family history of depressive disorder), compared to children whose depressions might be "secondary" consequences of the impairments associated with disruptive behavior disorders. Or, there might be etiological distinctions between children with true depressive disorders emerging in childhood, and other children with diffuse, nonspecific emotional and behavioral dysregulation who are diagnosed as having depression and comorbid conditions. The relative paucity of longitudinal studies of depressed children into adulthood suggests the need for further investigation (an exception is Weissman et al., 1999).

A related issue concerns whether depressions first arising in childhood, adolescence, or late life are really etiologically similar. It might be that disorders of childhood onset arise primarily either as severe forms of a genetically transmitted disorder or as reactions to severe adversity or environmental stressors interacting with a biologically sensitive or compromised stress-response system. The relatively dramatic upsurge in rates of depression in early adolescence, especially for females, also suggests that there may be unique processes involved with this developmental stage. Relatedly, Nolen-Hoeksema poses the question of whether adolescent-onset depressions result from preexisting vulnerabilities intersecting with adolescent changes, or whether there are processes that occur uniquely in adolescence, promoting depression if they come together in the right combinations. Powers and colleagues note that late-life onset of depression may often reflect possible indicators of neurological disorders. All the authors of the developmental chapters emphasize that there are marked gaps in our understanding of the etiological processes, and imply that understanding of depression in one age group may not necessarily generalize to all others.

Demographic trends underscore the importance of increasing our knowledge of the unique aspects of child–adolescent and late-life depressions: growing numbers of young people who are depressed and increasing proportions of older adults in the population (and who may be vulnerable to depression). Although mentioned in several chapters in this volume, treatment considerations, whether pharmacotherapy or psychotherapy, have been considerably less well developed in these populations than in adults. Clearly, there are compelling needs—and opportunities—for expansion of appropriate and effective interventions for children and older adults.

Suicidality Risk and Treatment

Finally, no discussion of depression is complete without recognition of the most fatal consequences of depression—suicide. Stolberg, Clark, and Bongar's chapter on suicide (Chapter 25) serves to remind us of the extent of suicidal risk and its close, but not specific, association with depression. The chapter is particularly helpful to clinicians, for despite the obvious need for further research to refine our understanding of risk factors, ultimately it is clinician judgment that may be called upon to recognize and intervene in potentially suicidal situations.

REFERENCES

Daley, S., Hammen, C., & Rao, U. (2000). Predictors of first onset and recurrence of major depression in young women during the five years following high school graduation. *Journal of Abnormal Psychology, 109,* 525–533.

Hammen, C., Rudolph, K., Weisz, J., Rao, U., & Burge, D. (1999). The context of depression in clinic-referred youth: Neglected areas in treatment. *Journal of the American Academy of Child and Adolescent Psychiatry, 38,* 64–71.

Jacobson, N. S., Dobson, K. S., Truax, P. A., Addis, M. E., Koerner, K., Gollan, J. K., Gortner, E., & Prince, S. E. (1996). A component analysis of cognitive-behavioral treatment for depression. *Journal of Consulting and Clinical Psychology, 64,* 295–304.

Lewinsohn, P. M., Allen, N. B., Seeley, J. R., & Gotlib, I. H. (1999). First onset versus recurrence of depression: Differential processes of psychosocial risk. *Journal of Abnormal Psychology, 108,* 483–489.

Weissman, M. M., Wolk, S., Wickramaratne, P., Goldstein, R. B., Adams, P., Greenwald, S., Ryan, N. D., Dahl, R. E., & Steinberg, D. (1999). Children with prepubertal-onset major depressive disorder and anxiety grown up. *Archives of General Psychiatry, 56,* 794–801.

Index

"f" indicates a figure; "t" indicates a table; "n" indicates a note

613